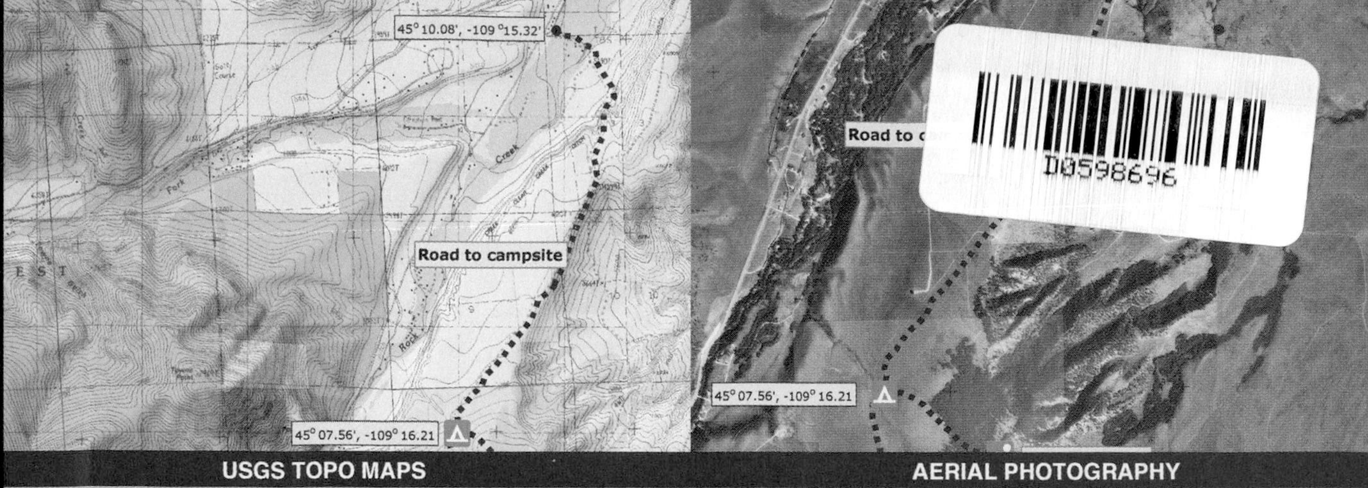
45° 10.08', -109° 15.32'
Road to campsite
45° 07.56', -109° 16.21
Road to c
D0598696
45° 07.56', -109° 16.21
USGS TOPO MAPS
AERIAL PHOTOGRAPHY

Shooter's Bible

No. 95 2004 Edition

Stoeger Publishing Company, Accokeek, Maryland

STOEGER PUBLISHING COMPANY
is a division of Benelli U.S.A.

Benelli U.S.A.
Vice President and General Manager: Stephen Otway
Director of Brand Marketing and Communications: Stephen McKelvain

Stoeger Publishing Company
President: Jeffrey K. Reh
Publisher: Jay T. Langston
Managing Editor: Harris J. Andrews
Design and Production Director: Cynthia T. Richardson
Photography Director: Alex Bowers
Imaging Specialist: Williams Graves
Sales Manager Assistant: Julie Brownlee
Editorial Assistant: Christine Lawton
Administrative Assistant: Shannon McWilliams

Published by:
Stoeger Publishing Company
17603 Indian Head HIghway, Suite 200
Accokeek, Maryland 20607-2501

Soft Cover: ISBN:0-88317-244-5 BK0301
Hard Cover: ISBN:0-88317-274-7 BK0411
Soft Cover: Library of Congress Control Number: 2002110062
Hard Cover: Library of Congress Control Number: 2003106089
Manufactured in the United States of America
Distributed to the book trade and the sporting goods trade by:
Stoeger Industries, Stoeger Publishing Company
17603 Indian Head HIghway, Suite 200
Accokeek, Maryland 20607-2501
301 283-6300 *Fax:* 301 283-6986

Note: Every effort has been made to record specifications and descriptions of guns, ammunition and accessories accurately, but the Publisher can take no responsibility for errors or omissions. The prices shown for guns, ammunition and accessories are manufacturers' suggested retail prices (unless otherwise noted) and are furnished for information only. These were in effect at press time and are subject to change without notice. Purchasers of the book have complete freedom of choice in pricing for resale.

Front Cover: This year's front cover showcases three firearms from Ruger chambered for the .17 Hornaday Magnum Rimfire cartridge: the new Ruger K77/17 VBBZ Bolt Action Rifle with laminated stock and Target Grey matte finish, fitted with a Leupold Vari-X III scope; the K77/17RM in blued steel with a walnut stock and Burris Black Diamond scope; and Ruger's new Model Single-Six revolver with a blued finish and Rosewood grips. The polymer tip of Hornady's .17 HMR V-Max bullet delivers dramatic expansion on impact and powerful new propellants confer a flat trajectory for long-range accuracy.

OTHER PUBLICATIONS:

Gun Trader's Guide – 25th Edition
"Complete Fully Illustrated Guide to Modern Firearms with Current Market Values"

Hunting & Shooting
Advanced Black Powder Hunting
Archer's Bible
Hounds of the World
Hunting Whitetails East & West
Hunt Club Management Guide
The Turkey Hunter's Tool Kit: Shooting Savvy
Complete Book of Whitetail Hunting
Hunting and Shooting with the Modern Bow
The Ultimate in Rifle Accuracy
Labrador Retrievers
Hunting America's Wild Turkey
Taxidermy Guide
The Truth About Turkey Hunting According to "Cuz"
The Whole Truth About Turkey Hunting According to "Cuz"

Collecting Books
Sporting Collectibles
The Working Folding Knife
The Lore of Spices

Firearms
Antique Guns
P-38 Automatic Pistol
The Walther Handgun Story
Complete Guide to Compact Handguns
Complete Guide to Service Handguns
America's Great Gunmakers
Firearms Disassembly with Exploded Views
Rifle Guide
Gunsmithing at Home
The Book of the Twenty-Two
Complete Guide to Modern Rifles
Complete Guide to Classic Rifles
Legendary Sporting Rifles
FN Browning Armorer to the World
Modern Beretta Firearms
How to Buy & Sell Used Guns
Heckler & Koch: Armorers of the Free World
Spanish Handguns

Reloading
The Handloader's Manual of Cartridge Conversions
Modern Sporting Rifle Cartridges
Complete Reloading Guide

Fishing
Ultimate Bass Boats
Bassing Bible
The Flytier's Companion
Deceiving Trout
The Complete Book of Trout Fishing
The Complete Book of Flyfishing
The Flytier's Manual
Flytier's Master Class
Handbook of Fly Tying
The Fly Fisherman's Entomological Pattern Book
Fiberglass Rod Making

Motorcycles & Trucks
The Legend of Harley-Davidson
The Legend of Indian
Great Trucks
4X4 Vehicles

Cooking Game
Fish & Shellfish Care & Cookery
Game Cookbook
Dress 'Em Out
Wild About Venison
Wild About Game Birds
Wild About Fresh Water Fish

CONTENTS

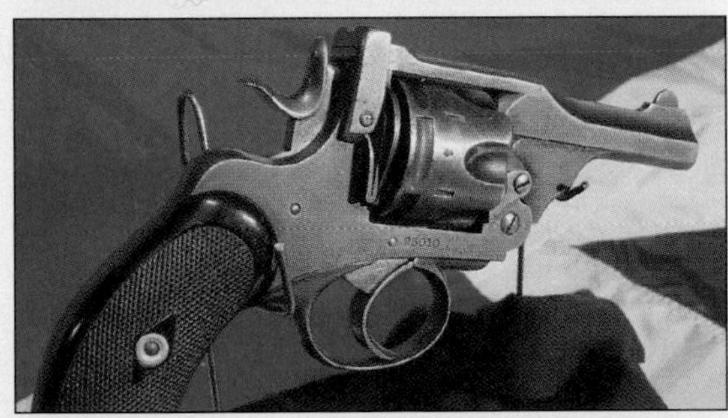

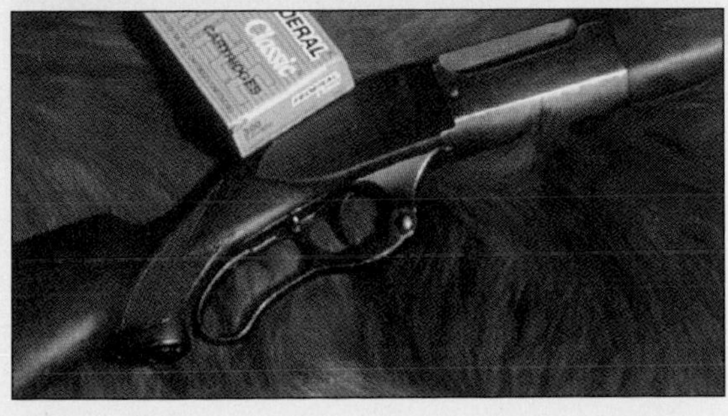

INTRODUCTION

Publisher Jay Langston puts a Ruger M-77 to the test with a Hornaday .17 HMR V-Max.

Welcome, fellow shooting enthusiasts....

You'll find plenty of new guns, cartridges and shooting accessories in this 2004 Shooter's Bible. Plus the most complete, reader-friendly ballistics tables anywhere. There's a new look to the pages too, so you can better compare items and get important specs in a jiffy. A New Products Section highlights the latest and greatest from the shooting industry.

Look to *Shooter's Bible* for tips on marksmanship and shotgunning in the illustrated article section, and also packed between gun descriptions. Here you'll learn little-known facts about gun design and history, and about the eccentric, brilliant, determined people who gave American shooters the best sporting arms in the world. Get the real story on how your bullets perform downrange and bone up on what's a must-have for your handloading bench. You can't shoot any better than you can see, so we cover sights, too, from "irons" to the most sophisticated range-finding scopes with adjustable objectives and illuminated reticles.

O.K. So you have a stack of *Shooter's Bibles* on the shelf. Do you need one every year? Yup for the same reason last week's newspaper won't do for today. You'll want to keep the old books; they're valuable references. But you won't be up to date in the shooting world without this edition. Its feature articles are jam-packed with useful information you won't find anywhere else. And the specifications section tells you all about the newest hardware. From Winchester's new SuperShort .223 to the thumb-size .500 Smith & Wesson, you'll become an expert on fascinating new cartridges and the guns engineered specifically for them. Want a rundown on what's available in non-toxic shot? Look here. The scoop on an affordable Zeiss varmint scope? Look here. A new load for the .17 HMR? A soup can-shaped shotgun slug that prints rifle-like groups? You have the source in your hand. If you're like me, you'll keep *Shooter's Bible* on the bench all year long. I hope you turn to it as you would an old friend. We've worked hard to make it worth more than a second look.

Wayne van Zwoll, Specifications Editor

About the cover

I've long been a fan of Sturm, Ruger and Company firearms. I fondly recall earning enough money mowing lawns to purchase my first Ruger, a Mark I .22 pistol. From that point several more Ruger models have found their way to the Langston house. The introduction of a hot new cartridge is just the excuse I need to add a few more.

Hot on the heels of the bullet-maker's introduction of the .17 Hornady Magnum Rimfire (HMR), Ruger added five new models to their lineup in this fascinating cartridge. Highlighted on the cover of this Shooter's Bible are two M-77 models and a Single Six single-action revolver. In addition to the stainless laminated and walnut M-77 versions, Ruger offers a stainless synthetic, a M-96/17 lever-action, and soon-to-be released semi-auto 10/17. Plinking with this new cartridge is just plain fun, and they perform well on pint-sized varmints, too.

Check out the new StoegerPublishing.com web site. Once there, you'll find lots of information about other Stoeger books on shooting, hunting, cooking, collecting, fishing and more. Log on to find out what's happening in the shooting industry and share shooting tips on the Stoeger Publishing bulletin board.

Good Shooting!
Jay Langston, Editor & Publisher

Special thanks to the National Rifle Association, for access to their image archives.

FEATURE ARTICLES

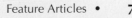

Beanfield Rifles Abroad: Kenny Jarrett's Original Long-Range Rifle Has Found a Place Beyond the Soybean Patch

By Wayne Van Zwoll

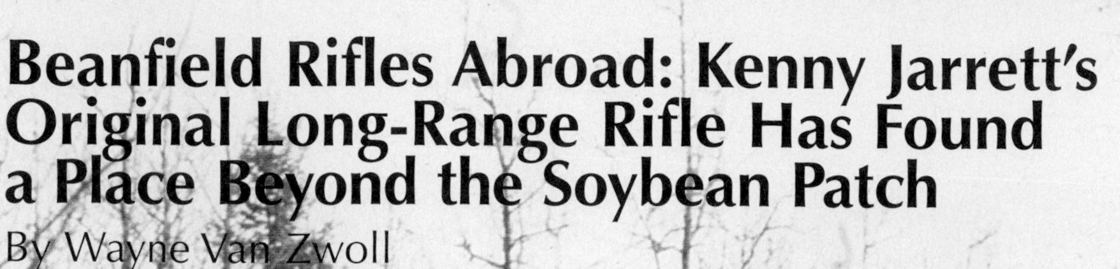

While Kenny Jarrett developed his rifles for shooting across southern beanfields, they work as well on cutlines in the north woods. He guarantees half-minute accuracy in sub-30-caliber rifles. Kenny prefers Remington Model 700 *(above)* actions, which he trues and tunes and rebarrels.

When shooters talk about accurate rifles, or long-range rifles, or beanfield rifles, Kenny Jarrett's name comes up. The burly, red-haired gun guru who looks and talks like an archetypal Bubba would just as soon keep it that way. His expanding line of rifles, including a bolt action he designed and manufactures, certainly provides fodder for conversation.

A fourth-generation farmer from Jackson, South Carolina, Jarrett grew up on the 10,000-acre Cowden Plantation owned by his uncle J. M. Brown. There he hunted whitetail deer and began tinkering with rifles. Soon he found that most rifles were woefully inaccurate—at least by his standards. Kenny had no use for rifles that wouldn't consistently hit a tennis ball at 200 yards. "Sure, a lot of deer are shot up close, where any rifle will work," he'd say later. "But when the buck is on the other side of a soybean field, you need artillery that shoots tight groups."

Kenny's view of what constitutes good accuracy evolved during his early years on the benchrest circuit, where competitors routinely shot one-hole groups. Texas gunmaker Harold Broughton took young Jarrett under his wing to show Kenny how to build fine accuracy into a rifle. After a time at Broughton's shop, he returned to South Carolina determined to build hunting rifles that delivered benchrest precision.

Barrels are crucial to accuracy. Jarrett uses only the best. Even his light-contour tubes shoot well.

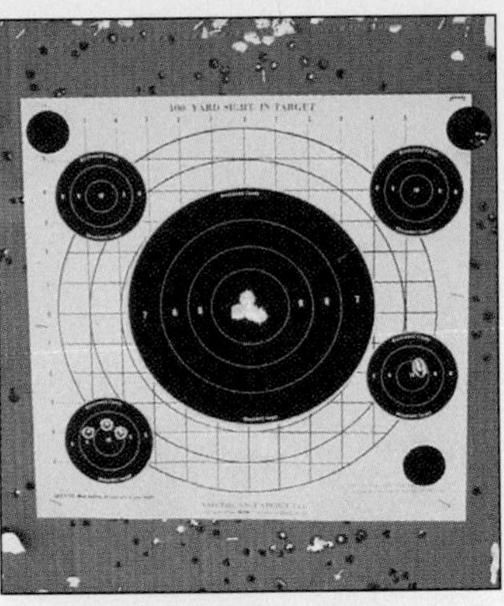

One-hole groups are not an anomaly at Jarrett Rifles; they're expected.

For that task, Jarrett needed barrels. Jerry Hart, whose barrels had earned a stellar reputation among target shooters, shared some of his expertise. By the mid-1970s, Kenny had garnered business from local riflemen who wanted their hardware "accurized." In 1979 he gave up farming to launch a career in gunsmithing. "The first year, we grossed $17,000," he recalls, "Not bad for a country boy." Kenny found his country-boy image and earthy aphorisms to be assets as he cultivated business around the United States. His aim: to get out of the accurizing and gun repair work altogether, replacing it with custom stocking and barreling on receivers he'd reworked. "I wanted to give my customers Jarrett rifles, not rifles I'd fixed."

Kenny Jarrett, owner and founder of Jarrett Rifles Inc., began his career as a country gunsmith and developed a small business into a major producer of custom quality rifles. For Jarrett, "the heart of the rifle is the barrel."

The problem was pricing. Accurate rifles aren't cheap to build. Besides the requisite truing and honing of actions, the hand bedding and installation of expensive barrels, Kenny had capital cost to think about—tooling up. Few deer hunters had expressed a need for rifles that would shoot benchrest groups, and few hunters had the shooting skill to test the half-minute rifles that Jarrett envisioned in his catalog. "I could have tried to build rifles that other riflemakers were marketing," he says. "Instead, I tried to create a market for more accurate rifles."

And, more quickly than anyone expected, he did. Invitations to knowledgeable gun writers put the Jarrett "beanfield" rifle in major publications. A flood of orders followed. By the end of a decade in the business, Kenny was employing 13 people and grossing more than half a million dollars annually. The original 2,200-square-foot shop, built of cypress lumber sawn on the farm and roofed with cedar shakes, had grown to encompass 6,000 square feet. It held five lathes and a full complement of milling machines, belt sanders, surface grinders and precision measuring instruments. Outside, Jarrett extended his target range, so he'd be able to test rifles

No gunsmith here. Jarrett prides himself in building rugged, accurate, weather-proof rifles.

at "beanfield distances."

The beanfield moniker became a signature name for Jarrett rifles, a fortuitous mix of brevity, corn-pone South and field savvy that resonated with deer hunters. If you owned a Jarrett, no buck was safe, no matter how long the shot. "At least, that's the image we marketed," says Kenny. "Truth is, our rifles were and are the most accurate you can buy. We still do guarantee half-inch groups at 100 yards from barrels of less than 30 caliber, and three-quarter-inch groups from the Big-Bores. But of course you have to hold the rifle still and dope the wind and estimate distance accurately to hit consistently at long range. We don't advocate long shooting. If you make a poor hit, a follow up at long range is most likely impossible. It's irresponsible to shoot at game farther than you can make center hits on paper—even if you're using one of our rifles."

Then what's the advantage of a super-accurate smokepole? "Confidence that the rifle will perform better than you will," says Kenny. "Assurance that you don't ever have to worry about a bad shot because your equipment failed. If you're shooting a Jarrett rifle and do everything right, the animal hits the deck. Every time. Shooters with confidence in their equipment can extend their reach through practice and make shots in the field that would be risky for other hunters."

Kenny shoots plenty of paper himself. Active as a benchrest competitor, he's punched out six world-record groups, and his rifles have accounted for 15 world records. In 1988 one of his bench guns won the Super Shoot, the most prestigious event in the game. Every one of his rifles is tested on the range. If after tuning it does not meet Jarrett's strict standards, it's rebarreled. Once, a rifle resisted all efforts to make it perform. Kenny matter-of-factly took a band saw to the receiver. He hung the halves on his shop wall to remind both employees and customers that a Jarrett rifle must not simply shoot well; it must shoot superlatively. "Or it doesn't leave."

Reliability and accuracy matter when a hunter is bound for remote places.

Big mule deer have become scarce and wary. A Jarrett rifle boosts your odds at long range.

When I first interviewed Kenny a decade ago, he'd built rifles for cartridges ranging in size from the .17 Remington to the .50 BMG. With more than 68 chamber reamers in inventory, he could fill orders for most popular wildcats as well as rifles in standard chamberings. The choice has grown substantially since, but his personal favorites still include the .280 Ackley Improved, a blown-out, sharp-shouldered .280 Remington. "It nearly matches the ballistic performance of the 7mm Remington Magnum," Kenny points out, "in a smaller case." He favors the .300 Winchester Magnum too, but has also developed his own .300 Jarrett. It's a necked-down 8mm Remington Magnum with a 35-degree shoulder. "We get 3600 fps with a 150-grain bullet, 3450 with a 165, 3250 with a 180 and 3050 with a

Kenny likes long barrels because they deliver more velocity. That means longer reach.

Namibia is the place to go for gemsbok. Long shots are the rule.

Long shooting intrigues riflemen. They respond with good optics and heavy rifles on bipods.

200," he says. "It's an ideal all-around pick if you expect long shooting at big game." Kenny has put it to use in the field. During the last decade, he's taken at least 17 deer with that big .30—at more than 600 yards.

Other wildcats have also emerged from the Jarrett shop. There's the .220 Jaybird, a super-fast .22 on the .308 case, and the .338 Kubla-Kahn, a reformed .378 Weatherby that according to Kenny sends 250-grain bullets out the muzzle at 3385 fps. It appeared long before the similar .338-378 Weatherby.

Most Jarrett rifles are built on Remington Model 700 actions, trued and squared so that the bolt face is perpendicular to the chamber and that bore, chamber and receiver are in axial alignment. The lugs must bear evenly too. For extra-large cartridges, the shop substitutes Weatherby Mark V actions, also tuned. Pillar bedding of all receivers is standard. Hart and Schneider have been the barrel brands of choice for Jarrett rifles, though you can specify others. Kenny has a strong preference for McMillan synthetic stocks and "won't do wood at all." Wood moves as temperature and humidity change, affecting the rifle's bedding and, consequently, its accuracy. (I have seen Jarrett rifles stocked in wood; they're anomalies.)

Metal finish is generally up to the customer. Because Kenny likes stainless steel barrels, that's the default material, and it looks good bead-blasted with no coating. However, he'll use electroless nickel or NP3 nickel-Teflon on the steel if you prefer. Chrome-moly receivers can be blued.

Whitetail bucks stay near the edge of southern fields. Wayne killed this one near dusk.

The Jarrett shop has made a specialty of switch-barrel rifles. The option can be had at extra cost on Remington 700 receivers. A twist with a wrench then gives you a choice of chamberings in one rifle.

Kenny typically adjusts Remington triggers down to a let-off weight of 2 pounds. If a particular trigger resists, or if the customer requests, he'll install an aftermarket Shilen or Jewell trigger. "If you disturb the rifle with your finger, you'll never get the accuracy we demand from our products," Kenny preaches a sermon steeped in benchrest shooting. To milk benchrest accuracy from the hunting-weight rifles that comprise 85 percent of his business, Kenny develops handloads that he shares with the customer. He also provides 20 rounds of loaded

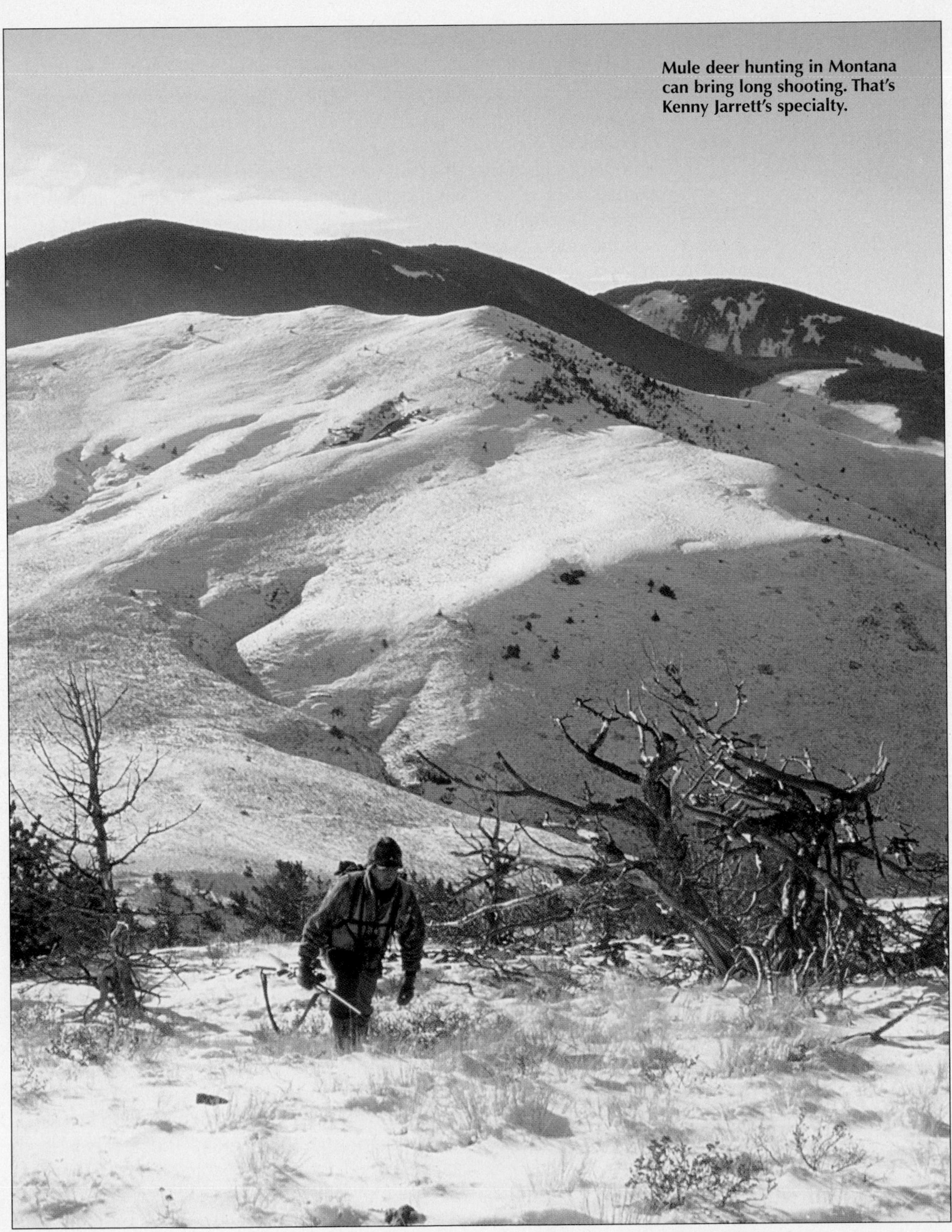

Mule deer hunting in Montana can bring long shooting. That's Kenny Jarrett's specialty.

ammunition and a test target with each rifle.

Expanding his line of rifles from the original "beanfield" design, Kenny has come up with nimble, lightweight sporters like the 6-pound "Walk-About" (that, yes, rountinely shoots into half an inch). He's developed his own muzzle brake to tame the recoil of powerful cartridges. And he has fashioned his own stock, produced by McMillan. Kenny has also assembled a custom shotgun on a Remington 870 action and offered custom pistol-smithing on revolvers, single and double action. His products include a "competition package" for the Colt 1911 autoloading pistol, with all the gingerbread a target shooter could want.

While versatility no doubt helps keep the lights on at the Jarrett shop, Kenny's first love is still the accurate rifle that made him famous. He still puts them to work in the field—he once shot a goundhog at 723 yards—and is as dedicated as ever to making them available to shooters.

"Because our rifles cost a lot to build, we have to charge more than many deer hunters are willing to spend on a rifle for the woods," Kenny explains, pinching another wad of tobacco from the ever-present tin. He eases the wad, as big as a field mouse, into his cheek. Somehow, his speech is not affected. "But I like to see average fellows step up for one of our tack-drivers. I think they appreciate it more than the man—one of our better customers—who's spent $46,000 on Jarrett rifles over the years. Long ago, one local youngster saved up hay money for three seasons to buy a Jarrett rifle. I threw in a Leupold scope on that deal." He smiles.

Long shooting can make the difference in places like the Kalahari Desert.

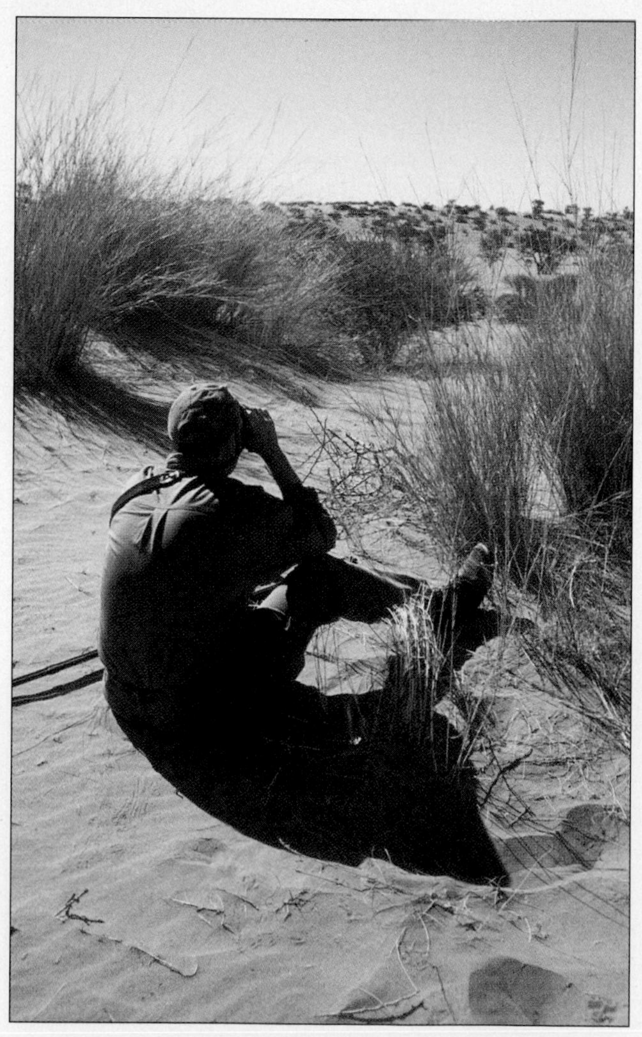

Speaking of optics, the best is none too good for a beanfield rifle. "I like Schmidt & Bender and Swarovski scopes," says Kenny. "Leupolds are a favorite of customers and a great buy in a hunting scope."

The most ambitious project of Kenny Jarrett's is his own rifle action. After building up to 140 rifles in a year based on other mechanisms, he decided in the mid-1990s to fashion his own. "It was to be the best bolt action anyone could make," he tells me. "And in my view, it is." He concedes that it also cost a lot more to produce than he'd anticipated, and that perfection is not always easy to market. But the Jarrett rifle action is a reality. And you can order one. Here's what you get:

A receiver and tang contoured to match the Remington 700s, so you can fit the action to a stock designed for the Remington. The receiver is of stainless steel, bolt and extractor of 4340 nickel chrome-molybdenum. A spiral-fluted bolt reciprocates within a unique sleeve or "bolt bushing." The

When a hunt hinges on one shot, says Kenny, his rifles suddenly become worth their cost!

Not pretty? Kenny Jarrett cares little for cosmetics. Accuracy gets all his attention.

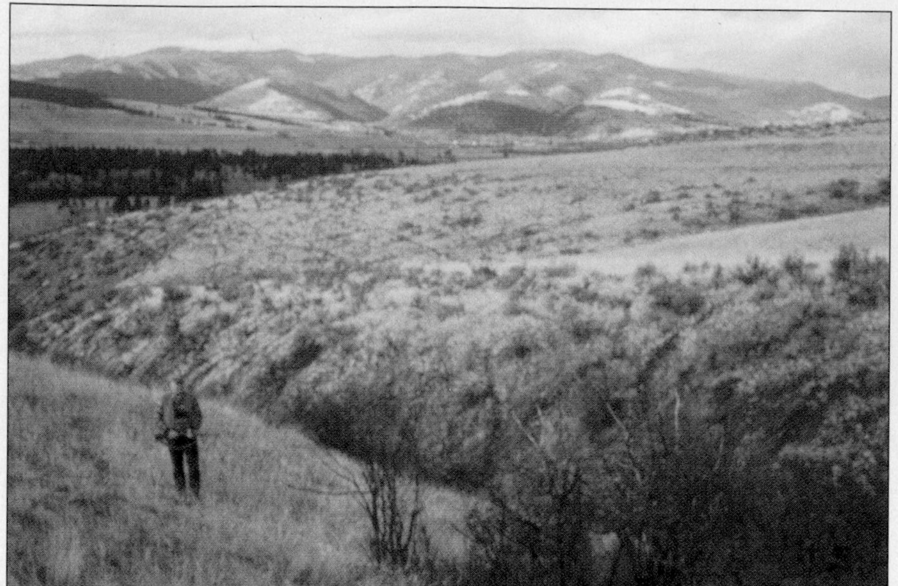

Shots can be beanfield-long on the skirts of Montana's Sapphire range.

sleeve is held captive in the receiver bridge; you don't even know it's there until you slide the bolt free. The bushing not only smoothes bolt travel, but serves as safety stop in the unlikely event of gas escape around the bolt body.

The two-piece bolt has no welding or brazing to fail—the bolt handle is threaded onto the body; then a cross pin secures it. Right-hand models have a left-hand bolt thread to prevent the handle from coming loose during difficult extraction. The cam surface for the cocking piece is integral with the handle so the bolt must be closed before the rifle can be fired. In lockup, the three lugs yield as much bearing surface as the standard two-lug bolt of a Remington 700, but they permit a low 60-degree bolt lift. Tested to pressures of more than double what you'd expect from maximum safe loads, the action has remained intact, sealing gas from rear escape. In the event of gas blowback, four holes in the bolt body channel the blast into the magazine well. The bolt sleeve limits any rearward movement of the striker. A side-mounted bolt release is an improvement over the Remington 700's trigger release.

The striker is exceptionally lightweight, resulting in fast lock time. Its shaft diameter is held to tight tolerances, preventing buckling of the mainspring. Flats on the striker shaft and head reduce contact with the spring and bolt, minimizing friction. The extractor, inside the bolt face but of substantial bite, allows for total enclosure of the case head by multiple rings of steel. It is cleverly designed to pull sticky cases authoritatively from the chamber. The floating ejector button enables you to tip the spent case gently into your hand or toss it briskly several feet from the rifle; the response depends on your hand movement. The floating button also lets

Even when shots aren't long, Jarrett's accuracy guarantee can inspire shooter confidence.

each cartridge enter the barrel without sideways pressure and a feed insert further smoothes chambering. It's essentially a removable rail, and replaceable with inserts of different dimensions so you can "tune" feeding to your specific cartridge.

You may not need a new rifle, or want a bolt action that nobody else on the block has discovered, but if you're a serious rifleman, you'll appreciate the level of accuracy that Jarrett rifles deliver. "It's hardly what you'd expect from any rifle, let alone a lightweight," enthused one customer whose trim 7-08 drilled out one group under .30 inch. "You see this surprised look," chuckles Kenny. "When a customer visits and tries his rifle out on our range, odds are he's never shot groups that small. It's a revelation." So it follows that nearly a quarter century after deciding to build more accurate rifles, Kenny Jarrett is still the undisputed "Baron of the Beanfield." The next time you plan a big game hunt, you might take to heart his observation that an expensive rifle can look mighty cheap when it helps you make good your only shot at a trophy-class animal.

It's worth pondering, even if you don't wear overalls, chew tobacco or hail from South Carolina.

For more information on Jarrett rifles, phone 803-471-3616.

Kenny prefers 30 magnums and the .280 Improved for much of his big game hunting.

Many hunters like to hunt whitetails by sitting at woods' edge and watching fields.

Swamp Rabbits: Small Game Hunting's Biggest Challenge

By Keith Sutton

Standing ankle-deep in the blackwater bayou, I watch the swamp rabbit. I can hear, in the distance, two beagles hot on his track, but this bottomland creature seems unconcerned. He hip-hops to the icy water's edge and slides in like a muskrat heading to the Cattail Diner.

I see a strong resemblance between this rabbit and the cottontails I often hunt. Each sports a powder-puff tail, long ears and big hind legs. Each wears a camo-brown coat peppered with black. In size, however, this swamp rabbit differs from a cottontail as much as a beagle from a Chihuahua. A big cottontail weighs perhaps three pounds; this swamper is pushing ten.

The rabbit swims as fluidly as an otter, with only his nose showing above the water. Then suddenly he dives and disappears. I wait, thinking soon he will surface. This mammal may have webbed feet but he certainly has no gills. After five minutes, however, the swamp rabbit still has not reappeared. Puzzled, I wade closer to the spot where I last saw him and focus on the scene. Where has the rabbit gone?

The dogs arrive ten minutes later, bawling loudly on the hot track. Rebel, a handsome lemon-colored beagle, appears first, followed closely by his littermate Bear. The rabbit's scent trail ends at the water's edge, but the beagles are undeterred. They vacuum the loam with noses that could track an ant through the Gobi Desert, determined to find their quarry.

It is Bear who solves the mystery of the disappearing rabbit. He stops beside a brushy top of a bush half-submerged at the water's edge, looks at it intently, and then yelps as if zapped by a cattle prod. I can see the rabbit now—his nose, at least. Bear sees it, too. The rabbit has swum into the brush and hidden, or so he thinks. Bear leaps at him from the bank, followed by Reb.

Once again, the chase is on—like two crocodiles swimming after Tarzan. The three animals cross the slough and bail out, the swamp rabbit running like the demons of hell are on his tail.

People who have not hunted swamp rabbits may not appreciate my enthusiasm, for there are subtle complexities to the game the uninitiated may not see. The swamp rabbit, you see, is more than just an overgrown bunny. A

The swamp rabbit looks much like its cousin, the cottontail, but adult swampers may be twice the size of adult cottontails.

Inset:
Swamper dogs and swamper hunters need webbed feet to keep up with swamp rabbits in their wetland homes.

Below:
Swamper dogs, hot on the trail of a big canecutter, race across a flooded bottomland logging road.

swamper running before a dog has more wits than a coyote, more speed than a fox. A swamper doesn't run a tight circle like a cottontail but traces huge ellipses, parabolas and figure eights through the bottoms, often taking an hour or more to make a single round through his home territory. A swamp rabbit may make two circles on the same track, then, for no good reason, head straight for the Mexican border.

To make things even more difficult, swamp rabbits are excellent swimmers. They'll swim downstream then exit the water in thick cover to throw dogs off the track. They'll dive and hide nose-up under root wads and log jams. A swamp rabbit is truly a fascinating animal.

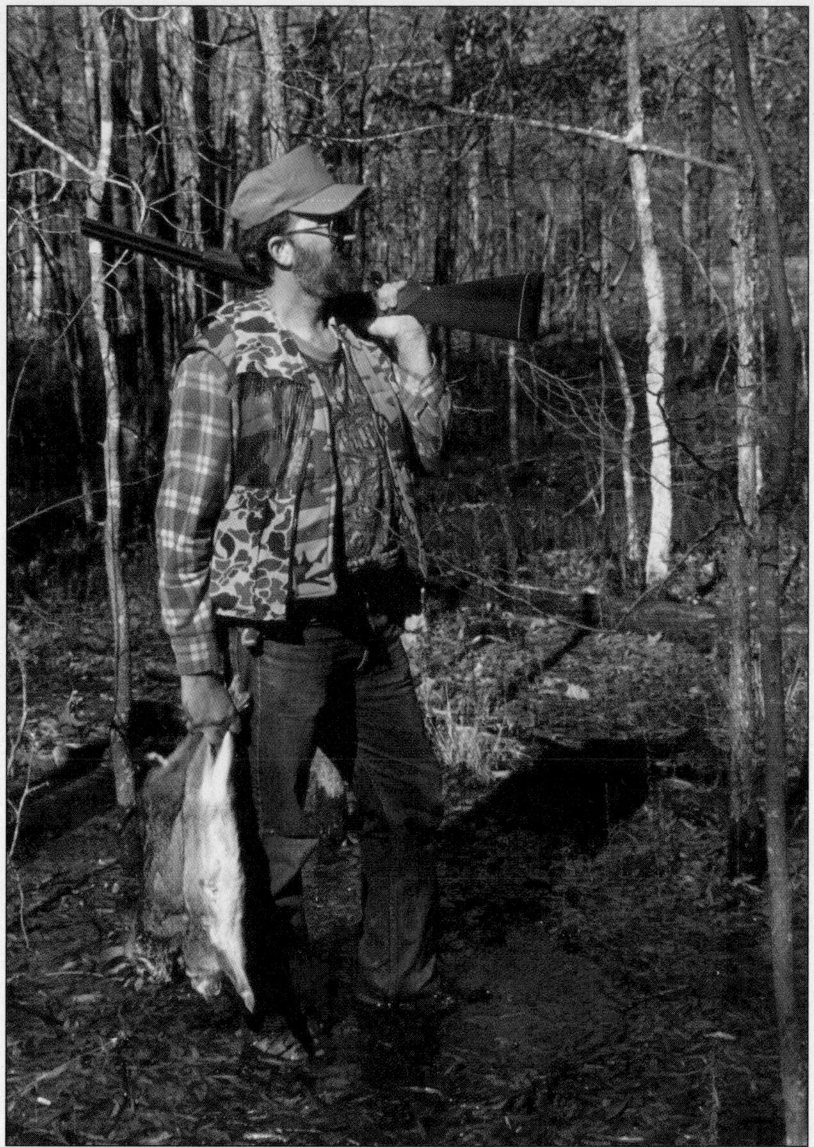
Orange headgear and bodywear help your partners keep you safely in mind when hunting the dense cover swamp rabbits frequent.

So is a fine swamper dog. On a good day, a beagle like Reb or Bear will work five times as hard as the best cottontail dog. A swamper hound would rather run rabbits than eat or sleep. He has a Labrador retriever's affinity for cold water. He'll go till his voice gives out, then he'll go some more, giving out feeble, laryngitic cries every few minutes until the sun goes down or the master calls. It's not uncommon to hear someone say they have good rabbit dogs, but not many can truly say they have good swamper dogs.

The swamp rabbit, the largest member of the cottontail family, lives where he can keep his feet wet. He can't thrive without abundant water and bottomland vegetation. Transplants to drier habitats have proven unsuccessful.

Fortunately for me, the river floodplains of Arkansas still have plenty of these elusive rabbits. The species occurs from extreme southeastern Kansas, southern Missouri, southern Illinois and extreme southwestern Indiana, south through eastern Oklahoma, eastern Texas, Arkansas, Louisiana, Mississippi, Alabama, northwestern Georgia and extreme western South Carolina. Throughout much of its range, however, the swamp rabbit suffers as streams are channeled, wetlands are drained and bottomland hardwoods are cleared. Here is an animal that can cope with unrelenting natural predators and the seasonal pressure of beagles and hunters, but it is no match for the bulldozer. Finding a huntable population is perhaps the biggest challenge swamper fans face.

The swamp rabbit goes by many descriptive nicknames. Throughout his range, he is called "canecutter" because of his fondness for young cane shoots. In other areas he's known as "cane jake," "swamp hare," "water rabbit" or simply "swamper." Some people refer to swamp rabbits as "bucks" because they think they're seeing big buck cottontails.

Swamp rabbits closely resemble eastern cottontails, but the two species are easily distinguished by size and habitat. The smallest mature swamp rabbit is about the size of the largest mature cottontail. The latter usually weighs two to three pounds, but the swamper tips the scales at four to eleven. And while cottontails usually prefer drier upland habitat, the swamp rabbit inhabits half-flooded timberlands and swamp thickets where hunters need webbed feet to have a sporting chance. Canebrakes, elderberry thickets and dense stands of honeysuckle and catbriar in stream floodplains provide ideal cover.

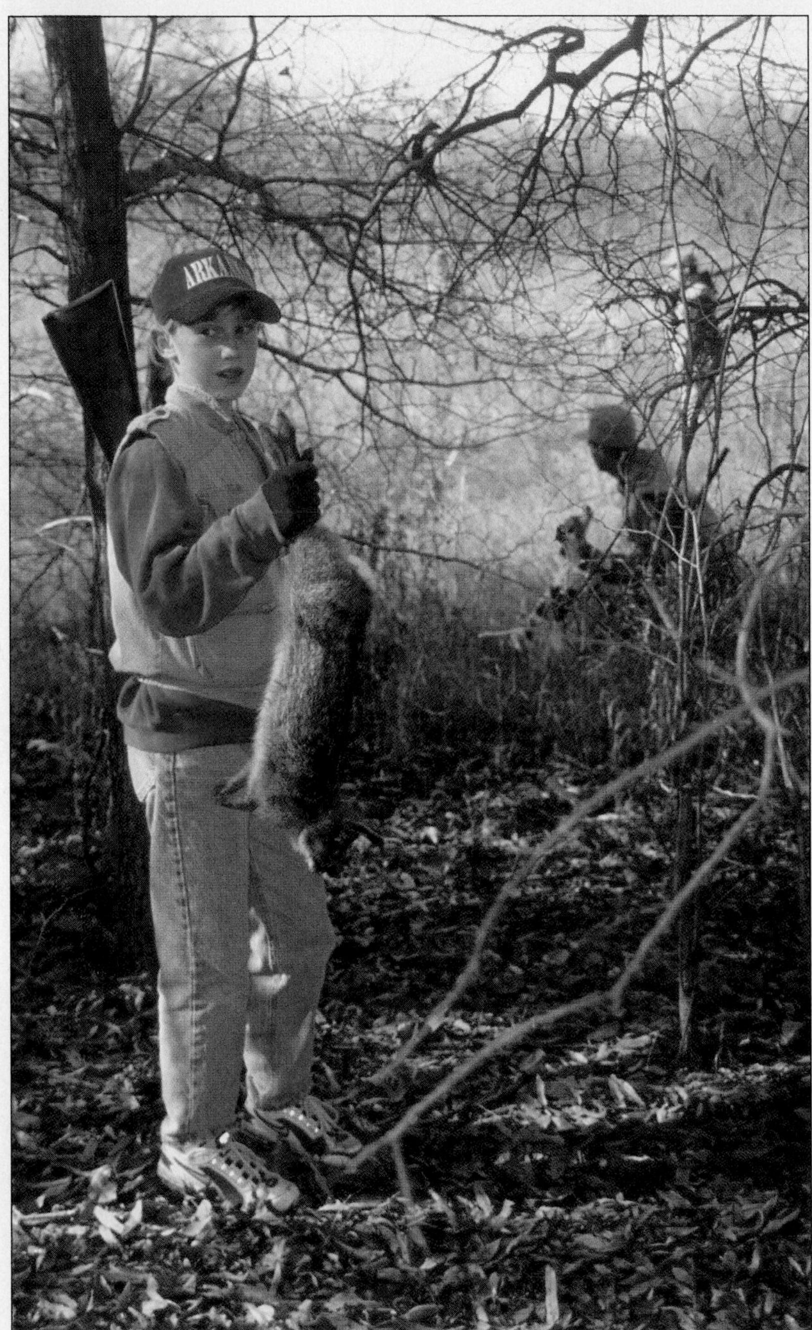

A full-grown swamp rabbit may look half as big as the youngster who bagged it, but most weigh in around six to eight pounds.

The swamp rabbit prefers an elevated perch. He rests on logs or stumps, a habit acquired from his semi-aquatic existence, and it's always surprising to jump a rabbit from a log or stump projecting out of shallow water and have the animal go splashing away through the water. Fresh rabbit pellets atop a log or stump are a sure sign swamp rabbits are using an area.

The successful hunter requires an in-depth knowledge of swamper habits. He must interpret his dogs' baying to predict the course of the rabbit and, when all is right, position himself to intercept the swamper within shooting distance. Then he must stand motionless, lest the quarry see him and flee for cover, and when the canecutter moves into range—a brown ghost on a brown background covering six feet, sometimes more, with each bound—the hunter must pinpoint his prey, shoulder his gun and shoot.

Consider all these factors and you may see why some hunters are smitten with a passion for swamp rabbits. It's a sport demanding the strategy of a war general, the shooting skill of a woodcock hunter, the intuition of a riverboat gambler, the lungs and legs of a marathon runner, the dog-handling talents of a professional trainer and the patience of Job. Unless you and your dogs are prepared for the challenge, swamp rabbits will get the best of you every time.

Here are more helpful tips to remember. Don't go in under-gunned. The light-load No. 7-1/2 or 8 shotshells you use for cottontail-only hunts just won't cut it when canecutters are also on the menu. Canecutters are tougher than their upland cousins, and the cover you'll be shooting through is more substantial. This combination calls for heavy loads of big shot. Most veteran swamper fans opt for modified or full-choke shotguns, usually in 12 gauge, and load them with No. 4, 5 or 6 heavy-load shells.

Don't be misled into thinking you've missed a swamper just because it keeps running after you've shot. Even when hit with heavy load No. 4 shot, these super-bunnies often keep on running for several yards before expiring, lending the impression that they might not have been hit at all. If your dogs stop running a short distance from the spot where you fired on the rabbit, chances are they've found a dead swamper, so move in and check it out. And finally, learn to interpret the course of the rabbit by the sounds of the chase. Cottontails and swampers each exhibit distinct running patterns that will help you prepare for a shot.

Cottontails usually make a fairly short circle, and you'll be able to hear the baying dogs clearly throughout their pursuit. Find a position close to the spot where the rabbit was started, and when the yelping beagles draw near, get ready—Br'er Cottontail will usually be just ahead of them.

A swamp rabbit chase is vastly different, but equally—if not more—exciting. When the dogs jump him, ol' canecutter takes off in high gear, pouring on the coals until he has established a substantial lead

Swamp rabbits like extremely dense thickets of honeysuckle, sweetgums and other bottomland plants.

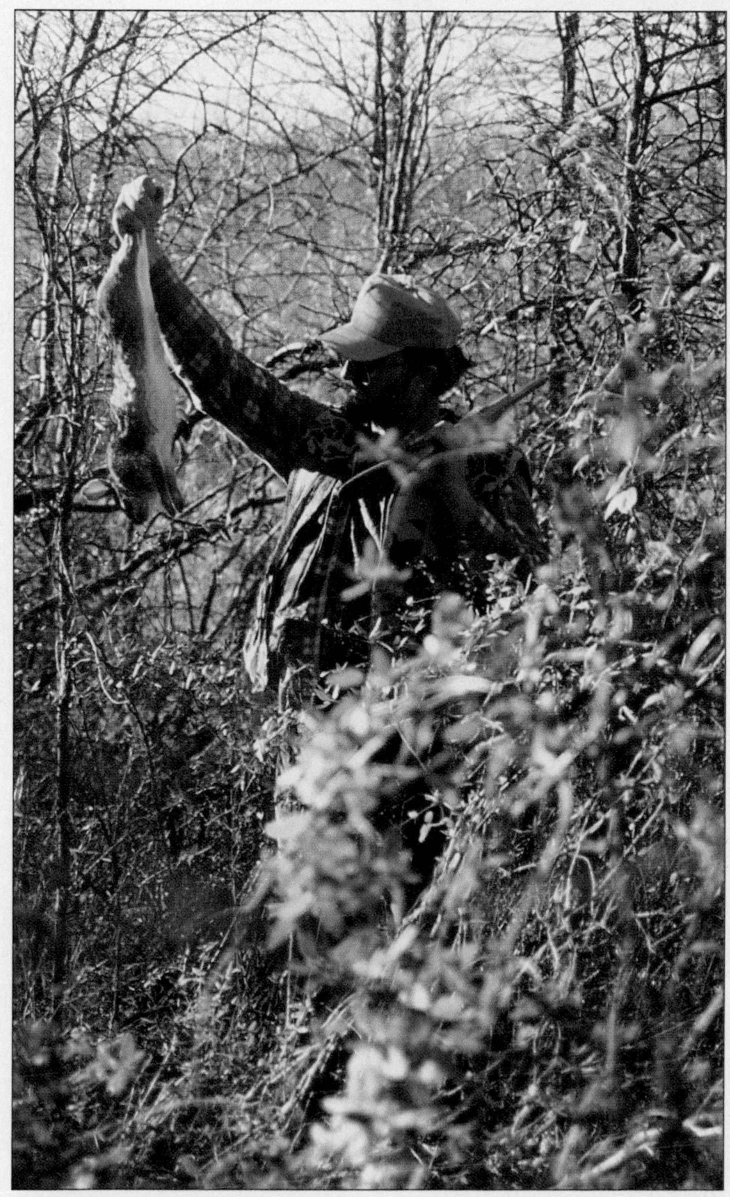

over the slow, ground-sniffing pack of beagles. He, too, will usually return to the point where first jumped, but not until he's taken the hounds completely—or at least nearly—out of earshot. When the dogs begin to turn back, even though they may still be quite distant, that's when you had better be on your toes, because the swamper will be far out in front of the beagles. If you and your hunting buddy are chewing the fat instead of scrutinizing your surroundings, the swamper will slip by undetected, and the dogs will have to make another complete circle before you're presented a shot. Being ready long before the dogs draw near is the hardest thing most novice canecutter hunters must learn.

Finally, proper clothing is a must. A good pair of rubber boots and brush-buster pants are indispensable in bottomland hunting territory, and for safety's sake, everyone in your hunting party should wear hunter-orange headgear and bodywear at all times. Always clearly identify your target before shooting, and keep in constant contact with your hunting buddies by whistling or shouting every couple of minutes. There's simply no room for mistakes when hunting dense lowland thickets.

In this successful hunter's hand are a swamp rabbit and a cottontail. The swamp rabbit is easily recognized by its much larger size.

I shoulder my gun and lean against a tree, content to listen to the dogs. The throaty aria of the two beagles rings through the bottomlands like a favorite hymn through a country chapel.

Reaching behind me, touching my game bag, I feel the shapes of two swamp rabbits taken earlier in the day. When younger, I might have stayed until I bagged a limit of eight, then struggled from the woods beneath the weight of all those giant rabbits. These days, however, two are enough. I can only eat so much fried rabbit and stockpile so many lucky feet. But I never tire of watching and listening as rabbits run and beagles bawl.

If the rabbits also swim, so much the better.

Jewels in the Rough

By Stan Warren

New gun prices scare you? Why not consider using a little time and elbow grease to refurbish a "previously owned" model that probably has a lot of life left? Call it a hunch. I was shopping for a new varmint rifle in one of the country's largest retail outlets (the boss is a good friend) when I came across an ugly specimen that had once been a pureblood. Bull barrel Model 70 Winchester, synthetic stock—the whole package.

The manager explained that it had belonged to a friend, a Nebraska prairie dog shooter who had traded it when the barrel became "shot out." As he said so, my friend raised his eyebrows. He couldn't urge me to buy the skinned-up rig, but he was not going to try and dissuade me

On a Wyoming prairie dog hunt, the author's resurrected Savage varmint rifle proved capable of dispatching sod poodles at ranges in excess of 500 yards. Newer and more expensive rifles could only deliver near misses.

Top:
Glass bedding the stock where the rear of the receiver's recoil lug makes contact, while relieving the receiver on the front often helps accuracy. Although this is primarily done on wooden versions, some synthetic stocks will benefit from this procedure.

Bottom:
When screws that attach the stock to the action are loose or improperly tightened, a rifle can display erratic accuracy and poor performance. The author once ran across a beautiful Mauser sporter that had a badly bowed action due to improper seating and tension.

either. Suffice to say I bought it for the proverbial song and toted it back to the homestead. For the next four nights cleaning sessions produced once-white patches that came out black, blue/green and gray. On the fifth night a clean patch emerged and hope was reborn.

In the company of my old Cabela's buddy, Joe Arterburn, I headed for the range with an adequate supply of Winchester's excellent Supreme varmint fodder. That supposedly worn-out chunk of iron equipped with a top-notch Bausch & Lomb scope took on a new life. It was nigh infallible. During our annual prairie dog hunt I got carried away and blazed along until it got so hot that the bolt would not open, all without any great loss in accuracy. Hey, if you don't believe me ask Joe. He has an honest job and is not a gun writer in hopes of making a buck here and there.

The urge to trade guns, buy something nicer and faster, more potent or whatever is one of the fun parts of being a gun nut. However, the idea that the average person is going to "shoot out" a barrel is a stretch. That well-traveled Winchester is a good example. I shot it for three years before selling it at a huge profit. Fast-stepping rounds require that the shooter give the tube a good scrubbing now and then so I gave it the proper attention and a retired oil company executive who shot with us on one occasion carried it home and made us both happy.

Another time, same store. An acquaintance, who could best be described as a casual shooter, had talked himself into buying a Savage bolt action .25-06 figuring that he would have a cheap and effective pronghorn and deer rifle while taking potshots at a distant coyote now and then. Since I was the one who had worked up the handloads that he was using, I had a fair amount of range time with the Savage and when he explained that he was getting rid of it because he could not keep his shots on paper at 100 yards, I had one of those rare moments of clarity. The rifle had a typically bad trigger pull and the owner had trouble dealing with it.

To cut to the chase, he traded for a used .30-06 Weatherby and lost a sizable chunk of his hip pockets in the process. Because the shop had little in the Savage, I picked it up for $100, added a quality after-market trigger and wound up with a truly delightful sporter. With 115- to 120-grain bullets it will deliver the mail way out there and with lighter stuff it will make a coyote wish that he was still chasing the roadrunner and falling off of cliffs.

Sometimes the trick to turning a sow's ear into a purse of some sort is not as simple as cleaning or adding a part. On one occasion I spied a rifle on the used rack at a local sports shop and recognized it instantly. There was a time when Remington made some of the most wonderfully accurate and totally ugly rifles in the industry, notably the Model 700 ADL with the weird, undercut forearm. There was no mistaking this one because the owner had gashed the stock on a barbed wire fence and finagled me into

Always check the screws on bases, mounts, rings and any other type of sighting equipment prior to test firing. Not even a .22 rimfire is immune to screws that work loose and wreck accuracy.

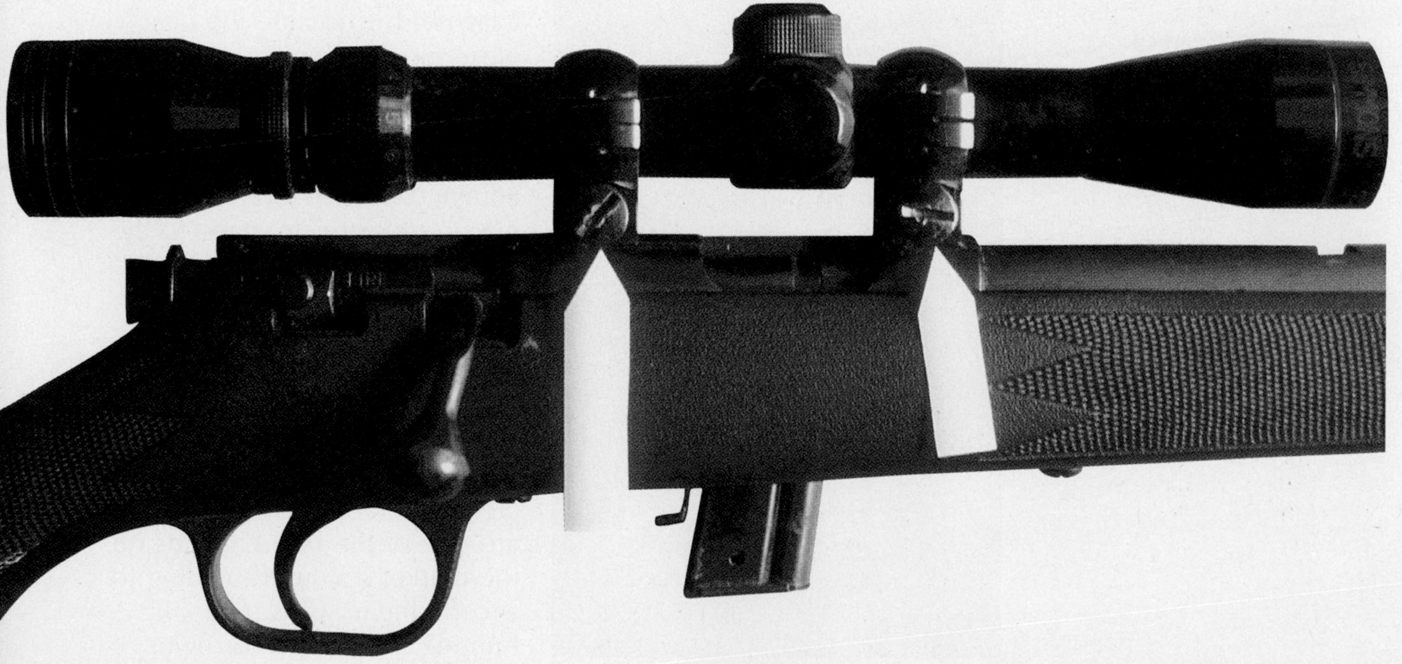

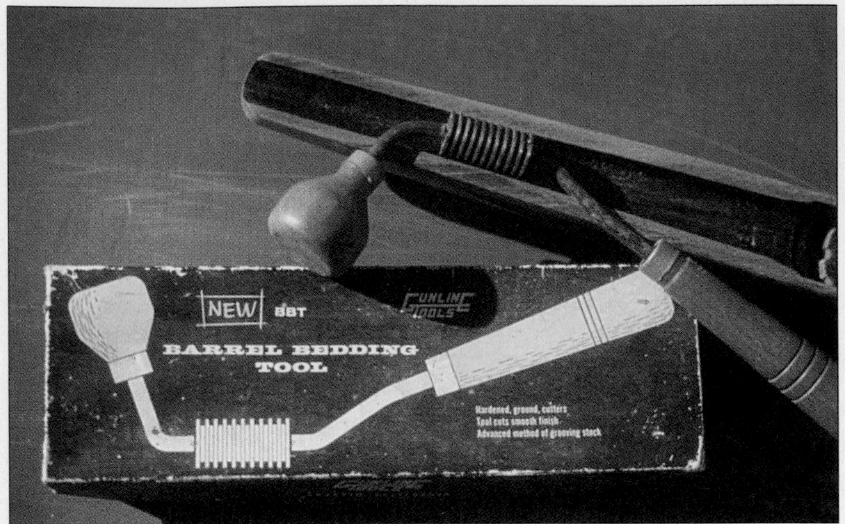

The "stringing" of consecutive shots meant that this stock had warped slightly and was putting uneven pressure on the barrel. Use of a channel-cutting tool permitted the option of free-floating the barrel or glassing the rig.

touching it up. My handiwork is not that great, so the repair was easy to spot.

Also on hand that day was a buddy who was getting ready to make his first elk hunt and wanted a 7 mm Remington magnum, the very caliber of the rifle on the rack. Now understand that this was a specimen that I had seen stick 175-grain Nosler Partitions almost in the same hole so there was no wishful thinking involved. With 160-grain Sierra Game King bullets, it would put everything that one wanted to throw downrange in one ragged opening.

It was the same story: the rifle just would not group anymore. Knowing how good it had been I talked my friend Dave, a fellow writer and capable of getting even with me if I goofed, into buying it. The first range session strained our friendship but also provided a critical bit of information because the rifle would not only not group, it produced "stringers." That thing would start on target and steadily walk the point of impact upward and to the right, an obvious bedding problem. A short session with a set of barrel channel cutters and some Brownell's Accra-Glass and it became the deadly piece of long-range, big game hardware that it had been in the beginning. For those who care about such things, accuracy was enhanced when we added a piece of electrician's tape to the barrel just back of the fore end. It seems to have added just enough pressure to get things on track.

Sometimes the addition of a small amount of pressure at the tip of the forearm can turn a modest performer into a real shooter. The author settled on a couple of strips of electrician's tape when working with this Savage 111.

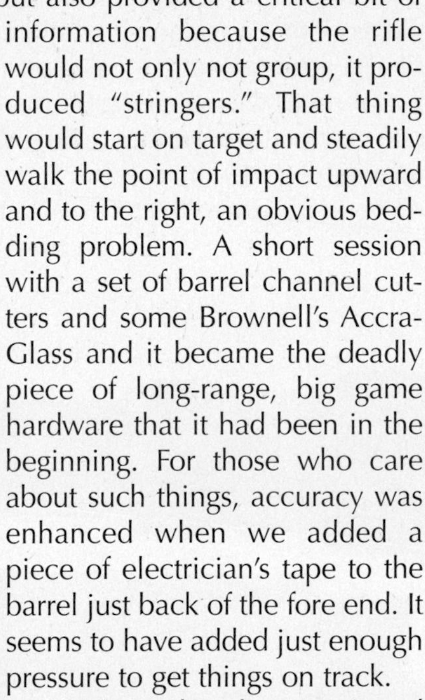

Having already mentioned the Savage big game rifles and their unpleasant trigger pulls, I must state something before progressing—for my money they are one of the best bargains on the market if you are willing to accept them warts and all. A hunting partner who owns a

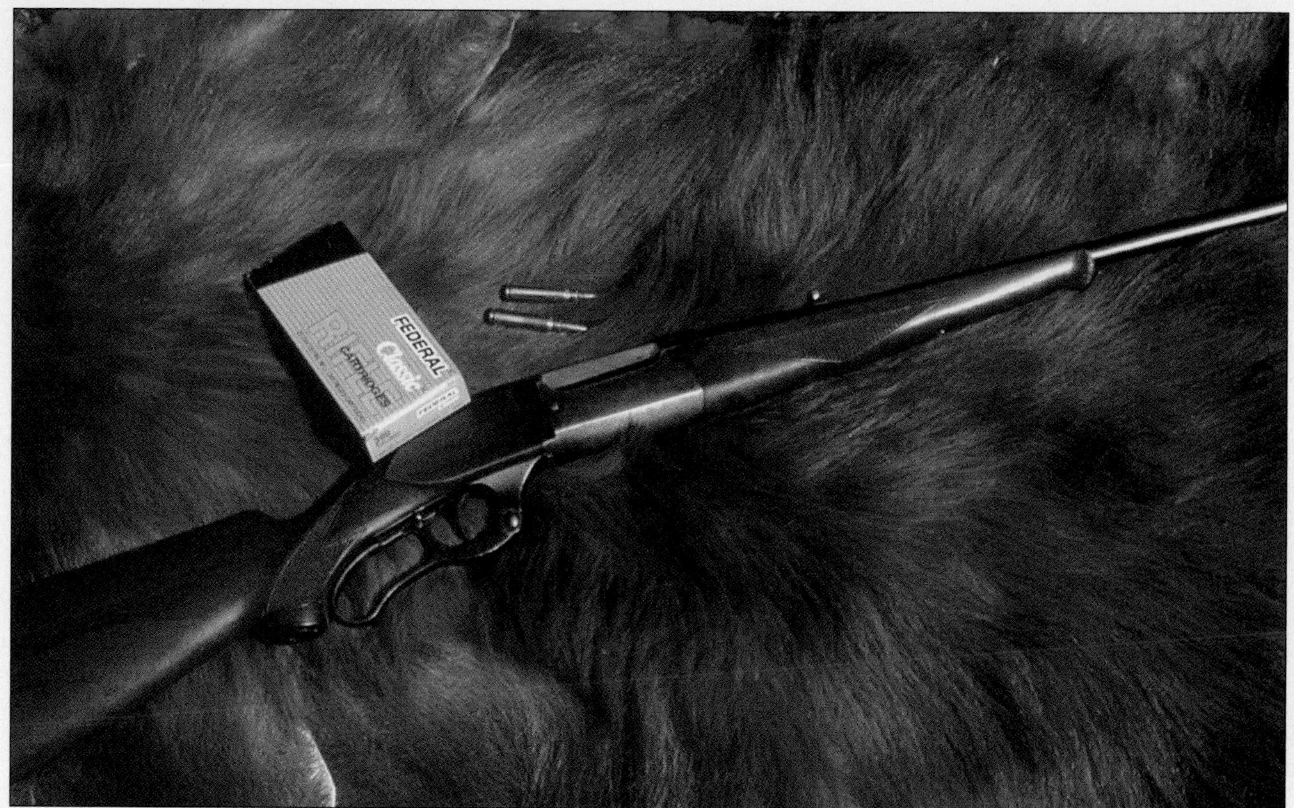

Sometimes you get lucky! This vintage Savage Model 1899 was purchased as nearly inoperable but its only defect was an accumulation of dirt and fouling that made operation of the action difficult.

pawnshop wound up a rack filled with various 110s, 111s and 112s, which are pretty much the same beast with different names. He tossed down what passes for a gauntlet, saying that since I seemed to be able to get the "the ugly things" to perform, why didn't I shoot some targets, sign my name to them, and he would run a special to get rid of the rifles just before hunting season?

In the space of one night I had taken all of them apart, glass bedded the stocks behind the recoil lugs and opened up the area in front of the lugs. Not being a professional target shooter I have no idea why a little gap ahead of the lug makes a difference but it does. Over the next few days we had the triggers adjusted or replaced and he wound up with a waiting list for his accurized Savage rifles. At the same time he encountered a serious drought in merchandise of that type. It seems that the locals who owned such rifles decided to take a second look before getting rid of their guns.

On another occasion the same shop owner called to say that he had taken in a rifle that might be of interest. It was a premium Model 1898 Mauser military rifle in as good a condition as any collector could ever want. Since the 8x57 round is a very efficient and deadly one, I grabbed the thing even though the stock, a beautiful piece of walnut from Reinhart Fajen was split right down the wrist. The idiot who tried to fit the pieces together obviously got tired of trying to do things right and just hogged out any wood that got in his way. The only things hold-

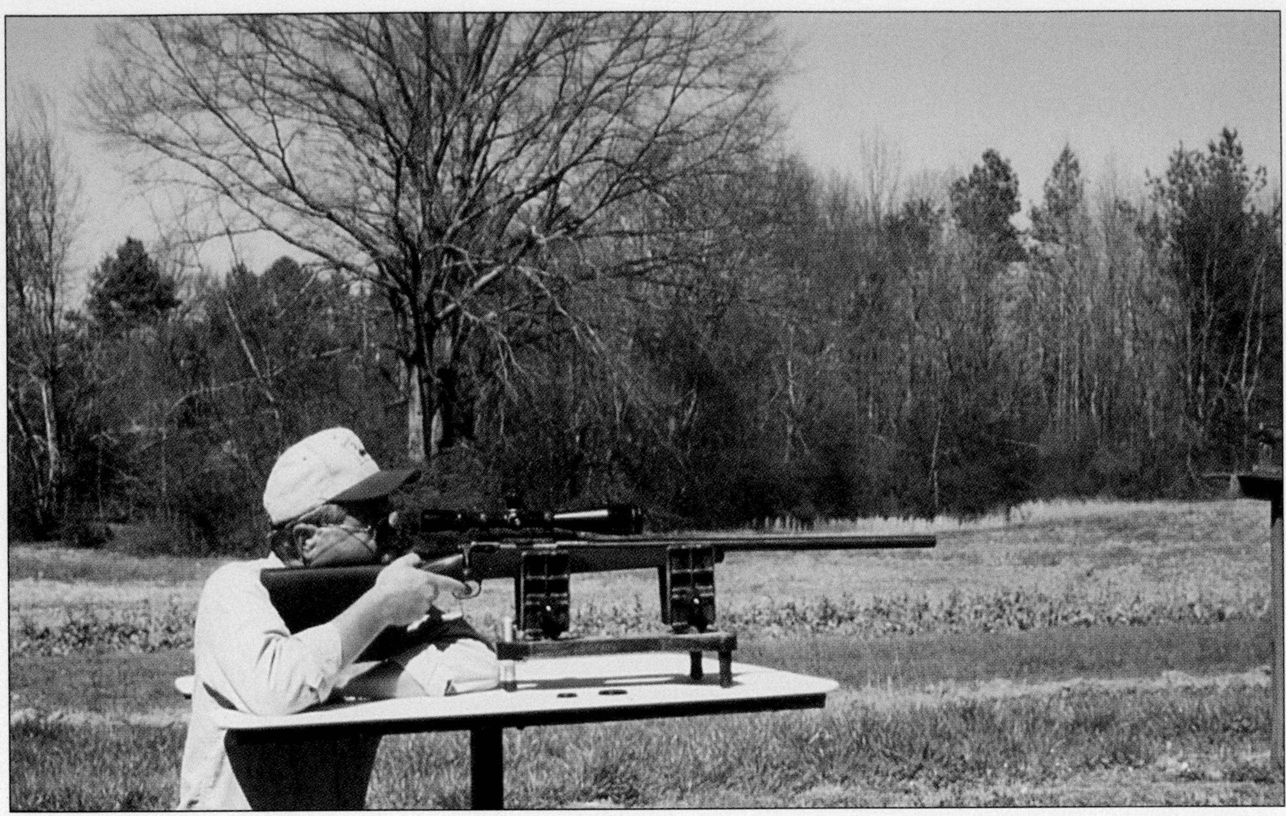

Nicknamed the Sow's Ear by the author's shooting buddies, this .22-250 varmint rifle showed extensive signs of heavy use and abuse. After four evenings worth of cleaning sessions, the Savage 112V proved that it could outperform shooting irons costing several times the price.

ing the stock and barrel together were the screws and when the first shot was turned loose, something had to give. The stock broke.

Once again I went the Accra-Glass route because the stock was just too pretty to scrap. Atop the receiver I stuck a Williams Receiver Sight and oversized front bead and went out to check my new toy. A light, cold and memorable drizzle was falling when I uncased the Mauser, then I realized that the usual supply of targets behind the seat of the pickup had dried up. The only thing available was a gallon paint can in the back that I had neglected to drop in the trash. At 80 paces the first offhand shot flipped the can backwards and I had a favorite woods-walking companion for several years. Using bullets in the 150- to 170-grain class it made numerous whitetails and a couple of elk go "all limber." If that doggone pawnshop owner had not bought it back I would still have the rifle.

When cruising the used gun racks, bear in mind that there are people out there who are dumber than you and I and this sometimes includes the store clerks. Being a chronic firearms shopper I dropped into a midwestern dealer's operation and eyeballed a good-looking, scoped Remington 700 that just somehow did not seem right. The young fellow behind the counter explained that he had sold the rifle but the new owner could not get it to shoot and the store had a 100 percent guarantee on everything they sold and thus it was his duty to make the customer happy. I was 20 miles down the interstate before the answer hit me and I made a U-turn. The scope was mounted 90 degrees off! Horizontal was where vertical was supposed to be! Of course it would not shoot because every adjustment made things worse.

Another visit to a major gun shop resulted in one of my favorite personal rifles. I have an abiding love for the 7x57 Mauser cartridge and a revamped Model 95 Mauser that should have been on the custom rack was sitting out for the masses to look at, dry fire and generally abused. When I asked what was wrong I was informed that it just would not group and therefore did not deserve a substantial price tag.

Closer examination showed that the barrel was a replacement job from Shilen, and friends if anybody tells you that a Shilen barrel will not shoot they have been eating too many of those funny mushrooms. That company never made a bad tube as far as I can find out and has won tons of titles to prove the point.

This one was not a skinny job but rather a medium sporter that had enough weight up front to hold well on distant targets. Another look explained that the 22-inch barrel had been cut back to 20 inches by somebody with a dull hacksaw. There was no indication that either lapping or crowning had ever been attempted. The previous owner must have read too many old articles about sheep rifles or whatever—mountains to be climbed—and so forth. This one may have had the same overall length as Remington's delightful Mountain Rifle and qualified as a semi-custom offering, but it had some serious flaws.

Since my gunsmith pal was off chasing elk, I decided to challenge this one on my own. After using a file to get things reasonably straight—it took nothing more than valve grinding compound on a round-headed screw that seemed to be about the right size—I chamfered the muzzle

Gun shop owners tend to agree that lack of proper cleaning probably causes more shooters to conclude that their barrel is "shot out" than any other cause. All firearms, even the big flame-throwing magnums, take a long time to develop problems if properly cleaned and maintained.

and got rid of the rough, ugly look. Emery paper was used to produce the outside contour but please don't spread that around since the professionals might take exception. The whole job took less than half an hour.

Now if any bullet is perfect for that cartridge it is the 140-grain Sierra, Nosler, or whatever. The 139-grain Hornady is no slouch either, but I digress. All that I had in the rack was a supply of Sierra 160-grain stuff so that is what went into the test work. Using 46 grains of IMR 4350 in the abused Mauser, I easily shot about one and a half minutes of angle every time that I tacked up a target.

The use of valve grinding compound does not end with barrel chamfering. I once watched my gunsmith friend use it to slick up a barrel that had a rusted spot in it thanks to the nest of a mud dauber wasp. The critters are notorious for such, at least in my part of the country, and not long ago I had to imitate my friend's technique on a .22 Contender barrel and the cylinder of a .36 caliber percussion revolver. It takes some time and is not going to guarantee that the thing will shoot as well as ever but it beats trying to deal with the rust.

For those who like the idea of getting a bargain but do not want to get involved in working on a shooting iron, take a tip from a gun shop owner I knew for many years. The first thing that he would do when a new rifle came into the shop was to check the tension on the stock screws. On a fair number of occasions one or more were loose, which can not only play hob with your accuracy, but can eventually wind up causing a cracked stock unless you're using one of the synthetic versions.

If the rifle has a scope attached, check the mount and base screws. If you can detect even a slight wiggle something is not right. Also examine the scope tube carefully. If recoil has caused the thing to slide even a minor bit you can spot marks on the tube. I once had a .300 Winchester magnum that would be remarkable for two or three shots and then things would start going sour. All of the screws were snug and had it not been for a "polished" spot on the tube I would have replaced the scope or gotten rid of the rifle. Instead all that it needed was a bit of tape placed inside the rings. It shot so well after that I picked it to make an African hunt and it performed great.

All of the rifles mentioned here are bolt actions of course. They are easiest to check out and work on, plus, as a rule, they are the most accurate of all the designs. I do not have the expertise to tinker with autoloaders, lever guns and pumps and to date I have not run across a used single-shot that I could not resist.

Ditto on shotguns although I have owned enough secondhand smoothbores to stock a modest store. That is not to say that I have not made some "adjustments" to a stock now and then. When a hunting partner asked me if my Labrador had been chewing on the butt, I gave up that sort of woodworking, but that's another story.

Like a ghost out of nowhere, suddenly he's there and you're face to face with the biggest buck in the county. For a once in a lifetime shot like this, there's just no such thing as overkill. You need all the bullet you can get - one with the knockdown power to drop him right where he stands. That's the idea behind **Federal® Premium® Trophy Bonded Bear Claw**. With its fusion–bonded core, this bullet delivers 95% of its weight during penetration. The bullet jacket features a hard, solid, copper base tapering to a soft, copper nose section for controlled expansion. Trophy Bonded Bear Claw–the ultimate big game bullet.

FOR YOUR NEAREST FEDERAL DEALER AND TO CONTACT US VISIT WWW.FEDERALCARTRIDGE.COM.

NO EXCUSES

FEDERAL Premium CARTRIDGES

THE ULTIMATE BIG GAME BULLET

Deer Hunting Mistakes You'll Want to Make

By Wayne van Zwoll

The kid stumbled into the woods long before daylight, hands clenched tight around his .30-30. He made lots of noise, and when he got to his stand he shivered. Northern Michigan can be cold in November. The smell of frost on leaves came sharp. A grouse thundered off in the distance as dawn seeped through the poplars. What had alarmed it? His thumb played on the hammer, at half cock. He could still feel it.

The deer came after the dull thuds of rifle shots had sifted his way. There were two, a doe and a fawn. By now he was very cold, and he'd put a numb hand in his mackinaw pocket to thaw. His teeth chattered as a breeze throttled up over Lake Superior. The deer moved off. They'd been just a few steps away. His whole body was shaking now. Maybe it wasn't just the cold.

Persevere in bad weather and tough country.

But he couldn't feel his feet, and to get them warm he got off the stump and stamped noisily along the track he'd taken into the woods. Just a few yards, he thought. He pushed through a copse of cedars and suddenly his heart stopped. A huge whitetail buck stood, wide-eyed. How in the world? The hammer spring felt like the rear leaf on a dump truck, the rifle like a lead pipe. The sights shuddered. Miraculously the deer stood, and he yanked the trigger.

The kid's buck was the biggest taken from that camp. Veteran hunters hauled in yearlings or went home without venison. "You won't soon beat that deer," one told him. "Helluva trophy for a first-timer."

Oddly enough, many big deer fall to beginners. It happens often enough that it can hardly be good fortune alone. What do beginners do that experienced hunters don't? Well, they make mistakes. More to the point, they do things that are out of character for the top guns of the deer woods. Some of the bungling is beyond redemption—you'll hardly ever see a big deer if you constantly hunt downwind or trot briskly along the horizon like a fashion model on a runway. On the other hand, some mistakes beget opportunity. Mature bucks get that way by figuring out what hunters are likely to do, then staying a step ahead. An unpredictable hunter is a dangerous hunter and there's nobody more unpredictable than a beginner.

Long ago, after a month of unsuccessful deer hunting, I tramped at dawn along a fence line. My destination was a woodlot that had swallowed a buck I'd missed the day before. Fat chance of finding that deer

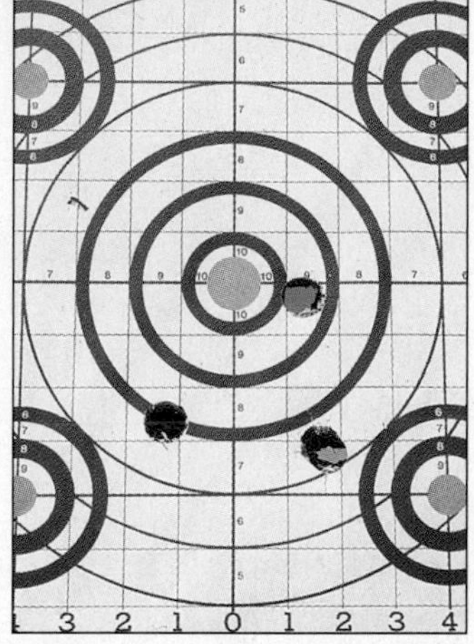

Top:
Small scopes like this 2.5x Leupold are out of vogue, but they give you a brighter sight picture and wider field than powerful scopes do—an advantage in the woods where most deer are shot.

Bottom:
Shoot before season from hunting positions. Tight groups from a bench won't help you kill deer.

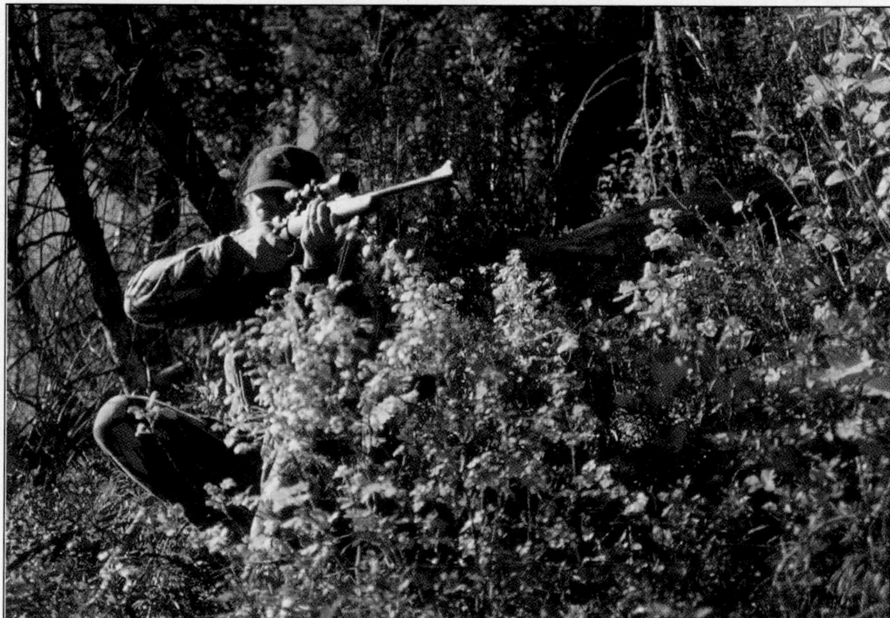

Hunt at noon. Even in the bright light of day, bucks move. Be where they are, near thick cover.

Go where you've seen deer. Wayne spotted this Kansas buck one evening and ambushed him the next morning.

again, I mused. To my astonishment, I spied the animal almost immediately, not in the woods but in a stubble field on its flank. I shot too quickly, missing twice. The deer looked about in mild bewilderment. The third bullet found its mark. I thought myself lucky. Of course, I was lucky, but my direct approach along an open fence line was unexpected. The buck had sneaked through a drive the day before and knew how to dodge bullets, but he hadn't anticipated some tyro marching up across the stubble. He wasn't looking my way and the sonic crack of the bullets didn't tell him which way to flee.

Another time, hunting mule deer, I pushed through a ridgeline thicket after bouncing several deer from its hem. They'd streamed downhill on either side of me and it was pretty evident the thicket was now empty. Imagine my surprise when I emerged on the far side to find a heavy-antlered buck staring at me. He apparently assumed I'd follow the other deer or take the easy path around the thicket. I shot him. With seven points per side, it was obvious that he'd had some time to study

hunters. My behavior, quite by accident, had not been according to the textbook. Deer pattern hunters, just as hunters attempt to pattern deer.

Most popular deer hunting tactics are popular because they work. For the most part you'll do well to hew to the fundamentals: Hunt early and late, move against the wind or crosswind, stay on deer trails, keep the sun to your back, look more than you move, stay clean, pay attention to scrape lines during rut. There are others. But to see deer most hunters don't see, you might also consider doing something offbeat.

For example, the hunter described in the opening paragraphs of this article broke a rule by leaving his stand to calm himself and restore circulation. By so doing, however, he appeared where the big buck did not expect him. No matter how carefully you conceal yourself, no matter how unobtrusive your stand, older bucks may skirt it. Reason: they've encountered hunters in that place or similar places. They've had close calls in the openings that hunters like to watch. Staying to cover, this particular buck happened along just when the young hunter decided to move. The delayed, I-can't-believe-this-is-a-hunter reaction is not uncommon. Sometimes a deer doesn't believe what it sees and waits for a whiff of scent to confirm.

Here are other rules you might want to break. They're not mistakes if you do them on purpose, and they just could show you a deer nobody else will ever see.

Top:
Before season, practice bolting in a second round quickly. You may have to.

Bottom:
In open country, get above deer early, even if you have to climb in the dark.

Offhand is unsteady, but it may be the only position you can use. Practice it!

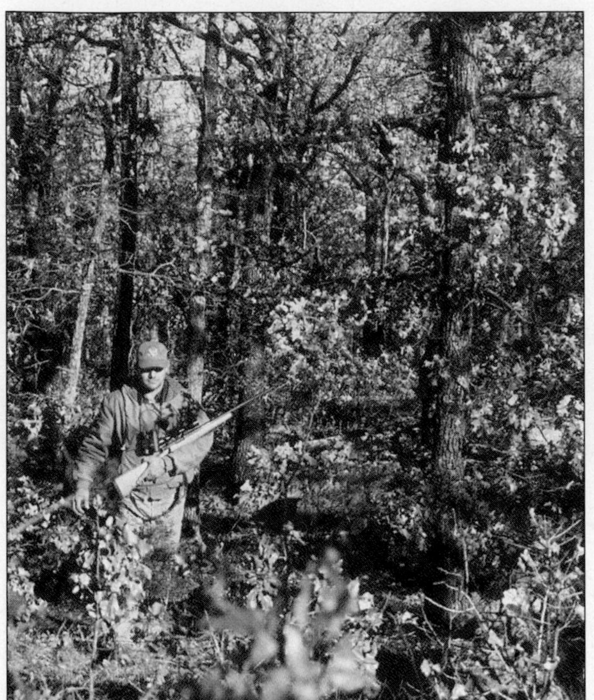

Play novice. Dry leaves may make still-hunting difficult, but deer make noise here too, and if you move like one, you may surprise a buck.

Hunt at noon

Bucks that forage at night often like to get up for a snack or a drink at midday. Sit near a pond or a patch of something a deer might eat. While they usually get adequate moisture from food, deer still enjoy sipping water, especially late in the season, when plants have dried out. And while they're classified as browsers, they relish green wheat and other succulent plants that bloom after fall rains. Also, a noon stakeout can show you bucks disturbed by hunters traveling back to camp for lunch.

Look in little places

A prairie that appears featureless isn't. A patch of brush that looks too small to hide a deer may hold several. Scrutinize cover the way deer do. Concentrate on spots that deer might choose to avoid hunters or shelter themselves from sun, wind or rain. Remember that bucks prefer places with excellent wind coverage, several escape routes and a line of visibility to likely hunter approaches. Glass these places thoroughly instead of mechanically perusing all that's in front of your lenses.

Investigate country that's hard to reach or otherwise deters other hunters. If it's posted, look up the landowner and ask anyway. The worst you can expect is a "No." But a courteous question can open gates. The landowner might suggest another place—or be so taken by your enterprising spirit that he lets you hunt. You could even find that the signs do not apply. Perhaps he's a new owner or once had cattle where hunters shot deer, or put the signs up to discourage an obnoxious neighbor. You don't know until you ask. Posted ground attracts deer.

Hunt roads

That is, walk them—especially abandoned logging trails and little-used farm roads. When snow flies, and even before, deer find these thoroughfares easygoing. So will you. Even if you don't see deer on the road, you'll move more quietly than through leaves and grass. You can spend more time looking around than watching your feet. In the woods, look for deer "highways" to scrapes and forage. A bonus: deer expect commotion where there's typically lots of traffic, and you won't alert them as easily.

Rest often

Hunting hard boosts your chances for a shot, but if you're tired or hungry, you can't be fully "switched on." In cold weather, you need to drink more than you think because the cold suppresses your thirst. Incipient dehydration dulls your senses. Frequent snacks keep your energy high. If you're on stand, leave briefly once in a while to restore circulation and give your eyes a rest. A fresh perspective can show you deer that

This buck didn't expect a hunter to be above him on this steep, remote ridge.

Look in little places. Deer don't take a landscape view; they move on trails and bed near bushes.

might otherwise escape notice. Make sure you're physically in top form at dawn and dusk.

In the woods, keep your field glasses to your eye. Many whitetail hunters think binoculars are useful only in open places. Truth is, they help you pick out details at close range too. A high-quality binocular of modest power is more important than a high-quality riflescope. Focus it for the distance you'll look most often. Look low. Keep the glass still as you move only your eyes. A riflescope needs focusing too. With the tube pointed to the northern sky, turn the eyepiece until the reticule is tack-sharp. You shouldn't have to focus the scope for distance.

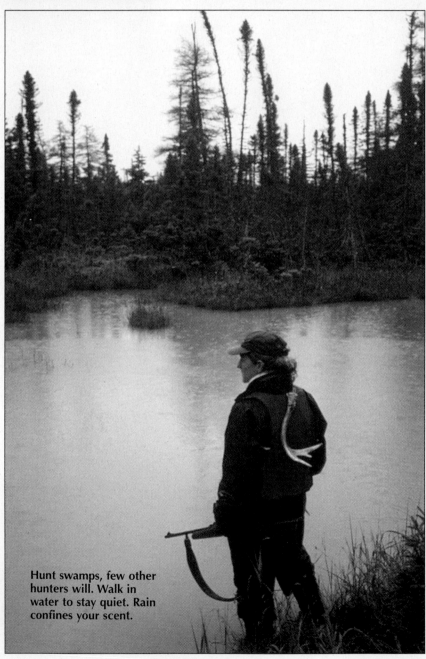

Hunt swamps, few other hunters will. Walk in water to stay quiet. Rain confines your scent.

Hunt the impossible places

Deer sometimes stay where almost any approach is doomed to fail, because of crusty snow, brittle leaves, a lack of approach cover or shifty wind. But if the deer are there and you can't reasonably expect to wait them out, play the low odds. Bucks holed up where a hunter is at a disadvantage don't expect disturbance. They may be less alert and less likely to sneak out far ahead. The closer you get, the better your odds for a shot. Deer may even think that a hunter making lots of noise is a lesser threat. Fool 'em!

Play the novice

Experienced hunters sometimes fail because they put their egos on the line. They dismiss a tactic because it might make them look foolish, or because they're not adept at it. If you want to move through the woods quietly in the dark, mark your trail, whether Leatherstocking did or not. Try rattling up a buck, even if you haven't practiced the technique. Wade into swamps or creeks if the travel there is quieter. Sit near a barnyard if

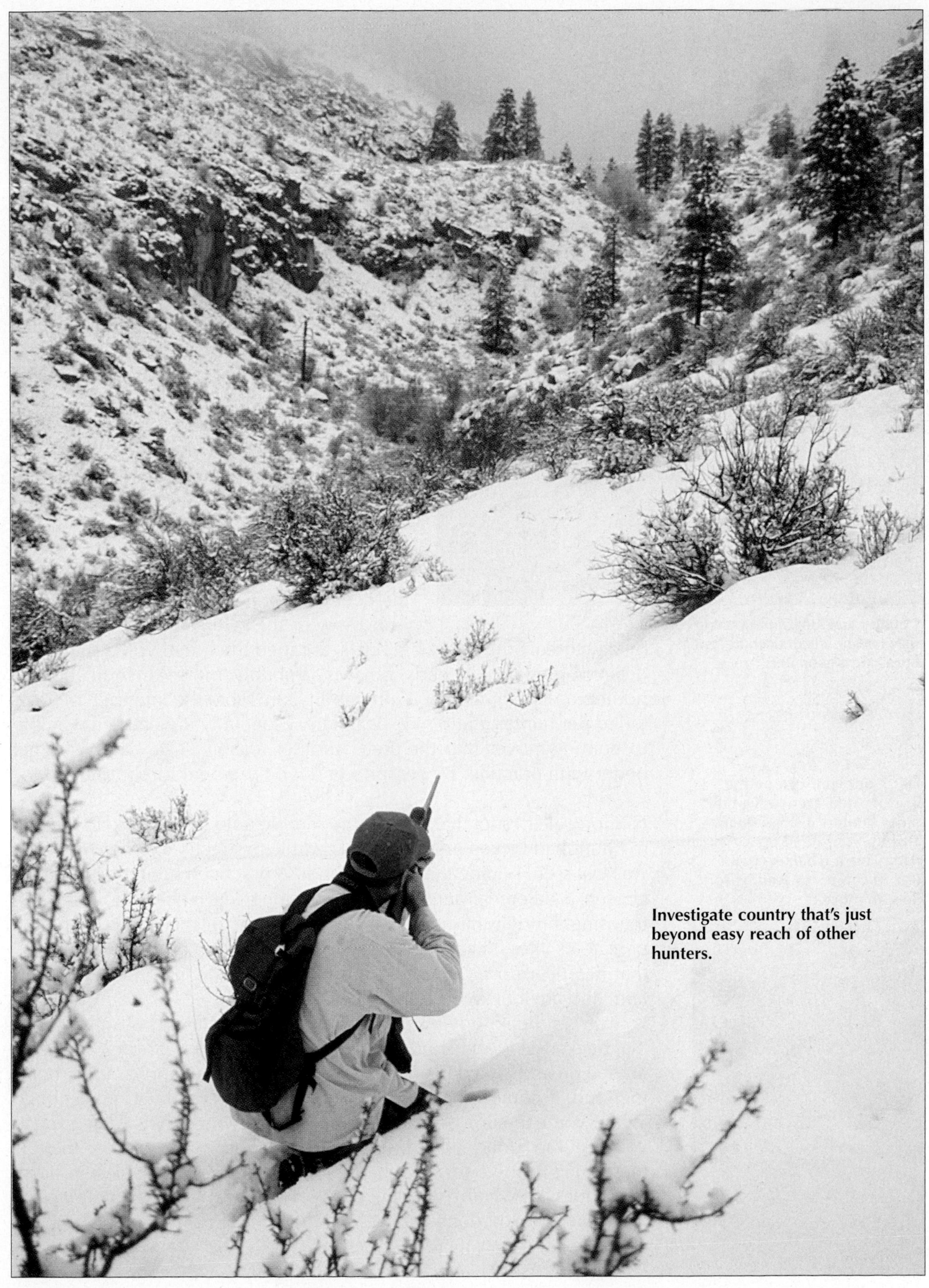

Investigate country that's just beyond easy reach of other hunters.

scrape evidence tells you that's where a buck might visit.

Take advantage of hunter activity to ambush deer. Going where hunters aren't, you may run into a buck doing exactly the same thing. After all, a food plot or a hot doe is of no use to a buck that's stumbled into the sights of some hunter. To mature deer, security is first priority. You're smart to play off the pressure in heavily hunted areas. Climb early to get above waves of hunters pushing deer uphill. Kick through grass fields fringing woodlots, to find bucks tired of dodging bullets in the trees. Sit at the junctures of travel lanes when hunters are probing coverts.

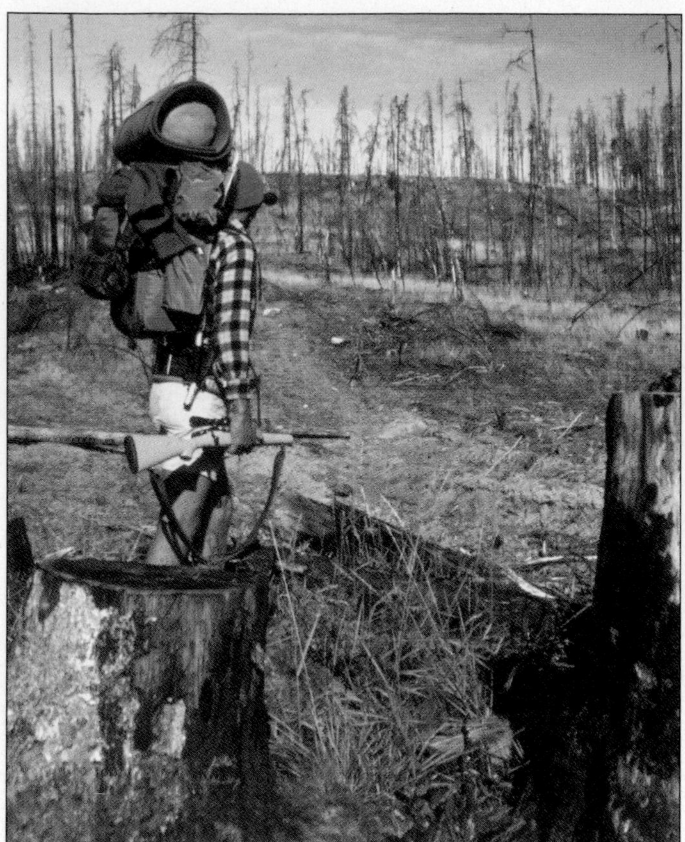

Country that looks inhospitable may harbor lots of deer. Recent burns are a good bet.

Persevere late in the season

In Michigan, where I grew up, about half the deer harvest happened on opening day. And most of the whitetails taken later fell by day three. Still, many big bucks escaped the initial volleys, and the disproportionate kill early on was probably more an indication of hunter traffic than deer vulnerability. In fact, the number of deer killed per hunter afield may peak late, especially if weather favorable to hunting moves into the area. Another reason to stay at it: you get better with practice. By season's end, you're a real threat to deer!

Not long after I shot that buck in the stubble field, it occurred to me that my hunt had lacked any strategy. I'd walked directly to where the deer was last seen, hoping that I'd get a shot. A practiced hunter would have chosen a different route, or sneaked along the fence line instead of traipsing through the field as if he were a tractor mechanic fetching a part. Years later it came to me that mechanics don't threaten deer, and that deer learn over time who is and who isn't dangerous. Act the villain, and any buck will respond accordingly.

Just last week, driving through an orchard, a friend of mine saw a big buck. The deer stood as my amigo stopped the truck, got out, loaded up and aimed his rifle. To the deer, he didn't appear to be hunting (and, it could be argued, his actions hardly qualified as hunting). While you can surprise deer by popping up where they don't expect, you can also fool deer by behaving as if shooting a deer were the furthest thing from your mind. In fact, that's often the best plan in noisy conditions, or where you can't conceal yourself. If there's no place to hide, act as if you don't care.

Don't put your ego on the line. Try new tactics even if other hunters dismiss them. This hunter rattled up a dandy buck when everyone else in camp was waiting for deer to move.

One final tip: Stay ready to shoot as long as you're afield. When the odds of seeing deer dwindle, many hunters relax. A savvy buck will pick that moment to slip away or, if cornered, burst from cover. A few years ago, emerging from a woodlot on a deer drive, a hunter levered the rounds from his Winchester carbine. As the last cartridge fell into his hand, a buck rocketed from a patch of grass at roadside. Another time, as hunters came together at the end of a drive and laid rifles down to break for lunch, a buck sprinted from behind a bush and escaped. Sometimes you'll want to follow the lead of experienced hunters. And sometimes you won't!

In the woods, keep glass to your eye. Binoculars are not just for long-distance viewing!

Hunt early and late, even if it

The Rifles Crash and the Bayonets Flash: Small Arms of the Irish Nationalist Movement

By Kenneth L. Smith-Christmas

Those who frequent Irish pubs and are familiar with Irish ballads will recognize the title of this article in the lyrics of a song, "To the Echo of a Thompson Gun." That rollicking tune gives the impression that Thompson submachine guns were in general use during the 1919-1921 Irish War for Independence, when in fact their only use in that conflict occurred just before the Truce of 1921, and they were not widely used until the Irish Civil War of 1922-1923. Indeed, many arms enthusiasts today encounter confusion when studying the weapons used by both sides of the Irish "troubles," and it is hoped that this article will help clear up the subject. In order to dispel some commonly held misconceptions about the small arms used in the last 50 years of the Irish nationalist movement, it is necessary to start the story some years before the mid-19th Century.

A figure representing young Ireland waves his green harp banner in this patriotic lithograph printed during the 1860s.

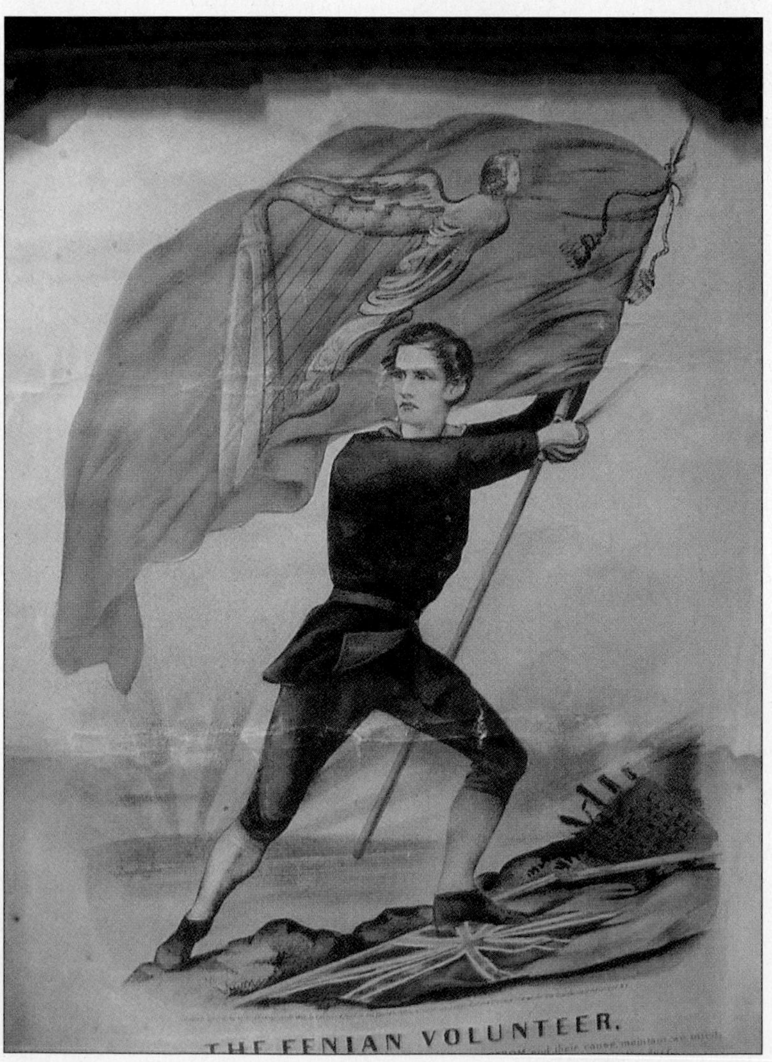

King William III of Great Britain finally established British rule over Ireland at the Battle of the Boyne in 1690. For four preceding centuries, England had periodically acted to extend control over various parts of the island, and for the next century and a quarter, Great Britain totally dominated Ireland deeply alienating most of the native population. For much of this time, interestingly enough, the preferred weapon of both the rulers and the ruled was the blunderbuss, sometimes fitted with a spring bayonet.

In 1798, a coalition of Protestant reformers and Catholic peasants initiated a bloody uprising, pitting pikes against yeomanry carbines and infantry muskets. The rising failed, and the British response was to dissolve the Irish parliament in Dublin and to rule Ireland directly from London. In order to prevent further insurrections, a national police force was formed in 1815. Fully armed with flintlock carbines, this force evolved into the Irish Constabulary by 1836. With recruits drawn from both the Protestant and Catholic population, and operating out of barracks, this force easily dominat-

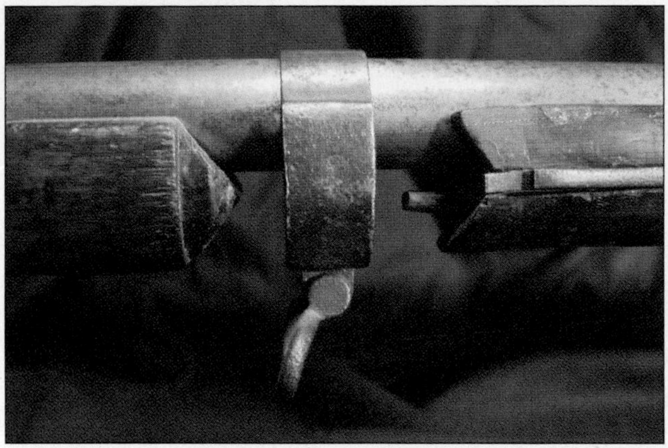

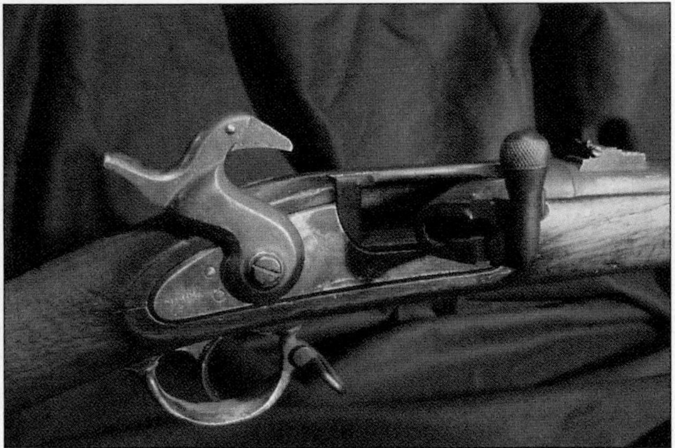

This .58 caliber Needham breechloader—converted from a Bridesburg 1863 rifle musket—was carried by the Fenians during their 1870 invasion of Canada.

ed the Irish scene. By the late 1840s, this paramilitary police force was armed with a unique single-shot cap lock pistol and a double-barreled cap lock Lovell-designed carbine. The carbine was similar to other variants carried by police forces in the spreading Empire, most notably the Cape Colony (South African) Mounted Constabulary. This carbine was unusual, in that it was fitted for a sword bayonet.

With the failure of land reforms under the Young Ireland movement of the 1840s and the devastating effects of the great potato famine, a new movement, known as the Fianna Fail (Irish Gaelic for "Army of Destiny") was founded. The name was anglicized into "Fenian," and this movement soon spread to America, attracting Irish veterans of both the Union and Confederate armies at the end of the Civil War. The Fenians planned to invade Canada, which at that time was a fragmented collection of provinces, and hold it for ransom for Ireland's release from British rule. Prior to forming their forces on the border near Niagara Falls in 1866, the Fenian leaders had purchased thousands of surplus Bridesburg contract military rifle-muskets from the firm of Alfred Jenks in Philadelphia. Despite their initial successes in action against the Canadian militia, the Fenians, many of them Irish-American veterans of the Civil War, were forced to retreat across the border in the face of opposition from the Canadians, British regulars, and pressure from the U.S. government. U.S. federal agents detained most of the Fenians once they re-crossed the border, and their muskets were seized and put in storage.

Bowing to pressure from the Irish-American voting bloc in 1868, the government returned the weapons to the Fenians, who promptly had them converted into Needham pattern breechloaders in a former railway engine shop in Trenton, New Jersey. Many of these Bridesburg-Needhams were altered so that they could be secretly shipped to points along the border in preparation for another incursion into Canada. This alteration consisted of cutting the wooden fore end under the middle band, and pinning the sections with a wooden dowel. The musket could then be disassembled and shipped in small containers, no longer than the length of the barrel. A short-lived Fenian raid near St. Albans, Vermont, in 1870 also failed, and the Fenians' weapons were once again confiscated by the U.S.

This brass property disk, dated 1904 and marked to the RIC, is affixed to the butt stock of a British Enfield .303 caliber bolt-action carbine issued for police use. The impressed mark to the right is a crown acceptance stamp.

government, which sold them as surplus many years later.

A Fenian "rising" in Ireland in the 1860s was quickly quelled. In appreciation for their service in suppressing the rising, Queen Victoria granted the title "Royal" to the police, so from 1867, the force was known as the Royal Irish Constabulary, commonly referred to as the "R.I.C." The response to the latest uprising on the part of the British Crown was to provide the constabulary with the most modern weapon available, the Webley center-fire revolver. The new revolver, a compact .450-caliber double-action weapon was dubbed the "RIC" Webley. While only those revolvers actually issued to the RIC were marked as such on the front of the frame, thousands were produced. With its success, Webley began its rise to the forefront of British handgun manufacturers.

The RIC were also rearmed with the most modern breechloading shoulder arm in the British service, the .577 caliber Snider-Enfield. Those rifles issued to the RIC had their barrels shortened to a length of 27 inches. RIC constables carried these carbine-length conversions up to the turn of the century. Later, smoothbore versions of the familiar Martini-Henry rifle were acquired to supplement the Sniders, to be used for guard purposes and riot control. The Martini-Henry smoothbores, were fitted with rudimentary rear sights and fired shot-shell cartridges. Those Martini-Henrys carried by the RIC had the appropriate markings stamped into a brass disk inset into the butt stock. The property disks were also used on subsequent models of RIC shoulder arms.

In 1905, the RIC decided to replace its Snider-Enfields and Martini-Henrys with .303 caliber bolt-action carbines, placing an initial order for 10,000 carbines from the Royal Small Arms factory at Enfield. For RIC purposes the decision was made to adapt the standard British cavalry carbine to a new configuration. A major exception to the cavalry carbine configuration was the rifle fore end and bayonet lug, which was installed for the M1888 knife bayonet. The carbines also carried the RIC brass disk, and all of them were stamped on the side of the stock with the date of their conversion. Subsequently, several hundred Lee-Metford carbines were also converted to the RIC configuration.

In 1905 the Royal Irish Constabulary issued Enfield .303 caliber bolt-action carbines based on the standard British cavalry carbine. The shorter weapons were handier for a constable mounted on a bicycle.

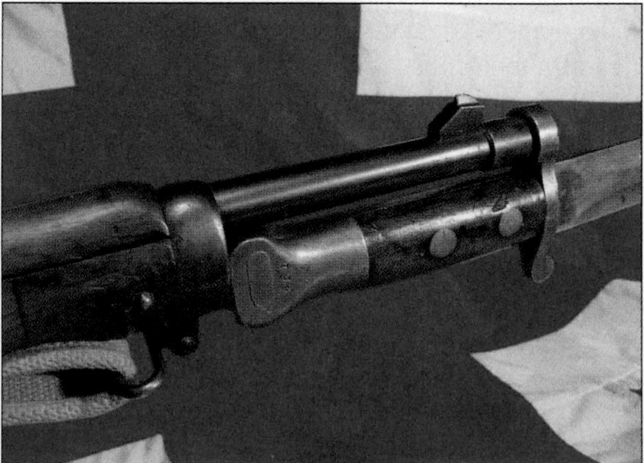

Youthful cadets of the Royal Irish Constabulary pose outside their barracks at Curragh in 1920. Attacks by the IRA and pressure from neighbors had forced the resignation of large numbers of experienced constables.

By the late 19th century the movement for home rule in Ireland was gaining momentum, and with each passing year, it looked as if it would become a reality. The concept would allow all of Ireland to enjoy the same status as the overseas dominions, notably Canada and Australia, instead of being ruled directly from London. This movement was an anathema both to the mostly Protestant landowners throughout Ireland (a group known as the Anglo-Irish) and to the Protestant Scots-Irish population of the industrialized northernmost province of Ulster. Both groups feared subjugation by a largely agrarian Catholic population if a system of home rule by popular vote was instituted, and politicians on both sides played the religious factions off against each other. However, with a liberal government in power at Westminster, home rule was practically assured passage.

In 1912, the Ulster Protestants, commonly referred to as "Orangemen" from their historic association with King William III—the Prince of Orange—formed their own paramilitary organization, the Ulster Volunteer Force (UVF), and vowed to resist home rule by force. By the thousands, the members of the UVF signed a covenant, in which they pledged to fight any attempt to give home rule to Ireland – symbolically many signed it in their own blood. An illegal shipment of arms consisting mainly of M1904 7.92mm Steyr-Mannlicher rifles was secretly run into Ulster from Germany and distributed to the membership, along with quantities of M1888 German Mauser "Commission" rifles and obsolete Italian 10.4mm Vetterli-Vitali magazine rifles. The

Mannlichers were overruns from a Rumanian contract and, with minor differences and the addition of a UVF stock stamping, were nearly identical to the 6.5mm Rumanian-issue rifles of the First World War. The Ulster Volunteers carried a variety of other arms, such as .303 Martini-Henry carbines and Lee-Enfield rifles, which had been covertly obtained in Great Britain.

In response to the Ulster movement, a pro-home rule organization, the Irish Volunteers, was formed in Dublin, and men and women throughout the other three provinces of Ireland joined in anticipation of a possible civil war. In 1914, on the eve of World War I, the Volunteers also received a shipment of obsolete M1871 German Mauser rifles from Hamburg, Germany, shipped aboard a private yacht. The guns were landed at the seaport town of Howth and were unloaded by Irish Boy Scouts, a new organization with political leanings toward the home rule faction. While the British government had winked at the earlier UVF importation of rifles, British troops intercepted Irish Volunteers moving the rifles from Howth into Dublin and opened fire killing several. At the same time, a small shipment of the same type of Italian Vetterli-Vitali rifles that the UVF had smuggled into Ulster was landed at the harbor of Kilcoole, some miles south of Howth.

Men of the Irish Republican Army defend the General Post Office in Dublin during the Easter Rising of 1916. Most were armed with German 1871 Mauser "Howth" rifles.

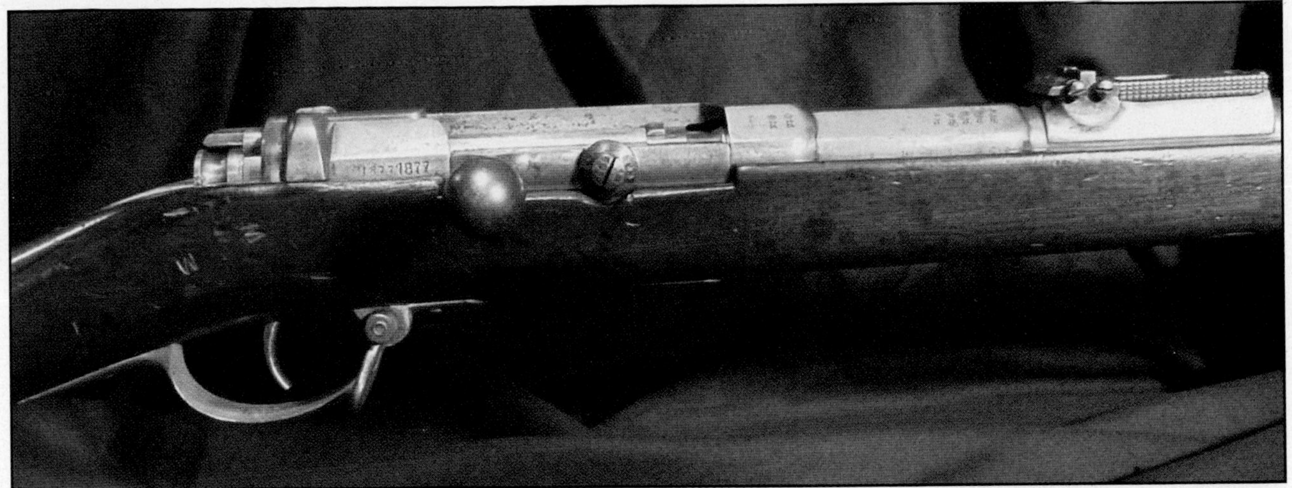

The German M7/84 rifle, carried by the IRA, fired an 11mm blackpowder cartridge and used an 8 round tubular magazine.

By midsummer of 1914, with conservative and liberal politicians at loggerheads over the future of Ireland, Great Britain was poised on the brink of a civil war that could threaten the very existence of the Empire itself. However, with the outbreak of World War I, both sides of the Irish question took a conciliatory course and agreed to shelve the settlement of the "Irish Question" until the end of hostilities. Over the next two years, Irishmen drawn from all ranges of the political spectrum volunteered and served with distinction in the British military, with the Ulster Volunteer Force enlisting en masse in 1914. The Ulstermen were formed into the 36th ("Ulster") Division, which was practically wiped out on the Somme in 1916.

During this period, there was a split in the ranks of the Volunteers. While the majority waited for home rule to be granted at the successful conclusion of the war, a small group dreamed of outright independence and the establishment of an Irish republic. By 1916, this group had gained enough strength to convince themselves that an insurrection against the war-weary and overextended British military would, with German assistance, force Britain to simply give up and grant independence to Ireland. The Germans, locked in a death struggle with Great Britain, took the opportunity to send 20,000 captured Russian M1891 7.62mm Mosin-Nagant rifles and a dozen Maxim machine guns to Ireland on a clandestine "mystery" ship in April 1916. The stocks on these rifles were stamped with both Russian and German markings. Surprised by the British Navy, the German captain scuttled his ship, with all of the arms going to the bottom of Cork harbor. Despite this setback, a splinter group of the Irish Volunteers (now calling themselves the "Irish Republican Army") took and held several key points in Dublin on Easter Monday, 1916, in league with a socialist trade-union organization, the Irish Citizen's Army. After a week of bitter street fighting, the rising was put down by reinforcements from England.

During the fighting, one of the most noticed leaders was the Countess Constance Markievicz, a member of an Anglo-Irish family from Sligo, the Gore-Booths. She carried a commercial 7.63mm M1896 Mauser semi-automatic "broomhandle" pistol, a weapon that came to figure prominently in the coming strife. Several other Republicans carried broomhandles, and one used his to great effect in

The "Royal Irish Constabulary" .450 revolver appeared in 1867, in response to the Fenian risings in Ireland.

the defense of the Mount Street bridge, arguably the most notable success of the insurrection. Known in Britain and Ireland as "Peter the Painter" after a notorious anarchist whose followers carried them, Mauser "broomhandle" pistols in both 7.63mm and 9mm became a favorite weapon of the IRA.

Although initially despised by the common people, many of whom had relatives fighting overseas with the British Army, the insurrectionists were elevated to hero status as a result of British mistakes in judgment and strategy in the aftermath of the Easter rising. By the end of World War I, the Republicans were in full rebellion in the three southern provinces of Leinster, Munster, and Connaught. The War for Irish Independence lasted from 1919 to 1921, with most of the fighting being a shadowy brutal war of ambushes, assassinations, reprisals, and counterreprisals. Few citizens were safe from the excesses of both sides. British troops in Ireland were armed with both the Short Magazine Lee-Enfield (SMLE) rifle, while the officers carried the standard Mark VI .455 Webley revolver. The plain-clothes detectives of the RIC carried .38 caliber Webley pocket revolvers.

Most of the RIC constables had resigned under pressure from their neighbors or out of disgust with the tactics of the British government, and British authorities devised a new system to replace them. The Crown recruited ex-enlisted men into the RIC, and they quickly became known as "Black and Tans" because of the assortment of Army khaki and dark green RIC coats and breeches they wore. The RIC was also augmented by the services of "Auxiliary Cadets," ex-officers who carried specially-designed short-barreled Mark VI Webley revolvers, in addition to their SMLE rifles. At this time, the RIC was also armed with Winchester lever-action rifles and M1897 Winchester riot shotguns. Long Lee-Enfields, the now-obsolescent magazine rifles that had been used by the British Army during the Boer War, were also pressed into service. These long Lee-Enfields were also marked with the standard brass disk, bearing "RIC" markings. While these long rifles were unsuited for police work, especially for constables on bicycles, they were used effectively by the Black and Tans and the Auxiliaries, when patrolling in trucks or armored cars. Both groups gained legendary notoriety in the southern three provinces.

Many IRA members used weapons captured from the RIC and the British Army, in addition to civilian sporting weapons stolen or commandeered from the owners of large estates. Several shipments of pistols were also acquired from Germany, including M1906 Navy Lugers and military M1912 Mauser broomhandles. A famous shootout in Dublin featured a long-barreled Luger in the hands of the celebrated republican, Sean Tracey. Both Colt and Smith & Wesson revolvers in

The compact .38 caliber Webley revolver *(above left)* was issued to RIC detectives and plain-clothes officers. Uniformed constables and men of the "Black and Tans" and the Auxiliaries carried the larger .455 Webley Mark VI short-barreled pistol *(above)*.

.455 caliber are also known to have been carried by both sides.

With the adoption of a truce in 1921, the British forces withdrew from the southern three provinces, but as a condition of the truce, reinforced the RIC in Ulster. The peace treaty, adopted by a slim majority of the insurgents, stipulated that Ulster would determine its own course, either with the new Irish Free State, or remain part of the United Kingdom. The question of whether to accept the partition of Ireland plunged the south into a bitter and bloody civil war, with former comrades of the IRA now fighting each other. Great Britain supported the Free State forces, supplying weapons and equipment and the Short Magazine Lee-Enfield (SMLE) Mark III rifles, supplied to the Free State troops, were marked with an "FF" in a flaming circle on the breech, the same Fianna Fail name used by the original Fenians. The Thompson submachine guns that had been smuggled into the country in 1921, and had seen very brief debut in an attack on a British troop train just before the truce, were now being used with a vengeance by the antagonists. By 1923, the Free State forces had prevailed.

The former leader of the outlawed IRA, Eamon de Valera, was voted into the presidency in the late 1930s and declared the Irish Free State a republic in 1948. After years of struggling with its economic and social programs, the Republic of Ireland is now a prosperous and vibrant country. Tourists have to look hard to find obvious mementos of the centuries of strife, although reminders of recent bombings and burnings are sadly still very much in evidence in Northern Ireland. For the past 35 years, Armalite and Kalashnikov rifles have dueled with British SLR rifles over the fate of this troubled land, and one can only hope that these weapons will one day be reduced to the status of the historical curiosities that have been examined here.

PASS ALONG THE TRADITION
Learn the thrill of speed
The hunter who pursues grouse or woodcock needs a gun that can be carried all day and then move like lightning to a fast-disappearing target.
The Franchi Veloce Squire is for those who never stop chasing the most elusive game.
It's a no-compromise speedster whose very name means "fast." An aluminum receiver, reinforced on the breech face with steel, is fitted with 20-ga. and 28-ga. barrel sets that keep weight a just 5 1/2 pounds. It's no slowpoke in the looks department, with select walnut stock, gold-embellished game scenes, a rugged monobloc, even a filigreed top lever.
Veloce: learn the thrill of speed!
VELOCE SQUIRE & VELOCE
THINK SAFETY!
NEW! Veloce Squire™ 28-ga. and 20-ga. set
Veloce™ English Stock
Franchi
Veloce Squire™ two gauge set
Imported by BenelliUSA.
For a catalog or nearest dealer, phone: 301-283-6981
WWW.FRANCHIUSA.COM

Shotgunning

By John M. Taylor

Originally, shotguns were simply smoothbored muskets loaded with "findings" that were mainly pebbles and small bits of iron. Shooters would sneak up on game and shoot it sitting on the ground. Today, there are only two instances in which a shotgun is actually aimed: when shooting slugs at big game—white-tailed deer and black bear—and spring gobblers, otherwise we're shooting at flying birds, clays or running rabbits. As shotguns evolved, shooting flying birds became accepted as sport, and today, when filling the pot to feed our family is much less of a concern, shotgunning has become a pastime that involves hand and eye coordination and practice and is a great deal of fun. Shotguns, too, have evolved from simple pot-fillers into a fairly complicated maze of designs. In this article we'll traverse that maze and, instead of finding the proverbial cheese, perhaps we can unravel some of the techno speak that has now become part of shotgunning.

Actions

Shotguns are available in six basic actions: single barrel, side-by-side, over/under, bolt-action, pump and semi-automatic. Although inexpensive, let's dismiss the single barrels and bolt-actions as being too slow for good wing shooting. That leaves us with the doubles and repeaters.

A bouquet of mallards on a cold morning bagged by this duck hunter's gas-operated semi-automatic.

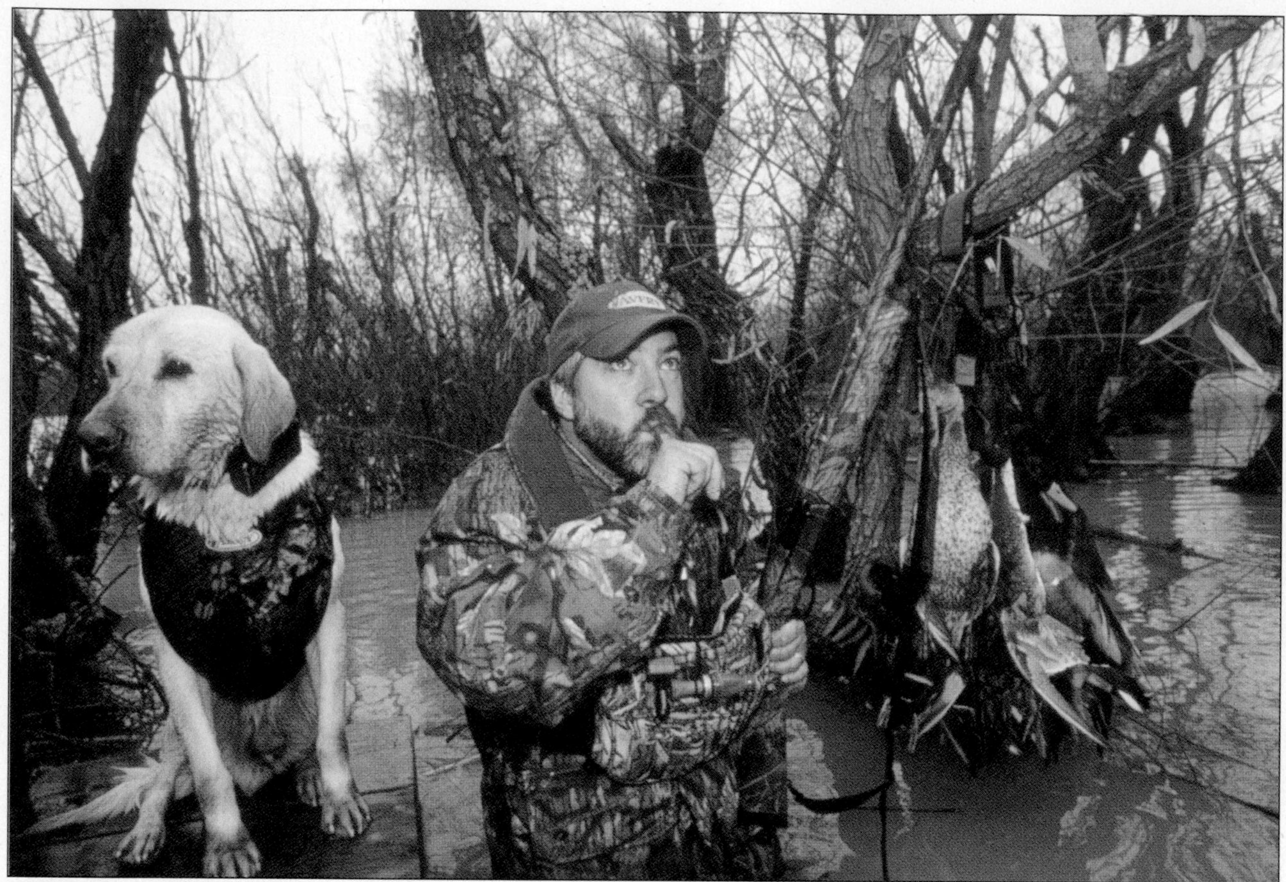

Calling 'em in is Avery Outdoors' Bili Cooksey. He favors a gas-operated semi-auto for his duck shooting.

As the modern shotgun evolved, the side-by-side was the first shotgun capable of firing more than one shot. They currently come in all price ranges from inexpensive, utilitarian guns to exquisite custom-made game guns produced by the likes of James Purdey and Holland & Holland in Britain and Ithaca Classic Doubles on these shores. During the last bit of the 19th century, the over/under also came into being. First by the august British firm of Boss & C., but now by manufacturers such as Ruger, Perazzi, Beretta and many others. As a clay-target and field gun, the over/under is an excellent choice. Like double, it offers the shooter the instant choice of two different chokes and excellent handling.

In 1905, firearm genius John Browning introduced his Automatic-5, recoil-operated semi-automatic shotgun. It harnessed the forces of recoil to cycle the action, sold in the millions, and gave hunters five shots with no more effort than pulling the trigger. Later limited to three shots by law, the Browning semi-auto is reliable and offers an extra shot that the twin-tubed guns don't provide, although through one choke. However, the Browning's rule wasn't undisputed. Following the end of World War Two, returning GIs had become very familiar with semi-automatic weapons, and firearm manufacturers were more than happy to accommodate them by adapting the gas-operating system used in machine guns and semi-automatic rifles to shotguns. High Standard's Flight King was the first, but Remington the most successful. Like its recoil-operated brother, the gas-operated semi-auto offers three or more shots with but the touch of a finger, but even more endearing is that the gas-operated semi-auto spreads out the sensation of recoil, making it seem more pleasant to shoot.

Perhaps the best loved, and certainly most versatile shotgun is the pump-action. The first pump-action shotgun was produced in 1882 by Christopher Spencer of Civil War repeating rifle fame, and later manufactured and sold by Francis Bannerman in New York. However, the introduction of the Browning-designed Winchester Model 1893, and then the 1897, quickly eclipsed the clumsy and heavy Spencer. Since then, the Winchester Model 12, Remington 31 and venerable 870 Wingmaster have set the standard for pump guns. Not only can these guns easily shoot any cartridge for which they are chambered, pumps point very well. I have a friend—a notoriously bad shot—who has become quite a good shot by simply buying and shooting a Benelli Nova, which, like most pumps, handles and points well. The slight weight-forward balance of a good pump makes for good marksmanship. Also, the time required to manually cycle the action allows the mind to reset, and redirects concentration back to the target. The thought that a pump is slower to cycle than a semi-auto is quickly dispelled by watching exhibition shooter Tom Knapp break a whole stack of clays with a pump-action shotgun before any hits the ground.

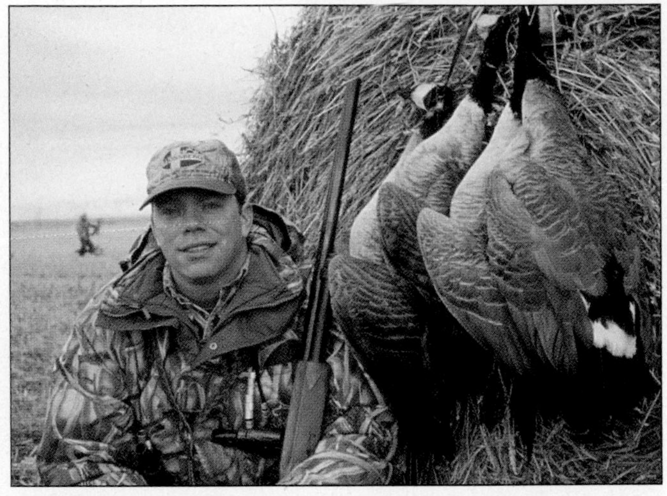

Mossberg's VP of marketing Dennis Kendall with a nice bag of Canada geese bagged in Alberta with a Mossberg 500, which celebrated its 40th anniversary in 2002.

The author in Manitoba with a snow and eagle-headed blue goose he bagged with a side-by-side; in this case, a classic Winchester Model 21.

Recommended Loads for Various Game

GAME	SHOT	RECOMMENDED SHOT SIZE	CHOKE	GAUGE
Large Geese	Steel	T, BBB, BB	Modified	10, 12
Large Geese	Bismuth	BB, 2	Mod., Full	10, 12
Large Geese	Tung./Polymer	1	Mod., I. Mod., Full	12
Small Geese	Steel	BB, 1	Mod., I. Mod.	10, 12
Small Geese	Bismuth	2, 4	Mod., I. Mod., Full	12
Small Geese	Tung./Polymer	1, 2	Mod., I. Mod., Full	12
Ducks	Steel	1, 2, 3	I.C., Mod., I. Mod.	10, 12, 20
Ducks	Bismuth	2, 4, 5, 6	I.C., Mod.	10, 12, 20
Ducks	Tung./Polymer	2, 3, 4, 5, 6	I.C., Mod.	12, 16, 20
Turkey	Lead	4, 5, 6	Full, Extra Full	10, 12, 16, 20
Pheasant	Steel	4	I.C., Mod., Full	12, 20
Pheasant	Lead	4, 5, 6, 7½	I.C., Mod., Full	12, 16, 20
Pheasant	Bismuth	2, 4, 6	I.C., Mod., Full	12, 20
Pheasant	Tung./Polymer	4, 5, 6	I.C., Mod., Full	12, 16
Grouse/Partridge	Lead	6, 7½, 8	I.C., Mod.	12, 16, 20, 28
Woodcock	Steel	4, 6, 7	I.C., Mod.	12, 16, 20
Woodcock	Bismuth	6, 7½	Skeet, I.C., Mod.	12, 16, 20, 28
Woodcock	Tung./Polymer	6	Skeet, I.C., Mod.	12, 16
Woodcock	Lead	6, 7½, 8	Skeet, I.C., Mod.	12, 16, 20, 28
Snipe/Rail	Steel	6, 7	Skeet, I.C.	12, 20
Snipe/Rail	Bismuth	6, 7½	Skeet, I.C.	12, 16, 20, 28
Snipe/Rail	Tung./Polymer	6	Skeet, I.C.	12, 16, 20
Quail	Lead	7½, 8	Skeet, I.C.	12, 16, 20, 28
Quail	Bismuth	7½	Skeet, I.C.	12, 16, 20, 28
Quail	Tung./Polymer	6	Skeet, I.C.	12, 16, 20
Dove	Lead	7½, 8	I.C., Mod., I. Mod.	12, 16, 20, 28
Dove	Steel	6, 7	Skeet, I.C., Mod.	12, 20
Dove	Bismuth	7½	I.C., Mod., I. Mod.	12, 16, 20, 28
Dove	Tung./Polymer	6	I.C., Mod., I. Mod.	12, 16, 20
Rabbit	Lead	4, 5, 6	I.C., Mod.	12, 16, 20, 28, .410
Squirrel	Lead	4, 5, 6	Mod., I. Mod., Full	12, 16, 20, 28, .410

Choke Abreviations:
I.C. = Improved Cylinder; Mod. = Modified; I. Mod. = Improved Modified

The above are based on manufacturers' recommendations and experience. In any situation, a more open choke is probably the best choice since it provides a little more room for error. Only in the case of turkey should extremely tight full chokes be used, and in this case they are highly recommended to put the maximum number of pellets possible into the small, tennis-ball-size head.

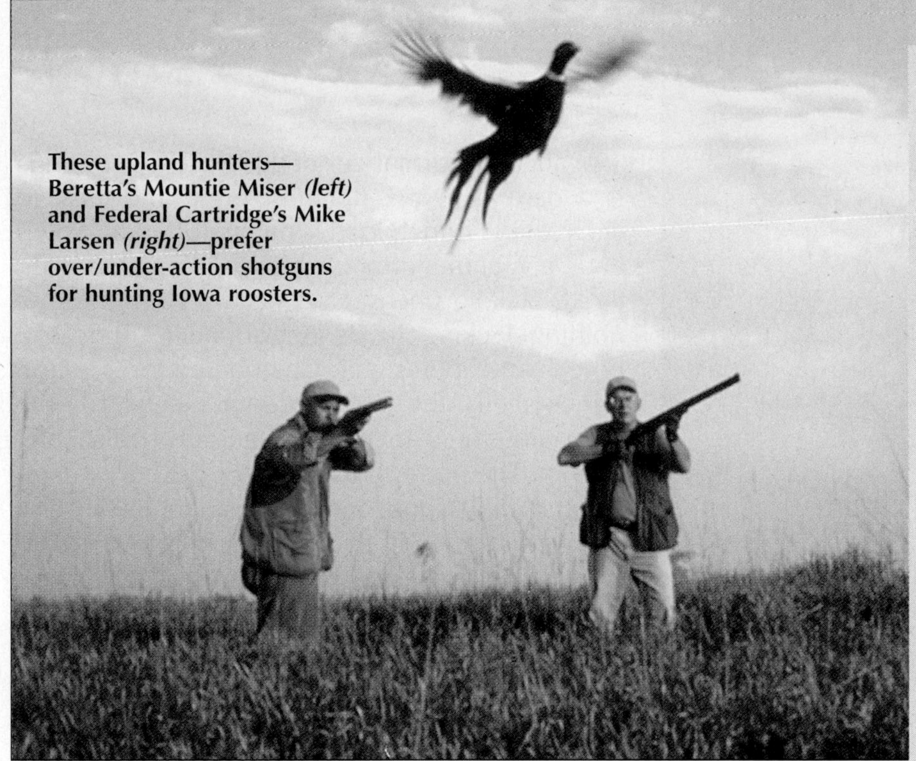

These upland hunters—Beretta's Mountie Miser *(left)* and Federal Cartridge's Mike Larsen *(right)*—prefer over/under-action shotguns for hunting Iowa roosters.

Gauges

As shotguns evolved, there needed to be a method to standardize them from gunmaker to gunmaker. How this system came about seems lost in history, but originally, shotgun bores—and indeed most smoothbore weapons—were designated by the number of equally sized balls that would tightly pass through the bore that could be cast from one pound of lead. The easiest to visualize is the 16 gauge, whose bore will accommodate 16, one-ounce lead balls. The 12 gauge takes 12, etc. The only exception is the .410, which is a caliber, and if designated as a gauge would be a 67 gauge. Today, we commonly use shotguns in 10, 12, 16, 20, 28 and .410-bore. The 10 is solely a waterfowl and turkey gun. The 12 is the most versatile in that when chambered for the various lengths of shells made, can be matched to about any game or clay-target application imaginable. The standard U.S. chambers for all the gauges, save the .410, are 2¾ inches. However, some 10- and 12-gauge shotguns are chambered for 3½-inch shells, and more commonly the 12-gauge can be chambered for 3-inch cartridges. Both are magnums, and intended for waterfowl and turkey. Cartridges shorter than the shotgun's chamber length can be safely fired, but never longer shells than those for which the shotgun is chambered. British-made 12-gauge shotguns are most often chambered for 2½-inch shells and a few for a tiny 2-inch shell. The 16 gauge suffers from lack of ammunition selection, primarily because, while a wonderful upland gun, its sales don't justify manufacturers producing a wide variety of ammo. The 2¾-inch chambered 20 gauge is a great upland and dove gun, but very limited for waterfowl. The 3-inch chambered 20 gauge is a good idea on paper, but the shells are a ballistic bastard, and although it promises

Shot

For generations, shotgunners used only one type of shot—lead—and the main decision was which size. As early as the 1940s, however, biologists began to identify lead poisoning in waterfowl and ultimately nontoxic shot was mandated for hunting waterfowl nationwide. Nontoxic shot is also specified for upland hunting on many state and federal lands that host waterfowl. The main alternative shot metal was and remains soft steel. With shot nearly as hard as the gun barrel, problems were initially encountered when steel shot was fired in older shotguns. Today, newer tubes are manufactured with steel shot in mind. Still, many hunters wished to shoot their older shotguns.

The first nontoxic alternative to steel shot was bismuth. The prime ingredient of patent stomach remedies, bismuth is the heaviest of the heavy metals and the only one that is nontoxic. Bismuth shot was exhaustively tested and finally approved as a nontoxic shot. Because bismuth is only slightly harder than lead, it became the primary choice for those wishing to hunt waterfowl with their Parkers, A. H. Foxes, and Belgian-made Brownings.

Shortly after bismuth hit the market, the British Kent Cartridge Company developed a viable nontoxic shot using tungsten/polymer technology. This pellet blends micro-fine tungsten into a stiff but elastic polymer that is an ideal candidate for shooting through older shotguns.

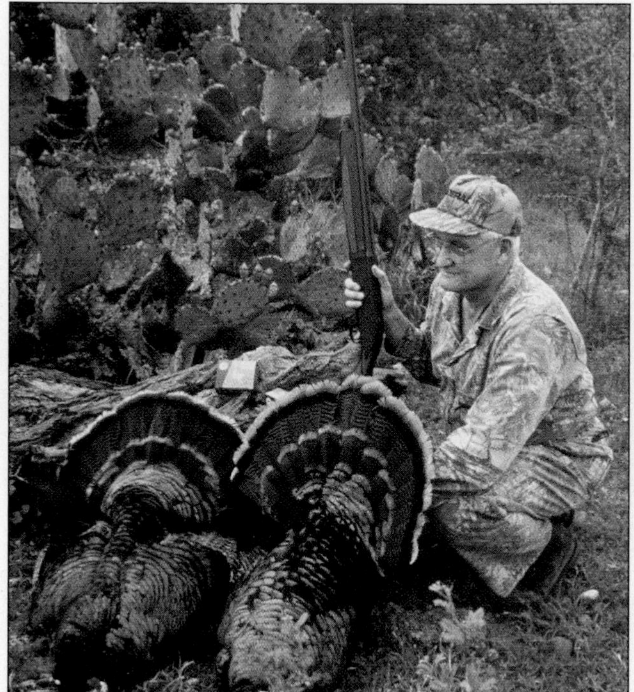

Federal Cartridge's Bill Stevens with two fine Rio Grande gobblers he called in and shot with a Beretta Xtrema. This gas-operated shotgun is designed to shoot extra-heavy loads used to hunt waterfowl and turkey.

12 gauge performance, does not. The 28 gauge is a darling in the uplands: Light and easy to carry, the 3/4-ounce load is plenty for quail, doves and any game-farm bird alive. I've shot wild South Dakota pheasants with my 28 and found nothing lacking in its performance. The .410 bore is an expert's gun. Chambered for 2½- and 3-inch shells, the former are for skeet while the latter, like the 3-inch 20-gauge, are ballistically inferior. The puny shot charge is just not enough to get the job done, and the idea that because of its negligible recoil the .410 is a beginner's gun is folly. To start a beginner with a shotgun whose load carries so little shot as to be ineffective is too great a handicap to overcome. Far better the 28 gauge, which can get the job done.

Shooting a Shotgun

Pointing is what shotgunning is all about. Point your finger at the television, a moving car or truck, a flying bird, it's easy, it's natural. Shooting a shotgun is little more than pointing it at the target, swinging along the flight path, moving the gun ahead of the target, pulling the trigger and following through. What is difficult is developing a smooth swing and understanding how much space in front? How far in front? This getting in front of the target is called lead, and there are many ways to achieve it. However, the biggest hurdle is that of perception.

Primarily, shotguns are short-range firearms. Although some write and talk about shooting and bagging birds at 50 and 60 yards and beyond, in truth, the practical range of a shotgun is about 40 yards. Certainly, skilled shots can consistently kill birds beyond that range, but for all realistic purposes 40 yards is it. The problem is that 40 yards to one person is 30 to another and 50 to yet another. But let's not get hung up with that. The fact is that if we correctly perceive lead, the getting ahead of the target part of wing shooting, the range is not as critical as we might think. The plot thickens when we get into unfamiliar territory. For example, the hunter who shoots bobwhite quail in close cover may want to blaze away at big Canada geese that are far out of range.

Advice around gun clubs and from fellow hunters and shooters is cheap, and although well intentioned, is often more confusing than helpful. All too often, we hear experienced shooters advise, "Shoot three feet in front of it." But how far is three feet? From where is it measured? At the gun? Or out where the target is? And what does three feet look like at 20, 30 or 40 yards? The late Robert Churchill authored a book called *Game Shooting* that details his system of wing shooting that is used and taught worldwide. In it is an interesting illustration that demonstrates the perception of lead. Churchill took three boards, one three feet long, one six feet long and another nine feet long. He placed them 10 yards apart with the three-foot board 10 yards from the shooter, the six-foot 10 yards beyond the three-foot board, etc. From the perspective of the shooter, they all appear identical in length! Certainly, each person perceives lead differently, but from the aspect of the shooter, three feet of lead at 20 yards, about right for a crossing target, looks the same as six feet at 30 yards, but both appear much less than three feet at the gun, and therein lies much of the confusion of describing lead. Yet without lead, we cannot hit a flying or running target. Lastly and most simply, if we clear our heads of calculations, and allow our natural ability to simply point at an object, move with it and move in front of it, much of the difficulty will be taken out of wing shooting.

Choke

Part of successful shotgunning involves the use of choke. Choke is a constriction at the muzzle of the shotgun that influences how wide the shot pattern will spread and also affects the length of the shot string. A swarm of shot is shaped like a sausage, and has both length and width. One without the other would make successful wing shooting impossible. What we want to do is to place this sausage-shaped cloud of shot in front of our target so that the two intersect. In other words, the bird or clay flies into the shot string. The width, actually a circle made by the shot charge, allows us room for error up and down and front to back, as does the charge's length, and choke controls the whole thing.

In the early days of choke—and no, it wasn't invented by Illinois duck hunter Fred Kimble, although legend ascribes it to him—ammunition was far less refined than what we shoot today and the soft lead pellets were far more susceptible to deformation than today's high-tech ammo. To keep the maximum number of pellets in the pattern, full choke, the maximum constriction, was applied to the barrel. A 12-gauge shotgun bored full choke has a constriction measuring about .036 inch; some go .040 and occasionally tighter as is witnessed

Shotgunners can keep sharp during the year by shooting clay targets. Normally, over/under and semi-automatic shotguns are favored for clays, but this shooter is using a side-by-side.

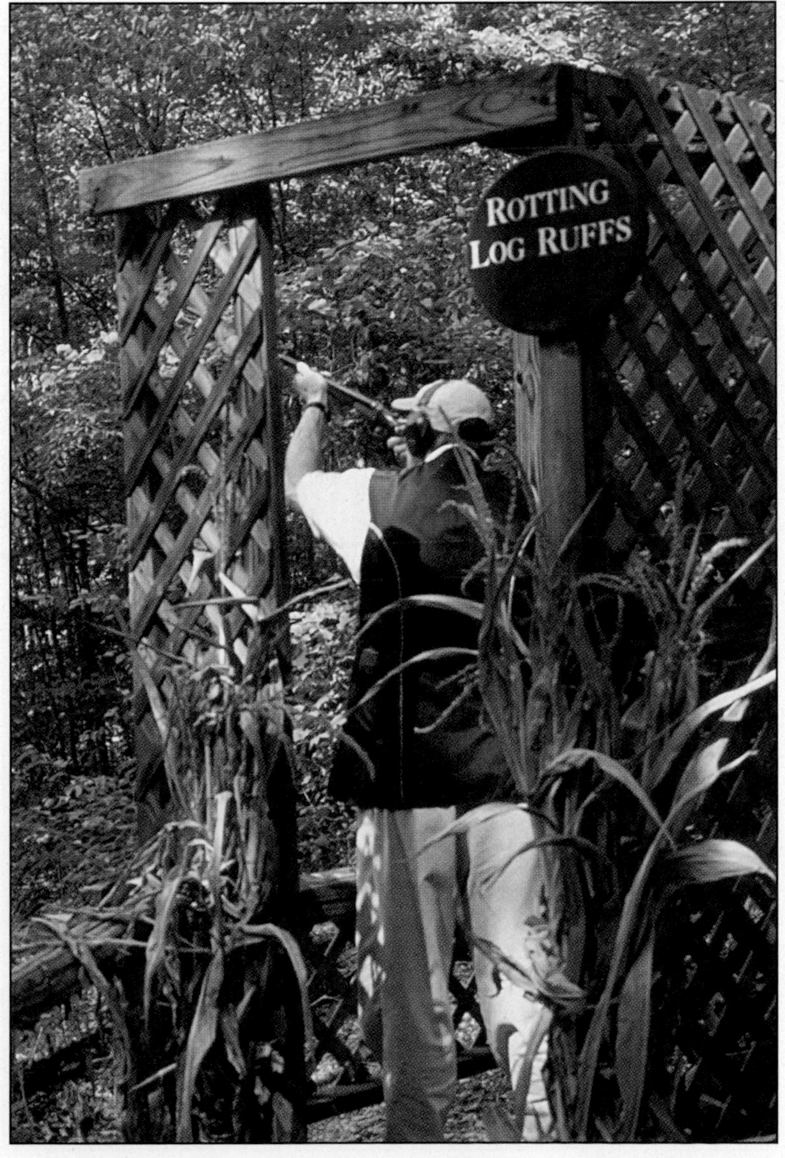

by the current crop of ultra-tight turkey chokes that go .060 or more. However, advances in powders, plastic shot-protecting cups, ground plastic buffer, extra-hard shot, plated shot, steel shot, etc. have pretty well rendered full choke a specialized tool now reserved almost exclusively for turkey hunting. In fact for steel shot, which is required for waterfowl hunting and even upland game hunting on many public lands, open chokes are required.

When combined with modern ammunition the modern shotgunner is perhaps best served with an improved cylinder choke for all-around use. Running about a .010-inch constriction in the 12 gauge, this choke will provide nice even patterns that will place about 70 percent of the pellets from a lead load into a 30-inch circle at 30 yards. Improved cylinder shoots steel shot very well for ducks, but if geese are on the menu, then modified is dictated. For upland game, improved cylinder is perfect. For close flushing quail, a light one-ounce load is all that's needed. Game-farm pheasants will consistently drop to 1 1/8-ounce loads, and if you're hunting wild pheasants or far flushing chukars, then move up to 1 1/4-ounce loads to thicken the pattern. Certainly, there are uses for modified and full choke beyond these very basic parameters, but with today's ammunition, improved cylinder is about all the choke you really need. Experience, either your own or that of a well-schooled buddy may dictate differently, but good old "I.C." provides maximum pattern spread, and that helps compensate for lots of shooting errors. All of this is very simplistic, since individual barrel/choke/ammunition combinations can vary greatly, but as a rule of thumb, you can't go far wrong. The fact that virtually every shotgun sold today comes with interchangeable, screw-in choke tubes provides the needed versatility to quickly and easily adjust to any situation.

Today's shotguns are truly advanced, yet retain the simplicity of the very first shotgun—that of shooting a controlled cloud of shot at a moving target and bringing it to bag. They come in various types and finish from utilitarian to exquisite, but for challenge and enjoyment they have few peers.

The basic shotgun actions (left to right): single barrel, side-by-side, over/under, pump, gas-operated semi-auto and recoil-operated semi-auto. Not pictured is the bolt-action, whose role in shotgunning is limited.

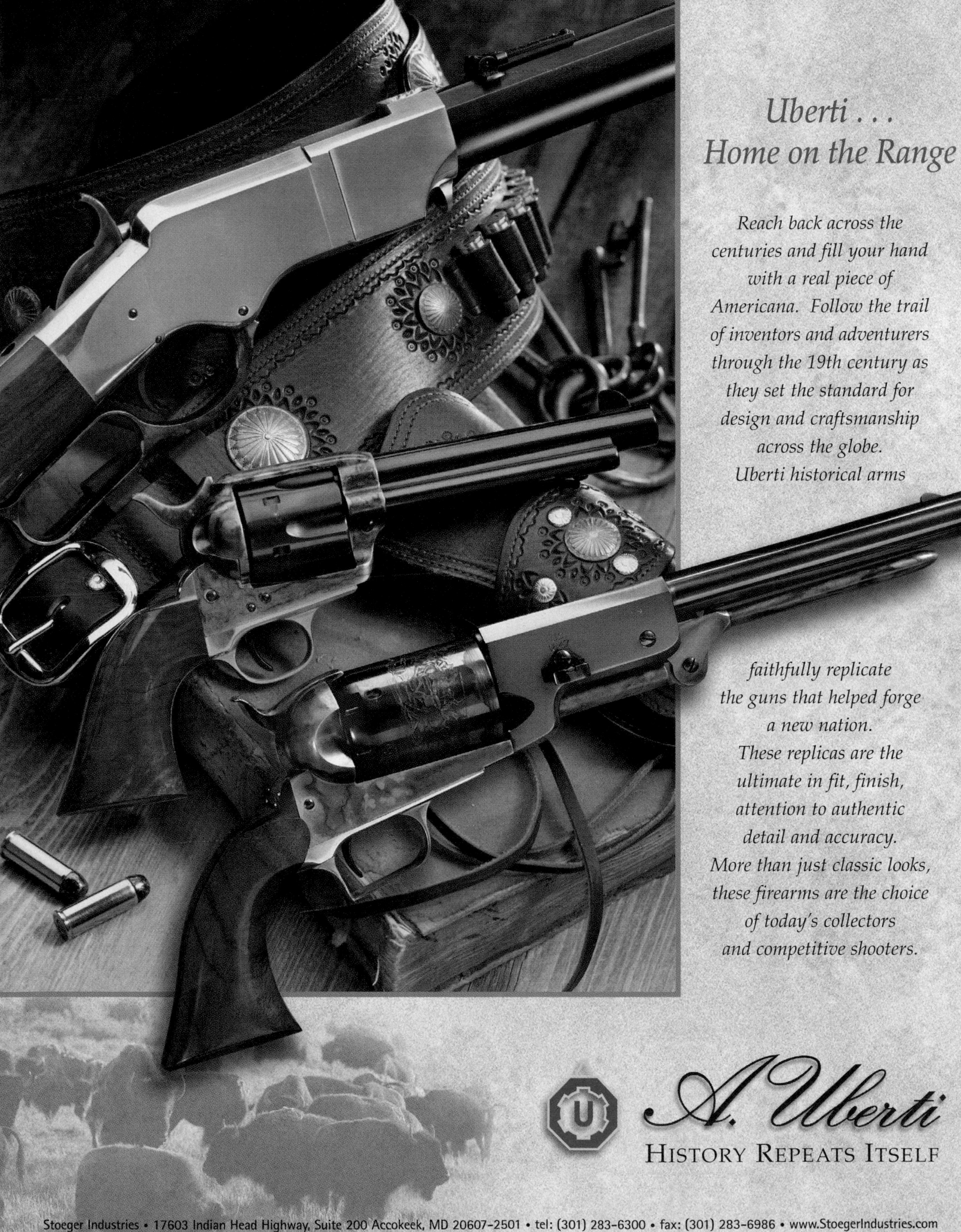
Uberti . . .
Home on the Range
Reach back across the centuries and fill your hand with a real piece of Americana. Follow the trail of inventors and adventurers through the 19th century as they set the standard for design and craftsmanship across the globe. Uberti historical arms faithfully replicate the guns that helped forge a new nation.
These replicas are the ultimate in fit, finish, attention to authentic detail and accuracy.
More than just classic looks, these firearms are the choice of today's collectors and competitive shooters.
A. Uberti
HISTORY REPEATS ITSELF
Stoeger Industries • 17603 Indian Head Highway, Suite 200 Accokeek, MD 20607-2501 • tel: (301) 283-6300 • fax: (301) 283-6986 • www.StoegerIndustries.com
Imported by Stoeger Industries® Part of the Benelli USA® family

Nash Buckingham: A Wingshooter for the Ages

by Jim Casada

Buckingham in later years on a hunt at Winchester's Nilo Farms.

Mr. Buck waits in the background while his horse for a day of quail hunting is readied.

Nash Buckingham was born in Memphis, Tennessee, on May 31, 1880, the son of Miles Sherman and Annie (Gyfford) Buckingham. From earliest childhood he was exposed to the ideals of gentility and humanity that characterized Southern society at its best, and these praiseworthy attributes were to be the essence of the man throughout his career. An innate courtesy, respect for his fellow man , and a deep appreciation for the genteel way of life into which he was born lay at the heart of Buckingham's very being.

During Buckingham's adolescent years, Memphis was the commercial heart of a region where cotton long had reigned as undisputed king, but within a short distance of this commercial hub of the upper Mississippi delta there were marvelous hunting opportunities. Though we know less than we might wish about Buckingham's development during this period, his writings suggest that as a boy he spent a great deal of time afield. In all likelihood his parents were quite comfortable, because both his autobiographical recollections of his youthful hunting experiences and the nature of his formal education suggest affluence.

A decoy that once belonged to Buckingham, with a weight (railroad spike from the line that ran to Beaver Dam) sits atop magazines containing his stories.

Furthermore, in some of his tales, most notably the poignant piece entitled "The Prodigal Years," we gain a glimpse of what these halcyon days must have been like. Prior to the turn of the century ducks and geese poured down the Mississippi Flyway each fall in a seemingly unending stream. Similarly, every back 40 acres, every pea field corner, and unkempt fence rows and ditches without end held quail. Sharecroppers kept hawks in check, killed egg-eating snakes, trapped 'coons and 'possums, and in general formed the finest cadre of friends the bobwhite has ever had. For a wingshooter with the right connections, good dogs, and sufficient financial wherewithal, it was a glorious time. Without question, Buckingham became enamored of the shooting life at an early age, and that love was one that dominated his entire life.

An individual whose bonhomie was matched by a powerful intellect, Buckingham enjoyed the opportunities to expand and develop his mental abilities as an undergraduate first at Harvard University and subsequently at the University of Tennessee in Knoxville. At the latter institution he also displayed the athletic skills that would later earn him a national reputation as an exceptional wingshooter. In truth, even at the dawn of manhood Buckingham evinced the Renaissance-like diversity of interests and talents that would typify his later years. While a student at Harvard he had his introduction to the pugilistic arts at the hands of no less authority than the renowned heavyweight champion, James J. Corbett. This was in an age when boxing, unlike today, when hype and hoopla rule, was considered preeminently a gentleman's sport. Teddy Roosevelt's fondness for the sport, for example, was such that he only gave it up, and reluctantly at that, after almost losing an eye. Buckingham's interest in boxing continued for many years, and he took a quiet but justifiable pride in the fact that he garnered heavyweight championship laurels in the Amateur Athletic Union's Southern Open Tournament held in New Orleans in 1910.

Buckingham at age 54 with his springer spaniel Chubby getting ready for a dove hunt.

Buckingham's size and strength (he stood over six feet, with powerful shoulders and arms and a body devoid of so much as a hint of fat) lent themselves to his

prowess as a boxer, but as an athlete he was a sterling example of what was known at the time as a true "all rounder." He demonstrated this in his college days in Knoxville. After leaving Harvard at the end of his freshman year, probably because of the homesickness of a heart harkening back to the Southland but possibly due to financial concerns as well, he completed his studies at the University of Tennessee. He lettered in four sports—baseball, boxing, track, and football—and in the latter Buckingham displayed tremendous versatility by playing all positions except center.

His athletic abilities naturally figured prominently in the duck blind, dove field, or when following a savvy pointer amidst golden waves of frost-tipped broom sedge. Gifted with marvelous hand-eye coordination, from an early age Buckingham was a first-rate wing shot. The original introduction to his most famous book, The Shootinest Gent'man quotes the gun editor of Field & Stream, Captain Paul Curtis, on Buckingham's abilities, and the author of the piece, Colonel Harold Sheldon, also praises his shooting prowess. Without question, he ranks as one of finest shots in the field that this country has ever produced. Though Buckingham was a master with the shotgun, he would eventually make even more of a mark as a writer, field trial judge, and consultant on shooting sports. Surprisingly, he pursued a variety of occupations, even though the first of them was as a journalist, before eventually concluding that writing was his métier. In retrospect, it might also be added that writing, more than any other pursuit, offered him the ability to spend a great deal of time hunting and rubbing elbows with those who shared his passions for fine guns, fine dogs, and first-rate sport.

Buckingham's medal-bedecked hat and other memorabilia.

Buckingham's *The Shootinest Gent'man* remains one of the great classics of American sporting literature.

His apprenticeship as a sporting scribe came immediately after college with a stint on the staff of the *Memphis Commercial Appeal,* where his forte was not outdoors coverage but football. His marriage in 1910 to Irma Lee Jones, to whom (along with the memory of his parents) he dedicated his first book, *The Shootinest Gent'man,* ended his work with the newspaper. Doubtless feeling an increased sense of responsibility as a result of his new marital status (although it brought him a tidy sum), Buckingham tried his hand at a number of occupations over the ensuing two decades. All related in some way to the sporting instincts that were so deeply ingrained in his being. These pursuits included, among others, ownership of a sporting goods business in Memphis from 1919 to 1925, a directorship with the Western Cartridge Company, and an associate editor's position with *Field & Stream* magazine. The latter position, together with a growing string of published articles to his credit, led directly to the publication of his first book. He never made a great deal of money from any of his books, all but one of which involved collections of previously published stories, but they did form the primary basis of Buckingham's literary legacy.

Once Buckingham reached a juncture in life where he possessed sufficient introspection to realize just how much the sporting life meant to him, he abandoned all pretense of pursuing other careers and gave himself fully to his first love—hunting. In the course of his long life he exhausted not one but two small fortunes (his inheritance and that of his wife), and in his final years the threat of impoverishment hung as a dark cloud on his personal horizon. However, if ever an individual lived the shooting life to the fullest it was the individual who, as his fame grew and his popularity expanded, many came to know as "Mr. Buck."

While he hunted a great deal, visited a lot of fine places, watched countless dogs work their canine wizardry, and shared the camaraderie of most everyone who was anyone in the bird hunting and waterfowling worlds, no one should make the mistake of thinking Nash Buckingham was lazy. Rather, he consciously chose a lifestyle many of us can only envy. His prolific pen produced a steady stream of articles for the best sporting journals of the day, and his knack of crafting sprightly, well-told tales made him one of the most popular writers of his time.

Almost without exception, Buckingham's work drew heavily on his own personal experiences or those of individuals with whom he was familiar. In fact, one of the finest ways to grasp the measure of the man lies in reading his works and recognizing the pronounced autobiographical strain they contain. He was a master of dialect, especially that of the Blacks who served as cooks, dog handlers, and sporting jacks-of-all-trades in the real-life world he knew, and he makes outstanding use of this ability in his writings. Similarly, Buckingham had a real flair for capturing a moment or setting a scene. To join him vicariously in his description of a hunt lunch is to find your salivary glands flowing of their own volition, and when he describes a staunch point at sunset you can almost envision the dog quivering as the heady scent of bobwhites wafts through the damp air of approaching evening.

Buckingham has been criticized on more than one occasion for his extensive use of dialect, but to my way of thinking that is misguided political correctness at its worst. His reliance on dialect brings life and reality to his writings. For anyone with Southern roots (such as this writer), his words soon come to have an almost uncanny audibility—as if they were actually being spoken—and even the untrained ear easily adjusts to their rhythmic quality. I know of no better way to sense and savor the sporting

Buckingham the Conservationist

Although few realize it today, Buckingham played a key role in fostering the conservation movement in this country. He realized, to his great regret, that he and countless others like him had been in part responsible for the precipitous decline in waterfowl numbers. Joining forces with Ding Darling and a few others, Mr. Buck played a key role in getting the Federal Duck Stamp program enacted, and he tirelessly preached the conservation message over the final decades of his life. He played a pivotal role in getting the Migratory Bird Treaty passed. A founding member of the Outdoor Writers Association of America, in 2002 he was belatedly but fittingly honored by that organization with its lifetime Excellence in Craft award.

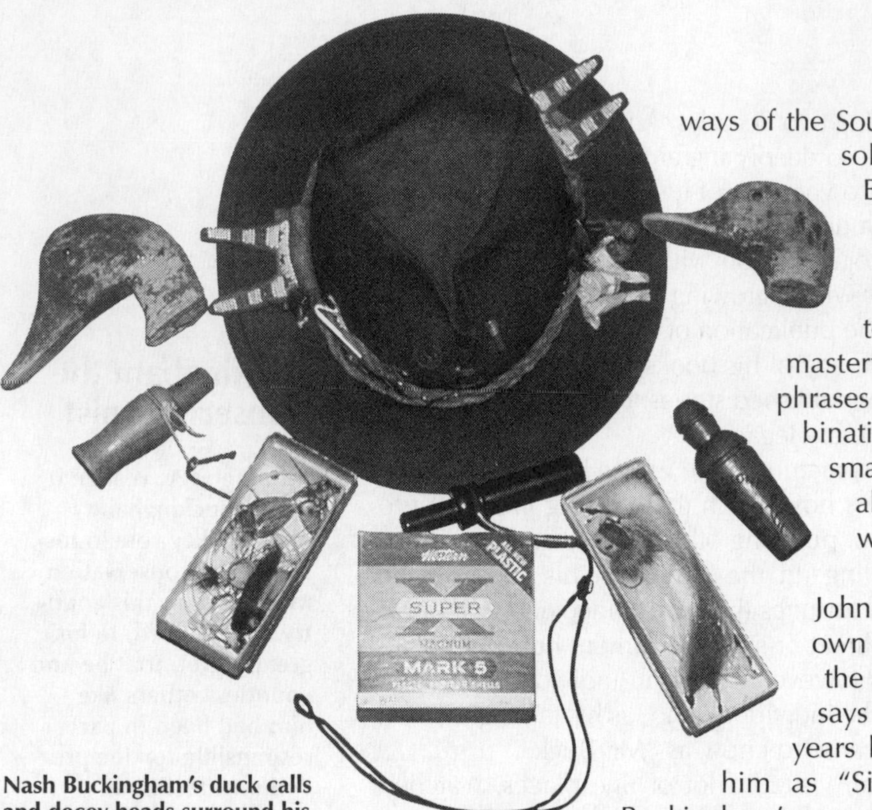

Nash Buckingham's duck calls and decoy heads surround his well-worn hunting hat.

ways of the South in yesteryear than through a solid armchair session with Mr. Buck as your guide down darkening avenues into a world we have largely, and sadly, lost. Of course, one should also hasten to add that Buckingham was masterful in producing well-turned phrases in normal English, and the combination of abilities explain in no small measure why he today is almost a cult figure with those who treasure fine writing.

The recollections of the late John Madson, a superb writer in his own right, help capture the nature of the man and his craftsmanship. He says that Buckingham, though 50 years his senior, invariably addressed him as "Sir." In particular, he recalled Buckingham's acceptance speech, delivered without the benefit of so much as a single note card, when he received Winchester's "Man of the Year" award. "He spoke of the gunmakers ('the armourers,' he called them) and their role in the establishment of our republican government, our defense of freedom, the settlement of wilderness, and the preservation of rural arts and their honorable traditions. He took us from the rockbound Pilgrim coast down to the Blue Ridge and beyond, through the Cumberland Gap and past the Dark and Bloody Ground into the fathomless grasslands that reached to the Stony Mountains. Beyond, the grim and waterless sinks that test men and their aspirations, over to the lofty Sierra Nevada and down into a gold land that ended in a vast and pacific seas. Through all this great westering odyssey, men were brothers-in-arms, and brothers to their arms, and still are." Chub Andrews characterizes the man in less eloquent but telling fashion. "He was the most powerful personality it has ever been my privilege to know."

Dr. William F. "Chubby" Andrews, Buckingham's best friend in later years, with his second Burt Becker magnum (the original "Bo Whoop" was lost).

Ever the athlete and a man of surpassing physical fitness, Buckingham eased into old age with grace. When well into his 60s he was featured in a delightful quail hunting piece in *Life* magazine, the locale being his cousin's massive 12,000-acre estate in Buckingham's beloved Grand Junction area along Tennessee's southwestern border. Even later, through his 70s and on into four score plus years he remained active in the field and continued to write, albeit not at the same rate of productivity that characterized the 1930s and 1940s. Financial worries and the need to care for his wife, who had suffered a debilitating stroke, troubled these years.

Buckingham died on March 10, 1971, just two months short of his

91st birthday. Death came in Knoxville, at the home of his daughter. More than two decades earlier a journalist had said that Buckingham was "one of a disappearing American strain," and one might simply add that there is no question that he stands well to the forefront among our great sportsmen and sporting writers. To see him in a goose blind working magic with the big Burt Becker magnum he called "Bo Whoop" (after the sound it made), to walk beside him as he made a crisp double on a whopping covey rise, or to watch him consistently tumble windblown doves from the sky at distances greater than 50 yards was to be in the presence of greatness.

The pages of his books positively exude gentility; not the crass, "money bought" elitism so common today but a deeper, more meaningful approach to and appreciation of sport. As John Madson described him, he was "a writer who read a great many things and listened to a great many good and thoughtful conversations." From those experiences came "a certain kind of grace, a courtliness of style that is somehow lost to us in this age of careless and hasty writing, when we seem to absorbed by canned entertainment to either read well or converse well." A gentleman in the original and finest sense of the word ("gentle man"), Mr. Buck left posterity his own memorial. His books capture forever the flavor of the man and his milieu, and to join him for a spate of armchair adventure is to know hunting, wingshooting, and the camaraderie of the field at its finest.

Top:
The second "Bo Whoop," two of Mr. Buck's calls, and two of his decoys.

Bottom:
Photo of Buckingham and Chub Andrews after a day of duck hunting at the Beaver Dam Club, Nash's beloved waterfowl retreat.

Handgun Metallic Silhouetting—Expanding Your Options

By Ken Horowitz

Hitting anything at 200 meters with a handgun is an exhilarating experience and the thrill of seeing a 55-pound metal ram toppling that long moment after you squeeze the trigger never gets tiresome. Even the "close in" chickens, set a "mere" 50 meters distant, present a daunting target for even the best of casual paper punchers who, for some inexplicable reason, have not yet stepped up to the challenging world of adult plinking. Yet, handgun metallic silhouetting is perhaps the easiest entry organized target sport available in this country and, to some extent, around the world.

Organized for just over a quarter of a century, IHMSA, the International Handgun Metallic Silhouette Association, has standardized the sport and devised a simple set of rules that allow shooters with diverse abilities and guns of different capabilities to compete. IHMSA rules encourage competition on a very friendly basis, within categories that don't unfairly give the edge to expertise—by stratifying classifications based on known shooter ability—or deep pockets. In other shooting sports, the best shooters always trounce the upcoming, or casual players, and the imprimatur of moneybags is frequently evident in the

Have it your way for Big Bore. The Thompson Center Contender *(middle)* has already been shown and discussed. At top is a Thompson Center Encore with a 15-inch barrel in 7mm BR Remington that can be used in Big Bore Unlimited, Unlimited Any Sights, Unlimited Half Scale or Unlimited Half Scale Any Sights. The bottom gun, a Smith and Wesson 44 Magnum Model 629 Classic can still topple rams, albeit with a lot of recoil and an ungainly trajectory. With its Weaver 4x scope, it can be used in a number of silhouette classifications.

gear of the pros.

Each IHMSA match entry is very simple, consisting of 40 targets, 10 each of chickens, pigs, turkeys and rams, set at increasing standard distances. For scoring either you topple a target or you don't—a ringer, where a target is hit but does not fall, is the same as a miss. For each target toppled, the shooter gets one point. A perfect score is 40 and to settle ties of the more proficient shooters (or shooters that want an extra set of fun targets), there are an additional 10 smaller shoot-off targets. Each IHMSA member keeps a personal classification card that is used to measure shooters among one another according to relative abilities.

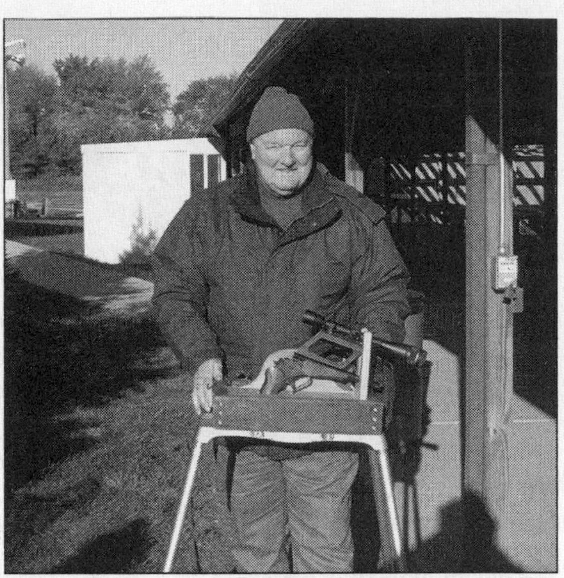

Many silhouette shooters fashion their own accessories or improvise. Here, Jerry Rinehart is setting up a custom gun box on a projector table. Note the gun resting in a cradle. Jerry, who has broken several records shooting metallic silhouettes, moves the whole rig from station to station during the course of fire.

Of the 40 metal animal targets, the shooter with the highest score wins. However, the win is only within that shooter's classification, both as to skill and type of gun used. Therefore, the "expert" shooter, with an INT (International) shooter classification, using an "Unlimited" gun, would win the match only with respect to similar shooters, similarly equipped. At the same competition, another shooter, with more modest capability and an off-the-shelf production gun, would also be the winner in a classification so defined by capabilities and hardware.

Within the three main divisions (Big Bore, including full size and half-scale, Small Bore and Field Pistol), shooters are classified as to ability in each discipline covering up to six strata (INT, AAA, AA, A, B and C), plus several gun classifications according to type of shooting; anyone would be hard pressed to not find a niche for ability and gun. To be sure, there are some rigs that would not get you into the game because they are overly long, overly heavy or that would do too much target damage, but such handguns are far and few between. Designed to accommodate the average shooter, IHMSA rules are geared toward the "shoot what you have crowd" with easy entry and few barriers, either skill based or economic. New shooters are encouraged to try shooting in a match before joining IHMSA. If you try it, you'll probably like it and join. The experience sells itself.

Once into the game with their general-purpose firearms, many shooters choose to expand their options by using Unlimited guns, or specialized silhouette cartridges, or a combination of both. For these shooters, the "everyone's included" approach encouraged by the IHMSA fosters a welcome environment, by classifying him or her into like-kind categories.

For Big Bore categories, production handguns are limited to barrels of 10¾ inches or shorter, with a weight not to exceed four pounds. Minor changes are permitted, using drop-in, readily available parts. Unlimited guns may have barrels up to 15 inches in length and can weigh up to five pounds. There are additional Any Sights categories that allow up to an additional pound that may be added by optical sights and mounts. The production gun rule is not overly restrictive and is

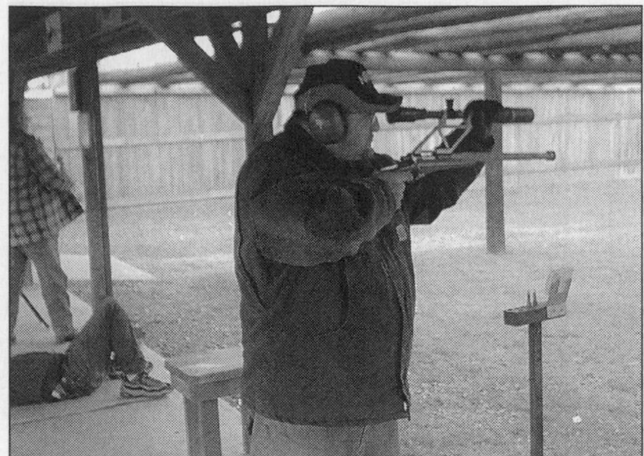

Bill Robinson, Pennsylvania State Director and holder of several records, uses a high-rise mount to shoot in the standing position. This type of mount reduces strain and shooter fatigue and is very popular in handgun silhouetting. Due to the distance between the scope and the barrel, extra care must be taken in determining sight settings for the various targets.

quite liberal in terms of which guns are allowed. Unlimited guns raise the ceiling since very few guns are disqualified from shooting in the Big Bore events.

The general rules for determining Production or Unlimited guns in Small Bore are about the same as those for Big Bore, with a few minor differences. For example, in Small Bore, reflecting the availability of good 22 Long Rifle pistols in a variety of actions, there are separate Production classes for semi-automatics, single shot pistols and revolvers. Field Pistol has only two categories, Production and Production Any Sights.

Category determination is also affected by shooting position, either standing or an all-inclusive freestyle, which allows the shooter extreme latitude, short of using an artificial rest. One of the more popular freestyle positions is Creedmoor, where the shooter lays backside down with feet toward the targets and knees drawn up, resting the gun alongside one leg, with the muzzle well forward to avoid danger to the shooter.

Perhaps the major draw to specialized silhouette guns, both in Production and Unlimited categories, is to the specialized Big Bore silhouette cartridges. While the rules permit just about any center-fire cartridge that won't do target damage, some cartridges are better than others for achieving the dynamics required in shooting targets ranging from those you could hit with a rock to those out to 200 meters.

The heaviest most distant target is the 55-pound regulation ram. In the IHMSA's infancy, using the handguns available at the time, standard pistol cartridges were shot at matches. Even hot loaded, the 357 Magnum is marginal for consistently toppling the rams and may leave

Spotters can help a shooter know where the bullets are going so that minor adjustments can be made while shooting the course of fire. Here, Bill is calling the shots for Wes to tell him exactly where he is hitting the targets, or, in the event of a miss, the location of the miss. All IHMSA members are more than happy to help a shooter and it is just as likely that Wes will be calling for someone else when not actually shooting a relay.

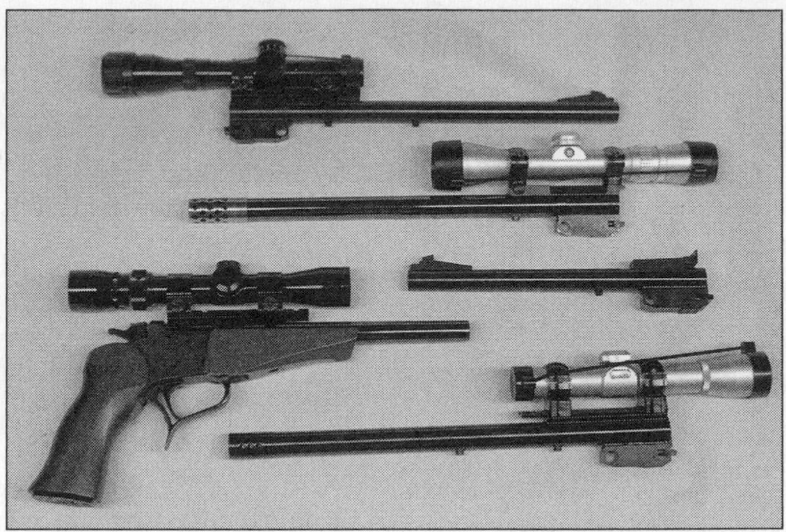

The versatility of a Thompson Center Contender can be demonstrated using this simple photo. The barrel on the gun is a 22LR in 10 inches, sporting a Weaver 2-4x variable scope that the author uses in Small Bore Unlimited Any Sights competition. The separate barrels, from top to bottom are a 14 inch 22 Hornet barrel for use in Big Bore Unlimited Half Scale Any Sights; a 14 inch 7mm TCU with muzzle brake topped by a Bausch & Lomb 2-6x Elite 3000 scope for use in Big Bore Unlimited Any Sights or Big Bore Unlimited Half Scale Any Sights; a Production barrel, also in 7mm TCU, for Production and Standing; and, for purposes of using a non-specialized silhouette cartridge, a 14 inch barrel with muzzle brake in the common 30-30 Winchester chambering, wearing a Nikon 2x pistol scope for use in Big Bore Unlimited Any Sights or Big Bore Unlimited Half Scale Any Sights.

too many ringers (a hit target that does not fall, thereby considered a miss). While properly loaded 41 Magnums, 44 Magnums and 45 Long Colts are adequate from a power perspective, the trajectories and attendant sighting problems make these cartridges less than ideal. Out to the turkeys (150 meters), these cartridges are acceptable, but after that, they have as much "svelteness" as an elephant jumping from a diving platform! Additionally, the cumulative effects of recoil after shooting many rounds can be daunting.

Shortly after the beginning of IHMSA, the popularity of handgun hunting began to rise. Seizing the opportunity, many handgun silhouetters turned to the new breed of handguns which chambered traditional rifle cartridges. Firing a Winchester 30-30 from a Thompson Center Contender or a 308 Winchester from a Remington XP-100 all but eliminated the trajectory issues of the large handgun cartridges, but these rifle calibers were housed in just about anything other than Production guns. Longer barrels, some with muzzle brakes plus heavier guns more or less pushed all these choices into the Unlimited categories. To be sure, you can fire a 30-30 Winchester from a shorter Production gun barrel, but you wouldn't want to do it too many times—and, shooting the 40 rounds of an IHMSA match would certainly fit the description of too many! Even with heavier, longer-barreled, Unlimited guns, rifle cartridge recoil is unpleasantly high and is happily avoided by all but a few shooters whose recoil lust borders on gluttonous.

So, a quest began to find the "ideal" cartridge for silhouetting, one that had just the right amount of energy to topple the most stubborn of metal critters, whose trajectory deviated the least from the sightline, and whose recoil was tolerable, if not modest. This "just enough, but not too much" approach spawned a whole family of specialty cartridges that continues to grow.

The more popular (though by no means exclusively so) silhouette cartridges use 7mm (.284) bullets, partly because of their excellent flight characteristics and partly because of the plethora of offerings by several quality manufacturers (perhaps only 30 caliber bullets have more choices). That there is more choice in this bore size goes hand in hand with the capabilities of these bullets; since they work so well, the manufacturers have offered them in the most varieties.

Mid-weight 7mm bullets, when thrown at modest speeds straddling 2000+/- feet per second, retain enough power to knock down the rams, have really nice trajectory, and don't beat up the shooter with undue recoil. A number of packages do this, but three of the more popular silhouette cartridges that launch 7mm bullets in this range are the 7mm

TCU, 7mm BR Remington and 7mm IHMSA. Common recipes can easily achieve the following results for a 150-grain bullet:

Cartridge	Barrel Length	Velocity Range
7mm TCU	14″	1650-2000
7mm BR Remington	15″	1900-2150
7mm IHMSA	15″	1900-2350

The 7mm TCU is based on a necked-up and fire-formed Remington 223 case (see side-bar on page 74). The parent brass puts a pretty low limit on the amount of powder that can fit in the case and generally explains why the 7mm TCU has relatively lower velocities than the other two rounds listed in the chart. The 7mm BR Remington is based on the Remington Universal Benchrest cartridge case, which in turn is a shortened Remington 308 case necked down to 7mm with a specially made small primer pocket. The 7mm IHMSA is based on a necked-down 300 Savage case, retaining the large primer pocket.

Perhaps you're wondering why there are multiple cartridges that do the same thing. There are many reasons, some based on rational criteria while others are based on less lofty ideals. Without judging the worthiness of the reasons and without any claim to completeness, consider the following: While 2000 feet per second might be a fairly typical muzzle velocity for toppling silhouettes with a 150-grain bullet, it is somewhat arbitrary. We could just have easily assumed 1900 feet per second, or 2100 feet per second. Assuming 2000 feet per second, there is no upward mobility with the 7mm TCU. The 7mm IHMSA is more flexible.

Alan Olsen, current IHMSA match director at Falls Township Rifle and Pistol Association, uses the Creedmoor position to fire at his bank of targets while other shooters in the background, choose to use the standing position. Note the rounds that Alan conveniently keeps available on cartridge loops around his thigh. Also, he is wearing a blast shield, an essential for revolver competition, even though he is using a single shot Thomson Center Contender for this relay. The muzzle must be kept well ahead of the shooter at all times.

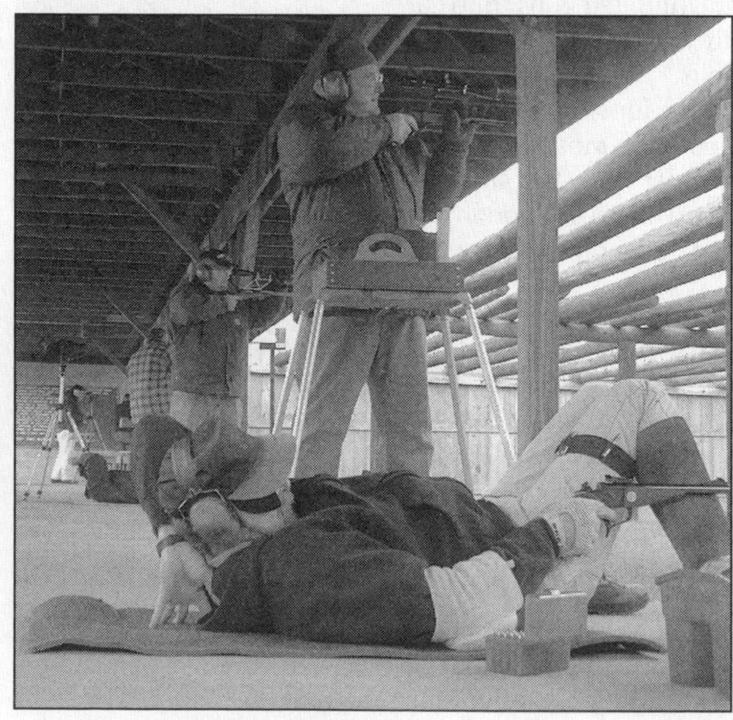

A question to ask is how much flexibility do you need, both for the purposes of silhouette shooting and for any other uses to which you may put the gun. Often, a casual silhouette shooter will use a multipurpose hunting/silhouette gun. If that's what you have in mind, you may also want to consider other bullet weights for which there are published recipes. The 7mm IHMSA handles a wider range of bullet weights, going from 100 grains up to 175 grains. The 7mm BR Remington and 7mm TCU usually go to 160 grains (although you can find recipes for both of these up to 175 grains in some manuals).

Personally, I like to start with a cartridge and then find a gun to shoot the cartridge I like. Not everyone approaches things that way; further, you may not find a gun that fires your cartridge of choice. Sometimes, the gun drives the decision. Since not all guns come in all chamberings, your cartridge choice may be limited to the standard offerings of the gun manufacturers. Sometimes, the popularity of a cartridge can be driven by the chamberings available in a particular firearm. For example, in the earlier days of IHMSA, threaded and chambered barrels for the then new 7mm IHMSA cartridge became available for the Remington XP-100, making it a relatively low cost Unlimited option. The move gave a boost both to the gun and to the cartridge.

In this photo, Jerry Greg fires a falling block action with open sights (hooded front sight to avoid glare) at the far distant rams. Note the timer on top of the makeshift ammo stand. Jerry places the five rounds required for the relay so that they are ready and sets the timer. Each relay allows two minutes to dispatch five targets, more than ample time.

Interestingly, sometime after the XP-100 was offered in a 7mm BR Remington chambering, Remington introduced a factory load. The immediate impact was to overshadow the 7mm IHMSA that was in use. Currently, there is no factory loading offered for either caliber, so if a shooter chooses to handload, it could just as easily be one or the other once a supply of brass is on hand.

Some cartridge designs are better used in certain action types. Falling block actions and some break-open actions favor rimmed cartridges. If a shooter determines on a particular cartridge design, such as rimmed or semi-rimmed, that factor may decide which cartridge will be used to propel the same weight of bullet downrange. Some shooters prefer rimmed cartridges for the ease of maintaining headspace during reloading, while, for others, it's simply a habit. Countless shooters have cut their center-fire teeth on the ubiquitous 30-30 Winchester and in their minds always envision a rim as a proper trapping for any self-respecting piece of brass.

Then there's the matter of cost. The ability to use a common cartridge or, at least, a wildcat easily formed from a commonly available case might mean the difference between shooting a lot or a little, or at all. The 7mm BR Remington brass is much more expensive than 223 Remington brass, which is used to form the 7mm TCU. At its least expensive option, 223 Remington brass can be free, whether it is your own or scrounged.

An "opportunity gun" can sometimes help make the decision on a particular cartridge. Suppose you come across an acceptable silhouette cartridge that shoots the bullet you want but you're unsure about the cartridge. Well, if it's at an offering price you can't refuse, and chances are that a fortuitous event such as this will help you make the decision.

What about using a downloaded version of a larger, more standard rifle cartridge? This may or may not be a good idea. Potential problems include overpower and/or low-density load. For example, assume the 7mm-08 Remington is your favorite rifle cartridge, or better yet, you've already picked up a Thompson Center Encore for hunting purposes cham-

Metamorphosis—Creating the 7mm TCU

The 7mm TCU cartridge is one of the easiest of the so-called "wildcat" rounds—cartridges that fail to achieve sufficient popularity for a major manufacturer to offer them as a standard catalog item—to make. It is simply a 223 Remington case that has been expanded to accept a 7mm bullet and then finished to final dimensions by fire forming.

The process starts with a 223 Remington case, preferably new and commercial, not used military. New brass is more malleable than fired brass, which has been work hardened and has had its temper changed by the heat of the firing process. While it is possible to use fired 223 Remington cases, the case life will be shorter and in the conversion process to 7mm TCU you will suffer more casualties due to cracked case mouths. Nevertheless, due to the cheapness of once-fired brass, many shooters choose to use them, accepting the potential losses. Military 5.56mm brass (the military version of the 223 Remington) has thicker walls and therefore less case capacity. As a consequence, loading data prepared for commercial brass will generate different results, including higher pressures, if applied to military cases.

Using a full-length sizing die with a tapered expander on a well (but not overly) lubricated case, the mouth of the 223 Remington case is opened to accept a 7mm bullet. The die should be carefully adjusted so that the resulting case fits properly in the 7mm TCU chamber, without too much or too little headspace.

The case can now be loaded using a safe published recipe, but will lack the sharp shoulders that will come upon fire forming. Firing this first load will force the shoulders to their final dimensions. To assure maximum case life, subsequent resizing of these cases should be done with a neck-only sizing die, until the case no longer will chamber, in which case they may be resized using a full-length sizing die.

bered in the 7mm-08. Further, suppose that for silhouettes, you decide you would rather load and shoot a cartridge that you have on hand.

Standard factory loads will be overpowered, but even if they don't damage the targets and you can safely handle them without excessive muzzle rise, you need to ask yourself whether the greater recoil is worth it. Perhaps that doesn't faze you, but keep in mind that as a hunting piece, you only fire it a few times during a hunt. As a silhouette gun, you'll be firing it at least 40 times per entry, up to 50 times with shoot-offs. The results will be multiplied by the number of entries you shoot in a match resulting in a cumulative amount of unnecessary punishment.

Downloading below safe published load recipes to more suitable silhouette speeds is a bad idea. Using currently acceptable powders for the 7mm-08 Remington would give low-density loads. Low density, particularly in slower burning rifle powders, may give erratic performance, defeating the purpose of selecting a high performance bullet such as the 150-grain 7mm in any design. More important are the safety considerations. There has been much written about the potential explosions which can result from light load detonations. Although there have been some challenges to the theories which have historically been used to explain this controversial phenomenon, it's just plain stupid to take the chance. When reloading, there's no payoff that's worth any chance of a catastrophe.

With all the preceding discussion about handloads, it is apparent that while not absolutely necessary, rolling your own does widen your options for shooting silhouettes. This is an area that can be developed gradually, after a shooter has gained a better idea of likes and dislikes.

While there are several really good choices out there for silhouette handguns—both Production and Unlimited—a really good option is

The metamorphosis of a cartridge begins with the Norma brand 223 Remington case on the left. In the center is an expanded case, with its mouth opened to accept a 7mm (.284) bullet. The right cartridge is a finished 7mm TCU; this one sporting a Sierra 140-grain Spitzer BT.

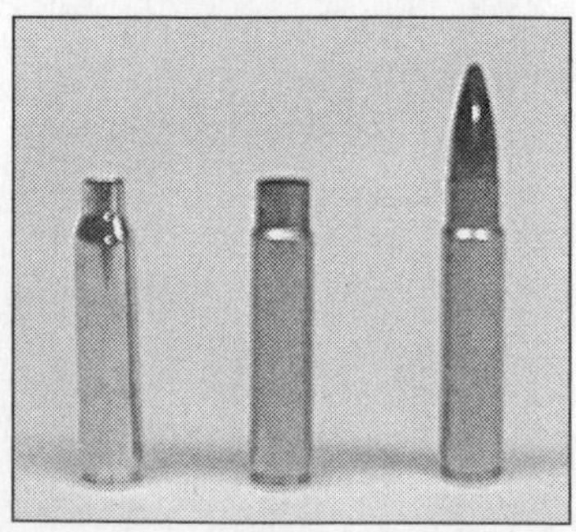

the system popularized by Thompson Center Arms with its switch-barrel Contender, Encore, or G2 Models. Beyond the convenience of quick-switch caliber changes, these guns are excellent for handgun metallic silhouette competitions even if you don't use the barrel change feature. It is not uncommon for even the best silhouetters to choose a Contender or other model just because it's a great gun. The switch-barrel option adds flexibility, while containing cost. In the event the shooter chooses a barrel and really doesn't like it, there is a robust aftermarket for most barrels. Not only is a new barrel not all that expensive, but you may also realize a good return on the old barrel.

Presently, I use the same Contender frame for a 7mm TCU 14-inch barrel with muzzle brake and scope in Big Bore Unlimited Any Sights and Unlimited Any Sights Half Scale; a 10 3/4-inch barrel in the same chambering for Production and Standing; two 22LR Production barrels, one with scope and one without for shooting various Small Bore options and a 10 3/4-inch 22 Hornet barrel for Field Pistol, with a longer 22 Hornet barrel for Big Bore Half Scale. All of this flexibility with only one frame!

I also have multiple barrels for a single Encore frame, most notably Production and Unlimited barrels in 7mm BR Remington configuration. It's little wonder that the Thompson Center line is so popular in handgun silhouetting. Whatever the perspective, performance or pocketbook, it's a tough act to follow.

For those who are certain of cartridge selection, there are some very solid choices ranging from bolt actions to falling blocks, albeit without the flexibility of quick barrel changes. It is a matter of personal choice and there are some shooters who prefer these actions and there are others who still go the break-action route. It is not uncommon to find shooters at matches who bring a whole box full of Contenders, each with its own dedicated barrel.

In the end, the matter is choice and expansion of your shooting horizons. Silhouetting is an easy game to enter. But if specialized equipment and cartridges draw your attention, you can move in that direction at your own pace, with your own pocketbook. Fortunately, this is still an every-shooter's sport, not a money game and not a fashion show. So, if you're tired of punching paper and want some real action, pick up your favorite pistol and find a silhouette match in your area.

The field of fire at Falls Township Rifle and Pistol Club (Falls Township, Pennsylvania) includes the close up chickens (50 meters), extending to the pigs (100 meters), turkeys (150 meters) and barely visible rams (200 yards, partly obscured due to the early morning shadow on the berm). Although the other animals are set in meters, the rams may be set in yards to accommodate those clubs whose ranges commonly extend only to 200 yards.

Model 92 Type M: The Forgotten Beretta

By Gene Gangarosa Jr.

The Model 92 Type M *(top)* is not Beretta's first compact 8-shot pistol: efficient Model 951 *(bottom)* 9mm pistol has been one of popular models for decades and remains in production in Egypt.

Two years before the Type M appeared, the Beretta company unveiled its first compact Model 92 variant. Note the straight front gripstrap, inherited from the full-size Model 92SB (photo courtesy Pietro Beretta SpA).

Beretta introduced the Model 92 series in 1976, and within a few years it had made significant inroads in the international military and police market. Several improved models followed, one of which, the Model 92S-1, attracted favorable notice in 1979 U.S. Air Force testing, but for five years all Model 92 variants were full-size pistols. Due to the large 15-shot, double-column magazine used, the Model 92 remained a large, bulky pistol poorly suited to concealed carry or to use by shooters with smaller hands.

The Model 92SB Compact appeared in 1981 as a companion to the company's updated Model 92SB. Compared to the full-size Model 92SB, the Model 92SB Compact featured a shortened barrel/slide assembly and a shortened magazine with a capacity reduced to 13 rounds. For the first time in the Model 92 series Beretta offered a reduced-size variant of the basic design. The Model 92SB Compact retained all the parent pistol's accuracy and reliability, only in a more compact package. Meanwhile, the full-size Model 92SB began to attract attention in U.S. military and police circles as the state police of Connecticut adopted it. Entered in still another round of U.S. military pistol testing in 1981, the 92SB again performed impressively, though the coveted U.S. service-pistol contract still remained tantalizingly out of reach.

Though the 13-round Model 92SB Compact offered the Model 92's excellent performance in a slightly smaller package, it was still a rather large pistol. While the 92SB-C made the Beretta pistol design available to many shooters who found the full-sized Model 92 too bulky, the pistol remained large for some missions, such as concealed carry. There remained a need for a truly compact pistol sharing the Model 92's desirable design features but reduced in size to allow concealed carry. To meet this need, Beretta introduced the Type M at the end of 1982. The Type M consists of a Model 92SB Compact top end (barrel and slide) attached to a new frame.

Early Type M pistols featured a traditional rounded triggerguard and, in this example, one of Beretta's first-ever Type Ms, checkered wooden grips. The Type M features a curved front gripstrap, the first Model 92 variant to do so. All Model 92s have this feature since Beretta standardized the Model 92F in 1985 (photo courtesy Pietro Beretta SpA).

The heart of the redesign that created the Type M centered around an 8-round magazine. Compared to the 15-shot magazine of the full-size model or even the 13-round magazine of the original compact model, the Type M's magazine is radically slimmed down. This slim magazine allows Beretta to make the Type M with an appreciably slimmer, handier grip. Many shooters who find the full-size Model 92 pistols bulky and clumsy will be pleasantly surprised by the Type M. The numbers tell part of the story: whereas the standard Model 92FS is 8.5 inches long, has a 4.9-inch barrel, and weighs 34 ounces unloaded, the Type M is only 7.8 inches long, has a 4.3-inch barrel, and weighs 31 ounces unloaded. However, the numbers aren't entirely suggestive of the Type M's potential. While the two guns are equally wide across the slide, the Type M's grip is .3 inch narrower than the full-size Model 92FS's grip. While this reduction may not sound like much, it gives the Type M an entirely different feel in the hand. Whereas the Model 92FS feels bulky to all but the largest-handed shooters, the Type M feels handy and graceful. It offers possibilities to police or military forces as a standard service pistol as well as for concealed carry.

Naturally, the Type M's similarity to the standard Model 92 works to the good, as it retains all the parent model's desirable features and incorporates identical operating controls, thereby simplifying training. The Type M does sacrifice the reversible magazine release of the thicker-framed models, but this is a small price to pay for the improved handling it offers.

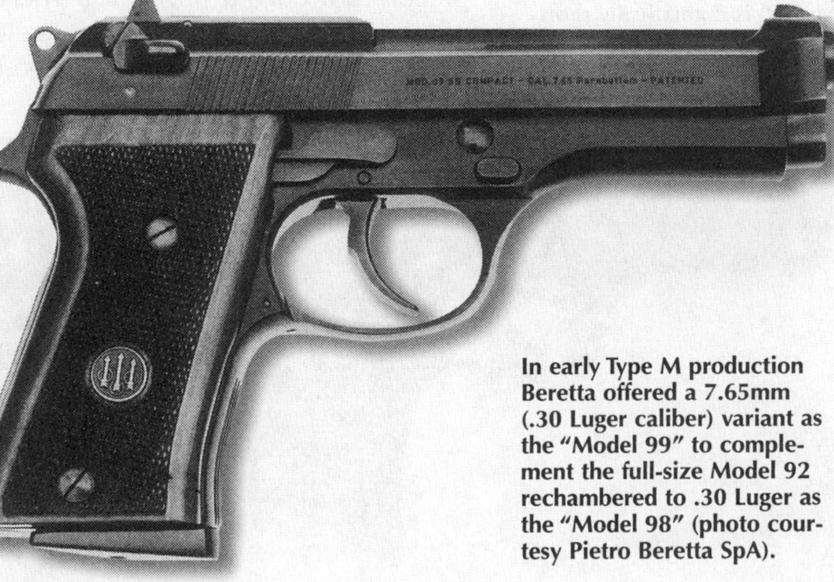

In early Type M production Beretta offered a 7.65mm (.30 Luger caliber) variant as the "Model 99" to complement the full-size Model 92 rechambered to .30 Luger as the "Model 98" (photo courtesy Pietro Beretta SpA).

The first Type M, called the Model 92SBCM, featured a high-polish blued finish and rounded triggerguard, both

features inherited from the Model 92SB. The Model 92 Type M replaced Beretta's first 8-shot 9mm service pistol, the Model 951. Introduced in 1951 with an aluminum-alloy frame, this was re-engineered in a steel frame and placed into series production in 1955. The Model 951 went on to become one of the company's most popular models for decades. It became a service pistol in Egypt, Israel, Nigeria, Haiti and Iraq. With the Type M's introduction Beretta decided to halt Model 951 production in May 1983 but licensed versions, the "Maadi Helwan" and "Maadi Cadet," remained in production in Egypt for many years. The major advantages of the Type M over the Model 1951 were the former's inclusion of a modern double-action trigger and a safety lever allowing mechanical decocking of the hammer.

Compared to a full-size Beretta Model 92FS *(top)*, the Type M *(bottom)* is smaller, shorter and lighter.

Despite the Type M's advanced design, sales were disappointingly low for years. Between 1983 and 1989, when Beretta quit making the Model 92SBCM, Beretta USA imported only about 2,000 of these pistols into the United States. Overseas sales, though greater, remained far below those of the full-size and 13-round variants. Indeed, even the full-size Model 92SB was not a best-seller in the United States in the early 1980s. But that was about to change.

After the 1981 armed forces testing, Beretta had continued refining the Model 92SB to bring it more in line with U.S. requirements. Interestingly, changes made to the SB's frame to create the winning Model 92SB-F came from the Type M: the toe (forward lower portion) of the frame was slightly extended, and the magazine floorplate received a curved finger rest. The hard work paid off in yet another round of testing in 1984, when Beretta finally won the coveted M9 pistol contract for the U.S. armed forces. The first M9 pistol contract, signed

Shown back to back with the parent Model 92FS, the Type M *(left)* is dramatically shorter thanks to its abbreviated grip section.

in January 1985, turned out to be one of the most prestigious handgun contracts in history. The U.S. armed forces' seal of approval put Beretta Model 92-series pistols on the map as far as U.S. sales were concerned. From this event Beretta dates the "arrival" of the Model 92 series in military, police and civilian sales in the all-important U.S. market. This is when the floodgates opened.

The M9 contract was also highly controversial, especially after slide separations occurred in military service, injuring some shooters. To address this serious safety concern, Beretta enlarged the head of the hammer axis pin so that it would lock in a groove cut into the underside of the slide in the event the slide's rear end broke free. This "slide retention device," placed in production in 1990, prevented the slide from flying off the rear end of the frame. The letter "S" added to the model designation denotes this slide retention feature.

Beretta's Type M *(top)* offers 8 rounds of 9mm Parabellum in an efficient, modern locked-breech design in a package hardly larger than the less powerful Makarov pistol shown underneath it.

In 1989 Beretta finally updated the Type M by incorporating the Model 92FS standards developed for the U.S. government. This involved switching from a high-polish blued finish to the matte Bruniton finish, chrome-plating the barrel bore, squaring off the front of the triggerguard, and installing the slide retention feature. Thus updated, the Type M received the designation "Model 92FM." The Type M was the last Beretta service pistol to receive the M9/M10 updates; the rest of the Model 92 pistol line, and even the lowly .380-caliber Models 84 and 85, had preceded the Type M by several years.

The Beretta Model 92 Type M retains all the parent Beretta Model 92FS's desirable features, including its easy disassembly procedure.

Despite the updated features, Type M sales remained disappointingly low. While sales of the 15-shot, full-size Model 92FS and even the 13-shot 92FC soared, the Type M sold so slowly that Beretta USA discontinued its importation for several years except by special order. It's not too difficult to figure out why the Type M fell on hard times. Most shooters of 9mm pistols in the United States favored high-capacity models in those days, which constricted the market for 8-shot models from the outset. Although Beretta sold the Type M at a reasonable price, it competed against even less expensive pistols in the Smith & Wesson Model 3913 series. On the higher-priced end, if one desired an exotic European 9mm compact pistol, the excellent SIG P225, joined by the P239 in 1996, proved formidable competition for the Type M. In the same commercial niche,

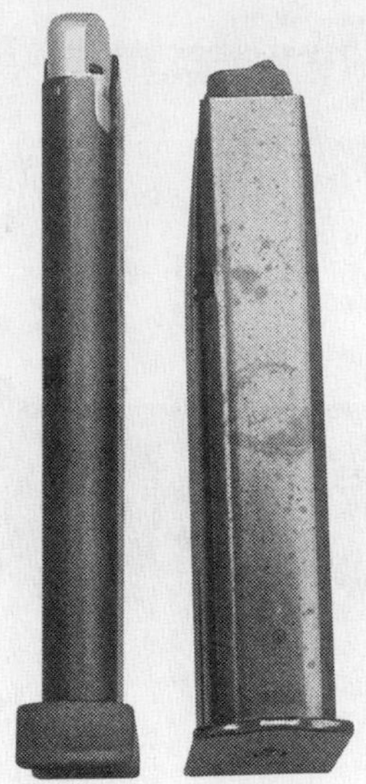

The Type M's magazine (left) is dramatically narrower than the high-capacity magazines used in the parent Model 92 and in such pistols as the FN High Power (right). The Type M's slim magazine allows Beretta to incorporate an appreciably handier grip in its design than is possible with most high-capacity pistols.

the Carl Walther Waffenfabrik offered the well-made P5, popular in police service overseas, and the even more sensational P5 Compact. Also in the higher-priced range, Heckler & Koch's P7 delivered sensational performance and a stellar reputation in foreign military and police use. All these pistols diverted business from the Type M.

The Type M's fortunes began to turn around when Beretta USA began to build it in the United States in 1998. The decision to do so had its roots in events dating back more than a decade. As a stipulation mandated by the government, Beretta USA had begun building full-size Model 92s at their factory in Accokeek, Maryland, shortly after winning the coveted M9 contract. In 1992 Beretta introduced the "Centurion" variation of the Model 92 in a bid to attract police sales. The Centurion featured the full-sized frame of the standard 125-shot Model 92, combined with a shorter barrel and slide. Throughout the mid-1990s, what little demand existed in the United States for the Type M could easily be met by modest importation of Italian-built guns. Then came the U.S. Congress' passage of the Crime Bill in September 1994. As of January 1, 1995, no more high-capacity magazines (over 10 rounds) could be manufactured for civilian sale in the United States. Now, by a stroke of the pen, the full-size Model 92 held only two more rounds than the appreciably less bulky Type M. In the wake of this restriction the Type M's eight shots looked much better than before.

By 1998 Beretta had sold over two million Model 92-type handguns to police and military units around the world. Civilian sales had also been strong, especially in the United States, riding the M9's coattails. The various factors: magazine-capacity restrictions, strong reputation of the Model 92 series, and an increasing interest in concealed carry legislation around the United States—seemed to suggest that the time was ripe to restore the Type M to the product line. When Beretta USA decided to reintroduce the Type M in early 1998, however, they sensibly decided to combine a Centurion upper half with a narrow Type M frame to reduce manufacturing costs. Thus the early "reborn" Type M featured Centurion markings on the slide. Incorporating the maximum number of parts from another pistol design also served as a hedge in case Beretta USA had misjudged the moment and the Type M again failed to catch on. And indeed, the Type M sales encountered what the company hopes is its last stumble. By 2000 the Type M was again reduced to special-order status. At this writing it appears sales are rebounding to a respectable level.

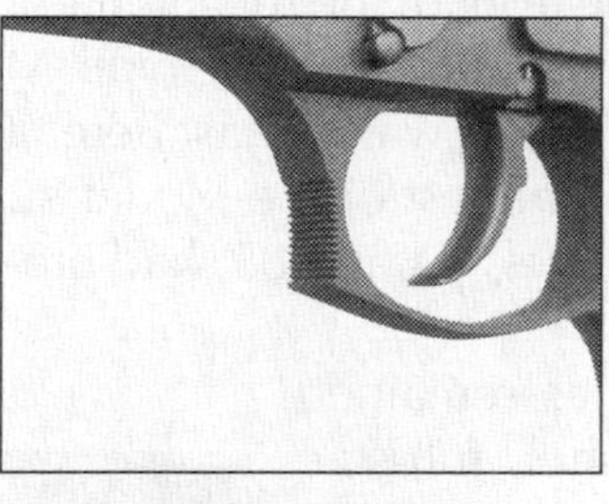

The earliest Type Ms built by Beretta USA featured a slide and barrel taken directly from the company's Centurion model, leading to the slide designation shown, reflecting the firm's continuing uncertainty regarding the Type M's prospects.

As the Type M garners increased attention, Beretta USA has given it its own slide designation and also offers it in an "Inox" stainless steel model as well as in the company's standard Bruniton finish.

The popularity of Beretta's full-size Model 92FS service pistol caused Beretta to redesign the Type M to incorporate some of its features, notably the distinctive recurved triggerguard developed at the U.S. Army's request.

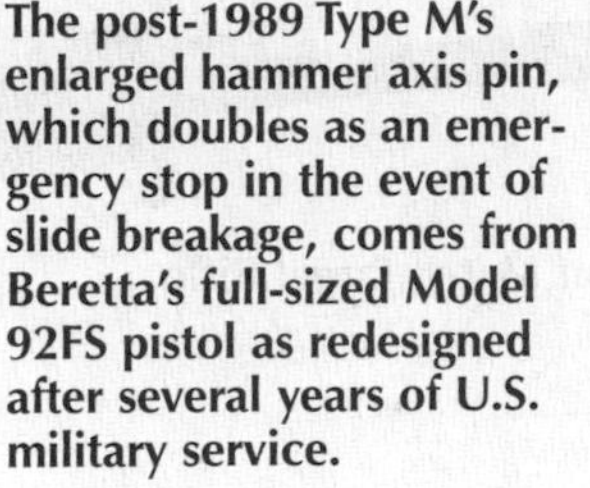

The post-1989 Type M's enlarged hammer axis pin, which doubles as an emergency stop in the event of slide breakage, comes from Beretta's full-sized Model 92FS pistol as redesigned after several years of U.S. military service.

Since 1998 the Type M has caught on well enough for Beretta USA to give it its own purpose-built slide, designated "Compact L." "TYPE M" is stamped on the right side of the frame. The standard Type M features the company's proprietary "Bruniton" matte black finish as developed for its U.S. military pistol. Bruniton is a no-nonsense, nonreflective finish more durable than bluing.

With the Type M's increasing success, Beretta USA has also begun to offer the model in an "Inox" finish. This consists of a stainless steel barrel and slide combined with a silver-anodized aluminum frame. The Type M Inox performs identically to the standard Bruniton-finished model and all parts interchange. The chief advantage of the Inox finish is its superior corrosion resistance compared to Bruniton. On the debit side of the ledger is greater cost and more visibility, possibly complicating concealed carry.

Other Type M options currently offered by Beretta include a standard trigger mode, offering a double-action first shot followed by single-action shots, and a "D" variant which fires double-action for every shot. The Type M-D also dispenses with the ambidextrous combination manual safety/decocking lever found on the standard Type M (inherited from the full-size models since 1979), in favor of a lower-profile "slick slide" configuration. However, the Type M-D retains the loaded-chamber indicator on the extractor, a useful and popular safety feature.

The Type M has suffered a checkered past through no fault of its own. Its superb design offers excellent performance. It successfully combines the outstanding accuracy and reliability of the full-size Model 92 in a package that is easier to handle and readily concealable. The Type M makes a promising service pistol and an outstanding choice for concealed carry. It's one of the most versatile modern automatic pistols currently in production, yet it's withstood the test of time. The Beretta Model 92 Type M represents both a classic and a thoroughly modern pistol design at the same time.

The Type M retains the excellent accuracy and reliability of Beretta's full-size Model 92 pistols.

A 1.9-inch group fired offhand with a Type M pistol shows the gun's excellent accuracy potential. Though the double-action trigger pull is heavier than the single-action pull, both are so smooth that the effect on accuracy is only slight.

A 2.1-inch 25-yard group represents excellent results for a service pistol.

America's Rifle—The AR 15: From Vietnam to the Fields and Woods of America

By Bob Campbell

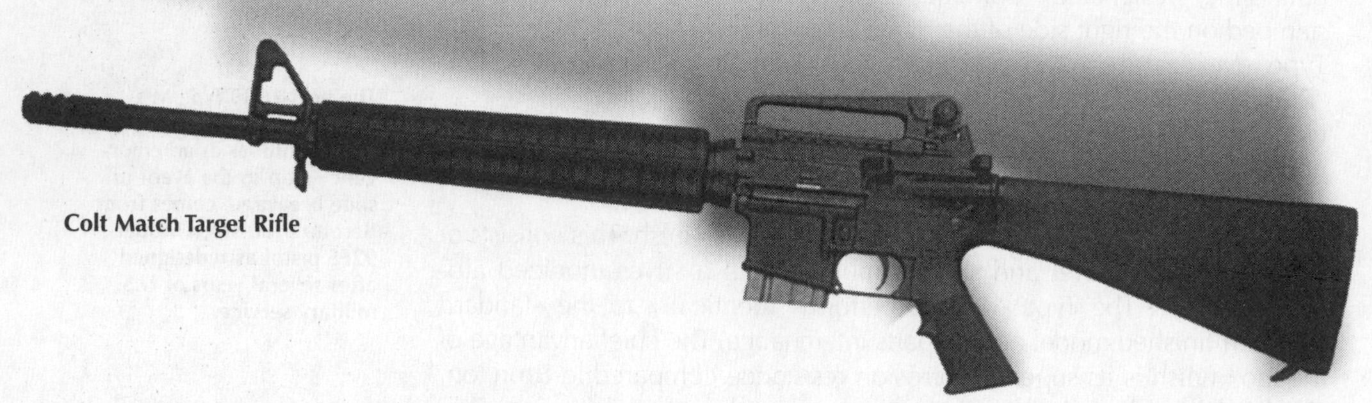

Colt Match Target Rifle

When you look at the firearms in use by American troops and some police agencies, you have to realize that many of these weapons achieved acceptance only after periods of intense criticism. Many weapons, among them the Beretta 92, the Glock and the AR 15, have survived linguistic slings and arrows and have not only soldiered on but have also flourished. The history of the AR 15/M 16 rifle is a long one. Few of the soldiers now deploying with this rifle realize that the basic design is 50 years old. The fact remains that in modern times, rifles—good rifles—tend to be long lived. Who would have thought that the Lee-Enfield's career would stretch from fighting the Zulus in Southern Africa to Communists in Korea? The record of the AK 47 speaks for itself.

America's AR 15 system may be squarely in middle age, but the refinements are quite fresh. The modern M 16 is a sophisticated system well suited to military requirements. It is a simple weapon to clean, maintain and use, and gives good results in the hands

An NCO of the 23d Infantry Division shouts to his men after receiving sniper fire near Chu Lai in Vietnam early in 1971.

of its user after relatively quick training. The opinions of several recent graduates of basic training at the U.S. Army training center at Fort Jackson, South Carolina, were unanimous—they were impressed with the rifle. Matthew Campbell, who was Soldier of the Cycle, liked the way the gun worked. He remarked that the rifles used were "old, really old." I am sure they were. The top marksman was a young man from Montana who had learned to shoot ridding the landscape of coyote and jackrabbit. There are lessons there, and good ones. One lesson is that none of the top shots of the class were target shooters, not one. They shot when hunting. Range work was zeroing the gun in, confirming the zero, and then getting down to business. Another lesson there.

The men and women who will use the rifle in battle are most important, but we need to give them something to fight with. Thank God our young warriors are not saddled with ironmongery such as the British SAR 80. It breaks and does not work, and the hue and cry from the ranks is met with scorn from the government. By any standards our people are better armed by leagues. The AR 15 is a compromise in some regards but when weighed in the balance, the trade-offs are reasonable. There are indeed criticisms, but when we look at the choices of professional operators worldwide, including top-paid security personnel, special weapons teams, and even Israeli troops, we find that the AR 15 is often chosen by those who can have their choice of any weapon. While there are weapons that seem more reliable than the AR 15—the AK 47 is one of these—the AR 15 is more accurate and easier to handle than the AK and overall the cartridge is superior.

The AR 15 has undergone numerous improvements over the years. The original weapon did indeed experience reliability problems, but these cannot be laid upon the gun itself. Poor liaison and ineptitude in military ranks were the culprits. Some variations of the rifle, especially short barrel types, did not prove as reliable as the full size rifle. Overall, the rifle's reputation was sullied for no good reason.

The AR 15—I use AR 15 as the term for the original rifle and the civilian version, the M 16, and now the M 4, are military rifles—is a gas-operated weapon as is every semi-automatic rifle I am aware of in current military use. A problem in any such system is that powder ash can find its way into the rifle's action, but the AR 15 is prone to dumping ash into the chamber. Armalite Corporation originally developed the AR 15 with ammunition loaded with IMR propellants.

The author saved this target before continuing to sight in this particular AR 15. Note the small group just above the Shoot N C bull.

Reliability was excellent. Maintenance was much lower than in previous service weapons, and the gun was light and easy to use well. While the AR 15 might suffer in comparison to the M 14 in long-range fire, it was far superior to M 1 and M 2 carbines and to any submachine gun. This was the real goal, to have an all-around weapons system. When the Army adopted the M 16, the powers that be decided to standardize on cartridges loaded with ball powder. This ammunition had a different pressure curve than IMR loaded ammunition. The rifle malfunctioned; sometimes exhibiting stuck case malfunctions. The cyclic rate was affected and ball powder tended to clog the weapon's gas cylinder.

Unfortunately the Army did not withdraw this ammunition from service in Vietnam despite damning field reports. Congress found that the Army's decisions led to the loss of lives and "bordered on criminal negligence." The Army tried to blame the problems on lax cleaning and maintenance in the field, despite the fact that they had not issued cleaning kits with the weapon. An extraordinary situation considering that even the bolt-action 1903 Springfield had been issued with a pull-through, brush and oil bottle. The Army issued the famous M 16 "comic book" cleaning manual that showed how to properly service the M 16, and eventually issued cleaning kits.

When Colt engineers were contracted to fix the M 16 problems, they saw that the Army was slow in changing ammunition and tried to adapt the gun to ball powder use. A special recoil-buffering device that featured an "internal plurality of masses" was developed and rushed to Vietnam. This device altered the M 16 cyclic rate and allowed the use of ball powder. Another development was a type of bushing or wedge that

The author found the Bushmaster carbine is as good an AR 15 type as he has ever fielded.

While the author makes use of his own handloads for many reasons, it is difficult to equal the accuracy and performance of Black Hills factory ammunition.

increased extractor tension, resulting in more forceful extraction.

This probably reduced malfunctions caused by cases stuck in the chamber. With a change of ammunition and the issue of cleaning kits, as well as strict maintenance requirements, the M 16 turned in good service. I have seen translations of NVA dispatches in which they spoke of the fear the enemy had of the "black gun." I am not sure that is where the term "black gun" comes from but this is as good a source as any. The "black gun" is something to be feared in the hands of our young warriors.

Since the end of the Vietnam War, the M 16 has performed well in various conflicts and our allies have found the rifle capable and reliable. The Israelis appreciate the M 16 and seem to prefer it to the home produced Galil. Some nations have adopted the M 16 or rifles based on the M 16 system. Others, who are not used to warfare, have adopted

The Winchester 64-grain jacketed softpoint offers excellent performance, out of proportion for the caliber.

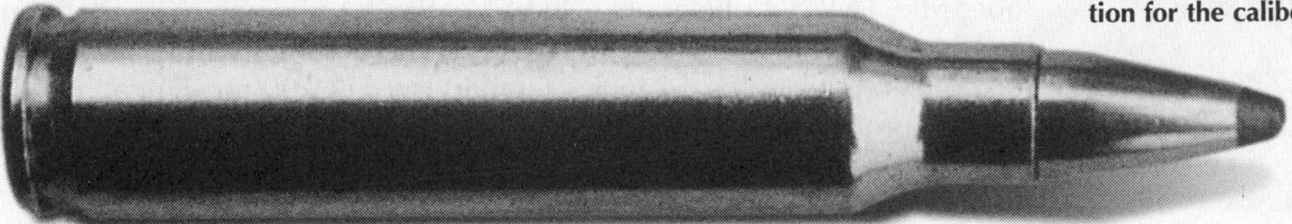

Many GIs fighting in the humid jungles and uplands of Vietnam kept an improvised rifle cleaning kit—a bottle of cleaning solution and a toothbrush—handy in the elastic band on their helmets. In fact M 16 malfunctions were more likely to be the result of the type of ammunition in use.

more complex and expensive systems and regretted it. Along the way, there have been M 16 programs that resulted in modification and development of the weapon. All have not been successful. Some were sent into action prematurely, and their shortcomings affected the rifle's reputation. Among the failures were various short barrel rifle programs.

The development of a submachine gun version of the M 16 was not long coming, but has been a process fraught with problems. Making a pistol cartridge perform adequately in a carbine is one thing—it is simple to design a blowback action—but attempting to make a rifle cartridge perform adequately in a short barrel format is quite another. The 11.5-inch barrel variants were known as the XM 177. These were the first M 16s to use folding stocks with various positions. This gun exhibited stupendous muzzle flash and a general lack of reliability. The necessary push and gas to properly actuate the action was simply not there in such a short barrel. Sufficient gas volume was not reliably generated. After many tests and developmental problems with short barrel AR 15 variants, the M 4 program finally proved successful. This rifle standardized the 14.5-inch barrel. This barrel length has been found to be the minimum length required to ensure the full 3000 fps in muzzle velocity necessary to retain effective wound ballistics in the .223 caliber rifle. The M 4 rifle appears to be headed toward universal adoption as the Army's rifle-submachine gun do-everything shoulder arm. My experience shows the 16-inch barrel adds a full 100 fps. Since the 16-inch barrel is the shortest civilians can legally purchase, this length looks even better! The 16-inch carbine is indeed a good compromise, long on handling but not giving up a lot of performance.

Sights and Sighting

Many shooters prefer the flat top model AR 15 in order to use optical sights. I still use most of these rifles with open sights, but the flat top does make mounting a scope much easier. There are many scopes that have been proven in hard use with the AR 15. Among the most reliable is the Leupold type used by active duty units. I have limited experience with this scope, but it has been used by ham-handed cops in various agencies and continues to have a good generation. Leupold's reputation is solid and I feel that this is a good scope.

The AR 15 can be quite effective in sniper suppression or in a police marksman's role. The optical sight is a must-have in this situation. Among the better all-around scopes that I have experience with comes from ATN. This scope features an illuminated reticule. Unlike some scopes, if the battery dies the reticule remains visible. This is a good feature.

When using the ATN scope, the rifle should be sighted for the most appropriate range. The scope can then be adjusted for range by setting a dial. In other words, the scope could be sighted for 100 yards for close-in predator calling and then instantly flipped to 200 yards if a longer shot was needed. The ATN's reticule is very clear for long-range shots. I have fired perhaps 1,250 rounds with an ATN scope mounted on my Bushmaster. This is a fine combination, one that I appreciate very much.

For those who favor the red dot type sight, the Bushnell HoloSight II works well. This sight is quick on target with an excellent field of view. While the HoloSight does not fit my personal needs, many will find that it is the quickest of all sights for ranges up to perhaps 50 yards. Range is an important consideration when deciding which sight equipment you will use on your AR. If I were still a peace officer, this might well be my first choice.

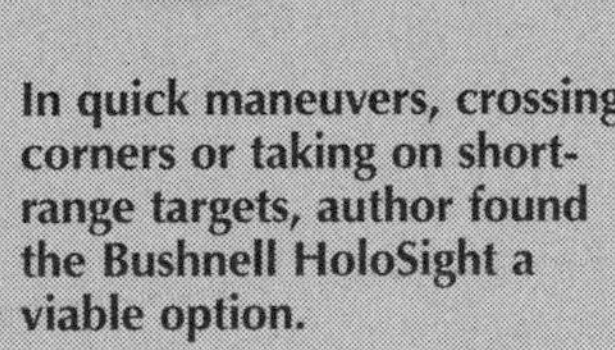

In quick maneuvers, crossing corners or taking on short-range targets, author found the Bushnell HoloSight a viable option.

When sighting in the AR 15 rifle—if the rifle is intended for personal defense—understanding the short-range zero is imperative. For example, if you attempt to make a precision shot at point blank range to about 10 yards you will find that the point of impact in relation to the sight picture can be about 4 inches low or even more. The sights are mounted above the line of sight, which results in considerably low strikes in relation to the point of aim at short range. Takeover robberies are depressingly common, and a large portion of my practice relates to attempting hostage rescue shots. This is simply shooting a bad guy off someone's back. If you are not familiar with the rifle's point of aim, that bullet will crash into the hostage, not the hostage taker. This is where the men in black earn their pay.

This is the long-range aperture for use at 100 yards or more.

At this point it is well to consider 5.56mm cartridge performance. The 55-grain military load is known to violently fragment or break apart at the cannelure—at least inside 100 yards. At 150 yards and beyond, its effect is more problematical. In civilian and police use in America, the .223 has proven to be extraordinarily effective, producing severe wounds and quickly putting adversaries down. Unlike handgun rounds, the .223 actually produces voids in tissue.

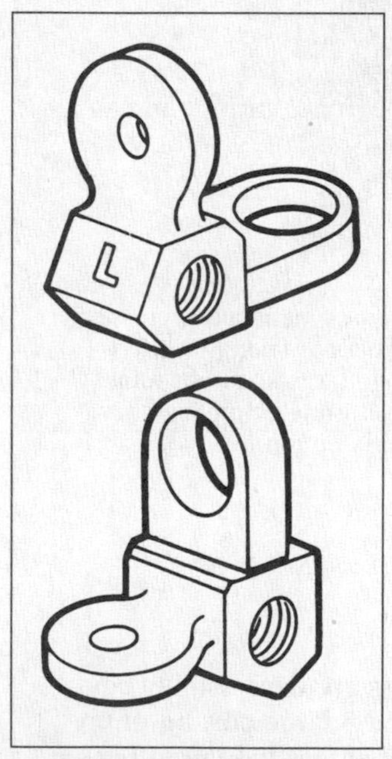

The low light level flip-sight for the M 16 has two apertures, a 7-mm opening for situations with limited visibility and a smaller, 2-mm aperture for normal conditions. The M 16 front sight is illuminated with a split post containing tritium.

While the performance of the cartridge is based on bullets and powder to a considerable extent, there are other factors. In a vehicle, the gearing of the rear end can affect performance, and similarly, in a rifle, the barrel has an effect upon the bullet. While bullet twist is far from an arcane science, it is not clearly understood by many users. When first introduced, the AR 15 used a one in fourteen-inch barrel twist. This resulted in a bullet that was not well stabilized, but performed with acceptable accuracy. When the bullet struck animate targets—usually members of the Viet Cong—it produced severe wounds. Early reports concluded that the rifle was more effective at short range than was the lower velocity .308 caliber M 14 rifle. Likewise .30 caliber carbine and pistol caliber submachine guns were simply not in the same class with the "black gun." However, these conclusions were drawn from the experience of jungle combat. The M 16 was originally intended to be a short-range weapon, intended for a specialized mission. After Vietnam, the Army standardized the M 16 cartridge. The M 16 would have to fight in Europe and at longer ranges and a cartridge capable of penetrating Soviet web gear was needed. The lightly clad Viet Cong did not present this problem. A heavier bullet with greater penetration was needed. Rounds heavier than the standard 55-grains required bullet twists of one in nine inches to one in seven inches in order to stabilize the long, heavy bullets. After testing most of the available loadings for the 5.56mm gun, I found the heavy bullet loads do offer longer range and greater penetration, while the lighter bullets have superior short range wound ballistics. I will not use bullets below 52 grains since 40-grain bullets seem prone to disintegration before reaching the target. In semi-auto rifles, function with these bullets can be a bit sluggish. I prefer 55- to 64-grain bullets.

Loading the .223

I have used 52- to 60-grain bullets with fine results. I no longer experiment with bullets lighter than 52 grains, having enjoyed good results in all rifles with the heavier bullets. For certain special applications I have loaded 68- to 77-grain bullets but just feel that a 60 grain 3200 fps is about right for the .223. Since 90 percent of my shooting has been with the AR 15, this has been the correct course. I have found that finer grained powders which meter easily into the .223's small case mouth work best for me, both in loading and in shooting. What surprised me is that almost all powders and bullets loaded gave at least satisfactory results. Others have outstanding to amazing results. I will not tell you I ran to the laboratory and worked these loads up just for this report. I have a well-equipped 1200 square foot loading area that is well laid out and filled with good equipment, but this type of research takes time. These loads were worked up and fired over a period of many months. Some entries represent the first try, with little load development, while others are more highly developed. But the most accurate have much in common—they are the most recent. I have invested in a number of items that are used by match shooters. Whether or not they are worthwhile for varmint hunters or casual shooters I cannot say. But I have coached my carbines beyond what I thought they were capable of with this equipment and careful loading practice. I have on hand from Russ Haydon's Shooters' Supply a set of special case preparation tools that ensure each case is uniform from the case mouth to the primer pocket. (I use Winchester commercial brass primarily.) My loading dies are from Dillon Precision, but I have a special match-type seater from A. E. Wilson. This die ensures the bullet is seated concentrically with the cartridge case. A Haydon arbor press allows the full implementation of the dies. I use a Hornady scale to weigh each charge, and a Vibra Shine powder trickler for helping finish off that last tenth of a grain. When loading for precision I have used bullets from Berger, Bart's, and ZIA custom bullets with excellent results. Why go to so much trouble? The .223 is an accurate cartridge and the AR rifle can perform nearly as well as a bolt-action rifle. With the right sights, the right trigger and especially with a person with trigger time behind those sights, the AR 15 is an awesome game gun and truly America's rifle.

I have found a few loadings that give .223 users a good balance between penetration and expansion. The bullets used in these loads do not fragment but rather push a full-caliber mushroom and offer adequate penetration. One load uses the Winchester 64 grain jacketed softpoint; another uses the Black Hills 60-grain jacketed softpoint. It is a tossup in some ways, one may prove the more accurate in one rifle rather than the other, but both are good performers.

If you are an AR 15 shooter or collector, you are sure to face the question at one time or another of pre-ban and legal parts. According to federal regulations, folding stocks are not supposed to be added to new rifles. If you really need or desire such features as a bayonet lug, flash suppressor, or folding stock, and are not stationed at Fort Bragg, perhaps your best bet is to invest in a pre-ban rifle. While I agree that the crime bill serves no purpose save to inconvenience honest gun owners, it is nevertheless foolish to run afoul of it. My Bushmaster is perfectly serviceable and better made with quality material, than most pre-ban rifles. There is no profit in skirting the law. Our modern rifles

The performance of any AR 15 can be improved by the installation of an aftermarket trigger assembly such as the Compass Lake assembly at right.

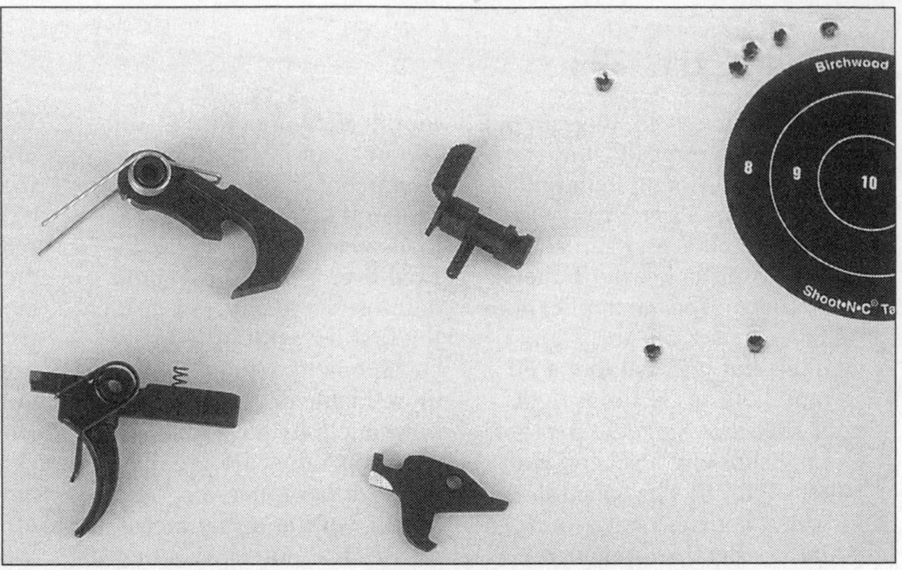

are quite good just as they are. I do not particularly care for ten round magazines but there are plenty of legal pre-ban twenty- and thirty-round magazines available at reasonable prices. Some appear not to have been used but constantly traded! In any case, the wise shooter would do well to carefully husband these magazines and use the inexpensive ten round magazines for practice.

When addressing the exact model of rifle a prospective AR 15 shooter might wish to purchase, the topic of which gun is a hot one. There are pre-ban and post-ban guns, and the law is the law, no matter how erroneous its precepts. While I really don't feel limited by owning a rifle with no bayonet lug—to each his own.

These bullets, from Zia bullets and Northwest Custom Projectile, have given fine results. The NWCP bullet is a rebated boat tail.

There are several profitable avenues that can be used to increase the accuracy of the AR 15 rifle. While ammunition selection is the simplest, tightening the action is another. There are various ways of accomplishing this. The AR 15 has an upper and lower receiver, and some models are much tighter than others. The factory Bushmaster is pretty tight as it comes from the factory, but it can be improved. Upper and lower halves can be glass bedded with standard bedding compounds available from Brownell's. Simply glass the upper and lower together carefully and, when first breaking the bond, pull the upper receiver straight up, being careful not to lever it unevenly. A surprisingly effective but simple little add-on is the Accu Wedge. I got mine from Mid South Supply. The Accu Wedge is a small plastic part that fits between the upper and lower receivers to tighten the action by a margin.

My personal rifle has been fitted with a Compass Lake trigger action. This is a very good feature, and relatively simple to install. After all, the linkage of the AR 15 is pretty simple. It is, however, possible to miss-install a trigger group. The usual result is a rifle that fires twice—once when the trigger is pressed and another when it is released. This is not a good thing! Take care in installing your trigger and you will find that you can control shot placement measurably better.

While the forte of the AR 15 rifle is rapid fire and quick, coarse shooting, my experience shows the rifle can be very accurate as well. Without the thrashing of heavy recoil, and with excellent human engineering as

AR 15 Cartridge Performance

The following loads have proven accurate and reliable in numerous AR 15 type rifles. Due care and reduction of powder charges by 10 per-cent is indicated before using these loads in your personal rifle, but none showed undue pressure signs. I have enjoyed firing these rifles very much and hope to do so for many years to come.

All loads fired in a Colt HRAR or a Bushmaster 20-inch barrel variant for accuracy unless otherwise noted. All Winchester primers. Remember, these groups were fired with open sights. The rifle is fitted with sights from KNS precision—this precision aperture allows excellent shooting.

Bullet	Powder Charge	Velocity	100 Yard Group
Speer 40 grain	28 Win. 748	3399 fps	2.0 inches
Sierra 40 grain	28.3 Win. 748	3427 fps	1.8 inches
Hornady 45 grain	22.0 IMR 4198	3367 fps	1.25 inches
Speer 50 grain TNT	26.5 AA 2495	3165 fps	2.25 inches
Barnes 50 grain VLC	26.5 IMR 3031	3290 fps	1.9 inches
Zia 52 grain	28.0 Win. 748	3299 fps	1.1 inches
Sierra 52 grain	25 IMR 3031	3333 fps	1.3 inches
Sierra 52 grain	28 Win. 748	3287 fps	1.4 inches
Sierra 52 grain	26 AA 2230	3321 fps	1.3 inches
55 grain Nosler	27.5 Win. 748	3290 fps	1.4 inches
55 grain Nosler	27 Varget	2788 fps	1.2 inches
60 grain Sierra	27 AA 2520	3056 fps	1.25 inches

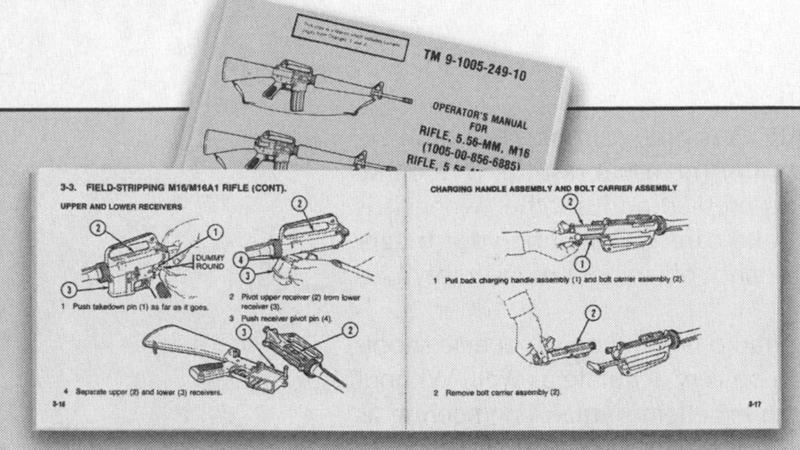

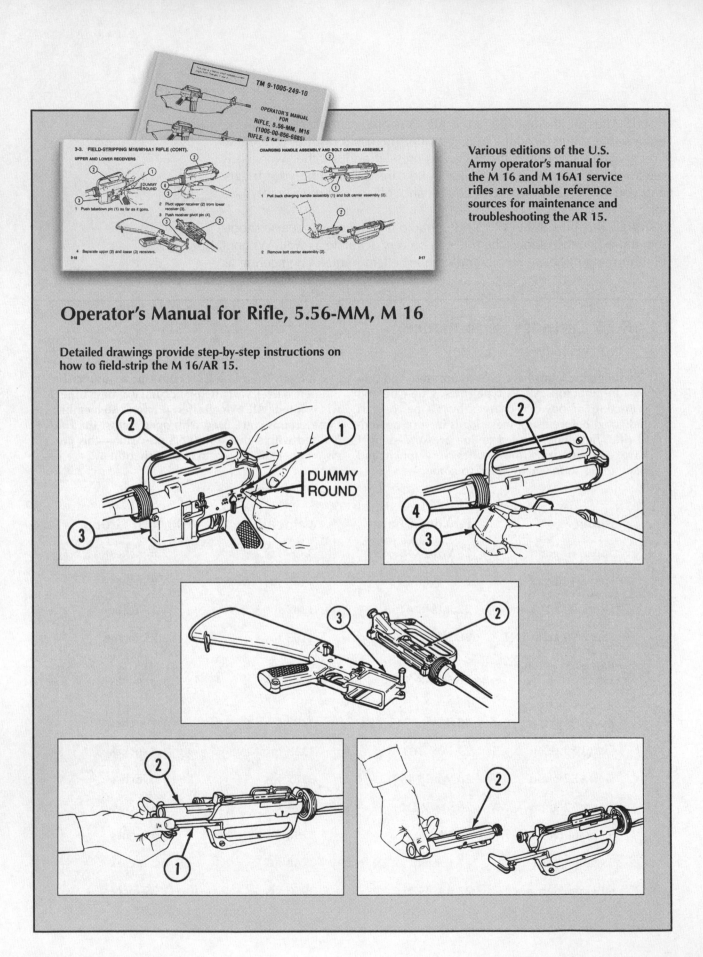

Various editions of the U.S. Army operator's manual for the M 16 and M 16A1 service rifles are valuable reference sources for maintenance and troubleshooting the AR 15.

Operator's Manual for Rifle, 5.56-MM, M 16

Detailed drawings provide step-by-step instructions on how to field-strip the M 16/AR 15.

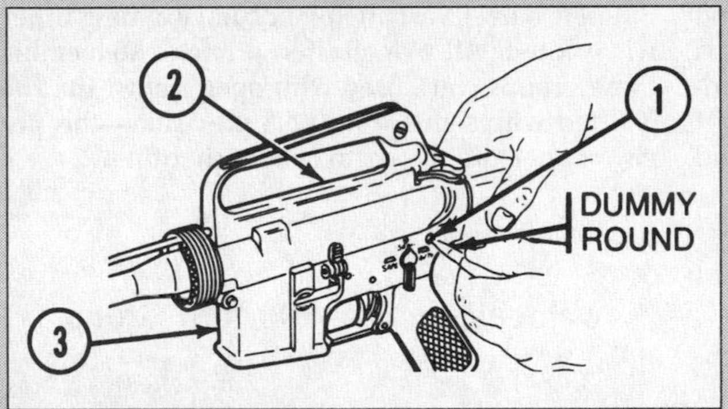

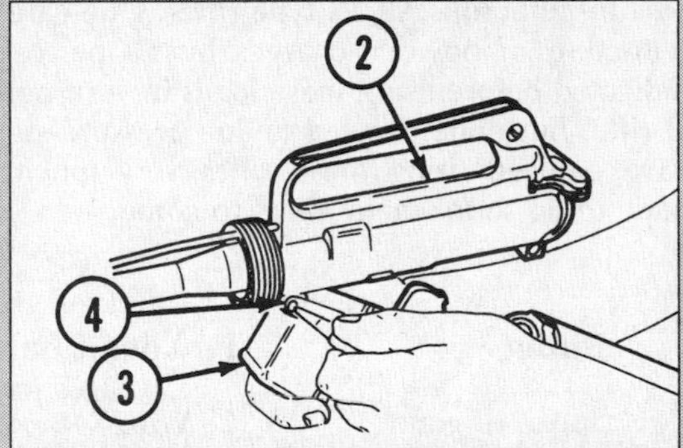

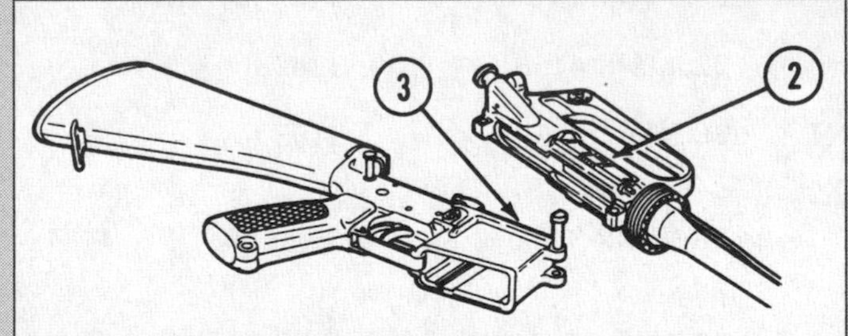

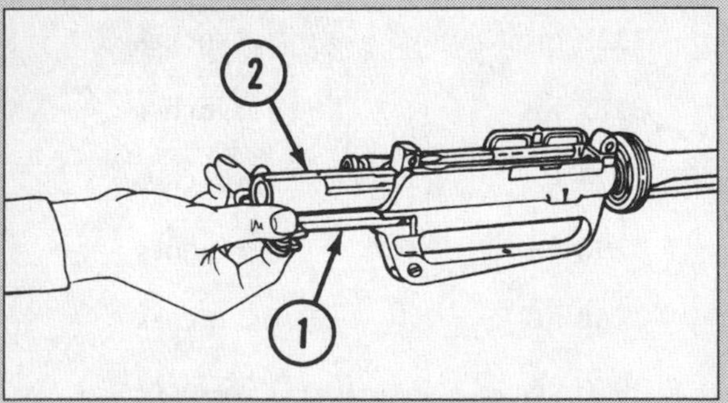

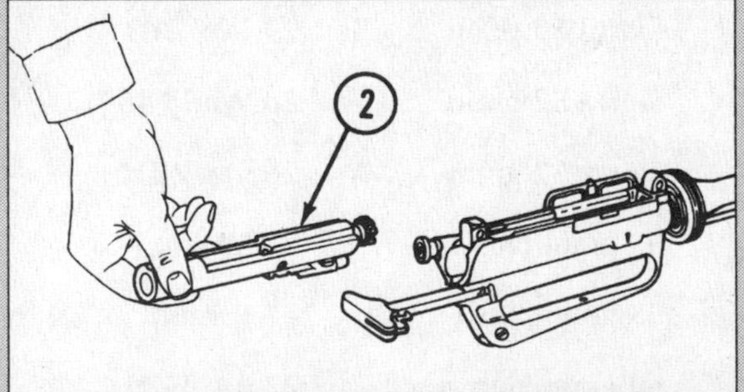

an aid—the controls are well located for rapid manipulation under stress —it is obvious the AR 15 is a rifle made with accuracy in mind.

The AR 15 is a popular choice for service rifle competition and is popular in three-gun "Combat Matches." But what many do not realize is that the rifle and cartridge have lived up to the promise of the original name Colt gave the gun when it was offered for civilian sale — the "Sporter."

The AR 15 in .223 caliber has taken its fair share of coyote, jackrabbit, polecat, crow and any other pest that fell under its sights. In addition, it has taken more than a few deer-size animals. While I am not sure that I advocate the taking of deer with a .224-inch bullet, even a fast centerfire, a friend of mine has used the .244 to take a string of 14 deer with single shot kills. It was a long, long time ago, but Charles Newton felt that his .22 Newton High Power would be a good game killer. However, the Newton cartridge was designed around a .227-inch 90-grain bullet at 3100 fps. This is a little beyond the .223's capabilities as commonly loaded, but I don't think a properly designed 80-grain bullet at 3200 fps or so is out of the question in a solid .223 caliber rifle. I have done just that in my Howa bolt action—but that is another story. These long bullets can be loaded in .223 cases, but are too long to feed properly in an AR 15 magazine. Suffice to say, for the man that can shoot straight, or for a slightly built woman or young boy, the .223 can be the ticket for deer-size game at moderate range. On smaller game, it is dynamite. For the larger animals, the factory load of choice seems to be Winchester's 64-grain jacketed softpoint.

The AR 15 remains primarily a military cartridge and a very popular one. The cartridge has many good points. Recoil is light and it shoots flat. Quite a few of my favorite loads, if sighted for 200 yards, are about 1.5 inches high at 100 yards and drop perhaps 7.5 inches at 300 yards. Try that with the .30-30! This is a fast stepping cartridge that is dynamite on varmints, very good on predators, and works well in good hands against larger animals. It is a wonderfully accurate match cartridge and a fine center-fire plinker. What more can we say? This is America's rifle cartridge.

MANUFACTURER'S SHOWCASE

VERSATILE RACK COMPANY

Maximize the space in your safe with handgun racks from Versatile Rack Co. Made with a welded steel wire frame for years of dependable use, then vinyl-coated to protect the finish of your expensive handguns. Available in versions to hold either 4 or 6 handguns. Visit us online to see our complete line of quality products. Dealer inquiries welcome.

Web Site Address:
www.versatilegunrack.com
Or call us at: 323-588-0137

Site-In-Clean Rest

Looking for a great value in a shooting rest?

MTM Case-Gard's Site-N-Clean is a rest so versatile, it makes sighting-in rifles, patterning shotguns, range cleaning, and even maintenance a breeze. The Site-N-Clean offers easy positioning using rubber padded shooting forks along with a handy, rear elevation dial. Available separately or as part of a Site-In-Clean Rest with Case combo, in which the rest rides inside a spacious, lockable range box. Shooters can carry the rest plus their shooting equipment in one handy, range-ready container.

MTM Molded Products Company
P.O. Box 13117, Dept. STB05 • Dayton, OH 45413
Tel: 937-890-7461 • www.mtmcase-gard.com

Specifications:
- Precision ground cast iron table: 10" x 34"
- Table travel: 17¾" longitudinal & 12¾" cross
- Spindle taper: R-8
- Spindle travel: 3½"
- Max. spindle to column: 17⅞"
- Max. spindle to table: 20⅛"
- 9 Speeds: 420-5000 RPM
- Motor: 1½ HP, Single-phase
- Approx. shipping wt: 1350 lbs.

Includes:
- Way chip protectors
- Drawbar

The **G9977** is **$2,195.00** and is shipped in the lower 48 states for $200.00.
Please check current pricing before ordering!

3 LOCATIONS
Bellingham, WA / Muncy, PA / Springfield, MO

514003658

Visit our Web site!

MEDIA CODE AD1762

TEL: 1-800-523-4777 • FAX: 1-800-438-5901

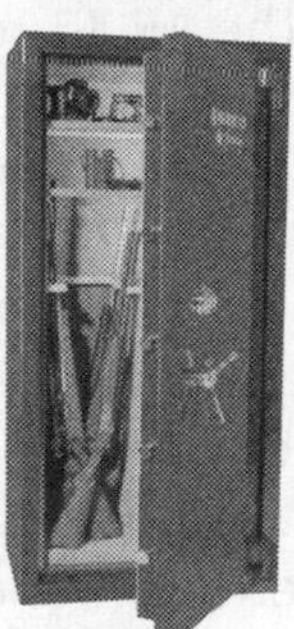

Think you own the best gun safe? Or are you interested in owning the best?

AMERICAN SECURITY PRODUCTS (AMSEC) offers you Better service, Better construction, Better interiors and the Best safety and fire protection available. AMSEC, the world's best known provider of security safes, offers more than 50 years of engineering in every safe we make! Our Gun Safe catalog provides complete details on our entire product line—and the best warranty on the market! Want to update or purchase the Best gun safe in the industry? It's easy, just contact your local sporting goods and gun retailer. Or call **AMSEC at (800) 421-6142.**

MANUFACTURER'S SHOWCASE

FORREST INC. OFFERS RIFLE/PISTOL MAGAZINES

Whether you're looking for a few spare magazines for that obsolete 22 rifle or pistol, or wish to replace a 10-shot with the higher-capacity pre-ban original, all are available from FORREST INC. With one of the largest selections of magazines, they offer competitive pricing especially for dealers who buy in quantity.

FORREST INC. also stocks parts and accessories for the Colt 1911 45 Auto Pistol, the SKS and MAK-90 rifles, and many U.S. military rifles. One of their specialty parts is firing pins for obsolete weapons.

Call or write for more information and a FREE brochure, DEALERS WELCOME! HIGH CAPS OUR SPECIALTY!

FORREST INC.
P.O. Box 326, Lakeside, CA 92040
Tel: 619-561-5800 Fax: 1-888-GUNCLIP
Web: www.GUNMAGS.com

Specifications:

- Precision ground cast iron table: 9½" x 39⅜"
- Table travel: 21⅞" longitudinal, 9¼" cross & 13½" vertical
- Spindle taper: R-8
- Spindle travel: 4⅞"
- Max. spindle to column: 26½"
- Max. spindle to table: 13½"
- 9 Vertical spindle speeds: 270-2950 RPM
- 8 Horizontal spindle speeds: 72-1300 RPM
- Motors: 2 HP (vertical), 1½ HP (horizontal), Single-phase,110/220V
- Table swivels side to side (not shown)
- Approx. shipping weight: 2360 lbs.

The **G3617** is **$2,995.00** and is shipped in the lower 48 states for $300.00.
Please check current pricing before ordering!

3 LOCATIONS
Bellingham, WA / Muncy, PA / Springfield, MO

grizzly.com **Visit our Web site!**

TEL: 1-800-523-4777 • FAX: 1-800-438-5901

MEDIA CODE **AD1762**

514003658

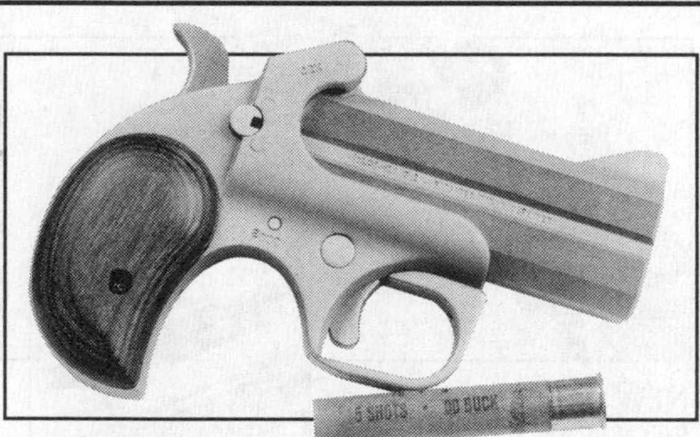

THE CENTURY 2000 DEFENDER "C2K" FROM BOND ARMS, INC.

The Century 200 Defender ("C2K") is the ultimate in self-defense. With its 3.5" double barrel, the C2K chambers the 3" .410 00 Buck Shot with five pellets. It also features a rebounding hammer, retracting firing pins, crossbolt safety, cammed locking lever, spring-loaded extractor and interchangeable barrels. Choice of caliber includes .410 with 3" chambers and .410/45LC with 2.5" chambers.

For further information, contact:

BOND ARMS, INC.
P.O. Box 1296 • Granbury, TX 76048
Tel: (817) 573-4445 • Fax: (817) 573-5636

Model ST1

TRIUS
"Setting the Standard for 45 Years"

The Trius 1-Step (shown) is almost effortless to use: (1) Set arm and place target on arm. (2) Step on pedal to put tension on arm and release target in one motion.

Birdshooter: quality at a budget price–now with high-angle retainer. **Model 92R:** the original "foot trap" **TrapMaster:** sit-down comfort plus pivoting action.

Trius traps are adjustable without tools; feature lay-on loading: singles, doubles, plus piggy-back doubles–offer unparalleled variety.

TRIUS PRODUCTS INC.
P.O. Box 25, Cleves, OH 45002
Tel: 513-941-5682
Web Site: www.trius.com

MANUFACTURER'S SHOWCASE

GLASER SAFETY SLUG, INC.

For over 25 years Glaser has provided a state-of-the-art personal defense ammunition used by the law enforcement and civilian communities Available in two bullet styles, the Glaser Blue is offered in a full range of handgun calibers from 25ACP to 45 Colt (including the 9MM Makarov and 357 Sig) and four rifle calibers; .223, 308, 30-06 and 7.62x39. The Glaser Silver is available in all handgun calibers from 380ACP to 45 Colt. A complete brochure is available on the internet @ www.safetyslug.com or contact:

GLASER SAFETY SLUG, INC.
1311 Industry Road
Sturgis, South Dakota 57785
Tel: 800-221-3489
Fax: 605-347-5055

Montana Hunter

GARY REEDER Custom Guns

Gary Reeder Custom Guns offers its 45 Long Colt: the **MONTANA HUNTER.** This new 5-shot beauty comes in the barrel length of your choice in either hi polish or satin stainless finish. The **MONTANA HUNTER** features our "Gunfighter Grip" in laminated walnut, interchangeable front sight blades, and our soft satin Vapor-Honed finish with contrasting high polish on the small parts. For the serious handgun hunter, the MONTANA HUNTER is hard to beat.

GARY REEDER CUSTOM GUNS
Tel: 520-526-3313
Web site: www.reedercustomguns.com

MODEL G9249 12" x 37" BELT DRIVE GAP BED LATHE

Specifications:
- Swing over bed: 12"
- Swing over gap: 18⅞"
- Distance between centers: 37"
- Spindle nose taper: MT#5
- Spindle bore: 1$\frac{7}{16}$"
- Speeds: 12
- Speed Range: 50-1200 RPM
- Tailstock barrel taper: MT#3
- Tailstock barrel travel: 3"
- Motor: 2 HP, Single-phase, 220V
- Approx. shipping weight: 790 lbs.

Includes:
- 6" 3-jaw chuck • 8" 4-jaw chuck
- 10" face plate • Steady rest
- Follow rest • Chip tray
- Heavy-duty stand • 4 way tool post
- Dual inch/metric dials

The **G9249** is **$1,895.00** and is shipped in the lower 48 states for $150.00.

Please check current pricing before ordering!

3 LOCATIONS
Bellingham, WA / Muncy, PA / Springfield, MO

514003658

Visit our Web site!

MEDIA CODE AD1762

TEL: 1-800-523-4777 • FAX: 1-800-438-5901

NEW — AO LEVER SCOUT MOUNT

Scout Scope Mount for lever guns w/8" Weaver-style rail and cross slots on ½" centers. Mounts scope ⅛" lower than previously possible for Marlin 1895 Guide Gun, 1894 & 336. Positions intermediate eye relief scope forward for extremely fast reticle acquistion, facilitates both eyes wide open for better target acquistion, and allows use of AO Ghost-Ring Sights without scope. Simple installation, no gunsmithing required, uses existing rear dovetail and front two mounting holes on receiver. AO Sight Systems: makers of AO Express/Pro Express Sights. Price: Lever Scout™ Mount: $50.00

AO SIGHT SYSTEMS
2401 Ludelle Street • Fort Worth, TX 76105
Tel: 817-536-0136 • Fax: 800-734-7939
Toll-free: 888-744-4880 • Website: www. aosights.com

MANUFACTURER'S SHOWCASE

MODEL G4016
13½" x 40"
GEAR-HEAD
LATHE
WITH STAND

Specifications:
- Swing over bed: 13½"
- Swing over gap: 19"
- Distance between centers: 40"
- Spindle: Camlock D1-4
- Spindle bore: 1 7/16"
- 8 Speeds: 78-2100 RPM
- Tailstock barrel taper: MT#3
- Tailstock barrel travel: 3½"
- Motor: 2 HP, Single-phase, 220V
- Approx. shipping weight: 1410 lbs.

Includes:
- 6" 3-jaw chuck • 8" 4-jaw chuck
- 12" Face plate
- 4-way turret tool post
- Two MT#3 dead centers
- Live center
- Steady rest • Follow rest
- Jog button & emergency stop
- Tool Box
- Stand, chip pan & splash guard

The **G4016** is **$2,695.00** and is shipped in the lower 48 states for $200.00.
Please check current pricing before ordering!

3 LOCATIONS
Bellingham, WA / Muncy, PA / Springfield, MO

514003658

grizzly.com **Visit our Web site!**

MEDIA CODE AD1762

TEL: 1-800-523-4777 • FAX: 1-800-438-5901

To feature your products in our Manufacturer's Showcase in the next edition of the Shooter's Bible contact:

SHOOTER'S BIBLE
STOEGER PUBLISHING

17603 Indian Head Highway
Accokeek, Maryland 20607
(301) 283-6300

BENCH MASTER® RIFLE REST

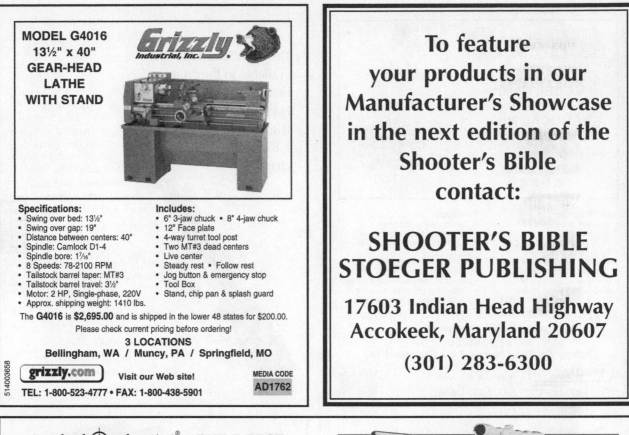

The Bench Master Rifle Rest is a rugged, compact and highly adjustable rifle-shooting accessory—one that offers precision line-up and recoil reduction when sighting in a rifle, testing ammunition or shooting varmints. It features three course positions totaling 5.5", with 1.5" fine adjustment in each course position, plus leveling and shoulder height adjustments for maximum control and comfort. Because of its unique design, the Bench Master can easily double as a rifle vise for scope mounting, bore sighting and cleaning. It comes with a LIFETIME Warranty and a list price of only $124.95. For a free brochure, call or write:

DESERT MOUNTAIN MFG.
2001 W. Fourth Plain • Vancouver, WA 98660
Tel: 360-693-5835 Fax: 360-693-7916

CNC Machined Trigger Guard

This is a complete CNC machined trigger guard eqipped with precision EDM parts. It features an internal pretravel adjustment that is set at the factory in order to greatly reduce pretravel. This new match trigger guard is CNC machined from a solid billet of high strength aircraft aluminum. The hammer is a precision ground 440C stainless steel. The sear and disconnector are EDM manufactured parts. The trigger is black anodized and equipped with an overtravel adjustment screw. The trigger is reset internally. An automatic bolt release and an extended magazine release are also included.

Volquartsen Custom Ltd.
24276 240th Street • P.O. Box 397 • Carroll, IA 51401
Telephone: 712-792-4238 Fax: 712-792-2542
E-mail: vcl@netins.net • Web Site: www.volquartsen.com

MANUFACTURER'S SHOWCASE

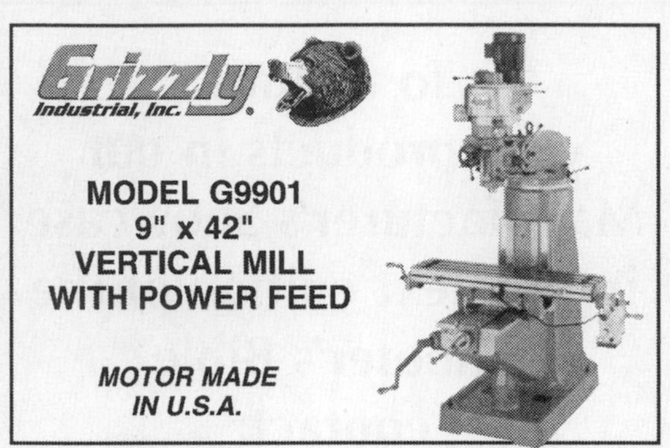

Specifications:
- Precision ground cast iron table: 9" x 42"
- Table travel (longitudinal): 25⅞"
- Table travel (cross): 12½"
- Max. dist. spindle to table: 18¼"
- Max. dist. spindle to column: 17½"
- 8 Speeds: 78-2000 R.P.M.
- Motor: 2 HP, Single-phase
- Approx. shipping weight: 2400 lbs.

Features:
- One-shot pump lubrication
- Power down feed • R-8 Spindle
- Quill Feeds/Spindle Rev.: .0019", .0035", .0058"
- Auto stop w/ micro adjustable stop
- Longitudinal power feed
- Adjustable micrometer quill depth stop
- Hardened & ground table surface
- Chrome plated, precision ground quill

The **G9901** is **$3,495.00** and is shipped in the lower 48 states for $375.00.

Please check current pricing before ordering!

3 LOCATIONS
Bellingham, WA / Muncy, PA / Springfield, MO

514003658

grizzly.com **Visit our Web site!**

MEDIA CODE AD1762

TEL: 1-800-523-4777 • FAX: 1-800-438-5901

The Lazz/Sako TRG-S is available in the "red hot" Lazzeroni 7.21 (.284) Firebird caliber along with the very popular 7.82 (.308) Warbird chambering.

This is one of the finest long range hunting rifles in the world, featuring a stainless steel barrel, precision three lug bolt action, detachable 3 round magazine box, heavy duty composite stock and a decelerator recoil pad.

Available exclusively from Lazzeroni Arms Co., PO Box 26696, Tucson, Arizona 85726-6696.

LAZZERONI ARMS COMPANY
Phone: 888-492-7247
Fax: 520-624-4250
E-mail: arms@lazzeroni.com
Web Site: www.lazzeroni.com

African Hunter

GARY REEDER Custom Guns

Gary Reeder Custom Guns presents the ultimate in a full custom hunting handgun. The **AFRICAN HUNTER,** a 5-shot single action handgun, is available in either 475 Linebaugh or 500 Linebaugh. As soon as we get an order, each gun is built the way you want it. You can have it in the caliber of your choice and the barrel length of your choice.

You can also have it in high polish stainless or in our own satin Vapor-Honed finish. If desired, the **AFRICAN HUNTER** can be equipped with a muzzle brake at no extra charge.

GARY REEDER CUSTOM GUNS
Tel: 520-526-3313
Web site: www.reedercustomguns.com

SERIES S MODEL L

HARRIS ENGINEERING, INC.

ULTRALIGHT BIPODS
- Versatile
- Sturdy
- Light
- Fast

SERIES S BIPODS
Pivoting Bipod with tension adjustment

Harris Bipods clamp quickly and securely to most stud equipped bolt-action rifles. Folding legs have completely adjustable spring-return telescoping extensions. Time proven design and quality manufacture. Thirteen models available plus adapters for various guns.

HARRIS ENGINEERING INC.
999 Broadway • Barlow, Kentucky 42024
Tel: 270-334-3633 • Fax: 270-334-3000

CUSTOM GUNMAKERS

This section of *Shooter's Bible* features custom guns from the most prestigious American small shops. Mass production of interchangeable parts and the factory manufacture of small arms came about in the 19th century. Before that, all guns were essentially unique unto themselves, though basic mechanisms and styles were shared among many makers. The custom gun survives because connoisseurs of firearms want something better than can be had from factory assembly lines, and they're willing to pay for the hand labor.

In its true sense, "custom" means built-to-order, with the customer dictating the gun's features and dimensions. There are practical limits to custom orders, of course. Few shops will offer an action to the buyer's specifications. They are constrained by the costs of designing and building actions (as well as by patents and the fact that most of the best actions are already in production) to use what is already available from major arms suppliers. To say that a rifle is not really a custom rifle because it employs a Remington 700 action is being too severe.

The gunmakers featured in this section are some of the most competent craftsmen in the field. Indeed, there are gunmakers, stockers, metalsmiths and engravers practicing today whose work is the best of its kind ever seen. Quality standards (and prices) continue to climb. In future editions of *Shooter's Bible,* you'll continue to find the best of the best in custom guns.

American Hunting Rifles

A few years ago, well-known firearms experimenter Ken Howell designed 12 rimless cases based on the .30-06 case. Well, not quite. The case looked like the '06 and had the same head dimensions, but it was 2.600 overall, or .106 longer than a .30-06 hull. At 2.058, head-to-shoulder measure was .110 greater than on the .30-06; and the Howell hull had a .455 shoulder —bigger by .014.

The Howell necks accepted common bullets: .224, .243, .257, .264, .277, .284, .308, .323, .338, .358, .375 and .411. Ken established all shoulders at 25 degrees and kept the necks .375 in length (head-to-shoulder measure on formed cases thus varied slightly with caliber). The Stevensville, Montana, gun enthusiast says they deliver near magnum performance with magnum recoil.

Ken and local entrepreneur Ed Plummer wanted to offer a semi-custom rifle for these cartridges. Ed went first to Winchester for Model 70 actions. Nothing came of it. He then visited the Czech Republic, where he made a deal with CZ for its Model 550. Ed went to renowned Kalispell gunmaker Jerry Fisher for a stock design, engaging a Bitterroot valley craftsman to fit and finish the walnut. The result was a delightful rifle with a clean, slim look and excellent balance. Reshaping trigger and bolt handle improved function and appearance. Ed called his firm American Hunting Rifles.

AHR rifles feature Mauser-type extractors, two-position thumb safeties, barrels from McGowan and Wilson (button rifled) and Lawrence (with cut rifling). Synthetic stocks are McMillans. Jim Weisner supplies replacement triggers and three-position safeties.

"Our metalwork is done right here in the Valley," says Ed. That includes truing the receiver and bolt face, lapping the lugs and ironing out the ribs on the CZ magazine boxes so they accept the AHR cases. A standard AHR bolt gun holds four in the magazine; magnum models hold three. Magnum rifles, incidentally, feature an additional recoil lug on the barrel and double crossbolts at the magazine well. Instead of a forend swivel stud, magnums have a barrel-band stud.

There are two other AHR models, built on the double-square-bridge CZ 550 magnum action. The Safari 550 offers a medium-fancy quarter-sawn walnut stock cut to your specified length of pull, oil finished and capped with a black Decelerator pad. Checkering is 22 lines per inch in four panels. Chambering: almost any common belted round, plus the .350 Rigby. The Safari 550 DGR (Dangerous Game Rifle) includes a custom trigger and Weisner three-position safety, an extra-fancy grade of walnut. Ordinarily bored for the likes of the .416 Rigby, .458 Lott, and .450 and .500 AHR, the DGR can be had in a host of standard and wildcat chamberings that require a long action and big bolt face. NECG supplies custom rear swivel studs for the Safari rifles, as well as fixed-and-folding rear open sights and barrel-band front sights. All are standard features. A quarter rib is available so too a muzzle brake. When I last visited Ed, he was working on three new cartridges of his own design: a .450, .500 and .585 AHR. The .500 AHR is an Ed Plummer original, similar in form to the potent .500 Jeffery but with a longer neck, 25-degree shoulder and full-diameter (not rebated) rim. Ballistically, it matches the Jeffery and the .505 Gibbs.

Axtell Rifle Company

Sheridan, Montana

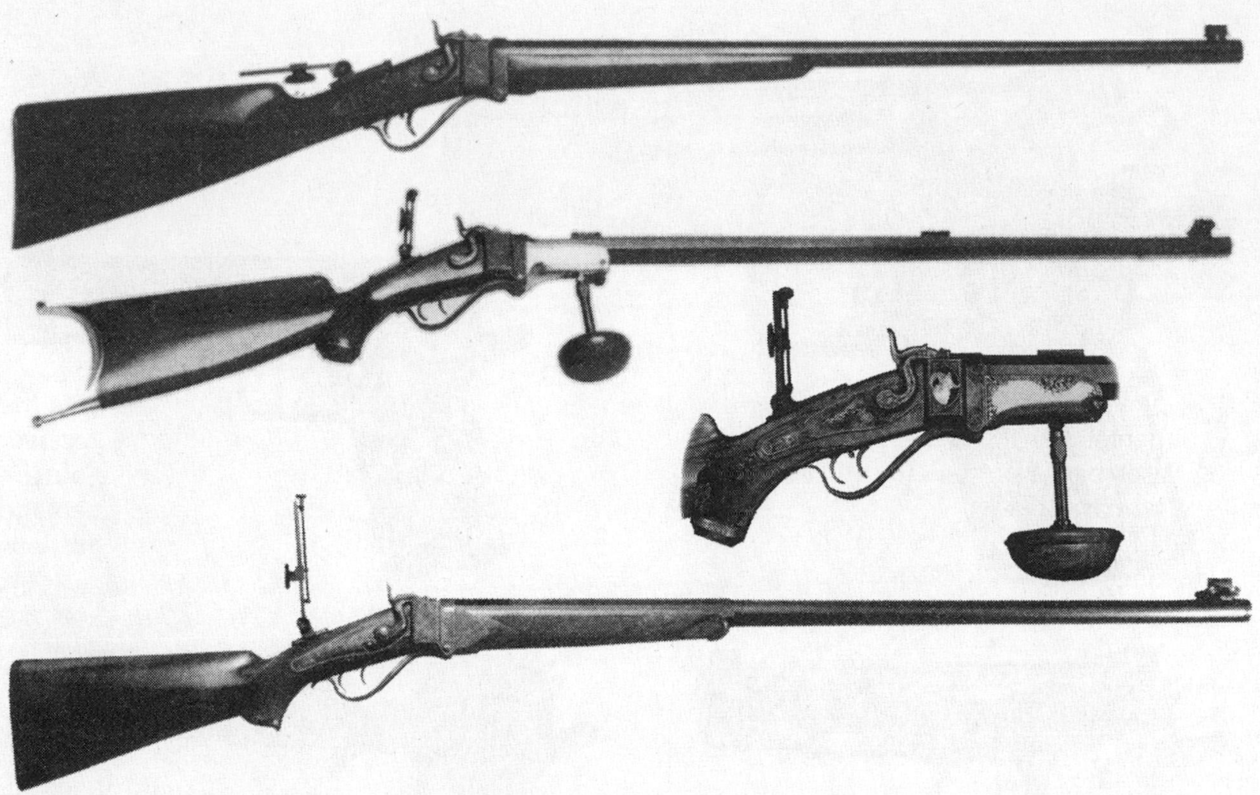

"Anybody can make a rifle. You don't have to be a man," says Carmen Axtell of Axtell Rifle Company ... and with one look at any Sharps 1877 rifle from her Sheridan, Montana, shop, all doubts vanish. It's artistry, remarkable not only for the authenticity of line, balance and mechanism, but for the meticulous care evident in the fitting and finishing of parts. The case coloring is exquisite, wood and metal finish ... well, better than the original.

In 1973, Riflesmith, Incorporated began manufacturing exact replicas of the late 19th-century sights used on Sharps rifles and others capable of long shooting. In 1989 the Axtell Rifle Company was formed to manufacture the New Model 1877 Sharps.

The original is not well known to casual gun enthusiasts, who for the most part are much more familiar with the 1874 Sharps rifles—the "buffalo guns" of books and films. Truth is, the Model 1877 is better. It evolved from a need for a more accurate long-range target rifle, about the time the famous Creedmoor Rifle Range was established on Long Island. The 1874 Sharps had proven its mettle in a match pitting Americans against the Irish. But shooters wanted faster lock time and a heavier barrel. The 1877 incorporated both.

"It's not a cheap rifle to produce," explains Carmen. "Our prices reflect cost more than profit. And you'll never be disappointed."

Axtell Rifle Company makes several variations of the 1877 Sharps: Custom Express, No. 1 Creedmoor, No. 2 Long Range, Lower Sporter, Lower Business, and Overbaugh Scheutzen. All 10 chamberings are original Sharps rounds, from the .45-70, .45-90 and .45-100 Express to the various 40- and 45-caliber cartridges only students of the period remember.

Axtell offers all manner of appropriate accouterments, from tang sights (included on all models) to the palm rest on the Schuetzen version. A variety of tang and globe sights are listed for sale separately. Like the rifles, all ring true in looks and function, and show the highest level of craftsmanship. In the rifle-making business, Carmen Axtell has deftly carved her own space.

Les Baer Custom

Hillsdale, Illinois

Les Baer, a well-known name among pistol shooters, and the first stop for competitors seeking a superior .45 self-loading pistol, is as committed to street-worthy guns as to National Match equipment.

His custom 1911-style .45s have earned their reputation in the hands of many national pistol champions as well as people like Clint Smith, who runs a training facility for both police and civilian shooters. Les Baer offers the standard-size 1911 pistols, and more compact Comanche and Stinger versions. You can also buy the frames in steel, stainless steel and alloy form, and slides and barrels are available as well. Other components include safeties, triggers, bushings, sights, magazines ... the list is long.

Les Baer Custom also markets custom-built autoloading "AR" series rifles and components for tactical shooters, service rifle competitors and anyone who simply wants one of the best .223 rifles on the market. The NRA Match rifle has a 30-inch, hand-lapped fast-twist barrel, floating handguard, two-stage Jewell trigger, titanium striker and many other refinements. The Picatinny rail, available on other Baer .223s, accommodates both scope rings and a receiver sight. You can also find rifle components in the Baer catalog, from handstops and stocks to barrels, bolts and upper and lower receivers. Les Baer has a versatility that has proven to be rare in the custom gun trade.

Mark Bansner

Adamstown, Pennsylvania

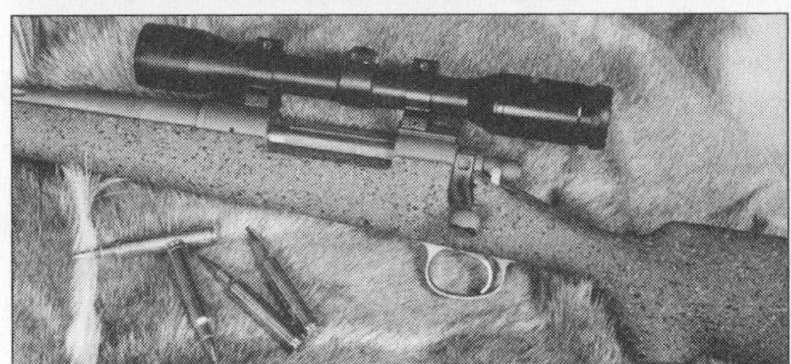

"Hardware that shoots." Mark Bansner has a practical perspective when it comes to building guns. He started with shotgun modifications that wowed turkey hunters, then gradually changed his focus to rifles. Now, with over 20 years of experience under his belt, Mark specializes in sleek, lightweight bolt-action rifles, for which he furnishes his own synthetic stocks (produced under the name "High Tech").

Four employees help Mark ship about 120 custom-built rifles a year from his 3,000-square foot shop in Adamstown, Pennsylvania. "We do no over-the-counter business," Mark explains. "While we have standard rifle configurations and options, each order is individual, and the customer can make his rifle truly personal." Though his rifles are each in fact one-of-a-kind, they cost much less than what many hunters would expect: between $2,200 and $3,700.

Some things come standard in Mark's rifles: match-grade Lilja barrels, hand-lapped, are fitted to actions trued from centerline to ensure concentric chambering. Tuned or replacement triggers deliver a crisp, consistent pull, and the stocks of graphite, epoxy and fiberglass cloth are hand-bedded to cradle the metal securely and without imposing any stresses.

Bansner rifles are guaranteed to deliver fine accuracy. "These rifles are for discriminating hunters who expect a high level of field performance. We—the people who build the rifles—are hunters too. I want my rifle to shoot a half-minute group, so that's what I offer prospective customers. A Bansner rifle will print half-minute 3-shot groups, or I'll make it right."

Shuffling through stacks of proof targets Mark has saved, even the most suspicious buyer has to be impressed. One-hole groups are common. These rifles do shoot well, even the 6-pound Sheep Hunter model. They look good too, with trim, functional lines and stock finishes that vary in color to taste. When ordered, speckling and spider-webbing is expertly applied. Stock-to-steel fit is skin-tight except on the barrel, which Mark provides in both fluted and conventional form. He even makes his own muzzle brakes. "They reduce recoil by up to 45 percent."

Mark keeps busy building rifles—but not too busy to take them afield on hunts. "Somebody has to test 'em," he grins.

The Biesens
Spokane, Washington

The basement, its dark north end a repository of aging walnut blanks, was never neat. Gun parts and tools lay scattered below faded photos of Biesen rifles in the hands of hunters behind trophy game. If you talked with Al, you had to do it on your feet while he worked. He liked to talk. For decades a sanctuary for people who dreamed of fine rifles, the Spokane, Washington, shop was also a first stop for those able to buy them. Jack O'Connor visited here, and carried a pair of lightweight Biesen .270s on hunts all over the world.

Now 86 and throttling back on his gunmaking, Al has turned his shop over to son Roger, who makes no apology for incorporating his father's style in the new Biesen rifles. Roger's daughter, Paula, has even turned her hand to the business, as an engraver. She's good at it.

"Dad didn't force me into this. I got plenty of encouragement but no push. My idea was to cut into steel what I painted in school—mostly animals." She grins.

Paula was up against stiff competition. "Grandpa would show me a Terry Wallace floorplate and tell me to try something like that! Sheesh!" But this pretty, vivacious blond refined her talent on gold and German silver nameplates, then started cutting grip caps and bottom metal. Meanwhile, she had been courted by David Malicki, a native of Napa, California. They married in 1992. David worked as a plumber in Spokane, while Paula began embellishing rifles.

"It was difficult starting," she confides. "I didn't know if I could succeed. But Grandpa was patient, and eventually I lost my fear of ruining a rifle." Paula's work has appeared on rifles commissioned for auction by the National Rifle Association, the Rocky Mountain Elk Foundation and Safari Club International. Her most daunting project was a rifle Al Biesen built for himself. "It's a Model 70 Winchester in .30-06," she tells me. "The wood was a gorgeous piece of French walnut that Grandpa salted away in 1968. It's a privilege to work on rifles like that; but there's also a lot of pressure. Grandpa could have gone to the best of engravers for that job."

Paula's modesty belies her clean rendering of detail and the lifelike appearance of the animals she scribes into steel. Her artistry shows in their facial expressions and musculature. "You learn tricks," she says, shrugging. "Like never setting an animal face-on so you have to duplicate details right and left. But just knowing what not to do isn't enough. Engraving game scenes is hard! Achieving fluid forms with a chisel is much tougher than with a brush."

Six years ago, just weeks before delivering her first baby, 29-year-old Paula Biesen was accepted as a member of the Custom Gunmakers Guild at the group's 1998 convention in Reno. As Al's rifles, and now Roger's continue to delight shooters, so Paula's work keeps the Biesen basement a popular shrine for rifle enthusiasts.

Kent Bowerly
Redmond, Oregon

Since his early retirement from the boatbuilding industry in 1985, Kent Bowerly has been busy building rifle stocks. But his gun work really started in 1958, the year Winchester announced its .338 Magnum and shortly after Weatherby came up with the Mark V rifle. Kent mated a Springfield 03-A3 to a Roberts semi-inletted stock. Friends admired his craftsmanship, and they offered to pay him for stockwork on their rifles. So began the hobby that would turn into a late career.

During the 1960s, Bowerly studied under Al Biesen and Earl Milliron, both masters of the trade and both living close by in the Pacific Northwest. He applied their techniques to classic hunting rifle stocks he shaped, fitted and finished.

"Mostly, I built handles for Winchester Model 70s," he says. "In those days, you could still get the early ones for a reasonable price, and a lot of hunters preferred them." He emphasizes that his stocks are of utilitarian design, though they carry the lines and detailing that sophisticated gun enthusiasts admire. "If a rifle won't shoot well in your hands, if it's not responsive, if it lacks the fine balance to point itself and put your eye behind the sight automatically, it's not stocked properly, no matter the quality of wood or workmanship."

Now, Bowerly works as a full-time stockmaker, applying his hand to both rifles and shotguns. He still likes the Model 70, but he's fitted walnut to Mausers as well, and the occasional Dakota 76 (a Model 70 look-alike). He has fashioned stocks for Ruger Number Ones, a rifle that adds variety to his workbench in Redmond, Oregon. Photographs of Bowerly rifles have appeared on rifle magazine covers and in the Nikon sports optics catalog, appropriate showcases for such a skill.

David Christman

Delhi, Louisiana

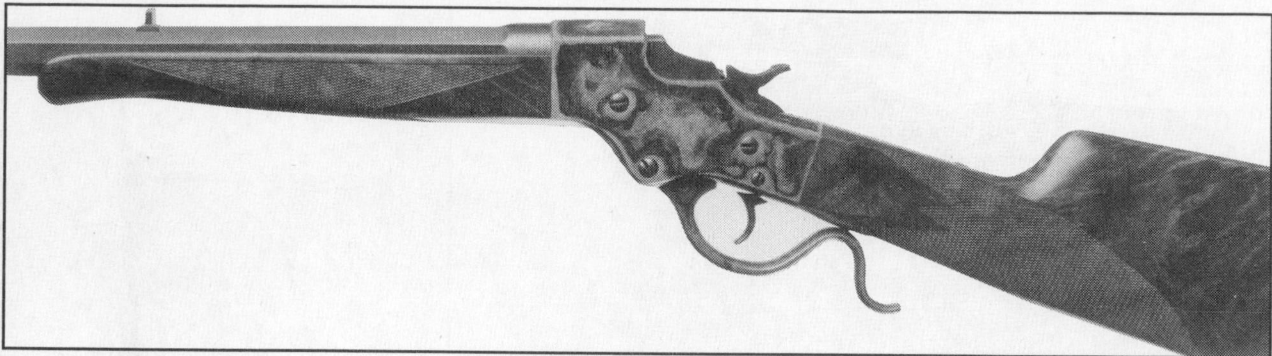

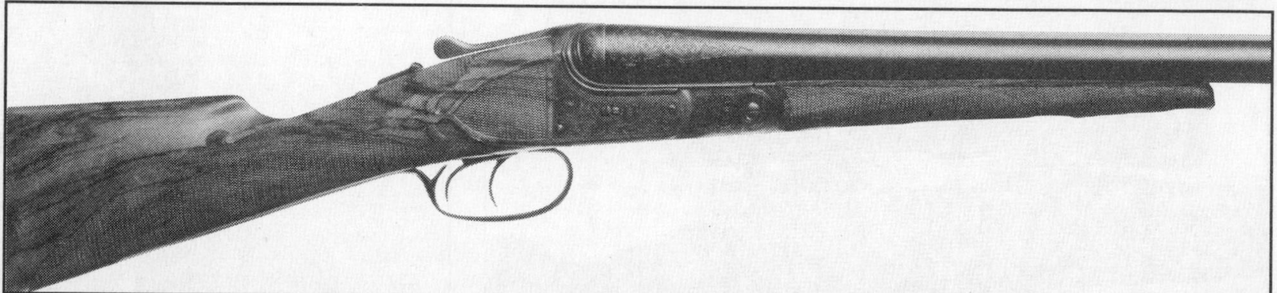

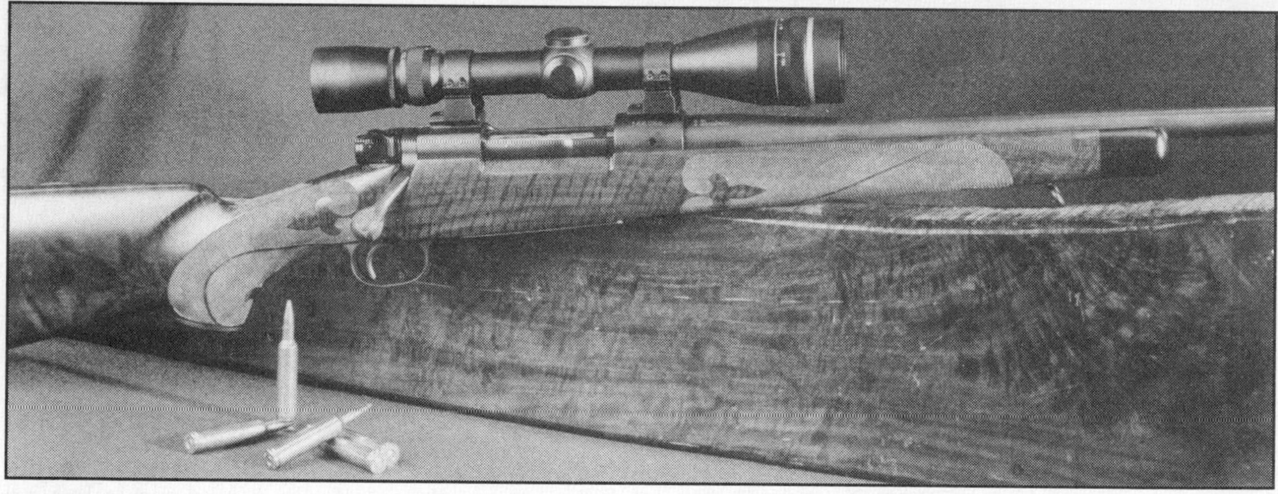

A corporate job kept David Christman in Colville, Washington, for 20 years. But after a U.S. West downsize, he decided it was time to go home. It may have been the move he needed. Now, back in Louisiana, David has restocked Parker double shotguns and Stevens single-shot rifles, besides building the bolt-action rifles so popular with custom makers. David isn't limited to one component or operation, and his versatility shows. He does both wood and metalwork, farming out only engraving.

"I suppose my favorite project is a bolt rifle on a Mauser 98 or Winchester 70 action. It should get a piece of English walnut, but Don Cantwell's high-grade Claro makes me almost as happy. Given the right parts and a little metalwork, the Remington 700 can blossom into a handsome custom rifle too. Right now I'm finishing up a four-gun set on Searcy actions. Hard metal in those!"

David offers a full suite of restocking and refinishing services, including rust bluing, in the same shop that turns out complete custom shotguns and rifles.

Jim Clark, Jr.

Princeton, Louisiana

In 1950 Jim Clark Sr. became the fifth pistol shooter—and the first civilian—to break a score of 2600 in bull's-eye competition. A decade later he became the fourth shooter to reach 2650. Jim Clark became the first president of the American Pistolsmiths Guild, bringing his match experience to the bench. There, for many years, he built handguns to outshoot the competition. In 1985 he received the Pistolsmith of the Year Award, and five years later the coveted Outstanding American Handgunner Award.

Jim Clark Sr. passed away two years ago, but his son has continued in the family tradition, not only turning out first-class custom pistols but earning the accolades of fellow shooters. Jim Clark Jr. was named Pistolsmith of the Year in 2000—the year he won the Soldier of Fortune Sniper Match competition. He repeated that victory in 2001. Clark has topped the field in the Buckmasters World Pistol Championship and Kenneyathalon (both in 1997), twice emerged as Steel Safari Champion, three times as Buckmasters World Rifle Champion and five times as Soldier of Fortune Champion.

While the Clark enterprise began as an "accurizing" service, making service and .22 pistols shoot better, the company has expanded to include revolvers, rifles and Clark's own aftermarket accessories. There's even a Clark tactical shotgun. Sights, mounts, triggers, safeties, magazines, grips, even the hardware to help install them—all are available from the Clark shop in Princeton, Louisiana. Conversion work remains a specialty. The Clark team draws from half a century of pistol know-how. Tap into it.

D'Arcy Echols
Providence, Utah

Trained as a gunmaker in Colorado, D'Arcy Echols established himself as a riflemaker at his shop in Providence, Utah. His elegant bolt guns stocked in fine walnut showed a fine eye for line and detail. D'Arcy has a rare, almost uncanny ability to carry out the most intricate work in wood and metal. But he avoids gingerbread.

"I like to build rifles you'd hunt with," he says. "The profile of a great rifle must serve a purpose, not just attract attention on a rack." Rather than incorporate novel ideas for the sake of novelty, D'Arcy achieves superiority the hard way: with perfectly straight lines and a mating of wood to metal that looks impossibly tight. His checkering, remarkable for its symmetry and uniformity, adorns a grip and forend that all but grab your hands. Cast-off is standard, and D'Arcy's pantograph is set up to deliver the requisite difference in "bend" between toe and heel. The classic rifles from D'Arcy's shop point like fine English shotguns.

The problem is, they're very expensive.

When in 1997 a customer suggested that D'Arcy build a less costly rifle with a synthetic stock, the affable gunmaker asked, "Why?" The answer: "so you can build more than five rifles a year and sell them to more hunters." Since then, the Echols "Legend" rifle has given D'Arcy more clients (and headaches) than he had before. "It helps to have a sense of humor if you're a gunmaker," quips D'Arcy. "Crying drives the customers away." But D'Arcy needs neither wit nor humor to keep the customers coming. His rifles do just that.

Built on new Winchester 70 Classic actions, mainly for belted magnum cartridges, the Legend wears a McMillan stock that D'Arcy designed in his shop. He overhauls the action, first modifying the magazine box to hold an extra cartridge. He lengthens the loading port and bores out scope base holes, tapping them for 8-40 screws. When fitting the Krieger cut-rifled barrel, he remachines then laps the lug seats and lugs, and squares up the receiver face and bolt face. He also repins the trigger and bolt stop and grinds the sear surface for a crisp, consistent 3-pound pull. After hand-bedding the matte-blued metal, D'Arcy shoots each rifle at least 40 times to break in the barrel and make sure the rifle meets his accuracy standards. "I don't guarantee half-minute accuracy," he says, "but most of my long-range rifles in .300 Weatherby will deliver groups smaller than that." D'Arcy also builds a Dangerous Game Rifle with a barrel-mounted sling swivel and action work to accommodate round-nose bullets. It's available with iron sights.

Kent "Buzz" Fletcher

Alamosa, Colorado

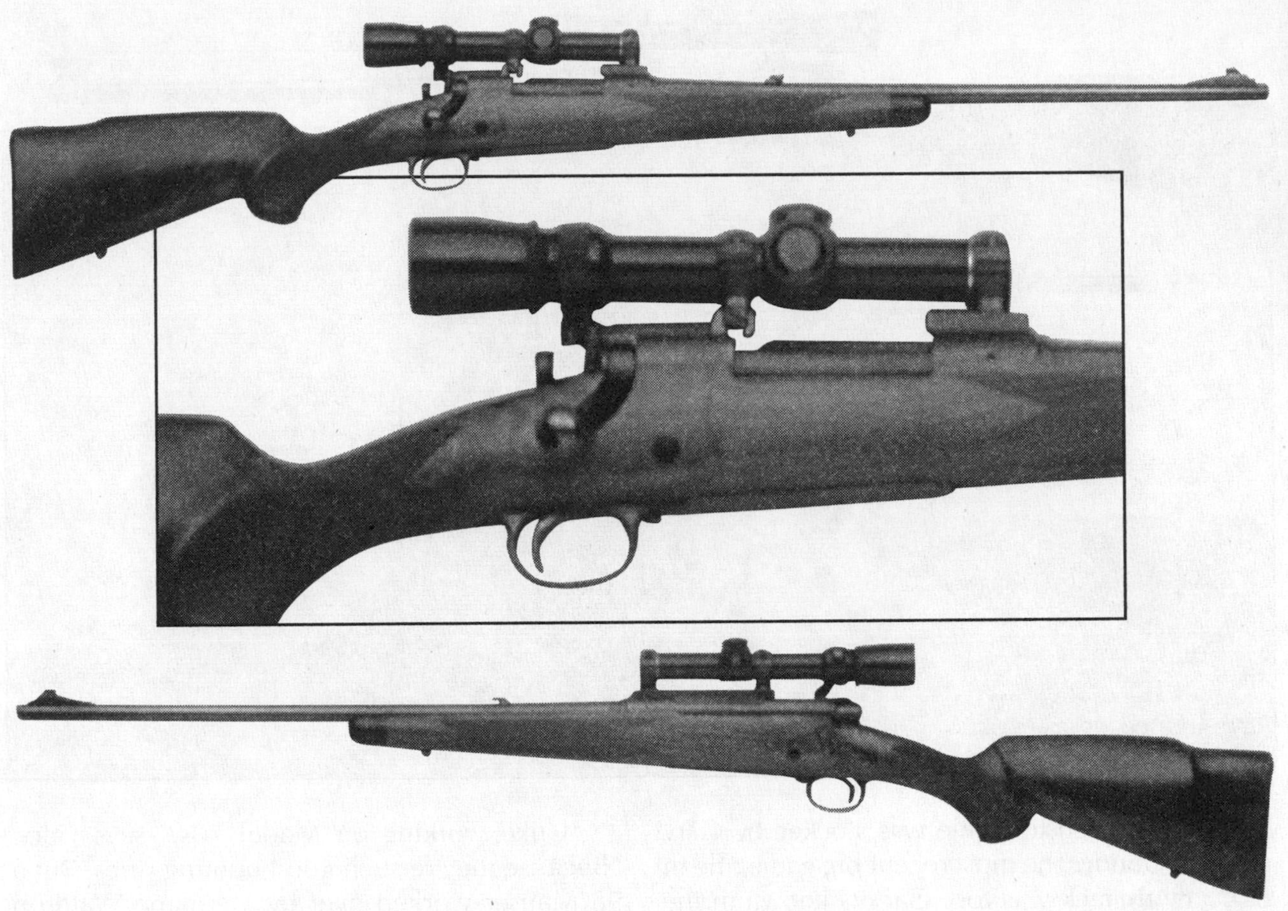

"I grew up on the writings of men like Kennedy, Dunlop, and Francis Sell," says Kent Fletcher. The youngest of 10 children, Buzz longed to accompany his six older brothers in the field. Like most youngsters, he wanted to hunt. But when brother Phil pointed him to writings of hunters who favored custom rifles and books by those who built them, "… the notion that I could build fine rifles suddenly had great appeal. It even seemed possible!"

Buzz enrolled in gunsmithing school at Trinidad State Junior College, studying with the likes of Maurice Ottmar, Chuck Grace, Jim Turtin and others who later would establish themselves as premier gunmakers. After graduating in 1972, Buzz left for Austria, where he worked in a gun shop for a year. Then he returned to Colorado, setting up his own shop in Alamosa.

While Buzz has an American's affinity for the classic bolt-action sporting rifle, he's also an accomplished shotgun stocker. "The British got it right," he says. "And I've worked hard to understand the foundations of their designs. My quail guns have British lines." Their weight and balance, and the cast, pitch and drop of the buttstock, result from painstaking study of the British game gun. Buzz also builds rifles after British patterns. Whatever the style, he strives to make a firearm handle like an extension of the shooter's body. "Fit is very important. If the gun doesn't point naturally, it's not acceptable."

Fletcher rifles and shotguns are typically checkered 22 lines per inch. "My rifles and shotguns are for shooting, not for show," Buzz says, though he does cut some patterns at 24 lpi. He uses various fillers to get the stock surface he wants, but finishes only with Tung Oil. Buzz Fletcher's attention to quality and detail shows in every aspect of his work.

Gary Goudy
Dayton, Washington

My first custom rifle was stocked by Gary Goudy. The most recent big game rifle in my rack was too. Gary is known in the trade as one of the most talented and productive of his fraternity. After 37 years as a stockmaker, it's not surprising. "I'm 65 now, retired from the airline industry but working as hard as ever on guns," he chuckles. "Hunting's expensive. I can't afford to quit!"

Not that he would if he could. Gary is a charter member of the American Custom Gunmakers Guild, and now its vice president. His work belies a perfectionist's obsession, and a genuine affinity for fine guns and the best walnut. "I work mainly with California English," he says. "Or Bastogne. I've not had such good luck with European blanks." Unlike many of his colleagues, Gary buys most of his wood green, preferring to dry it himself. "Most blanks need a couple of years, but I like to give them four seasons before inletting." Gary is renowned not only for skintight wood-to-metal fit, but impossibly detailed checkering that leaves ribbons the width of a pencil line and even as a lightbeam.

"I like working on Model 70s," says Gary. "Because they're such good hunting rifles. But a 98 Mauser worked over by Hermann Waldron or Tom Burgess is every bit their equal. I've worked on shotguns from time to time—almost all of them side-by-sides. He concedes that two of the most recent double-gun projects are his own. "Dakotas. A 12 and a 20. They took a long time to finish, they're true exhibition-grade guns." Gary is also working on a Dakota take-down rifle for his own use. But he still hunts with the Winchester Model 70 Featherweight that he's been carrying for years. "It doesn't have one of my stocks," he laughs. "It shoots just fine in the factory wood, and I've been too busy to change it." Gary's taken all manner of North American big game with that rifle, and plans to take more.

"Last year I hunted the River of No Return Wilderness in Idaho," he says. "And I drew a Wyoming elk tag. Shot a big bull near home a couple of years ago ...." Gary lives in Dayton, Washington, and tends to his stockmaking in the shadow of the Blue Mountains.

Chuck Grace
Trinidad, Colorado

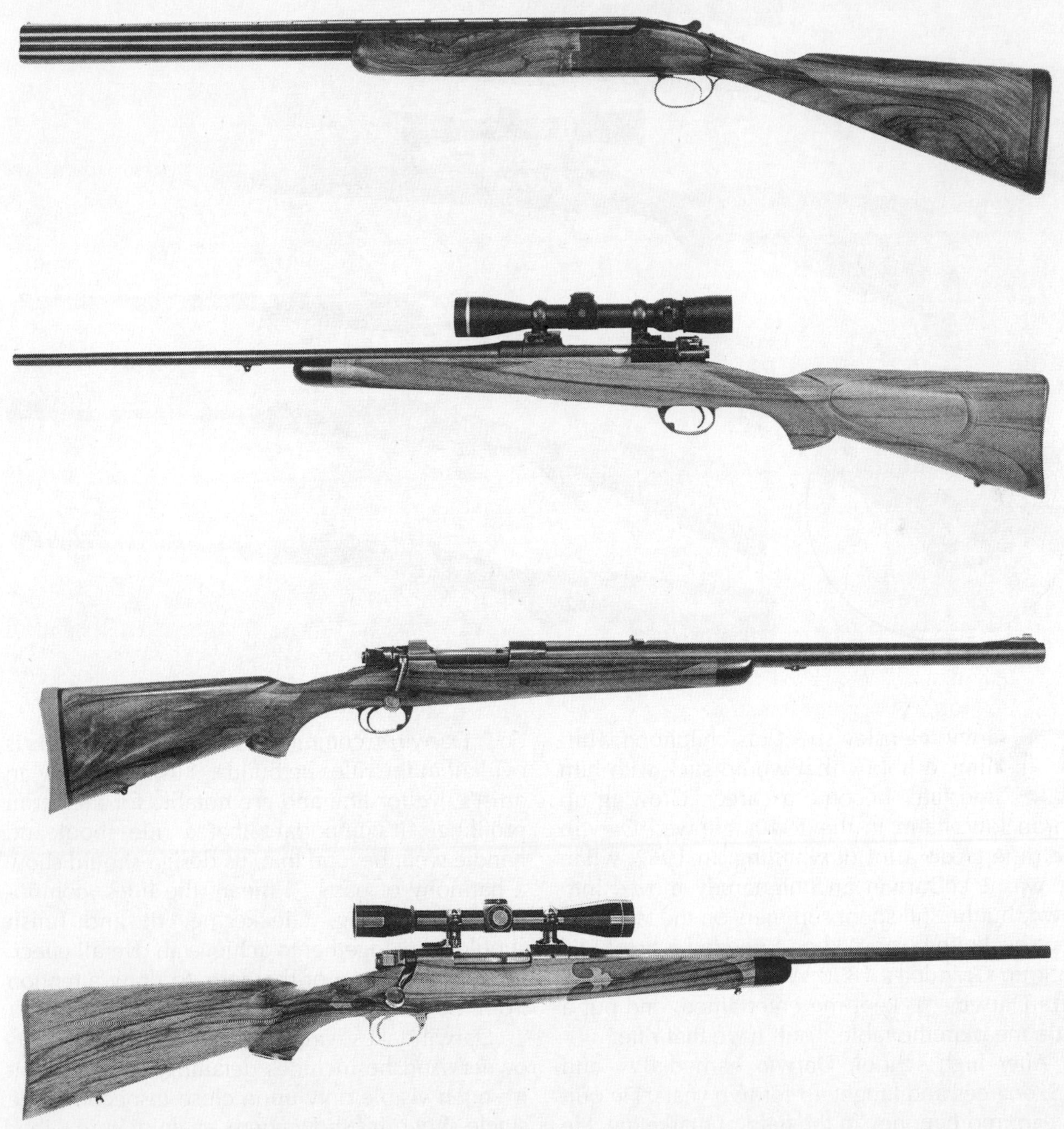

Clean, trim lines and expertly rendered forend tips—aren't easy to deliver. Ask Chuck Grace, who in 1971 left his Michigan home for gunsmithing school in Colorado. He stayed there.

Since 1980, Chuck has been a full-time stockmaker, and in 1983 became a charter member of the American Custom Gunmakers Guild. His considerable talent was most recently shown on the ACGG's 16th annual fund-raising project: a Winchester Model 70 rifle in 7x57. His rifles have sleek, open grips that make for fast handling. Chuck also takes on rifle restoration and custom metalwork in his Trinidad shop. Grace rifles boast both high quality and affordability.

Darwin Hensley
Brightwood, Oregon

Darwin Hensley spent his childhood whittling, a hobby that would stick with him and later become a career. Growing up on an Iowa farm in the 1940s allowed Darwin the time to do a lot of whittling. In 1952, when he was 10, Darwin and his family moved into town, but he still spent summers on the farm and kept his knife busy. "When I needed a break, I'd pick up Grandpa's 1890 Winchester .22 pump," says Darwin. "It kept me entertained, and put a little meat on the table. I still have that rifle."

After high school, Darwin earned B.A. and B.S. degrees and taught art for two years. He quit to earn more money in the field of marketing. He stayed with it for 25 years, raising a family. Darwin still whittled on gunstocks. He also bought and sold high-grade firearms. Then in 1985 he gave up "real work" and became a full-time stockmaker. He doesn't regret it.

"I've been blessed with wonderful clients. I wake up every day eager to go to work. It's not the life for everyone, but there's nothing I'd rather do." Darwin's commitment to superior work is evident in the rifles he builds. His rifles show an artist's eye for line and are notable for their trim profiling. "It's important that a rifle shoot and handle well; beyond that, its design should show a harmony of parts. I mean, the lines, components, engraving, checkering, fit and finish should work together to achieve an overall effect. It's wrong for one of the parts to draw attention from the whole."

Darwin takes care to fit each rifle stock to its owner. And he includes detailing so subtle that it's often visible only upon close inspection. The single-shot rifles shown here—a miniature Gibbs Farquharson in .17 Hornet, a miniature Jeffery Farquharson in 2R Lovell and a miniature Alex Henry in .218 Bee—show the sleek, spare profiles that Darwin Hensley somehow turns into elegance. Metalwork on the first two (and on the featured bolt rifles) is by Steve Heilmann. The .218 Bee proves that Darwin is also an accomplished metalsmith. Engraving: Terry Wallace.

Hill Country Rifle Company

New Braunfels, Texas

Established in 1996, Hill Country Rifle Company specializes in high-quality bolt-action rifles built to order on commercial actions. Customers can choose a McMillan synthetic stock or French, English or Turkish walnut. Clarao and Bastogne walnut are also available. Lilja, Hart and Krieger barrels remain the top choices from this New Braunfels, Texas, firm. Actions are pillar-bedded and barrels free-floating. For most calibers, 1-inch three-shot groups are guaranteed.

J. Earl Bridges, in charge of stockmaking and metalsmithing, has worked in the trade for 18 years, is a longtime member of the American Custom Gunmakers Guild and has owned and operated the Colorado Gunsmithing Academy.

A typical Hill Country rifle includes:

- Winchester M70 action
- Exhibition-grade English walnut stock
- Ebony for-end tip
- Lilja #6 chrome-moly barrel
- Sunny Hill drop-box bottom metal
- Biesen steel buttplate
- Fisher skeleton grip cap
- Contoured crossbolts
- Barrel band front sight, single-leaf adjustable rear
- Custom extended extractor
- Checkered bolt handle and bolt release
- HCR blueprinting and accurizing

Bob Hisserich

Mesa, Arizona

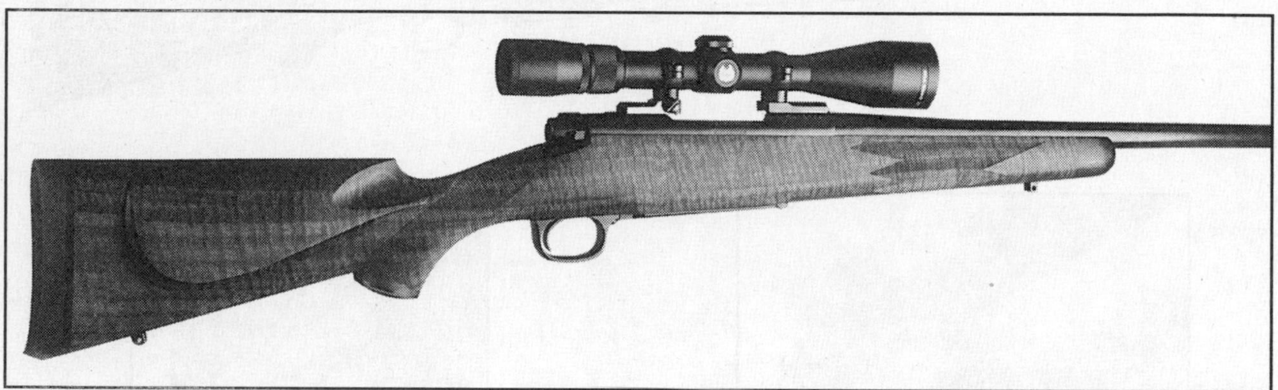

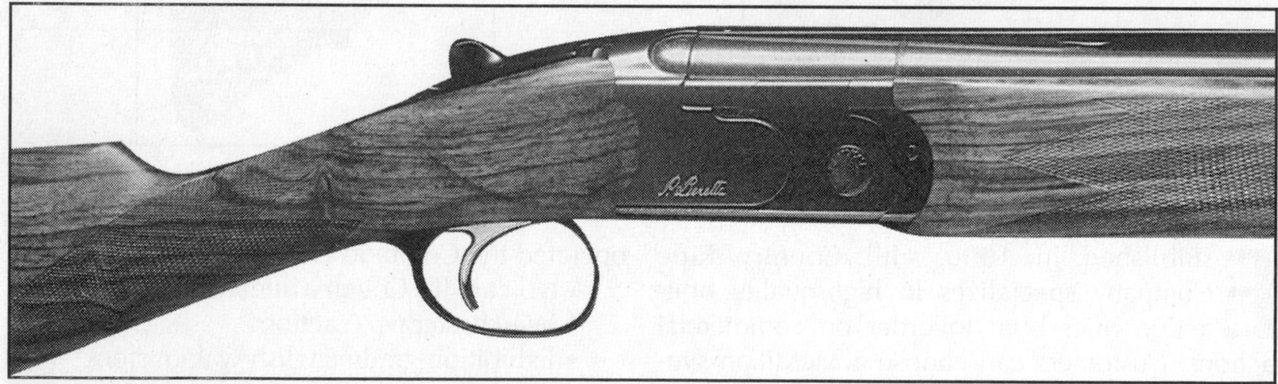

Some gunmakers struggle to make a handsome rifle shoot well, but Bob Hisserich claims, "It's tough to build a rifle that looks as good as it shoots." Bob is only 17 years into his career as a gunmaker, but the rifles and shotguns coming out of his Mesa, Arizona, shop show a high level of craftsmanship and a good eye for line. "Accuracy is mainly a function of installing a good barrel on an action that's square with the barrel axis," he says. "The bolt face must be true and the lugs made to bear evenly. Of course, the stock can't be allowed to interfere."

Bob uses a Honig/Rodman stock duplicator (pantograph) capable of .0001 precision. His rifle stocks—laminates as well as traditional walnut versions—are all on classic patterns, though Bob also builds crossover models for shooters with an off-side dominant eye. You'll find his work on shotguns as well.

Patrick Holehan

Tucson, Arizona

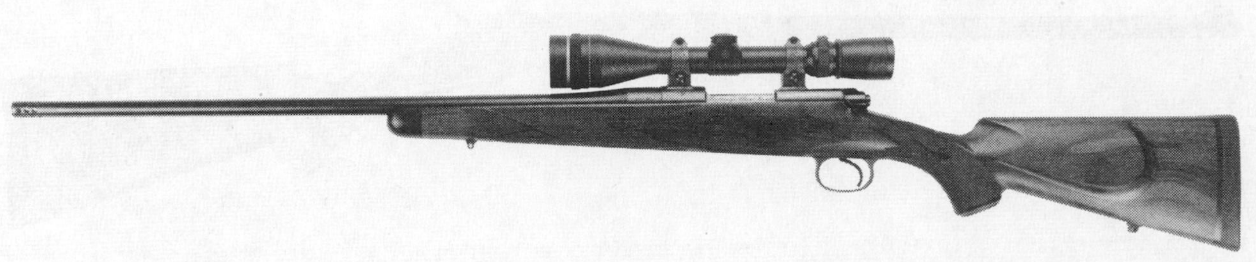

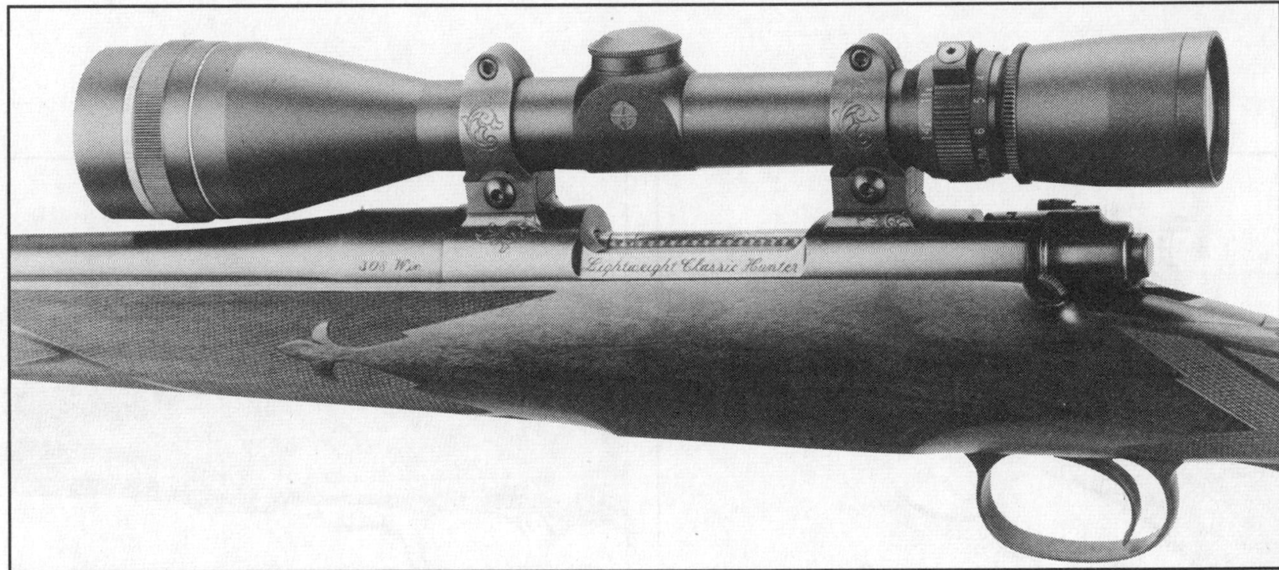

Many gunmakers toil for years to gain national recognition. Patrick Holehan's name has risen quickly to the attention of rifle connoisseurs, and the innovative young riflemaker continues to earn his reputation. For example, Patrick makes what he calls his Arizona square bridge actions. "I start with Model 70 Winchester metal, then add the blocks, contouring them into the receiver. They're machined on top to accept quick-detachable scope rings." This Holehan touch is just one of many that make his rifles unique, as well as pleasing to the eye. "I hew to classic lines," says Pat. "But I also try hard to make my rifles distinctive. Of course, they must shoot well and function perfectly. I'm an avid hunter; my rifles are made for the field."

Named the "Hunter" series, Patrick's M70 bolt rifles include Long Range, Lightweight and Safari versions, with walnut or high-quality synthetic stocks pillar-bedded to the actions. Patrick trues barrel seating surfaces, laps the locking lugs and hones and polishes the feed ramp and bolt face. Customers can order from a long list of options; Patrick offers most standard and wildcat chamberings in cryogenically treated barrels. His Tucson-made rifles are more affordable than those of established makers, but no less appealing to hunters who want higher performance and classier looks than are available from factory-built rifles.

One of a small number of gunmakers who complete the entire rifle, stock and metal in their own shops, Patrick admits he's not the fastest gunmaker around. "But you don't order a handmade rifle because you need a rifle right away. You order it because you want a rifle done just right." And his are.

Steven Dodd Hughes
Livingston, Montana

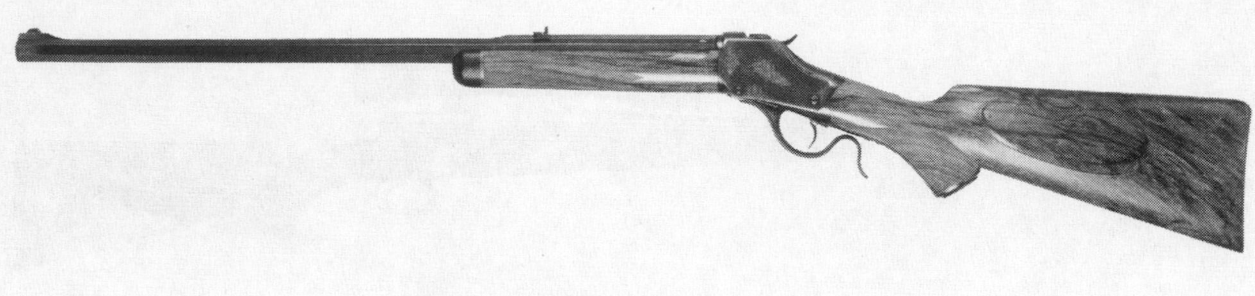

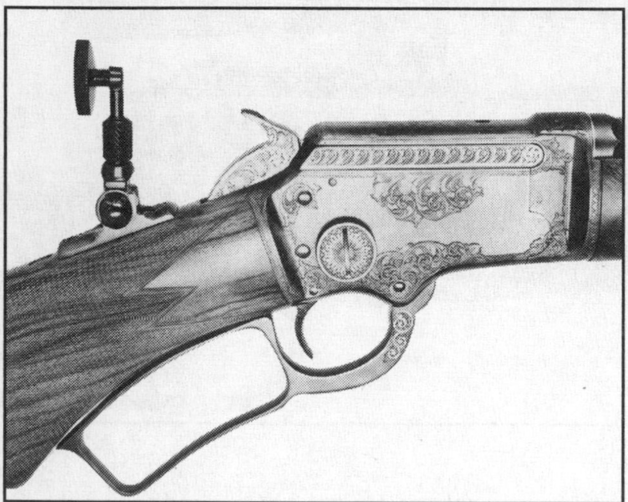

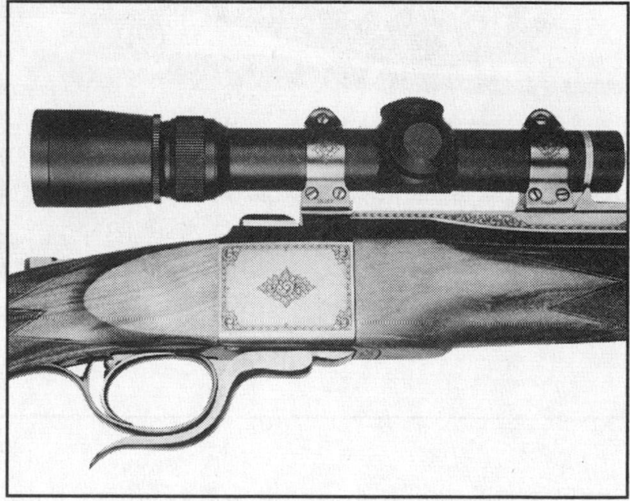

Steven Hughes has built lever-action and single-shot rifles, and first-class double shotguns; he also writes a "Fine Gunmaking" column for *Shooting Sportsman* magazine. He photographs guns with the skill of a pro, and has authored a couple books as well. But this multi-talented man still considers himself primarily a gunmaker.

For a decade after starting his career in 1978, he focused on building muzzleloading firearms faithful to 18th- and 19th-century patterns. Now he works almost exclusively on cartridge guns, like the Marlin Model 39 rimfire lever rifle shown here with the Steven Hughes 1920s-pattern High Wall. William Gamradt, of Missoula, Montana, engraved the .280 Dakota Model 10 that Steven rebuilt with a new trigger and guard as well as an elegant stock.

"I leave the bolt rifles to the masses," jokes Steven, who points out that there are dozens of craftsmen building custom turnbolt guns for every one keen to tackle a single-shot. "I also like the old lever-actions. One of my favorite projects was an original Winchester 1873, refitted with new parts, many of which I made. I stocked it like one of the original 1-of-1,000 rifles. It came out nice."

So have his two books, *Fine Gunmaking: Double Shotguns* (Krause Publishing) and *Custom Rifles in Black and White* (Fandango Press). Steven is currently working on a third—between gun projects and photography—from his Livingston, Montana, home.

David Miller
Tucson, Arizona

The David Miller booth is an institution at Safari Club International conventions, serving as plush background to his custom rifles, and long enough to display his collection of outstanding Coues deer bucks. Last year David spent 45 days in Mexico hunting Coues deer. "It's something of an obsession," he shrugs. Then, chuckling: "It's not the worst vice a man can have." And it hasn't yet affected the superior quality of the rifles he and partner Curt Crum ship from their Tucson shop.

A savvy marketer, David decided early on that rifles built to the highest standards and peddled to the wealthiest people would always sell. "I don't sell lots of them," he says. "But they're not production-class rifles. They can't be stamped out like cookies, and I don't sell `em cheap." Miller Classic rifles have justly earned the spotlight at several SCI conventions.

Some years ago, David assembled a rifle for his own use, a .300 Weatherby on a Model 70 Winchester action, with a long, fluted barrel and a laminated stock. The rifle wore a Leupold 6.5-20x scope in David's own bombproof mount. This outfit had the same clean lines as David's Classic rifle, but not the hand-checkering and expensive wood. As soon as other hunters heard of the project, they beat a path to Miller's Tucson shop. Now David and Curt offer their Marksman rifle at about half the price of a Classic.

"It's still not a cheap rifle," David says without apology. "We don't build cheap rifles. We build very accurate rifles that look good, for people who want the best there is." And those people are not disappointed.

Steve Nelson

Corvallis, Oregon

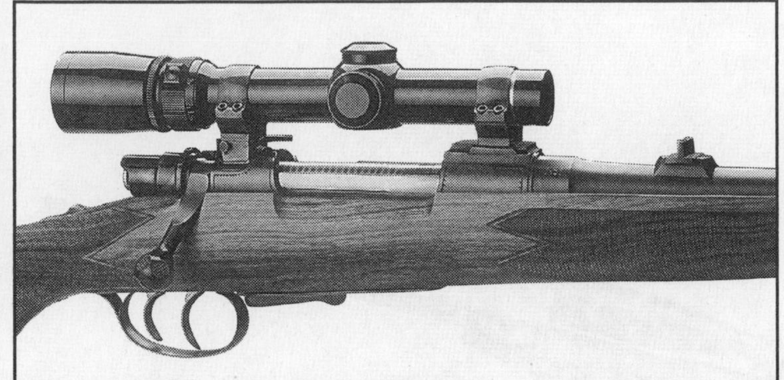

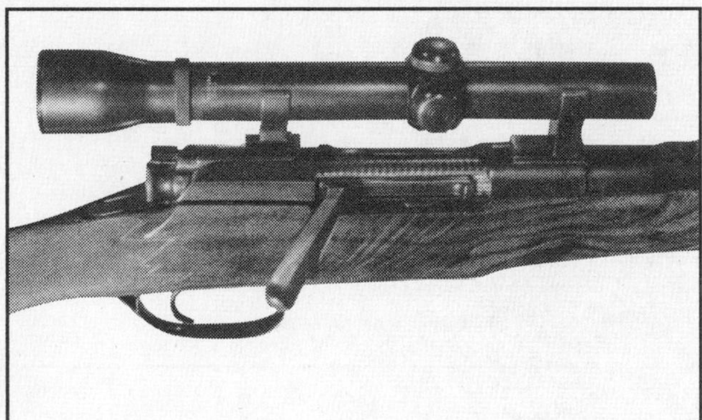

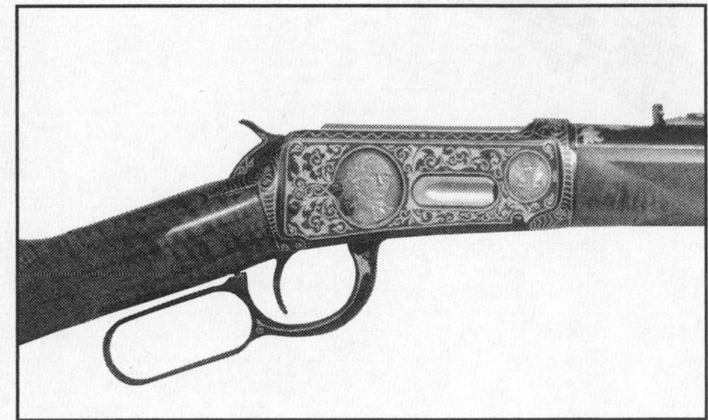

In 1974, Steve Nelson stumbled upon a career. He wanted a better rifle than he could afford, so he figured he'd build one.

"The result wasn't quite what I had in mind, but the process taught me a great deal. Enough, anyway, to prompt a follow-up," says Steve. "But before I bungled again, I signed up for one of Jerry Fisher's NRA summer seminars at Trinidad, Colorado. Then I attended the annual meeting of the American Custom Gunmakers Guild. What an eyeopener! I had no idea such flawless, sophisticated work was even possible. And I determined to come as close as I could to the craftsmanship presented there." Steve eagerly accepted tips and encouragement from Al Lind, Mark Lee, Dale Goens and other luminaries in the custom gun trade. A decade later, after much hard work and steady progress as a gunmaker, he was accepted as a member of ACGG.

"Strictly defined, a custom firearm is one built for an individual. The rifle or shotgun has a stock fitted specifically for its owner, who also decides chambering, barrel dimensions, choke, sights, trigger and all the options that might make the product perform better or give the customer the look he or she wants. Of course, you can buy a custom rifle secondhand and shoot well with it even though it is no more built for your hands than is a factory rifle. And you can buy custom rifles from makers who insist on incorporating their own ideas, independent of your wishes. I like to think I'm a consultant as well as a gunbuilder. My aim is to deliver a rifle that meets the client's needs specifically. I do all the work on a rifle or shotgun—wood and metal—except the engraving."

Dave Norin

Waukegan, Illinois

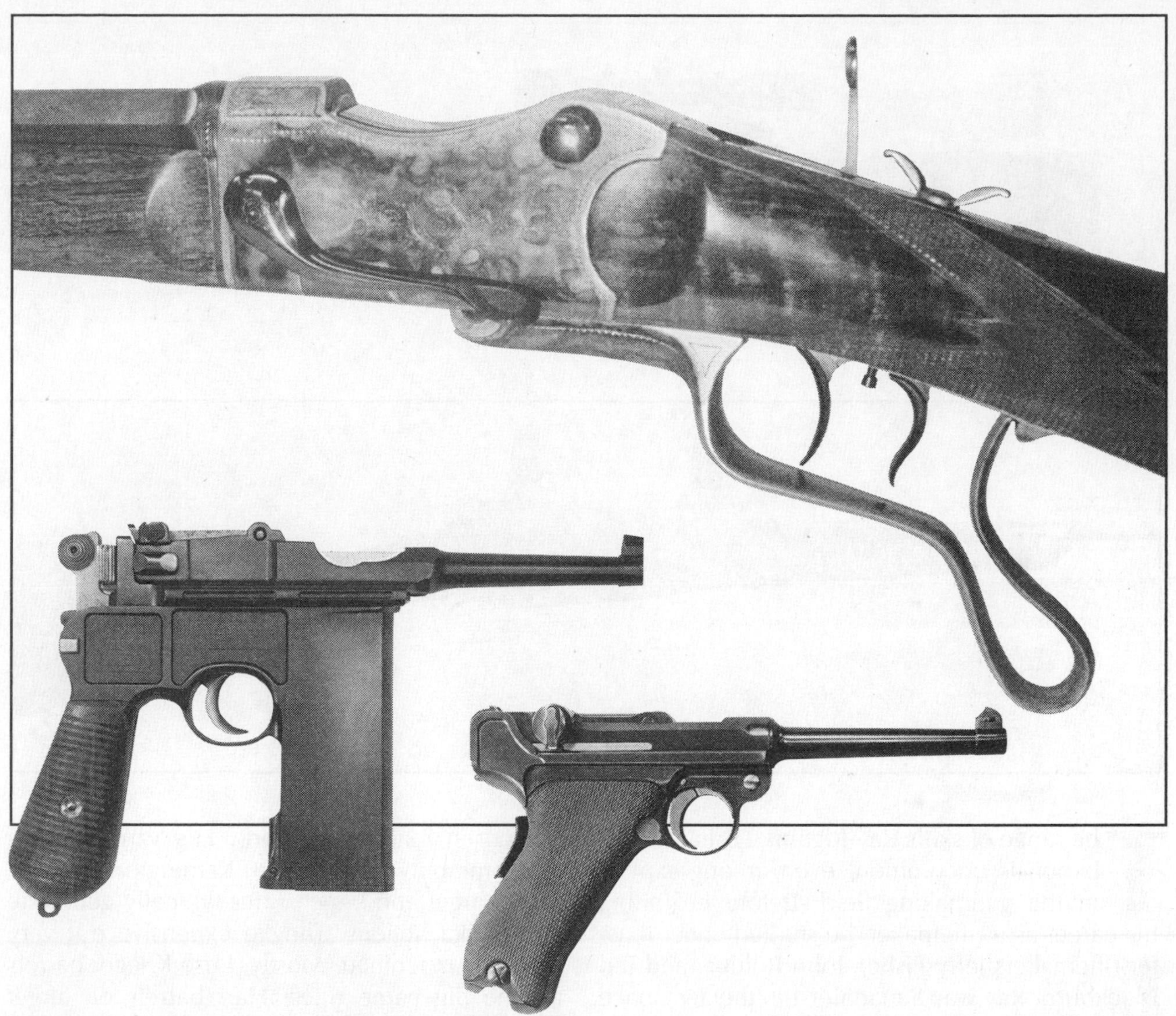

A whitetail hunter first and an upland bird hunter second, Dave Norin lives where both abound: in Waukegan, Illinois. He and his wife have four children and a grandchild. "Even without the shop and my hunting, I'd be busy!"

Dave graduated in 1972 from Trinidad State College in Colorado and joined a large fraternity in the gunmaking industry with that alma mater. But he has since distinguished himself by steering toward work less commonly done by custom gunmakers. "I have a broad range of interests," he admits. "I collect pre-1945 self-loading pistols, Winchesters, any nice double I can afford...."

Dave's specialty these days is restoration of collector-quality firearms, and fine custom gunsmithing—like rebuilding a German 8x46R takedown target rifle and bringing an ultra-rare Farrow rifle back to life. He has restored Luger, Mauser and Mannlicher pistols, lever-action Winchester rifles "and of course the bolt-action rifles everybody else works on." But few other custom shops boast the suite of services available at the Norin digs: rust bluing, Niter bluing, color case hardening, stocking from blanks and vintage wood finishes. Dave's work shows an artist's attention to detail, and a faithfulness to original color and form that keeps his services in demand among sophisticated gun people.

Ray Riganian
Glendale, California

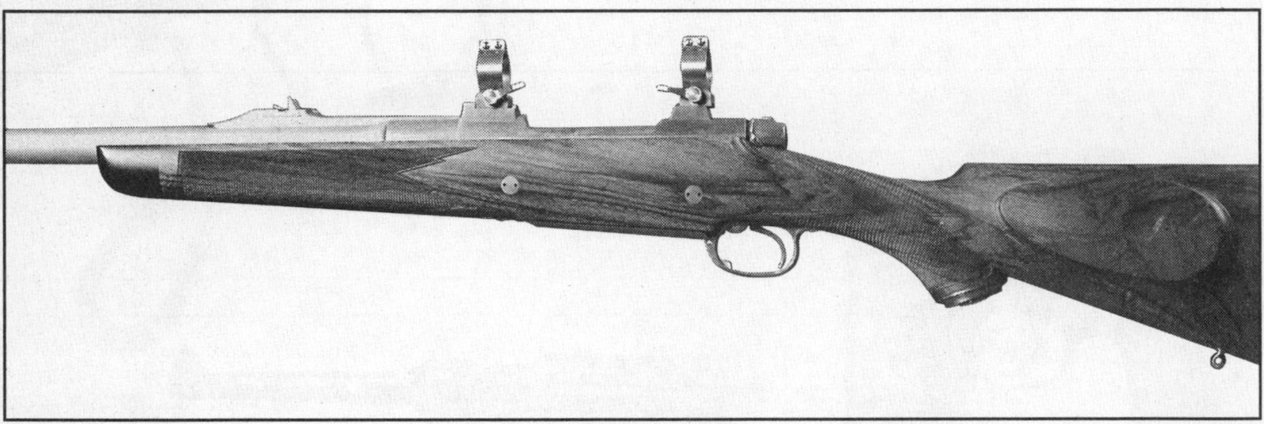

The range of skills Ray Riganian brings to the bench is uncommon, even among experts in the gunmaking field. Before beginning his career as a riflemaker, he studied under master riflemakers Jerry Fisher, John Bolliger and Ted Blackburn. Ray was a machinist in the aerospace industry, and he does "almost all the work" in his benchrest and hunting rifles. "I machine my own sight and scope bases from bar stock, my own swivel bands too," he says. "Of course, I true up the bolt and receiver with the barrel shank, recutting threads when necessary and squaring the lug bearing surfaces."

Some components come from other sources: sights and his rifles' elegant Blackburn bottom metal, for example. He uses Talley scope rings. "Everything is carefully matched to the other components and to the use the customer expects to make of his rifle." Ray likes the Model 70 Winchester for hunting rifles, because of its beefy extractor—"also the 98 Mauser, but it requires a lot of work to finish." He favors Searcy and Johannsen magnum actions. His varmint rifles are commonly built on 700 Remingtons. "Long-range target and bench rifles typically get Stolle or Nishika actions. They're expensive but very precisely machined. Mostly, I use Krieger barrels for the big game rifles, Hart barrels on target guns." He sends the metal out for cold rust-bluing or a "special treatment that's more durable than Teflon and sticks better to the steel." Ray pillar-beds the actions to the stocks.

Ray's stocks show the same attention to detail and sensible line that he lavishes on metal. "I prefer to work on California English, but Circassian walnut is a close second choice. I buy dry blanks and will not start work on any with more than 8 percent moisture. Though on high-quality wood I sometimes cut checkering as fine as 28 lines per inch, most of my checkering is 22 or 24 lpi, because hunters find it easier to grip. Function is as important to me as showcasing my abilities in technical tours de force."

Tony Schuelke

Glencoe, Minnesota

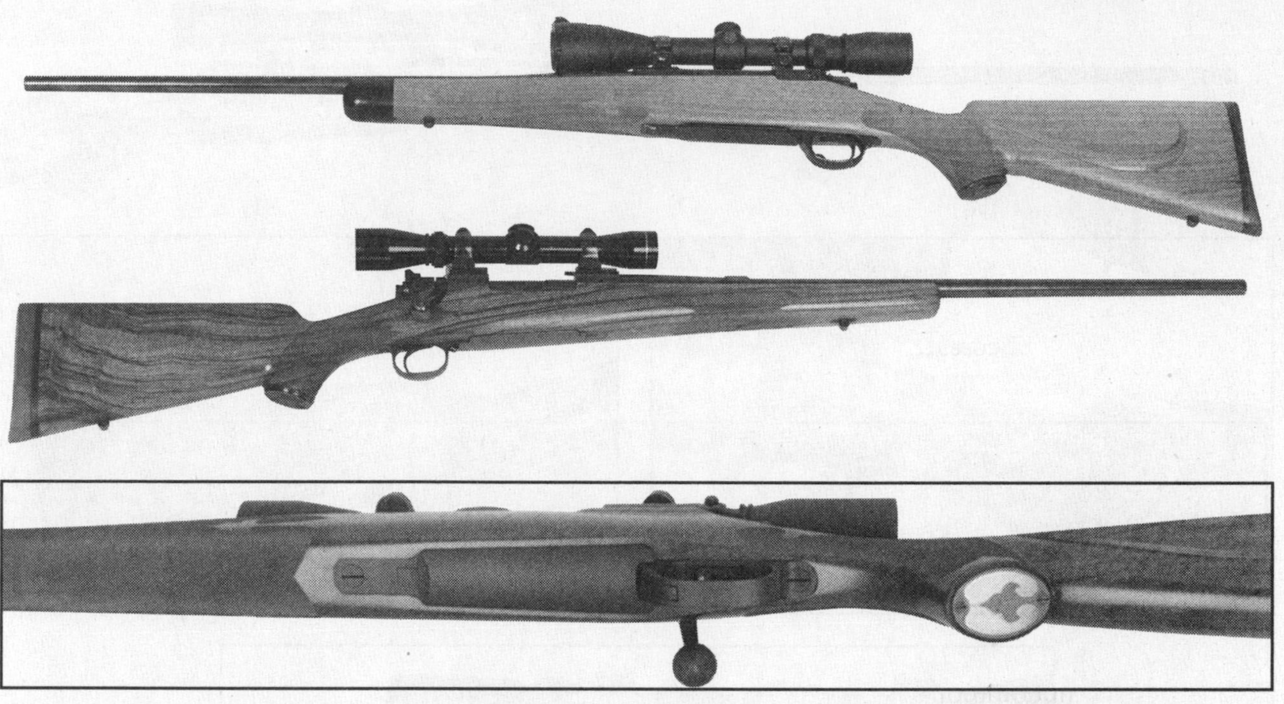

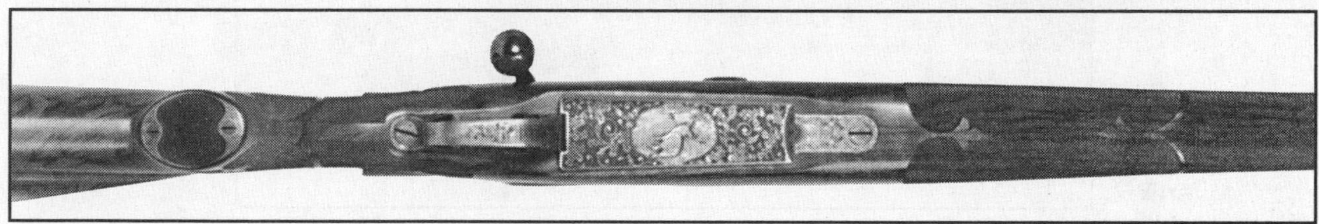

A self-taught craftsman, Tony Schuelke tackles some of the toughest jobs in custom gun-building. But he started with a straightforward project. At age 16, he stripped the stock on a Remington autoloading shotgun and tried to refinish the wood as recommended by Jack O'Connor in a book. It became the first of many gun projects for Tony.

Despite his early affinity for firearms, Tony didn't start building guns until very late in life. He worked as a certified auto mechanic, then ran a life insurance business. A stint in banking followed, then one in real estate. He's a machinist now, he says modestly. But that label is inadequate. Tony is an accomplished man with a file, checkering not only stocks but bolt handles, and fabricating skeleton grip caps. While he doesn't imitate anyone, Tony takes every opportunity to study the work that he admires. He's constantly innovating. "If you're not a creative kind of a guy, there's not much interesting about building guns," he says.

Tony solicits the customer's ideas. He'd rather respond to them than recommend his own design. "Custom guns—especially side-by-sides—are more like art than implements. Customers have their own tastes, and they're paying the freight. So I listen." He adds that individuality can be important to gun people, and little details that have no bearing on performance often matter a great deal. Untested ideas intrigue him, though he says that a lot of what does make sense in gun design has already been tried—"at least on traditional double-barrel frames." Tony Schuelke's shop is in Glencoe, Minnesota, where he says winters "are just right for working on guns."

Gene Simillion

Gunnison, Colorado

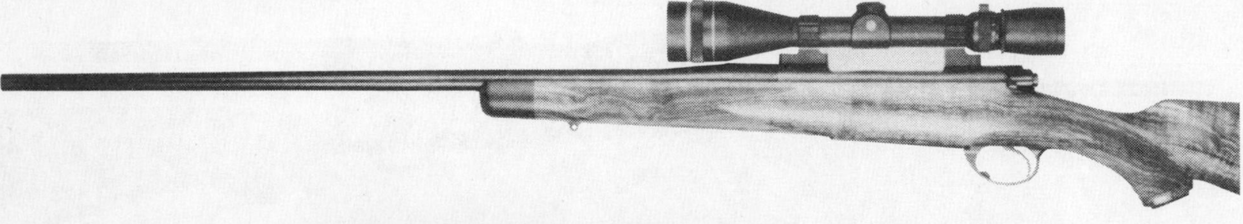

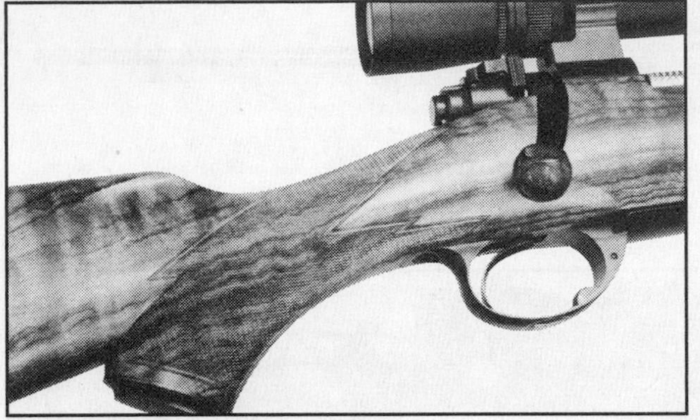

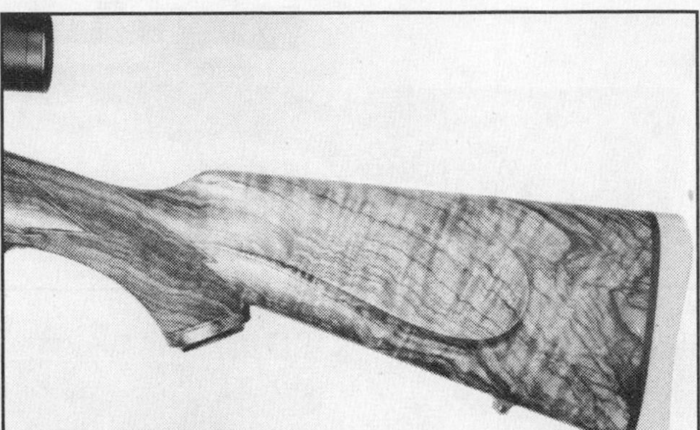

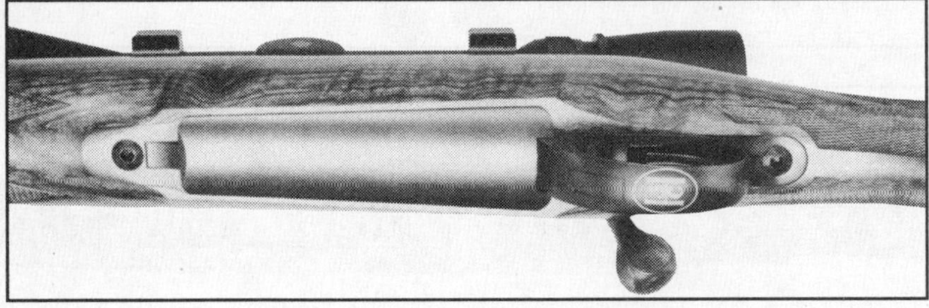

When not hunting in the Mountain West or northern Canada, Gene Simillion builds rifles in his Gunnison, Colorado, shop. But 20 years ago, Gene was headed in a different direction: learning to teach industrial arts. He soon realized that "If you teach, you have to be in school during hunting season." So he switched occupations—a move he wouldn't regret.

Gene worked for a year in Kalispell, Montana, under the tutelage of ace stockmaker Jerry Fisher. "Not very far down the road was Tom Burgess," grins Gene. "He's forgotten more about metalsmithing than most gunmakers will ever learn. I got the best education a young fellow could hope for." He also credits exposure to the work of D'Arcy Echols, Monte Mandarino and Don Klein.

A veteran rifle-builder now, Gene affirms that the classic bolt rifle is not only his favorite but a product with timeless appeal. "It still sells, and the best of contemporary makers build them better than they've ever been built before." Gene's aim is to produce a rifle with "fine accuracy, flawless function and elegant beauty." He points out that the main difference between custom rifles and the best factory-built guns is in the detailing—"things like checkered bolt knobs and and screwless sling swivel studs" (both standard on Simillion rifles).

The "Premier" rifle is Gene's best, built to each customer's specifications. Gene prefers to work with new Model 70 Classic rifles but will substitute early Model 70s, Mauser 98s and Remington 700s. Gene installs his own scope bases. Magnums get a second recoil lug and a crossbolt in front of the magazine well. Quarter ribs and drop-box magazines are two of the options. The less costly Classic Hunter comes only on the new M70 action. It has fewer options and less detailing, but its cut-rifled barrel, hand-bedded to a checkered walnut stock, delivers the same level of performance.

Charlie Sisk

Dayton, Texas

Talking is one of Charlie Sisk's evident strengths—he keeps in close touch with the people who order his super-accurate rifles. But Charlie has other talents, refined since he built his first gun in a high-school machine shop. "It was a .257 Roberts on a 98 Mauser action. It's still in the rack." But the rack has filled up these days, mainly with modern synthetic-stocked guns. "I'd say they can all shoot half inch, because I've managed half-inch groups," he grins. "But I have two-inch days."

Such candor endears Charlie to his customers, who are for the most part a pretty critical lot. Charlie's rifles don't wear handsome wood or engraving. They're meant to be shot. "Beauty is as beauty does—or somethin' like that," he drawls. Charlie works almost exclusively on bolt-action rifles but has lately tackled Marlin 1895 rifles in .45-70, smoothing up the action and installing a black leather cartridge band on the butt. He adds a Teflon finish to the metal, a soft black decelerator pad to the stock, and a black Latigo sling. "A great gun for thick places." And handsome. In bolt rifles, Charlie prefers Model 700 Remingtons but says Winchester 70s come in close behind. He uses barrels from several top-brand suppliers but air-gauges them to cull any that vary more than .0001. "I also inspect each barrel with a bore-scope. And my chambering is done with match-grade live-pilot reamers to ensure concentricity." Charlie's standard rifle jobs include "blue-printing" the action to square up the bolt with the bore. He thinks most rifles will shoot about as well as they can shoot if the forend tip puts some pressure on the barrel. However, he will free-float barrels on request.

Bench accuracy isn't enough for hunters who must control lightweight rifles under field conditions. Charlie installs and adjusts aftermarket triggers (he likes Jewell and Timney), and he takes care that his synthetic stocks fit each client perfectly. Rifle balance and weight matter to Charlie; he makes his own muzzle brakes and commonly works up loads for his customers. Charlie prides himself in doing all the work personally from his Dayton, Texas, shop.

Dale A. Storey

Casper, Wyoming

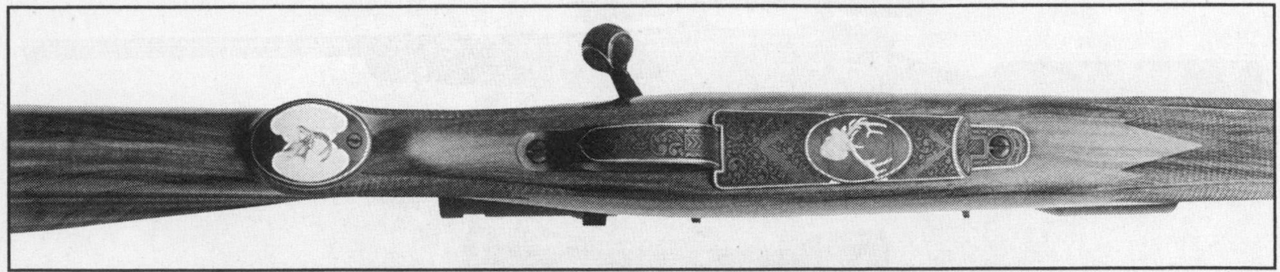

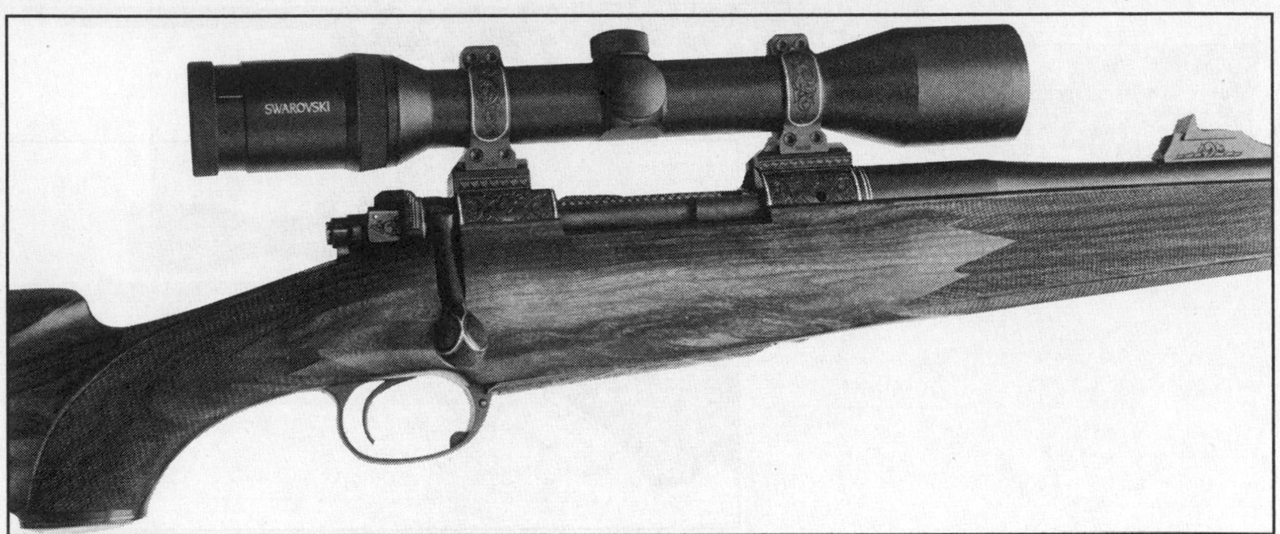

"In high school, I knew I wanted to be a gunbuilder." And Dale Storey is doing just that. He started working on guns soon after graduating from the Colorado School of Trades in 1962, but didn't commit to the craft full time until 1981. "Uncle Sam used my talents for a while," he says. After military service and two degrees from Montana State University, Dale bankrolled his gun shop by teaching for 11 years at a high school and post-secondary schools.

Dale's high-school enthusiasm still runs high at his current bench in Casper, Wyoming, where he works on a variety of rifles, from the black-powder muzzleloaders that were his early love to modern bolt guns. For the most part, he builds modern hunting rifles, taking pains to give each the perfect balance he says is so crucial to good shooting. His economy of line emphasizes balance too. "No one thing should dominate a rifle in form or function," he says. "A rifle should point quickly and shoot accurately from any hunting position." He concedes that high-quality parts are essential but adds that putting them together is what distinguishes an expert craftsman from a mere assembler. Dale says he can do "almost everything" in building a rifle, but he leaves the engraving and inlay work to others.

One of Dale's favorite rifle styles is the half-stock black-powder pattern he followed on a recent project. The result: an exquisite rifle true in form and function to an original Alex Henry. It is most elegant, with engraving by Liz Dolbare. Dale traces his interest in muzzleloaders to mentor V. M. Starr, who taught him about their history and how they should be built. Starr was instrumental in bringing shotgun shooting to the annual black-powder rendezvous at Friendship, Indiana.

Among Dale's latest projects are matched bolt rifles in .300 and .375 H&H Magnums. "I can't tell you what's next," he grins. "I expect to throttle back one of these days. But it's still fun to build rifles. And," he adds with a twinkle, "customers say I'm getting better at it."

Mark Stratton

Lynnwood, Washington

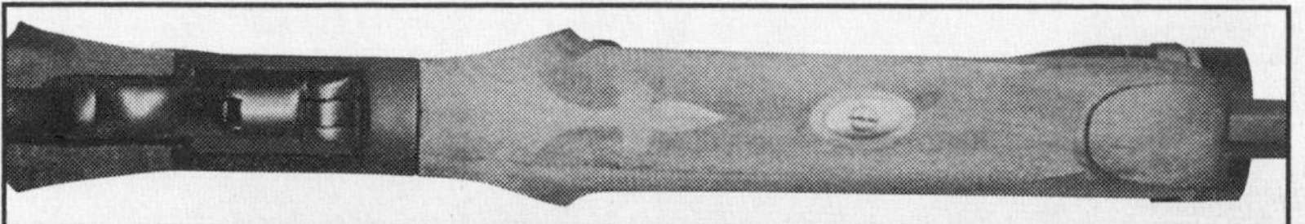

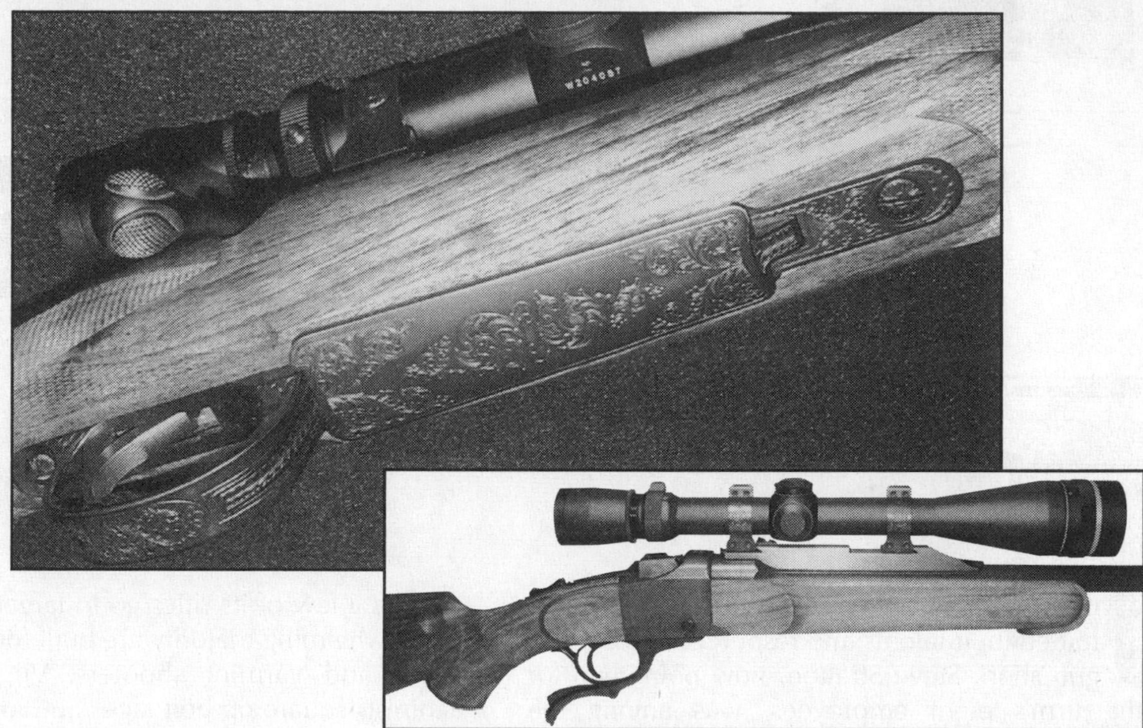

After Mark Stratton spent two years in gunsmithing school in Trinidad, Colorado, and a few days in a gun shop in his native southern California, he discovered that gun work didn't pay the bills. So in 1971 he went to work as a machinist for an electronics firm, but in his spare time started building rifles. He sold his first in 1974 to a friend, "for the cost of the parts."

Mark moved to Seattle, where he continued building rifles in his off-hours. But still he lacked the confidence to abandon his "real" job. Then, a decade later, at the 1988 American Custom Gunmakers Guild show in Reno, Mark saw the products of the country's finest craftsmen. He marveled. "I'd become pretty adept at metalwork," he recalls. "But these fellows were way beyond me in the wood." Inspired, Mark set out to improve his stockmaking. In the meantime, though, he found that his moonlighting had taught him some techniques worth marketing.

"In 1991 a Guild member asked me about making an octagon barrel. I'd developed the tooling for making my octagon barrels years before, so decided to write it up. The article was very well received, and since then I've published 15 other technical tips. Later I was invited to write regularly for an industry magazine. I still do."

Even after his first writing on metalsmithing, Mark didn't join ACGG. "I didn't think it appropriate when my work was still essentially a hobby." But in 1994 he started advertising his work. It brought kudos from buyers, and shortly thereafter Mark was asked to present a seminar on rifle-building at his alma mater in Trinidad. Full-time commitment to his hobby followed, and in 2001 Mark joined the Guild.

Now each year he closes his Lynnwood, Washington, shop for a trip to Trinidad. He has also delivered seminars at other schools. Says Mark of his new career, "If there's anything more rewarding than rifle-building, it's sharing your techniques with others who love the craft."

Virgin Valley Guns

Hurricane, Utah

Just five years ago a group of investors committed their talents and resources to a custom gun shop. Steve Stratton, now point-man for the firm's eight employees, was among the founders. "We've grown fast," he says. "Partly that's because we're so versatile."

Indeed. Virgin Valley's craftsmen, working in wood and metal, turn out custom rifles on actions ranging from Martinis to the Nisika Bay. "We've built something of a reputation with the T/Cs," Steve tells me. "It still accounts for about half our business. The Encore has overtaken the Contender; three of every four Thompsons we build have Encore frames." Other single-shots like the Ruger Number One are also favored by Virgin Valley customers.

"We have our own sawmill," says Steve. "Much of our wood is American walnut bought on the stump, then cut and seasoned here. We live in a dry climate, so a blank can be ready for cutting in as little as a year." Virgin Valley also buys walnut from a California supplier and now offers its own (subcontracted) fiberglass stocks for customers who value durability and stability over aesthetic appeal. The company will also stock rifles in wood laminates.

While a few of its rifles go to target shooters, the overwhelming majority are built for big game hunters and varmint shooters. Virgin Valley machinists square up bolt faces and locking lugs as part of any rebarreling job. Complete tooling is on hand for "blueprinting" the popular Remington 700 action and a few others. A custom rifle normally includes a Shilen match-grade barrel, though Steve says "select" barrels are available on request, and the company also installs some Douglas barrels. "We prefer Jewell triggers for most of our work," he adds. But Canjar and Timney products are available too.

What's the most popular chambering at Virgin Valley? "Well, right now the new short magnums have brought us a lot of work. We've built quite a few Encores for cartridges derived from both the Winchester and Remington short magnums. The .17 Hornady Magnum Rimfire is another hot number. The beauty of the Encore is its versatility. We've chambered this rifle for the likes of the 7 STW, as well."

Virgin Valley Guns offers a suite of gunsmithing services, including scope mounting and zeroing, even load development from its home in Hurricane, Utah (vvcguns@infowest.com).

NEW PRODUCTS

NEW Products: **Anschutz Rifles**

Model 1517

Action: bolt
Stock: walnut
Barrel: target-grade sporter, 22 in.
Sights: none
Weight: 6.0lbs.
Caliber: .17 HMR
Magazine: 4
Features: M64 action, heavy and sporter barrels, Monte Carlo and Classic stocks available; target-grade barrel, adjustable trigger (2.5 lbs.)

Classic $699
Monte Carlo. $797

Model 1710

Action: bolt
Stock: walnut
Barrel: target-grade sporter, 22 in.
Sights: none
Weight: 6.7lbs.
Caliber: .22 LR
Magazine: 5
Features: M54 action; two-stage trigger, Monte Carlo stock; silhouette stock available

Model 1710 . . . . $1298
with fancy wood. $1477
Silhouette Model 1712 . . . . . . $1358

NEW Products: **Barrett Rifles**

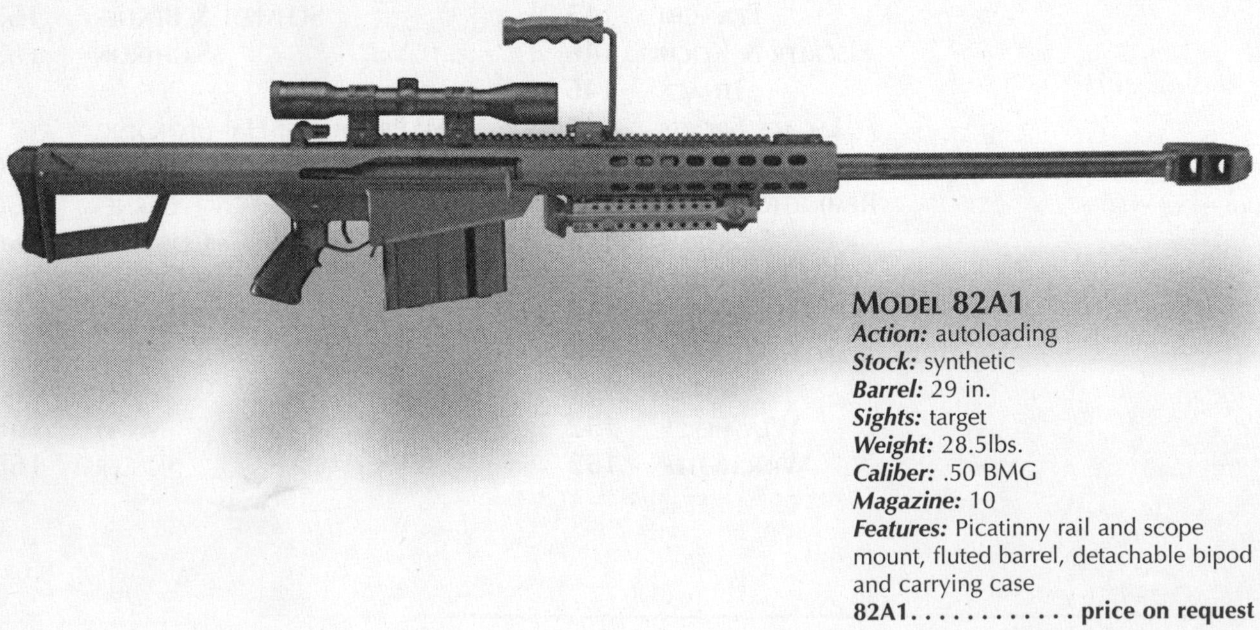

Model 82A1

Action: autoloading
Stock: synthetic
Barrel: 29 in.
Sights: target
Weight: 28.5lbs.
Caliber: .50 BMG
Magazine: 10
Features: Picatinny rail and scope mount, fluted barrel, detachable bipod and carrying case

82A1. . . . . price on request

NEW Products: **Barrett Rifles**

Model 95, Model 99
Action: bolt
Stock: synthetic
Barrel: 29 in. or 33 in. (M99)
Sights: none
Weight: 25.0lbs.

Caliber: .50 BMG
Magazine: 5 (M95) or none (M99)
Features: Picatinny rail, detachable bipod, M95 has fluted barrel and weighs 22 lbs.
M95, M99 . . . . price on request

NEW Products: **Benelli Rifles**

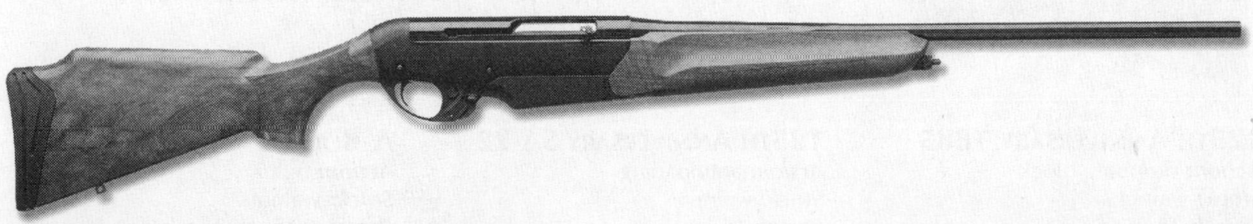

R-1 Rifle
Action: autoloading
Stock: walnut
Barrel: 22 in. (Standard Rifle); 20 in. (Standard Carbine); 24 in. (Magnum Rifle) 20 in. (Magnum Carbine) . . . . .
Sights: none
Weight: 7.1 lbs. (Standard Rifle); 7.0 lbs. (Standard Carbine); 7.2 lbs. (Magnum Rifle) 7.0 lbs. (Magnum Carbine) . . . .
Caliber: Standard 30-06; Magnum .300 Win. Mag.
Magazine: 3-4 shot detachable box

Features: auto-regulating gas-operated system; three lugged rotary bolt; select satin walnut stock; receiver drilled and tapped for scope mount;
Standard Rifle & Carbine: 1065
Magnum Rifle & Carbine: 1080

125TH ANNIVERSARY 1885

125TH ANNIVERSARY SA-22

A-BOLT HUNTER

A-BOLT MEDALLION

A-BOLT MICROHUNTER

125TH ANNIVERSARY 1885

Action: dropping block
Stock: walnut
Barrel: 28 in.
Sights: open and tang peep
Weight: 8.8lbs.
Caliber: .45-70
Magazine: none
Features: high-grade walnut, octagon barrel, 24-K gold accents; only 500 to be made
Anniversary Model. . price on request

125TH ANNIVERSARY SA-22

Action: autoloading
Stock: walnut
Barrel: 16 in.
Sights: open
Weight: 5.5lbs.
Caliber: .22 LR
Magazine: 11
Features: high-grade walnut, gray-finish receiver, 24-K gold accents, only 500 to be made
Anniversary SA-22. . price on request

A-BOLT

Action: bolt
Stock: walnut
Barrel: 23 in. (22 in. Micro Hunter)
Sights: none
Weight: 6.6lbs.
Caliber: .270 WSM, 7mm WSM, .300 WSM; standard calibers also
Magazine: 4
Features: also: Micro Hunter and left-hand
Hunter. $706
MicroHunter $701
MicroHunter in standard calibers $673
Medallion $824

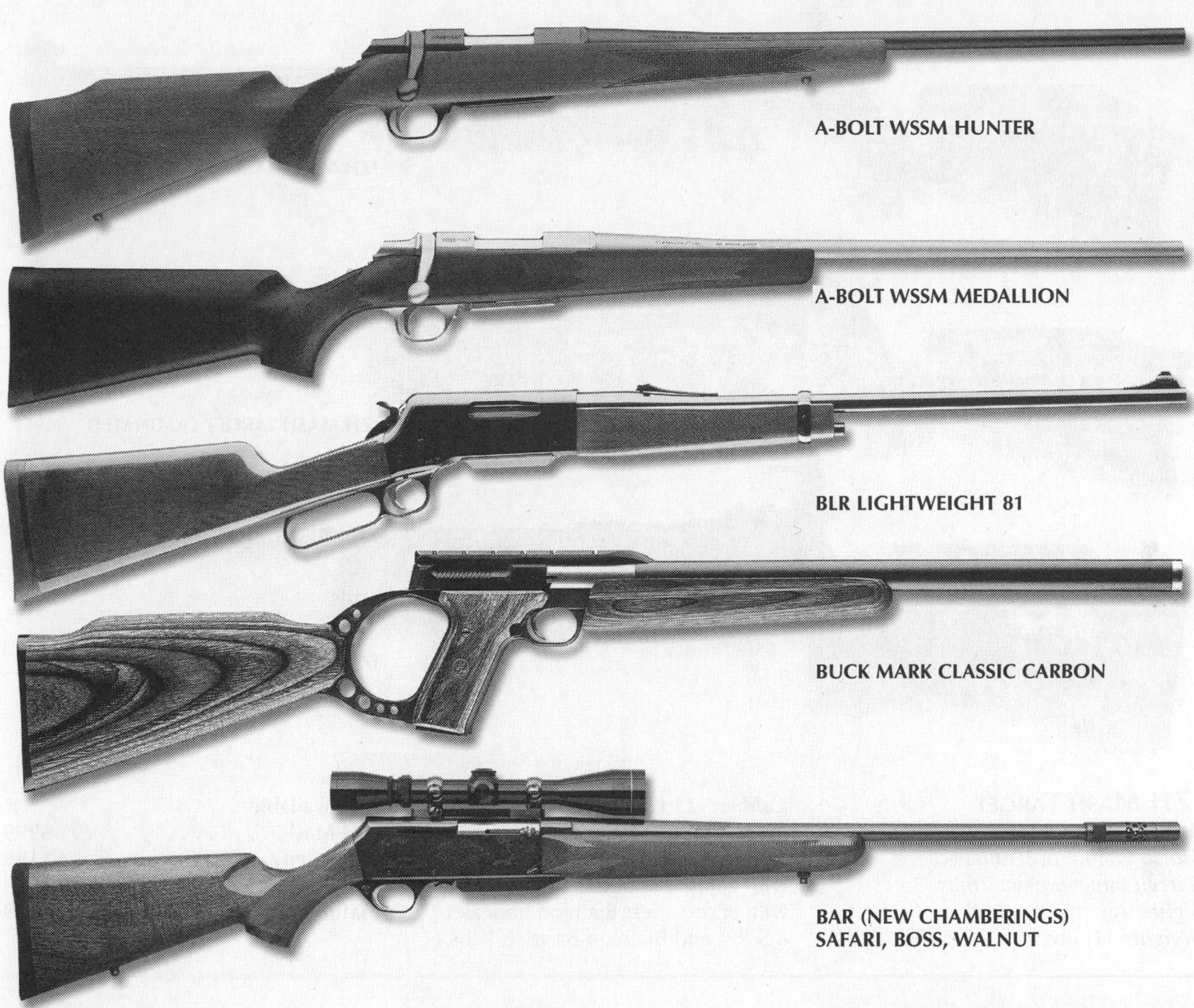

A-BOLT WSSM HUNTER

A-BOLT WSSM MEDALLION

BLR LIGHTWEIGHT 81

BUCK MARK CLASSIC CARBON

BAR (NEW CHAMBERINGS)
SAFARI, BOSS, WALNUT

A-Bolt WSSM

Action: bolt
Stock: walnut or synthetic
Barrel: 21 in.
Sights: none
Weight: 6.06lbs.
Caliber: .223 WSSM, .243 WSSM
Magazine: 4
Features: short, short action, classic-style stock or Monte Carlo, (stainless: 6.1 lbs.)
Hunter $678
Classic Hunter $761
Stainless Stalker $881
Composite Stalker $719
Medallion $795

BAR

Action: autoloading
Stock: walnut or synthetic
Barrel: 23 in.
Sights: open or none
Weight: 8.2lbs.
Caliber: .270 WSM or 7mm WSM
Magazine: 3
Features: Lightweight has synthetic stock, weighs 7.5 lbs., open sights or BOSS attachment
Lightweight, sights $901
Lightweight, BOSS $981
Safari, BOSS, walnut. $1007

BLR Lightweight 81

Action: lever
Stock: straight-grip walnut
Barrel: 20, 22 or 24 in.
Sights: open
Weight: 6.5 lbs. or 7.3lbs.
Caliber: .22-250, .243, 7mm-08, .308, .358, .450 Marlin, .270, .30-06 (22"), 7mm Rem. Mag., .300 Win. Mag. (24")
Magazine: 5 and 4 (magnums)
Features: short action alloy receiver, front-locking bolt, rack-and-pinion action
BLR $737
BLR Lightweight 81 . . . . $696
WSMs $764

Buck Mark Classic Carbon

Action: autoloading
Stock: laminated
Barrel: 18 in.
Sights: none
Weight: 3.6lbs.
Caliber: .22 LR
Magazine: 10
Features: composite carbon barrel with steel liner, integral scope rail
Buck Mark Classic Carbon $615

NEW Products: **European American Armory Rifles**

IZH MASH TARGET WOOD HW 660

IZH MASH TARGET LAMINATED

IZH MASH TARGET BIATHLON

IZH Mash Target

Action: bolt
Stock: walnut or laminated
Barrel: target-weight 26 in.
Sights: Anschutz
Weight: 11.3lbs.
Caliber: .22 LR
Magazine: none
Features: match-grade barrel, stock with adjustable butt, comb; front rail with accessories; Biathlon (repeater 8.5 lbs) and Biathlon Basic (6.1 lbs.)

also available
IZH Mash. $999
laminated. $1199
Biathlon. $979
Biathlon Basic $339

NEW Products: **Henry Rifles**

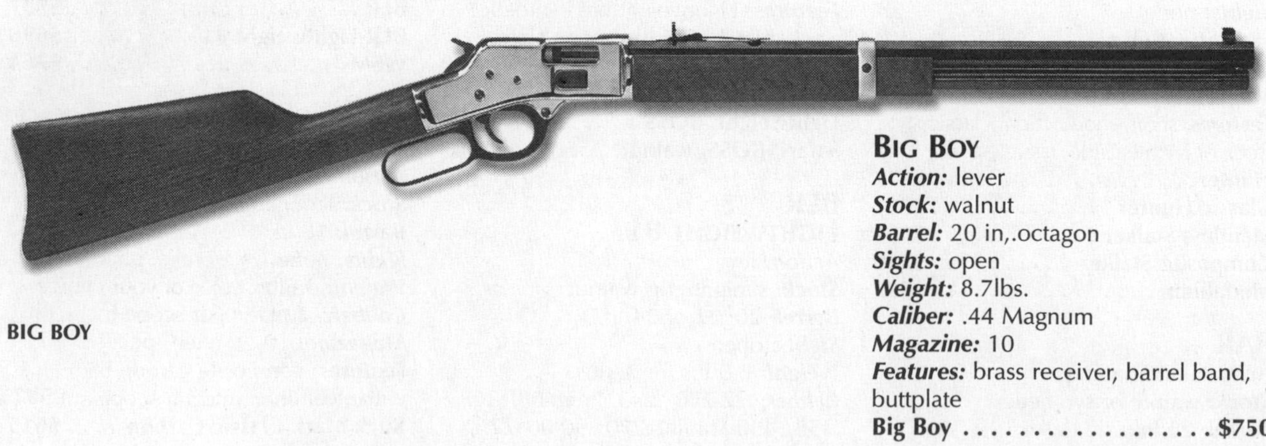

BIG BOY

Big Boy

Action: lever
Stock: walnut
Barrel: 20 in,.octagon
Sights: open
Weight: 8.7lbs.
Caliber: .44 Magnum
Magazine: 10
Features: brass receiver, barrel band, buttplate
Big Boy $750

NEW Products: **Henry Rifles**

LEVER VARMINT EXPRESS

Lever Varmint Express

Action: lever
Stock: walnut
Barrel: 20 in.
Sights: none
Weight: 5.8lbs.
Caliber: .17 HMR
Magazine: 11
Features: Monte Carlo stock; scope mount included
Varmint Express $460

NEW Products: **Jarrett Rifles**

PROFESSIONAL HUNTER

SERIES RIFLE

Professional Hunter

Action: bolt
Stock: synthetic
Barrel: 24 in.
Sights: open
Weight: 9.0lbs.
Caliber: any popular standard or wildcat chambering
Magazine: 5 or 3
Features: muzzle brake, also, two Leupold 1.5-5x scopes zeroed in Talley QD rings
Professional Hunter $8040

Series Rifle

Action: bolt
Stock: synthetic
Barrel: 24 in.
Sights: none
Weight: 7.2lbs.
Caliber: any popular standard or wildcat chambering
Magazine: 5 or 3
Features: muzzle brake, phenolic metal finish in color of your choice, Swarovski or similar scope included; all features most often specified on orders
Series Rifle. $5025

NEW Products: **Kimber Rifles**

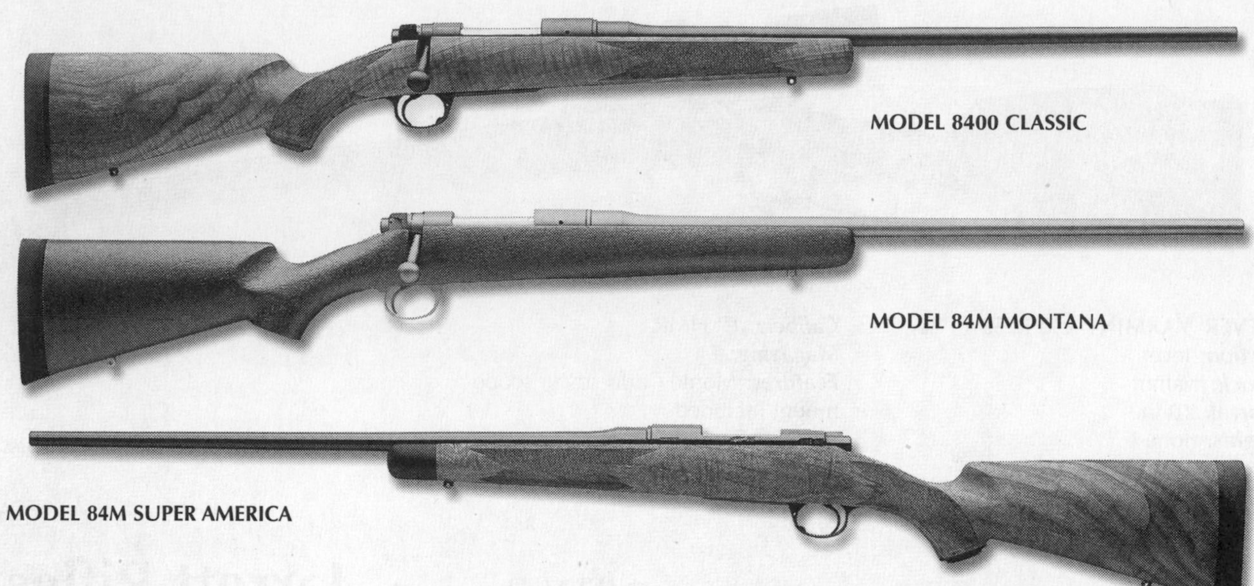

Model 8400 Classic

Action: bolt
Stock: walnut
Barrel: 24 in.
Sights: none
Weight: 6.6lbs.
Caliber: .270, 7mm and .300 WSM
Magazine: 3
Features: also left-hand
8400 Classic. $950
8400 Classic left-hand $1018

Model 84M Montana

Action: bolt
Stock: synthetic
Barrel: 22 or 24 in.
Sights: none
Weight: 6.1lbs.
Caliber: .270 WSM, 7mm WSM, .300 WSM
Magazine: 5 or 3
Features: stainless steel
84M Montana, standard calibers . . . $1053
Montana, WSMs $1086

Model 84M Super America

Action: bolt
Stock: walnut
Barrel: 24 in.
Sights: none
Weight: 6.6lbs.
Caliber: .270 WSM, 7mm WSM, .300 WSM
Magazine: 3
Features: wrap checkering on select wood
84M Super America $1764

NEW Products: **Legacy Sports Rifles**

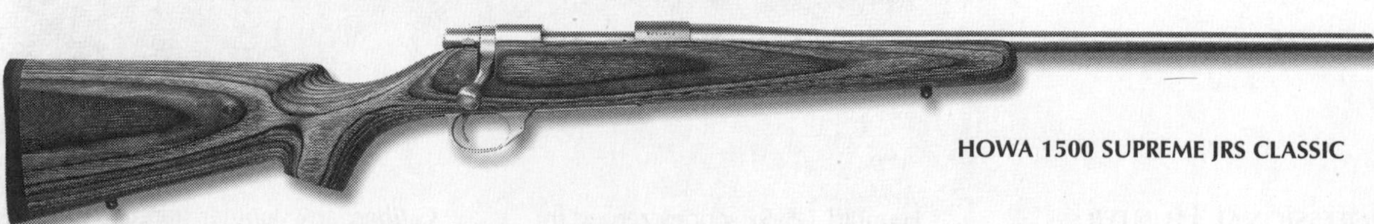

HOWA 1500 SUPREME JRS CLASSIC

Howa 1500 Supreme JRs Classic

Action: bolt
Stock: laminated
Barrel: 22 or 24 in.
Sights: none
Weight: 7.6lbs.
Caliber: .223, .22-250, .243, 6.5x55, .270, .308, .30-06, 7mm Rem. Mag., .300 Win. Mag., .338 Win. Mag., .270 WSM, 7mm WSM, .300 WSM
Magazine: 5 or 3
Features: stainless or blue, nutmeg or pepper stock; also: Hunter rifles with walnut stock
blue. $641
stainless $714
Hunter, blue. $539
Hunter, stainless. $714

NEW Products: **Legacy Sports Rifles**

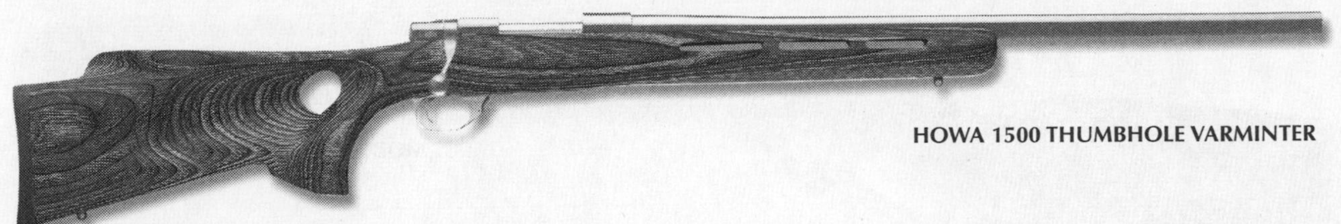

HOWA 1500 THUMBHOLE VARMINTER

Howa 1500 Thumbhole Varminter

Action: bolt
Stock: laminated
Barrel: heavy 22 in.
Sights: none
Weight: 9.9lbs.
Caliber: .223, .22-250, .308
Magazine: 5
Features: nutmeg or pepper stock color, blued or stainless; also: new Sporter thumbhole version (7.6 lbs.) in 13 calibers including WSMs
blue $692
stainless $794
stainless Sporter $764

NEW Products: **Marlin Rifles**

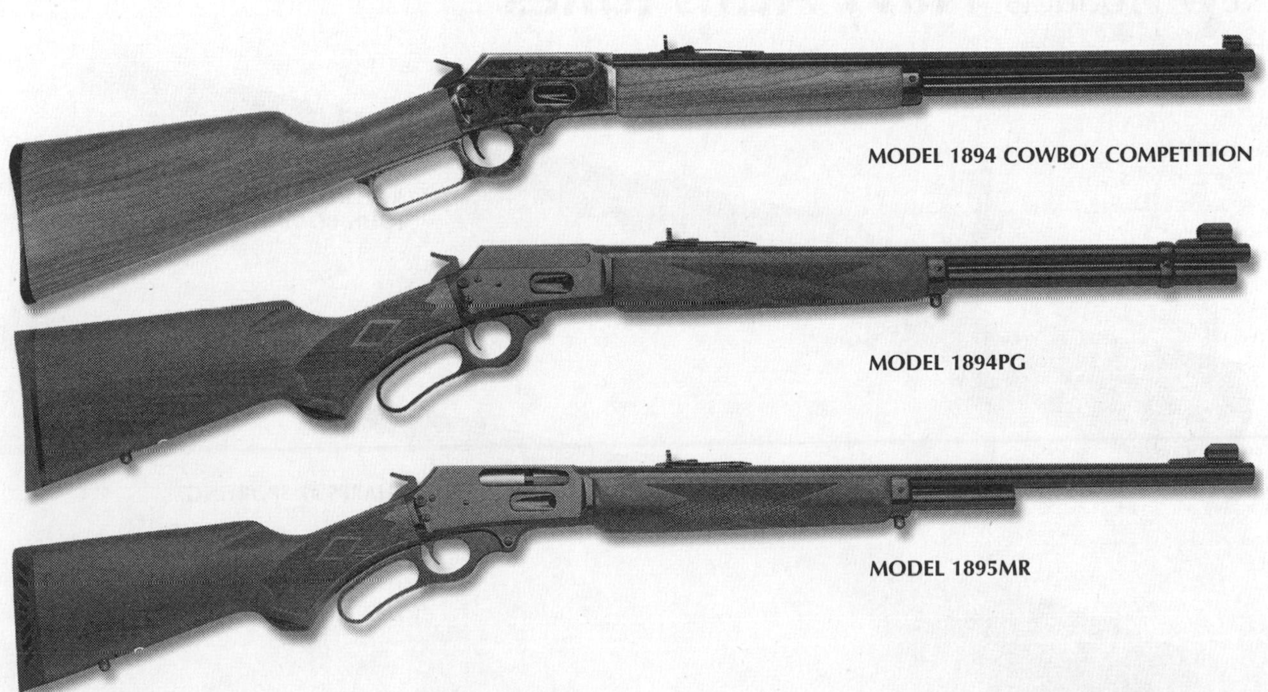

MODEL 1894 COWBOY COMPETITION

MODEL 1894PG

MODEL 1895MR

Model 1894 Cowboy Competition

Action: lever
Stock: walnut
Barrel: 20 in.
Sights: open
Weight: 7.0lbs.
Caliber: .45 Long Colt
Magazine: 10
Features: case-colored receiver, also in .38 Spl.
1894 Cowboy Competition $986

Model 1894FG and 1894PG

Action: lever
Stock: walnut
Barrel: 20 in.
Sights: open
Weight: 6.5lbs.
Caliber: .44 Magnum (PG) and .41 Magnum (FG)
Magazine: 10
Features: pistol grip stock
1894 . . . . $610

Model 1895MR

Action: lever
Stock: walnut
Barrel: 22 in.
Sights: open
Weight: 7.5lbs.
Caliber: .450 Marlin
Magazine: 4
Features: pistol-grip stock
1895 . . . . $761

NEW Products: **Marlin Rifles**

MODEL 336Y SPIKEHORN

MODEL 336Y SPIKEHORN
Action: lever
Stock: walnut
Barrel: 16.5 in.
Sights: open
Weight: 6.5lbs.
Caliber: .30-30
Magazine: 5
Features: pistol grip stock; 12.5-inch pull for small shooters
336Y Spikehorn $536

NEW Products: **Navy Arms Rifles**

ROLLING BLOCK #2
JOHN BODINE

SHARPS #2 SPORTING

ROLLING BLOCK #2 JOHN BODINE
Action: dropping block
Stock: walnut
Barrel: 30 in.
Sights: adjustable tang
Weight: 12.0lbs.
Caliber: .45-70
Magazine: none
Features: double set triggers, nickel-finish breech
John Bodine $1426

SHARPS #2 SPORTING
Action: dropping block
Stock: walnut
Barrel: 30 in.
Sights: target
Weight: 10.0lbs.
Caliber: .45-70
Magazine: none
Features: also #2 Silhouette Creedmoor and Quigley (with 34 in. barrel)
Sporting, Silhouette and Creedmoor $1339
Quigley $1432

NEW Products: **New England Firearms Rifles**

HANDI-RIFLE YOUTH

Handi-Rifle Youth

Action: hinged breech
Stock: hardwood
Barrel: 22 in.
Sights: none
Weight: 7.0lbs.
Caliber: 7mm-08
Magazine: none
Features: single-shot; scope rail included; also: Youth model with shorter (11.8 in.) stock (6.8 lbs.)
Handi-Rifle in 7mm-08 . . . . $274

NEW Products: **Remington Arms Rifles**

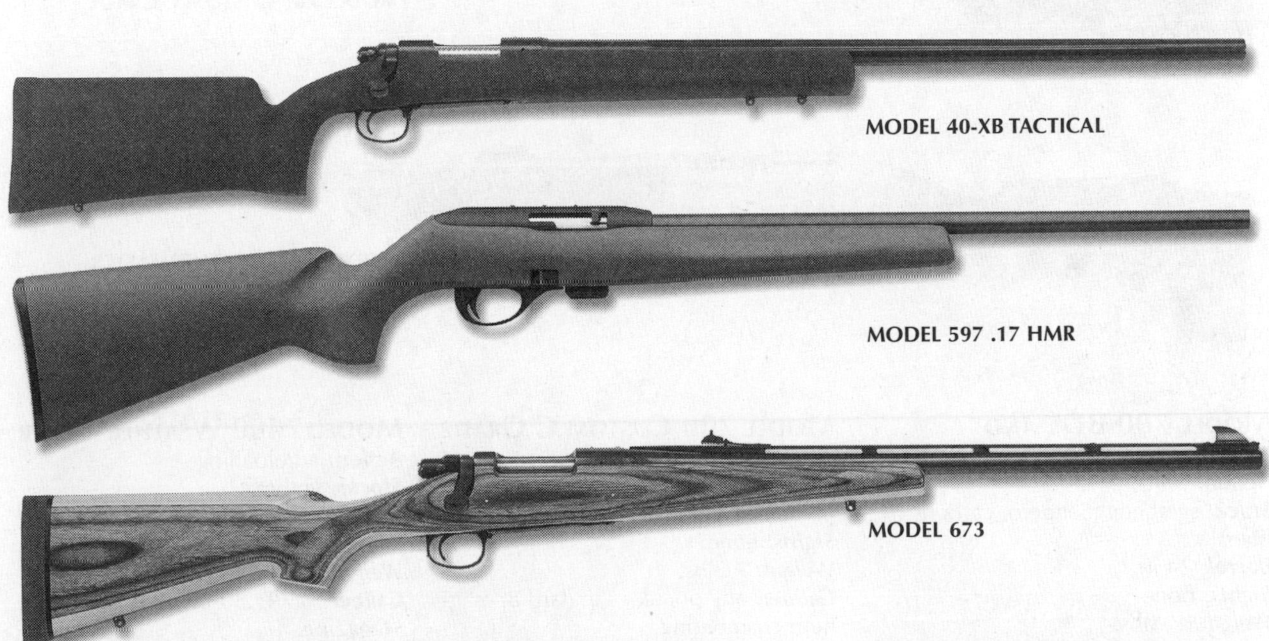

MODEL 40-XB TACTICAL

MODEL 597 .17 HMR

MODEL 673

Model 40-XR and 40-XB

Action: bolt
Stock: walnut
Barrel: 24 or 26 in.
Sights: none
Weight: 6.5lbs.
Caliber: .22 LR (LR series), any popular centerfire cartridge (XB series)
Magazine: 5 shot, detachable box
Features: single-shot or repeater, built to order; target and tactical weigh 10 lbs.
.22 XR Sporter $3383
.308 XB Tactical $2108

Model 597 .17 HMR

Action: autoloading
Stock: synthetic
Barrel: 20 in.
Sights: open
Weight: 6.0lbs.
Caliber: .17 HMR
Magazine: 8
Features: detachable box magazine
Model 597 .17 HMR. $305

Model 673

Action: bolt
Stock: laminated
Barrel: 22 in.
Sights: open
Weight: 7.5lbs.
Caliber: .350 Rem. Mag., .300 SUM
Magazine: 3 + 1
Features: vent rib, Model Seven action
Model 673 . . . . $825

NEW Products: Remington Arms Rifles

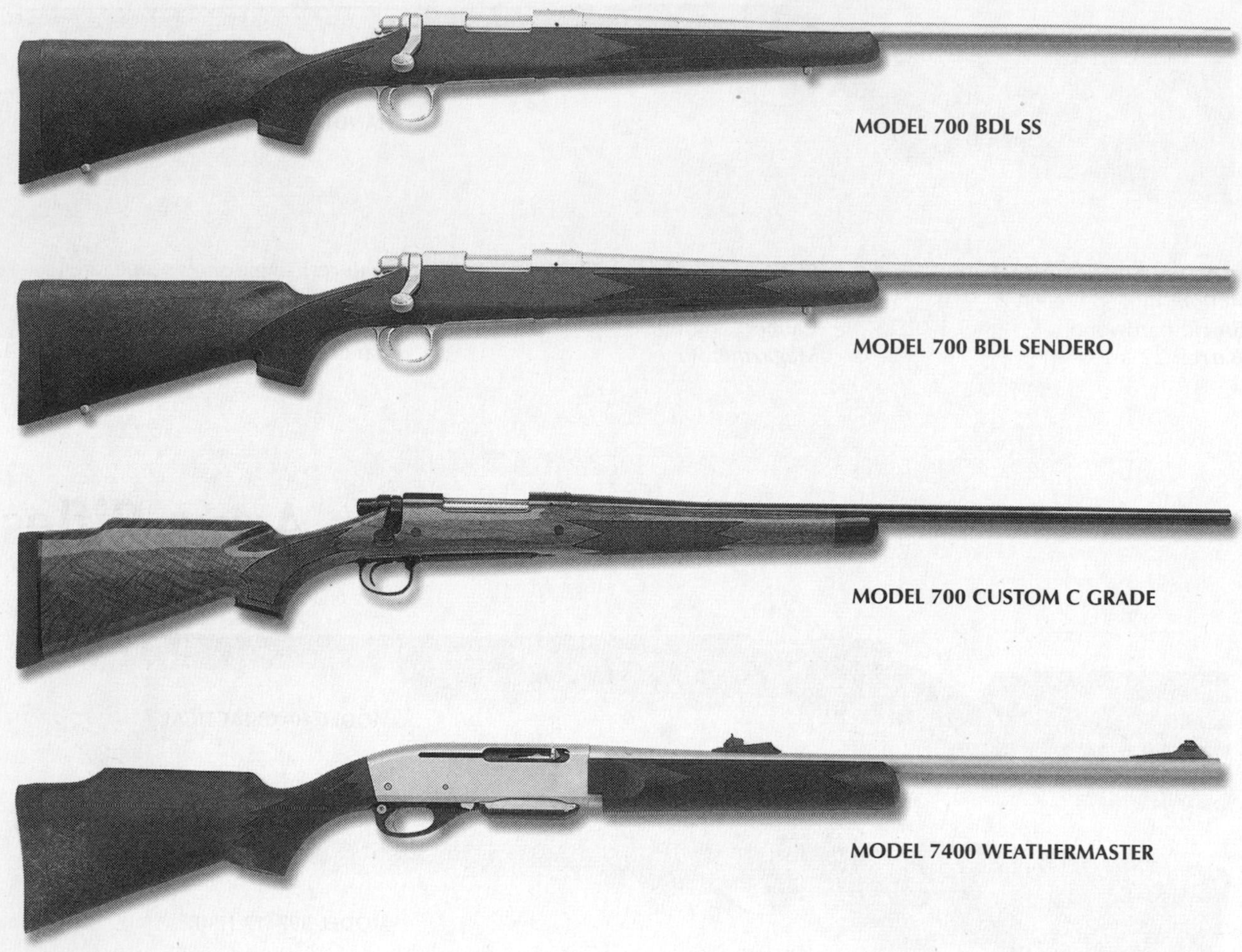

MODEL 700 BDL SS

MODEL 700 BDL SENDERO

MODEL 700 CUSTOM C GRADE

MODEL 7400 WEATHERMASTER

MODEL 700 BDL AND SENDERO

Action: bolt
Stock: synthetic (Sendero, carbon fiber)
Barrel: 24 in.
Sights: none
Weight: 7.5lbs.
Caliber: 7mm SUM, .300 SUM
Magazine: 3 + 1
Features: stainless short actions and barrels; 8.5 lbs. for Sendero
BDL $775
Sendero $1016

MODEL 700 CUSTOM C GRADE

Action: bolt
Stock: walnut
Barrel: 24 in.
Sights: none
Weight: 7.5lbs.
Caliber: any popular standard or magnum chambering
Magazine: 3 to 5
Features: some custom-shop options available
Model 700 Custom C Grade . . $1733

MODEL 7400 WEATHERMASTER

Action: autoloading
Stock: synthetic
Barrel: 22 in.
Sights: open
Weight: 7.5lbs.
Caliber: .270, .30-06
Magazine: 4
Features: nickel plated
Weathermaster $624

NEW Products: **Rossi Rifles**

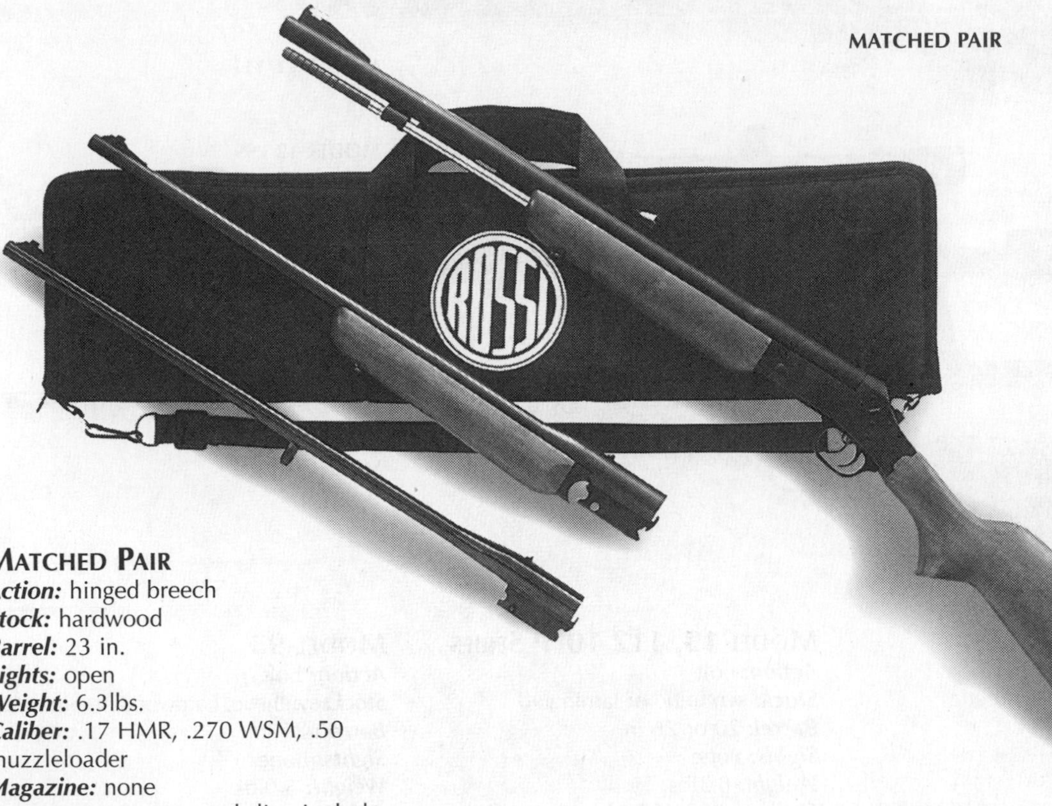

MATCHED PAIR

Matched Pair

Action: hinged breech
Stock: hardwood
Barrel: 23 in.
Sights: open
Weight: 6.3lbs.
Caliber: .17 HMR, .270 WSM, .50 muzzleloader
Magazine: none
Features: carry case and sling included; adjustable sights
Matched Pair $350

NEW Products: **Sako Rifles**

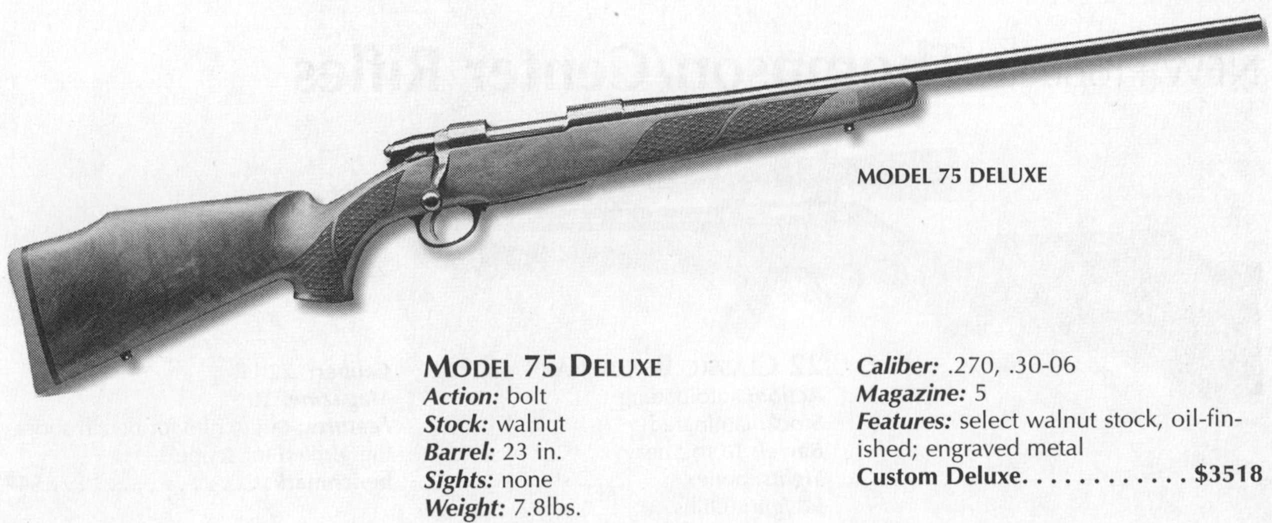

MODEL 75 DELUXE

Model 75 Deluxe

Action: bolt
Stock: walnut
Barrel: 23 in.
Sights: none
Weight: 7.8lbs.
Caliber: .270, .30-06
Magazine: 5
Features: select walnut stock, oil-finished; engraved metal
Custom Deluxe. $3518

NEW Products: Savage Arms Rifles

Model 11/111

Action: bolt
Stock: hardwood or synthetic
Barrel: 24 in.
Sights: none
Weight: 7.0lbs.
Caliber: .270 WSM, 7mm WSM, .300 WSM, 7mm SUM, .300 SUM (all new for 2003 in various configurations)
Magazine: 3
Features: top tang safety; adjustable sights available
from **$428**

Model 12, 112 10FP Series

Action: bolt
Stock: synthetic or laminated
Barrel: 20 or 26 in.
Sights: none
Weight: 8.3lbs.
Caliber: .223, .22-250, .243, .25-06, 7mm Rem. Mag., .308, .30-06, .300 WSM, .300 Win. Mag.
Magazine: 3 or 4
Features: single-shot or box magazine; new in these rifles for 2003 is the Savage AccuTrigger
12 youth **$515**
12 VSS Stainless single-shot. . . . $934

Model 93

Action: bolt
Stock: synthetic, hardwood or laminated
Barrel: 21 in.
Sights: none
Weight: 5.0lbs.
Caliber: .17 HMR
Magazine: 5
Features: scope bases included; eight versions with stainless or C-M steel, different stocks; varmint models weigh 6.0 lbs.
synthetic F **$184**
camo **$214**
hardwood GV or GLV........ **$221**
laminated stainless BVSS...... **$306**

NEW Products: Thompson/Center Rifles

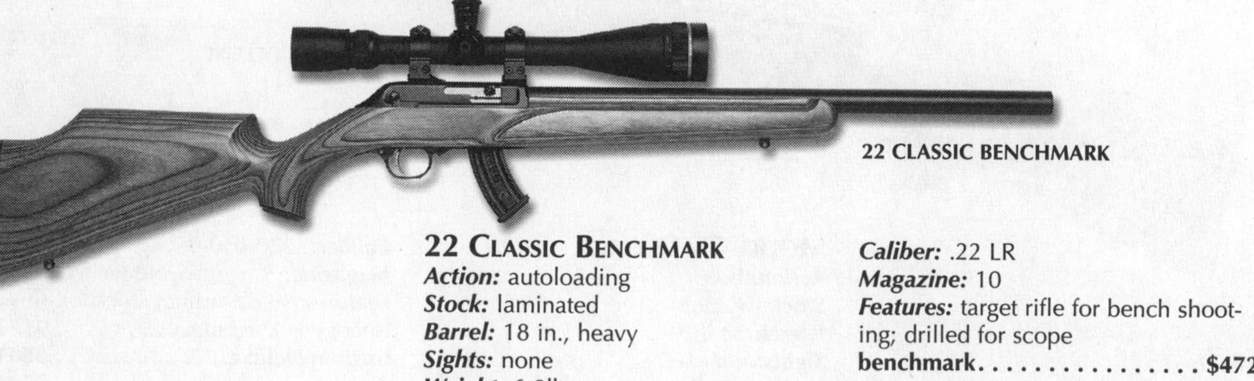

22 Classic Benchmark

Action: autoloading
Stock: laminated
Barrel: 18 in., heavy
Sights: none
Weight: 6.8lbs.
Caliber: .22 LR
Magazine: 10
Features: target rifle for bench shooting; drilled for scope
benchmark................ **$472**

NEW Products: **Weatherby Rifles**

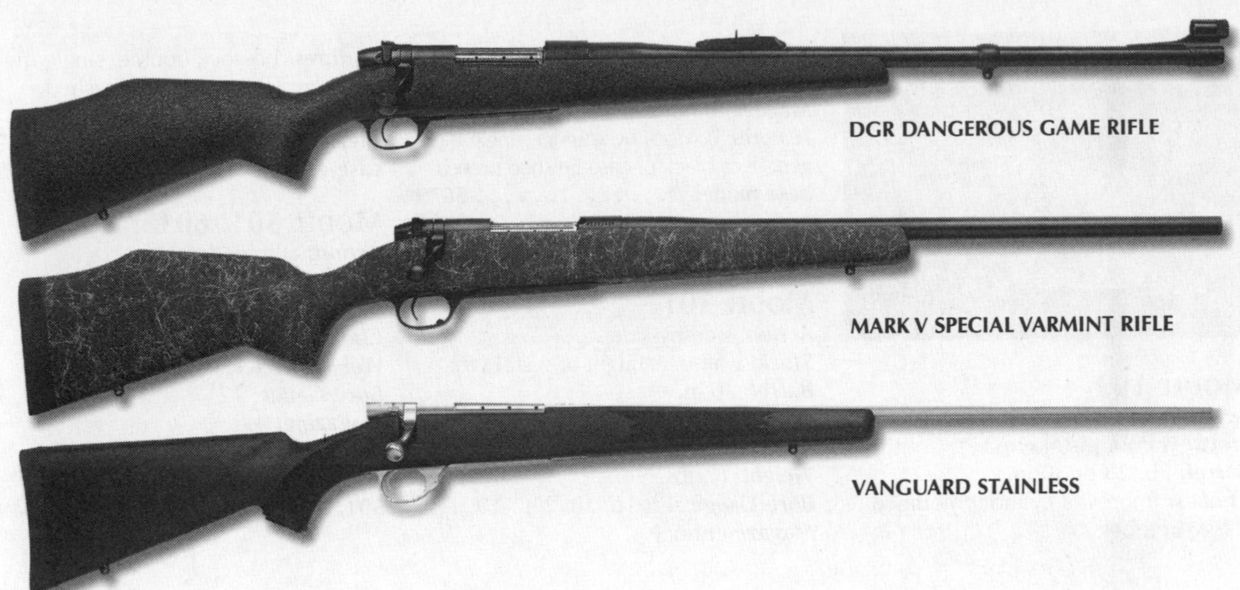

DGR DANGEROUS GAME RIFLE

MARK V SPECIAL VARMINT RIFLE

VANGUARD STAINLESS

Mark V DGR Dangerous Game Rifle

Action: bolt
Stock: composite
Barrel: 24 in. Krieger
Sights: adjustable open
Weight: 8.8lbs.
Caliber: .458 Lott
Magazine: 3
Features: black oxide metal finish, Mark V 9-lug bolt; Pachmayr Decelerator pad, aluminum bedding dock
DGR $2892

Mark V Special Varmint Rifle

Action: bolt
Stock: composite
Barrel: 22 in.
Sights: none
Weight: 7.3lbs.
Caliber: .223, .22-250
Magazine: 5 and 4
Features: 6-lug action, made in USA; barrel #3 contour, lapped, fluted, floated; 1½-inch factory guarantee for 3-shot group
SVR $999

Vanguard

Action: bolt
Stock: composite
Barrel: 24 in.
Sights: none
Weight: 7.8lbs.
Caliber: .223, .22-250, .243, .270, .308, .30-06, 7mm Rem. Mag., .300 Win. Mag., .300 WSM, .300 Wby. Mag., .338 Win. Mag.
Magazine: 5 to 3
Features: 6-lug action, made in USA, 1½-inch factory guarantee for 3-shot group
synthetic $476
stainless $595

NEW Products: **Winchester Rifles**

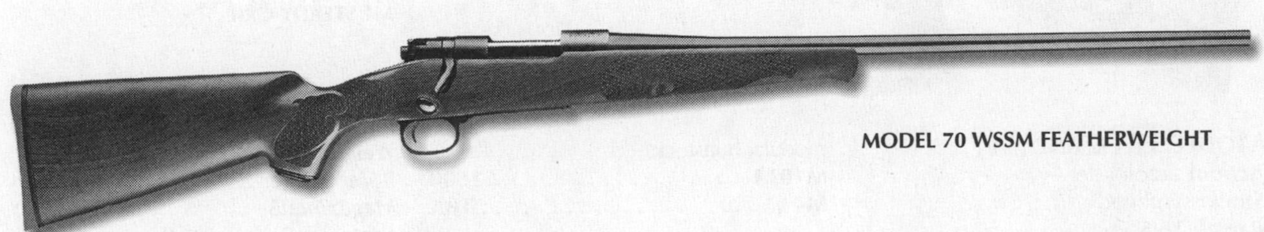

MODEL 70 WSSM FEATHERWEIGHT

Model 70 WSSM

Action: bolt
Stock: walnut, synthetic or laminated
Barrel: 24 in.
Sights: none
Weight: 6.0lbs.
Caliber: .223 WSSM, .243 WSSM
Magazine: 3
Features: shortened M70 action, new synthetic shadow stock with grip inserts; laminated Coyote weighs 9 lbs.
Shadow $543
Featherweight $769
Coyote $734

NEW Products: Armsco Shotguns

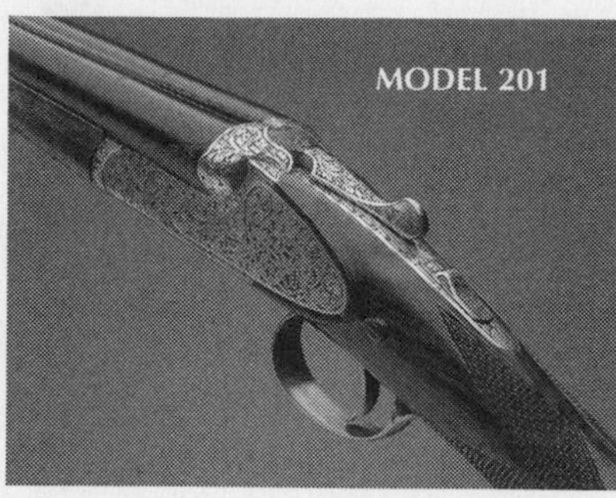

Model 103
Action: over/under
Stock: walnut pistol grip
Barrel: 26, 28 or 30 in.
Chokes: improved cylinder/modified, screw-in tubes
Weight: 7.0lbs.
Bore/Gauge: 12, 16, 20, 28, 410
Magazine: none
Features: boxlock over/under, single trigger, silver, black or case-finished breech
base model $679
mid-grade $999
high-grade $1299

Model 201
Action: side-by-side
Stock: walnut, straight or pistol grip
Barrel: 26 in.
Chokes: improved cylinder/modified, screw-in tubes
Weight: 6.3lbs.
Bore/Gauge: 12, 16, 20, 28, 410
Magazine: none
Features: boxlock double, single trigger, silver, black or case-finished breech; IC/M in 16 ga. and .410
silver or black $899
case-colored................ $999

Model 501, 601
Action: autoloader
Stock: walnut
Barrel: 24, 26 or 28 in.
Chokes: screw-in tubes
Weight: 7.0lbs.
Bore/Gauge: 12
Magazine: 4
Features: matte or polished metal; also 20 gauge 701
501, 601 .... $499

NEW Products: Benelli Shotguns

MODEL 1014

M4 STANDARD OR PISTOL GRIP

M1 STEADY GRIP

Model 1014 and M4
Action: autoloader
Stock: synthetic
Barrel: 18.5 in.
Chokes: improved cylinder, modified, full
Weight: 8.0lbs.
Bore/Gauge: 12
Magazine: 4 + 1
Features: M4 has pistol grip or field stock; gas operated, ghost-ring sight, modular buttstocks
M1014................. $1600
M4 .... TBA

M1 Field, Super Black Eagle Steady Grip
Action: autoloader
Stock: synthetic with vertical pistol grip
Barrel: 24 in.
Chokes: I.C., X-full
Weight: 7.3lbs.
Bore/Gauge: 12
Magazine: 3
Features: Benelli inertia-system mechanism; Super Black Eagle also handles 3½-inch shells
M1 Field $1175
Super Black Eagle......... $1465

NEW Products: **Benelli Shotguns**

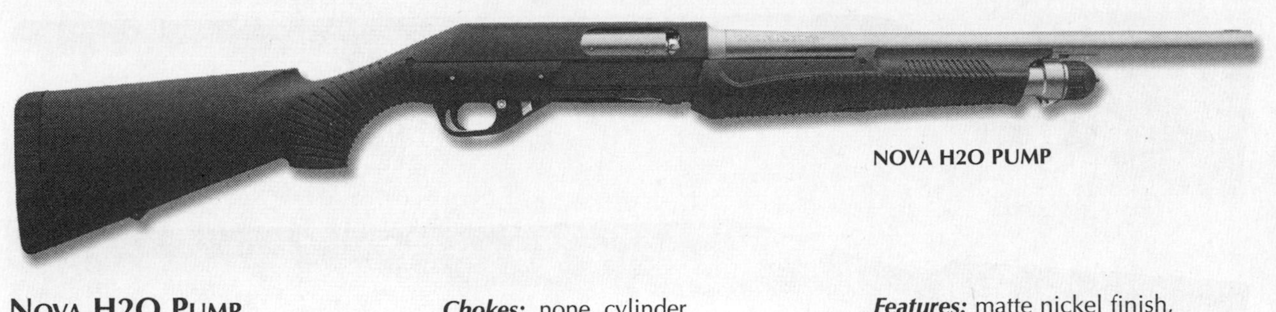
NOVA H2O PUMP

Nova H2O Pump
Action: pump
Stock: synthetic
Barrel: 18½ in.
Chokes: none, cylinder
Weight: 7.2 lbs.
Bore/Gauge: 12
Magazine: 4 + 1
Features: matte nickel finish, open rifle sights
synthetic $465

NEW Products: **Bernardelli Shotguns**

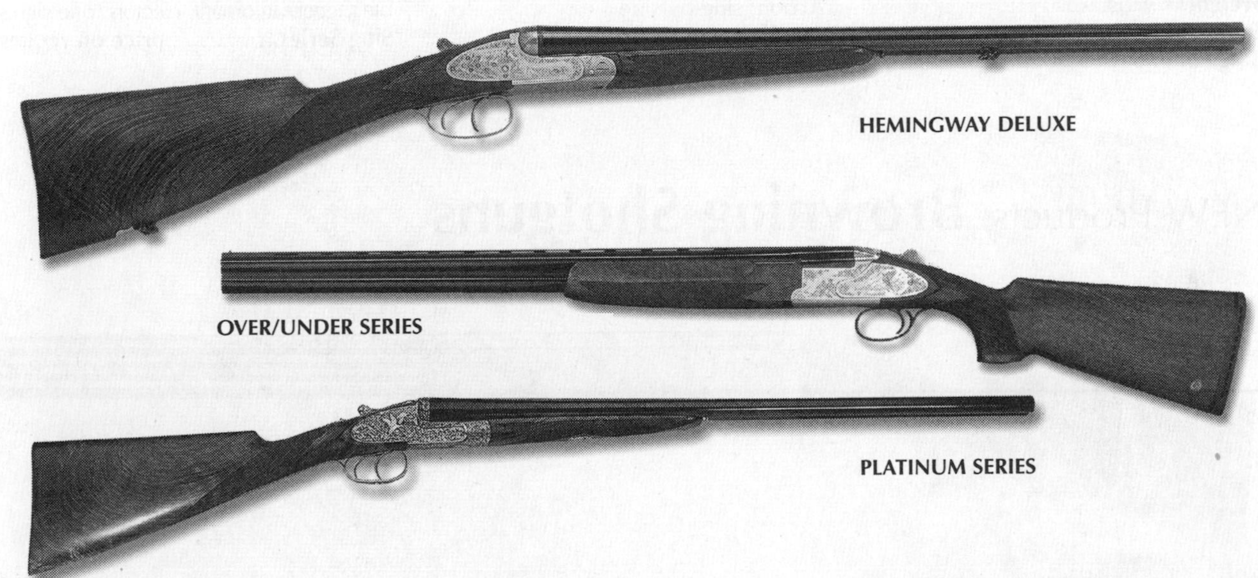
HEMINGWAY DELUXE

OVER/UNDER SERIES

PLATINUM SERIES

Hemingway Deluxe
Action: side-by-side
Stock: walnut, straight grip
Barrel: 26 in.
Chokes: modified, improved modified, full
Weight: 6.25lbs.
Bore/Gauge: 16, 20, 28
Magazine: none
Features: boxlock double, single or double trigger, automatic ejectors
Hemingway Deluxe . . price on request

Over/Under Series
Action: over/under
Stock: walnut, pistol grip
Barrel: 26 or 28 in.
Chokes: modified, improved modified, full, screw-in tubes
Weight: 7.2lbs.
Bore/Gauge: 12, 20
Magazine: none
Features: boxlock over/under, single or double triggers, vent rib, various grades
Over/Under . . . . . . price on request

Platinum Series
Action: side-by-side
Stock: walnut, straight or pistol grip
Barrel: 26 or 28 in.
Chokes: modified, improved modified, full
Weight: 6.5lbs.
Bore/Gauge: 12
Magazine: none
Features: sidelock double; articulated single selective or double trigger, triple-lug Purdey breeching automatic ejectors, various grades
Platinum Series . . . . price on request

NEW Products: Bernardelli Shotguns

SEMI-AUTOMATIC SERIES

SLUG SERIES

SEMI-AUTOMATIC SERIES
Action: autoloader
Stock: walnut, synthetic or camo
Barrel: 24, 26 or 28 in.
Chokes: screw-in tubes
Weight: 6.7lbs.
Bore/Gauge: 12
Magazine: 5
Features: gas-operated, concave top rib, ABS case included
Semi-Automatic. . . . price on request

SLUG SERIES
Action: side-by-side
Stock: walnut, pistol grip
Barrel: 24 in.
Chokes: modified, improved modified, full
Weight: 7.0lbs.
Bore/Gauge: 12
Magazine: none
Features: boxlock double, single or double trigger, automatic ejectors, rifle sights
Slug Series. . . . . . . price on request

NEW Products: Browning Shotguns

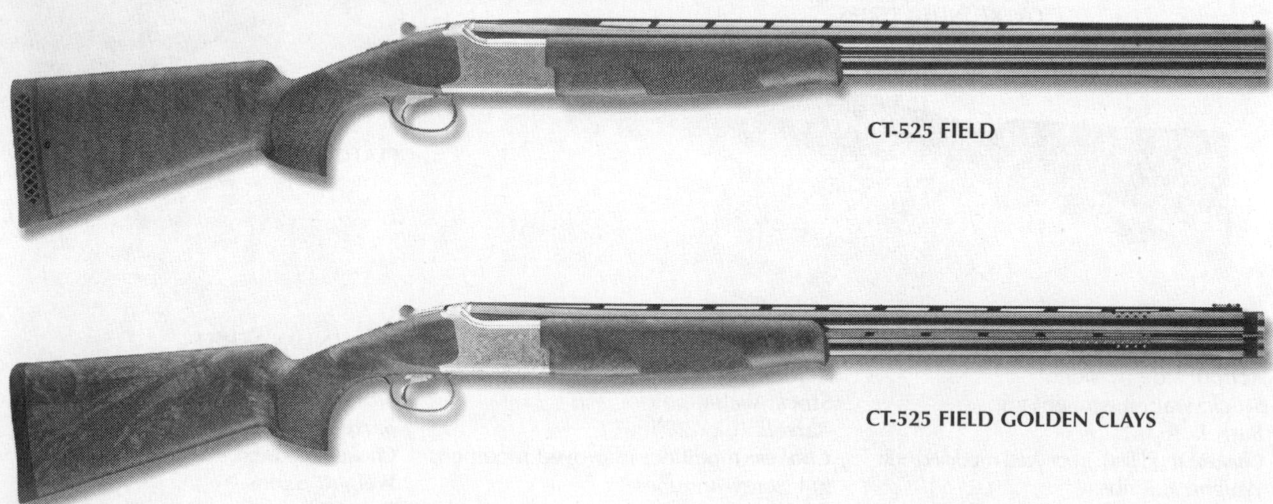
CT-525 FIELD

CT-525 FIELD GOLDEN CLAYS

CT-525 FIELD
Action: over/under
Stock: walnut
Barrel: 26 or 28 in.
Chokes: screw-in tubes
Weight: 6.7lbs.
Bore/Gauge: 28, 410
Magazine: none
Features: small-gauge additions to existing 525 Citori series; also available in CT-525 Sporting and CT-525 Golden Clays
Field $1858
Sporting. $2575
Golden Clays $4300

NEW Products: **European American Armory Shotguns**

DOUBLE HUNTER

SAIGA

Double Hunter

Action: side-by-side
Stock: walnut
Barrel: 24, 26 or 28 in.
Chokes: screw-in tubes
Weight: 6.8lbs.
Bore/Gauge: 12, 16, 20, 28, 410
Magazine: none
Features: hinged breech boxlock; ejectors, single selective trigger, automatic safety, chrome-lined, hammer forged barrels, choke in .410 IM/F and 28 ga. IC/M; also, exposed-hammer "Cowboy" model, 12-gauge rifle barrel inserts available

12 ga. $389
other gauges $439
English stock in .410. . . . . $480
20 and 28 ga. two-barrel set . . . $630
rifle barrel inserts .45/70 . . . . . $159

Saiga

Action: autoloader
Stock: synthetic
Barrel: 19, 21, 22 or 24 in.
Chokes: screw-in tubes
Weight: 7.4lbs.
Bore/Gauge: 12, 20, 410
Magazine: 5 + 1 (4 + 1 .410)
Features: AK-47 mechanism, detachable box magazine

12 ga. $429
20 ga. $389
.410. $239

NEW Products: **Franchi Shotguns**

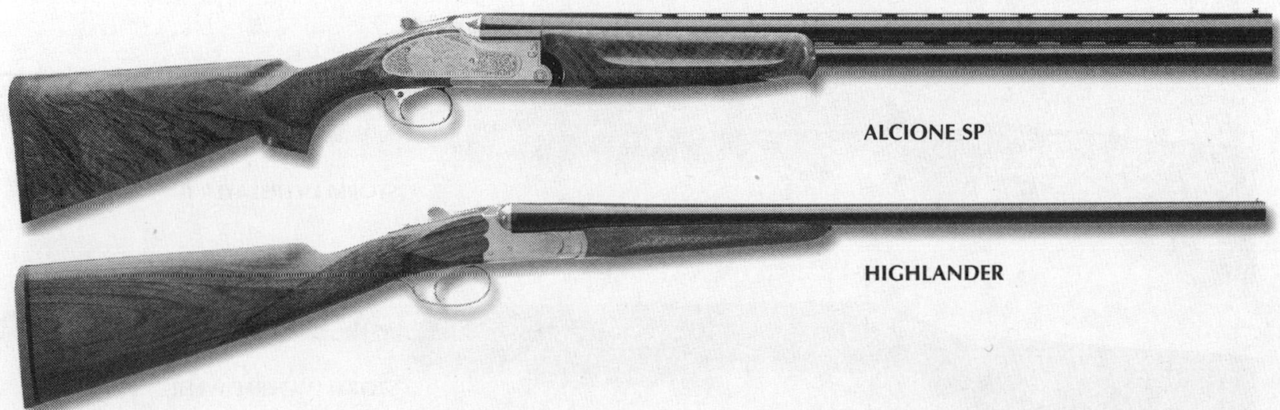

ALCIONE SP

HIGHLANDER

Alcione SP

Action: over/under
Stock: walnut
Barrel: 28 in.
Chokes: improved cylinder, modified, full
Weight: 7.5lbs.
Bore/Gauge: 12
Magazine: none
Features: boxlock, engraved, coin-finish sideplates, fitted hard case

Alcione SP $2700

Highlander

Action: side-by-side
Stock: walnut, straight grip
Barrel: 26 in.
Chokes: improved cylinder, modified
Weight: 6.4lbs.
Bore/Gauge: 12, 20, 28
Magazine: none
Features: boxlock, fitted hard case, single selective trigger, coin finish receiver

Highlander. $1800
28 gauge $1950

NEW Products: Heckler & Koch Shotguns

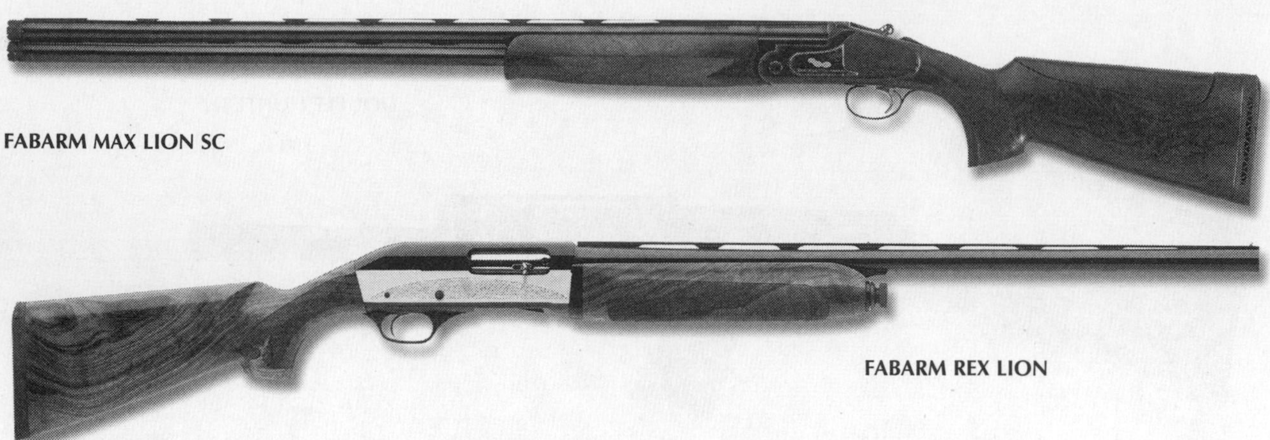

FABARM MAX LION SC

FABARM REX LION

FABARM PARADOX LION

Action: over/under
Stock: walnut
Barrel: 24 in.
Chokes: screw-in tubes
Weight: 7.6lbs.
Bore/Gauge: 12, 20
Magazine: none
Features: boxlock; choke tube on top barrel and rifled below; case-colored receiver; 6.6 lbs for 20 gauge; also, new Max Lion Sporting Clays with adjustable stock and 32 in. tube-choked barrels (7.9 lbs.)
Paradox Lion $1129
Max Lion SC. $1799

FABARM REX LION AND GOLD LION

Action: autoloader
Stock: walnut
Barrel: 26 or 28 in.
Chokes: screw-in tubes
Weight: 7.7lbs.
Bore/Gauge: 12
Magazine: 2
Features: gas operated, Turkish walnut stock, chrome-lined barrel
Rex Lion. $1049
Gold Lion. $939

NEW Products: Ithaca Shotguns

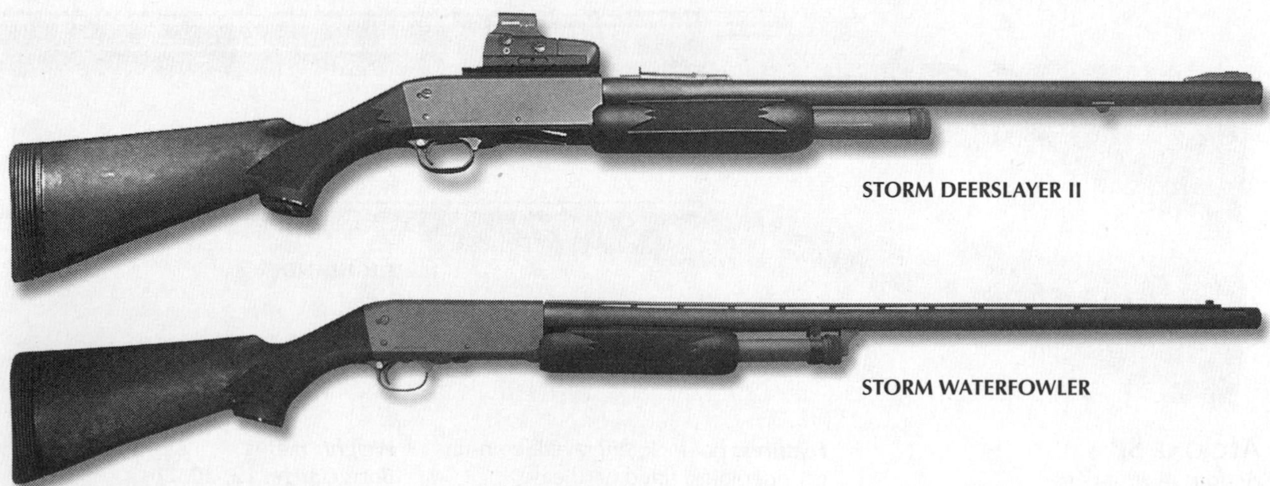

STORM DEERSLAYER II

STORM WATERFOWLER

STORM SERIES

Action: pump
Stock: solid synthetic
Barrel: 24 or 28 in.
Chokes: screw-in tubes
Weight: 5.5lbs.
Bore/Gauge 12, 20
Magazine: 4
Features: parkerized steel finish; ported 24 in. Turkey barrel with Tru-Glo sights, rifled 24 in. Deerslayer II barrel with Tru-Glo sights, or 28 in. Waterfowler barrel; camo available
from $499

NEW Products: **Legacy Sports Shotguns**

ESCORT FIELD, CAMO

ESCORT FIELD, AIM-GUARD

ESCORT
Action: pump
Stock: synthetic and camo
Barrel: 24 or 28 in.
Chokes: screw-in tubes
Weight: 7.0lbs.
Bore/Gauge: 12
Magazine: 4
Features: also vent rib Aim-Guard defense model with 7-shot magazine, 20 in. plain barrel, cylinder choke
field $200
field, camo. $220
Aim-Guard (6.4 lbs.). $190

NEW Products: **Marlin Shotguns**

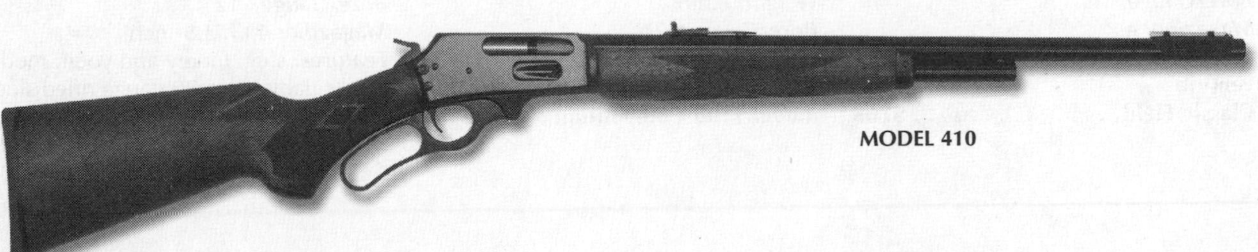

MODEL 410

MODEL 410
Action: pump
Stock: walnut
Barrel: 22 in.
Chokes: none
Weight: 7.3lbs.
Bore/Gauge: 410
Magazine: 4
Features: hamamer block safety; 2 1/2- inch only
Marlin 410. . . . . $536

NEW Products: **Remington Arms Shotguns**

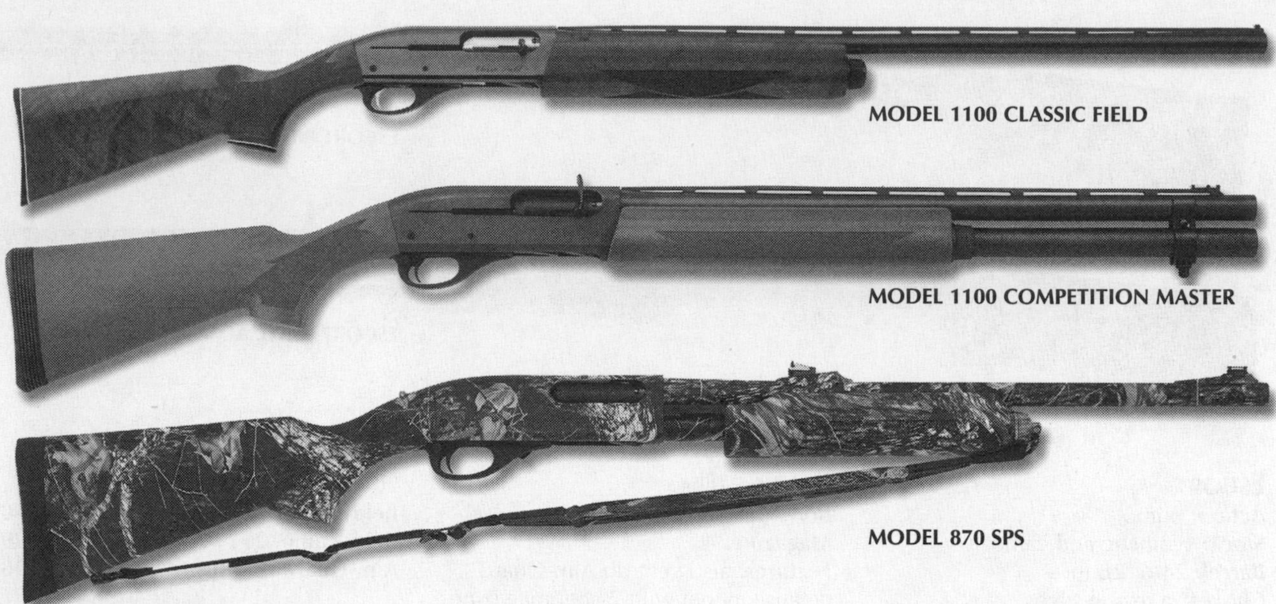

Model 1100 Classic Field

Action: autoloader
Stock: walnut
Barrel: 26 or 28 in.
Chokes: screw-in tubes
Weight: 7.1lbs.
Bore/Gauge: 16
Magazine: 4
Features: gas-operated autoloading, vent rib
Classic Field $765

Model 1100 Competition Master

Action: autoloader
Stock: synthetic
Barrel: 22 in.
Chokes: screw-in tubes
Weight: 8.0lbs.
Bore/Gauge: 12
Magazine: 8 + 1
Features: vent rib, fiber optic sight
model 1100 Competition Master $932

Model 870 SPS Shotguns

Action: pump
Stock: camo
Barrel: 20, 21 or 23 in.
Chokes: screw-in tubes
Weight: 7.3lbs.
Bore/Gauge 12
Magazine: 4 (3: 3.5-inch)
Features: slug, turkey and youth models available; also 20 gauge rifled slug
Turkey $595
Slug $595
Cantilever slug $609

NEW Products: **Sig Arms Shotguns**

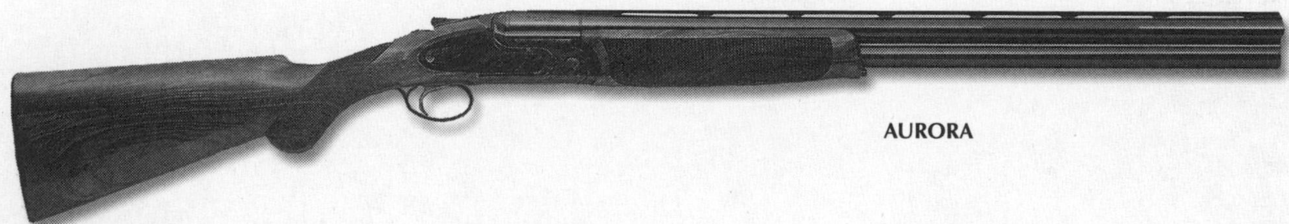

Aurora

Action: over/under
Stock: walnut
Barrel: 26 or 28 in.
Chokes: screw-in tubes
Weight: 7.3lbs.
Bore/Gauge: 12, 20, 28, 410
Magazine: none
Features: boxlock, single selective trigger, automatic ejectors, replaceable hingepin; 20 gauge weighs 6.3 lbs., 28 ga. and .410 6.0 lbs.

Series 20 . . . . $1935
New Englander $2161
Series 30 . . . . $2301
Compeition $2073

NEW Products: **Stevens Shotguns**

MODEL 411

Model 411

Action: side-by-side
Stock: walnut
Barrel: 26 or 28 in.
Chokes: screw-in tubes
Weight: 6.8lbs.
Bore/Gauge: 12, 20, 410
Magazine: none
Features: boxlock; single selective trigger, automatic safety; 6.5 lbs for 20 ga. and .410
12 ga. $395
20 ga. and .410 . . . . $432

NEW Products: **Stoeger Shotguns**

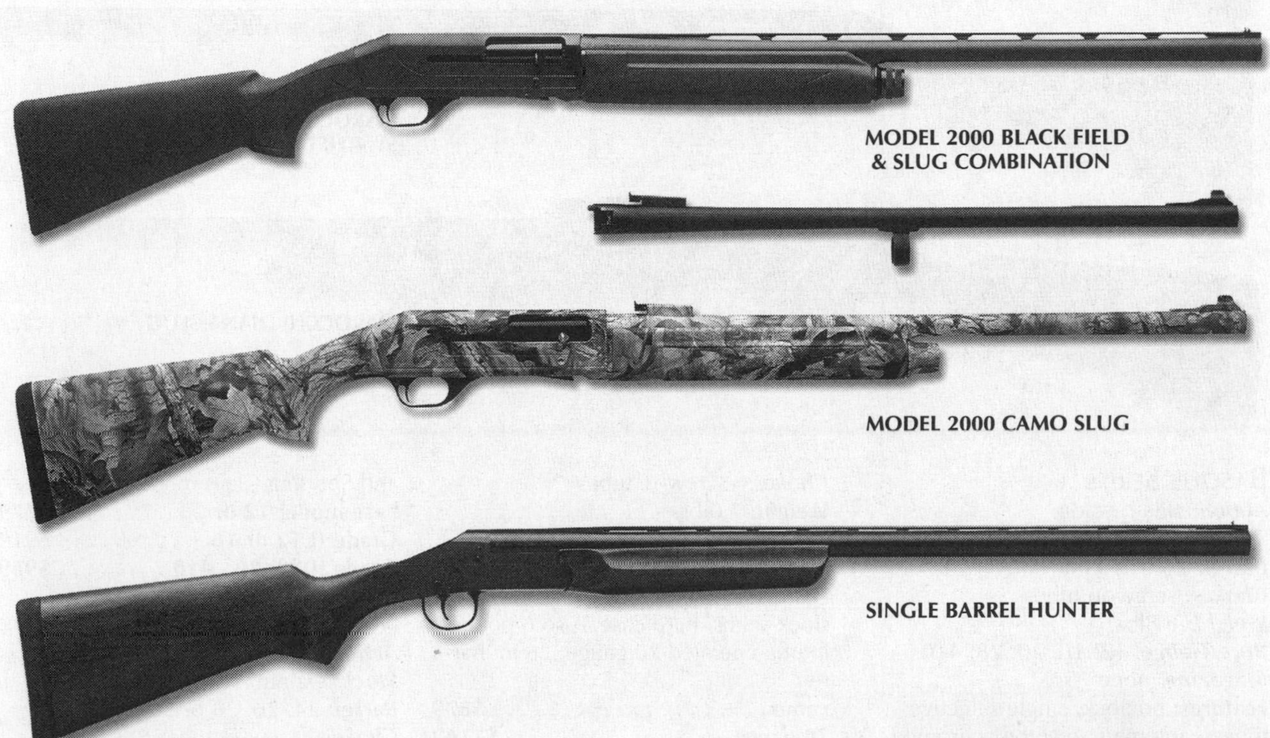

MODEL 2000 BLACK FIELD & SLUG COMBINATION

MODEL 2000 CAMO SLUG

SINGLE BARREL HUNTER

Model 2000

Action: autoloader
Stock: walnut, synthetic or camo
Barrel: 24-30 in.
Chokes: screw-in tube
Weight: 6.7-7.2 lbs.
Bore/Gauge: 12
Magazine: 4
Features: 24 in. smooth-bore slug barrel, proofed for steel shot; fires both 2¾- and 3-in. shells.
Model 2000: . . . . $435 to $495
Model 2000 Combo: . . $495 to $580
Model 2000 Slug: . . . . $430 to $505

Single Barrel Hunter

Action:
Stock: walnut
Barrel: 26 in.
Chokes: screw-in tube
Weight: 5.4 lbs.
Bore/Gauge: .410, 20, 12
Magazine: none
Features: ventilated grooved rib,
Price:. $199

NEW Products: **Tristar Sporting Arms Shotguns**

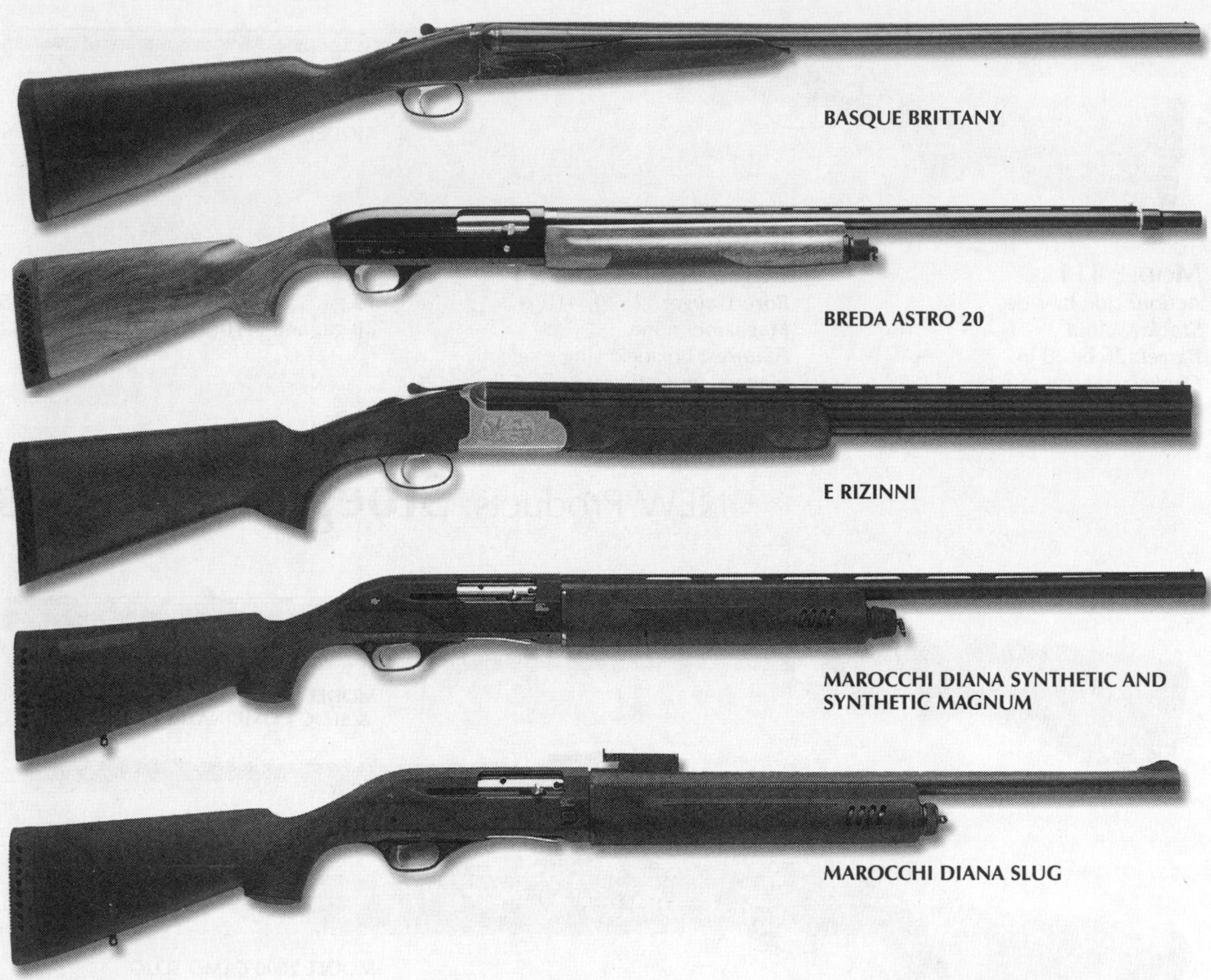

BASQUE BRITTANY

BREDA ASTRO 20

E RIZINNI

MAROCCHI DIANA SYNTHETIC AND SYNTHETIC MAGNUM

MAROCCHI DIANA SLUG

BASQUE SERIES

Action: side-by-side
Stock: walnut, straight or pistol grip
Barrel: 26 or 28 in.
Chokes: screw-in tubes
Weight: 6.8lbs.
Bore/Gauge: 12, 16, 20, 28, 410
Magazine: none
Features: boxlock, single selective trigger, automatic ejectors, chromed bores, also: 20-inch Coach gun; chokes in 16 gauge: M/F and IC/M in 28 gauge and .410.

Gentry $679
Brittany $749
Brittany Sporting $866

BREDA

Action: autoloader
Stock: walnut or camo
Barrel: 28 or 30 in.
Chokes: screw-in tubes
Weight: 7.0lbs.
Bore/Gauge: 12
Magazine: 4
Features: gas-operated, rotary bolt, stock shims, hard case. Also 6 pound inertia-operated 20 gauge, 26 in. barrel

camo $879
20-gauge $1142
12-gauge black and walnut . . . $1259

E. RIZINNI

Action: over/under
Stock: walnut
Barrel: 24, 26 or 28 in.
Chokes: screw-in tubes
Weight: 7.3lbs.
Bore/Gauge: 12, 16, 20, 28, 410
Magazine: none
Features: boxlock, camo and magnum and Sporting Clays models available

base model 12 or 20. . . . . $779
Grade II 12 or 16. . . . . $919
Grade II 20, 20, .410 . . . . $969

MAROCCHI DIANA

Action: autoloader
Stock: walnut, synthetic or camo
Barrel: 24, 26, 28 or 30 in.
Chokes: screw-in tubes
Weight: 7.0lbs.
Bore/Gauge: 12, 20, 28
Magazine: 4
Features: gas-operated, stock shims, slug model has sights, scope mount on rifled barrel

synthetic $399
walnut $425
synthetic magnum $487
camo magnum $576
slug $425

NEW Products: **Verona Shotguns**

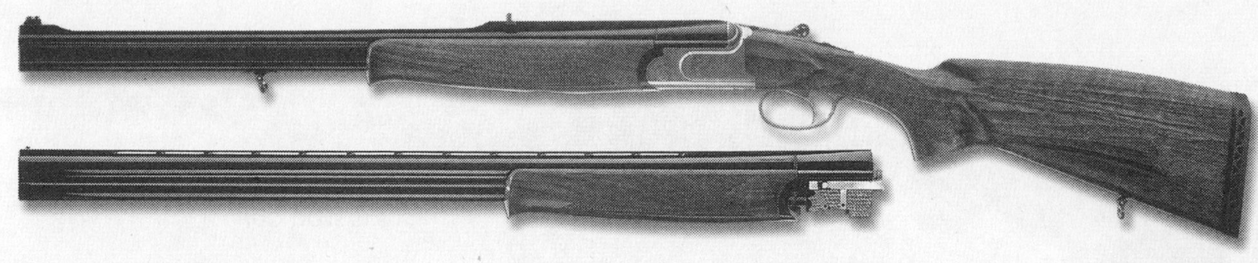

LX 1001-308/20 EXPRESS COMBO

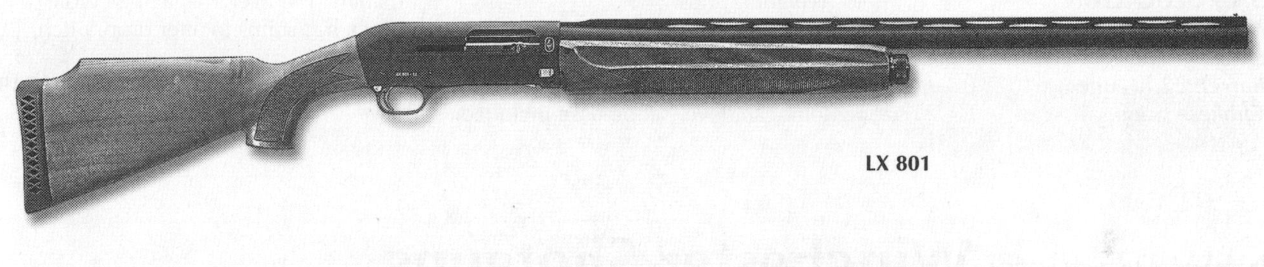

LX 801

SX 405

LX 980 COMPETITION

LX 1001-308/20 Express Combo

Action: over/under
Stock: Turkish walnut
Barrel: 28 in.
Chokes: screw-in tubes
Weight: 8.0lbs.
Bore/Gauge 20
Magazine: none
Features: top barrel in .223, .243, .270, .308, .30-06; single selective tirgger, automatic ejectors; also 28 over .410
Express Combo . . . . price on request

LX 801

Action: autoloader
Stock: walnut
Barrel: 28 or 30 in.
Chokes: screw-in tubes
Weight: 6.8lbs.
Bore/Gauge 12
Magazine: 3
Features: gas-operated, alloy receiver, sporting and competition models available; also model SX405: synthetic or camo, 22 in. slug or 26 in. field
Verona LX 801. . . . . price on request
Verona SX 405. . . . . price on request

LX 980 Competition

Action: over/under
Stock: Turkish walnut
Barrel: 30 in. 932 on Trap Model)
Chokes: screw-in tubes
Weight: 7.5lbs.
Bore/Gauge 12
Magazine: none
Features: boxlock; removable competition trigger, ported barrels, deluxe case; also multiple-barrel sets
Verona LX 980. . . . . price on request

NEW Products: **Weatherby Shotguns**

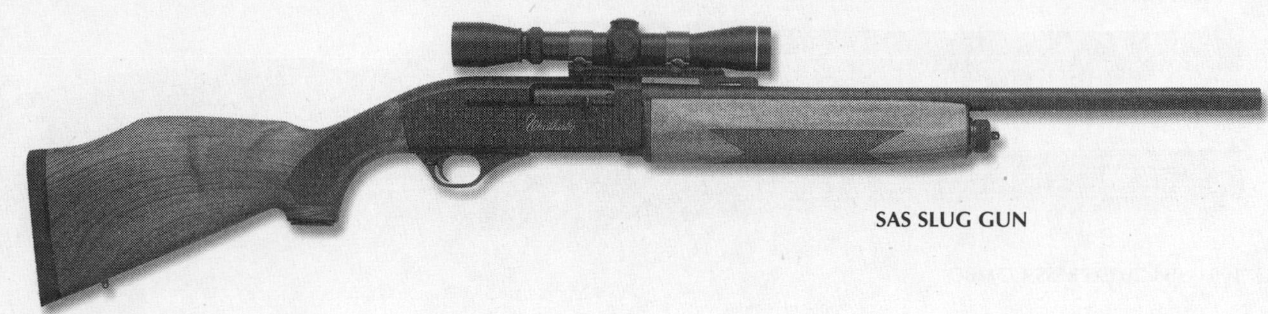

SAS SLUG GUN

SAS Slug Gun

Action: autoloader
Stock: walnut
Barrel: 22 in. rifled
Chokes: none
Weight: 7.3lbs.
Bore/Gauge: 12
Magazine: 4
Features: self-compensating gas system; cantilever scope base included; "smart" follower, magazine cutoff, stock has shims to alter drop, pitch, cast-off
SAS Slug Gun. $749

NEW Products: **Winchester Shotguns**

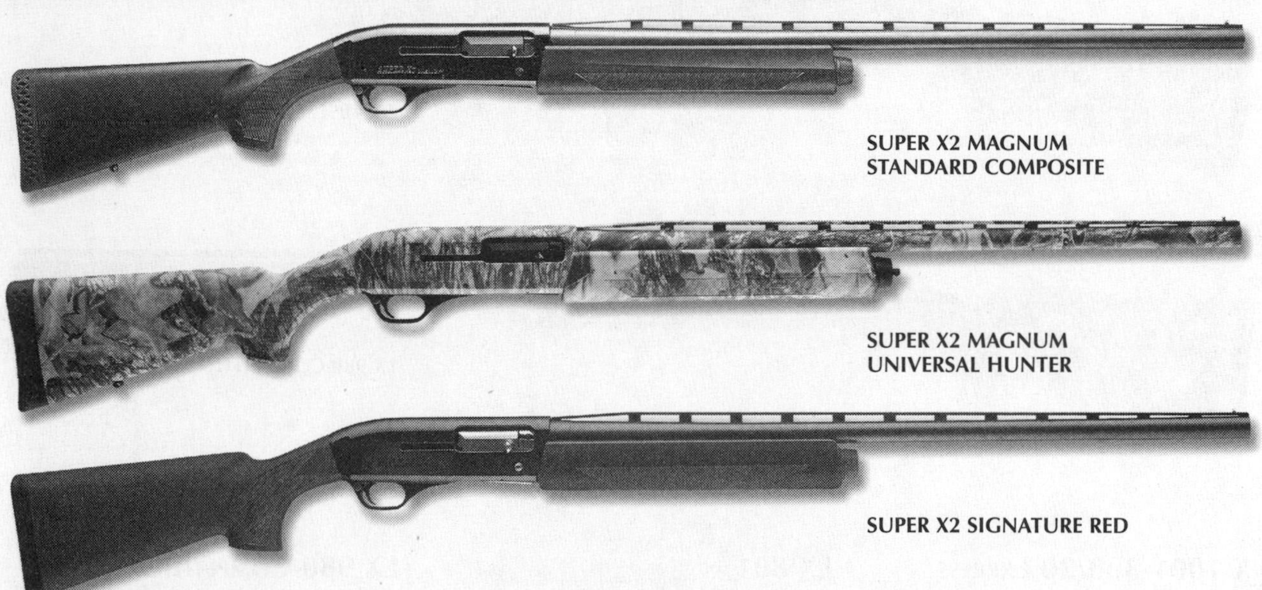

SUPER X2 MAGNUM STANDARD COMPOSITE

SUPER X2 MAGNUM UNIVERSAL HUNTER

SUPER X2 SIGNATURE RED

Super X2 3½-inch Magnums

Action: autoloader
Stock: synthetic
Barrel: 24, 28 or 30 in.
Chokes: screw-in tubes
Weight: 7.8lbs.
Bore/Gauge: 12
Magazine: 3
Features: weight to 8.0 lbs. depending on barrel length; Universal Hunter, Greenhead, Turkey and other versions available, all with "Dura-Touch" finish, some with Tru-Glo sights
standard. $969
Greenhead $976
Waterfowl and Universal Hunter $1116
Turkey $1130

Super X2 Signature Red

Action: autoloader
Stock: hardwood, "Dura-Touch" finish
Barrel: 30 in.
Chokes: screw-in tubes
Weight: 8.0lbs.
Bore/Gauge: 12
Magazine: 4
Features: shims adjust buttstock; back-bored barrel; "Dura-Touch" armor coating now available on many other Winchesters
Signature Red. $957

NEW Products: **Comanche Handguns**

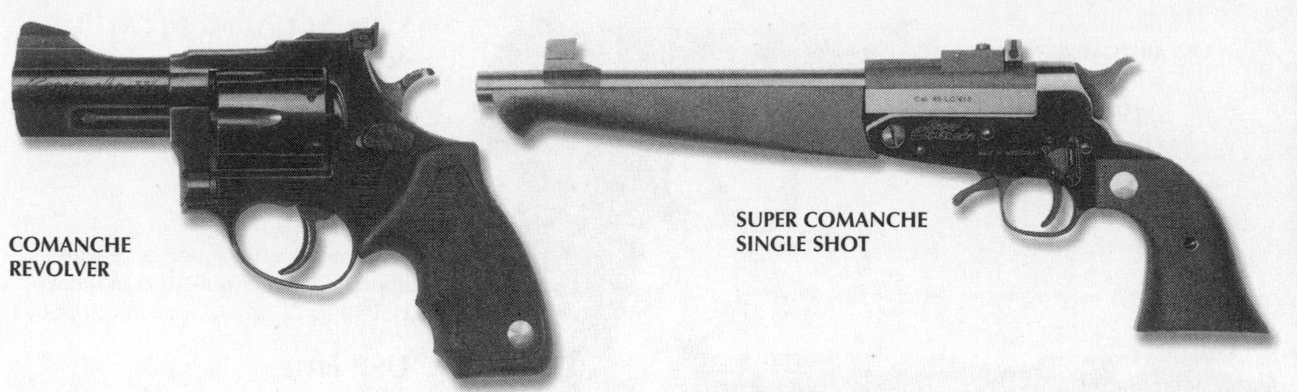

COMANCHE REVOLVER

SUPER COMANCHE SINGLE SHOT

Comanche Revolver

Action: double-action revolver
Grips: rubber
Barrel: 3 or 6 in.
Sights: target
Weight: 22.0oz.
Caliber: .38 Spl. (also in.357)
Capacity: 6
Features: stainless or blue
blue. $220
stainless $237
.357 blue $254
.357 stainless $275

Super Comanche Single Shot

Action: hinged breech
Grips: composite
Barrel: 10 in.
Sights: target
Weight: 48.0oz.
Caliber: .45 LC/.410
Capacity: 1
Features: satin nickel finish (also in blue)
nickel. $192
blue. $175

NEW Products: **Glock Handguns**

G-36 Slimline

Action: autoloader
Grips: synthetic
Barrel: 3.8 in.
Sights: fixed open
Weight: 21.0oz.
Caliber: .45 ACP
Capacity: 6 + 1
Features: single-stack magazine for thinner grip
G36 . . . . price on request

G-37 Slimline

Action: autoloader
Grips: synthetic
Barrel: 24-30 in.
Sights:fixed open
Weight:
Caliber: .45 Glock
Capacity: 10 + 1
Features: chambered for .45 Glock shortened 45 ACP cartridge
G-37: . . . . price on request

G36 SLIMLINE

G37 SLIMLINE

NEW Products: **Heckler & Koch**

USP 40 COMPACT LEM

USP ELITE

USP 40 Compact LEM

Action: autoloader
Grips: composite
Barrel: 3.6 in.
Sights: fixed open
Weight: 24.0oz.
Caliber: .40 S&W
Capacity: 10
Features: double-action only with improved trigger pull; also in 9mm
USP40 . . . . $821

USP Elite

Action: autoloader
Grips: composite
Barrel: 6.2 in.
Sights: target
Weight: 36.0oz.
Caliber: 9mm, .45 ACP
Capacity: 10
Features: short recoil action, fiber-reinforced polymer frame; universal scope mounting groves, ambidextrous magazine release
USP Elite $1533

NEW Products: **Heritage**

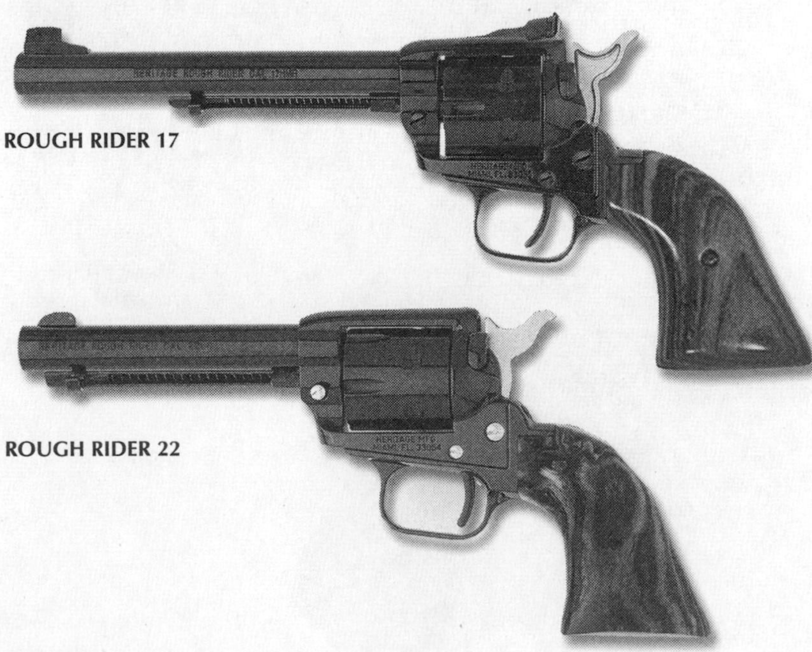
ROUGH RIDER 17

ROUGH RIDER 22

Rough Rider

Action: single-action revolver
Grips: laminated
Barrel: 4.8 or 6.0 in.
Sights: fixed open
Weight: 38.0oz.
Caliber: .22 LR, .22 WMR, .17 HMR
Capacity: 6
Features: adjustable sights available, also case-colored frame
Rough Rider. $185
with adjustable sights $240

NEW Products: **Navy Arms**

Gunfighter Series
Action: single-action revolver
Grips: walnut
Barrel: 4.8, 5.5, 7.5 in.
Sights: fixed open
Weight: 47.0oz.
Caliber: .357, .44-40, .45 Colt
Capacity: 6
Features: case-colored frames, after 1873 Colt design
Gunfighter $415
stainless $510

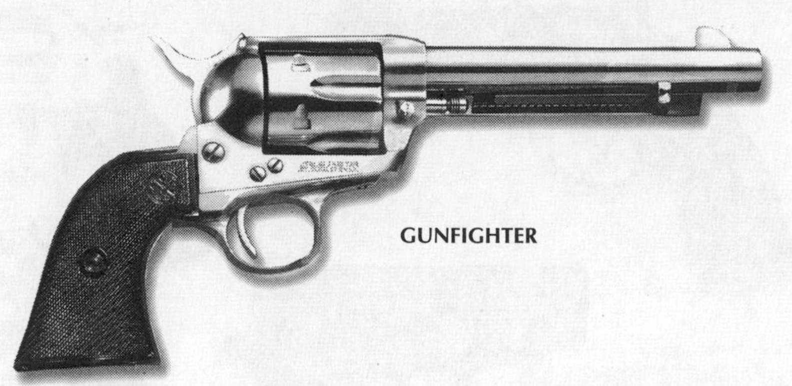

GUNFIGHTER

NEW Products: **North American Arms Handguns**

Guardian.380
Action: autoloader
Grips: composite
Barrel: 2.5 in.
Sights: fixed open
Weight: 18.8oz.
Caliber: .380
Capacity: 6
Features: manufactured with Kahr Arms
Guardian $449

GUARDIAN.380

NEW Products: **Para Ordnance**

Tac-Four
Action: autoloader
Grips: rubber
Barrel: 4.3 in.
Sights: low-profile combat
Weight: 36.0oz.
Caliber: .45 ACP
Capacity: 13
Features: 1911-style stainless-steel
Tac-Four $939

TAC-FOUR

NEW Products: **Smith & Wesson Handguns**

NEW PRODUCTS

Model 329 PD

Action: double-action revolver
Grips: wood
Barrel: 4 in.
Sights: adjustable fiber optic
Weight: 27.0oz.
Caliber: .44 Mag.
Capacity: 6
Features: scandium frame, titanium cylinder
329 PD $900

Model 4040 PD

Action: double-action revolver
Grips: Hogue rubber
Barrel: 3.5 in.
Sights: 3-dot
Weight: 25.6oz.
Caliber: .40 S&W
Capacity: 7 + 1
Features: first scandium-frame pistol
4040 PD $788

Model 500

Action: double-action revolver
Grips: Hogue Sorbathane
Barrel: ported 8.4 in.
Sights: target
Weight: 72.5oz.
Caliber: .500 S&W
Capacity: 5
Features: X-Frame, double-action stainless revolver
Model 500 . . . . $990

Model 647

Action: double-action revolver
Grips: rubber
Barrel: 8.4 in.
Sights: target
Weight: 52.5oz.
Caliber: .17 HMR
Capacity: 6
Features: stainless, full-lug, K-frame
Model 647 . . . . $677

Model 658

Action: double-action revolver
Grips: rubber
Barrel: 6 in.
Sights: target
Weight: 45.0oz.
Caliber: .22 WMR
Capacity: 6
Features: stainless, full-lug, K-frame
Model 648 . . . . $659

SW1911

Action: autoloader
Grips: rubber
Barrel: 5 in.
Sights: low-profile combat
Weight: 39.0oz.
Caliber: .45 ACP
Capacity: 8 + 1
Features: stainless, extended beavertail, match trigger; single action
SW 1911 . . . . $932

SW99

Action: autoloader
Grips: polymer
Barrel: 4.3 in.
Sights: low-profile combat
Weight: 25.6oz.
Caliber: .45 ACP
Capacity: 9 + 1
Features: double action pistol made in collaboration with Walther; also new: 23-ounce compact version in 9mm and .40 S&W, 3.5 in. barrel
Model 99 . . . . $688

NEW Products: **Springfield Armory Handguns**

Model XD 9801

Action: autoloader
Grips: composite
Barrel: 3 in.
Sights: fixed open
Weight: 20.5oz.
Caliber: 9mm
Capacity: 10
Features: lightweight polymer frame, stainless magazines
XD 9801 . . . . $489
with Tritium sights $549

MODEL XD 9801

NEW Products: **Taurus Handguns**

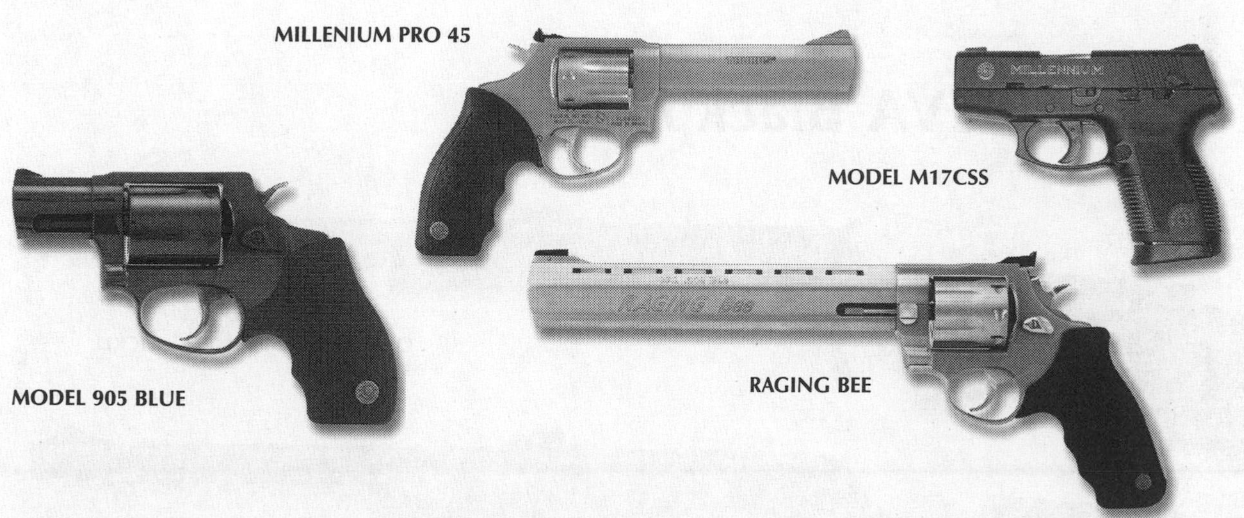

MILLENIUM PRO 45

MODEL M17CSS

MODEL 905 BLUE

RAGING BEE

Model 905, 405 and 455

Action: double-action revolver
Grips: rubber
Barrel: 2 in.
Sights: fixed open
Weight: 21.0oz.
Caliber: 9mm, .40 S&W, .45 ACP 9with 2, 4 or 6.5 inch barrel)
Capacity: 5
Features: stellar clips furnished; UltraLite weighs 17 oz.
blue $383
stainless $430
UltraLite, blue $414
UltraLite, stainless $461
.45 ACP $523

Model M17CSS

Action: double-action revolver
Grips: composite
Barrel: 2, 4, 5, 6.5 or 12 in.
Sights: target
Weight: 18.5oz.
Caliber: .17 HMR
Capacity: 7 or 8
Features: 10 models available in blued and stainless steel; weight varies with barrel length to 49.8 oz.
blue, 2, 4 or 5 in. barrel $359
most stainless models $391
12 in. barrel. $430

Millenium Pro

Action: autoloader
Grips: composite, wood, mother of pearl
Barrel: 3.5 in.
Sights: low-profile combat
Weight: 18.7oz.
Caliber: .40 S&W, .45 ACP
Capacity: 10 + 1
Features: double action, polymer frame; also comes with night sights (add $78); .45 ACP weighs 23 oz.
.40 blue/composite. $461
.40 stainless/composite. $477
.45 blue/composite. $484
.45 stainless/composite. $500

Raging Series

Action: double-action revolver
Grips: rubber
Barrel: 10 in.
Sights: target
Weight: 50.0oz.
Caliber: .22 Hornet, .218 Bee, .30 Carbine
Capacity: 8
Features: stainless, .30 comes with stellar clips
Raging Series $898

NEW PRODUCTS

NEW Products: **Thompson/Center Handguns**

CONTENDER G2 PISTOL

Contender G2 Pistol

Action: hinged breech
Grips: walnut
Barrel: 12 or 14 in.
Sights: target
Weight: 56.0oz.
Caliber: many popular rimfire and centerfire calibers, from .17 HMR to .45-70
Capacity: 1
Features: can recock the G2 without opening; rifle in .17 HMR, .22 LR, .223, .30-30, .45/70

G2, 12 in. $555
14 in.. . . . . $561
rifle with buttsotck, 23 in. barrel . . . $600
209x.45 muzzleloading rifle . . . $636

NEW Products: **CVA Blackpowder**

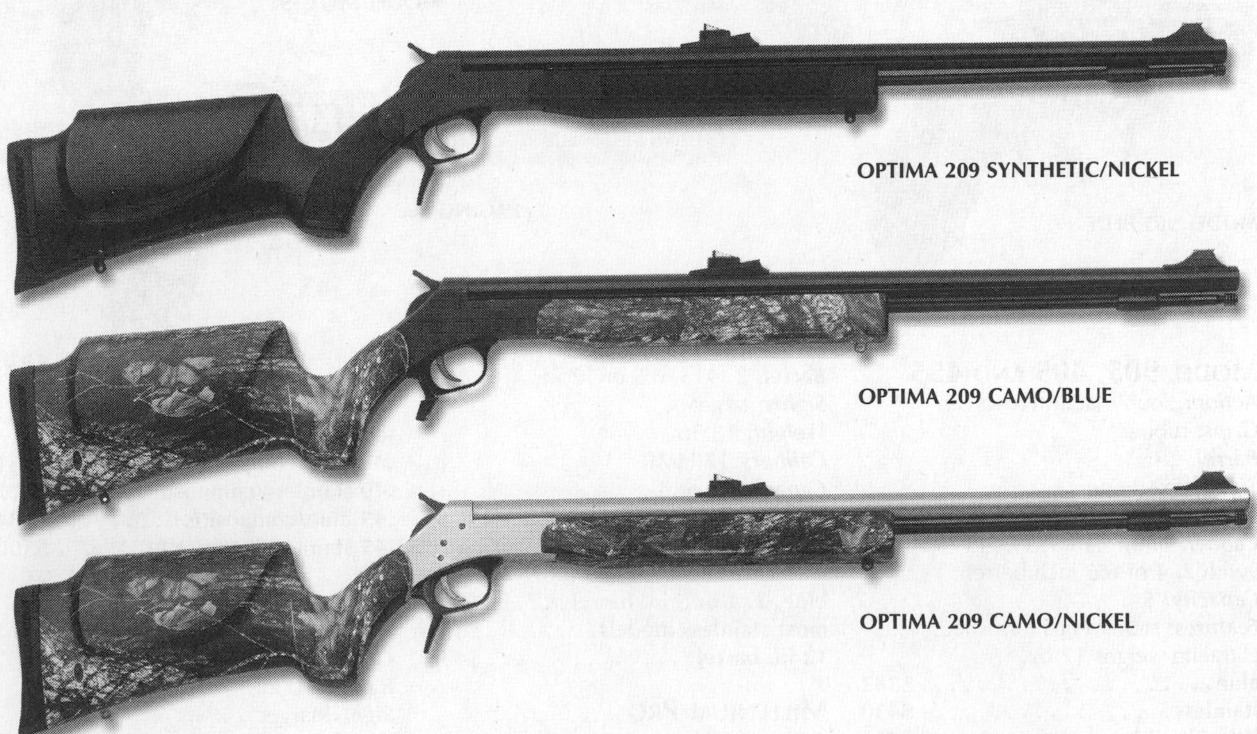

OPTIMA 209 SYNTHETIC/NICKEL

OPTIMA 209 CAMO/BLUE

OPTIMA 209 CAMO/NICKEL

Optima and Optima Pro

Lock: traditional caplock
Stock: synthetic or camo
Barrel: 26 in. (29 in. on Pro), 1:28 twist
Sights: adjustable fiber optic
Weight: 8.2lbs.
Caliber/Bore: .45 or .50
Features: stainless steel 209 breech plug, ambidextrous stock; add $65 for Pro (8.8 lbs.)

Optima, synthetic/blue. $200
synthetic/nickel $215
camo/blue $234
camo/nicket. $250

NEW Products: **Traditions Blackpowder**

EVOLUTION SYNTHETIC

EVOLUTION WALNUT

Evolution Premier Series

Lock: in-line
Stock: hardwood, synthetic, camo or laminated
Barrel: 26 in., 1:28 twist, internally ported
Sights: fiber optic
Weight: 7.0lbs.
Caliber/Bore: .50
Features: stainless steel 209 priming; "LD" Long Distance Models have Tru-Glo instead of Williams sights, cost less; standard models have 24 in. barrels, laminated version weighs 7.8 lbs.

synthetic **$269**
hardwood **$329**
camo **$359**
laminated. **$439**

NEW Products: **White Rifles Blackpowder**

Hunter Series

Lock: in-line
Stock: synthetic or laminated
Barrel: stainless, 22 in. (24 in. Elite)
Sights: fiber-optic
Weight: 7.7lbs.
Caliber/Bore: .45 or .50
Features: Elite weighs 8.6 lbs., aluminum ramrod with bullet extractor, also: Thunderbolt bolt action with 209 ignition, 26 in. barrel

Whitetail **$450**
Blacktail and Elite. **$600**
Thunderbolt **$700**

NEW Products: **Winchester Blackpowder**

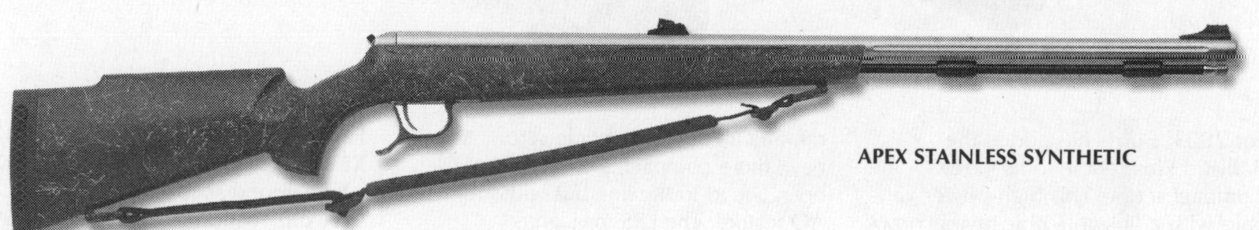

APEX STAINLESS SYNTHETIC

Apex Muzzleloader

Lock: in-line
Stock: synthetic or camo
Barrel: 30 in., 1:28 twist
Sights: fiber optic
Weight: 8.4lbs.
Caliber/Bore: .45 or .50
Features: "swing-action" breech

blue synthetic **$345**
blue camo **$390**
stainless synthetic. **$420**
stainless camo **$470**

NEW Products: **BSA Optics**

HUNTSMAN 3-9X40

For 2003, BSA has announced a new line of modestly priced riflescopes. The Huntsman series includes three 3-9x and a 6-18x AO, plus fixed-power and low-power variable models. A 3-12x and 4-16x have 50mm objectives. All tubes are 1-inch alloy, of one-piece construction. They feature finger-adjustable windage and elevation dials and generous eye relief. Multi-coated lenses are standard. Huntsman scopes are warranted waterproof, fog proof and shockproof. Among other new BSA offerings: 4x32 and 3-9x32 scopes designed expressly for .22 rim fire rifles. Parallax-corrected at 50 yards, they feature quarter-minute adjustments and 1-inch alloy tubes sealed against fogging. To complement these sights, BSA has come up with "Sweet 17" scopes designed for the new .17 HMR rifles. Both the 4x32 and 2-7x32 have adjustable objectives and feature a range-compensating elevation dial "calibrated to match the ballistic trajectory of the .17 HMR cartridge." A plex reticle, one-piece alloy tube and limited lifetime warranty complete the package.

Huntsman series scopes: $90 to $172
.22 rim fire riflescopes: . $40 and $90
"Sweet 17" rifle scopes:

NEW Products: **Burris Optics**

4X12X COMPACT

1X4X COMPACT

6X24X BD

For 2003, Burris has added the Ballistic Plex reticle to its 4-12x Compact scope. This high-power variable with adjustable objective is properly configured for big game rifles. The firm has also brought out a pair of shotgun/muzzleloader scopes: a 2.5x Full field II and a 1-4x XER. Also from Burris is a trio of new Black Diamond scopes. The 4-16x, 6-24x and 8-32x all wear 50mm objectives and side-mounted parallax adjustments. These scopes have resettable dials on the turret, and a Posi-Lock reticle screw. A new, more compact, 2.5-10x44 has been added to the line but without the AO feature. The LRS, or Lighted Reticle Scopes, now offer Ballistic Plex range-finding capability. Burris offers lighted Ballistic Plex reticles in its 3-9x40 and 3.5-10x50 Full field II scopes. There's also a lighted Fast Plex in the 1.75-5x Signature Safari scope.

MSR: Compact 4-12x
w/Ballistic Plex reticle $552
Shotgun/muzzleloader scopes:
Full field II 2.5x $307
XER 1-4x $397
Black Diamond scopes:
4-16x50 . . . . $969
6-24x50 . . . . $1076
8-32x50 . . . . $1126
2.5-10x44. . . . . $892
Full field II w/ lighted
Ballistic Plex reticles:
3-9x40 . . . . $558
3.5-10x50 . . . . $672
Signature Safari 1.75-5x
w/ lighted Fast Plex reticle . . $769

NEW Products: **Bushnell Optics**

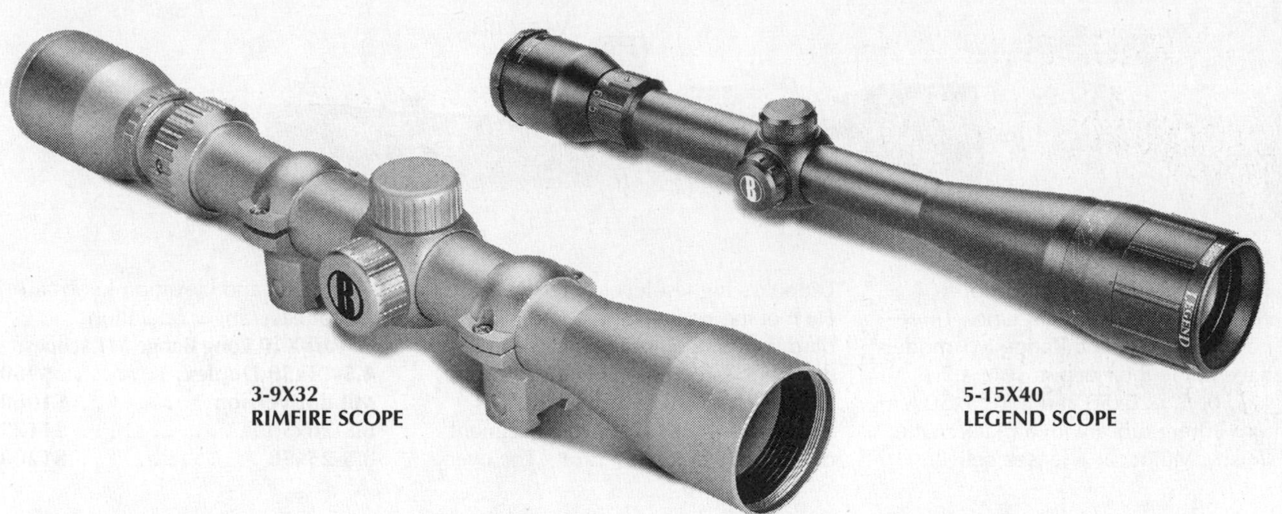

3-9X32 RIMFIRE SCOPE

5-15X40 LEGEND SCOPE

The Bushnell line has several changes this year. Most intriguing is the new Firefly reticle now available in Elite 3200 scopes, from 1.5-4.5x32 to 3-9x50. Firefly requires no batteries. You "energize" it by shining a flash-light beam into the scope for a minute. The reticle glows green for a short time, then fades to black. As shooting light diminishes, even hours later, the green glow returns, enabling you to see the reticle more clearly. Also from Bushnell is the new Legend mid-priced series, with 3-9x40, 3-9x50 and 5-15x40 models. They weigh 15, 16 and 14.4 ounces and have wide ranges of adjustment (80 inches at 100 yards for the 3-9s and 50 inches for the 5-15. Bushnell is bringing a bullet drop compensator to its popular Banner 3-9x40. For rim fire shooters, the Bushnell line has expanded to include a 4x32 and 3-9x32 designed just for rim fire rifles. They feature 1-inch tubes (silver or matte black) and plex reticles.

NEW Products: **Kaps Optics**

A 50-year-old German company headquartered in Asslar/Wetzlar, Kap has manufactured optics for military and police units, and for hunters. It now brings its riflescope line Stateside, with 4x36, 6x42 and 8x56 fixed-power models and five variables: 1-4x22, 1.5-6x42, 1-8x42, 2.5-10x50, 2.5-10x56. Pick illuminated reticles in 8x56, 2.5-10x50 and 2.5-10x56. The 30mm alloy tubes wear a satin finish. High-quality glass and state-of-the-art coatings complement reticles in the first focal plane – traditional in European scopes.

KAPS SCOPES

NEW Products: Leupold Optics

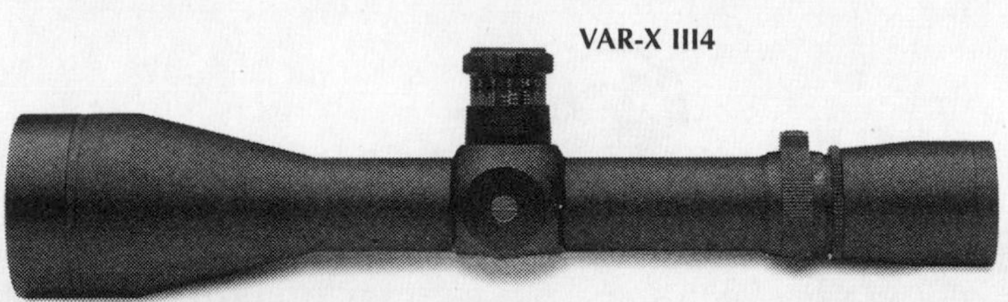
VAR-X III4

This year the big news in scopes comes from the Tactical Line. Three new Vari-X III Long Range M1 models have made their debut. The 4.5-14x50, 6.5-20x50 and 8.5-25x50 feature 30mm tubes with a black matte finish. Multicoat 4 lenses deliver Leupold's highest level of resolution. Each of the new scopes comes standard with range-finding mil dot reticle, though the 4.5-14x50 is also available with a Duplex. These are all "AO" scopes, with the objective adjustment on the left side of the turret. The oversize windage and elevation knobs are made for easy finger operation.

MSR: Vari-X III Long Range M1 scopes:

4.5-14x50 Duplex........ $960
Mil dot version $1060
6.5-20x50 .... $1125
8.5-25x50 .... $1200

NEW Products: Nikon Optics

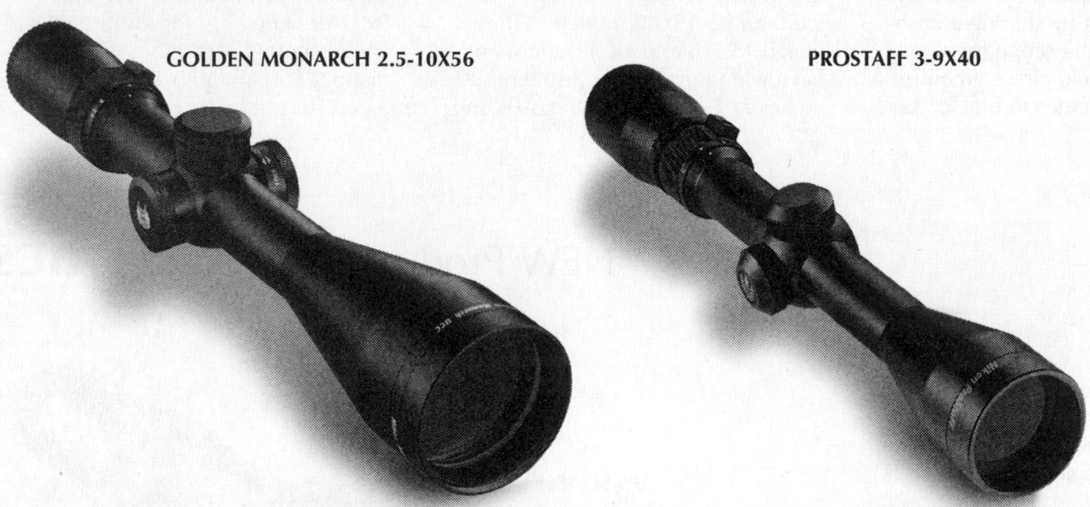
GOLDEN MONARCH 2.5-10X56

PROSTAFF 3-9X40

Nikon's news for 2003 includes the Prostaff line — 4x32, 2-7x32 and 3-9x40 scopes. The 4x is parallax-corrected at 50 yards. It measures 11.2 inches long and weighs just 11.6 ounces. Order it in silver, matte black or Realtree camo finish. The 2-7x, parallax-free at 75 yards, is a 12-ounce scope available in matte black or camo. You can get the 13-ounce 3-9x in all three finishes. It has been zeroed-out for parallax at 100 yards. The Prostaff scopes have multicoated lenses and quarter-minute adjustments. They're waterproof, fog proof and carry Nikon's Full Lifetime Warranty. Also from Nikon this year: the company's first 30mm scopes. The Golden Monarch line includes a 1.5-6x42, a 2.5-10x50 and a 2.5-10x56. All feature quick-focus European eyepieces and low-profile quarter-minute click adjustments. Choose from a standard Nikoplex reticle, or the German #4.

MSR: Prostaff scopes:

4x32 .... $100
2-7x32 .... $130
3-9x40 .... $150

Golden Monarch 30mm scopes:

1.5-6x42............... $500
2.5-10x50.............. $600
2.5-10x56.............. $700

NEW Products: **Pentax Optics**

Pentax has introduced a new 3-9x40 rifle scope for 2003. The Pioneer offers fully coated optics in a one-piece, 1-inch alloy tube. It comes in matte black finish with a Penta-Plex reticle. Weighing just 13 ounces, the scope offers 50 inches of elevation adjustment in quarter-minute graduations.

MSR: $310

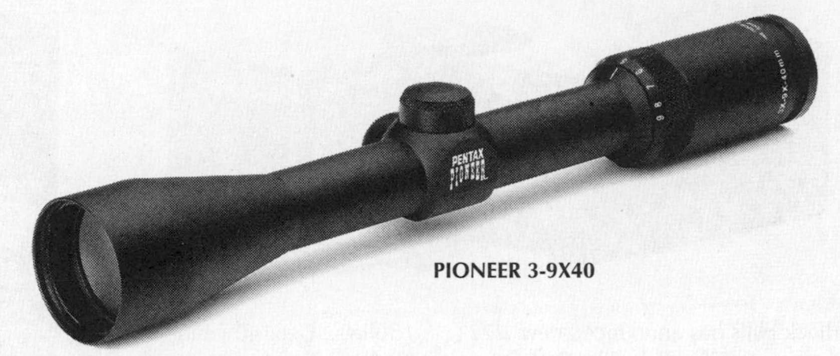

PIONEER 3-9X40

NEW Products: **Schmidt & Bender Optics**

Schmidt & Bender has announced two new premium-quality 30mm scopes for 2003. The Zenith 2.5-10x56 and 3.5-12x50 are relatively short, at 13 and 13.4 inches, and come with #7, 8 and 9 reticles. A unique feature in the Zenith is the "Posicon" reticle position indicator that shows you how much windage or elevation adjustment you have to work with.

MSR: $1490
with illuminated reticle. . . . $1795

ZENITH

NEW Products: **Sightron Optics**

SI 3.510X50

Three new SI scopes have popped up in the Sightron line: 3-9x40, 3-9x50 and 3.5-10x50. The 3-9x40MD features a mil dot range-finding reticle. All have multi-coated optics and come with Sightron's Lifetime Replacement Warranty. The company has also announced its first scopes with illuminated reticles. The SII 3-9x42IR and 4.5-14x42IRMD have a three-position brightness switch. Battery life ranges from 100 to 400 hours, depending on intensity. The 3-9x features a plex reticle with a lighted center. The 4.5-14x has a mil dot reticle.

MSR: Sightron scopes
3-9x40 . . . . $233
3-9x50 . . . . $235
3.5-10x50 . . . . $260
SII 3-9x42IR $504
4.5-14x42IRMD $689

NEW Products: **Black Hills Ammunition**

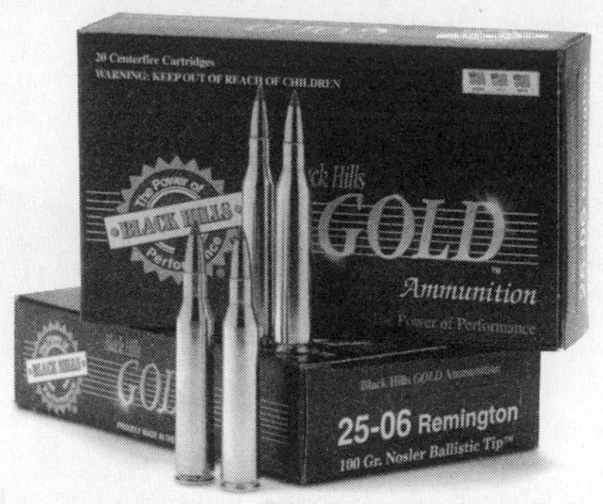

Black Hills has announced new .223 ammunition loaded with 60-grain Nosler Partition bullets, for hunters who use the little 5.56 for deer-size game. Velocity is 3150 fps from a 24-inch barrel. You'll also find new additions to the Black Hills Gold big game series. The .25-06 comes with 100-grain Nosler Ballistic Tips and 115-grain Barnes X-Bullets. Get 140-grain Ballistic Tips and X-Bullets in 7mm Remington Magnum cartridges. Another new offering at Black Hills augments the Cowboy line, which includes modern and traditional rounds from the .32 H&R to the .45-70. The latest entry is a .38-55 with 255-grain lead bullets at 1250 fps.

NEW Products: **Federal Ammunition**

For 2004 Federal offers Speed-Shok steel ammo in 12 and 20 gauge, with shot sizes from #7 to BB and Ultra-Shok shells with zinc-plated pellets, in 10, 12, 16 and 20 gauges, shot sizes #6 to T. Consistent with its enduring partnership with Speer/CCI, Federal has announced a new line: Power-Shok. These cartridges, from .243 to .300 Winchester Magnum, feature Speer Grand Slam bullets.

NEW Products: **Fiocchi Ammunition**

As it courts bird hunters in North America, Fiocchi expands its high-octane lines. This Italian company has turkey loads that include a $2\frac{3}{8}$-ounce charge in $3\frac{1}{2}$-inch 12-gauge shells. Velocity: 1210 fps. There's a $1\frac{1}{2}$-ounce 3-inch load, and a $1\frac{1}{2}$-ounce $2\frac{1}{2}$-inch. Same speed. These shells feature nickel-plated shot and magnum primers. For 2003, Fiocchi also offers #7 steel shot at 1200 fps for clay target events where lead shot is not welcome. A low-recoil slug for practice and law enforcement work is available; and the Golden Pheasant line of field loads now includes 3-inch shells in both 12 and 20 gauge. Choose from #4, 5 or 6 shot, nickel-plated with a relatively soft core.

NEW Products: **Hornady Ammunition**

New loads from Hornady this year include a 265-grain .444 Marlin that clocks 2335 fps at the muzzle, and the first .458 Lott ammo to be factory loaded. The 500-grain softpoints leave at 2300 fps and generate nearly 5900 foot-pounds of energy at the muzzle. Hornady also offers a 500-grain solid bullet with the same punch.

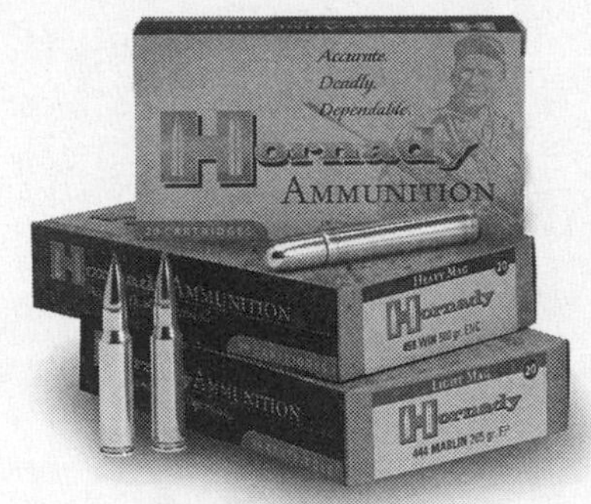

NEW Products: **Magtech Ammunition**

Guardian Gold law enforcement ammunition tops the list of new offerings at Magtech. Guardian Gold features jacketed hollow point bullets in .38 Spl., .380 Auto, 9mm, .357 Magnum, .40 S&W and .45 Auto. Also from Magtech this year: CleanRange target loads with fully encapsulated bullets to reduce or eliminate free lead residue on indoor ranges.

NEW Products: **Winchester Ammunition**

Winchester's new pair of Super Short Magnums — the .223 and .243 — are based on the Short Magnum series but are considerably shorter – so short, in fact, that new rifle actions (Winchester M70 and Browning A-Bolt) were developed to accommodate them. The .223 is loaded with three bullets: the 55-grain Ballistic Silvertip, the 55-grain Pointed Soft Point and 64-grain Power-Point. Winchester handgun ammunition now includes the new Platinum Tip bullet with a notched, reverse-taper jacket with a two-step nose cavity. Supreme Platinum Tip hunting ammo is available in .41 Magnum, .44 Magnum and .454 Casull. In shotshells, Winchester announces Xpert High-Velocity steel loads, with #4, 3, 2 and BB shot. They're available in all 12-gauge shell lengths, clocking 1550 fps.

NEW PRODUCTS

NEW Products: **Alliant Powder Handloading**

Alliant's Reloder family of sporting rifle powders has a new member. RL-10 was developed for the .223 and .22-250, the 6mm and other small-bore rounds with relatively small cases. It's being marketed to benchrest and varmint shooters. In other Alliant news, there's 410 powder, aptly named for the shotshell that will most benefit. It's the only flake powder, says Alliant, formulated for the .410.

NEW Products: **Barnes Handloading**

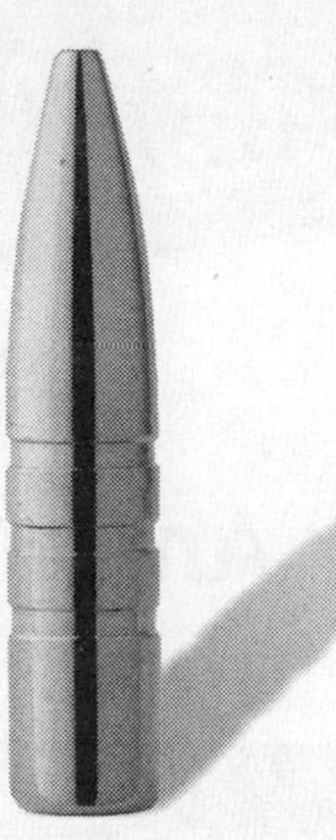

The new Barnes Triple-Shock X-Bullet is a copper bullet with a hollow nose. Three circumferential grooves on the shank reduce bearing surface. Four-petal expansion ensures a wide wound channel but penetration the company says is 28 percent deeper than that of jacketed soft points. The new Barnes Triple-Shock bullets come in 6mm, .257, .270, 7mm and .308 diameters, from 95 to 180 grains.

NEW Products: **Cor-Bon Handloading**

You might have heard the name in connection with the firm's own .400 Cor-Bon cartridge. Specializing in high-performance handgun ammo, Cor-Bon collaborated with Smith & Wesson last year to develop a super-potent revolver round for a giant new S&W revolver. The .500 S&W is now loaded exclusively by Cor-Bon. From the S&W X-Frame revolver, it easily outperforms the .454 Casull. A 275-grain Barnes X-Bullet clocks 1665 fps – about the same speed as a 400-grain Hawk Softpoint, which turns up 2500 foot-pounds of energy. The 440 lead bullet from Cast Performance leaves at 1625 fps, to generate 2580 foot-pounds. The newest in Cor-Bon's line is ammunition loaded with Pow'Rball, a controlled expansion bullet with a polymer ball in the nose. It's designed to penetrate glass and light sheet metal but expand readily in flesh.

NEW Products: **Hodgdon Handloading**

Hodgdon Powder Company now offers its popular sulfur-free Triple Seven powder in 50-grain pellets. Formulated for use with 209 shotshell primers, Triple Seven leaves no rotten egg smell, and the residue is easy to clean from the bore with water only. The new pellets are sized for 50-caliber muzzleloaders and can be used singly (for target shooting or small game) as well as two at a time (for a 100-grain big game charge).

NEW Products: **Hornady Handloading**

The Hornady SST bullet is now available for black powder shooters. The 200-grain .40 and 250- and 300-grain .45 bullets are meant for use in sabot sleeves. They feature a jacketed lead core with the signature red polymer tip. The SST has lead also to Hornady's newest big game bullet, the Interbond. Essentially, it's an SST with a thicker jacket that has an inner "expansion control ring" near the front of the shank. Jacket and core are also bonded to ensure deep penetration and high weight retention. Though it typically opens to double its initial diameter, the Interbond bullet can be expected to hold 90 percent of its weight in the animal.

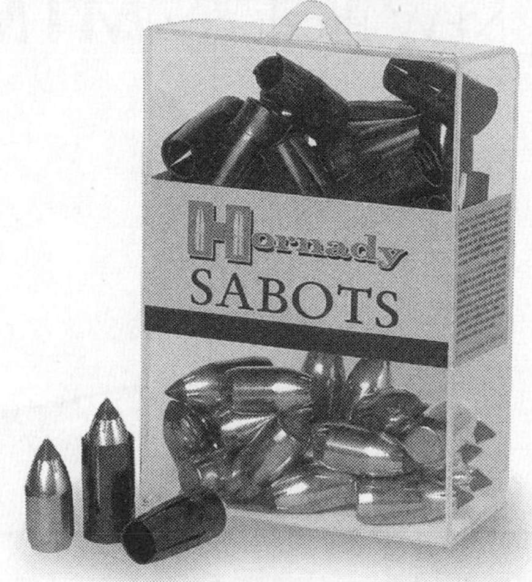

NEW Products: **Lapua Handloading**

Lapua, offers the Naturalis, a solid-copper expanding bullet, with a hollow, polymer-capped nose. It comes loaded in these forms: 130-grain 6.5x55, 180-grain .308 Winchester, 180-grain .30-06 and 270-grain 9.3x62. Lapua Aficionado center fire target loads are available in .223 and .308, feature 69-grain and 167-grain match bullets. A line of .22 rim fire rounds carries the Lapua Signum bullet, whose tiny lube grooves on the front of a driving band minimize gumming in bore and chamber. The bullet's design reduces pressure by 15 percent, say the people who've tested them. Lapua offers 13 kinds of .22 ammo, including specialty rounds for pistol and biathlon competition.

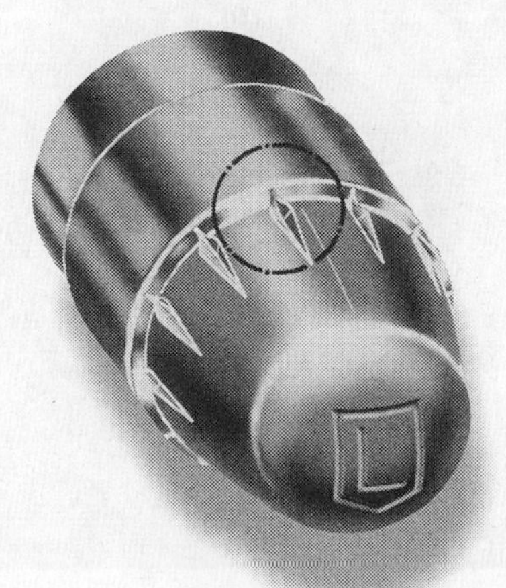

NEW Products: **Lyman Handloading**

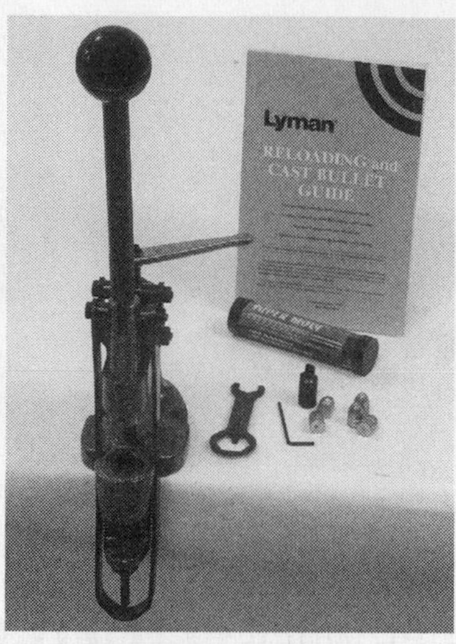

The 1200 DPS (Digital Powder System) from Lyman dispenses powder quickly, with .1-grain precision. Another new Lyman product is the 4500 Lube Sizer, with a one-piece base casting and a built-in heating element (choose 110- or 220-volt). The long ball-knob handle offers the leverage for sizing and lubricating big bullets. It comes with a gas check seater. Prep your cases with a new Lyman 2500 Pro Magnum tumbler. The bin handles up to 900 .38 Special cartridges at once.

MSR: 1200 DPS $333
4500 Lube Sizer $167
2500 Pro Magnum tumbler. . . . $100
with Auto Flow feature $133

NEW Products: **MTM Handloading**

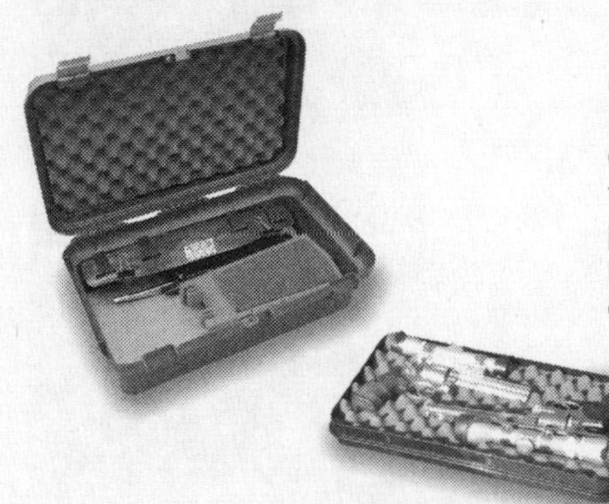

MTM, known for molded plastic handloading trays and ammo boxes, now offers a kit for the hand gunner to take to the range. A hard-sided, foam-padded utility case holds pistols or revolvers in a top tray, a "jammit" compact target stand and a 20-position pistol rest in the well below. There's also an all-weather target backer. The Handgunner Range Combo will accommodate long-barreled magnums.

MSR: $54

NEW Products: **Nosler Handloading**

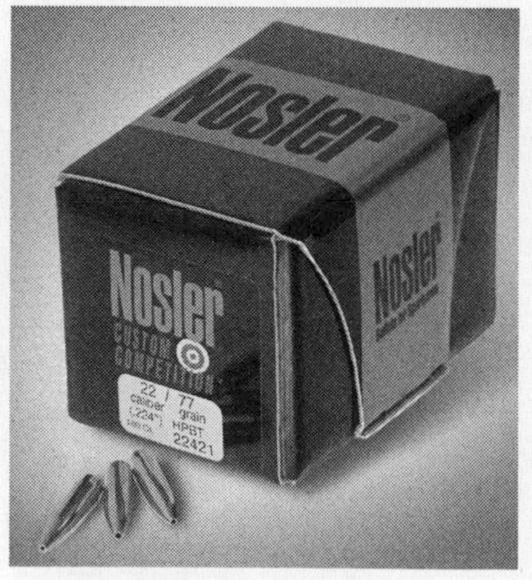

Nosler offers the new AccuBond, a bonded-core bullet without a partition. The polymer tip gives AccuBond the sleek profile of Nosler's Ballistic Tip bullets and in many ways resembles the Swift® Scirocco. Order AccuBond component bullets in these configurations: 140-grain .270, 160-grain 7mm, 200-grain .308, 225-grain .338, 260-grain .375. Nosler is also offering a new 150-grain .270 Ballistic Tip, and a 140-grain .270 Partition. The firm's Custom Competition line now has a 77-grain .22 boat-tail hollow point with a ballistic coefficient of .340 made for fast-twist (1-in-8) barrels in .223 match rifles.

RIFLES

Anschutz Rifles

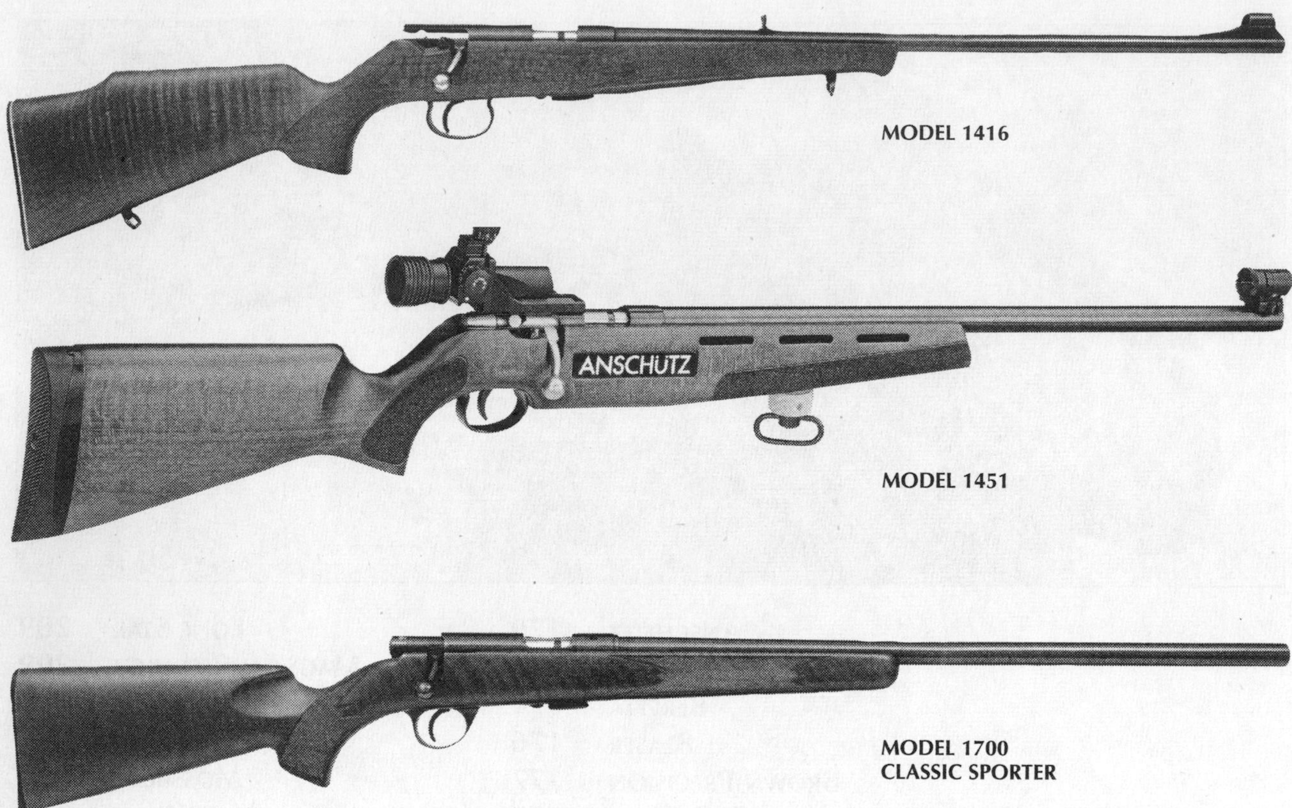

MODEL 1416

MODEL 1451

MODEL 1700
CLASSIC SPORTER

J.G. ANSCHUTZ began as a company in 1856, making pistols, rifles and shotguns. Since its rebirth following World War II, the firm has been best known for its fine rim-fire target rifles. There is also a line of bolt-action target pistols that have put Anschutz in the winner's circle more often than any other rim-fires in recent times.

Julius Gottfried Anschutz, son of a German gunsmith, founded J.G. Anschutz to build pocket pistols, shotguns and rifles. In 1896 the firm moved out of its small workshop into a factory and by 1911 there were 200 people working at the Anschutz plant. Growth came to an abrupt halt in 1945, when the factory was shut down pursuant to Germany's surrender in World War II. Five years later J.G. Anschutz GmbH was founded to make air pistols and repair firearms. Soon it turned to target rifles and even resumed manufacture of the Flobert-type guns that had been among the firm's original products. Anschutz target rifles began to build a solid reputation among the world's elite shooters.

An ultramodern plant in Ulm, Germany, produces what have become recognized world wide as the standard against which all rim-fire target rifles and pistols are judged. Anschutz rifles captured all of the gold medals, and all but two of the silver medals in the Barcelona Olympic Games.

Model 1416

Action: bolt
Stock: checkered walnut
Barrel: 22 in.
Sights: open
Weight: 5.5
Caliber: .22LR, .22 WMR
Magazine: detachable box, 5-round .22 LR, 4-round .22 WMR
Features: M64 action; 2-stage match trigger; stock available in classic, MC and Mannllicher
Classic: $656
Monte Carlo: $689
Mannlicher: $1014

Model 1451

Action: bolt
Stock: Sporter Target, hardwood
Barrel: heavy 22 in.
Sights: open
Weight: 6.3
Caliber: .22 LR
Magazine: detachable box, 10-round
Features: M64 action
1451:. $515

Model 1700 Series Classic Sporter

Action: bolt
Stock: sporter, walnut
Barrel: 23 in.
Sights: none
Weight: 7.3
Caliber: .22 LR, .22 Hornet, .222
Magazine: detachable box, 5-round
Features: M54 action; Meister grade about $180 additional
1710 .22 LR: $1214
1710 with heavy barrel. $1214
1730 .22 Hornet: $1272
1730 with heavy barrel. $1272
1740 .222:. $1341
1740 with heavy barrel. $1341

Anschutz Rifles

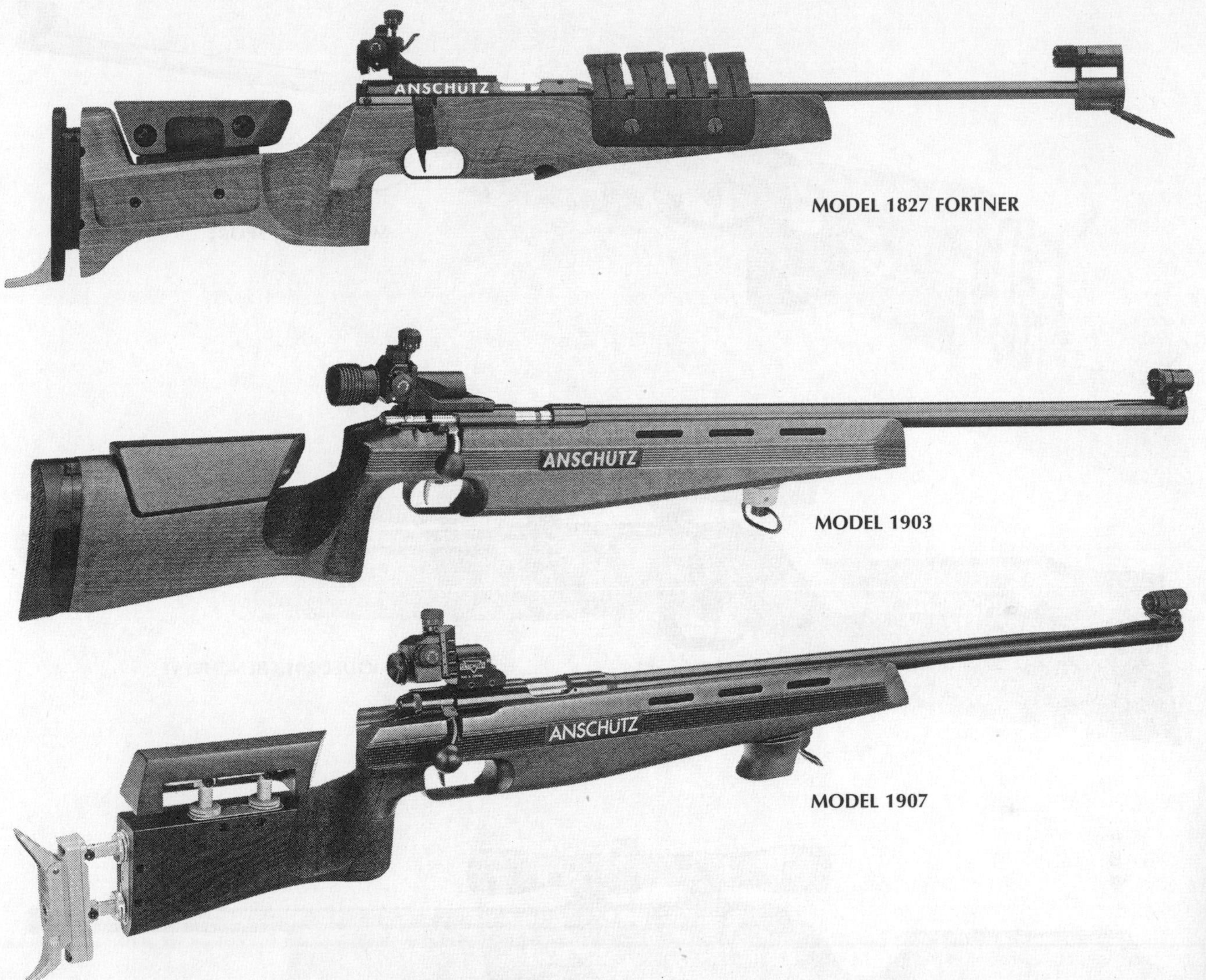

MODEL 1827 FORTNER

MODEL 1903

MODEL 1907

Model 1827 Fortner

Action: bolt
Stock: Biathlon, walnut
Barrel: medium 22 in.
Sights: none
Weight: 8.8
Caliber: .22 LR
Magazine: detachable box, 5 rounds
Features: M54 action, stock has holder for four magazines
1827: $1850
with thumbhole stock: $1940

Model 1903

Action: bolt
Stock: Standard Rifle, hardwood
Barrel: heavy 26 in.
Sights: none
Weight: 10.5
Caliber: .22 LR
Magazine: none
Features: M64 action, adjustable cheekpiece, forend rail
1903: $690
left-hand: $730

Model 1907

Action: bolt
Stock: Standard Rifle, walnut
Barrel: heavy 26 in.
Sights: none
Weight: 10.5
Caliber: .22 LR
Magazine: none
Features: M54 action, adjustable cheekpiece and butt, forend rail
1907: $1375
left-hand: $1475

Anschutz Rifles

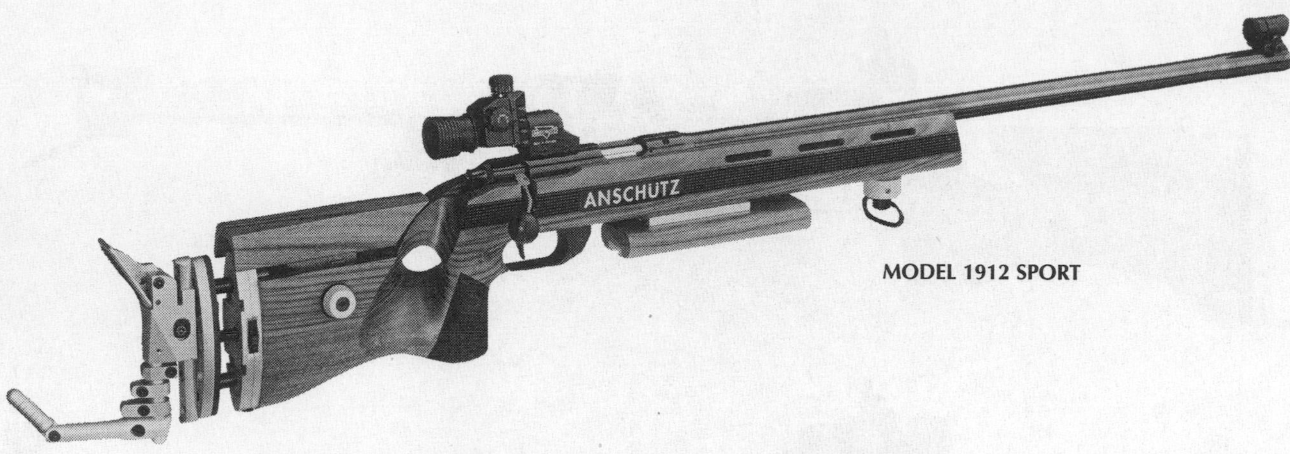

MODEL 1912 SPORT

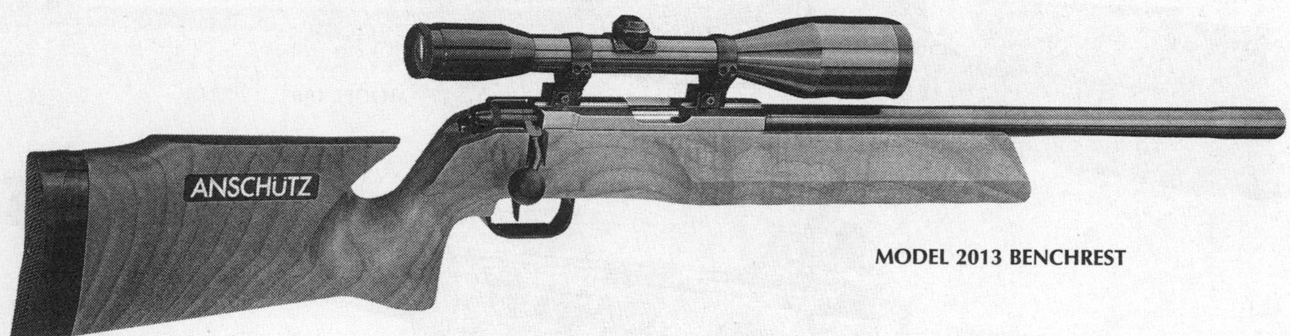

MODEL 2013 BENCHREST

MODEL 54.18 MS R "SILHOUETTE"

Model 1912 Sport

Action: bolt
Stock: International, laminated
Barrel: heavy 26 in.
Sights: none
Weight: 11.4
Caliber: .22 LR
Magazine: none
Features: M54 action, adjustable cheekpiece and butt, forend rail
1912:. $1690
left-hand:. $1785

Model 2013 Benchrest

Action: bolt
Stock: Benchrest (BR-50) walnut
Barrel: heavy 20 in.
Sights: none
Weight: 10.3
Caliber: .22 LR
Magazine: none
Features: M54 action
2013:. $1575

Model 54.18 MS

Action: bolt
Stock: Silhouette, walnut
Barrel: heavy 22 in.
Sights: none
Weight: 8.1
Caliber: .22 LR
Magazine: none
Features: M54 action
54.18: $1225
with thumbhole stock: $1350

Auto-Ordnance Rifles

MODEL 1927 A1
COMMANDO

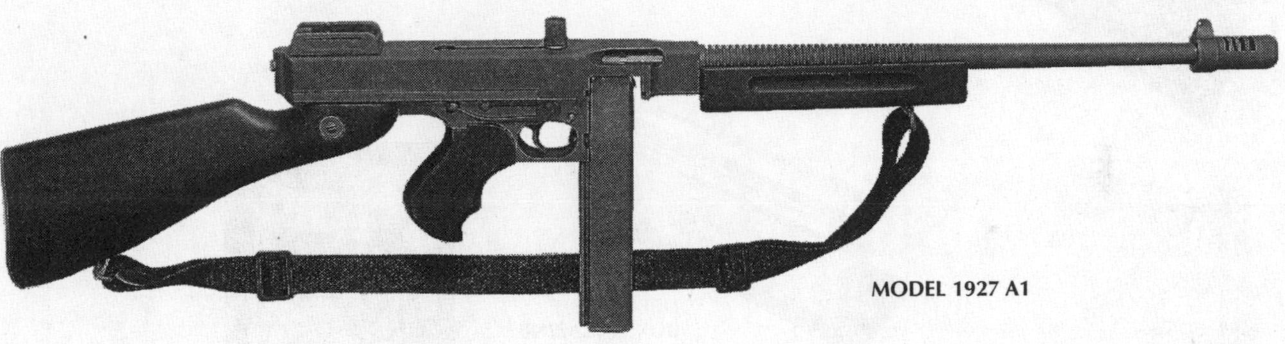

MODEL 1927 A1

THIS VETERAN design, the Thompson Submachine Gun, became famous during the "Roaring Twenties" and World War II.These replicas are legal autoloaders, not machine guns.

Model 1927 A1 Commando

Action: autoloading
Stock: walnut, horizontal fore-grip
Barrel: 16 in.
Sights: open
Weight: 13.0
Caliber: .45 ACP
Magazine: detachable box 20-round
Features: Top-cocking, autoloading blowback; carbine version with side-cocking lever, 11.5 lbs.
1927:. $950
carbine:. $925

Model 1927A1

Action: autoloading
Stock: walnut, vertical foregrip
Barrel: 16 in.
Sights: open
Weight: 13.0
Caliber: .45 ACP
Magazine: detachable box, 20-round
Features: top-cocking, autoloading blowback; lightweight version 9.5 lbs.
standard: $950
lightweight: $950

RIFLES

Heavy barrels are not intrinsically more accurate than lightweight barrels. But they are typically more consistent when shooting long strings because they don't "walk" as readily when they heat.

Beretta Rifles

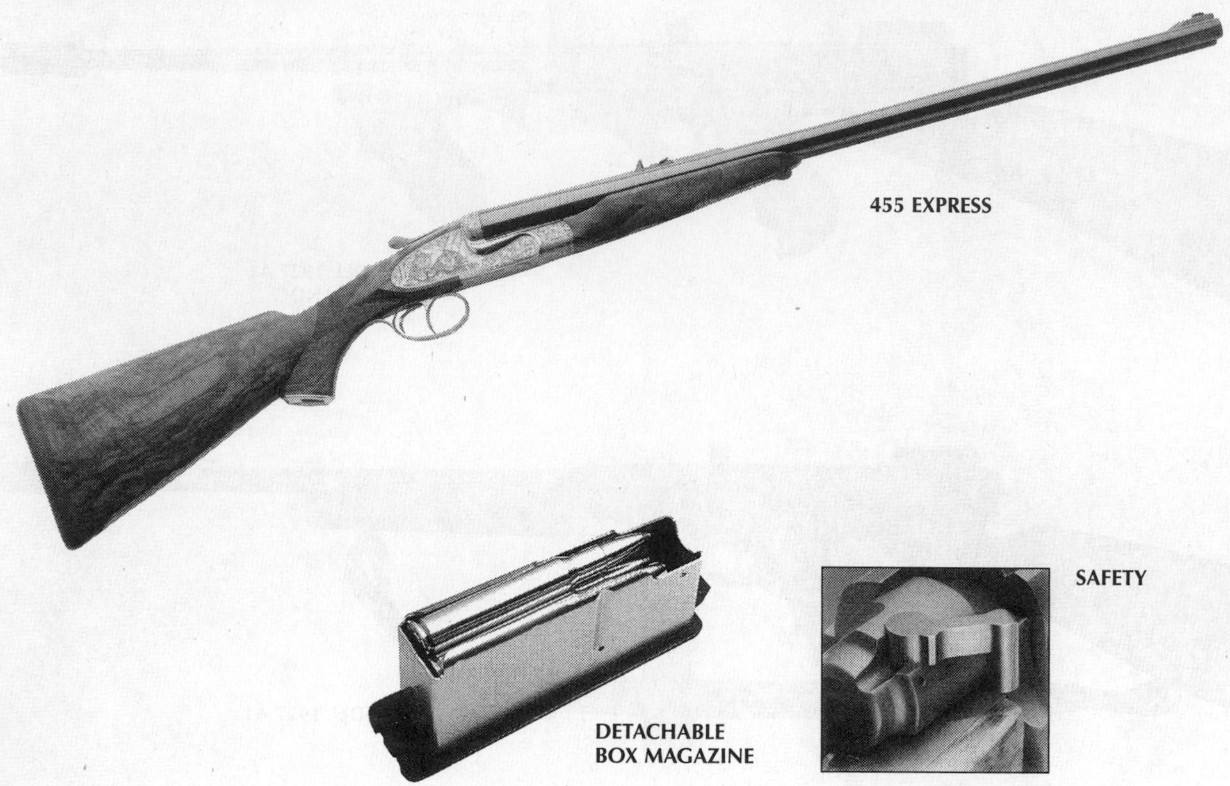

455 EXPRESS

DETACHABLE BOX MAGAZINE

SAFETY

RIFLES

EXPRESS DOUBLE RIFLES require strong, precisely-fitted actions to handle large, high pressure cartridges. Barrels must be joined with absolute precision for optimum convergence. The SS06 and SS06EELL Over-and Under Express Rifles offer rifled barrels of special cold-hammered steel. An extra set of matching 12 gauge barrels is available. Hand-finished, hand-checkered stocks and forends are made from select walnut or walnut briar. A special trap door compartment for extra cartridges is fitted inside the stock, and a cavity under the pistol-grip cap holds a set of spare front sights. The SS-06 is finished with light engraving on the color case-hardened receiver. The SS06 EELL sports a receiver hand-engraved with game scenes, or a color case-hardened version with gold inlaid animals.

The 455 Side-by-Side Express Rifle action is made of special high-strength steel and forged with an elongated 60mm plate. This increases the distance between the hinge pin and the three-lug locking system to compensate for stress when shooting. To withstand the pressure of high-powered cartridges, the sealed receiver has reinforced sides, and the top tang extends fully up to the stock comb to strengthen attachment of the stock. An articulated front trigger and automatic blocking device eliminate the possibility of simultaneous discharge. The safety (automatic on request) provides for quick, reliable and positive on/off operation. The Boehler steel barrels are joined with a Demibloc chamber system.

Model 455 SxS Express

Action: hinged breech
Stock: select walnut, hand-checkered
Barrel: 24 in.
Sights: open
Weight: 11.0
Caliber: .375 H&H, .416 Rigby, .458 Win. Mag., .470 N.E., .500 N.E.
Magazine: none
Features: articulated front trigger; dimensions and embellishments to order on EELL
455: $53,000

Beretta Rifles

SABLE O/U

CARRYING CASE

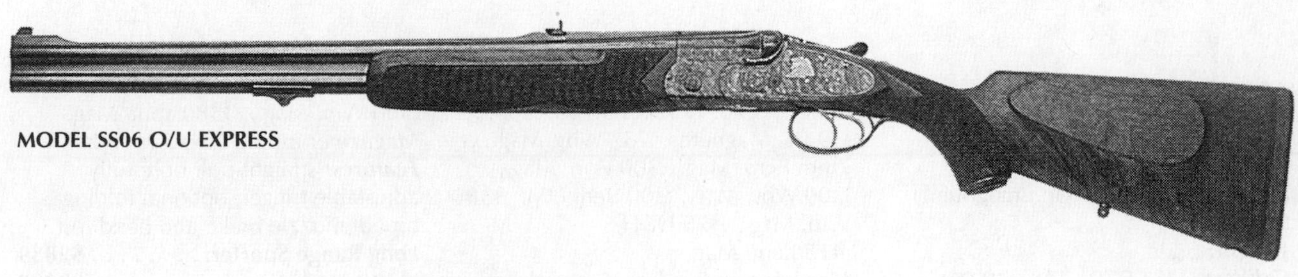

MODEL SS06 O/U EXPRESS

Sable O/U

Action: hinged breech
Stock: select walnut, hand-checkered
Barrel: 24 in.
Sights: open
Weight: 7.7
Caliber: .30-06, 9.3x74R and .444 Marlin
Magazine: none
Features: articulated front trigger; Silver Sable has nickeled engraved receiver; Gold Sable has case-colored engraved receiver
Silver Sable: $3850
Gold Sable: $5750

Model SS06 O/U Express

Action: hinged breech
Stock: select walnut, hand-checkered
Barrel: 24 in.
Sights: open
Weight: 11.0
Caliber: 9.3x74R, .375 H&H, .458 Win.
Magazine: none
Features: spare sights in grip compartment; dimensions and embellishments to order on EELL
SS06: $39500

RIFLES

Blaser Rifles

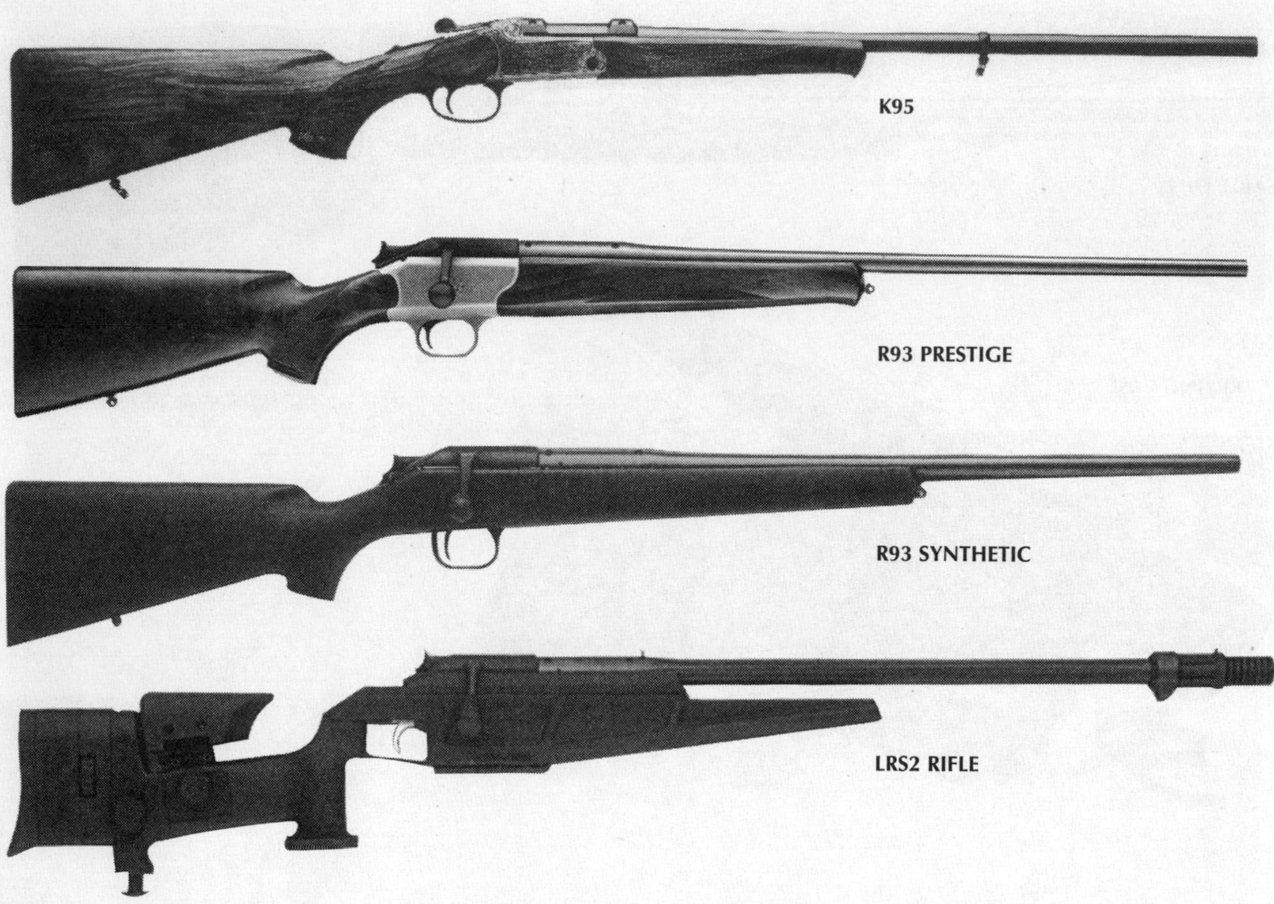

RIFLES

Model K95

Action: hinged breech
Stock: walnut
Barrel: 24 in. and 26 in. (magnum)
Sights: none
Weight: 5.5
Caliber: .243, .270, .308, .30-06; magnum: 7mm Ren., .300 Win., .300 Wby.
Magazine: none
Features: easy takedown with no loss of zero; magnum calibers weigh 5.8 lbs.; Luxus has hand engraving on receiver
Prestige:. $3460
Luxus: $3000

Model R93

Action: bolt
Stock: walnut or synthetic
Barrel: 22 in.
Sights: none
Weight: 6.5
Caliber: .22-250, .243, .25-06, 6.5x55, .270, 7x57, 7mm/08, .308, .30-06; Magnums: .257 Wby. Mag., 7mm Rem. Mag., .300 Win. Mag., .300 Wby. Mag., .300 Rem UM, .338 Win. Mag., .375 H&H, .416 Rem. Mag.
Magazine: in-line box, 5 rounds
Features: straight-pull bolt with expanding collar lockup; higher grades available; magnums weigh 7 lbs.; left-hand versions available, add $141
Prestige:. $2339
Synthetic:. $1831
Luxus: $3109
Attache $4392

Model R93 Long Range Sporter 2

Action: bolt
Stock: tactical composite
Barrel: heavy, fluted 26 in.
Sights: none
Weight: 8.0
Caliber: .223 Rem., .22-250,.308, .300 Win. Mag., .338 Lapua Mag.
Magazine: in-line box, 5 rounds
Features: straight-pull bolt; fully adjustable trigger; optional folding bipod, muzzle brake and hand rest
Long Range Sporter: $2839
.338 Lapua: $3288

Model R93 LRS2 Tactical Rifle Package

Action: bolt
Stock: synthetic tactical with adjustments
Barrel: heavy, fluted 26 in.
Sights: none
Weight: 10
Caliber: .308, .300 Win. Mag., .338 Lapua
Magazine: in-line box, 5 rounds
Features: package includes bipod, sling, Leupold Tactical scope, mirage band, muzzle brake
Long Range Tactical: $4095
.338 Lapua: $4972

Brown Precision Rifles

CUSTOM TEAM CHALLENGER

HIGH COUNTRY RIFLE

HIGH COUNTRY YOUTH RIFLE

RIFLES

DESIGNED FOR THE SERIOUS game hunter or guide, this custom version of Brown Precision's Pro-Hunter rifle begins life as a Winchester Model 700 Super Grade action with controlled feed claw extractor. The trigger is tuned to a crisp let-off at each customer's specified weight. A Shilen Match-Grade stainless-steel barrel is custom crowned and hand fitted to the action.

The Pro-Hunter Elite features choice of express rear sight or custom Dave Talley removable peep sight and banded front ramp sight with European dovetail and replaceable brass bead. An optional flip-up white night sight is also available, as is a set of Dave Talley detachable T.N.T. scope mount rings and bases installed with Brown's Magnum Duty 8X40 screws.

All metal parts are finished in either matte electroless nickel or black Teflon. The barreled action is glass bedded to a Brown Precision Alaskan-configuration fiberglass stock, painted according to customer choice and fitted with a premium 1" buttpad and Dave Talley trapdoor grip cap. Weight ranges from 7 to 15 lbs., depending on barrel length, contour and options.

Custom Team Challenger

Action: autoloading
Stock: composite
Barrel: heavy Shilen match grade 18 in.
Sights: open
Weight: 7.0
Caliber: .22 LR
Magazine: rotary, 10 rounds
Features: also available with stainless barrel
Team Challenger: $1395
stainless: $1495

High Country

Action: bolt
Stock: composite classic stock
Barrel: choice of contours, lengths
Sights: none
Weight: 6.0
Caliber: any popular standard caliber
Magazine: box, 5 rounds
Features: Remington 700 barreled action; tuned trigger; choice of stock colors and dimensions
High Country: $2795

High Country Youth

Action: bolt
Stock: composite sporter, scaled for youth
Barrel: length and contour to order
Sights: none
Weight: 5.0
Caliber: any popular standard short action
Magazine: box, 5 rounds
Features: Remington Model 700 or Model 7 barreled action; optional muzzle brake, scopes, stock colors and dimensions; included: package of shooting, reloading, and hunting accessories
Youth: $1435

Brown Precision Rifles

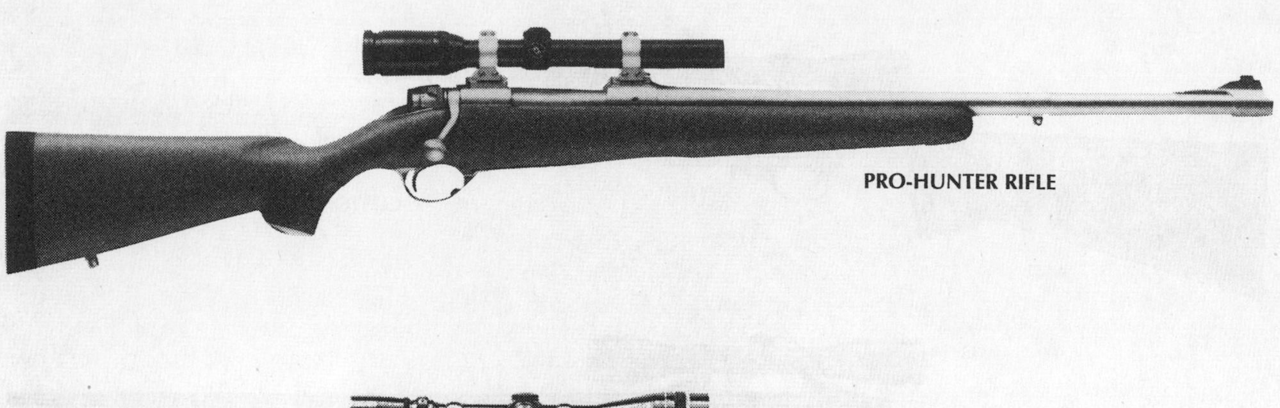
PRO-HUNTER RIFLE

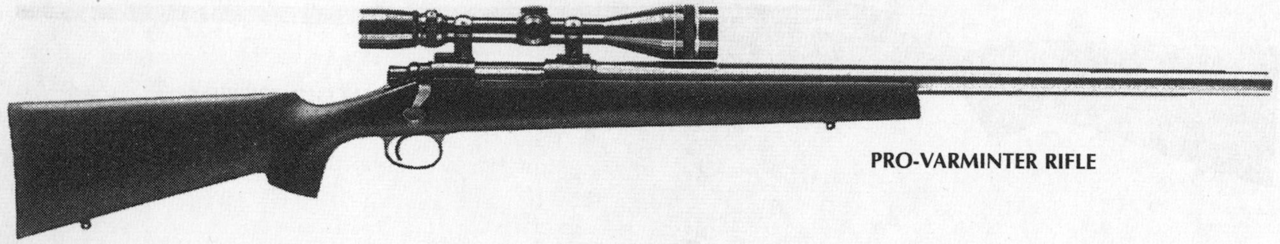
PRO-VARMINTER RIFLE

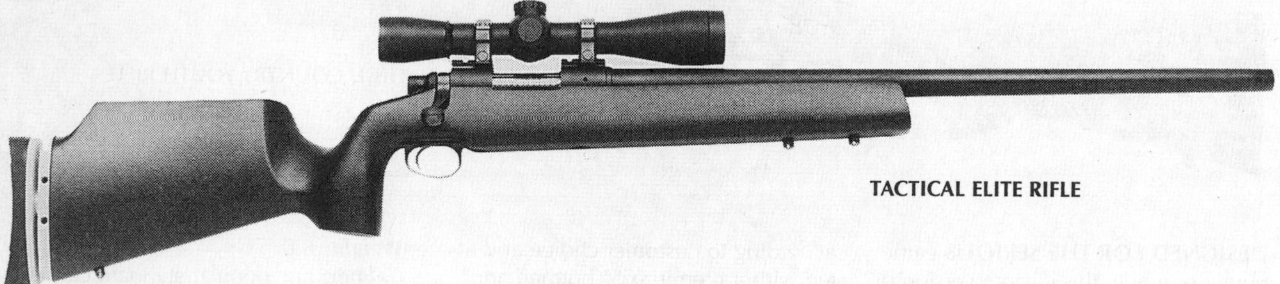
TACTICAL ELITE RIFLE

PRO HUNTER

Action: bolt
Stock: composite sporter
Barrel: Shilen match grade stainless
Sights: none
Weight: 8.0
Caliber: any standard and belted magnum caliber up to .375 H&H
Magazine: box, 3 to 5 rounds
Features: Model 70 action with Mauser extractor; tuned trigger; optional Talley peep sight and banded ramp front sight or Talley mounts with 8-40 screws; optional muzzle brake, Mag-Na-Porting, Americase aluminum hard case
Pro Hunter: $3495
in left-hand: $3695

PRO VARMINTER

Action: bolt
Stock: composite, varmint or bench rest
Barrel: heavy stainless match grade 26 in.
Sights: none
Weight: 9.0
Caliber: all popular calibers
Magazine: box (or single shot)
Features: Remington 40X or 700 action (right or left-hand); bright or bead-blasted finish; optional muzzle brake; after-market trigger; scope and mounts optional
Model 700, right-hand: $2495
Model 700, left-hand: $2695
Rem. 40X (with target trigger): $3195

TACTICAL ELITE

Action: bolt
Stock: composite tactical
Barrel: Shilen match-grade, heavy stainless
Sights: none
Weight: 9.0
Caliber: .223, .308, .300 Win. Mag., (others on special order)
Magazine: box, 3 or 5 rounds
Features: Remington 700 action, Teflon metal finish; adjustable butt plate; tuned trigger; optional muzzle brakes, scopes
Elite: $3195

Browning Rifles

.22 SEMI-AUTOMATIC

IN 1869 JOHN M. BROWNING and his brother Matt established a gun shop in Ogden, just 50 miles from Promontory Point. The shop's crossroads location brought plenty of business. In 1878 at age 23, John Browning designed his own breech-loading mechanism, and fashioned a working prototype with no blueprints or milling machines. On October 7, 1879, Browning received his first patent for a single-shot breech-loader, an immensely strong gun with large, simple parts that were easy to make and hard to break.

By 1879 John and his brother Ed bought a 30-foot lot at the edge of Ogden's business district. Within two years the brothers had formed a partnership, and John had designed another dropping-block rifle -- this one with a fixed trigger guard and forward-mounted operating lever. By 1882 he'd patented a repeating rifle with a tubular magazine and immediately set to work on a second repeating mechanism. John received patents for both rifles, but shelved the designs until he could improve upon them.

In 1883 Winchester salesman Andrew McAusland sent a used Browning rifle to company president Thomas G. Bennett in New Haven, Connecticut. While Winchester had a firm grip on the market for lever-action repeaters, it had no guns stout enough to handle heavy cartridges like the Army's .45-70. Rights to Browning's rifle would give Winchester a competitive gun. In 1883, Bennett bought the rights for Browning breech-loader for $8,000.

John, no longer permitted to build his single-shot, quickly resurrected his lever-action designs. In 1884 he and brother Matt visited Winchester's headquarters with a new repeater, the Winchester Model 1886. The following year John designed the Model 1887 lever-action shotgun -- widely considered to be the first practical repeating shotgun.

After a two-year hiatus as a Mormon missionary John was back at his bench by 1889, setting a blistering pace, netting 20 patents in less than four years. During the next 17 years Winchester bought 44 designs from the Browning shop. Among John Browning's most famous designs was the Model 1897 pump shotgun, which immediately smothered all competition and stayed in production for 60 years. When Bennett turned to Browning to replace Winchester's outdated Model 1873, a prototype of the Model 1892 arrived within 30 days.

Ironically, John Browning's next achievement scuttled his relationship with Bennett. John had long been intrigued by automatic guns; but unlike R.J. Gatling who had used multiple barrels and a hand-operated mechanism, he sought to use the firing force of one round to manipulate the action to fire another round.

In 1890 John offered Colt, the manufacturer of the Army's Gatling guns, an "Automatic Machine Gun" that could be built "as cheaply as a common sporting rifle." In tests John fired 200 .45-70 rounds without a hitch.

In 1893 tests Browning demonstrated an action which vented gas through a port in the barrel to operate the spring-loaded bolt. The bolt ejected the spent case on its rearward stroke, then chambered and fired another round as it slammed home. Colt started production for the Navy in 1895.

John adapted his autoloading principle to shotguns. When Thomas Bennett refused Browning's terms for a long-recoil shotgun, the productive relationship dissolved. Browning marketed his design, the Auto 5, in Belgium and through Remington, in the U.S. Even more famous was Browning's military pistol, the powerful Colt Model 1911.

John continued to work on military designs, completing a water-cooled machine gun in 1910 and, soon after, developing an infantry weapon called the Browning Automatic Rifle, or BAR.

Rumblings of war in Europe revived interest in John Browning's machine gun. In tests at Springfield Armory he triggered 20,000 rounds without malfunction and, in a second demonstration, fired another 20,000 cartridges! In the fall of l9l7, ordnance officers tendered $750,000 for manufacturing rights for the Model 19l17 machine gun, the BAR and Colt's Model 1911pistol. It was about $12 million less than he could have received from private royalties, but he accepted. "Had I been 20 years younger," he stated, "I might have been ducking German bullets in French mud, wishing for a better gun."

In l926, on a trip to the F.N. plant in Belgium, John felt chest pains and retired to the office. A couple of minutes later his heart stopped beating. John Browning was 71.

No gun designer in American history has contributed as much to firearms development. In nearly 50 years at the bench he was issued 128 patents on 80 distinct mechanisms, from single-shots to selfloaders.

RIFLES

.22 Semi-Automatic

Action: autoloading
Stock: walnut
Barrel: 19 in.
Sights: open
Weight: 5.2
Caliber: .22 LR
Magazine: tube in stock, 11 rounds
Features: Grade VI has high grade walnut, finer checkering, engraved receiver
Grade I: $504
Grade VI: $1080

Browning Rifles

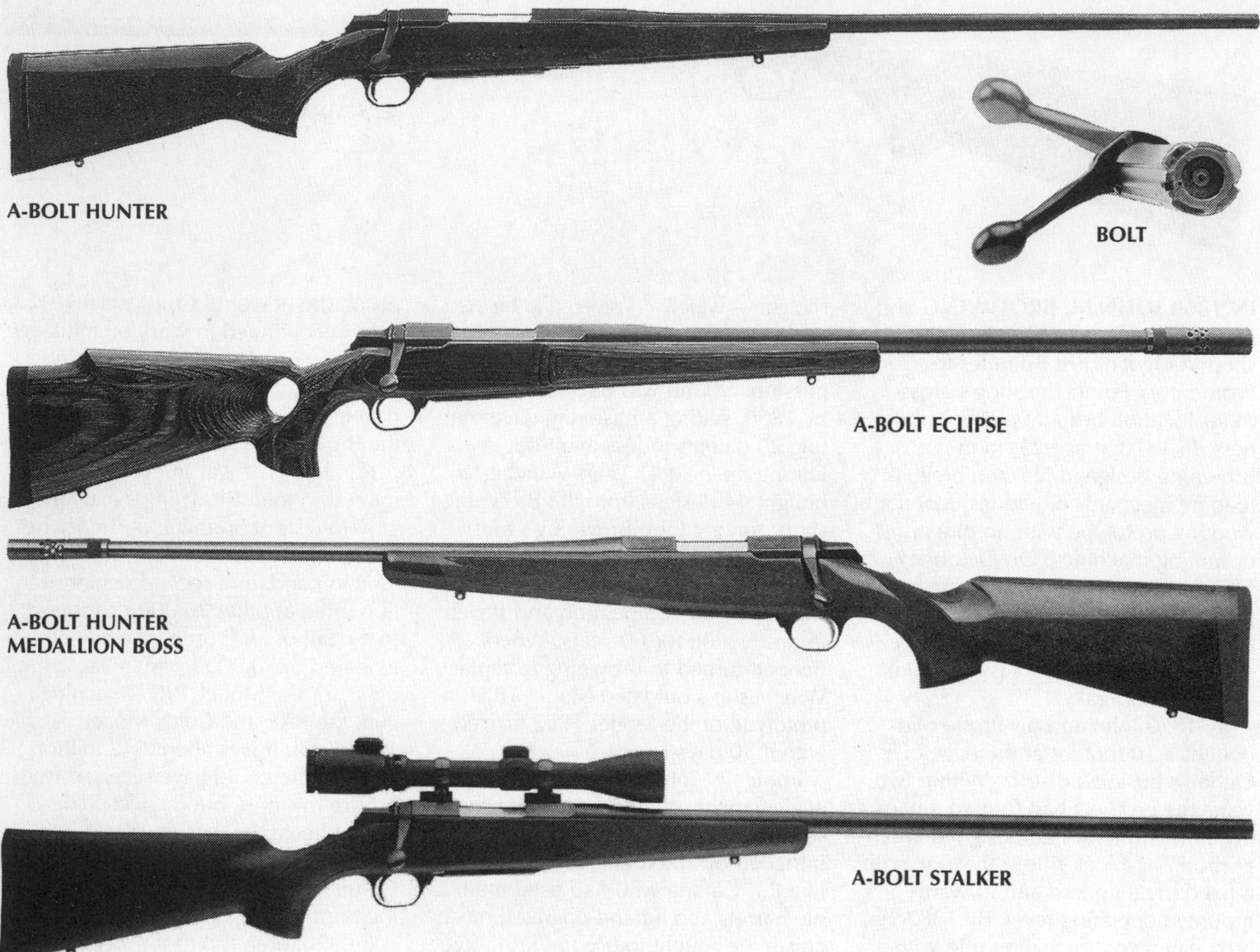
A-BOLT HUNTER

BOLT

A-BOLT ECLIPSE

A-BOLT HUNTER MEDALLION BOSS

A-BOLT STALKER

A-Bolt Hunter

Action: bolt
Stock: walnut
Barrel: 20 and 22 in.
Sights: none
Weight: 7.0
Caliber: all popular cartridges from .22 Hornet to .30-06. i
Magazine: detachable box, 4 to 6 rounds
Features: BOSS (ballistic optimizing shooting system) available; Micro Hunters weigh 6.3 lbs. with 20 in. barrel and shorter stock. Left-hand Medallion available. Eclipse thumbhole stock available with light or heavy barrel (9.8 lbs.) and BOSS.

Hunter: $652
Medallion: $767
Medallion BOSS: $847
Micro Hunter: $645
Eclipse Hunter:........... $1061

A-Bolt Hunter Magnum

Action: bolt
Stock: walnut
Barrel: 23 and 26 in.
Sights: none
Weight: 7.5
Caliber: popular magnums from 7mm Rem. to .375 H&H, including .270, 7mm and .300 WSM.
Magazine: detachable box, 3 rounds
Features: rifles in WSM calibers have 23 in. barrels and weigh 6.5 lbs.; BOSS (Ballistic Optimizing Shooting System) available; left-hand available.

Magnum: $678
Medallion Magnum: $795
Medallion Magnum BOSS: $875

A-Bolt Stalker

Action: bolt
Stock: synthetic
Barrel: 22, 23 and 26 in.
Sights: none
Weight: 7.5
Caliber: most popular calibers and magnums, including .270, 7mm and .300 WSMs.
Magazine: detachable box, 3 to 6 rounds
Features: BOSS (Ballistic Optimizing Shooting System) available; stainless option. Rifles in WSM calibers have 23 in. barrels and weigh 6.5 lbs.

Stalker: $671
BOSS: $751
Stainless :................. $854
Stainless, BOSS: $934
Stainless, left-hand: $880
Stainless, left-hand, Boss: $960

Browning Rifles

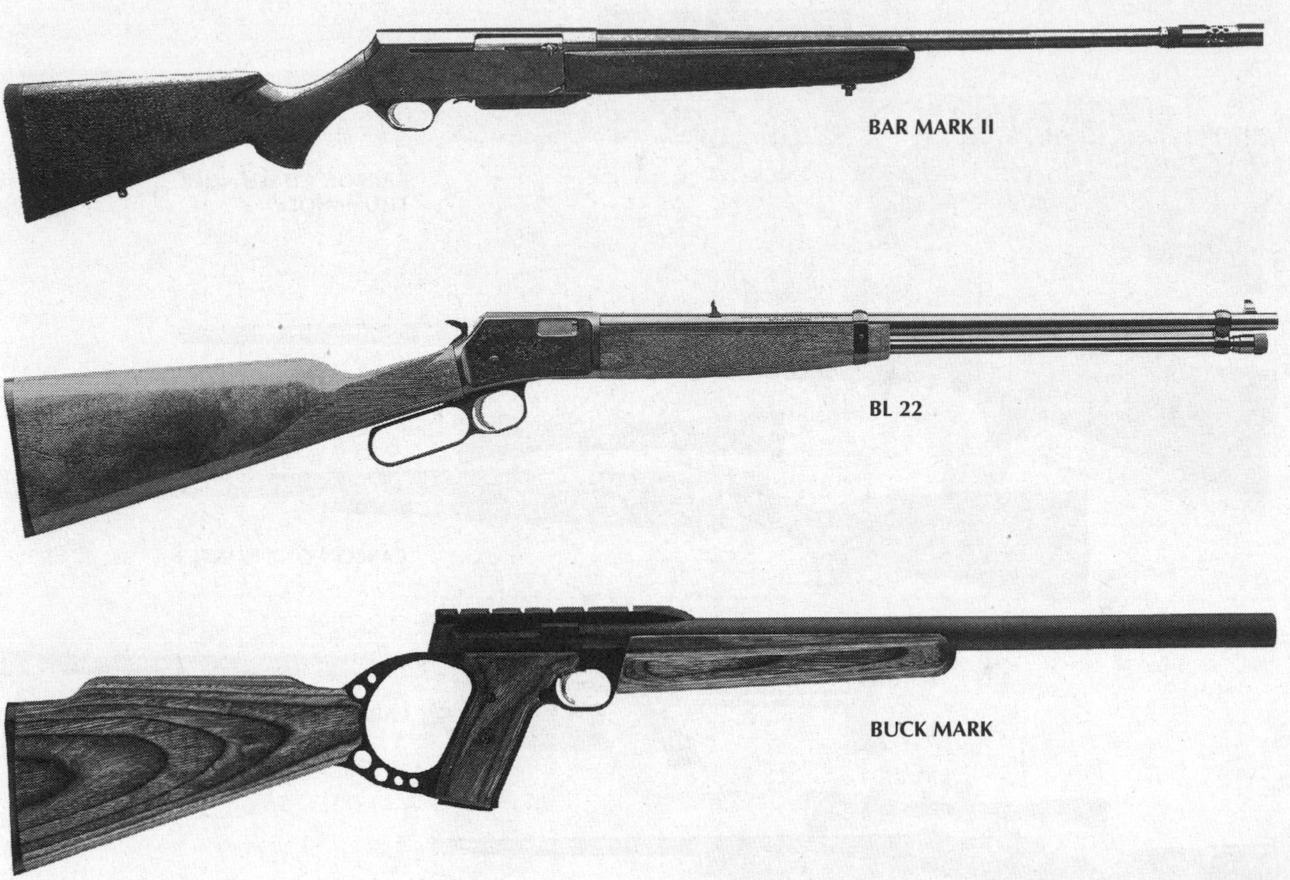

BAR MARK II

BL 22

BUCK MARK

BAR Mark II

Action: autoloading
Stock: walnut or synthetic
Barrel: 20, 22, and 24 in.
Sights: open
Weight: 7.5
Caliber: .243, .25-06, .270, .308, .30-06, 7mm Rem. Mag., .300 Win. Mag., .300 WSM, .338 Win. Mag.
Magazine: detachable box, 3 and 4 rounds
Features: gas operated; lightweight model with alloy receiver and 20 in. barrel weighs 7.1 lbs.; magnum with 24 in. barrel weighs 8.4 lbs. \BOSS (Ballistic Optimizing Shooting System) available; higher grades also available.

Mark II: $831
open sights: $850
no sights, BOSS: $930
magnums: $908
magnums, open sights: $927
magnum, no sights, BOSS:. . $1007
lightweight, open sights: $850
lightweight, no sights, BOSS:. $927

BL 22

Action: lever
Stock: walnut
Barrel: 20 in.
Sights: open
Weight: 5.0
Caliber: .22 LR
Magazine: under-barrel tube, 15 rounds
Features: short stroke, exposed hammer, lever action; straight grip; also available in Grade II with fine checkered walnut.

Grade I:. $436
Grade Ii: $494

Buck Mark

Action: autoloading
Stock: laminate
Barrel: 18 in.
Sights: open
Weight: 5.2
Caliber: .22 LR
Magazine: detachable box, 10 rounds
Features: also in target model with heavy barrel

Sporter: $539
Target, heavy barrel:. $555

Christensen Arms Rifles

RIFLES

Carbon Challenger Thumbhole

Action: autoloading
Stock: synthetic or wood thumbhole
Barrel: graphite sleeved 20 in.
Sights: none
Weight: 4.0
Caliber: .22 LR
Magazine: rotary, 10 rounds
Features: 10/22 Ruger action; custom trigger and bedding
Challenger: $1150

Carbon One Custom

Action: bolt
Stock: synthetic or wood sporter
Barrel: graphite sleeved 26 in.
Sights: none
Weight: 6.0
Caliber: all popular magnums
Magazine: box, 3 rounds
Features: Remington 700 action; optional custom trigger
Custom: $2950

Carbon One Hunter

Action: bolt
Stock: synthetic
Barrel: graphite sleeved 26 in.
Sights: none
Weight: 7.0
Caliber: any popular
Magazine: box, 3 or 5 rounds
Features: Remington 700 action
Hunter: $1499

Carbon Ranger

Action: bolt
Stock: retractable tactical skeleton
Barrel: graphite sleeved, up to 36 in.
Sights: none
Weight: 10.0
Caliber: .50 BMG
Magazine: box, 5 rounds
Features: Omni Wind Runner action; custom trigger; guaranteed 5 shots in 8 in. at 1000 yds.
Ranger: $4999

Carbon Tactical

Action: bolt
Stock: synthetic
Barrel: graphite sleeved, 26 in.
Sights: none
Weight: 7.0
Caliber: most popular calibers
Magazine: box, 3 or 5 rounds
Features: guaranteed accuracy 1/2 in. at 100 yards; optional custom trigger, muzzle brake
Tactical: . . . . price on request

Cimarron Firearms Rifles

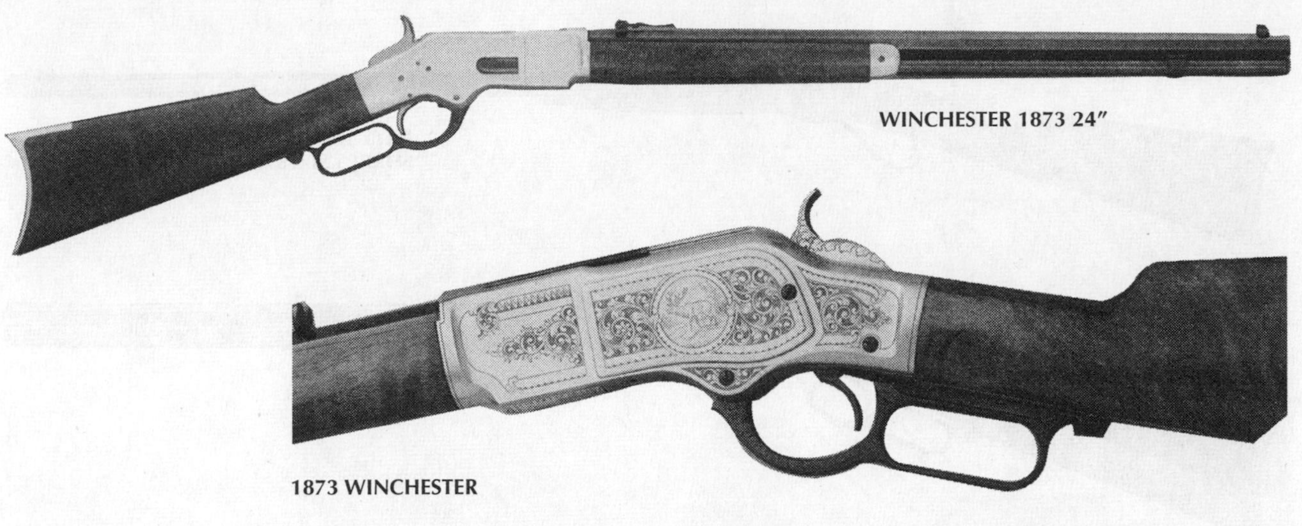

WINCHESTER 1873 24"

1873 WINCHESTER

1873 "DELUXE" SPORTING RIFLE

1885 HIGH WALL

1873 Winchester

Action: lever
Stock: walnut, straight grip
Barrel: 24 in.
Sights: open
Weight: 7.5
Caliber: .45 Colt, .44 WCF, .357-38 Special, .32-20, .44 Special, .38-40
Magazine: under-barrel tube, 11 rounds
Features: Available: "Sporting" model, "Deluxe" model, "Long Range" model (30 in. barrel), and carbine (19 in. barrel); Deluxe model has pistol grip
Sporting: $949
Deluxe: $1089
Long Range: $999
Long Range Deluxe: $1149
Carbine: $949

1885 High Wall

Action: dropping block
Stock: walnut, straight grip
Barrel: octagon 30 in.
Sights: open
Weight: 9.5
Caliber: .45-70, .45-90, .40-65, .38-55
Magazine: none
Features: reproduction of the Winchester single shot hunting rifle popular in the 1880s
1885: $995

When shooting, keep your head erect, the buttplate high on your shoulder so you look directly into the sight. You see best when looking straight ahead, not from the corner of your eye.

Cimarron Firearms Rifles

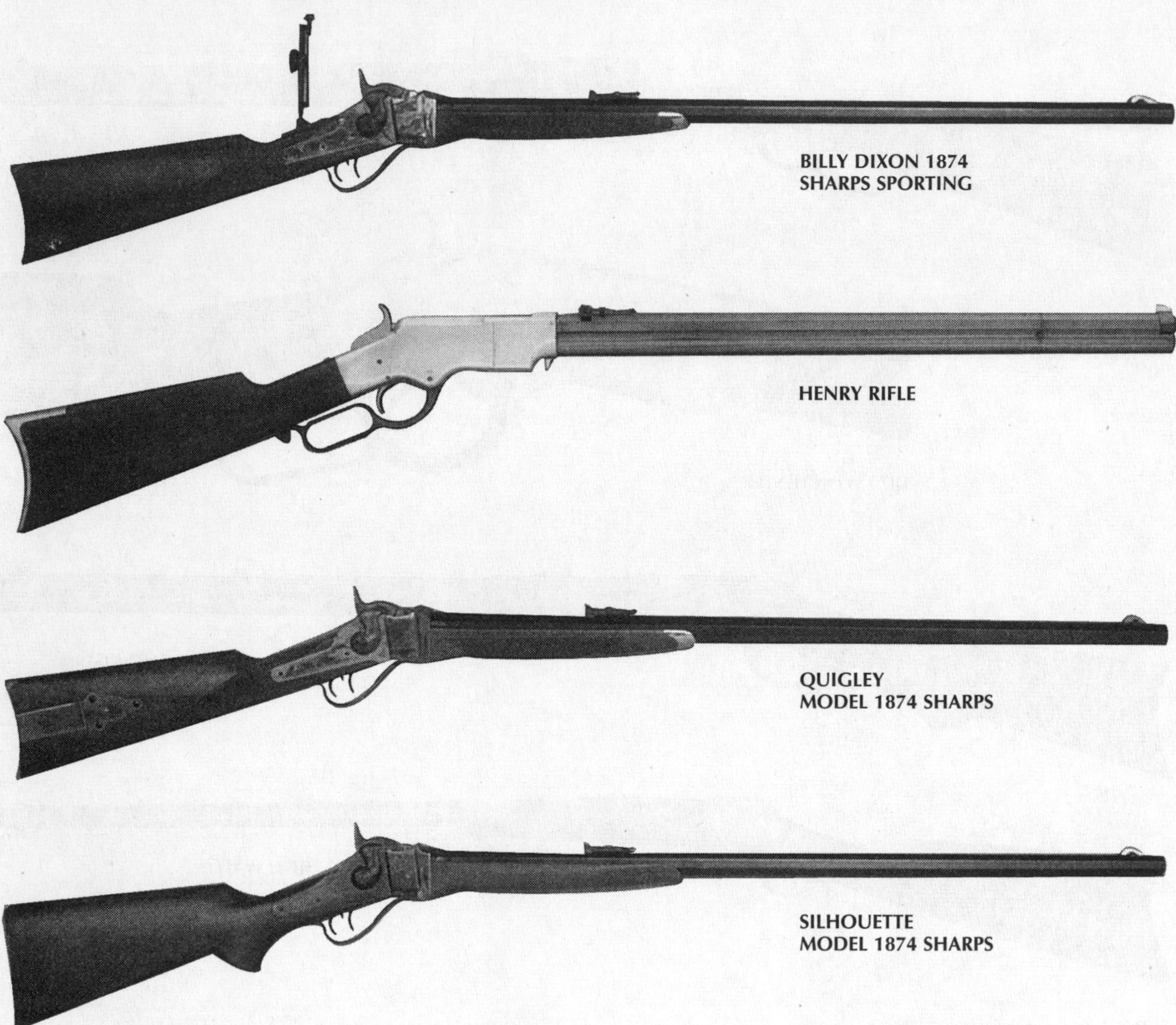

BILLY DIXON 1874
SHARPS SPORTING

HENRY RIFLE

QUIGLEY
MODEL 1874 SHARPS

SILHOUETTE
MODEL 1874 SHARPS

Billy Dixon 1874 Sharps Sporting

Action: dropping block
Stock: walnut, straight grip
Barrel: octagon 32 in.
Sights: open
Weight: 10.5
Caliber: .45-70, .45-90, .45-110, .50-90
Magazine: none
Features: Single-shot reproduction
Billy Dixon: $1295

Henry Rifle

Action: lever
Stock: walnut, straight grip
Barrel: 24 in.
Sights: open
Weight: 7.5
Caliber: .44 WCF, .45 LC
Magazine: under-barrel tube, 11 rounds
Features: replica of the most famous American rifle of the Old West
Henry: $1029

Quigley Model 1874 Sharps

Action: dropping block
Stock: walnut, straight grip
Barrel: octagon 34 in.
Sights: open
Weight: 10.5
Caliber: .45-70, .45-90, .45-120
Magazine: none
Features: single-shot reproduction
Quigley: $1350

Silhouette Model 1874 Sharps

Action: dropping block
Stock: walnut, pistol grip
Barrel: 32 in. octagon
Sights: open
Weight: 10.5
Caliber: .45-70, .50-70
Magazine: none
Features: single-shot reproduction; shotgun style buttplate; barrel features cut rifling, lapped and polished
Silhouette: $1299

Colt Rifles

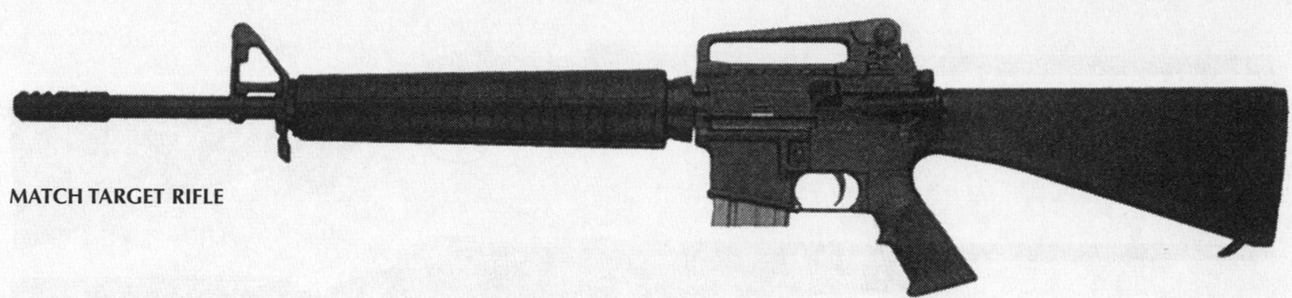
MATCH TARGET RIFLE

MATCH TARGET RIFLE
Action: autoloading
Stock: combat-style, synthetic
Barrel: 16 or 20 in.
Sights: open
Weight: 8.0
Caliber: .223
Magazine: detachable box, 9 rounds
Features: suppressed recoil; accepts optics; 2-position safety; available with heavy barrel, compensator
Target: $1194

Cooper Arms Rifles

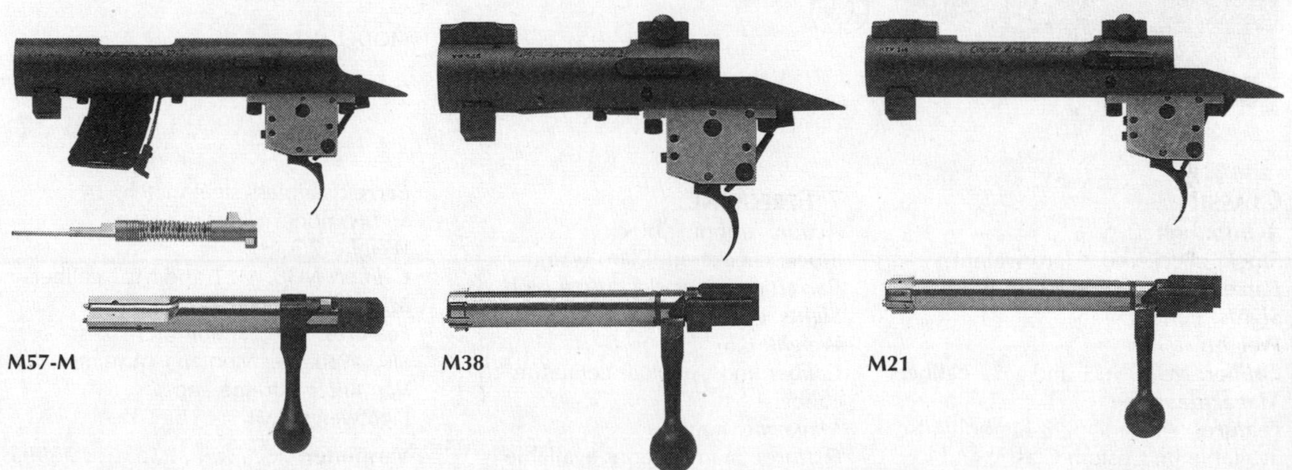
M57-M M38 M21

RIFLES

COOPER ARMS was founded in 1990 by Dan Cooper and has since become famous for producing some of the world's most accurate and beautifully hand-crafted rifles. Four action sizes are available in any of six stock configurations. Cooper Arms offers varmint and traditional configurations.

Cooper Arms employs 20 artisans who produce a line of bolt-action single-shot centerfire and bolt-action repeating rimfire rifles. Finished barreled actions are hand fitted to each individual rifle. for a custom wood to metal fit. The actions are glass bedded behind the recoil lug and 1" forward of the breech. The barrels are free-floated. Cooper guarantees their accuracy to ½ MOA.

M57-M CALIBERS:
22LR, 22WMR, 17HMR

M38 CALIBERS:
17 Ackley Hornet, 22 Hornet, 22 K-Hornet, 218 Bee, 218 Mashburn Bee

M21 CALIBERS:
17 Rem, 17 Mach IV, Tactical 29, 221 Fireball, 222 Rem Mag, 223, 223 AI, 22 PPC, 6 PPC

M22 CALIBERS:
22-250 Rem, 22-250 AI, 25-06 AI, 243 Win, 243 Win, 243 AI, 220 Swift, 257 Roberts, 257 AI, 7-08, 6mm Rem, 6x284, 22 BR, 6 BR, 308 Win, 20 Rem

Cooper Arms Rifles

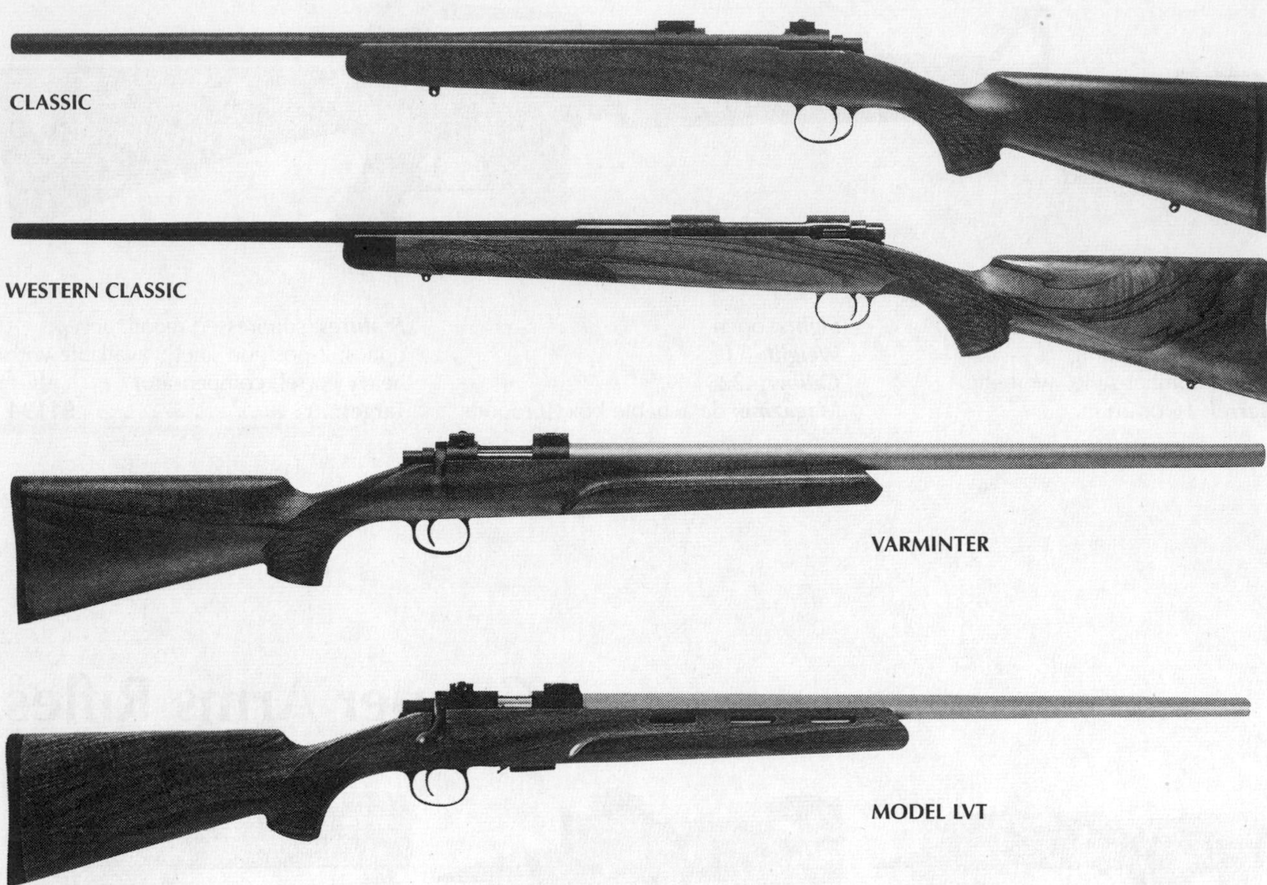

CLASSIC
Action: bolt
Stock: checkered, Claro walnut
Barrel: match grade 22 in.
Sights: none
Weight: 6.5
Caliber: M38, M21 and M22 calibers
Magazine: none
Features: single shot; 3-lug bolt; also available in: Custom Classic and Western Classic with upgraded wood
Classic: $1100
Custom Classic: $1895
Western Classic: $2495

7 PEREGRINE
Action: dropping block
Stock: checkered, Claro walnut
Barrel: match-grade, crome-moly
Sights: open
Weight: 6.5
Caliber: most popular centerfire calibers
Magazine: none
Features: many options available
Peregrine:. $1995

VARMINTER
Action: bolt
Stock: checkered, Claro walnut
Barrel: stainless steel match, 24 in.
Sights: none
Weight: 7.5
Caliber: M38, M21 and M22 calibers
Magazine: none
Features: 3-lug action in 3 sizes; also available: Montana Varminter, Varminter Extreme and Lightweight LVT
Varminter: $995
Montana Varminter: $1295
Varminter Extreme:. $1795
LVT: $1295

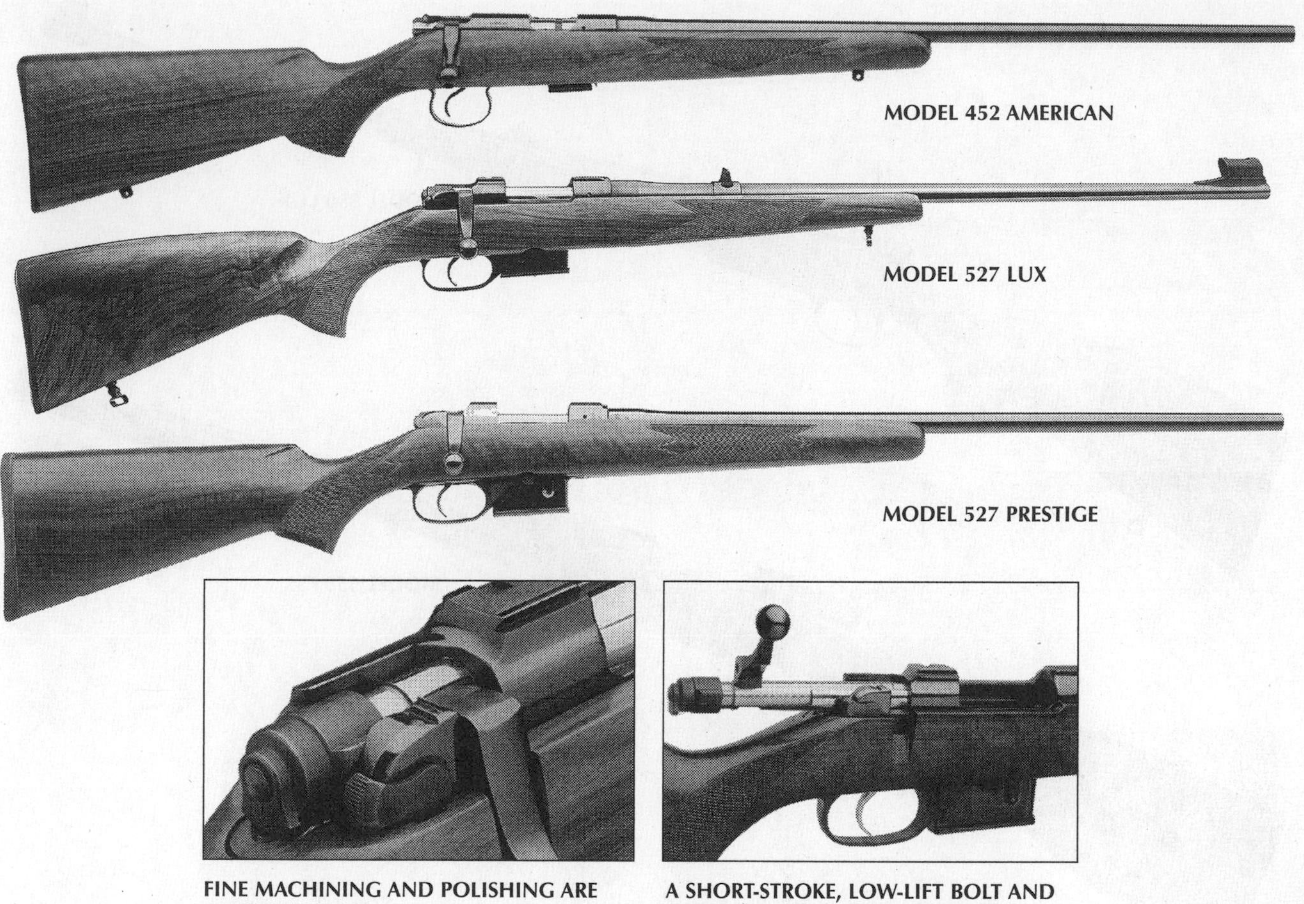

MODEL 452 AMERICAN

MODEL 527 LUX

MODEL 527 PRESTIGE

FINE MACHINING AND POLISHING ARE CZ TRADEMARKS

A SHORT-STROKE, LOW-LIFT BOLT AND DETACHABLE BOX MAGAZINE ARE DESIGNED FOR SMOOTH FEEDING.

THE RIMFIRE RIFLES produced by Ceska Zbrojovka Uhersky Brod are ranked among the best of their kind. Quality, long service life, accuracy and safety are the main virtues of these firearms. The CZ 452 rimfire rifles offer a compact design with a robust Mauser-type action. The rifles feature a tangent rear sight adjustable for elevation and windage. The receiver is factory milled for telescopic sight mounts. The CZ 452 rifles are supplied with a 5-shot magazine.

The CZ 550 series rifles represent a line of elegant, aesthetic and ergonomically designed firearms. The diversified range of CZ 550 rifles feature two-lug bolts with long claw extractors, and adjustable single-stage trigger and two-position thumb safety.

The CZ 527 is a precision repeating rifle, designed for sport shooting and hunting. The single set trigger mechanism is adjustable for both pull and trigger travel. The safety is a two-position rotary lever which locks the trigger mechanism, while simultaneously locking the bolt closed.

Model 452 American

Action: bolt
Stock: checkered walnut sporter
Barrel: 22 in.
Sights: none
Weight: 6.0
Caliber: .22 LR, .22 WMR
Magazine: detachable box, 5 rounds
Features: adjustable trigger; Model 452 Lux has European-style stock and open sights on 24 in. barrel; Varmint version has heavy 22 in. barrel, both weigh 7 lbs. Youth Scout rifle has shortened stock, 16 in. barrel, single loading device and weighs 4 lbs..

American and Lux, .22 LR: $378
.22 WMR $407
.17 HMR $420

Model 527 Lux

Action: bolt
Stock: checkered, walnut sporter
Barrel: 24 in.
Sights: open
Weight: 6.2
Caliber: .22 Hornet, .222, .223
Magazine: detachable box, 5 rounds
Features: single-set, adjustable trigger; also available: CZ 527 Carbine in .223, CZ 527 full stock (FS) in .22 Hornet, .222 and .223 with 20 in. barrel and 527 Prestige in .22 Hornet and .223 with 22 in. barrel

Lux : $582
carbine: $588
FS: $670
Prestige: $854

CZ Rifles

Model 550 Lux

Action: bolt
Stock: checkered walnut sporter
Barrel: 24 in.
Sights: open
Weight: 7.3
Caliber: .243, 6.5x55, .270, 7x57, 7x64, .308, .30-06, 9.3x62
Magazine: box, 5 rounds
Features: adjustable trigger; detachable magazine optional; full-stocked model (FS) available; CZ 550 Safari Magnum has magnum length action, express sights in calibers: .375 H&H, .416 Rigby, .458 Win.

Lux: **$588**
FS: **$684**
Safari magnum: **$833**

Model 550 Varmint

Action: bolt
Stock: walnut
Barrel: heavy varmint 24 in.
Sights: open
Weight: 8.5
Caliber: .308 Win., 22-250
Magazine: box, 5 rounds
Features: laminated stock optional; detachable magazine optional; also available: CZ 550 medium magnum in .7mm Rem. Mag. and .300 Win. Mag.

Varmint: **$633**
Varmint Laminate: **$727**
Medium Magnum: **$670**

Dakota Arms Rifles

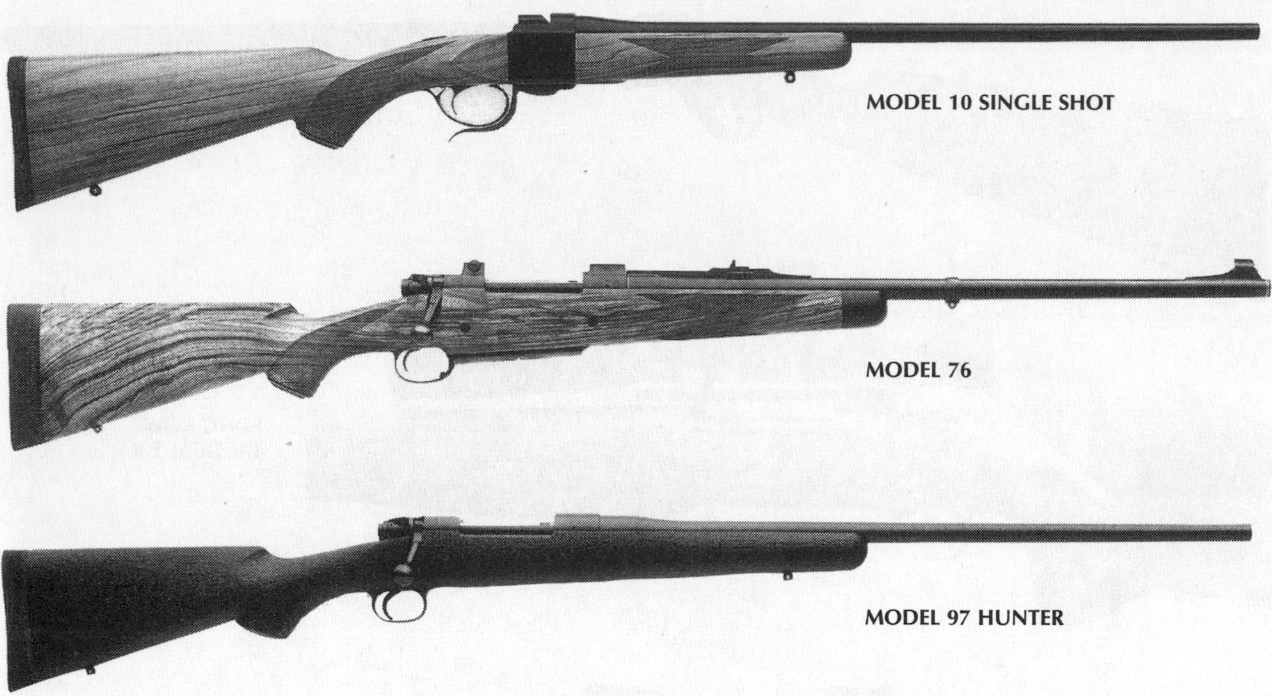

MODEL 10 SINGLE SHOT

MODEL 76

MODEL 97 HUNTER

Model 10 Single Shot

Action: dropping block
Stock: select walnut
Barrel: 23 in.
Sights: none
Weight: 5.5
Caliber: from .22 LR to .375 H&H: magnum: .338 Win. to .416 Dakota
Magazine: none
Features: receiver and rear of breech block are solid steel; removable trigger plate

standard or magnum: $3795
barreled actions: $2050
action only: $1675

Model 76

Action: bolt
Stock: select walnut
Barrel: 23 to 24 in.
Sights: none
Weight: 6.5
Caliber: Safari: from .257 Roberts to .458 Win. Mag. Classic: from ..22-250 through .458 Win. Mag.(inc. WSM). African: .404 Jeffery, .416 Dakota, .416 Rigby, .450 Dakota
Magazine: box, 3 to 5 rounds
Features: three-position striker-blocking safety allows bolt operation with safety on; stock in oil-finished English, Bastogne or Claro walnut; African model weighs 9.5 lbs. and the Safari is 8.5 lbs.

Classic: $3795
Safari: $4795
African: $5495

Model 97 Hunter

Action: bolt
Stock: walnut or composite
Barrel: 24 in.
Sights: open
Weight: 7.0
Caliber: Hunter; .25-06 through .375 Dakota; Lightweight Hunter: .22-250 through .330; Varmint hunter: .17 Rem. through .22-250
Magazine: blind box, 3 to 5 rounds
Features: 1 in. black recoil pad, 2 sling swivel studs; Varmint model has #4 chrome-moly barrel, adjustable trigger, ½ in. black pad and weighs 8 lbs.

Hunter: $2195
97 with semi-fancy wood stock:$2495
action only: $1000
barreled action: $1300

Before taking a shot, inhale deeply, then let your lungs relax. A surge of oxygen improves your vision and sight picture; but if you hold your breath, you tense up and pulse becomes a problem.

Dakota Arms Rifles

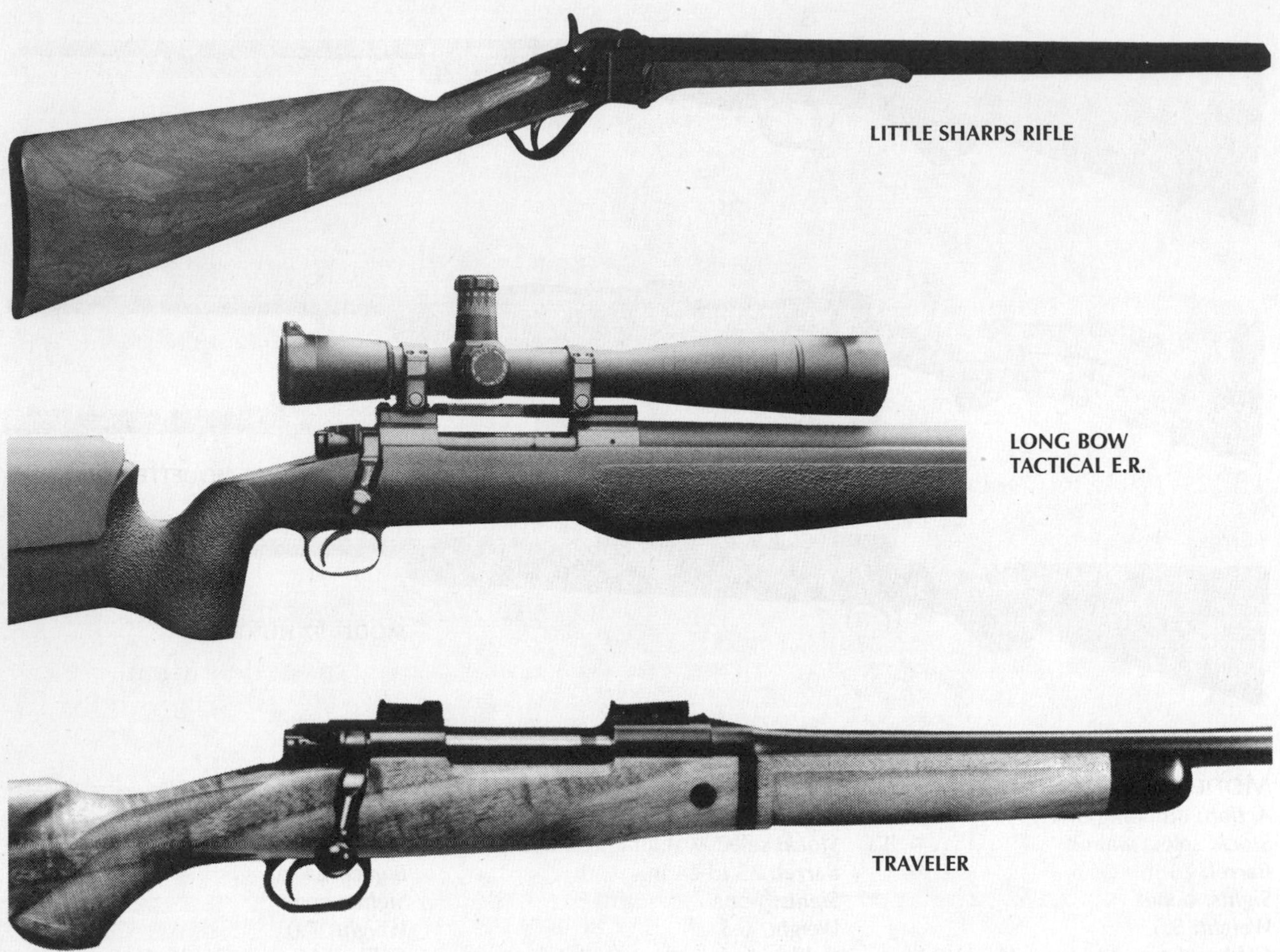

LITTLE SHARPS RIFLE

LONG BOW TACTICAL E.R.

TRAVELER

RIFLES

Double Rifle

Action: hinged breech
Stock: exhibition walnut, pistol grip
Barrel: 25 in.
Sights: open
Weight: 9.5
Caliber: most common calibers
Magazine: none
Features: round action, elective ejectors, recoil pad, Americase
Double Rifle: $25000

Little Sharps Rifle

Action: dropping block
Stock: walnut, straight grip
Barrel: octagon 26 in.
Sights: open
Weight: 8.0
Caliber: .17 HRM to .30-40 Krag
Magazine: none
Features: small frame version of 1874 Sharps
Little Sharps: $3100

Long Bow Tactical E.R.

Action: bolt
Stock: McMillan fiberglass, matte finish
Barrel: stainless, 28 in.
Sights: open
Weight: 13.7
Caliber: .338 Lapua, .300 Dakota and .330 Dakota
Magazine: blind, 3 rounds
Features: Adjustable cheekpiece; 3 sling swivel studs; bipod spike in forend; controlled round feeding; one-piece optical rail; 3-position firing pin block safety; deployment kit; muzzle brake
Tactical E.R.: $4500
Action only: $2400

Traveler

Action: bolt
Stock: take-down, checkered walnut
Barrel: choice of contours, lengths
Sights: none
Weight: 8.5
Caliber: all popular cartridges
Magazine: box, 3 to 5 rounds
Features: The Dakota Traveler is based on the Dakota 76 design. It features threadless disassembly. Weight and barrel length depend on caliber and version.
Classic: $4695
Safari: $5795
African: $6495

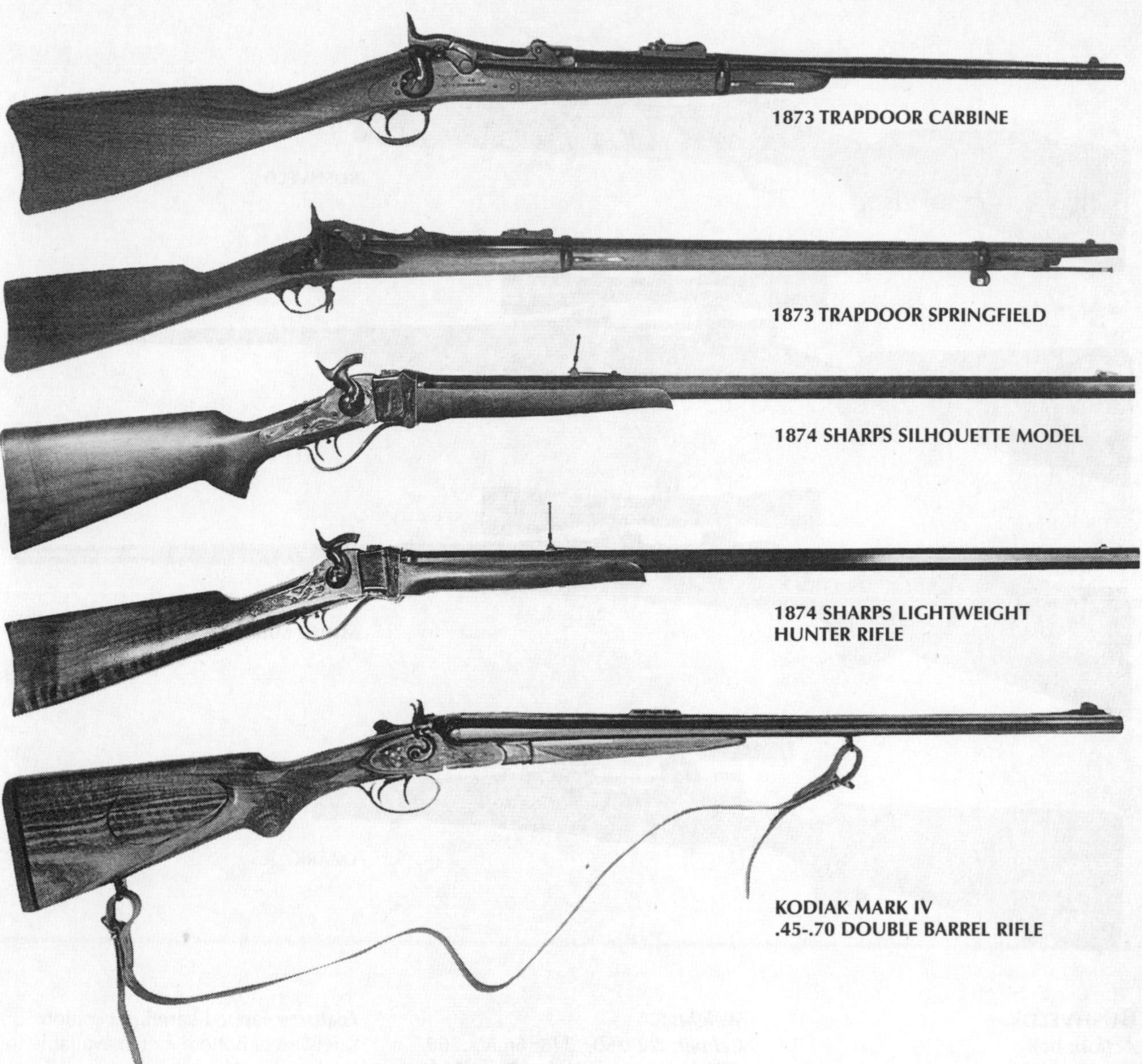

1873 Springfield "Trapdoor"

Action: hinged breech
Stock: walnut
Barrel: 26 or 32 in. (22 in carbine)
Sights: adjustable
Weight: 8.0lbs.
Caliber: .45-70
Magazine: none
Features: single shot rifle, first cartridge rifle of U.S. Army; Officer's Model (26 in.) has checkered stock; weight with 32 in. barrel: 8.5 lbs. and 7.5 lbs. for carbine
1873 Springfield "Trapdoor" . . . $895
Officer's Model $995

1874 Sharps Lightweight Hunter

Action: dropping block
Stock: walnut
Barrel: 30 in.
Sights: ajustable
Weight: 10.0lbs.
Caliber: .45-70
Magazine: none
Features: case-colored receiver, drilled for tang sights; also 1874 Sharps Silhouette Hunter in .40-65 or .45-70
Hunter. $925
Silhouette. $1025

Kodiak Double Rifle

Action: hinged breech
Stock: walnut
Barrel: 24 in.
Sights: open, folding leaf
Weight: 10.0lbs.
Caliber: .45-70
Magazine: none
Features: double-barrel rifle with exposed hammers
Kodiak Double Rifle $2500

Ed Brown Rifles

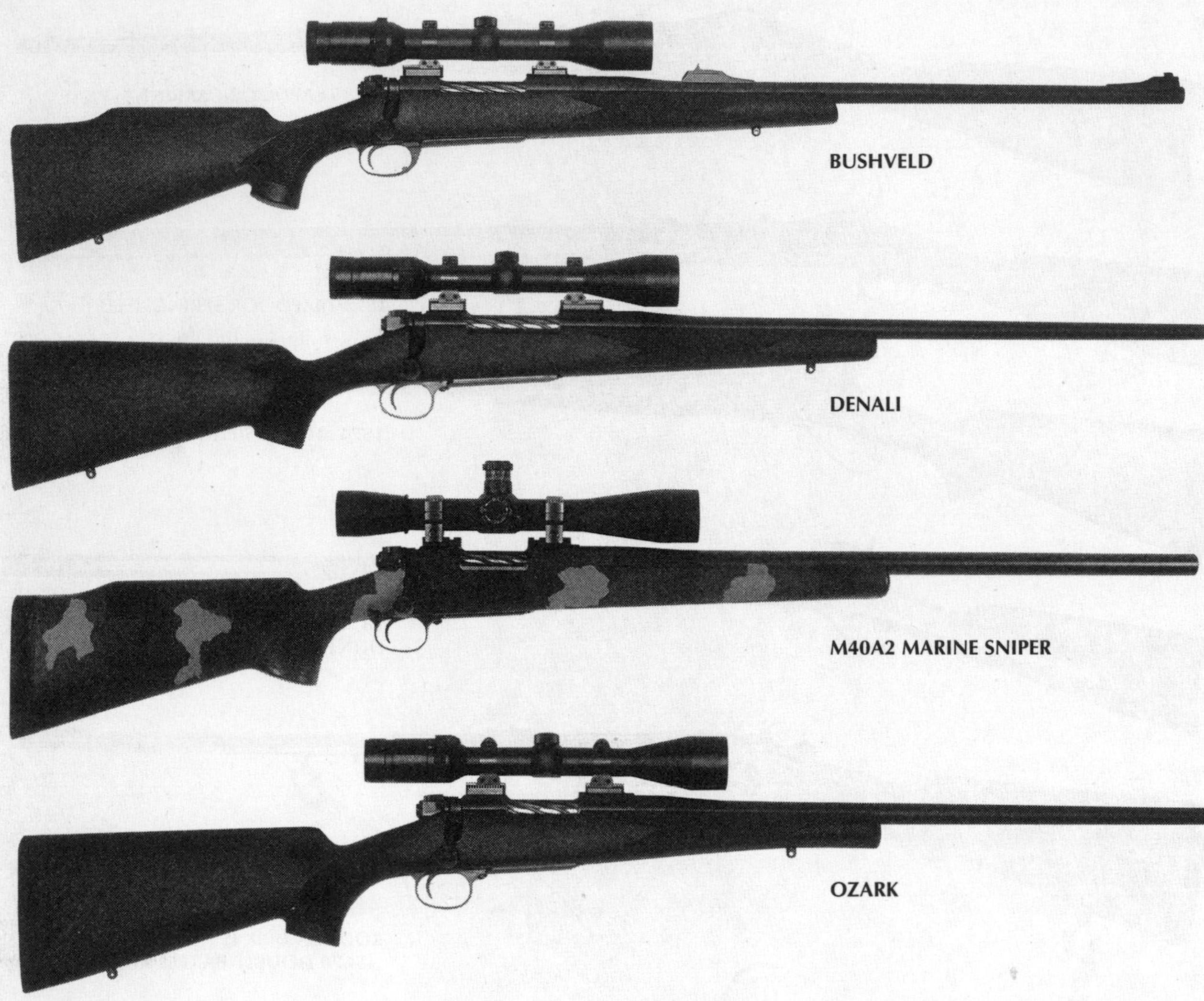

BUSHVELD

DENALI

M40A2 MARINE SNIPER

OZARK

RIFLES

Bushveld

Action: bolt
Stock: McMillan composite
Barrel: medium to heavy 24 in.
Sights: open
Weight: 8.5
Caliber: .338 Win., .375 H&H, .416 Rem., .458 Win. Mag.
Magazine: deep box, 4 rounds
Features: lapped barrel, 3 position safety, steel bottom metal, Talley scope mounts with 8-40 screws; optional QD scope rights, barrel-mounted swivel
Bushveld: $2900

Denali

Action: bolt
Stock: McMillan composite
Barrel: 22 or 23 in.
Sights: none
Weight: 6.8
Caliber: .22-250, .243, 6mm, .260, .270 WSM, 7mm WSM, 7mm/08, .308, .300 WSM
Magazine: box, 3 or 4 rounds
Features: Short action; lapped barrel, 3 position safety, steel bottom metal, Talley scope mounts with 8-40 screws. Also available: Long-action version in .25-06, .270, .280, .30-06, 7mm Rem. Mag.
Denali: $2800

Model 40A2 Marine Sniper

Action: bolt
Stock: McMillan composite tactical
Barrel: heavy match 24 in.
Sights: none
Weight: 9.3
Caliber: .308, .30-06
Magazine: box, 5 rounds
Features: lapped barrel, 3 position safety, steel bottom metal; available in left-hand
Marine Sniper: $2900

Ozark

Action: bolt
Stock: McMillan composite
Barrel: #2 21 in.
Sights: none
Weight: 6.5
Caliber: .223, .243, 6mm, .260, 7mm/08, .308
Magazine: box, 5 rounds
Features: lapped barrel, 3 position safety, steel bottom metal; Talley scope mounts with 8-40 screws
Ozark: $2800

Ed Brown Rifles

SAVANNA

TACTICAL

LIGHT TACTICAL

VARMINT

RIFLES

Savannah

Action: bolt
Stock: McMillan composite
Barrel: #3 lightweight 24 in.
Sights: open
Weight: 8.0
Caliber: .223, .22-250, .243, 6mm, .260, .270 WSM, 7mm/08, 7mm WSM, .308, .300 WSM
Magazine: box, 3 or 5 rounds
Features: short action; lapped barrel, 3 position safety, steel bottom metal; long-action model in .25-06, .270, .280, 7mm Rem. Mag., 7STW, .30-06, .300 Win. Mag., .300 Wby. Mag., .338 Win. Mag. with 26 in. #4 barrel in magnums, 8.5 lbs.
Savannah:. $2800

Tactical

Action: bolt
Stock: McMillan composite tactical
Barrel: heavy 26 in.
Sights: none
Weight: 11.3
Caliber: .308, .300 Win. Mag.
Magazine: box, 3 or 5 rounds
Features: Jewell trigger; Talley scope mounts with 8-40 screws. Also available: Lightweight Tactical with sporter stock, 21 in. medium barrel, 8.8 lbs. in .223 and .308
Tactical:. $2900
Light Tactical:. $2800

Varmint

Action: bolt
Stock: McMillan composite varmint
Barrel: medium 24 in. or heavy 24 in.
Sights: none
Weight: 9.0
Caliber: .223, .22-250, .220 Swift, .243, 6mm, .308
Magazine: none
Features: lapped barrel, 3 position safety, steel bottom metal; optional 2 oz. trigger
Varmint:. $2500

EMF Replica Rifles

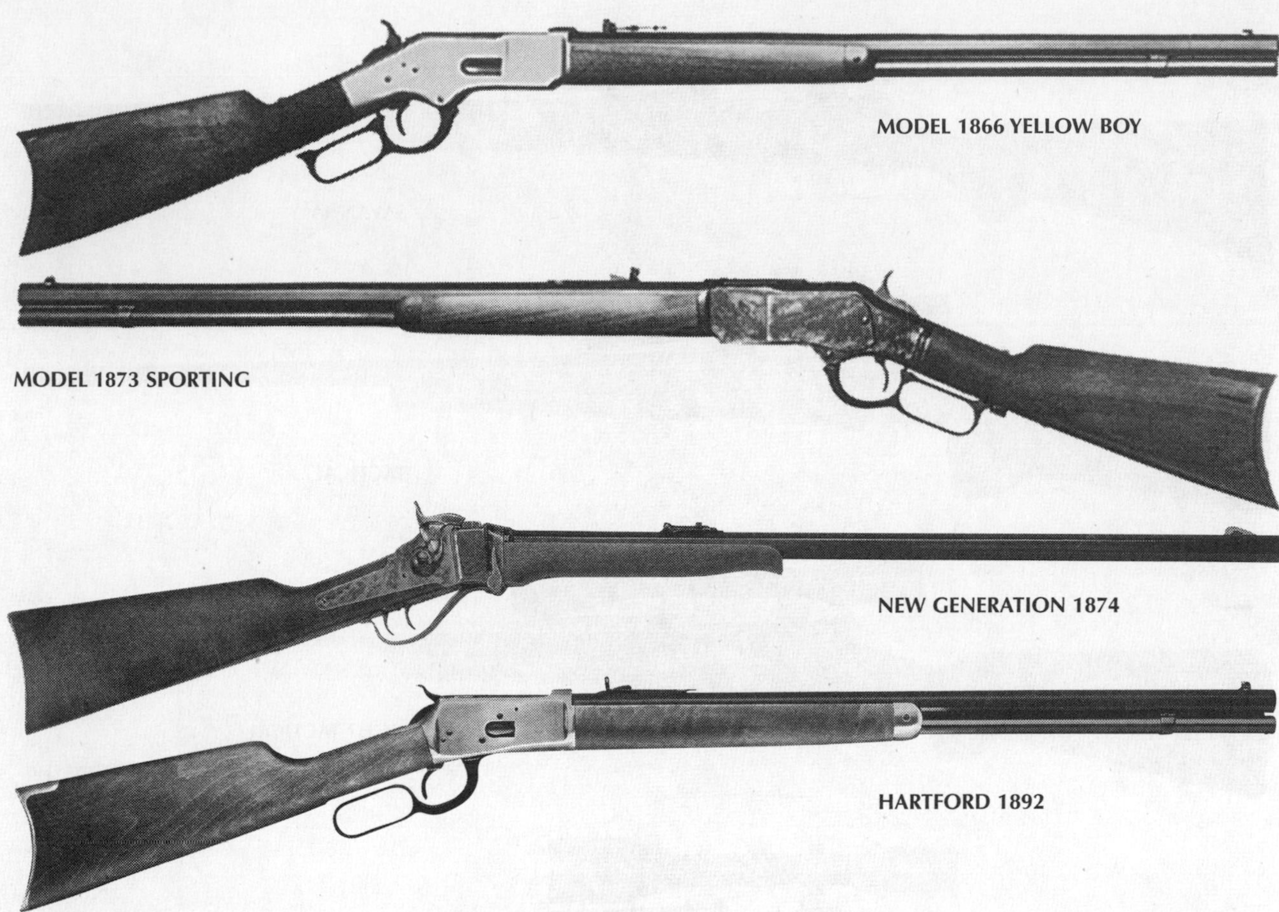

MODEL 1866 YELLOW BOY

MODEL 1873 SPORTING

NEW GENERATION 1874

HARTFORD 1892

RIFLES

MODEL 1860 HENRY

Action: lever
Stock: walnut
Barrel: 24 in.
Sights: open
Weight: 9.3
Caliber: .44-40 and .45 LC
Magazine: under-barrel tube, 11 rounds
Features: blued barrel, brass frame
1860 Henry:. $1100

MODEL 1866 YELLOW BOY

Action: lever
Stock: walnut
Barrel: 24 in.
Sights: open
Weight: 8.0
Caliber: .45 LC, .38 Special and .44-40
Magazine: under-barrel tube, 11 rounds
Features: blued barrel, brass frame
Yellow Boy: $840
carbine:. $800

MODEL 1873 SPORTING

Action: lever
Stock: walnut
Barrel: octagon 24 in.
Sights: open
Weight: 8.1
Caliber: .32-20, .357, .38-40, .44-40, .45 LC; carbine: .32-30, .357, .45LC
Magazine: under-barrel tube, 11 rounds
Features: Magazine tube in blued steel; frame is casehardened; carbine has 20 in. barrel
standard: $1000
carbine: $960

HARTFORD 1892

Action: lever
Stock: walnut
Barrel: octagon or round 24 in.
Sights: open
Weight: 7.5
Caliber: .357 and .45 LC
Magazine: under-barrel tube, 11 rounds
Features: blued, casehardened or stainless steel; carine has 20 in. barrel
blued: $480
case-hardened:. $490
stainless: $530
Carbine, blued, round barrel: . . $400
Carbine, case-hardened, round barrel: $420
Carbine, stainless, round barrel: $460

NEW GENERATION 1874 SHARPS

Action: dropping block
Stock: walnut
Barrel: octagon 28 in.
Sights: open
Weight: 9.0
Caliber: .45-70
Magazine: none
Features: Created by Christian Sharps, this rifle played a major role in the Civil War. Single shot, double-set triggers, Schnabel forearm, barrel in blue, white or brown patina.
1874 Sharps: $880
with brown patina:. $900
with white patina:. $1000
Carbine model: $750

Gibbs Rifle Company

GIBBS RIFLE COMPANY'S Sport Specialty rifles include the Quest II Extreme Carbine. The Quest II is built around on a modern 2A Chrome Vanadium steel barreled action and is chambered for the popular, powerful .308 Winchester. The Quest II's electroless nickel finish protects against the elements and is fitted with a compensator/flash-hider that tames recoil and reduces muzzle jump. Pre-fitted see-through scope mount allows open sights to be used and accepts Weaver-based optics and accessories. The butt trap houses a waterproof survival kit with Brunton liquid-filled compass.

Gibbs Rifle Company's newest addition to its line of historical re-makes includes the arsenal reconditioned Mauser M71/84, the first bolt-action repeating rifle ever built by Paul and Wilhelm Mauser. The M71/84 was adopted by Germany in 1871 and upgraded to an 8-round tubular magazine repeater in 1884. It saw combat in the colonial wars of Africa and in World War I.

These rifles have been reconditioned with original and reproduction parts and returned to arsenal refinished condition.

Model 71/84 (Refurbished)

Action: bolt
Stock: full-length walnut
Barrel: 29 in.
Sights: open
Weight: 8.5
Magazine:
Features: arsenal refurbished metal fitted to new stocks
M71/84:. $300

Quest II Extreme Carbine

Action: bolt
Stock: walnut
Barrel: 19 in. with flash-hider
Sights: open
Weight: 7.0
Caliber: .308
Magazine: detachable box, 10 rounds
Features: British SMLE design; pre-fitted scope mount for Weaver rings; trap buttplate with survival kit
Quest II: $280

Harrington & Richardson Rifles

BUFFALO CLASSIC

ULTRA HUNTER

Buffalo Classic
Action: hinged breech
Stock: checkered walnut
Barrel: 28 and 32 in.
Sights: target
Weight: 8.0
Caliber: .45-70 and .38-55 Target
Magazine: none
Features: single-shot, break-open action; steel buttplate; Williams receiver sight; Lyman target front sight; antique color case-hardened frame
standard or target: $418

Ultra
Action: hinged breech
Stock: hand-checkered, laminate
Barrel: 22, 24, and 26 in.
Sights: none
Weight: 7.0
Caliber: .22 WMR, .223 Rem. and .243 (Varmint), .25-06, .308 Win., .450 Marlin
Magazine: none
Features: Single-shot with break-open action and side lever release. Monte Carlo stock with sling swivels on stock and forend; scope mount included. Weight varies to 8 lbs. with bull barrel. Also available: Ultra Comp with camo stock in .30-06 and .270
Ultra:. $332
Ultra in .22 WMR: $193
Ultra Comp:. $376

RIFLES

Heckler & Koch Rifles

SL8-1 RIFLE

Model SL8-1 .223 Rifle
Action: autoloading
Stock: polycarbonate, combat-style
Barrel: 21 in.
Sights: open
Weight: 8.5
Caliber: .223
Magazine: detachable box, 10 rounds
Features: Picatinny rail for scope mounts; ambidextrous safety and bolt cocking lever; clear polymer magazine; gas operated
SL8-1: $1249

Heckler & Koch Rifles

SLB 2000

USC CARBINE

SLB 2000

Action: autoloading
Stock: polycarbonate sporter-style
Barrel: 22 in.
Sights: open
Weight: 8.0
Caliber: .308, .30-06,
Magazine: detachable box, 5 rounds
Features: gas operated
SLB 2000: $1299

USC .45 ACP Carbine

Action: autoloading
Stock: polycarbonate, combat-style
Barrel: 16 in. hammer-forged
Sights: open
Weight: 6.0
Caliber: .45 ACP
Magazine: detachable box, 10 rounds
Features: Picatinny rail for scope mounting; ambidextrous safety; oversized trigger guard; blow-back action
Carbine:. $1249

Henry Rifles

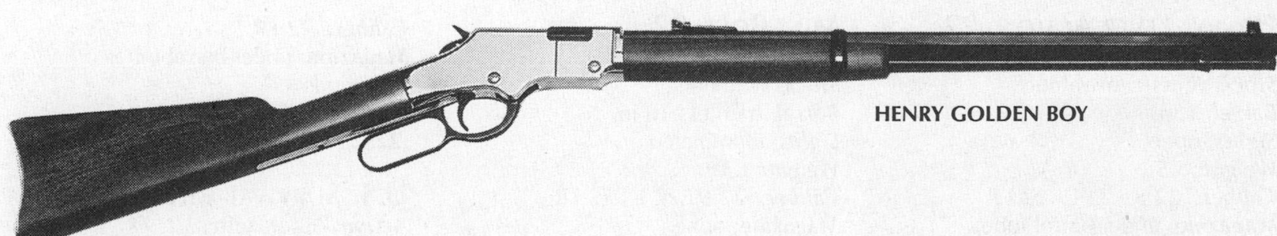

HENRY GOLDEN BOY

Big Boy .44

Action: lever
Stock: walnut, straight grip
Barrel: octagon 20 in.
Sights: open
Weight: 8.7
Caliber: .44 Magnum
Magazine: under-barrel tube, 10 rounds
Features: brass receiver
Big Boy:. $750

Henry Golden Boy

Action: lever
Stock: walnut, straight-grip
Barrel: octagon 20 in.
Sights: open
Weight: 6.8
Caliber: .22 S, .22 L, .22 LR
Magazine: under-barrel tube, 16 to 22 rounds
Features: brass receiver and buttplate per Winchester 66
Golden Boy:. $400

Henry Rifles

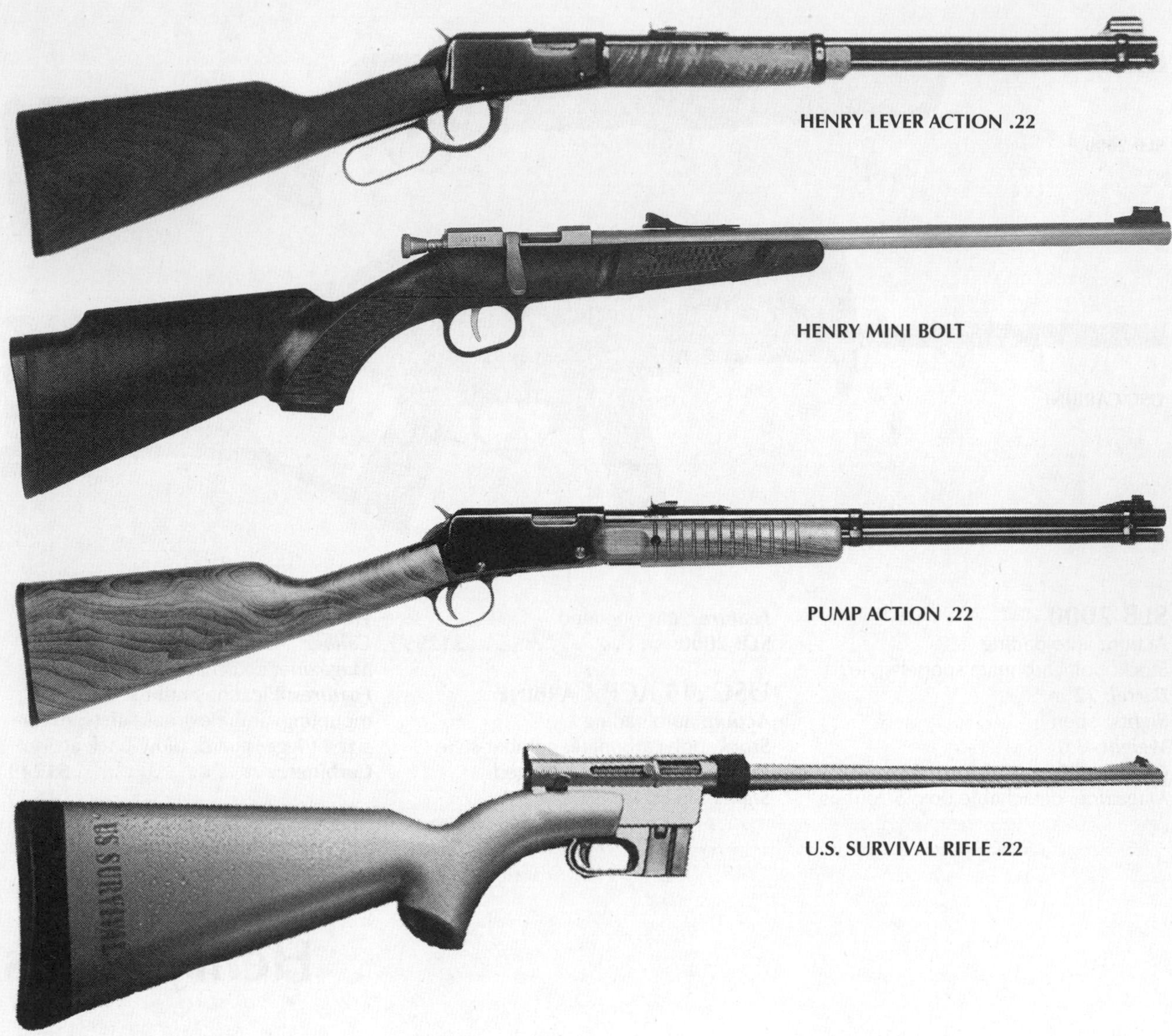

Henry Lever Action .22

Action: lever
Stock: American walnut
Barrel: 18 in.
Sights: open
Weight: 5.5
Caliber: .22 S, .22 L, .22 LR
Magazine: under-barrel tube, 15 to 21 rounds
Features: also available: carbine and youth model, .22 WMR with checkered stock, 19 in. barrel; Varmint Express in .17 HMR with 20 in. barrel and cantilever scope mount
rifle, carbine or youth: $260
magnum: $380
Varmint Express:. $475

Mini Bolt .22

Action: bolt
Stock: synthetic
Barrel: stainless 16 in.
Sights: illuminated
Weight: 3.3
Caliber: .22 S, .22 L, .22 LR
Magazine: none
Features: single-shot; designed for beginners
Mini Bolt:. $200

Pump-Action .22

Action: pump
Stock: walnut
Barrel: 18 in.
Sights: open
Weight: 5.5
Caliber: .22 LR
Magazine: under-barrel tube, 15 rounds
Features: alloy receiver
.22: $300

U.S. Survival Rifle

Action: Autoloading
Stock: synthetic butt stock
Barrel: 16 in.
Sights: open
Weight: 4.5
Caliber: .22 LR
Magazine: detachable box, 8 rounds
Features: barrel and action stow in water-proof, floating stock
Survival Rifle:. $190

H-S Precision Rifles

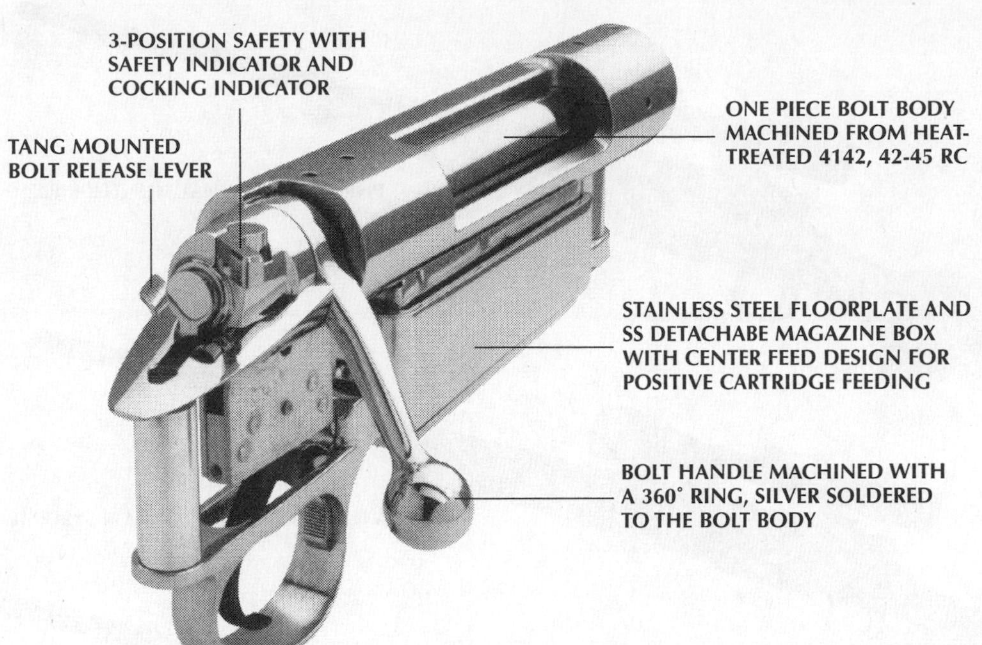

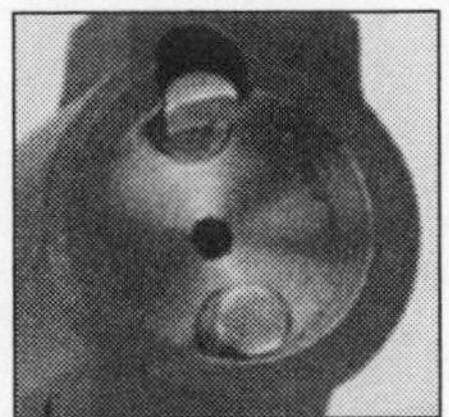

HARDENED STEEL-TIPPED FIRING PIN WITH SPEED LOCK SPRING

IN 1978 TOM HOUGHTON had a degree in chemistry. Instead of getting a job, he started a gun company. "Of course, I couldn't offer a diverse line of guns like Remington or Winchester. And there's no economy of scale with a start-up company." Tom hoped a few shooters would pay a premium for exceptionally accurate rifles. H-S tapped quickly into the tactical and varmint-shooting market and now manufactures big game rifles as well. H-S offers a broad array of synthetic gunstocks, and barrels that have won the allegiance not only of competitive shooters, but ballistics laboratories. "We're the world's leading supplier of pressure, velocity and accuracy test barrels," says Tom proudly. H-S Precision also offers ballistic test equipment, including universal receivers, return-to-battery assemblies, and a laser aiming system. You can get an H-S muzzle brake and scope rings, and after-market bottom metal for your Remington 700.

When visiting H-S Precision's plant in Rapid City, South Dakota some years ago, I was impressed by its cleanliness and efficiency. It was clear that the focus was on quality and attention to tolerances. H-S barrels are all cut rifled in 416R stainless steel and so accurate that all Pro-Series 2000 rifles up to 30-caliber come with a half-minute accuracy guarantee. Most other firms cringe at the thought of any accuracy pledge. It means using the best barrels and ensuring close-tolerance, on-axis assembly of bolt, receiver and barrel. It means bedding the stock securely in a channel that won't shift. "In short, it means doing what we do to give the customer superior accuracy," laughs Tom's daughter, Tricia Hoeke.

I ran ammunition tests with an H-S Precision rifle. This Pro Series 2000, chambered in .223 (1-in-12 twist) routinely drilled out dime-size groups. Like all Pro-Series rifles, my .223 was built around a stainless action with a two-lug bolt. The bolt handle is silver-soldered to a one-piece bolt body. Its semi-cone head incorporates a face-mounted extractor.

A barrel with .0002 uniformity from breech to muzzle is part of the accuracy formula (H-S 10x barrels are given a slight radius at the juncture of land and groove as an additional gas seal). Another ingredient is a rigid H-S fiberglass, Kevlar and carbon fiber stock. "H-S is not really a custom shop," Tricia says, "and we're leaning more and more to producing stock rifles. But we've always tried to accommodate special orders within reason."

RIFLES

H-S Precision Rifles

PHR (PROFESSIONAL HUNTER RIFLE)

VTD (VARMINT TAKE-DOWN SYSTEM)

VAR (VARMINT RIFLE)

PHR (Professional Hunter Rifle)

Action: bolt
Stock: composite
Barrel: 24 to 26 in.
Sights: none
Weight: 8.0
Caliber: all popular magnum calibers up to .375 H&H and .338 Lapua
Magazine: detachable box, 3 rounds
Features: Pro series 2000 action: full-length bedding block, optional 10x Model with match-grade stainless, fluted barrel, muzzle brake, built-in recoil reducer; Lightweight SPR rifle is chambered in standard calibers
PHR: $2200
SPR:. $1950

Take-Down Rifles

Action: bolt
Stock: 2-piece composite
Barrel: any contour and weight 22 to 26 in.
Sights: none
Weight: 8.0
Caliber: any popular standard or magnum chambering
Magazine: detachable box, 3 or 4 rounds
Features: rifle disassembles in front of action and reassembles to deliver identical point of impact; price includes carrying case, TD versions with sporter or tactical stocks; customer's choice of barrels and chambering; left-hand model: add $200
Take-Down: $2500

VAR (Varmint)

Action: bolt
Stock: composite
Barrel: heavy 24 in.
Sights: none
Weight: 11.0
Caliber: all popular varmint calibers
Magazine: detachable box, 4 rounds
Features: Pro-series 2000 action; full-length bedding block; also 10x version with fluted, stainless barrel, optional muzzle
VAR: $1975

Jarrett Custom Rifles

JARRETT 50 CALIBER

SQUIRREL KING HUNTING RIFLE

STANDARD HUNTING RIFLE

WALKABOUT

RIFLES

.50 Caliber

Action: bolt
Stock: McMillan composite
Barrel: 30 to 34 in.
Sights: none
Weight: 35.0
Caliber: .50 BMG
Magazine: none
Features: single-shot; choice of barrel length and contours; rifle comes with load data and 20 rounds of ammunition, military scope mounts and muzzle brake; repeater available
Single shot: $8050
Repeater: $8350

Squirrel King

Action: autoloading
Stock: Brown Precision composite
Barrel: match grade 18 in.
Sights: none
Weight: 6.0
Caliber: .22 LR
Magazine: rotary, 10 rounds
Features: built on Ruger 10/22 action; target and hunting configurations available; Talley rings and bases included; guaranteed 1/2″ groups at 50 yards
Hunting model: $2150
Target model: $2400

Standard Hunting Rifle

Action: bolt
Stock: McMillan synthetic
Barrel: #4 match grade, 24 in.
Sights: none
Weight: 8.5
Caliber: any popular standard or magnum
Magazine: box, 3 or 5 rounds
Features: Shilen trigger; Remington 700 or Winchester 70 action; Talley scope mounts, case, sling, load data and 20 rounds of ammunition; Wind Walker has skeletonized 700 action (7.3 lbs.), muzzle brake. Professional Hunter rifle has additional options
Standard: $4625
Wind Walker: $5300
Professional Hunter: $5300

Walk About

Action: bolt
Stock: synthetic
Barrel: 20 in.
Sights: none
Weight: 7.5
Caliber: any popular short-action
Magazine: box, 3 or 5 rounds
Features: Remington Model 700 short action; includes Talley scope mounts, choice of scope plus case, sling, load data and 20 rounds of ammunition
Walk About: $4625

Johannsen Express Rifles

TRADITION

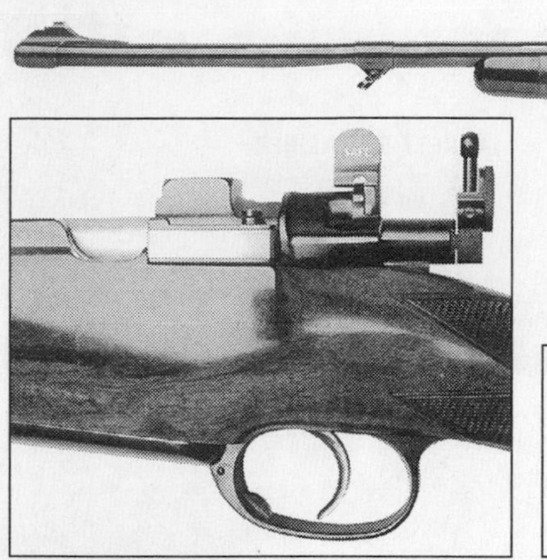

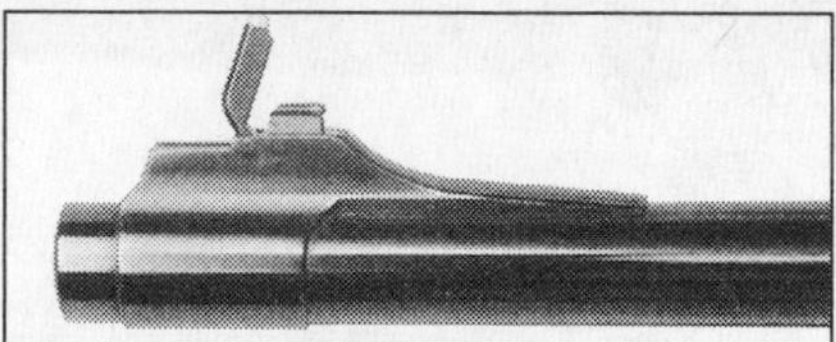

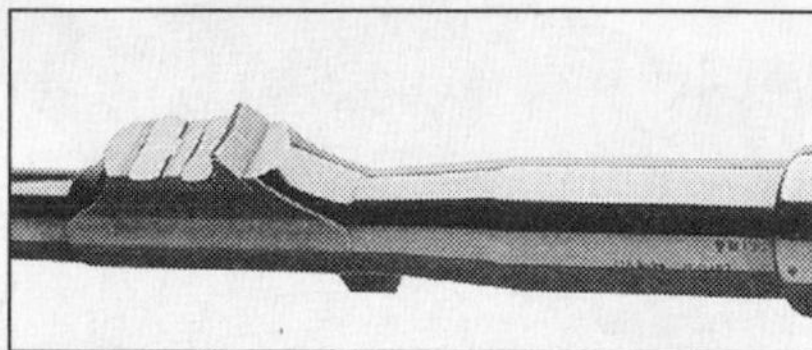

WING SAFETY
The "Classic Safari" features a wing safety with "safe" and "fire" clearly indicated in gold.

PEEP SIGHT
For precision sighting with open sights - or to compensate for less than perfect vision - the peep sight mounted on the cocking piece can be raised into position.

HOLLAND & HOLLAND-TYPE NIGHT SIGHT
The "Classic Safari" and "Safari" models come with a 4-mm ivory bead that can be flipped up to cover the 2-mm silver bead under poor light conditions.

EXPRESS SIGHT
The rear sight with its two leaves fits into a special ring base. The rear sight base extends around the barrel and has the second recoil shoulder on the underside, which is important for large-bore rifles.

SAFARI MAGAZINE CAPACITIES, MAXIMUM:

Normal Caliber	Rigby Floorplate	Floorplate
.300 Weatherby Magnum	4	5
.338-378 Weatherby Magnum	3	4
.375 H & H Magnum	4	5
.416 Rigby	3	4
.450 Dakota	3	4
.500 Jeffery	3	4

Other calibers upon request.

THREE MODELS of this rifle are available - the "Classic Safari", the "Safari" and the "Tradition". The "Classic Safari", is the choice of hunters after African big game. The "Safari" is designed for scope use as well. The "Tradition" is ideal for the globe-trotting big-game hunter. All models are available in several chamberings with standard and custom features, and each rifle is produced individually. A Johannsen Express Rifle represents true custom work.

Safari

Double square bridge action without thumbcut. 4-lb. double-pull trigger. Three-position safety with horizontal lever. Bolt handle close to side of action. Especially suitable for EXPERT scope mount. 2-mm silver bead combined with fold-away 4-mm Holland & Holland-type ivory bead. Express sight with two leaves. Safari-style stock with 1¾"/2½" drop. Oil finish. 26" barrel. Length overall 47". Weight from approx. 8 lbs. 6 oz. depending upon caliber. **Standard calibers:** .375 H & H Magnum, 4-shot, or .416 Rigby, 3-shot.
Price: $10,250

Classic Safari

Single square bridge action with thumbcut. 4-lb. double-pull trigger. Three-position wing safety. Traditional bolt handle. 2-mm silver bead combined with a fold-away 4-mm Holland & Holland-type ivory bead. Express sight with two leaves. Safari-style stock with 1¾"/2½" drop. Oil finish. 24" barrel. Length overall 45". Weight from approx. 8 lbs. 3 oz. depending upon caliber. **Standard calibers:** .375 H & H Magnum, 4-shot, or .416 Rigby. 3-shot.
Price: 9,500

Tradition

Double square bridge action without thumbcut. Adjustable-pull single-set trigger. Three-position safety with horizontal lever. Low bolt handle. Especially suitable for EXPERT scope mount. "Masterpiece" front sight base with 2.5-mm fluorescent bead. Express sight with two leaves. Stock with straight comb and 1¾"/2" drop. Oil finish. 26" barrel. Length overall 47". Weight from approx. 8 lbs. depending upon caliber. **Standard calibers:** .300 Weatherby Magnum, 4-shot, .375 H & H Magnum, 4-shot.
Price: 10,550

KBI/Charles Daly Rifles

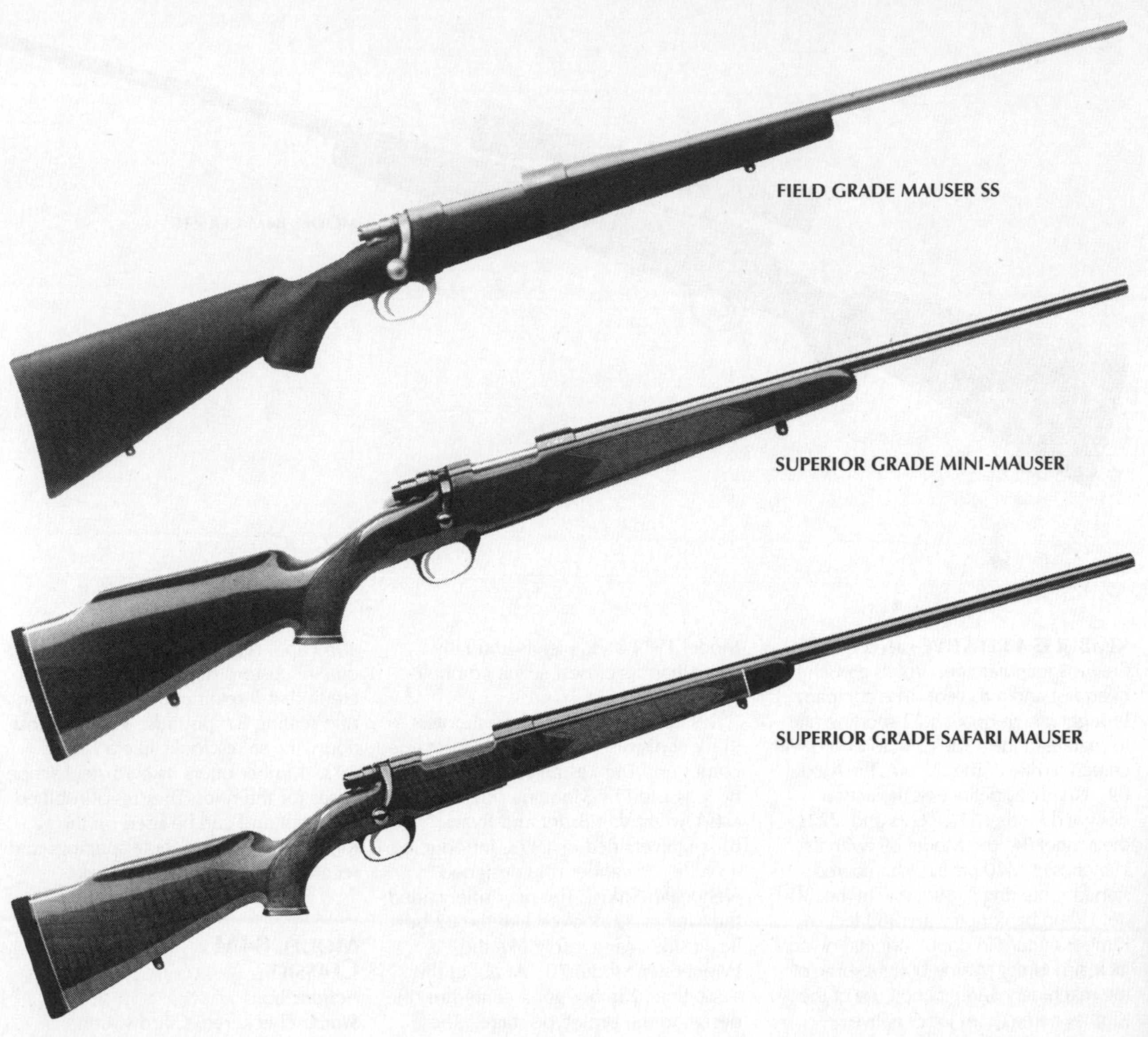

FIELD GRADE MAUSER SS

SUPERIOR GRADE MINI-MAUSER

SUPERIOR GRADE SAFARI MAUSER

FIELD GRADE MAUSER
Action: bolt
Stock: synthetic
Barrel: 22 or 24 in.
Sights: none
Weight: 7.0
Caliber: .22-250, .243, .25-06, .270, 7mm Rem. Mag., .308, .30-06, .300 Win. Mag.
Magazine: box, 3 or 5 rounds
Features: Mauser 98 action; stainless barrel available; also Superior grade with walnut stock and high-polish blue and Superior grade Mini Mauser in .22 Hornet, .223, 7.62x39 with 20 in. barrel; superior grade Safari available in .375 H&H and .458 Win.

field grade:. $459
stainless: $509
magnum: $499
magnum stainless: $539
Superior grade and superior mini: $529
Superior magnum: $559
Superior safari:. $729

Kimber Rifles

MODEL 84M CLASSIC

KIMBER IS A RELATIVE late-comer to firearms manufacture. But its growth has been fast and turbulent. The company brought a high-quality .22 sporting rifle to market in the 1980s and followed with centerfire rifles. The .22 was the Model 82. Nearly as petite was the action designed for the .17s, .222s and .223s -- the Model 84. The Model 89, with its Winchester M70 profile, chambered standard hunting cartridges like the .30-06. When bankruptcy in 1989 left Kimber's future in doubt, original owners Jack and Gregg Warne bought some of the machinery and retained use of the Kimber name (from Jack's native Australia). By 1992 a revamped .22, the 82C, was in production.

RIFLES

Les Edelman emerged from the bankruptcy proceedings as majority stakeholder in a new gun company. In 1995, handgun sports were becoming more popular, and many people were concerned with the effect of stricter regulations on the availability of handguns. Les Edelman thought there'd be a market for high-quality pistols based on the 1911 Colt. He enlisted both the reputation and expertise of ace pistol shooter Chip McCormick, bought a factory in Yonkers and began turning out pistols, projecting a run of 5000. His projection proved conservative; now the Kimber plant makes 44,000 Model 1911-style pistols annually, more than its closest seven competitors combined.

It's no wonder that some shooters think of pistols when the Kimber name comes up. But Les and his company, now assisted by Montana rifle enthusiasts Dwight Van Brunt and Ryan Busse, diversified in 1998, introducing a svelte .22 caliber rifle designed by Nehemiah Sirkis. The new rifle, called the Kimber 22, looked like the 82 but has a side-swing safety like the Winchester Model 70. At about the same time, Kimber got a centerfire rifle design to the prototype stage. The Model 770, designed by Jack Warne and Pete Grisel, never made it to market, but now there's an 84M, also designed by Sirkis. Initially bored for the .243, .260, 7mm-08 and .308 (as well as the .22-250), it weighs 5½ pounds with a 22-inch barrel and classic-style walnut stock designed by Darwin Hensley. The stock is trim, with conservative lines. It is glassed and pillar-bedded to the action. The barrel floats and an A 1-inch Pachmayr decelerator pad is standard.

This Kimber lightweight has a match-grade trigger and match-grade barrel. There's a Mauser-style extractor, steel bottom metal (a floorplate with release button in the guard) and a steel grip cap – refinements you see on best-quality custom rifles. It is to Kimber's credit that it retained these features in a rifle scaling 5½ pounds. The two-position wing safety looks like a Model 70's. Kimber offers its own steel scope bases for the rifle. They're satin-blued to match and can be used on the Kimber 22, because hole spacings and receiver diameters are the same.

Model 84M Classic

Action: bolt
Stock: checkered, Claro walnut
Barrel: light sporter, 22 in.
Sights: none
Weight: 5.6
Caliber: .243, .260, 7mm-08, .308
Magazine: box, 5 rounds
Features: also Varmint model (7.4 lbs.) in .22-250 with 26 in. stainless, fluted barrel; Long Master Classic (7.4 lbs) in .308 with 24 in. stainless, fluted barrel and Long Master VT (10 lbs.) in .22-250 with stainless, bull barrel, laminated target stock

Classic: **$917**
Varmint : **$1001**
Long Master Classic:. **$1001**
Long Master VT: **$1122**
Long Master Pro. **$1189**
Super America **$1764**

Kimber

Classic

Action: bolt
Stock: checkered, Claro walnut
Barrel: 22 in. match grade
Sights: none
Weight: 5.5
Caliber: .22 LR
Magazine: detachable box, 5 rounds
Features: Model 70-type safety; bead blasted finish; deluxe checkering, hand-rubbed finish; 50-yard groups less than .4 in.; also available: no-frills Hunter model and Youth Hunter with shorter barrel; Super America with fancy Claro stock with wrap-around checkering
Classic: $1085
Hunter: $678
Super America:. $1764

HS (Hunter Silhouette)

Action: bolt
Stock: high-comb walnut
Barrel: medium-heavy, half-fluted 24 in.
Sights: none
Weight: 7.0
Caliber: .22 LR
Magazine: detachable box, 5 rounds
Features: designed for NRA rimfire silhouette competition
HS: $813

SVT (Short Varmint Target)

Action: bolt
Stock: heavy, competition style
Barrel: extra heavy, fluted, stainless 18 in.
Sights: none
Weight: 7.5
Caliber: .22 LR
Magazine: detachable box, 5 rounds
Features: bead-blasted blue; gray laminated stock
SVT:. $949

Krieghoff Rifles

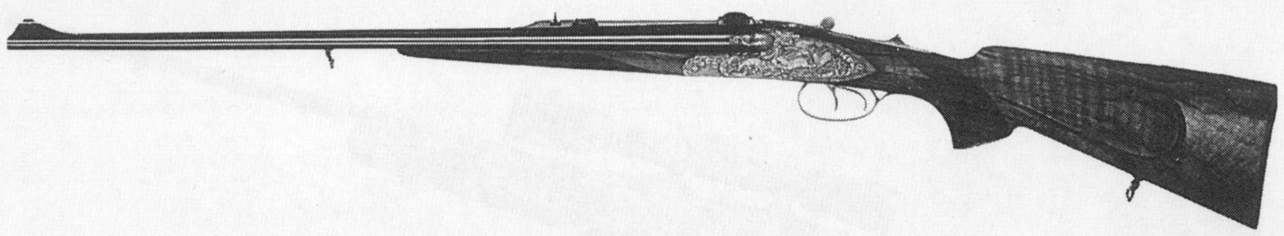

CLASSIC SIDE-BY-SIDE DOUBLE RIFLE

Classic Side-by-Side

Action: hinged breech
Stock: select walnut
Barrel: 23.5 in.
Sights: open
Weight: 8.0
Caliber: 7x65R, .308, .30-06, .30R Blaser, 8x57, 9.3x74, .375 H&H, .416 Rigby, .458 Win., .470 N.E., .500 N.E.
Magazine: none

Features: thumb-cocking, break-action; double triggers; optional 21.5 in. barrel; engraved side plates; weight depends on chambering and barrel contour

standard calibers:.......... $7850
magnum calibers:.......... $9450
extra barrels with forearm (fitted): $4500
magnum barrels:.......... $5500

L.A.R. Rifles

RIFLES

GRIZZLY BIG BOAR

Grizzly Big Boar

Action: bolt
Stock: all steel sleeve with rubber butt pad
Barrel: 36 in.
Sights: none
Weight: 30.4
Caliber: .50 BMG
Magazine: none
Features: Bull Pup single-shot; descending pistol grip; bi-pod; finish options

Grizzly:................. $2195
Parkerized:.............. $2295
nickel-frame: $2445
full nickel: $2545

Lazzeroni Rifles

MODEL L2000DG

MODEL L2000SA

MODEL L2000SP

MODEL L2000ST

RIFLES

Model L2000DG

Action: bolt
Stock: composite
Barrel: 24 in.
Sights: none
Weight: 8.0
Caliber: 10.57 (.416) Meteor
Magazine: box, 4 rounds
Features: matchgrade, stainless steel barrel; fully adjustable trigger, aluminum pillar block bedding; barrel mounted swivel stud
L2000DG: $5500

Model L2000SA

Action: bolt
Stock: composite
Barrel: 24 in.
Sights: none
Weight: 6.8
Caliber: 6.17 (.243) Spitfire, 6.71 (.264) Phantom, 7.21 (.284) Tomahawk, 7.82 (.308) Patriot, 8.59 (.338) Galaxy
Magazine: box, 4 rounds
Features: match-grade, stainless steel barrel, fully adjustable trigger; aluminum pillar block bedding; left-hand available.
L2000SA: $5500

Model L2000SP

Action: bolt
Stock: thumbhole (right hand only), composite
Barrel: 25 in.
Sights: none
Weight: 7.8
Caliber: 6.53 (.257) Scramjet, 7.21 (.284) Firebird, 7.82 (.308) Warbird, 8.59 (.338) Titan
Magazine: box, 4 round
Features: matchgrade, stainless steel barrel; fully adjustable trigger; aluminum pillar block bedding
L2000SP: $5500

Model L2000ST

Action: bolt
Stock: composite
Barrel: 27 in.
Sights: none
Weight: 8.1
Caliber: 6.53 (.257) Scramjet, 7.21(.284) Firebird, (.308) 7.82 Warbird, (.338) 8.59 Titan
Magazine: box, 4 rounds
Features: stainless steel matchgrade barrel; fully adjustable trigger; aluminum pillar block bedding; left-hand stock available
L2000ST: $5499

Legacy Sports

HOWA

MODEL 1500 LIGHTNING
Action: bolt
Stock: Black Polymer (Hunter) Walnut
Barrel: 22 in.
Sights: none
Weight: 7.6 lbs.
Caliber: Popular standard and magnum calibers from .223 Rem. to.300 WSM
Magazine: box, 5 rounds
Features: choice of blue or stainless; 22 in. (standard) or 24 in. (magnum) barrels; barreled actions are available
blue finish standard: $479
magnum: $502
stainless standard: $585
magnum: $612

MODEL 1500 HUNTER
Action: bolt
Stock: American walnut
Barrel: 22 in.
Sights: none
Weight: 7.6 lbs.
Caliber: popular standard and magnum calibers from .223 Rem. to.300 WSM
Magazine: box, 5 rounds
Features: choice of blue or stainless; 22 in. (standard) or 24 in. (magnum) barrels; varmint model in .223, .22-50 and .308;
blue finish standard: $539
magnum: $560
stainless: standard: $638
magnum: $662

MODEL 1500 VARMINT
Action: bolt
Stock: Black Polymer or American walnut
Barrel: 22 in.
Sights: none
Weight: 9.3 lbs.
Caliber: .223, .22-50 and .308
Magazine: box, 5 rounds
Features: choice of blue or stainless; 24 in. barrels; wood stocks with weather-resistant finish and laser-stippled grip and forearm panels
blue finish black polymer:. $517
walnut:. $575
stainless black polymer: $626
walnut:. $677

MODEL 1500 ULTRALIGHT
Action: bolt
Stock: Black texture wood
Barrel: 20 inches
Sights: none
Weight: 6.4 lbs.
Caliber: .243 Win.
Magazine: box, 5 rounds
Features: mill-cut lightweight receiver; wood stock with textured flat black finish, blue finish
1500 Ultralight. $511

MAUSER

MAUSER M98 RIFLE
Action: bolt
Stock: American walnut
Barrel: 24 in.
Sights: none
Weight: 8.4 lbs.
Caliber: .300 WinMag. (Big Five available in choice of magnum calibers)
Magazine: box, 5 round
Features: large, non-rotating extractor; one-piece machined bolt with low-profile handle; three-position thumb safety mounted on the cocking piece; fully adjustable trigger; integral scope-mounting rails on square-bridge receiver; fully adjustable trigger.
M98 Rifle: $955
Big-Five Ultramag: $3,056

Lone Star Rifles

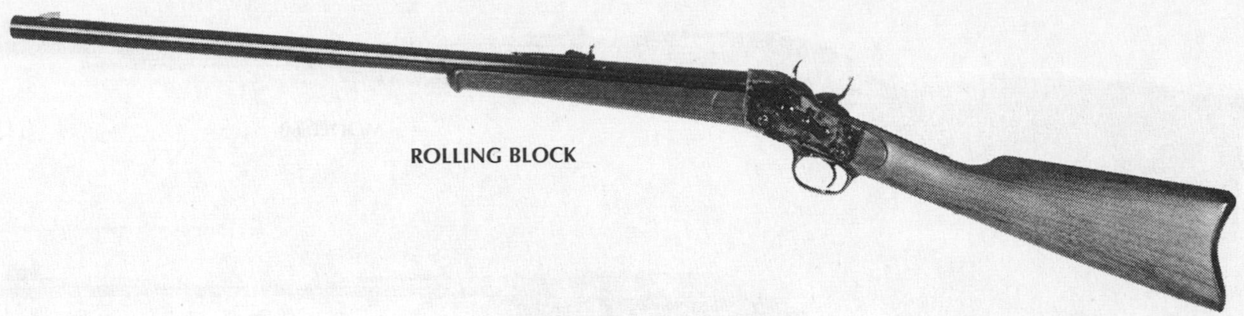

ROLLING BLOCK

ROLLING BLOCK
Action: dropping block
Stock: walnut
Barrel: all standard lengths
Sights: open
Weight: 7.0
Caliber: ..25-35, .30-30, 30-40, 32-40, .38-55, .40-65, .40-70, .45-70, .45-90, .45-110, .50-70, .50-90.
Magazine: none
Features: true-to-form replicas of post-Civil War Remington rolling blocks; single trigger, case-colored actions on Blackpowder Silhouette, Creedmoor, Sporting, Deluxe Sporting, Buffalo Rifle, Custer Commemorative, Gove Underlever and Cowboy
standard: $1595

Magnum Research Rifles

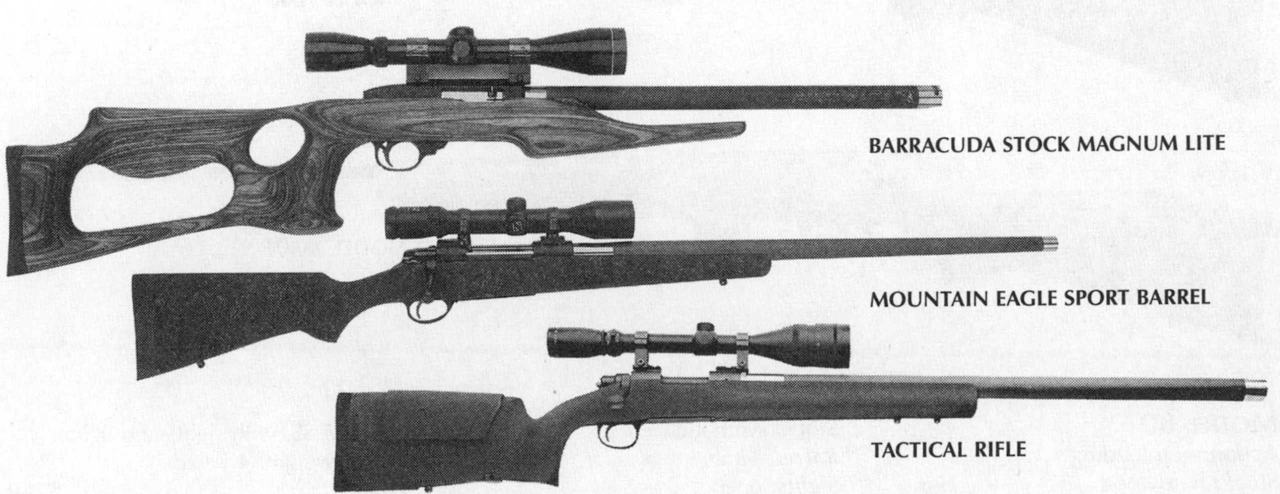

BARRACUDA STOCK MAGNUM LITE

MOUNTAIN EAGLE SPORT BARREL

TACTICAL RIFLE

MAGNUM LITE RIMFIRE
Action: autoloading
Stock: Hogue composite or Turner laminated
Barrel: graphite sleeved, 18 in.
Sights: none
Weight: 5.2
Caliber: .22LR and .22 WMR
Magazine: rotary, 10 rounds
Features: Ruger 10/22 action; carbon-fiber barrel sleeve (75% lighter than steel); muzzle porting
with composite stock:. $599
with laminated stock: $799
magnum with composite: $799
magnum with laminated: $999

MOUNTAIN EAGLE
Action: bolt
Stock: composite
Barrel: graphite, sleeved 24 or 26 in.
Sights: none
Weight: 7.8
Caliber: .280, .30-06, 7mm Rem. Mag., .300 Win. Mag.,
Magazine: box, 3 or 4 rounds
Features: adjustable trigger, free-floating match-grade barrel; platform bedding system; steel bottom metal; left-hand available
Mountain Eagle: $2295
Varmint model: $2295

TACTICAL RIFLE
Action: bolt
Stock: H-S Precision, synthetic tactical
Barrel: graphite sleeved 26 in.
Sights: open
Weight: 8.3
Caliber: .223, .22-250, .300 WSM, .308, .300 Win. Mag.
Magazine: box, 3 or 5 rounds
Features: accurized Rem. 700 action; adjustable comb; adjustable trigger
Tactical: $2400

Marlin Rifles

MODEL 60

MODEL 70PSS "PAPOOSE"

MODEL 7000

MODEL 25MN

Model 60

Action: autoloading
Stock: hardwood
Barrel: 19 in.
Sights: open
Weight: 5.5lbs.
Caliber: .22 LR
Magazine: under-barrel tube, 14 rounds
Features: last shot hold-open device; stainless, synthetic and laminated stocked versions available; also available with camo-finished stock

standard **$185**
stainless **$235**
stainless, synthetic **$257**
stainless, laminated **$297**

Model 70 PSS Papoose

Action: autoloading
Stock: synthetic
Barrel: 16 in.
Sights: open
Weight: 3.3lbs.
Caliber: .22 LR
Magazine: detachable box, 7 rounds
Features: take-down rifle; nickel-plated swivel studs; floatable, padded carrying case included

Papoose **$3094**

Model 7000

Action: autoloading
Stock: synthetic
Barrel: target weight, 28 in.
Sights: none
Weight: 5.3lbs.
Caliber: .22 LR
Magazine: detachable box, 10 rounds
Features: also available as Model 795 and 795 SS, with sights and lighter barrel (weight: 4.5 lbs.)

7000 . . . . **$249**
795 . . . . **$176**
795 SS **$235**

Model 25MN

Action: bolt
Stock: hardwood
Barrel: 22 in.
Sights: open
Weight: 6.0lbs.
Caliber: .22 WMR
Magazine: detachable box, 7 rounds
Features: Micro-Groove barrel; also available with Mossy Oak camo-finish stock

25MN **$241**
25MNC (camo) **$278**

Marlin Rifles

MODEL 25MN CAMO

MODEL 81TS

MODEL 83TS

MODEL 17VS

LITTLE BUCKAROO

Model 25N

Action: bolt
Stock: hardwood
Barrel: 22 in.
Sights: open
Weight: 5.5lbs.
Caliber: .22 LR
Magazine: detachable box, 7 rounds
Features: Micro-Groove rifling; can be ordered with scope; also available with Mossy Oak camo stock finish

25N **$212**
25N with scope **$220**
25NC (camo) **$248**

Model 81TS

Action: bolt
Stock: synthetic
Barrel: 22 in.
Sights: open
Weight: 6.0lbs.
Caliber: .22 LR
Magazine: under-barrel tube, 17 rounds
Features: Micro-Groove rifling

81TS **$213**

Model 83TS

Action: bolt
Stock: synthetic
Barrel: 22 in.
Sights: open
Weight: 6.0lbs.
Caliber: .22 WMR
Magazine: under-barrel tube, 12 rounds
Features: Micro-Groove rifling; available as Model 883 with walnut stock or laminated stock and stainless barrel

83TS **$259**
Model 883 . . . . **$337**
Model 883 SS **$358**

Model 17V

Action: bolt
Stock: hardwood
Barrel: heavy 22 in.
Sights: none
Weight: 6.0lbs.
Caliber: .17 HMR
Magazine: detachable box, 7 rounds
Features: 1-in. scope mounts provided; also available: 17VS stainless steel with laminated hardwood stock (7 lbs.)

17V **$269**
17VS **$402**

Little Buckaroo

Action: bolt
Stock: hardwood
Barrel: 16 in.
Sights: open
Weight: 4.3lbs.
Caliber: .22LR
Magazine: none
Features: stainless version available

Little Buckaroo **$209**
stainless **$233**

Marlin Rifles

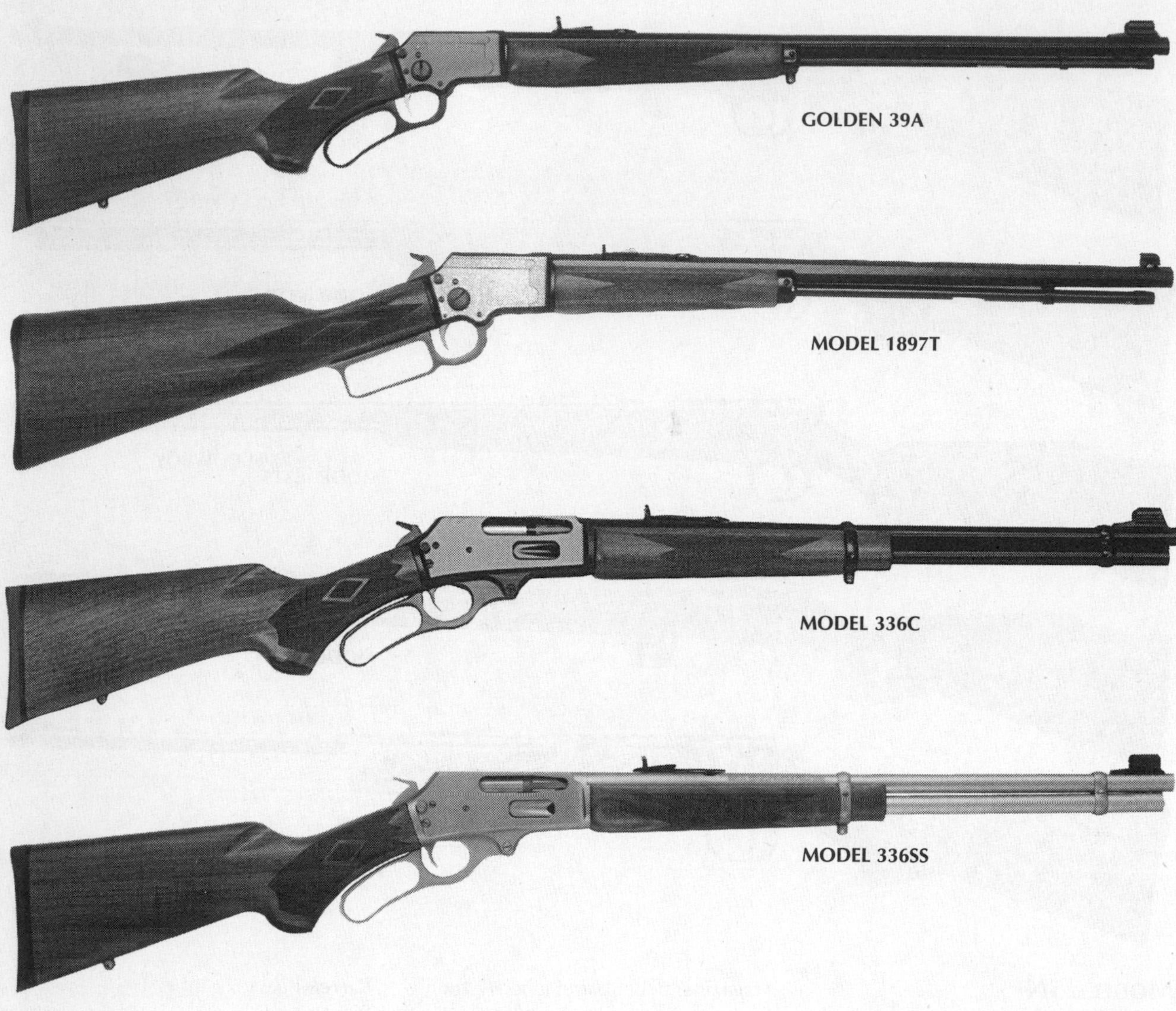

RIFLES

Golden 39A

Action: lever
Stock: checkered walnut, pistol grip
Barrel: 24 in.
Sights: open
Weight: 6.5lbs.
Caliber: .22 LR
Magazine: under-barrel tube, 19 rounds
Features: Micro-Groove rifling, single-screw take-down; swivel studs
Golden 39A $552

Model 1897T

Action: lever
Stock: checkered walnut, straight grip
Barrel: 21 in.
Sights: open
Weight: 6.0lbs.
Caliber: .22 LR
Magazine: under-barrel tube, 14 rounds
Features: Micro-Groove rifling; single-screw take-down
1897T $748

Model 336C

Action: lever
Stock: checkered walnut, pistol grip
Barrel: 20 in.
Sights: open
Weight: 7.0lbs.
Caliber: .30-30 Win., and .35 Rem.
Magazine: tube, 6 rounds
Features: blued, hammer-block safety, offset hammer spur for scope use
Model 336C. $529
Model 336A, .30-30 only, birch stock $451
Model 336W, .30-30 only, camo stock. $503
Model 336W, .30-30 only, gold-plated. $457
Model 336Y, .30-30 only, 16 in. bbl. $536

Model 336SS

Action: lever
Stock: checkered walnut, pistol grip
Barrel: 20 in.
Sights: open
Weight: 7.0lbs.
Caliber: .30-30
Magazine: under-barrel tube, 6 rounds
Features: offset hammer spur for scope use; Micro-Groove rifling
336SS $640

Marlin Rifles

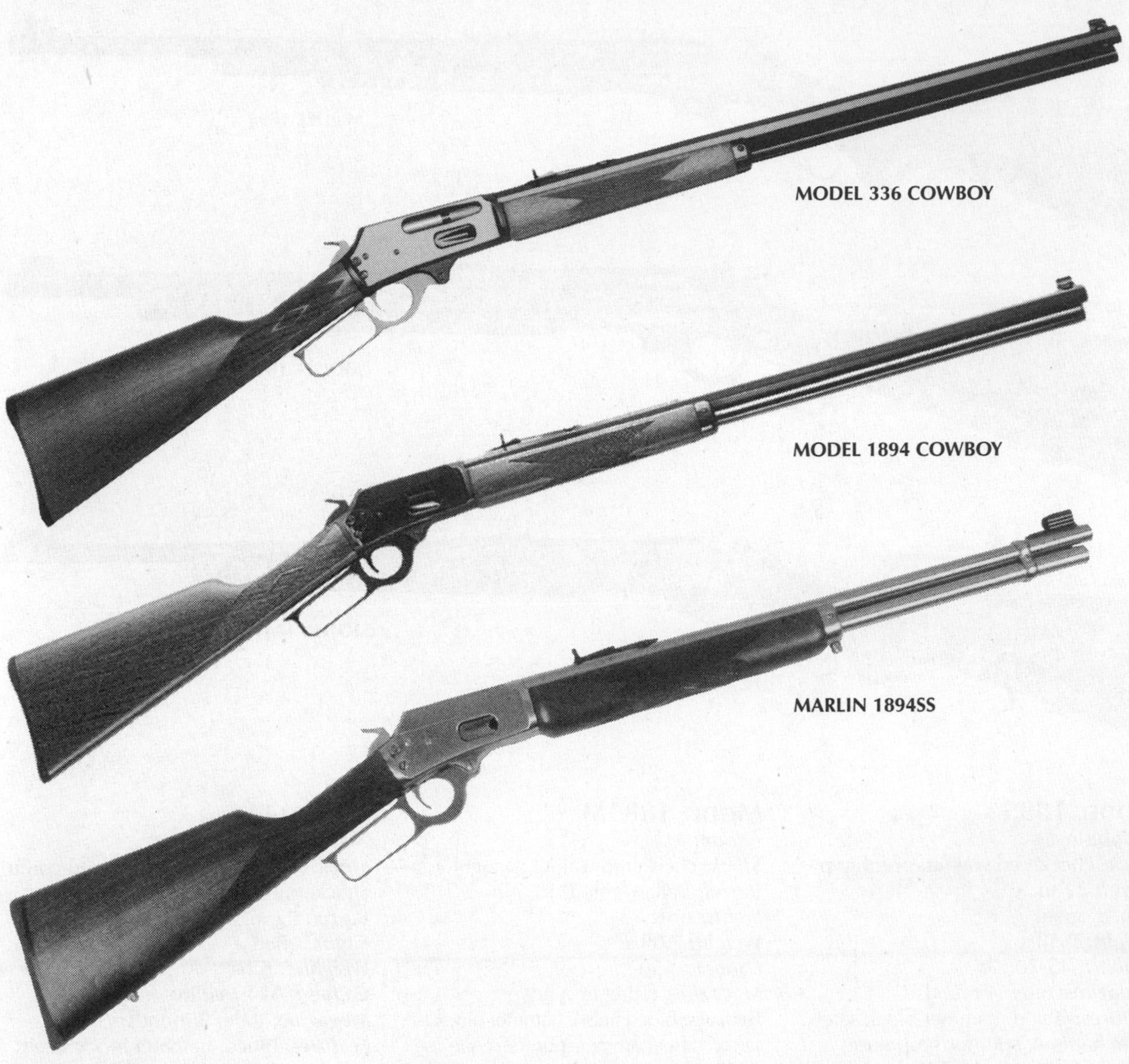

MODEL 336 COWBOY

MODEL 1894 COWBOY

MARLIN 1894SS

Model 336 Cowboy

Action: lever
Stock: walnut, straight grip
Barrel: octagon 24 in.
Sights: open
Weight: 7.5lbs.
Caliber: .38-55
Magazine: under-barrel tube, 8 rounds
Features: Ballard-style rifling
Cowboy $735

Model 1894 Cowboy

Action: lever
Stock: walnut, straight grip, checkered
Barrel: tapered octagon 24 in.
Sights: open
Weight: 7.5lbs.
Caliber: .357 Mag./38 Special, .44 mag./.44 Special and .45 Colt
Magazine: tube, 10 rounds
Features: blued finish, hammer-block safety, hard rubber buttplate; Competition model available in .38 Special or .45 Colt with 20 in. barrel (6.5 lbs.)
1894 Cowboy. $820
1894 Cowboy Competition $986

Model 1894 SS

Action: lever
Stock: checkered walnut, straight grip
Barrel: 20 in.
Sights: open
Weight: 6.0lbs.
Caliber: .44 Rem. Mag.
Magazine: under-barrel tube, 10 rounds
Features: Micro-groove rifling
1894 SS $680

Model 1894PG

Action: lever
Stock: checkered walnut, straight grip
Barrel: 20 in.
Sights: open
Weight: 6.5lbs.
Caliber: .44 Rem. Mag./.44 Special
Magazine: tube, 10 rounds
Features: solid-top receiver tapped for scope mount
Model 1894PG. $610
Model 1894FG
in .41 Rem. Mag. $610

Marlin Rifles

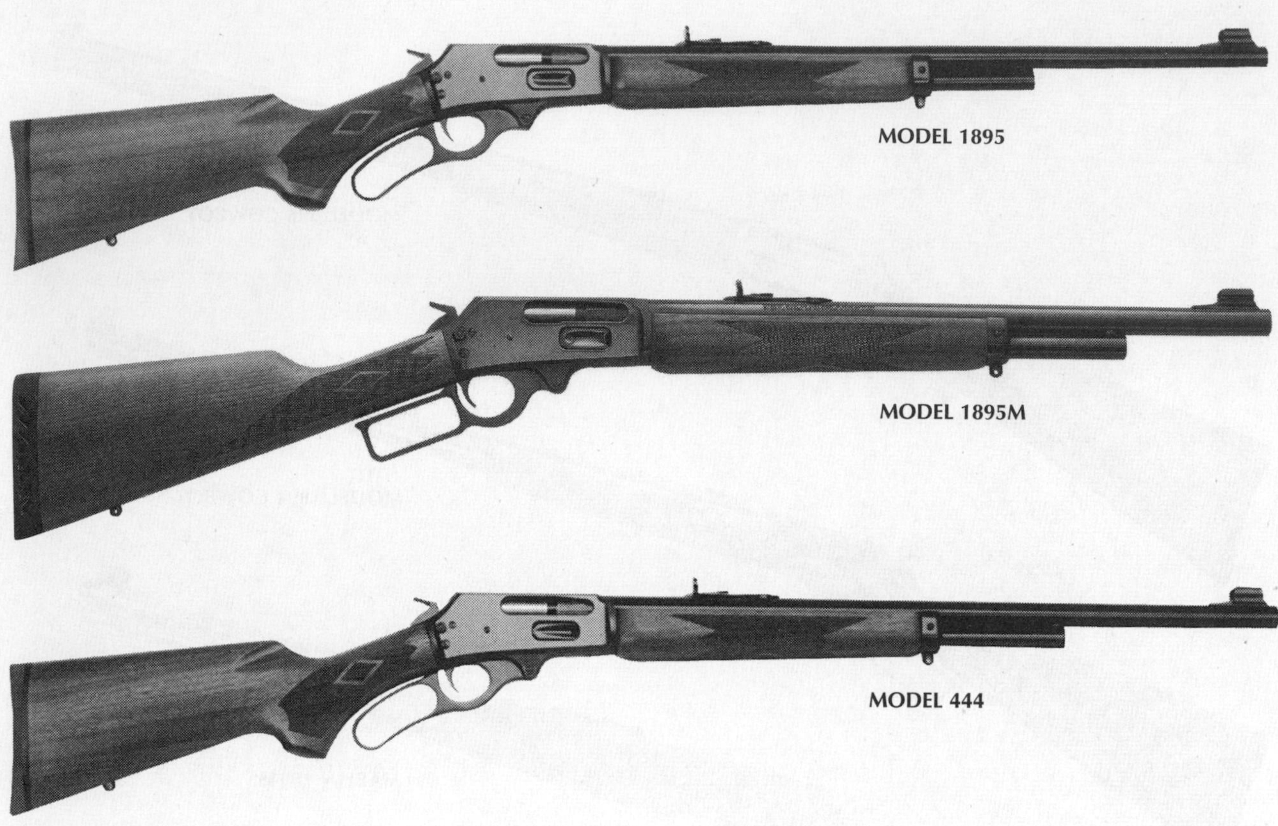

Model 1895

Action: lever
Stock: checkered walnut, pistol grip
Barrel: 22 in.
Sights: open
Weight: 7.5lbs.
Caliber: .45-70 Govt.
Magazine: tube, 4 rounds
Features: blued, hammer-block safety, offset hammer spur for scope use; Model 1895G has 18.5 in. barrel and straight grip.

1895 . . . . $631
1895G $646
1895GS in stainless steel $760

Model 1895M

Action: lever
Stock: checkered walnut, straight grip
Barrel: Ballard rifled, 18.5 in.
Sights: open
Weight: 7.0lbs.
Caliber: .450
Magazine: tube, 4 rounds
Features: blued finish, hammer-block safety, offset hammer spur for scope use.

1895M $695
1895 MR with 22 in. bbl. $761

Model 444

Action: lever
Stock: walnut, pistol grip, fluted comb, checkering
Barrel: 22 in.
Sights: open
Weight: 7.5lbs.
Caliber: .444 Marlin
Magazine: tube, 5 rounds
Features: blued, hammer-block safety, offset hammer spur for scope use.

444 . . . . $631

Adjust your trigger so it "breaks" at a comfortable weight. Heavy triggers require too much hand muscle in the squeeze. You'll move the rifle.

Merkel Rifles

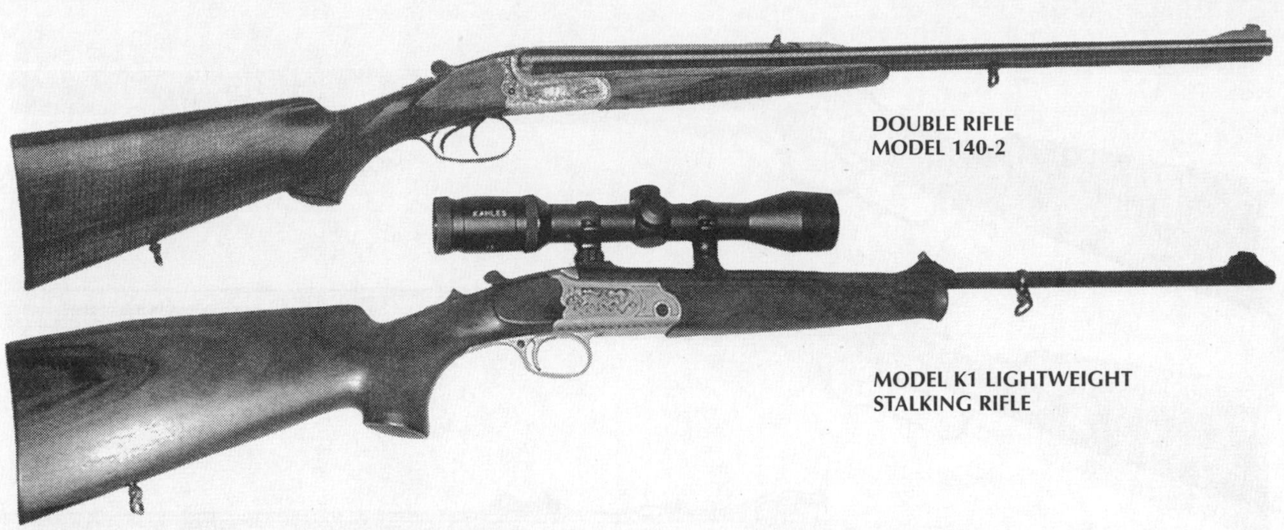

DOUBLE RIFLE
MODEL 140-2

MODEL K1 LIGHTWEIGHT
STALKING RIFLE

Model K1 Lightweight Stalking Rifle

Action: hinged breech
Stock: select walnut
Barrel: 24 in.
Sights: open
Weight: 5.6
Caliber: .243, .270, 7x57R, 7mm Rem. Mag., .308, .30-06, .300 Win. Mag., 9.3x74R
Magazine: none
Features: single-shot; Franz Jager action; also available: Premium and Jagd grades

Stalking Rifle: **$4095**
Premium: **$4395**
Jagd: **$4695**

Double Rifle Model 140-2

Action: hinged breech
Stock: select walnut
Barrel: length and contour to order
Sights: open
Weight: 9.0
Caliber: .375 H&H, .416 Rigby, .470 N.E.
Magazine: none
Features: Anson & Deely box-lock; double triggers; includes oak and leather luggage case; higher grade available; also Model 140-1, lightweight double in 7x57R, .308, .30-06, 9.3x74R

Safari Double: **$10195**
higher grade: **$11395**
Model 140-1: **$7195**

Mossburg Rifles

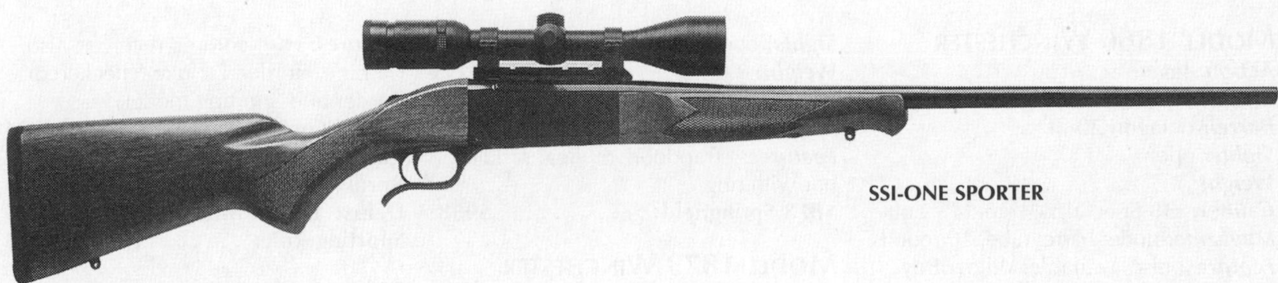

SSI-ONE SPORTER

Model SSI-1

Action: hinged breech
Stock: walnut
Barrel: interchangeable 24 in.
Sights: none
Weight: 8.0
Caliber: .223, .22-250, .243, .270, .308, .30-06, 12 ga., 3.5 in. chamber)
Magazine: none
Features: barrel drilled and tapped for scope; hammerless with top tang safety, selected ejector; also available: SSI-1 Varmint in .223, .22-250 with bull barrel (10 lbs.)

SSI-1: **$483**

RIFLES

Navy Arms Rifles

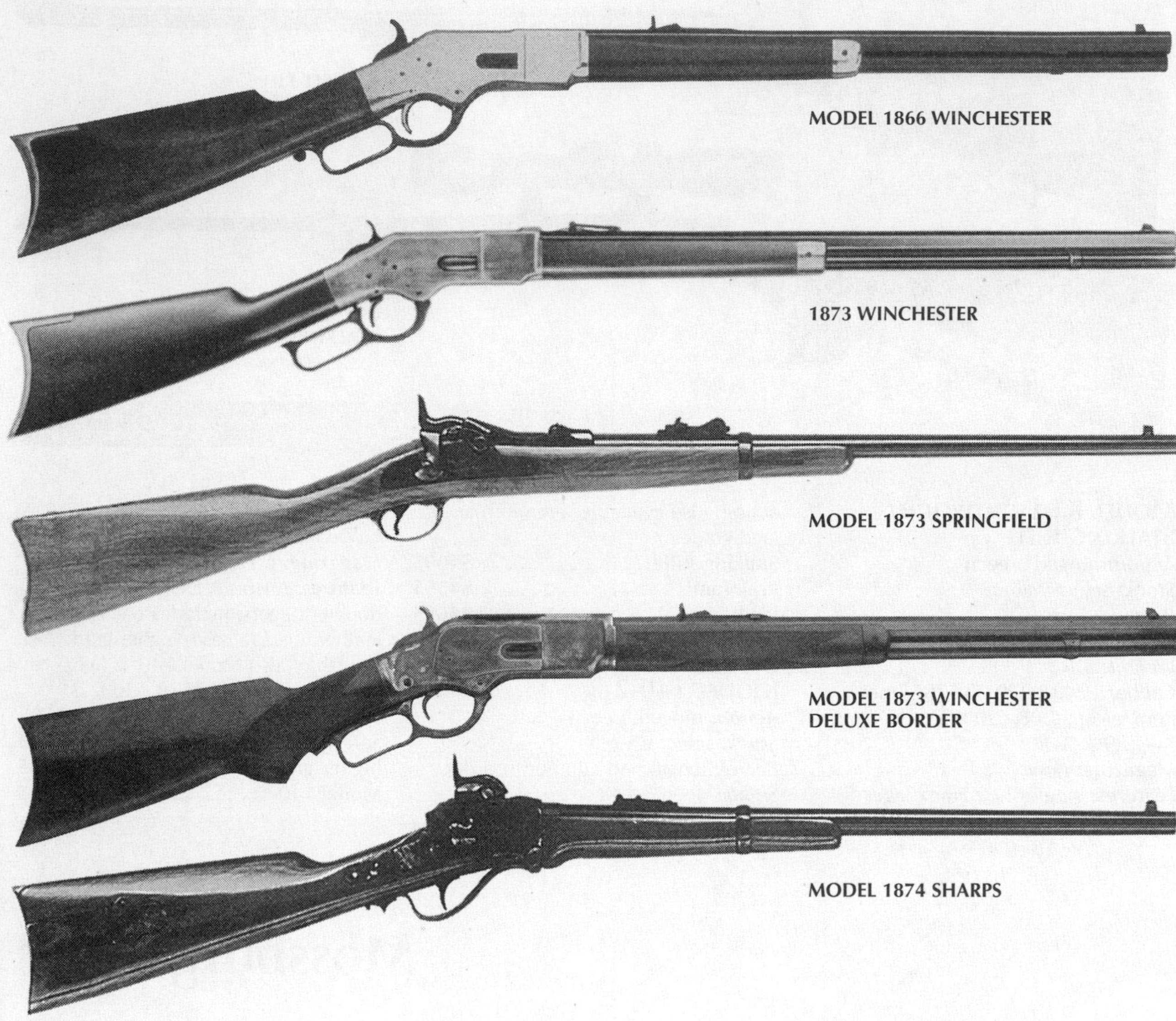

MODEL 1866 WINCHESTER

1873 WINCHESTER

MODEL 1873 SPRINGFIELD

MODEL 1873 WINCHESTER DELUXE BORDER

MODEL 1874 SHARPS

RIFLES

Model 1866 Winchester

Action: lever
Stock: walnut, straight grip
Barrel: octagon 20 in.
Sights: open
Weight: 7.5
Caliber: .38 Special, .44-40, .45 Colt
Magazine: under-barrel tube, 10 rounds
Features: also available: Yellow Boy with 24 in. barrel (8.3 lbs.)
1866:. $786
1866 Yellow Boy: $799

Model 1873 Springfield

Action: dropping block
Stock: walnut
Barrel: 22 in.
Sights: open
Weight: 7.0
Caliber: .45-70
Magazine: none
Features: "Trapdoor" replica, saddle bar with ring
1873 Springfield: $958

Model 1873 Winchester

Action: lever
Stock: walnut, straight grip
Barrel: 24 in.
Sights: open
Weight: 8.3
Caliber: .357 Mag., .44-40, .45 Colt
Magazine: under-barrel tube, 13 rounds
Features: case-colored receiver; also: Carbine, Border, Deluxe (checkered) Border and Sporting models
1873 Winchester:. $934
Carbine:. $912
Border Model: $934
Deluxe Border Model: $1055
Sporting Rifle: $1055

Model 1874 Sharps

Action: dropping block
Stock: walnut
Barrel: 22 in.
Sights: open
Weight: 7.8
Caliber: .45-70
Magazine: none

Navy Arms Rifles

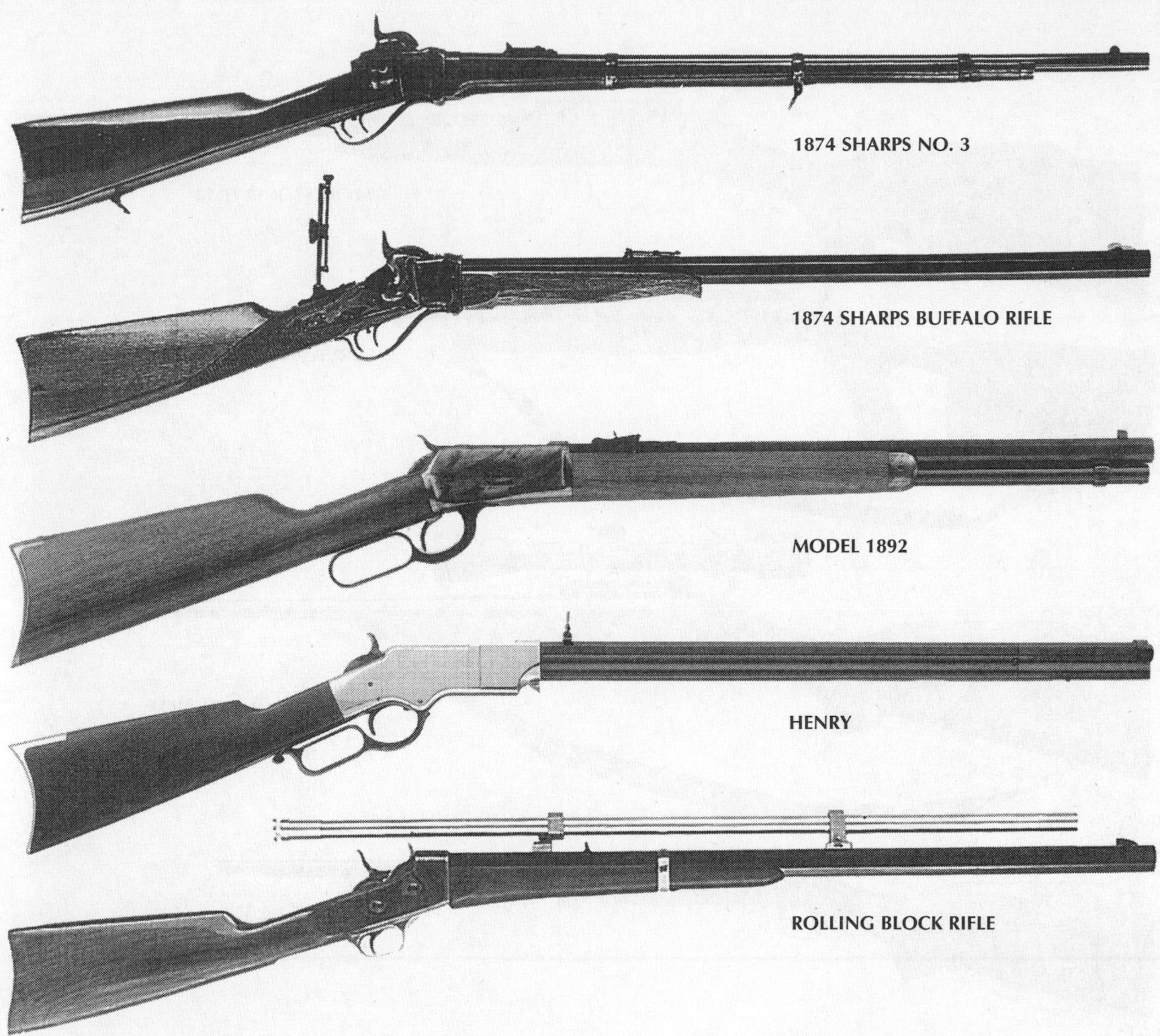

1874 SHARPS NO. 3

1874 SHARPS BUFFALO RIFLE

MODEL 1892

HENRY

ROLLING BLOCK RIFLE

Features: also: No. 3 Long Range Sharps with double set triggers, 34 in. barrel (10.9 lbs.) and Buffalo Rifle with double set triggers, 28 in. octagon barrel (10.6 lbs.)
Carbine:.................. $1030
No. 3:................... $1942
Buffalo Rifle:............. $1242

Model 1892

Action: lever
Stock: walnut, straight grip
Barrel: octagon 20 in.
Sights: open
Weight: 6.3
Caliber: .357 Mag., .44-40, .45 Colt
Magazine: under-barrel tube, 20 rounds
Features: case-colored or blued receiver; also available in stainless steel and full-length rifle with 24 in. barrel (7 lbs.)
short or full-length rifle:...... $561
stainless short:............. $530
stainless rifle:.............. $603

Henry

Action: lever
Stock: walnut, straight grip
Barrel: 24 in.
Sights: open
Weight: 9.0
Caliber: .44-40, .45 Colt
Magazine: under-barrel tube, 13 rounds
Features: blued or case-colored receiver
Henry:.................. $1087
Military Henry............ $1083

Rolling Block Rifle

Action: dropping block
Stock: walnut
Barrel: 26 or 30 in.
Sights: open
Weight: 9.0
Caliber: .45-70
Magazine: none
Features: case-colored receiver; optional brass telescopic sight; drilled for Creedmoor sight; also; checkered Creedmore model with tang and globe sights
Rolling Block:............. $815
Creedmoor:............... $995

New England Firearms Rifles

SPORTSTER 17 HMR

SURVIVOR

SYNTHETIC HANDI-RIFLE

HARDWOOD HANDI-RIFLE

RIFLES

Sportster 17 HMR

Action: hinged breech
Stock: synthetic
Barrel: heavy varmint 22 in.
Sights: none
Weight: 6.0
Caliber: .17 Hornady Magnum Rimfire
Magazine: none
Features: Monte Carlo stock; sling swivel, recoil pad; Sportster Youth available with 20 in. barrel (5.5 lbs.), in .22 LR

Sportster: $180
Youth: $149

Survivor

Action: hinged breech
Stock: lightweight synthetic
Barrel: light sporter, 20 in.
Sights: open
Weight: 5.5
Caliber: .22 Hornet, .223, .243
Magazine: none
Features: single-shot; tapped for scope mount; sling swivels; recoil pad; also: Survivor in .223 and .308 with 22 in. bull barrel, hollow synthetic stock, thumbscrew take down

Superlight: $281
Survivor: $284

Hardwood Handi-Rifle

Action: hinged breech
Stock: Monte Carlo synthetic
Barrel: 22 or 26 in.
Sights: none
Weight: 7.0
Caliber: .223, .243, .270, .280, .30-06
Magazine: none
Features: single-shot; scope base included; offset hammer; open-sight version of Handi-Rifle in .22 Hornet, .30-30, .357 Mag., .44 Mag., .45-70 Govt. Youth and stainless models in .223 and .243

Handi-Rifle: $281
with hardwwod stock: $270
Synthetic stainless
(.223, .and .243): $337
Youth Synthetic: $270

New Ultra Light Arms

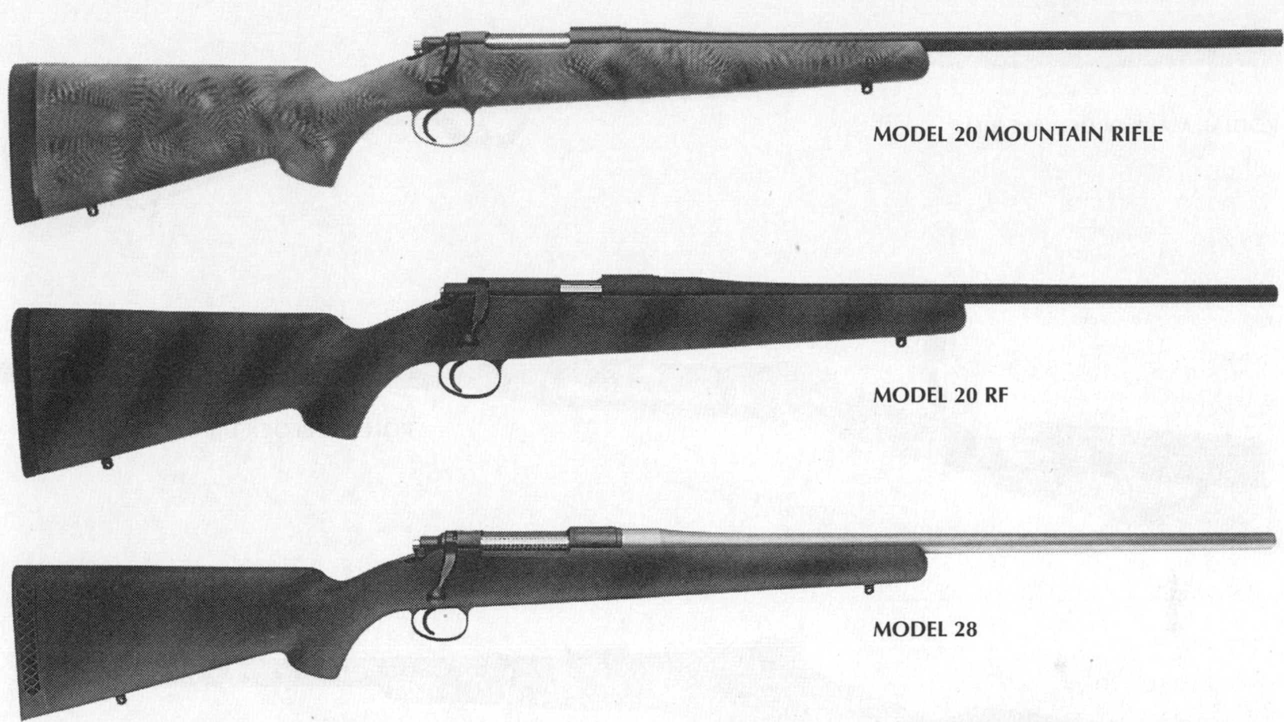

MODEL 20 MOUNTAIN RIFLE

MODEL 20 RF

MODEL 28

SLIM, LIGHTWEIGHT rifles appeal to anyone who hikes a lot. Short-range saddle guns are easy to carry but lack the reach or accuracy many shooters want. A new breed of super-light rifles dates to about 1984, when Melvin Forbes designed, from the ground up, his Model 20 Ultra Light. This bolt-action looks like a Remington 700. But close up you'll notice a lot of differences. First, the bolt and receiver diameters are smaller.

To keep weight down, Melvin made efficient use of steel. The receiver has standard wall thickness, but a slimmer bolt made for less receiver wall. The Model 20 wasn't conceived as a universal mechanism, for cartridges of all sizes. It was made for relatively short cartridges. In a fit of brilliance, Melvin chose to make the magazine box 3.00 inches long, not the 2.85 inches common in short-action rifles, to accommodate the 7x57 Mauser and its derivatives, and the .284 Winchester.

He didn't want to skeletonize anything or shorten the barrel to shave ounces. So after configuring the action, Melvin chose synthetic material to further reduce weight. Walnut was too heavy. Besides, it could warp, and he wanted this rifle to be fly-speck accurate under field conditions.

Model 20 Mountain Rifle

Action: bolt
Stock: Kevlar/graphite composite
Barrel: 22 in.
Sights: none
Weight: 4.75
Caliber: short action: 6mm, .17, .22 Hornet, .222, .222 Rem. Mag., .22-250, .223, .243, .250-3000 Savage, .257, .257 Ackley, 7x57, 7x57 Ackley, 7mm-08, .284, .300 Savage, .308, .358
Magazine: box, 4, 5 or 6 rounds
Features: two-position safety; choice of 7 or more stock colors; available in left-hand
Mountain Rifle: $2700
left-hand: $2800

Model 20 RF

Action: bolt
Stock: composite
Barrel: Douglas Premium #1 Contour 22 in.
Sights: none
Weight: 5.25
Caliber: .22 LR
Magazine: none (or detachable box, 5 rounds)
Features: single shot or repeater; drilled and tapped for scope; recoil pad, sling swivels; fully adjustable Timney trigger; 3-position safety; color options
single-shot: $1150
repeater: $1200

Model 24

Action: bolt
Stock: Kevlar composite
Barrel: 22 in.
Sights: none
Weight: 5.25
Caliber: long action: .270, .30-06, .25-06, .280, .280 Ackley, .338-06, .35 Whelen; Magnum (Model 28): .264, 7mm, .300, .338, .300 WSM, .270 WSM, 7mm WSM; Model 40: (magnum) .300 Wby. and .416 Rigby
Magazine: box, 4 rounds
Features: Model 28 has 24 in. bbl. and weighs 5.5 lbs.; Model 40 has 24 in. bbl. (6.5 lbs.) All available in left-hand versions.
Model 24: $2800
Model 24, left-hand: $2900
Model 28 or Model 40: $3100
Model 28 or Model 40, left-hand: $3200

RIFLES

Pedersoli Replica Rifles

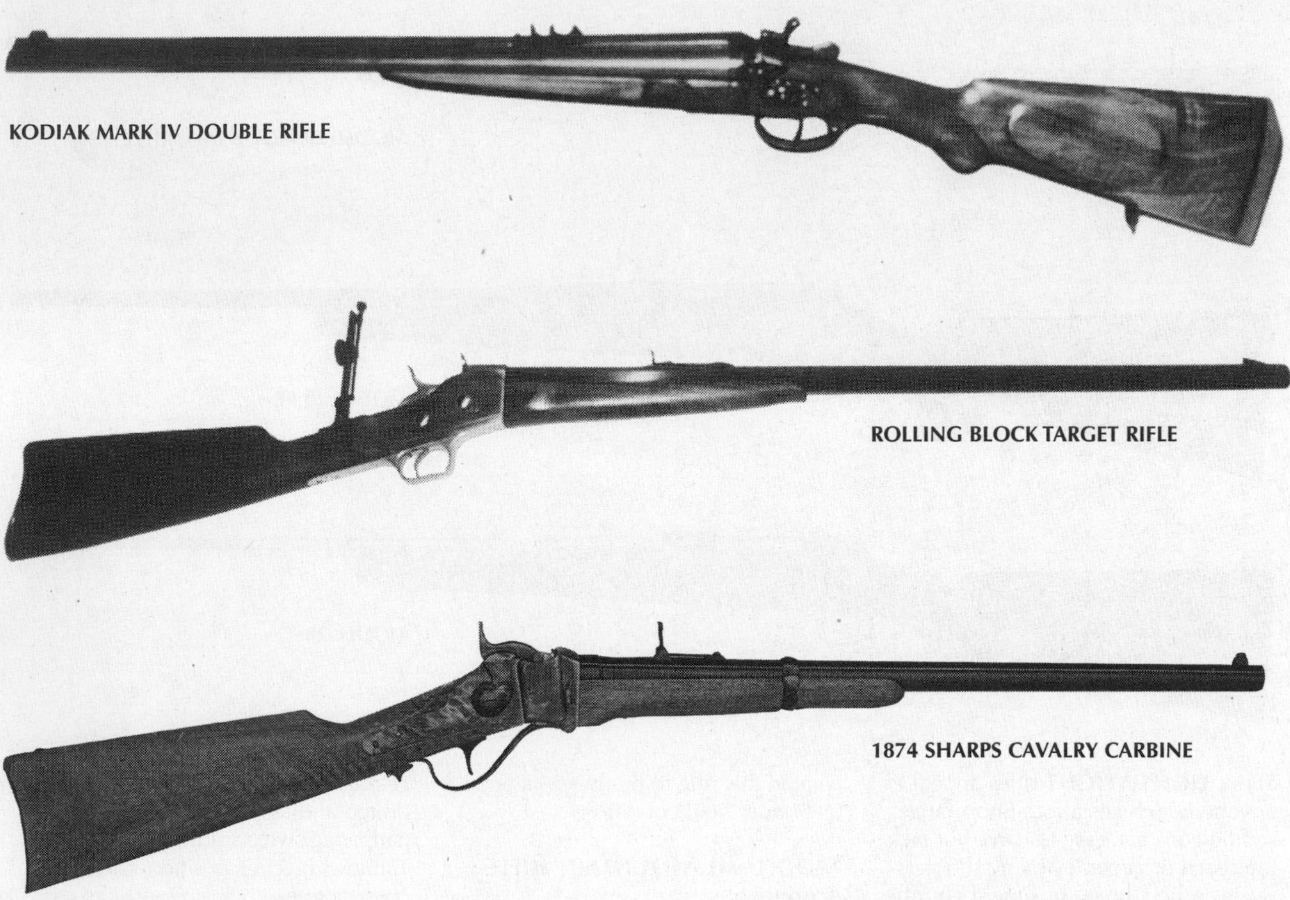

KODIAK MARK IV DOUBLE RIFLE

ROLLING BLOCK TARGET RIFLE

1874 SHARPS CAVALRY CARBINE

RIFLES

Kodiak Mark IV Double

Action: hinged breech
Stock: walnut
Barrel: 22 and 24 in.
Sights: open
Weight: 8.2
Caliber: .45-70, 9.3x74R, 8x57JSR
Magazine: none
Features: .45-70 weighs 8.2 lbs.; also available: Kodiak Mark IV with interchangeable 20-gauge barrel
45-70: $3250
8x57, 9.3x74: $3250
Kodiak Mark IV: $4495

Rolling Block Target

Action: dropping block
Stock: walnut
Barrel: octagon 30 in.
Sights: target
Weight: 9.5
Caliber: .45-70 and .357 (10 lbs.)
Magazine: none
Features: Creedmoor sights; Also available: Buffalo, Big Game, Sporting, Baby Carbine, Custer, Long Range Creedmoor
Rolling Block Target: $810

Sharps 1874 Cavalry Model

Action: dropping block
Stock: walnut
Barrel: 22 in.
Sights: open
Weight: 8.4
Caliber: .45-70
Magazine: none
Features: also available: 1874 Infantry (set trigger, 30 in. bbl.), 1874 Sporting (.40-65 or .45-70, set trigger, 32 in. oct. bbl.), 1874 Long Range (.45-70 and .45-90, .45-120, 34 in. half oct. bbl., target sights)
Cavalry: $1015
Infantry: $1195
Sporting: $1135
Long Range: $1555

Prairie Gun Works Rifles

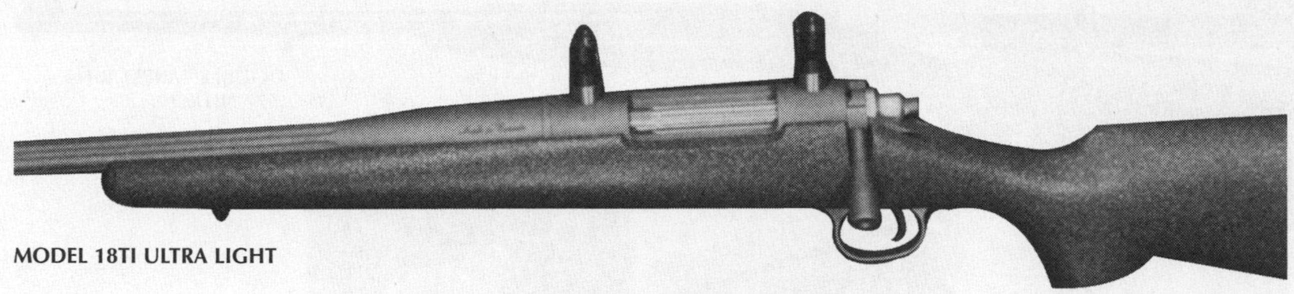

MODEL 18TI ULTRA LIGHT

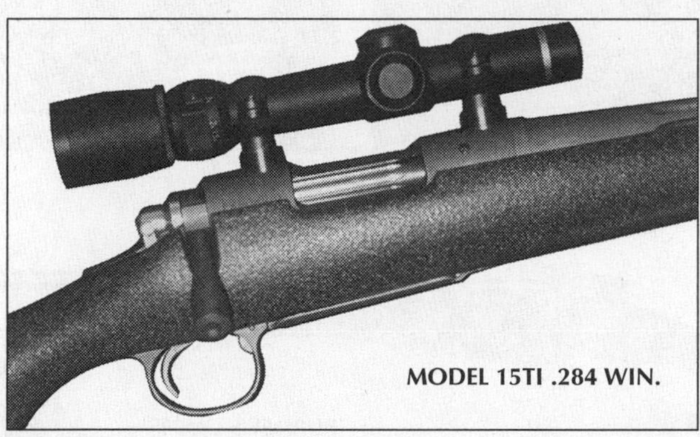

MODEL 15TI .284 WIN.

LIGHTWEIGHT RIFLES based on Ti series of Titanium rifle actions. These rifles feature match grade stainless barrels, kevlar/glass stocks, Titanium scope bases, fully adjustable triggers, and customer supplied specifications, such as length of pull, barrel length, and twist. The M15Ti rifle (short) is suitable for cartridges up to the size of the .284 Win. and its wildcats. The M18Ti rifle (long) is suitable for cartridges up to the Remington "Ultramag" and its wildcats. These rifles can be built from 4.25 lbs. to 6.25 lbs.

Some of the unique features found on the Ti series rifles: cone breech, ¼"-28 base/ring screw attachment, wire EDM lugways, one piece bolt, double plunger ejectors, Sako type extraction, left- or right-hand bolt/port configurations available, aluminum pillar bedding, removable muzzle brake with cap, barrel flutes X8.

Model 15Ti Ultra Light

Action: bolt
Stock: composite
Barrel: 22 in.
Sights: none
Weight: 5.0
Caliber: most short-action calibers
Magazine: box, 5 rounds
Features: Rem. 700 short action, custom alloy scope mounts, new firing pin and bolt shroud tuned; also: Model 18Ti with long 700 action
Model 15Ti: $2800
Model 18Ti: $2800

RIFLES

"Drop box" magazines that hold more cartridges makes sense for big dangerous-game rounds like the .416 Rigby. But for most cartridges and most hunting, they add unnecessary bulk and cost.

Purdey

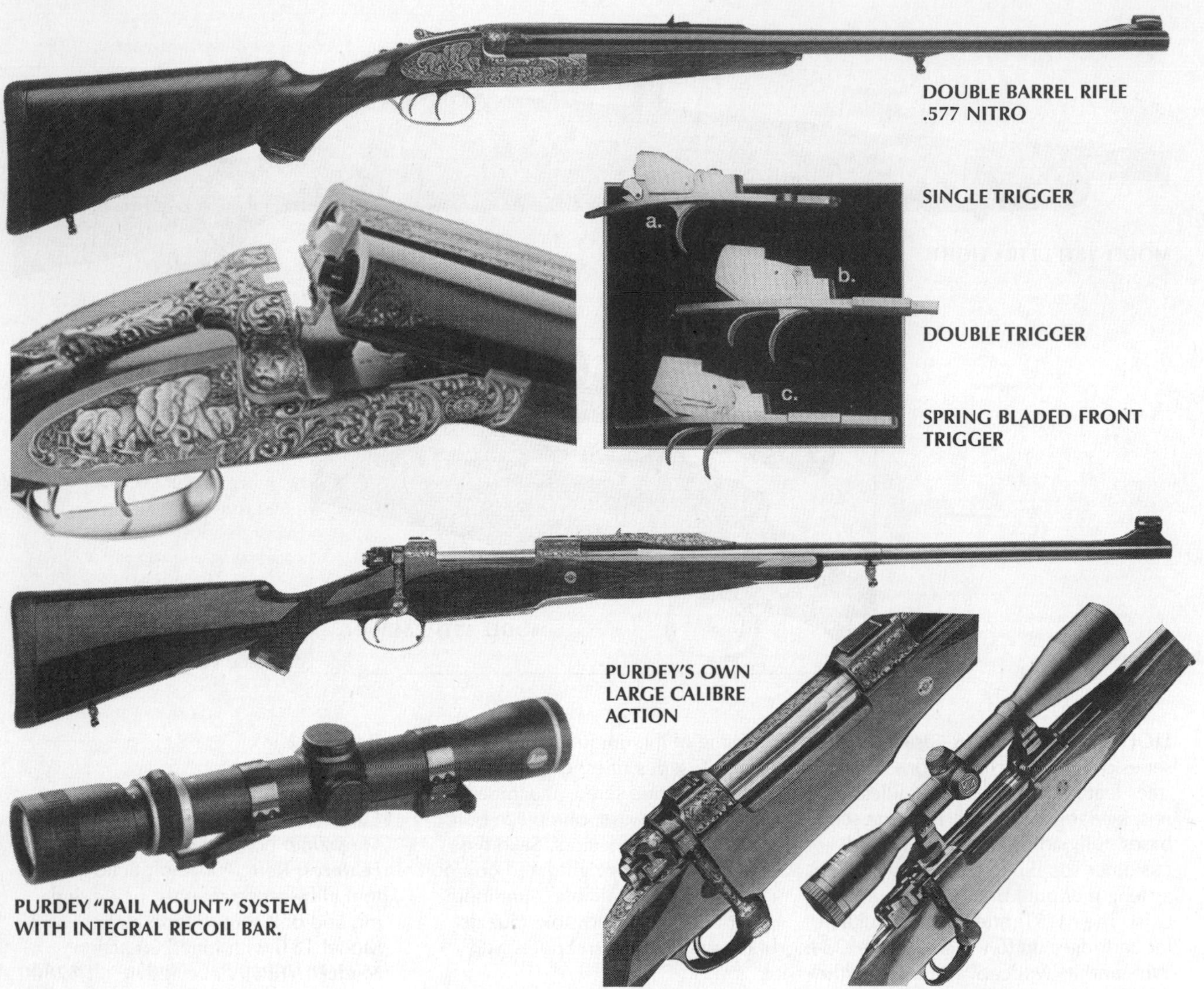

DOUBLE BARREL RIFLE .577 NITRO

SINGLE TRIGGER

DOUBLE TRIGGER

SPRING BLADED FRONT TRIGGER

PURDEY'S OWN LARGE CALIBRE ACTION

PURDEY "RAIL MOUNT" SYSTEM WITH INTEGRAL RECOIL BAR.

RIFLES

Double Barrel Rifle .577 Nitro

The word "Express" was coined by James Purdey the younger to publicize his rifles. He likened their performance to a railway or "Express" train, which was heavy, travelled with great velocity and had a flat trajectory.

Purdey's double-barrel Express rifles are built to customer specifications on actions sized to each particular cartridge. Standard chamberings include .375 H&H Magnum and .470, .577 and .600 Nitro Express. The Purdey side-by-side action patented in 1880 is still made now with only very minor changes. The action mechanism, designed by Frederick Beesley, retains a portion of the energy in the mainsprings to facilitate the opening of the gun.

The over-under is derived from the Woodward, patented in 1913. The action blocks for all guns are cut from certified forgings, for consistency of grain throughout, and are so fitted to the barrels as to give an absolute joint.

The actioner then fits the fore-part, the locks, the strikers and the safety work before finally detonating the action.

A – Single trigger

The Purdey single trigger works both by inertia and mechanically. It is simple, effective and fast. The firing sequence is fixed, therefore no barrel selection is possible.

B & C – Double Triggers

The standard double triggers (B) can be augmented with an articulated front trigger (C). This device alleviates damage to the back of the trigger finger on discharge.

Purdey makes its own dedicated actions for bolt rifles in the following calibers: .375 H&H, .416/450 Rigby or other, .500 and .505 Gibbs.

The action length is suited to cartridge length in each caliber. Mauser Square Bridge and Mauser '98 actions are available.

Rail Mount System

This is Purdey's own system for big bolt rifles. It is very secure and facilitates fast on/off. Rings and mounts are all made with an integral recoil bar from a single piece of steel. This system is recommended for Purdey actions and Mauser Square Bridge actions.

Remington Arms Rifles

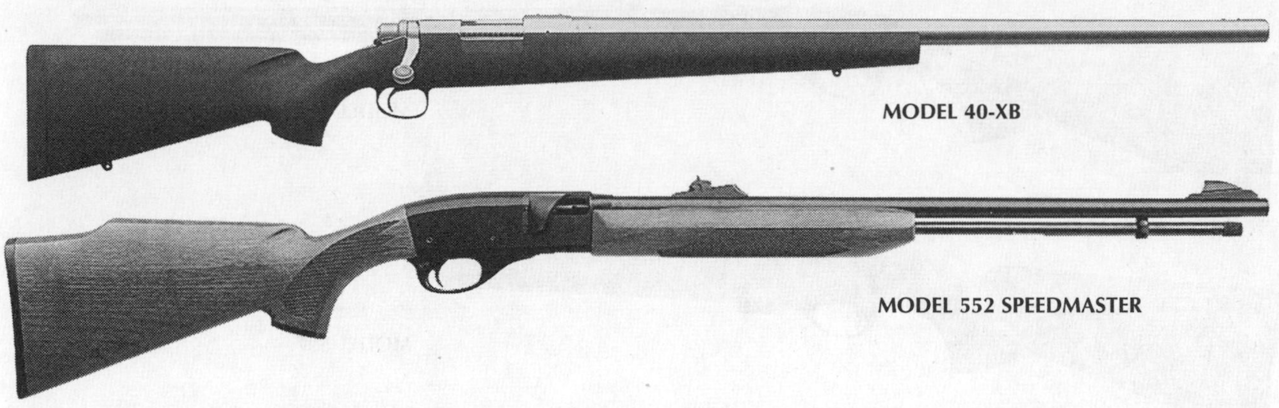

MODEL 40-XB

MODEL 552 SPEEDMASTER

JOHN D. PETERSON began working on a pump-action centerfire rifle in September, 1908. Crawford C. Loomis helped Pederson develop the rifle which would become the Remington Model 14. Chambered in .30 and .32 Remington, the Model 14was introduced in August 1912. The .35 Remington was added soon thereafter. Standard-grade rifles initially sold for $20. The 14R Carbine, with an 18-inch barrel and straight-grip stock listed for $18.

During this period, Remington also designed and marketed the Model 8 autoloading rifle. Initially called simply the Remington Autoloading Repeating Rifle, the Model 8 was bored for the .25, .30, .32 and .35 Remington. It had a box magazine that could be clip-charged. The barrel recoiled within a fixed jacket.

In 1922 Loomis began working on a small-frame centerfire that became the Model 25 a year later. Loomis' pump gun was really an adaptation of the Model 12 rimfire rifle, rather than a redesign of the Model 14. It came in .25-20 and .32-20; the tube magazine held 10 shots. A six-shot carbine followed. The 25 remained in production until it was replaced in 1936, by the Model 141 Gamemaster. Bored for the .30, .32 and .35 Remington, the Gamemaster proved a popular deer gun in both rifle and carbine version. A more powerful pump rifle, the Remington 760, supplanted it in 1950. Meanwhile, Remington's Model 8 autoloader had been replaced (in 1936) by the Model 81, essentially a beefy version of the Model 8.

In 1955 Remington introduced a fixed-barrel, gas-operated autoloader called the 740. It shared the 760's sleek profile and the buttstock, receiver and trigger group were, in fact, essentially the same. The Woodsmaster was replaced in 1960 by an improved version, the 742. Both it and the 760 Gamemaster remained in the line for two more decades.

In 1981 Remington changed them both internally and cosmetically. The new Model Four and 7400 autoloaders and Model Six and 7600 pumps featured fewer locking lugs than their predecessors, improved magazines, one-piece barrel extensions, rivetless extractors and a counterbore at the rear of the chamber to further enhance feeding. Chambered for such high-power rounds as the .30-06, .270, and .280, as well as for the .243 and .308 short-action rounds, the 7400 and 7600 remain favorites of many hunters today. The Models Four and Six were dropped in 1988.

In 1898, Roswell F. Cook patented a change to the Lee bolt-action rifle, moving the locking lugs from the bolt body to the head. The upshot: a Remington-Lee Small Bore Magazine Rifle. Chambered in 7X57, 7.65 Mauser, .236 Remington, .30-30 Winchester and .30-40 Krag, which stayed in the Remington line for a decade. The military rifles and carbines, in .30-40 Krag, armed Cuba as well as U.S. National Guard units. The next Remington bolt-action centerfire was conceived by Crawford C. Loomis and C.H. Barnes. Announced in 1921, the Model 30 had been several years in the making, the result of efforts to use surplus 1917 Enfield receivers. It was, predictably, a heavy rifle. It was also expensive and sold poorly. An improved version appeared in 1926. The 30 Express was chambered in .30-06 – and 25, .30, .32 and .35 Remington. It weighed 12 ounces less than its predecessor and had a better trigger. A carbine version followed in 1927. In 1931 Remington added the 7x57 to the list of chamberings and, in 1936, the .257 Roberts.

Model 40-XB Target Rifle

Action: bolt
Stock: target, benchrest or tactical
Barrel: heavy 24 in.
Sights: none
Weight: 9.0
Caliber: 16 popular standard and magnum calibers
Magazine: box, 3 or 5 rounds
Features: rimfire and single-shot versions available; walnut, laminated and composite stocks; forend rail, match trigger
40-X: $1636
Left-hand $1970

Model 552 Speedmaster

Action: autoloading
Stock: walnut
Barrel: 21 in.
Sights: open
Weight: 5.8
Caliber: .22 S, .22 L, .22 LR
Magazine: under-barrel tube, 15 rounds
Features: classic autoloader made 1966 to date
552: $393

RIFLES

Remington Arms Rifles

MODEL 572 FIELDMASTER

MODEL 597

MODEL 700 ADL

MODEL 700 AFRICAN BIG GAME

RIFLES

Model 572 Fieldmaster

Action: pump
Stock: walnut
Barrel: 21 in.
Sights: open
Weight: 5.5
Caliber: .22 S, .22 L, .22 LR
Magazine: under-barrel tube, 15 rounds
Features: grooved receiver for scope mounts
Fieldmaster: $407

Model 597

Action: autoloading
Stock: synthetic or laminated
Barrel: 20 in.
Sights: open
Weight: 5.5
Caliber: .22 LR
Magazine: detachable box, 10 rounds
Features: magnum version in .22 WMR and .17 HMR (both 6 lbs.); also: heavy-barrel model
597: $169
stainless: $224
stainless laminated: $279
magnum: $361
heavy-barrel: $265
heavy-barrel magnum: $399

Model 700 ADL

Action: bolt
Stock: synthetic or walnut
Barrel: 22 in.
Sights: none
Weight: 7.3
Caliber: .223, .22-250, .243, .270, 7mm Rem. Mag., .308, .30-06, .300 Win. Mag.
Magazine: box, 3 or 5 rounds
Features: walnut in .270 and .30-06 only; magnums with 24 in. barrels; youth model has short stock, 20 in. barrel and weighs 6.8 lbs.
ADL synthetic: $500
synthetic magnum: $527
Youth: $500
walnut: $580

Model 700 African Big Game

Action: bolt
Stock: laminated
Barrel: 26 in.
Sights: open
Weight: 9.0
Caliber: .375 H&H, .375 UM, .458 Win, .416 Rem.
Magazine: box, 3 rounds
Features: barrel-mounted front swivel
African Big Game: $1726

Remington Arms Rifles

MODEL 700 AFRICAN PLAINS RIFLE (APR)

MODEL 700 CLASSIC

MODEL 700 BDL DM

MODEL 700 KS MOUNTAIN RIFLE

Model 700 African Plains Rifle

Action: bolt
Stock: laminated
Barrel: 24 in.
Sights: none
Weight: 9.0
Caliber: all popular magnums
Magazine: box, 3 rounds
Features: barrel-mounted front swivel
African Plains Rifle: $1716

Model 700 Classic

Action: bolt
Stock: walnut
Barrel: 24 in.
Sights: none
Weight: 7.3
Caliber: .300 Savage
Magazine: box, 5 rounds
Features: one-year run per caliber
700 Classic: $683

Model 700 BDL

Action: bolt
Stock: walnut
Barrel: 22 in.
Sights: open
Weight: 7.5
Caliber: popular standard calibers from .17 Rem. to .375 UM
Magazine: box, 5 rounds
Features: magnums have 24 in. barrels; DM version features detachable magazine; left-hand bolt available on many 700s for $25 premium
BDL: $683
BDL Magnum: $709
BDL Ultra-Mags: $723
BDL Stainless: $735
BDL Stainless Magnum: $761
BDL Stainless Ultra-Mags:. $775
BDL Stainless DM: $801
BDL Stainless DM Magnum: . . . $828

Model 700 KS Mountain Rifle

Action: bolt
Stock: lightweight composite
Barrel: 22 in.
Sights: none
Weight: 6.5
Caliber: all popular standard calibers
Magazine: box, 3 or 5 rounds
Features: stainless or chrome-moly steel; also: magnum model with 24 in. barrel
standard: $1350
magnums: $1480

Model 700 Mountain Rifle DM

Action: bolt
Stock: walnut
Barrel: 22 in.
Sights: none
Weight: 6.5
Caliber: .260, .270, 7mm-08, .280, .30-06
Magazine: detachable box, 4 rounds
Features: also; LSS with laminated stock, stainless steel
Mountain DM: $749
LSS: $800

Remington Arms Rifles

MODEL 700 SENDERO

MODEL 700 SENDERO SF (STAINLESS FLUTED)

MODEL 700 VLS (VARMINT LAMINATED STOCK)

MODEL 710

RIFLES

MODEL 700 SENDERO SF

Action: bolt
Stock: composite
Barrel: 26 in. heavy stainless
Sights: none
Weight: 8.5
Caliber: 7mm Rem. Mag., .300 Ultra Mag., .338 Ultra Mag., 7 mm Rem Ultra Mag., 7mm & 300 Rem SA Ultra Mag. and .300 Win. Mag.
Magazine: box, 3 or 5 rounds
Features: full-length bedding block; fluted barrel
Sendero:. $1003
Ultra Magnum calibers: $1016

MODEL 700 TITANIUM

Action: bolt
Stock: synthetic
Barrel: stainless 22 in.
Sights: none
Weight: 5.5
Caliber: .260, .270, 7mm-08, .308, .306
Magazine: box, 5 rounds
Features: Titanium receiver; fluted bolt
Titanium: $1239

MODEL 700 VS

Action: bolt
Stock: synthetic
Barrel: 26 in.
Sights: none
Weight: 9.5
Caliber: .223, .22-250, .308
Magazine: box, 5 rounds
Features: SF has fluted barrel; also in .220 Swift (8.5 lbs.); VLS has laminated stock, also in .243, 6mm
VS: $811
VSSF:. $976
VLS:. $837

MODEL 710

Action: bolt
Stock: synthetic
Barrel: 22 in.
Sights: none
Weight: 7.3
Caliber: .270, .30-06
Magazine: detachable box, 4 rounds
Features: self-lubing nylon receiver insert; 60º bolt throw; includes mounted 3-9x40 Bushnell scope
710 with scope: $425

Remington Arms Rifles

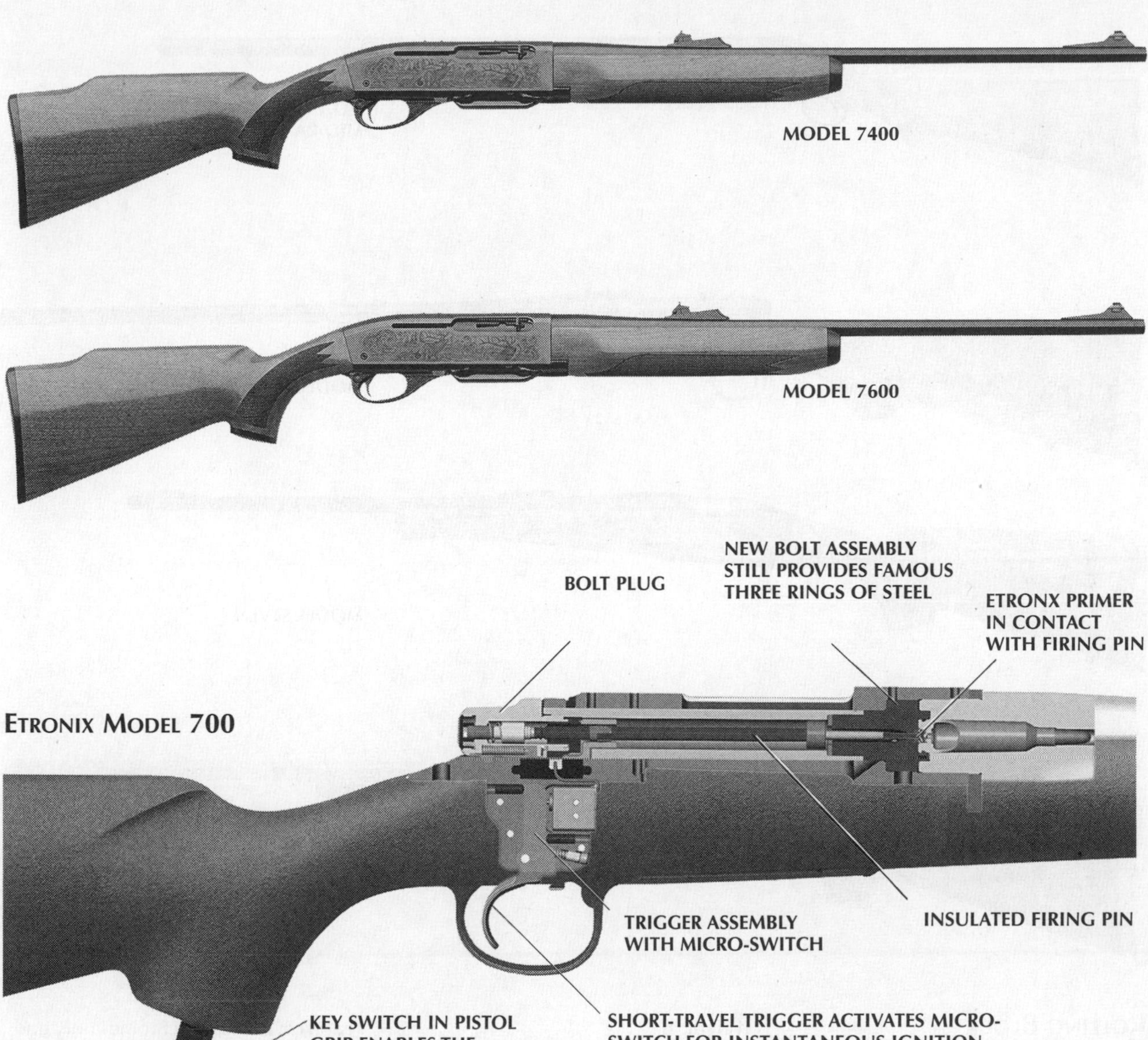

RIFLES

Model 7400

Action: autoloading
Stock: walnut or synthetic
Barrel: 22 in.
Sights: none
Weight: 7.5
Caliber: .243, .270, .308, .30-06
Magazine: detachable box, 4 rounds
Features: also; 7400 carbine with 18 in. barrel (7.3 lbs.)

walnut: $624
synthetic:................. $520

Model 7600

Action: pump
Stock: walnut or synthetic
Barrel: 22 in.
Sights: open
Weight: 7.5
Caliber: .243, .270, .308, .30-06
Magazine: detachable box, 4 rounds
Features: also: 7600 carbine with 18 in. barrel (7.3 lbs.)

walnut: $588
synthetic:................. $484

Etronix Model 700

Action: bolt
Stock: synthetic
Barrel: fluted 26 in.
Sights: none
Weight: 8.5
Caliber: .22-250, .220 Swift, .243
Magazine: box, 5 rounds
Features: requires special ammunition; fired by electronic pulse, not mechanical striker; switch in grip turns on the system

Etronix: $1332

Remington Arms Rifles

NO.1 ROLLING BLOCK
MID-RANGE SPORTER

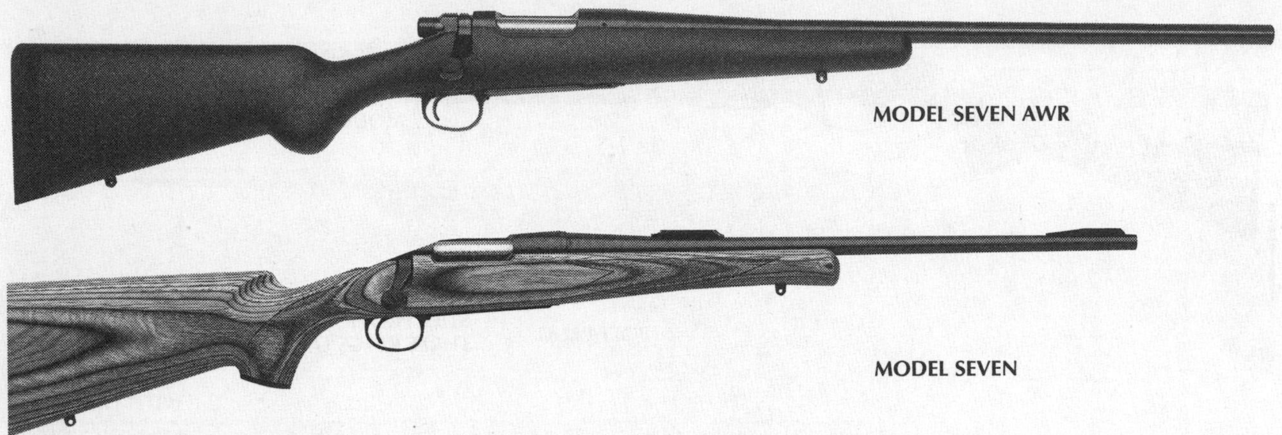

MODEL SEVEN AWR

MODEL SEVEN

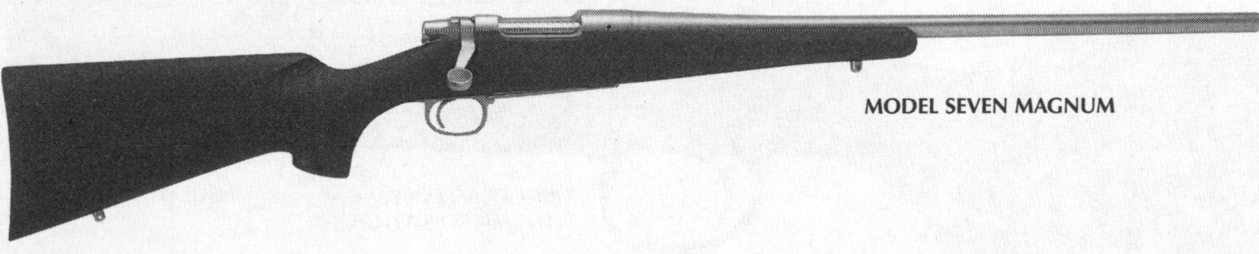

MODEL SEVEN MAGNUM

Rolling Block Mid-Range Sporter Rifle

Action: dropping block
Stock: walnut
Barrel: heavy 30 in.
Sights: none
Weight: 9.0
Caliber: .45-70
Magazine: none
Features: single set trigger; also: Mid-Range Sporter in other calibers
Mid-Range Sporter: $1450
Rolling Block Silhouette:. $1560

Model Seven AWR (Custom Shop)

Action: bolt
Stock: lightweight composite or laminated
Barrel: stainless 22 in.
Sights: open
Weight: 6.5
Caliber: 7mm SUM, .300 SUM
Magazine: box, 3 rounds
Features: Alaska Wilderness Rifle has lightweight composite stock; also: MS laminated, full-length stock (7.3 lbs.); Model Seven KS in standard short-action calibers has 20 in. barrel
Model Seven AWR:. $1546
MS: $1332
KS:. $1314

Model Seven LS (laminated)

Action: bolt
Stock: synthetic
Barrel: 20 in.
Sights: open
Weight: 6.5
Caliber: .223, .243, .260, 7mm-08, .308
Magazine: box, 5 rounds
Features: choice of chrome-moly and stainless steel; synthetic and laminated stocks; also: youth model with short hardwood stock
LS:. $701
Youth: $547
Stainless synthetic:. $729

Model Seven Magnum

Action: bolt
Stock: synthetic
Barrel: stainless 22 in.
Sights: open
Weight: 7.3
Caliber: 7mm SUM, .300 SUM
Magazine: box, 3 rounds
Features: also: laminated stock versions with chrome-moly steel
LS laminated:. $741
SS synthetic:. $769

CLASSIC

LIGHTWEIGHT STRATA STAINLESS MODEL

MASTER SERIES

SAFARI MODEL

CLASSIC

Action: bolt
Stock: laminated fiberglass
Barrel: stainless steel, match grade 24 to 26 in.
Sights: none
Weight: 6.5
Caliber: all popular chamberings up to .375 H&H
Magazine: box, 3 or 5 rounds
Features: Winchester 70 stainless steel, controlled-round feed action; lapped bolt; pillar glass bedded stock; adjustable trigger; hinged floor-plate; also: Signature Series, stainless Rem. 700 action, 27 in. fluted barrel, synthetic stock in .300 Rem. UM

Classic: $2500
Classic, left-hand:. $2600
Signature : $2800
Signature, left-hand: $2950

LIGHTWEIGHT STRATA STAINLESS

Action: bolt
Stock: laminated with textured epoxy
Barrel: stainless match grade 22 to 24 in.
Sights: none
Weight: 4.75
Caliber: all popular chamberings up to .375 H&H
Magazine: box, 3 or 5 rounds
Features: Stainless Rem. action, fluted tapped and handle-hollowed bolt; pillar glass bedded stock; stainless metal finish; blind or hinged floorplate; custom Protektor pad; also: Lightweight 70 (5.75 lbs.); Lightweight Titanium Strata

Lightweight Strata: $2850
Strata, left-hand:. $2950
Lightweight 70: $2750
70, left-hand: $2850
Titanium Strata: $3850

MASTER SERIES

Action: bolt
Stock: laminated fiberglass
Barrel: match grade 24 to 27 in.
Sights: none
Weight: 7.75
Caliber: all popular chamberings up to .300 Rem. Ultra Mag.
Magazine: box, 3 or 5 rounds
Features: Remington 700 action

Master Series:. $2950

SAFARI MODEL

Action: bolt
Stock: laminated fiberglass
Barrel: stainless match grade 23 to 25 in.
Sights: open
Weight: 9.0
Caliber: all popular chamberings
Magazine: box, 3 or 5 rounds
Features: Win. Model 70 action; drilled and tapped for 8-40 screws; Stainless Quiet Slimbrake; stainless or black Teflon finish; adjustable trigger; hinged floor-plate; express sights; barrel band; quarter rib

Safari: $3000
with options: $4100

Rogue Rifle Company

STD-DELUXE

Chipmunk
Action: bolt
Stock: walnut, laminated or camo
Barrel: 16 in.
Sights: target
Weight: 2.5
Caliber: Sporting rifle in .17 HMR; Target model in .22
Magazine: none
Features: single-shot; manual-cocking action; receiver-mounted rear sights; Target model weighs 5 lbs. and comes with competition-style receiver sight and globe front and adjustable trigger, extendable buttplate and front rail. Also: .22 WMR
standard: $194
Target with options: $279

Rossi Rifles

ROSSI MATCHED PAIR WITH BOTH .22 LONG RIFLE AND .410-BORE SHOTGUN BARRELS

SINGLE-SHOT

Matched Pair
Action: hinged breech
Stock: hardwood
Barrel: 18.5 in (rifle), 22 in. (shotgun)
Sights: open
Weight: 4.0
Caliber: .22 LR and .410 bore
Magazine: none
Features: single shot; stainless steel; single-stage trigger; also; Centerfire Rifle/Shotgun Matched Pair, full size 12 or 20 gauge with .223 or .243
blued: $152
stainless: $194
.410 and .17 HMR, blue: $180
.410 and .17 HMR, SS: $223
Centerfire Pair:. $230

Single Shot
Action: hinged breech
Stock: hardwood
Barrel: 24 in.
Sights: open
Weight: 5.5
Caliber: .17 HMR, .22 LR, .22 Mag., .357 Mag., .44 Rem Mag., 223, 243, .45/410, .308, .30-06, .270, .270 WSM
Magazine: none
Features: single shot; recoil pad; sling swivels; extra-wide positive-action extractor; good rifle for first time shooters
.17 HMR or .22 LR, .22 Mag. blue: . . $158
.17 HMR or .22 LR, .22 Mag. stainless,/black: $202
.357 or .44 Rem. Mag, blue: . . . $173
.357 or .44 Rem. Mag., stainless/black:. $216
.223, .243, .308, .30-06, .270, .270 WSM blue: $202
.410/.45 Colt, blue: $187
.410/.45 Colt, stainless: $230
Youth w/Monte Carlo stock: . . . $202

RIFLES

Ruger Rifles

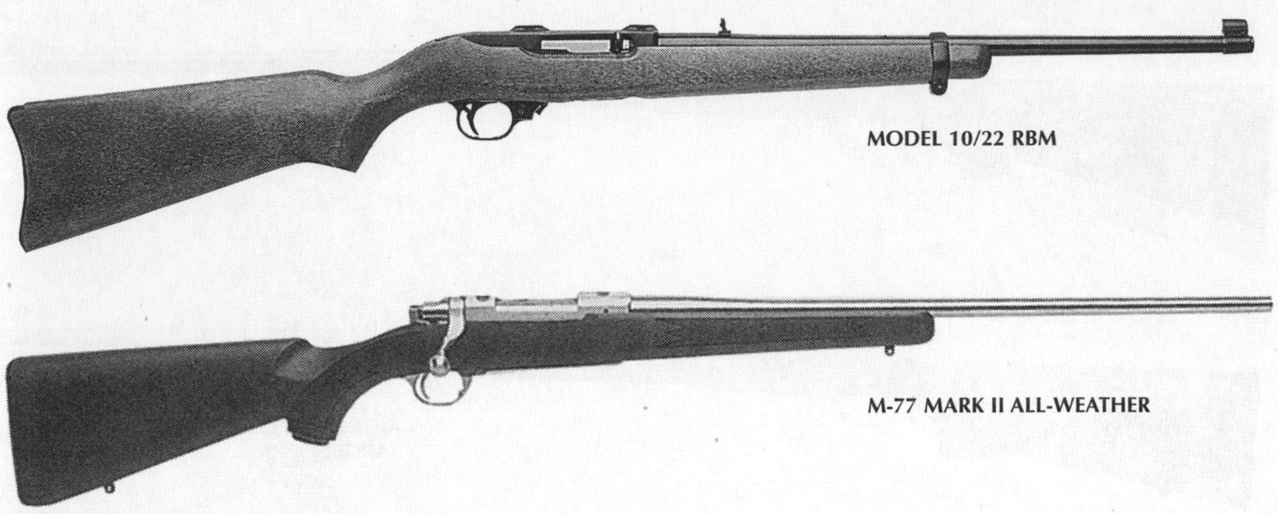

MODEL 10/22 RBM

M-77 MARK II ALL-WEATHER

WILLIAM BATTERMAN RUGER, founder and Chairman Emeritus of Sturm, Ruger & Company, died at his home July 6, 2002, at age 86. He was certainly the most prominent gun designer in the U.S. during the last half of the 20th century.

Born June 21, 1916 in Brooklyn, New York, Ruger discovered a passion for guns when he received a rifle from his father at age 12. As a student at the University of North Carolina, he converted an empty room into a machine shop, and, 1938 came up with initial designs for what eventually became a light machine gun for the Army. Ruger executed the drawings on his in-laws' dining room table. Ordnance officials liked the gun, which launched Ruger to become a full-time gun designer. Over the next 53 years he helped invent and patent dozens of models of sporting firearms.

Ruger teamed with Alexander McCormick Sturm to establish Sturm, Ruger & Company in 1949. After Sturm's death in 1951, Ruger took full control of the Company, whose first firearm, a stylish .22 caliber target pistol, is still one of the most popular target pistols in the U.S. Bill Ruger had a hand in the original design and styling of every firearm his company produced, and continued to work on new products up until his death.

When not involved with his firearms operations, Ruger indulged his life-long passions: collecting antique firearms and early Western American art. His antique car collection of more than 30 vehicles included Bentleys, Rolls-Royces, Bugattis, Stutzes, and a 1913 Mercer Raceabout. In 1970, Ruger commissioned the design and construction of a sports tourer automobile. Called the Ruger Special, it was based on the 1929 Bentley 4½ liter.

Bill Ruger's philanthropy helped fund several charities, and the Buffalo Bill Historical Center in Cody, Wyoming, where he served as a member of the Board of Trustees for over 15 years.

Ruger is survived by his son William B. Ruger, Jr., who is the current Chairman of the Company.

Sturm, Ruger & Company, is the largest firearms manufacturer in the U.S., and has produced more than 20 million firearms for hunting, target shooting, collecting, self-defense, law enforcement and military use. Plants are located in Newport, New Hampshire, and Prescott, Arizona, with corporate headquarters in Southport, Connecticut. Sturm, Ruger precision investment castings are made for a wide variety of applications, including aero-space, automotive, general manufacturing and the golf market.

Model 10/22

Action: autoloading
Stock: walnut, birch, synthetic or laminated
Barrel: 18 in.
Sights: open
Weight: 5.0
Caliber: .22 LR
Magazine: rotary, 10 rounds
Features: blowback action; also: International with full-stock, heavy-barreled Target and stainless steel versions; Magnum with 9-shot magazine

10/22: **$239**
walnut: **$299**
stainless: **$279**
International: **$279**
stainless International: **$299**
Target: **$425**
Target stainless, laminated: **$485**
magnum: **$499**

Model 77 RFP Mark II

Action: bolt
Stock: synthetic
Barrel: 22 in.
Sights: none
Weight: 7.0
Caliber: most popular standard and magnum calibers
Magazine: box, 5 rounds
Features: stainless steel barrel and action, (magnums with 24 in. barrel); scope rings included; also: RSFP with sights

RFP: **$675**
RSFP: **$729**

Ruger Rifles

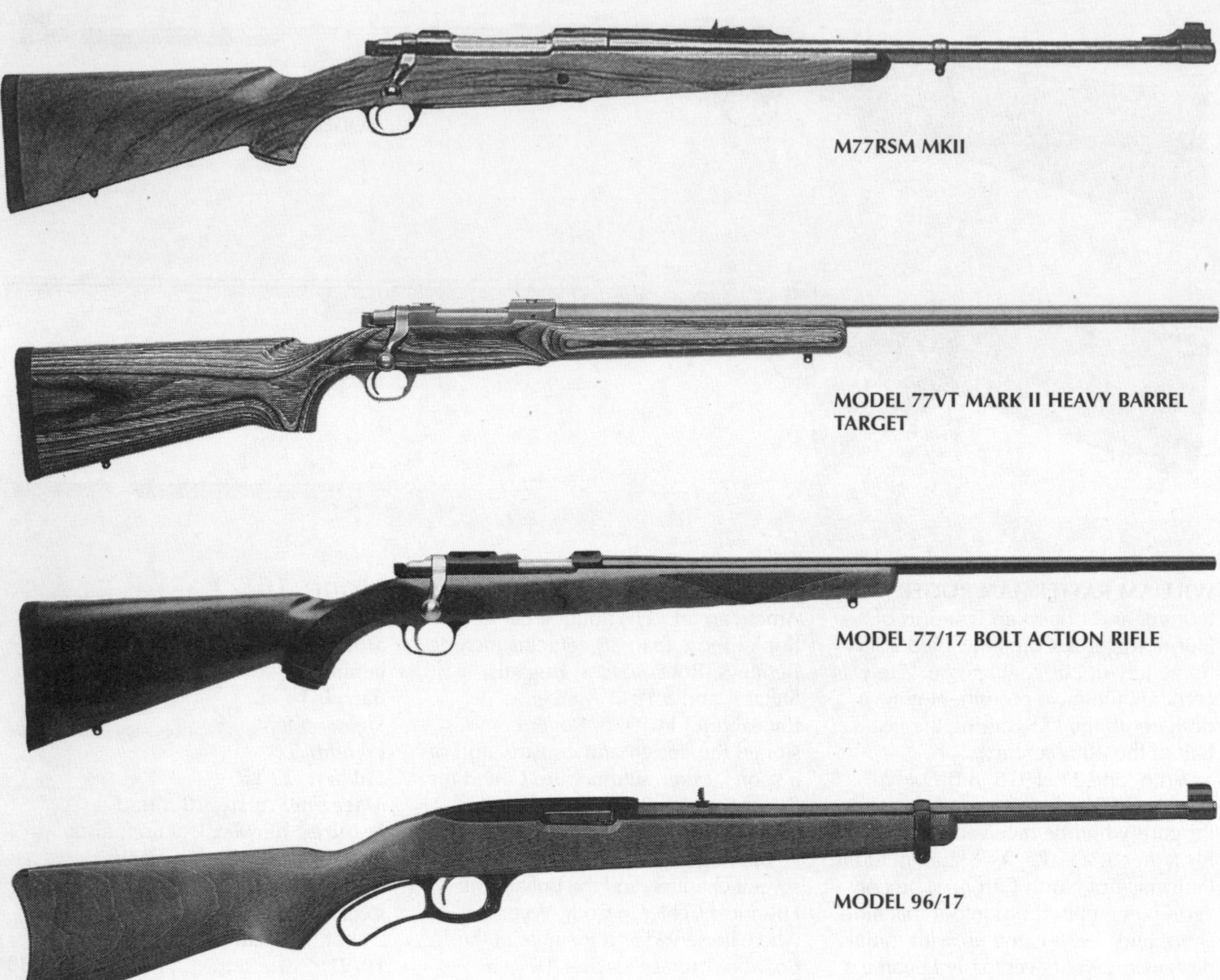

M77RSM MKII

MODEL 77VT MARK II HEAVY BARREL TARGET

MODEL 77/17 BOLT ACTION RIFLE

MODEL 96/17

Model 77 RSM

Action: bolt
Stock: Circassian walnut
Barrel: 23 in. with quarter rib
Sights: open
Weight: 9.3
Caliber: .375 H&H, .416 Rigby (10.3 lbs.)
Magazine: box, 4 rounds
Features: barrel-mounted front swivel; also: Express rifle in popular standard and magnum long-action calibers
Price:. $1695
Express: $1625

Model 77 VT Mark II

Action: bolt
Stock: laminated
Barrel: heavy stainless 26 in.
Sights: none
Weight: 9.8
Caliber: .223, .22-250, .220 Swift, .243, .25-06, .308
Magazine: box, 5 rounds
77 VT: $819

Model 77/17

Action: bolt
Stock: walnut, synthetic or laminated
Barrel: 22 in.
Sights: none
Weight: 6.5
Caliber: .17 HMR
Magazine: 9 rounds
Features: also: stainless (P) and stainless varmint with laminated stock (VMBBZ), 24 in. barrel (6.9 lbs.)
77/17 RM: $580
77/17 RMP: $580
K77/17 VMBBZ: $645

Model 96/17M Lever Action Rifle

Action: Lever
Stock: Hardwood
Barrel: 18½ inches blued
Sights: Adjustable rear sight
Weight: 5.25 lbs.
Caliber: .17 HMR
Magazine: 9 round rotary magazine
Features: Enclosed short-throw lever action; cross bolt safety; standard tip-off scope-mount base.
Price: . . . . $ 375.00

Ruger Rifles

MODEL 77/22VBZ VARMINT

MODEL 77/44 RS

MODEL M-77R MKII

MODEL M-77RL MKII ULTRA LIGHT

Model 77/22 Rimfire Rifle

Action: bolt
Stock: walnut
Barrel: 20 in.
Sights: none
Weight: 6.0
Caliber: .22 LR
Magazine: rotary, 10 rounds
Features: also: Magnum (M) and stainless synthetic (P) versions; scope rings included for all; sights on S versions. VBZ has 24 in. medium stainless barrel (6.9 lbs.)

77/22R: **$580**
77/22RM: **$580**
K77/22RP: **$580**
K77/22 RMP: **$580**
K77/22RSP: **$605**
K77/RSMP: **$605**
K77/22VBZ: **$645**

Model 77/44RS

Action: bolt
Stock: walnut
Barrel: 18 in.
Sights: open
Weight: 6.0
Caliber: .44 Magnum
Magazine: rotary, 6 rounds
Features: also: stainless synthetic (P) version

77/44RS: **$605**
K77/44 RSP: **$605**

Model 77R Mark II

Action: bolt
Stock: walnut
Barrel: 22 in.
Sights: none
Weight: 7.0
Caliber: most popular standard and magnum calibers
Magazine: box, 5 rounds
Features: scope rings included; RS Model has open sights; RBZ has stainless steel, laminated stock; RSBZ with sights

77R: **$675**
RS: **$759**
RBZ: **$729**
RSBZ: **$799**

Model 77RL Mark II Ultra Light

Action: bolt
Stock: walnut
Barrel: 20 in.
Sights: none
Weight: 6.0
Caliber: .223, .243, .257, .270, .308, .30-06
Magazine: box, 5 rounds
Features: RSI International Model has full-length stock, 18 in. barrel

77RL Ultra Light: **$729**
International Model: **$769**

Ruger Rifles

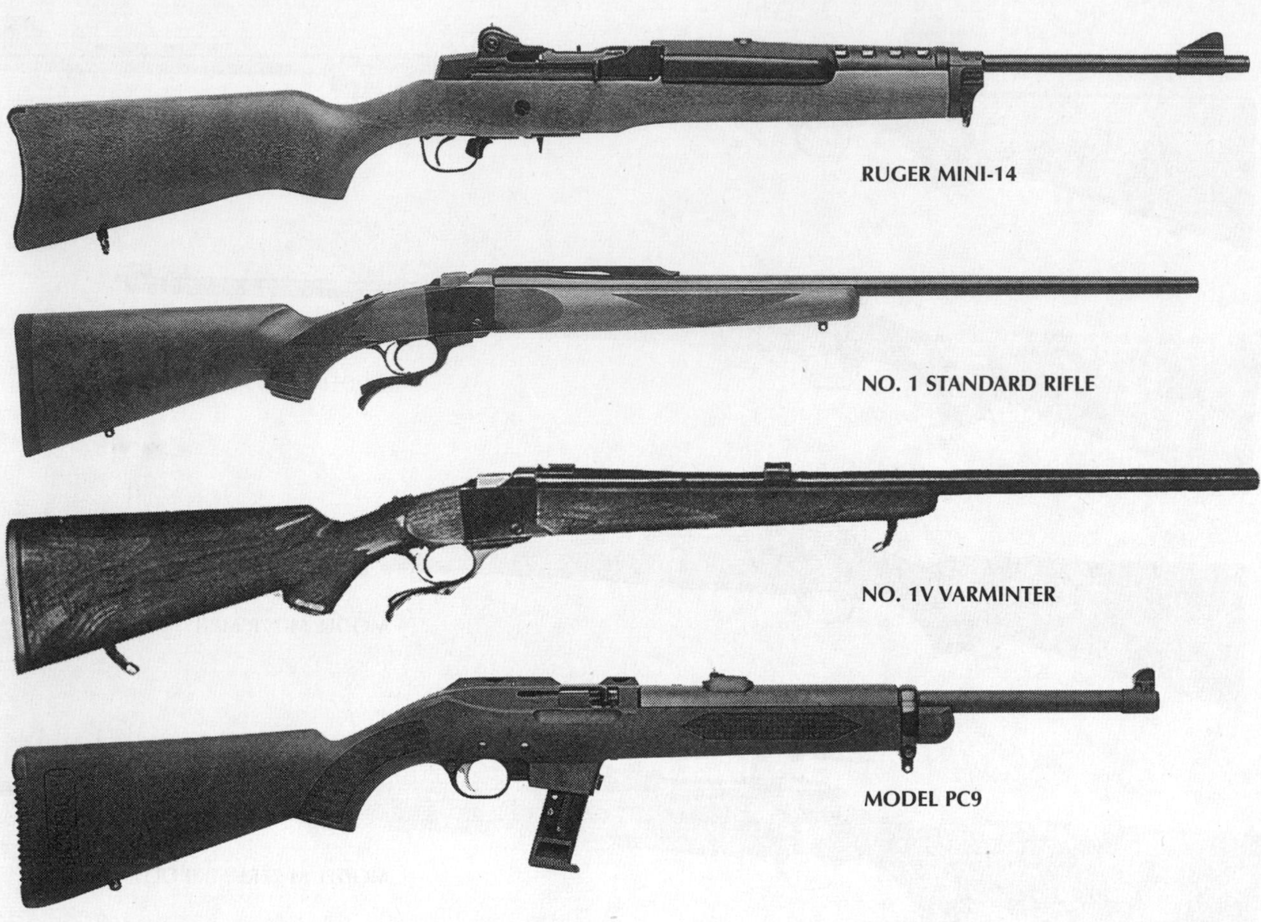

Mini-14 Carbine

Action: autoloading
Stock: hardwood
Barrel: 18 in.
Sights: target
Weight: 6.5
Caliber: .223
Magazine: detachable box, 5 rounds
Features: also: stainless, stainless synthetic versions of Mini-14/5; Ranch Rifle (with scope mounts) and Mini-thirty (in 7.62x39)

Mini 14:. $655
stainless Mini 14: $715
stainless synthetic Mini 14:. . . . $715
Ranch Rifle: $695
Ranch rifle, stainless: $770
Ranch rifle, stainless synthetic: . $770
Mini-Thirty: $695
Mini-thirty, stainless: $770
Mini-Thirty, stainless synthetic: . $770

No. 1 Single-Shot

Action: dropping block
Stock: select checkered walnut
Barrel: 22, 24, or 26 in.
Sights: open
Weight: 7.25
Caliber: all popular chamberings in Light Sporter, Medium Sporter, Standard Rifle
Magazine: none
Features: pistol grip; all rifles come with Ruger 1″ scope rings; Medium Sporter weighs 8 lbs. and 45-70 is available in stainless; Standard Rifle weighs 8 lbs. No. 1 Stainless comes in .243, .25-06, 7mm Rem. Mag., 7mm STW, .30-06, .308

No. 1: $875
Stainless steel: $910

No. 1V (Varminter)

Action: dropping block
Stock: select checkered walnut
Barrel: heavy 24 or 26 in. (.220 Swift)
Sights: open
Weight: 9.0
Caliber: .22-250, .220 Swift, .223, .25-06, 6mm
Magazine: box, 5 rounds
Features: Ruger target scope block, stainless available in .22-250; also: No. 1H Tropical (heavy 24 in. bbl.) in .375 H&H, .416 Rigby, .45 Lott, .405; No.1 RSI International (20 in. light bbl. and full-length stock) in .243, .270, .30-06, 7x57

Varmint:. $875
Tropical: $875
International:. $890

Model PC9 Carbine

Action: autoloading
Stock: synthetic
Barrel: 16
Sights: open
Weight: 6.3
Caliber: 9mm, .40 auto
Magazine: detachable, 10 rounds
Features: delayed blowback action; optional ghost ring sight

Carbine:. $605
with ghost ring sights:. $628

Sako Rifles

SAKO 75 HUNTER

KEY

SAKO ACTIONS

LOCKED

READY

THUMB SAFETY, DOVETAILED RECEIVER

SAKO 75 ACTIONS are renowned for their graceful lines, strength and reliability. Each of the four action sizes is manufactured for a specific range of calibers. The Sako 75 is the first to offer a bolt with three locking lugs and a mechanical ejector while maintaining a bolt lift of only 70°. Five guiding surfaces prevent the bolt from binding and provide ultra smooth-operation. The two-position thumb safety is located conveniently behind the bolt handle. A separate button in front of the safety allows the bolt to be opened while the safety is on. The detachable magazine can be loaded through the ejection port. Both carbon steel and stainless steel actions are available.

The three largest Sako actions now feature "key concept", a mechanism on the cocking piece that locks or unlocks the striker. You can thus render the 75 absolutely safe, disabling it with a turn of the key. Three keys are provided with each rifle, and others can be ordered by rifle serial number from the 7500 patterns. All Sako Model 75 rifles except those built on the smallest actions will soon come standard with the key concept lock.

"The key blends into the rifle contours when the lock is open and the gun is operational," explained Mr. Paul-Erik Tolvo, former president of Sako Ltd. "When the key is removed, the lock takes effect and the hunting rifle is completely safe and inoperative."

This revolutionary concept puts complete control of the safety and security of the rifle in the hands of its owner. "When the key is removed, there is no way to operate the gun, even accidentally. Any attempts to pick the lock will render the rifle unusable," said Mr. Tolvo. He also noted that the Sako 75 is considered the very best bolt action rifle in the industry. "The Sako 75 is the best hunting rifle in the world. It is only natural that we wanted to offer it with added security and safety for its owner and society in general. We believe this will become the new standard in gun safety."

Model 75 Hunter

Action: bolt
Stock: walnut or synthetic
Barrel: hammer-forged 22, 24 or 26 in.
Sights: none
Weight: 7.0
Caliber: most popular standard and magnum calibers from .222 Rem. to .375 H&H and new .300 WSM
Magazine: detachable box, 4 to 6 rounds
Features: barrel length depends on caliber; 4 action lengths; also: stainless synthetic and short-barreled Finnlight versions, Deluxe Grade with fancy walnut stock

Hunter: **$1129**
Magnum: **$1163**
Stainless synthetic: **$1212**
Left-hand (.25-06, .270, .30-06): . . **$1198**
Magnum stainless: **$1246**
Finnlight: **$1267**
Magnum Finnlight: **$1301**
Deluxe: **$1653**
Deluxe Magnum: **$1688**
.416 Rem: **$1967**
.375 Hunt Mag with iron sights . . . **$1757**

RIFLES

Sako Rifles

SAKO 75 VARMINT RIFLE

FINNFIRE TARGET22 LONG RIFLE

TRG 42

TRG S

Model 75 Varmint

Action: bolt
Stock: varmint-style walnut
Barrel: heavy 24 in.
Sights: none
Weight: 9.0
Caliber: most popular standard and magnum calibers from .17 Rem. to .375 H&H
Magazine: detachable box, 4 to 6 rounds
Features: also: 75 Varmint Laminated Stainless in .222, .223, 6PPC, .22-250, .243, 7mm-08, .308
Varmint:. $1337
Varmint LS: $1448

Finnfire Target 22

Action: bolt
Stock: walnut
Barrel: 22 in.
Sights: none
Weight: 5.3
Caliber: .22 LR
Magazine: detachable box, 5 or 10 rounds
Features: adjustable trigger; 2-lug, 50-degree bolt; available with open sights; also: varmint (heavy) and Sporter (adjustable target) versions
Hunter: $854
Varmint:. $896
Target: $951

Model TRG-22

Action: bolt
Stock: synthetic
Barrel: 26 in.
Sights: none
Weight: 10.3
Caliber: .308
Magazine: detachable box, 10 rounds
Features: 3-lug bolt; fully adjustable trigger; optional bipod, brake; also: TRG 42 in .300 Win. Mag. and .338 Lapua (5-round magazine, 27 in. barrel, 11.3 lbs.)
TRG-22:. $2898
TRG-42:. $2829

Model TRGS M995

Action: bolt
Stock: synthetic
Barrel: 27 in.
Sights: none
Weight: 8.2
Caliber: .30-378 Wby., .338 Lapua
Magazine: detachable box, 3 rounds
Features: 60-degree bolt throw; sporting version of UIT Model 22
TRGS M995: $896

Sauer Rifles

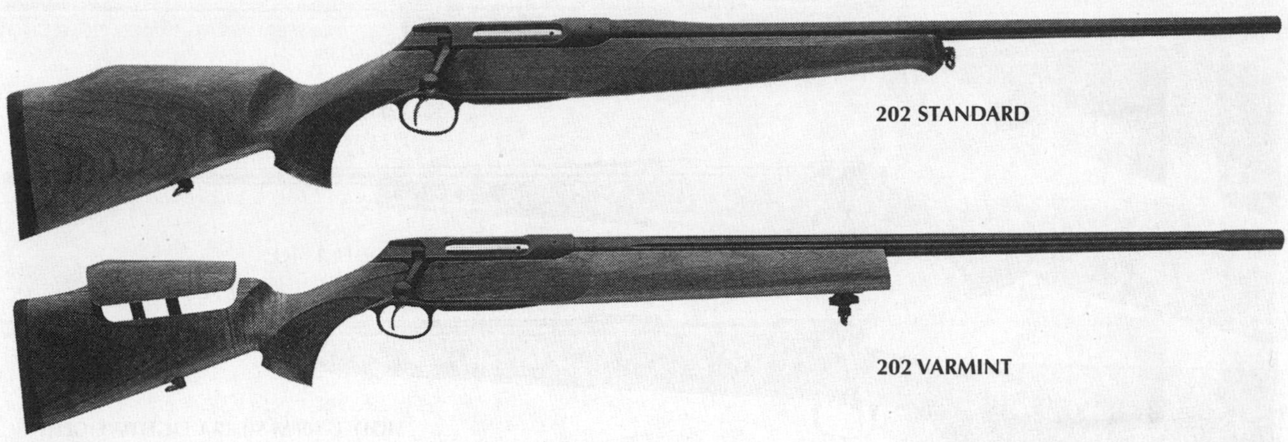

202 STANDARD

202 VARMINT

MODEL 202
Action: bolt
Stock: Claro walnut
Barrel: 24 in.
Sights: none
Weight: 7.7
Caliber: .243, .25-06, 6.5x55, .270, .308, .30-06
Magazine: detachable box, 5 rounds
Features: adjustable trigger; quick-change barrel; also: Supreme Magnum with 26 in. barrel in 7mm Rem., .300 Win., .300 Wby., .375 H&H; Varmint and Tactical versions too

Model 202: **$1233**
Magnum: **$1445**
Synthetic: **$1288**
Lightweight: **$1449**
Varmint: **$1544**
Left-hand (.30-06, walnut): . . . **$2732**
SSG 3000 Tactical: **$1612**

Savage Rifles

MODEL 12FV

THE LAST HALF OF the l9th century witnessed a flood of new gun designs from American inventors. Beginning in l849 with Christian Sharps's dropping-block rifle and the Hunt Volitional Repeater, manufacturers found ways to marry mass production with powerful cartridges in order to build rapid-fire guns that worked every time. Like many of his predecessors, Arthur William Savage used one successful gun design to found a company that would become a household name in American gun design.

Born June l3, l857 in Kingston, Jamaica, Arthur Savage went to school in England and the United States. His father was England's Special Commissioner to the British West Indies. Young Savage had an adventurous streak and immediately after college sailed for Australia, where he found work on a cattle ranch. Arthur also found a wife (Annie Bryant) and started a family. One of his sons was born in a wagon on a wilderness trek. Eventually the Savages would have four sons and four daughters. An astute businessman, Arthur quickly built himself a stake in cattle. After an 11-year stay, he was said to own the biggest ranch in Australia.

The Outback had provided fortune and thrills (Aborigines once captured him and held him for several months), but Savage itched for new frontiers. He sold his ranch, moved back to Jamaica and bought a coffee plantation. There he tinkered with machinery and pursued an interest in firearms and explosives. With another inventor, he developed the Savage-Halpine torpedo. It got good reviews from the U.S. Navy, but no contract came. Later the design was sold to the Brazilian government. Savage also worked on plans for recoilless rifles.

In l892, when Savage was just 35 years old, he finished the blueprint for a new lever-action repeating rifle – a hammerless gun with a rotary magazine. It was a daring design in the wake of analyses that blamed the failure of the similar Model l878 Sharps-

RIFLES

Savage Rifles

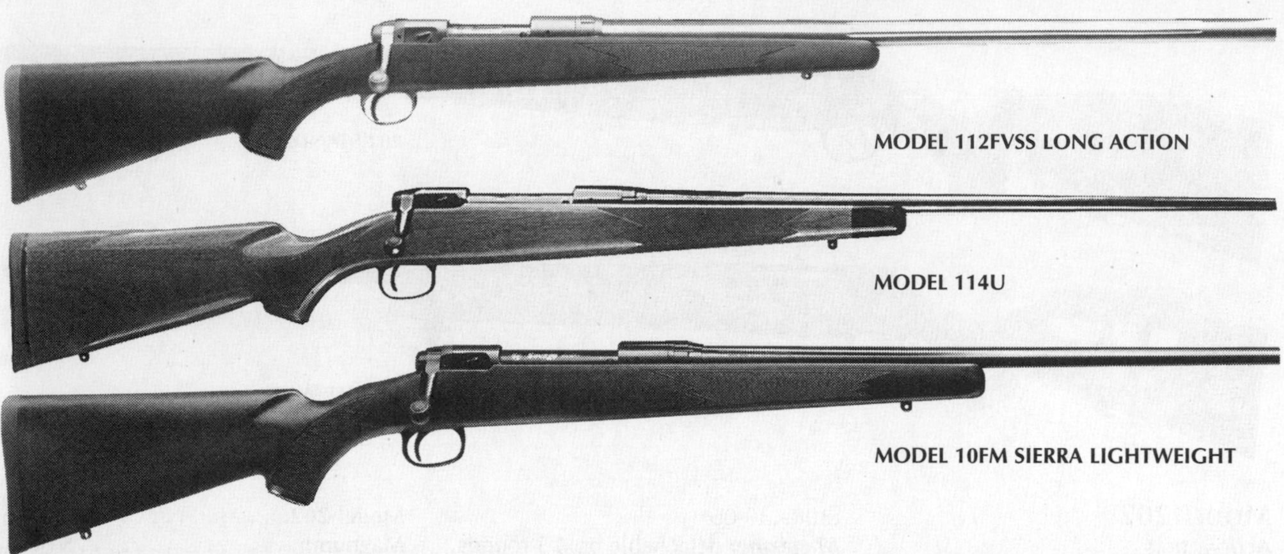

MODEL 112FVSS LONG ACTION

MODEL 114U

MODEL 10FM SIERRA LIGHTWEIGHT

Borchardt on its lack of a visible hammer. By this time Savage was living in the U.S. and he submitted his rifle for testing at the l892 ordnance trials on Governor's Island, New York. It was beaten by the Krag-Jorgensen, and Savage turned to sportsmen. Arthur Savage redesigning his gun, paring magazine capacity to five and altering the lever to accommodate three fingers. He also developed a new cartridge for the rifle and in l894 formed the Savage Arms Company in Utica, New York. Factory operations began within a year.

Savage's first commercial rifle was called the Model l895. Its rear-locking bolt abutted a steel web machined into the tail of a streamlined receiver milled from a forging. There were no openings rearward to allow the escape of gas from a ruptured case. Side ejection kept cases out of the line of sight and would later permit low scope mounting.

Savage's action was less vulnerable to water and debris than were Marlin and Winchester lever guns of the day. It had a coil mainspring (the first of its kind on a commercial lever gun) and a through-bolt to join buttstock and receiver. The through-bolt made for a stronger union than tiny wood screws applied through a tang extension. But the most exciting part of this gun was its magazine, a spring-loaded brass spool with a visible cartridge counter that showed how many rounds remained.

Savage's spool magazine design was better protected than any under-barrel tube, and smoother in operation. It didn't affect rifle balance, because the weight stayed between your hands. Winchesters became muzzle-heavy with full tubes. Secondly, the Savage magazine didn't affect barrel vibrations as tubular magazines did. Accuracy was thus enhanced. Most importantly, pointed bullets were safe to use in the Model 95 because the cartridges did not rest primer-to-bullet tip. So a hunter could use more powerful ammunition with greater reach.

Model 12FV (Short Action)

Action: bolt
Stock: synthetic
Barrel: varmint 26 in.
Sights: none
Weight: 9.0lbs.
Caliber: .223, .22-250, .243, .308
Magazine: box, 5 rounds
Features: also: 12VSS with fluted stainless barrel, Choate adjustable stock (11.3 lbs.) and V2BVSS with stainless fluted barrel, laminated or synthetic stock (9.5 lbs.)

FV $515
VSS $934
VBSS laminated $675
VBSS synthetic $626

Model 112 FVSS (Long-Action)

Action: bolt
Stock: lightweight composite
Barrel: fluted stainless 26 in.
Sights: none
Weight: 10.3lbs.
Caliber: .25-06, 7mm Rem. Mag., .30-06, .300 Win. Mag.
Magazine: box, 4 rounds
Features: also: 112BVSS with laminated stock

FVSS $626
BVSS $675

Model 114U

Action: bolt
Stock: walnut
Barrel: 22 in.
Sights: none
Weight: 7.0lbs.
Caliber: .270, .30-06
Magazine: box, 5 rounds
Features: also Magnum in 7mm Rem., .300 Win. (3-round magazine)

114U $552

Model 10FM Sierra

Action: bolt
Stock: lightweight composite
Barrel: 20 in.
Sights: none
Weight: 6.3lbs.
Caliber: .243, .270 WSM, 7mm-08, .308, .300 WSM
Magazine: box, 5 rounds
Features: open sights available; LE (Law Enforcement) version with heavy 20 or 26 in. barrel; FCM Scout with ghost ring sight, detachable box magazine and forward scope mount

FM. $495
LE $566
FCM . . . . price on request

RIFLES

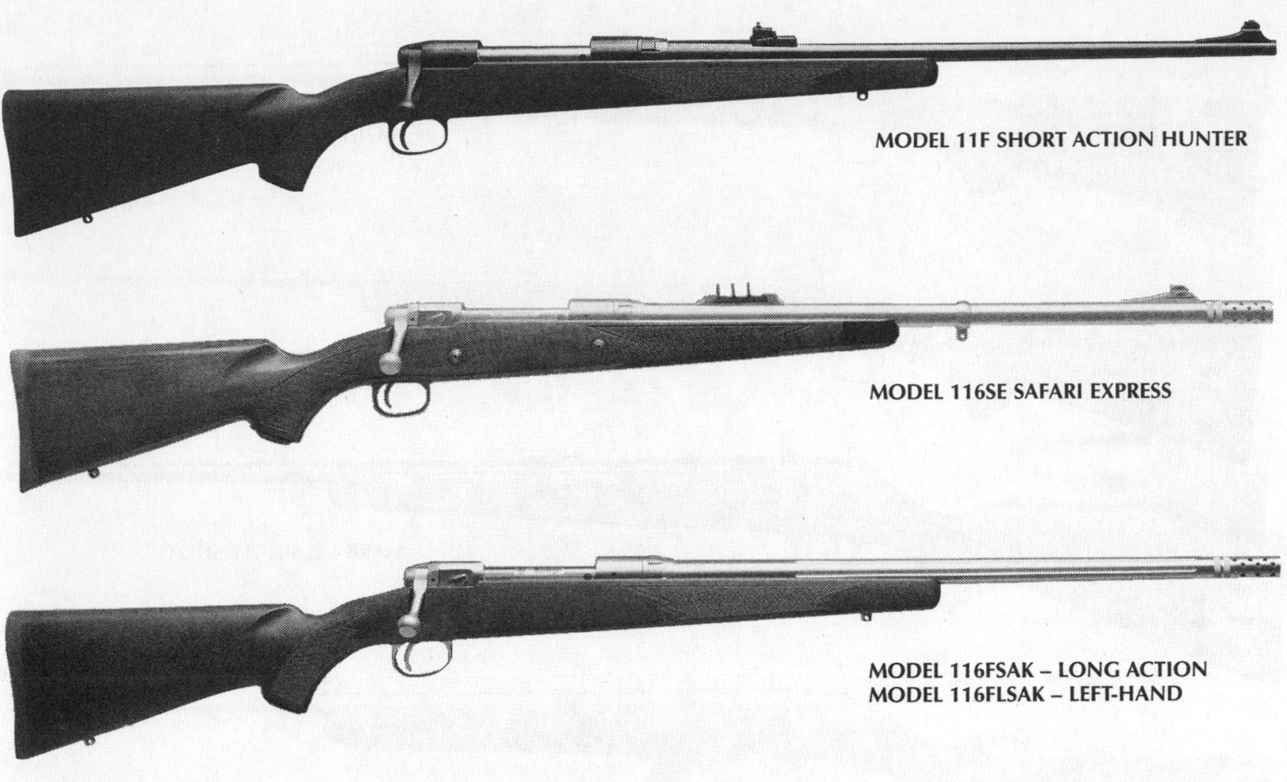

MODEL 11F SHORT ACTION HUNTER

MODEL 116SE SAFARI EXPRESS

MODEL 116FSAK – LONG ACTION
MODEL 116FLSAK – LEFT-HAND

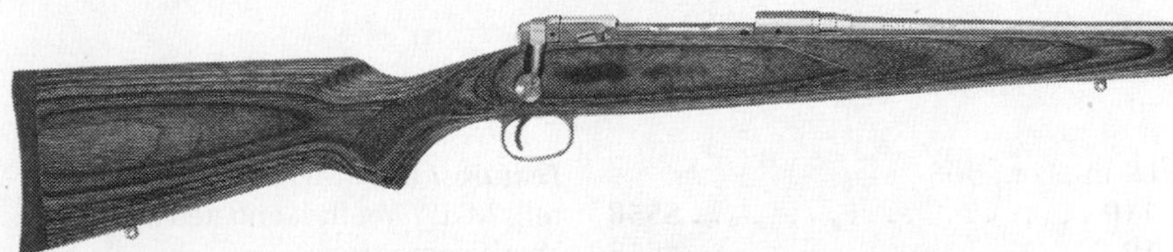

MODEL 116BSS — LONG ACTION

Model 11F

Action: bolt
Stock: synthetic
Barrel: 22 in.
Sights: none
Weight: 6.8lbs.
Caliber: .223, .22-250, .243, 7mm-08, 7SUM, .308, .270 WSM, 7mm WSM, .300 WSM, 7mm RSUM, .300 RSUM
Magazine: box, 5 rounds
Features: open sights available; also 11G with walnut stock, 10 GY Youth with short stock in .223, .243, and .308

11F $461
11G. $436

Model 116 SE Safari Express

Action: bolt
Stock: walnut with cut checkering, ebony tip
Barrel: stainless 24 in.
Sights: open
Weight: 8.5lbs.
Caliber: .375 H&H, .300 Rem. Ultra Mag., .458 Win. Mag.
Magazine: box, 4 rounds
Features: Classic-style stock with select-grade wood, stainless-steel crossbolts, internally vented recoil pad

Safari Express $1013

Model 116FSAK

Action: bolt
Stock: synthetic
Barrel: stainless, fluted 22, 24, and 26 in.
Sights: none
Weight: 6.8lbs.
Caliber: .270, .30-06 (22 in.), 7mm Rem. Mag., .300 Win. Mag. (24 in.), .300 RUM (26 in.)
Magazine: box, 4 rounds
Features: included: adjustable muzzle brake

116 FSAK. $601

Model 116FSS (Long Action)

Action: bolt
Stock: synthetic
Barrel: stainless 22, 24, or 26 in.
Sights: none
Weight: 6.5lbs.
Caliber: .270, .30-06 (22 in.), 7mm Rem. Mag., .300 Win. Mag., .338 Win. Mag., 7mm RUM, .300 RUM (26 in.)
Magazine: box, 3 or 4 rounds
Features: also: 116BSS with checkered laminated stock

116FSS. $520
116BSS $668

Savage Rifles

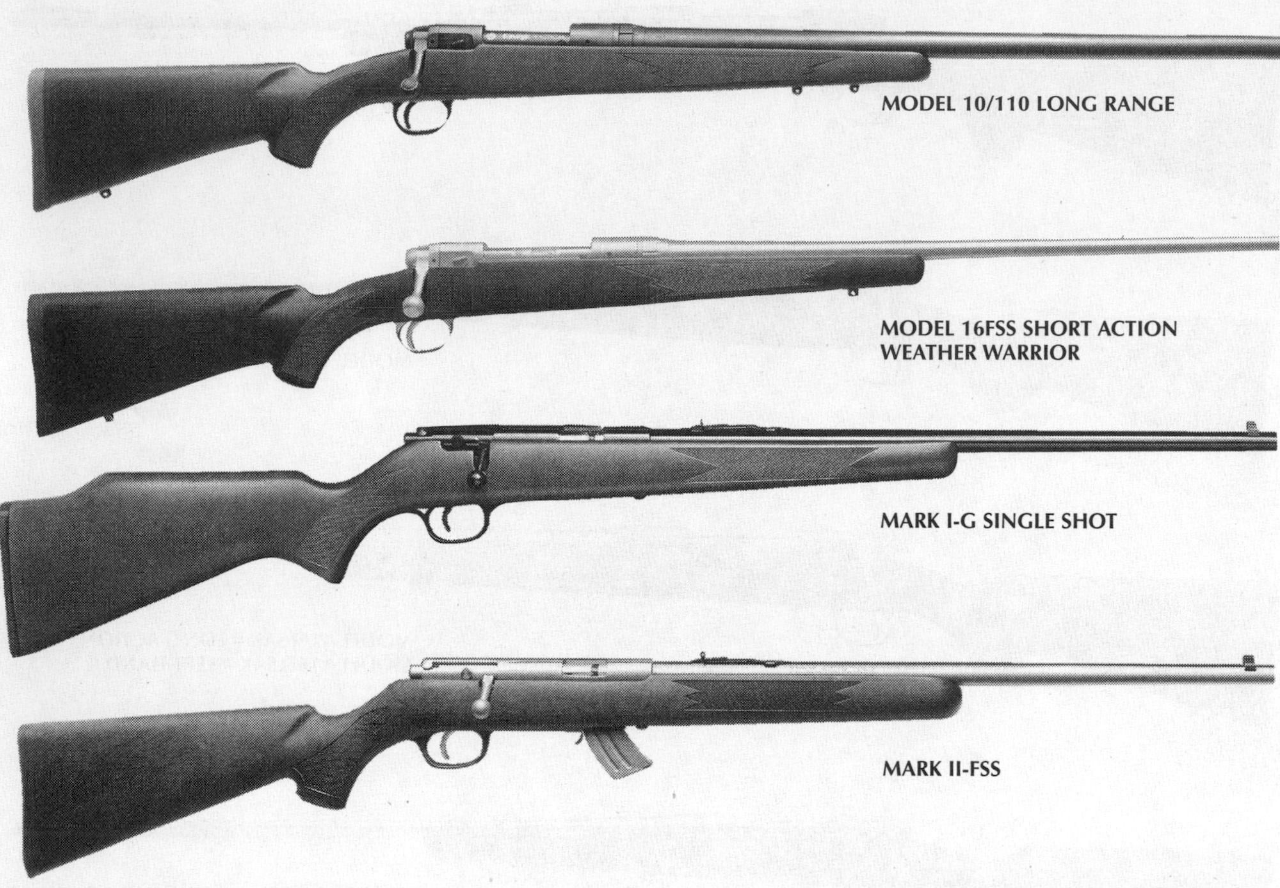

MODEL 10/110 LONG RANGE

MODEL 16FSS SHORT ACTION WEATHER WARRIOR

MARK I-G SINGLE SHOT

MARK II-FSS

RIFLES

Model 10/110

Action: bolt
Stock: checkered synthetic
Barrel: 24 in. with recessed target-style muzzle
Sights: none
Weight: 8.5lbs.
Caliber: .223, .25-06, .30-06, 7mm Rem. Mag., .308, .300 Win. Mag.
Magazine: box, 5 rounds
Features: Black matte finish on metal; black graphite stock; drilled and tapped for scope mount, bases included. Left-hand available.
Model 10/110 . . . . $558

Model 110 Long Range

Action: bolt
Stock: lightweight composite
Barrel: heavy 24 in.
Sights: none
Weight: 8.5lbs.
Caliber: .25-06, 7mm Rem. Mag., .30-06
Magazine: box, 4 rounds
Features: also short-action Model 10 LR in .223, .308
110 . . . . $558
10 . . . . $558

Model 16FSS (Short Action)

Action: bolt
Stock: synthetic
Barrel: stainless 22 in.
Sights: none
Weight: 6.0lbs.
Caliber: .223, .243, 7-08, 7 SUM, .308, .300 SUM
Magazine: box, 3 or 4 rounds
Features: also: 16BSS with checkered laminated stock in .300 WSM only
16FSS. $520
16BSS $668

Mark I

Action: bolt
Stock: hardwood
Barrel: 21 in.
Sights: open
Weight: 5.5lbs.
Caliber: .22 S, .22 L, .22 LR
Magazine: none
Features: also: MkIG Youth (19 in. barrel), MkILY Youth laminated stock, MIY Youth camo stock
Mark I G $144
G Youth $144
LY $175
Y Camo $174

Mark II F

Action: bolt
Stock: synthetic
Barrel: 21 in.
Sights: open
Weight: 5.0lbs.
Caliber: .22 LR
Magazine: detachable box, 5 rounds
Features: also: MkIIG with hardwood stock, MkIIFSS stainless, MkIIGY with short stock and 19 in. barrel
F $144
G. $156
FSS $205
GY. $156
GXP (with scope) $164
camo $174

Savage Rifles

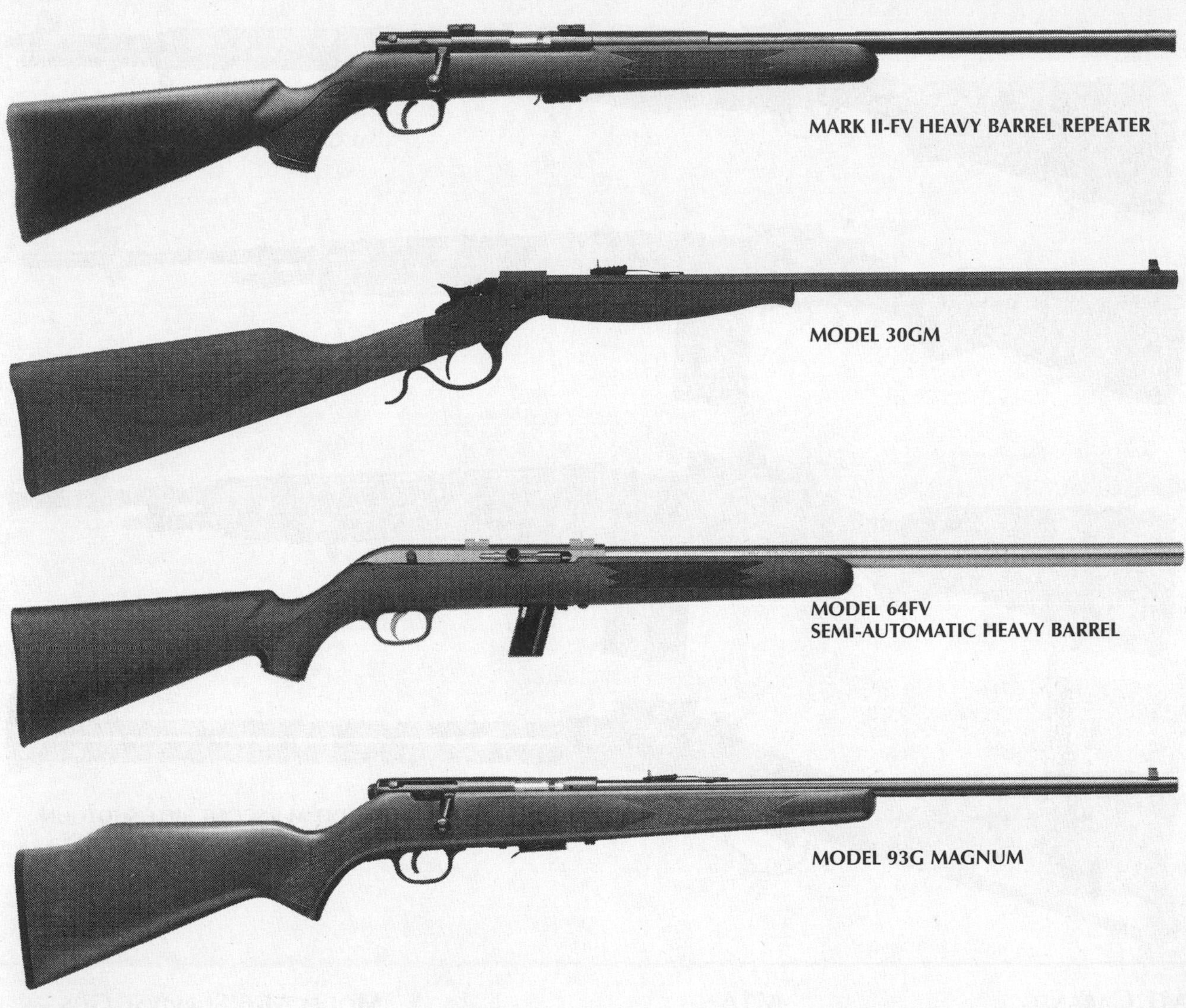

MARK II-FV HEAVY BARREL REPEATER

MODEL 30GM

MODEL 64FV
SEMI-AUTOMATIC HEAVY BARREL

MODEL 93G MAGNUM

Mark II FV Heavy-Barrel

Action: bolt
Stock: synthetic
Barrel: heavy 21 in.
Sights: none
Weight: 6.0lbs.
Caliber: .22 LR
Magazine: detachable box, 5 or 10 rounds
Features: Weaver scope bases included; also: MkII LV with laminated stock (6.5 lbs.)

FV **$216**
BV **$248**
FVXP (with scope) **$252**

Model 30

Action: dropping block
Stock: walnut
Barrel: octagon 21 in.
Sights: open
Weight: 4.3lbs.
Caliber: .22 LR, .22 WMR, .17 HMR
Magazine: none
Features: re-creation of Steven's Favorite

30G **$221**
30GM **$258**
30R17 . . . . **$284**

Model 64F

Action: autoloading
Stock: synthetic
Barrel: 21 in.
Sights: open
Weight: 5.5lbs.
Caliber: .22 LR
Magazine: detachable box, 10 rounds
Features: also; 64 FSS stainless, 64FV and FVSS heavy barrel, 64G hardwood stock

64F **$135**
64FV **$182**
64FVSS **$235**
64G **$151**

Model 93G

Action: bolt
Stock: synthetic
Barrel: 21 in.
Sights: open
Weight: 5.8lbs.
Caliber: .22 WMR, .17 HMR
Magazine: detachable box, 5 rounds
Features: 93G with hardwood stock; 93 FSS stainless, 93FVSS with heavy barrel, 93G with hardwood stock

G **$182**
GV in .17 HMR **$221**

Springfield Rifles

M1 GARAND

M1A STANDARD

M1A-A1 SCOUT RIFLE

MODEL M-6 SCOUT RIFLE/SHOTGUN COMBO FOLDING SURVIVAL GUN

RIFLES

M1 Garand

Action: autoloading
Stock: walnut
Barrel: 24 in.
Sights: target
Weight: 9.5
Caliber: .30-06
Magazine: clip-fed, 8 rounds
Features: gas-operated; new stock, receiver, barrel; other parts mil-spec

M1 Garand .308: $1129
M1 Garand .30-06: $1099

M1A

Action: autoloading
Stock: walnut
Barrel: 22 in.
Sights: target
Weight: 9.2
Caliber: .308
Magazine: detachable box, 5 or 10 rounds
Features: also with fiberglass stock and M1A/Scout with 18 in. barrel and scope mount (9.0 lbs.)

M1A: $1448
M1A fiberglass: $1319
M1A Scout Rifle: $1639
M1A Scout Rifle, fiberglass: . . $1529

Model M-6 Survival Gun

Action: hinged breech
Stock: synthetic
Barrel: 16 in.
Sights: open
Weight: 4.0
Caliber: .22LR and .410 or .22 Hornet and .410
Magazine: none
Features: over/under combination gun; lockable plastic case; also: stainless M-6

M-6: $185
M-6 stainless: $219

Szecsei & Fuchs Rifles

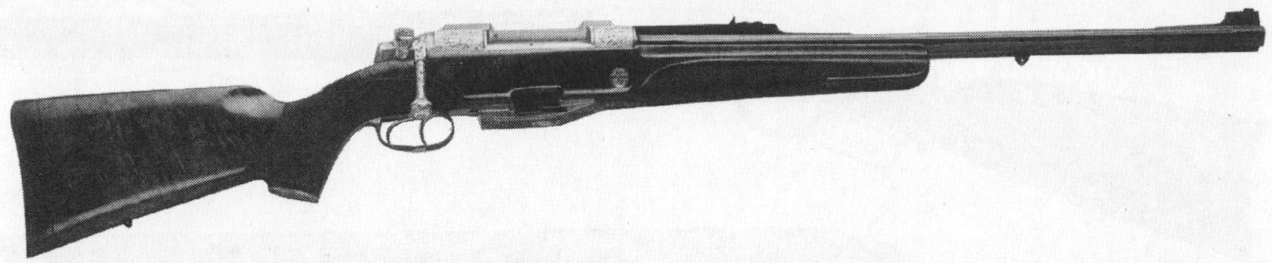

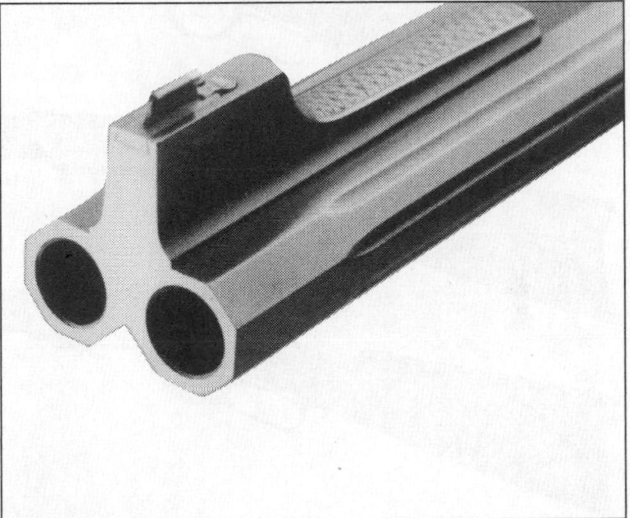

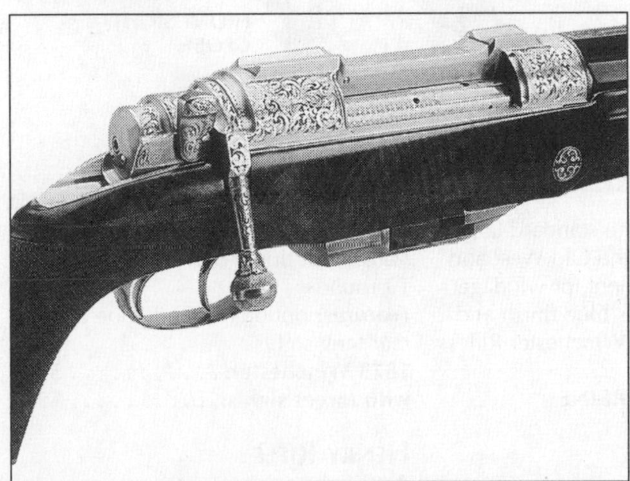

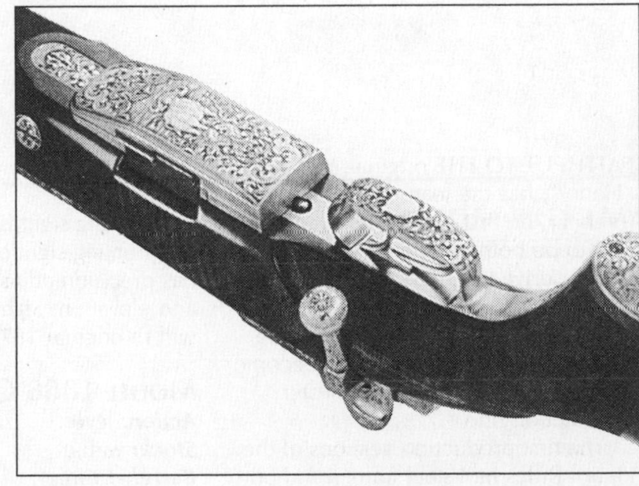

RIFLES

THE SZECSEI & FUCHS double-barrel bolt action rifle may be the only one of its kind. Built with great care and much handwork from the finest materials, it follows a design remarkable for its cleverness. And while the rifle is not light-weight, it can be aimed quickly and offers more large-caliber firepower than any competitor. The six-shot magazine feeds two rounds simultaneously, both of which can then be fired by two quick pulls of the trigger.

Specifications

Chamberings: .300 Win, 9.3 x 64, .358 Norma, .375 H&H, .404 Jeff, .416 Rem., .458 Win., .416 Rigby, .450 Rigby, .460 Short A-Square, .470 Capstick, .495 A-Square, .500 Jeffery

Weight: 14 lbs. with round barrels, 16 with octagon barrels.

Price: . . . . Available on request

Taylor's Rifles

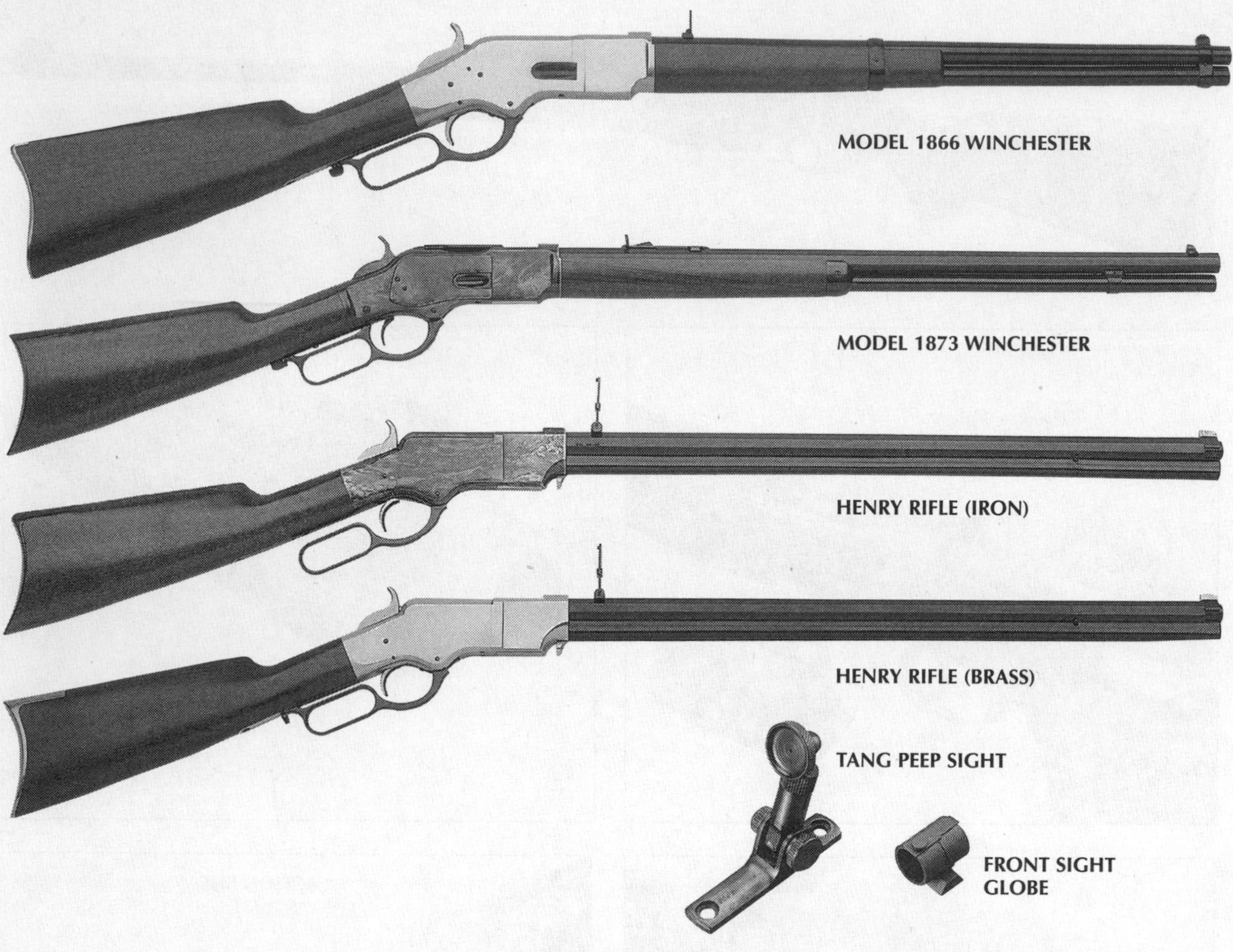

RIFLES

FAITHFUL TO THE original, the Taylor "Henry", has the features that made its forebear the first lever-action repeating rifle to be both practical and reliable. It was derived from the Volcanic carbines of Walter Hunt, and was named after B. Tyler Henry, who refined the rifle. The Henry design would become the cornerstone of the Winchester lever-action line.

The first production versions of the Henry Rifles had steel frames and butt plates with a total production of around 400 rifles. These first models also lacked the lever latch. Only a few specimens are available now and they are highly prized by collectors around the world.

The original Winchester 73 had a long life, from 1873-1927. Its steel frame enabled the use of .44/40 ammunition, a more powerful round than the .44 Henry. Demand quickly pushed production into the hundreds of thousands.

This tang sight is the standard target and hunting sight of the Old West and has precision adjustment for windage and elevation. Sight is blue finish and will fit original 1873 Winchester Rifles.

Model 1866 Carbine

Action: lever
Stock: walnut
Barrel: 19 in.
Sights: open
Weight: 6.5
Caliber: .44-40, .45 Long Colt
Magazine: under-barrel tube, 9 rounds
Features: brass frame
Carbine:. $725

Model 1873 Winchester Rifle

Action: lever
Stock: walnut
Barrel: 24 in.
Sights: open
Weight: 7.5
Caliber: .44-40, .45 Long Colt
Magazine: under-barrel tube, 13 rounds
Features: optional: front globe and rear tang sights
1873 Winchester:. $875
with target sights:. $981

Henry Rifle

Action: lever
Stock: walnut
Barrel: 24 in.
Sights: open
Weight: 7.5
Caliber: .44-40, .45 Long Colt
Magazine: under-barrel tube, 13 rounds
Features: brass frame; also: original-type steel-frame in .44-40 only
Henry:. $945
.44-40 Steel frame:. $1020

Thompson & Campbell Rifles

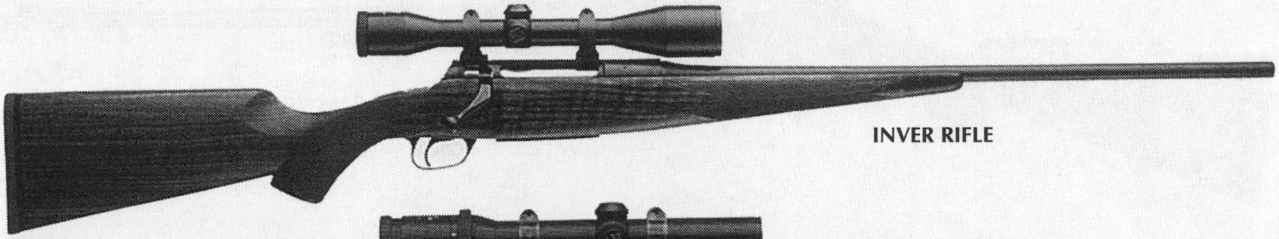

INVER RIFLE

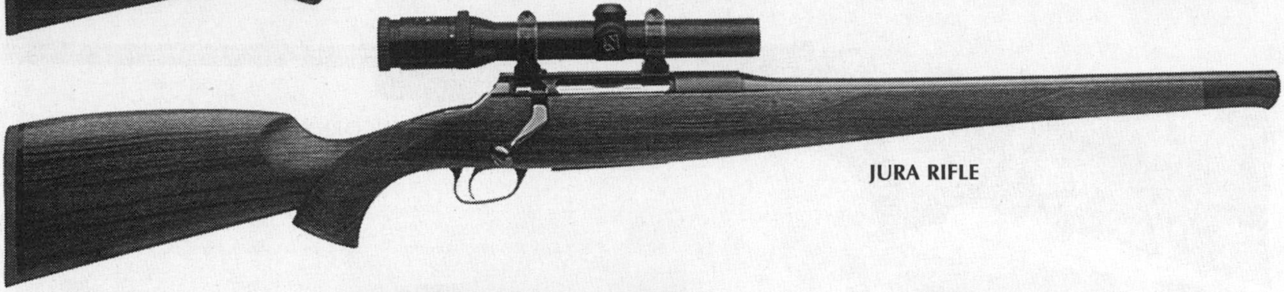

JURA RIFLE

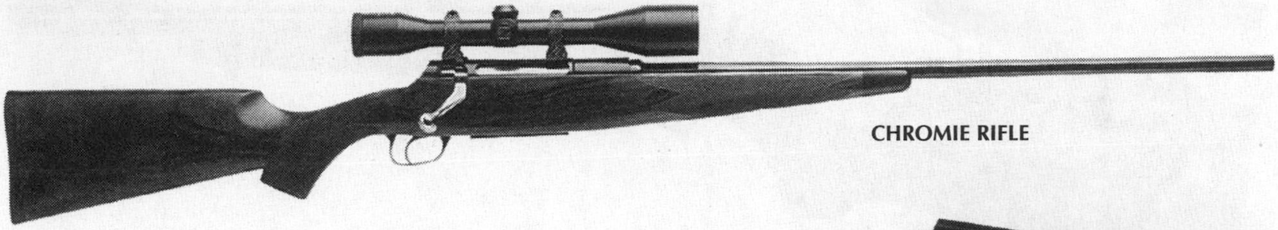

CHROMIE RIFLE

PATENTED
INVER ACTION SHOWING
BEDDING PLATE.

Inver
Action: bolt
Stock: select walnut
Barrel: 22 in.
Sights: none
Weight: 8.0
Caliber: all popular standard calibers
Magazine: detachable box, 4 rounds
Features: takedown barrels; optional removable sights and two-stage trigger; also: Chromie deluxe version
Inver: . . . . price on request

Jura
Action: bolt
Stock: full length walnut
Barrel: 17 in.
Sights: none
Weight: 7.5
Caliber: all popular standard calibers
Magazine: detachable box, 4 rounds
Features: optional removable sights, two-stage trigger
Jura: . . . . price on request

Learn to use a sling for shooting as well as carrying. Brownell's Latigo sling is a fine example of one designed for shooting. It's leather, with an adjustable loop. Carrying straps don't qualify.

Thompson/Center Rifles

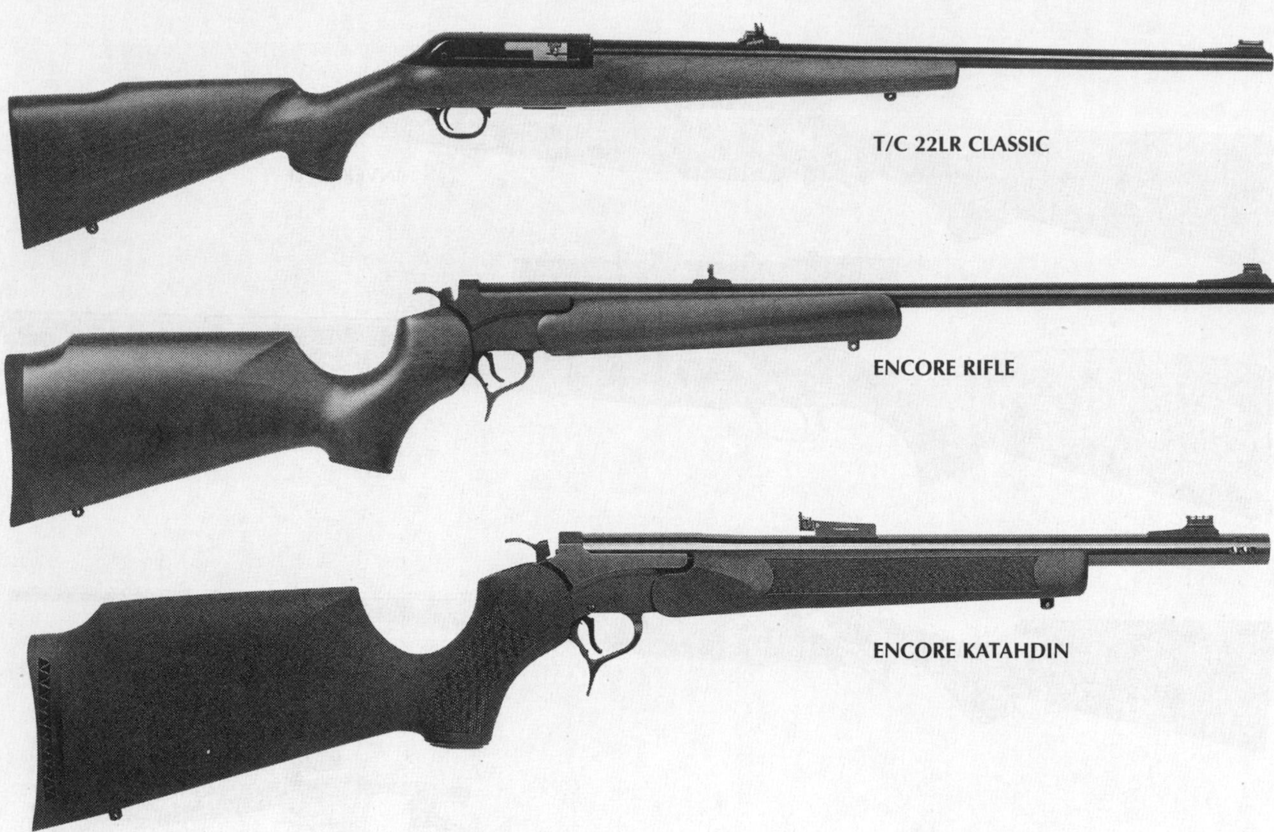

T/C 22LR CLASSIC

ENCORE RIFLE

ENCORE KATAHDIN

T/C.22LR Classic
Action: autoloading
Stock: walnut
Barrel: 22 in.
Sights: illuminated
Weight: 5.5
Caliber: .22 LR
Magazine: detachable box, 8 rounds
.22 Classic: $369

Encore
Action: hinged breech
Stock: walnut
Barrel: 24 and 26 in.
Sights: open
Weight: 6.8
Caliber: most popular calibers, from .22 Hornet to .300 Win. Mag. and .45-70
Magazine: none
Features: also: synthetic and stainless versions; Hunter package with .308 or .300 includes 3-9x40 T/C scope and hard case
walnut: $626
synthetic: $599
stainless: $669

Katahdiin Carbine
Action: hinged breech
Stock: synthetic
Barrel: 18 in.
Sights: illuminated
Weight: 6.6
Caliber: .444, .450, .45-70
Magazine: none
Features: integral muzzle brake
Carbine: $618

Short barrels leak velocity. How much depends on the cartridge and load and starting length. For standard-size rounds, a 22-inch barrel is adequate; small-bore magnums need longer barrels.

RIFLES

Uberti Rifles

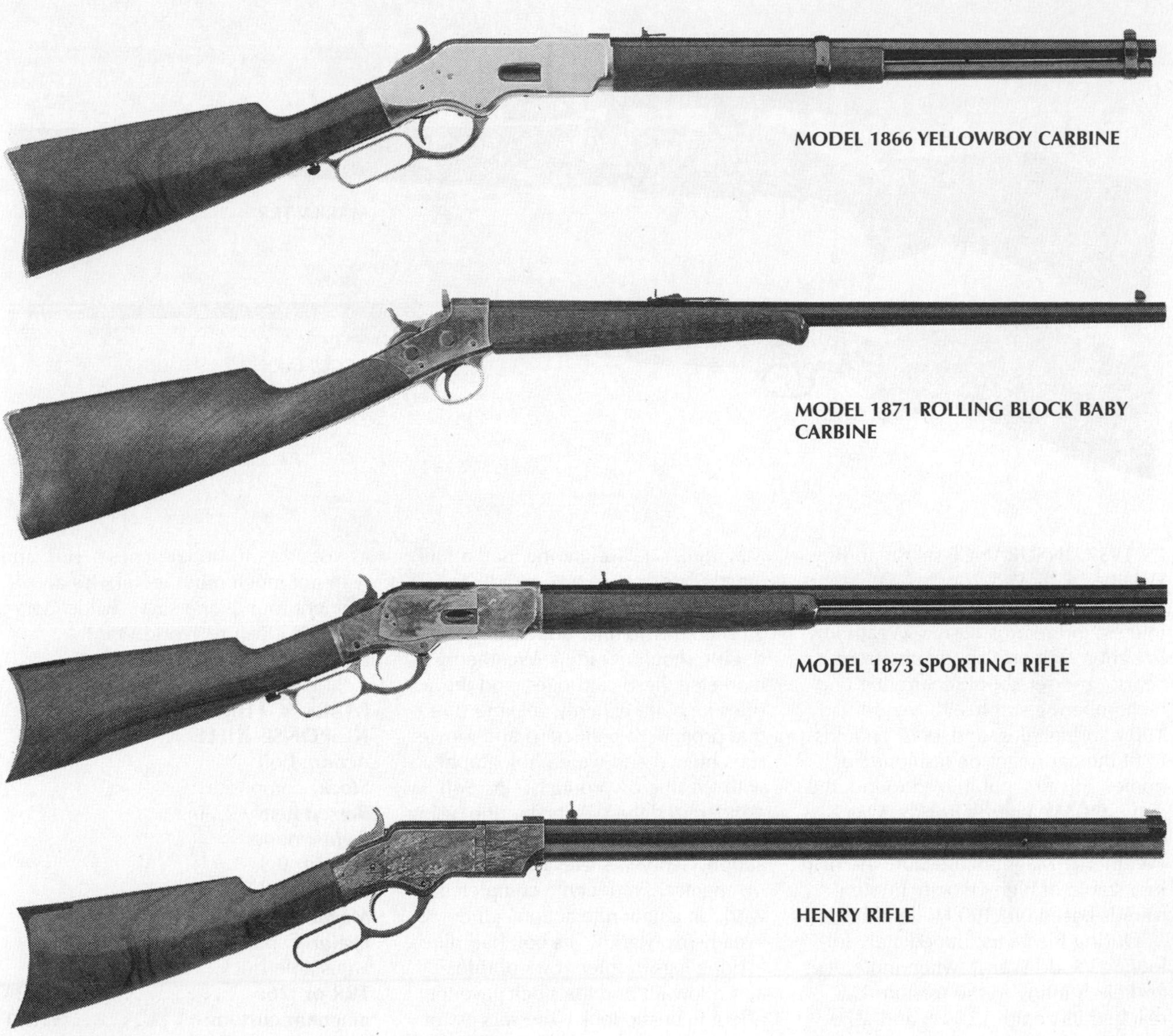

MODEL 1866 YELLOWBOY CARBINE

MODEL 1871 ROLLING BLOCK BABY CARBINE

MODEL 1873 SPORTING RIFLE

HENRY RIFLE

RIFLES

Model 1866 Winchester Carbine

Action: lever
Stock: walnut, straight grip
Barrel: 19 in.
Sights: open
Weight: 7.4
Caliber: .22 LR, .22 WMR, .38 Spl., .44-40, .45 Long Colt
Magazine: under-barrel tube
Features: brass frame
1866 Winchester Carbine: $755
1866 Rifle (24" BBL): $775

Model 1871 Remington Baby Carbine

Action: dropping block
Stock: walnut, straight grip
Barrel: 22 in.
Sights: open
Weight: 4.9
Caliber: .22 LR, .22 WMR, .22 Hornet, .357 Magnum
Magazine: none
Features: case-colored receiver
Baby Carbine: $515
1871 Rifle (26" BBL): $580

Model 1873 Winchester Sporting Rifle

Action: lever
Stock: checkered walnut, straight grip
Barrel: octagon 20, 24 or 30 in.
Sights: open
Weight: 7.5
Caliber: .32-20, .357 Mag., .44-40, .45 Long Colt
Magazine: under-barrel tube, 10 rounds
Features: optional pistol grip
straight grip (20" BBL): $930
(24" BBL): $930
pistol grip: $1015

Henry Rifle

Action: lever
Stock: walnut, straight grip
Barrel: octagon 18, 22 and 24 in.
Sights: open
Weight: 7.9
Caliber: .44-40, .45 Long Colt
Magazine: under-barrel tube, 9 rounds
Features: brass or steel frame
brass frame: $995
steel frame: $1085

Weatherby Rifles

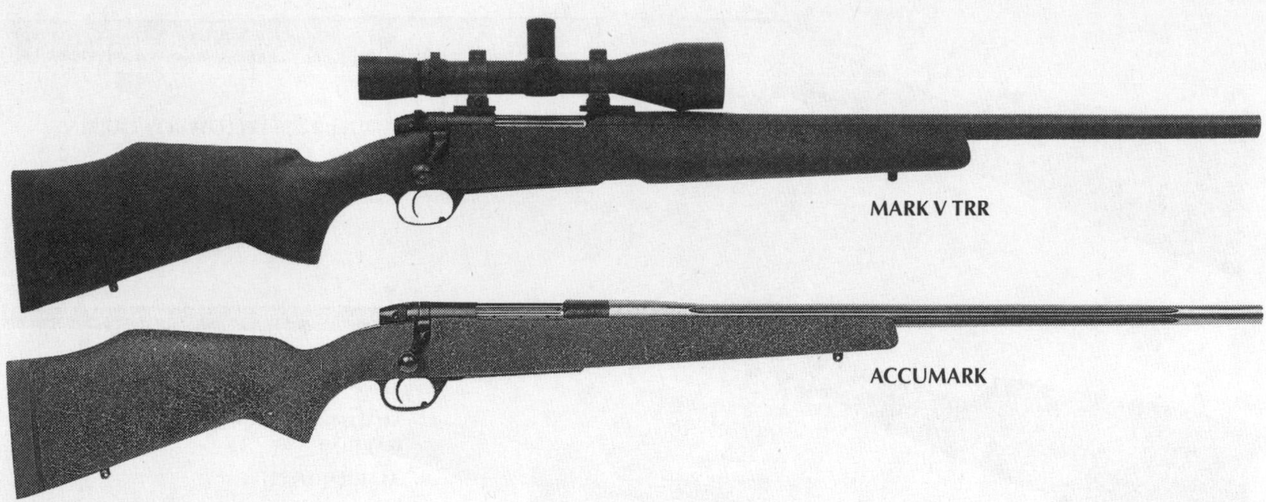

MARK V TRR

ACCUMARK

IN 1937, INSURANCE salesman Roy Weatherby moved from his native Kansas to California. To pursue his interest in firearms design, Weatherby bought a drill press and lathe from Sears. and set about rebarreling and rechambering surplus 98 Mausers, 1903 Springfields, and 1917 Enfields to fit the cartridges he fashioned at home. His first publicized round, the racy .220 Weatherby Rocket, was a blown-out Swift. His next, the .270 Weatherby Magnum, became the first in a stable of high-velocity hunting rounds based on .300 Holland brass.

During the years immediately following World War II, when mule deer and elk hunting in the western U.S. reached its zenith, .30-06 and .270 cartridges became increasingly popular. In fact the .30-06 had already supplanted the .30-30 as the most popular U.S. deer cartridge. A 1947 survey reported by *The American Rifleman*, stated that hunters "want bolt actions and fast loads!" and Roy Weatherby set out to accommodate riflemen who craved even higher performance.

Weatherby quickly made a business of his avocation, promoting high velocity rounds as the way to make lightning-like kills at long range. His .270 Magnum drove bullets 300 feet-per-second faster than a .270 Winchester. The .257 and 7mm Weatherby Magnums that followed were based on a shortened Holland & Holland case cut to fit .30-06-length actions. The .300 Weatherby Magnum, a 1946 offering, had a full-length case.

All Weatherby rounds were distinguished by minimal body taper and a double shoulder radius. Weatherby marketed these cartridges (and the rifles he built) expertly, making sure that prominent politicians and movie stars hunted and were photographed with Weatherby products. In 1948 he standardized the Weatherby rifle, using a commercial Fabrique Nationale (FN) action. Ten years later he and company engineer Fred Jennie completed work on a new rifle action -- the Weatherby Mark V. Its bolt had nine locking lugs in three rows of three, and a low lift and the stock gave the rifle a futuristic look. The success of Weatherby rifles were limited by their expense, unique chamberings, and availability of Weatherby ammunition, loaded only by Norma of Sweden.

In 1997 Weatherby introduced the 6½-pound Lightweight Mark V rifle chambered for standard cartridges. It featured a smaller receiver and trimmer bolt, with six lugs instead of the Magnum Mark V's nine. This rifle's 24-inch barrel ensured good balance and kept velocity up. A year later Weatherby announced a 5½-pound Ultra Lightweight, also wearing a 24-inch barrel. Additional fluting and some alloy parts trimmed ounces.

In 2001 the Ultra Lightweight became the first rifle from a commercial firm to chamber the .338-06. This powerhouse drives a 200-grain bullet as fast as a .30-06 launches a 180, and with not much more recoil. It's an efficient round, and savvy wildcatters adopted it before World War II.

Mark V Threat Response Rifle

Action: bolt
Stock: composite
Barrel: heavy 22 in.
Sights: none
Weight: 9.5
Caliber: .223, .308
Magazine: box, 3 or 5 rounds
Features: magnum custom has adjustable stock, 26 or 28 in. barrel
TRR or .26: $1624
magnum custom: $2861

Mark V Accumark

Action: bolt
Stock: composite
Barrel: 24, 26 and 28 in. barrels
Sights: none
Weight: 7.0
Caliber: .223, .22-250, .243, .25-06, .270, .280, 7-08, 7mm Rem. Mag., 7mm STW, 30-06, .308, .300 Win. Mag.; Wby. Magnums: .257, .270, 7mm, .300, .340, .30-378, .338-378
Magazine: box, 3 or 5 rounds
Features: lightweight and standard MK V actions; weight depends on caliber
Accumark: $1557
magnums: $1613
.30-378, .338-378: $1845
left-hand: $1668
magnum, left-hand: $1913

Weatherby Rifles

MARK V DANGEROUS GAME RIFLE

MARK V DELUXE

MARK V FIBERMARK STAINLESS

Mark V Dangerous Game Rifle

Action: bolt
Stock: composite
Barrel: 24 or 26 in.
Sights: open
Weight: 9.0
Caliber: .300 Win., .300 Wby., .338 Win., .340 Wby., .375 H&H, .375 Wby., .416 Rem., .458 Win., .458 Lott; also: .378, .416, .460 Wby.
Magazine: box, 3 rounds
Features: express sights, barrel band swivel

Dangerous Game Rifle: **$2892**
.378, .416: **$3053**
.460: **$3140**

Mark V Deluxe

Action: bolt
Stock: Claro walnut
Barrel: 24, 26 and 28 in.
Sights: none
Weight: 8.5
Caliber: .22-250, .243, .240 Wby., .25-06, .270, .280, 7-08, .30-06, .308; Wby. Magnums: .257, .270, 7mm, .300, .340, .278, .416, .460
Magazine: box, 3 or 5 rounds
Features: 26 in. barrels for most magnum calibers; 28 in. barrel for .378, .416, .460 (with brake)

standard: **$1835**
magnum: **$1891**
.378, .416: **$2224**
.460: **$2614**

Mark V Fibermark

Action: bolt
Stock: composite
Barrel: 24 and 26 in.
Sights: none
Weight: 8.0
Caliber: popular standard and magnum chamberings from .22-250 to .30-378 Wby.
Magazine: box, 3 to 5 rounds
Features: stainless versions available

Price: **$1145**
magnum: **$1200**
.30-378: **$1441**
stainless: **$1247**
magnum, stainless: **$1339**
.30-378 stainless: **$1528**

Weatherby Rifles

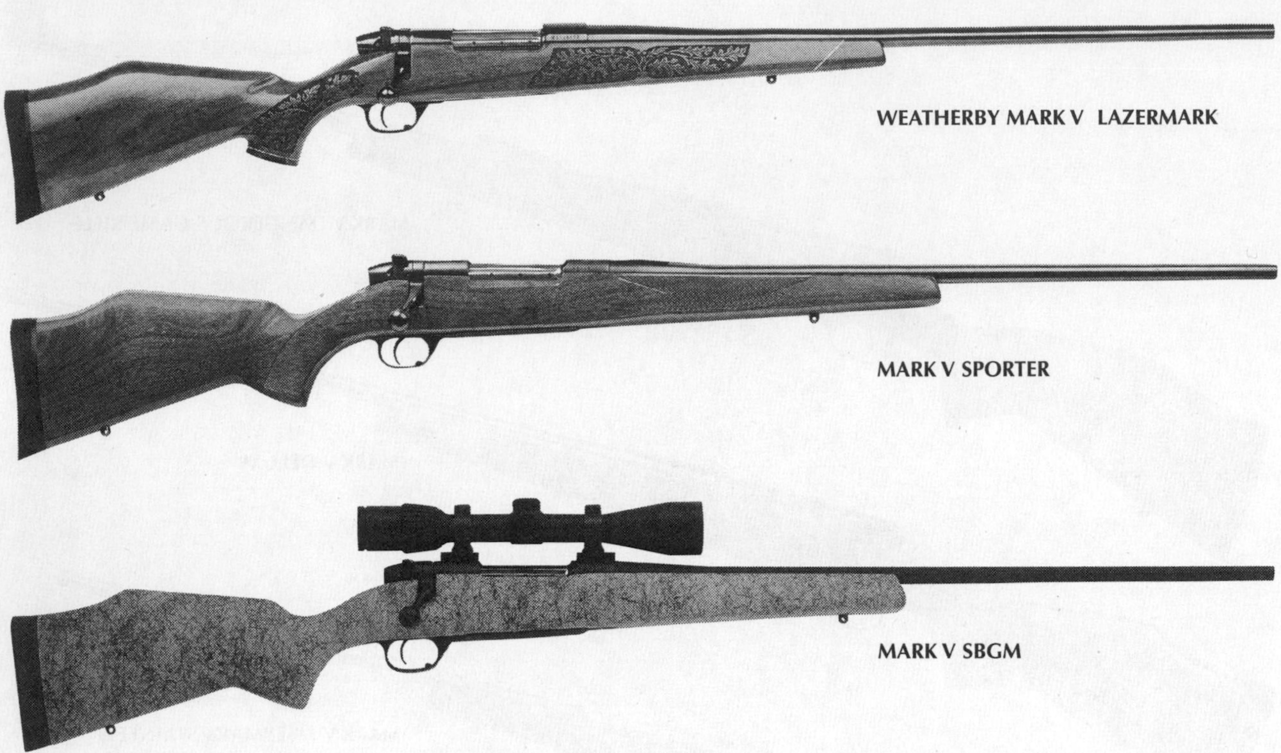

WEATHERBY MARK V LAZERMARK

MARK V SPORTER

MARK V SBGM

Mark V Lazermark

Action: bolt
Stock: walnut
Barrel: 26 in.
Sights: none
Weight: 8.5
Caliber: Wby. Magnums from .257 to .340
Magazine: box, 3 rounds
Features: laser-carved stock, hammer-forged Krieger barrel
Lazermark:. $2058

Mark V Sporter

Action: bolt
Stock: walnut
Barrel: 24 and 26 in.
Sights: none
Weight: 8.0
Caliber: popular standard and magnum chamberings from .22-250 to .340 Wby. and .375 H&H
Magazine: box, 3 or 5 rounds
Features: also available: Eurosport with oil stock finish, SLS stainless laminated
Mark V Sporter: $1167
magnums: $1223

Mark V Super Big Game Master

Action: bolt
Stock: composite
Barrel: 24 and 26 in.
Sights: none
Weight: 6.8
Caliber: .240 Wby., .25-06, .270, .280, 7mm Rem. Mag., .30-06, .300 Win. Mag., .338-06; Wby. Magnums: .257, .270, 7mm, .300
Magazine: box, 3 or 5 rounds
Features: hammer-forged Krieger barrel
Super Big Game Master:. $1561
magnums: $1623

Zero a big game rifle so the bullet strikes between 3 inches above point of aim at mid-range. That way, you'll achieve greatest "point-blank" range. For the .30-06 and kin, try a zero of 200 yards.

Weatherby Rifles

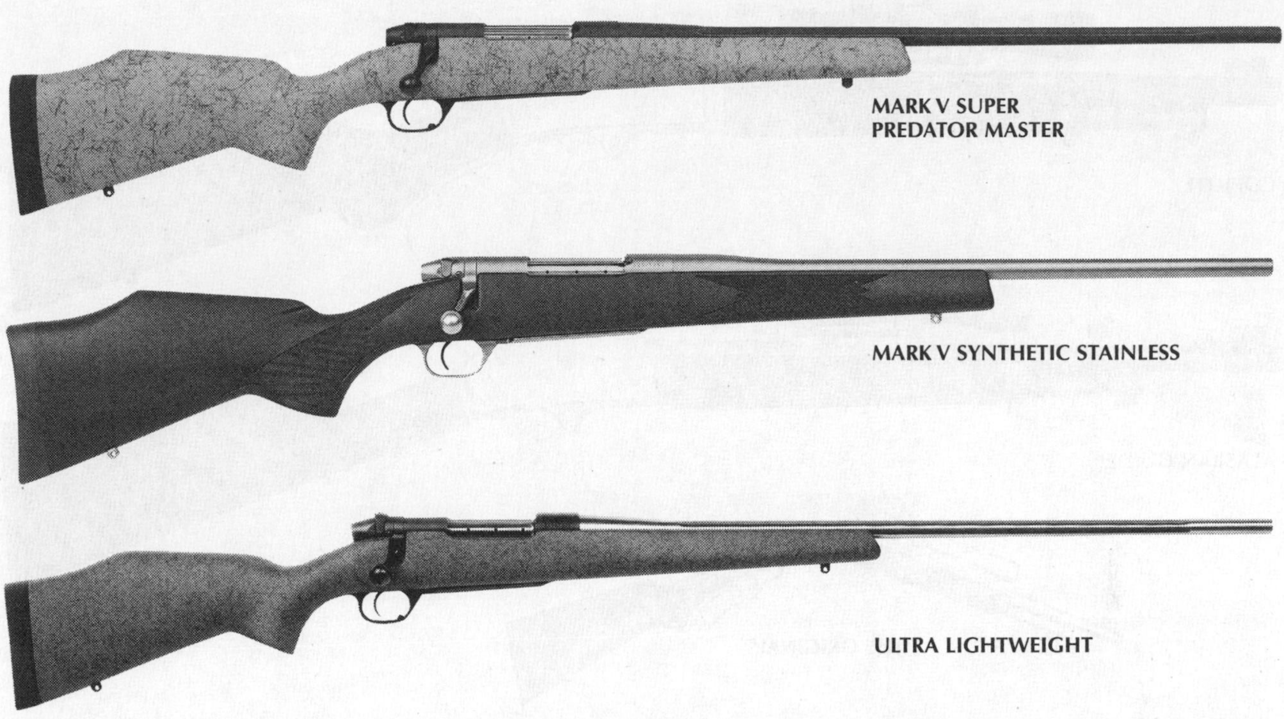

MARK V SUPER PREDATOR MASTER

MARK V SYNTHETIC STAINLESS

ULTRA LIGHTWEIGHT

Mark V Super Predator Master

Action: bolt
Stock: composite
Barrel: 24 in.
Sights: none
Weight: 6.3
Caliber: .223, .22-250, .243, 7-08, .308
Magazine: box, 5 rounds
Features: Super Varmint master has heavy 26 in., fluted stainless barrel, flat-bottomed stock (8.5 lbs.)
SPM: $1561
SVM: $1624

Mark V Synthetic

Action: bolt
Stock: synthetic
Barrel: 24, 26 and 28 in.
Sights: none
Weight: 8.5
Caliber: popular standard and magnum calibers from .22-250 to .338-378 Wby.
Magazine: box, 3 or 5 rounds
Features: also: stainless version, carbine in .243, 7-08 and .308
Mark V Synthetic: $988
magnum: $1043
.30-378, .338-378: $1232
stainless: $1089
magnum, stainless: $1199
.30-378, .338-378 stainless: . . $1385

Ultra Lightweight

Action: bolt
Stock: composite
Barrel: 24 and 26 in.
Sights: none
Weight: 6.0
Caliber: .243, .240 Wby., .25-06, .270, 7-08, .280, 7mm Rem. Mag., .308, .30-06, .300 Win. Mag., .338-06; Wby. Magnums: .257, .270, 7mm, .300
Magazine: box, 3 or 5 rounds
Features: lightweight action; 6-lug bolt
Ultra Lightweight: $1561
magnums: $1638
left-hand: $1668

Mount scopes low so they don't adversely affect the rifle's balance, and so when you cheek the stock you're looking right down the scope's axis.

Wild West Guns

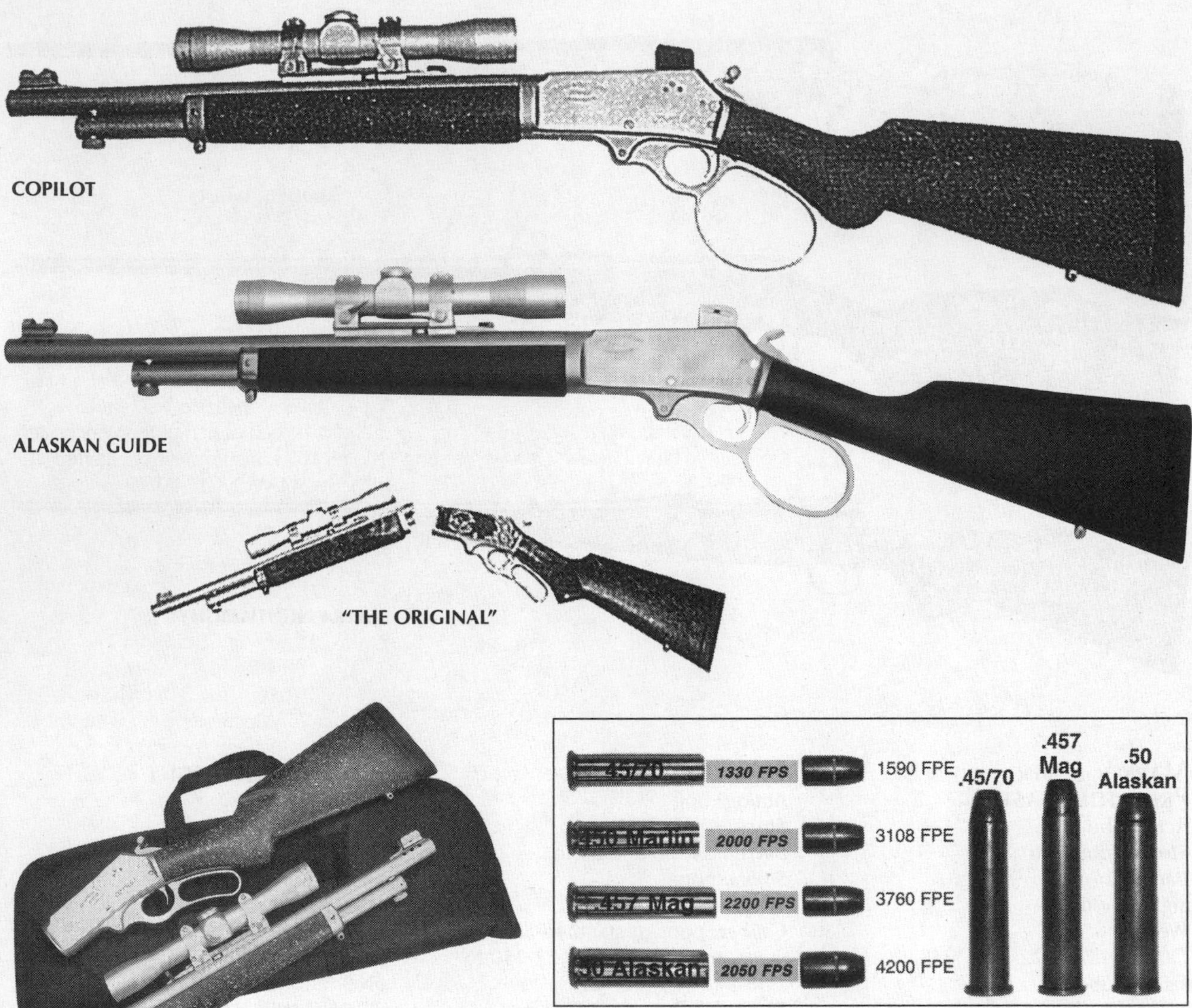

BIG GUNS FOR BIG STUFF

Co-Pilot

Action: lever
Stock: walnut
Barrel: 16, 18 or 20 inch
Sights: illuminated
Weight: 7.0
Caliber: .45-70, .457 Magnum, .50 Alaskan
Magazine: under-barrel tube
Features: 1895 Marlin action; ported barrels; take-down feature; Alaskan Guide similar, not take-down

Co-Pilot: $1799
on supplied 1895 Marlin: $1449
.50 Alaskan conversion: $200
Alaskan Guide:. $1199
Alaskan on supplied 1895 Marlin: $849
.50 Alaskan conversion: $200
Master Guide Take-Down:. . . . $1699
Take-Down on supplied 1895G: $1349

Winchester Rifles

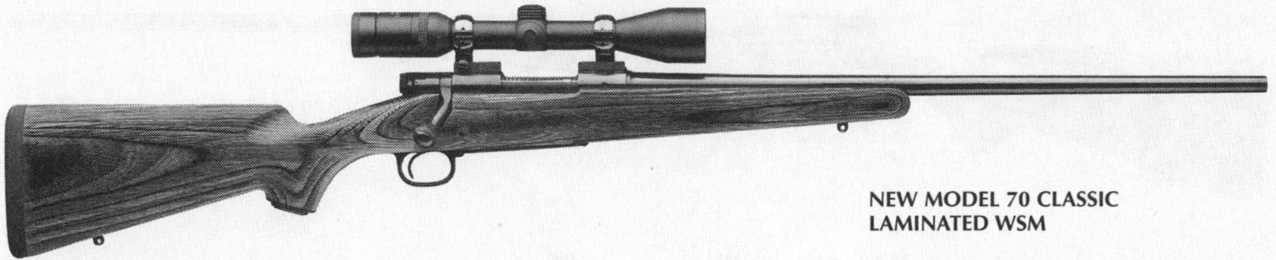

NEW MODEL 70 CLASSIC LAMINATED WSM

WINCHESTERS WERE NOT the first lever-actions, nor were lever-actions the first successful repeaters. When war with Mexico threatened to drain U.S. arsenals in 1845, armsmakers scrambled to build more rifles. Looking for more production capacity, Eliphalet Remington II traveled to Chicopee Falls, Massachusetts. There he found the N.P. Ames Company – and bought it for $2581. Included in the bargain was a new breech-loading rifle and the services of its inventor, a young Welshman named William Jenks. Remington fitted the flintlock Jenks rifles with Edward Maynard's tape-primer percussion lock and a Merrill breech mechanism.

About that time, another notable rifle appeared. Called the "Volition Repeater" by its inventor Walter Hunt, it used a 54-caliber conical "rocket ball." The base of the bullet was hollow and a charge of fulminate nearly filled the cavity. The cavity was covered by a cork cap which had a hole in its center that was sealed by paper. Priming pellets were fed under the hammer by a pill-lock mechanism as the rocket balls advanced from a tube magazine. Beset by numerous defects, Hunt sold his design to George Arrowsmith of New York.

Arrowsmith hired Lewis Jennings to improve the Volitional rifle – which he did by combining two operating levers into one and installing a rack-and-pinion gear. Arrowsmith then sold the rifle to New York financier Courtland Palmer who contracted with Robbins and Lawrence of Windsor, Vermont, for 5000 Jennings rifles. The mechanism proved hard to make and unreliable and early guns were marketed as single-shots.

Horace Smith and Benjamin Tyler Henry added improvements and in l855, a group of 40 New York and New Haven businessmen formed the Volcanic Repeating Arms Company and bought out Smith, Wesson and Palmer. Among the group was Oliver F. Winchester, a 45-year-old shirt-maker, who soon became the company director. Winchester moved Volcanic Repeating Arms from Norwich to New Haven. Daniel Wesson stayed on as shop superintendent until l856, when he joined Horace Smith to start another firm. Sales of Volcanic guns slumped, however, and early in 1857, creditors forced receivership. Winchester purchassed all of the assets for $40,000.

Winchester saw a bright future for the lever-action repeater. In April, l857, he reorganized Volcanic Repeating Arms into the New Haven Arms Company. Benjamin Tyler Henry, then 36, became shop foreman. From his work with the Volitional Repeater emerged a lever-action rimfire rifle with a l5-round, under-barrel magazine and a two-pronged firing pin. Some of the early Henrys had iron frames, but brass soon became standard. The $40 Henry used 26 grains of black powder to push 44-caliber 216-grain bullets to 1025 fps. Anemic by modern standards, the .44 Henry developed 10 times the energy of Volcanic bullets! The rifle's main fault was a slotted magazine. Dents rendered the follower unreliable, and debris clogged the slot. But the rifle had advantages over the Spencer (which the U.S. Army proclaimed sturdier): It held l5 rounds to the Spencer's seven, and one motion of the lever would load and cock the gun.

By mid 1860s, Winchester Repeating Arms Company had swallowed New Haven Arms, and B. Tyler Henry had left the company. In 1866 shop foreman Nelson King redesigned the Henry's magazine, adding a spring-loaded port in the receiver. These changes, along with with a forend, resulted in the Winchester 1866. This rifle became an immediate hit.

In 1870 Thomas G. Bennett began work for Winchester. He became company secretary the following year and, later, Oliver Winchester's son-in-law. Bennett helped design of the Winchester Model 1873, the firm's first centerfire rifle. Its .44 WCF (.44-40) cartridge struck with nearly nearly 30 percent more energy than the .44 Henry – over 12 times the payload of the old Volcanic bullet. The brass frame of the l866 became forged iron on the 73 and iron was replaced with steel in l884.

The next Winchester lever gun, the Model l876, was just a big Model l873. The .45-75 Winchester, with its 350-grain bullet, doubled the energy of the .44 WCF. Later Winchester added the .50-95 Express, .45-60 WCF and .40-60 WCF. The 1876 became the official rifle of Canada's Royal Canadian Mounted Police. One day in 1883 Bennett was shown a used dropping-block rifle picked up by a Winchester salesman. He traced the barrel stamping to a Utah gunshop – and booked train passage there. He found a handful of young men, barely out of their teens, designing and building rifles. Bennett secured manufacturing rights to two Browning rifles. One would become the Model l885 single-shot, the other the Model l886 lever-action. John Browning would later sell Winchester the plans for more than 40 mechanisms.

MODEL 70 BLACK SHADOW

Action: bolt
Stock: synthetic, varmint-style
Barrel: 22 and 24 in.
Sights: none
Weight: 7.3
Caliber: .270, .30-06 (22 in.), 7mm Rem. Mag. and .300 Win. Mag. (24 in.)
Magazine: box, 3 or 5 rounds
Features: push-feed
Black Shadow: $523
magnum: $553

RIFLES

Winchester Rifles

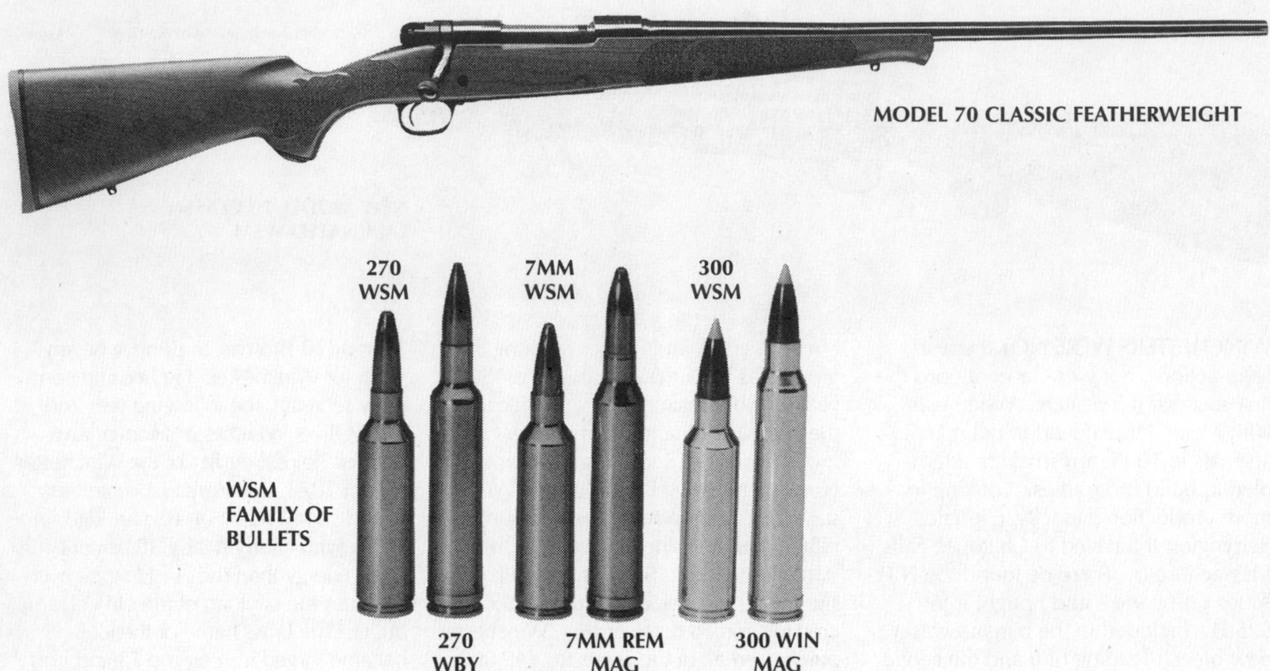

Model 70 Classic Compact

Action: bolt
Stock: walnut
Barrel: 20 in.
Sights: none
Weight: 6.5
Caliber: .243, 7-08, .308
Magazine: box, 4 rounds
Features: features 13-in. pull for small-frame people
Compact: $740

Model 70 Classic Featherweight

Action: bolt
Stock: walnut
Barrel: 22 and 24 in.
Sights: none
Weight: 7.0
Caliber: .22-250, .243, 6.5x55, .270, .270 WSM, 7-08, 7mm WSM, .308, .30-06, .300 WSM
Magazine: box, 3 or 5 rounds
Features: stainless available in .22-250, .243, .270, .308, .30-06
Classic Featherweight: $740
magnum: $769
stainless: $803

Model 70 Classic Sporter

Action: bolt
Stock: walnut
Barrel: 24 and 26 in.
Sights: none
Weight: 7.8
Caliber: .25-06, .270, 7mm Rem. Mag., 7STW, .30-06, .300 Win. Mag., .338 Win. Mag.
Magazine: box, 3 or 5 rounds
Features: also in .270, 7mm and .300 WSM with laminated stock
Classic Sporter: $727
magnum: $756
WSM: $793

Model 70 Classic Stainless

Action: bolt
Stock: synthetic
Barrel: 24 and 26 in.
Sights: none
Weight: 7.3
Caliber: .270, .270 WSM, .30-06, 7STW, 7mm Rem. Mag., 7mm WSM, .300 Win. Mag., .300 UM, .300 WSM, .338 Win. Mag., .375 H&H
Magazine: box, 3 or 5 rounds
Features: open sights on .375 H&H
Classic Stainless: $800
magnum: $829
.375: $924

The harder the walnut, the easier it is to checker – and, typically, the more it costs. French and English, Turkish and Circassian walnuts are all regional forms of Juglans regia.

Winchester Rifles

MODEL 70 CLASSIC SUPER GRADE

MODEL 70 COYOTE

MODEL 70 STEALTH

MODEL 94 TRADITIONAL

Model 70 Classic Super Grade

Action: bolt
Stock: walnut
Barrel: 24 and 26 in.
Sights: none
Weight: 7.8
Caliber: .25-06, .270, .30-06, 7mm Rem. Mag., .300 Win. Mag., .338 Win. Mag.
Magazine: box, 3 or 5 rounds
Features: also; Safari Express in .375 H&H (8.5 lbs.), .416 Rem. Mag. and .458 Win. with open sights
Classic Super Grade:........ $1015
magnum: $1044
Safari express: $1124

Model 70 Coyote

Action: bolt
Stock: laminated
Barrel: 24 in.
Sights: none
Weight: 9.0
Caliber: .223, .22-250, .243, .308; also .270 WSM, 7mm WSM, .300 WSM
Magazine: box, 3 to 6 rounds
Features: push-feed action
Coyote: $705
magnum: $734

Model 70 Stealth

Action: bolt
Stock: synthetic
Barrel: 26 in.
Sights: none
Weight: 10.8
Caliber: .223, .22-250, .308
Magazine: box, 5 or 6 rounds
Features: push-feed action
Stealth: $800

Model 94 Traditional

Action: lever
Stock: walnut, straight grip
Barrel: 20 in.
Sights: open
Weight: 6.25
Caliber: .30-30, .480 Ruger
Magazine: under-barrel tube, 6, 10 or 11 rounds
Features: also available: TraditionalCW in .30-30, .44 Rem. Mag., .480 Ruger; Ranger with hardwood stock; Trails End with large-loop option in .357, .44 Mag., .45 Long Colt
Traditional in .30-30: $426
Traditional in .480 Ruger:..... $469
Traditional-CW in .30-30:..... $461
Traditional in .44 Rem. Mag.: . . $482
Traditional-CW in .480 Ruger: . $531
Ranger: $371
Trails End: $465

Winchester Rifles

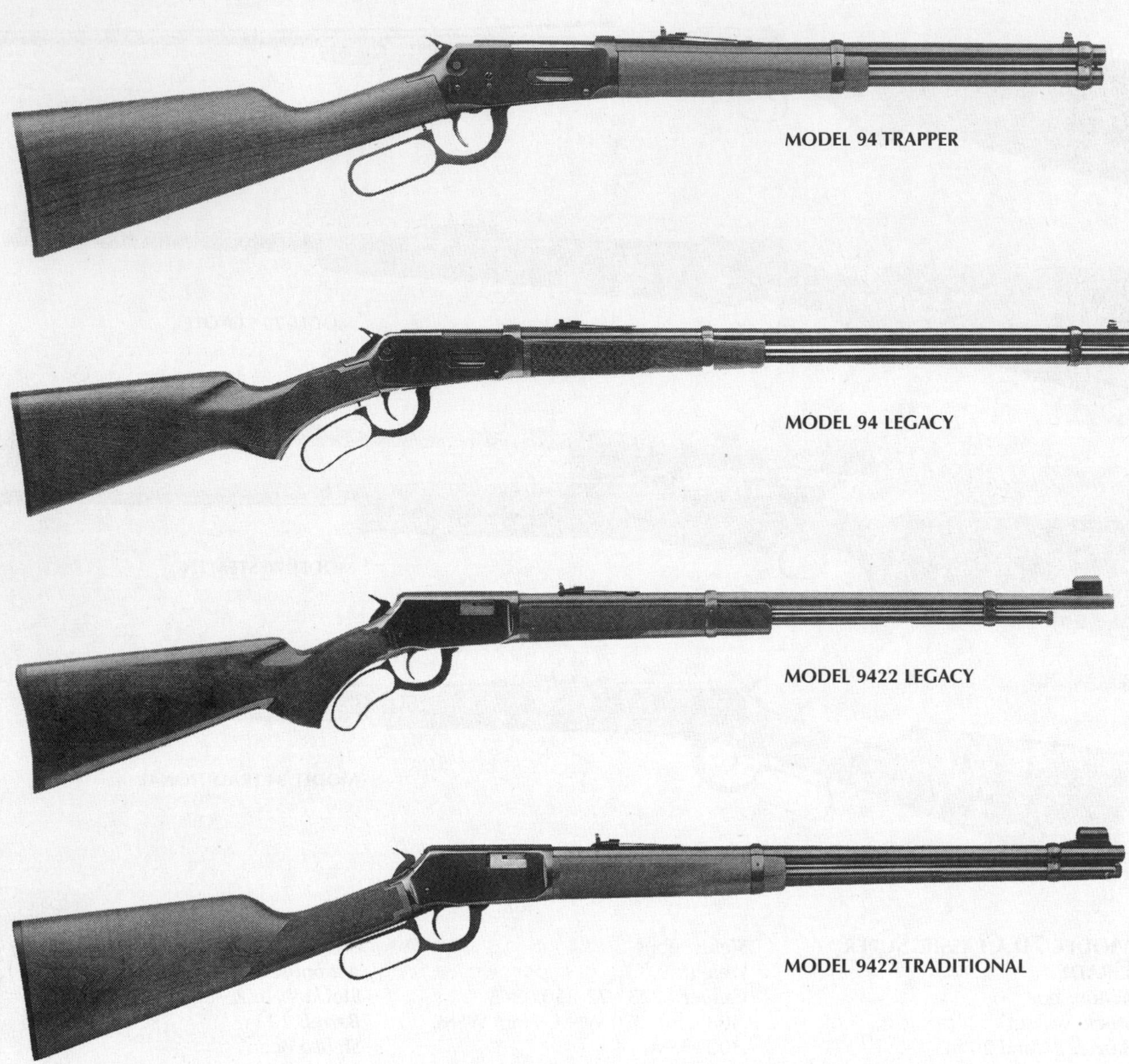

RIFLES

Model 94 Trapper

Action: lever
Stock: walnut
Barrel: 16 in.
Sights: open
Weight: 6.0
Caliber: .30-30, .357 Mag., .44 Mag., .45 Long Colt
Magazine: under-barrel tube, 5 or 8 rounds
Features: saddle ring; 8rounds only in .357, .44, .45
.30-30:. $426
.357, .44, .45: $451

Model 94 Legacy

Action: lever
Stock: checkered walnut, pistol grip
Barrel: 20 or 24 in.
Sights: open
Weight: 6.8
Caliber: .30-30, .357 Mag., .44 Mag., .45 Long Colt
Magazine: under-barrel tube, 6 rounds
Features: deluxe version of 94; 11 rounds only in .357, .44, .45
Legacy: $477

Model 9422 Rifles

Action: lever
Stock: checkered walnut, straight grip
Barrel: 20 in.
Sights: open
Weight: 6.0
Caliber: .22 LR or .22 WMR
Magazine: under-barrel tube, 15 round (11 in WMR)
Features: also available: legacy with pistol grip, 22 in. barrel
9422:. $465
Magnum: $487
Legacy: $498
Legacy, magnum: $521

SHOTGUNS

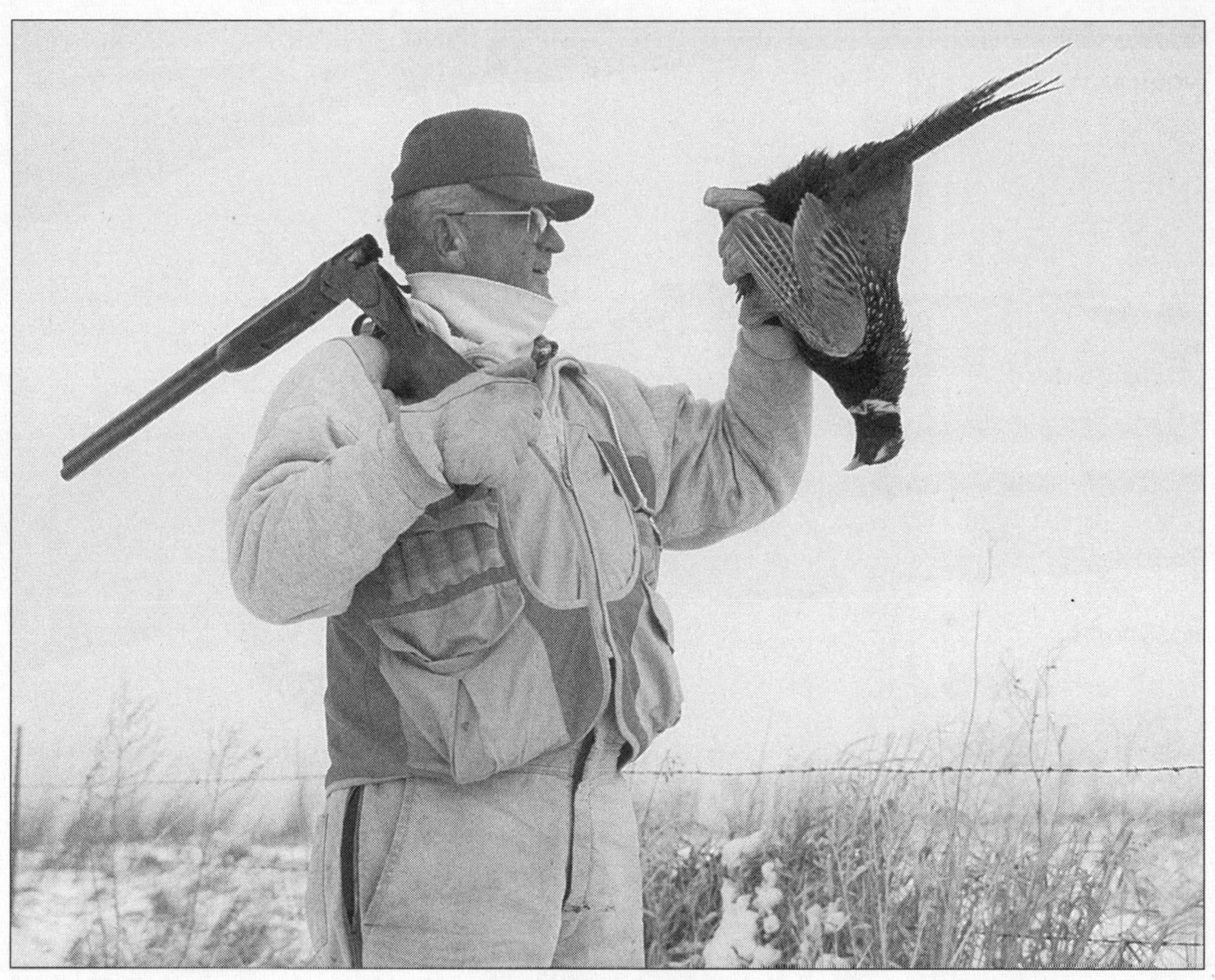

AYA Shotguns

MODEL 4/53

COUNTRYMAN

Model 4/53

Action: side-by-side
Stock: walnut, straight grip
Barrel: 26, 27 or 28 in.
Chokes: improved cylinder, modified, full
Weight: 7.0lbs.
Bore/Gauge 12, 16, 20, 28, .410
Magazine: none
Features: boxlock; chopper lump barrels, bushed firing pins, automatic safety and ejectors
Model 4/53 . . . . $2095

Countryman

Action: side-by-side
Stock: walnut, straight grip
Barrel: 26, 27, 28, 29 or 32 in.
Chokes: improved cylinder, modified, full
Weight: 7.0lbs.
Bore/Gauge 12, 16, 20
Magazine: none
Features: Holland sidelock design, chopper lump barrels, bushed firing pins, automatic safety and ejectors, replaceable hinge pin; deluxe wood on order
Countryman $3495

When shopping for an autoloader, mind its mechanism. Some these days accept loads of various lengths and recoil interchangeably, without adjustment. And asset if you'll change ammo often.

Benelli Shotguns

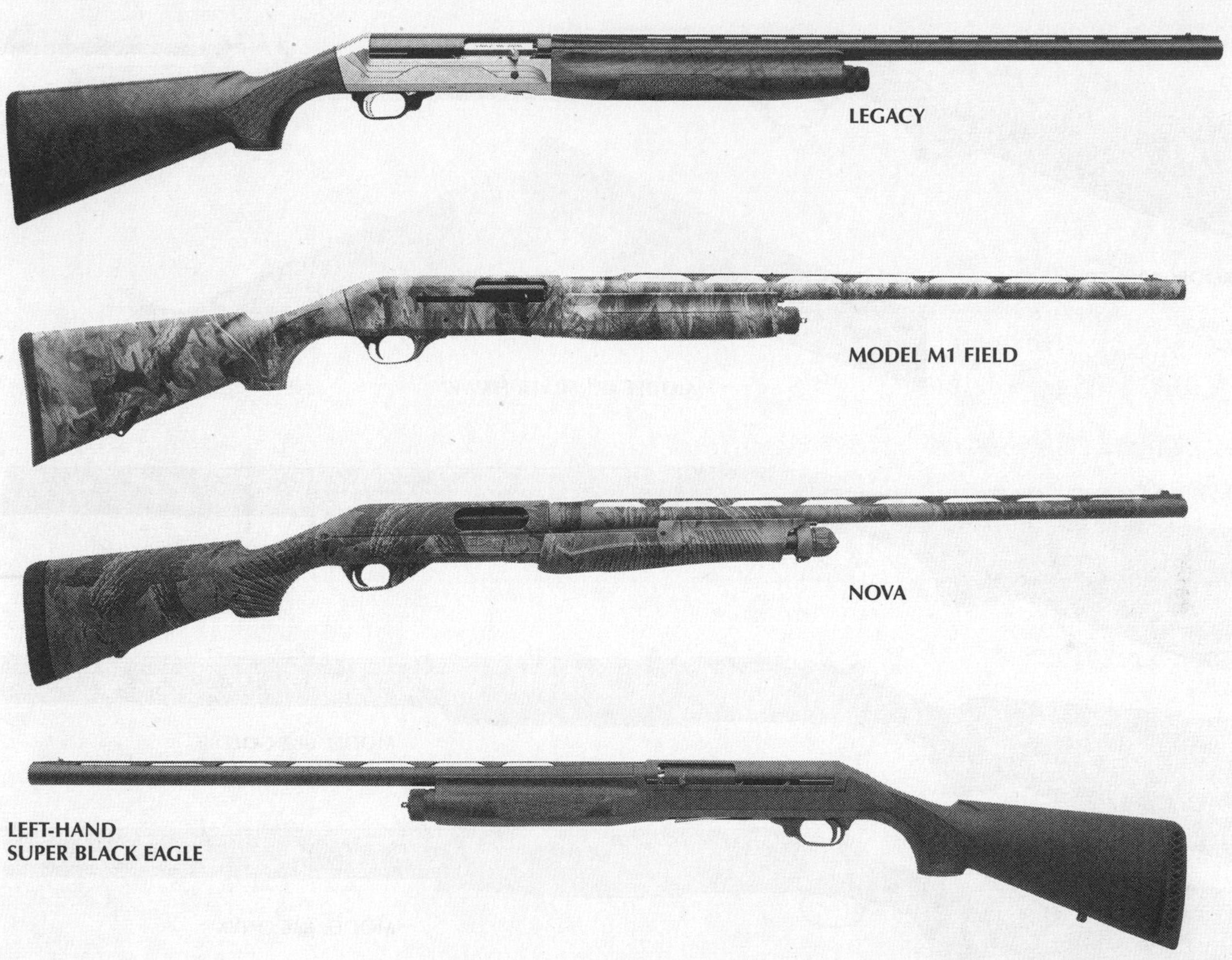

LEGACY

MODEL M1 FIELD

NOVA

LEFT-HAND SUPER BLACK EAGLE

Legacy

Action: autoloader
Stock: walnut
Barrel: 24, 26 or 28 in.
Chokes: screw-in tubes
Weight: 7.5lbs.
Bore/Gauge: 12, 20
Magazine: 3
Features: 3-inch chambers, inertia recoil system, rotating bolt with dual lugs; Executive series, Grades I, II and III at extra cost
Legacy $1400

Model M1 Field

Action: autoloader
Stock: walnut, synthetic or camo
Barrel: 21, 24, 26, 28 or 30 in.
Chokes: screw-in tubes
Weight: 7.3lbs.
Bore/Gauge: 12, 20
Magazine: 3
Features: 3-inch chambers, inertial recoil system, rotating bolt with dual lugs, rifled slug (12-gauge) about $80 more; Sport: 8 pounds, walnut, 12 ga.; Montefeltro: walnut, 5.3 to 7.1 pounds.
synthetic $985
wood $1000
camo $1085
tactical. $1030
Sport $1400
Montefeltro $1005

Nova

Action: pump
Stock: synthetic
Barrel: 24, 26 or 28 in.
Chokes: screw-in tubes
Weight: 8.1lbs.
Bore/Gauge 12, 20
Magazine: 4
Features: molded polymer (steel reinforced) replaces traditional stock and receiver; bolt locks into barrel
Nova synthetic $335
camo $400
rifled slug. $500
rifled slug, camo $575

Super Black Eagle

Action: autoloader
Stock: walnut or synthetic
Barrel: 24, 26 or 28 in.
Chokes: screw-in tubes
Weight: 7.3lbs.
Bore/Gauge: 12
Magazine: 3
Features: 3½" chamber, inertial recoil system; rotating bolt with dual lugs; rifles slug and left-hand versions about $50 extra
synthetic $1290
walnut $1300
camo $1385

Beretta Shotguns

MODEL 1201 FP

MODEL 471 SILVER HAWK

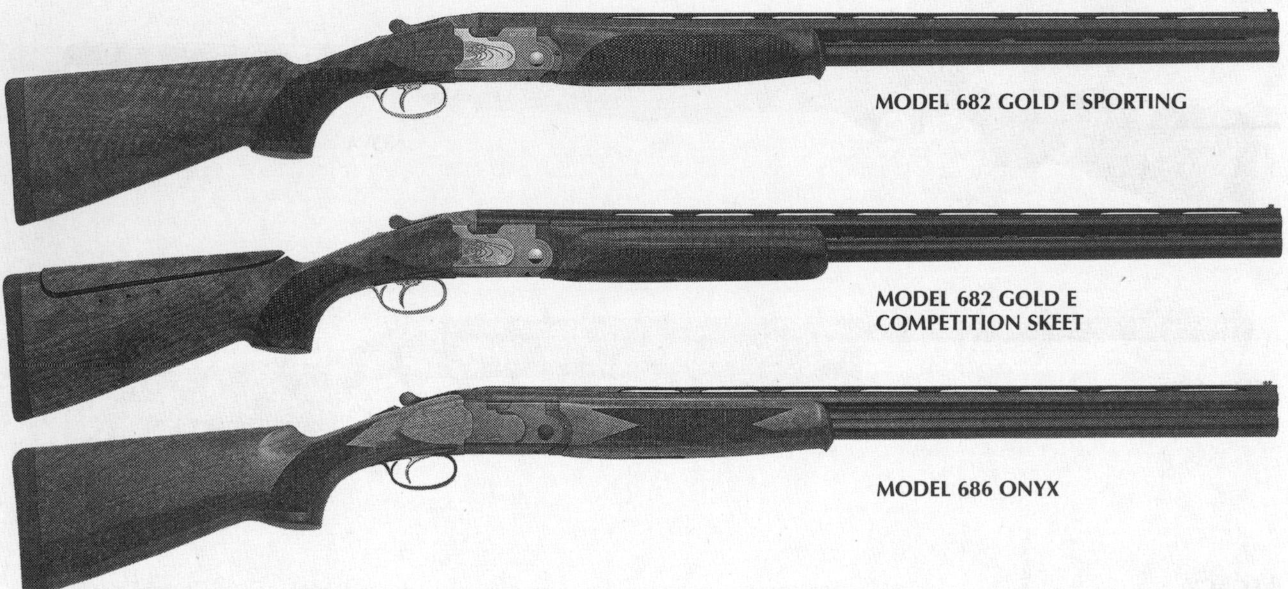

MODEL 682 GOLD E SPORTING

MODEL 682 GOLD E COMPETITION SKEET

MODEL 686 ONYX

Model 1201 FP

Action: autoloader
Stock: synthetic
Barrel: 18 in.
Chokes: cylinder
Weight: 6.3lbs.
Bore/Gauge: 12
Magazine: 6
Features: Tritium sights, short recoil action, special weather-resistant finish
FP $890

Model 471 Silver Hawk

Action: side-by-side
Stock: walnut
Barrel: 26 or 28 in.
Chokes: imp.cyl/mod or mod/full
Weight: 6.5lbs.
Bore/Gauge: 12, 20
Magazine: none
Features: boxlock; satin chromed receiver, single selective trigger, automatic ejectors; EL has case-colored receiver, gold inlays
12 gauge $2596
20 gauge $2726
EL $5980

Model 682 Silver Pigeon Sporting

Action: over/under
Stock: walnut
Barrel: 28, 30 or 32 in.
Chokes: screw-in tubes
Weight: 6.8lbs.
Bore/Gauge: 12
Magazine: none
Features: boxlock; single selective adjustable trigger; automatic ejectors
Silver Pigeon $1931
Gold E $3850
Skeet $4320
Trap $4320
Combo Trap $5305

Model 686 Onyx

Action: over/under
Stock: walnut
Barrel: 26 or 28 in.
Chokes: screw-in tubes
Weight: 6.8lbs.
Bore/Gauge: 12, 20
Magazine: none
Features: boxlock; 3-inch chambers; single selective trigger; automatic ejectors; Waterfowler has 3½-inch chambers
686 Onyx. $1583
Waterfowler. $1648

Beretta Shotguns

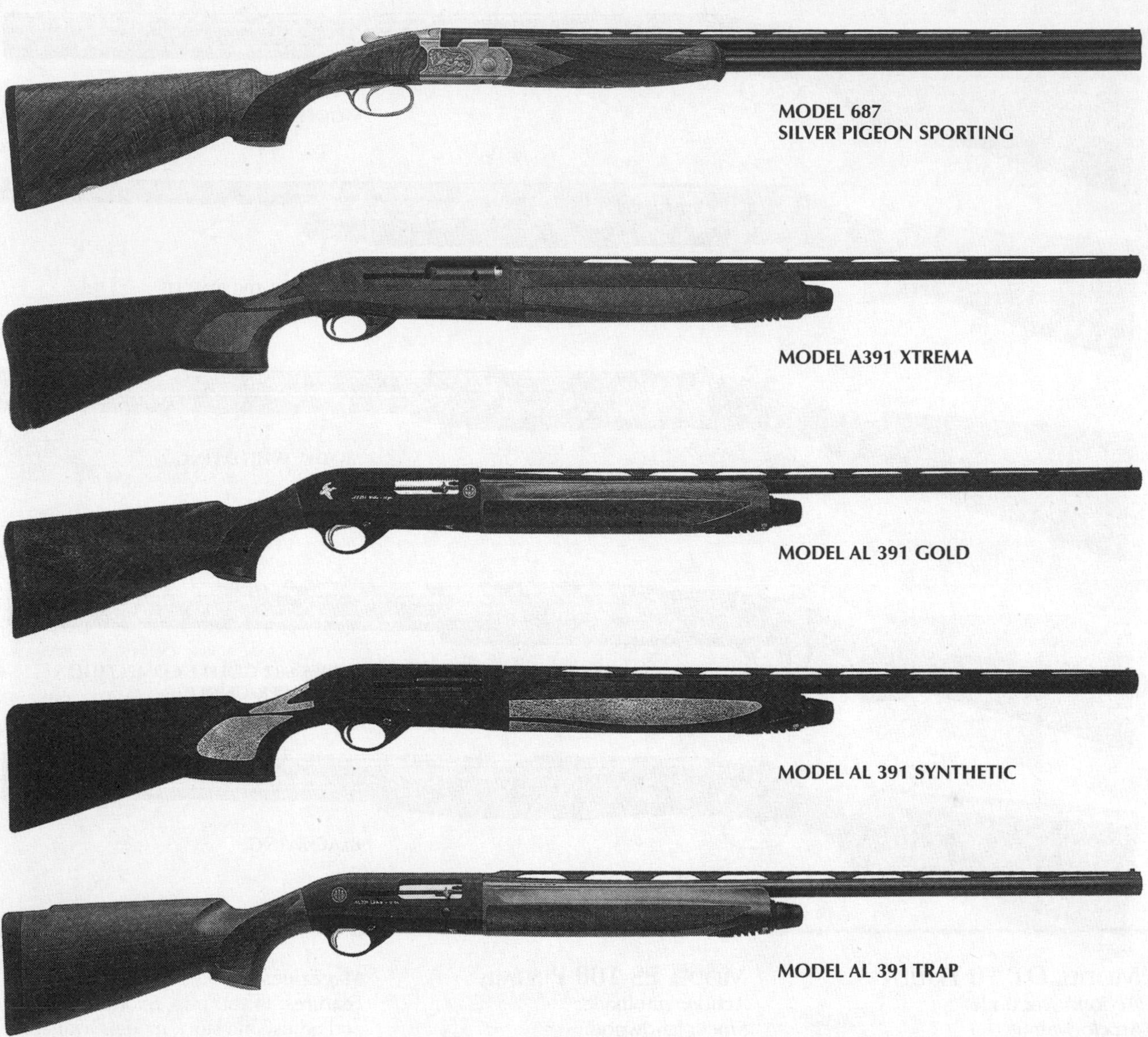

MODEL 687
SILVER PIGEON SPORTING

MODEL A391 XTREMA

MODEL AL 391 GOLD

MODEL AL 391 SYNTHETIC

MODEL AL 391 TRAP

Model 687 Silver Pigeon Sporting

Action: over/under
Stock: walnut
Barrel: 26 or 28 in.
Chokes: screw-in tubes
Weight: 6.8lbs.
Bore/Gauge: 12, 20
Magazine: none
Features: boxlock; 3-inch chambers; single selective trigger; automatic ejectors; Ultralight (12 ga. only) has alloy receiver; higher grades available

687 . . . . $2196
Ultralight $1931
Ultralight Deluxe $2323
Combo $3151

Model A391 Xtrema

Action: autoloader
Stock: synthetic
Barrel: 28 in.
Chokes: screw-in tubes
Weight: 7.8lbs.
Bore/Gauge: 12
Magazine: 3
Features: 3½-inch chambers; gas-operated rotating bolt

synthetic $1143
camo $1260

Model AL 391

Action: autoloader
Stock: walnut or synthetic
Barrel: 24, 26, 28 or 30 in.
Chokes: screw-in tubes
Weight: 7.4 lbs.
Bore/Gauge: 12, 20
Magazine: 3
Features: gas-operated action; alloy receiver, shims supplied for stock adjustment; high-grade "Gold" versions available

wood or synthetic $984
camo $1090
Youth $984
Trap $1027
Sporting $1027
Gold $1213
Gold Lightweight $1254

Beretta Shotguns

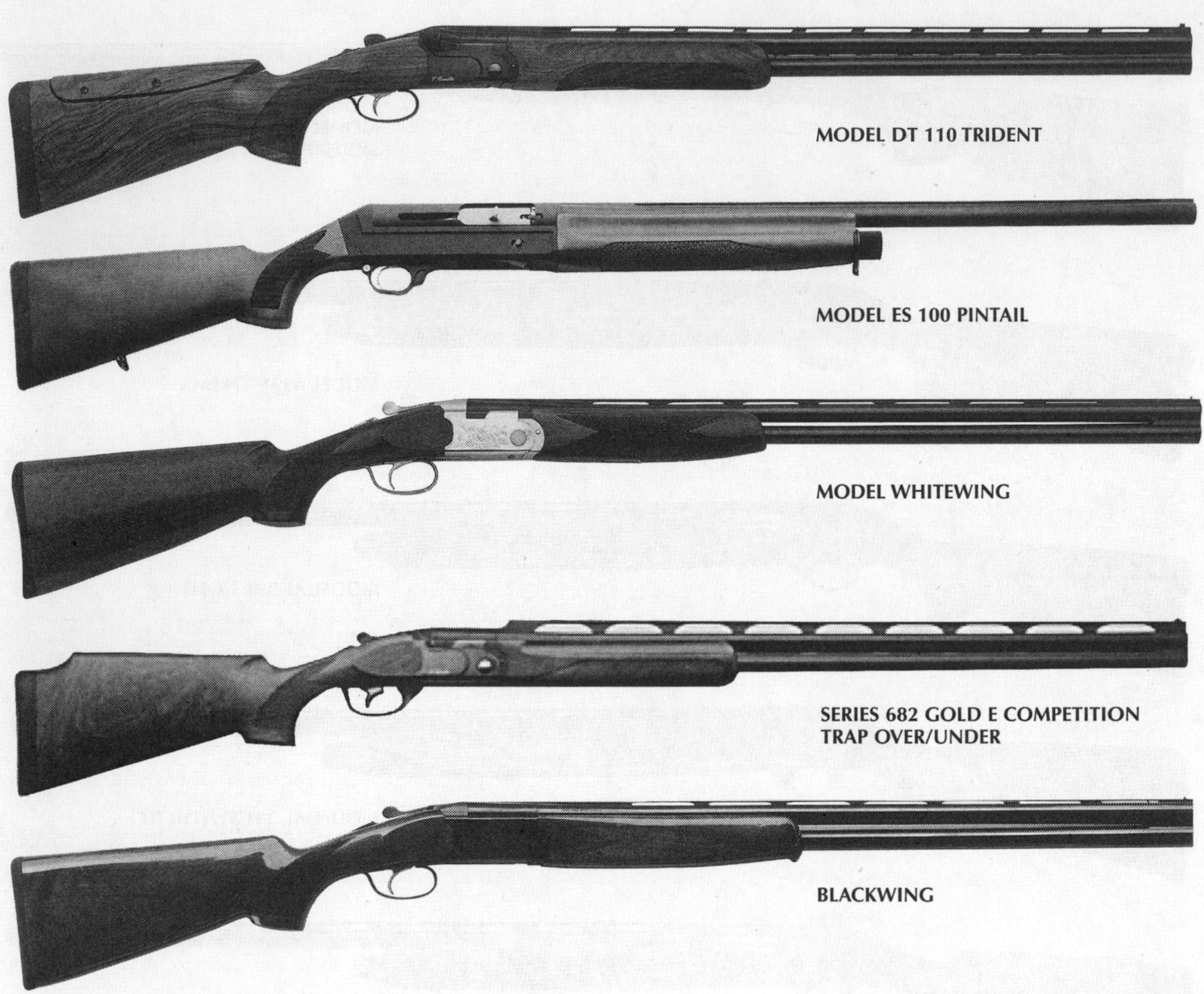

MODEL DT 110 TRIDENT

MODEL ES 100 PINTAIL

MODEL WHITEWING

SERIES 682 GOLD E COMPETITION TRAP OVER/UNDER

BLACKWING

Model DT 10 Trident

Action: over/under
Stock: walnut
Barrel: 28, 30, 32 or 34 in.
Chokes: screw-in tubes
Weight: 7.5lbs.
Bore/Gauge: 12
Magazine: none
Features: boxlock; single selective trigger, automatic ejectors; Skeet, Trap and Sporting models are Beretta's best competition guns. Combo with top single or bottom single; Trap versions available

Sporting $7850
Skeet $8030
Trap $8500
Trap, Top Single $8500
Trap, Combo Top Single $10790

Model ES 100 Pintail

Action: autoloader
Stock: hardwood
Barrel: 24, 26 or 28 in.
Chokes: screw-in tubes
Weight: 7.3lbs.
Bore/Gauge: 12
Magazine: 3
Features: short recoil action; slug gun has fully rifled 24-inch barrel

Pintail $682
camo $777
slug $749

Model 682

Action: over/under
Stock: walnut
Barrel: 28, 30 or 32 inches
Chokes: screw-in tubes
Weight: 7.6lbs.
Bore/Gauge: 12
Magazine: none
Features: Skeet, Trap, Sporting, Combo and adjustable-stock models available

Sporting: $3436
Skeet, Trap: $3905
Combo: $4940

Whitewing, Blackwing

Action: over/under
Stock: walnut
Barrel: 26 or 28 in.
Chokes: screw-in tubes
Weight: 6.7lbs.
Bore/Gauge: 12, 20
Magazine: none
Features: boxlock, 3-inch chamber,; single selective trigger, automatic ejectors; reciever finishes differ; same action as on 686

Whitewing $1332
Blackwing $1332

Browning Shotguns

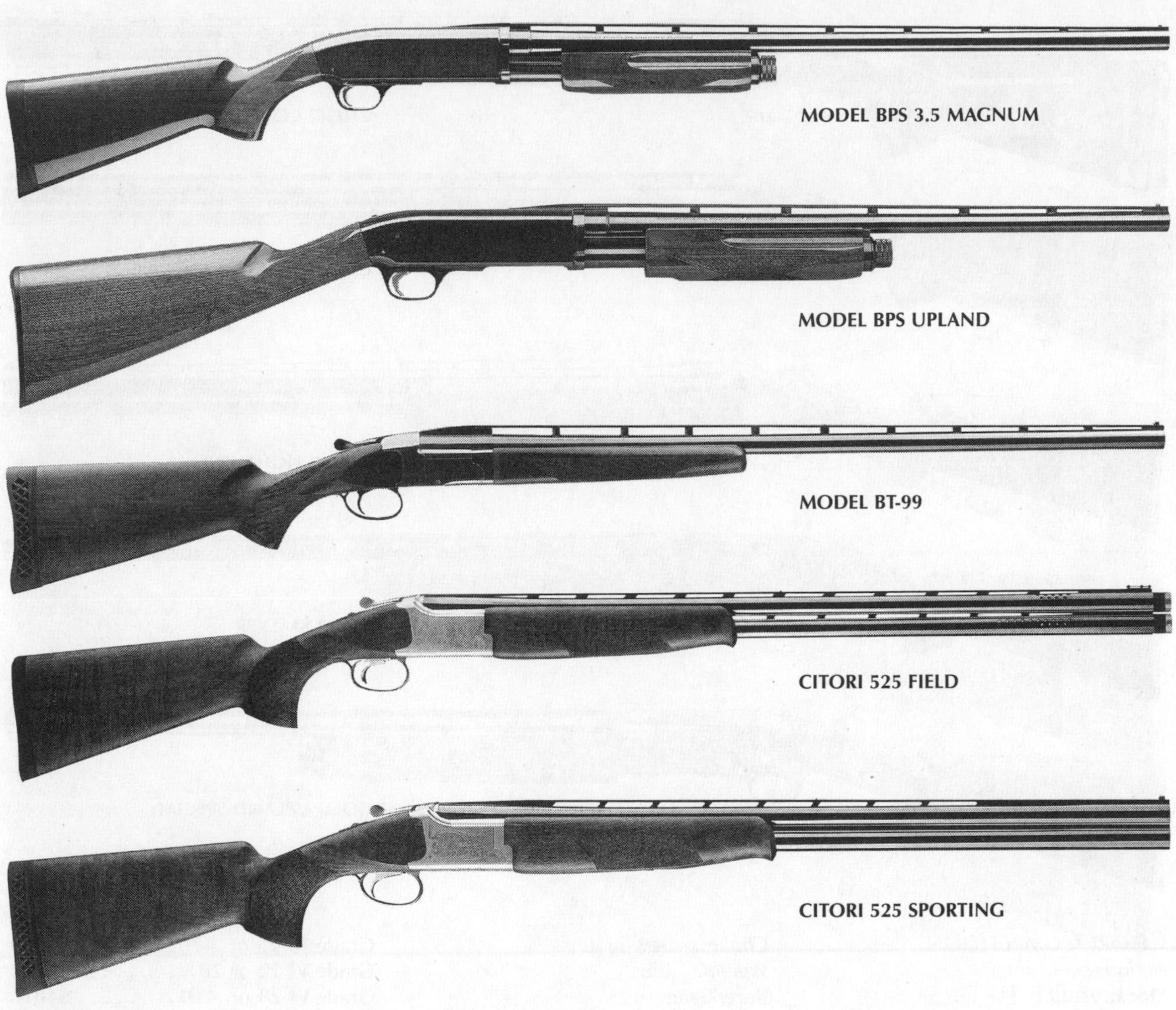

Model BPS

Action: pump
Stock: walnut or synthetic
Barrel: 20, 22, 24, 26, 28 or 30 in.
Chokes: screw-in tubes
Weight: 8.0lbs.
Bore/Gauge: 10, 12, 20, 28, .410
Magazine: 4
Features: Both 10 and 12 gauge available with 3.5-inch chambers; Upland Special has short barrel, straight grip; Deer Special has rifled barrel; Micro BPS has short barrel, stock

Hunter (walnut) **$482**
Stalker (synthetic) **$466**
Camo synthetic **$652**
28 or .410 . . . . **$515**
Magnum (3.5-inch). **$548**
Magnum Camo. **$652**
Upland (12, 20) **$482**
Micro (20) **$482**

Model BT-99

Action: hinged single-shot
Stock: walnut, trap-style
Barrel: 30 or 32 in.
Chokes: screw-in tubes
Weight: 8.0lbs.
Bore/Gauge: 12
Magazine: none
Features: boxlock single-shot competition gun with high-post rib

BT-99. . . . . **$1265**
with adjustable comb **$1508**

Citori 525

Action: over/under
Stock: walnut
Barrel: 26, 28 or 30 in.
Chokes: screw-in tubes
Weight: 7.3lbs.
Bore/Gauge: 12, 20
Magazine: none
Features: boxlock; European-style stock, pronounced pistol grip, floating top and side ribs; Golden Clays has gold inlays

Field **$1830**
Sporting. **$2568**
Golden Clays **$4113**

Browning Shotguns

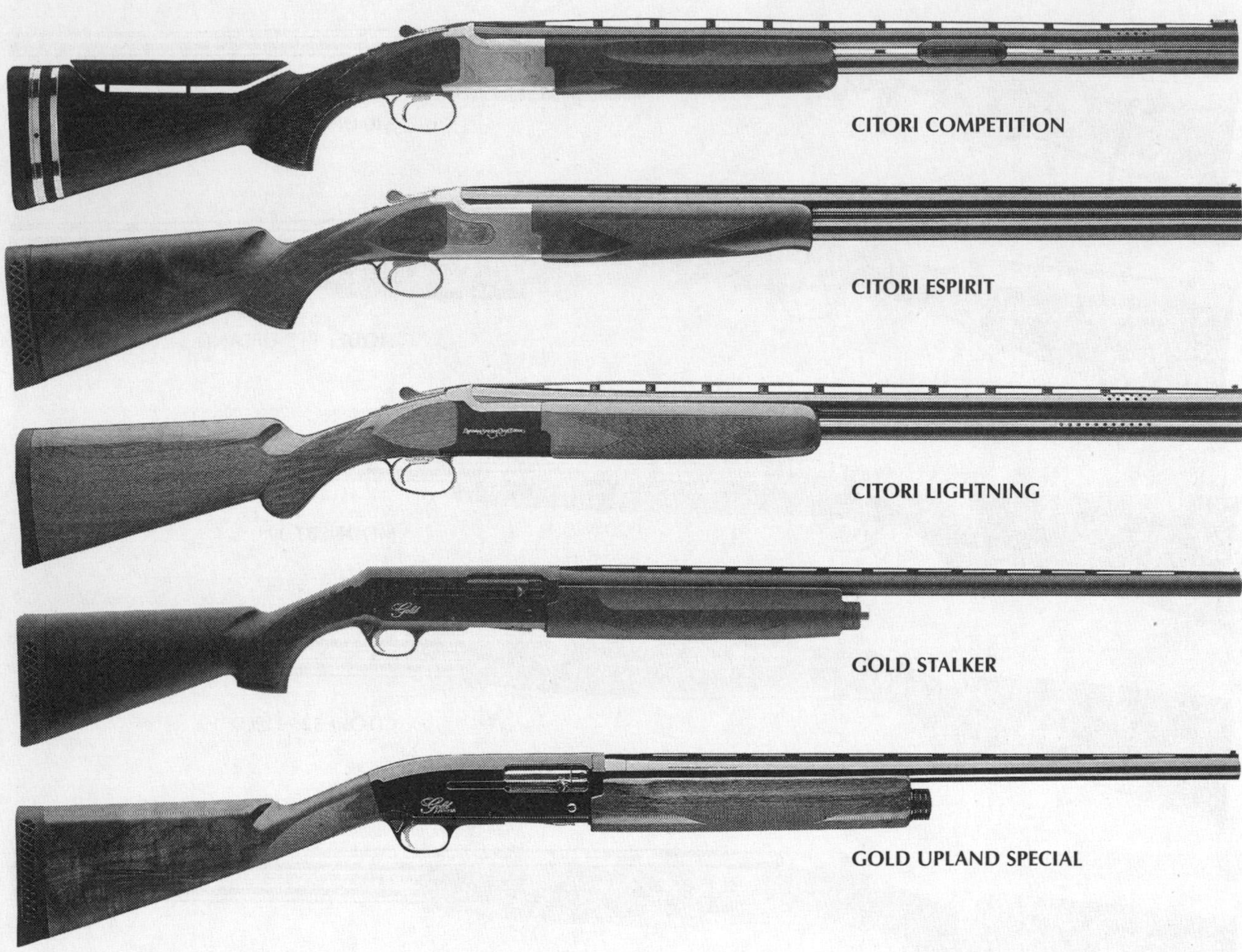

CITORI COMPETITION

CITORI ESPIRIT

CITORI LIGHTNING

GOLD STALKER

GOLD UPLAND SPECIAL

Citori Competition

Action: over/under
Stock: walnut
Barrel: 26, 28 or 30 in.
Chokes: screw-in tubes
Weight: 8.0lbs.
Bore/Gauge: 12
Magazine: none
Features: boxlock; XS Pro-Comp has ported barrels, adjustable stock comb, GraCoil recoil reducer; Trap and Skeet Models are stocked and barreled accordingly

XS Pro-Comp $3910
Trap $2145
Trap with adjustable comb . . . $2405
Skeet $2294
Skeet with adjustable comb . . $2525

Citori Espirit

Action: over/under
Stock: walnut
Barrel: 28 in.
Chokes: screw-in tubes
Weight: 7.0lbs.
Bore/Gauge: 12
Magazine: none
Features: boxlock; schnable forend, high-grade wood, satin metal finish; White Lightning has 24 inch barrel, straight-grip stock, also in 20 gauge (6 pounds)

Espirit $2502

Citori Lightning

Action: over/under
Stock: walnut
Barrel: 26, 28 or 30 in.
Chokes: screw-in tubes
Weight: 6.0lbs.
Bore/Gauge: 12, 20, 28, .410
Magazine: none
Features: boxlock; single selective trigger, automatic ejectors; higher grades available; ported barrels optional

Grade I Sporting. $1742
Grade III 12 or 20 . . . . $2416
Grade III 28 or .410 . . . . $2700
Grade VI 12 or 20 . . . . $3723
Grade VI 28 or .410 . . . . $4010

Gold

Action: autoloader
Stock: walnut (Hunter) or synthetic (Stalker)
Barrel: 24, 26, 28 or 30 in.
Chokes: screw-in tubes
Weight: 8.0lbs.
Bore/Gauge: 10, 12, 20
Magazine: 3
Features: gas-operated, 3½-inch chambers on 10 and one 12 gauge version; Youth and Ladies versions available

Stalker $873
Hunter. $912
Sporting Clays $984
Upland Special. $915
Rifled Deer Stalker. $967
Rifled Deer Hunter. $1007
3 ½-inch Hunter. $1022

Charles Daly Shotguns

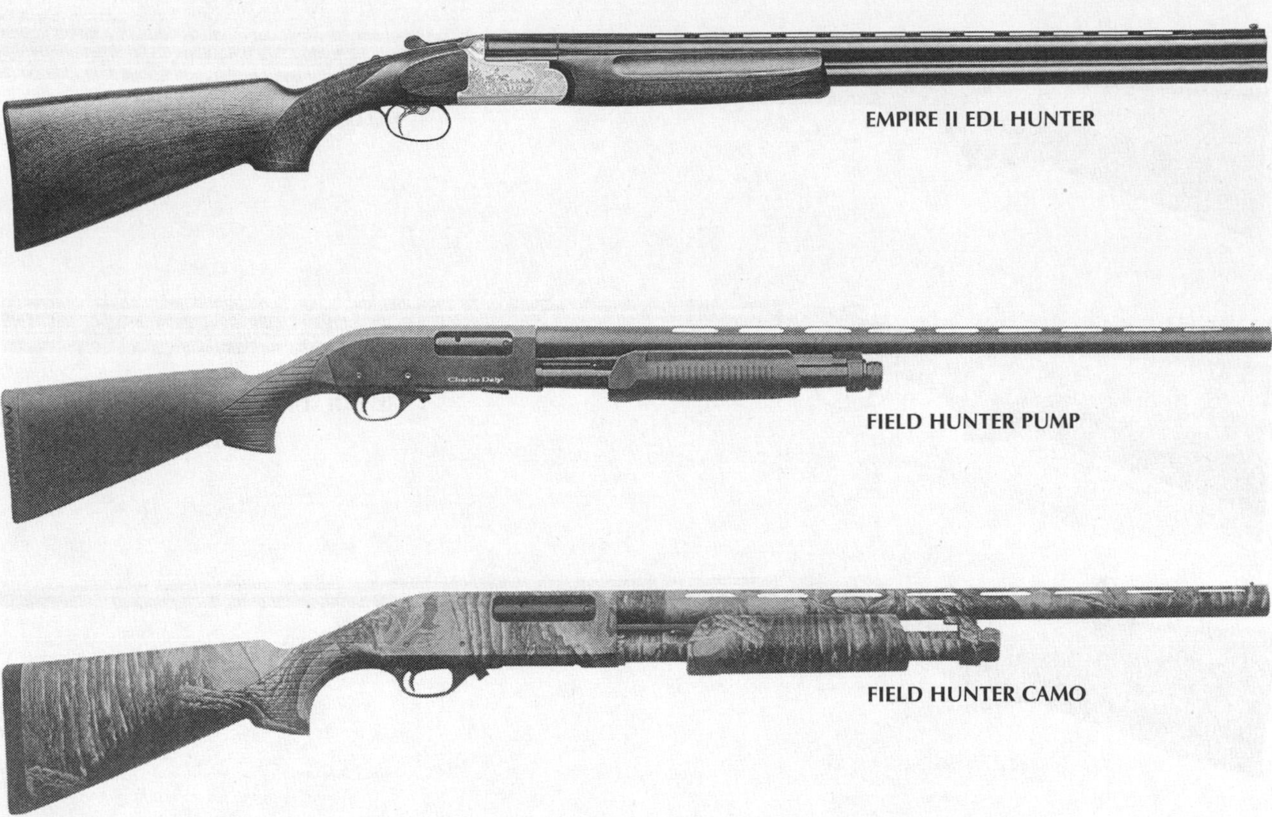

EMPIRE II EDL HUNTER

FIELD HUNTER PUMP

FIELD HUNTER CAMO

Empire II EDL Hunter

Action: over/under
Stock: walnut
Barrel: 26 or 28 in.
Chokes: screw-in tubes
Weight: 7.2lbs.
Bore/Gauge: 12, 20, 28, .410
Magazine: none
Features: boxlock; single selective trigger, automatic safety, automatic ejectors

12 or 20 ga. $1639
28 ga. $1625
.410 . . . . $1625
Trap $1689

Field Hunter Autoloader

Action: autoloader
Stock: synthetic
Barrel: 22, 24, 26, 28 or 30 in.
Chokes: screw-in tubes
Weight: 7.5lbs.
Bore/Gauge: 12, 20, 28
Magazine: 4
Features: ventilated rib; Superior II Grade has walnut stock, ported barrel

12 or 20 ga. $399
28 ga. $459
camo $489
3.5-in. magnum synthetic $589
3.5-in. magnum camo. $685
Superior Field. $539
Superior Trap $579

Field Hunter Pump

Action: pump
Stock: synthetic
Barrel: 26 or 28 in.
Chokes: screw-in tubes
Weight: 7.0lbs.
Bore/Gauge: 12, 20
Magazine: 4
Features: ventilated rib

Field Hunter. $269
camo $359
3.5-in. magnum synthetic $335
3.5-in. magnum camo. $435

Pattern your shotgun not only to determine pellet-strike percentages in 30-inch circles at 40 yards but to find the center of impact relative to your sightline. The gun must shoot where you look!

Charles Daly Shotguns

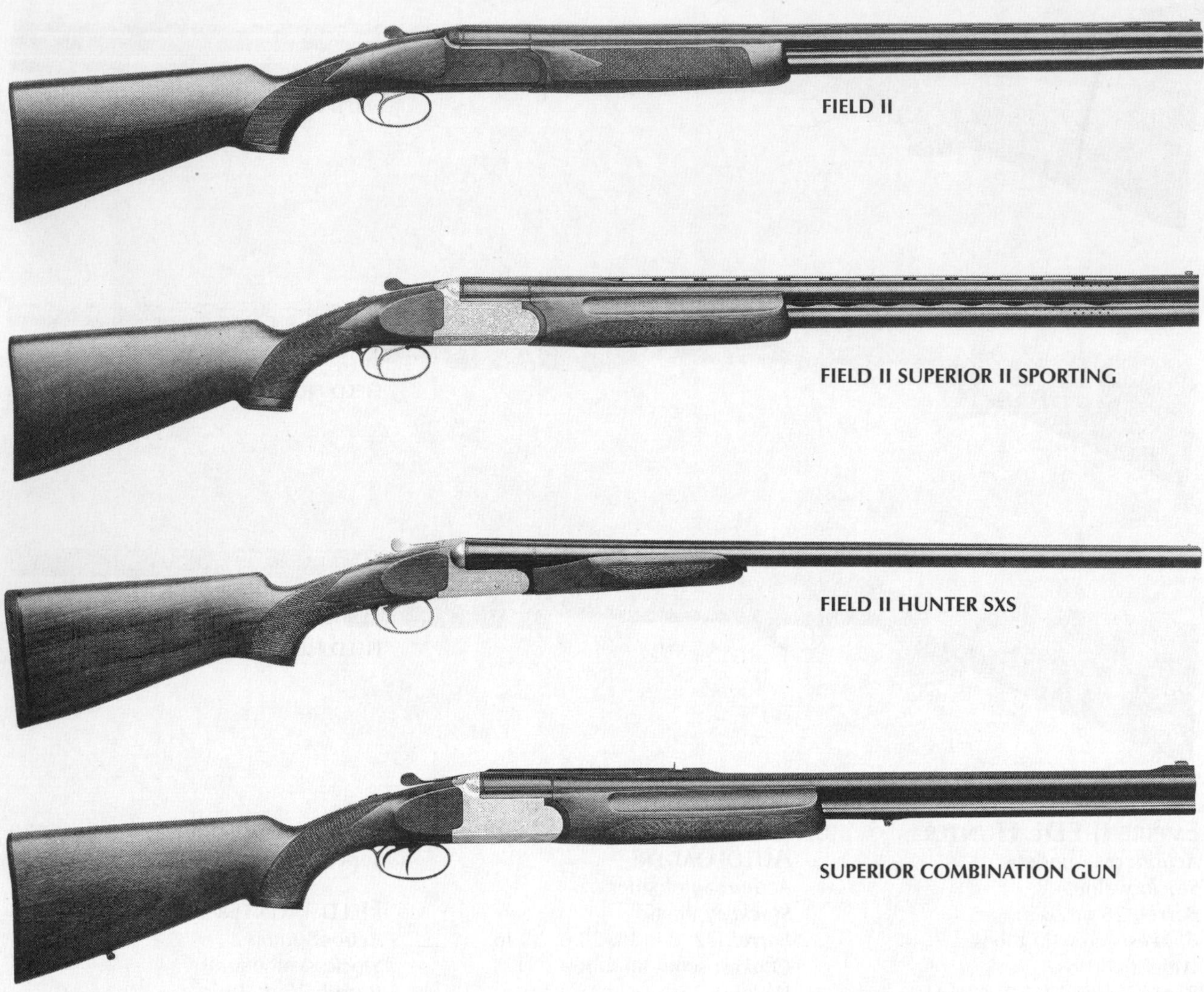

FIELD II

FIELD II SUPERIOR II SPORTING

FIELD II HUNTER SXS

SUPERIOR COMBINATION GUN

Field II

Action: over/under
Stock: walnut
Barrel: 26 or 28 in.
Chokes: mod/full (28 in.), imp.cyl/mod (26 in.), full/full (.410)
Weight: 7.2lbs.
Bore/Gauge: 12, 16, 20, 28, .410
Magazine: none
Features: boxlock; single selective trigger, automatic safety

Field II $799
28-gauge $879
.410. $879
Ultra-Light (12, 20) $919
Field (12, 20)
w/ 5 choke tubes $999
Superior II $1289
Superior II Trap $1339

Field II Hunter SxS

Action: side-by-side
Stock: walnut
Barrel: 26, 28 or 30 in.
Chokes: imp.cyl/mod (26 in.), mod/full (28, 30 in.), full/full (.410)
Weight: 10.0lbs.
Bore/Gauge: 12, 20, 28, .410
Magazine: none
Features: boxlock; single selective trigger, automatic safety

12 or 20 ga. $799
28 ga. or .410 . . . . $729
Superior Grade. $1059

Superior Combination Gun

Action: side-by-side
Stock: walnut
Barrel: 24 in.
Chokes: improved cylinder
Weight: 7.5lbs.
Bore/Gauge: 12
Magazine: none
Features: boxlock drilling; 12 gauge over .22 Hornet, .223 or .30-06 rifle; double triggers, sling swivels

Superior. $1119
Empire Grade. $1739

Flodman Shotguns

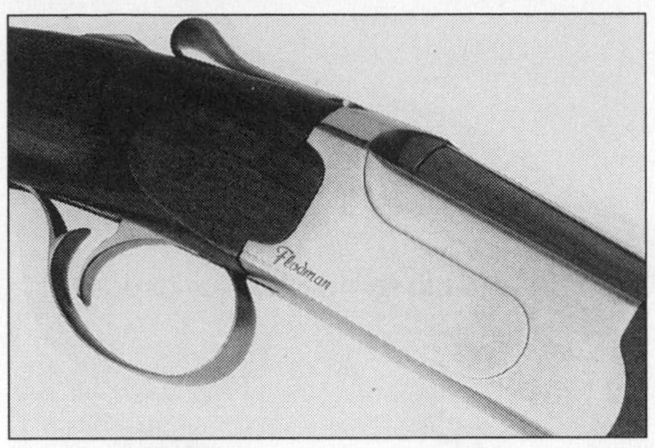

FLODMAN STAINLESS STEEL AND TITANIUM

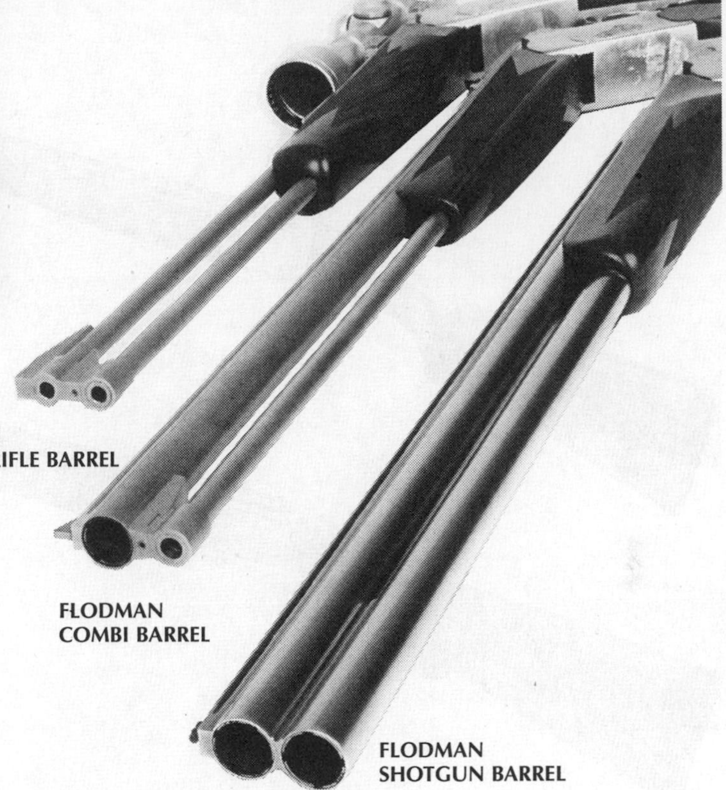

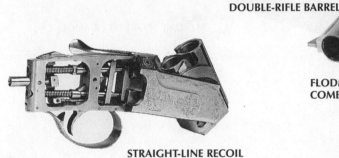

FLODMAN DOUBLE-RIFLE BARREL

FLODMAN COMBI BARREL

FLODMAN SHOTGUN BARREL

STRAIGHT-LINE RECOIL

FLODMAN GUNS is a family business and part of the Skullman Enterprise AB Group (est 1978).

The company's founder, Sixten Skullman, was originally an airplane mechanic and previously built racing engines. In 1992 Skullman Enterprises AB took over Flodman Guns.

In 1993 Flodman Guns began manufacturing combi and double-barreled shotguns. At the time they offered the option of titanium barrels.

Exquisite walnut wood is a standard fitting on the Flodman, which is self-opening. In contrast to other over-and-under weapons, the barrels are not used to break the weapon. When the mechanism is cocked with the top lever, the barrels fall in place under their own weight. The system's opening angle is larger for quick reloading.

During manufacture it is tested under gas pressure three times greater than a standard cartridge.

Flodman shotgun barrels are of ss2377, a stainless steel. Barrels are available in titanium (grade 5) from Sandvik Steel (www.sandvik.com) giving superiority in relation to strength and weight. Flodman has changeable chokes, but may be ordered with fixed chokes.

The ejector mechanism is released by the cartridge expansion on firing for dry firing without ejector movement.

No hammer, rather a primed firing pin that moves perpendicularly, the shortest way to the detonator. This gives an action (lock) time of approximately 2 thousandths of a second from pulling the trigger to detonating the cartridge.

If you need to change a firing pin or firing spring, it takes approximately 1 minute with the accompanying tool.

Flodman is delivered with automatic safety, which can easily be changed to manual.

Flodman Shotguns

Action: over/under
Stock: walnut, fitted to customer
Barrel: any standard length
Chokes: improved cylinder, modified, full
Weight: 7.0lbs.
Bore/Gauge: 12, 20
Magazine: none
Features: boxlock offered in any standard gauge or rifle/shotgun combination; true hammerless firing mechanism, single selective trigger, automatic ejector
Flodman shotguns $10,500

Franchi Shotguns

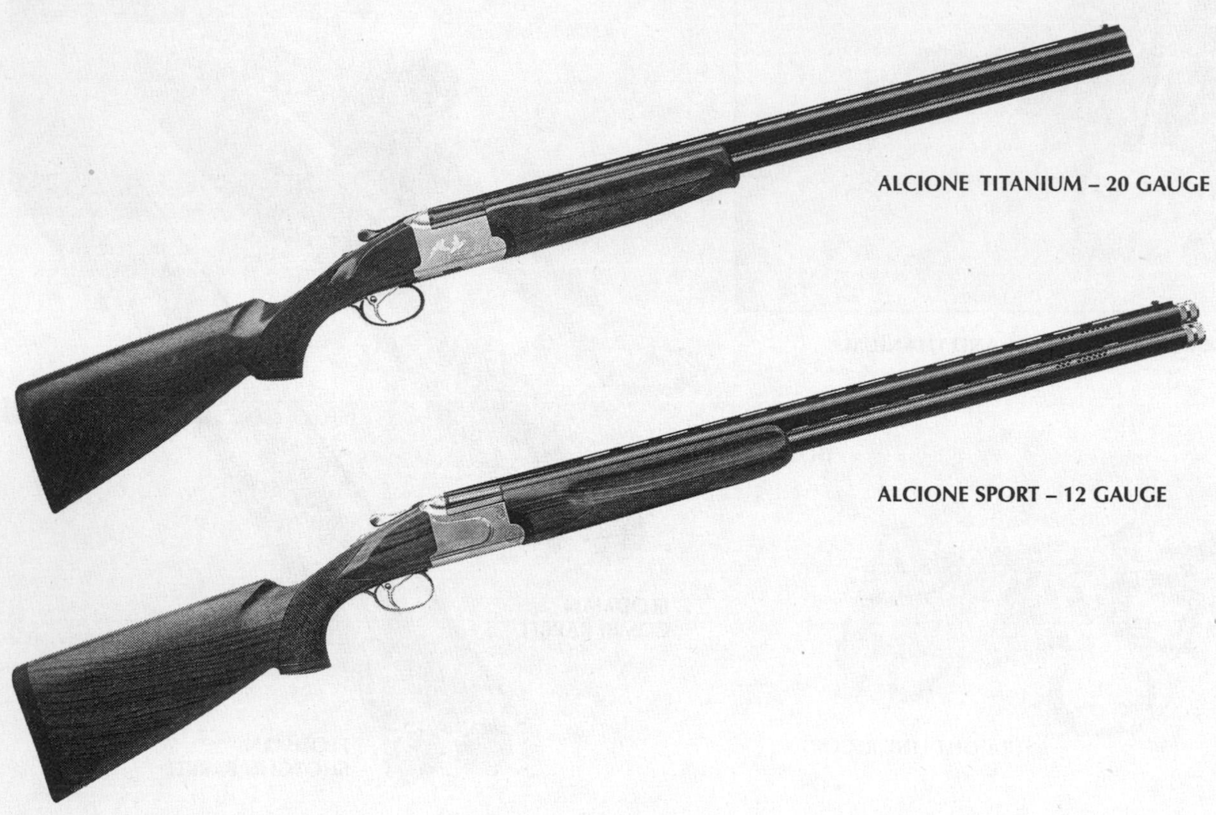

ALCIONE TITANIUM – 20 GAUGE

ALCIONE SPORT – 12 GAUGE

THE ALCIONE SPORT over-under is available in 12 ga. with 30″ ported barrels and extended knurled choke tubes. It is chambered for 2¾″ target loads. A 10mm-wide rib quickly pulls the eye to targets and builds scores. A manual safety complements mechanical triggers, which do not require recoil from the first barrel to fire the second barrel.

The Alcione Sport and SX have removable receiver sideplates. The stock and forend are shaped from high-grade walnut and have special dimensions for the serious competitor. The Alcione Sport and Field offer left-handed stock dimensions.

The Alcione SX has a high-grade walnut stock with fine checkering. The receivers are highly polished and feature delicate etchings. Unique to the Alcione product line is the ability to interchange barrels without the need for fitting. Simply swap any barrel set (12 or 20 gauge) onto any other frames and forend. No gunsmithing is required.

Alcione

Action: over/under
Stock: walnut
Barrel: 26 or 28 in.
Chokes: screw-in tubes
Weight: 5.4lbs.
Bore/Gauge: 12, 20
Magazine: none
Features: boxlock; mechanical single selective trigger

Alcione $1275
titanium. $1425
Sport model $1650
SX Lightweight $1800

SHOTGUNS

Remington's "Hevi-Shot" isn't round or even uniform in size, but it's 10 percent denser than lead and delivers tight patterns, even from open chokes. Use it only in barrels that handle steel shot.

Franchi Shotguns

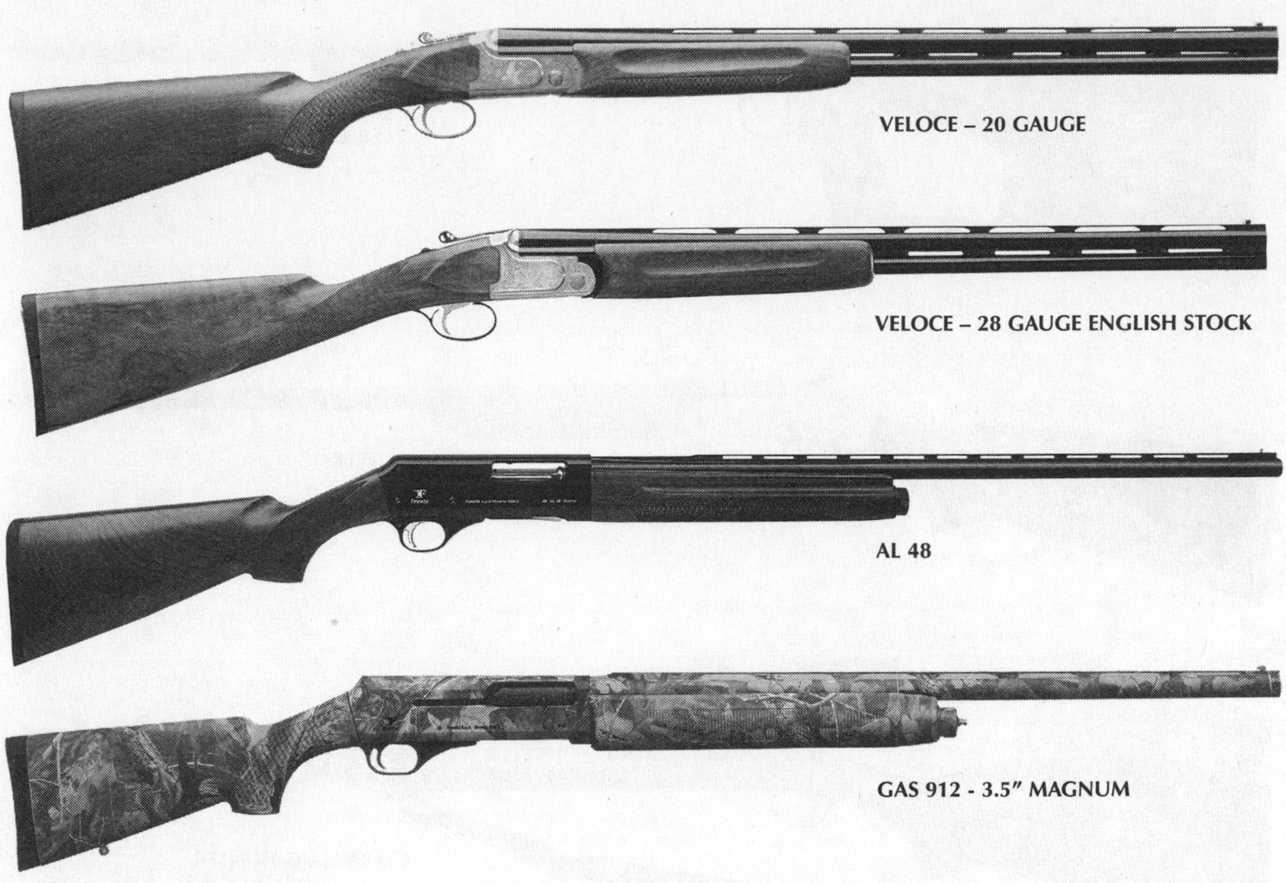

VELOCE – 20 GAUGE

VELOCE – 28 GAUGE ENGLISH STOCK

AL 48

GAS 912 - 3.5″ MAGNUM

THE LIGHTWEIGHT VELOCE is available in 20 ga. and 28 ga. only, and is built on its own aluminum alloy scaled-down frame. This mechanism allows the receiver to be quite shallow, adding to the balance and feel. A steel insert in the breech face adds further strength. The Veloce features engraved sideplates with gold-embellished game scenes. The trigger is mechanical for added reliability. The barrel selector doubles as a safety. Stocks and forends are beautifully-figured walnut and expertly checkered. The stock features a straight English or round pistol grip for natural pointing and the forend has a fluted design. The barrels have 3″ chambers in 20 ga. and 2¾″ chambers in 28 ga. All are chrome-lined for increased durability. A set of choke tubes in CYL, IC and MOD is included. The monoblock is jeweled for both a pleasing appearance and added resistance to wear. "Veloce" means "fast" in Italian, and at only 5½ pounds, this fast-swinging speedster is the perfect companion for a long day's hunt.

Veloce

Action: over/under
Stock: walnut, straight or English pistol grip
Barrel: 26 or 28 in.
Chokes: screw-in tubes
Weight: 5.5lbs.
Bore/Gauge: 20, 28
Magazine: none
Features: boxlock; alloy frame, steel breech insert, mechanical single selective trigger

20 ga. $1425
28 ga. $1500

Model AL 48

Action: autoloader
Stock: walnut
Barrel: 24, 26 or 28 in.
Chokes: screw-in tubes
Weight: 5.6lbs.
Bore/Gauge: 20, 28
Magazine: 4
Features: long recoil action

20 ga. $715
28 ga. $825
Deluxe 20 . . . . $940
Deluxe 28 . . . . $990

Model 612, 620

Action: autoloader
Stock: walnut or synthetic
Barrel: 18, 24, 26, 28, or 30 in.
Chokes: screw-in tubes
Weight: 9.0lbs.
Bore/Gauge: 12, 20
Magazine: 4
Features: gas-operated, rotary bolt; Model 912 chambered for 3.5-inch shells

walnut $675
synthetic $660
camo $765
defense (18 in.) $635
Sporting $975
Model 912 3.5-inch, walnut . . . $825
Model 912, synthetic $765
Model 912, camo $885

SHOTGUNS

Harrington & Richardson Shotguns

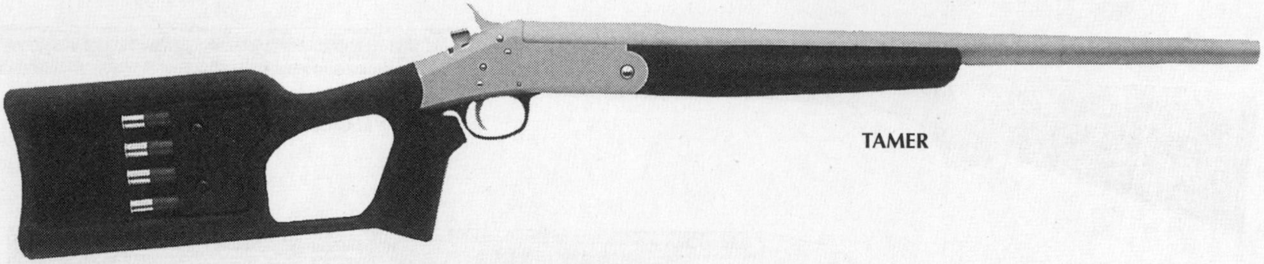

TAMER

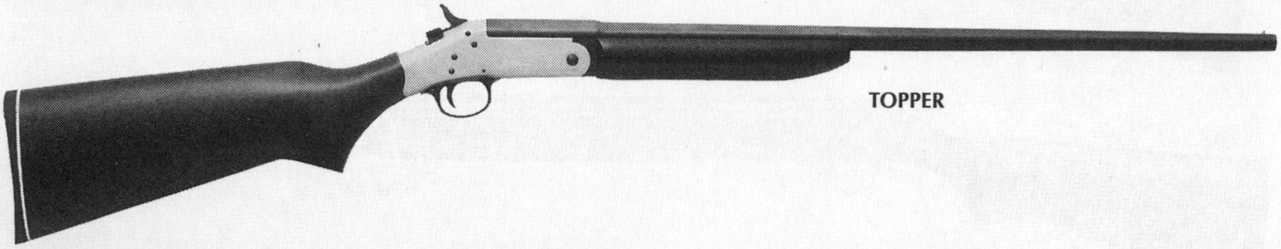

TOPPER

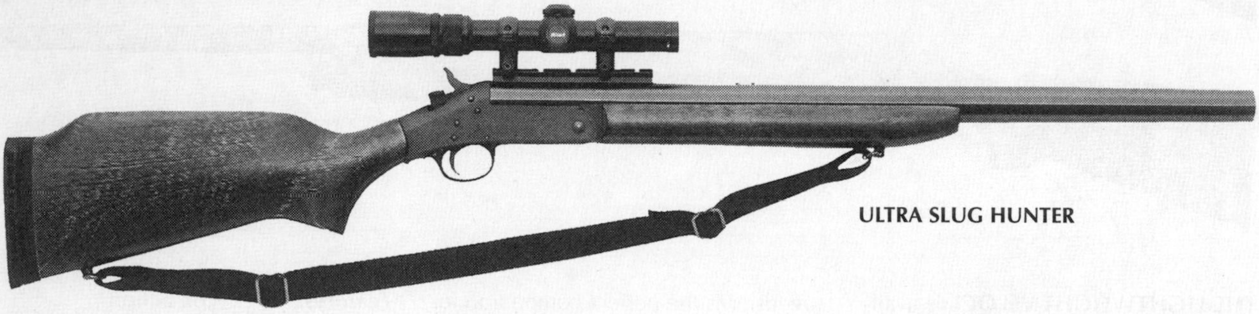

ULTRA SLUG HUNTER

TAMER
Action: hinged single-shot
Stock: synthetic
Barrel: 20 in.
Chokes: full
Weight: 5.5lbs.
Bore/Gauge: .410
Magazine: none
Features: thumbhole stock with recessed cavity for ammo storage
Tamer $161

TOPPER
Action: hinged single-shot
Stock: hardwood
Barrel: 26 or 28 in.
Chokes: screw-in tubes
Weight: 6.0lbs.
Bore/Gauge: 12, 20, 28, .410
Magazine: none
Features: hinged-breech with side lever release, automatic ejection
Topper $143
12 gauge 3.5-inch. $167
Junior with walnut stock. $184
NWTF Special with camo stock $216
Youth, 20 ga., 22-in. barrel, mod. choke $207

ULTRA SLUG HUNTER
Action: hinged single-shot
Stock: hardwood
Barrel: 24 in., rifled
Chokes: none
Weight: 7.5lbs.
Bore/Gauge: 12, 20
Magazine: none
Features: factory-mounted Weaver scope base, swivels and sling
Ultra Slug Hunter. $255
with checkered laminated wood $313

Turkey and heavy waterfowl loads extend your reach but batter your gums. More power doesn't always add birds to the bag. Standard loads in lighter guns can help you shoot sooner.

Heckler & Koch Shotguns

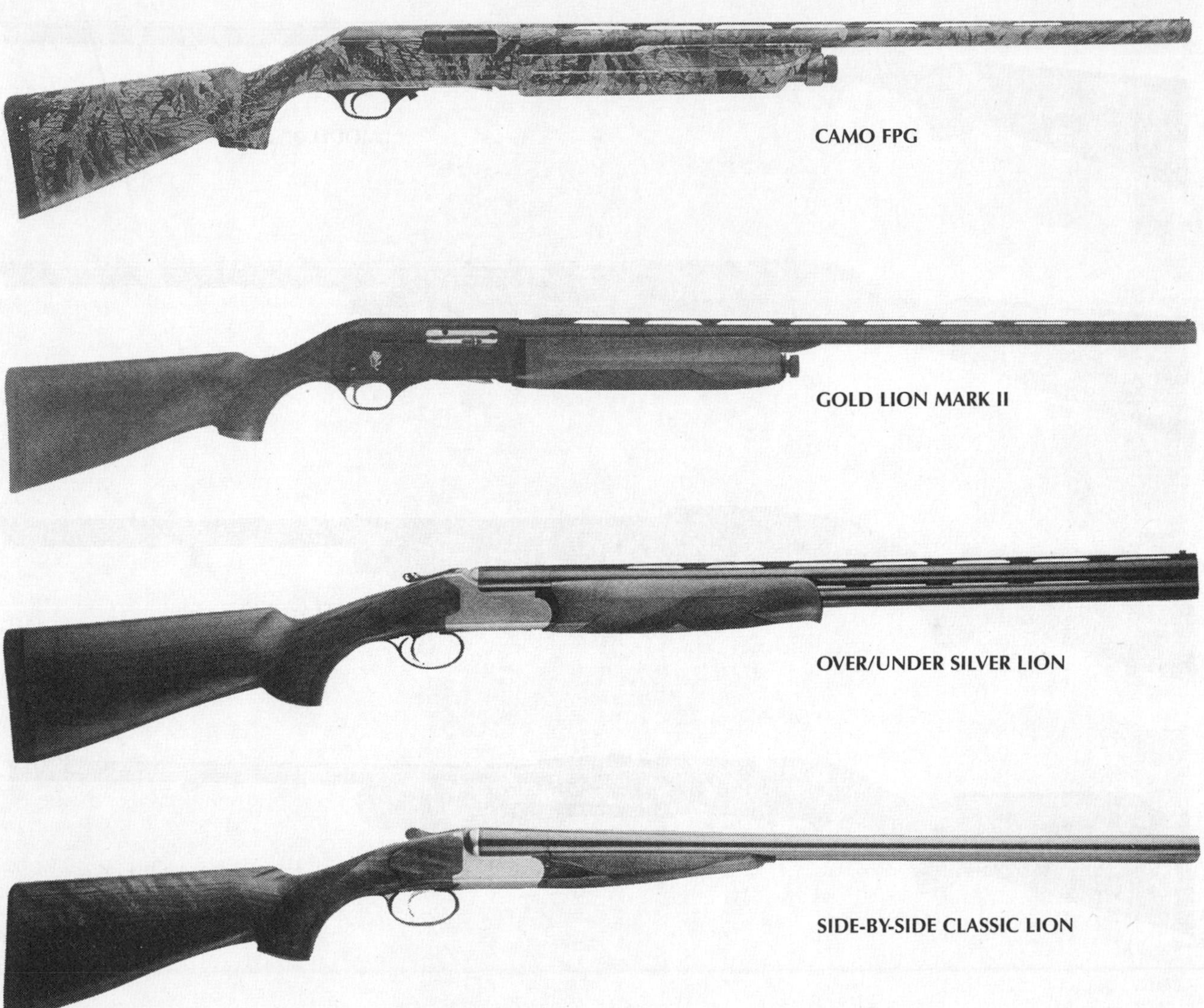

CAMO FPG

GOLD LION MARK II

OVER/UNDER SILVER LION

SIDE-BY-SIDE CLASSIC LION

Model FP6

Action: pump
Stock: walnut
Barrel: 26 or 28 in.
Chokes: screw-in tubes
Weight: 7.0lbs.
Bore/Gauge: 12
Magazine: 4
Features: back-bored barrel
FP6 . . . . **$399**
camo **$469**

Golden Lion Mark II

Action: autoloader
Stock: walnut or synthetic
Barrel: 24, 26 or 28 in.
Chokes: screw-in tubes
Weight: 7.0lbs.
Bore/Gauge: 12
Magazine: 4
Features: gas-operated actions, shim-adjustable buttstock
Golden Lion Mark II **$939**
Sporting Clays **$1249**

Over/Under

Action: over/under
Stock: walnut
Barrel: 26 or 28 in.
Chokes: screw-in tubes
Weight: 7.0lbs.
Bore/Gauge 12, 20
Magazine: none
Features: boxlock; back-bored barrels, single selective trigger
Over/Under **$1129**
Silver Lion **$1229**
Sporting Clays **$1749**

Side-by-Side

Action: side-by-side
Stock: walnut
Barrel: 26 or 28 in.
Chokes: screw-in tubes
Weight: 7.0lbs.
Bore/Gauge: 12
Magazine: none
Features: boxlock; back-bore barrels, single selective trigger
Grade I **$1499**
Classic Lion **$1689**
Classic Lion Grade II **$2099**

Ithaca Shotguns

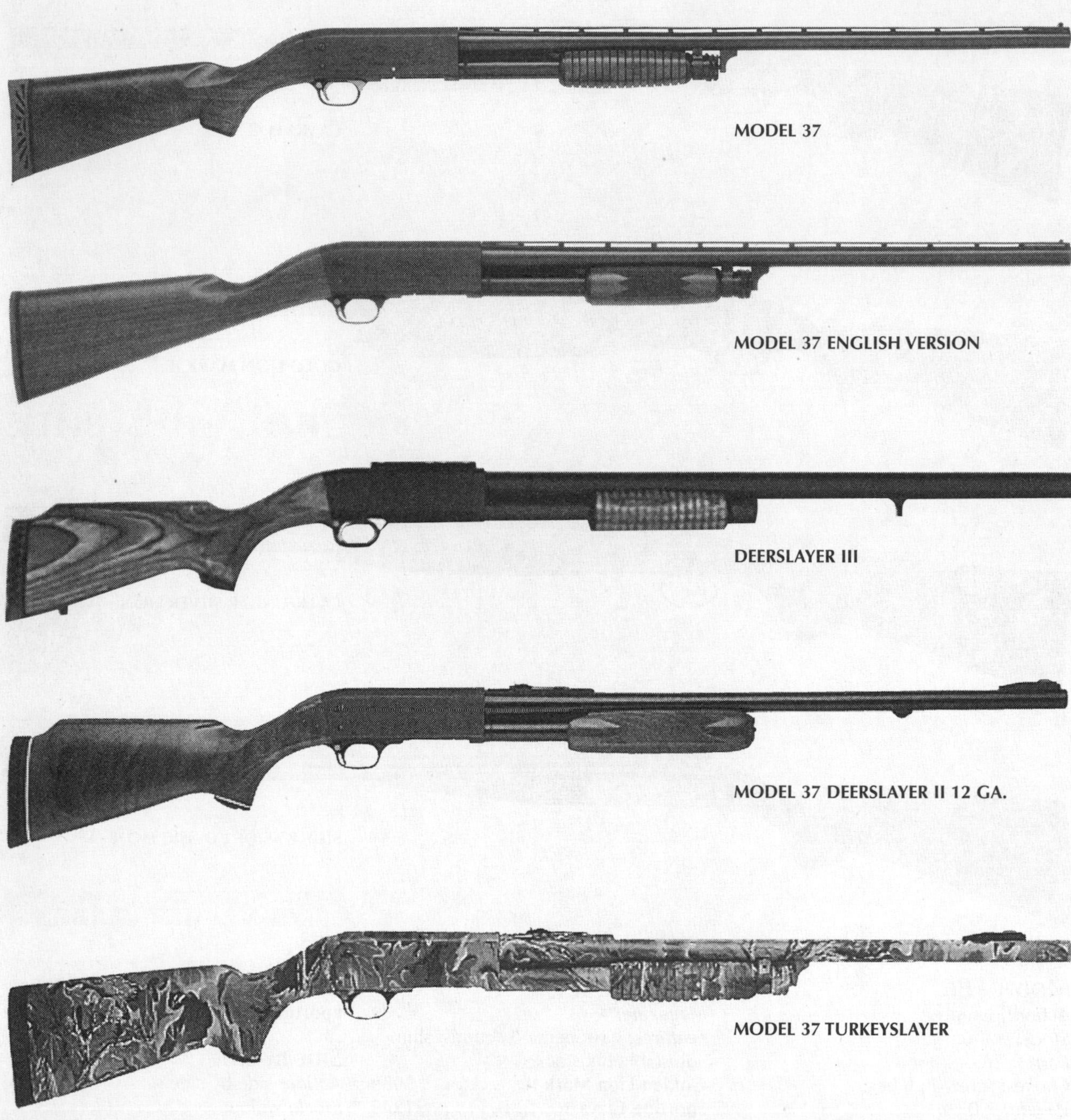

MODEL 37

MODEL 37 ENGLISH VERSION

DEERSLAYER III

MODEL 37 DEERSLAYER II 12 GA.

MODEL 37 TURKEYSLAYER

Model 37

Action: pump
Stock: walnut or synthetic
Barrel: 20, 22, 24, 26 or 28 in.
Chokes: screw-in tubes
Weight: 7.0lbs.
Bore/Gauge: 12, 16, 20
Magazine: 4
Features: bottom ejection
Model 37 . . . . $510
Ultralight 16 or 20 ga., straight-grip $803
Trap or Sporting Clays with Briley tubes. $1185

Model 37 Deerslayer II

Action: pump
Stock: walnut
Barrel: 20 or 25 in. rifled or smoothbore
Chokes:
Weight: 7.0lbs.
Bore/Gauge: 12, 16, 20
Magazine: 4
Features: open sights; receiver fitted with Weaver-style scope base; also available: Deerslayer III with 26-in. heavy rifled barrel and Turkeyslayer (12 or 20) with 22 in. barrel, extra-full tube
Deerslayer II $582
Deerslayer III. $900
Turkeyslayer. $654

Kimber Shotguns

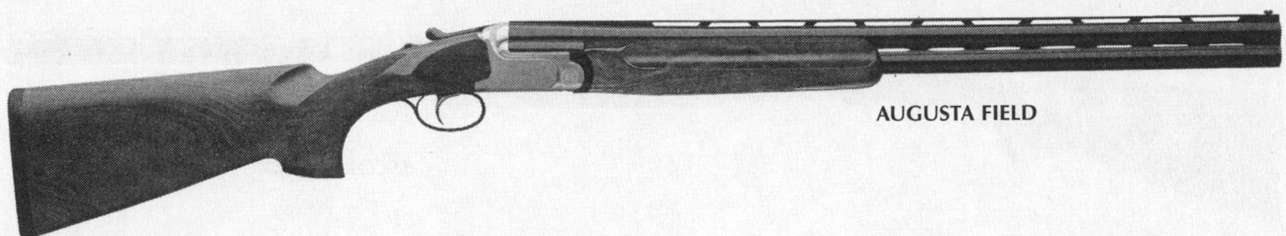

AUGUSTA FIELD

Augusta Field

Action: over/under
Stock: walnut
Barrel: 26, 28 and 30 in.
Chokes: screw-in tubes
Weight: 8.5lbs.
Bore/Gauge: 12
Magazine: none
Features: boxlock; backbored barrel with long forcing cones; adjustable single trigger, automatic ejectors, Hi-Viz sights (Sporting, Field, Trap and Skeet models available)
Augusta $4500

Krieghoff Shotguns

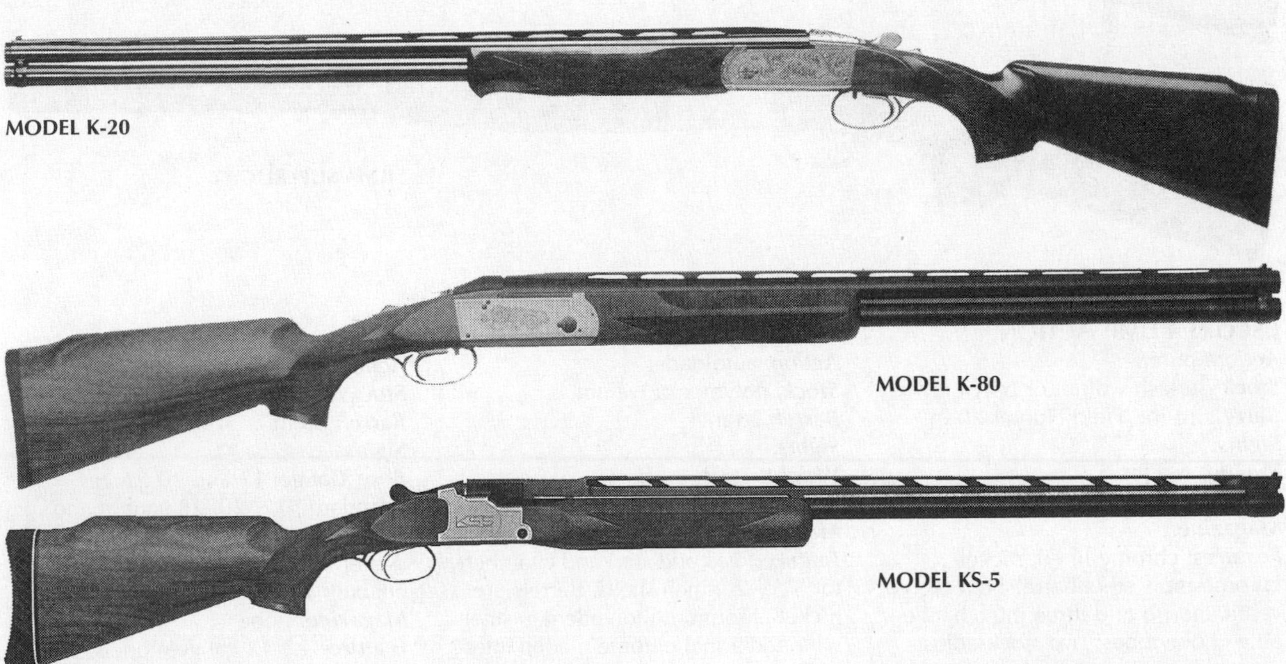

MODEL K-20

MODEL K-80

MODEL KS-5

Model K-20

Action: over/under
Stock: walnut
Barrel: 28 or 30 in.
Chokes: screw-in tubes
Weight: 7.2lbs.
Bore/Gauge: 20, 28, .410
Magazine: none
Features: boxlock; single selective trigger, automatic ejectors, tapered rib, choice of receiver finish; fitted aluminum case
K-20 . . . . price on request

Model K-80

Action: over/under
Stock: walnut
Barrel: 28 or 30 in.
Chokes: screw-in tubes
Weight: 8.0lbs.
Bore/Gauge: 12
Magazine: none
Features: boxlock; single selective trigger, automatic ejectors, tapered rib, choice of receiver finish; (Sporting Clays, Live Bird, Trap and Skeet models available)
K-80 . . . . price on request

Model KS-5

Action: hinged single-shot
Stock: walnut
Barrel: 30 in. or length to order
Chokes: screw-in tubes
Weight: 8.0lbs.
Bore/Gauge: 12
Magazine: none
Features: boxlock; adjustable trigger (release trigger available), step rib, case-colored receiver, optional fronthangers to adjust point of impact, optional adjustable comb
KS-5 . . . . price on request

Legacy Sports Shotguns

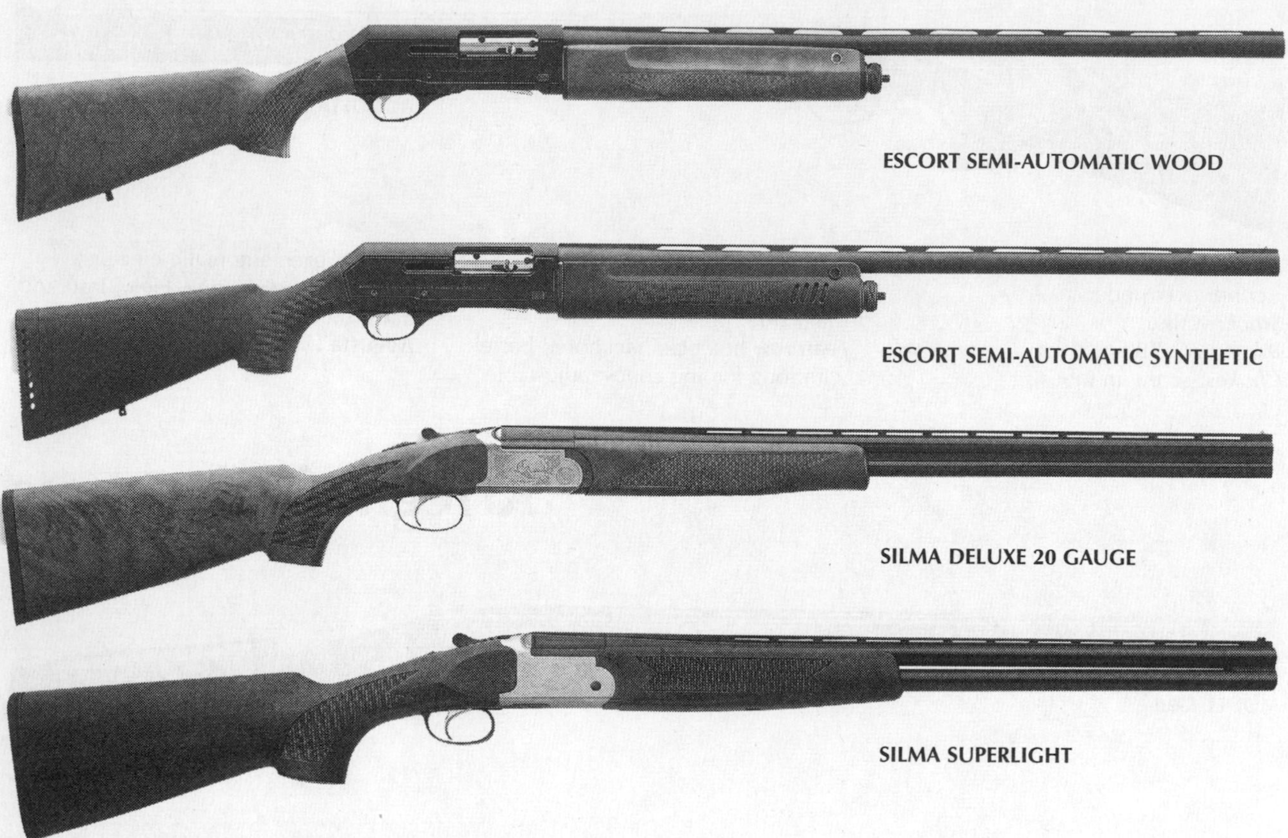

ESCORT SEMI-AUTOMATIC WOOD

ESCORT SEMI-AUTOMATIC SYNTHETIC

SILMA DELUXE 20 GAUGE

SILMA SUPERLIGHT

Escort Pump Action

Action: pump
Stock: Turkish walnut or polymer
Barrel: 28 in. (Field Hunter 20 in.)
Sights:
Weight: 6.4 lbs.
Bore/Gauge: 12
Magazine:
Features: chrome lined, nickel-chrome-moly steel barrels; checkered ventilated rib and three interchangeable choke tubes; two stock-adjustment shims, sling-swivel studs, ventilated recoil pad, migratory waterfowl magazine plug, and 7-shot magazine extender; Field Hunter series with matte blue or camo finish; Aim Guard extras include a polymer pistol grip and stock drop adjusting spacers.

Escort AS (walnut) $386
Escort PS (polymer) $364
Field Hunter. $199
Aim Guard. $189
Field Hunter Mossy Oak $219

Escort Semi-Automatic

Action: autoloader
Stock: polymer or walnut
Barrel: 28 in.
Sights:
Weight: 7 lbs.
Bore/Gauge: 12
Magazine:
Features: gas operated and chambered for 3" or 2¾-inch shells. Barrels are nickel-chromium-molybdenum steel with additional chrome plating internally and a ventilated anti-glare checkered rib. Bolts are chrome plated. Extras include three chokes, a migratory plug, and two spacers to adjust the slope of the stock. Camo waterfowl and turkey combo available in Mossy Oak Break-Up with Hi Viz sights.

Escort AS polymer: $386
Escort PS walnut: $364
Camo waterfowl & turkey: $479

Silma

Action: box lock
Stock: walnut
Barrel: 28 in.
Sights:
Bore/Gauge: 12 and 20 gauges (Standard); 12, 20, 28 gauges and .410 bore (Deluxe); 12 & 20 gauge (Superlight);12 gauge (Superlight deluxe); 12 and 20 (Clays)
Magazine: none
Features: all 12 gauge models, except Superlight, come with 3.5 inch chambers, high grade steel barrels and are proofed for steel shot. All models come with mechanical single trigger, automatic safety, automatic ejectors, ventilated rib, and recoil pad.

Standard: $765
Deluxe
12 & 20gauge: $823
28 gauge & .410: $961
Superlight: $1004
Superlight Deluxe: $1004
Clays:. $1237

SHOTGUNS

Marocchi Shotguns

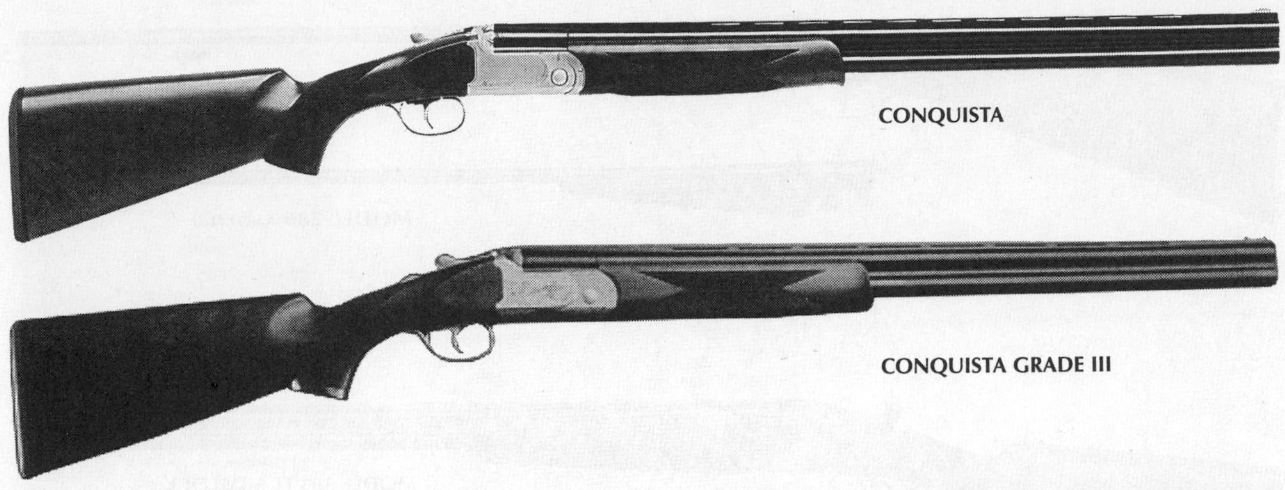

CONQUISTA

CONQUISTA GRADE III

Conquista
Action: over/under
Stock: walnut
Barrel: back-bored 28, 29, 30 or 32 in.
Chokes: screw-in tubes
Weight: 8.0lbs.
Bore/Gauge: 12
Magazine: none
Features: boxlock; single adjustable trigger, automatic ejectors (other grades in Sporter, Trap and Skeet available)
Sporter. $1490
other grades, from $2350

Merkel Shotguns

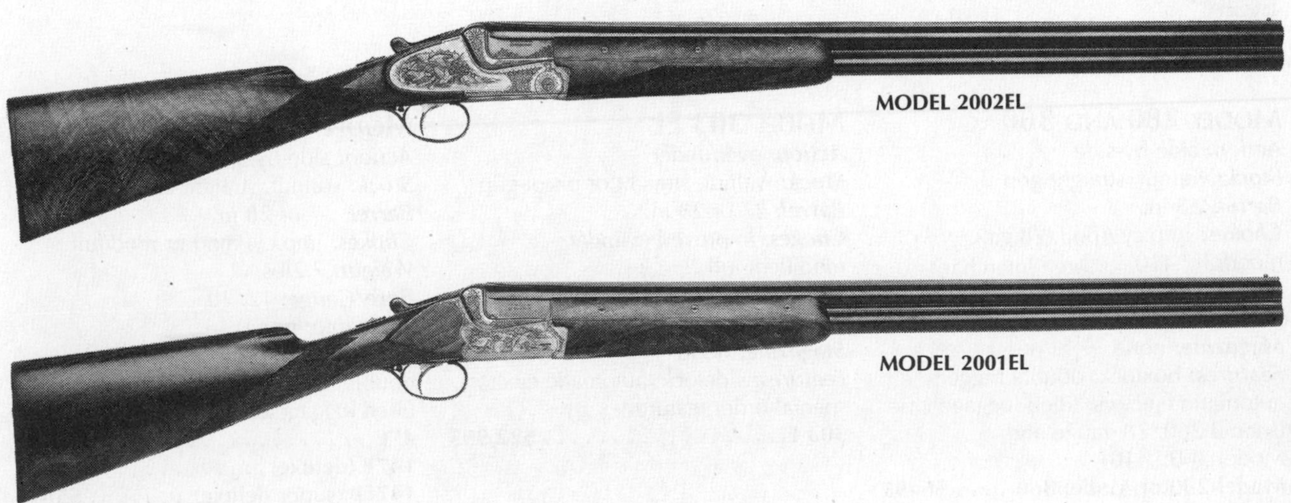

MODEL 2002EL

MODEL 2001EL

Model 2000 EL
Action: over/under
Stock: walnut, straight or pistol grip
Barrel: 27 or 28 in.
Chokes: improved cylinder, modified, full
Weight: 7.3lbs.
Bore/Gauge: 12, 20, 28
Magazine: none
Features: boxlock; single selective or double trigger; three-piece forend, automatic ejectors
2000 EL $5795
2001 EL (deluxe) $7295
2002 EL (with sideplates) . . . $10,995

SHOTGUNS

Merkel Shotguns

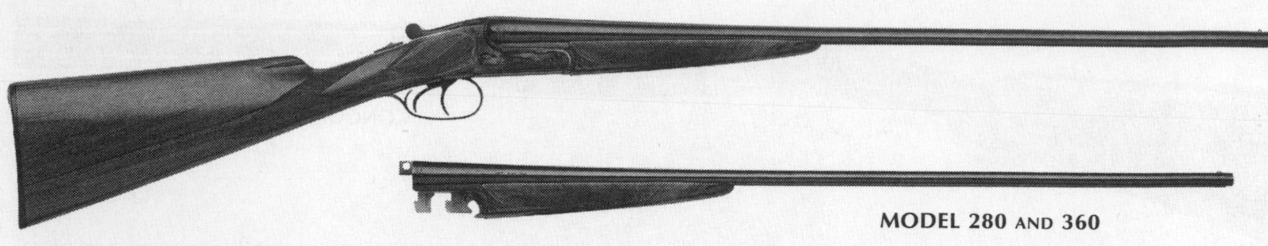

MODEL 280 AND 360

MODEL 303 EL SIDELOCK

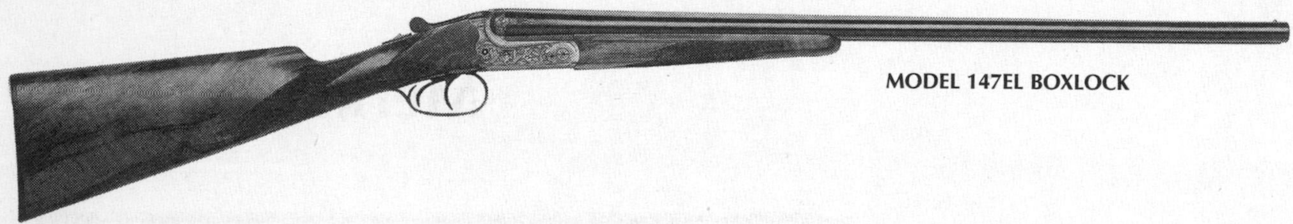

MODEL 147EL BOXLOCK

Model 280 and 360

Action: side-by-side
Stock: walnut, straight grip
Barrel: 28 in.
Chokes: imp.cyl/mod (28 ga.), mod/full (.410)
Weight: 6.0lbs.
Bore/Gauge: 28, .410
Magazine: none
Features: boxlock; double triggers, automatic ejectors; fitted luggage case (Model 280: 28 gauge and Model 360: .410)

Model 280 or Model 360 . . . . $6495
two-barrel sets $9395
S models with sidelocks, all gauges, from $6595

Model 303 EL

Action: over/under
Stock: walnut, straight or pistol grip
Barrel: 27 or 28 in.
Chokes: improved cylinder, modified, full
Weight: 7.3lbs.
Bore/Gauge: 16, 20, 28
Magazine: none
Features: sidelock; automatic ejectors, special-order features

303 EL. $22,995

Model 47E

Action: side-by-side
Stock: walnut, straight or pistol grip
Barrel: 27 or 28 in.
Chokes: imp.cyl/mod or mod/full
Weight: 7.2lbs.
Bore/Gauge: 12, 20
Magazine: none
Features: boxlock; single selective or double triggers; automatic ejectors; fitted luggage case

47E $3795
147E (deluxe). $4495
147EL (super deluxe) $5695

Mossberg Shotguns

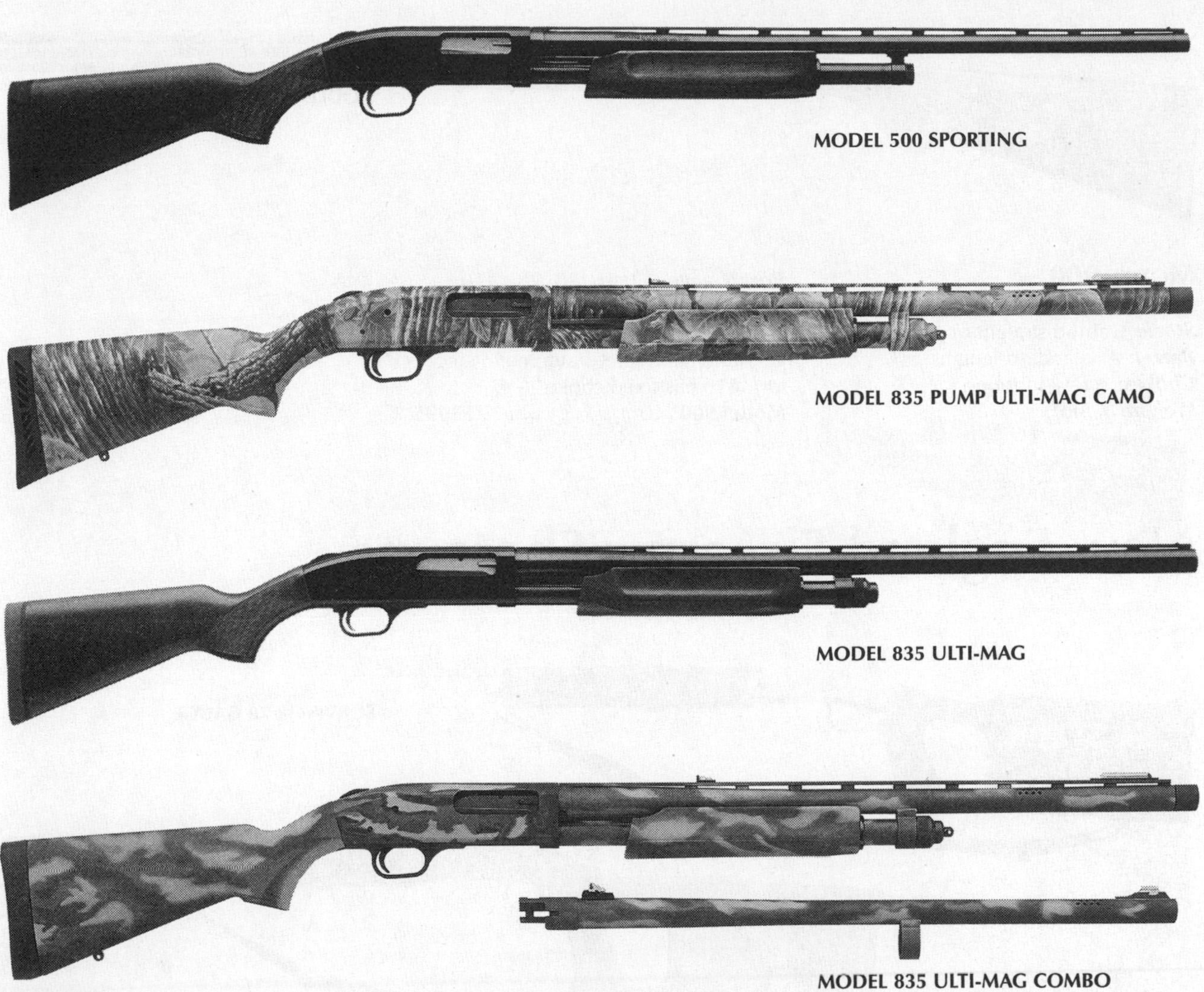

MODEL 500 SPORTING

MODEL 835 PUMP ULTI-MAG CAMO

MODEL 835 ULTI-MAG

MODEL 835 ULTI-MAG COMBO

Model 500

Action: pump
Stock: wood or synthetic
Barrel: 18, 22, 24, 26 or 28 in.
Chokes: screw-in tubes
Weight: 7.5lbs.
Bore/Gauge: 12, 20, .410
Magazine: 5
Features: barrels mostly vent rib, some ported; top tang safety; camouflage stock finish options; 10-year warranty
Model 500 . . . . $316
Slugster Ported 24" bbl: $361
two-barrel combo set $376

Model 500 Mariner

Action: pump
Stock: synthetic
Barrel: 18 or 20 in.
Chokes: cylinder
Weight: 7.0lbs.
Bore/Gauge: 12
Magazine: 5
Features: top tang safety; 12-gauge has "Marinecote" metal and 10-year warranty; 20 gauge and .410 variations available in blued finish
Mariner $497
20 gauge and .410 . . . . $513

Model 835 Ulti-Mag

Action: pump
Stock: synthetic or camo
Barrel: 24 or 28 in.
Chokes: full
Weight: 7.0lbs.
Bore/Gauge: 12
Magazine: 4
Features: barrel ported, back-bored with vent rib; 3.5-inch chamber; top tang safety; rifled slug barrel and combination sets available; 10-year warranty
Model 835 . . . . $450
Combo: $556

New England Arms (FAIR) Shotguns

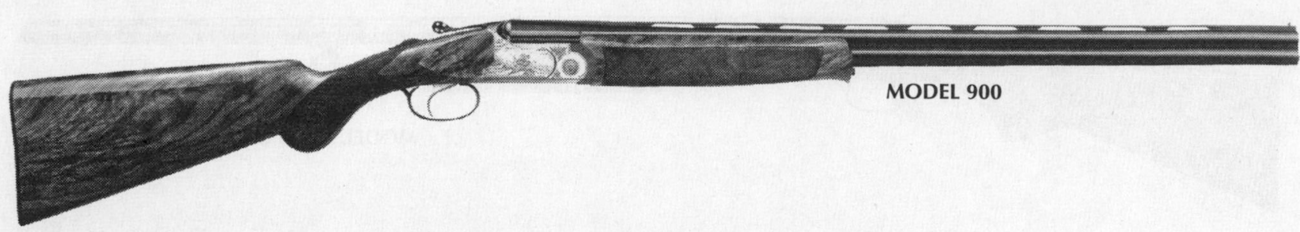

MODEL 900

Model 900

Action: over/under
Stock: walnut, straight or pistol grip
Barrel: all standard lengths
Chokes: screw-in tubes
Weight: 7.5lbs.
Bore/Gauge: 12, 16, 20, 28, .410
Magazine: none
Features: boxlock; single selective trigger, automatic safety, automatic ejector; .410 has fixed choke
Model 900 . . . . $3995

New England Firearms Shotguns

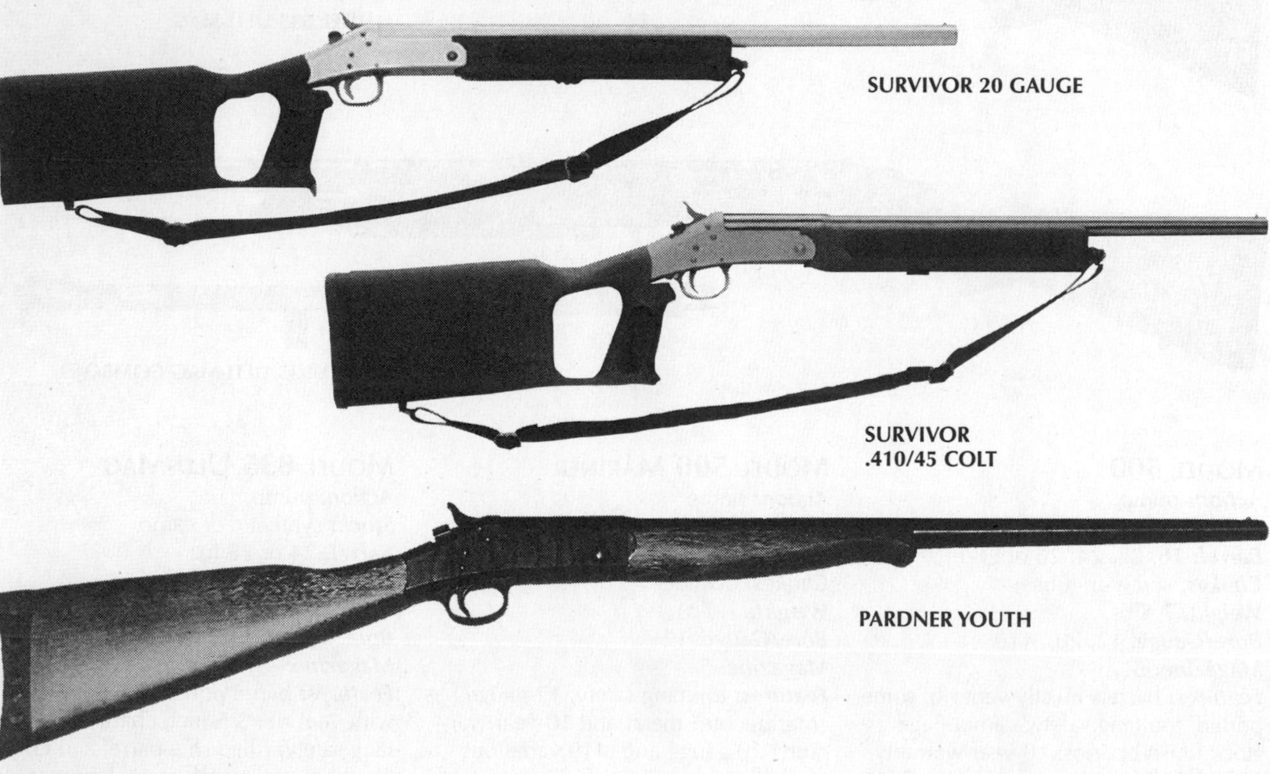

SURVIVOR 20 GAUGE

SURVIVOR .410/45 COLT

PARDNER YOUTH

Model Survivor and Pardner

Action: hinged single-shot
Stock: synthetic
Barrel: 22, 26, 28 or 32 in.
Chokes: modified, full
Weight: 6.0lbs.
Bore/Gauge: 12, 16, 20, 28, .410
Magazine: none
Features: Youth and camo-finish Turkey models available; Survivor has hollow pistol-grip buttstock for storage, chambers .41 and .45 Colt
Survivor $161
Pardner $131
Pardner Youth. $140
Pardner Turkey Camo Youth . . . $187

SHOTGUNS

New England Firearms Shotguns

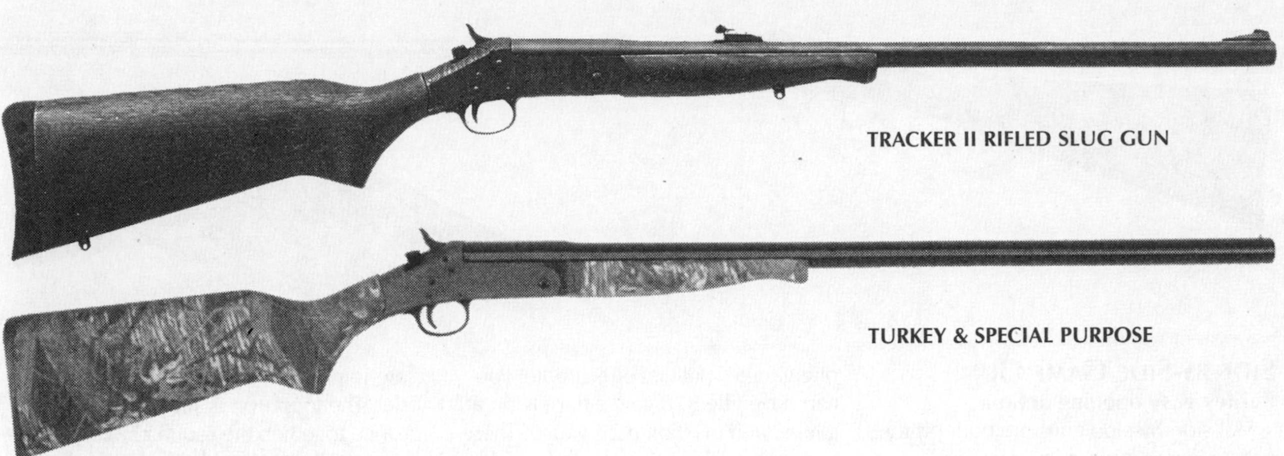

TRACKER II RIFLED SLUG GUN

TURKEY & SPECIAL PURPOSE

Tracker II Rifled Slug Gun

Action: hinged single-shot
Stock: hardwood
Barrel: rifled 24 in.
Chokes: none
Weight: 6.0lbs.
Bore/Gauge 12, 20
Magazine: none
Features: camo finish available, adjustable rifle sights, swivels and sling standard
Tracker II $183

Turkey & Special Purpose

Action: hinged single-shot
Stock: hardwood
Barrel: 24 in. (Turkey) or 28 in. (Waterfowl)
Chokes: full, screw-in tubes
Weight: 9.5lbs.
Bore/Gauge: 10, 12
Magazine: none
Features: Turkey and Waterfowl models available with camo finish, swivels and sling standard
Turkey Gun (camo, full choke) . $187
Turkey Gun (black, tubes). $177
Special Purpose Waterfowl 10 ga.. . . . . $268
with 28 in. barrel, walnut $212
Special Purpose Waterfowl 12 ga.. . . . . $165

Perazzi Shotguns

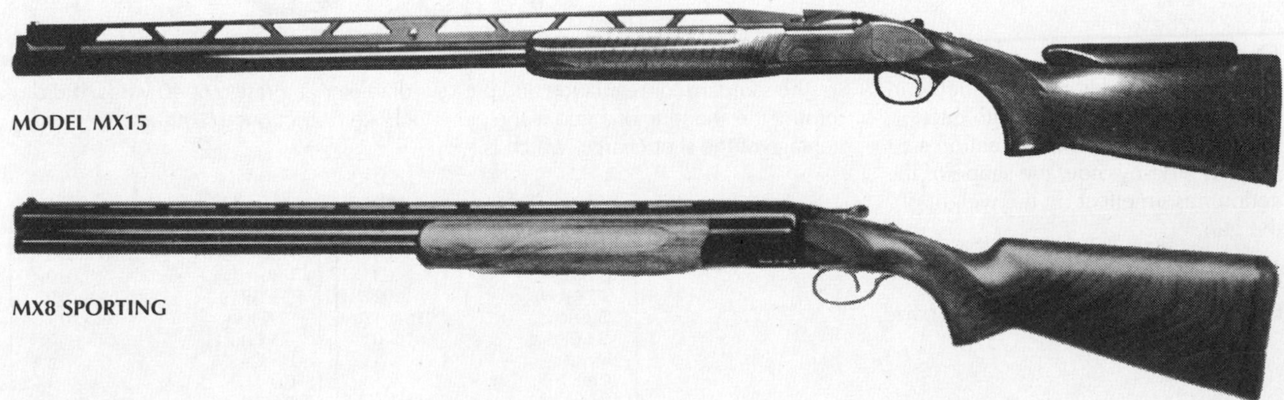

MODEL MX15

MX8 SPORTING

Model MX15

Action: hinged single-shot
Stock: walnut, adjustable comb
Barrel: 32 or 34 in.
Chokes: full
Weight: 8.4lbs.
Bore/Gauge: 12
Magazine: none
Features: high trap rib
MX15. . . . . $8140

Model MX8

Action: over/under
Stock: walnut
Barrel: 26 or 28 in.
Chokes: screw-in tubes
Weight: 7.3lbs.
Bore/Gauge: 12, 20, 28, .410
Magazine: none
Features: hinged-breech action; double triggers or single selective or non-selective trigger; Sporting, Skeet and Trap models available
MX8. . . . . $9560

SHOTGUNS

Purdey Shotguns

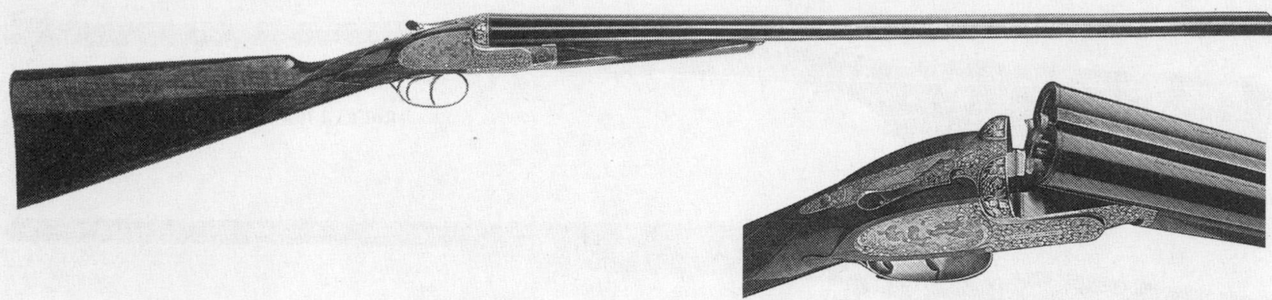

Side-by-Side Game Gun

Purdey easy opening action:

All side-by-side guns are built on the easy opening system invented by Frederick Beesley. This system is incorporated in guns built from 1880 onwards.

Purdey offers dedicated action sizes for each of the bores 10, 12, 20, 28 & .410 cores. An extra pair of barrels can be ordered, even if you want a barrel set one gauge smaller. For example, you can have fitted 28 gauge barrels on a 20 gauge, and .410 on a 28 gauge. These guns are made with a single forend for both bores.

All Purdey barrels, both SxS and O/U, are of chopper lump construction. Each individual tube is hand filled and then "struck up" using striking files. This gives the tube the correct Purdey profile.

Once polished, the individual tubes are joined at the breech using silver solder. The loop iron is similarly fixed. Once together, the rough chokes can be cut and the internal bores finished using a traditional lead lapping technique.

Ribs are hand-filed to suit the barrel contour exactly, and then soft-soldered in place, using pine resin as the fluxing agent. Pine resin provides extra water resistance to the surfaces enclosed by the ribs.

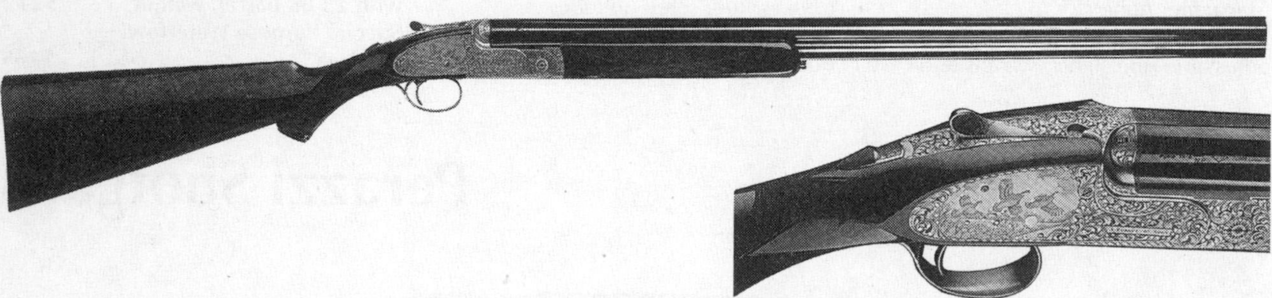

Over/Under Gun

The Over-Under gun is available in 12, 16, 20, 28 and .410, with each bore made on a dedicated action size. As with Side-by-Side, the shape of the action has an effect on the weight of the gun.

Conventionally, the Purdey over-under will shoot the lower barrel first, but can be made to shoot the top barrel first if required. All prices on request.

The standard for regulating and patterning the shooting of a gun is the percentage of the shot charge, which is evenly concentrated in a circle of 30" diameter at a range of 40 yards. (Purdey choke restrictions 1/1000 inch.)

12 Bore 2.75" 1.25 oz No.6	
Full Choke	.038 - .040
Choke	.035
.75 (mod)	.022
.5 Choke	.016-.017
.25 Choke	.010-.01
Imp Cyl	7-8
Cyl	3
Skeet	Open Bore

20 Bore 2.75"	
Full Choke	.038 - .040
Choke	.030
.75 (mod)	.018-.019
.5 Choke	.012-.013
.25 Choke	7-8
Imp Cyl	6
Cyl	3
Skeet	Open Bore

The Choke Section

The Percentages Of Choke	
Cylinder	45%
Improved Cylinder	50%
1/4 Choke	55%
1/2 Choke	60%
3/4 or Modified Choke	65%
Choke	70%
Full Choke	75%
Skeet (2)	45%
Skeet (1)	40%

12 Bore 2.5" 1 oz. No. 6	
Full Choke	.038 - .040
Choke	.030
.75 (mod)	.018-.019
.5 Choke	.012-.013
.25 Choke	6-7
Imp Cyl	3
Cyl	2

28 Bore 2.75"	
Full Choke	.026
Choke	.020
.75 (mod)	.018
.5 Choke	.015
.25 Choke	.011
Imp Cyl	7
Cyl	3
Skeet	Open

Remington Shotguns

MODEL 1100 SPORTING 12

MODEL 11-87 PREMIER AUTOLOADER

MODEL 11-87 PREMIER DEER GUN

MODEL 11-87 SPS-T TURKEY GUN

MODEL 11-87 SPS SUPER MAGNUM CAMO & 3″ MAGNUM

Model 1100

Action: autoloader
Stock: walnut or synthetic
Barrel: 21, 26 or 28 in.
Chokes: screw-in tubes
Weight: 7.0lbs.
Bore/Gauge: 12, 16, 20
Magazine: 4
Features: chambered for 2 3/4-inch shells; available in Deer, Youth and Youth Turkey variations with 21-inch barrels, Sporting Clays and Trap versions

1100 . . . . **$549**
Cantilever Deer **$629**
Youth Turkey **$612**
Sporting Clays or Skeet. **$868**
Trap. **$895**

Model 11-87

Action: autoloader
Stock: walnut or synthetic
Barrel: 26, 28 or 30 in.
Chokes: screw-in tubes
Weight: 7.5lbs.
Bore/Gauge: 12
Magazine: 5
Features: gas-operated, handles 2 3/4 and 3-inch shells interchangeably; deer gun has cantilever scope mount, rifled bore; Upland Special has straight grip; SPS Super Magnum chambers 3.5-inch shells

11-87. **$777**
Deer Gun. **$824**
Upland Special. **$777**
SPS Turkey Gun **$905**
Camo Turkey Gun. **$963**

Remington Shotguns

MODEL 332 O/U

MODEL 870 EXPRESS

MODEL 870 EXPRESS "YOUTH" GUN

MODEL 870 EXPRESS TURKEY CAMO

MODEL 870 EXPRESS COMBO

Model 332

Action: over/under
Stock: walnut
Barrel: 26, 28 or 30 in.
Chokes: screw-in tubes
Weight: 7.3lbs.
Bore/Gauge: 12
Magazine: none
Features: boxlock; ventilated rib; Model 332 patterned after classic Model 32
Model 332 . . . . $1624

Model 870

Action: pump
Stock: walnut, synthetic or hardwood (Express)
Barrel: 26, 28 or 30 in.
Chokes: screw-in tubes
Weight: 7.3lbs.
Bore/Gauge: 12, 16, 20, 28, .410
Magazine: 5
Features: Super Magnum chambered for 3.5-inch shells; deer gun has rifled barrel, open sights

standard or 6.5 lb. Lightweight $584
Super Magnum or 28 ga. $665
Express $332
Express Super Magnum. $376
Express Lightweight Youth 20 ga.. . . . . $332
Turkey Camo 3.5-inch $500
Combo with shot barrel and slug barrel $523

Remington Shotguns

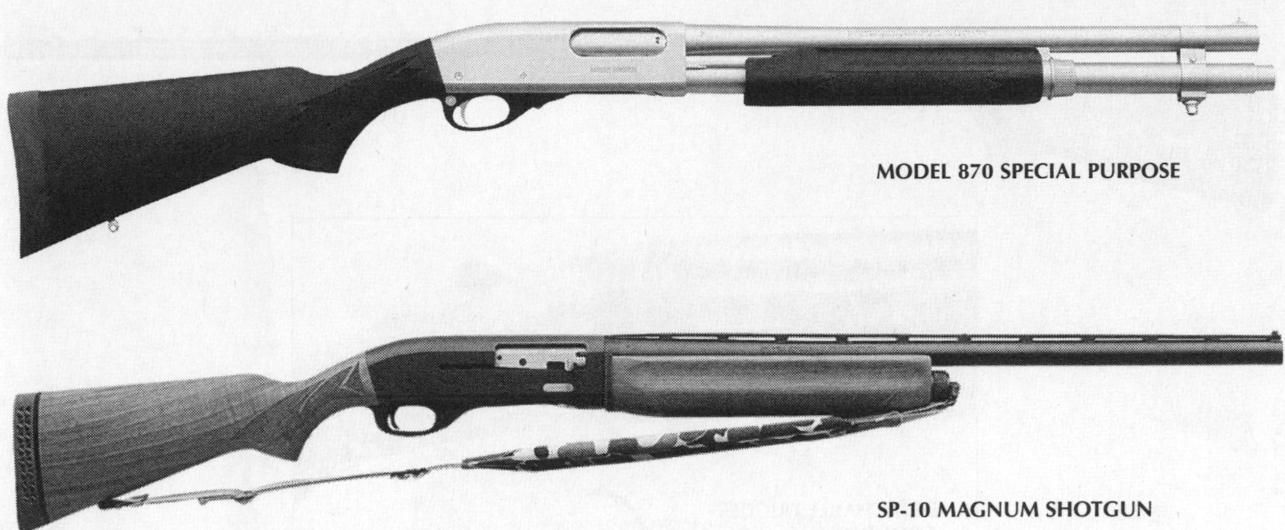

MODEL 870 SPECIAL PURPOSE

SP-10 MAGNUM SHOTGUN

Model 870 Marine Magnum

Action: pump
Stock: synthetic
Barrel: 18 in.
Chokes: none
Weight: 7.5lbs.
Bore/Gauge: 12
Magazine: 7
Features: nickel-plated exterior metal
Marine Magnum............ $573

Model SP-10

Action: autoloader
Stock: walnut or synthetic
Barrel: 26 or 30 in.
Chokes: screw-in tubes
Weight: 11.0lbs.
Bore/Gauge: 10
Magazine: 4
Features: the only gas-operated 10 gauge made; stainless piston and sleeve
SP-10.................. $1317
camo.................. $1453

Slim grips allow the shotgun to float in your hand, so as you point at a bird the weight of the muzzle carries the bore into line with the target. A bulky, tight, restrictive grip slows you down.

SHOTGUNS

Renato Gamba Shotguns

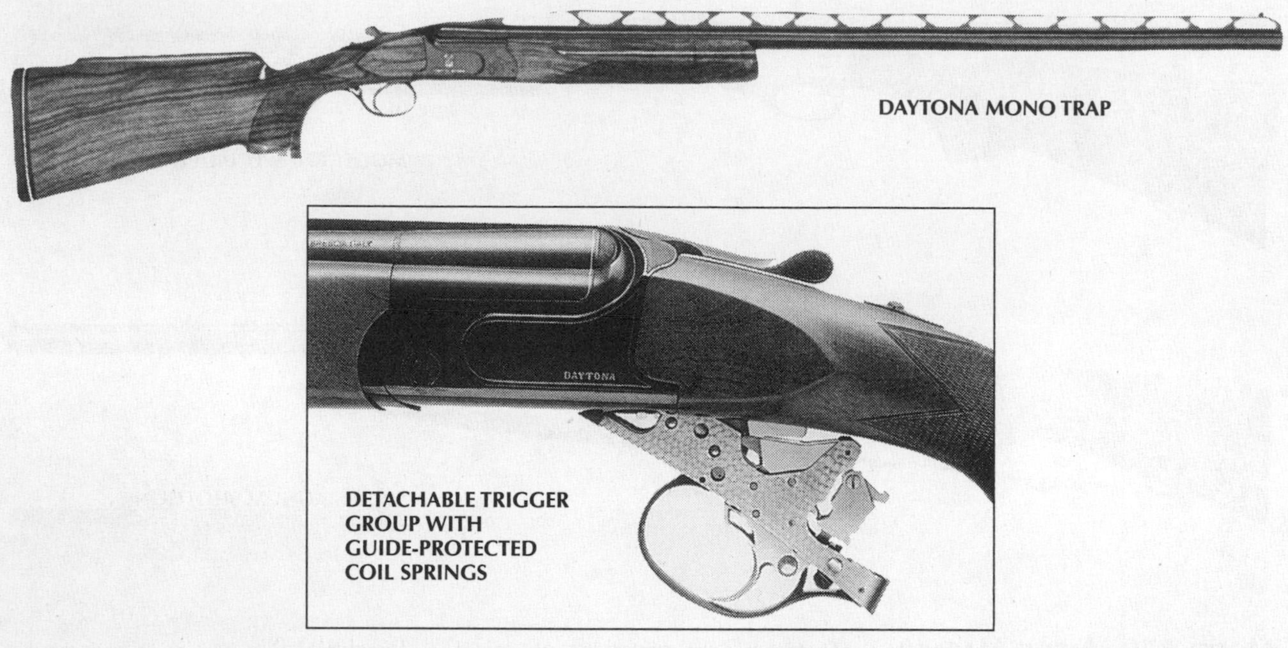

DAYTONA MONO TRAP

DETACHABLE TRIGGER GROUP WITH GUIDE-PROTECTED COIL SPRINGS

	TRAP	DOUBLE TRAP	SKEET	SPORTING CLAYS	HUNTING	MONO TRAP
GAUGE	12 - 20					
BARRELS	heat treated special chrome-nickel-molybdenum steel					
CHANBER	mm 70 (2"3/4) • mm 79 (3") on request					
BARRELS LENGTH	cm. 76 - cm.81 30" - 32"	cm. 76 30"	cm. 68-71 26"3/4 - 28"	cm. 71-74cm 76 - cm.81 28"- 29"- 30"- 32"	cm. 68- cm. 71 26"3/4 - 28"	cm. 81- cm. 86 32" - 34"
CHOKES	imp. mod/ full-mac/full	imp. cil./full	SK/SK	mod./full	imp. cit./imp.mod. mod./full	full
INTERCH. CHOKES	5 screw-in choke tubes set available on request					

The Daytona Shotgun

The Daytona shotgun is available in several styles oriented specifically to American Trap, International Trap, American Skeet, International Skeet, and Sporting Clays. The Daytona SL, (the side plate model), and the Daytona SLHH, (the side lock model), are the top of the Daytona line.

All employ the Boss locking system in a breech milled from one massive block of steel.

The trigger group: The trigger group is detachable and is removable without the use of tools. The frame that contains the hammers, sears and springs is milled from a single block of special steel and jeweled for oil retention. On special order, an adjustable trigger may be produced with one inch of movement that can accomodate shooters with exceptionally large or small hands. Internally, the hammer springs are constructed from coils that are contained in steel sleeves placed directly behind the hammers. With the fail safe capsule surrounding the springs, the shotgun will fire even if breakage occurs.

Hunter o/u. . . . . from $1390
Le Maus o/u. . . . . from 1580
Concorde o/u. . . . . from 6100
Daytona 2K o/u . . . . from 7600

Back-bored barrels are simply those with oversize dimensions forward of the chamber. The advantage: less friction as the shot charge leaves, less pellet deformation. Also, lower pressures.

E. Rizzini Shotguns

PREMIER SPORTING EL (12 GAUGE)

UPLAND EL (20 GAUGE)

OVER/UNDER TR I, II, & PLUS

OVER/UNDER TR-MAG
MOSSY OAK BREAK-UP

Rizzini Sporting and Upland EL

Rizzini builds a well-finished boxlock ejector over/under that is available in all gauges and in many different configurations.

The Artemis and Premier are production guns built to standard specifications. The EL models, which include the Upland EL, the Sporting EL and the High Grades, feature higher grade wood, checkering and hand finishing.

Field guns are available with case-colored or coin-finish actions with straight grips or round knob semi-pistol grips. Also available are multi-gauge field sets with .410, 28 or 20 gauge barrels in any combination. These sets are available in EL or High Grade level guns. On custom orders, stock dimensions, chokes and barrel length may be specified. Screw-in chokes are available on 12 and 20 gauge guns.

Sporting guns, in 12 and 20 gauge only, feature heavier weight and a target-style rib, stock and forearm. The Sporting models are available in three versions: Premier Sporting, Sporting EL and S790EL.

High Grade models, with or without sideplates, come in four engraving styles, including game scenes and gold inlays.

Sporting El (12 gauge) $3,600
Upland El (20 gauge) $2,800
S790 EMEL High Grade $7,800
Artemis El High Grade $12,650

Emilio Rizzini Over/Unders

The TR-I, TR-I Plus, and TR-II Emilio Rizzini boxlocks have walnut stocks, 3″ chambers (except the 28 & 16 gauge models: 2 3/4″ chamber) and ventilated ribs. The TR-1 has a fixed choke and extractors, the new TR-I-Plus two choke tubes and extractors, and the TR-II three choke tubes (IC/M/F) and auto ejectors. The TR-MAG series has 3" magnum chambers, choke tubes, extractors (All 10GA, & 12GA.WF) or ejectors (12GA. MOB & 12 GA. MOS) and a ventilated 7mm top rib in three handsome models: The standard matte blue finish with walnut stock, Mossy Oak Break-up camouflage pattern, and Mossy Oak Shadow Grass camouflage pattern.

Weight: 6.75-7.5 lbs. (10 ga., 9.75 lbs.)
Barrel Length: 24-28"

TR-I (fixed chokes) $687
TR-I Plus (choke tubes) $748
TR-II 12, 16 ga. $879
TR-II 20, 28, .410 . . . . $924
TR-MAG 12 ga. $764
12 ga. camo $942
10 ga. camo $1132

Rossi Shotguns

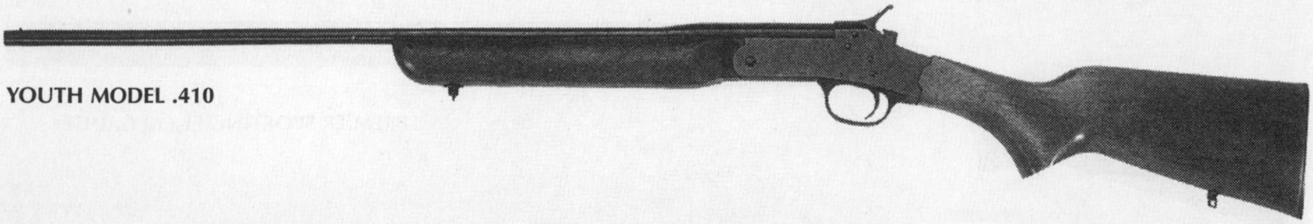

YOUTH MODEL .410

FIELD GRADE 12 GAUGE

MATCHED PAIR

SINGLE BARREL SHOTGUNS

Action: hinged single-shot
Stock: hardwood
Barrel: 28 in.
Chokes: modified, full
Weight: 5.3lbs.
Bore/Gauge: 12, 20, .410
Magazine: none
Features: exposed-hammer, transfer-bar action; Youth model available; rifle barrels have open sights

Single-Shot $106
Youth, 22" barrel $106
two-barrel sets with 12 ga/.22 WMR, 12/.22 LR, 20/.22LR,
two barrel set with stainless bbl.
.410/.22LR $194
.410/.17HMR $223
two-barrel set with
.410/.22LR $144
12 ga/.17 HMR or
20ga/.17 HMR $180

Some shooters prefer mechanical single triggers on double guns because they work even if you have a misfire in the first barrel. A recoil-operated trigger won't switch unless the round fires.

SHOTGUNS

Ruger Shotguns

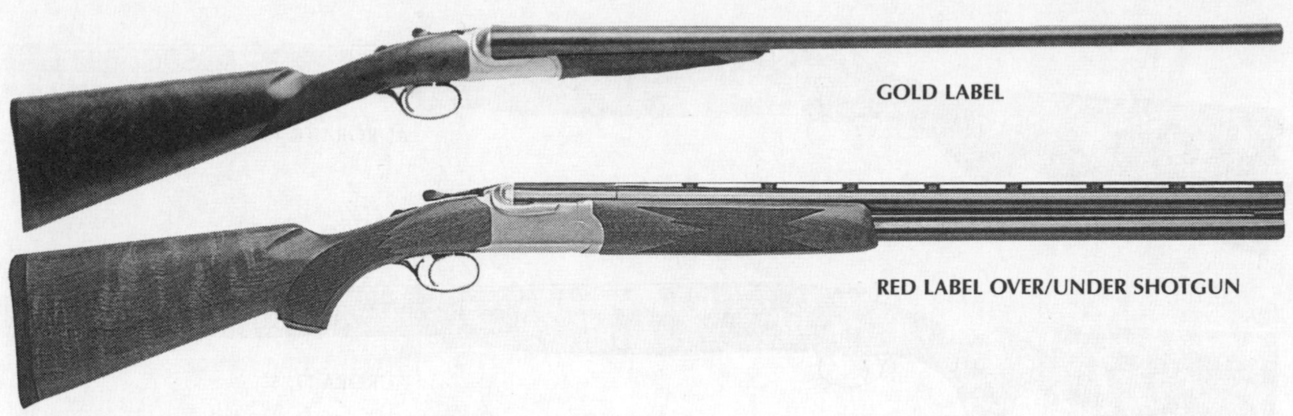

GOLD LABEL

RED LABEL OVER/UNDER SHOTGUN

Gold Label

Action: over/under
Stock: walnut, straight or pistol grip
Barrel: 28 in.
Chokes: screw-in tubes
Weight: 6.5lbs.
Bore/Gauge: 12
Magazine: none
Features: boxlock; round stainless frame
Gold Label $1950

Red Label Shotguns

Action: over/under
Stock: walnut or synthetic, straight or pistol grip
Barrel: 26, 28, 30 or 34 in.
Chokes: screw-in tubes
Weight: 7.4lbs.
Bore/Gauge: 12, 20, 28
Magazine: none
Features: boxlock; All-Weather version has stainless steel, synthetic stock
standard or All-Weather $1489
with 30-in. barrel $1545
engraved $1650

Savage Shotguns

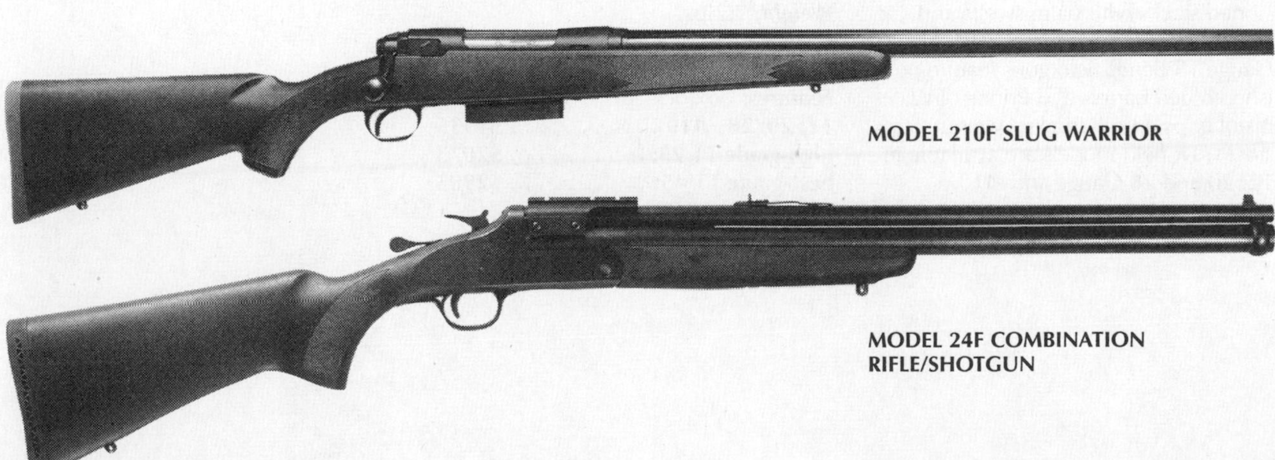

MODEL 210F SLUG WARRIOR

MODEL 24F COMBINATION RIFLE/SHOTGUN

Model 210F Slug Warrior

Action: bolt
Stock: synthetic
Barrel: rifled, 24 in.
Chokes: none
Weight: 7.5lbs.
Bore/Gauge: 12
Magazine: 2
Features: top tang safety, no sights, new camo version available
210F $440
Camo. $472

Model 24F

Action: hinged single-shot
Stock: synthetic
Barrel: rifle over shotgun, 24 in.
Chokes: none
Weight: 8.0lbs.
Bore/Gauge: 12, 20
Magazine: none
Features: open sights, hammer-mounted barrel selector; available in 20 ga./.22LR, 20/.22 Hornet, 20/.223, 12 ga./.22 Hornet, 12/.223, 12/.30-30
20 gauge $556
12 gauge $586

SIG Arms Shotguns

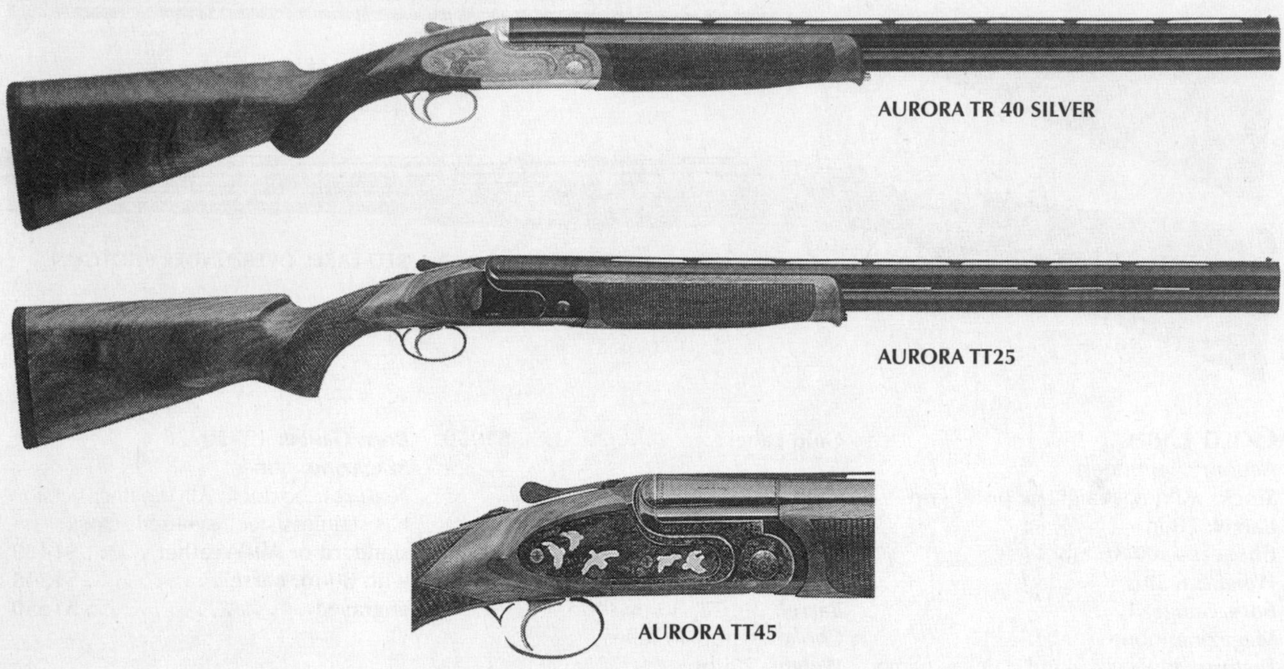
AURORA TR 40 SILVER

AURORA TT25

AURORA TT45

THE AURORA FAMILY of field and competition over-and-unders are available in a wide range of receiver styles. Competition TT25 models include Seminole choke tubes, specialty dimensioned stocks with palm swells and more. TT25s are available in 12 and 20 Gauge.TR Series field guns feature polished blued barrels and Prince of Wales pistol grips on oiled select walnut stocks. TR field models are available in 12, 20 and 28 Gauge and .410.

AURORA
Action: over/under
Stock: walnut
Barrel: all standard lengths
Chokes: screw-in tubes
Weight: 7.2lbs.
Bore/Gauge: 12, 20, 28, .410
Magazine: none
Features: boxlock
12, 20, 28, .410 . . . . $1935
high-grade TT 25: $2073
best-grade TT 45: $2905

SHOTGUNS

Recoil – or anticipation of it – can cause flinching and missing. A soft, thick recoil pad can pay big dividends, especially if you insist on shooting very lightweight guns with heavy loads.

SKB Shotguns

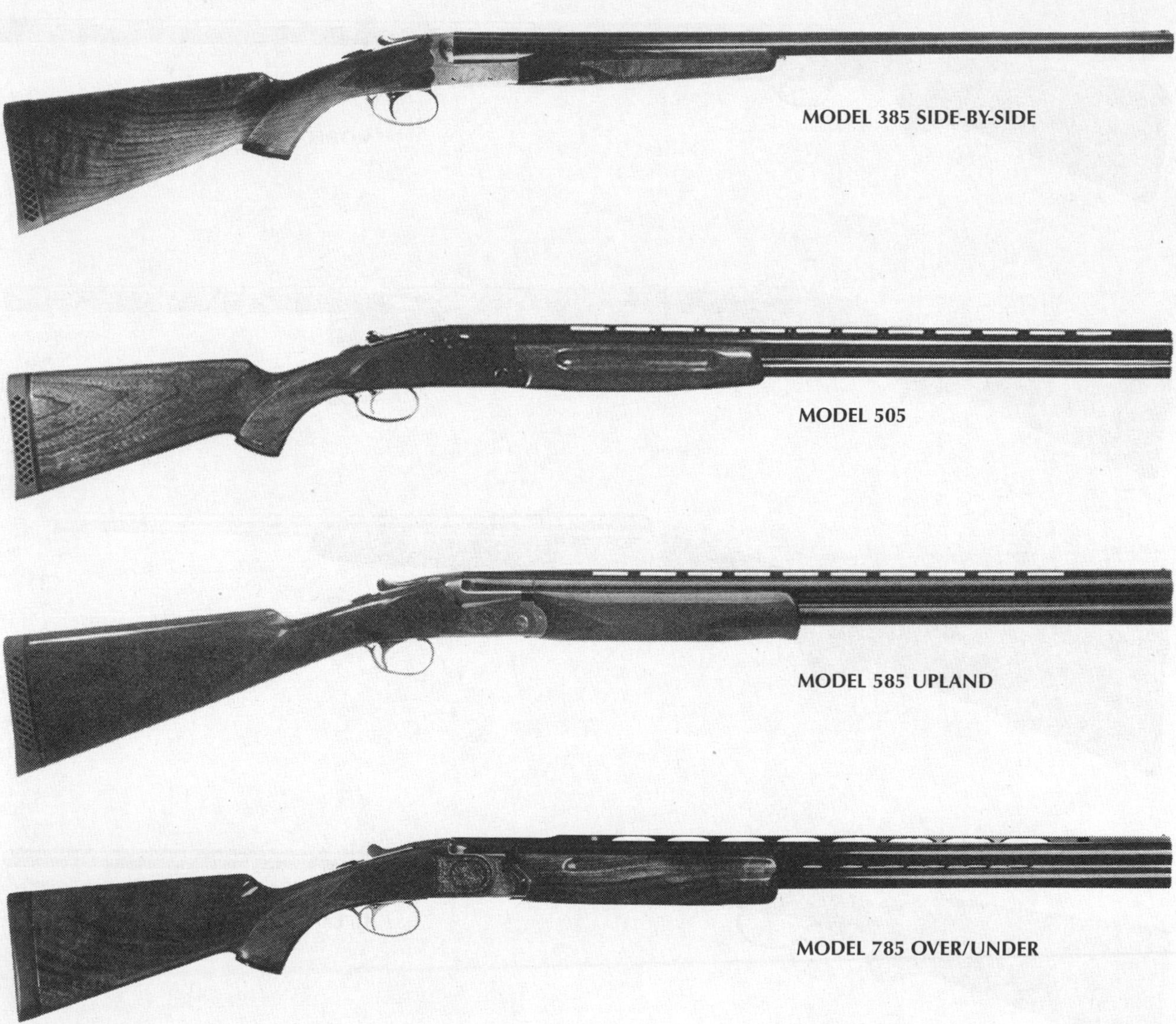

MODEL 385 SIDE-BY-SIDE

MODEL 505

MODEL 585 UPLAND

MODEL 785 OVER/UNDER

Model 385 and 485

Action: side-by-side
Stock: walnut, straight or pistol grip
Barrel: 26 or 28 in.
Chokes: screw-in tubes
Weight: 7.2lbs.
Bore/Gauge: 12, 20, 28
Magazine: none
Features: boxlock; single selective trigger, automatic ejectors; two-barrel sets also available
standard. $2049
Model 485 deluxe. $2769
two-barrel set. $2929

Model 505

Action: over/under
Stock: walnut
Barrel: 26, 28 or 30 in.
Chokes: screw-in tubes
Weight: 8.4lbs.
Bore/Gauge: 12, 20
Magazine: none
Features: boxlock; ventilated rib, automatic ejectors
Model 505 . . . . $1189
Sporting Clays $1299
Sporting Clays ported $1429

Model 585

Action: over/under
Stock: walnut, straight or pistol grip
Barrel: 26, 28, 30, 32 or 34 in.
Chokes: screw-in tubes
Weight: 9.0lbs.
Bore/Gauge: 12, 20, 28, .410
Magazine: none
Features: boxlock; Field, Upland, Youth, Sporting Clays, Skeet and Trap versions available
Field, Upland, Youth
(12 and 20 ga.). $1499
28 ga. $1569
Skeet and Trap
(12 and 20 ga.). $1619
Sporting Clays (12 and 20 ga.)
Skeet (28 and .410). $1679
Field Set. $2399

SHOTGUNS

Stoeger Shotguns

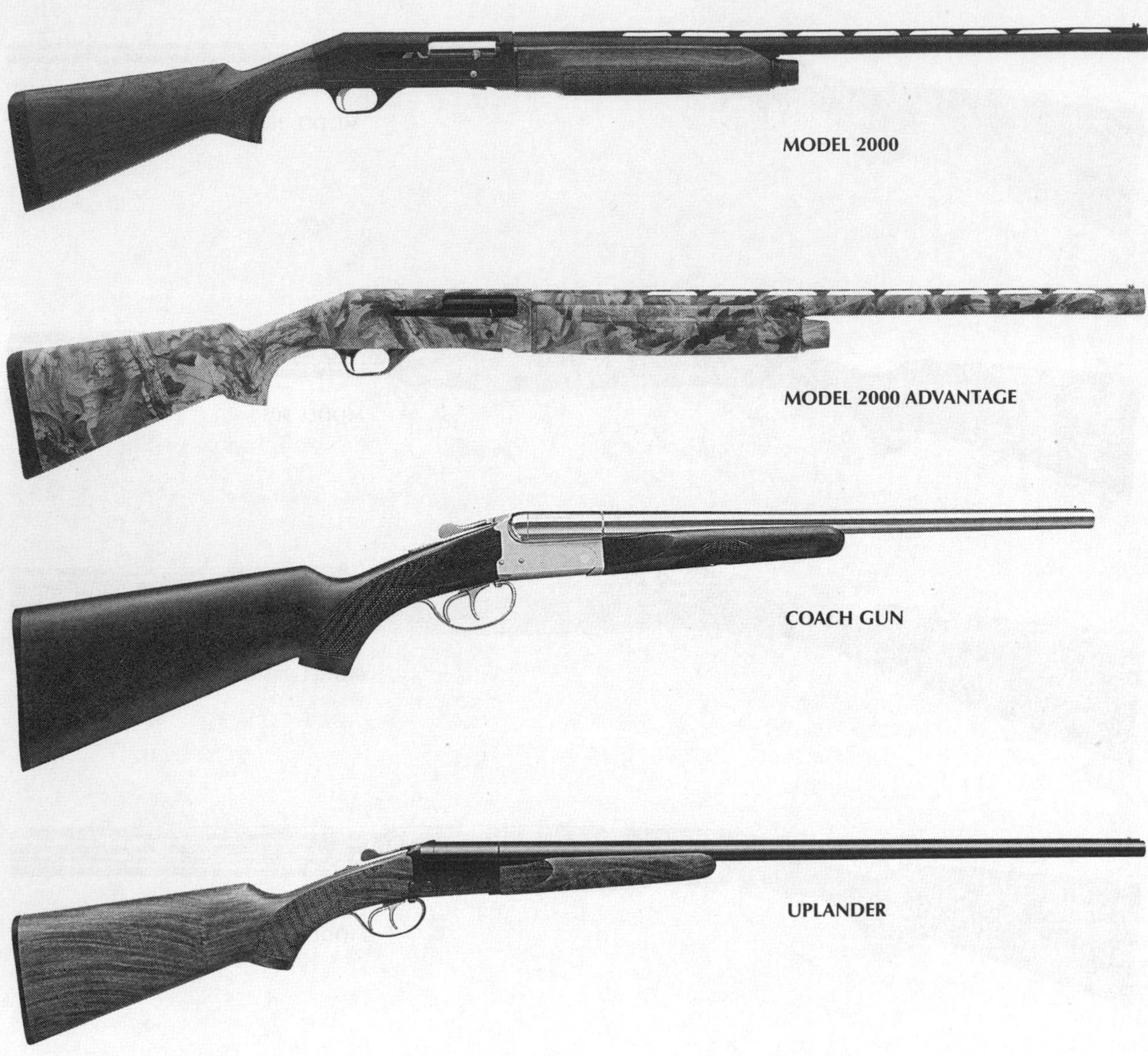

MODEL 2000

MODEL 2000 ADVANTAGE

COACH GUN

UPLANDER

Model 2000

Action: autoloader
Stock: walnut or synthetic
Barrel: 24, 26, 28 or 30 in.
Chokes: screw-in tubes
Weight: 7.0lbs.
Bore/Gauge: 12
Magazine: 4
Features: inertia-recoil system, ventilated rib, add $10 for slug barrel instead

walnut $435
synthetic $420
camo $495
walnut shot/slug barrel combo $495
camo shot/slug barrel combo $580

Coach Gun and Uplander

Action: side-by-side
Stock: hardwood
Barrel: 20 in. (Uplander 26 or 28 in.)
Chokes: improved cylinder, modified
Weight: 6.4lbs.
Bore/Gauge: 12, 20, .410
Magazine: none
Features: boxlock; double triggers, automatic safety, nickel and matte nickel breech finish available; Uplander similar (also in 16 ga.) and available with choke tubes, Youth stock; Uplander Supreme with automatic ejectors, single selective trigger, walnut stock

Coach Gun. $320
nickel finish $375
Uplander $335
Uplander Youth $335
Uplander with choke tubes. . . . $350
Uplander Supreme $445

Stoeger Shotguns

CONDOR

CONDOR SUPREME DELUXE

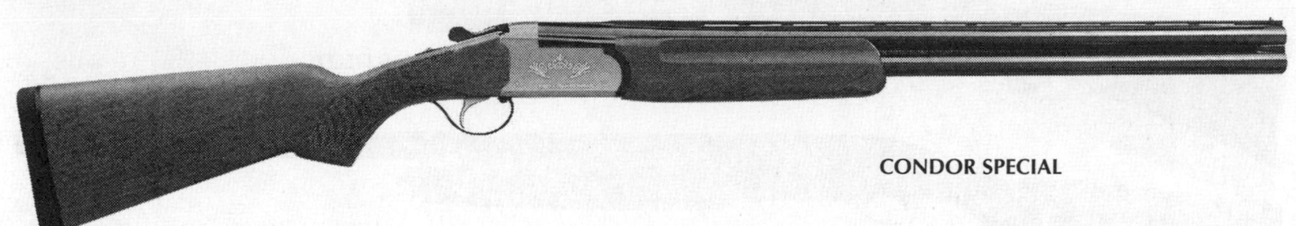

CONDOR SPECIAL

CONDOR

Action: over/under
Stock: hardwood
Barrel: 26 or 28 in.
Chokes: improved cylinder, modified
Weight: 7.7lbs.
Bore/Gauge: 12, 20
Magazine: none
Features: boxlock; single trigger
Condor $390
Special with nickel breech $440
Supreme Deluxe with walnut stock, automatic ejectors $500

SINGLE-BARREL SHOTGUN

Action: hinged single-shot
Stock: hardwood
Barrel: 22, 24 or 28 in.
Chokes: screw-in tubes
Weight: 5.4lbs.
Bore/Gauge: 12, 20, .410
Magazine: none
Features: transfer bar mechanism, crossbolt safety; .410 has fixed choke
standard or Youth $109
hammerless version (26 or 28") $119

Some crack shotgun competitors lay their left center finger under the forend, pointing it at the target instead of wrapping it around the gun. The pointing and loose grip both help you hit.

SHOTGUNS

Weatherby Shotguns

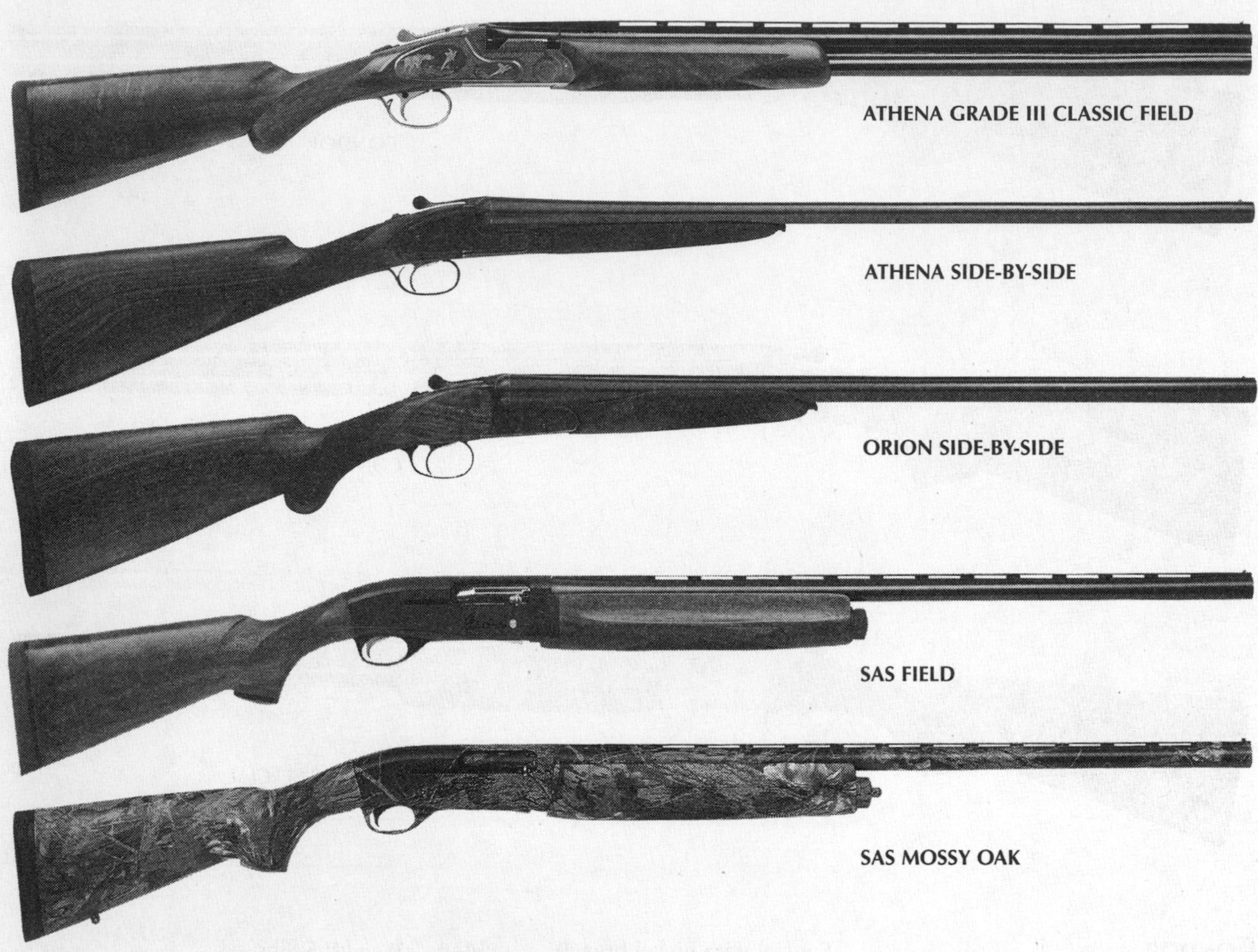

ATHENA GRADE III CLASSIC FIELD

ATHENA SIDE-BY-SIDE

ORION SIDE-BY-SIDE

SAS FIELD

SAS MOSSY OAK

Athena
Action: over/under
Stock: walnut
Barrel: 26, 28 or 30 in.
Chokes: screw-in tubes
Weight: 8.0lbs.
Bore/Gauge: 12, 20, 28
Magazine: none
Features: boxlock; single selective mechanical trigger, automatic ejectors
Grade III $2173
Grade V $3037

Athena Side-by-Side
Action: side-by-side
Stock: Turkish walnut, straight grip
Barrel: 26 or 28 in.
Chokes: screw-in tubes
Weight: 7.0lbs.
Bore/Gauge: 12, 20
Magazine: none
Features: boxlock; single selective trigger, case-colored receiver with false sideplates
Athena Side-by-Side $1599

Orion
Action: over/under
Stock: walnut, straight or pistol grip
Barrel: 26, 28 or 30 in.
Chokes: screw-in tubes
Weight: 8.0lbs.
Bore/Gauge: 12, 20
Magazine: none
Features: boxlock; single selective trigger, automatic ejectors
Upland. $1299
Grade II $1622
Sporting Clays $2059
Grade III $1955

Orion Side-by-Side
Action: side-by-side
Stock: Turkish walnut, Prince of Wales grip
Barrel: 26 or 28 in.
Chokes: screw-in tubes
Weight: 7.0lbs.
Bore/Gauge: 12, 20, 28, 410
Magazine: none
Features: boxlock; single selective trigger
Orion Side-by-Side $1149

SAS
Action: autoloader
Stock: walnut or synthetic
Barrel: 26, 28 or 30 in., vent rib
Chokes: screw-in tubes
Weight: 7.8lbs.
Bore/Gauge: 12
Magazine: 4
Features: gas-operated, 3-inch chamber, magazine cutoff
walnut $699
synthetic $649
camo $749
Sporting Clays $799
Slug gun (22" rifled bbl.). $749

Winchester Shotguns

MODEL 1300 UNIVERSAL HUNTER

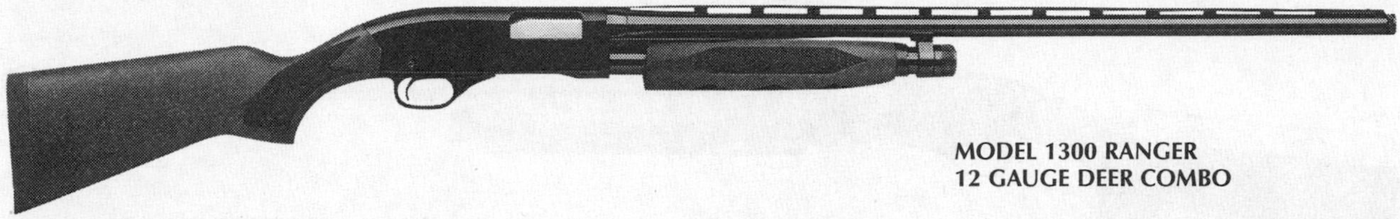

MODEL 1300 RANGER
12 GAUGE DEER COMBO

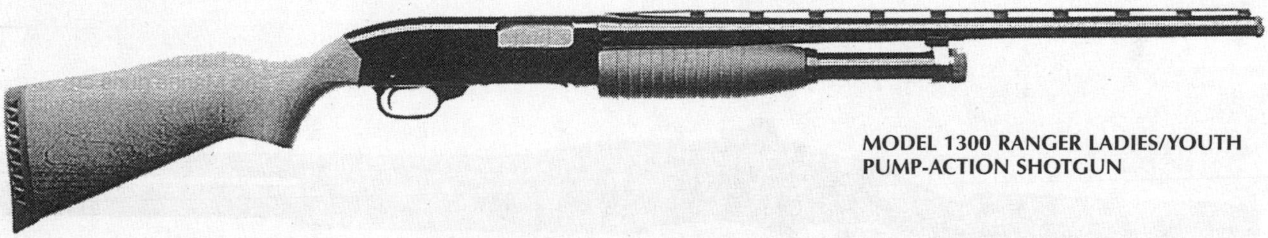

MODEL 1300 RANGER LADIES/YOUTH
PUMP-ACTION SHOTGUN

MODEL 9410 PACKER SHOTGUN

MODEL 1300

Action: pump
Stock: walnut or synthetic
Barrel: 18, 22, 24, 26 or 28 in.
Chokes: screw-in tubes
Weight: 7.5lbs.
Bore/Gauge: 12, 20
Magazine: 4
Features: Deer versions feature either smooth or rifled 22-inch barrels, rifle sights

synthetic $346
walnut $409
Ranger, hardwood $360
Turkey, camo $550
Deer, synthetic. $370
Deer, synthetic
with cantilever mount. $413

MODEL 9410

Action: lever
Stock: walnut
Barrel: 20 or 24 in.
Chokes: full
Weight: 7.0lbs.
Bore/Gauge: 410
Magazine: 9
Features: 2.5-inch chamber; Truglo front sight, shallow V rear
9410 . . . . $567
Packer with 20-inch barrel $589

Pull the shotgun firmly into your shoulder with your right hand; let the left gently and smoothly guide the muzzle.

Winchester Shotguns

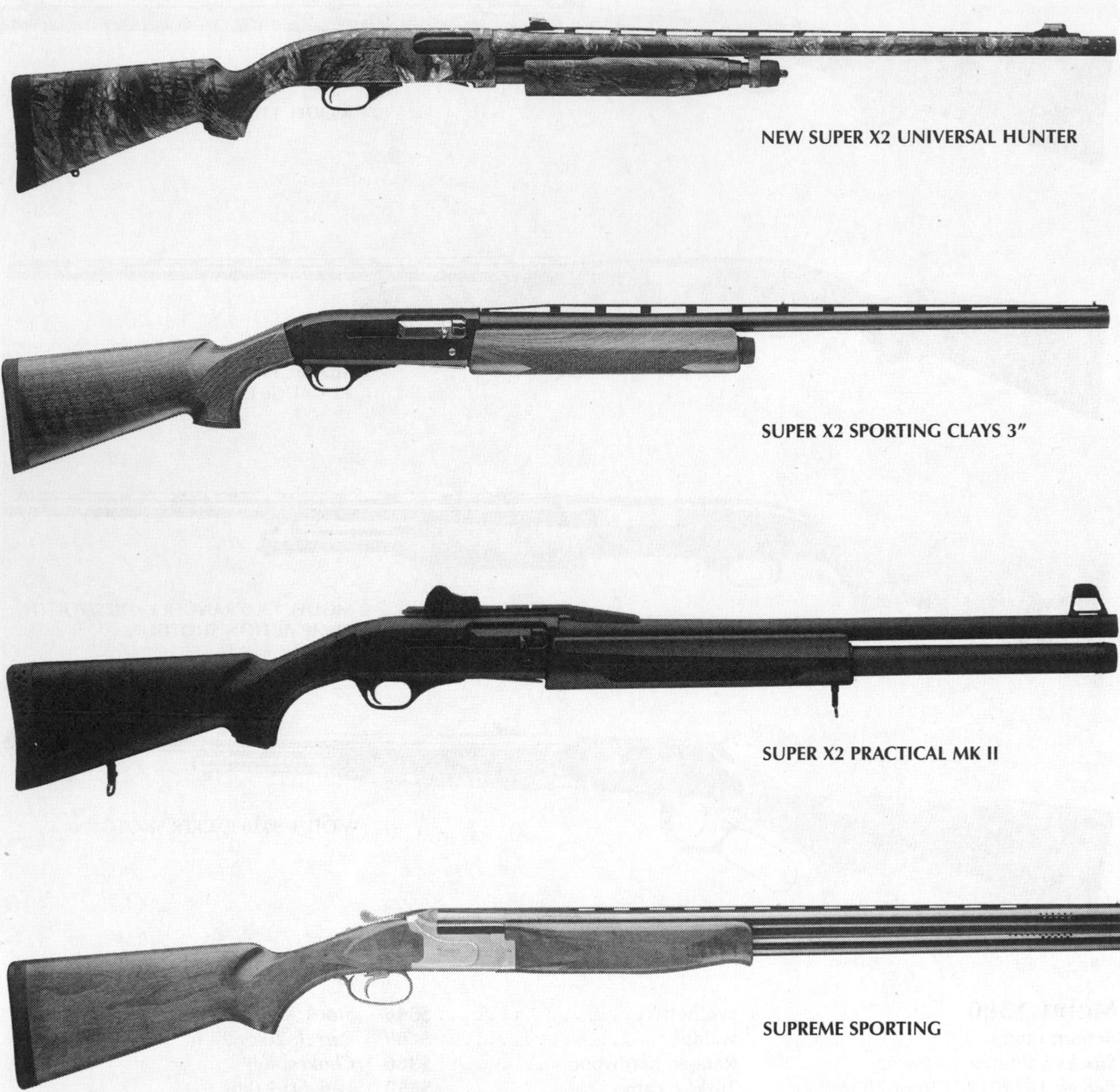

NEW SUPER X2 UNIVERSAL HUNTER

SUPER X2 SPORTING CLAYS 3″

SUPER X2 PRACTICAL MK II

SUPREME SPORTING

Super X2

Action: autoloader
Stock: walnut or synthetic
Barrel: 22, 24, 26, 28 or 30 in.
Chokes: screw-in tubes
Weight: 8.0lbs.
Bore/Gauge: 12
Magazine: 4
Features: gas-operated mechanism, back-bored barrels; Turkey version has 3.5-inch chamber, Truglo sights

Super X2 . . . . $835
Sporting Clays $940
Deer, rifled barrel with sights . . $880
Practical MK II, extended magazine $1212
3.5-inch synthetic. $969
3.5-inch camo $1116

Supreme

Action: over/under
Stock: walnut
Barrel: back-bored, 26, 28 or 30 in.
Chokes: screw-in tubes
Weight: 7.3lbs.
Bore/Gauge: 12
Magazine: none
Features: boxlock; chromed chambers, vent rib, single selective trigger, automatic ejectors

Supreme Field $1239
Sporting with ported barrel. . . $1406
Elegance $1987

HANDGUNS

American Derringer Handguns

MODEL 4

MODEL 4

Action: hinged breech
Grips: stag
Barrel: 4 in.
Sights: fixed open
Weight: 16.5oz.
Caliber: .32 H&R, .38 Spl., .357 Mag., .357 Max., .44 Mag., .45 Colt/.410, .45-70
Capacity: 2
Features: over/under Derringer also available with .45-70 over .45 Colt/.410

.38 Spl **$385**
.357 Mag. **$430**
.357 Max. **$440**
.44 Mag. **$540**
.45 Colt/.410 . . . . **$460**

Auto Ordnance Handguns

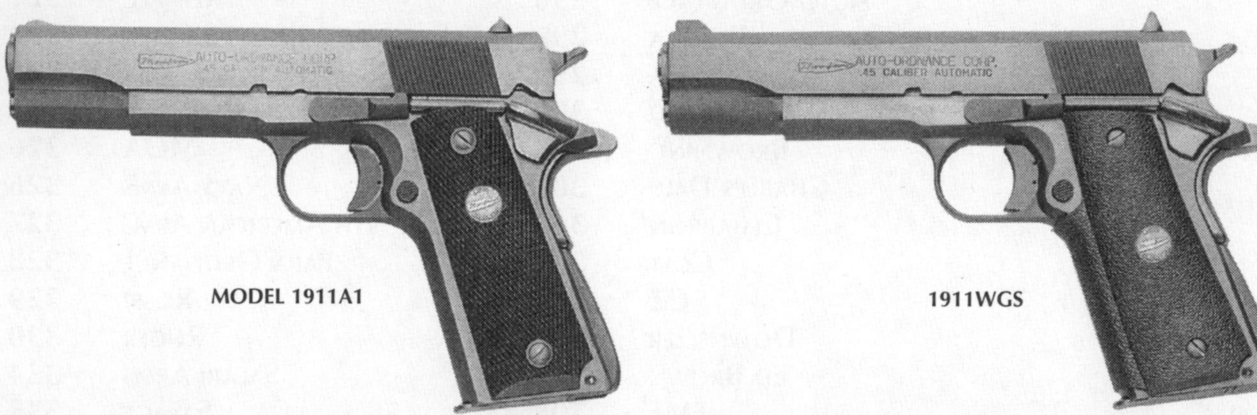

MODEL 1911A1

1911WGS

MODEL 1911A1

Action: autoloader
Grips: plastic
Barrel: 5 in.
Sights: fixed open
Weight: 39.0oz.
Caliber: .45 ACP
Capacity: 7 + 1
Features: single-action 1911 Colt design; Deluxe version has rubber wrap-around grips, 3-dot sights

standard **$540**
WWII Parkerized **$546**
Deluxe **$557**

Beretta Handguns

MODEL 21 BOBCAT

MODEL 8000 SERIES COUGAR

MODEL 3032 TOMCAT

MODEL U22 NEOS

Model 21 Bobcat

Action: autoloader
Grips: plastic or walnut
Barrel: 2.4 in.
Sights: fixed open
Weight: 11.5oz.
Caliber: .22 LR, .25 Auto
Capacity: 7 (.22) or 8 (.25)
Features: double action, tip-up barrel, alloy frame, walnut grips extra

matte **$259**
blued **$292**
stainless **$315**

Model 8000 Series Cougar

Action: autoloader
Grips: composite
Barrel: 3.6 in.
Sights: fixed open
Weight: 32.6oz.
Caliber: 9mm, .357 Sig, .40 S&W, .45 ACP
Capacity: 10 + 1 and 8 + 1 (.45 ACP)
Features: locked-breech, rotating barrel mechanism, double action, chrome-lined bore; also mini-Cougar (27.5 oz.) with 8-shot magazine in 9mm, .40 S&W

Cougar **$709**
.45 ACP **$745**

Model 3032 Tomcat

Action: autoloader
Grips: plastic
Barrel: 2.5 in.
Sights: fixed open
Weight: 14.5oz.
Caliber: .32 Auto
Capacity: 7 + 1
Features: double action; tip-up barrel

matte **$349**
blue **$379**
stainless **$428**
Titanium **$589**

Model U22 Neos

Action: autoloader
Grips: plastic
Barrel: 4.5 or 6 in.
Sights: target
Weight: 31.7oz.
Caliber: .22 LR
Capacity: 10 + 1
Features: single action; removable colored grip inserts; model with 6 in. barrel weighs 36.2 oz.; Deluxe model features adjustable trigger, replaceable sights; optional 7.5-iinch barrel

U22 Neos **$265**
Deluxe **$336**

Beretta Handguns

MODEL 92

MODEL 92/96 VERTEC

MODEL 96

MODEL 84 CHEETAH

MODEL 92

Action: autoloader
Grips: wood or plastic
Barrel: 4.3
Sights: 3-dot
Weight: 34.4oz.
Caliber: 9mm and .40 S&W
Capacity: 10 + 1 (8 + 1 compact)
Features: chrome-lined bore; double action tritium sights available; reversible magazine catch

Model 92 . . . . $691
stainless $748
compact stainless $748
Brigadier $748
Brigadier stainless $798

MODEL 92/96 VERTEC

Action: autoloader
Grips: thin, vertical, dual-textured panels
Barrel: 4.7
Sights: fixed open
Weight: 32.2oz.
Caliber: 9mm and .40 S&W
Capacity: 10 + 1
Features: double action, accessory rail for laser sight, flashlight

Vertec $726

MODEL 96

Action: autoloader
Grips: composite
Barrel: 5.9 in.
Sights: target
Weight: 40.0oz.
Caliber: .40 S&W
Capacity: 10 + 1 (8 + 1 compact)
Features: double action, rubber magazine bumpers, competition-tuned trigger; tool set and ABS case

Model 96 . . . . $748
stainless $798
compact $691
compact stainless $748

MODEL 84 CHEETAH

Action: autoloader
Grips: plastic or wood
Barrel: 3.8 or 4.4 in. (M86)
Sights: fixed open
Weight: 23.3oz.
Caliber: .380 Auto
Capacity: 10 + 1
Features: double action, ambidextrous safety

Cheetah 84 . . . . $599
M85 with 8-round single-stack magazine $563

Beretta Handguns

MODEL 87 TARGET

MODEL 9000 D

Model 87 Target

Action: autoloader
Grips: plastic or wood
Barrel: 3.8 or 5.9 in. (Target)
Sights: fixed open
Weight: 20.1oz.
Caliber: .22 LR
Capacity: 10 + 1
Features: blowback design; Target weighs 40.9 oz. with target sights
Model 87 . . . . $599
Target $682

Model 9000 D

Action: autoloader
Grips: soft polymer
Barrel: 3.5 in.
Sights: fixed open
Weight: 27.0oz.
Caliber: 9mm and .40 S&W
Capacity: 10 + 1
Features: double action, polymer frame, firing pin block
9000 D $558
B-Lok with keyed lock $582

Bersa Handguns

Model 380 Thunder

Action: autoloader
Grips: composite
Barrel: 3.5 in.
Sights: fixed open
Weight: 23.0oz.
Caliber: .380 ACP
Capacity: 7 + 1
Features: double action; also Thunder .45
.380. . . . . $267
.380 nickel. $292
.380, 9-shot $300
.45. . . . . $401
.45 Duo Tone $425
.45 nickel. $442

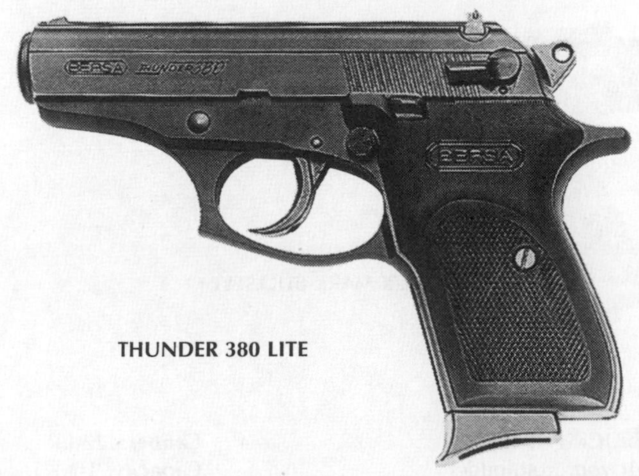

THUNDER 380 LITE

Bond Arms Handguns

MODEL 450 SUPER DEFENDER

Model 450 Super Defender
Action: hinged breech
Grips: composite
Barrel: 3 in.
Sights: fixed open
Weight: 21.0oz.
Caliber: .450 Autobond, .45 Colt/.410, 21 other calibers
Capacity: 2
Features: over/under Derringer, stainless steel
Super Defender $369
.45/.410. . . . . $389
extra barrels. $139

Browning Handguns

BUCK MARK STANDARD (5.5″ BARREL)

BUCK MARK CLASSIC

BUCK MARK BULLSEYE

BUCK MARK 5.5 TARGET

Buck Mark
Action: autoloader
Grips: composite, laminated or wood
Barrel: 5.5 in.
Sights: target
Weight: 32.0oz.
Caliber: .22 LR
Capacity: 10 + 1
Features: standard, camper, target, bullseye models available with various grips, barrel contours
Buck Mark $301
nickel. $355
Camper $271
Camper nickel $302
Bullseye $441
Target $569

Charles Daly Handguns

FIELD TARGET

FIELD GRADE

Model 1911

Action: autoloader
Grips: walnut
Barrel: 3.5, 4.0 or 5.0 in.
Sights: target
Weight: 33.0oz.
Caliber: .45 ACP
Capacity: 7 + 1
Features: stainless and target models available (weights vary to 39 oz.)

Model 1911 . . . . $459
Target $539
Target stainless. $629

SUPERIOR GRADE

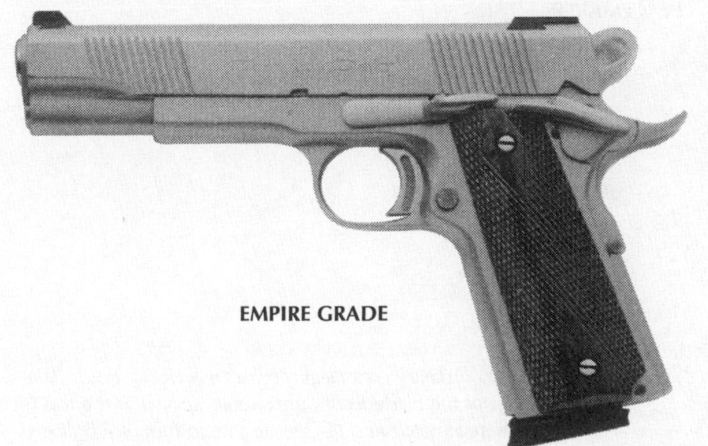

EMPIRE GRADE

Cimarron Handguns

1858 ARMY

Model 1858 Army

Action: single-action revolver
Grips: walnut
Barrel: 7.5 in.
Sights: fixed open
Weight: 50.0oz.
Caliber: .44
Capacity: 6
Features: black powder single action revolver also available in .36 Paterson
1858 Army $269
Paterson $399

1872 OPEN TOP

Model 1872 Open Top

Action: single-action revolver
Grips: walnut
Barrel: 5.5 and 7.5 in.
Sights: fixed open
Weight: 40.0oz.
Caliber: .38 Colt and S&W, .44 Colt and Russian, .45 Schofield
Capacity: 6
Features: modern steel, traditional design; weight varies up to 46 oz.
1872 . . . . $529

MODEL P JR. 1873
PEACEMAKER

Model P Jr. 1873 Peacemaker

Action: single-action revolver
Grips: composite
Barrel: 3.5 and 4.8 in.
Sights: none
Weight: 44.0oz.
Caliber: .38 Spl.
Capacity: 6
Features: fashioned after the 1873 Colt SAA but 20 percent smaller
Peacemaker $419

Zero ordinary pistol sights for a "6-o'clock" hold. The top of the blade front sight should appear at the top of the rear notch and tangent to the bottom of a bullseye.

Colt Handguns

GOVERNMENT 1991 MATTE

XSE COMMANDER

GOLD CUP

DEFENDER

Series 70
Action: autoloader
Grips: walnut
Barrel: 5 in.
Sights: fixed open
Weight: 39.0oz.
Caliber: .45 ACP
Capacity: 7 + 1
Features: single-action M1911 design
Model 70 . . . . $599

.38 Super
Action: autoloader
Grips: rosewood or composite
Barrel: 5 in.
Sights: fixed open
Weight: 39.0oz.
Caliber: .38 Super
Capacity: 9 + 1
Features: M1911 stainless models available, aluminum trigger
blue $864
stainless $943
bright stainless $1152

1991 Series
Action: autoloader
Grips: rosewood or composite
Barrel: 5 in.
Sights: fixed open
Weight: 39.0oz.
Caliber: .45 ACP
Capacity: 7 + 1
Features: M1911 Commander with 4.3 in. barrel available; both versions in stainless or chrome moly
1991 . . . . $699
stainless $800

Model XSE
Action: autoloader
Grips: rosewood
Barrel: 5 in.
Sights: 3-dot
Weight: 39.0oz.
Caliber: .45 ACP
Capacity: 8 + 1
Features: stainless, M1911 with extended ambidextrous safety, upswept beavertail, slotted hammer and trigger; also available as 4.3-in. barreled Commander
XSE $950

Gold Cup
Action: autoloader
Grips: black composite
Barrel: 5 in.
Sights: target
Weight: 39.0oz.
Caliber: .45 ACP
Capacity: 8 + 1
Features: stainless or chome-moly; Bo-Mar or Eliason sights
Gold Cup, blue. $1050
stainless $1116

Defender
Action: autoloader
Grips: rubber finger-grooved
Barrel: 3 in.
Sights: 3-dot
Weight: 30.0oz.
Caliber: .45 ACP
Capacity: 7 + 1
Features: stainless M1911, extended safety, upswept beavertail, beveled magazine well
Defender $842

Colt Handguns

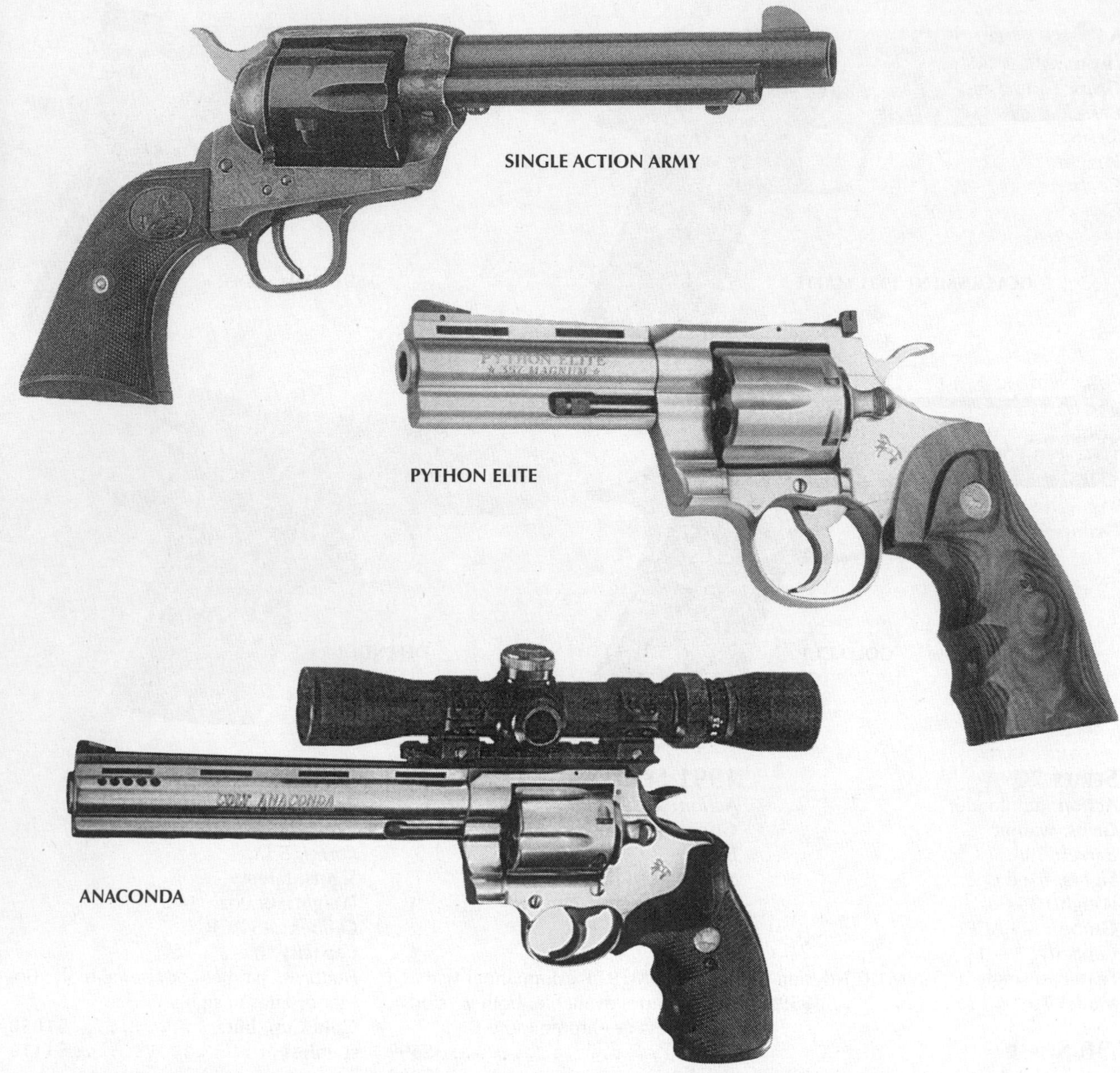

SINGLE ACTION ARMY

PYTHON ELITE

ANACONDA

Single Action Army

Action: single-action revolver
Grips: composite
Barrel: 4.3, 5.5 or 7.5 in.
Sights: fixed open
Weight: 46.0oz.
Caliber: .357 Mag., .44-40, .45 Colt
Capacity: 6
Features: case-colored frame, transfer bar, weight for .44-40, 48 oz. and 50 oz. for .45 Colt
Single Action Army $1380

Python Elite

Action: double-action revolver
Grips: wood
Barrel: 4 or 6 in. (47 oz.)
Sights: target
Weight: 44.0oz.
Caliber: .357 Mag.
Capacity: 6
Features: stainless or chrome-moly;
Python Elite $1150

Anaconda

Action: double-action revolver
Grips: rubber combat-style
Barrel: 4, 6 or 8 in. (ported)
Sights: target
Weight: 47.0oz.
Caliber: .44 Mag.
Capacity: 6
Features: ventilated rib, target trigger and hammer (weight depends on barrel length)
4 or 6 in. $1000
8 in. ported $1050

CZ Handguns

Model 100
Action: autoloader
Grips: composite
Barrel: 3.9 in.
Sights: target
Weight: 24.0oz.
Caliber: 9mm, .40 S&W
Capacity: 10 + 1
Features: single or double action, decocking lever
Model 100 . . . . $436

Model 75
Action: autoloader
Grips: composite
Barrel: 4.7 in.
Sights: 3-dot
Weight: 35.0oz.
Caliber: 9mm or .40 S&W
Capacity: 10 + 1
Features: single or double action
9mm $494
.40 S&W $510

Model 75 Champion
Action: autoloader
Grips: composite
Barrel: 4.5 in.
Sights: target
Weight: 35.0oz.
Caliber: 9 mm or .40 S&W
Capacity: 10 + 1
Features: also available: IPSC version with 5.4-in. barrel
Champion $1598
IPSC. $1118

Model 83
Action: autoloader
Grips: composite
Barrel: 3.8 in.
Sights: fixed open
Weight: 26.0oz.
Caliber: 7.65mm Browning, 9mm Makarov, 9mm Browning
Capacity: 10 + 1
Features: single or double action
Model 83 . . . . $408

MODEL 100

MODEL 75

MODEL 75 CHAMPION

MODEL 75 IPSC

CZ 83

CZ Handguns

MODEL 85 COMBAT

MODEL 97

MODEL 75 COMPACT

KADET MODEL 75

THE KADET ADAPTER IN ITS REAR (COCKED) POSITION

Model 85 Combat

Action: autoloader
Grips: composite
Barrel: 4.7 in.
Sights: target
Weight: 35.0oz.
Caliber: 9 mm
Capacity: 10 + 1
Features: single or double action
Combat $582

Model 97

Action: autoloader
Grips: composite
Barrel: 4.8 in.
Sights: fixed open
Weight: 41.0oz.
Caliber: .45 ACP
Capacity: 10 + 1
Features: single or double action
Model 97 . . . . $644

Compact Model

Action: autoloader
Grips: composite
Barrel: 3.9 in.
Sights: fixed open
Weight: 32.0oz.
Caliber: 9 mm
Capacity: 10 + 1
Features: double action
Compact $523

Kadet Model 75

Action: autoloader
Grips: composite
Barrel: 4.9 in.
Sights: target
Weight: 38.0oz.
Caliber: .22 LR
Capacity: 10 + 1
Features: double action
Kadet. $491
.22 conversion kit for CZ 75/85 . . . . $291

Downsizer Handguns

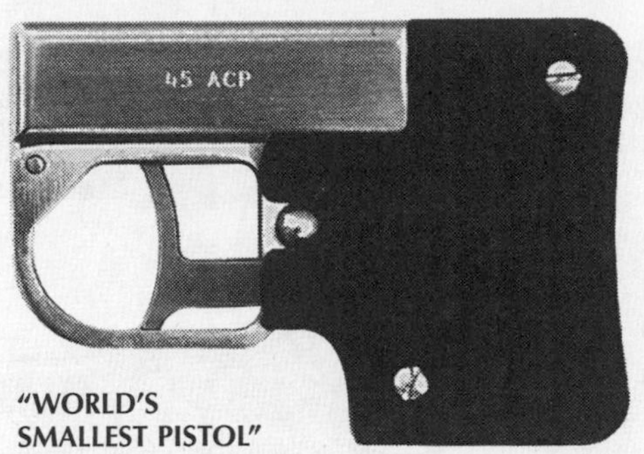

"WORLD'S SMALLEST PISTOL"

WSP
Action: hinged breech
Grips: composite
Barrel: 2.1 in.
Sights: none
Weight: 11.0oz.
Caliber: .357 Mag., .45 ACP
Capacity: 1
Features: double action only, stainless steel
WSP $499

HANDGUNS

Ed Brown Handguns

CLASS A LTD.
Action: autoloader
Grips: Hogue wood
Barrel: 5 in.
Sights: to order
Weight: 34.0oz.
Caliber: 9 mm, 9x23, .38 Super, .357 Sig, .40 S&W, 10 mm, .400 Cor-Bon, .45 ACP
Capacity: 7 + 1 or more
Features: custom-grade M1911 Colt with many options to order
base model. $2250

CLASS A LTD.

CLASSIC CUSTOM
Action: autoloader
Grips: Hogue wood
Barrel: 5 in.
Sights: target
Weight: 39.0oz.
Caliber: .45 ACP
Capacity: 7 + 1
Features: single action, M1911 Colt design, Bo-Mar sights; checkered fore-strap, ambidextrous safety
Classic Custom. $2895

CLASSIC CUSTOM

COMMANDER BOBTAIL

COMMANDER BOBTAIL
Action: autoloader
Grips: Hogue exotic wood
Barrel: 4.3 in.
Sights: low-profile combat
Weight: 34.0oz.
Caliber: 9mm, .38 Super, .357 Sig, .40 S&W, .400 Cor-Bon, .45 ACP
Capacity: 7 + 1
Features: Bob-tail butt, checkered forestrap, stainless optional
Commander Bobtail $2300

Ed Brown Handguns

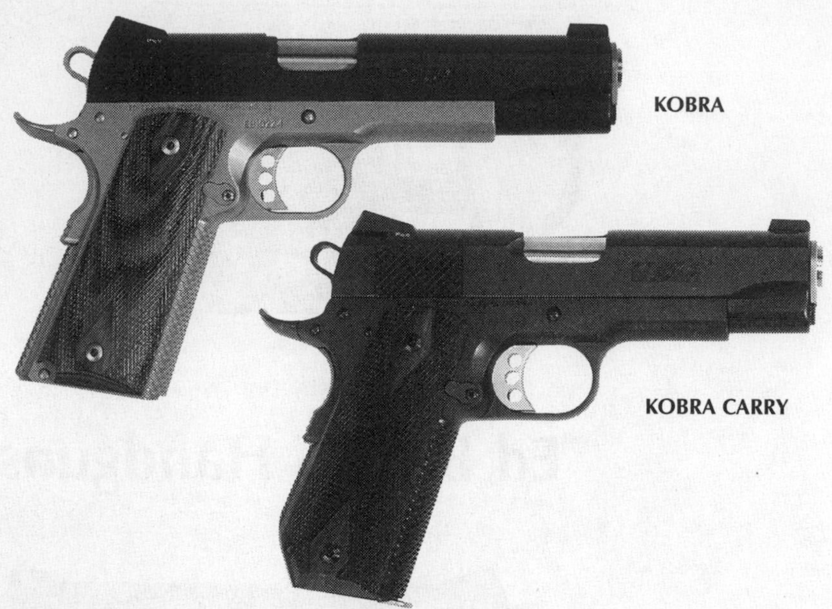

KOBRA

KOBRA CARRY

Kobra

Action: autoloader
Grips: Hogue wood
Barrel: 5 in.
Sights: low-profile combat
Weight: 39.0oz.
Caliber: .45 ACP
Capacity: 7 + 1
Features: single-action M1911 Colt design, stainless models available
Kobra. $1795
Kobra Carry
with 4.3-in. barrel. $1995

EMF Handguns

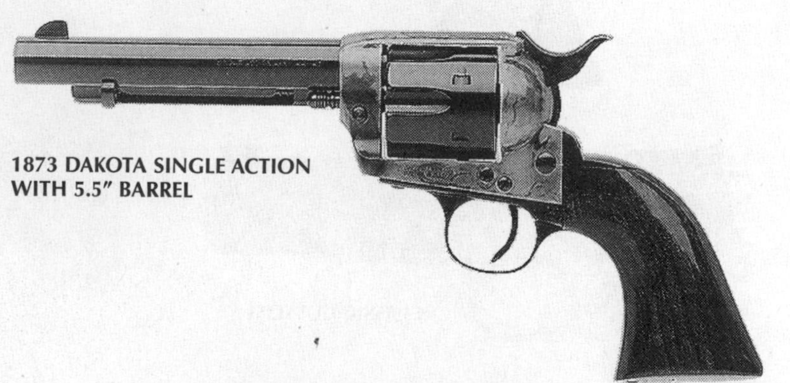

1873 DAKOTA SINGLE ACTION WITH 5.5" BARREL

Model 1873 Dakota

Action: single-action revolver
Grips: walnut
Barrel: 4.8, 5.5 and 7.5 in.
Sights: fixed open
Weight: 46.0oz.
Caliber: .357 Mag., .44-40, .45 Colt
Capacity: 6
Features: case-colored frame; barrel length determines weight
1873 Dakota $400
Buntline with
12 in. barrel, 55 oz. $510

1873 HARTFORD "BUNTLINE"

Model 1875 Remington

Action: single-action revolver
Grips: walnut
Barrel: 7.5 in.
Sights: fixed open
Weight: 48.0oz.
Caliber: .357 Mag., .45 Colt
Capacity: 6
Features: case-colored frame
Model 1875 . . . . $500
engraved $750

Model 1890 Remington Police

Action: single-action revolver
Grips: walnut
Barrel: 5.8 in.
Sights: fixed open
Weight: 48.0oz.
Caliber: .357 Mag., .44-40, .45 Colt
Capacity: 6
Features: lanyard loop, case-colored frame
Model 1890 . . . . $500
engraved $750

Hartford Pinkerton

Action: single-action revolver
Grips: walnut, birds-head
Barrel: 4 in.
Sights: fixed open
Weight: 44.0oz.
Caliber: .357, .45 Colt
Capacity: 6
Features: case-colored frame
Hartford Pinkerton $480

MODEL 1875 REMINGTON

MODEL 1890 REMINGTON POLICE

HARTFORD PINKERTON

Pistoleers concentrate on three things: sight alignment, sight alignment and sight alignment. A bit of wobble, slight movement of the sight off target matter little. Poor sight alignment is fatal.

Enterprise Arms Handguns

BOXER P500

TACTICAL P325 PLUS

Model 500 Boxer

Action: autoloader
Grips: composite
Barrel: 5 in.
Sights: target
Weight: 44.0oz.
Caliber: .40 S&W, .45 ACP
Capacity: 10 + 1
Features: match-grade components and fitting, stainless one-piece guide rod, lapped slide, flared ejection port
.45 ACP $1399
.40 S&W $1499

Medalist

Action: autoloader
Grips: composite
Barrel: 5 in.
Sights: target
Weight: 44.0oz.
Caliber: .40 S&W, .45 ACP
Capacity: 10 + 1
Features: up-turned beavertail, stainless hammer and sear, flared ejection port, match trigger, lapped slide
.45. . . . . $979
.40 S&W $1099

Tactical P325 Plus

Action: autoloader
Grips: composite
Barrel: 3.3 in.
Sights: low-profile combat
Weight: 37.0oz.
Caliber: .45 ACP
Capacity: 10 + 1
Features: extended ambidextrous safety, lapped slide, up-turned beavertail, skeleton trigger and hammer; Tactical Ghost Ring or Novak sights; (also available with 4.3 and 5.0-inch barrels)
Tactical $979
with 3-dot sights, fewer refinements. $740

Tournament

Action: autoloader
Grips: composite
Barrel: 5 in.
Sights: target
Weight: 44.0oz.
Caliber: .38 Super, .40 S&W, .45 ACP
Capacity: 10 + 1
Features: up-turned beavertail, extended thumb safety, front cocking grooves, checkered front strap, all match components; 2-lb. trigger
TI with stainless bull barrel. . . $2300
TII with long slide $2000
TIII ported, hard chromed, fashioned for scope use $2700

European American Armory Handguns

WITNESS

BIG BORE BOUNTY HUNTER SINGLE ACTION

SMALL BORE BOUNTY HUNTER

WITNESS P COMPACT

WINDICATOR REVOLVER

BIG BORE BOUNTY HUNTER

Action: single-action revolver
Grips: walnut
Barrel: 4.5 or 7.5 in.
Sights: fixed open
Weight: 37.0oz.
Caliber: .357 Mag., .44 Mag., .45 Colt
Capacity: 6
Features: case-colored or blued or nickel frame; version with 7.5 in. barrel weighs 42 oz.
Bounty Hunter $379
nickel. $399

WINDICATOR

Action: double-action revolver
Grips: rubber
Barrel: 2 or 4 in.
Sights: fixed open
Weight: 36.0oz.
Caliber: .357 Mag., .38 Special
Capacity: 6
Features: transfer bar
.38, 2-inch $249
.38, 4-inch; .357, 2-inch $259
.357, 4-inch $279

WITNESS

Action: autoloader
Grips: rubber
Barrel: 4.5 in.
Sights: 3-dot
Weight: 33.0oz.
Caliber: 9mm, .38 Super, .40 S&W, 10 mm, .45 ACP
Capacity: 10 + 1
Features: double action, polymer frame available
steel. $449
polymer $429
"Wonder" finish. $459

WITNESS COMPACT

Action: autoloader
Grips: rubber
Barrel: 3.6 in.
Sights: 3-dot
Weight: 29.0oz.
Caliber: 9mm, .38 Super, .40 S&W, 10 mm, .45 ACP
Capacity: 10 + 1
Features: double action, polymer frame and ported barrels available
steel. $449
polymer $429
"Wonder" finish or polymer ported. $459
"Wonder" finish, ported $479

Firestorm Handguns

MODEL 380

MODEL 45

MINI

Model 380

Action: autoloader
Grips: rubber
Barrel: 3.5 in.
Sights: 3-dot
Weight: 23.0oz.
Caliber: .380
Capacity: 7 + 1
Features: double action, also available in .22 LR, 10-shot magazine
Model 380 . . . . $265
Duotone $275

Model 45

Action: autoloader
Grips: rubber
Barrel: 4.3 or 5.2 in.
Sights: 3-dot
Weight: 34.0oz.
Caliber: .45 ACP
Capacity: 7 + 1
Features: single action, 1911 Colt design, from cocking grooves
Model 45 . . . . $325
Duotone $334

Mini

Action: autoloader
Grips: polymer
Barrel: 3.5 in.
Sights: target
Weight: 24.5oz.
Caliber: 9mm, .40 S&W, .45 ACP
Capacity: 10 + 1 (7 + 1 in .45)
Features: double action
Mini. $384
Duotone $392
Duotone .45. . . . . $400
nickel $409
.45 nickel $417

Freedom Arms Handguns

Model 83

Action: single-action revolver
Grips: Pachmayr rubber or hardwood
Barrel: 4.8, 6.0, 7.5 or 10 in.
Sights: target
Weight: 50.0oz.
Caliber: .357 Mag., .41 Mag., .44 Mag., .454 Casull, .45 Colt, .45 Win. Mag., .475 Linebaugh, .50 AE
Capacity: 5
Features: sights and scope mounts and extra cylinders optional
field grade $1527
field grade, adjustable sights . . $1591
premier grade. $1976
premier grade, adjustable sights $2058

Model 83 Rimfire

Action: single-action revolver
Grips: Micarta or laminated
Barrel: heavy 5.1, 7.5 or 10 in.
Sights: target
Weight: 50.0oz.
Caliber: .22 LR
Capacity: 6
Features: dual firing pin, version with 7.5 in. barrel weighs 58 oz., 10-inch barrel, 63 oz.; magnum cylinder available
Model 83 . . . . $1828
with 10-inch barrel. $1902

Model 97 Premier

Action: single-action revolver
Grips: Micarta or laminated
Barrel: 4.5, 5.5, 7.5 or 10 in.
Sights: target
Weight: 36.0oz.
Caliber: .357 Mag., .41 Mag., .44 Mag.
Capacity: 5
Features: weight varies to 42 oz. depending on barrel length; .22 rimfire version available
Premier $1668
.22. . . . . $1782

MODEL 83
454 CASULL FIELD GRADE

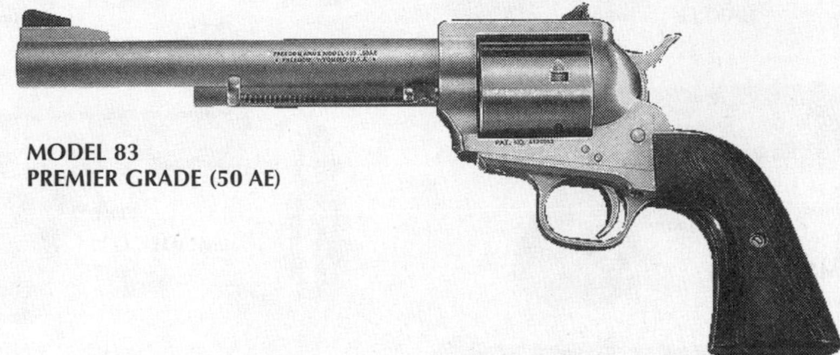

MODEL 83
PREMIER GRADE (50 AE)

MODEL 83 RIMFIRE
SILHOUETTE CLASS 10″ BARREL

MODEL 97
PREMIER GRADE

Glock Handguns

MODEL G19

MODEL G23

PORTED BARREL

MODEL G26

9X19

MODEL G17

MODEL G27

.40

MODEL G22

MODEL G33

.357

MODEL G31

9X19

MODEL G34

MODEL G29

10MM

MODEL G20

MODEL G30

9X19

MODEL G17

.40

MODEL G35

Compact Pistols

Action: autoloader
Grips: composite
Barrel: 3.8 in.
Sights: fixed open
Weight: 21.2oz.
Caliber: 9mm, .40 S&W, .357 Mag., 10 mm, .45 ACP
Capacity: 9, 10, 13, 15 depending on cartridge, magazine
Features: trigger safety, double action, 10 mm and .45 ACP weigh 24.0 oz.
Compact Pistols. . . . price on request

Full-Size Pistols

Action: autoloader
Grips: composite
Barrel: 4.5 in.
Sights: fixed open
Weight: 22.3oz.
Caliber: 9 mm, .40 S&W, .357 Mag., 10 mm, .45 ACP
Capacity: 10, 13, 15, 17 depending on cartridge
Features: trigger safety, double action, 10 mm and .45 ACP weigh 26.3 oz.
Full-Size . . . . price on request

Subcompact Pistols

Action: autoloader
Grips: composite
Barrel: 3.5 in.
Sights: fixed open
Weight: 19.8oz.
Caliber: 9mm, .40 S&W, .357, .45
Capacity: 9, 10, 6, depending on cartridge, magazine
Features: trigger safety, double action
Subcompact . . . . . . price on request

Hammerli Handguns

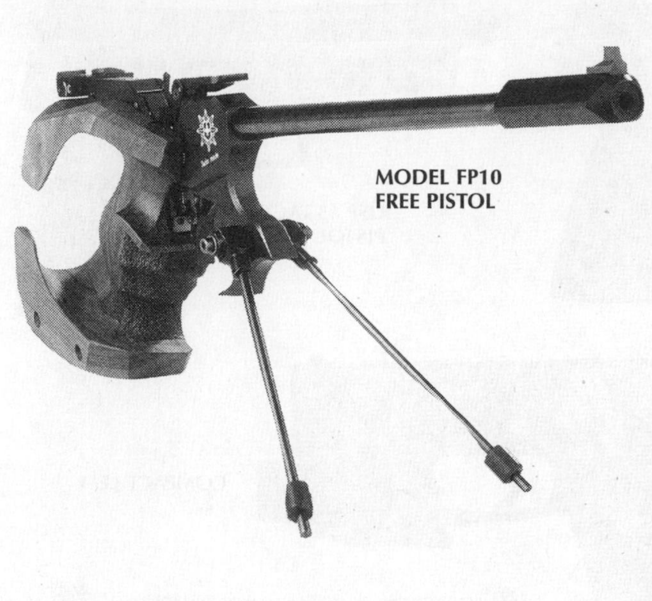

MODEL FP10
FREE PISTOL

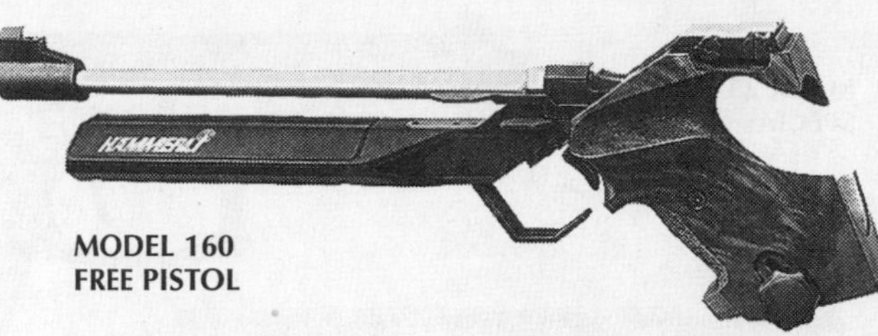

MODEL 160
FREE PISTOL

HAMMERLI SP 20

X-ESSE .22 L.R.
WITH LONG BARREL

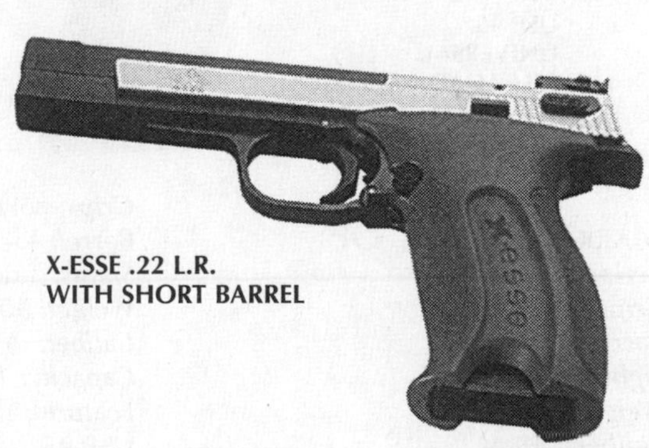

X-ESSE .22 L.R.
WITH SHORT BARREL

Model 160 Free Pistol

Action: Martini
Grips: walnut target
Barrel: 11.3 in.
Sights: target
Weight: 45.0oz.
Caliber: .22 LR
Capacity: 1
Features: side-mounted locking lever, fully adjustable trigger
Model 160 . . . . $2410
Model FP10 with integral compensator $2041

Model SP20

Action: autoloader
Grips: synthetic
Barrel: 4.6 in.
Sights: target
Weight: 40.0oz.
Caliber: .22 LR, .32 S&W
Capacity: 5
Features: front-end magazine
.22. . . . . $1668
.32. . . . . $1743

Model X-ESSE Sport

Action: autoloader
Grips: composite
Barrel: 4.5 or 5.5 in.
Sights: target
Weight: 36.0oz.
Caliber: .22 LR
Capacity: 10
Features: single action
X-ESSE. . . . . price on request

Heckler & Koch Handguns

MARK 23 SPECIAL OP

USP 45 TACTICAL PISTOL

MODEL P7M8

COMPACT LEM

USP 45 UNIVERSAL SELF-LOADING PISTOL

USP EXPERT

Mark 23 Special OP

Action: autoloader
Grips: polymer
Barrel: 5.9 in.
Sights: 3-dot
Weight: 42.0oz.
Caliber: .45 ACP
Capacity: 10 + 1
Features: military version of USP
Mark 23 Special OP $2444

Model P7M8

Action: autoloader
Grips: polymer
Barrel: 4.1 in.
Sights: target
Weight: 28.0oz.
Caliber: 9mm
Capacity: 8 + 1
Features: blue or nickel finish
Model P7M8 . . . . $1472

USP 45

Action: autoloader
Grips: polymer
Barrel: 4.4 in.
Sights: 3-dot
Weight: 30.0oz.
Caliber: .45 ACP
Capacity: 10 + 1
Features: short-recoil action
USP 45 . . . . $827

USP 9 & 40

Action: autoloader
Grips: polymer
Barrel: 4.25 in.
Sights: 3-dot
Weight: 27.0oz.
Caliber: 9mm, .40 S&W
Capacity: 10 + 1
Features: short-recoil action, also in kit form
USP $766
kit $1124

USP Compact

Action: autoloader
Grips: polymer
Barrel: 3.6 in.
Sights: fixed open
Weight: 25.0oz.
Caliber: 9mm, .357 Sig, .40 S&W (also .45 ACP)
Capacity: 10 + 1
Features: LEM (law enforcement model) available with laser attachment
Compact $786
stainless $878
LEM $821
.45 ACP $857
.45 stainless $909

USP Expert

Action: autoloader
Grips: polymer
Barrel: 6 in.
Sights: 3-dot
Weight: 39.0oz.
Caliber: 9mm, .40 S&W, .45 ACP
Capacity: 10 + 1
Features: short-recoil action
USP Expert. $1533

Heritage Handguns

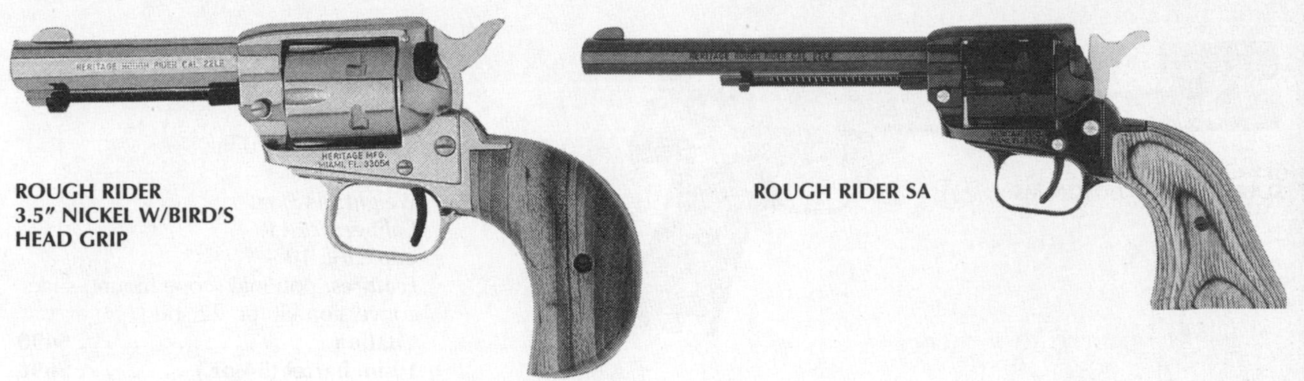

ROUGH RIDER
3.5" NICKEL W/BIRD'S
HEAD GRIP

ROUGH RIDER SA

Rough Rider
Action: single-action revolver
Grips: hardwood, regular or birds-head
Barrel: 3.8, 4.8, 6.9 or 9.0 in.
Sights: fixed open
Weight: 31.0oz.
Caliber: .22 LR (.22 WMR cylinder available)
Capacity: 6
Features: action on Colt 1873 pattern, transfer bar, satin or blued finish, weight to 38 oz. dependent on barrel length

Rough Rider $145
with WMR cylinder $160
satin, with WMR cylinder $200
satin, adjustable sights, WMR cylinder $240

High Standard Handguns

Olympic military
Action: autoloader
Grips: walnut
Barrel: 5.5 in.
Sights: target
Weight: 44.0oz.
Caliber: .22 LR
Capacity: 10 + 1
Features: single action, blowback mechanism
Olympic Military $625

Olympic Rapid-Fire
Action: autoloader
Grips: walnut
Barrel: 4 in.
Sights: target
Weight: 46.0oz.
Caliber: .22 short
Capacity: 5
Features: push-button take-down, adjustable match trigger
Rapid-Fire $1027

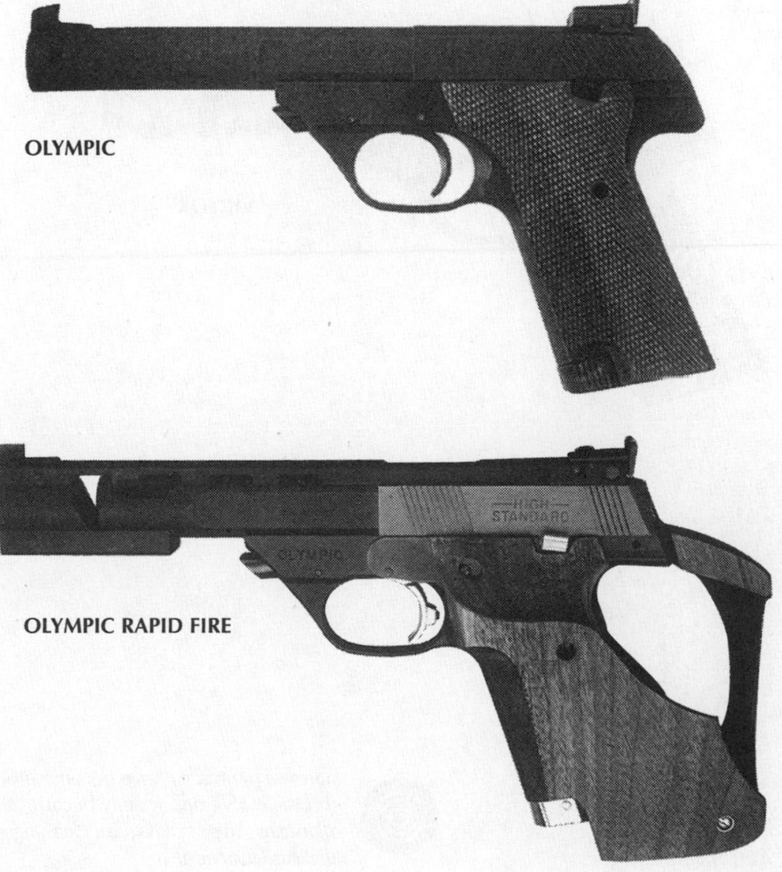

OLYMPIC

OLYMPIC RAPID FIRE

High Standard Handguns

HANDGUNS

SUPERMATIC CITATION MS

SUPERMATIC TROPHY

VICTOR

Supermatic Citation

Action: autoloader
Grips: walnut
Barrel: 5.5 or 10 in.
Sights: target
Weight: 44.0oz.
Caliber: .22 LR
Capacity: 10 + 1
Features: optional scope mount, slide conversion kit for .22 short

Citation $490
10-in. barrel (54 oz.) $696
slide conversion kit $317

Supermatic Trophy

Action: autoloader
Grips: walnut
Barrel: 5.5 (bull) or 7.3 (fluted) in.
Sights: target
Weight: 44.0oz.
Caliber: .22 LR
Capacity: 10 + 1
Features: left-hand grip optional

5.5 in. barrel $603
7.3 in barrel (46 oz.) $689

Victor

Action: autoloader
Grips: walnut
Barrel: 4.5 or 5.5 in.
Sights: target
Weight: 45.0oz.
Caliber: .22 LR
Capacity: 10 + 1
Features: optional slide conversion kit for .22 Short

4.5 in. barrel $564
5.5 in. barrel (46 oz.) $625
.22 Short conversion kit $317

Stainless handguns have become more popular than chrome-moly guns, mainly because they're easier to maintain. They still require cleaning for best accuracy and sure function!

Hi-Point Handguns

380 Polymer

Action: autoloader
Grips: polymer
Barrel: 3.5 in.
Sights: 3-dot
Weight: 30.0oz.
Caliber: .380
Capacity: 8 + 1 (10-shot magazine available)
Features: last-round lock-open; comp model has 4 in. barrel

380 Polymer. $100
comp. $125
with laser sight. $190

9mm Polymer

Action: autoloader
Grips: polymer
Barrel: 3.5 in.
Sights: 3-dot
Weight: 30.0oz.
Caliber: 9mm
Capacity: 8 + 1 (10-shot magazine available)
Features: last-round lock-open, comp model has 4 in. barrel

9mm Polymer. $137
comp. $159
with laser sight. $219

Big Bore Pistol

Action: autoloader
Grips: polymer
Barrel: 4.5 in.
Sights: 3-dot
Weight: 32.0oz.
Caliber: .45 ACP, .40 S&W
Capacity: 9 + 1, 10 + 1
Features: last-round lock-open

Big Bore. $169

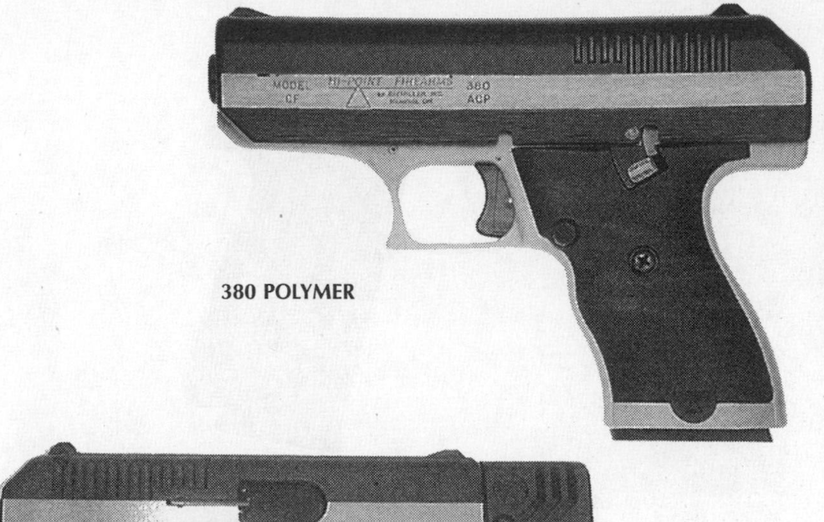

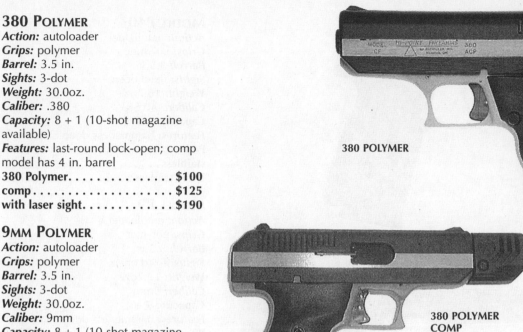

380 POLYMER

380 POLYMER COMP

9MM COMPACT POLYMER

9MM COMP GUN

Kahr Handguns

MODEL P40

MODEL P9

Model P40

Action: autoloader
Grips: polymer
Barrel: 3.5 in.
Sights: fixed open
Weight: 18.7oz.
Caliber: .40 S&W
Capacity: 6 + 1
Features: hammerless double action
P40 . . . . $631
stainless $672
Elite stainless $730

Model P9

Action: autoloader
Grips: polymer
Barrel: 3.5 in.
Sights: fixed open
Weight: 17.7oz.
Caliber: 9mm
Capacity: 7 + 1
Features: hammerless double action
P9 . . . . $631
stainless $672
Elite black $694
Elite stainless $730
PM9
(black frame, stainless slide) . . . $660

Unlike rifle or target pistol shooting, in which line of fire may be 30 degrees from a line across your feet or shoulders, defensive or combat pistol work is done at right angles to your stance.

Kel-Tec Handguns

P-11 CALIBER

P-32 CALIBER .32 AUTO

SUB RIFLE 2000 (READY TO FIRE)

SUB RIFLE 2000 CALIBERS 9MM & 40 S&W

Model P-11

Action: autoloader
Grips: polymer
Barrel: 3.1 in.
Sights: fixed open
Weight: 14.4oz.
Caliber: 9mm
Capacity: 10 + 1
Features: locked-breech mechanism
P-11 $314
parkerized $355
chrome $368

Model P-32

Action: autoloader
Grips: polymer
Barrel: 2.7 in.
Sights: fixed open
Weight: 6.6oz.
Caliber: .32 Auto
Capacity: 7 + 1
Features: locked-breech mechanism
P-3AT $300
parkerized $340
chrome $355

Model P-3AT

Action: autoloader
Grips: polymer
Barrel: 2.8 in.
Sights: fixed open
Weight: 7.3oz.
Caliber: .380
Capacity: 6 + 1
Features: locked-breech mechanism
P-3AT $305
parkerized $345
chrome $355

Sub Rifle 2000

Action: autoloader
Grips: polymer
Barrel: 16 in.
Sights: target
Weight: 64.0oz.
Caliber: 9mm and .40 S&W
Capacity: 10 + 1
Features: take-down, uses pistol magazines
Sub Rifle $383
SU-16 in .223 $640

Kimber Handguns

CUSTOM CDP II

COMPACT II & PRO CARRY II

CUSTOM II & CUSTOM TARGET II

ECLIPSE TARGET II

In 1995, following bankruptcy proceedings at Kimber, handgun sports were becoming more popular, and many people were concerned with the effect of stricter regulations on the availability of handguns. Kimber owner, Les Edelman thought there'd be a market for high-quality pistols based on the 1911 Colt. He enlisted the reputation and expertise of ace pistol shooter Chip McCormick, bought a factory in Yonkers and began turning out pistols, projecting a run of 5000. His projection proved conservative; now the Kimber plant makes 44,000 Model 1911-style pistols annually, more than its closest seven competitors combined.

It's no wonder that some shooters think of pistols when the Kimber name comes up. But Les and his company, now assisted by Montana rifle enthusiasts Dwight Van Brunt and Ryan Busse, diversified in 1998, with a svelte .22 rifle designed by Nehemiah Sirkis. The new rifle, called the Kimber 22, looked like the 82 but has a side-swing safety like the Winchester Model 70.

CDP Series

Action: autoloader
Grips: rosewood
Barrel: 5 in.
Sights: low-profile combat
Weight: 38.0oz.
Caliber: .40 S&W, .45 ACP
Capacity: 7 + 1
Features: alloy frame, stainless slide; also in 4 in. (Pro Carry) and 3 in. (Ultra) configurations

CDP. $1141

Compact II

Action: autoloader
Grips: synthetic
Barrel: 4 in.
Sights: low-profile combat
Weight: 34.0oz.
Caliber: .38 Super, .45 ACP
Capacity: 7 + 1
Features: shortened single action 1911 Colt design; also Pro Carry with alloy frame at 28 oz.; match-grade bushingless bull barrel

Compact II. $870
Pro Carry $773
Pro Carry stainless $845

Custom II

Action: autoloader
Grips: composite or rosewood
Barrel: 5 in.
Sights: target
Weight: 38.0oz.
Caliber: .38 Super, .40 S&W, .45 ACP
Capacity: 7 + 1
Features: single action, 1911 Colt design, front cocking grooves, skeleton trigger and hammer

Custom II. $730
stainless $832
Target $837
Target stainless. $945

Eclipse II

Action: autoloader
Grips: laminated
Barrel: 5 in.
Sights: 3-dot
Weight: 38.0oz.
Caliber: .45 ACP
Capacity: 7 + 1
Features: matte-black oxide finish polished bright on flats; also 3-inch Ultra and 4-inch Pro Carry versions; sights also available in low profile combat or target

Eclipse II $1071
Target $1153
Ultra $1052

Kimber Handguns

GOLD COMBAT II

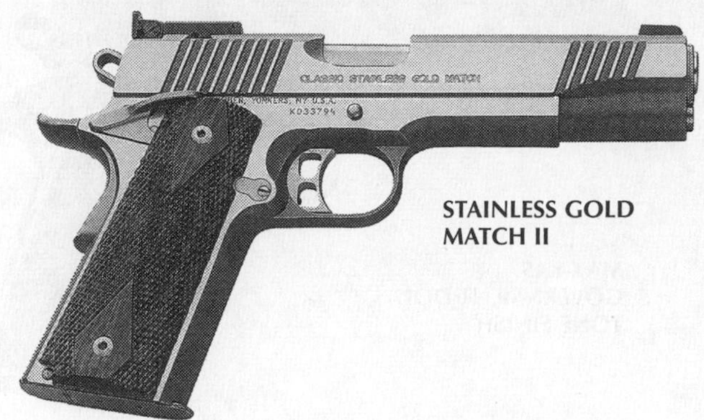

STAINLESS GOLD MATCH II

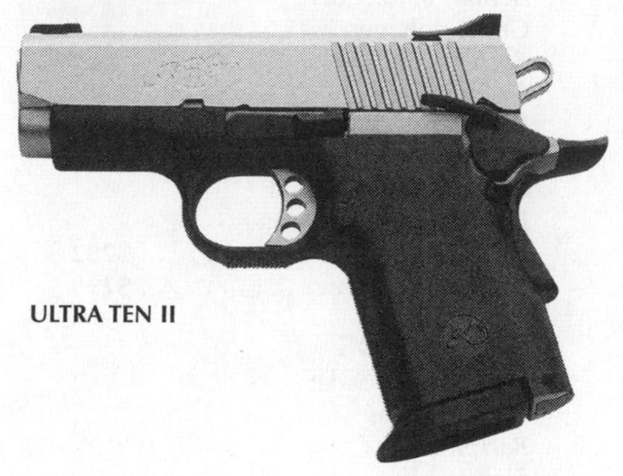
ULTRA TEN II

STAINLESS ULTRA CARRY II

Gold Combat II

Action: autoloader
Grips: rosewood
Barrel: 5 in.
Sights: low-profile combat
Weight: 38.0oz.
Caliber: .45 ACP
Capacity: 7 + 1
Features: M1911 Colt design with many refinements: checkered front strap, match bushing, ambidextrous safety, stainless match barrel
Gold Combat II $1681

Gold Match II

Action: autoloader
Grips: rosewood
Barrel: 5 in.
Sights: target
Weight: 38.0oz.
Caliber: .45 ACP
Capacity: 7 + 1
Features: single action 1911 Colt design; match components, ambidextrous safety
Gold Match II $1168
stainless $1315
stainless in .40 S&W. $1345

Ten II High Capacity

Action: autoloader
Grips: synthetic
Barrel: 5 in.
Sights: low-profile combat
Weight: 34.0oz.
Caliber: .45 ACP
Capacity: 10 + 1
Features: double-stack magazine, polymer frame; also in 4 in. (Pro Carry) and 3 in. (Ultra) configurations, from 24 oz.
stainless. $755
Pro Carry. $770
Ultra $790

Ultra Carry II

Action: autoloader
Grips: synthetic
Barrel: 3 in.
Sights: low-profile combat
Weight: 25.0oz.
Caliber: .40 S&W, .45 ACP
Capacity: 7 + 1
Features: smallest commercial 1911-style pistol
Ultra Carry II. $767
stainless. $841
stainless in .40 S&W. $884

Llama Handguns

MAX-I 45
GOVERNMENT DOU-
TONE FINISH

MICROMAX .380
MATTE FINISH

MINIMAX .45 SATIN
CHROME FINISH

Maxi-I Government

Action: autoloader
Grips: rubber
Barrel: 5 in.
Sights: 3-dot
Weight: 38.0oz.
Caliber: .45 ACP
Capacity: 7 + 1
Features: single action M1911 Colt design; extended safety, beavertail, Duotone finish
Maxi-I $389

Micromax .380

Action: autoloader
Grips: polymer
Barrel: 4 in.
Sights: 3-dot
Weight: 29.0oz.
Caliber: .380, .32 ACP
Capacity: 7 + 1, 8 + 1
Features: extended safety
matte. $282
satin chrome $299

Minimax .45

Action: autoloader
Grips: rubber
Barrel: 3 in.
Sights: 3-dot
Weight: 28.0oz.
Caliber: .40 S&W, .45 ACP
Capacity: 7 + 1 (.40), 6 + 1 (.45)
Features: single-action M1911 Colt design; extended beavertail grip
matte. $334
Duo-Tone. $343
satin chrome $350

Magnum Research Handguns

Baby Eagle

Action: autoloader
Grips: polymer
Barrel: 4 in.
Sights: fixed open
Weight: 28.0oz.
Caliber: 9mm, .40 S&W, .45 ACP
Capacity: 7 + 1 (6 + 1, .45)
Features: squared, serrated guard
Baby Eagle $499

Mark XIX Desert Eagle

Action: autoloader
Grips: composite
Barrel: 6 or 10 in.
Sights: fixed open
Weight: 70.0oz.
Caliber: .357 Mag., .44 Mag., .50 AE
Capacity: 9 + 1, 8 + 1, 7 + 1
Features: gas operated, universal frame accepts optional barrels; all with polygonal rifling, integral scope bases
Desert Eagle, 6 in. barrel $1199
10 in. barrel (79 oz.) $1299
6 in. chrome or nickel $1424
6 in. Titanium. $1699

Single Action Hunter

Action: single-action revolver
Grips: rubber
Barrel: 6.5, 7.5 or 10 in.
Sights: target
Weight: 48.0oz.
Caliber: .45/70, .444, .450 (long cylinder), .480 Ruger, .475 Linbaugh, .22 Hornet, .45 Colt/.410
Capacity: 5
Features: both short and long-cylinder models entirely of stainless steel
Single Action Hunter $999

BABY EAGLE

DESERT EAGLE PISTOL
MARK XIX .50 MAGNUM
TITANIUM FINISH

MARK XIX
COMPONENT SYSTEM

SINGLE-ACTION
HUNTER

MOA Handguns

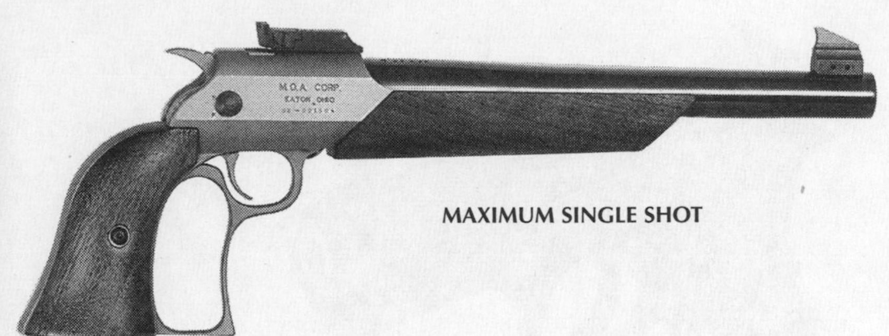

MAXIMUM SINGLE SHOT

Maximum
Action: hinged breech
Grips: walnut
Barrel: 8.5, 10.5 or 14 in.
Sights: target
Weight: 56.0oz.
Caliber: most rifle chamberings from .22 Hornet to .375 H&H
Capacity: 1
Features: stainless breech, Douglas barrel; extra barrels, muzzle brake available
Maximum. $823
with stainless barrel $919
extra barrels. $269

Navy Arms Handguns

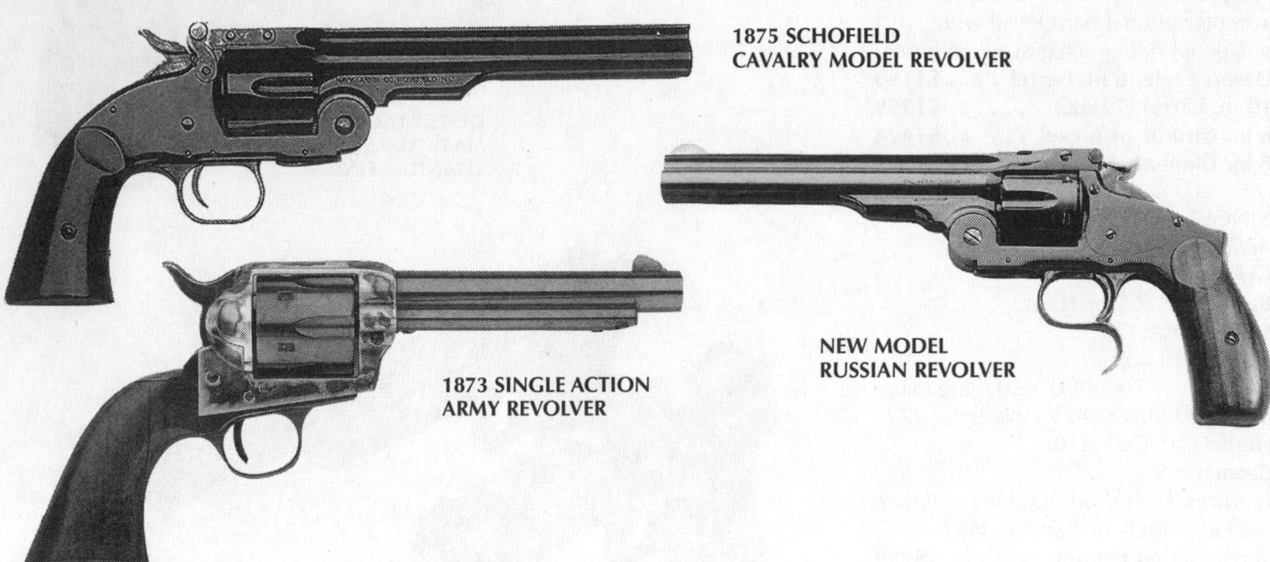
1875 SCHOFIELD CAVALRY MODEL REVOLVER

NEW MODEL RUSSIAN REVOLVER

1873 SINGLE ACTION ARMY REVOLVER

Model 1873 SAA
Action: single-action revolver
Grips: walnut
Barrel: 4.8, 5.5, 7.5 in.
Sights: fixed open
Weight: 36.0oz.
Caliber: .357 Mag., .44-40, .45 Colt
Capacity: 6
Features: case-colored frame; weight varies with caliber to 39 oz.
1873 SAA. $415
U.S. Cavalry Model (7.5 in.) . . . $500
Flat Top target (7.5 in.) $464

Model 1875 Schofield
Action: double-action revolver
Grips: walnut
Barrel: 3.5, 5.0 or 7.0 in.
Sights: fixed open
Weight: 35.0oz.
Caliber: .44-40, .45 Colt
Capacity: 6
Features: top-break action, automatic ejectors; 5 in barrel (37 oz.) and 7 in. barrel (39 oz.)
1874 Schofield $716

Bisley
Action: single-action revolver
Grips: walnut
Barrel: 4.8, 5.5 or 7.5 in.
Sights: fixed open
Weight: 45.0oz.
Caliber: .44-40, .45 Colt
Capacity: 6
Features: Bisley grip case-colored frame; weight to 48 oz.
Bisley. $445

New Model Russian
Action: double-action revolver
Grips: walnut
Barrel: 6.5 in.
Sights: fixed open
Weight: 40.0oz.
Caliber: .44 Russian
Capacity: 6
Features: top-break action
New Model Russian $792

North American Arms Handguns

Guardian .32
Action: autoloader
Grips: polymer
Barrel: 2.5 in.
Sights: fixed open
Weight: 12.0oz.
Caliber: .32 Auto
Capacity: 6 + 1
Features: stainless, double action
Guardian $408
.380. . . . . $449

Mini Revolver
Action: single-action revolver
Grips: laminated rosewood
Barrel: 1.2 in.
Sights: fixed open
Weight: 5.0oz.
Caliber: .22 Short, .22 LR, .22 WMR
Capacity: 5
Features: holster grip, adjustable sight available
.22 Short or .22 LR. $256
with adjustable sight. $274
.22 Magnum. $286
.22 Magnum with adjustable sight. $304

GUARDIAN 32

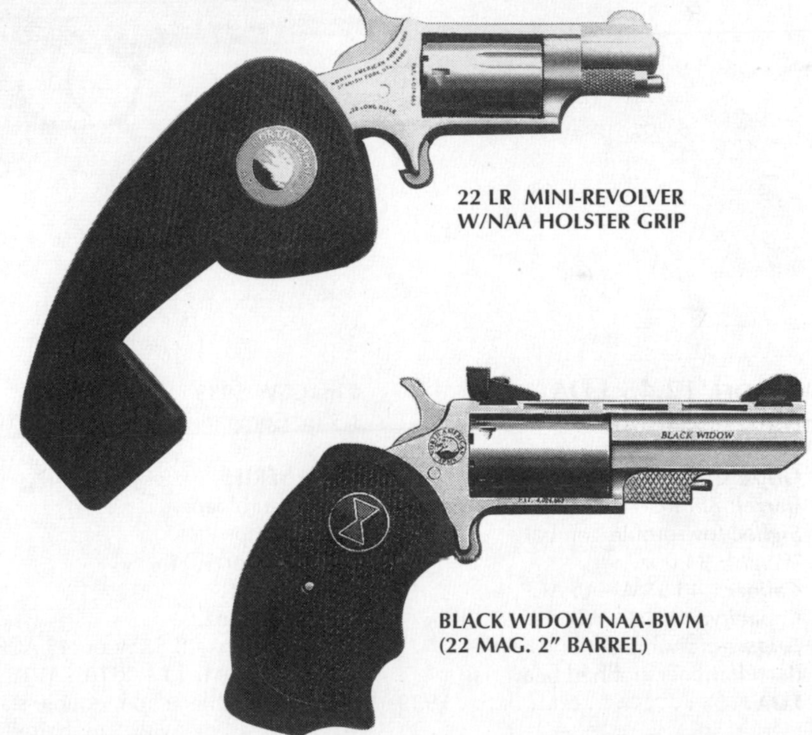

22 LR MINI-REVOLVER W/NAA HOLSTER GRIP

BLACK WIDOW NAA-BWM (22 MAG. 2" BARREL)

Red dot sights and the Bushnell Holo-Sight are particularly useful on handguns because they're lightweight and don't require your eye to be "on-axis" for an accurate shot.

Para Ordnance Handguns

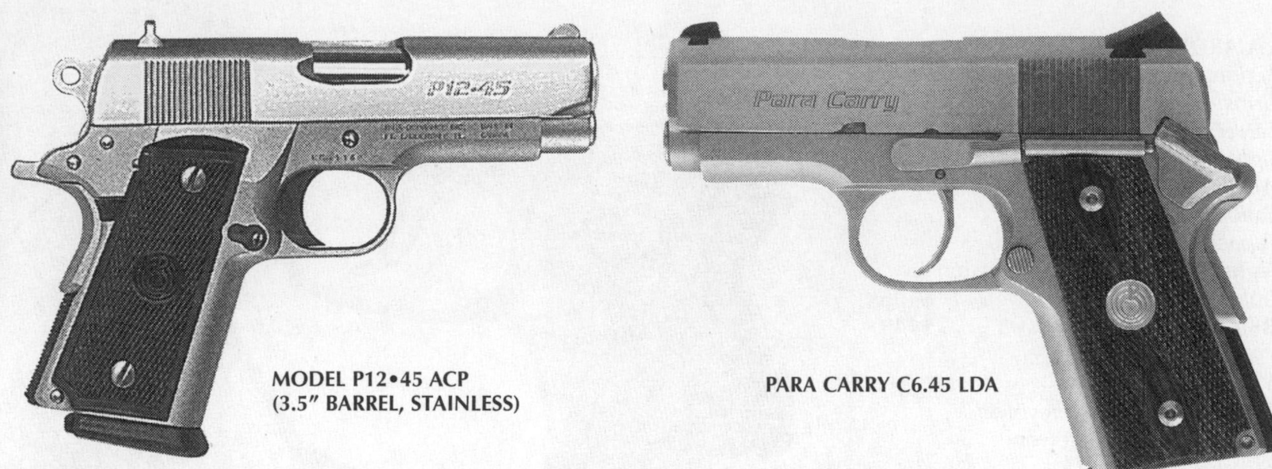

MODEL P12•45 ACP
(3.5" BARREL, STAINLESS)

PARA CARRY C6.45 LDA

LDA

MODEL 12.45 LDA AND 14.40 LDA

Action: autoloader
Grips: Cocobolo
Barrel: 3.5 in.
Sights: low-profile combat
Weight: 34.0oz.
Caliber: .40 S&W, .45 ACP
Capacity: 14 + 1 (.40), 12 + 1 (.45)
Features: double action, stainless, flush hammer, bobbed beavertail

LDA $939

CCW AND COMPANION CARRY

Action: autoloader
Grips: rosewood
Barrel: 3.5 or 4.3 in.
Sights: low-profile combat
Weight: 32.0oz.
Caliber: .45 ACP
Capacity: 7 + 1
Features: double action, stainless; Tritium night sights available

4 in. CCW $939
3.5 in. Companion Carry $1009

LDA SERIES

Action: autoloader
Grips: composite
Barrel: 3.5 or 5.0 in.
Sights: target
Weight: 34.0oz.
Caliber: 9mm, .40 S&W or .45 ACP
Capacity: 12 + 1, 14 + 1, 16 + 1, 18 + 1
Features: double action, double-stack magazine; 40 oz. with 5 in. barrel

LDA $859

P-SERIES

Action: autoloader
Grips: composite
Barrel: 3.0, 3.5, 4.3, or 5.0 in.
Sights: fixed open
Weight: 24.0oz.
Caliber: 9mm, .40 S&W, .45 ACP
Capacity: 10 + 1
Features: customized 1911 Colt design, beveled magazine well, polymer magazine; also available with 3-dot or low-profile combat sights; weight to 40 oz. depending on barrel length

.45 ACP $829
stainless .45 . . . . $899
9mm $960
"Limited" .40 or .45 with adj. sights $949
stainless "Limited" $999

TAC-FOUR

Action: autoloader
Grips: Cocobolo
Barrel: 4.3 in.
Sights: low-profile combat
Weight: 36.0oz.
Caliber: .45 ACP
Capacity: 13 + 1
Features: double action, stainless; flush hammer, bobbed beavertail

Tac-Four. $939

Rossi Handguns

MODEL R352

MODEL R461

MODEL R972 .357
MAGNUM 6-SHOT

Model R352

Action: double-action revolver
Grips: rubber
Barrel: 2 in.
Sights: fixed open
Weight: 24.0oz.
Caliber: .38 Spl.
Capacity: 6
Features: stainless; R351 chrome-moly also available

R352 . . . . $345
R351 . . . . $298
R851, 4 in. barrel. $298

Model R462

Action: double-action revolver
Grips: rubber
Barrel: 2 in.
Sights: fixed open
Weight: 26.0oz.
Caliber: .357 Mag.
Capacity: 6
Features: stainless; R461 chrome-moly also available

R462 . . . . $345
R461 . . . . $298

Model R972

Action: double-action revolver
Grips: rubber
Barrel: 6
Sights: target
Weight: 34.0oz.
Caliber: .357 Mag.
Capacity: 6
Features: stainless after S&W M19 pattern; also R971 chrome-moly with 4 in. barrel

R972 . . . . $391
R971 . . . . $345

Short pistol barrels may be handy and quick, but they increase blast, sometimes to uncomfortable levels. They also reduce sight radius (distance between sights) and thus impair precision.

Ruger Handguns

REDHAWK REVOLVER

STAINLESS REDHAWK

SUPER REDHAWK STAINLESS

STAINLESS REDHAWK W/SCOPE RINGS

VAQUERO SINGLE ACTION

VAQUERO STAINLESS

Redhawk

Action: double-action revolver
Grips: walnut
Barrel: 5.5 or 7.5 in.
Sights: target
Weight: 49.0oz.
Caliber: .44 Mag.
Capacity: 6
Features: stainless model available; 7.5 in. version weighs 54 oz.; scope rings available

Redhawk $585
with rings. $625
stainless $645
stainless with rings $685

Super Redhawk

Action: double-action revolver
Grips: walnut
Barrel: 7.5 or 8.5 in.
Sights: target
Weight: 53.0oz.
Caliber: .44 Mag., .454 Casull, .480 Ruger
Capacity: 6
Features: gray finish; 9.5 in. version weighs 58 oz.

.44 Magnum. $685
.454, .480 Ruger $775

Vaquero

Action: single-action revolver
Grips: Micarta or rosewood
Barrel: 4.6 or 7.5 in.
Sights: fixed open
Weight: 40.0oz.
Caliber: .357, .44-40, .44 Mag., .45 Colt
Capacity: 6
Features: Bisley, birds-head grips also available

Vaquero $535
Bisley. $555
birds-head grips $576

Ruger Handguns

New Model Super Blackhawk

Action: single-action revolver
Grips: walnut
Barrel: 4.6, 5.5, 7.5 or 10.5 in.
Sights: target
Weight: 45.0oz.
Caliber: .44 Mag.
Capacity: 6
Features: weight to 51 oz. depending on barrel length; also available: Super Blackhawk Hunter, stainless with 7.5 in. barrel, black laminated grips, rib, scope rings
chrome-moly $519
stainless $535
Super Blackhawk Hunter $639

New Model Single Six

Action: single-action revolver
Grips: rosewood or Micarta
Barrel: 4.6, 5.5, 6.5 or 9.5 in.
Sights: fixed open
Weight: 33.0oz.
Caliber: .22 LR, .22 WMR, .17 HMR, .32 H&R
Capacity: 6
Features: adjustable sights available; weight to 38 oz. depending on barrel length
Single Six $389
stainless $469
.32 H&R $576

NEW SUPER MODEL BLACKHAWK SINGLE-ACTION REVOLVER

SUPER BLACKHAWK

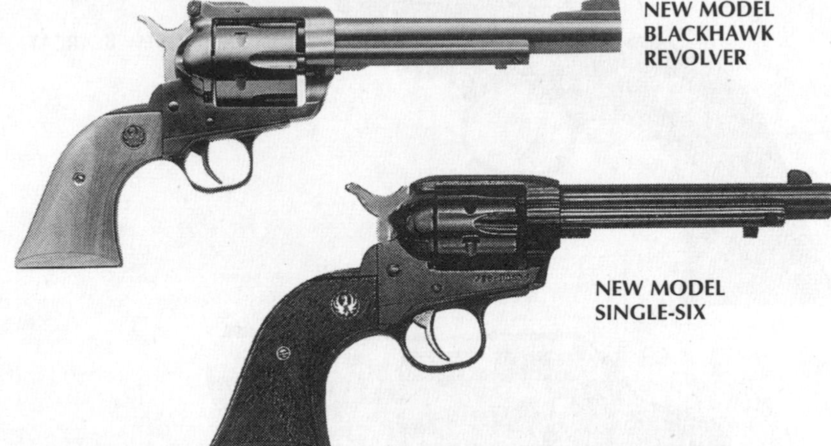

NEW MODEL BLACKHAWK REVOLVER

NEW MODEL SINGLE-SIX

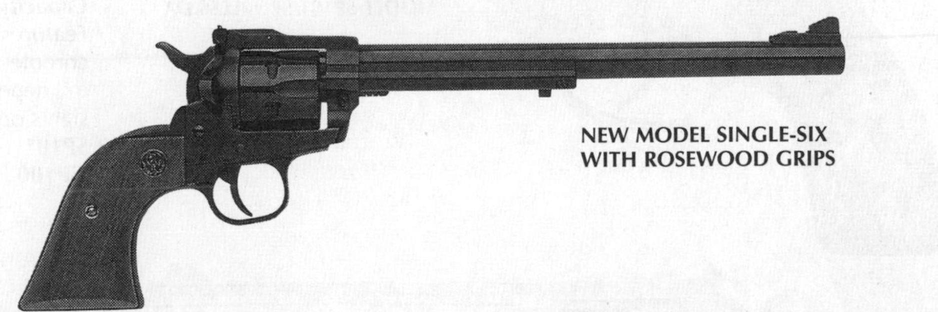

NEW MODEL SINGLE-SIX WITH ROSEWOOD GRIPS

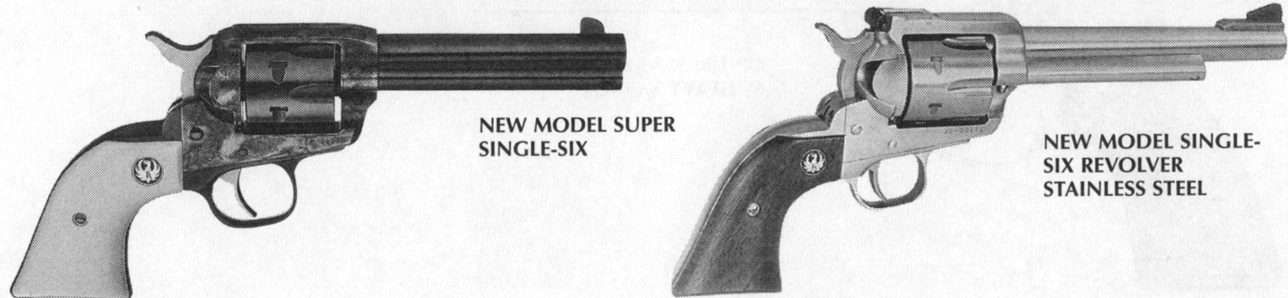

NEW MODEL SUPER SINGLE-SIX

NEW MODEL SINGLE-SIX REVOLVER STAINLESS STEEL

Ruger Handguns

HANDGUNS

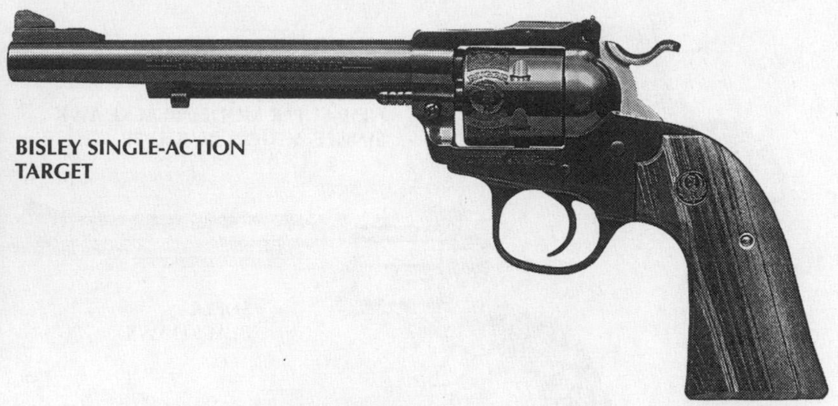
BISLEY SINGLE-ACTION TARGET

MODEL SBC-4 NEW BEARCAT

MODEL SP101 SPURLESS DA

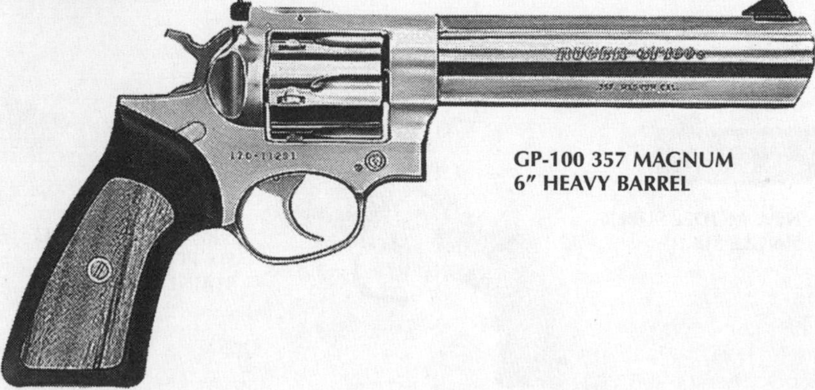
GP-100 357 MAGNUM 6″ HEAVY BARREL

Bisley

Action: single-action revolver
Grips: walnut
Barrel: 6.5 or 7.5 in.
Sights: target
Weight: 41.0oz.
Caliber: .22 LR, .357 Mag., .44 Mag., .45 Colt
Capacity: 6
Features: rimfire and centerfire (48 oz.); low-profile hammer
.22. . . . . $422
.357, .44, .45 . . . . $535

Model SBC-4 New Bearcat

Action: single-action revolver
Grips: rosewood
Barrel: 4 in.
Sights: fixed open
Weight: 24.0oz.
Caliber: .22 LR
Capacity: 6
Features: transfer bar
New Bearcat $379
stainless $429

Model SP101 and GP100

Action: single-action revolver
Grips: composite and walnut
Barrel: 2.3, 3.0, 4.0 or 6.0 in.
Sights: fixed open
Weight: 25.0oz.
Caliber: .22 LR, .32 H&R, .38 Spl., .357
Capacity: 6 (5 in some SP101s)
Features: SP101 stainless, GP100 chrome-moly or stainless; weight to 46 oz. depending on barrel length; target sights on GP100
SP101 . . . . $495
GP100 . . . . $555

Ruger Handguns

MARK II

MARK II 22/45 W/ZYTEL FRAME

22/45 TARGET MODEL P-512

MODEL P95D

MODEL P94

MODEL P89D

Mark II

Action: autoloader
Grips: polymer
Barrel: 4 to 10 in.
Sights: target
Weight: 28.0oz.
Caliber: .22 LR
Capacity: 10 + 1
Features: blowback, Mark I and .22/.45 designs, many barrel options; bull barrels extra

Mark I **$289**
stainless **$379**
Target stainless **$439**

P-Series

Action: autoloader
Grips: polymer
Barrel: 3 in.
Sights: fixed open
Weight: 30.0oz.
Caliber: 9mm, .40 S&W, .45 ACP
Capacity: 10 + 1 (8 + 1 in .45)
Features: double action, ambidextrous grip, safety; decocker on some models, manual safety on others. Price range; $425-$575

blued **$475**
stainless **$525**
blued .45 . . . . **$525**
stainless .45 . . . . **$565**

Safari Arms Handguns

COHORT

ENFORCER

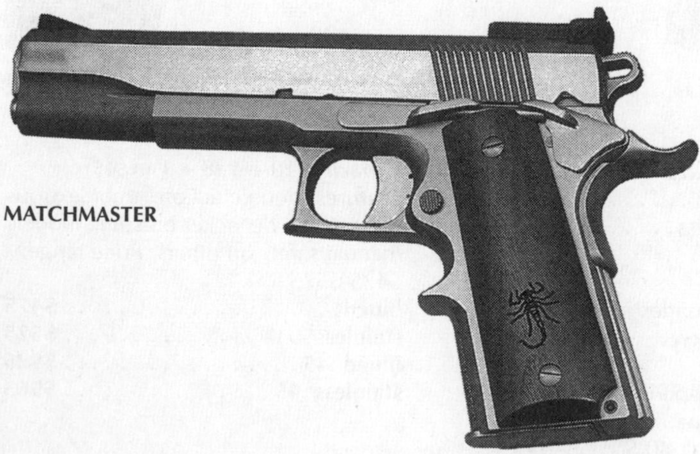

MATCHMASTER

COHORT
Action: autoloader
Grips: walnut
Barrel: 4 in.
Sights: target
Weight: 38.0oz.
Caliber: .45 ACP
Capacity: 7 + 1
Features: single action on 1911 Colt design, extended beavertail, stainless or parkerized
Cohort $649

ENFORCER
Action: autoloader
Grips: walnut
Barrel: 4.8 in.
Sights: low-profile combat
Weight: 36.0oz.
Caliber: .45 ACP
Capacity: 6 + 1
Features: single action on 1911 Colt design; extended beavertail, stainless or parkerized
Enforcer. $625

MATCHMASTER
Action: autoloader
Grips: walnut
Barrel: 5 or 6 in.
Sights: target
Weight: 40.0oz.
Caliber: .45 ACP
Capacity: 7 + 1
Features: single action on 1911 Colt design; extended beavertail, stainless or parkerized
Matchmaster $595
6 in. barrel (44 oz.) $645

Savage Handguns

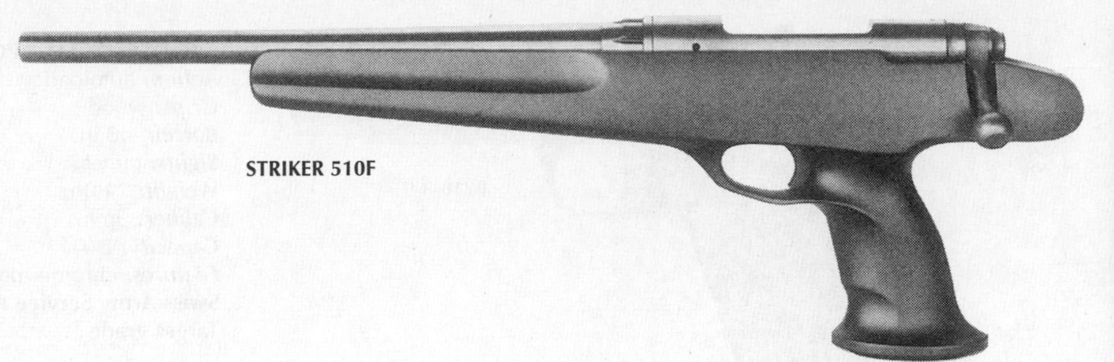
STRIKER 510F

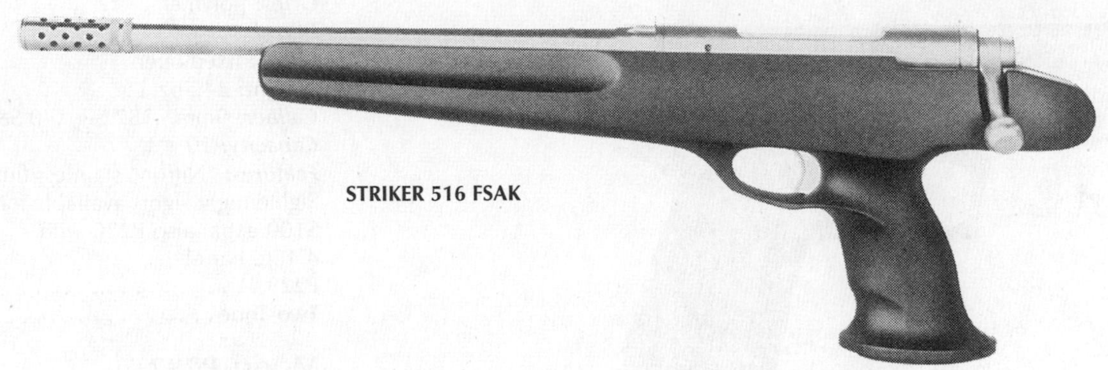
STRIKER 516 FSAK

STRIKER 516 FSAK CAMO

Striker 501, 502, 503

Action: bolt
Grips: synthetic
Barrel: 10 in.
Sights: none
Weight: 64.0oz.
Caliber: .22 LR, .22 WMR, .17 HMR
Capacity: 5 + 1
Features: left-hand bolt, right-hand ejection

.22 LR $227
.22 WMR $249
.17 HMR $274
.17 HMR stainless $321

Striker 510F

Action: bolt
Grips: synthetic
Barrel: 14 in.
Sights: none
Weight: 78.0oz.
Caliber: .223, .243, 7mm-08, .308
Capacity: 2 + 1
Features: chrome-moly steel; left-hand bolt, right-hand ejection

Striker $469

Striker 516 FSAK

Action: bolt
Grips: synthetic
Barrel: 14 in.
Sights: none
Weight: 78.0oz.
Caliber: .243, 7mm-08, .308, .270 WSM, 7mm WSM, .300 WSM
Capacity: 2 + 1
Features: stainless, with muzzle brake

FSAK $562

Sig Handguns

P210-8-9

MODEL P226

MODEL P229

MODEL P232

Model P210 Sport

Action: autoloader
Grips: wood
Barrel: 4.8 in.
Sights: target
Weight: 24.0oz.
Caliber: 9mm
Capacity: 8 + 1
Features: chrome-moly, single action
Swiss Army Service Model . . . $1680
Target grade $1089

Model P229

Action: autoloader
Grips: polymer
Barrel: 3.9 in.
Sights: fixed open
Weight: 24.5oz.
Caliber: 9mm, .357 Sig, .40 S&W
Capacity: 10 + 1
Features: "Nitron" stainless finish; Siglite night sights available for about $100 extra; also P226 with 4.4 in. barrel
P229 . . . . $840
Two-Tone $896

Model P232

Action: autoloader
Grips: polymer
Barrel: 3.6 in.
Sights: fixed open
Weight: 16.2oz.
Caliber: .380
Capacity: 7 + 1
Features: double action, available with Siglite night sights
P232 . . . . $516
stainless $559

Model P239
Action: autoloader
Grips: polymer
Barrel: 3.6 in.
Sights: target
Weight: 27.0oz.
Caliber: 9mm, .357 Sig, .40 S&W
Capacity: 7 + 1
Features: stainless, double action
P239 . . . . $642
with Siglite night sights. $745

Model PL22 Trailside
Action: autoloader
Grips: rubber or walnut
Barrel: 4.5 or 6.0 in.
Sights: target
Weight: 26.0oz.
Caliber: .22 LR
Capacity: 10 + 1
Features: all versions have a top rail for scope mounts
4.5 in. standard $455
4.5 in. target $534
6.0 in. target $559
6.0 in. competition. $710

Pro
Action: autoloader
Grips: polymer
Barrel: 3.9 in.
Sights: fixed open
Weight: 29.0oz.
Caliber: .357 Sig, .40 S&W
Capacity: 10 + 1
Features: polymer frame, stainless slide, double action; Siglite night sights available
Pro $641
Two-Tone $671

MODEL P239

MODEL PL 22 TRAILSIDE COMPETITION

PRO PISTOL

Smith & Wesson Handguns

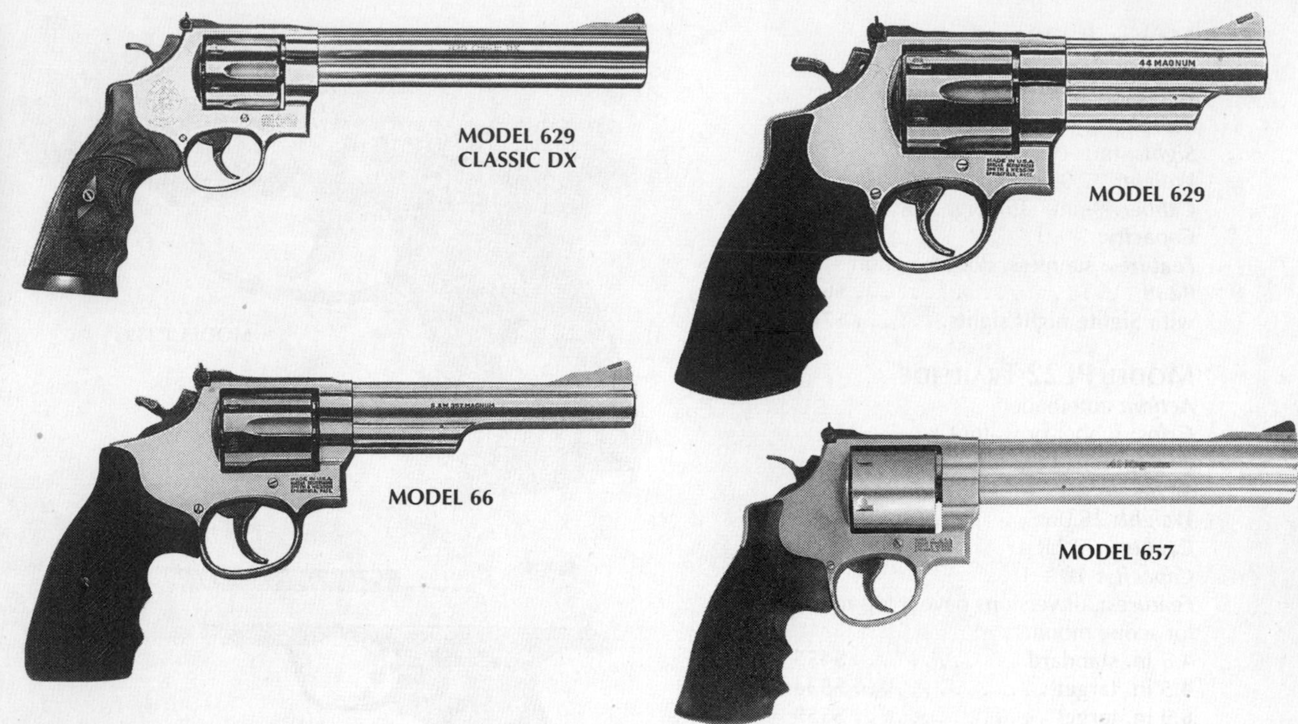

MODEL 629 CLASSIC DX

MODEL 629

MODEL 66

MODEL 657

Model 625

Action: double-action revolver
Grips: Hogue rubber, round butt
Barrel: 4 or 5 in.
Sights: target
Weight: 49.0oz.
Caliber: .45 ACP
Capacity: 6
Features: N-frame, stainless; also in Model 610 10mm with 4 in. barrel; 5 in. barrel: 51 oz.
Model 625 . . . . $767
10 mm $808

Model 629

Action: double-action revolver
Grips: Hogue rubber
Barrel: 4 or 6 in.
Sights: target
Weight: 44.0oz.
Caliber: .44 Mag.
Capacity: 6
Features: N-frame, stainless; 6 in. weighs 47 oz.
4 in. $738
6 in. $760

Model 629 Classic

Action: double-action revolver
Grips: Hogue rubber
Barrel: 5.0, 6.5 or 8.4 in.
Sights: target
Weight: 51.0oz.
Caliber: .44 Mag.
Capacity: 6
Features: N-frame, stainless, full lug; weight to 54 oz. depending on barrel length
5.0 or 6.5 in. $791
8.4 in. $817

Model 66

Action: double-action revolver
Grips: Uncle Mike's Combat
Barrel: 2.5 or 4 in.
Sights: target
Weight: 30.5oz.
Caliber: .357 Mag.
Capacity: 6
Features: stainless K-frame; 4 in. barrel: 36 oz.
4 in. $596
2.5 in. $607

Model 657

Action: double-action revolver
Grips: Hogue rubber
Barrel: 7.5 in.
Sights: target
Weight: 52.0oz.
Caliber: .41 Mag.
Capacity: 6
Features: N-frame stainless
Model 657 . . . . $726

"Fanning" a single-action revolver is probably the least accurate way to shoot it, despite what you see on television. And it can be dangerous, because it reduces your control of the pistol.

Smith & Wesson Handguns

Model 686

Action: single-action revolver
Grips: combat or target
Barrel: 2.5, 4, 6, 8.4 in.
Sights: target
Weight: 34.5oz.
Caliber: .357 mag.
Capacity: 6
Features: stainless, K-frame 686 Plus holds 7 rounds; to 48 oz. depending on barrel length

2.5 in. $625
4 in.. . . . . $651
6 in.. . . . . $657
6 in. ported $701
2.5 in. Plus. $649
4 in. Plus $672
6 in. Plus $682

Model 65

Action: double-action revolver
Grips: Uncle Mike's Combat
Barrel: 4 in.
Sights: fixed open
Weight: 34.0oz.
Caliber: .357 Mag.
Capacity: 6
Features: K-frame; also as LadySmith with 3 in. barrel, rosewood grips

Model 65 . . . . $547
LadySmith $600

Model 10

Action: double-action revolve
Grips: Uncle Mike's Combat
Barrel: 4.0 in. heavy
Sights: fixed open
Weight: 33.5oz.
Caliber: .38 Spl.
Capacity: 6
Features: "military and police" model; also in stainless, K-frame

Model 10 . . . . $511
stainless Model 64 . . . . $547
stainless with 2 iin. barrel, round butt $537

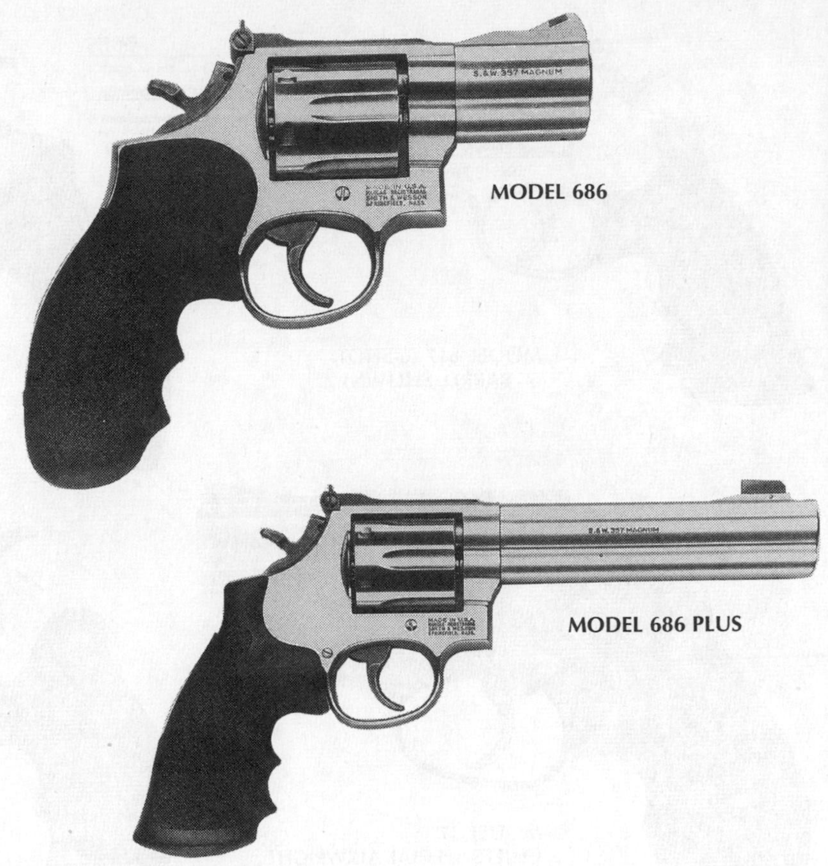

MODEL 686

MODEL 686 PLUS

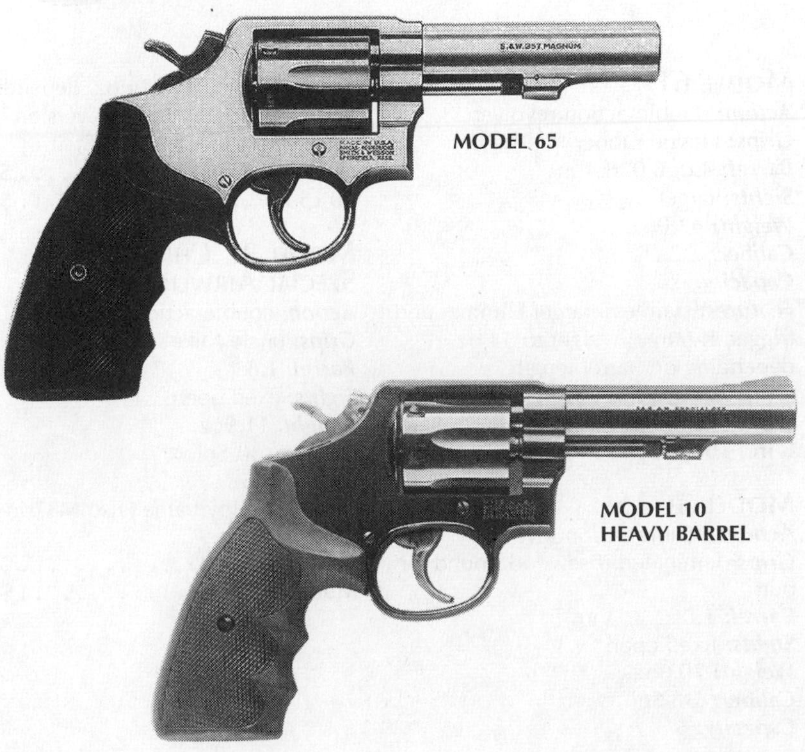

MODEL 65

MODEL 10 HEAVY BARREL

Smith & Wesson Handguns

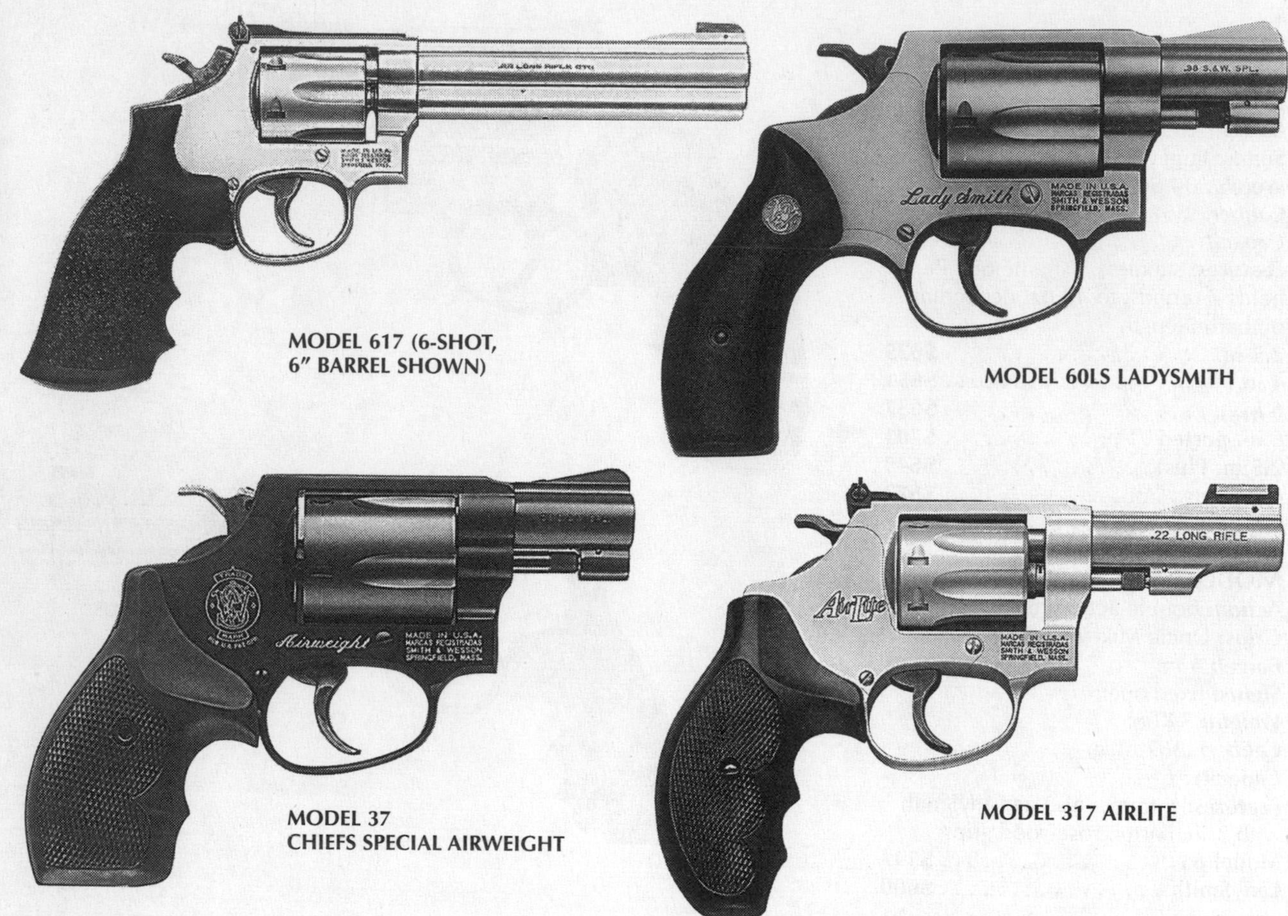

MODEL 617 (6-SHOT, 6" BARREL SHOWN)

MODEL 60LS LADYSMITH

MODEL 37 CHIEFS SPECIAL AIRWEIGHT

MODEL 317 AIRLITE

Model 617

Action: double-action revolver
Grips: Hogue rubber
Barrel: 4.0, 6.0, 8.4 in.
Sights: target
Weight: 42.0oz.
Caliber: .22 LR
Capacity: 6
Features: stainless, target hammer and trigger, K-frame; weight to 54 oz. depending on barrel length
4 in.. . . . . $663
6 in.. . . . . $643
6 in., 10-shot $688

Model 36-LS

Action: double-action revolver
Grips: laminated rosewood, round butt
Barrel: 1.8, 2.2, 3 in.
Sights: fixed open
Weight: 20.0oz.
Caliber: .38 Spl.
Capacity: 5
Features: weight to 24 oz. depending on barrel length; stainless version in .357 Mag. available (60 LS)
Model 36 LS. $533
60 LS $583

Model 37 Chief's Special Airweight

Action: double-action revolver
Grips: uncle Mike's boot
Barrel: 1.8
Sights: fixed open
Weight: 11.9oz.
Caliber: .38 Spl.
Capacity: 5
Features: alloy frame (also M37 in blue finish)
Model 637 . . . . $450
Model 37 . . . . $538

Model 68 Chief's Special Stainless

Action: double-action revolver
Grips: Uncle Mike's Combat
Barrel: 2.2 or 3 in.
Sights: low-profile combat
Weight: 23.5oz.
Caliber: .357 Mag. or .38 Spl.
Capacity: 5
Features: stainless
2.5 in. .357 . . . . $557
3 in. .38 Spl. $591

Model 317

Action: double-action revolver
Grips: rubber
Barrel: 1.8 or 3 in.
Sights: fixed open
Weight: 10.5oz.
Caliber: .22 LR
Capacity: 8
Features: alloy frame
1.8 in. $565
3 in.. . . . . $618

Smith & Wesson Handguns

Model 442 Airweight
Action: double-action revolver
Grips: rubber
Barrel: 1.8 in.
Sights: fixed open
Weight: 15.0oz.
Caliber: .38 Spl.
Capacity: 5
Features: stainless Model 642 and 442 are concealed-hammer, double-action only
Model 442 . . . . $563
stainless $614
LadySmith model $677

Model 640 Centennial
Action: double-action revolver
Grips: rubber
Barrel: 2.2
Sights: fixed open
Weight: 23.0oz.
Caliber: .357
Capacity: 5
Features: stainless, concealed-hammer, double-action-only; also M649 Bodyguard single or double-action
M640. $617
M649. $611

Model 386
Action: double-action revolver
Grips: rubber
Barrel: 3.2 in.
Sights: low-profile combat
Weight: 18.5oz.
Caliber: .357 Mag.
Capacity: 7
Features: Scandium alloy frame, titanium cylinder
Model 386 . . . . $822
with Hi-Viz sight $839

Model 360 Airlite
Action: double-action revolver
Grips: rubber
Barrel: 1.8 in.
Sights: fixed open
Weight: 12.0oz.
Caliber: .357 Mag.
Capacity: 5
Features: Scandium alloy frame, titanium cylinder
Model 360 . . . . $767
with Hi-Viz sight $805
3.2 in. Kit Gun
with Hi-Viz sight. $812

MODEL 442

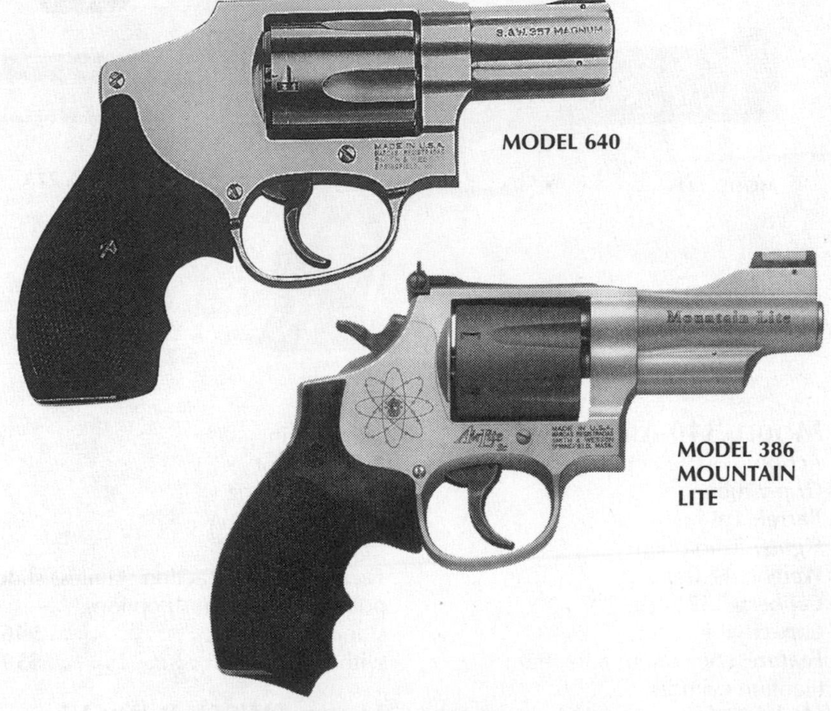

MODEL 640

MODEL 386 MOUNTAIN LITE

MODEL 360 PD AIRLITE

Smith & Wesson Handguns

MODEL 340 AIRLITE
SIGMA SERIES MODEL SW9VE FULL SIZE DA
MODEL 3913 LADYSMITH
MODEL 41
MODEL 22A SPORT

Model 340 Airlite

Action: double-action revolver
Grips: rubber
Barrel: 1.8 in.
Sights: fixed open
Weight: 12.0oz.
Caliber: .357 Mag.
Capacity: 5
Features: Scandium alloy frame, titanium cylinder
Model 340 . . . . $786
with Hi-Viz sight $823

Model 3913 LadySmith

Action: autoloader
Grips: Hogue rubber
Barrel: 3.5 in.
Sights: low-profile combat
Weight: 24.8oz.
Caliber: 9mm
Capacity: 8 + 1
Features: double action, stainless
Model 3913 . . . . $805

Model SW40E, P and VE

Action: autoloader
Grips: polymer
Barrel: 4 in.
Sights: 3-dot
Weight: 24.4oz.
Caliber: .40 S&W
Capacity: 10 + 1
Features: double action stainless slide, polymer frame, finish options
standard. $460
with night sights. $598

Model SW9G, P and VE

Action: autoloader
Grips: polymer
Barrel: 4 in.
Sights: 3-dot
Weight: 24.7oz.
Caliber: 9mm
Capacity: 10 + 1
Features: double action, stainless slide, polymer frame, finish options
standard. $648
with night sights. $767

Model 41

Action: autoloader
Grips: walnut
Barrel: 5.5 or 7 in.
Sights: target
Weight: 41.0oz.
Caliber: .22 LR
Capacity: 12 + 1
Features: adjustable trigger; 7 in. barrel: 44 oz.
Model 41 . . . . $996

Model 22A Sport

Action: autoloader
Grips: polymer
Barrel: 4, 5.5 or 7 in.
Sights: target
Weight: 28.0oz.
Caliber: .22 LR
Capacity: 10 + 1
Features: scope mounting rib; 5.5 in. bull barrel available
4 in.. . . . . $275
5.5 in. (31 oz. $304
5.5 in. bull $382
5.5 in. bull, Hi-Viz sights $402
5.5 in. bull, stainless, Hi-Viz sights. $471
7 in. (33 oz.) $345
7 in. stainless $411

Smith & Wesson Handguns

MODEL 3913TSW

MODEL 4013TSW

MODEL 4513TSW

MODEL 5906 DA STAINLESS

Model 3913 TSW

Action: autoloader
Grips: rubber
Barrel: 3.5 in.
Sights: 3-dot
Weight: 24.8oz.
Caliber: 9mm
Capacity: 8 + 1
Features: alloy frame, stainless slide; also: 3953TSW double-action-only
Model 3913TSW $783

Model 4013TSW

Action: autoloader
Grips: rubber
Barrel: 3.5 in.
Sights: 3-dot
Weight: 26.8oz.
Caliber: .40 S&W
Capacity: 9 + 1
Features: alloy frame, stainless slide, ambidextrous safety; also: 4053TSW double-action-only
Model 4013TSW $912

Model 4513TSW

Action: autoloader
Grips: rubber
Barrel: 3.5 in.
Sights: 3-dot
Weight: 28.6oz.
Caliber: .45 ACP
Capacity: 7 + 1
Features: alloy frame, stainless slide, ambidextrous safety
Model 4513TSW $952

Model 5903TSW

Action: autoloader
Grips: rubber
Barrel: 4 in.
Sights: 3-dot
Weight: 29.0oz.
Caliber: 9mm
Capacity: 10 + 1
Features: alloy frame, stainless slide; also 5906 with stainless frame, 38.3 oz.
Model 5903 . . . . $866
Model 5906 . . . . $931

Model 4003TSW

Action: autoloader
Grips: rubber
Barrel: 4 in.
Sights: 3-dot
Weight: 28.5oz.
Caliber: .40 S&W
Capacity: 10 + 1
Features: alloy frame, stainless slide; also 4006 with stainless frame, 37.8 oz.
Model 4003 . . . . $935
Model 4006 . . . . $972

Smith & Wesson Handguns

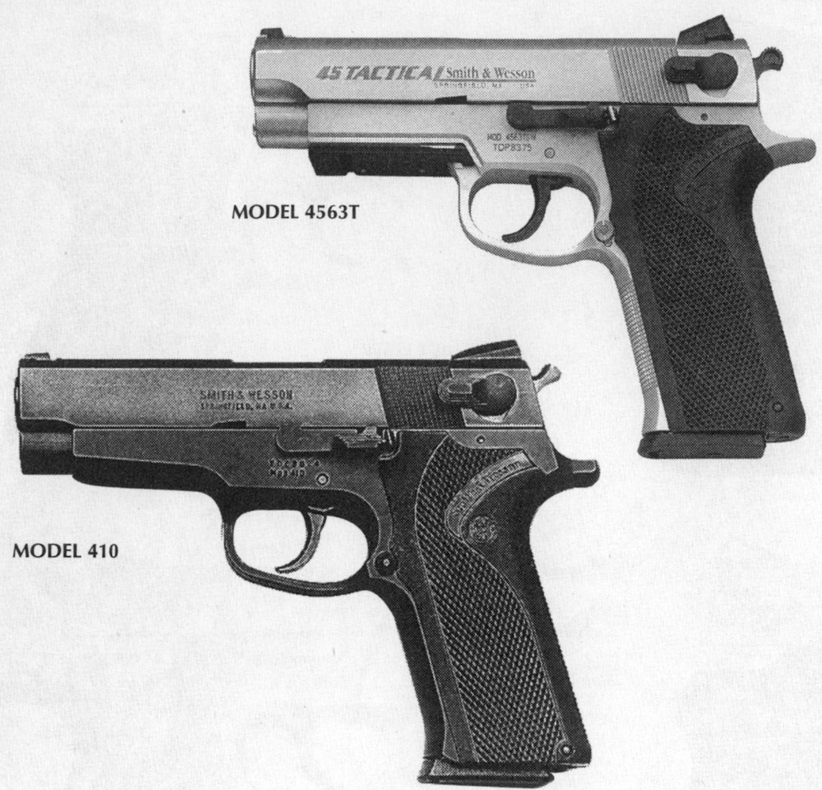

MODEL 4563T

MODEL 410

Model 4563

Action: autoloader
Grips: rubber
Barrel: 4 in.
Sights: 3-dot
Weight: 30.6oz.
Caliber: .45 ACP
Capacity: 8 + 1
Features: alloy frame, stainless slide; also 4566 with stainless frame, 39.1 oz.
Model 4563 . . . . $948
Model 4566 . . . . $971

Model 910, 410

Action: autoloader
Grips: rubber
Barrel: 4 in.
Sights: 3-dot
Weight: 28.5oz.
Caliber: 9mm, .40 S&W
Capacity: 10 + 1
Features: alloy frame, chrome-moly slide, decocking lever; also M457 in .45 ACP, 7 + 1 capacity; Hi-Viz sights extra
Model 910 . . . . $551
Model 410 . . . . $609
Model 457 . . . . $609

When handloading powerful pistol cartridges, be sure to crimp! Heavy bullets, stiff recoil and a short gripping surface within the case can lead to slippage, "tying up" revolver cylinders.

Springfield Handguns

HANDGUNS

MODEL 1911-A1
CHAMPION
4-INCH

MODEL 1911-A1
TROPHY MATCH

MICRO
COMPACT
1911-A1

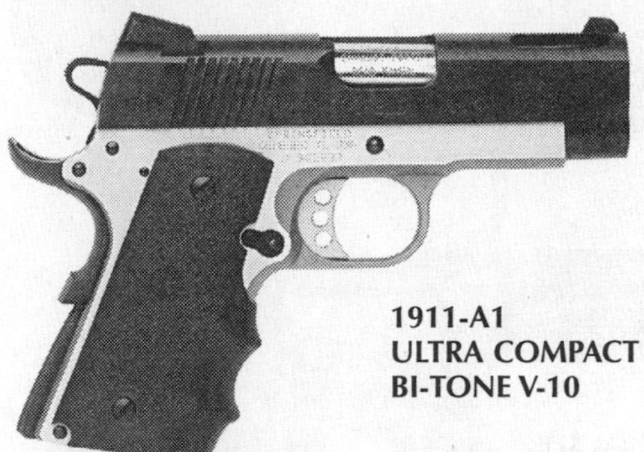

1911-A1
ULTRA COMPACT
BI-TONE V-10

MODEL 1911-A1
STANDARD &
LIGHTWEIGHT

X-TREME DUTY (XD)

Model 1911 Champion

Action: autoloader
Grips: walnut
Barrel: 4 in.
Sights: fixed open
Weight: 34.0oz.
Caliber: .45 ACP
Capacity: 7 + 1
Features: also: Ultra Compact with 3.5 in. barrel, Novak sights, Bi-Tone finish option
Champion $849
Ultra Compact $849

Model 1911 Trophy Match

Action: autoloader
Grips: Cocobolo
Barrel: match-grade, 5 in.
Sights: target
Weight: 40.0oz.
Caliber: .45 ACP
Capacity: 7 + 1
Features: Videcki speed trigger, serrated front strap
Trophy Match $1248
stainless $1452

Model 1911-A1

Action: autoloader
Grips: Cocobolo
Barrel: 5 in.
Sights: fixed open
Weight: 38.5oz.
Caliber: .45 ACP
Capacity: 7 + 1
Features: also Lightweight (31.5 oz.) and 3 in. Micro Compact (24 oz.) with alloy frames
M199-A1 . . . . $829
stainless, ported $737
Lightweight $877
Micro Compact $1021

X-Treme Duty

Action: autoloader
Grips: walnut
Barrel: 4 in.
Sights: fixed open
Weight: 22.8oz.
Caliber: 9mm, .357 Sig, .30 S&W
Capacity: 10 + 1
Features: short recoil, single action
X-Treme Duty. $489

Taurus Handguns

MODEL PT 22

MODEL PT-945

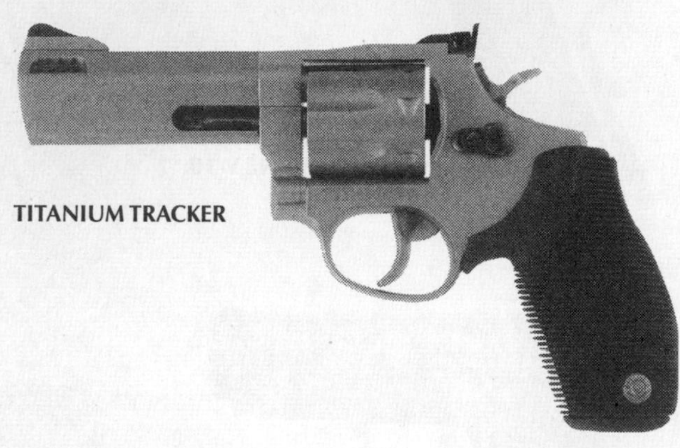
TITANIUM TRACKER

MODEL PT-92

Model PT22

Action: autoloader
Grips: rosewood
Barrel: 2.8 in.
Sights: fixed open
Weight: 12.3oz.
Caliber: .22 LR
Capacity: 8 + 1
Features: double action only, blue, nickel or DuoTone finish; also in .25 ACP (PT25)
PT22 . . . . $219
with gold trim $234

Model PT945

Action: autoloader
Grips: rubber or rosewood
Barrel: 4.3 in.
Sights: 3-dot
Weight: 29.5oz.
Caliber: .45 ACP
Capacity: 8 + 1
Features: double action; also PT940 in .40 S&W (28.2 oz., 10 + 1 capacity)
blue. $563
stainless $578
blue with porting $602
stainless with porting $617
Model 940 blue $523
Model 940 stainless $539

Titanium Tracker

Action: double-action revolver
Grips: rubber
Barrel: 4 or 6 in.
Sights: target
Weight: 21.0oz.
Caliber: .357 Mag or .42 Mag. (4 in. only)
Capacity: 7 (.357) or 5 9.41)
Features: Titanium frame; 23 oz. with 6 in. barrel
Tracker $688

Model PT911 Compact

Action: autoloader
Grips: polymer
Barrel: 4 in.
Sights: 3-dot
Weight: 28.2oz.
Caliber: 9mm
Capacity: 10 + 1
Features: double action only; ambidextrous decocker
blue. $523
stainless. $539
Price:. $422
Price:. $438

Model PT92

Action: autoloader
Grips: walnut
Barrel: 5 in.
Sights: fixed open
Weight: 34.0oz.
Caliber: 9mm
Capacity: 15 + 1
Features: double action; also PT99 with adjustable sights
blue. $578
stainless. $594
blue with adjustable sights $594
stainless with adjustable sights . $609

Taurus Handguns

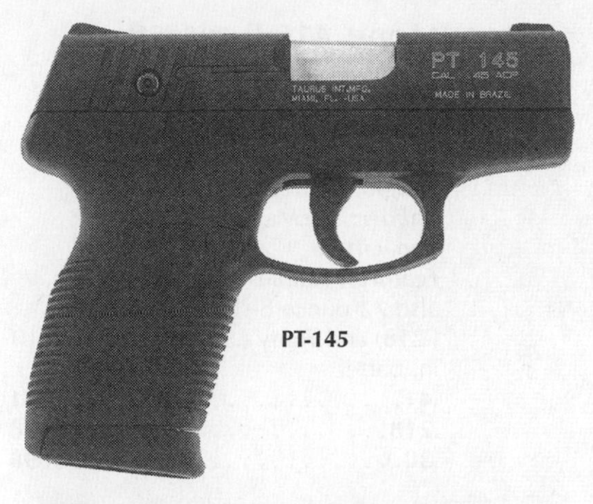

PT-145

MODEL 44

454 CASULL
"RAGING BULL" DA

MODEL 82

Model PT145

Action: autoloader
Grips: polymer
Barrel: 1.8 in.
Sights: fixed open
Weight: 22.0oz.
Caliber: .45 ACP
Capacity: 10 + 1
Features: double action, double-stack magazine
blue $484
stainless $500
blue with night sights $563
stainless with night sights $578

Model PT938 Compact

Action: autoloader
Grips: rubber
Barrel: 3 in.
Sights: fixed open
Weight: 27.0oz.
Caliber: .380
Capacity: 10 + 1
Features: double action only
blue $516
stainless $531

Model 44

Action: double-action revolver
Grips: rubber
Barrel: 4, 6 or 8.4 in.
Sights: target
Weight: 44.0oz.
Caliber: .44 Mag.
Capacity: 6
Features: vent rib, porting; weight to 57 oz. depending on barrel length
blue, 4 in. $500
stainless, 4 in. $563
blue, 6 or 8.4 in. $523
stainless, 6 or 8.4 in. $578

Model 454 Raging Bull

Action: double-action revolver
Grips: rubber
Barrel: 6.5 or 8.4 in.
Sights: target
Weight: 53.0oz.
Caliber: .454 Casull
Capacity: 5
Features: stainless or chrome-moly, vent rib, ported; 8.4 in. weighs 63 oz.
blue $797
stainless $859

Model 82

Action: double-action revolver
Grips: rubber
Barrel: 4 in.
Sights: fixed open
Weight: 34.0oz.
Caliber: .38 Spl.
Capacity: 6
Features: also, 21-ounce model 85 in .38 Spl and .32 H&R, with 2 or 3 in. barrel, grip options
Model 82, blue. $352
Model 82, stainless. $398
Model 85, blue. $375
Model 85, stainless. $422

Protector

Action: double-action revolver
Grips: rubber
Barrel: 2 in.
Sights: fixed open
Weight: 24.5oz.
Caliber: .357 Mag.
Capacity: 5
Features: shrouded but accessible hammer; also Titanium and UltraLight versions to 17 oz.
blue $406
stainless $453

Taurus Handguns

MODEL 416
RAGING BULL

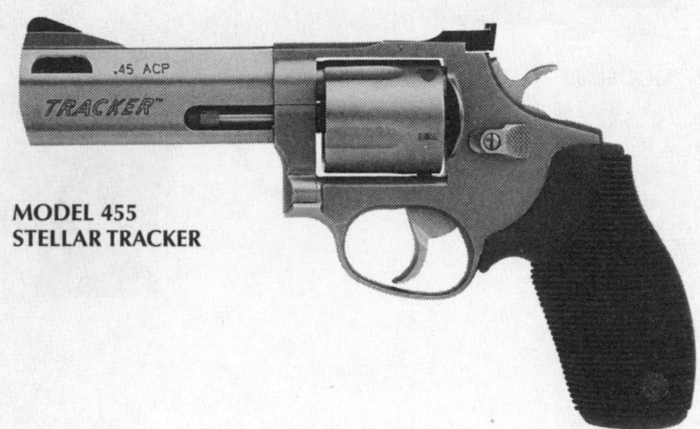

MODEL 455
STELLAR TRACKER

MODEL 941

Model 416 Raging Bull

Action: double-action revolver
Grips: rubber
Barrel: 6.5 in.
Sights: target
Weight: 62.0oz.
Caliber: .41 Mag.
Capacity: 6
Features: stainless vent rib, ported; also 72-ounce 8-shot Raging Bee (.218) and Thirty (.30 Carbine) with 10 in. barrel

.41. . . . . $641
.218. . . . . $898
.30. . . . . $898

Model 455 Stellar Tracker

Action: double-action revolver
Grips: rubber
Barrel: 2, 4 or 6 in.
Sights: target
Weight: 28.0oz.
Caliber: .45 ACP
Capacity: 5 (full-moon clips)
Features: ported barrel, to 38 ounces depending on barrel length; also M460 Tracker in .45 Colt with 4 or 6 in. barrel

Model 455 . . . . $523
Model 460 . . . . $516

218 Target Silhouette

Action: double-action revolver
Grips: rubber
Barrel: 12 in.
Sights: target
Weight: 52.3oz.
Caliber: .218 Bee
Capacity: 7
Features: vent rib, stainless

Model 218 . . . . $461

Model 94

Action: double-action revolver
Grips: hardwood
Barrel: 2, 4 or 5 in.
Sights: target
Weight: 25.0oz.
Caliber: .22 LR
Capacity: 9
Features: solid rib; also .22 WMR with 8-shot cylinder

blue. $328
stainless. $359
Magnum, blue $344
Magnum, stainless $391

Taurus Handguns

Model 608

Action: double-action revolver
Grips: rubber
Barrel: 4, 6.5 or 8.4 in.
Sights: target
Weight: 49.0oz.
Caliber: .357 Mag.
Capacity: 8
Features: transfer bar, weight to 53 oz. depending on barrel length

blue, 4 in. $469
stainless, 4 in. $523
blue, 6.5 or 8.4 in. $484
stainless, 6.5 or 8.4 in. $544

Model 445

Action: double-action revolver
Grips: rubber
Barrel: 2 in.
Sights: fixed open
Weight: 28.3oz.
Caliber: .44 Spl.
Capacity: 5
Features: solid rib, transfer bar, porting optional; also 445CH with concealed hammer

Model 445 . . . . $359
stainless $406

Model 605

Action: double-action revolver
Grips: rubber
Barrel: 2.3 in.
Sights: fixed open
Weight: 24.5oz.
Caliber: .357 Mag.
Capacity: 5
Features: transfer bar; porting optional; also 605CH with concealed hammer

Model 605 . . . . $375
stainless $422

**MODEL 608
DOUBLE ACTION**

**MODEL 445
BRIGHT BLUE
STEEL 2" BARREL,
PORTED**

MODEL 605

Keep both eyes open when shooting any firearm, squinting slightly or using a patch or tape only if you must to avoid "doubling" the sight picture. A severe squint impairs vision in the open eye.

Thompson/Center Handguns

HANDGUNS

CONTENDER G2

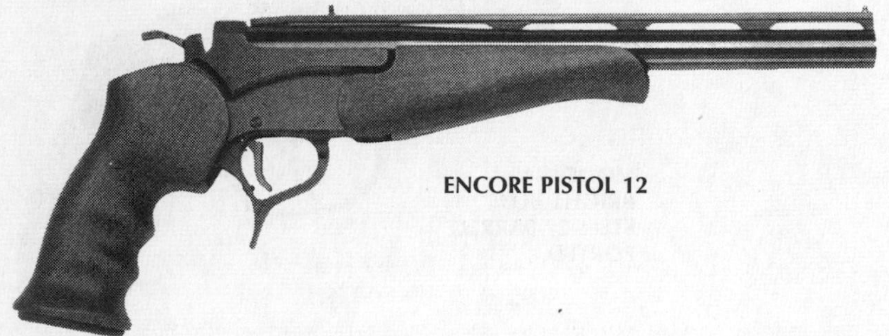
ENCORE PISTOL 12

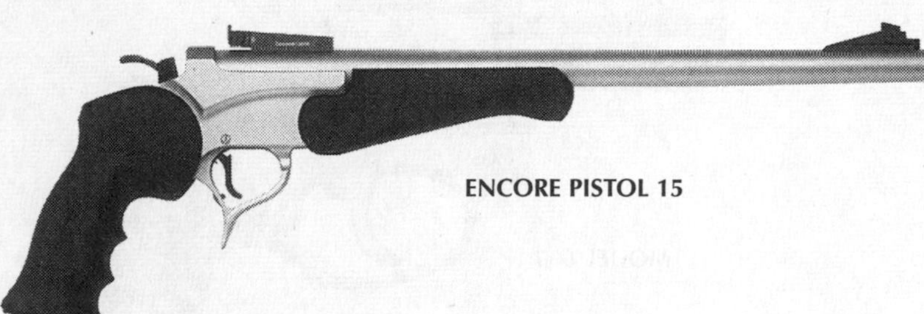
ENCORE PISTOL 15

ENCORE HUNTER PACKAGE

CONTENDER G2

Action: hinged breech
Grips: walnut
Barrel: 12 or 14 in.
Sights: target
Weight: 60.0oz.
Caliber: .22 LR, .22 Hornet, .357 Mag., .44 Mag., .45/.410 (12 in.), .17 HMR, .22 LR, .22 Hornet, .223, 7-30, .30-30, .44 Mag., .45/.410, .45-70 (15 in.)
Capacity: 1
Features: improved, stronger version of Contender

12 in. $555
15 in. (64 oz.) $561

ENCORE

Action: hinged breech
Grips: walnut or rubber
Barrel: 12 or 15 in.
Sights: target
Weight: 68.0oz.
Caliber: many popular rifle and big-bore pistol rounds, from the .22 Hornet to the .30-06 and .45-70, the .454 Casull and .480 Ruger
Capacity: 1
Features: also in package with 2-7x scope, carry case; prices vary with caliber, options

12 in. $583
15 in. (72 oz.) $588
.45/.410 with rib $607
stainless with rubber grips $646

Uberti Handguns

Model 1871 Rolling Block Pistol

Action: rolling block
Grips: walnut
Barrel: 14 in.
Sights: target
Weight: 45.0oz.
Caliber: .22 LR, .22 WMR, .22 Hornet, .357 Mag.
Capacity: 1
Features: case-colored breech, brass guard
1871 Rolling Block $410

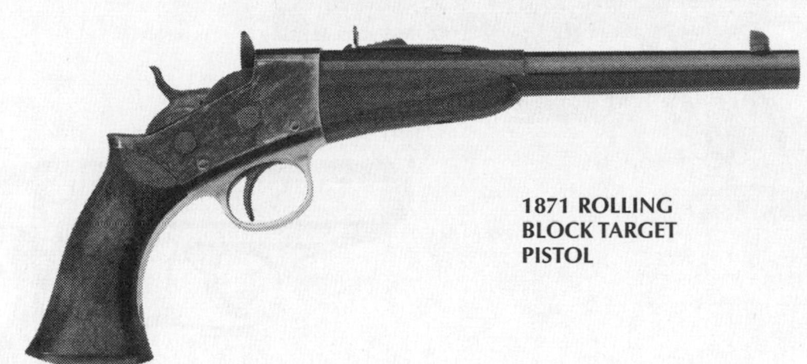

1871 ROLLING BLOCK TARGET PISTOL

Model 1873 Single Action Revolver

Action: single-action revolver
Grips: walnut
Barrel: 4.8, 5.5 or 7.5 in.
Sights: fixed open
Weight: 37.0oz.
Caliber: .38-40, .357 Mag., .44-40, .44 Spl., .45 Colt
Capacity: 6
Features: case-colored frame, weight to 42 ounces depending on barrel length; 18 in. buntline also available
1873 . . . . $395
with birds-head grips $430
nickel finish $470

1873 CATTLEMAN

Even the most powerful pistol cartridges have less energy than ordinary rifle cartridges, and their bullets are less efficient at long range. When hunting with a handgun, keep shot ranges short!

Walther Handguns

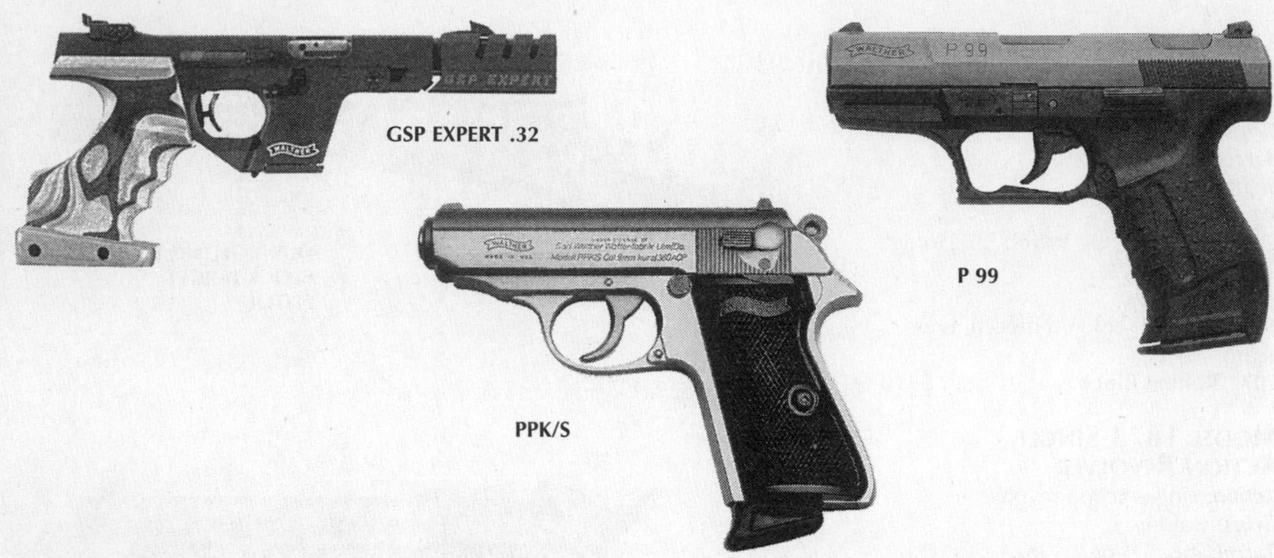
GSP EXPERT .32

PPK/S

P 99

GSP Expert
Action: autoloader
Grips: laminated wood
Barrel: match-grade compensated 4.2 in.
Sights: target
Weight: 29.0oz.
Caliber: .22 LR, .32 S&W
Capacity: 5
Features: forward magazine
.22. . . . . $1240
.32. . . . . $1420

P22
Action: autoloader
Grips: polymer
Barrel: 3.4 or 5 in.
Sights: 3-dot
Weight: 19.6oz.
Caliber: .22 LR
Capacity: 10 + 1
Features: double action; 20.3 ounces with 5 in. barrel
P22 . . . . $249

P99 Compact
Action: autoloader
Grips: polymer
Barrel: 4 in.
Sights: low-profile combat
Weight: 25.0oz.
Caliber: 9mm, .40 S&W
Capacity: 10 + 1
Features: double action, ambidextrous magazine release, high-capacity magazines available
P99 Compact $644

PPK and PPK/S
Action: autoloader
Grips: polymer
Barrel: 3.4 in.
Sights: fixed open
Weight: 22.0oz.
Caliber: .380 and .32 ACP
Capacity: 7 + 1
Features: double action, blue or stainless, decocker
PPK $543

Wildey Handguns

Wildey Automatic Pistol
Action: autoloader
Grips: composite
Barrel: 5, 6, 7, 8, 10, 12 or 14 in.
Sights: target
Weight: 64.0oz.
Caliber: .45 Win. Mag., .45 and .475 Wildey
Capacity: 7 + 1
Features: gas operated, ribbed barrel
starting at $1385

BLACKPOWDER

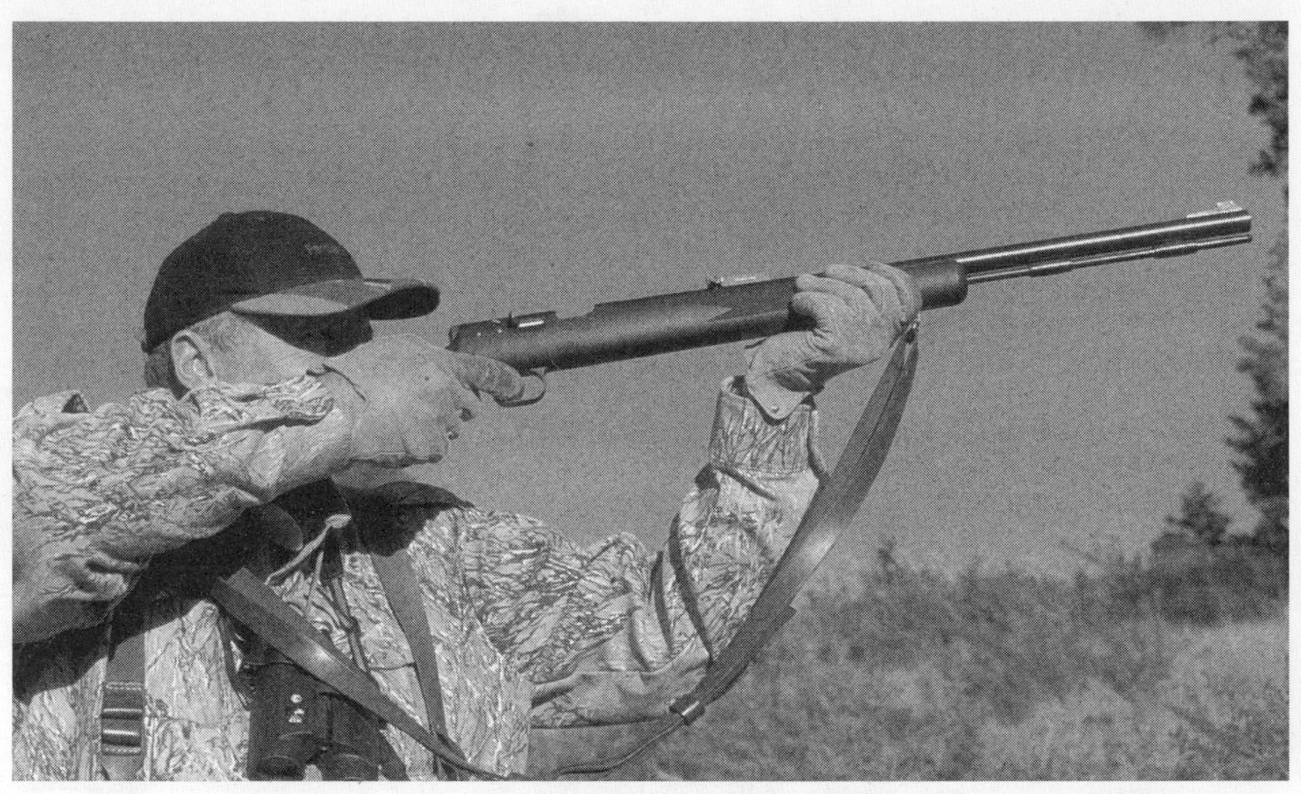

Austin & Halleck Blackpowder

MODEL 320 REALTREE-HARDWOODS CAMO

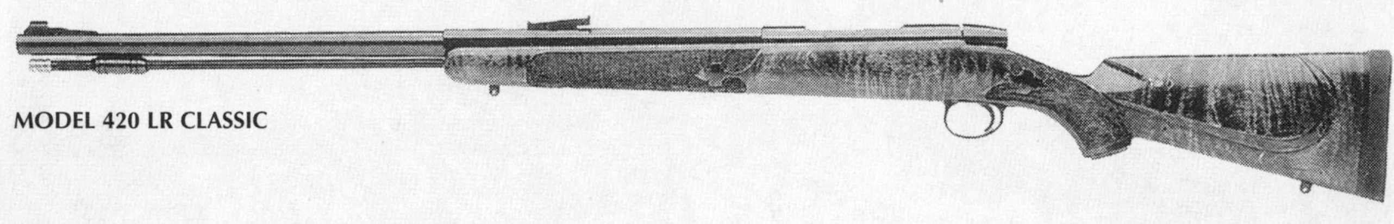

MODEL 420 LR CLASSIC

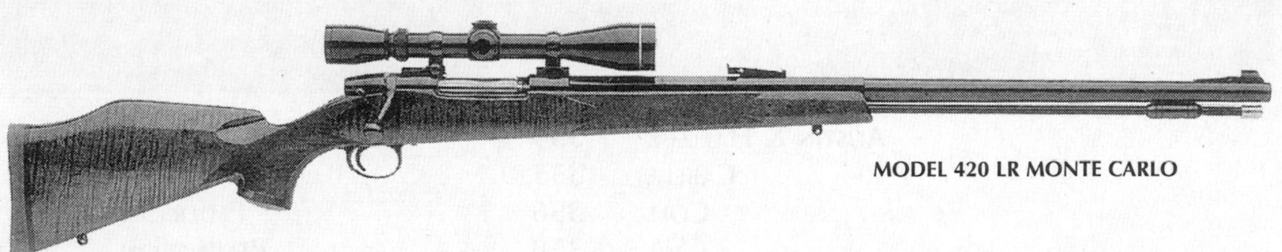

MODEL 420 LR MONTE CARLO

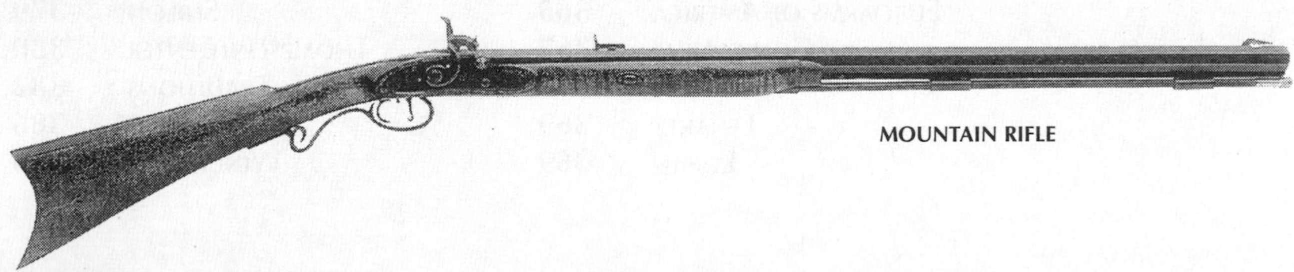

MOUNTAIN RIFLE

Bolt Action M328, 420

Lock: in-line
Stock: curly maple, synthetic, camo
Barrel: 26 in., 1:28 twist
Sights: adjustable open
Weight: 7.8lbs.
Bore/Caliber: .50
Features: match trigger

synthetic $399
stainless synthetic. $439
camo $439
stainless camo $469
maple $509
stainless maple $539

Mountain Rifle

Lock: traditional cap or flint
Stock: curly maple
Barrel: 32 in., 1:66 or 1:28 twist
Sights: fixed
Weight: 7.5lbs.
Bore/Caliber: .50
Features: double set triggers

percussion $589
select percussion $719
flint $639
select percussion $769

Cabela's Blackpowder

TRADITIONAL HAWKEN RIFLE

BLUE RIDGE RIFLE

KODIAK EXPRESS DOUBLE RIFLE

BLACK POWDER

HAWKEN
Lock: traditional cap or flint
Stock: walnut
Barrel: 24 in., 1:28 twist
Sights: adjustable open
Weight: 9.0lbs.
Bore/Caliber: .50 or .54
Features: brass furniture, double-set trigger
percussion (right or left-hand). . $250
flint $280

BLUE RIDGE
Lock: side-hammer caplock
Stock: walnut
Barrel: 39 in., 1:48 twist
Sights: none
Weight: 7.8lbs.
Bore/Caliber: .32, .36, .45 and .50
Features: double set triggers, case-colored locks
caplock $479
flint $499

KODIAK EXPRESS DOUBLE RIFLE
Lock: traditional caplock
Stock: walnut, pistol grip
Barrel: 28 in., 1:48 twist
Sights: folding leaf
Weight: 9.3lbs.
Bore/Caliber: .50, .54, .58 and .72
Features: double triggers
from $799

DOUBLE SHOTGUN
Lock: traditional caplock
Stock: walnut
Barrel: 27, 28 or 30 in.
Sights: none
Weight: 7.0lbs.
Bore/Caliber: 20, 12 or 10 ga.
Features: screw-in choke tubes: X-Full, Mod, IC, double triggers; weight to 10 lbs. depending on gauge
from $639

Pyrodex pellets make loading faster and easier than measuring black powder or granular Pyrodex (a black powder substitute).

Colt Blackpowder

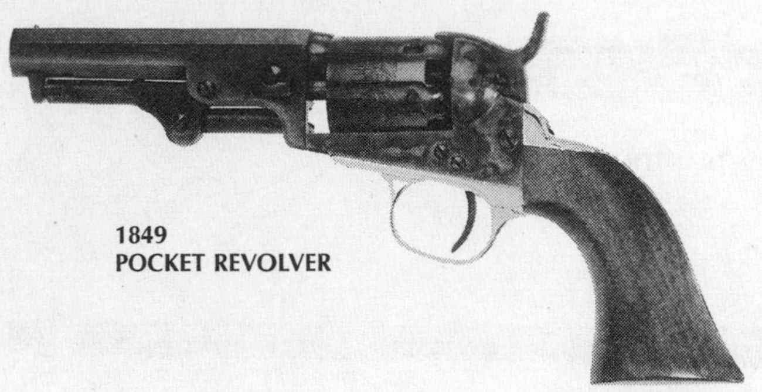

1849
POCKET REVOLVER

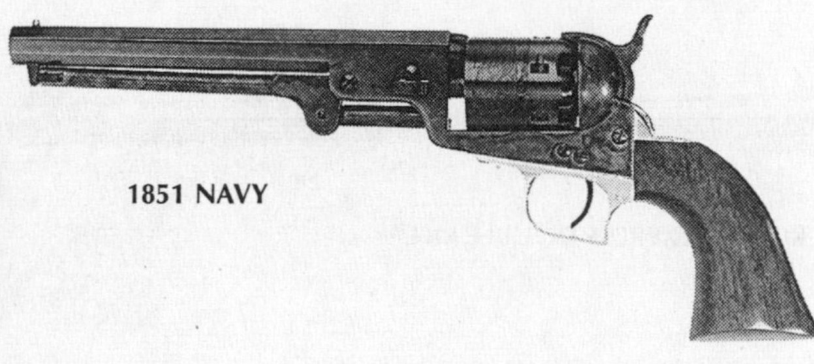

1851 NAVY

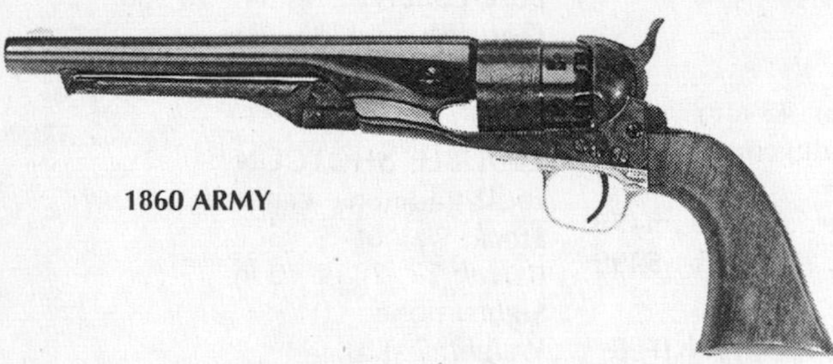

1860 ARMY

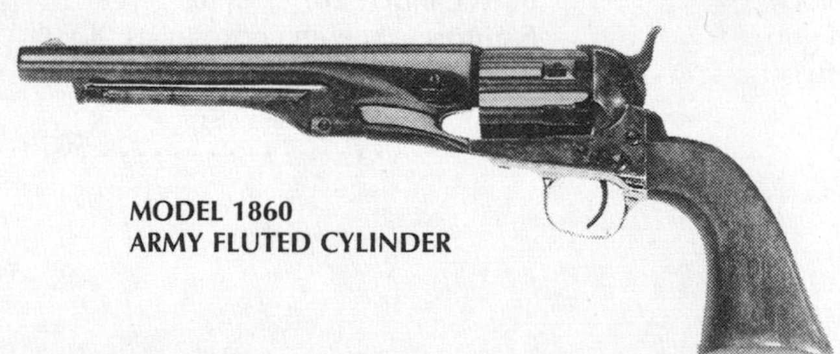

MODEL 1860
ARMY FLUTED CYLINDER

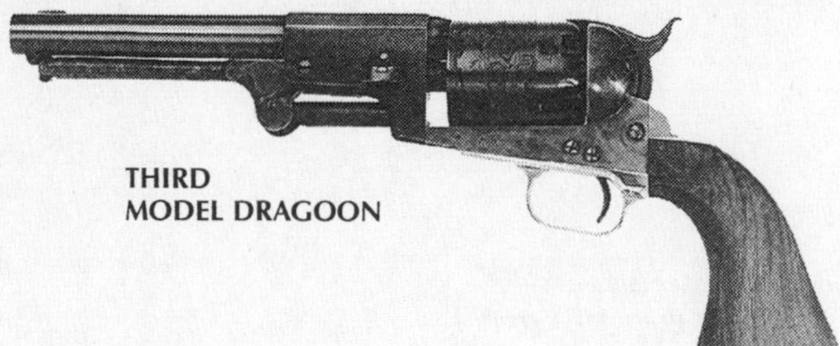

THIRD
MODEL DRAGOON

BLACK POWDER

1849 Pocket Revolver

Lock: caplock revolver
Stock: walnut
Barrel: 4 in.
Sights: fixed
Weight: 1.5lbs.
Bore/Caliber: .31
Features: case-colored frame
Pocket Revolver $430

1851 Navy

Lock: caplock revolver
Stock: walnut
Barrel: 7.5 in.
Sights: fixed
Weight: 2.5lbs.
Bore/Caliber: .36
Features: case-colored frame
1851 Navy $450

1860 Army

Lock: caplock revolver
Stock: walnut
Barrel: 8 in.
Sights: fixed
Weight: 2.6lbs.
Bore/Caliber: ..44
Features: case-colored frame, hammer, plunger; also with fluted cylinder and adapted for shoulder stock
1860 Army $450

Third Model Dragoon

Lock: caplock revolver
Stock: walnut
Barrel: 7.5 in.
Sights: fixed
Weight: 4.1lbs.
Bore/Caliber: .44
Features: case-colored frame, hammer, lever, plunger
Dragoon $500

Colt Blackpowder

Walker
Lock: caplock revolver
Stock: walnut
Barrel: 9 in.
Sights: fixed
Weight: 4.6lbs.
Bore/Caliber: .44
Features: case-colored frame, authentic remake of 1847 Walker
Walker $500

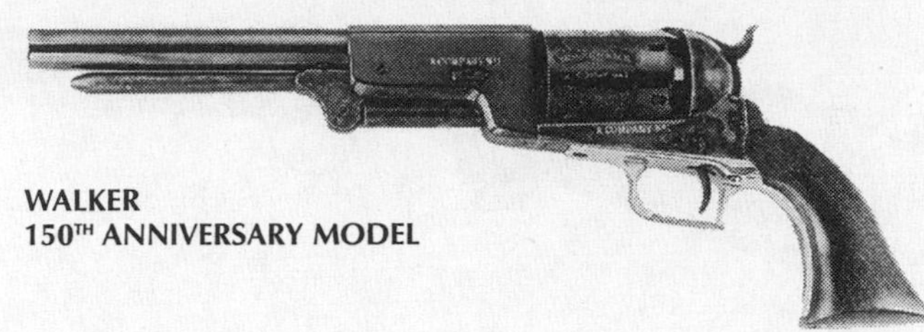

WALKER
150TH ANNIVERSARY MODEL

1861 Navy
Lock: caplock revolver
Stock: walnut
Barrel: 7.5 in.
Sights: fixed
Weight: 2.6lbs.
Bore/Caliber: .36
Features: revolver with case-colored frame, hammer, lever, plunger
1861 Navy $450

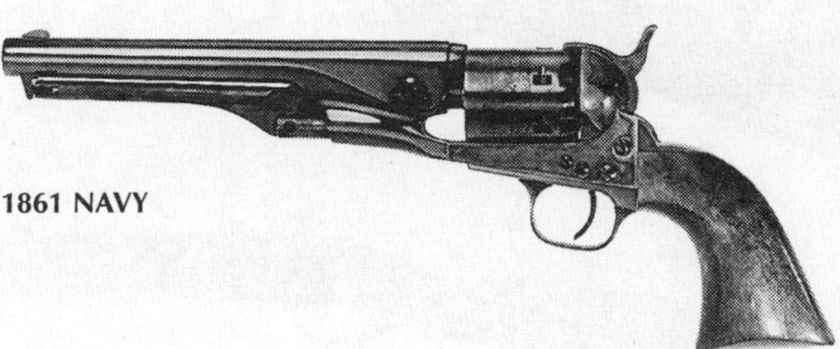

1861 NAVY

Trapper 1862 Pocket Police
Lock: caplock revolver
Stock: walnut
Barrel: 3.5 in.
Sights: fixed
Weight: 1.25lbs.
Bore/Caliber: .36
Features: revolver with case-colored frame, separate brass ramrod
Pocket Police $430

TRAPPER
1862 POCKET POLICE

Colt 1861 Rifle
Lock: traditional caplock
Stock: walnut
Barrel: 40 in.
Sights: folding leaf
Weight: 9.2lbs.
Bore/Caliber: .58
Features: authentic reproduction of 1861 Springfield
1861 Musket. $800

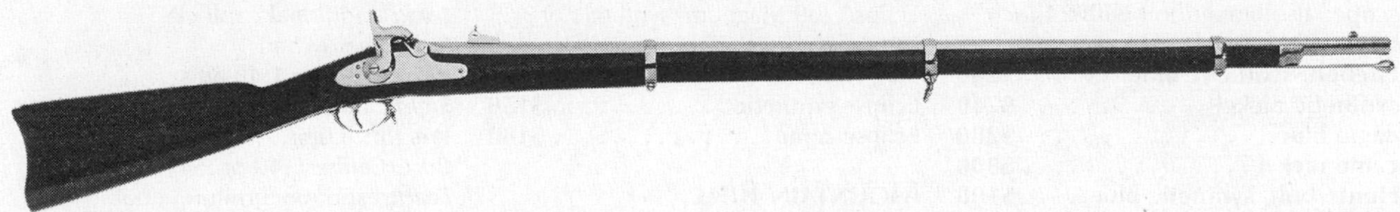

COLT 1861 RIFLE

CVA Blackpowder

BLACK POWDER

FIREBOLT ULTRAMAG RIFLE

STAG HORN MAGNUM RIFLE

MOUNTAIN RIFLE

ST. LOUIS HAWKEN II

Firebolt Ultramag Rifle

Lock: inline
Stock: synthetic or camo
Barrel: 26 in., fluted
Sights: none
Weight: 7.0lbs.
Bore/Caliber: .45 or .50
Features: uses 209 primers, drilled for scope; also Hunterbolt with 24-inch barrel, fiber optic sights

Firebolt, synthetic blue $240
synthetic nickel $240
camo blue $280
camo nickel $300
Hunterbolt, synthetic blue $190
synthetic nicke. $205
camo blue $225
camo nickel $240

Stag Horn

Lock: traditional caplock
Stock: synthetic
Barrel: 24 in., 1:28 twist
Sights: adjustable open
Weight: 6.0lbs.
Bore/Caliber: .45 or .50
Features: uses 209 primers; also Eclipse 209 Magnum, synthetic or camo

Stag Horn $122
Eclipse synthetic $150
Eclipse camo. $180

Mountain Rifle

Lock: traditional caplock
Stock: maple
Barrel: 32 in., 1:66 twist
Sights: adjustable open
Weight: 9.0lbs.
Bore/Caliber: .50
Features: browned steel hardware, limited production; also Mountain Hunter, blued with hardwood stock

Mountain Rifle $400
Mountain Hunter $260

St. Louis Hawken II

Lock: traditional caplock
Stock: hardwood
Barrel: 28 in.; 1:48 twist
Sights: adjustable open
Weight: 8.0lbs.
Bore/Caliber: .40 or .54
Features: brass furniture, double set trigger

St. Louis Hawken II. $230
left-hand. $275

CVA Blackpowder

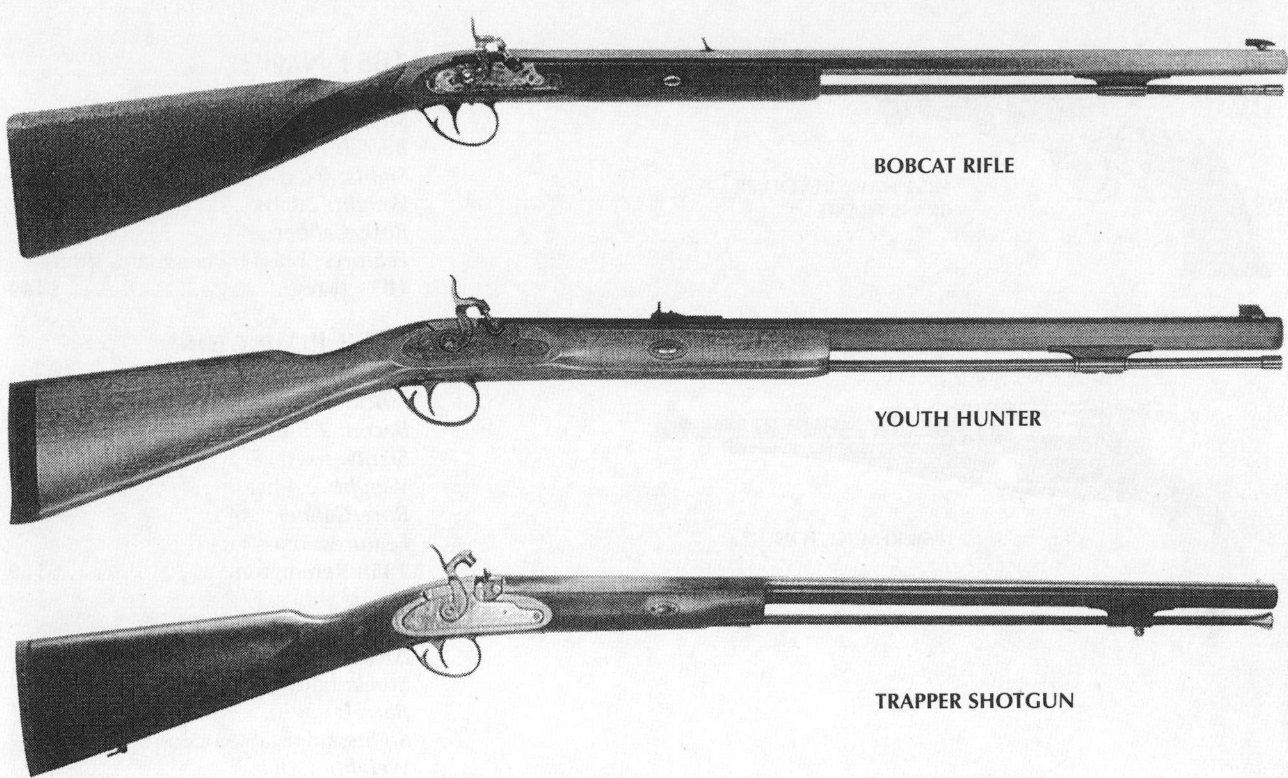

Bobcat

Lock: traditional caplock
Stock: hardwood or synthetic
Barrel: 26 in., 1:48 twist
Sights: fixed
Weight: 6.0lbs.
Bore/Caliber: .50
Features: basic muzzleloader with versatile deep-groove rifling; also, Plainsman flintlock with wood stock
synthetic.................. $105
hardwood $128
Plainsman.................. $288

Youth Hunter

Lock: traditional caplock
Stock: hardwood (short pull)
Barrel: 24 in., 1:48 twist
Sights: adjustable open
Weight: 5.0lbs.
Bore/Caliber: .50
Features: oversize guard, synthetic ramrod
Youth Hunter $136

Trapper Shotgun

Lock: traditional caplock
Stock: hardwood
Barrel: 28 in.
Sights: none
Weight: 6.0lbs.
Bore/Caliber: 12 ga.
Features: chrome-lined bore for steel shot; case-colored lock, modified choke, synthetic ramrod
Trapper.................... $288

Before loading a caplock rifle, hold the muzzle close to a patch of grass and fire a primer only. If the grass shudders, the nipple is clear and the gun ready for loading.

CVA Blackpowder

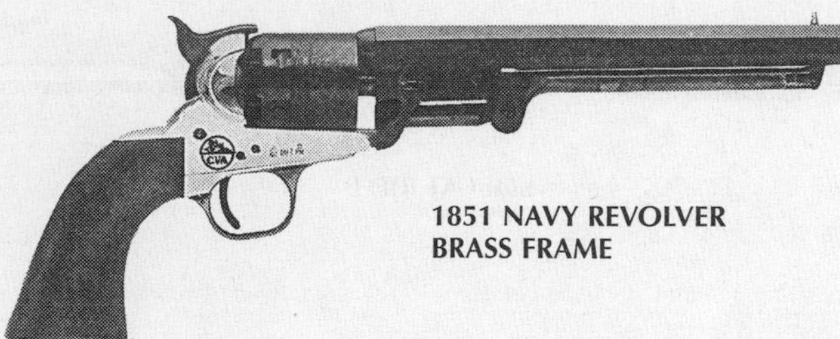

1851 NAVY REVOLVER
BRASS FRAME

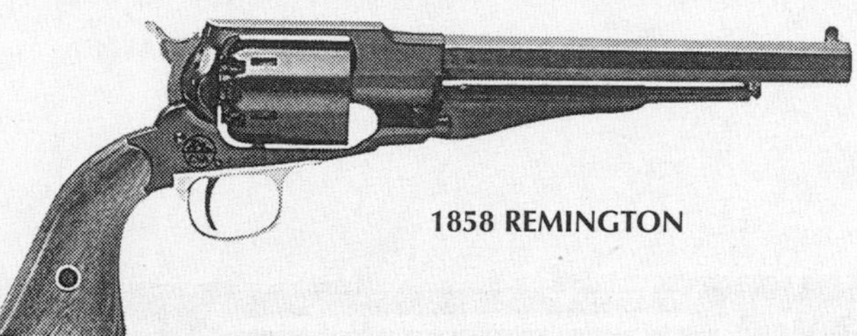

1858 REMINGTON

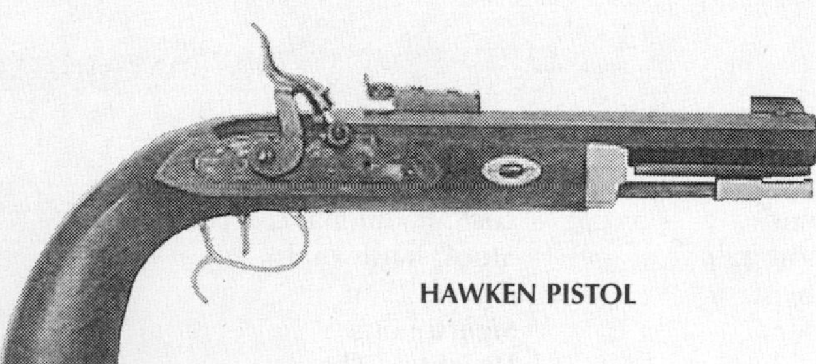

HAWKEN PISTOL

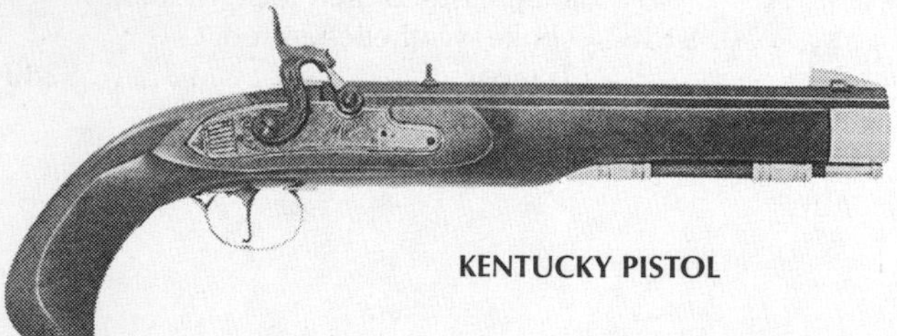

KENTUCKY PISTOL

1851 Navy

Lock: caplock revolver
Stock: walnut
Barrel: 7.5 in.
Sights: fixed
Weight: 2.8lbs.
Bore/Caliber: .44
Features: brass frame, guard, strap
1851 Navy $144

1858 Remington

Lock: caplock revolver
Stock: walnut
Barrel: 7.5 in.
Sights: fixed
Weight: 2.4lbs.
Bore/Caliber: .44
Features: brass guard
1858 Remington $160

Hawken Pistol

Lock: traditional caplock
Stock: hardwood
Barrel: 9.8 in.
Sights: adjustable open
Weight: 3.1lbs.
Bore/Caliber: .50
Features: brass furniture
Hawken Pistol. $168
unfinished kit $120

Kentucky Pistol

Lock: traditional caplock
Stock: hardwood
Barrel: 9.8 in.
Sights: fixed
Weight: 2.5lbs.
Bore/Caliber: .50
Features: brass-tipped hardwood ramrod
Kentucky Pistol $168
unfinished kit $120

Queen Anne Pistol

Lock: traditional flintlock
Stock: walnut
Barrel: 7.5 in.
Sights: none
Weight: 2.2lbs.
Bore/Caliber: .45
Features: brass furniture
Queen Anne Pistol $245
unfinished kit $195

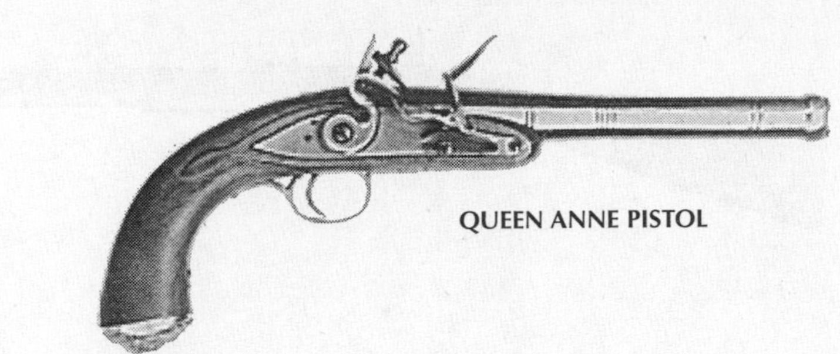

QUEEN ANNE PISTOL

Charles Moore Dueling Pistol

Lock: traditional cap or flint
Stock: walnut
Barrel: 11 in.
Sights: fixed
Weight: 2.8lbs.
Bore/Caliber: .45
Features: silver-plated furniture, case-colored
cap $375
flint $425

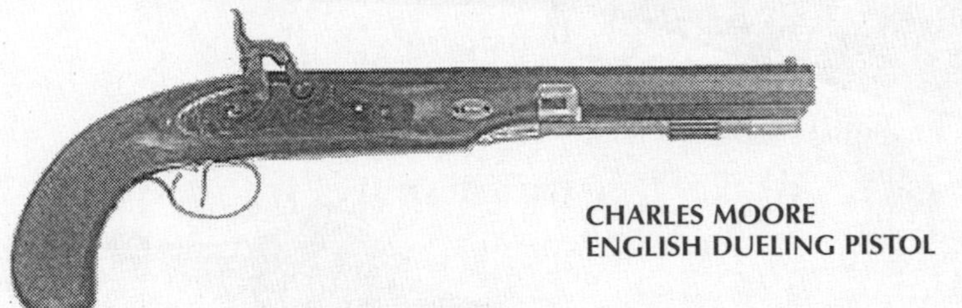

CHARLES MOORE
ENGLISH DUELING PISTOL

Mang Target Pistol

Lock: traditional caplock
Stock: hardwood
Barrel: 10.4 in., 1:15 twist
Sights: fixed
Weight: 2.5lbs.
Bore/Caliber: .38
Features: half-stock, finger rest on guard
Mang Target Pistol $895

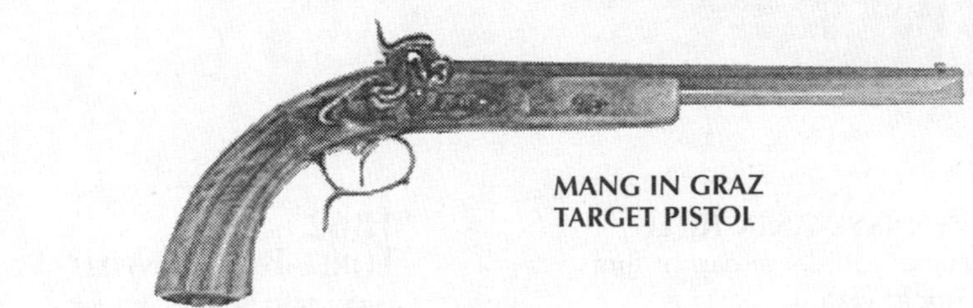

MANG IN GRAZ
TARGET PISTOL

LePage Dueling Pistol

Lock: traditional caplock
Stock: hardwood
Barrel: 9 in.
Sights: fixed
Weight: 2.5lbs.
Bore/Caliber: .45
Features: double set trigger
LePage Dueling Pistol $450

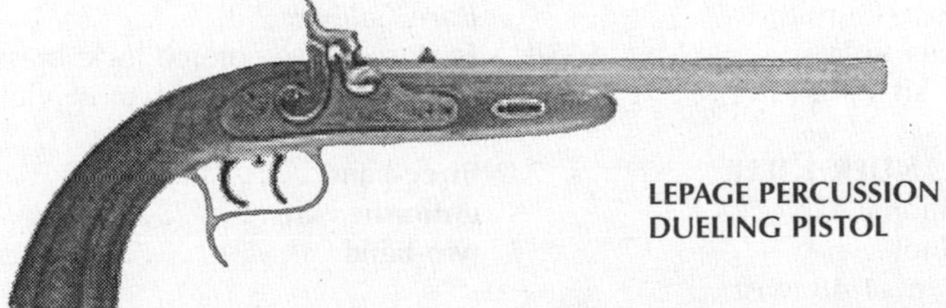

LEPAGE PERCUSSION
DUELING PISTOL

Screw Barrel Pistol

Lock: traditional caplock
Stock: hardwood
Barrel: 3 in.
Sights: none
Weight: 0.75lbs.
Bore/Caliber: .445
Features: barrel detaches for loading; folding trigger
Screw Barrel Pistol $115
unfinished kit $95

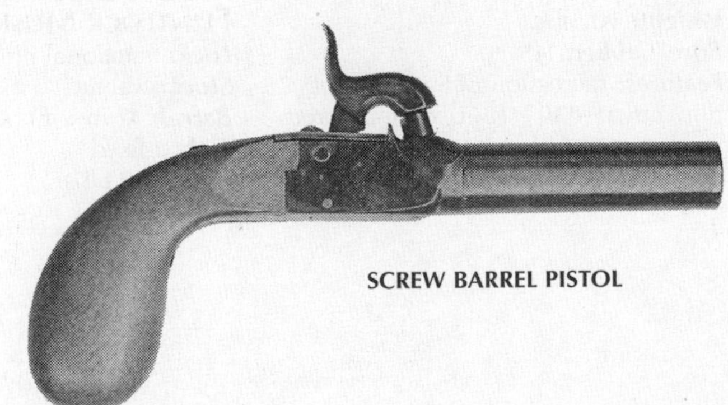

SCREW BARREL PISTOL

Dixie Blackpowder

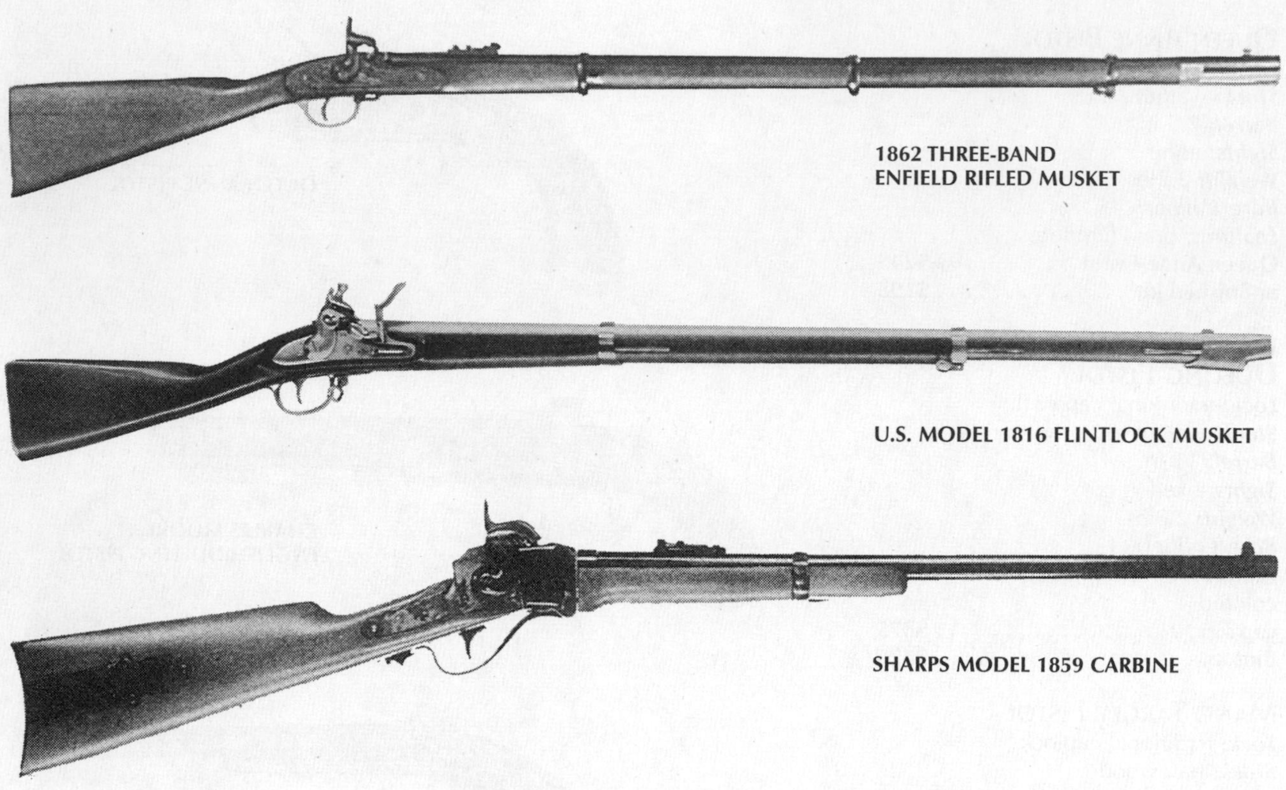

1862 THREE-BAND ENFIELD RIFLED MUSKET

U.S. MODEL 1816 FLINTLOCK MUSKET

SHARPS MODEL 1859 CARBINE

Pennsylvania Rifle

Lock: traditional cap or flint
Stock: walnut
Barrel: 41 in.
Sights: fixed
Weight: 8.0lbs.
Bore/Caliber: .45
Features: brass furniture
Pennsylvania Rifle $550
unfinished kit $450

Waadtlander Rifle

Lock: traditional caplock
Stock: walnut
Barrel: 31 in., 1;48 twist
Sights: aperture
Weight: 10.5lbs.
Bore/Caliber: .45
Features: recreation of Swiss Target rifle, circa 1839 - 1860, case-colored hardware, double set trigger
Waadtlander $1550

1862 Three-Band Enfield

Lock: traditional caplock
Stock: walnut
Barrel: 39 in.
Sights: fixed
Weight: 10.5lbs.
Bore/Caliber: .58
Features: case-colored lock, brass furniture; also 1858 two-band Enfield with 33 in. barrel
three-band $535
unfinished kit $495
two-band $525

Model U.S. 1816 Flintlock Musket

Lock: traditional flintlock
Stock: walnut
Barrel: 42 in. smoothbore
Sights: fixed
Weight: 9.8lbs.
Bore/Caliber: .69
Features: most common military flintlock from U.S. armories, complete with bayonet lug and swivels
Musket $825

Model 1859 Sharps Carbine

Lock: dropping block
Stock: walnut
Barrel: 22 in.
Sights: adjustable open
Weight: 7.8lbs.
Bore/Caliber: .54
Features: case-colored furniture, including saddle ring; also 1859 military rifle with 30-inch barrel (9 lbs.); both by Pedersoli
Sharps Carbine $815
with 30 in. barrel $965

EMF Hartford Blackpowder

1851 Sheriff's
Lock: caplock revolver
Stock: walnut
Barrel: 5 in.
Sights: none
Weight: 2.4lbs.
Bore/Caliber: .44
Features: brass guard, strap
1851 Sheriff's Model $140

1860 Army Revolver
Lock: caplock revolver
Stock: walnut
Barrel: 8 in.
Sights: fixed
Weight: 2.6lbs.
Bore/Caliber: .44
Features: case-colored frame, brass guard, strap
1860 Army $145

Hartford Model 1862 Police Revolver
Lock: caplock revolver
Stock: walnut
Barrel: 5.5 in.
Sights: fixed
Weight: 2.1lbs.
Bore/Caliber: .36
Features: 5-shot cylinder
1862 Police Revolver. $200

1851 Buntline Special
Lock: caplock revolver
Stock: walnut
Barrel: 12 in.
Sights: fixed
Weight: 3.4lbs.
Bore/Caliber: .44
Features: brass frame
1851 Buntline Special $165

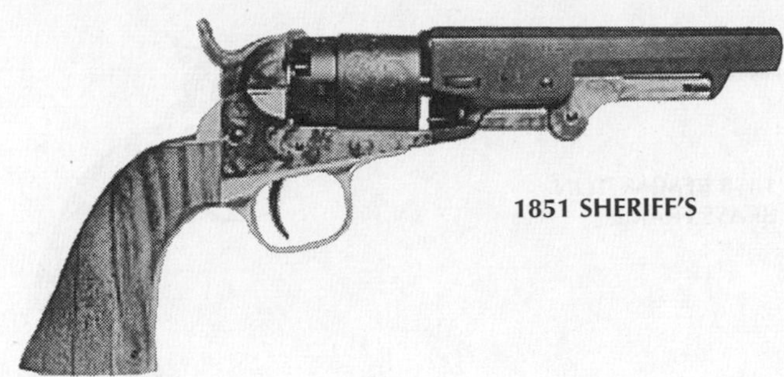
1851 SHERIFF'S

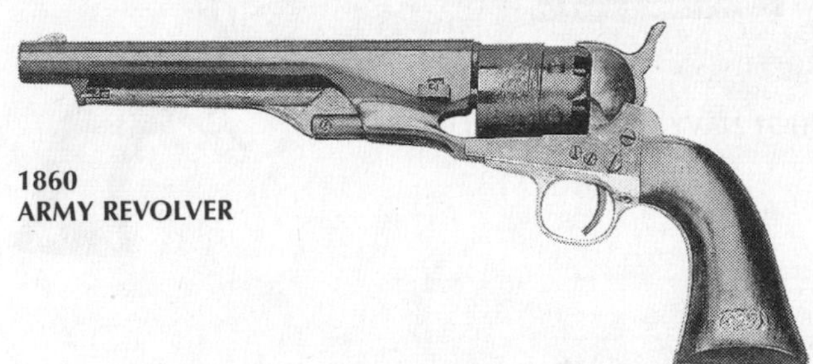
1860 ARMY REVOLVER

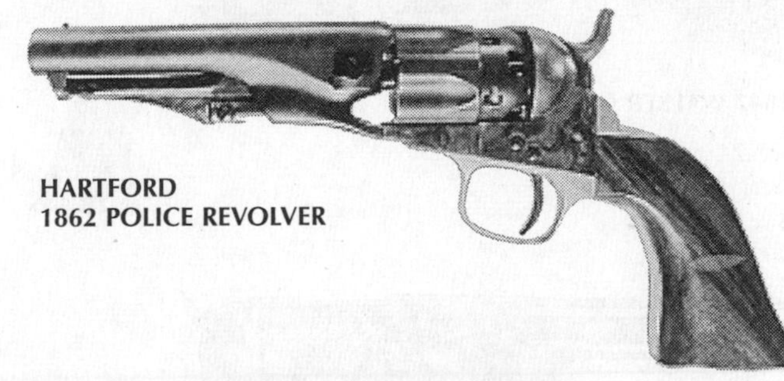
HARTFORD 1862 POLICE REVOLVER

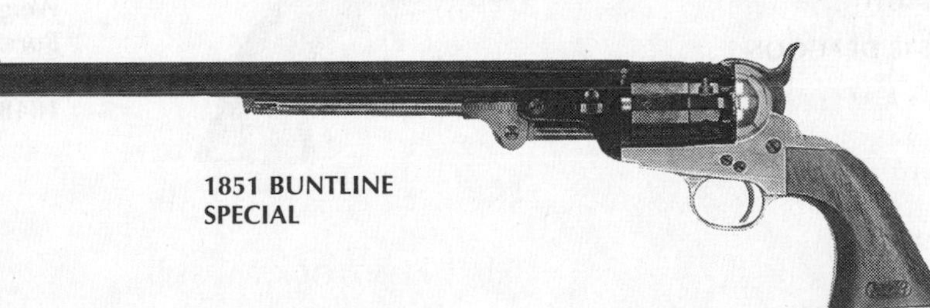
1851 BUNTLINE SPECIAL

BLACK POWDER

Conical lead bullets need fast-twist barrels: 1 turn in 28 inches. Patched balls typically shoot best with slow twist: 1 in 66. The popular compromise in many muzzleloaders: 1-in-48 twist.

EMF Hartford Blackpowder

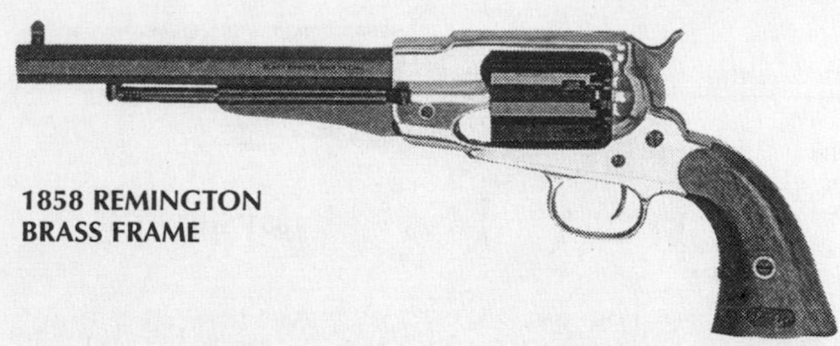

1858 REMINGTON
BRASS FRAME

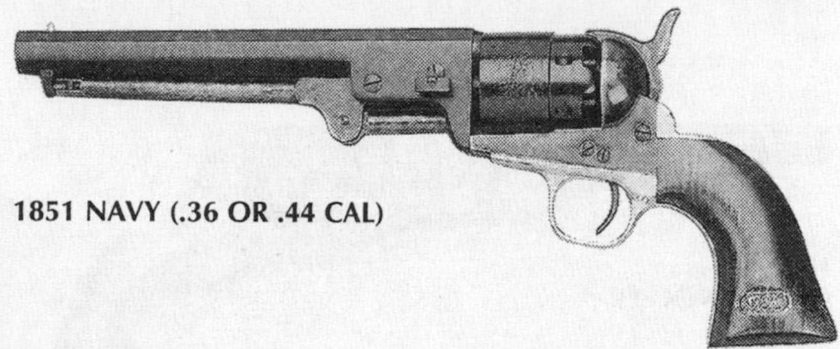

1851 NAVY (.36 OR .44 CAL)

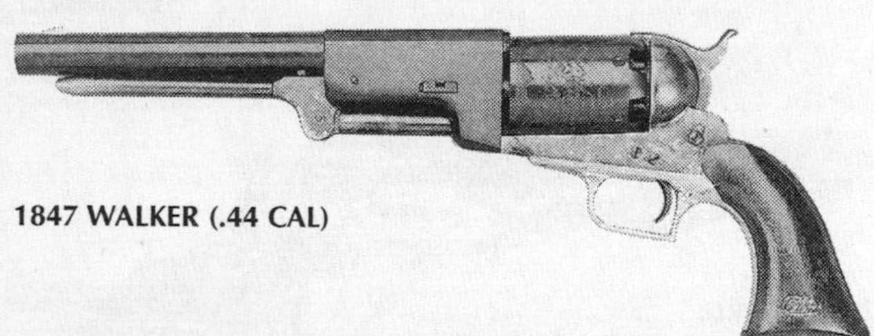

1847 WALKER (.44 CAL)

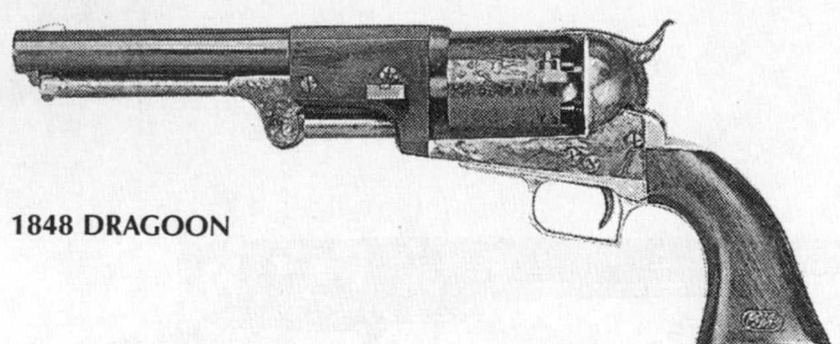

1848 DRAGOON

1858 Remington

Lock: caplock revolver
Stock: walnut
Barrel: 8 in.
Sights: fixed
Weight: 2.5lbs.
Bore/Caliber: .44
Features: brass or case-colored frame
brass.................... $180
case-colored............... $195

1851 Navy

Lock: caplock revolver
Stock: walnut
Barrel: 7.5 in.
Sights: fixed
Weight: 2.5lbs.
Bore/Caliber: .36 or .44
Features: brass frame
1851 Navy................ $150

1847 Walker

Lock: caplock revolver
Stock: walnut
Barrel: 9 in.
Sights: fixed
Weight: 4.6lbs.
Bore/Caliber: .44
Features: largest commercial Colt single-action, named after Texas Ranger
1847 Walker.............. $280

1848 Dragoon

Lock: caplock revolver
Stock: walnut
Barrel: 7.5 in.
Sights: fixed
Weight: 2.9lbs.
Bore/Caliber: .44
Features: case-colored frame
1848 Dragoon............. $260

Be sure you check state game regulations before buying an in-line muzzleloader or scoping your smokepole. Some states insist that "primitive weapons" be primitive!

Euroarms of America Blackpowder

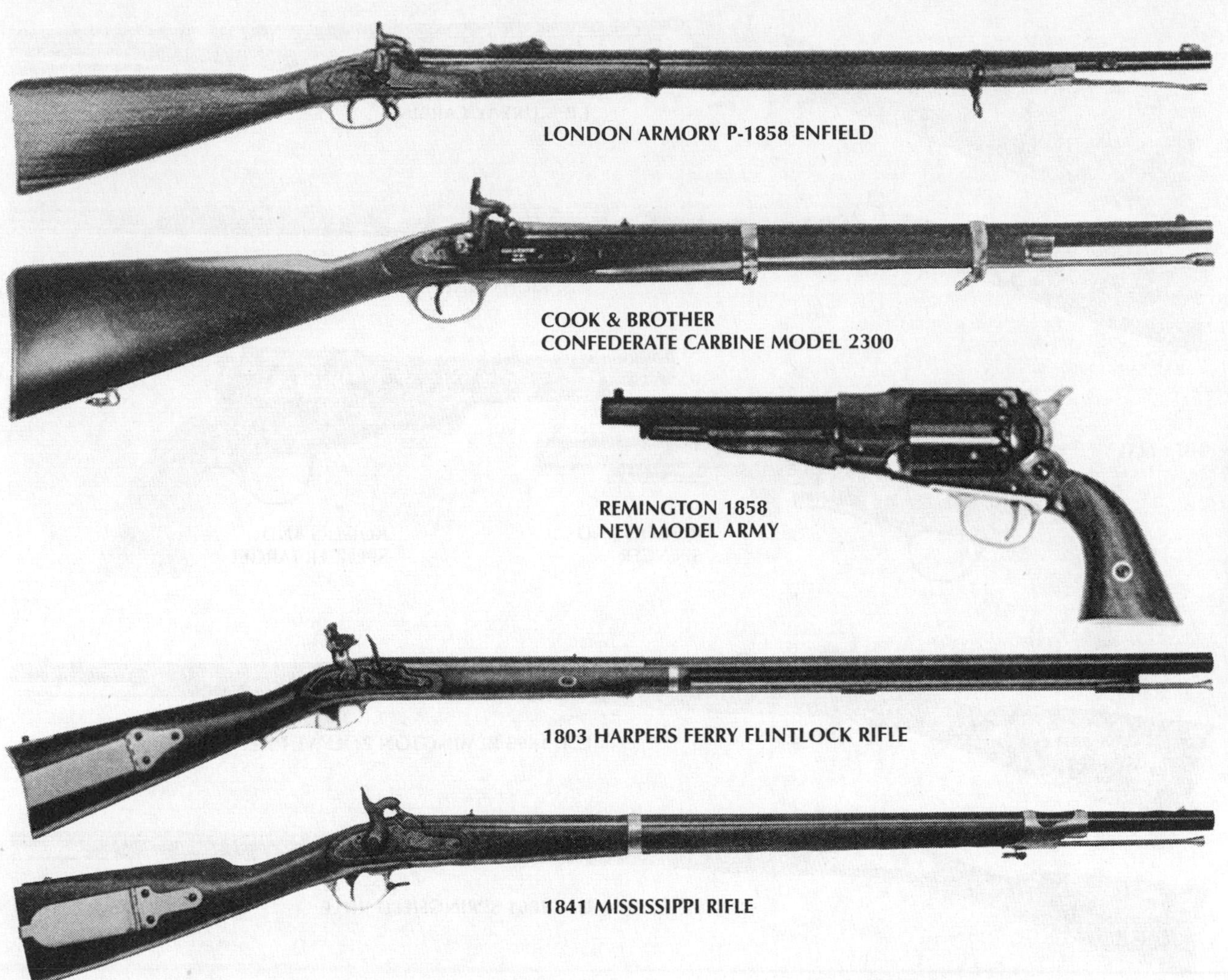
LONDON ARMORY P-1858 ENFIELD

COOK & BROTHER
CONFEDERATE CARBINE MODEL 2300

REMINGTON 1858
NEW MODEL ARMY

1803 HARPERS FERRY FLINTLOCK RIFLE

1841 MISSISSIPPI RIFLE

London Armory P1858 Enfield

Lock: traditional caplock
Stock: walnut
Barrel: 33 in.
Sights: adjustable open
Weight: 8.8lbs.
Bore/Caliber: .58
Features: steel ramrod, 2-band
P1858 Enfield $470

Cook & Brother Confederate

Lock: traditional caplock
Stock: walnut
Barrel: 24 in.
Sights: fixed
Weight: 7.9lbs.
Bore/Caliber: .577
Features: carbine; also rifle with 33 in. barrel
carbine $447
rifle $480

Remington 1858 New Model Army

Lock: caplock revolver
Stock: walnut
Barrel: 8 in.
Sights: fixed
Weight: 2.5lbs.
Bore/Caliber: .44
Features: brass guard; also engraved version
New Model Army $200
engraved.................. $275

1803 Harper's Ferry Flintlock

Lock: traditional flintlock
Stock: walnut
Barrel: 35 in.
Sights: fixed
Weight: 10.0lbs.
Bore/Caliber: .54
Features: half-stock, browned steel
1803 Harper's Ferry $640

1841 Mississippi Rifle

Lock: traditional caplock
Stock: walnut
Barrel: 33 in.
Sights: fixed
Weight: 9.5lbs.
Bore/Caliber: .54 or .58
Features: brass furniture
1841 Mississippi $500

Euroarms of America Blackpowder

J.P. Murray Carbine

Lock: traditional caplock
Stock: walnut
Barrel: 23 in.
Sights: fixed
Weight: 7.5lbs.
Bore/Caliber: .58
Features: brass furniture, replica of rare Confederate Cavalry Carbine
J.P. Murray Carbine $453

C.S. Richmond Musket

Lock: traditional caplock
Stock: walnut
Barrel: 40 in.
Sights: fixed
Weight: 9.0lbs.
Bore/Caliber: .58
Features: 3-band furniture, swivels
C.S. Richmond Musket $530

Rogers and Spencer

Lock: caplock revolver
Stock: walnut
Barrel: 7.5 in.
Sights: fixed
Weight: 2.9lbs.
Bore/Caliber: .44
Features: recommended ball diameter .451; also target model with adjustable sight
Rogers and Spencer. $227
with London gray finish. $245
Target $239

U.S. 1841 Mississippi Rifle

Lock: traditional caplock
Stock: walnut
Barrel: 33 in.
Sights: fixed
Weight: 9.5lbs.
Bore/Caliber: .54 or .58
Features: brass furniture; also 1863 Remington Zouave rifle
Mississippi $500
Zouave $430

U.S. 1861 Springfield

Lock: traditional caplock
Stock: walnut
Barrel: 40 in.
Sights: fixed
Weight: 10.0lbs.
Bore/Caliber: .58
Features: sling swivels; also London P-1852 rifled musket, London Enfield P-1861 (7.5 lbs.)
Springfield $530
1852 rifled musket $480
1861 London Enfield $415

Gonic Blackpowder

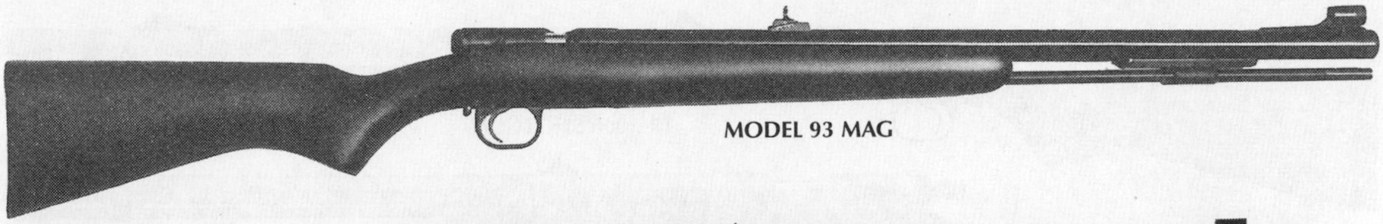

MODEL 93 MAG

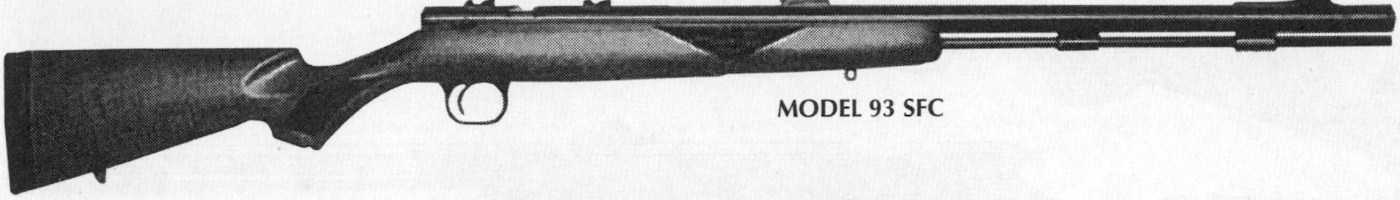

MODEL 93 SFC

STANDARD

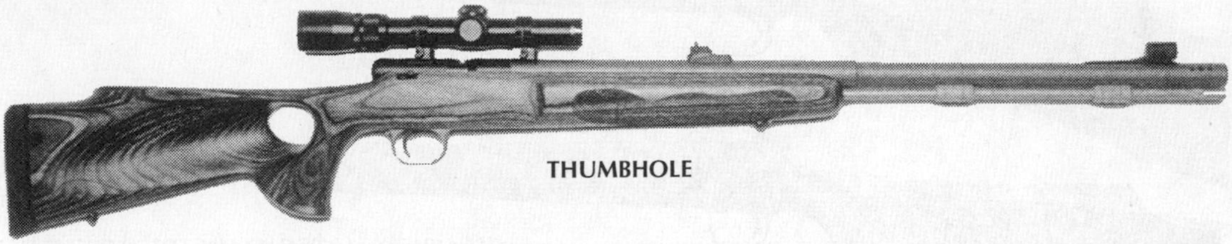

THUMBHOLE

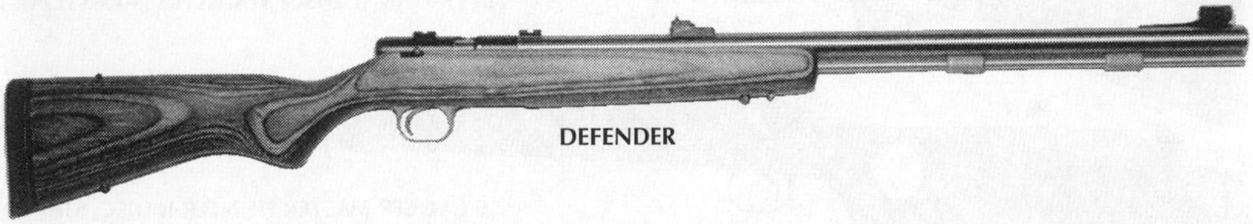

DEFENDER

Model 93

Lock: in-line
Stock: laminated or synthetic, pillar bedded
Barrel: 26 in. stainless, 1:24 twist
Sights: adjustable open
Weight: 7.0lbs.
Bore/Caliber: .50
Features: various stock configurations, including thumbhole; scope mounting provisions
Model 93 . . . . $999

Traditional #11 percussion caps are being replaced with musket caps and #209 shotshell primers because these options are "hotter" and provide surer ignition in guns that accept them.

Knight Blackpowder

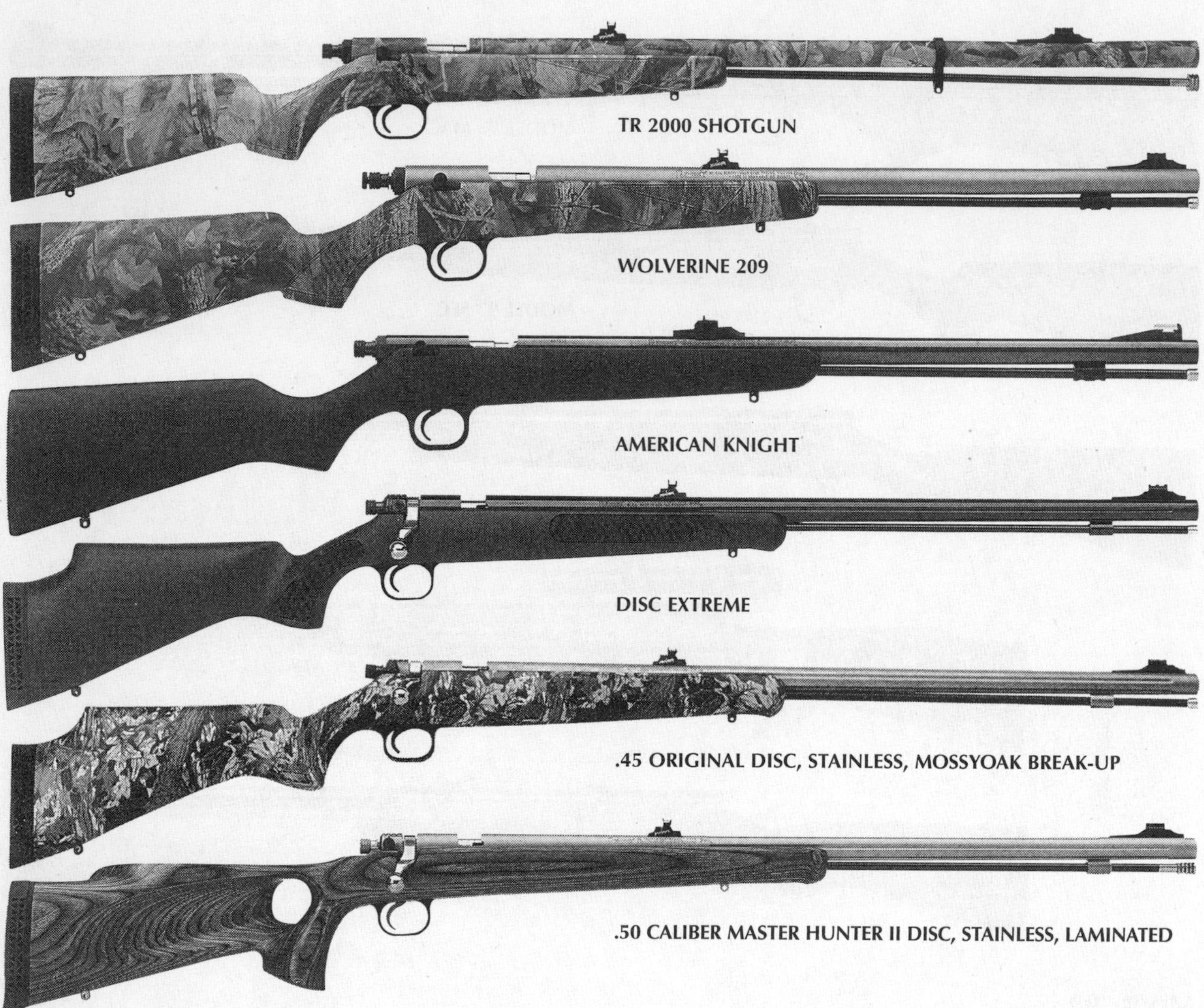
TR 2000 SHOTGUN
WOLVERINE 209
AMERICAN KNIGHT
DISC EXTREME
.45 ORIGINAL DISC, STAINLESS, MOSSYOAK BREAK-UP
.50 CALIBER MASTER HUNTER II DISC, STAINLESS, LAMINATED

BLACK POWDER

Model TR 2000 Shotgun

Lock: in-line
Stock: synthetic or camo
Barrel: 26 in.
Sights: fiber optic
Weight: 7.6lbs.
Bore/Caliber: 12 ga.
Features: adjustable trigger, screw-in choke tubes; uses 209 primers
synthetic $350
camo $400

Wolverine 209

Lock: in-line
Stock: synthetic or camo
Barrel: 22 in., 1:28 twist
Sights: fiber optic
Weight: 7.0lbs.
Bore/Caliber: .50
Features: Full Plastic Jacket ignition
Wolverine $336

American Knight

Lock: in-line
Stock: synthetic
Barrel: 22 in., 1:28 twist
Sights: fiber optic
Weight: 6.2lbs.
Bore/Caliber: .50
Features: basic Knight hunting rifle
American Knight $200

DISC Extreme

Lock: in-line
Stock: walnut or synthetic thumbhole
Barrel: 26 in., 1:28 twist air-gauged Green Mtn.
Sights: fiber optic
Weight: 7.3lbs.
Bore/Caliber: .45 or .50
Features: Full Plastic Jacket ignition, blue or stainless, adjustable trigger; also original DISC rifle with 1:20 twist (8.2 lbs.)
Extreme, walnut $550
blue/synthetic $460
blue/camo $510
stainless/synthetic $530
stainless/camo $580

Master Hunter II DISC

Lock: in-line
Stock: laminated thumbhole or synthetic
Barrel: 26 in., 1:28 twist
Sights: fiber optic
Weight: 7.5lbs.
Bore/Caliber: .45 or .50
Features: adjustable trigger, top of Knight line
Master Hunter II $1100

Lenartz Backpowder

MODEL RDI-50

Model RDI-5
Lock: in-line
Stock: walnut
Barrel: 26 in., 1:28 twist
Sights: adjustable open
Weight: 7.5lbs.
Bore/Caliber: .50
Features: adjustable trigger; uses 209 primers, converts to #11
RDI-5 . . . . price on request

Lyman Blackpowder

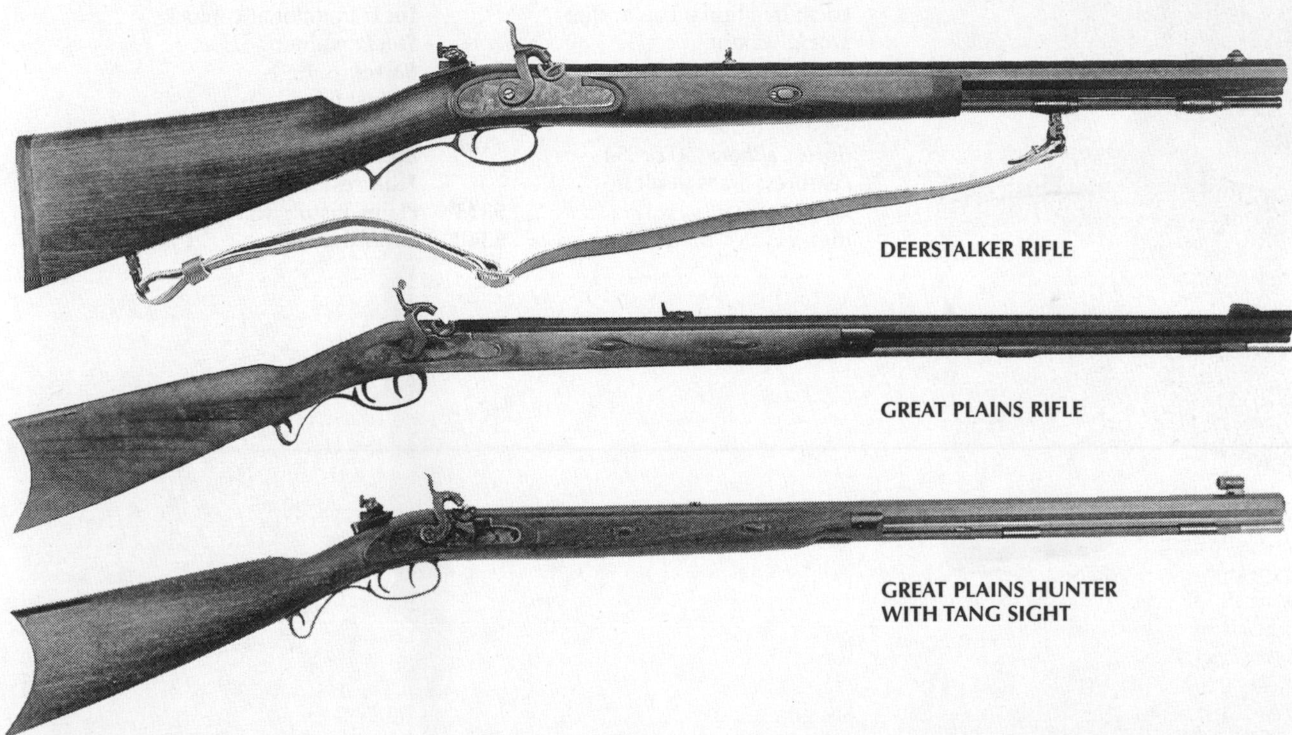

DEERSTALKER RIFLE

GREAT PLAINS RIFLE

GREAT PLAINS HUNTER WITH TANG SIGHT

Deerstalker
Lock: traditional cap or flint
Stock: walnut
Barrel: 24 in.
Sights: aperture
Weight: 7.5lbs.
Bore/Caliber: .50 or .54
Features: left-hand models available
caplock $305
left-hand $330
stainless caplock $395
flintlock. $350
left-hand $360

Great Plains Rifle
Lock: traditional cap or flint
Stock: walnut
Barrel: 32 in., 1:66 twist
Sights: adjustable open
Weight: 8.0lbs.
Bore/Caliber: .50 or .54
Features: double set triggers, left-hand models available; also Great Plains Hunter with 1:32 twist
caplock $475
unfinished kit. $365
flintlock. $500
unfinished kit $390

Lyman Blackpowder

LYMAN TRADE RIFLE

PLAINS PISTOL

BLACK POWDER

LYMAN TRADE RIFLE

Lock: traditional cap or flint
Stock: walnut
Barrel: 28 in., 1:48 twist
Sights: adjustable open
Weight: 8.0lbs.
Bore/Caliber: .50 or .54
Features: brass furniture
Lyman $315
flint $340

PLAINS PISTOL

Lock: traditional caplock
Stock: walnut
Barrel: 6 in.
Sights: fixed
Weight: 2.2lbs.
Bore/Caliber: .50 or .54
Features: iron furniture
Plains Pistol $245
unfinished kit $195

When you seat a ball or bullet, make sure it's in contact with the powder. Let the ramrod drop a few inches onto the charge. If it bounces, the ball or bullet is probably seated properly.

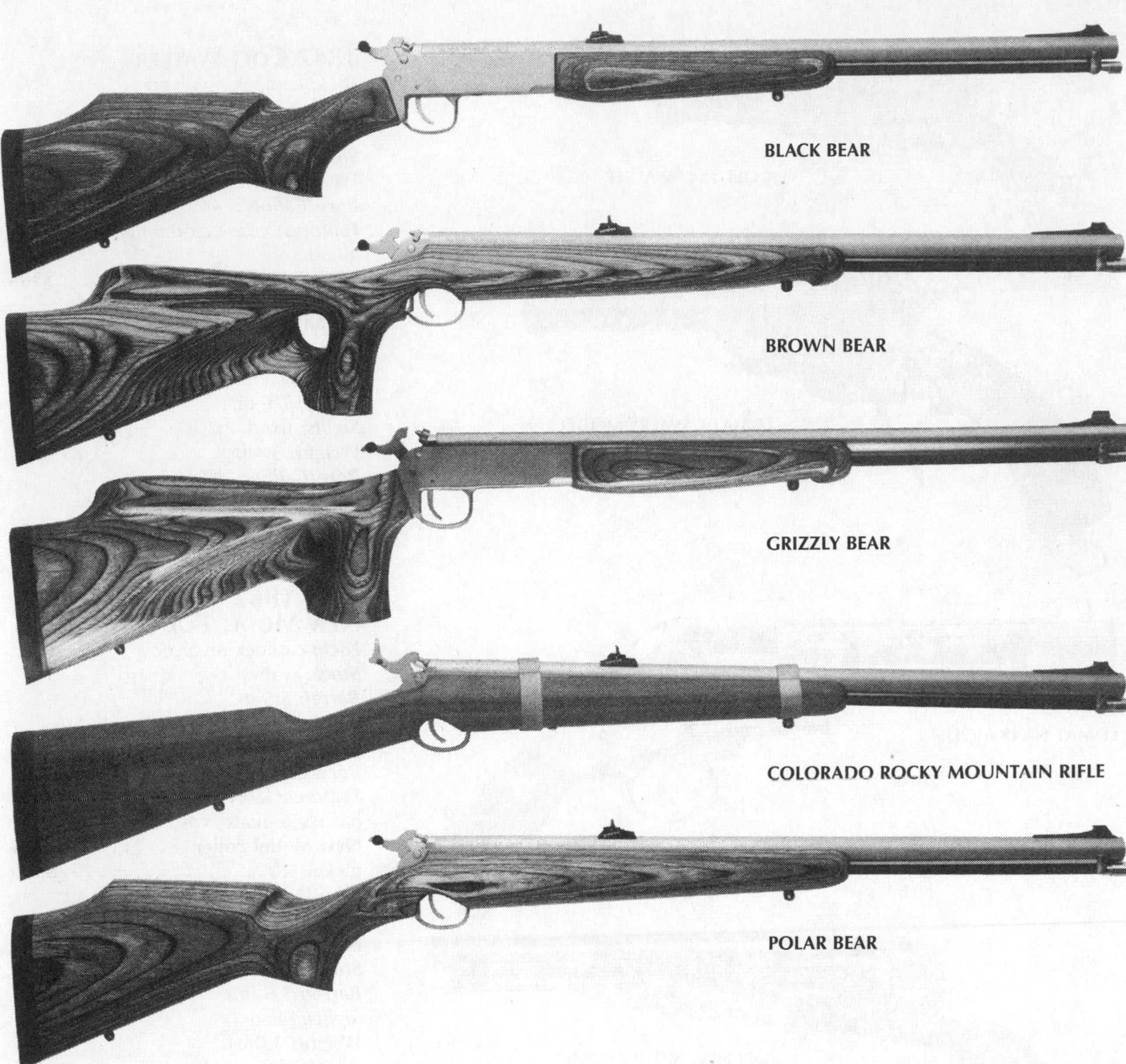

BLACK BEAR

BROWN BEAR

GRIZZLY BEAR

COLORADO ROCKY MOUNTAIN RIFLE

POLAR BEAR

Black Bear

Lock: in-line
Stock: two-piece laminated
Barrel: 24 in., 1:26 twist
Sights: adjustable open
Weight: 6.5lbs.
Bore/Caliber: .36, .45, .50, .54
Features: also Grizzly Bear with thumbhole stock, Brown Bear with one-piece thumbhole stock, both checkered, aluminum ramrod

Black Bear, blue $537
stainless $553
camo $557
camo stainless $573
Brown Bear $659
stainless $676
camo stainless $698
Grizzly Bear $643
stainless $665
camo stainless $684

Colorado Rocky Mountain Rifle

Lock: in-line
Stock: walnut, laminated
Barrel: 24 in., 1:26 twist
Sights: adjustable open
Weight: 7.0lbs.
Bore/Caliber: .36, .45, .50, .54
Features: #11 or magnum ignition

Rocky Mountain Rifle $549
stainless $567

Polar Bear

Lock: in-line
Stock: laminated
Barrel: 24 in., 1:26 twist
Sights: adjustable open
Weight: 7.8lbs.
Bore/Caliber: .36, .45, .50, .54
Features: one-piece stock

from $540

Navy Arms Blackpowder Handguns

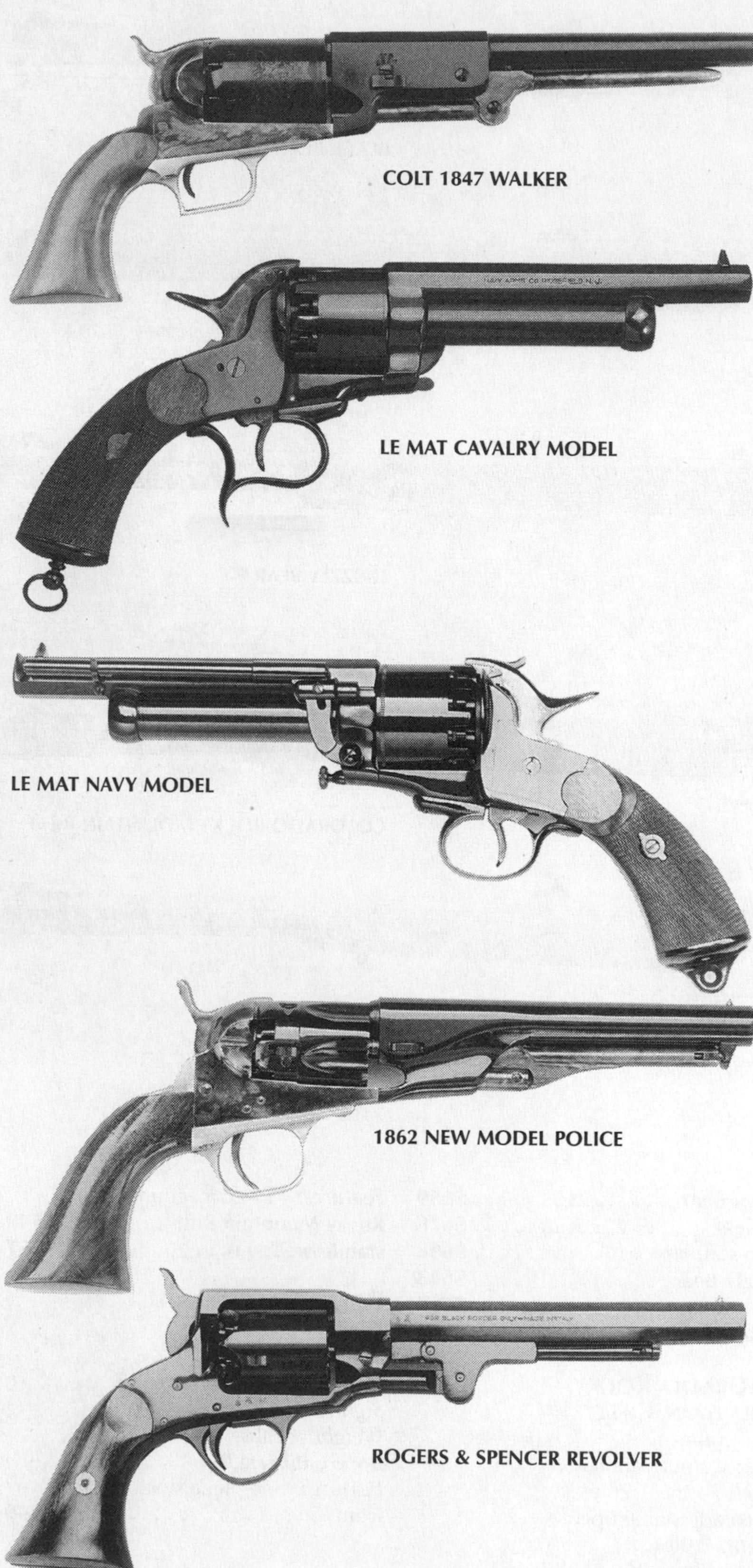

COLT 1847 WALKER

LE MAT CAVALRY MODEL

LE MAT NAVY MODEL

1862 NEW MODEL POLICE

ROGERS & SPENCER REVOLVER

BLACK POWDER

1847 Colt Walker

Lock: caplock revolver
Stock: walnut
Barrel: 9 in.
Sights: fixed
Weight: 4.5lbs.
Bore/Caliber: .44
Features: case-colored frame, brass guard
1847 Colt Walker $304

Le Mat Calvary Model

Lock: caplock revolver
Stock: walnut
Barrel: 7.6 in.
Sights: fixed
Weight: 3.4lbs.
Bore/Caliber: .44
Features: 9-shot cylinder; Navy, Cavalry, Army models available
Le Mat $685

Colt 1862 New Model Police

Lock: caplock revolver
Stock: walnut
Barrel: 5.5 in.
Sights: fixed
Weight: 2.7lbs.
Bore/Caliber: .36
Features: last of the percussion Colts, has brass guard, case-colored frame
New Model Police $324
nickel $309

Rogers and Spencer

Lock: caplock revolver
Stock: walnut
Barrel: 7.5 in.
Sights: fixed
Weight: 3.0lbs.
Bore/Caliber: .44
Features: octagonal barrel, 6-shot cylinder
Rogers and Spencer $271

Navy Arms Blackpowder Handguns

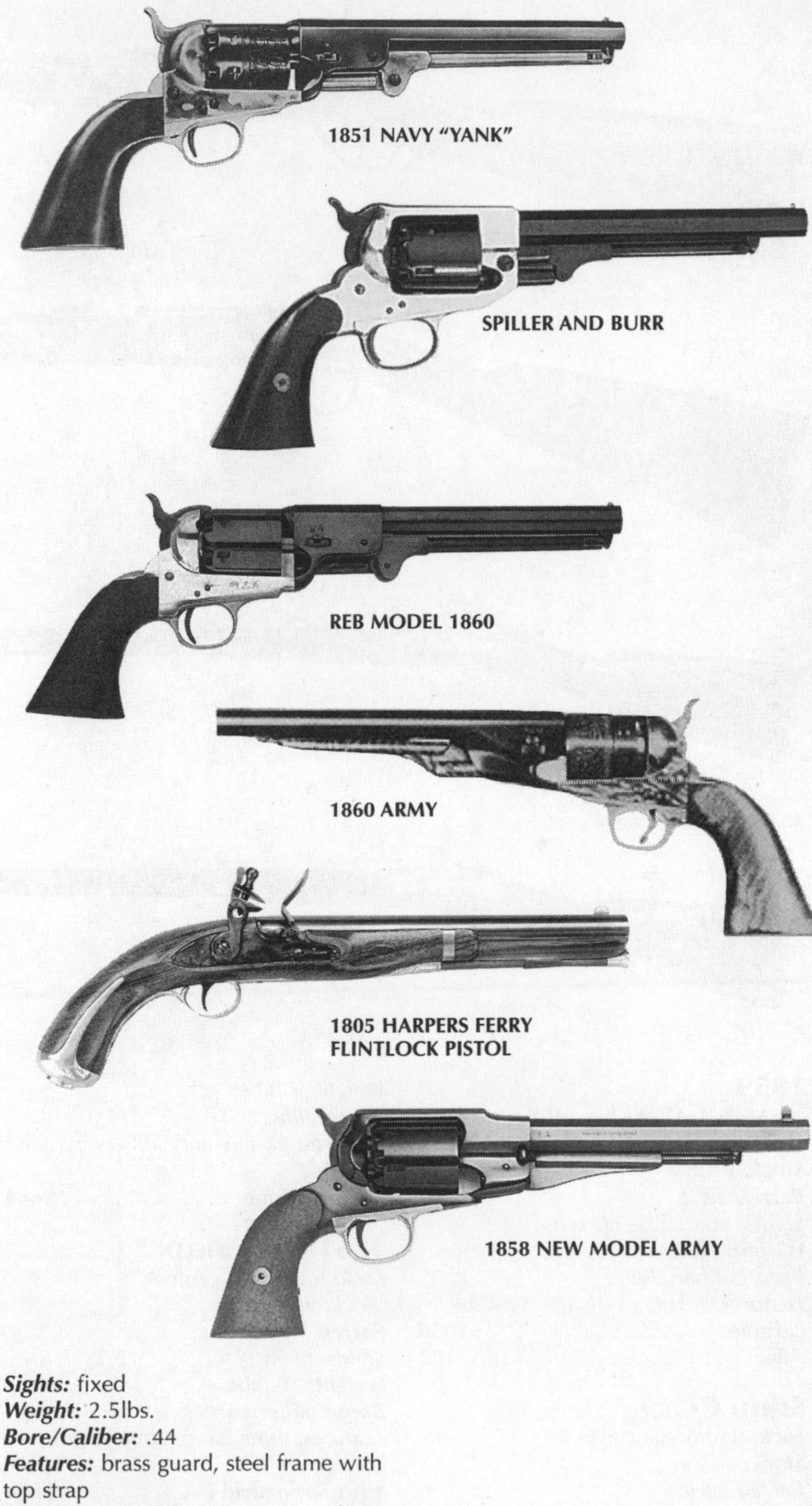
1851 NAVY "YANK"
SPILLER AND BURR
REB MODEL 1860
1860 ARMY
1805 HARPERS FERRY FLINTLOCK PISTOL
1858 NEW MODEL ARMY

1851 Navy
Lock: caplock revolver
Stock: walnut
Barrel: 7.5 in.
Sights: fixed
Weight: 2.7lbs.
Bore/Caliber: .36 and .44
Features: brass guard and strap
1851 Navy $170

Spiller and Burr
Lock: caplock revolver
Stock: walnut
Barrel: 7 in.
Sights: fixed
Weight: 2.6lbs.
Bore/Caliber: .36
Features: brass frame
Spiller and Burr $160

1860 Reb
Lock: caplock revolver
Stock: walnut
Barrel: 7.3 in.
Sights: fixed
Weight: 2.6lbs.
Bore/Caliber: .36 and .44
Features: brass frame; also Sheriff's Model with 5 in. barrel
1860 Reb $124

1860 Army
Lock: caplock revolver
Stock: walnut
Barrel: 8 in.
Sights: fixed
Weight: 2.6lbs.
Bore/Caliber: .44
Features: brass guard, steel backstrap
1860 Army $196

Harper's Ferry Flintlock Pistol
Lock: traditional flintlock
Stock: walnut
Barrel: 10 in.
Sights: fixed
Weight: 2.6lbs.
Bore/Caliber: .58
Features: case-colored lock, brass furniture, browned barrel
Harper's Ferry $355

1858 New Model Army Remington
Lock: caplock revolver
Stock: walnut
Barrel: 8 in.
Sights: fixed
Weight: 2.5lbs.
Bore/Caliber: .44
Features: brass guard, steel frame with top strap
1858 New Model Army Rem. . . $185
with brass frame $139
stainless $299

BLACK POWDER

Navy Arms Blackpowder Rifles

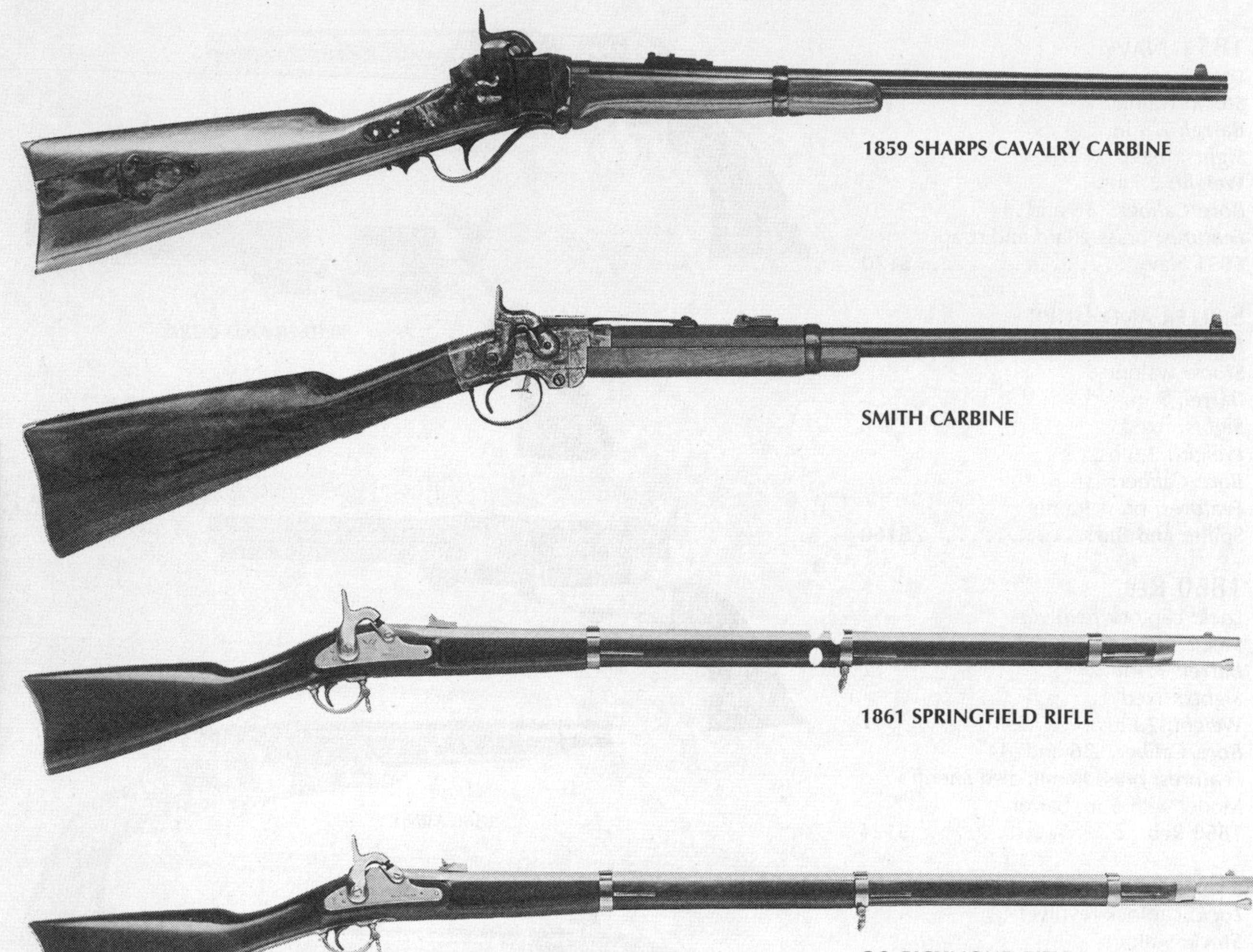

1859 Sharps Cavalry Carbine

Lock: traditional caplock
Stock: walnut
Barrel: 22 in.
Sights: adjustable open
Weight: 7.8lbs.
Bore/Caliber: .54
Features: infantry rifle also available
carbine **$1030**
rifle **$1133**

Smith Carbine

Lock: traditional caplock
Stock: walnut
Barrel: 22 in.
Sights: adjustable open
Weight: 7.8lbs.
Bore/Caliber: .50
Features: cavalry and artillery models available
Smith Carbine **$664**

1861 Springfield

Lock: traditional caplock
Stock: walnut
Barrel: 40 in.
Sights: fixed
Weight: 10.0lbs.
Bore/Caliber: .58
Features: three-band furniture polished bright
1861 Springfield **$608**

C.S. Richmond Rifle

Lock: traditional caplock
Stock: walnut
Barrel: 40 in.
Sights: fixed
Weight: 10.0lbs.
Bore/Caliber: .58
Features: polished furniture
C.S. Richmond **$608**

Navy Arms Blackpowder Rifles

PARKER-HALE 1858 ENFIELD RIFLE

PARKER-HALE MUSKETOON

BROWN BESS MUSKET

1803 HARPERS FERRY RIFLE

BERDAN 1859 SHARPS RIFLE

BLACK POWDER

Parker-Hale 1858 Enfield Rifle

Lock: traditional caplock
Stock: walnut
Barrel: 33 in.
Sights: adjustable open
Weight: 9.6lbs.
Bore/Caliber: .58
Features: brass furniture
Parker-Hale Enfield $618

Parker-Hale Musketoon

Lock: traditional caplock
Stock: walnut
Barrel: 24 in.
Sights: adjustable open
Weight: 7.5lbs.
Bore/Caliber: .58
Features: brass furniture
Parker-Hale Musketoon $530

Brown Bess Musket

Lock: traditional flintlock
Stock: walnut
Barrel: 42 in.
Sights: fixed
Weight: 9.5lbs.
Bore/Caliber: .75
Features: full stock without bands
Brown Bess Musket $922

1803 Harper's Ferry Rifle

Lock: traditional flintlock
Stock: walnut
Barrel: 35 in.
Sights: fixed
Weight: 8.5lbs.
Bore/Caliber: .54
Features: case-colored lock, brass patch box
1803 Harper's Ferry $695

Berdan 1859 Sharps Rifle

Lock: traditional caplock
Stock: walnut
Barrel: 30 in.
Sights: adjustable open
Weight: 8.5lbs.
Bore/Caliber: .54
Features: case-colored receiver, double set trigger
Berdan 1859 Sharps $1200

Pedersoli Blackpowder

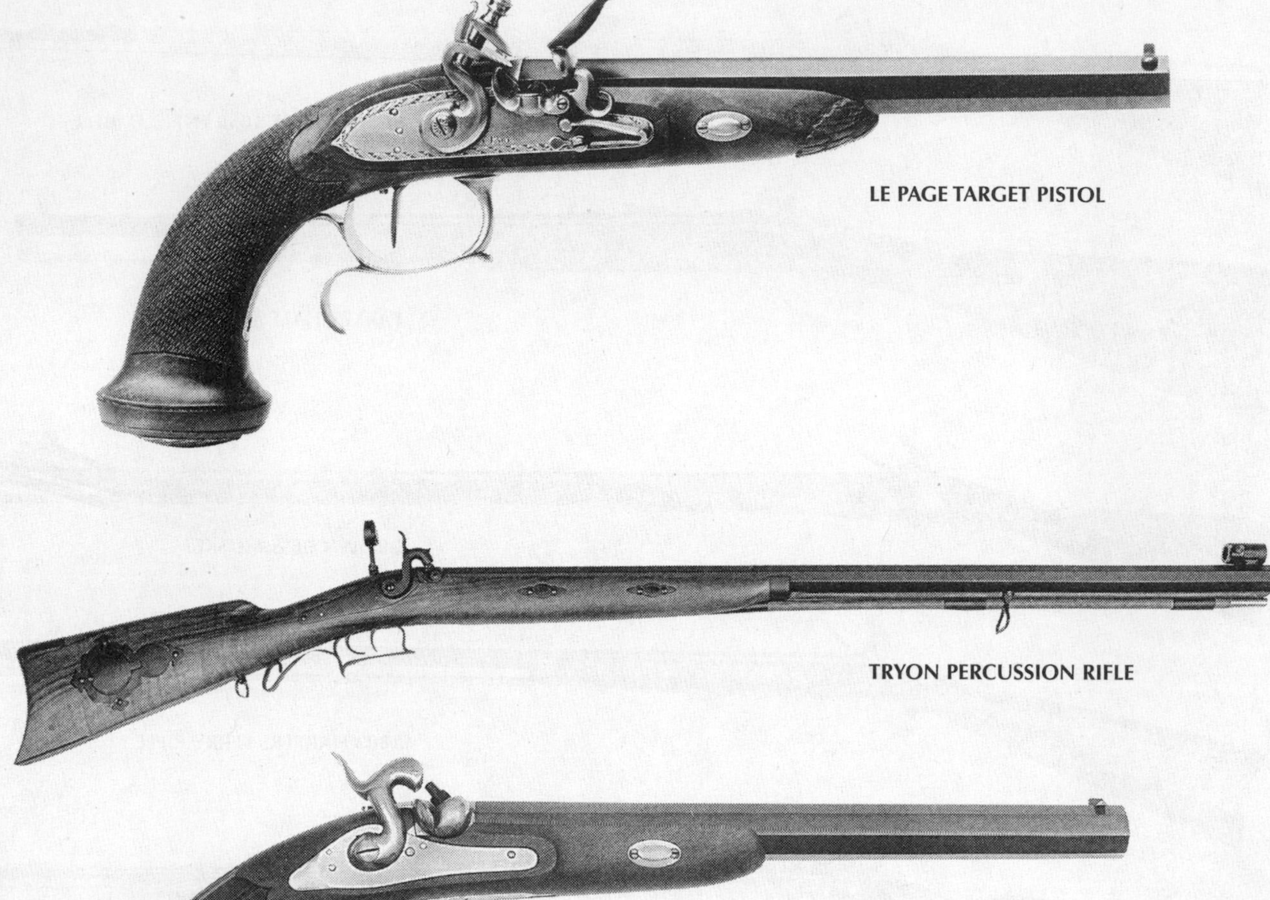

LE PAGE TARGET PISTOL

TRYON PERCUSSION RIFLE

MANG IN GRAZ

LePage Target Pistol

Lock: traditional flintlock
Stock: walnut
Barrel: 10.5 in., 1:18 twist
Sights: fixed
Weight: 2.5lbs.
Bore/Caliber: .44 or .45
Features: smoothbore .45 available
LePage $780
caplock in .36, .38, .44. . . . . $675

"Mang in Graz"

Lock: traditional caplock
Stock: walnut
Barrel: 11 in., 1:15 or 1:18 (.44) twist
Sights: fixed
Weight: 2.5lbs.
Bore/Caliber: .38 or .44
Features: grooved butt
Price:. $1095

Mortimer Target Rifle

Lock: flintlock
Stock: English-style European walnut
Barrel: octagon to round 36 in.
Sights: target
Weight: 8.8lbs.
Bore/Caliber: .54
Features: case-colored lock; stock has cheekpiece and hand checkering; 7-groove barrel
Mortimer Target $1075

Tryon-Percussion Rifle

Lock: traditional caplock
Stock: walnut
Barrel: 32 in., 1:48 or 1:66 (.54) twist
Sights: adjustable open
Weight: 9.5lbs.
Bore/Caliber: .45, .50, .54
Features: Creedmoor version with aperture sight available
Tyron-Percussion $650
Creedmoor $960

Remington Arms Blackpowder

MODEL 700 BLACKPOWDER

MODEL 700 MLS STAINLESS

BLACK POWDER

Model 700 Black Powder

Lock: in-line
Stock: synthetic
Barrel: 24 in.
Sights: open
Weight: 7.5lbs.
Bore/Caliber: .45, .50
Features: 1:28 twist, full set of nipples and loading and maintenance accessories included; also: magnum version with stainless 26 in. barrel
700 Black Powder . . price on request

When hunting with a traditional caplock blackpowder rifle in cold or wet weather, you can decrease the chance of a misfire by seating the percussion cap carefully and sealing it around the flange with a light coating of beeswax or bowstring wax.

Ruger Blackpowder

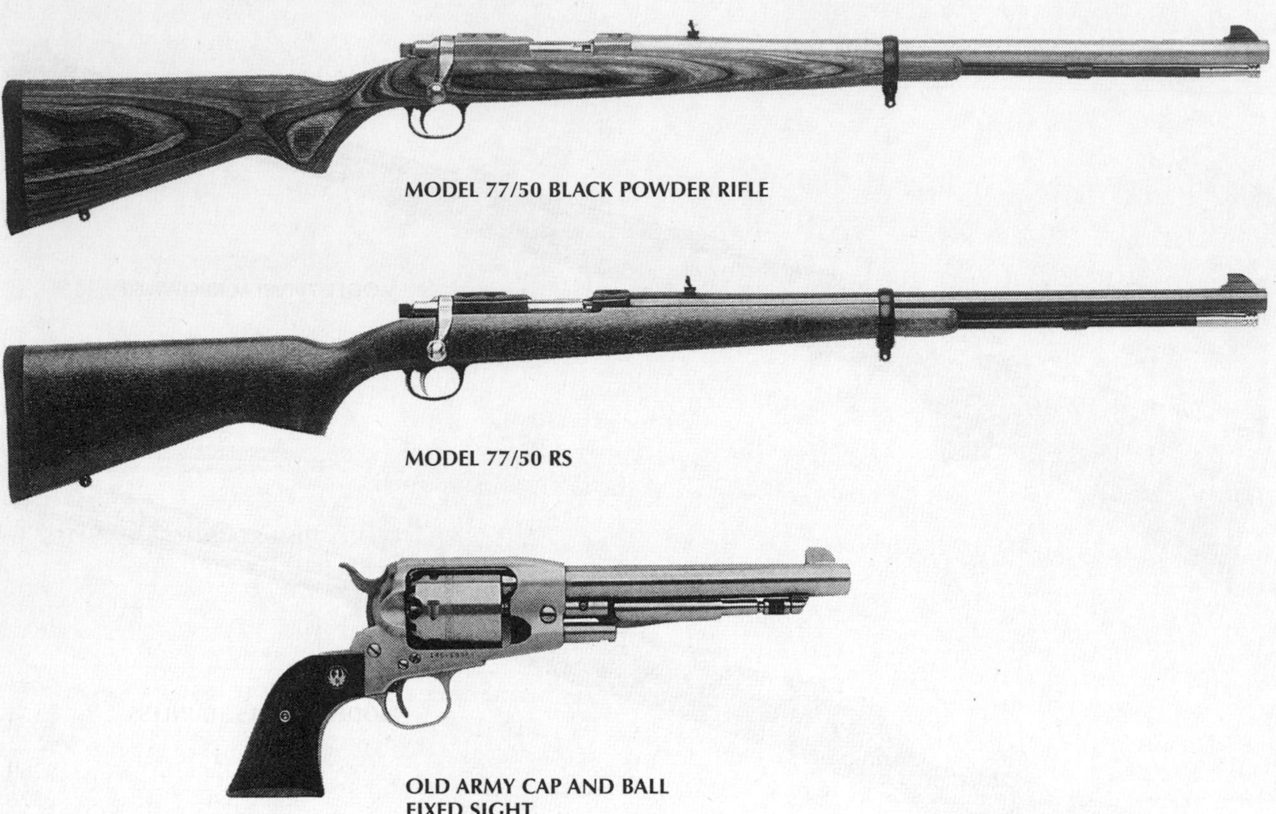

MODEL 77/50 BLACK POWDER RIFLE

MODEL 77/50 RS

OLD ARMY CAP AND BALL
FIXED SIGHT

Model 77/50 Black Powder Rifle

Lock: in-line
Stock: synthetic or laminated
Barrel: 22 in., 1:28 twist
Sights: folding leaf
Weight: 6.5lbs.
Bore/Caliber: .50
Features: comes with 1-inch scope rings
hardwood blue $434
walnut blue. $555
stainless synthetic $580
stainless laminated $601

Old Army Cap and Ball

Lock: caplock revolver
Stock: walnut
Barrel: 5.5 or 7.5 in.
Sights: fixed
Weight: 2.9lbs.
Bore/Caliber: .45
Features: Civil War-era reproduction in modern steel, music wire springs
blue $499
stainless $535

Whether you hunt with a traditional flintlock or caplock rifle, always remember to carry some kind of vent pick. A fouled touchhole or percussion cone can block a successful shot.

Savage Blackpowder

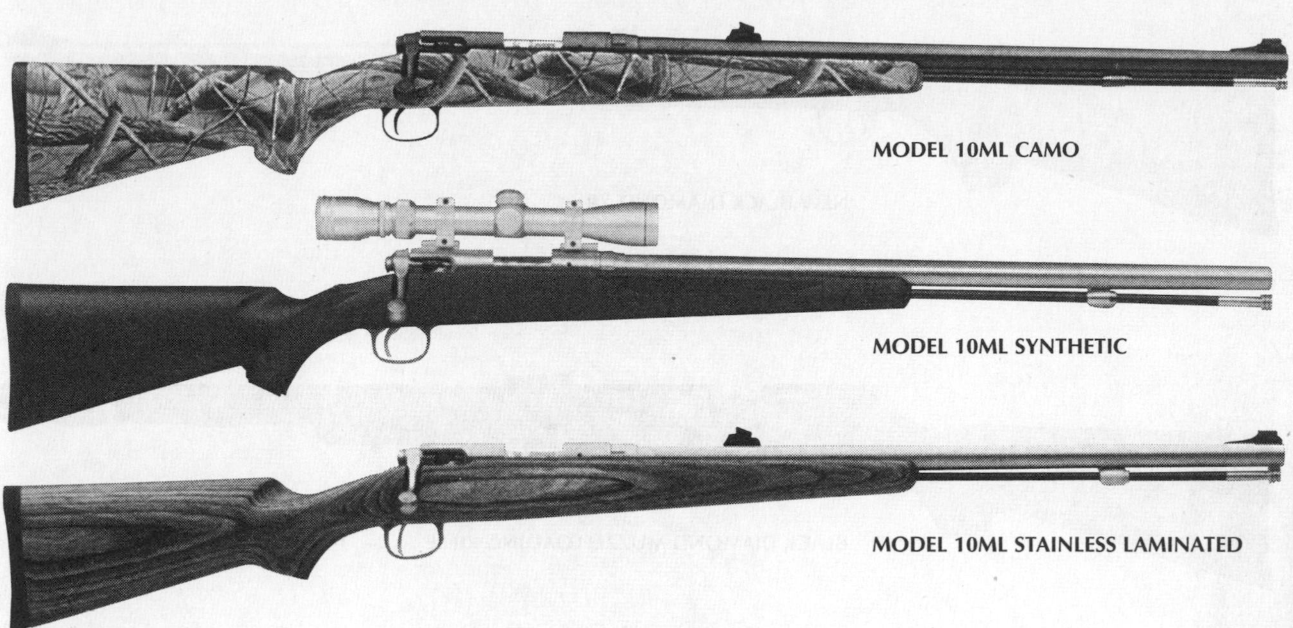

MODEL 10ML CAMO

MODEL 10ML SYNTHETIC

MODEL 10ML STAINLESS LAMINATED

BLACK POWDER

Model M10ML Muzzleloader

Lock: in-line
Stock: synthetic, camo or laminated
Barrel: 24 in.
Sights: adjustable fiber optic
Weight: 8.0lbs.
Bore/Caliber: .50
Features: bolt action mechanism, 209 priming

blue synthetic $496
stainless $554
blue camo. $533
stainless camo. $589
stainless laminated $626

Shiloh Blackpowder

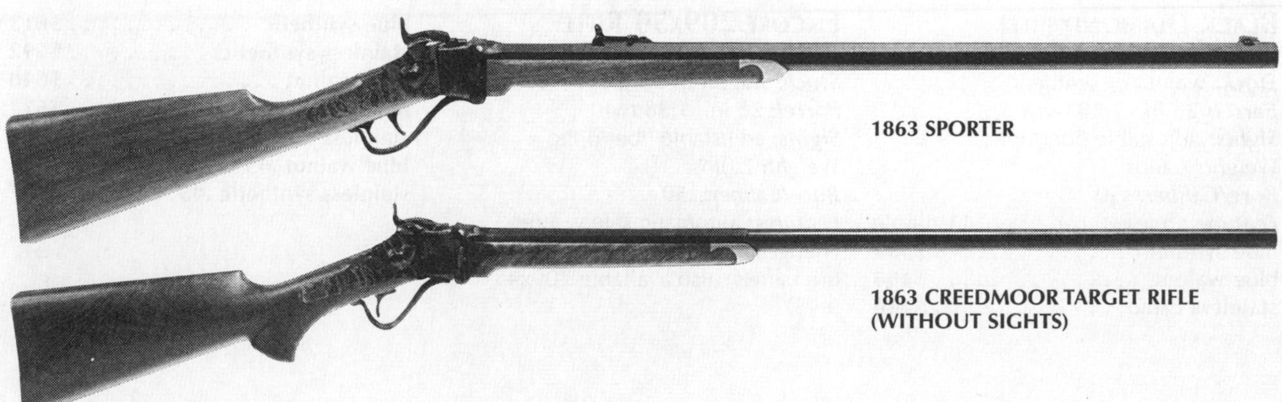

1863 SPORTER

1863 CREEDMOOR TARGET RIFLE (WITHOUT SIGHTS)

Model 1863 Sharps

Lock: traditional caplock
Stock: walnut
Barrel: 30 in.
Sights: adjustable open
Weight: 9.5lbs.
Bore/Caliber: .50 or .54
Features: sporting model with half-stock, double set trigger military model with 3-band full stock; also carbine with 22 in. barrel (7.5 lbs.)

sporting rifle and carbine $1504
military rifle $1750

Thompson/Center Blackpowder

NEW BLACK DIAMOND XR

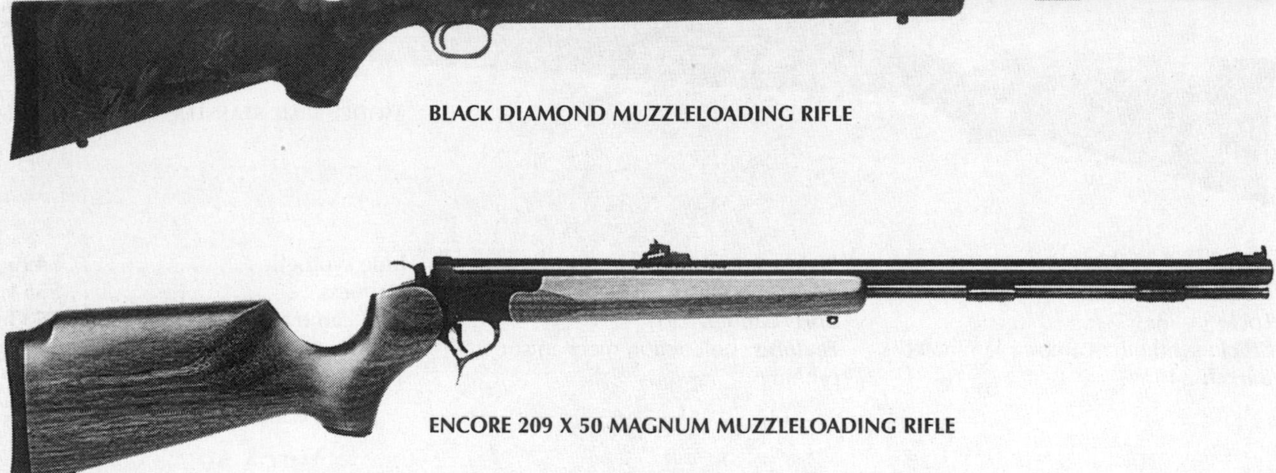

BLACK DIAMOND MUZZLELOADING RIFLE

ENCORE 209 X 50 MAGNUM MUZZLELOADING RIFLE

BLACK DIAMOND RIFLE
Lock: in-line
Stock: walnut or synthetic
Barrel: 26 in., 1:28 twist
Sights: adjustable fiber optic
Weight: 6.6lbs.
Bore/Caliber: .50
Features: musket, cap or no. 11 nipple
blue synthetic $334
blue walnut. $404
stainless camo. $440

ENCORE 209X50 RIFLE
Lock: in-line
Stock: walnut or synthetic
Barrel: 26 in., 1:28 twist
Sights: adjustable fiber optic
Weight: 7.0lbs.
Bore/Caliber: .50
Features: automatic safety, interchangeable barrel with Encore centerfire barrels; also available 209x45 9.45)
blue synthetic $613
stainless synthetic. $692
blue walnut $640
blue camo $672
stainless camo $751
blue walnut .45 . . . . $665
stainless synthetic .45. . . . . $707

Thompson/Center Blackpowder

BLACK POWDER

Fire Storm
Lock: traditional cap or flint
Stock: synthetic
Barrel: 26 in., 1:48 twist
Sights: adjustable fiber optic
Weight: 7.0lbs.
Bore/Caliber: .50
Features: aluminum ramrod
blue **$415**
stainless **$464**

Hawken Rifle
Lock: traditional cap or flint
Stock: walnut
Barrel: 26 in., 1:28 twist
Sights: adjustable open
Weight: 8.5lbs.
Bore/Caliber: .45, .50, .54
Features: brass furniture
caplock **$545**
flintlock **$569**

New Omega 50
Lock: in-line
Stock: synthetic or laminated
Barrel: 28 in., fast twist
Sights: adjustable fiber optic
Weight: 7.0lbs.
Bore/Caliber: .50
Features: swinging breech block mechanism
blue synthetic **$413**
stainless synthetic **$465**
stainless laminated **$494**
stainless camo **$524**

Traditional blackpowder open choked shotguns perform best when loaded with a combination of wads rather than a modern one-piece plastic wad. One effective combination consists of a heavy over-powder card wad, a fiber cushion wad and a thin card over shot wad.

Traditions Blackpowder

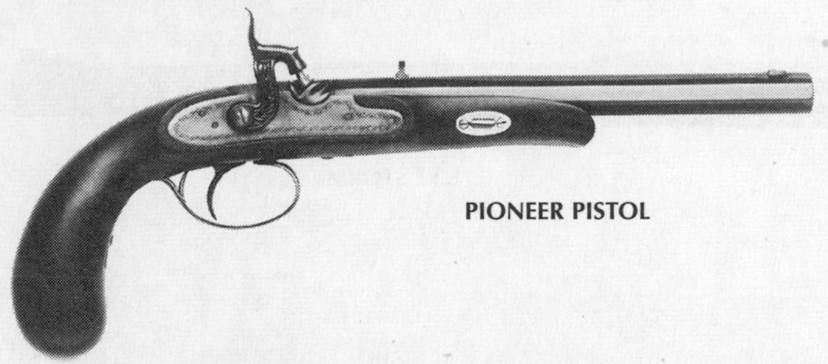

PIONEER PISTOL

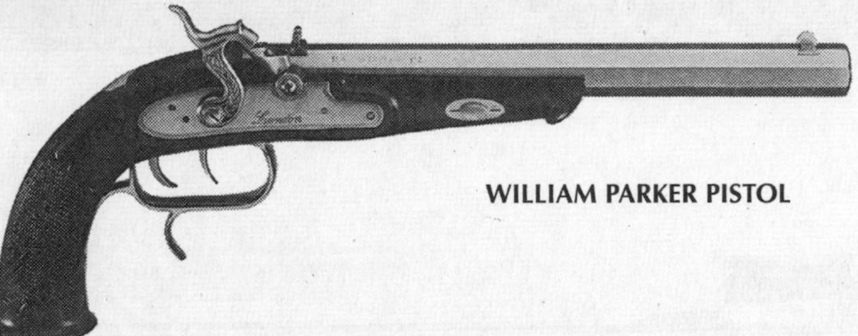

WILLIAM PARKER PISTOL

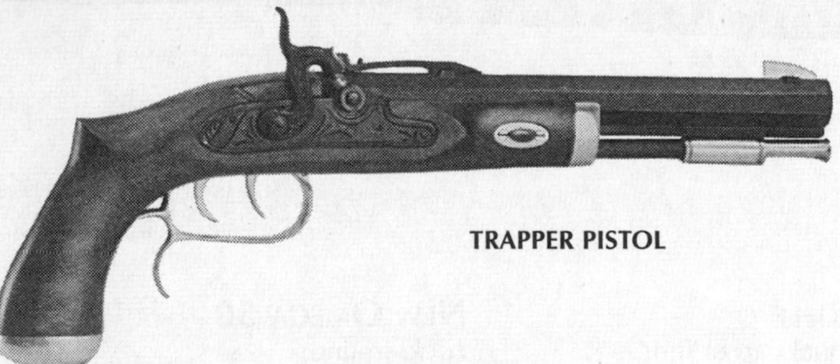

TRAPPER PISTOL

BUCKHUNTER PRO
ALL-WEATHER

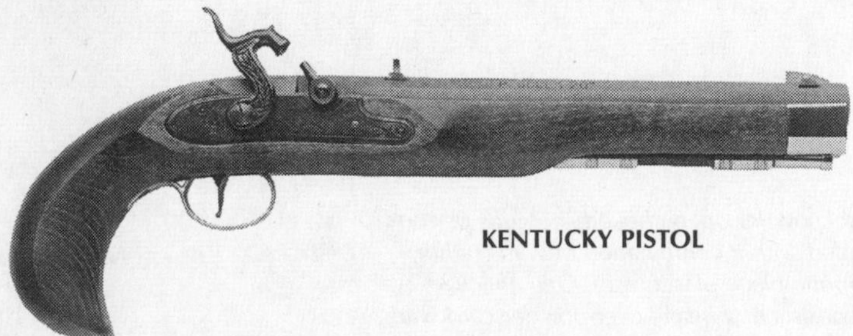

KENTUCKY PISTOL

PIONEER PISTOL

Lock: traditional caplock
Stock: walnut
Barrel: 9.6 in.
Sights: fixed
Weight: 1.9lbs.
Bore/Caliber: .45
Features: German silver furniture
Pioneer $149
unfinished kit $129

WILLIAM PARKER PISTOL

Lock: traditional caplock
Stock: walnut
Barrel: 10.4 in.
Sights: fixed
Weight: 2.3lbs.
Bore/Caliber: .50
Features: checkered with brass furniture
William Parker $269

TRAPPER PISTOL

Lock: traditional cap or flint
Stock: beech
Barrel: 9.8 in.
Sights: adjustable open
Weight: 2.9lbs.
Bore/Caliber: .50
Features: brass furniture
Trapper $189
flintlock $269
caplock unfinished kit. $149

IN-LINE PISTOLS (BUCKHUNTER)

Lock: in-line
Stock: walnut or synthetic
Barrel: 9.5 or 12.5 in.
Sights: adjustable open
Weight: 2.1lbs.
Bore/Caliber: .50
Features: blue or nickel furniture; also with extra-long barrel and brake
9.5 in.. . . . . $249
12.5 in. $269
14.8 in.
with brake (also in .45) $299

KENTUCKY PISTOL

Lock: traditional caplock
Stock: beech
Barrel: 10 in.
Sights: fixed
Weight: 2.5lbs.
Bore/Caliber: .50
Features: brass furniture
Kentucky Pistol. $149
unfinished kit $119

Traditions Blackpowder

DEERHUNTER

PANTHER RIFLE ALL-WEATHER

TRACKER 209 IN-LINE RIFLE

E-BOLT 209 RIFLE

BLACK POWDER

1863 Remington Pocket Revolver

Lock: caplock revolver
Stock: walnut
Barrel: 3.5 in.
Sights: fixed
Weight: 1.0lbs.
Bore/Caliber: .31
Features: brass frame
1863 Rem. Pocket Revolver $179

Deerhunter Rifle

Lock: traditional cap or flint
Stock: hardwood, synthetic or camo
Barrel: 24 in., 1:48 twist
Sights: fixed
Weight: 6.0lbs.
Bore/Caliber: .32, .50, .54
Features: blackened furniture; also economy-model Panther, 24 in .50 or .54
caplock blue,
flint nickel synthetic $189
flintlock blue hardwood $199
flintlock blue camo $229
Panther. $119

E-Bolt 209

Lock: in-line
Stock: synthetic or camo
Barrel: 22 in., 1:28 twist (1:20 .45)
Sights: fiber optic
Weight: 6.5lbs.
Bore/Caliber: .45 or .50
Features: 209 primer ignition
blue synthetic $169
nickel synthetic $179
blue camo $219
nickel camo $229

Panther Rifle

Action: traditional cap lock
Stock: synthetic
Barrel: 24 in., 1:48 twist
Sights: fixed
Weight: 6.0 lbs.
Bore/Caliber: 50, .54
Features: #11 Percussion ignition; sling swivels; synthetic ramrod.
5ocal Percussion Rifle: $119
54cal Percussion Rifle: $119

Tracker 209

Lock: in-line
Stock: synthetic or camo
Barrel: 22 in., 1:28 twist (1:24 .45)
Sights: fiber optic
Weight: 6.5lbs.
Bore/Caliber: .45 or .50
Features: 209 primer ignition
blue synthetic $139
nickel synthetic. $159
nickel camo $189

Traditions Blackpowder

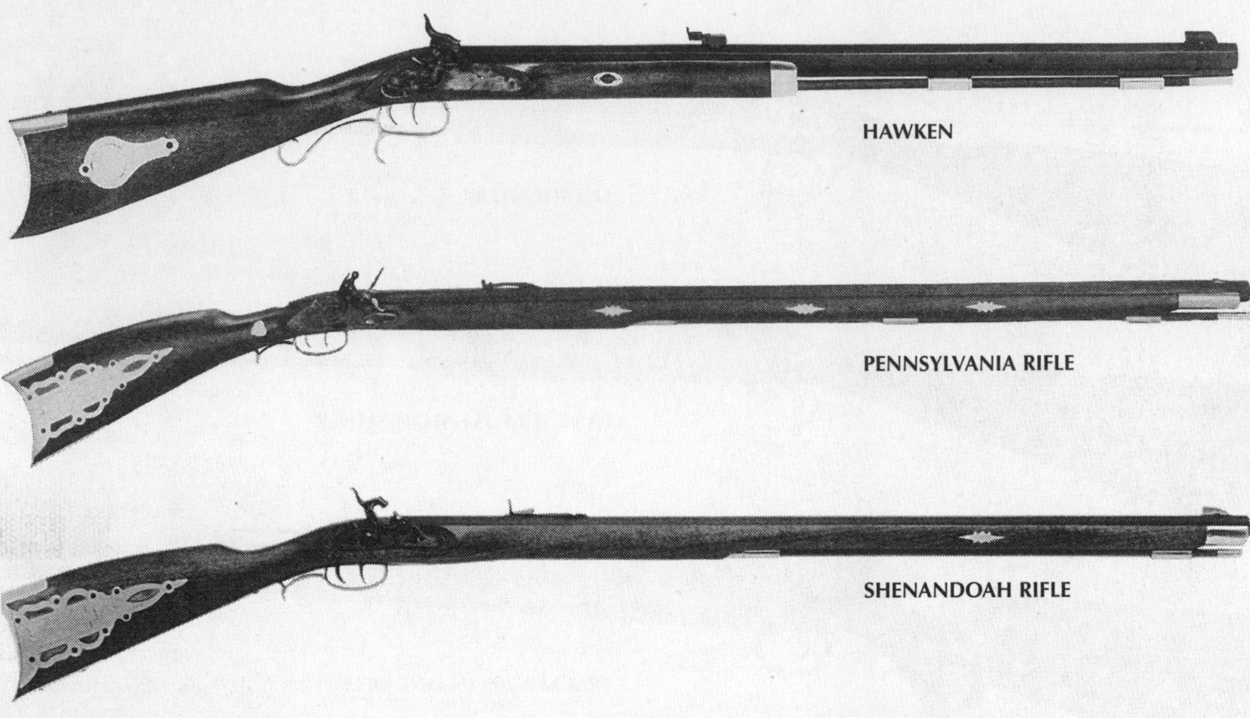

BLACK POWDER

Hawken

Lock: traditional cap or flint
Stock: beech
Barrel: 28 in., 1:48 twist
Sights: adjustable open
Weight: 7.7lbs.
Bore/Caliber: .50 or .54
Features: brass furniture

caplock. $249
lefthand caplock. $269
flintlock $279

Pennsylvania Rifle

Lock: traditional cap or flint
Stock: walnut
Barrel: 20 in., 1:66 twist
Sights: adjustable open
Weight: 8.5lbs.
Bore/Caliber: .50
Features: brass furniture

caplock $489
flintlock $509

Shenandoah Rifle

Lock: traditional cap or flint
Stock: beech
Barrel: 33 in., 1:66 twist
Sights: fixed
Weight: 7.2lbs.
Bore/Caliber: .50
Features: brass furniture; squirrel rifle in .36

caplock $379
flintlock $389
caplock .36 . . . . $379
flintlock .36 . . . . $429

Traditions Blackpowder

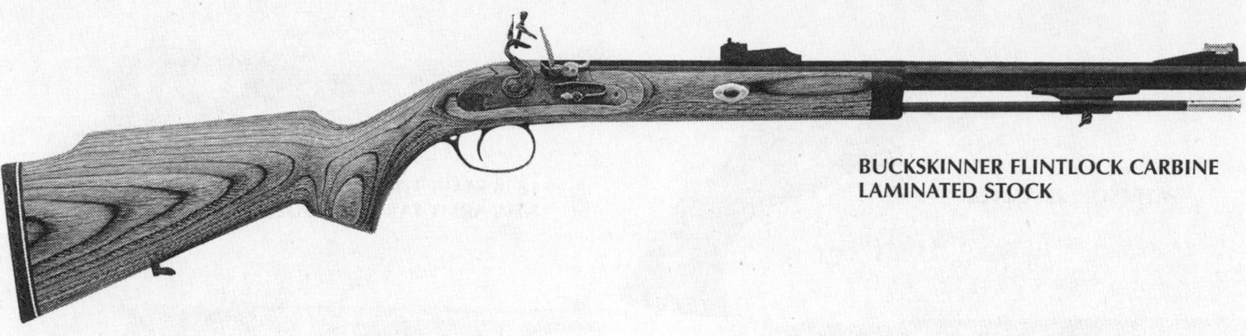

BUCKSKINNER FLINTLOCK CARBINE
LAMINATED STOCK

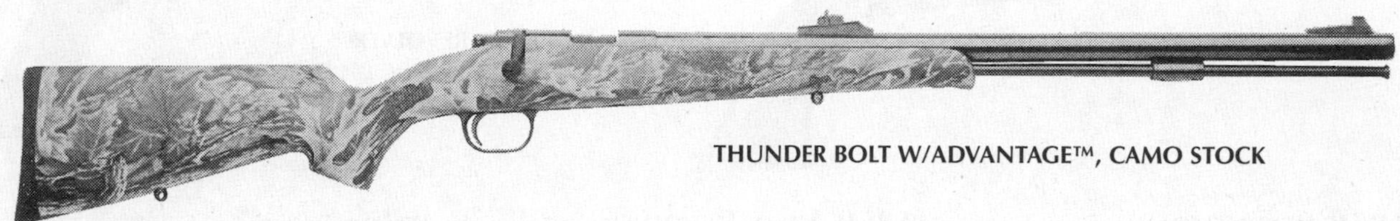

THUNDER BOLT W/ADVANTAGE™, CAMO STOCK

BLACK POWDER

BUCKSKINNER CARBINE

Lock: traditional flintlock
Stock: hardwood or laminated
Barrel: 21 in., 1:48 twist
Sights: fiber optic
Weight: 6.0lbs.
Bore/Caliber: .50
Features: German silver hardware
hardwood $239
laminated. $309

THUNDER BOLT

Lock: in-line
Stock: synthetic or camo
Barrel: 24 in., 1:28 twist
Sights: fiber optic
Weight: 6.8lbs.
Bore/Caliber: .45 or .50
Features: bolt action, 209 primer ignition; also 21 in. Youth Model
blue synthetic and Youth $179
nickel synthetic. $189
blue camo. $209
nickel camo $219

EVOLUTION

Lock: in-line
Stock: beech, walnut, synthetic or camo
Barrel: 24 in., 1:28 twist (1:48 .54)
Sights: fiber optic
Weight: 7.0lbs.
Bore/Caliber: .50 or .54 (with brake)
Features: 209 primer ignition, drilled for scope
blue synthetic $219
nickel synthetic $239
blue camo $249
nickel camo $279
blue beech $279
blue walnut $299
fluted stainless synthetic .54 . . . $299
fluted stainless camo .54 . . . . . $301

A CO2 bullet discharger will remove an unfired load safely by blowing it out of the bore with a blast of compressed gas. The device, which contains a CO2 cartridge, screws into the percussion bolster.

Uberti Blackpowder

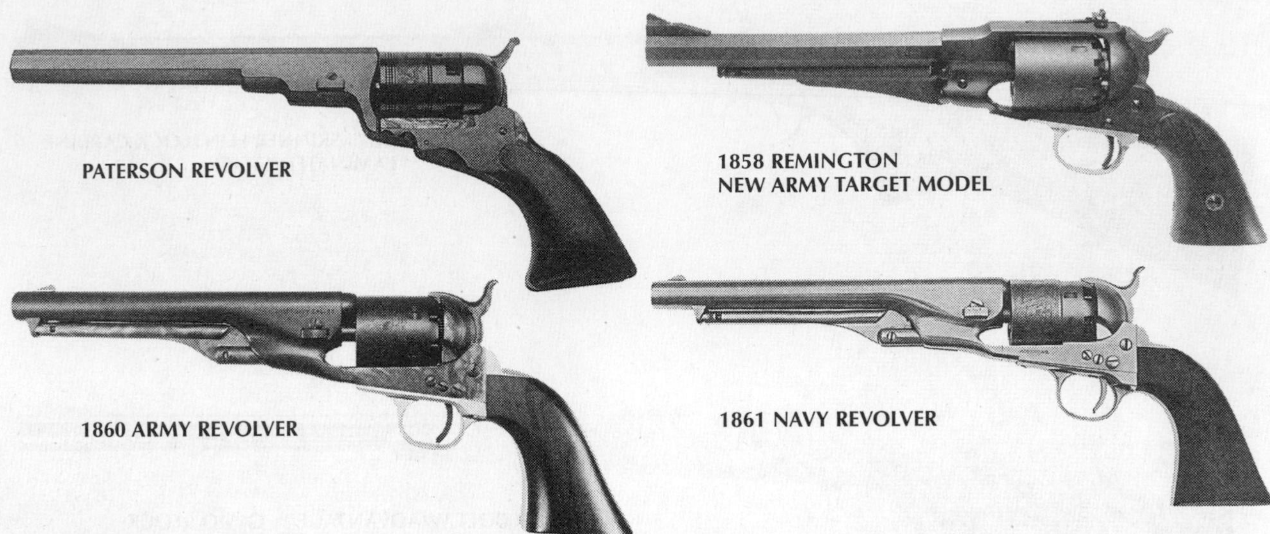

PATERSON REVOLVER

1858 REMINGTON NEW ARMY TARGET MODEL

1860 ARMY REVOLVER

1861 NAVY REVOLVER

1858 Remington New Army Target

Lock: caplock revolver
Stock: walnut
Barrel: 8 in.
Sights: fixed
Weight: 2.8lbs.
Bore/Caliber: .44
Features: octagonal barrel, brass guard
Target $255
stainless $305
with 18 in. barrel, carbine stock $395

1860 Army Revolver

Lock: caplock revolver
Stock: walnut
Barrel: 8 in.
Sights: fixed
Weight: 2.6lbs.
Bore/Caliber: .44
Features: case-colored frame
1860 Army $255
with fluted cylinder $260

1861 Navy Revolver

Lock: caplock revolver
Stock: walnut
Barrel: 7.5 in.
Sights: fixed
Weight: 2.8lbs.
Bore/Caliber: .36
Features: case-colored frame; also Model 1851 Navy
1861 Navy $260
1851 Navy $235

Paterson Revolver

Lock: caplock revolver
Stock: walnut
Barrel: 7.5 in.
Sights: none
Weight: 2.6lbs.
Bore/Caliber: .36
Features: 5-shot cylinder
Paterson $390

Winchester Blackpowder

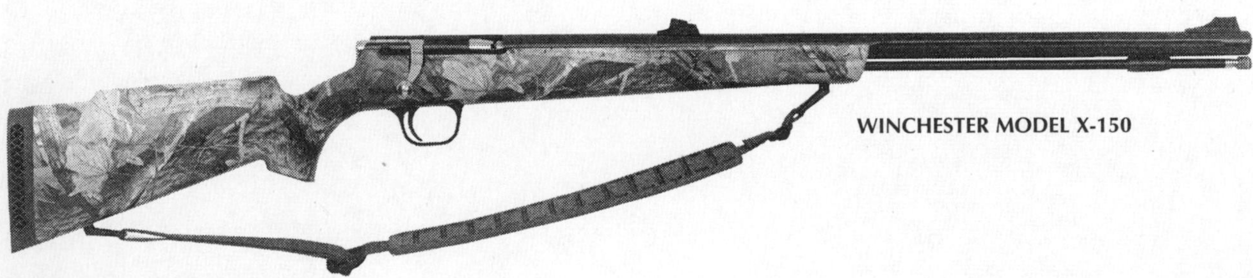

WINCHESTER MODEL X-150

Model X-150 Muzzleloading Rifle

Lock: in-line
Stock: synthetic or camo
Barrel: 26 in. fluted, 1:28 twist
Sights: fiber optic
Weight: 8.2lbs.
Bore/Caliber: .45 or .50
Features: 209 primer ignition, stainless bolt action
blue synthetic $345
blue camo $390
stainless synthetic. $420
stainless camo $470

SIGHTS & SCOPES

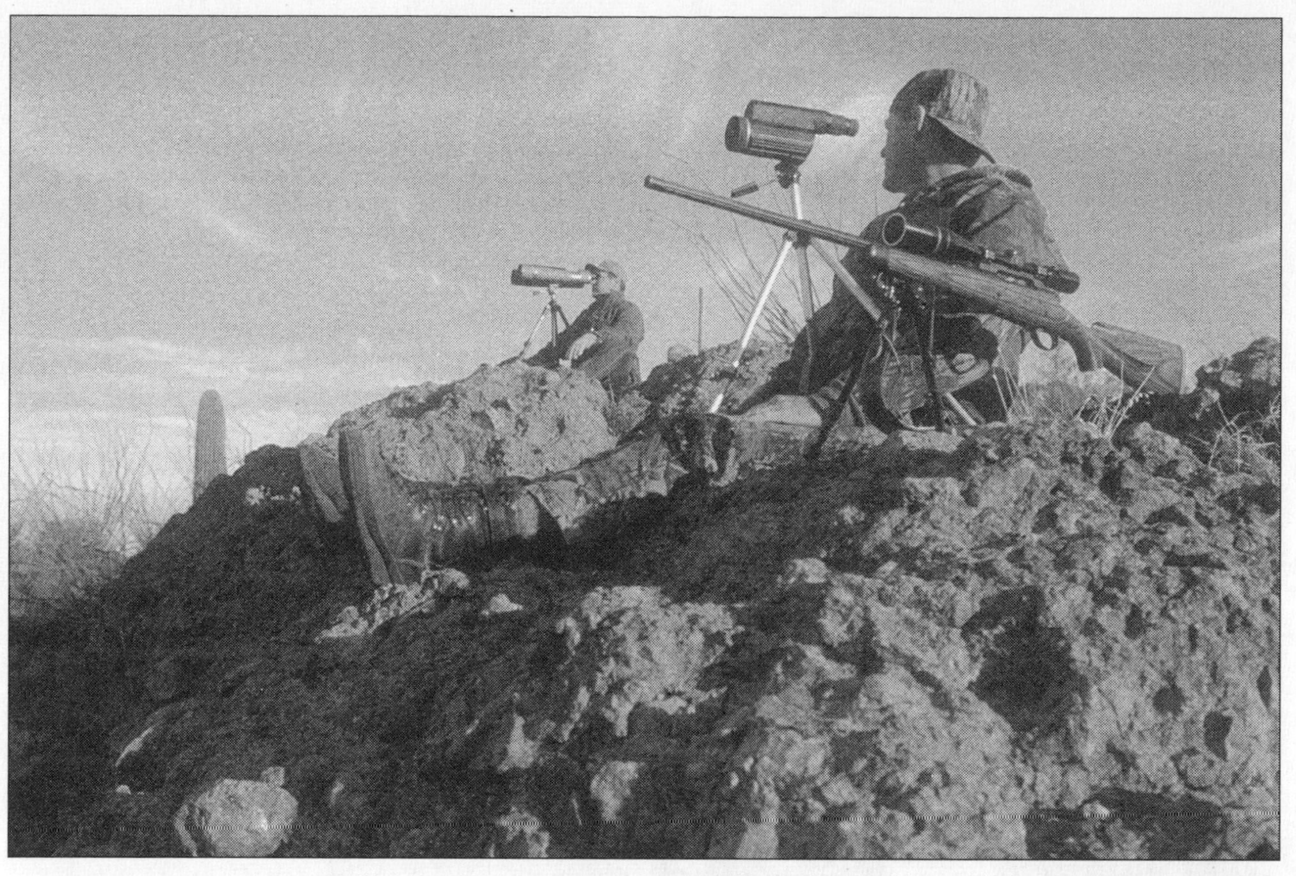

Aimpoint Sights

7000S SIGHT

COMP M2 AND
COMP ML2

SERIES 3000 UNIVERSAL

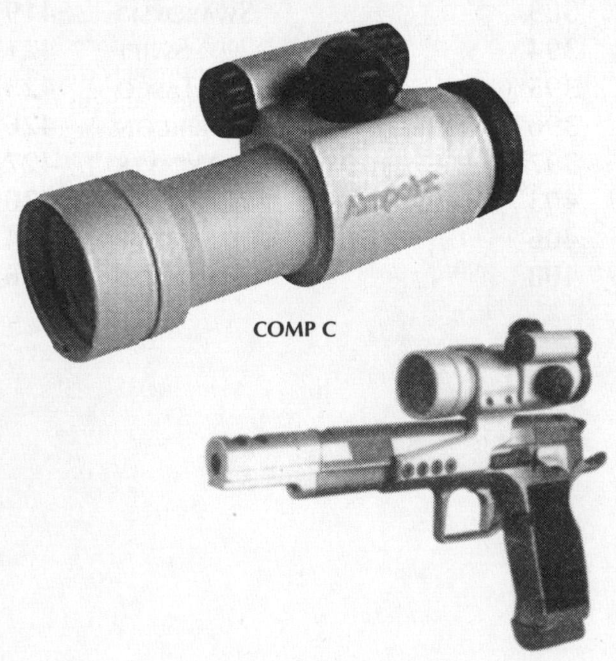

COMP C

7000S Sight

Specifications

System: Parallax free
Optical: Anti-reflex coated lenses
Adjustment: 1 click = ½ inch at 100 yards
Length: 6.3" *Weight:* 7.4 oz. *Objective diameter:* 36mm
Mounting system: 30mm rings *Magnification:* 1X
Material: Anodized aluminum; black finish
Diameter of dot: Red dot, 4 MOA
Price:. $298
Also Available:
7000L (length: 7.9") 298
7000S 2X (fixed 2X) 378
7000L 2X (fixed2X) 378

Comp C2X

Specifications

System: Parallax free Optical: Anti-reflex coated lens
Adjustment: 1 click = 1/2" at 100 yards Length: 4.7"
Weight: 6.5 oz.
Objective diameter: 36 mm
Diameter of dot: 2 MOA
Mounting system: 30mm ring
Magnification: 2X fixed
Material: Anodized aluminum; black finish
Price:
Comp ML2 368
Comp M2. 410
Comp M2 2X 521
Comp ML2 2X 467

Series 3000 Universal

Specifications

System: 100% parallax free
Weight: 6 oz.
Length: 6.25"
Magnification: 1X
Scope attachment: 3X
Eye relief: Unlimited
Battery choices: 2X Mercury SP 675 1X Lithium or DL ⅓N
Material: Anodized aluminum, black finish
Mounting: 1" Rings (Medium or High)
Price: Black 232

Comp C

Specifications

System: 100% Parallax free
Optics: Anti-reflex coated lenses
Eye relief: Unlimited Batteries: 3V Lithium
Adjustment: 1 click = ½-inch at 100 yards
Length: 4¾" Weight: 6.5 oz.
Objective diameter: 36mm
Dot diameter: 4 MOA
Mounting system: 30mm ring *Magnification:* 1X
Material: Black or stainless finish
Price:. 324
Also Available: heavy-duty, hard anodized, graphite gray, submersible to 80' **411**

SIGHTS & SCOPES

BSA Scopes

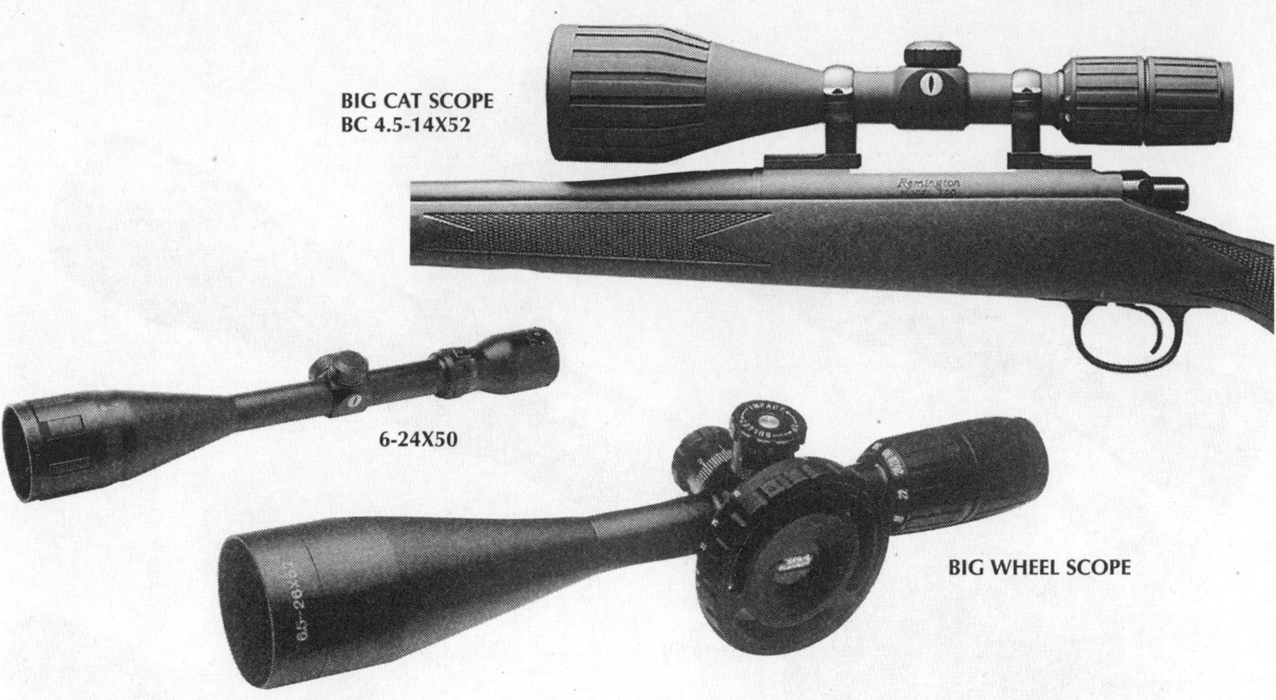
BIG CAT SCOPE BC 4.5-14X52

6-24X50

BIG WHEEL SCOPE

BSA Scopes

The BSA name once reserved for superior rifles and motorcycles is now appearing on rifle scopes. The Catseye line, with multi-coated objective and ocular lenses and a European-style reticle for shooting in dim light, includes two new looks for 2001. The PowerBright has the features of a BSA Catseye plus a PowerBright reticle that lights up bright red against dark backgrounds. The Big Cat has all the features wanted in a hunting scope: long eye relief, fully multicoated, very bright three piece objective lens.

Prices: Catseye
1.5-4x32 . . . . **$92**
3-10x44 . . . . **152**
3.5-10x50 . . . . **172**
4-16x50 AO **192**
6-24x50 AO **223**
Bigcat
2-7x42 . . . . **190**
3.5-10x42 . . . . **220**
4.5-14x52 AO **250**
1.5-4.5x42 . . . . **220**
3-9x42 . . . . **250**
3.5-10x42 . . . . **270**
Catseye Plus
1.5-4.5x32 . . . . **122**
3-10x44 . . . . **172**
3.5-10x50 . . . . **192**

BSA Catseye CE 6-24x50

Specifications

Magnification: 6x-24x ***Objective Lens Diameter:*** 50mm
Exit Pupil Range: 8.3-2.0 ***Field of View at 100 yd:*** 16-3'
Optimum Eye Relief: 4.5" ***Length/Weight:*** 16"/23 oz.
Price: **223**

Big Cat Scope BC 4.5-14x52

The Big Cat is an all new scope design, with a longer eye relief, finger adjustable windage, and elevation knobs. A three-piece objective lens system for sharper resolution, better color, and less distortion. And for extra brightness, the lenses are 14-layer, fully multi-coated. It is very compact and finished in Shadow Black. There are six BigCat models, 3 with large 30mm tubes.

BSA Platinum Target Scopes

BSA Platinum target scopes are fitted with finger-adjustable windage and elevation dials that move point of impact in 1/8-minute clicks. BSA's Big Wheel is for long distance shooting when parallax adjustments are extremely critical. It has a convenient sidewheel for extra-sensitive focusing. Actually the side wheel is two wheels in one. The larger outer wheel is best for off-hand or prone shooting, and the smaller wheel for benchrest. You just snap off the outer wheel to use the smaller focusing wheel. These new scopes are more compact than older models and have three-piece objective lens systems for sharper resolution, better color and less distortion.

Prices: PT 6-24x44 AO **$222**
PT 8-32x44 AO **242**
PT 6-24x44 AO Mildot reticle **200**
PT 8-32x44 AO Mildot reticle **230**

SIGHTS & SCOPES

BSA Scopes

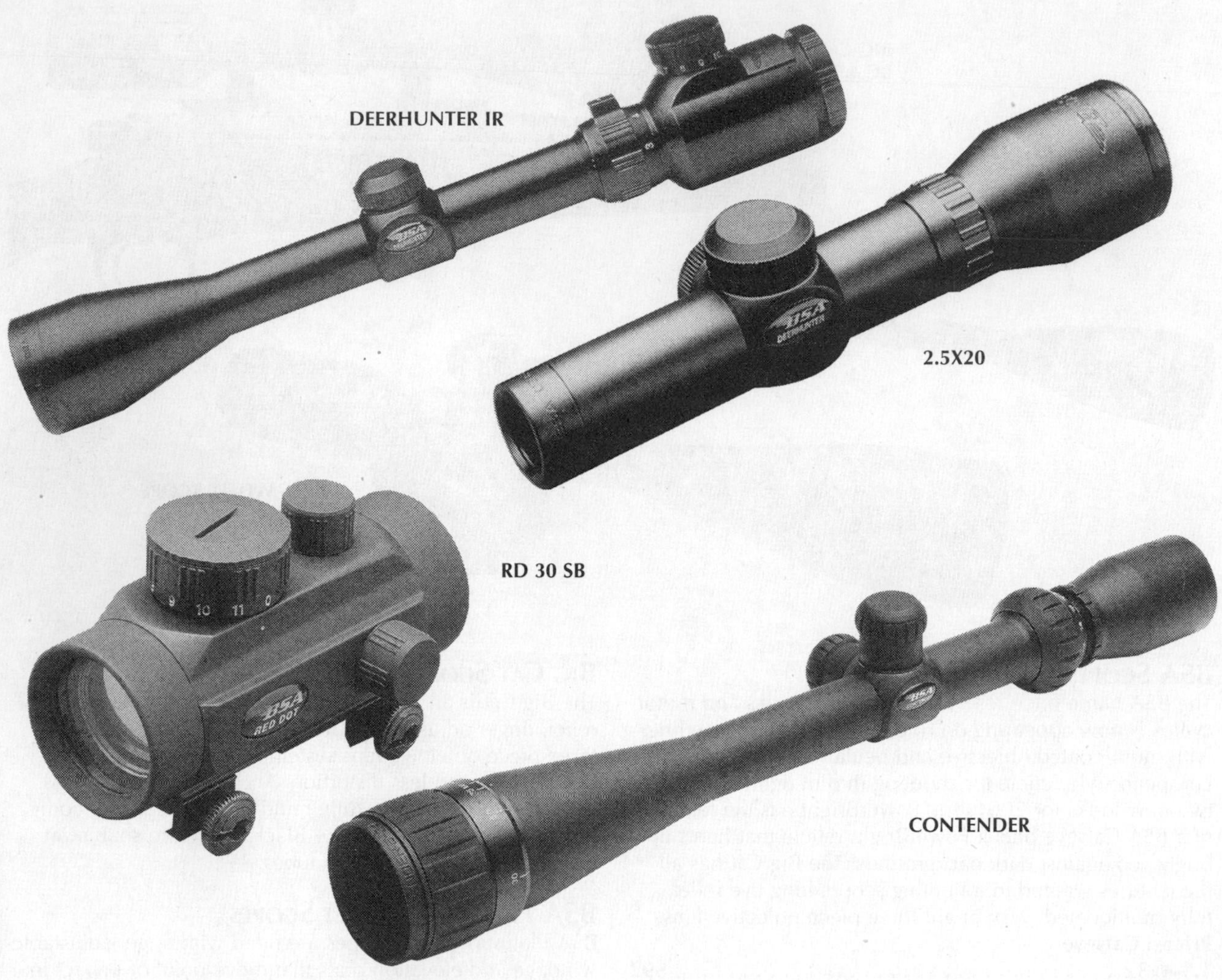

Deerhunter 3-9x40 Illuminated Reticle

Specifications

Magnification: 3x-9x ***Objective Lens Diameter:*** 40mm
Exit Pupil Range: 13.3-4.4 ***Field of View at 100 yd:*** 26'
Eye Relief: 4.5" ***Weight:*** 13 oz.
Price: **$130**

BSA Deer Hunter scopes, from a 2.5x20 (shown) to a 3-9x50 offer value for the big game hunter on a budget.
Prices: from . . . . **60 to 130**

Red Dot Scope

Prices: RD30 (30mm black matte or silver) 60
RD30SB (30mm shadow black) 70
RD42 (42mm black matte) 80
RD42SB (42mm shadow black) 90
RD50SB (50mm shadow black) 110

Deerhunter DH 2.5x20

Specifications

Magnification: 2.5x Objective Lens Diameter: 20mm
Exit Pupil Range: 8 Field of View at 100 yd: 72'
Optimum Eye Relief: 6" Length/Weight: 7.5"/7.5 oz.
Price: **$60**

Contender CT 6-24x40 TS

Specifications

Magnification: 6x-24x ***Objective Lens Diameter:*** 40mm
Exit Pupil Range: 6.7-1.7 ***Field of View at 100 yd:*** 16'-4'
Optimum Eye Relief: 3" ***Length/Weight:*** 15.5"/20 oz.
Price: **150**
Also Available: 3-12x40 130
4-16x40 132
8-32x40 172
3-12x50 132
4-16x50 152
6-24x50 172
8-32x50 192

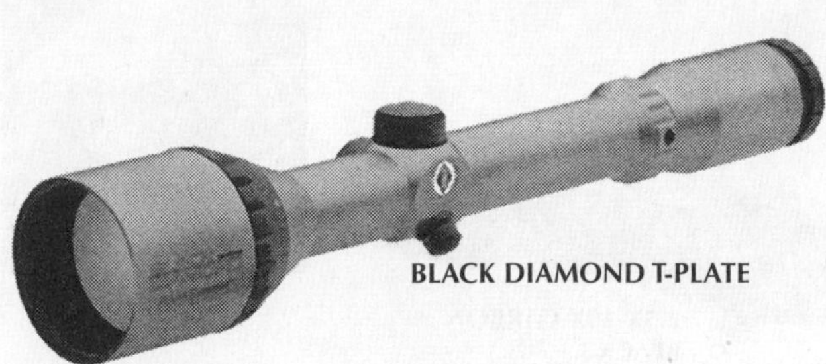

BLACK DIAMOND T-PLATE

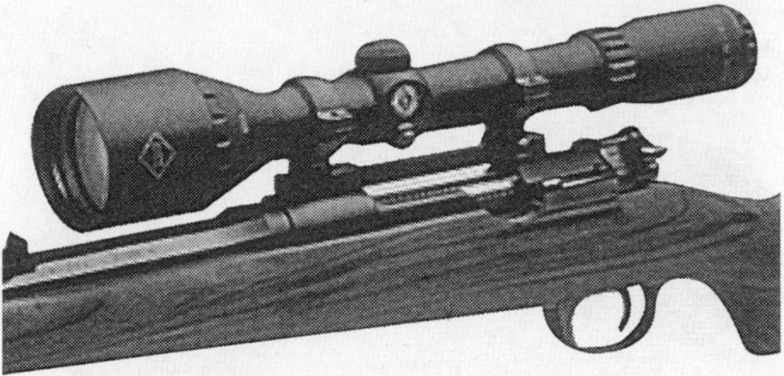

MODEL 3X-12X-50MM

Black Diamond™ T-Plate Scopes

The popularity of Black Diamond scopes and T-Plate lens coating technology on Mr. T riflescopes created a significant number of requests to apply T-Plate to Black Diamond riflescopes. Available in 2.5x-10x and 4x-16x, these scopes are essentially the same as the Mr. T offering, except Black Diamonds are built on a foundation of 6061-T6 Aluminum instead of Titanium.

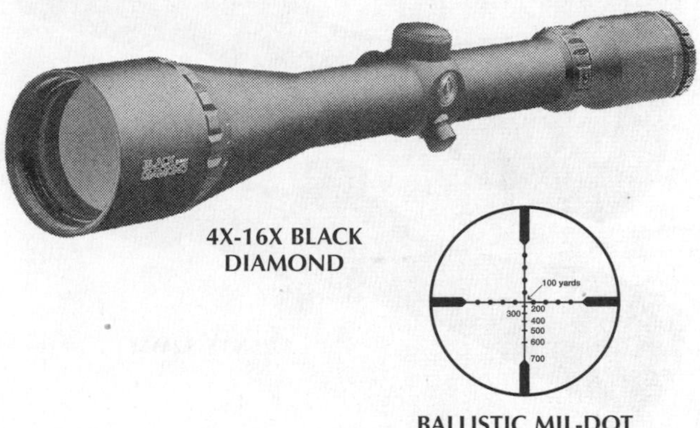

4X-16X BLACK DIAMOND

BALLISTIC MIL-DOT

4x-16x Black Diamond

The Burris Black Diamond is designed for long-range big game rifles and dual-purpose big game/varmint rifles, it has a 50mm objective and Burris' best optics. It is available with the trajectory-compensating Ballistic Mil-Dot reticle. The heavy 30mm tube is notable for its ruggedness.

Burris's Black Diamond line includes three models of a 30mm main tube 3-12X50mm with various finishes, reticles, and adjustment knobs. These riflescopes have easy-to-grip rubber-armored parallax-adjust rings, an adjustable and resettable adjustment dial, and an internal focusing eyepiece.

Specifications

Models: 3-12X50mm/4-16x50/6-24x50/8-32x50
Field of View (feet @ 100yds.): 34'-12'/18-6
Optimum eye relief: 3.5"-4.0"/3.5-4
Exit Pupil: 13.7mm-4.2mm/7.6-2.1
Click adjust value (@ 100 yds.): .25"/.125
Max. internal adj. (@ 100 yds.): 100"/52
Clear objective diameter: 50mm/50mm
Ocular end diameter: 42mm/42mm
Weight: 25 oz./25 oz.
Length: 13.8"/16.2"
Reticles available: Plex, Mil-Dot, Ballistic MDot, and Fine Plex

1X XER SCOUT

2.75X SCOUT

Scout Scopes

...for hunters who need a 7- to 14-inch eye relief for mounting in front of the ejection port; allows you to shoot with both eyes open. The 15-foot field of view and 2.75X magnification are ideal for brush guns and shotgunners. Rugged, reliable and fog proof.

SPEEDDOT 135

SpeedDot 135

1x35mm pistol and shotgun sight. Electronic red dot reticle, 3 moa or 11 moa

Burris Riflescopes

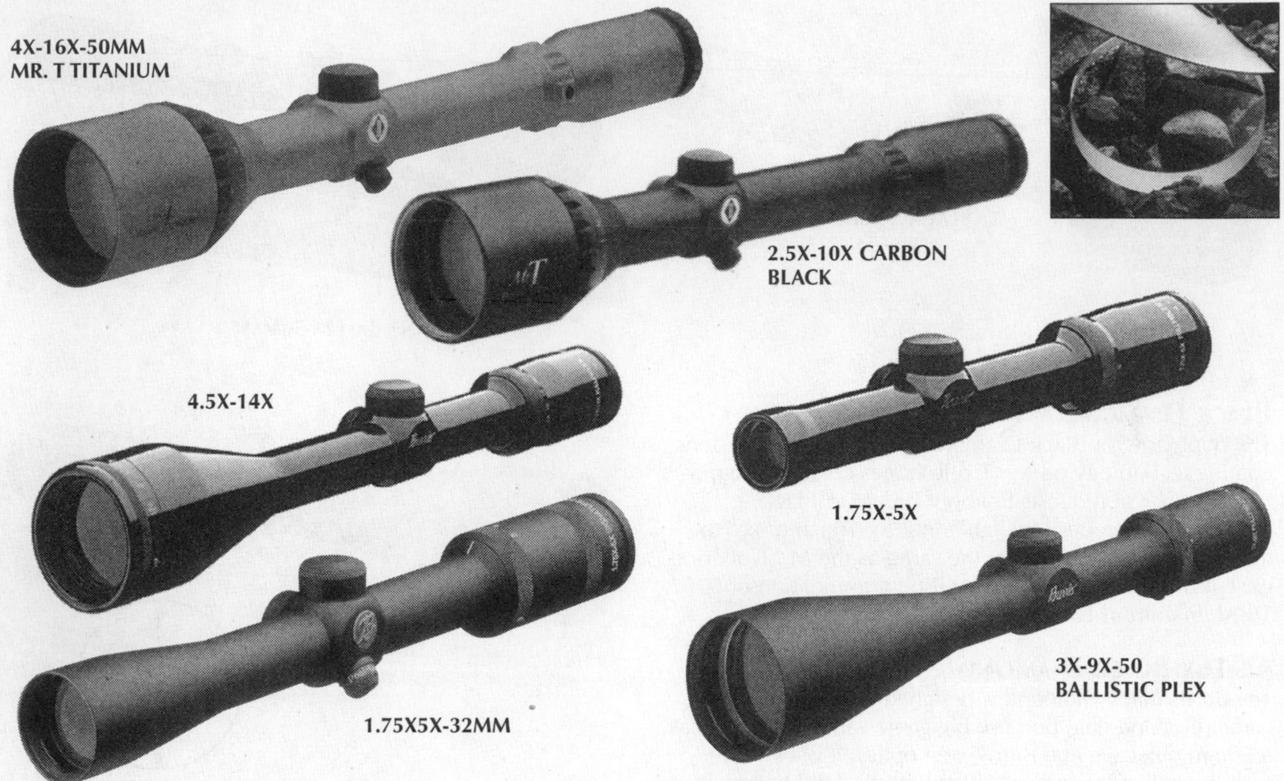

Burris "Mr T"
Titanium Black • Diamond Scopes

Substantially stronger than aluminum, and much lighter than steel, Mr. T is one scope worthy of the description 'tough'. Beyond the whole scope tube and eyepiece being made of solid titanium, each scope is coated with a nitride harder than carbide or hard chrome—such as titanium nitride, aluminum titanium nitride, or chrome nitride, depending on the color. These nitrides are molecularly bonded to the titanium through high intensity physical vapor deposition for maximum adhesion that will not blister, flake, or chip. The result is an ultra-hard (up to 85 Rockwell C), abrasion resistant surface. Also available in Autumn Gold.

1.75X-5X-32mm
Signature™ Safari

A whole new optic system was designed to integrate a host of features into the ultimate riflescope for heavy brush country, for heavy recoiling dangerous game rifles, and for magnum slug shotguns. The new 1.75X-5X Signature Safari™ provides ¾" additional eye relief to save your brow while shooting from awkward positions. The 32mm objective allows for ultra-flexibility in eye position. The eyepiece and power ring are combined into a single sturdy unit that makes changing magnifications faster. The Post and Crosshair reticle is the fastest and most instinctive reticle pattern available. Because of its size, shape, ruggedness, and lighter weight, the 1.75X-5X also makes a great scope for all the new short magnum rifles.

T-Plated Lenses

The toughness of this scope doesn't end with the metal work. The scratch-proof T-Plate coating applied to the objective and eyepiece lenses is remarkable. These lenses do not come with the warning of other "scratch-resistant" coatings about removing all dust before cleaning. T-plated lenses do not require a "soft clean lens cloth". Just knock the mud off the lens and wipe it clean with a dirty shirt tail. Ordinary dirt, dust, and grit won't touch it. This coating technology is prohibitively expensive for ordinary scopes. Mr. T is a premium - quality sight for discriminating hunters.

Burris Fullfield II Variable Scopes

The Fullfield II is now much more forgiving for eye positioning both fore and aft, and left and right. Burris has shaved roughly four ounces of weight on each model without effecting durability or optical performance. In fact, several areas are even stronger and more precisely fitted than before. Overall, the Fullfield is about one inch shorter than its predecessor for a more compact look and feel. Like the Fullfield, and unlike other scopes, Fullfield II eyepieces are sealed with special quad seals rather than old-tech O-rings. And the eyepiece is now part of the power ring. To change magnification, simply turn the entire eyepiece. A European-style adjustable eyepiece is easy to use and requires no locking mechanism. For 2002, Burris has added a 3X-9X-50mm to their Fullfield II line, as well as a fixed 6X for traditionalists, and a 6X-32mm HBRII for benchrest shooters.

Also available: 3.5-10x50, 4.5X-14X and 6.5-20x50

Burris Scopes

Signature Series

8X-32X SIGNATURE

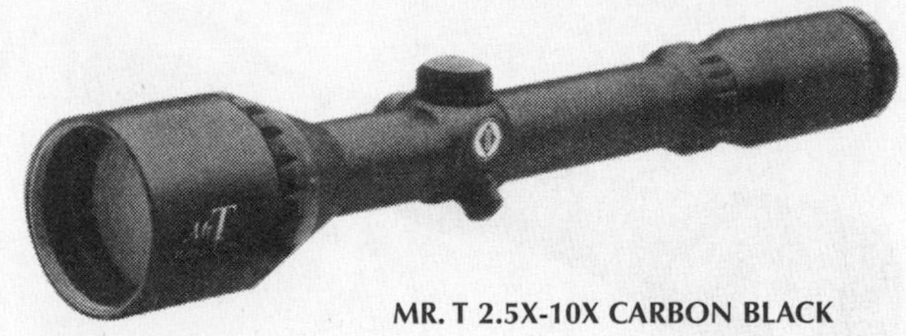

MR. T 2.5X-10X CARBON BLACK

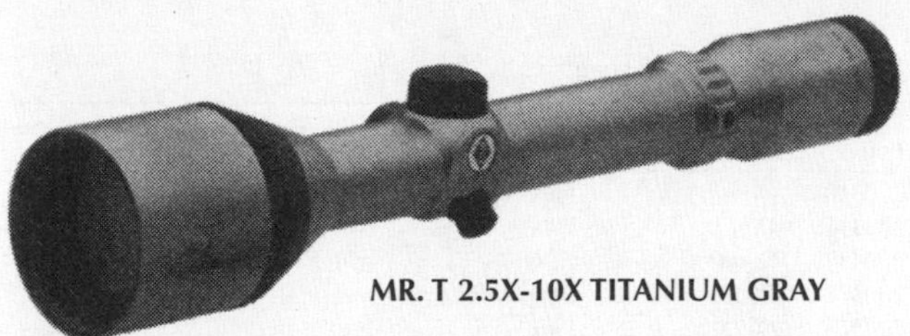

MR. T 2.5X-10X TITANIUM GRAY

All models in the Signature Series have Hi-Lume (multi-coated) lenses for maximum light transmission. Many models also feature Posi-Lock to prevent recoil shift and protect against loss of zero from rough hunting use. It allows the shooter to lock the internal optics of the scope in position after the rifle has been sighted in.

SIGNATURE SERIES SCOPES

Item	Model	Reticle	Finish	Features	List
200511	6X	Plex	mat		$463
200700	1.5X-6X	Plex	blk		518
200701	1.5X-6X	Plex	mat		538
200706	1.5X-6X	Plex	mat	Posi-Lock	588
200711	1.5X-6X	Electro-Dot	mat		667
200600	3X-9X	Plex	blk		$611
200601	3X-9X	Plex	mat		631
200597	3X-9X	Plex	blk	Posi-Lock	660
200598	3X-9X	Plexmat		Posi-Lock	681
200580	3X-9X	Electro-Dot	blk		763
200581	3X-9X	Electro-Dot	mat		763
200590	3X-9X	Electro-Dot	blk	Posi-Lock	794
200591	3X-9X	Electro-Dot	mat	Posi-Lock	815
200607	2.5X-10X	Plex	blk	PA	$647
200631	2.5X-10X	Plex	mat	Posi-Lock /PA	729
200614	3X-12X	Plex	blk	Posi-Lock /PA	$704
200707	1.75X-5X-Safari	Taper Plex	mat	-	$601
200708	1.75X-5X-Safari	Taper Plex	mat	Posi-Lock	649
200709	1.75X-5X-Safari	Post Crosshair	mat	Posi-Lock	667
200710	1.75X-5X-Sig LRS	LRS Fast Plex	mat	-	769
200603	3X-9X	Ballistic Plex	mat	-	640
200817	6X-24X	Plex	blk	Target /PA	756
200750	4X-16X	Plex	blk	PA	$738
200751	4X-16X	Plex	mat	PA	757
200767	4X-16X	Ballistic MDot	mat	PA	887
200756	4X-16X	Plex	mat	Posi-Lock /PA	810
200765	4X-16X	Electro-Dot	mat	PA	861
200766	4X-16X	Electro-Dot	mat	Posi-Lock /PA	914
200817	6X-24X	Plex	blk	PA	$756
200804	6X-24X	Plex	mat	PA	776
200803	6X-24X	Fine Plex	blk	Target /PA	$795
200806	6X-24X	Fine Plex	mat	Target /PA	813
200811	6X-24X	Fine Plex	nic	Target /PA	823
200816	6X-24X	Ballistic MDot	mat	Target /PA	947
200813	6X-24X	Plex	mat	Posi-Lock /PA	831
200850	8X-32X	Fine Plex	blk	Target /PA	$813
200860	8X-32X	Fine Plex	mat	Target /PA	833
200866	8X-32X	Fine Plex	nic	Target /PA	842
200861	8X-32X	Ballistic MDot	mat	Target /PA	965

MR. T BLACK DIAMOND TITANIUM SCOPES (30MM)

Item	Model	Reticle	Finish	Features	List
200920	2.5X-10X-50mm	Plex	titanium gray		$1,786
200928	4X-16X-50mm	Plex	titanium gray	PA	1,875
200956	4X-16X-50mm	Ballistic MDot	titanium gray	PA	1,964

BLACK DIAMOND T-PLATES SCOPES (30MM)

Item	Model	Reticle	Finish	Features	List
200912	2.5X-10X-55mm	Plex	mat	PA	$1,165
200956	4X-16X-50mm	Ballistic MDot	mat	PA	1,351

BLACK DIAMOND SCOPES (30MM)

Item	Model	Reticle	Finish	Features	List
200906	6X-50mm	Plex	mat		$756
200900	3X-12X-50mm	Plex	mat	PA	$974
200901	3X-12X-50mm	Plex	mat	Posi-Lock /PA	1,046
200954	4X-16X-50mm	Plex	mat	Side PA	969
200955	4X-16X-50mm	Ballistic MDot	mat	Side PA	1,119
200957	4X-16X-50mm	German 3P#4	mat	Side PA	1,155
200958	4X-16X-50mm	Ballistic MDot	mat	PLOCK/Side P	1,190
200933	6X-24X-50mm	Fine Plex	mat	Tar-Side /PA	1,076
200934	6X-24X-50mm	Ballistic MDot	mat	Tar-Side /PA	1,237
200942	8X-32X-50mm	Fine Plex	mat	Tar-Side /PA	1,126
200943	8X-32X-50mm	Ballistic MDot	mat	Tar-Side /PA	1,308

ELECTRO-DOT SCOPES

Item	Model	Reticle	Finish	Features	List
200167	3X-9X Fullfield II	Electro-Dot	mat		$520
200168	3X-9X FFII LRS	LRS Ball Plex	mat		558
200173	3.5X-10X-50 FFII LRS	LRS Ball Plex	mat		672
200710	1.75X-5X Sig LRS	LRS Fast Plex	mat		$769
200711	1.5X-6X Signature	Electro-Dot	mat		667
200712	1.5X-6X Signature	Electro-Dot	mat	Posi-Lock	719
200581	3X-9X Signature	Electro-Dot	mat		$763
200590	3X-9X Signature	Electro-Dot	blk	Posi-Lock	794
200591	3X-9X Signature	Electro-Dot	mat	Posi-Lock	815
200765	4X-16X Signature	Electro-Dot	mat	PA	$887
200766	4X-16X Signature	Electro-Dot	mat	Posi-Lock/PA	942

Burris Scopes

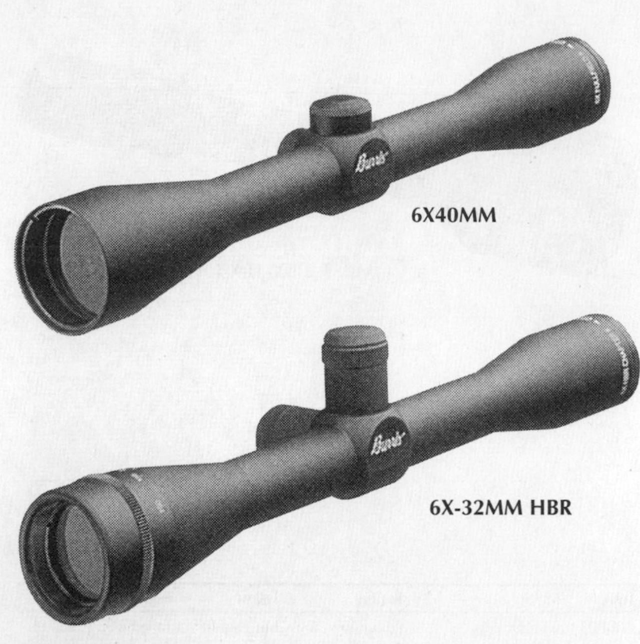

6X40MM

6X-32MM HBR

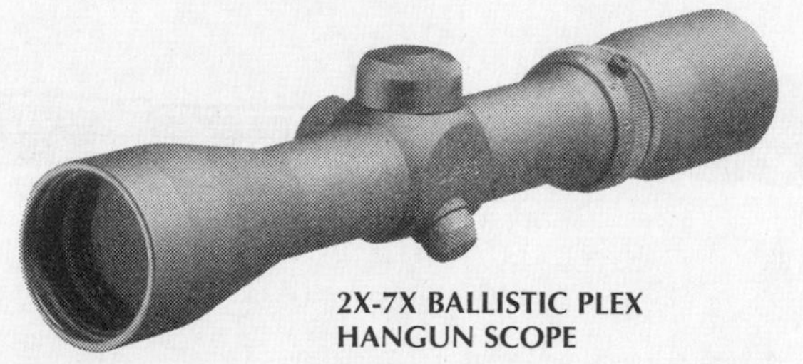

2X-7X BALLISTIC PLEX HANGUN SCOPE

FULLFIELD IITM SCOPES FIXED POWER WITH HI-LUME LENSES

FULLFIELD II SCOPES

ITEM	MODEL	RETICLE	FINISH	FEATURES	LIST
200052	6X-40mm	Plex	mat	-	$386
200057	6X-32mm HBRII	Superfine XHr	mat	Target /PA	515
200056	6X-32mm HBRII	.375 Dot	mat	Target /PA	538
200153	3X-9X-50mm	Plex	mat	-	481
200154	3X-9X-50mm	Ballistic Plex	mat	-	490
200086	1.75-5X	Plex	blk		$400
200087	1.75-5X	Plex	mat		420
200160	3X-9X-40mm	Plex	blk		$336
200161	3X-9X-40mm	Plex	mat		336
200162	3X-9X-40mm	Ballistic Plex	mat		$354
200163	3X-9X-40mm	Plex	nic		372
200164	3X-9X-40mm	German 3P#4	mat		372
200167	3X-9X-40mm	Electro-Dot	mat		520
200168	3X-9X-40LRS	LRS Ball Plex	mat	PA	558
200170	3.5X-10X-50mm	Plex	blk		$542
200171	3.5X-10X-50mm	Plex	mat		561
200172	3.5X-10X-50mm	Ballistic Plex	mat		$570
200173	3.5X-10X-50LRS	LRS Ball plex	mat		672
200180	4.5X-14X	Plex	blk	PA	$585
200181	4.5X-14X	Plex	mat	PA	585
200182	4.5X-14X	Fine Plex	mat	PA	$602
200183	4.5X-14X-42mm	Ballistic Plex	mat	PA	602
200184	4.5X-14X-42	German 3P#4	mat	PA	620
200190	6.5X-20X-50mm	Fine Plex	blk	PA	656
200191	6.5X-20X-50mm	Fine Plex	mat	PA	674
200192	6.5X-20X-50mm	Fine Plex	mat	Target /PA	715
200193	6.5X-20X-50mm	Ballistic MDot	mat	PA	808

FULLFIELD SCOPES

ITEM	MODEL	RETICLE	FINISH	FEATURES	LIST
200413	2.5X shotgun	Plex	mat		$307
200103	6X-18X	Fine Plex	blk	PA	$543
200109	6X-18X	Fine Plex	mat	PA	561
200104	6X-18X	Fine Plex	blk	Target /PA	581

COMPACT SCOPES

ITEM	MODEL	RETICLE	FINISH	FEATURES	LIST
200424	1X XER	Plex	mat		$320
200310	4X	Plex	blk		$302
200311	4X	Plex	mat		324
200432	1X-4X	XER	mat		397
200396	4X-12X	Ballistic Plex	mat	PA	552
200375	2X-7X	Plex	blk		409
200376	2X-7X	Plex	mat		431
200387	3X-9X	Plex	mat		442
200388	3X-9X	Plex	nic		450
200384	3X-9X	Plex	mat	PA	449
200390	4X-12X	Plex	blk	PA	$527
200395	4X-12X	Plex	mat	PA	534
200393	4X-12X	Fine Plex	blk	Target /PA	567
200394	4X-12X	Fine Plex	mat	Target /PA	586

RIMFIRE/AIRGUN SCOPES

ITEM	MODEL	RETICLE	FINISH	FEATURES	LIST
200384	3X-9X	Plex	mat	PA	$449
200390	4X-12X	Plex	blk	PA	527
200395	4X-12X	Plex	mat	PA	534
200396	4X-12X	Ballistic Plex	mat	PA	552
200393	4X-12X	Fine Plex	blk	Target /PA	567
200394	4X-12X	Fine Plex	mat	Target /PA	586
200858	8X-32X	Plex	blk	Target /PA	$835
200859	8X-32X	Fine Plex	mat	Target /PA	854

HANDGUN SCOPES

ITEM	MODEL	RETICLE	FINISH	FEATURES	LIST
200299	2X-7X	Ballistic Plex	mat	Posi-Lock	$527
200309	3X-12X	Ballistic Plex	mat	PA	586
200424	1X XER	Plex	mat		$320
200220	2X	Plex	blk		$286
200218	2X	Plex	mat		279
200229	2X	Plex	nic		306
200228	2X	Plex	mat	Posi-Lock	334
200235	4X	Plex	blk		$338
200263	10X Target /PA	Plex	blk	Target	$515
200214	1.5X-4X	Plex	nic		$411
200207	1.5X-4X	Plex	mat	Posi-Lock	449
200213	1.5X-4X	Plex	nic	Posi-Lock	450
200290	2X-7X	Plex	blk		$458
200291	2X-7X	Plex	mat		468
200293	2X-7X	Plex	blk	PA	506
200298	2X-7X	Plex	nic		479
200294	2X-7X	Plex	blk	Posi-Lock	501
200297	2X-7X	Plex	nic	Posi-Lock	520
200306	3X-12X	Plex	blk	PA	$558
200307	3X-12X	Plex	mat	PA	568
200308	3X-12X	Plex	blk	PA	577
200305	3X-12X	Fine Plex	blk	Target /PA	570
200303	3X-12X	Plex	mat	Posi-Lock	608

SPEEDDOT 135 SIGHTS

ITEM	MODEL	RETICLE	FINISH	FEATURES	LIST
300200	1X-35mm	3 MOA Dot	mat		$291
300201	1X-35mm	11 MOA Dot	mat		291

SCOUT SCOPES

ITEM	MODEL	RETICLE	FINISH	FEATURES	LIST
200424	1X XER	Plex	mat		$320
200269	2.75X	Heavy Plex	mat		349

Bushnell Riflescopes

ELITE 3200 RIFLESCOPES WITH RAINGUARD

Model	Special Feature	Actual Magni-fication	Obj. Lens Aperature (mm)	Field of View @ 100yds (ft.)	Weight (oz)	Length	Eye Relief (in.)	Exit Pupil (mm)	Click Value @ 100yds (in.)	Adjust Range @ 100yds (in.)	Selection	Suggested Retail
32-1040	Mil Dot Reticle, Target Turrets	10x	40	11	15.5	11.7	3.5	4	.25	100		$280
32-156M	Firefly Reticle	1.5X-4.5X	32	63-20	13	12.5	3.6	21-7.6	.25	100	Low power variable for close-in shadowing	308
32-2632M	Handgun (32-2632S Silver Finish)	2x-6x	32	10-4	10	9	20	16-5.3	.25	50	Constant 20" eye relief At all powers w/max. recoil resistance	390
32-2732M	Matte Finish	2x-7x	32	44.6-12.7	12	11.6	3	12.2-4.6	.25	50	Compact variable for close-in brush or med. range shooting. Excellent for shotguns	266
32-3940G	(32-3940M Matte Finish, 32-3940S Silver Finish)	3x-9x	40	33.8-11.5	13	12.6	3.3	13.3-4.4	.25	50	For the full range of hunting. From varmint to big game. Tops in versatility.	280
32-3943	Matte, 3-2-1 low light reticle	3x-9x	40	33.8-11.5	13	12.6	3.3	13.3-4.4	.25	50	All types of hunting	280
32-3944M	Fast-Focus Eyepiece	3x-9x	40	33.8-11.5	13	12.6	3.3	13.3-4.4	.25	50	For the full range of hunting. From varmint to big game. Tops in versatility.	280
32-3946M	Firefly Reticle	3X-9X	40	33.8-11.5	13	12.6	3.3	13.3-4.4	.25	40	Full range hunting	322
32-3954M	Matte	3x-9x	50	31.5-10-5	19	15.7	3.3	16-5.6	.25	50	All purpose variable with extra brightness.	336
32-3955E	European Reticle Matte Finish	3x-9x	50	31.5-10.5	22	15.6	3.3	16-5.6	.36	70	Large exit pupil and 30mm tube for max. brightness.	562
32-3956M	Firefly Reticle	3x-9x	50	31.5-10.5	22	15.6	3.3	16-5.6	.25	50		378
32-3957M	Firefly Reticle 30mm tube	3x-9x	50	31.5-10.5	22	15.6	3.3	16-5.6	.36	70	Large exit pupil & 30mm tube for brightness	604
32-3953	Matte, 3-2-1 low light reticle	3x-9x	50	31.5-10.5	19	15.7	3.3	16-5.6	.25	50	All purpose, extra bright	334
32-4124A	Adjustable Objective	4x-12x	40	26.9-9	15	13.2	3.3	10-3.33	.25	50	Medium to long-range variable makes a superb choice for varmint or big game	412
32-5154M	Matte adj. objective sunshade	5x-15x	40	21-7	19	14.5	4.3	9-2.7	.25	50	Long range, big game	440
32-5155M	Adjustable Objective	5x-15x	50	21-7	19	15.9	3.4	10-3.3	.25	40	Large objective for brightness	464

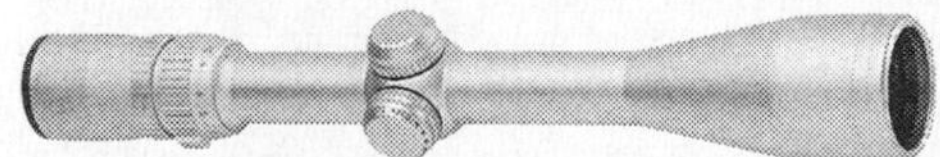

ELITE™ 4200 RIFLESCOPES WITH RAINGUARD™

Model	Special Feature	Actual Magni-fication	Obj. Lens Aperature (mm)	Field of View @ 100yds (ft.)	Weight (oz)	Length	Eye Relief (in.)	Exit Pupil (mm)	Click Value @ 100yds (in.)	Adjust Range @ 100yds (in.)	Selection	Suggested Retail
42-1636M	Matte Finish	1.5x-6x	36	61.8-16.1	15.4	12.8	3	14.6-6	.25	60	Compact wide angle for close-in & brush hunting. Max. brightness. Execel. for shotguns	$534
42-2104G	(42-2104M Matte Finish, 42-2104S Silver Finish)	2.5x-10x	40	41.5-10.8	16	13.5	3	15.6-4	.25	50	All purpose hunting scope w/4x zoom range for close-in brush & long range shooting	564
42-2105M	Matte Finish	2.5x-10x	50	40-10.8	18	14.3	3.5	15-2.5	.25	50	Ideal hunting and all purpose	670
42-2146M	Firefly Reticle	2.5X-10X	40	41.5-16.8	16	13.5	3	15.6-4	.25	.50	All purpose hunting scope w/4X 200mm range	606
42-2151M	Illum 1 Dot Reticle	2.5x-10x	50	40-10.8	18	14.3	3.5	15-2.5	.25	50	Ideal hunting and all purpose	700
42-4164M	Matte Adjustable Obj Sunshade	4x-16x	40	26-7	18.6	14.4	3.5	10-25	.25	40	Parallax focus from 10 yds to infinity	566
42-4165M	Matte Finish	4x-16x	50	26-7.2	22	15.6	3	12.5-3.1	.25	50	The ultimate varmint, airgun and precision shooting scope. Parallax focus from 10 meter to infinity.	732
42-6244M	Adjustable Objective, Sunshade Matte	6x-24x	40	18-4.5	20.2	16.9	3	6.7-1.7	.125	26	Varmint, target & silhouette long range shooting and airgun. Parallax focus adjust. for pinpoint accuracy. Parallax focus from 10 meter to infinity.	640
42-6243A	Adjustable Objective and 1/4" MOA dot reticle	6-24x	40	18-4.5	20.2	16.9	3	6.7-1.7	.125	26	Varmint, target and silhouette long range shooting and airgun. Parallax focus adjust for pinpoint accuracy. Parallax focus from 10 meter to infinity.	640
42-6242M	Matte w/Mil Dot	6x-24x	40	18-6	20.2	16.9	3	6.7-1.7	.125	26	Long range varmint or target	660
42-8324M	Matte finish, adj. objective sunshade	8x-32x	40	14-3.75	22	18	4-3.5	5-1.25	.125	20	Long range varmint, bench	704

Bushnell Riflescopes

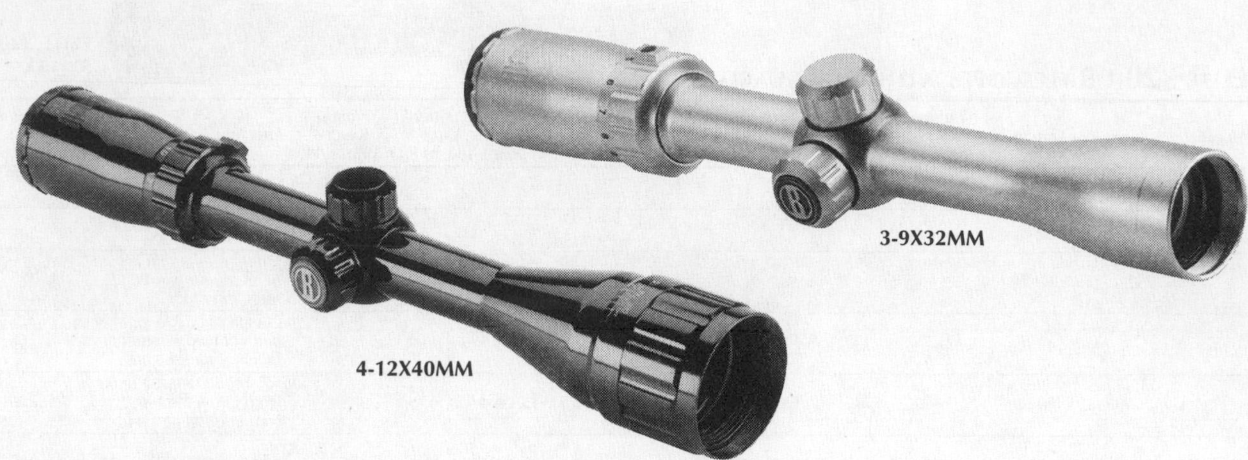

Sportsman Riflescopes

Sportsman Riflescopes have multi-coated optics, plus a long list of standard features, including a fast-focus eyepiece and 1/4 M.O.A. fingertip windage and elevation adjustments. The easy-grip power change ring makes changing magnifications fast and easy. The rigid one-piece 1" tube is waterproof, fogproof and shockproof. 3-9x32mm: Gloss, 72-1393; Silver, 72-1393S; Matte, 72-13984-12x40mm: Gloss, 72-0412

Bushnell Sportsman® Riflescopes

Model	Finish	Features/Selection	Actual Magnification	Obj. Lens Aperture (mm)	Field of View Ft@100 yds	Weight (oz)	Length (in)	Eye Relief (in)	Exit Pupil (mm)	Click Value In@100yds	Adj. Range In@100yds	Price
72-0038		For High-Velocity Break Barrel Airguns. 50 Feet Parallax Setting	3x-9x	32	37 14	13.5	12	3.5	10.6-3.6	.25	100	$70
72-0039	G	Adjustable Objective. Rings. Air Rifle, Rimfire with Range Focus Adjustments 10yd-Infinity.	3x-9x	32	13.1	163	12.2	3	3.6-11	.25	100	102
72-0130	M	Red Dot Sight. 6 M.O.A. Dot. Ideal for Handgun, Shotgun and Competitive Shooting.	1x	23	60	4.9	5.5	Unlimited	2.3@1x	.5	50	74
72-0412	G	Adjustable Objective. Long Range.	4x-12x	40	8.5 25.8	14.6	13.75	3	10-3.3	.25	90	124
72-1393 72-1393S 72-1398	G S M	All-Purpose Variable	3x-9x	32	14 41	13.5	12	3	10-3.6	.25	100	60
72-1403	M	General Purpose	4x	32	29	11	11.7	3	8	.25	110	50
72-1545	M	Shotgun/Muzzle Loader. Low Power Variable Ideal for Close-In or Medium-Range Shooting.	1.5x-4.5x	21	24 69	11.7	10.1	3	10-3.6	.25	210	80
72-1548R	Camo	Circle-X Reticle. Turkey Hunting Shotgun Slugs and Muzzle Loading.	1.5x-4.5x	32	19.3 46.2	13.5	11.7	3	7.1-123	.25	100	96
72-3940 72-3940M	G M	Excellent for Use at Any Range.	3x-9x	40	12 37	15	13	3.5	13-4.4	.25	100	84
72-3943	M	3-2-1 Low-Light Reticle. Improved Crosshair Visibility for Low-Light Shooting.	3x-9x	40	12 37	15	13	3.5	13-4.4	.25	100	84

Bushnell Riflescopes

3X-9X (40MM) TROPHY®
WIDE ANGLE RIFLESCOPE

BUSHNELL TROPHY® RIFLESCOPES

MODEL	SPECIAL FEATURE	ACTUAL MAGNI-FICATION	OBJ. LENS APERATURE (MM)	FIELD OF VIEW @ 100YDS (FT.)	WEIGHT (OZ)	LENGTH	EYE RELIEF (IN.)	EXIT PUPIL (MM)	CLICK VALUE @ 100YDS (IN.)	ADJUST RANGE @ 100YDS (IN.)	SELECTION	SUGGESTED RETAIL
73-0131	Red Dot Sight 6 M.O.A. Dot	1x	28	68	6	5.5	-	28	.5	50	Ideal for handgun, shotgun, competitive	$90
73-0134	Red Dot Sight w/ 4 Dial in Reticles	1x	28	68	6	5.5	Unlimited	28	.5	50	Handgun and Shotgun	120
73-1500	Wide Angle	1.75x-5x	32	68-23	12.3	10.8	3.5	18.3-1.75x	.25	120	Shotgun, black powder or center-fire. Close-in brush hunting.	156
73-3940	Wide angle (73-3940S Silver)	3x-9x	40	42/14-14/5	13.2	11.7	3	13.3-4.44	.25	60	All purpose variable, excellent for use from close to long range. Circular view provides a definite advantage over "TV screen" type scopes for running game uphill or down.	140
73-3946	All Purpose Mil Dot Reticle	3x-9x	40	42	13.2	11.7	3.4	13.3	.25	60		150
73-3949	Wide angle with Circle-x™ Reticle	3x-9x	40	42-14	13.2	11.7	3	13.3-4.4	.25	60	Matte finish, Ideal low light reticle.	150
73-3948	Matte finish Wide Angle	3x-9x	40	42-14	13.2	11.7	3	13.3-4.4	.25	60	Ideal for game running uphill or down	140
73-4124	Wide angle, adjustable objective (73-4124M Matte)	4x-12x	40	32-11	16.1	12.6	3	10-3.3	.25	60	Medium to long range variable for varmint and big game. Range focus adjustment. Excellent air riflescope.	264
73-6184	Semi-turret target adjustments, adjustable objective	6x-18x	40	17.3-6	17.9	14.8	3	6.6-2.2	.125	40	Long-range varmint centerfire or short range air rifle target precision accuracy.	332
TROPHY® HANDGUN SCOPES												
73-0232S	(73-0232S Silver)	2x	32	20	7.7	8.7	9	16	.25	90	Designed for target and short to med. range hunting. Magnum recoil resistant.	192
73-2632	(73-2632S Silver)	2x-6x	32	11-4	10.9	9.1	18	16-5.3	.25	50	18 inches of eye relief at all powers	252
TROPHY® SHOTGUN/HANDGUN SCOPES												
73-1421	Brush Scope/Turkey with Circle-x™ Reticle	1.75x-4x	32	73-30	10.9	10.8	3.5	18-8	.25	120	Ideal for turkey hunting, slug guns or blackpowder guns. Matte finish.	150
TROPHY® AIR RIFLESCOPES												
73-4124	Wide angle, adjustable objective (73-4124M Matte)	4x-12x	40	32-11	16.1	12.6	3	10-3.3	.25	60	Medium to long range variable for varmint and big game. Range focus adjustment. Excellent air riflescope.	264
73-6184	Semi-turret target adjustments, adjustable objective	6x-18x	40	17-6	17.9	14.8	3	6.6-2.2	.125	40	Long-range varmint centerfire or short range air rifle target precision accuracy.	332

Bushnell Riflescopes

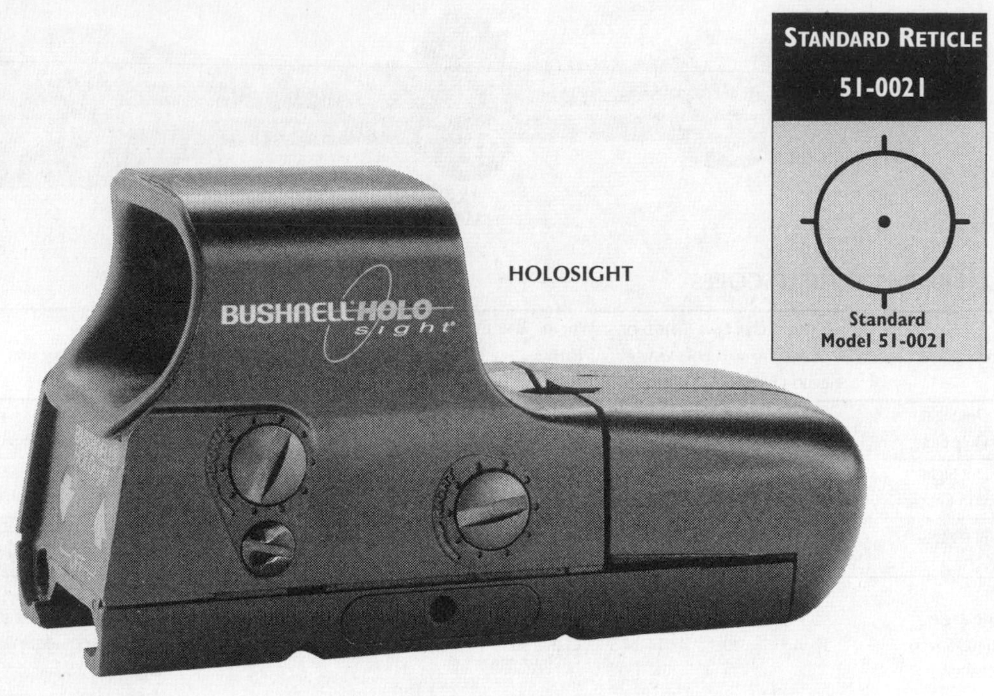

HOLOsight®

The BUSHNELL® HOLOsight® is the world's fastest sight. Advanced holographic technology lets you zero in on your target as quickly as you raise your firearm. Unlike conventional sights, HOLOsight® projects the appearance of an illuminated crosshair 50 yards in front of your gun, yet no forward light is projected. Sight from any distance behind the gun - without taking both eyes off the target. Offers unlimited field of view and eye relief. Shockproof, waterproof and fogproof. Half the length and weight of conventional scopes. Fits easily on handguns, shotguns and rifles with a standard Weaver® style mount. Uses 2 common N batteries.

Bushnell Holosight® Specifications

Optics	Magnification @ 100 yds	Field of View ft @ 100 yds	Weight (oz/g)	Length (in/mm)	Eye Relief (in/mm)	Batteries	Windage Click value in @100 yds mm@ 100m	Elevation Click Value in @100 yds mm@ 100m	Brightness adjustment settings
Holographic	1x	Unlimited	6.4/181	4.125/104.8	½" to 10 ft. 13 to 3045 mm	2 Type N 1.5 Volt	.25 M.O.A./ 7mm @100m	.5 M.O.A./ 14mm@100m	20 levels

Model	Reticle	Description	Uses	
HOLOsight®				
51-0021	Standard	2-Dimensional 65 M.O.A. ring with one M.O.A. dot and tick marks.	General all-purpose handguns, rifles, slug guns, and wing shooting	$390

Bushnell Riflescopes

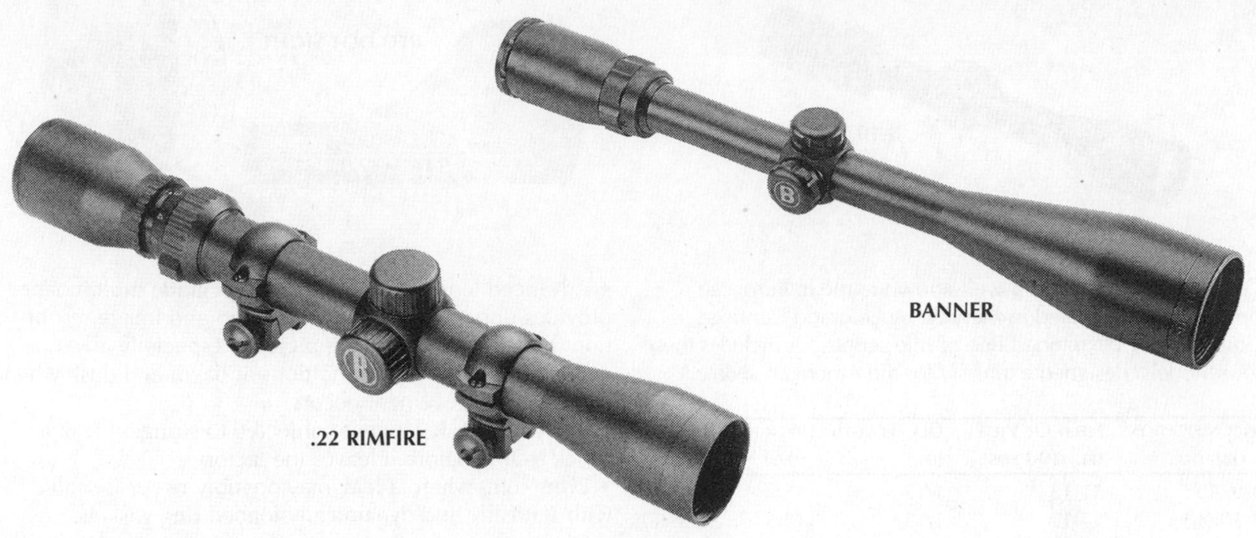

.22 Rimfire

Bushnell .22 Rimfire scopes are designed specifically for .22 Rimfire rifles, with 50-yard parallax setting. Includes rings, fully coated optics for low-light shooting and easy-grip power change ring. One-piece 1" tube is waterproof and fogproof. 1/4 M.O.A. fingertip windage and elevation adjustments.

Banner

Banner Dusk & Dawn riflescopes feature DDB multi-coated lenses to maximize dusk and dawn brightness for clarity in low and full light. A fast-focus eyepiece and wide-angle field of view focus on and follow game easily. One-piece tube for durability under all conditions. Features ¼" M.O.A. fingertip resettable windage and elevation adjustments. An easy-grip power change ring allows fast and easy zoom changes. Fully waterproof, fogproof and shockproof.

.22 Rimfire

Model	Special Features	Actual Magnification	Obj. Lens Aperature (mm)	Field of View ft @ 100yds/m	Weight (oz/g)	Length (in/mm)	Eye Relief (in/mm)	Eye Pupil (mm)	Click Value in @ 100yds mm @ 100m	Adjust Range in @ 100 yds m@ 100m	Selection	Suggested Retail
76-2239	Multix Reticle w/ rings	3x-9x	32	40	11.2	11.75	3	10.6-3.6	.25	40		$54
76-2243	Multix Reticle w/ rings	4	32	30	10	11.5	3	8	.25	40		46

Bushnell Banner Riflescopes

Model	Special Features	Actual Magnification	Obj. Lens Aperature (mm)	Field of View ft @ 100yds/m	Weight (oz/g)	Length (in/mm)	Eye Relief (in/mm)	Eye Pupil (mm)	Click Value in @ 100yds mm @ 100m	Adjust Range in @ 100 yds m@ 100m	Selection	Suggested Retail
71-0432	Shotgun/.22 scope Circle-x reticle, matte finish	4x	32	31.5	11.1	11.3	3.5	8	.25	50	Ideal for .22S/shotgun	$90
71-1432	Circle-x reticle Matte finish	1x-4x	32	78.5-24.9	12.2	10.5	3.8	16.9	.25	50	Ideal for .22S/shotgun	108
71-1545	Wide Angle	1.5x-4.5x	32	67-23	10.5	10.5	3.5	17-7	.25	60	Ideal Shotgun and median to short range scope.	102
71-1436	Provides long eye relief	1.75x-4x	32	35-16	12.1	10.8	6	18.3-6.4	.25	100	For cantilever shotguns	102
71-3944	Black powder scope w/extended eye relief and Circle-x@ reticle	3x-9x	40	36-13	12.5	11.5	4	13-4.4	.25	60	Specifically designed for black powder and shotguns	110
71-3948	Ideal scope for multi purpose guns	3x-9x	40	40-74	13	12	3	13.3-4.4	.25	60	General purpose	106
71-3950	Large objective for extra brightness in low light	3x-9x	50	31-10	19	16	3	16-5.6	.25	50	Low light conditions	164
71-3951	Matte finish low light reticle	3x-9x	50	26-12	19	16	3.5	16-5.6	.25	50	Good for low-light	164
71-4124	Adjustable objective	4x-12x	40	29-11	15	12	3	10-3.3	.25	60	Ideal scope for long-range shooting.	139
71-6185	Adjustable objective	6x-18x	50	17-6	18	16	3	8.3-2.8	.25	40	Long range varmint and target scope.	184

Docter Sports Optics

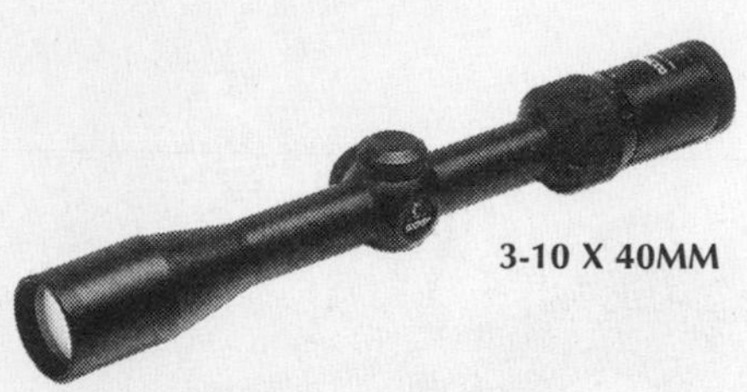

3-10 X 40MM

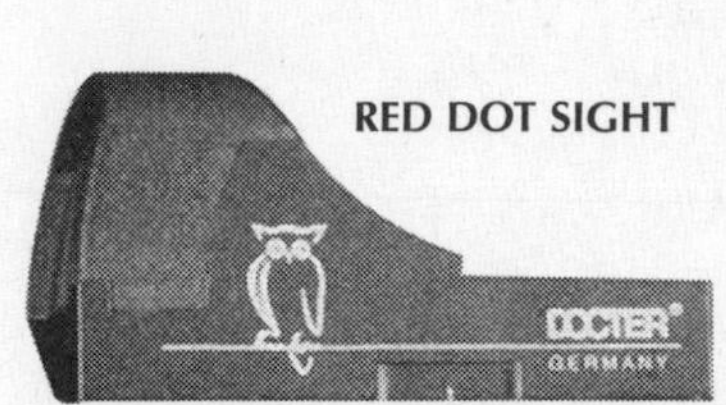

RED DOT SIGHT

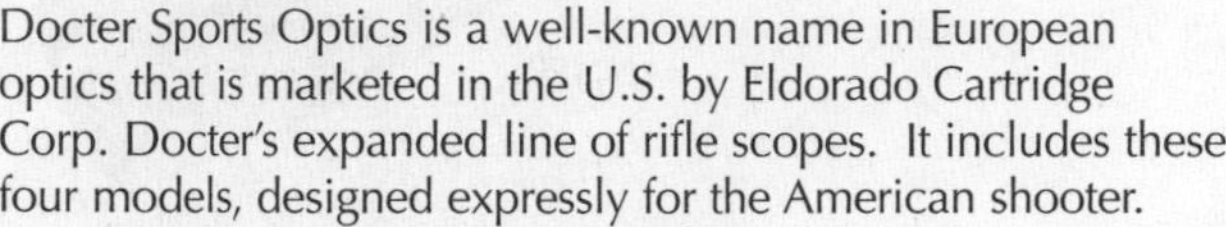

Docter Sports Optics is a well-known name in European optics that is marketed in the U.S. by Eldorado Cartridge Corp. Docter's expanded line of rifle scopes. It includes these four models, designed expressly for the American shooter.

MAGNIFICATION X OBJ. DIA.	FIELD OF VIEW (FT., 100 YDS)	DIA./LENGTH (IN.)	WEIGHT (OZ.)	PRICE
3-9x40	31-13	1/12.5	17	$378.00
3-10x40	34-12	1/13	18.5	626.00
4.5-14x40	23-8	1/13.5	21.5	652.00
8-25x50	13-4	1/16	26.5	901.00

Some of Docter Optic 30mm scopes feature aspherical lenses, as do the company's binoculars. All Docter scopes offer these advantages:

RIFLE SCOPE SPECIFICATIONS

• High strength, one-piece tube construction of aircraft-grade aluminum eliminates weak screw-together joints that can leak or break, won't rust or corrode in adverse weather.
• Precise click-stop adjustments of ¼" at 100 yards for windage and elevation. Wide range of adjustment (50") makes it easier to compensate for mounting errors.
• Advanced lens technology and high grade multi-coating provides unparalled light transmission and image resolution for crisp, clear sighting picture - especially advantageous during low light conditions at dawn and dusk when most animal movement occurs.
• Every DOCTER scope is subjected to stringent leak and shock testing before it leaves the factory.
• Every joint where a leak may possibly occur is sealed with statically and dynamically loaded ring gaskets.
• Diopter focusing adapts the focus to your particular needs.
• Eye relief of over 3 inches, plus a wide rubber ring on the eye-piece protects the shooter from half-moon cuts, even with heavy calibers.

DOCTOR RED DOT SIGHT

A red dot sight is now available from Docter Sports Optics. Weighing just one ounce, it is not much bulkier than a standard rear sight, yet it offers the advantage of a single sighting plane. A red dot appears to project itself on the target—there's nothing to line up. You can shoot more quickly than with any other type of sight. Coated, high-quality lenses ensure a clear sight picture. There is no battery switch; batteries last up to five years without rest. Available in 3.5 or 7 M.D.A.

DESCRIPTION	MAGNIFICATION	OBJECTIVE LENS DIA.	COLOR	RETICLE
ONE-INCH TUBE SCOPES				
3-9 x 40 Variable	3x to 9x	40 mm	Matte Black	Plex
3-9 x 40 Variable	3x to 9x	40 mm	Matte Black	German #4
3-10 x 40 Variable	3x to 10x	40 mm	Matte Black	Plex
3-10 x 40 Variable	3x to 10x	40 mm	Matte Black	German #4
4.5-14 x 40 Variable	4.5x to 14x	40 mm	Matte Black	Plex
4.5-14 x 40 Variable	4.5x to 14x	40 mm	Matte Black	Dot
8-25 x 50 Variable	8x to 25x	50 mm	Matte Black	Dot
8-25 x 50 Variable	8x to 25x	50 mm	Matte Black	Plex
30 mm TUBE SCOPES				
1.5-6 x 42 Variable	1.5x to 6x	42 mm	Matte Black	Plex
1.5-6 x 42 Variable	1.5x to 6x	42 mm	Matte Black	German #4
1.5-6 x 42 Var., Aspherical Lens	1.5x to 6x	42 mm	Matte Black	Plex
1.5-6 x 42 Var., Aspherical Lens	1.5x to 6x	42 mm	Matte Black	German #4
2.5-10 x 48 Variable	2.5x to 10x	48 mm	Matte Black	Plex
2.5-10 x 48 Variable	2.5x to 10x	48 mm	Matte Black	German #4
2.5-10 x 48 Var., Aspherical Lens	2.5x to 10x	48 mm	Matte Black	Plex
2.5-10 x 48 Var., Aspherical Lens	2.5x to 10x	48 mm	Matte Black	German #4
3-12 x 56 Variable	3x to 12x	56 mm	Matte Black	Plex
3-12 x 56 Variable	3x to 12x	56 mm	Matte Black	German #4
3-12 x 56 Var., Aspherical Lens	3x to 12x	56 mm	Matte Black	Plex
3-12 x 56 Var., Aspherical Lens	3x to 12x	56 mm	Matte Black	German #4

Kahles Riflescopes

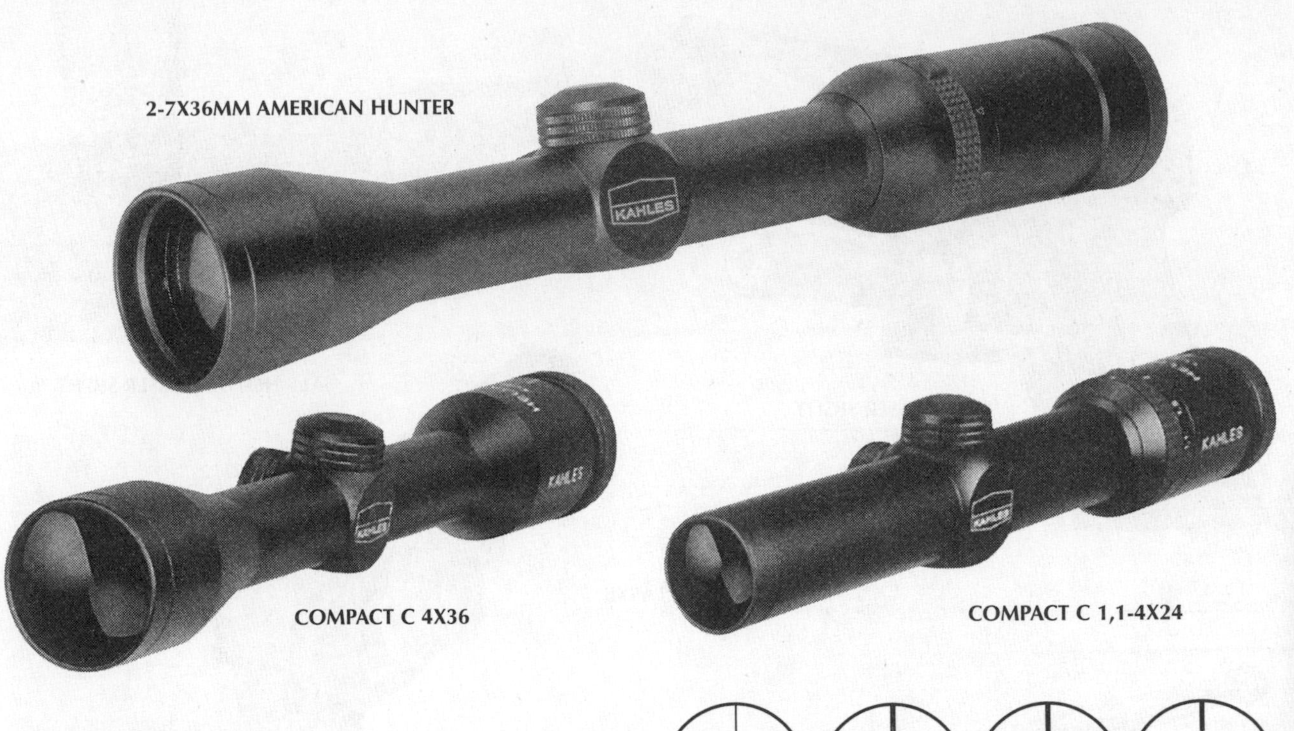

2-7X36MM AMERICAN HUNTER

COMPACT C 4X36

COMPACT C 1,1-4X24

American Hunter

Kahles rifle scopes with a 1" main tube are compact and lightweight with excellent optical performance. One piece construction, generous eye relief, hard anodized, scratch resistant finish, shockproof and fogproof. The AH's reticle is mounted in the second image focal plane, so the reticle appears the same size at every power setting.

Prices: AH 2-7x36 (4A)....................... $554
AH 2-7x36 (Plex)........................... 554
AH 2-7x36 (Turkey)......................... 556
AH 2-7x36 (TDS)............................ 610
AH 2-7x36RF (Rimfire) 4A................... 554
AH 2-7x36RF (Rimfire) Plex................. 554
AH 3-9x42 (4A)............................. 654
AH 3-9x42 (Plex)........................... 654
AH 3-9x42 (TDS)............................ 710
AH 3.5-10x50 (4A).......................... 710
AH 3.5-10x50 (Plex)........................ 710
AH 3.5-10x50 (TDS)......................... 777

Compact

Kahles AMV-multi-coatings transmit up to 99.5% per air-to-glass surface. This ensures optimum use of incident light, especially in low light level conditions or at twilight.

Kahles rifle scopes are rugged, shockproof, waterproof and fogproof. Nitrogen purged several times to assure the absolute elimination of any moisture. 30mm tube.

Prices:C 1.1-4x24 (4A or 7A)................ $777
C 1.5-6x42 (4A or 7A)...................... 877
C 2.5-10x50 (7A or Plex).................. 1077
C 3-12x56 (7A, Plex or 4A)................. 1188
C 4x36 (1" tube, 4A or 7A)................. 610
C 6x42 (1" tube, 4A or 7A)................. 744

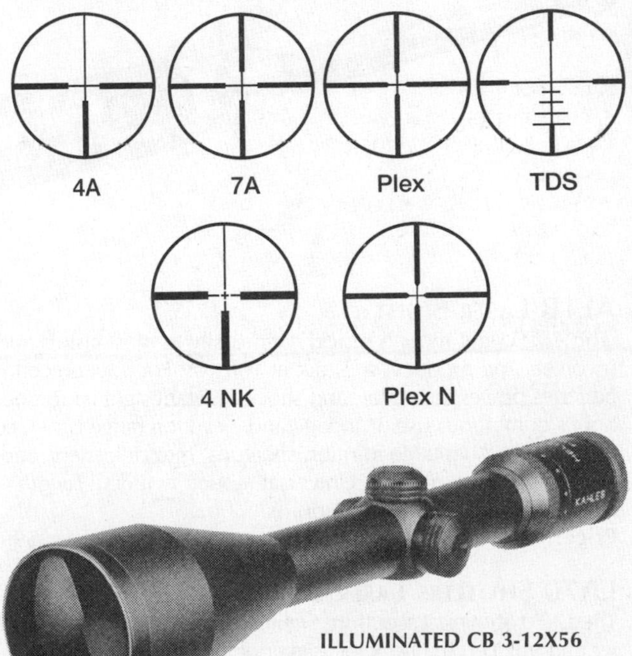

ILLUMINATED CB 3-12X56

Illuminated

Bright reticle is adjustable for illumination, 30mm tube (1" tube on 8x50). Optimum illumination. Minimized straylight. Battery life - 110 hours.

Prices: CB 1.5-6x42 (4NK or PlexN)........... $1321
CB 2.5-10x50 (4NK or PlexN)................. 1432
CB 3-12x56 (PlexN or 4NK)................... 1543

Laseraim Technologies Inc. Sights

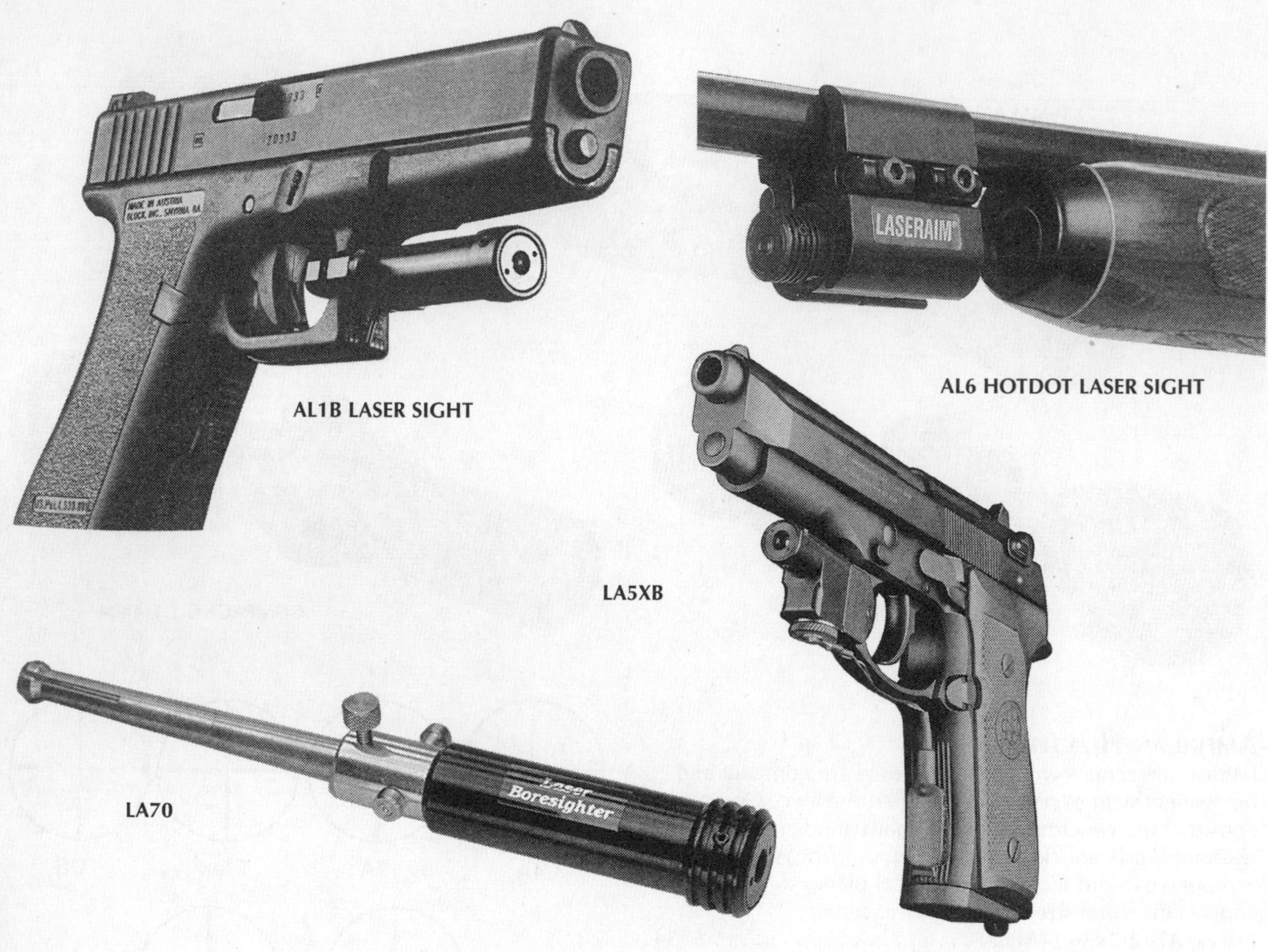

AL1B LASER SIGHT

AL6 HOTDOT LASER SIGHT

LA5XB

LA70

AL1B Laser Sight

The AL1B sight mounts quickly and easily to most pistols and revolvers and produces a 2" dot at 100 yds. Four button cell batteries power the water- and shock-resistant sight up to one hour's continuous use. Windage and elevation range is 9 feet at 25 yards. Adaptable to rifles, shotguns, muzzleloaders, and bows. Available in black. Universal mount included. ***Length***: 2.75" ***Diameter***: ⅝" ***Weight*** (approx.): 2 oz.

Price:. $99

LA70 Shotless Laser Bore Sighter™

The LA70 Shotless Laser Bore SighterTM makes sighting in easier and quicker. To check the center of the bore, simply rotate the laser on axis of the gun bore. The LA70 is equipped with a rotational Laseraim™ with constant ON switch and six arbors fitting calibers 22 thru 45, 12-gauge shotguns and muzzleloaders (50 and 54 cal.). ***Length:*** 8" (w/laser and arbor).

Price:. 169

AR15 Custom Laser Sight

The AR15 laser sight is custom designed to fit all AR15/M16 rifles equipped with triangular front sight post. Laser provides three hours of continuous battery life with convenient replaceable battery. Machined from aircraft grade alminum. ***Weight:*** 3 oz. ***Length:*** 2"

Price:. $190

AL6 Hotdot Laser Sight

Ten times brighter than many other laser sights, this laser produces a 2-inch dot at 100 yards. The remote pressure switch provides operation for up to 2 hours of continuous power. The laser features Laseraim's unique 3-way micro-lock windage and elevation adjustment. Fits Laseraim mounts with no gunsmithing required and is suitable for handguns, rifles, shotguns, muzzle loaders, and bows. Uses convenient replaceable watch batteries.

Price: AL6 Hotdot laser sight 99

LA5XB
Hotdot Mighty Sight

Up to 10 times brighter than other laser sights, Laseraim's Hotdot Lasersights include a rechargeable NICad battery and in-field charger. Produce a 2" dot at 100 yards with a 500-yard range. ***Length:*** 2". ***Diameter:*** .75". Can be used with handguns, rifles, shotguns and bows. Fit all Laseraim mounts. Available in black or satin.

Price:. 139

Leupold Riflescopes

Vari-X III Line

The Vari-X III scopes feature a power-changing system that is similar to the sophisticated lens systems in today's finest cameras. Improvements include an extremely accurate internal control system and a sharp sight picture. All lenses are coated with Multicoat 4. Reticles are the same apparent size throughout the power range and stay centered during elevation/windage adjustments. Eyepieces are adjustable and fog-free. Reticles include German #1, German #1 European, German #4, Post and Duplex, and Leupold Dot.

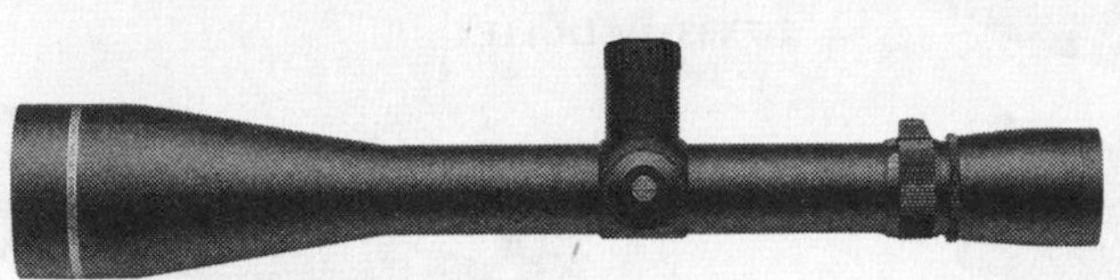
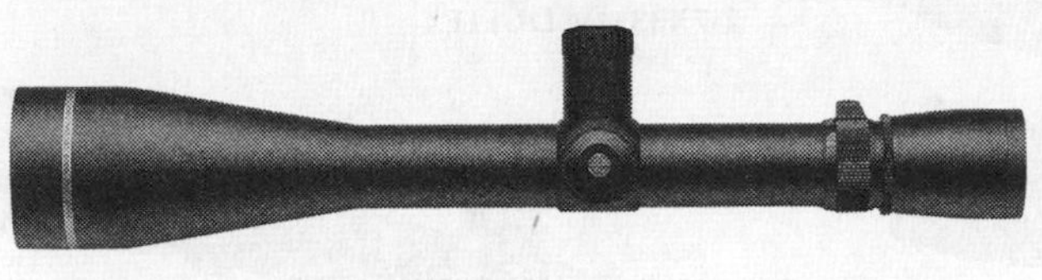
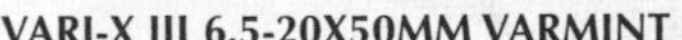

VARI-X III 6.5-20X50MM VARMINT

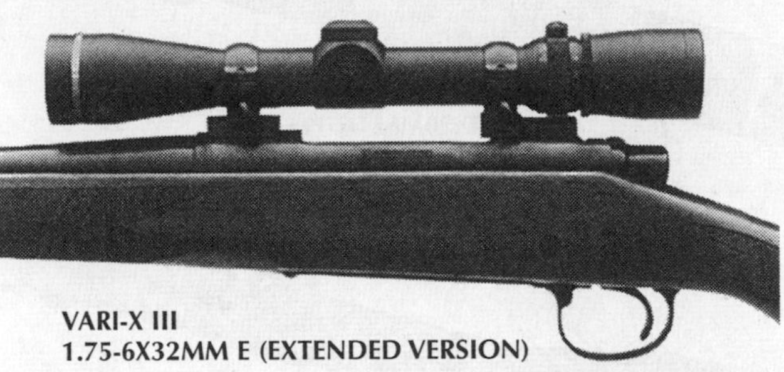

VARI-X III
1.75-6X32MM E (EXTENDED VERSION)

VARI-X III 1.5-5X20MM

This selection of hunting powers is for ranges varying from very short to those at which big game is normally taken. The field at 1.5X lets you get on a fast-moving animal quickly. With magnification at 5X, medium and big game can be hunted around the world at all but the longest ranges.

Duplex or Heavy Duplex, Gloss $520
In black matte finish. 540
German #4 (Gloss). 560
German #1 or #4 (Matte) 580
Also available:
VARI-X III 1.75-6X32mm. Matte finish 560
German Reticles 600

VARI-X III 2.5-8X36MM

This is an excellent range of powers for almost any kind of big game hunting. The top magnification provides enough resolution for varmint shooting.

Duplex. $550
In matte or silver finish 550
Mil Dot (Matte) 690
German #4 (Matte) 600
Post & Duplex (Gloss) 550

VARI-X III 3.5-10X40MM

The extra power range makes these scopes the optimum choice for year-around big game and varmint hunting. The adjustable objective model, with its precise focusing at any range beyond 50 yards, also is an excellent choice for some forms of target shooting.

Duplex. $560
With matte or silver finish 575
Leupold Dot, German #4 610
German #4 or #1 (Matte) 625

VARI-X III 3.5-10X50MM

The hunting scope is designed specifically for low-light situations. The 3.5X10-50mm scope, featuring lenses coated with Multicoat 4, is ideal for twilight hunting because of its efficient light transmission. The new scope delivers an exit pupil that transmits all the light the human eye can handle in typical low-light circumstances, even at the highest magnification.

Duplex or Heavy Duplex $625
With matte or silver finish 650
#4 German (Gloss). 690
Matte or Silver (Dot or German #4) 710

VARI-X III 4.5-14X40MM (ADJ. OBJECTIVE)

This model has enough range to double as a hunting scope and as a varmint scope.

Duplex, Fine or Heavy Duplex $625
With matte finish 660
German #1 or #4 675
Matte. 700
Same as above with 50mm adj. obj., Duplex, Fine or Heavy Duplex; matte finish only 740
German #1 or #4 775

VARI-X III 6.5-20X40MM (ADJ. OBJECTIVE)

This scope has a wide range of power settings, and can be used for any kind of big-game hunting where higher magnifications are useful. Side-focus adjustment allows shooters to eliminate parallax while in shooting position without taking their eyes off the target.

Gloss finish (duplex). $675
Leupold Dot. 720
With matte or silver finish 690
Also available:
6.5-20X50mm Adj. Obj. w/Duplex matte finish 775
6.5-20X50mm Adj. Obj. w/Mil Dot matte finish 875
w/Leupold Dot or German #4 810

VARI-X III 6.5-20X40MM E.F.R. TARGET

For those situations, such as air rifle or rimfire silhouette, where normal adjustable objective ranges are simply too distant, Leupold offers the EFR (Extended Focus Rifle) model of the 6.5-20. With this model, parallax distances as close as 10 meters can be set.

Fine Duplex (Matte) 750
Target Dot (Matte) 795

Leupold Scopes
VXII Line

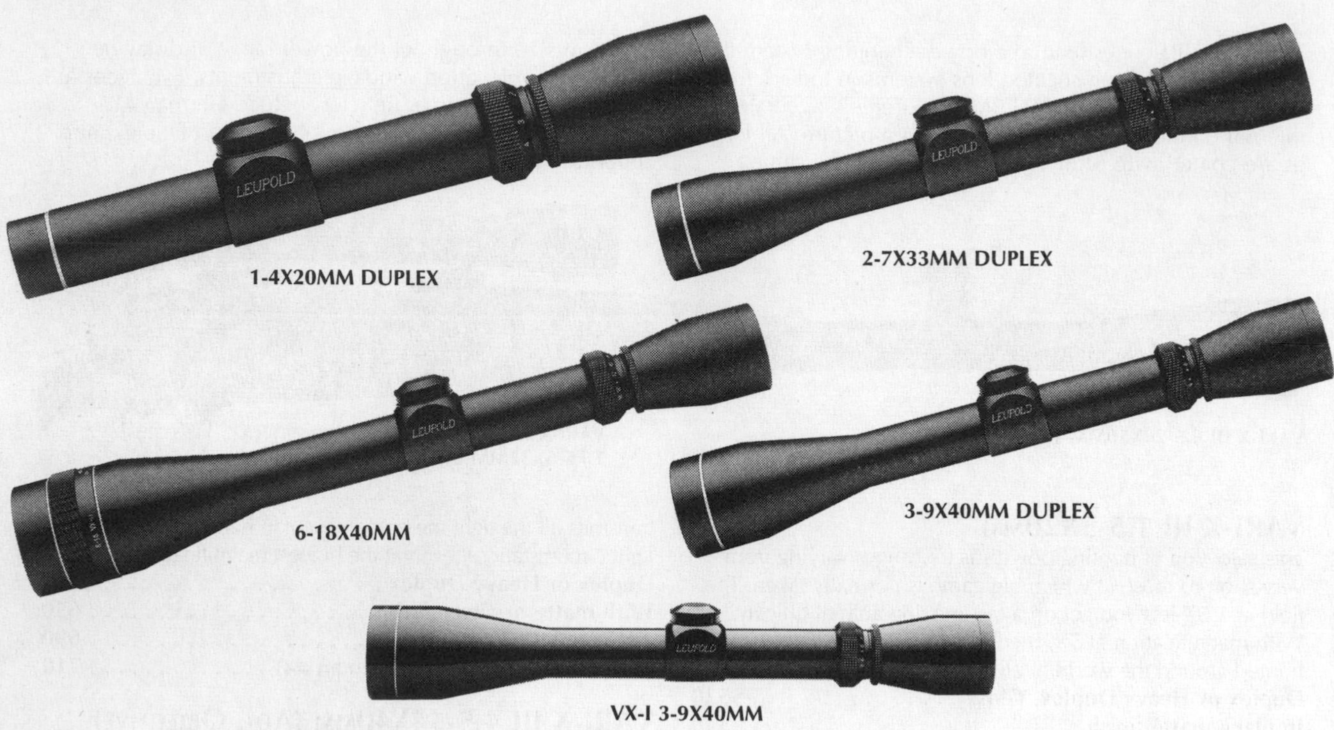

The VXII line offers multi-coated 4 exterior lenses and magnesium fluoride-coated interior lenses for improved light transmission, ¼ M.O.A. click, a locking eyepiece for reliable ocular adjustment, and a sealed, nitrogen-filled interior for fog-free reliability.

VX-II 1-4X20MM DUPLEX

This scope, the smallest of Leupold's VARI-X II line, is noted for its large field of view: 70 feet at 100 yards.

Matte finish only(Duplex) $310
CPC 350

VX-II 2-7X33MM DUPLEX

A compact scope, no larger than the Leupold M8-4X,offering a wide range of power. It can be set at 2X for close ranges in heavy cover or zoomed to maximum power for shooting or identifying game at longer ranges.

VX II 2-7x 33 Shotgun (Duplex) matte $325
Leupold Dot. 360

VX-II 3-9X50MM

This LOV scope delivers a 5.5mm exit pupil for low-light visibility: Gloss (Duplex). 410
Matte finish (Leupold Dot or Duplex) 410
German reticles (Matte) 450

VX-II 3-9X40MM DUPLEX

A wide selection of powers offers the right combination of field of view and magnification to fit most hunting conditions. Many hunters use the 3X or 4X setting most of the time, cranking up to 9X for positive identification of game or for extremely long shots. The adjustable objective eliminates parallax and permits precise focusing on any object from less than 50 yards to infinity for extra-sharp definition.

Gloss finish $340
In matte, silver (Duplex). 340
Matte (CPC, Leupold Dot, German) 375

VX-II 4-12X40MM (ADJ. OBJECTIVE)

The ideal answer for big game and varmint hunters alike. At 12.25 inches, the 4X12 is virtually the same length as Vari-X II 3X9. New fixed objective has same long eye relief and is factory-set to be free of parallax at 150 yds.

Matte or silver finish (Leupold Dot) $550
Mil. Dot (Gloss) German 4, Post, or Duplex 560

VX-II 6-18X40MM ADJ. OBJ. TARGET

Features target-style click adjustments, fully coated lenses, adj. objective for parallax-free shooting from 50 yards to infinity.

In matte, Fine Duplex. 500
Target Dot 540
Dot w/Target knobs 575
Fine Duplex w/Target knobs 540

VX-I SERIES

A tough, gloss black finish and Duplex reticle. Leupold's high quality at an affordable price. Available in 2-7x33, 3-9x40 and 4-12x40mm

from 199

SIGHTS & SCOPES

Leupold Scopes

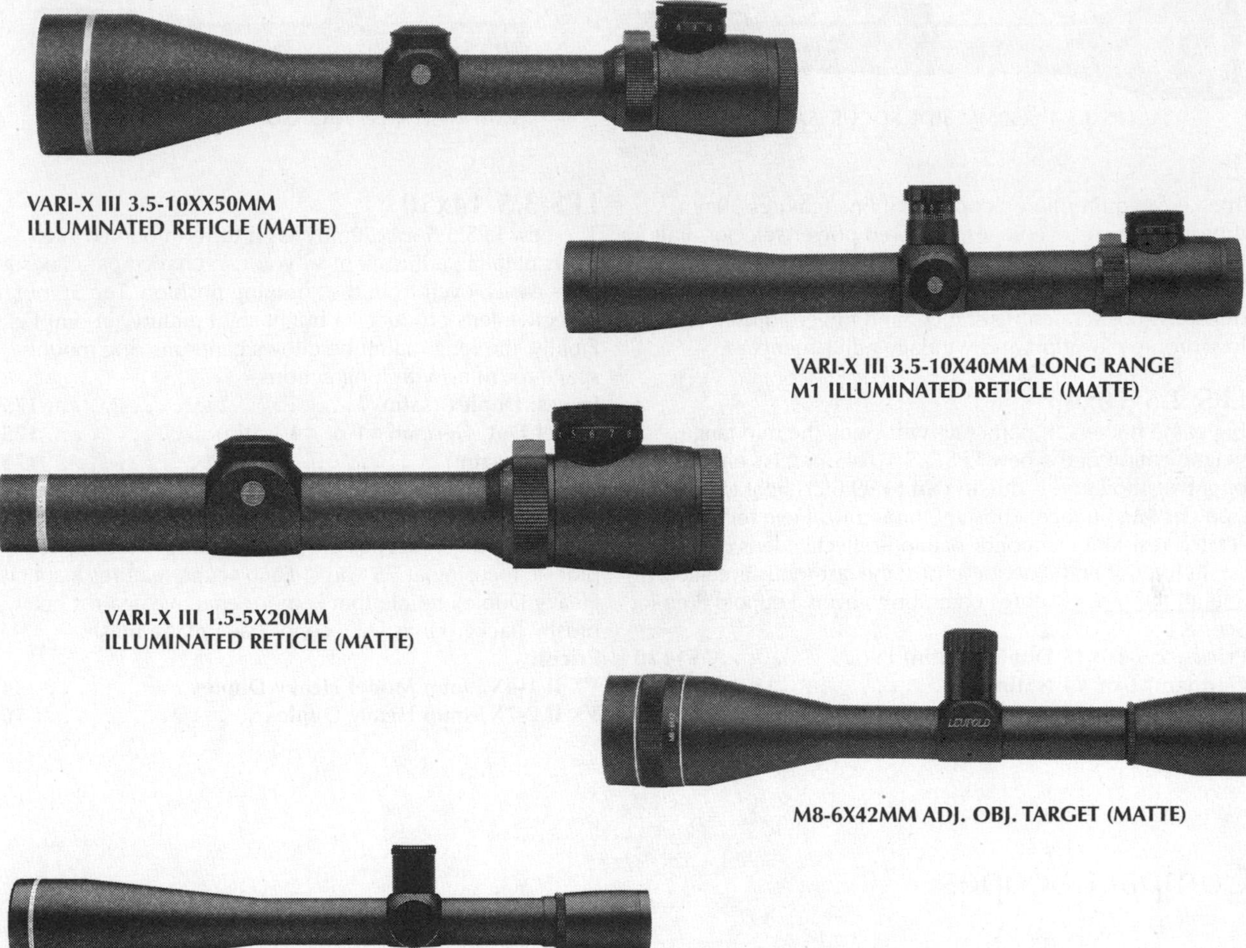

VARI-X III 3.5-10XX50MM ILLUMINATED RETICLE (MATTE)

VARI-X III 3.5-10X40MM LONG RANGE M1 ILLUMINATED RETICLE (MATTE)

VARI-X III 1.5-5X20MM ILLUMINATED RETICLE (MATTE)

M8-6X42MM ADJ. OBJ. TARGET (MATTE)

COMPETITION SERIES 45X45MM

Illuminated Reticle

Acquire targets and place shots quickly and accurately in even the most extreme low-light conditions. Adjust between 11 intensity settings to match the light - even the brightest setting won't overpower your target or affect your low-light vision. Switch the reticle off in daylight and it reverts to black. Choose from three different reticle designs: Illuminated Duplex, Illuminated German #4 Dot, or Illuminated Circle Dot. Each scope, meets the Leupold standard for waterproofing and durability.

Price: 1.5-5x20. . . . . **$750**
3.5-10x50 . . . . **850**
4.5-14x50 . . . . **950**
3.5-10x40 M1+M3 . . . . **1125**

Leupold 6 x 42 AO Target Scope

The Leupold M8 6x42mm Adjustable Objective Target Scope offers all the features needed by hunters and benchrest shooters. Both the elevation and windage dials of this scope feature ¼ minute of angle, target-style click adjustments. An adjustable objective dial offers the ability to correct parallax from a distance of 50 yards to infinity.

Price: Matte w/Duplex **500**

Competition Series Scopes

Leupold's new Competition series includes the 35x45mm, 40x45mm and 45x45mm. Shooters get a bright, crisp sight picture with outstanding contrast, at extremely high magnification. The side-focus parallax adjustment knob allows you to adjust your scope to be parallax-free at distances from 40 yards to infinity. Available in matte finish with target dot or target crosshair reticle.

Price **1190**

Leupold Scopes

Leupold Premier Scopes (LPS)

LPS 3.5-14X50MM SIDE FOCUS (SATIN FINISH)

VX-II 1-4X20MM SHOTGUN/MUZZLELOADER

The Leupold Premiere Scope (LPS) line features 30mm tubes, fast-focus eyepieces, armored power selector dials that can be read from the shooting position, 4-inch constant eye relief, Diamondcoat lenses for increased light transmission, scratch resistance, and finger adjustable, low-profile elevation and windage adjustments.

LPS 2.5-10x45

Big game hunters in particluar will enjoy the mid-range magnification of the new LPS 2.5-10x45mm. It's unusually bright sight picture is due in part to 99.65% light transmission per lens surface; constant, non-critical eye relief; scratch resistant DiamondCoat anti-reflective lens coating on all interior and exterior lenses; the fast-focus eyepiece; and all the other features common to every Leupold Premier Scope.

Prices: 2.5-10x45 Duplex (satin) $1120
German #1 or #4 (satin). 1120

LPS 3.5-14x50

The new LPS 3.5-14x50mm has a turret-mounted side-focus parallax adjustment so you can change parallax settings easily, even from the shooting position. The 50mm objective lens produces a bright sight picture, in dim light. Finally, the long maintube allows generous ring mount space for rifles with long actions.

Prices: Duplex (satin) 1750
Target Dot, German #1 or #4 (satin) 1750
Mil Dot (satin) 1750

Shotgun & Muzzleloaders Scopes

Leupold shotgun scopes are parallax-adjusted to deliver precise focusing at 75 yards. Each scope features a special Heavy Duplex reticle that is more effective against heavy, brushy backgrounds. All scopes have matte finish.

Prices:
VX II 1-4X20mm Model Heavy Duplex 340
VX II 2-7X33mm Heavy Duplex 360

Compact Scopes

M8 - 2.5X20MM COMPACT

M8 4X28 COMPACT RF SPECIAL

VARI-X 2-7X28 & RF SPECIAL

VARI-X 3-9X33 COMPACT

M8 2.5-20mm Compact

This small scope presents the shooter with an enormous field of view for fast target acquisition. It also features generous elevation and windage adjustment. Standard models are parallax adjusted to 100 yards. The Turkey Ranger model, with a special Post & Duplex reticle designed to subtend 9 inches from the post to crosswire at 40 yards, is parallax adjusted to 40 yards. Offered in a matte finish.

Duplex or Heavy Duplex (matte) $250
M8 4x28mm Compact Rimfire Special
Fine Duplex (gloss) 310

Vari-X 2-7x28mm Compact
Duplex (gloss). $390
Vari-X 2-7x28mm Compact Rimfire Special
Fine Duplex (gloss) 390
Vari-X 3-9x33mm Compact Duplex
(matte, silver) 430

Vari-X 3-9x33mm Compact E.F.R.

With an adjustable objective capable of correcting parallax as close as 10 meters, this scope is perfectly suited to .22 rimfire silhouette and air rifle shooting.

Duplex (gloss) 435

SIGHTS & SCOPES

Leupold Scopes

Leupold Tactical Scopes
Fixed and Variable Power.
Repeatable accuracy on all powers. 1/4 MOA audible click windage and elevation adjustments (Except M-3s). Superior image quality and excellent light transmission. Duplex or Mil Dot reticle. Waterproof.

M8-2.5x28mm

For all the shooters wirldwide who are rediscovering the classic lever-action rifle, the M8-2.5x28mm IER Scout is the ideal choice. Designed specifically for lever-action and scout-style rifles, it offers 9 to 17 inches of eye relief (IER stands for "Intermediate Eye Relief"). The Scout is mounted on the barrel, in front of the receiver.
Matte finish (Duplex) **$240**
Matte or silver (Duplex) **240**

M8-4X

The 4X delivers a widely used magnification and a generous field of view **(Gloss)** **325**
In black matte finish (Duplex). **438**

M8-6X

The 6X extends the range for big-game hunting and doubles in some cases as a varmint scope **(Gloss)** **340**

M8-6x42mm

Large 42mm objective lens features a 7mm exit pupil for increased light-gathering capability. Recommended for varmint shooting at night.
Duplex or Heavy Duplex **425**
In matte finish **470**

M8-12x40mm STANDARD (Adj. Obj.)

Outstanding optical qualities, resolution and magnification make the 12X a natural for the varmint shooter. Adjustable objective is standard for parallax-free focusing.
Fine Duplex **475**
Leupold Dot. **500**

Mark 4 M1 10X40 (Matte)/Mark 4 M1 16X40 (Matte)
Duplex. **1510**
  Mil Dot **1610**
VX II 3-9x40 (Matte)
  Duplex **450**
  Mil Dot **540**
Vari-X III 3.5-10x40 (Matte)
  Duplex. **655**
  Mil Dot **750**
Vari-X III 4.5-14x40 AO (Matte)
  Duplex. **720**
  Mil Dot **825**

Fixed Power Scopes

M8-2.5X28MM IER SCOUT

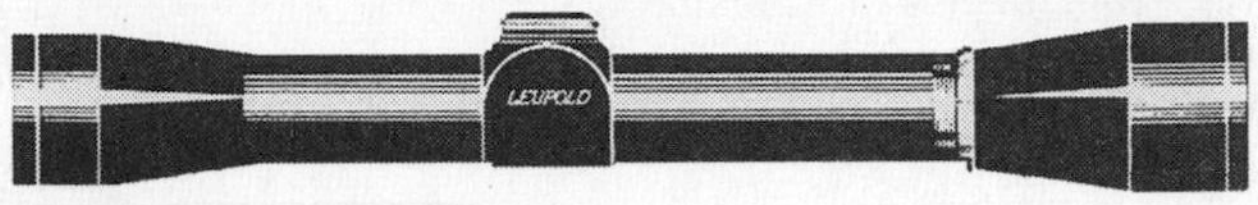

M8-4X33

M8-6X36

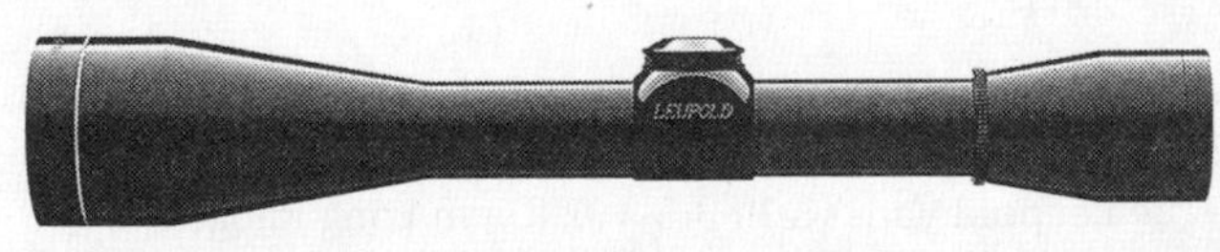

M8-6X42MM

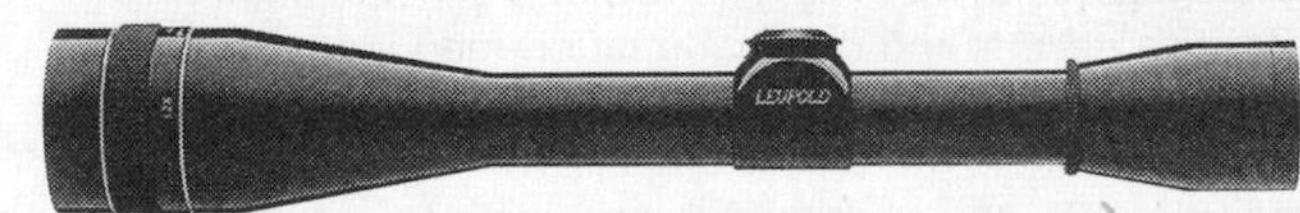

M8-12X40MM STANDARD

Tactical Scopes

MARK 4 M1-16X40MM

SIGHTS & SCOPES

Leupold Scopes
Long-Range Models

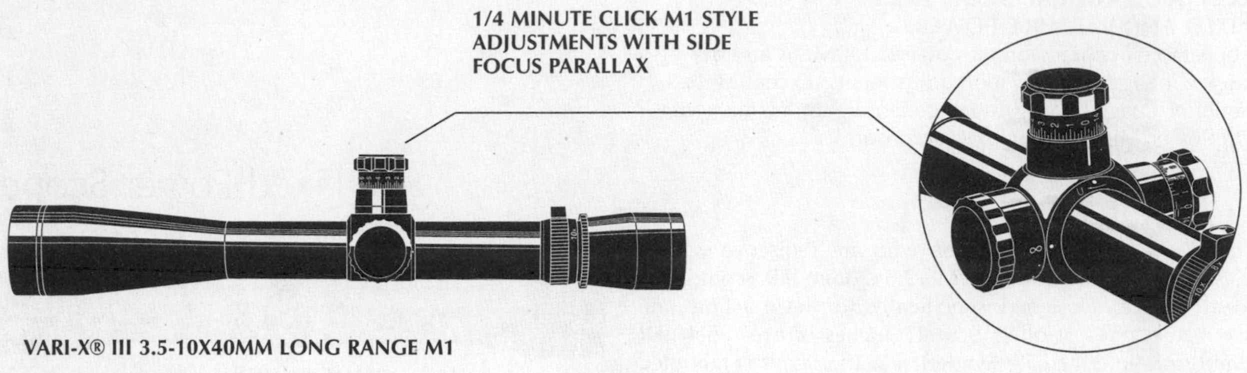

VARI-X® III 3.5-10X40MM LONG RANGE M1

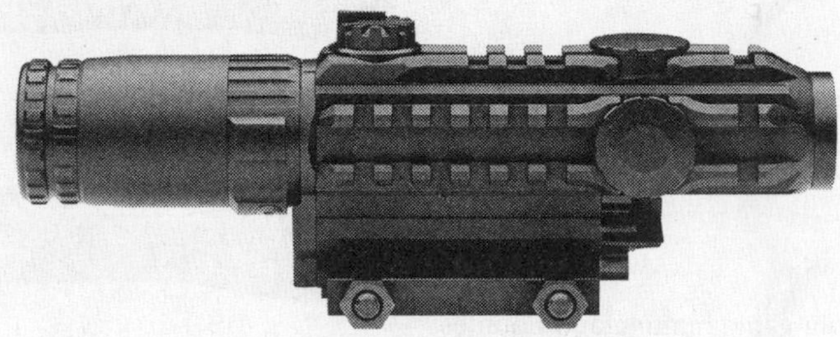

MARK 4 CQ/T 1-3X14MM

SIGHTS & SCOPES

Vari-X III 3.5-10x40mm Long Range Tactical M1

The Leupold Vari-X® III 3.5-10x40mm Long Range M1 scope features easy-to-grip, M1 style finger-adjustable windage, elevation, and side focus parallax adjustment dials that make them easy to use in any field condition. Positive detents and clear calibration markings greatly enhance the simplicity of field adjustments. The 30mm maintube offers increased range of windage and elevation adjustments, and Multicoat 4 lens coatings ensure exceptional brightness, clarity, and contrast. Available in either the traditional Leupold Duplex or "round dot" Mil Dot reticle designs. Like all Leupold Tactical products, it is offered in a full black matter finish.

Duplex (matte) **$940**
Mil. Dot (matte) **1050**

Vari-X III 4.5-14x50mm Long Range Tactical

The 4.5-14x50mm Long Range models with their 30mm maintubes, target style adjustment knobs, and side mounted parallax dials offer the shooter everything necessary to achieve success at great distances.

Vari-X III 4.5-14x50mm Long Range Target Duplex or Fine Duplex (matte) . . . . **P.O.R.**
Vari-X III 4.5-14x50mm Long Range Tactical Mil. Dot (matte) . . . . **P.O.R.**

Vari-X III 6.5-20x50mm Long Range Target

Designed with a 30mm maintube to provide additional elevation and windage adjustment, and featuring target style adjustment dials and a side-mounted parallax dial, this scope offers the long range shooter impressive magnification and convenient adjustment mechanisms.

Fine Duplex (matte, silver) **$955**
Target Dot (matte,silver) **1000**
¾ Min. Mil. Dot (matte) **1060**

Vari-X III 8.5-25x50mm Long Range Target

With a 30mm maintube to provide additional elevation and windage adjustment, target style adjustment dials, and a side mounted parallax dial, this scope offers the long range shooter impressive magnification and convenient adjustment mechanisms.

Fine Duplex (matte) **1030**
Target Dot (matte) **1075**

New Mark 4 CQ/T

The Leupold Mark 4 CQ/T 1-3x14mm is a revolutionary optical sight for tactical firearms. It combines the strengths of a red dot sight and variable-power riflescopes. Ten illumination settings match any light conditions; two low-intensity settings work with night-vision devices.

Price **825**

Nikon Monarch Scopes

6.5-20X44 AO

2-7X32

1.5-4X20

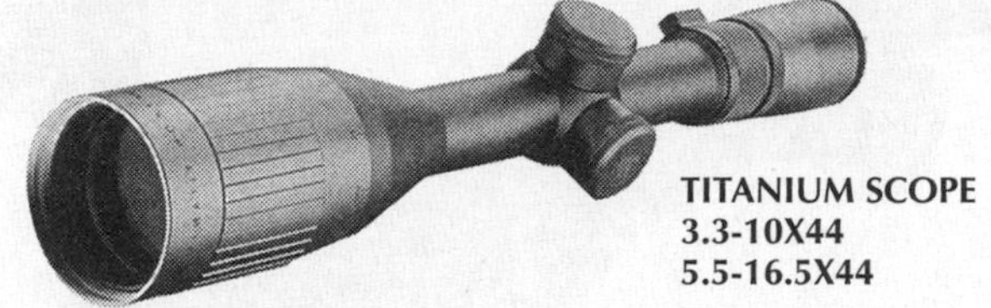

TITANIUM SCOPE
3.3-10X44
5.5-16.5X44

Rifle Scopes

Model 6500 4x40 Lustre $351
Model 6505 4x40 Matte 371
Model 6506 6x42 Lustre 371
Model 6508 6x42 Matte 391
Model 6510 2-7x32 Lustre.................... 407
Model 6515 2-7x32 Matte.................... 427
Model 6520 3-9x40 Lustre.................... 431
Model 6525 3-9x40 Matte.................... 451
Model 6528 3-9x40 Silver Matte 471
Model 6530 3.5-10x50 Lustre 665
Model 6535 3.5-10x50 Matte 685
Model 6537 3.3-10x44AO Lustre.............. 579
Model 6538 3.3-10X44AO Matte (Mildot) 599
Model 6539 3.3-10x44AO Matte.............. 599
Model 6540 4-12x40 AO Lustre................ 573
Model 6545 4-12x40 AO Matte................ 593
Model 6580 5.5-16.5x44 AO Black Lustre......... 603
Model 6585 5.5-16.5x44 AO Black Matte........ $623
Model 6550 6.5-20x44 AO Lustre............... 705
Model 6555 6.5-20x44 AO Matte 725
Model 6570 6.5-20x44 HV.................... 705
Model 6575 6.5-20x44 HV.................... 725
Model 6630 3.3-10x44 AO (Titanium)............ 899
Model 6680 5.5-16.5x44 AO (Titanium) 939

Handgun and Shotgun Scopes

Model 6560 2x20 EER Black Lustre.............. 269
Model 6562 2x20 EER Matte.................... 279
Model 6565 2x20 EER Silver 289
Model 6590 1.5-4.5x20 Shotgun Black Matte 385
Model 6595 1.5-4.5x20 Sabot/Slug Black Matte 385

Also Available:
Illuminated Scopes
3.5-10x50 (Nikoplex or Mildot)............... 865
6.5-20x44 (Nikoplex or Mildot)............... 981

MONARCH™ UCC RIFLESCOPE SPECIFICATIONS

Model	4x40	1.5-4.5x20	2-7x32	3-9x40	3.5-10x50	4-12x40AO	5.5-16.5x44AO	6.5-20x44AO	2x20EER
Lustre	6500	N/A	6510	6520	6530	6540	6580	6550/6556	6560
Matte	6505	6595	6515	6525	6535	6545	6585	6555/6558	6562
Silver	N/A	N/A	N/A	6528	N/A	N/A	N/A	N/A	6565
Actual Magnification	4x	1.5x-4.5x	2x-7x	3x-9x	3.5x-10x	4x-12x	5.5x-16.5x	6.5x-19.46x	1.75x
Objective Diameter	40mm	20mm	32mm	40mm	50mm	40mm	44mm	44mm	20mm
Exit Pupil (mm)	10	13.3-4.4	16-4.6	13.3-4.4	14.3-5	10-3.3	8-2.7	6.7-2.2	11.4
Eye Relief (in)	3.5	3.7-3.5	3.9-3.6	3.6-3.5	3.9-3.8	3.6-3.4	3.2-3.0	3.5-3.1	26.4-10.5
FOV @ 100 yds (ft)	26.9	50.3-16.7*	44.5-12.7	33.8-11.3	25.5-8.9	25.6-8.5	19.1-6.4	16.1-5.4	22
Tube Diameter	1 in.	1 in.	1 in.	1 in.	1 in.	1 in.	1 in.	1 in.	1 in.
Objective Tube(mm/in)	47.3-1.86	25.4/1	39.3-1.5	47.3-1.86	57.3-2.2	53.1-2.09	54-2.13	54-2.13	25, 4/1
Eyepiece O.D. (mm)	38	38	38	38	38	38	38	38	38
Length (in)	11.7	10	11.1	12.3	13.7	13.7	13.4	14.6	8.1
Weight (oz)	11.2	9.3	11.2	12.6	15.5	16.9	18.4	20.1	6.6
Adjustment Gradation	1/4 MOA	1/4 MOA	1/4 MOA	1/4 MOA	1/4 MOA	1/4 MOA	1/4 MOA	1/8 MOA	1/4 MOA
Max Internal Adjustment	120 MOA	120 MOA	70 MOA	55 MOA	45 MOA	45 MOA	40 MOA	38 MOA	120 MOA
Parallax Setting (yds)	100	75	100	100	100	50 to ∞	50 to ∞	50 to ∞	100

*FOV @ 75 yds (ft) *FOV @ 50 yds (ft)

Nikon Buckmaster Scopes

SPECIAL LIMITED EDITION 3-9X40

4.5-14

Teamed with Buckmasters, Nikon has produced a limited edition riflescope line. Built to withstand the toughest hunting conditions, the scopes integrate shockproof, fogproof and waterproof construction, plus numerous other features seldom found on riflescopes in this price range. Nikon's Brightvue™ anti-reflective system of high-quality, multicoated lenses provides over 93% anti-reflection capability for high levels of light transmission and optical clarity required for dawn-to-dusk big game hunting. These riflescopes are parallax-adjusted at 100 yards and have durable matte finishes that reduce glare while afield. They also feature positive steel-to-brass, quarter-minute-click windage and elevation adjustments for instant, repeatable accuracy and a Nikoplex® reticle for quick target acquisition.

Prices:

Model 6465 1x20 . . . . $241
Model 6405 4x40 249
Model 6425 3-9x40 Black Matte 303
Model 6415 3-9x40 Silver 325
Model 6435 3-9x50 463
Model 6450 4.5-14x40 AO Blck Matte 431
Model 6455 4.5-14x40 AO Silver 451
Model 6466 4.5-14X40AO Matte Adj. Mildot 431

SIGHTS & SCOPES

BUCKMASTERS SCOPES

Model	1x20	4x40	3-9x40	3-9x50	4.5-14x40AO
Matte	6465	6405	6425	6435	6450
Silver	N/A	N/A	6415	N/A	6455
Actual Magnification	1x	4x	3.3-8.5x	3.3-8.5x	4.5-13.5x
Objective Diameter	20mm	40mm	40mm	50mm	40mm
Exit Pupil (mm)	20	10	12.1-4.7	15.1-5.9	8.9-2.9
Eye Relief (in)	4.3-13.0	3.5	3.5-3.4	3.5-3.4	3.6-3.4
FOV @ 100 yds (ft)	52.5	30.6	33.9-12.9	33.9-12.9	22.5-7.5
Tube Diameter	1 in.	1 in.	1 in.	1 in.	1 in.
Objective Tube (mm/in)	27/1.06	47.3/1.86	47.3/1.86	58.7/2.3	53/2.1
Eyepiece O.D. (mm)	37	42.5	42.5	42.5	38
Length (in)	8.8	12.7	12.7	12.9	14.8
Weight (oz)	9.2	11.8	13.4	18.2	18.7
Adjustment Gradation	1/4: 1 click	1/4: 1 click	1/4: 1 click	1/4: 1 click	
Max Internal Adjustment	50	80	80	70	40
Parallax Setting (yds)	75	100	100	100	50 to ∞

Nikon Scopes

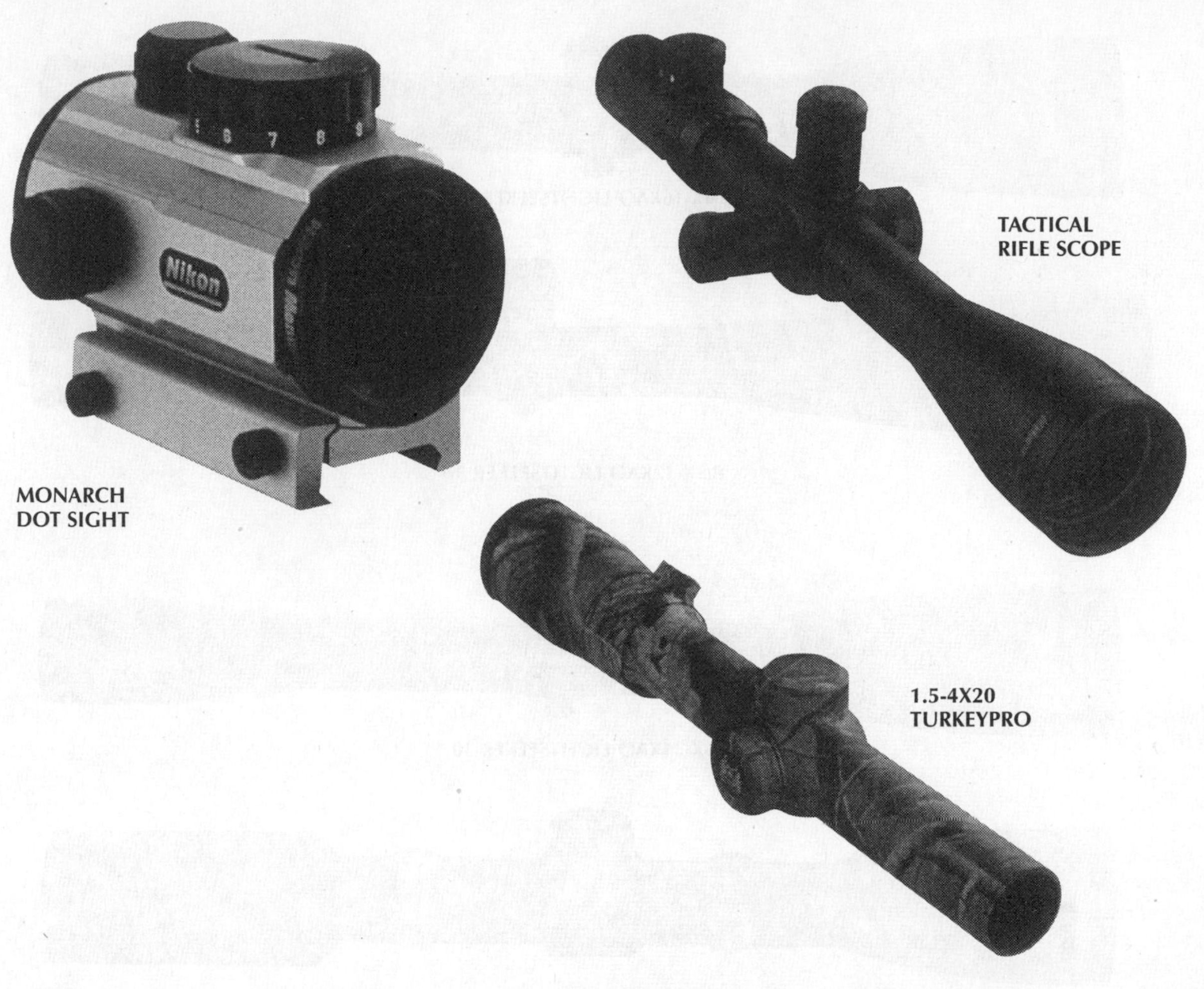

MONARCH DOT SIGHT

TACTICAL RIFLE SCOPE

1.5-4X20 TURKEYPRO

SIGHTS & SCOPES

Tactical Riflescope

Nikon's Tactical Riflescopes are available in 2.5-10x44 and 4-16x50. The 2.5-10x44 features a choice of reticles: Nikoplex, Mildot, and Dual Illuminated Mildot. The 4-16 is offered with Nikoplex or Mildot. Both are equipped with turret mounted parallax adjustment knobs, have a tough, black-anodized matte finish and have easy-to-grip windage and elevation knobs for accurate field adjustments.

Prices:

Tactical 2.5-10x44 (Nikoplex or Mildot) $1361

With Illuminated Mildot 1561

Tactical 4-16x50 (Mildot or Nikoplex) 1461

Monarch Dot Sight

The Monarch Dot Sights are fully waterproof, fogproof and shockproof. Objective and ocular lenses are 30mm diameter and are fully multicoated. The Dot sights have zero magnification, providing unlimited eye relief and a 47.2' field of view at 100 yards, perfect for close up, fast shots. Brightness is controlled by a lithium battery. The standard Monarch Dot Sight is available in silver and black and has a 6 MOA dot. It is also available in Realtree camouflage.

Price: Standard $401

VSD 461

VSD in camo 491

1.5-4.5x20 TurkeyPro

The 1.5-4x20 Monarch TurkeyPro is now available in Realtree Hardwoods camo. It is parallax-free at 50 yards for great shotgun shooting.

Price: 415

2.5-8x28 EER Handgun Scope

Nikon's 2.5-8x28 EER (Extended Eye Relief) is a highly flexible variable handgun scope that should find favor with a wide assortment of hunters, varminters and competitors. It has a wide field of view at low power, but a twist of the power ring instantly supplies 8x magnification for long range shots.

Price: Matte 425

Silver 445

Pentax Scopes

4X-16XAO LIGHTSEEKER 30

8.5X-32XAO LIGHTSEEKER 30

6X-24XAO LIGHTSEEKER 30

WHITETAILS UNLIMITED

Pentax Lightseeker Series

Features:

- ***Scratch-resistant outer tube.*** Under ordinary wear and tear, the outer tube is almost impossible to scratch.
- High Quality cam zoom tube. No plastics are used. The tube is made of a bearing-type brass with precision machined cam slots. The zoom control screws are precision-ground to ½ of one thousandth tolerance.
- ***Leak Prevention.*** Power rings are sealed on a separate precision-machined seal tube. The scopes are then filled with nitrogen and double-sealed with heavy-duty "O" rings, making them leak-proof and fog-proof.
- ***Optics.*** Fully multi-coated, Lightseekers' optics are among the best in the industry, giving you a bright, sharp picture even in poor light.

THE LIGHTSEEKER-30 has the same features as the Lightseeker II, but with a 30mm tube.

The purchase of every Pentax Whitetails Unlimited rifle or shotgun scope includes a free one-year membership in Whitetails Unlimited, and a portion of the purchase price goes to the organization to support its conservation efforts.

PENTAX CORPORATION expands its extensive line of scopes by adding a Ballistic Plex reticle option to two of its Whitetail Unlimited models. Ballistic Plex reticles are available on the 3X-9X and 6.5X-20X Whitetails Unlimited Scopes.

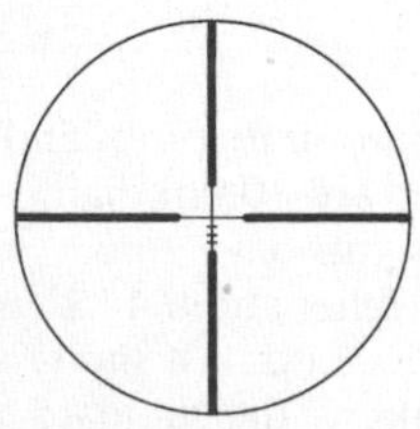

THE BALLISTIC PLEX RETICLE is a copyrighted design on the lower vertical crosshair that compensates for bullet drop. The Ballistic Plex reticle is set to provide dead-on aiming from 100 yards to 500 yards for many of the most common hunting cartridges.

Pentax Rifle Scopes

LIGHTSEEKER 2.5xSG PLUS
MOSSY OAK® BREAK-UP SCOPE

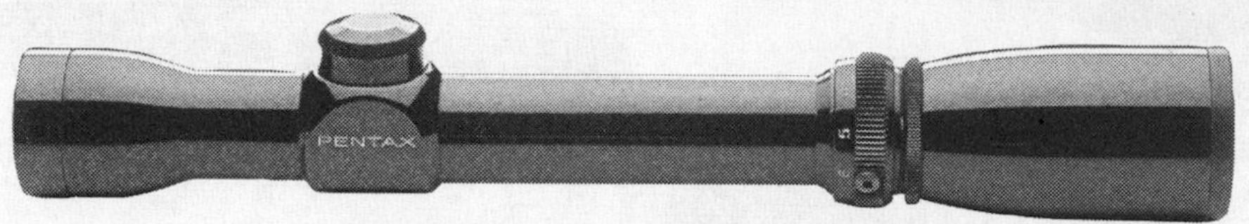

LIGHTSEEKER 1.75X-6X

Lightseeker Riflescope and Whitetails Unlimited

	Tube Diameter (in)	Objective Diameter (mm)	Eyepiece Diameter (mm)	Exit Pupil (mm)	Eye Relief (in)	Field of View (ft@100 yd)	Adjustment Graduation (in@100 yd)	Maximum Adjustment (in@100 yd)	Length (in)	Weight (oz)	Reticle	Price
Rifle Scopes												
Lightseeker 1.75X - 6X	1	35	39	15.3-5	3.5-4.0	71-20	1/2	110	10.75	13	P, TW	$455
Lightseeker 3X - 9X	1	43	39	12.0-5.0	3.5-4.0	36-14	1/4	50	12.7	15	P, MD	495-523
Lightseeker 3X - 9X	1	50	39	16.1-5.6	3.5-4.0	35-12	1/4	50	13.0	19	TW, BP	582
Lightseeker 2.5X - 10X	1	50	39	16.3-4.6	4.2-4.7	35-10	1/4	100	14.1	23	TW	665
Lightseeker 4X - 16X	1	44	36	10.4-2.8	3.5-4.0	33-9	1/4	35	15.4	23.7	BP	682
Lightseeker 2.5X SG Plus	1	25	39	7.0	3.5-4.0	55	1/2	60	10.0	9	DW	292-303
Lightseeker-30												
4X-16X AO	30mm	50	42	12-3.1	3.3-3.8	27-7.5	1/4	74	15.2	23	TW, MD	$714-798
6X-24X AO	30mm	50	42	7.6-2.1	3.2-3.7	18-5	1/8	52	16.9	27	MD, FP	746-832
8.5X-32X AO	30mm	50	42	6.2-1.7	3.0-3.5	14-4	1/8	39	18.0	27	MD, FP	786-865
Whitetails Unlimited												
2X-5X WTU	1	20	39	11.1-4.2	3.1-3.8	65-23	1/2	70	10.7	10	TW	332-348
3X-9X WTU	1	40	39	12.9-4.7	3.1-3.8	31-13	1/4	50	12.4	13	TW	332-348
3.5X-10X WTU	1	50	39	13-5.1	3.1-3.8	28-11	1/4	50	13.1	15	LBP	582
3.7X-11X WTU	1	42	39	13-5.1	3.1-3.8	28-11	1/4	50	13.1	15	TW	465
4.5X-14X WTU	1	50	39	9.1-3.1	3.1-3.8	25-9	1/4	40	14.1	15	TW	582
6.5X-20X WTU	1	50	39	7.6-2.6	3.1-3.6	17-6	1/4	30	14.6	19	BP	598
3X-9X WTU	1	50	39	16.0-5.3	3.1-3.8	32-13	1/4	50	13.2	17	BP	398

Scopes are available in high gloss black, matte black, or camouflage, depending on model.
P=Penta-Plex, FP=Fine-Plex, DW=Deepwoods Plex, MD=Mil-Dot, CP=Comp-Plex, TW=Twilight Plex, BP=Ballistic Plex, LBP=Laser Ballistic Plex

Redfield Scopes

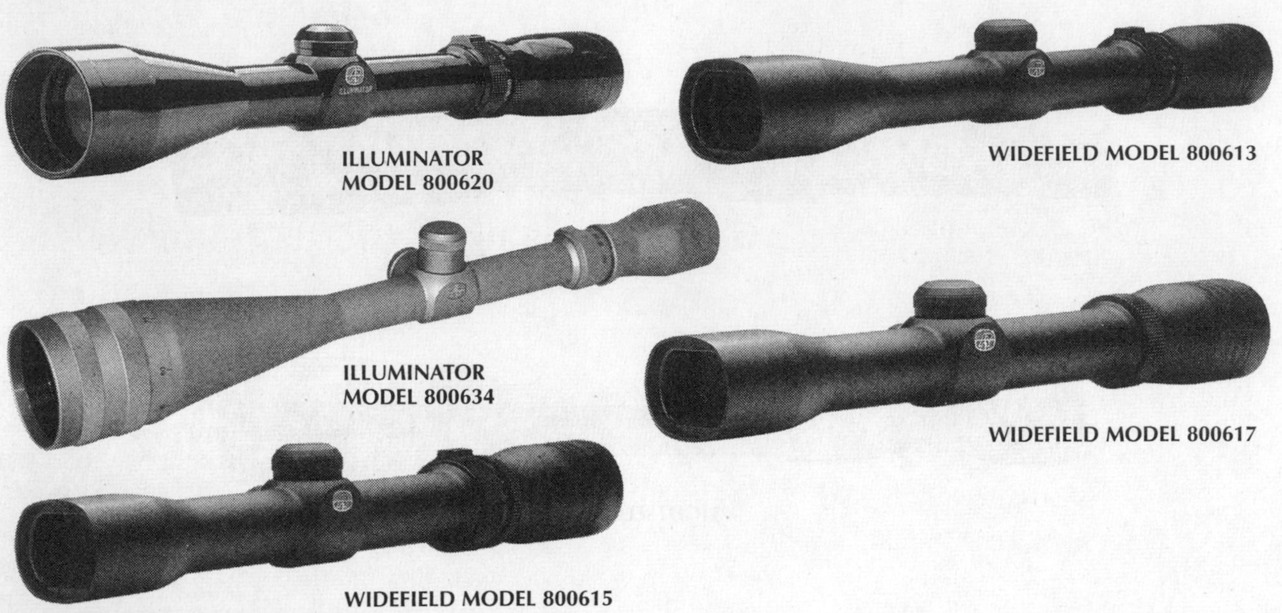

ILLUMINATOR MODEL 800620

WIDEFIELD MODEL 800613

ILLUMINATOR MODEL 800634

WIDEFIELD MODEL 800617

WIDEFIELD MODEL 800615

Illuminator

Illuminator is Redfield's best scope - made for the hardest of the hardcore hunters. Its large objective lens transmits maximum contrast and target definition to the eye, giving an edge in the uncertain light of dawn and dust. Crank up the magnification and Illuminator holds zero. The 3-9 variable with a 42mm objective lens comes in gloss, matte or brushed silver finish. The 3-10 variable with 50mm objective lens is available in gloss or matte black.

Widefield

Widefield's field of view is 30% wider than that of conventional scopes - over 40 feet at 100 yards on two models. It helps scan more area to detect the flick of an ear, or to pick the best shooting lane on running game. It's also designed to mount low on the receiver, a quicker sight picture when mounting the rifle. Choose a 2-7 power, 3-9 power or a fixed 4 power, in gloss or matte finish.

Redfield Illuminator

Model	Magnification Object Lens Dia-mm	Finish	Exit Pupil Range In Variable MM	Field of View in Feet @ 100 yds	Optimum Eye Relief Inches	Overall Length Inches	Weight Ounces	Reticle	Price
800619	3-9x42	Black matte	13-4.6	31x24-12.1x9.6	3.25-3.13	12.63	14.9	Truplex TV	$669
800620	3-9x42	Black polished	13-4.6	31x24-12.1x9.6	3.25-3.13	12.63	14.9	Truplex TV	669
800621	3-9x42	Silver matte	13-4.6	31x24-12.1x9.6	3.25-3.13	12.63	14.9	Truplex TV	675
800622	3-10x50	Black matte	12-5	34.5x24.5-11.3x8.7	3.125-3	14.75	1 lb 2.1 oz.	Truplex TV	752
800623	3-10x50	Black polished	12-5	34.5x24.5-11.3x8.7	3.125-3	14.75	1 lb 2.1 oz.	Truplex TV	752
800634	6-20x50 AO	Silver Matte	8.3-2.5	20.5-6.3	3.125-3.25	16	24	MX Dot	806
800635	6-20x50 AO	Black Matte	8.3-2.5	20.5-6.3	3.125-3.25	16	24	MX Dot	795
800636	6-20x50 AO	Black Matte	8.3-2.5	20.5-6.3	3.125-3.25	16	24	CH Dot	795
800637	6-20x50 AO	Black Polished	8.3-2.5	20.5-6.3	3.125-3.25	16	24	MX Dot	806

Redfield Widefield

Model	Magnification Object Lens Dia-mm	Finish	Exit Pupil Range In Variable MM	Field of View in Feet @ 100 yds	Optimum Eye Relief Inches	Overall Length Inches	Weight Ounces	Reticle	Price
800612	3-9x27x36	Black gloss	12x10-4x3	42.5x33-14.3x10.9	3.25-3	12.38	15	Truplex TV Oval	$443
800613	3-9x27x36	Black matte	12x10-4x3	42.5x33-14.3x10.9	3.25-3	12.38	15	Truplex TV Oval	443
800614	2-7x22x30	Black gloss	9x75x11.75-3.1x4	43.27x57.78-13.53x18.34	3.75-2.88	11.5	13.7	Truplex TV Oval	412
800615	2-7x22x30	Black matte	9x75x11.75-3.1x4	43.27x57.78-13.53x18.34	3.75-2.88	11.5	13.7	Truplex TV Oval	412
800616	4x22x30	Black gloss	5.3x7.4	29.75x35.95	2.88	11.38	12.4	Truplex TV Oval	360
800617	4x22x30	Black matte	5.3x7.4	29.75x35.95	2.88	11.38	12.4	Truplex TV Oval	360

Redfield Scopes

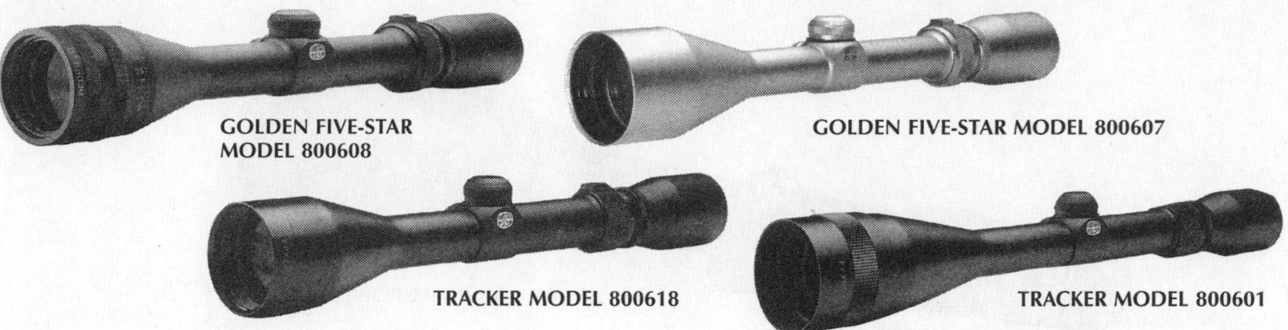

GOLDEN FIVE-STAR MODEL 800608

GOLDEN FIVE-STAR MODEL 800607

TRACKER MODEL 800618

TRACKER MODEL 800601

Golden Five Star

The Golden Five Star is purely practical. Its fully multi-coated optics give bright, clear sight pictures. The 3-9 power comes with 40 or 50mm objective lenses. A 40mm objective is standard on the 4-12 and 6-18 power.

Tracker

The Tracker is designed for the value-conscious hunter who wants a rugged Redfield scope at a modest price. Each Tracker is built from strong, lightweight aircraft aluminum and fine optical glass for maximum performance and clear bright images. The popular 3-9 power gives you a choice of 40 or 50m objective lens. Each scope has a black matte finish and is covered by the Redfield limited lifetime warranty.

Redfield Golden Five Star

Model	Magnification Object Lens Dia-mm	Finish	Exit Pupil Range In Variable MM	Field of View in Feet @ 100 yds	Optimum Eye Relief Inches	Overall Length Inches	Weight Ounces	Reticle	Price
800602	3-9x40	Black matte	13.3-4.4	34-11.3	3-2.88	12.75	13.5	Truplex	$309
800603	3-9x40	Black gloss	13.3-4.4	34-11.3	3-2.88	12.75	13.5	Truplex	309
800604	3-9x40	Silver matte	13.3-4.4	34-11.3	3-2.88	12.75	13.5	Truplex	319
800605	3-9x50	Black matte	11.85-5.1	36.7-12.66	3.63-3.38	13.13	1 lb. 2.7 oz.	Truplex	381
800606	3-9x50	Black gloss	11.85-5.1	36.7-12.66	3.63-3.38	13.13	1 lb. 2.7 oz.	Truplex	381
800607	3-9x50	Silver matte	11.85-5.1	36.7-12.66	3.63-3.38	13.13	1 lb. 2.7 oz.	Truplex	386
800608	4-12x40	Black matte	10.3-3.3	27-9.1	3-2.88	12.63	16	Truplex	443
800609	4-12x40	Black gloss	10.3-3.3	27-9.1	3-2.88	12.63	16	Truplex	443
800610	6-18x40	Black matte	6.6-2.22	17.8-6.1	3-2.88	13.5	16.3	Truplex	484
800611	6-18x40	Black gloss	6.6-2.22	17.8-6.1	3-2.88	13.5	16.3	Truplex	484

Redfield Tracker

Model	Magnification Object Lens Dia-mm	Finish	Exit Pupil Range In Variable MM	Field of View in Feet @ 100 yds	Optimum Eye Relief Inches	Overall Length Inches	Weight Ounces	Reticle	Price
800631	3-9x40	Black matte	13.3-4.5	35-11.3	3.25-3.13	12.75	13.5	Truplex	$216
800632	3-9x40	Black matte	15.8-6.3	35-11.75	3.25-3	13	1 lb. 2.5 oz.	Truplex	237
800618	3-12x44	Black matte	5.5-3.0	33-8.7	3-2.75	12.38	13.5	Truplex	268
800601	3-12x44	Black matte	5.5-2.7	26.2-7.42	3-2.625	14.375	16	Truplex	299

ESD MODEL 800624

Redfield ESD (Electronic Sighting Device)

Model	Objective	Description	Finish	Overall Length (Inches)	Weight (oz.)	Price
800624	28mm	Vari-Dot 4,8,12 &16 MOA	Black Matte	5.5	6.5	$395
800625	28mm	Vari-Dot 4,8,12 &16 MOA	Silver	5.5	6.5	400
800626	28mm	Multi-Reticle/16MOA Peep Plex/10 MOA DOT 3 MOA Center DOT/Standard Crosshair	Black Matte	5.5	6.5	388
800627	28mm	Multi-Reticle/16MOA Peep Plex/10 MOA DOT 3 MOA Center DOT/Standard Crosshair	Silver	5.5	6.5	395
800629	28mm	Compact ESD	Black Matte	4.25/5.5	5.25/5.6	286
800630	28mm	Compact ESD	Silver	4.25/5.5	5.2/5.6	291

Schmidt & Bender Rifle Scopes

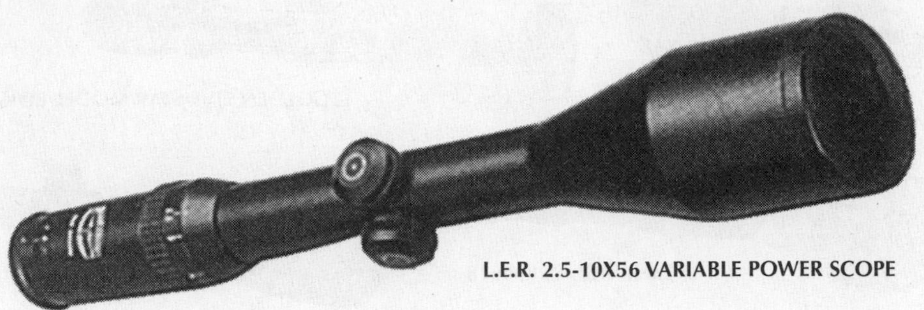

L.E.R. 2.5-10X56 VARIABLE POWER SCOPE

L.E.R. 2.5-10X56 VARIABLE POWER SCOPE

Price:.................................$1390

Also available:

1.25-4X20 Variable Power Scope 995

1.5-6X42 Variable Power Scope................. 1125

3-12X42 Variable Power Scope 1290

3-12X50 Variable Power Scope 1360

4-16X50 Variable Power Scope 1595

Note: All variable power scopes have glass reticles and aluminum tubes.

Also available:

4X36 FIXED POWER SCOPE

1" Steel Tube w/o Mounting Rail $760

6X42 Fixed Power 835

8X56 Fixed Power 960

10X42 Fixed Power............................ 955

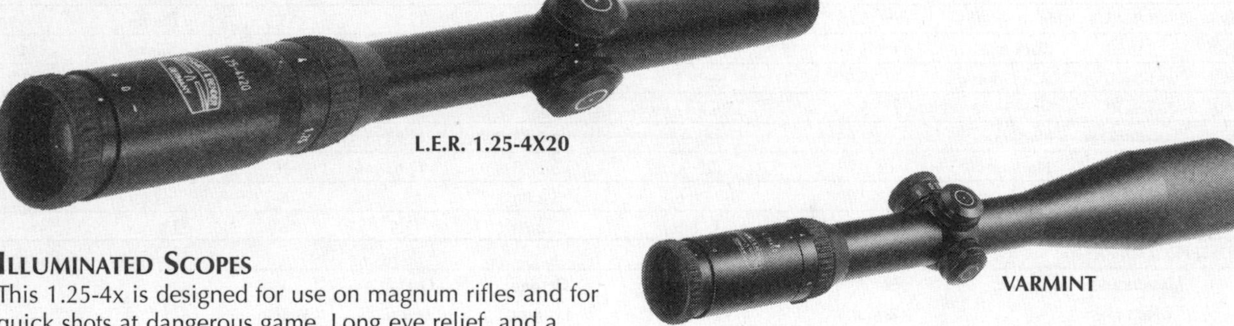

L.E.R. 1.25-4X20

VARMINT

ILLUMINATED SCOPES

This 1.25-4x is designed for use on magnum rifles and for quick shots at dangerous game. Long eye relief, and a wide field of view (31.5 yards at 200 yards) speed your aim. The Flash Dot reticle shows up bright against the target at the center of the crosswire.

Magnification: 1.25-4X

Objective lens diameter: 12.7-20mm

Field of view at 100m: 32m-10m; at 100 yards: 96'-16'

Objective housing diameter: 30mm

Scope tube diameter: 30mm

Twilight factor: 3,7-8,9 Lenses: hard multi-coating

Click value 1 click @100 meters: 15mm; @100 yards: .540"

Price:.................................$1480

Also available:

Illuminated reticles

1.5-6x42 1525

3-12x50 or 3-12X42....................... 1640

2.5-10x56 1725

Zenith Series (not shown)

3-12x50 or 2.5-10X56 1490

2.5-10x56 Illuminated or 3-12X50 Ill.......... 1795

Designed for long-range target shooters and varmint hunters, Schmidt & Bender 4-16X50 "Varmint" riflescope features a precise parallax adjustment located in a third turret on the left side of the scope, making setting adjustments quick and convenient. The fine crosshairs of Reticle No. 6 and 8 cover only 1.5mm at 100 meters (.053" at 100 yards) throughout the entire magnification range.

Magnification: 4-16X

Objective lens diameter: 50mm

Field of view at 100m: 7.5-2.5m; at 100 yards: 22.5'-7.5'

Objective housing diameter: 57mm

Scope tube diameter: 30mm

Twilight factor: 14-28

Lenses: Hard multi-coating

Click value 1 click @100 meters: 10mm; @100 yards: .360"

Price:.................................$1595

Schmidt & Bender Scopes

Police/Marksman II

PM II

Specifications

	10 x 42	3-12 x 50	3-12 x 50 w/parallax adj.	3-12 x 50 illuminated	4-16 x 50 w/parallax adj.
Price	$1085	1555	1785	1905	1870
Magnification	10x	3-12x	3-12x	3-12x	4-16x
Field of View	4m	11.1-4.2m	11.1-4.2m	11.1-4.2m	7.5-2.5m
(100m/100yd)	12'	33.3-12.6'	33.3-12.6'	33.3-12.6'	22.5-7.5'
Objective Diameter	42mm	50mm	50mm	50mm	5mm
Exit Pupil	4.2mm	14.3-4.3mm	14.3-4.3mm	14.3-4.3mm	12.5-3.1mm
(mm/inches)	.165"	.563-.169"	.563-.169"	.563-.169"	.492"-.122"
Twilight Factor	20.5	11.4-24.5	11.4-24.5	11.4-24.5	14-28
Eye Relief	95mm	995mm	95mm	95mm	95mm
(mm/inches)	3.74"	3.74"	3.74"	3.74"	3.74"
Middle Tube Diameter	30mm	34mm	34mm	34mm	34mm
Weight	520g	7600g	810g	780g	880g
(gram/lb., oz.)	1 lb. 2 oz.	1 lb. 2.5 oz.	1 lb. 12.5 oz.	1 lb. 11.5 oz.	1 lb. 15 oz.
Adj. Range @	*270 cm/97"	200 cm/72"	200 cm/72"	200 cm/72"	185 cm/67"
(100m/100 yd)	**250 cm/990"	180 cm/64.8"	180 cm/64.8"	180 cm/64.8"	170 cm/61.2"
	***130 cm/46.8"	130 cm/46.8"	130 cm/46.8"	130 cm/46.8"	130 cm/46.8"

**Using the very ends of the elevation adjustment will reduce the windage adjustment range **Sighting-in adjustment range without restriction of windage*
****With adjustment knob locked in place*

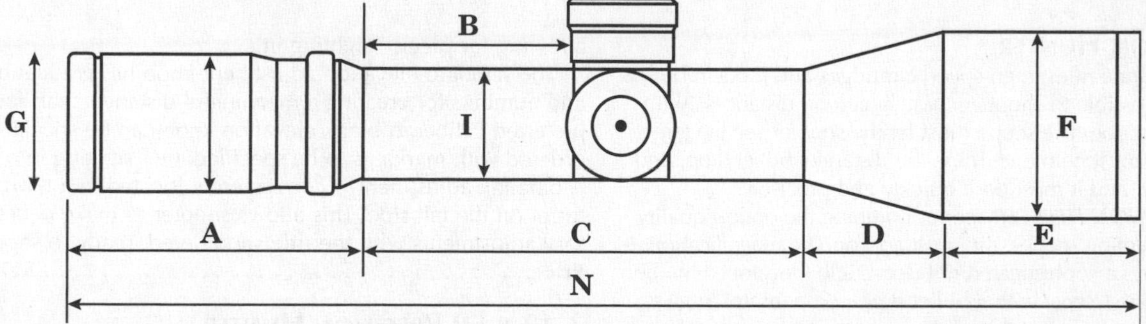

Dimensions

Model	A	B	C	D	E	F	G	I	N
10x42	98mm	56mm	139mm	55mm	54mm	50mm	43mm	30mm	346mm
	3.858″	2,204″	5.472″	2.165″	2.126″	1.969″	1.693″		13.622″
3-12x50	101.3mm	68.3mm	145.4mm	43.5mm	64.8mm	57mm	43mm	34mm	355mm
	3.988″	2.689″	6.076″	1.713″	3.354″	2.244″	1.693″		13.976″
4-16x50	101.3mm	68.3mm	145.4mm	85.2mm	75.5mm	57mm	43mm	34mm	405.7mm
	3.988″	2.689″	6.076″	1.713″	3.354″	2.244″	1.693″		15.972″

Schmidt & Bender Scopes

Scopes For Long Range Shooting

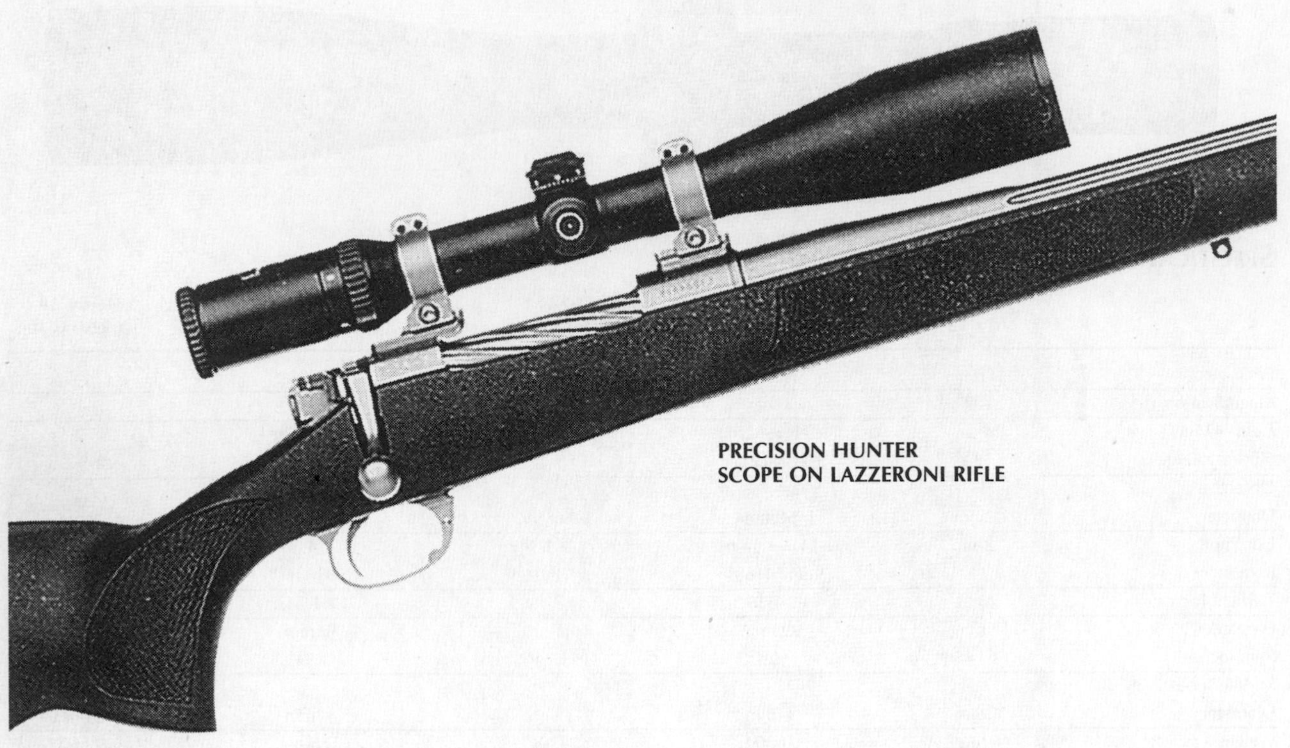

PRECISION HUNTER
SCOPE ON LAZZERONI RIFLE

Precision Hunter

Very accurate rifles, high-speed cartridges and modern bullets make it possible to shoot accurately at long distances...with the right scope. The scope must let the shooter see the target clearly. It must help determine the distance, bullet drop, and wind drift, and it must do it quickly and precisely.

PRECISION HUNTER scopes combine the optical quality of S&B hunting scopes, the most appropriate magnification ranges, and a sophisticated mil-dot reticle (developed by the U.S. Marine Corps) with a bullet drop compensator to give shooters the ability and confidence to place an accurate shot at up to 500 yards. Three different models are available:

4-16 x 50 Precision Hunter Scope with Parallax Adjustment

Set on 4 power, the mil-dot reticle with fine crosshairs and four posts allows quick target acquisition.

Turned up to 16 power, the mil-dots become visible and can be used for range, trajectory and windage calculations. The top-mounted bullet drop compensator has 5mm (1/5") clicks, permitting quick adjustments up to 500 yards. The windage adjustment also has 5mm (1/5") clicks, allowing for precise sighting in.

The standard elevation adjustment knob has graduations and numbers for creating a meaningful distance chart for preferred caliber. A blank elevation knob can be special-ordered with markings to be specified after sighting in rifle. A parallax adjustment is conveniently located in a third turret on the left side. This allows shooter to make necessary adjustments with the rifle shouldered, ready to shoot.

Price: **$1770**

3-12 x 50 Precision Hunter

Identical to the 4-16 x 50 with mil-dot reticle but 1cm (2/5") clicks and no parallax adjustment. It is factory-adjusted to be parallax free at 200 meters.

Price: **1535**

2.5-10 x 56 Precision Hunter

Identical to the 3-12 x 50, but with 1 cm (2/5") clicks for windage and elevation adjustment and with our Reticle No. 9, which makes it suitable for dangerous game.

Price: **1565**

Sightron Scopes

SIGHTRON SHOTGUN SCOPES

SIGHTRON BENCHREST SCOPES

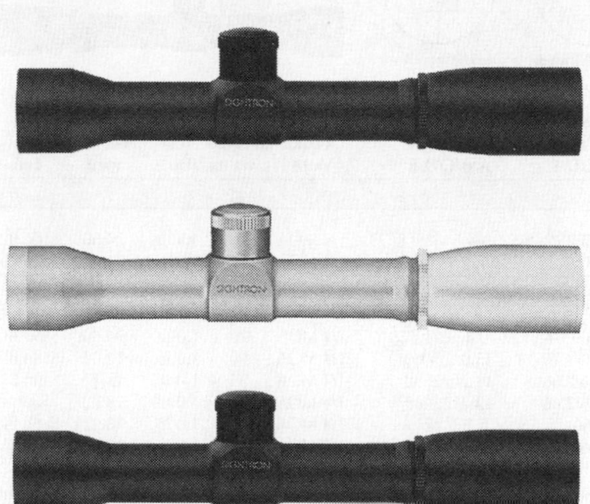

SIGHTRON PISTOL SCOPES

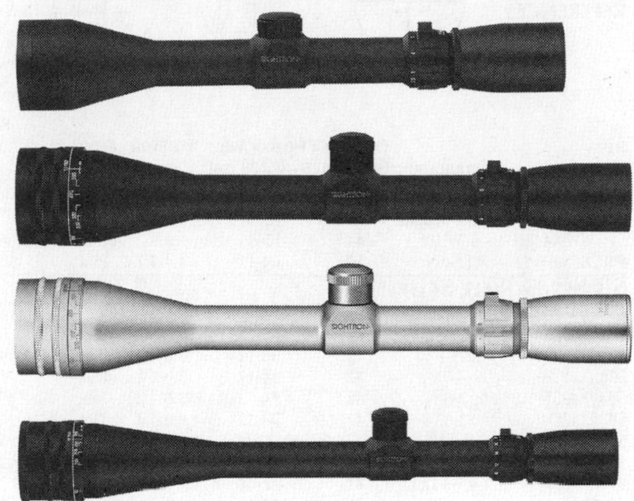

SIGHTRON HUNTING SCOPES

Sightron Series III 3.5-10x44 with Side-Mounted ("Saddle") Parallax Adjustment

Sightron's scope line offers nearly 40 models in fixed and variable power at modest prices. The SII series features 1-inch alloy tubes; the SIII series has 30 mm aluminum tubes, multicoated lenses, and "saddle" mounted parallax adjustments. Most target and competition scopes feature 1/8-minute clicks. Sightron offers stainless finish and a broad choice of reticles including the mil dot.

Prices:

SIII 3.5-10x44 mil dot $851
SIII 1.5-6x50 plex. 715
SII shotgun 2.5-7x32 297
SII hunting scopes:
3-9x42. 337
3-9x42 dot. 396
3-9x50. 415
1.5-6x42 352
3-12x42. 398
3-12x50. 418
3.5-10x42 398
3.5-10x50 422
4.5-14x42 454
4.5-14x50 447
SII target scopes:
4-16x42. 454
4-16x42 dot. 504
6-24x42. 481
6-24x42 dot. 532
SII competition scopes:
3-12x42 mil dot 404
4-16x42 mil dot. 537
4.5-14x42 mil dot 690
6-24x42 mil dot. 565
24x44 Dot 417
6x42 AO HBRD 417
6-24x42. 481
36x42 504
SII compact scopes:
4x32 252
2.5-10x32 320
2.5-7x32 297
6x42 275
12x42 Dot 447

Sightron Scopes

In conventional scopes a curved erector tube surface contacts the flat surface of the adjustment peg. This contact is only complete at zero adjustment. As the adjustments press the erector tube in any direction, the contact becomes imperfect, causing the reticle to drift from the optical center. In many cases, since the point of contact is less than what is required to hold the erector tube in position, point of impact can shift. Sightron has developed a new erector tube with an integral ring. ExacTrack will keep constant and perfect point-of-impact, at or off zero. This constant pressure point will ensure the accuracy of all Sightron scopes under heavy recoil and severe use afield.

Sightron Compact Scopes

RETICLE DIMENSION REFERENCES

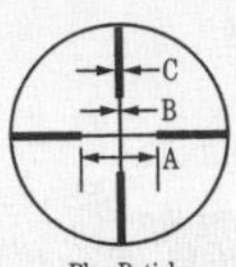

Plex Reticle

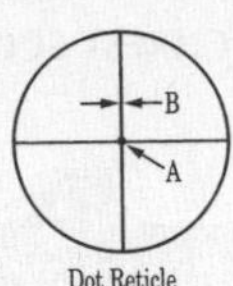

Dot Reticle

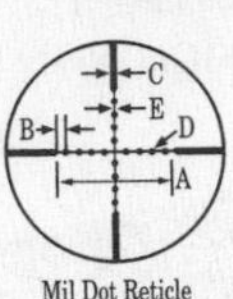

Mil Dot Reticle

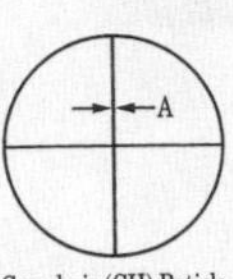

Crosshair (CH) Reticle

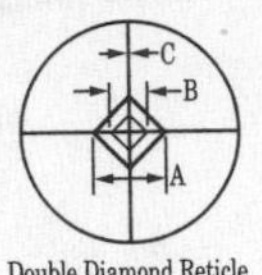

Double Diamond Reticle

Item Number	Magnification	Objective Dia. (mm)	Field of View (ft @ 100 yds)	Eye Relief (in.)	Reticle Type	Reticle Subtensions (in. @ 100 yds) Min. Power A/B/C/D/E	Max. Power A/B/C/D/E	Click Value	Windage/ Elevation Travel (in.)	Tube (Dia.)	Weight (oz.)	Finish
SIII Series Rifle Scopes												
30mm Side Saddle Rifle Scopes												
SIII3.510X44MD	3.5-10X	44	28-9.2	3.5	Mil-Dot	102.6/10.26/3.25/2.2/.69	36/3.6/1.15/.8/.23	1/4 MOA	80	30mm	24.60	Satin Black
SIII1.56X50MD	1.5-6X	50	64-17	4.3-3.7	Plex	79.0/1.33/5.32	19.8/.33/1.32	1/4 MOA	70	30mm	21.00	Satin Black
SII Series Rifle Scopes												
Variable Power Rifle Scopes												
SII1.56X42	1.5-6X	42	50-15	4.0-3.8	Plex	79.0/1.33/5.32	19.8/.33/1.32	1/4 MOA	70	1.0 in.	14.00	Satin Black
SII2.58X42	2.5-8X	42	36-12	3.6-4.2	Plex	48.0/.80/3.20	15.0/.25/1.0	1/4 MOA	90	1.0 in.	12.82	Satin Black
SII39X42	3-9X	42	34-12	3.6-4.2	Plex	39.9/.66/2.66	13.2/.22/.88	1/4 MOA	95	1.0 in.	13.22	Satin Black
SII39X42ST	3-9X	42	34-12	3.6-4.2	Plex	39.9/.66/2.66	13.2/.22/.88	1/4 MOA	95	1.0 in.	13.22	Stainless
SII39X42D	3-9X	42	34-12	3.6-4.2	Dot	4/.66	1.3/.22	1/4 MOA	95	1.0 in.	13.22	Satin Black
SII312X42	3-12X	42	32-9	3.6-4.2	Plex	39.9/.66/2.66	9.9/.16/.66	1/4 MOA	80	1.0 in.	12.99	Satin Black
SII3.510X42	3.5-10X	42	32-11	3.6	Plex	34.2/.57/2.28	12.0/.20/.80	1/4 MOA	60	1.0 in.	13.80	Satin Black
SII4.514X42	4.5-14X	42	22-7.9	3.6	Plex	26.4/.44/1.76	8.5/.14/.56	1/4 MOA	50	1.0 in.	16.07	Satin Black
SII39X50	3-9X	50	34-12	4.2-3.6	Plex	39.9/.66/2.66	13.2/.22/.88	1/4 MOA	*	1.0 in.	15.40	Satin Black
SII312X50	3-12X	50	34-8.5	4.5-3.7	Plex	39.9/.66/2.66	9.9/.16/.66	1/4 MOA	*	1.0 in.	16.30	Satin Black
SII3.510X50	3.5-10X	50	30-10	4.0-3.4	Plex	34.2/.57/2.28	12.0/.20/.80	1/4 MOA	50	1.0 in.	15.10	Satin Black
SII4.514X50	4.5-14X	50	23-8	3.9-3.25	Plex	26.4/.44/1.76	8.4/.14/.56	1/4 MOA	60	1.0 in.	15.20	Satin Black
SII6.525X50	6.5-25X	50	15-4.2	3.8-3.3	Plex	18.5/.3/1.2	4.8/0.1/.3	1/4 MOA	40	1.0 in.	20.70	Satin Black
Variable Power Target Scopes												
SII416X42	4-16X	42	26-7	3.6	Plex	30/.50/2.0	7.5/.125/.50	1/8 MOA	56	1.0 in.	16.00	Satin Black
SII416X42ST	4-16X	42	26-7	3.6	Plex	30/.50/2.0	7.5/.125/.50	1/8 MOA	56	1.0 in.	16.00	Stainless
SII416X42D	4-16X	42	26-7	3.6	Dot	1.7/.10	.425/.025	1/8 MOA	56	1.0 in.	16.00	Satin Black
SII416X42DST	4-16X	42	26-7	3.6	Dot	1.7/.10	.425/.025	1/8 MOA	56	1.0 in.	16.00	Stainless
SII624X42	6-24X	42	15.7-4.4	3.6	Plex	19.8/.33/1.32	4.8/.08/.32	1/8 MOA	40	1.0 in.	18.70	Satin Black
SII624X42ST	6-24X	42	15.7-4.4	3.6	Plex	19.8/.33/1.32	4.8/.08/.32	1/8 MOA	40	1.0 in.	18.70	Stainless
SII624X42D	6-24X	42	15.7-4.4	3.6	Dot	1.12/.066	.27/.016	1/8 MOA	40	1.0 in.	18.70	Satin Black
SII624X42DST	6-24X	42	15.7-4.4	3.6	Dot	1.12/.066	.27/.016	1/8 MOA	40	1.0 in.	18.70	Stainless
Competition/Tactical Scopes												
SII39X42MD	3-9X	42	34-14	3.6-4.2	Mil-Dot	150/15/10/4/1	50/5/3.3/1.3/.3	1/4 MOA	95	1.0 in.	13.22	Satin Black
SII312X42MD	3-12X	42	32-9	3.6-4.2	Mil-Dot	144/14/4.7/3.1/.7	36/3.6/1.2/.79/.1	1/4 MOA	80	1.0 in.	12.99	Satin Black
SII416X42MD	4-16X	42	26-7	3.6	Mil-Dot	144/14/4.7/3.1/.6	36/3.6/1.2/.79/.1	1/8 MOA	56	1.0 in.	16.00	Satin Black
SII416X42MDST	4-16X	42	26-7	3.6	Mil-Dot	144/14/4.7/3.1/.6	36/3.6/1.2/.79/.1	1/8 MOA	56	1.0 in.	16.00	Stainless
SII624X42MD	6-24X	42	15.7-4.4	3.6	Mil-Dot	144/14/4.7/3.1/.4	36/3.6/1.2/.79/.1	1/8 MOA	40	1.0 in.	18.70	Satin Black
SII624X42MDST	6-24X	42	15.7-4.4	3.6	Mil-Dot	144/14/4.7/3.1/.4	36/3.6/1.2/.79/.1	1/8 MOA	40	1.0 in.	18.70	Stainless
SII24X44D	24X	44	4.4	4.33	Dot	.27/.016		1/8 MOA	60	1.0 in.	15.87	Satin Black
SII6X42HBRD	6X	42	20	4.00	Dot	.375/.070		1/8 MOA	100	1.0 in.	16.00	Satin Black
SII6X42HBR	6X	42	20	4.00	CH	.33		1/8 MOA	100	1.0 in.	16.00	Satin Black
Compact Rifle Scopes												
SII4X32	4X	32	25	4.52	Plex	30/.50/2.0		1/4 MOA	120	1.0 in.	9.80	Satin Black
SII2.57X32	2.5-7X	32	41-11.8	3.8-3.2	Plex	48/.80/3.20	17.2/.29/1.2	1/4 MOA	120	1.0 in.	11.60	Satin Black
SII2.510X32	2.5-10X	32	41-10.5	3.8-3.5	Plex	48/.80/3.20	12/.20/.80	1/4 MOA	120	1.0 in.	10.93	Satin Black
SII6X42	6X	42	20	3.60	Plex	19.8/.33/1.32		1/4 MOA	100	1.0 in.	12.69	Satin Black
Shotgun Scopes												
SII2.5X20SG	2.5X	20	41	4.33	Plex	48.0/.80/3.201/4 MOA		160	1.0 in.	9.00	Satin Black	
SII2.57X32SG	2.5-7X	32	41-11.8	3.8-3.2	DD	48/24/.60	17/8.5/.26	1/4 MOA	120	1.0 in.	11.60	Satin Black
Pistol Scopes												
SII1X28P	1X	28	30	9-24	Plex	120.0/2.0/8.01/8 MOA		60	1.0 in.	9.30	Satin Black	
SII1X28PST	1X	28	30	9-24	Plex	120.0/2.0/8.01/8 MOA		60	1.0 in.	9.30	Stainless	
SII2X28P	2X	28	15	9-24	Plex	60.0/1.0/4.0		1/8 MOA	60	1.0 in.	9.30	Satin Black

*Specifications not available at press time

SIGHTS & SCOPES

Simmons Scopes
Aetec

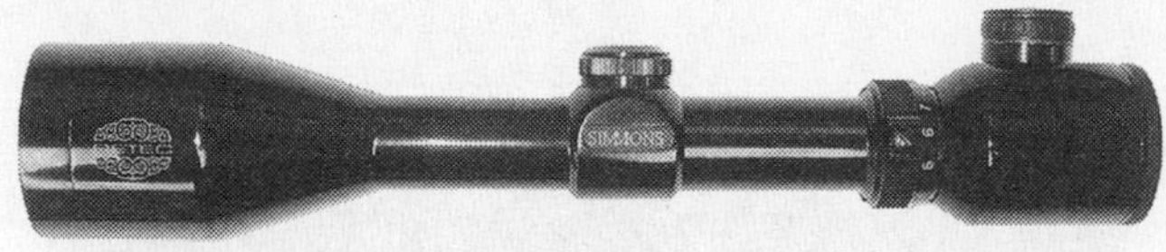

AETEC MODEL 800865

Model 2100/2101/2102
2.8-10X44 WA ***Length:*** 11.9" ***Weight:*** 15.5 oz. ***Reticle:*** Truplex
Price: $190
Model 2104 3.8-12x44mm AO 200

Model 800865/800866
Illuminated Reticle, black matte
Prices: Model 800865 (2.8-10x44) 210
Model 800866 (3.8-12x44) 230

44 Mag Riflescopes

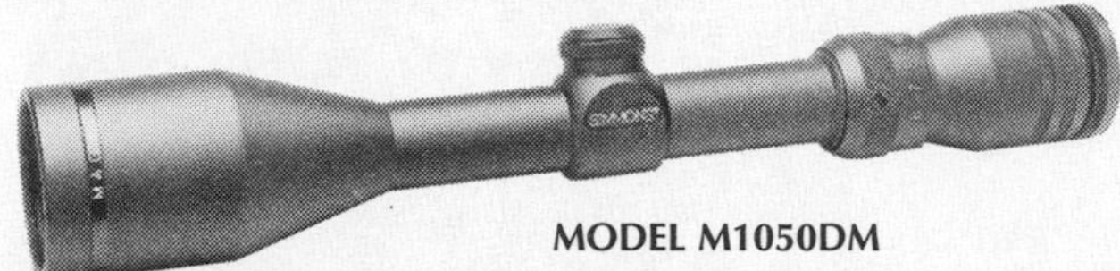

MODEL M1050DM

Model M1044 (black matte)
3-10X44mm ***Length:*** 12.75" ***Weight:*** 15.5 oz.
Price: $150

Model M1050DM 44 Diamond Mg (black matte) Range-Calculating Smart Reticle (black matte)
3.8-12X44mm ***Length:*** 13.08" ***Weight:*** 16.75 oz.
Price: $190

Model M1045 (black matte)
4-12X44mm ***Length:*** 13.2" ***Weight:*** 18.25 oz.
Price: 170

Model M1047 (black matte)
6.5-20X44mm ***Length:*** 12.8" ***Weight:*** 19.5 oz.
Price: 200
Also available:

Model M1048
6.5-20X44 Target Turrets
Black Matte (1/8" MOA) 220

Model M1055
3-10X44 Mildot 170

Model M1056
6.5-20X44 Mildot................................ 200

ProHunter Riflescopes

PRO 50 MODEL 8800

PROHUNTER SE MODEL 807729

Model 7710
3-9X40mm Wide Angle Riflescope
Length: 12.6"
Weight: 13.5 oz.
Features: Truplex reticle; silver matte finish
Price: $90
(Same in black matte or black polish, Models 7711 and 7712) Also available:
Model 7700 2-7X32 Black Matte 80
Model 7716 4-12X40 Black Matte AO............ 130
Model 7721 6-18X40 AO Black Matte............ 145
Model 7740 6X40 Black Matte 100
Model 7711 3-9X40 WA Matte..................... 90
Model 7702 3-9X40 Illum......................... 120
Model 7712 3-9X40 Gloss 90
Model 7703 6-24X42 Mildot...................... 160

Pro50
Pro 50's have all the features of the Prohunter models, only with a 50mm lens.

Prices:
Model 8800 4-12x50mm, AO Black Matte........ $180
Model 8810 6-18x50mm, AO Black Matte......... 175
Model 8830 2.5-10x50mm, Black Matte 180
Model 8825 3.5-10X50mm, Comp Matte 180

Prohunter SE
Sleek new design, one-piece body tube construction, Sure-grip power adjustments, Coated optics, ¼ MOA windage and elevation adjustments, waterproof, fogproof and shockproof.
Prices:
Model 807719 2-7x32 Black Matte............... 90
Model 807723 3-9x40 Black Matte............... 99
Model 807724 4x32 Black Matte 70
Model 807730 4-12x40 AO Black Matte.......... 120
Model 807726 4-12x50 AO Black Matte.......... 153
Model 807727 6-18x40 AO Black Matte.......... 138
Model 807728 6-18x50 AO Black Matte.......... 150
Model 807729 3.5-10x50 AO Black Matte........ 120

Simmons Scopes

1022T Rimfire Target Scope

Magnification: 3-9X32mm WA/AO ***Finish:*** Black matte
Features: Adjustable for windage and elevation; adjustable objective lens, target knobs
Price:. $170
Also available:
1022 4X32 black matte w/22 rings 50
1031 4X28 22 Mag Mini black matte w/22 rings 50
1032 4X28 22 Mag Mini silver matte w/22 rings 50
1033 4X32 silver matte w/22 rings 50
1037 3-9X32 silver matte w/22 rings 60
1039 3-9X32 black matte w/22 rings 60

1022T RIMFIRE TARGET SCOPE

Black Powder Scopes

MODEL BP2732M

Model BP2732M

Magnification: 2-7X32 Finish: Black matte
Field of view: 57.7'-16.6' 100 yards Eye relief: 3"
Reticle: Truplex Length: 11.6" Weight: 12.4 oz.
Price:. $130

Also available: Models BP400M/400S
4X20 Black Matte or Silver Matte, Long Body
Field of view: 28' ***Eye relief:*** 5.0" ***Length:*** 10.25"
Weight: 8.7 oz. ***Reticle:*** Truplex
Price:. $60

ProDiamond Shotgun Scopes

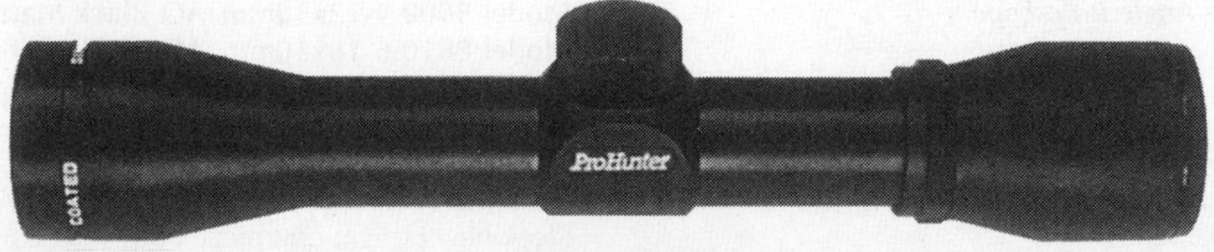

MODEL 7790D

Models 7790D

Magnification: 4X32 ***Finish:*** Black matte
Field of view: 17′ Eye relief: 5.5″ Reticle: ProDiamond
Length: 8.5″ ***Weight:*** 9.1 oz.
Prices:
Model 7790D $110

Also available:
Model 7789D 2X32 Black matte (ProDiamond reticle) 100
Model 7791D 1.5-5X20 WA Black matte (ProDiamond reticle) 130
Model 7792D 1.5-5X32 Camo Pro Diamond 130

SIMMONS 8 POINT
4X32 BLACK

The Simmons 8-Point series is aimed at the entry level or budget-minded shooter who needs a reliable scope at an affordable price. The 8-Point family includes seven scopes in popular configurations: 3-9x32mm, 3-9x40mm, 3-9x50mm, 4x32mm, 4-12x40mm AO, and 4x32 mm shotgun. All versions are offered in black matte finish, and the 3-9x40mm is also available in silver. Fully coated lenses enhance light transmission for low-light viewing and reduce reflections. Simmons' popular Truplex reticle is standard. Windage and elevation are adjusted in ¼-MOA increments. The new 8-Point scopes are shockproof, waterproof, and fogproof.

8-Point Scope 4-12x40mm AO

Magnification: 4-12X
Field of View: 29 - 10 ft. at 100 yards
Eye Relief: 3 inches at 4X and 2⅞ inches at 12X
Length: 13.5 inches
Weight: 15.75 oz.
Reticle: Duplex
Finish: Black Matte
Price: $100

8-point Scope 4x32mm

Magnification: 4X
Field of View: 28.75 ft. at 100 yards
Eye Relief: 3 inches
Length: 11.625 inches
Weight: 14.25 oz.
Reticle: Duplex
Finish: Black Matte
Price: 35

8-Point Scope 3-9x32 mm

Magnification: 3-9X
Field of View: 37.5 - 13 ft. at 100 yards
Eye Relief: 3 inches at 3X and 2⅞ inches at 9X
Length: 11.875 inches
Weight: 11.5 oz.
Reticle: Duplex
Finish: Black Matte
Price: $40

8-Point Scope 3-9x40mm

Magnification: 3-9X
Field of View: 37 - 13 ft. at 100 yards
Eye Relief: 3 inches at 3X and 2⅞ inches at 9X
Length: 12.25 inches
Weight: 12.25 oz.
Reticle: Duplex
Finish: Black Matte or Silver
Price: Black Matte or Silver 50
Camo 80

8-Point Scope 3-9x50mm

Magnification: 3-9X
Field of View: 32 - 11.75 ft. at 100 yards
Eye Relief: 3 inches at 3X and 2⅞ inches at 9X
Length: 13 inches
Weight: 15.25 oz.
Reticle: Duplex
Finish: Black Matte
Price:. 80

Simmons Scopes

Whitetail Expedition

SIMMONS 3-9X42MM WHITETAIL EXPEDITION SCOPE

Simmons introduced aspherical lenses to shooters with the AETEC series of riflescopes. Now, Simmons offers aspherical lenses in the Whitetail Expedition series. Because aspherical lenses eliminate minor aberrations found in regular spherical lens systems, these scopes produce a sharp, crisp view all the way to the edges of the lens. Field of view is 30% greater than that of other scopes of comparable magnification and objective lens size. All lens surfaces of the new Whitetail Expedition scopes, inside and out, are fully-multicoated for maximum edge-to-edge brightness and reflection reduction. The scopes have a Truplex reticle, the most versatile and popular in the marketplace, and are shockproof, waterproof, and fogproof. Configurations available in the Whitetail Expedition series are: 1.5-6x32mm WA, 3-9x42mm WA, 4-12x42mm WA, and 6-18x42mm WA. The two higher-range scopes have adjustable objective lenses for precision shooting at any range. Adjustments for windage and elevation are ¼-MOA increments.

Whitetail Expedition 1.5-6x32mm

Magnification: 1.5-6X ***Field of View:*** 72 - 19 ft. at 100 yards ***Eye Relief:*** 3 inches ***Length:*** 11.16 inches ***Weight:*** 15 oz. ***Reticle:*** Duplex ***Finish:*** Black Matte

Price:. $268

Whitetail Expedition 3-9x42mm

Magnification: 3-9X ***Field of View:*** 40 - 13.5 ft. at 100 yards ***Eye Relief:*** 3 inches ***Length:*** 13.2 inches ***Weight:*** 17.5 oz. ***Reticle:*** Duplex ***Finish:*** Black Matte

Price:. 278

Whitetail Expedition 4-12x42mm

Magnification: 4-12X ***Field of View:*** 29 - 9.6 ft. at 100 yards ***Eye Relief:*** 3 inches ***Length:*** 13.46 inches ***Weight:*** 21.25 oz. Reticle: Duplex ***Finish:*** Black Matte

Price:. 309

Whitetail Expedition 6-18x42mm

Magnification: 6-18X ***Field of View:*** 18.3 - 6.5 ft. at 100 yards ***Eye Relief:*** 3 inches ***Length:*** 15.35 inches ***Weight:*** 22.5 oz. ***Reticle:*** Duplex ***Finish:*** Black Matte

Price: 330

SIGHTS & SCOPES

Prohunter Handgun Scopes

MODEL 7732 (2X)

MODEL 7738 (4X)

Model #7732/7733 (Silver Matte)

Specifications

Magnification: 2X Field Of View: 22' ***Eye Relief:*** 9-17" ***Length:*** 8.75" ***Weight:*** 7 oz. ***Reticle:*** Truplex ***Finish:*** Black matte

Price:. $110

Model #7738/7739 (Silver Matte)

Specifications

Magnification: 4X ***Field Of View:*** 15' ***Eye Relief:*** 11.8-17.6" ***Length:*** 9" ***Weight:*** 8 oz. ***Reticle:*** Truplex ***Finish:*** Black matte

Price:. 130

Also: Prohunter 2-6X32, Matte or Silver 160

Swarovski Scopes

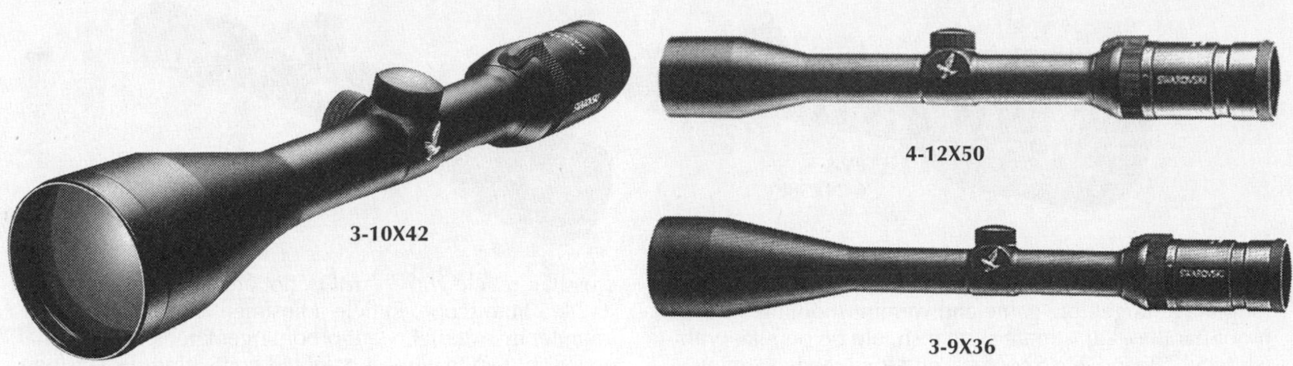
3-10X42

4-12X50

3-9X36

Swarovski A-Line Series Lightweight 1-inch Scopes

Developed for American hunters, the A-Line scopes feature constant-size reticles, lightweight alloy tubes and satin finish. Totally waterproof even with caps removed, these scopes have fully multi-coated lenses and the quality that has made Swarovski famous.

Prices:

AV 3-10 x 42 (4A, Plex) $854
AV 4-12 x 50 (4A, Plex) 888
AV 3-9 x 36 (4A, Plex) 777
AV 6-18x50 (4A, Plex) 932
AV 6-18x50 (TDS) 999
AV 4-12X50 (TDS) 954

6-18x50

Swarovski's 6-18x50 incorporates a parallex adjustment ring that insures parallex free accuracy from 50 yds to beyond 500. The objective bell, 1" tube, turret housing and ocular bell are machined out of one solid piece of alloy bar stock for strength, weight and waterproof integrity.

Price: 888

A-LINE RETICLES AVAILABLE:

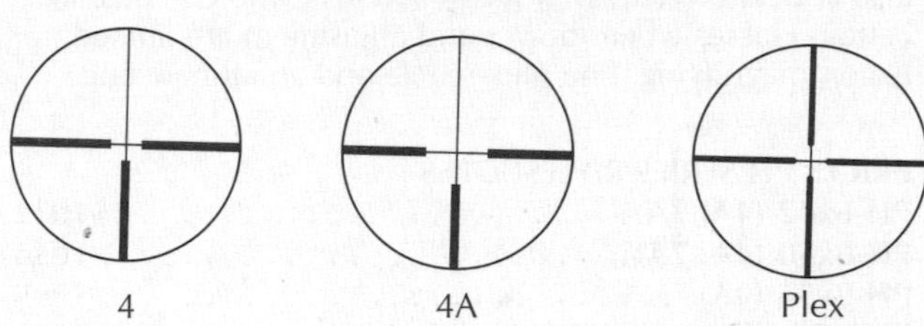

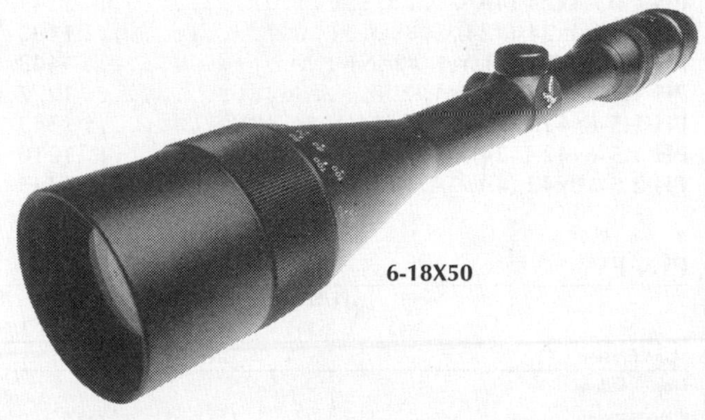
6-18X50

	3-9x36	3-10x42	4-12x50	6-18x50
Magnification	3-9x	3.3-10x	4-12x	6-18x
Objective lens diameter: mm	36	42	50	50
in	1.42	1.55	1.97	1.97
Exit pupil, diameter: mm	12-4	12.6-4.2	12.5-4.2	8.3-2.8
Eye relief: in	3.5	3.5	3.5	3.5
Field of view, real: m/100m	13-4.5	11-3.9	9.7-3.3	17.4-6.5
ft/100yds	39-13.5	33-11.7	29.1-9.9	17.4-6.5
Diopter compensation (dpt)	± 2.6	± 2.5	± 2.5	± 2.5
Transission (%)	94	94	94	92
Twilight factor (DIN 58388)	9-18	9-21	11-25	17-30
Impact Point correction per click: in/100yds	0.25	0.25	0.25	0.25
Max. elevation/windage adjustment range: ft/100yds	4.8	4.2	3.6	3.9
Length, approx: in	11.8	12.44	13.5	14.85
Weight, approx (oz.): L	11.6	12.7	13.9	20.3
LS	–	13.6	15.2	–

L=light alloy • LS=light alloy with rail

Swarovski Scopes

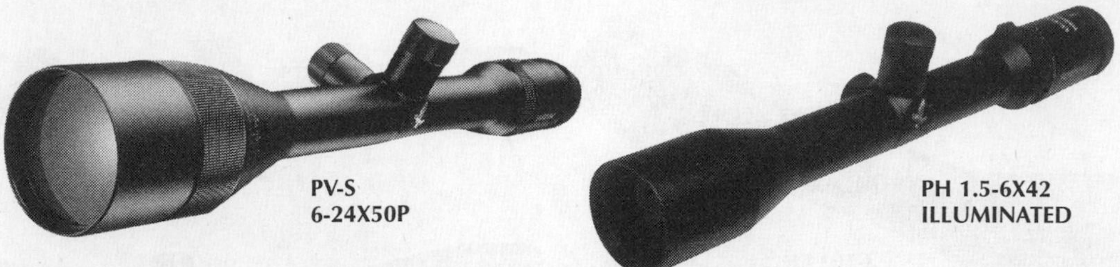

PV-S 6-24X50P

PH 1.5-6X42 ILLUMINATED

Swarovski's 6-24X50mm "PH" riflescope was developed for long-range target, big-game and varmint shooting. Its waterproof parallax adjustment system should be popular with whitetail "Bean Field Shooters" and long-range varmint hunters looking for a choice of higher powers in a premium rifle scope and still deliver accuracy. The scope will also appeal to many bench rest shooters who compete in certain classes where power and adjustment are limited. A non-magnifying, fine plex reticle and an all-new fine crosshair reticle with 1/8" MOA dot are available in the 6-24x50mm scope. Reticle adjustment clicks are 1/6" (minute) by external, waterproof target knobs. The internal optical system features a patented coil spring suspension system for dependable accuracy and positive reticle adjustment. The objective bell, 30mm middle tube, turret housing and ocular bell are machined from one solid bar of aluminum.

Price: **$1754**

PRICES PH SERIES RIFLESCOPES

PH 6x42 (4A, 7A) **$1032**
PH 8x50 (4A, 7A) **1054**
PH 8x56 (4A) **1099**
PH8x56 (Illum. ret. PLEXN) **1532**
PH 1.25-4x24 (4A) **1143**
PH 1.25-4x24 (#24) **1188**
PH 1.25-4x24 (Ill. ret. #24N) **1443**
PH 1.5-6x42 (4A, 7A) **1277**
PH 1.5-6x42 (Illum. ret. #24N, 4A-1K) **1543**
PH 1.5-6x42 (#24) **1310**
PH 2.5-10x42 (4A, 7A, PLEX) **1443**
illum reticle (4NK) **1754**
PH 2.5-10x56 (4A, 7A PLEX) **1488**
w/illum reticle (4NK, PLEXN) **1866**
PH 3-12x50 (4A, 7A, PLEX) **1488**
TDS reticle **1599**
w/illum reticle (4NK, PLEXN) **1877**
PH 6-24x50 (4A, PLEX) with low turret **1654**
PH 6-24x50 (low turrets, TDS) **1777**
PH 4-16x50 (4A, PLEX) **1554**
PH 4-16x50 (TDS) **1643**

PF& PV

	PF 6x42	PF/PF-N 8x50	PF/PF-N 8x56	PV/PV-1 1.25-4x24	PV 1.5-6x42	PV/PV-N 2.5-10x42	PV/PV-N 2.5-10x56	PV/PV-N 3-12x50	PV 4-16x50P	PV 6-24x50P	PV-S 6-24x50P
Magnification	6x	8x	8x	1.25-4x	1.5-6x	2.5-10x	2.5-10x	3-12x	4-16x	6-24x	6-24x
Objective lens diameter: mm	42	50	56	17-24	20-42	33-42	33-56	39-50	50	50	50
in	1.65	1.97	2.20	0.67-0.94	0.79-1.65	1.3-1.65	1.3-2.20	1.54-1.97	1.97	1.97	1.97
Exit pupil, diameter: mm	7	6.25	7	12.5-6	13.1-7	13.1-4.2	13.1-5.6	13.1-4.2	12.5-3.1	8.3-2.1	8.3-2.1
Eye relief: in	3.15	3.15	3.15	3.15	3.15	3.15	3.15	3.15	3.15	3.15	3.15
Field of view, real: m/100m	7	5.2	5	32.8-10.4	21.8-7	13.2-4.2	13.2-4.1	11-3.5	9.1-2.6	6.2-1.8	6.2-1.8
ft/100yds	21	15.6	15.6	98.4-31.2	65.4-21	39.6-12.6	39.6-12.3	33-10.5	27.3-7.8	18.6-5.4	18.6-5.4
Diopter compensation (dpt)	+2. -3	+2. -3	+2. -3	+2. -3	+2. -3	+2. -3	+2. -3	+2. -3	+2. -3	+2. -3	+2. -3
Transission (%)	94	94/92	93/91	93/91	93	94/92	93/91	94/92	90	90	90
Twilight factor (DIN 58388)	16	20	21	4-10	4-16	7-21	7-24	9-25	11-28	17-35	17-35
Impact Point correction per click: in/100yds	0.36	0.36	0.36	0.54	0.36	0.36	0.36	0.36	0.18	0.18	0.17
Max. elevation/windage adjustment range: ft/100yds	3.9	3.3	3.9	9.9	6.6	3.9	3.9	3.3	E:5.4/W:3	E:3.6/W:2.1	E:3.6/W:2.1
Length, approx: in	12.83	13.94	13.27	10.63	12.99	13.23	13.62	14.33	14.21	15.43	15.43
Weight, approx (oz.): L	12.0	14.8	15.9	12.7	16.2	15.2	18.0	16.9	22.2	23.6	24.5
LS	13.4	15.9	16.9	13.8	17.5	16.4	19.0	18.3	—	—	—

L=light alloy • LS=light alloy with rail

Swift Scopes

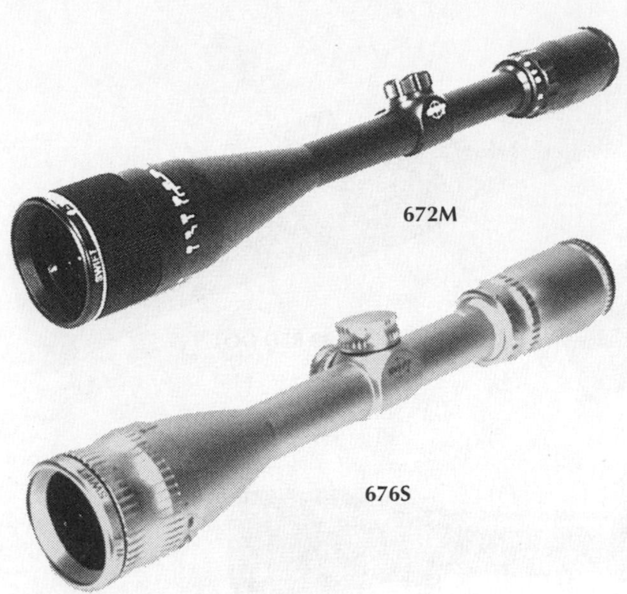

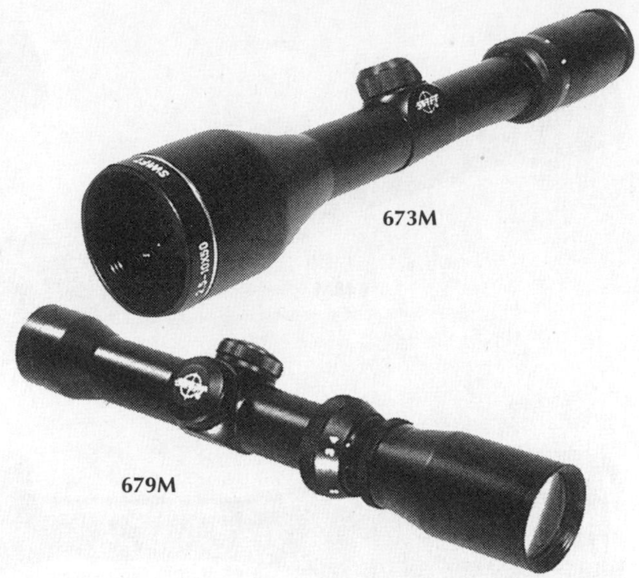

Swift Instruments, Inc., a prominent name in the optics industry since 1926, has four new scopes in its line: three rifle scopes that offer faster focusing with the Swift Speed Focus feature and one new shock resistant pistol scope. All four are waterproof, shock-tested and have multi-coated lenses for a bright image from dawn to dusk without glare.

Model 672M
Swift Premier Rifle Scope

6-18X, 50mm - WA - Multi-Coated - Waterproof - SPEED FOCUS

A great scope for varmint, silhouette and target shooters. The Speed Focus feature presents optimum focusing ability at any power setting. Multi-coated lenses with an adjustable objective to correct parallax. New longer tube body allows more eye relief adjustment in long action firearms. Black matte finish.

Price:. **$260**

Model 673M
Swift Premier Rifle Scope

Featuring a 30mm tube for a brighter image at dawn or dusk 2.5-10X, 50 - Wide Angle - Waterproof - Multi-Coated - SPEED FOCUS

This scope with a 30mm tube and a 50mm objective lens is brighter than other scopes under poor light condition. It has an extremely wide field. The objective adjustment allows accurate shooting from close up to distant ranges. Elevation and windage adjustments, full saddle hard anodized 30mm tube.

Price:. **295**

Model 676S
Swift Premier Rifle Scope

4-12X, 40 - WA - Waterproof -Multi-Coated - Speed Focus

With a parallax adjustment from 10 yards to infinity, this scope is highly adaptable and excellent for use as a varmint scope or on gas powered air rifles. Elevation and windage adjustments are mounted full saddle on the hard anodized 1-inch tube. Speed Focus adjustment brings shooters on target easily. The objectives are multi-coated; Quadraplex reticle is standard. Available in regular (676), matte (676M), and silver finish (676S).

Price:. **$190**
Gloss **180**
Matte. **185**

Model 679M Swift Pistol Scope

1.25-4X, 28mm - 8.2 oz.

An extremely versatile full saddle scope with excellent eye relief of 23 inches at 1.25x, 15 inches at 4x. This ruggedly made scope is shock resistant and waterproof. It has 7 magenta coated lens elements and weighs only 8.2 ounces. Matte finished.

Price:. **250**
Also available: **Pistol scopes 4x32, 2x20**
Price:. **130**

Premier Illuminated Reticle

Swift Instruments have three illuminated reticle rifle scopes in their line. All are waterproof, shock tested and have multi-coated lenses that provide a bright, sharp, glare-free image from dawn to dusk. Add to this variable-intensity red crosshairs in the center of the reticle that adjusts to make getting on target easier in low light conditions.

Model 680M 3-9x40. . . . . **400**
Model 681M 1.5-6x40 . . . . **400**
Model 682M 4-12x50. . . . . **500**

Swift Rifle & Pistol Scopes

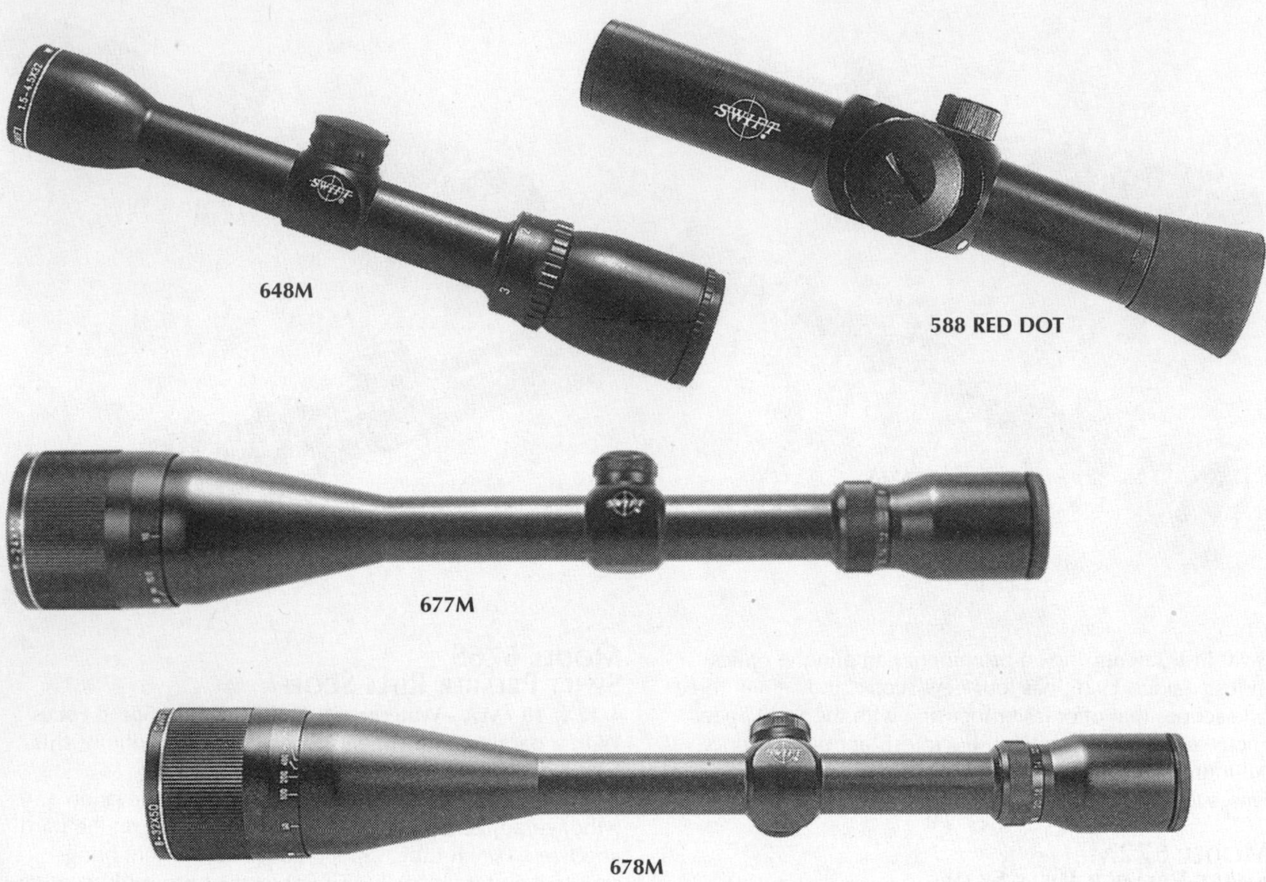

648M

588 RED DOT

677M

678M

SIGHTS & SCOPES

Model 648M Swift Premier
1.5-4.5x, 32mm - WA-Waterproof-Multi-coated-Speed Focus

Considered to be the most versatile scope in the Premier line, the 1.5-45x is ideal on shotguns and black powder rifles. Eye relief ranges from 3.05 to 3.27. Crosshair and circle reticle make this riflescope easy to focus on target, and ideal for turkey hunting. Black matte finish.**Price $180**

Model 677M Swift Premier
6-24x, 50mm - WA - Waterproof - Multi-coated - Speed Focus

With a magnification range of 6 to 24 power and a 50mm objective lens with sunshade, this scope is the one to use when you're after really tight groups. Elevation and windage adjustments are mounted full saddle on the hand anodized 1-inch tube. The objective may be adjusted for parallax.This is a fine scope for long-range big game hunting and varminting. **Price 280**

Model 678M Swift Premier
8-32x, 50mm - Waterproof - Multi-Coated - Speed Focus

With an ample field of view of 13 feet at 100 yards and eye relief of 3.13 inches, this scope can be used for bench rest shooting and long range hunting. It is very effective on prairie dogs. Parallax adjustment adds versatility. Elevation and windage adjustments are mounted full saddle on the hard anodized 1-inch tube. Equipped with sunshade.
Price $290

Model 588 Red Dot Scope
1x, 21mm - Fog-proof - Fully coated

Under any light conditions this Aerolite red dot electronic sight can be rapidly aligned for pinpoint accuracy. It has a field of view of 39 feet at 100 yards and unlimited eye relief. It is free of parallax from 5 meters to infinity. Body length is 6 1/4" to 7 1/8" with the rubber eyecup. Weighs only 5 ounces. These characteristics make it especially suitable for handgun shooting, shotguns and bows. CR-2032: 3-volt button battery is included.
Price 100
Also Available: Red Dot Fire Fly 1x30 Price 224

PROPOINT 1X25

Propoint Red Dot Sighting Device

Propoint Red Dot Sights have been the choice for competitive shooters, turkey hunters and slug gun enthusiasts for years. Built to last, the Propoint features solid construction, flawless tracking and a rheostat-controlled illuminated red dot. Included accessories: rings to fit standard 5/8″ bases, extension tubes, polarizing filter and one lithium battery.

Model	Power	Objective Diameter	Finish	Reticle	Field of View @ 100 Yds.	Eye Relief	Tube Diam.	Scope Length	Scope Weight	Prices
Propoint Scopes										
PDP2	1X	25mm	Black Matte	5 M.O.A. Dot	40'	Unlimited	30mm	5"	5.5 oz.	$118
PDP3	1X	25mm	Black Matte	5 M.O.A. Dot	52'	Unlimited	30mm	5"	5.5 oz.	138
PDP3ST	1X	25mm	Stainless	10 M.O.A. Dot	52'	Unlimited	30mm	5"	5.5 oz.	144
PDP3CMP	1X	30mm	Black Matte	10 M.O.A. Dot	68'	Unlimited	33mm	4.75"	5.4 oz.	156
Red Dot Sights										
BKRD30	1X	30mm	Black Matte AWF	Illum. Red Dot	57"	Unlimited	38mm	3.75"	6 oz.	$46
BKRD30/22	1X	30mm	Black Matte AWF	Illum. Red Dot	57"	Unlimited	38mm	3.75"	6 oz.	46
BKRD42	1X	42mm	Black Matte AWF	Illum. Red Dot	62"	Unlimited	47mm	3.75"	6.7 oz.	58

SIGHTS & SCOPES

Eye relief is the distance from your eye to the scope's rear or ocular lens. Mount the scope well forward, to protect your brow and speed your aim as you shove your face forward on the comb.

Tasco Scopes

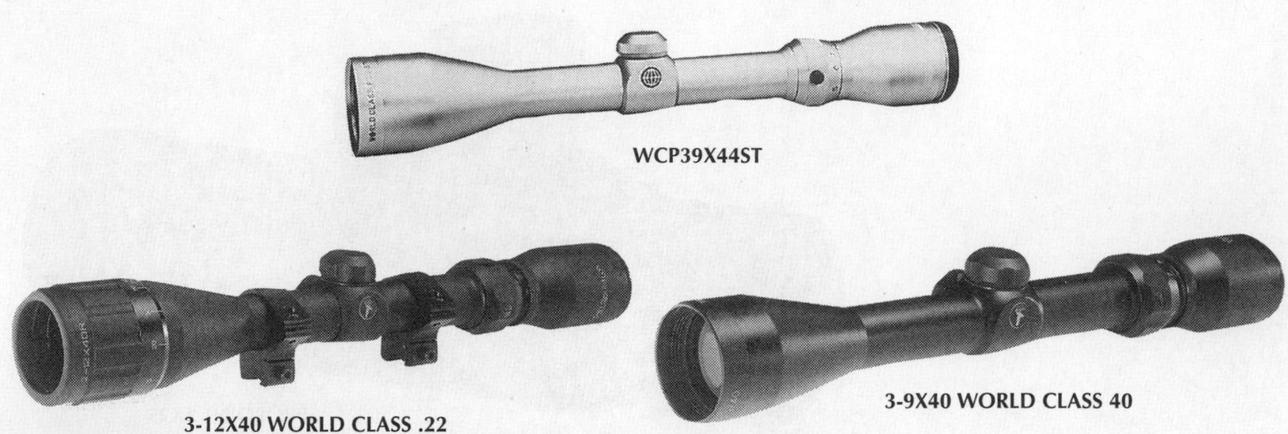

WCP39X44ST

3-12X40 WORLD CLASS .22

3-9X40 WORLD CLASS 40

World Class Riflescopes

Long a favorite with sportsmen, wide-angle World Class Riflescopes now have 1" Advanced Monotube Construction to make them even stronger and more shock resistant. SuperCon multi-layered coating on the objective and ocular lenses and fully-coated optics throughout increase light transmission. World Class Riflescopes are waterproof, fog-proof and shockproof.

Titan Riflescopes

The Titan riflescope features a wider field of view and more light gathering than 1" scopes. The scope is multi-coated, has finger adjustable windage and elevation controls and a fast-focus eyebell. Available with a 30/30 or German-style 4A reticle, the Titan is waterproof, fogproof and shockproof.

SIGHTS & SCOPES

Tasco Riflescopes

Model	Power	Objective Diameter	F.O.V. @ 100 Yd.s	Eye Relief (inches)	Length	Weight	Prices
Titan							
DWCP351050	3.5-10	50	30-10.5	3.75	13	17.1	$191.95
DWCP39X44	3-9	44	39-14	3.5	12.75	16.5	173.95
T156X42N	1.5-6	42	59-20	3.5	12	16.4	293.95
T14526N4A	1.5-6	42	59-20	3.5	12	16.4	293.95
T14526N4A	1.25-4.5	26	77.5-22	3.25	10.5	15.2	273.95
T312X52N	3-12	52	27-10	4.5	14	20.7	335.95
T312X52N4A	3-12	52	27—10	4.5	14	20.7	335.95
T39X42N	3-9	42	37-13	3.5	12.5	16	281.95
T39X42N4A	3-9	42	37-13	3.5	12.5	16	281.95
Target & Varmint							
VAR251042M	2.5-10	42	35-9	3	14	19.1	$ 89.95
MAG624x40	6-24	40	17-4	3	16	19.1	113.95
VAR624X42M	6-24	42	13-3.7	7	16	19.6	113.95
TG624X44DS	6-24	44	15-4.5	3	16.5	19.6	199.95
TG104050DS	10-40	50	11-2.5	3.25	15.5	25.5	211.95
DWC416X50	4-16	50	28-7	3	16	20.5	123.95
World Class							
BA1545X32	1.5-4.5	32	77-23	4	11.25	12	$59.95
DWC28X32	2-8	32	50-17	4	10.5	12.5	69.96
DWC39X40N	3-9	40	41-15	3.5	12.75	13	73.95
WA39X40N	3-9	40	41-15	3.5	12.75	13	73.95
WA39X40STN	3-9	40	41-15	3.5	12.75	13	73.95
DWC39X50N	3-9	40	41-13	3	12.5	15.8	87.95
DWC39X40N	3-9	40	41-15	3.5	12.75	13	73.95
Pronghorn							
PH39X40D	3-9	40	39-13	3	13	12.1	$53.95
PH39X32D	3-9	32	39-13	3	12	11	41.95
PH4x32D	4	32	32	3	12	11	35.95

Tasco Riflescopes

Varmint/Tactical Scopes

Long range shooting is easier with Tasco's True Mil-Dot system. SuperCon multi-layered lens coatings and fully coated optics throughout provide clear resolution. With extra large 42mm objectives, this line of Varmint riflescopes transmit more light than standard 40mm scopes.

New For 2002

Tasco's new LER (Long Eye Relief) combines a lightweight, compact scope with illuminated technology (IT) to make these riflescopes perfect for rifles, shotgun, black powder, slug and brush. Available in fixed 4 power and variable 1.5 to 6 power.

EXP 3-9X42/54

The Tasco EXP features an oval objective lens. This new technology allows low profile mounting with standard or low rings without sacrificing light transmission.

Mag IV Riflescopes

The large 40mm objective of MAG IV riflescopes delivers a full four times magnification with more zooming range than most variable scopes. In addition, a focusing objective provides valuable parallax correction. MAG IV scopes feature ¼-minute windage/elevation click stops and black matte finish. The result is a line of scopes that provide superior light transmission and clarity even at high magnifications. Waterproof, fogproof and shockproof.

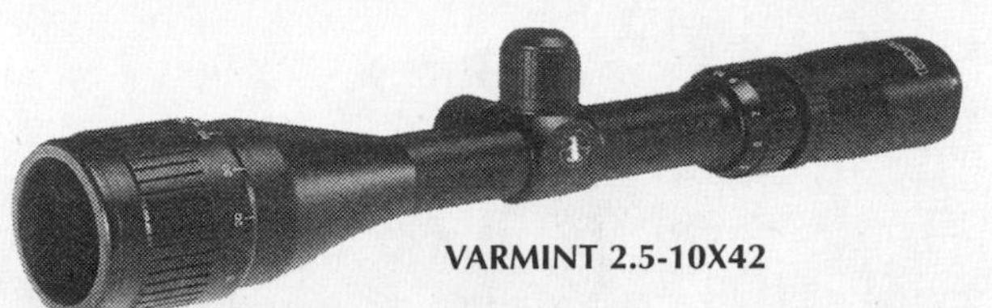

VARMINT 2.5-10X42

LER4X32

EXP 3-9X42/54

3-12X40

Tasco riflescopes

Model	Power	Objective Diameter	F.O.V. @ 100 Yd.s	Eye Relief (inches)	Length	Weight	Prices
.22 Riflescopes							
MAG39X32D	3-9	32	17.75-6	3	12.75	11.3	55.95
MAG38X32SD	3-9	32	17.75-6	3	12.75	11.3	55.95
MAG4X32SD	4	32	13.5	3	12.25	12.1	43.95
MAG4X32STD	4	32	13.5	3	12.25	12.1	43.95
Rimfire							
EZ01D	1	20	35	Unltd.	4.75	2.5	17.95
RF37X20D	3-7	20	24	2.5	11.5	5.7	23.95
RF4X15D	4	15	20.5	2.5	11	4	7.95
RF4X20WAD	4	20	23	2.5	10.5	3.8	9.95
ProPoint							
BKRD30	1	30	57	Unltd	3.75	6	45.95
BKR3022	1	30	57	Unltd.	3.75	6	45.95
BKRD42	1	42	62	Unltd.	3.75	6.7	57.95
PDP2	1	25	40	Unltd.	5	5.5	117.95
PDP3CMP	1	30	68	Unltd.	4.75	5.4	157.95
PDP3	1	25	52	Unltd.	5	5.5	137.95
PDP3ST	1	25	52	Unltd.	5	5.5	143.95
Golden Antler							
DMGA39X32T	3-9	32	39-13	3	13.25	12.2	49.95
DMGA4X32T	4	32	32	3	12.75	11.	37.95
GA3940	3-9	40	41-15	3	12.75	13	57.95

Trijicon Sights & Scopes
Fiber-Optic

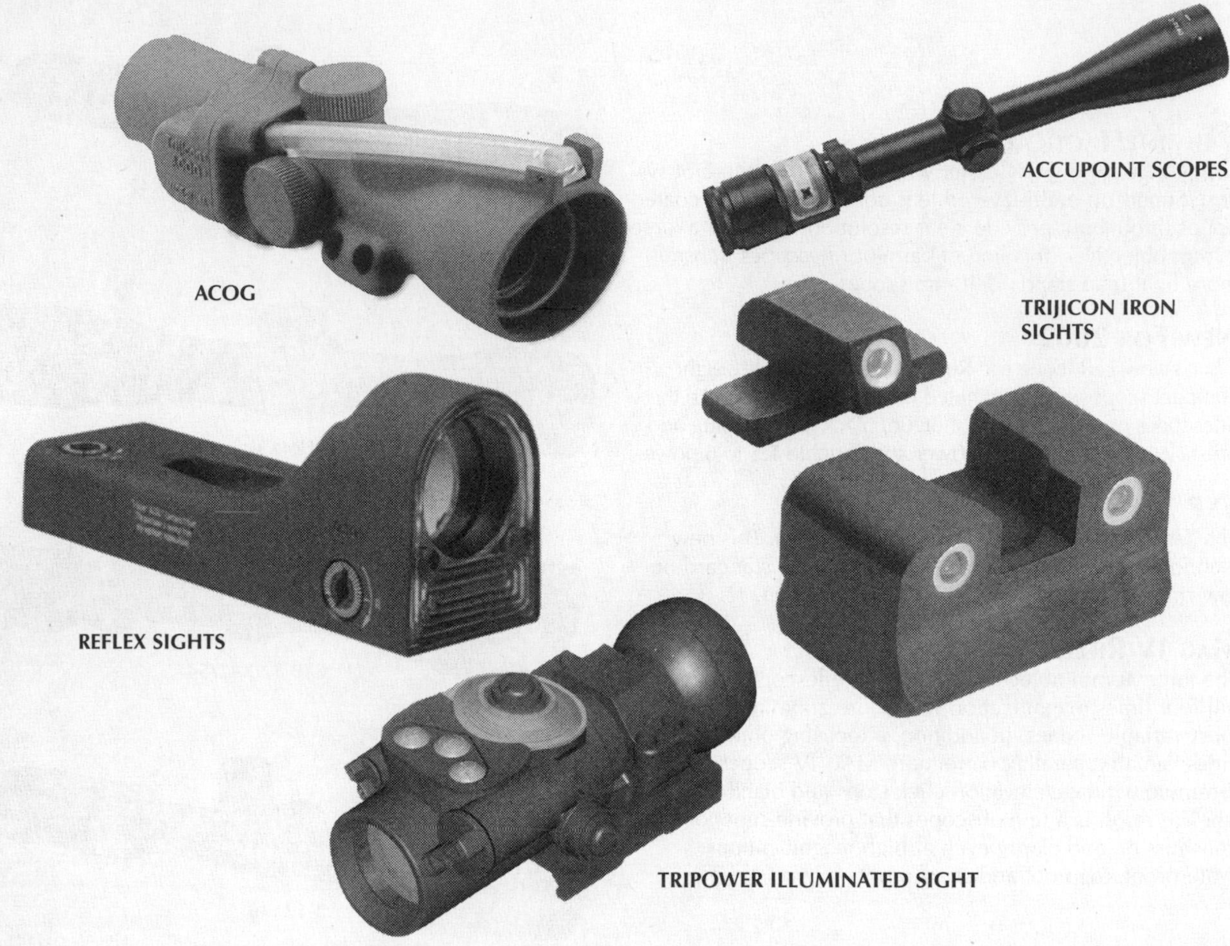
ACOG
ACCUPOINT SCOPES
TRIJICON IRON SIGHTS
REFLEX SIGHTS
TRIPOWER ILLUMINATED SIGHT

ACOG
The ACOGs are internally-adjustable, compact telescopic sights with tritium illuminated reticle patterns for use in low light or at night. Many models are dual-illuminated, featureing fiber optics which collect ambient light for maximum brightness in day-time shooting. The ACOGs combine traditional, precise distance marksmanship with close-in aiming speed.

Prices: . . . . **$950 to 1672**
Compact ACOG **950**

Accupoint Scopes
AccuPoint's dual-illuminated aiming point offers a major advancement over crosshairs that can disappear due to lack of contrast when aiming at a dark animal, or in low-light conditions. Reticle illumination is supplied by advanced fiber optics or, in low-light conditions, by a self-contained tritium lamp.

Prices: 3-9x40, red or amber triangle **720**
1.2-4x24, red or amber triangle **700**

Reflex Sights
The dual-illuminated, Trijicon Reflex sight gives shooters next-generation technology for super-fast, any-light aiming-without batteries.
Developed for the military for use in both-eyes-open Close Quarters Battle (CQB) situations, the Reflex sight features an amber aiming dot or triangle that is illuminated both by light from the target area and from a tritium lamp.

Price: . . . . **$350 to 599**

Trijicon Iron Sights
Trijicon self-luminous iron sights give shooters greater night fire accuracy-with the same speed as instinctive shooting. Trijicon Bright & Tough night sights are the first choice of major handgun manufacturers and standard issue with hundreds of municipal and county departments, numerous state and police departments and several Federal agencies.

Price: . . . . **99 to 119**

TriPower Illuminated Sight
The new TriPower features a red chevron-shaped reticle illuminated by three lighting sources: an integrated fiber optic system, a Tritium-Illuminated reticle and on-call battery backup. The TriPower has a 30mm tube, coated lenses, and is sealed for underwater use up to 100 feet. The TriPower is 5 inches long and weighs 6 oz.

Price: **550**

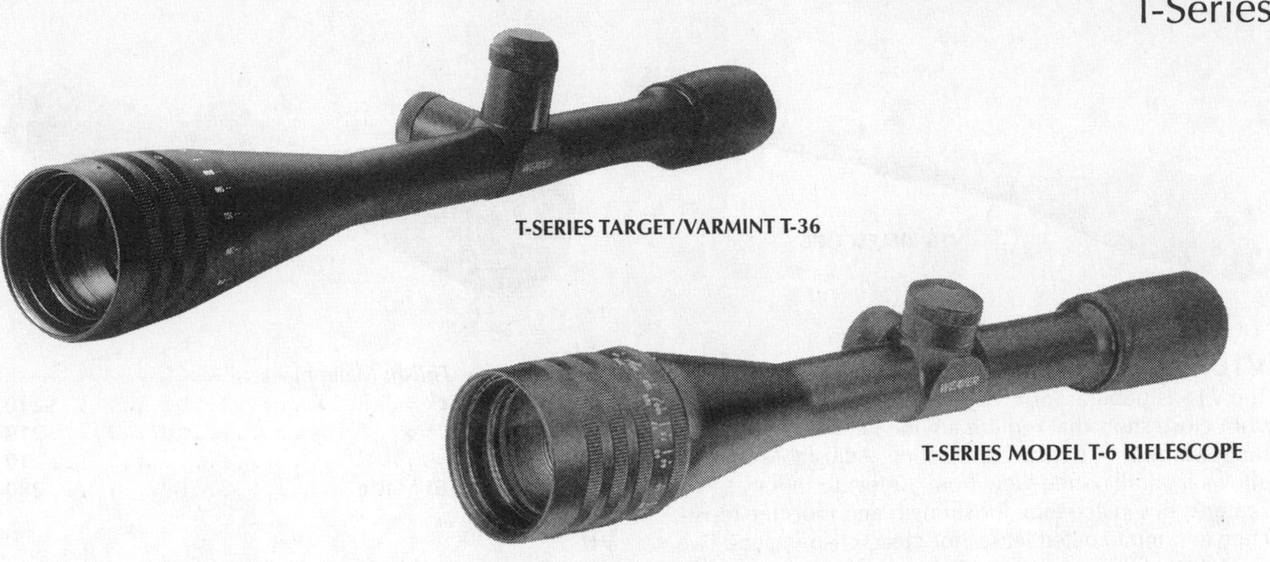

T-SERIES TARGET/VARMINT T-36

T-SERIES MODEL T-6 RIFLESCOPE

T-Series Target/Varmint T-36

T-Series Target/Varmint Scopes - These fixed-power scopes feature Weaver's patented Micro-Trac adjustment system utilizing a dual-spring, four-bearing contact design that allows independent movement of windage and elevation. Optics are fully multi-coated, delivering premium image clarity in virtually all light conditions. Adjustable objective lens allows for zero parallax from 50′ to infinity. Choice of fine crosshair or dot reticles. Scopes come with sunshade, extra pair of oversize benchrest adjustment knobs, and screw-in metal lens caps.

Model: T-36 ***Magnification/Objective:*** 36X40mm ***Field Of*** View: 3.0′ ***Eye Relief:*** 3.0" ***Length:*** 15.1" ***Weight:*** 16.7 oz. ***Reticle:*** 1/8 MOA Dot, Fine Crosshair ***Finish:*** Matte black or silver

Price: Matte **$480**
Silver or Matte Dot **490**
Silver Dot **500**

T-Series Model T-6 Riflescope

Weaver's T-6 competition 6x scope is only 12.7 inches long and weighs less than 15 ounces. All optical surfaces are fully multi-coated for maximum clarity and light transmission. The T-6 features Weaver's Micro-Trac precision adjustments in 1/8-minute clicks to ensure parallel tracking. The protected target-style turrets are a low-profile configuration combining ease of adjustment with weight reduction. A 40mm adjustable objective permits parallax correction from 50 feet to infinity without shifting the point of impact. A special AO lock ring eliminates bell vibration or shift. The T-6 comes with screw-in metal lens caps and features a competition matte black finish.

Reticles: dot, Fine Crosshair

Price: 6x40 Satin Black **$340**

Weaver Tactical Scopes (not shown)

These tactical scopes have a first-plane reticle, meaning the crosshair measurement maintains the same size relative to the size of the target at any power. The range-calculating reticle of the Tactical scope is etched into the glass in front of the adjustment housing.

At the center of the reticle is a small diamond that covers one inch outside. Marks beyond the diamond on the crosspieces can be used to bracket a target and determine range.

Tactical scopes have 1/8-minute-of-angle windage and elevation adjustments with target-style knobs. The knobs also offer a "guaranteed zero" feature that allows the shooter to move the reticle for a specific shooting need, then return the scope to zero without sighting in again. An adjustable objective lens is also included on the 4.5-14x44mm scope for precise parallax-free adjustments.

All air-to-glass lens surfaces are fully multi-coated, and the scopes are waterproof to 10,000 feet and to 120 degrees with 100% humidity. Weaver's Tactical scopes are offered in black matte finish.

Price: 4.5-14x44 . . . . **540**
Also: 3-9x40 . . . . **480**

SPECIFICATIONS

Magnification X Obj. Diam. (mm)	Exit Pupil (mm)	FOV (Ft. @ 100 Yds.)	Eye Relief (In.)	Overall Length (In.)	Weight (Oz.)	Reticle
3-9x40	13.3-4.4	33-14.5	4.17-3.02	12.5	17.0	Diamond
4.5-14x44	10-3	22-9.4	4.1-2.8	15.2	20.6	Diamond

Weaver Scopes

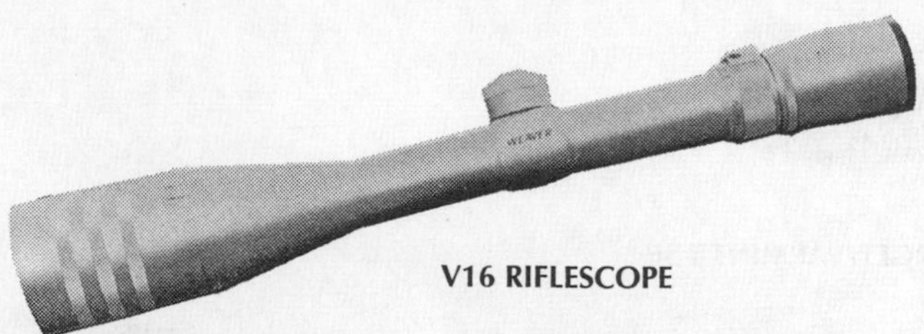
V16 RIFLESCOPE

CLASSIC V9

V16 Riflescopes

The V16 is popular for a variety of shooting applications, from close shots that require a wide field of view to long-range varmint or benchrest shooting. Adjustable objective allows a parallax-free view from 30 feet to infinity. Features one-piece tube for strength and moisture resistance and multicoated lenses for clear, crisp images. Two finishes and three reticle options.
Magnification/Objective: 4-16X42mm ***Field Of View:*** 26.8'-6.8' ***Eye Relief:*** 3.1" ***Length:*** 13.9" ***Weight:*** 16.5 oz.
Reticle: Choice of Dual-X, 1/4 MOA Dot, or Fine Crosshair
Finish: Matte black

Price: **$330**
V24 6-24x42 (not shown) black matte **380**

V10 (not shown)

Magnification/Objective: 2-10X38mm ***Field Of View:*** 38.5-9.5 ***Eye Relief:*** 3.5" ***Length:*** 12.2" ***Weight:*** 11.2 oz.
Reticle: Dual-X ***Finish:*** Matte black, silver

Price: Matte black **$210**
Silver **210**
In gloss black **210**
V10x50 (2-10x50) Matte **280**

V9

Magnification/Objective: 3-9x38 ***Field Of View:*** 34-11' ***Eye Relief:*** 3.5" ***Length:*** 12" ***Weight:*** 11 oz. ***Finish:*** Matte black, gloss

Price: Matte black **190**
Gloss **190**
V9XX50 (3-9x50) Matte **240**

V3 (not shown)

Magnification/Objective: 1-3x20 ***Field Of View:*** 100x34 ***Eye Relief:*** 3.5" ***Length:*** 9" ***Weight:*** 9 oz. ***Finish:*** Matte black

Price: Matte black **190**

CLASSIC HANDGUN 1.5-4X20

CLASSIC RIMFIRE RV7

Weaver Classic Handgun Scopes

Fixed-power scopes include 2x28 and 4x28 scopes in gloss black or silver. Variables in 1.5-4x20 and 2.5-8x28 come with a gloss black finish. The 2.5-8x28 is also available in black matte. One-piece tubes, fully multi-coated lenses and generous eye relief (4-29") make these scopes top performers on hunting handguns.

Prices: 2x28 .... **$161**
4x28 .... **175**
1.5-4x20 .... **216**
2.5-8x28 .... **229**
2.5-8x28 matte **229**

Classic Rimfire RV7

Lenses are multi-coated for bright, clear low-light performance and the one-piece tube design is shockproof and waterproof.

Prices:
2.5-7x28 Rimfire Matte **$149**
2.5-7x28 Rimfire Silver **149**

Rimfire Scope RV4 (not shown)

This fixed 4x scope is ideal for a variety of shooting applications. It's durable, light-weight and waterproof.

Prices:
Rimfire Matte Black 4x28 .... **127**

SIGHTS & SCOPES

Weaver Scopes

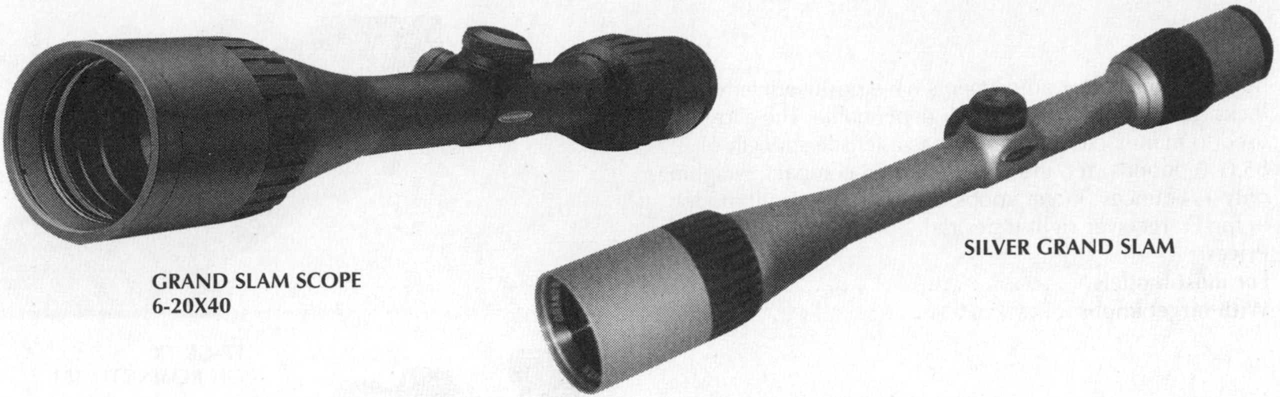

GRAND SLAM SCOPE
6-20X40

SILVER GRAND SLAM

Weaver Grand Slam Scopes

Among the advanced features of the Grand Slam series are a "sure-grip" power ring and AO adjustment that let you easily adjust the variable scopes, even while wearing heavy gloves, and an offset parallax indicator so you can remain in shooting position while adjusting the scope. Grand Slam scopes feature camera-quality, fully multi-coated lenses that ensure sharp, bright viewing. For quick focusing, the eyepiece has a fast-focus adjustment ring. Simply rotate the ring until the reticle becomes sharp.

Grand Slam scopes' solid, one-piece construction makes them not only rugged and reliable, but resistant to moisture and humidity. Configurations include: 4.75x40mm, a fixed-power scope with sufficient magnification for longer shots, yet a wide field of view for finding running game close in; 1.5-5x32mm, the ideal scope for short-range rifles and fast target acquisition in brushy country; 3.5-10x40mm, the traditional choice of big-game hunters for short- or long-range shooting; 3.5-10x50mm, which provides the brightest view in low-light situations; 4.5-14x40mm AO, possibly the most versatile Grand Slam scope, with a low range suitable for stand hunting and high enough magnification for target shooting or varmint hunting; and 6-20x40mm AO, two target/varminter models.

Windage and elevation knobs have target-type finger adjustments so 1/4-MOA adjustments can be made by gripping the rim of the knob between the thumb and index finger. The Grand Slam scopes are also equipped with Micro-Trac, Weaver's patented four-point adjustment system.

All Grand Slam scopes are offered with a plex reticle (except the 6-20x model, which is offered with a choice of Weaver's Varminter reticle or fine crosshairs with a dot). The scopes have a non-glare black matte or silver and black finish, featuring the new green and gold oval Weaver logo medallion on the scope saddle and green ring inside the objective lens hood.

Price:6-20x40 AO **$420**
4.5-14x40 AO **400**
3.5-10x50 . . . . **390**
3-10x40 . . . . **330**
1.5-5x32 . . . . **350**
4.75x40 . . . . **300**

SIGHTS & SCOPES

CLASSIC 2.5 2.5X20MM

Weaver Classic K Series

The K2.5, K4 and K6 have a long history in America's game fields. New logos distinguish these versatile hunting scopes at a glance. Reasonably priced and great values, K scopes–including the target model, KT-15–have one-piece tubes and bright optics.

Prices: KT-15 (15x40 gloss) **$281**
K6 (gloss) **155**
K6 (matte) **155**
K4 (gloss) **150**
K4 (matte) **150**
K2.5 (2.5x20 gloss) **133**

Williams Sights

FP Series

FP-GR-TK
ON REMINGTO 581

Internal micrometer adjustments have positive internal locks. The FP is strong, rugged, dependable. The alloy used to manufacture this sight has a tensile strength of 85,000 pounds. Yet, the FP is light and compact, weighing only 1½ ounces. Target knobs are available on all models of the FP receiver sight if desired.

Prices:

For most models. $68
With target knobs 80

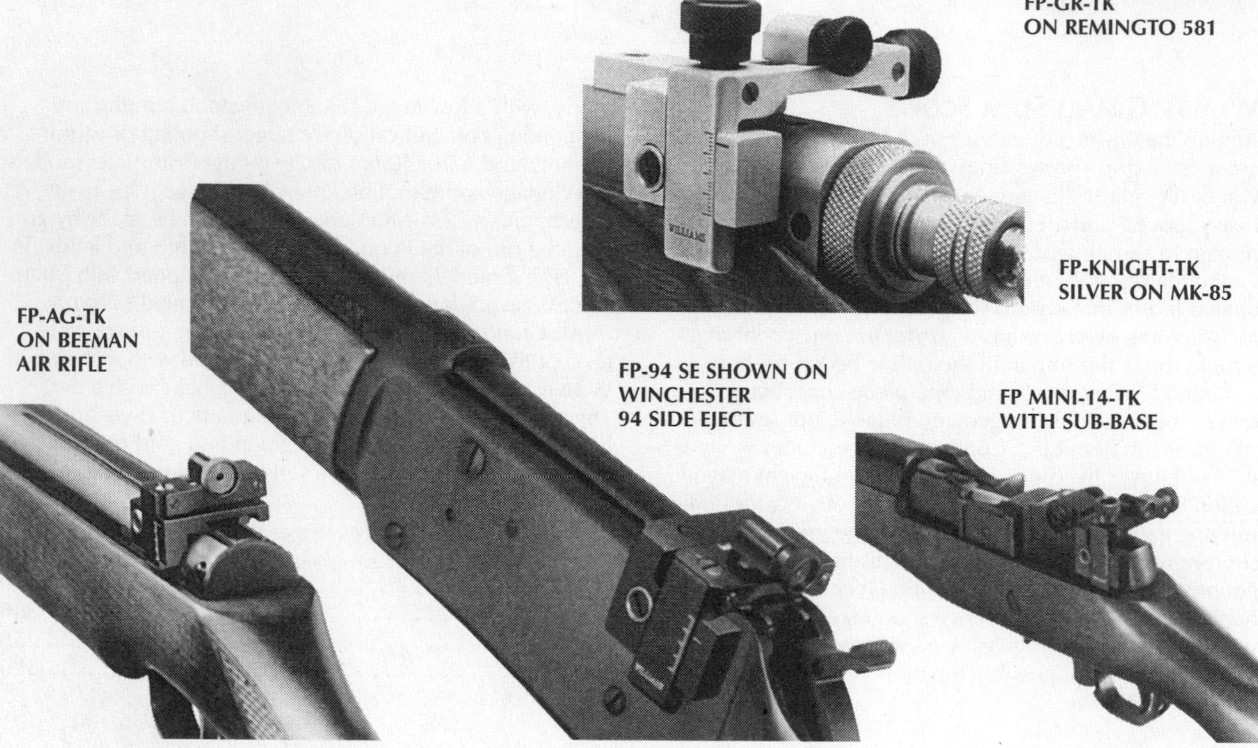

FP-KNIGHT-TK
SILVER ON MK-85

FP-AG-TK
ON BEEMAN
AIR RIFLE

FP-94 SE SHOWN ON
WINCHESTER
94 SIDE EJECT

FP MINI-14-TK
WITH SUB-BASE

FP Receiver Sight Options

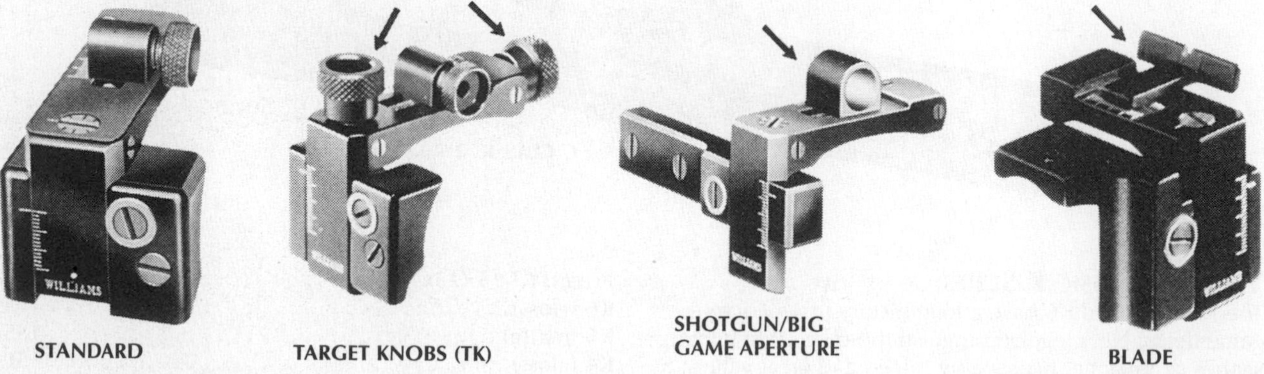

STANDARD

TARGET KNOBS (TK)

SHOTGUN/BIG
GAME APERTURE

BLADE

Williams Sights

Open Sights

WGOS Series

- Made from high tensile strength aluminum. Will not rust.
- All parts milled - no stampings.
- Streamlined and lightweight with tough anodized finish.
- Dovetailed windage and elevation - Easy to adjust, positive locks.
- Interchangeable blades available in four heights and four styles.

Price: $19-26

Blades are sold separately, except "U" blades are available installed on WGOS octagon T/C and CVA.

Price:. 7

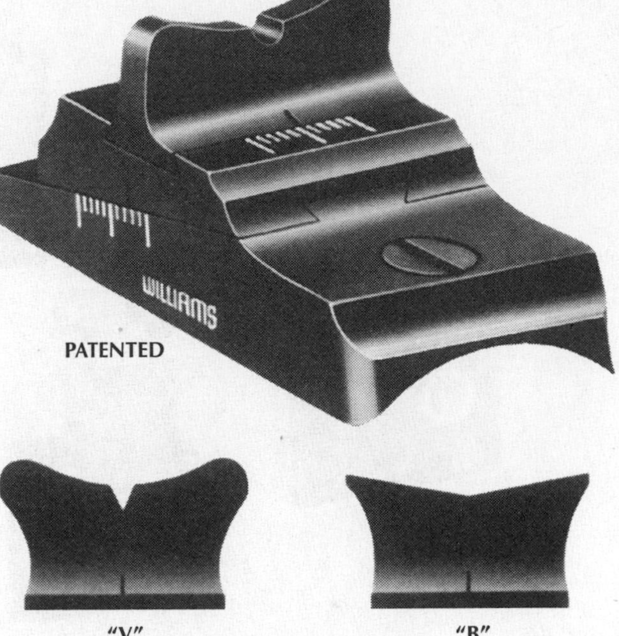

PATENTED

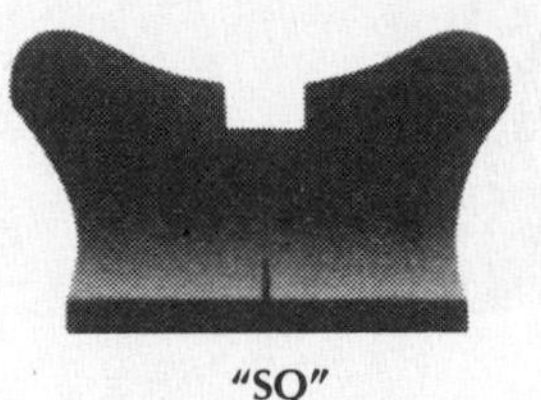
"SQ"

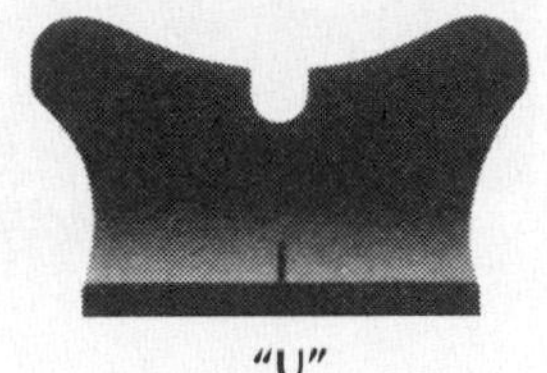
"U"

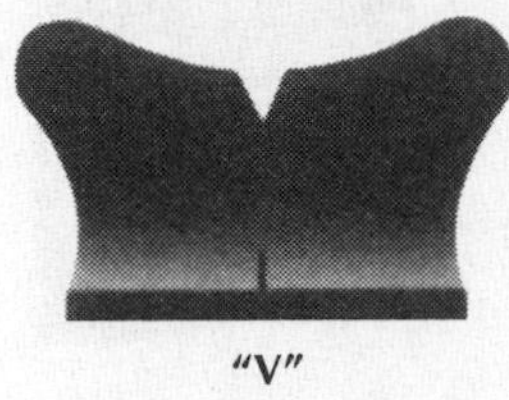
"V"

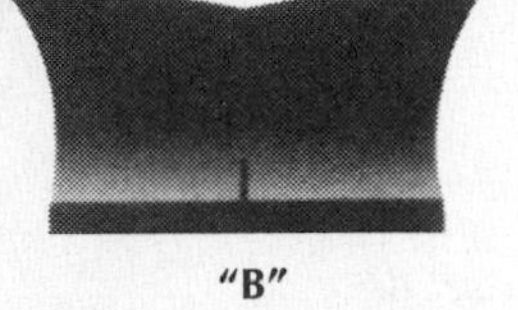
"B"

Receiver Sights

WGRS Series

- Compact Low Profile
- Lightweight, Strong, Rustproof
- Positive Windage and Elevation Locks

In most cases these sights utilize dovetail or existing screws on top of the receiver for installation. They are made from an aluminum alloy that is stronger than many steels. Light. Rustproof. Williams quality throughout.

Price: most models. $34

Fire Sights

Williams has introduced new "Fire Sights". These sights are machined from aircraft-strength aluminum and steel. This sight is lightweight, durable and brightens in low-light situations.

Prices:

Pistol Fire Sight Sets. 44
Shotgun Fire Sight Sets . . . . 29 to 37
Muzzleloader Fire Sight Sets . . . . 29 to 50
Rifle Fire Sight Sets . . . . 29 to 39
Peep Sets . . . . 40 to 79
Rifle Beads. 17

WGRS-CVA ON CVA APOLLLO

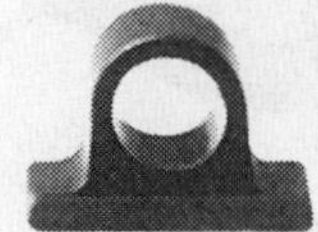

"GHOST RING" SHOTGUN APERTURE AVAILABLE FOR WGRS RECEIVER SIGHTS. SOLD SEPARATELY.

FIRE SIGHTS

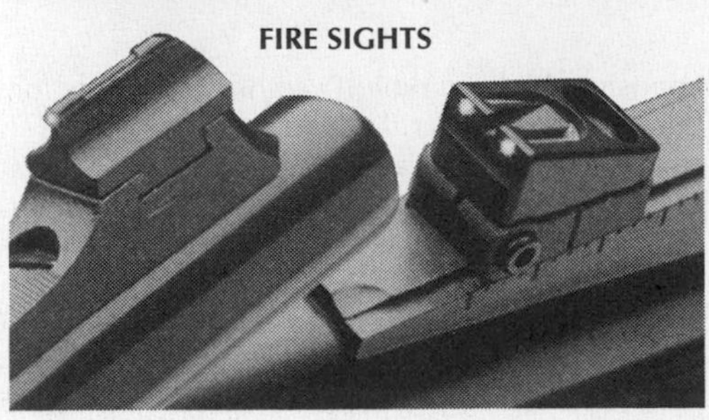

Williams Sights
5D Series

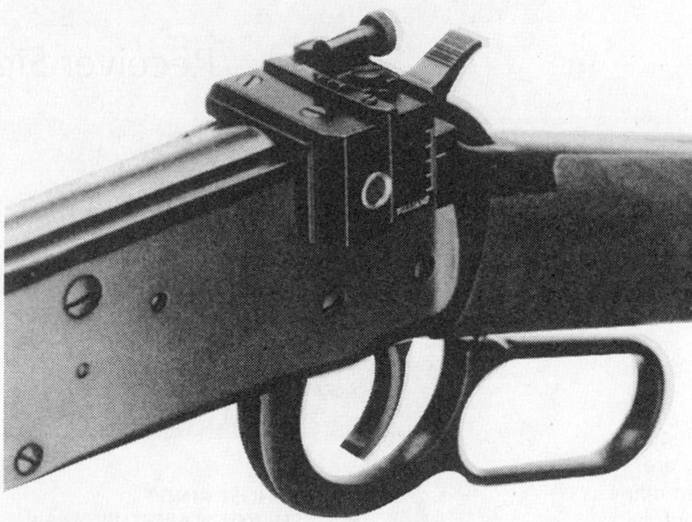

5D Series
- **FOR BIG GAME RIFLES, 22'S, SHOTGUNS**
- **POSITIVE WINDAGE AND ELEVATION LOCKS**
- **LIGHTWEIGHT, STRONG, ACCURATE**
- **WILLIAMS QUALITY THROUGHOUT - RUSTPROOF**

The inexpensive, high quality 5D sight is available for most of the more popular rifles and shotguns. These sights have the same strength, lightweight, and neat appearance, but without the micrometer adjustments. Designed for rugged hunting use, the 5D sights are dependable and accurate. Positive locks. Clear unobstructed vision. No knobs or side plates to blot out shooter's field of vision. Wherever possible, the manufacturers' mounting screw holes in the receivers of the guns have been utilized for easy installation. The upper staff of the Williams 5D sight is readily detachable. Just loosen one screw. The angular bushing locks this upper staff. A set screw is provided as a stop screw so that the sight will return to absolute zero after reattaching. The Williams 5D sight is made of one of the highest grade alloys obtainable. Laboratory tests show that the material used has a tensile strength approximately 25% greater than mild steels.

Price: Most 5D models. $36

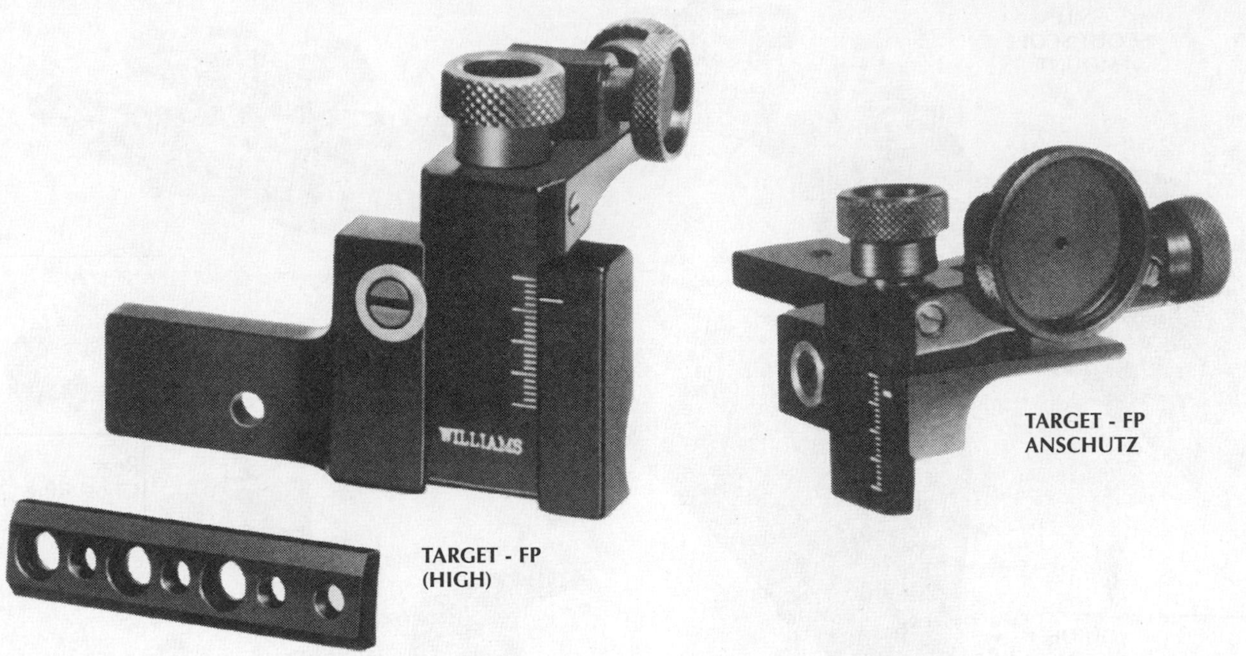

TARGET - FP
(HIGH)

TARGET - FP
ANSCHUTZ

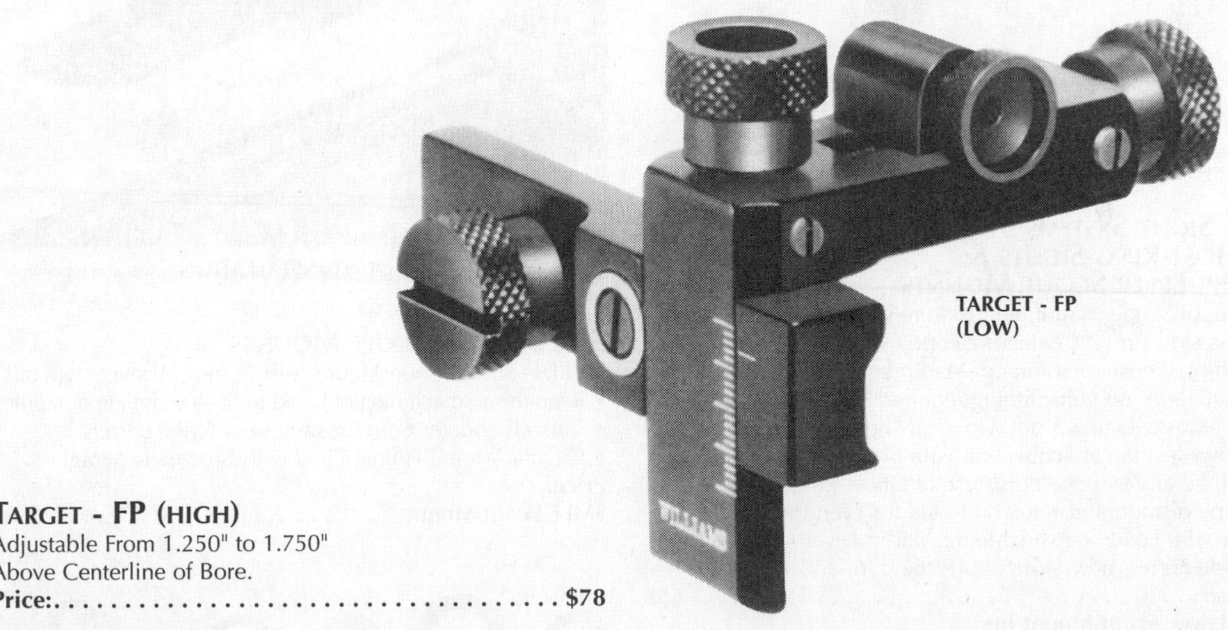

TARGET - FP
(LOW)

Target - FP (high)
Adjustable From 1.250" to 1.750"
Above Centerline of Bore.
Price:. $78

Target FP-Anschutz
Designed to fit many of the Anschutz Lightweight .22 Cal. Target and Sporter Models. No Drilling and Tapping required.
Price:. 76

Target - FP (low)
Adjustable From .750" to 1.250"
Above Centerline of Bore.
Price:. 78

XS Sight Systems

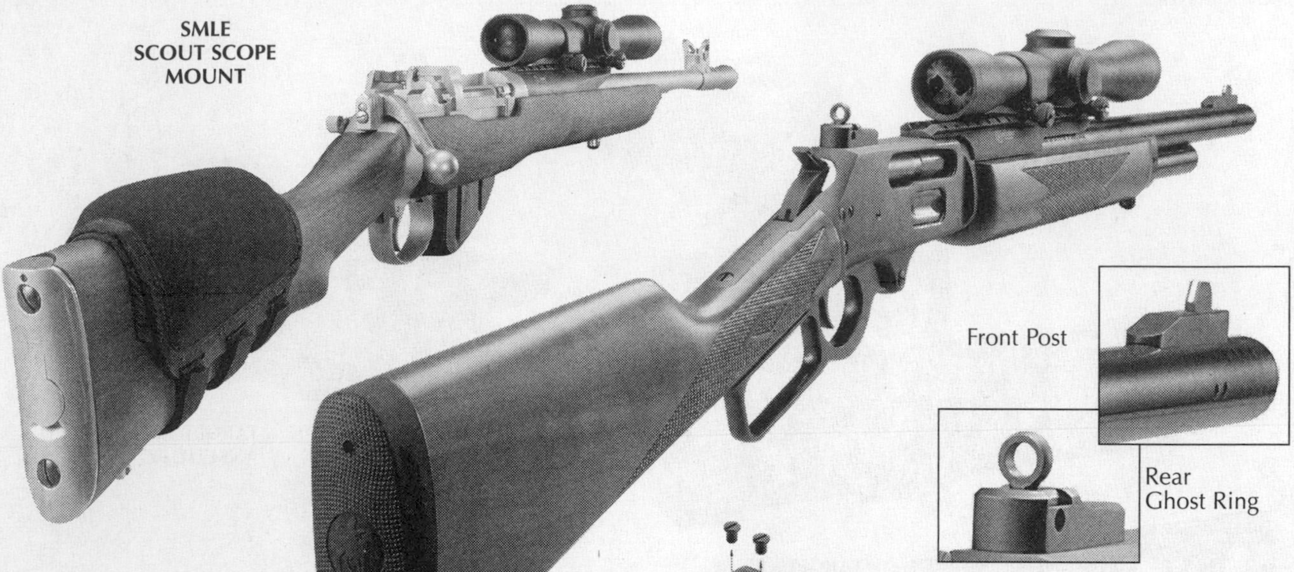

SMLE SCOUT SCOPE MOUNT

Front Post

Rear Ghost Ring

GUIDE GUN

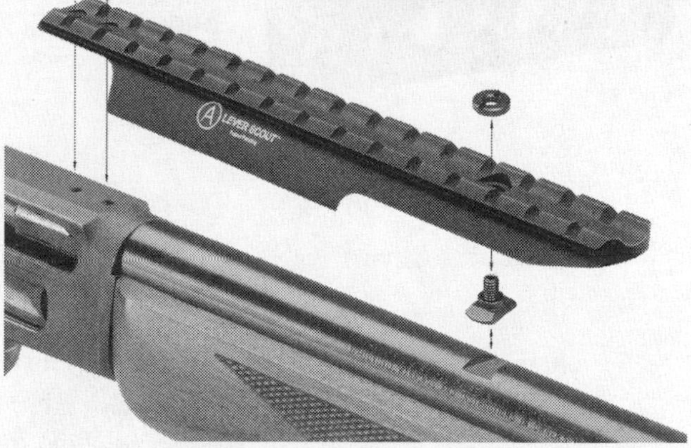

MOUNT INSTALLATION

SIGHTS & SCOPES

XS Sight Systems Ghost-Ring Sights & New Lever Scout Mounts

• Scout Scope Mount with 8" long Weaver-style rail and cross slots on ½" Centers • Scope mounts ⅛" lower than previously possible on Marlin Lever Guns • Drop-in installation, no gunsmithing required • Installs using existing rear dovetail & front two screw holes on receiver • Allows fast target acquisition with both eyes open—better peripheral vision • Affords use of Ghost-Ring Sights with Scope dismounted • Recoil tested for even the stout 45/70 and .450 Loads • Available for Marlin Lever Models: 1895 Guide Series, new .450, .444P, the 336, and 1894.

Price: **$50**

XS Lever Scout Mount for Win 94 . . . . **55**

XS Ghost-Ring Hunting Sights

• Fully adjustable for windage & elevation • Available for most rifles, including blackpowder • Minimum gunsmithing for most installations; matches most existing mounting holes • Compact design, CNC machined from steel and heat treated • Perfect for low light hunting conditions and brush/timer hunting, offers minimal target obstruction.

Price: AO Ghost-Ring Hunting Sight Set **90**

SMLE Scout Scope Mounts

• Offers Scout Scope Mount with 7" long Weaver style rail
• Requires no machining of barrel to fit—no drilling or tapping
• Tapered counter bore for snug fit of SMLE Barrels
• Circular Mount is final filled with Brownells Acraglass

Price:

SMLE Scout Mount **$60**

Ghost Ring Sights for Rifles and Carbines

Price: rear **60**

front **30**

XS Sight Systems

GLOCK 36
W/BIG DOT
TRITIUM

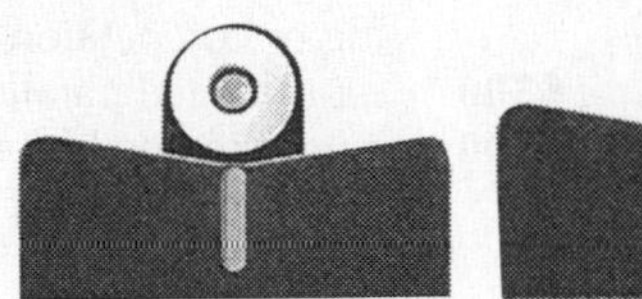

BIG DOT TRITIUM W/TRITIUM REAR

XS Express Sights

Extremely Fast Front Sight using proven Express Sight Principles. Low profile Shallow V Express rear with white vertical line, front white dot available with or without Tritium. Machined steel sights in matte black finish. Rear sight available in different heights. Made for most pistols, and limited styles of revolvers. Rear available in double set-screw for most installations.

Prices:
Big Dot Tritium Set **90**
Standard Dot Tritium Set **90**

XS 24/7 Express Sights

The original fast aacquisition sight. Now enhanced with new 24/7 tritium sight.

24/7 Express sights are the finest sights made for fast sight acquisition under any light conditions. Light or dark just "dot the i" and put the dot on the target.

- Enhances low light sight acquisition
- Improves Low Light accuracy
- Low profile, snag free design
- Available for most pistols

Prices: XS 24/7 Big Dot Express Sets **$120**
XS 24/7 Standard Dot Express Sets **120**

XS Adjustable Express Sight Sets

Incorporates Adjustable Rear Express Sight with a white stripe rear, or Pro Express Rear with a Vertical Tritium Bar, fits Bomar style cut, LPA style cut, or a Kimber Target cut rear sight. Affords same Express Sight principles as fixed sight models.

Prices:
Adjustable Express w/White Stripe Rear and Big Dot Front or Standard Dot Front **$120**
Adjustable Express w/White Stripe Rear and Big Dot Tritium or Standard Dot Tritium Front **150**
Adjustable Pro Express w/Tritium Rear and Big Dot Tritium or Standard Dot Tritium Front **150**

SIGHTS & SCOPES

Zeiss Scopes

CONQUEST 3-9X40

CONQUEST 3.5-10X44
STAINLESS STEEL FINISH

Conquest 3-9x40

The 3-9x40 Conquest is the most versatile scope in the series, featuring a 4-inch eye-relief with unique European quick focus and advanced internal design, enabling the widest windage/elevation adjustment to 64 inches. All this combined with a solid one-piece alloy body manufactured to German standards makes the 3-9x40 Conquest a practical hunting sight.

Price: 3-9x40 MC 500
Stainless. 530

Conquest 3-9x40S (not shown)

The 3-9x40S Conquest is designed to support sportsmen who demand a shotgun, airgun, or muzzleloader scope with heavy reticle. The 3-9x40S has the same glass and coating as the 3-9, with a safe 4-inch eye relief, etched glass reticle and one-piece alloy tube.

Price: 3-9x40S $500
w/turkey reticle 500

Conquest 3.5-10x44

The 3.5-10x44 Conquest, designed to replace Zeiss' Diavari C 3-9x36, is superior in design and has all the standard Conquest features. Additionally, the 3.5-10x44 Conquest offers a 22-percent larger objective and a 66-inch windage/ elevation adjustment. Combine these features with a weight of just 14 oz., the 3.5-10x44 Conquest makes it suitable for general big game hunting.

Price: 3.5-10x44 MC 600
Stainless. 630
Target 700

Conquest 4.5-14x44 (not shown)

The 4.5-14x44 Conquest offers the first turret-mounted parallax adjustment from Zeiss. The 64-inch windage/elevation adjustment coupled with the 25-foot to 8.3-foot field of view made the 4.5-14x44 Conquest the selection of choice. The objective clarity and light transmission exceeds most models that have larger objectives and provides for perfect balance without adding weight or requiring raised mounts.Conquest riflescopes are water- and fog-proof, are free of lead and arsenic, and are backed by Zeiss' lifetime transferable warranty.

Price: 4.5-14x44 AO. 750
w/crosshair reticle 750
Stainless. 770
Target 850

Conquest 6.5-20X50 MC (not shown)

The latest addition to the Conquest line of riflescopes is the 6.5-20X50. Developed for the American long-range shooter, this riflescope is ideal for big game hunting, varmint shooting or competition at great distances. Equipped with a turret-mounted parallax adjustment, the new 6.5-20X50 eliminates the need for the shooter to take his eye off the target. The external target turret knobs have no caps to lose and make it easier to view the windage and elevation. The riflescope does not require high mounts, allowing for a compact rifle profile and low line of sight.

Reticle: Z Plex or Fine Crosshair ***Eye Relief:*** 3.5"
F.O.V.: 17.6'-5.8' at 100 yds. ***Weight:*** 21.5 oz.

Price: Matte Black $950
Stainless. 970

Zeiss Conquest Series Riflescopes

The Conquest series has Zeiss' proprietary MC anti-reflective coating and is backed by a Lifetime Transferable Warranty. Couple this with Zeiss' world renowned low-light performance, new arsenic/lead-free glass technology, precision engineering, quick focus and constant eye relief design and you have one of the world's highest performance riflescope series.

Specifications	Zeiss Conquest 3-9x40	Zeiss Conquest 3-9x40S	Zeiss Conquest 3.5-10x44	Zeiss Conquest 4.5-14x44	Zeiss Conquest 6.5-20x50AO
Magnification	3-9x	3-9x	3.5-10x	4.5-14X	6.5-20X
Objective	40	40	44	44	50
Tube diameter	1"	1"	1"	1"	1"
Field of View(ft.@100yards)	11.01'-34'	11.01'-34'	11.61'-35.1'	8.31'-24.99'	17.6'-5.8'
Parallax (yards)	100	50	100	30-Infinity	50-Infinity
Exit Pupil (mm)	13.3-4.4	13.3-4.4	12.57-4.4	9.7-3.14	7.7-2.5
Eye Relief	4"	4"	3.5"	3.5"	3.5"
Length	13.15"	13.15"	12.7"	13.86"	15.6"
Weight	15 oz.	15 oz.	15.8 oz.	17.5 oz.	21.5 oz.
MOA	1/4	1/4	1/4	1/4	1/4

Diavari VM/V 3-9x42 T*

Over the years, the 3-9x power range has proven its staying power. It is still the favorite power range of North American hunters. The 42 mm objective, coupled with the Zeiss T* coating, extends the hunting day. Whether the quarry is elk, Dall sheep or Boone and Crockett white-tail, the VM/V Diavari 3-9 x 42T* offers top quality and the right magnification.

Power	3-9x
Effective Objective Diameter (mm)	30-42
Exit Pupil Diameter (mm)	10-4.7
Twilight Factor	8.5-18.4
Field Of View At 100 Yards (feet)	36-12.9
Minimum Square Adjustment Range At 100 Yards (inch)	49.7
Eye Relief (inch)	3.74
Center Tube Diameter (inch)	1
Objective Bell Diameter (inch)	1.89
Length (inch)	13.3
Weight (ounces)	15.2
Parallax Free (yards)	109.4
Price:	$1250

Diavari VM/V 5-15x42 T*

Precise windage and elevation adjustments make the Diavari VM/V 5 - 15 x 42 T* the perfect companion for a target or varmint rifle. The rugged adjustment system provides fast, accurate and repeatable adjustments. By aligning the optical and mechanical axes, Zeiss ensures full range of adjustment.

Power	5-15x
Effective Objective Diameter (mm)	42-42
Exit Pupil Diameter (mm)	8.4-2.8
Twilight Factor	14.1-25.1
Field Of View At 100 Yards (feet)	23.7-7.8
Minimum Square Adjustment Range At 100 Yards (inch)	30
Eye Relief (inch)	3.74
Center Tube Diameter (inch)	1
Objective Bell Diameter (inch)	1.89
Length (inch)	13.3
Weight (ounces)	14
Parallax Free (yards)	109.4
Price:	$1500

Diavari VM/V 3-12x56 T*

In the quiet haze of dawn or the fleeting light of sunset, a riflesope is put to the ultimate test. Under these conditions, the Diavari VM/V 3-12x56 T* excels. The patented Zeiss T* anti-reflection coating is designed to transmit the optimum percentage of light throughout the spectral range to take full advantage of your eye's sensitivity. Weighing in at 13.5 ounces, the VM/V 3-12x56 T* won't slow you down.

Power	3-12x
Effective Objective Diameter (mm)	44.0-56
Exit Pupil Diameter (mm)	14.7-4.7
Twilight Factor	8.5-25.9
Field Of View At 100 Yards (feet)	37.5-10.4
Minimum Square Adjustment Range At 100 Yards (inch)	36.7
Eye Relief (inch)	3.54
Center Tube Diameter (inch)	1.18
Objective Bell Diameter (inch)	2.44
Length (inch)	13.54
Weight (ounces)	17.8/16.8
Parallax Free (yards)	109.4
Price:	$1600
w/illuminated reticle	$2050

Sights & Scopes

Zeiss Scopes

Zeiss Premuim Sports Optics

1.1-4 X 24 T*

DIAVARI 1.1-4 X 24 T* VM/V

- Compact riflescope with 108 ft. field of view at 1.1 power
- Extremely lightweight - ideal for safari rifles
- With illuminated varipoint reticle for fast target acquisition clearly visible also in critical lighting conditions
- Especially designed for running shots and hunting in heavy brush
- Available with bullet drop compensator
- Eye relief: 3.74 in.

Price: **$1800**

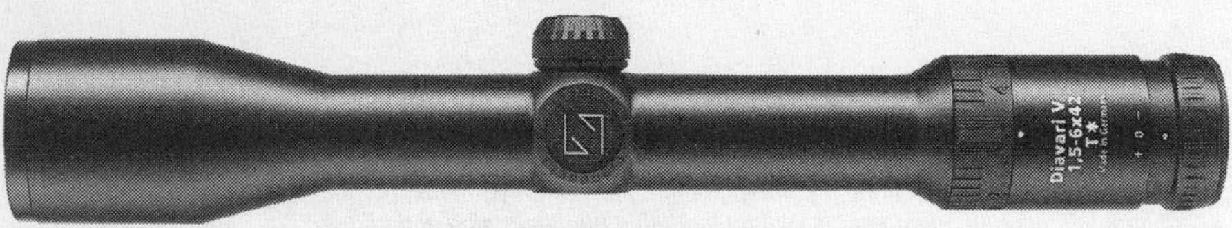

1.5-6 X 42 T*

DIAVARI 1.5-6 X 42 T* VM/V

- Excellent choice for white-tail or moose hunter
- Compact and easy to handle
- Lightest scope of its class
- 72 ft. field of view - largest field of view in premium class
- Easy-grip adjustment knob
- Available with bullet drop compensator
- Eye relief: 3.54 in.

Price: **$1350**
w/Varipoint, reticle **1850**
w/Varipoint 54 reticle **1900**

2.5-10 X 50 T*

DIAVARI 2.5-10 X 50 T* VM/V

- High powered riflescope with superior twilight performance
- Light, compact with a wide field of view
- Available with an illuminated reticle
- Easy-grip adjustment knob
- Excellent choice for world-wide all-round hunting
- Available with bullet drop compensator
- Eye relief: 3.54 in.

Price: **$1550**
w/illuminated reticle **2000**

Also Available (not shown)

DIAVARI 3-12X56 ZM/Z

Magnification: 3.12 ***Tube Diameter:*** 30mm ***Eye Relief:*** 3.2"
Field of view: 27.6' - 9.9' **Length:** 15.3" ***Weight:*** 27oz.

Price: Black matte **1100**
Stainless **1150**
w/illuminated reticle **1500**

SIGHTS & SCOPES

AMMUNITION

Remington
PREMIER COPPER SOLID
Sabot Slug 12 GAUGE 2 3/4 LENGTH MAX DR EQ 1oz. WEIGHT
FIVE HOLLOW POINT SLUGS

Black Hills Ammunition

Black Hills, aptly named for its South Dakota base of operations, offers an expanding line of factory-new and remanufactured ammunition for handguns and rifles. The Cowboy Action Line includes loads for the .32 H+R, .357 Magnum, .38-40, .44-40, .45 Colt, .32-20, .44 Colt, .44 Spl., .45 Schofield, .38 Spl, .38 Long Colt, .44 Russian, .45-70. Modern handgun ammunition, from .40 S+W to .44 Magnum, features a variety of bullet types. Black Hills rifle cartridges include the popular .223, .308, 6.5-284, .300 Win. Mag, and the potent long-range tactical round, the .338 Lapua. There's also specialty ammo, with frangible or moly-coated bullets. New for 2002 is Black Hills Gold ammunition, hunting rounds available in 243 Win, 270 Win, 308 Win, 30-06, and 300 Win Mag.

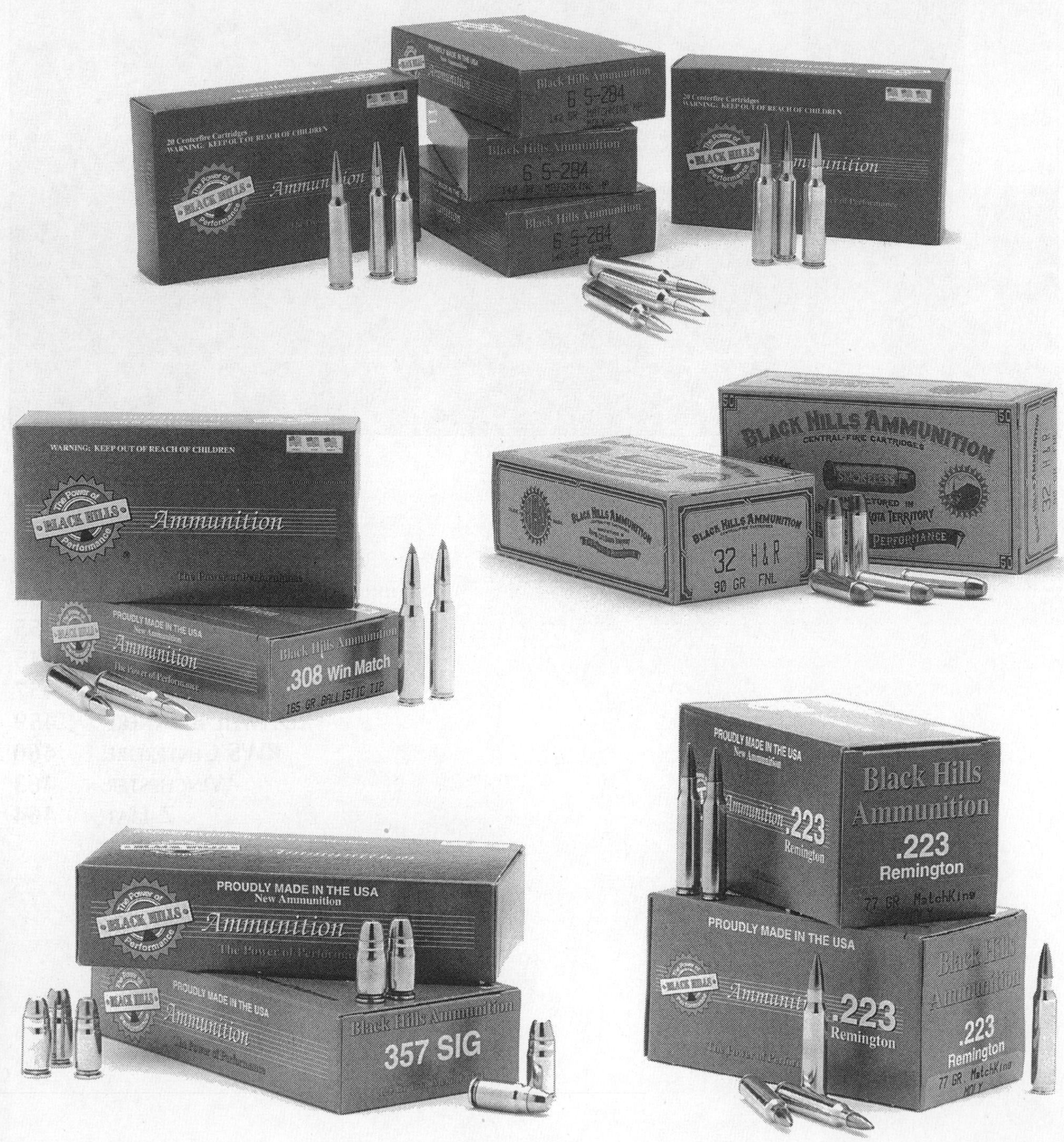

Federal Ammunition

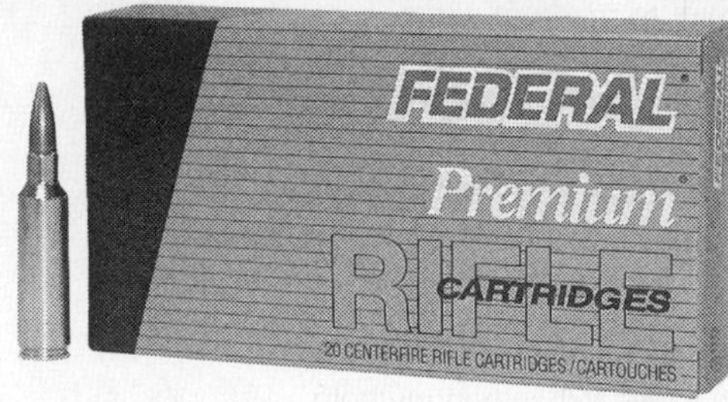

Premium Grand Slam Turkey Load

Features & Benefits

- High velocity provides increased downrange pellet energy and deep penetration
- Copper-plated extra hard shot for tight patterns
- Granulated plastic shot buffer cushions the shot for dense, uniform patterns
- Triple-Plus wad column provides positive gas sealing for uniform ballistics
- High base hull with high output 209A primer for consistant reliable ignition
- Portion of the proceeds from the sales go to the National Wild Turkey Federation

Classic Steel - Heavy High Velocity

Features & Benefits

- Increased shot payload with more downrange energy
- High velocity so it is quicker to target
- Three watertight seals at crimp, wad and primer
- High density shot cup prevents pellets from contacting bore surface
- High output 209A Primer provides consistent ballistic performance at all temperatures
- New box design
- Water resistant packaging

Premium Pistol Expanding Full Metal Jacket

Features & Benefits

- No hollowpoint to fill and block expansion, insuring consistent expansion through barriers
- Internally skived jacket gives consistent, symmetrical expansion with a large diameter
- Rubber front core performs well under a wide range of operating velocities and temperatures
- Works well in short barreled and standard barrel length handguns
- Low flash propellant for low light tactical use
- Reliable feed and function in semi-auto and automatic firearms

Premium Rifle 300 Win. Short Magnum

Features & Benefits

- Designed for short action rifles
- Beltless high capacity case provides ballistics equal to the longer 300 Win Magnum
- Available with Trophy Bonded Bear Claw or Speer Grand Slam bullets

Trophy Bonded Bear Claw:

- 100% fusion bonded jacket and core
- 95% weight return
- Reliable expansion from 25 yards to extreme ranges
- Better penetration through bone and muscle with no fragmentation

Speer Grand Slam:

- Exclusive hot core process insures reliable expansion and penetration
- Excellent retained weight and flat trajectory

American Eagle Pistol

Features & Benefits

- Gives price conscious customers top value for their money
- Federal brass for easy reloading
- Made in USA
- Quality components with reliable performance

Bullets in Federal Ammunition

Trophy Bonded Bear Claw®

This legendary Jack Carter design is ideal for medium to large dangerous game and is loaded exclusivly by Federal. The jacket and core are 100% fusion-bonded for reliable bullet expansion from 25 yards to extreme ranges. The bullet retains 95% of its weight, assuring deep penetration. The bullet jacket features a hard solid copper base tapering to a soft, copper nose section for controlled expansion.

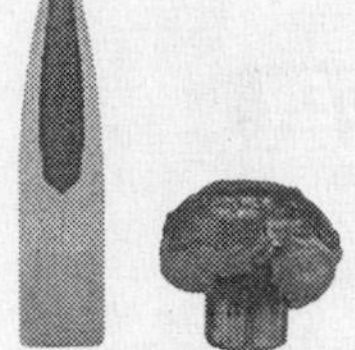

Trophy Bonded Sledgehammer®

Use it on the largest, most dangerous game in the world. This Jack Carter design maximizes stopping power and your confidence. It's a bonded bronze solid with a flat nose that minimizes deflection off bone and muscle for a deep, straight wound channel.

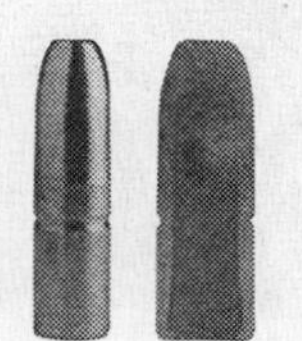

Sierra® GameKing® Boat-Tail

Long ranges are its specialty. With varying calibers, it's an excellent choice for everything from varmints to big game animals. The GameKings's tapered, boattail design provides extremely flat trajectories. The design also gives it a higher downrange velocity, so there's more energy at the point of impact. Reduced wind drift makes it a good choice for long-range shots.

Barnes® XLC™ Coated X-Bullet™

Recommended for medium to large game. A solid copper bullet provides reliable four-petal expansion and 100% weight retention for deep penetration. The outer heat-cured, dry film coating prevents copper-fouling in your barrel, reduces bore friction and won't rub off on your hands.

Woodleigh® Weldcore

Safari hunters have long respected this bonded Australian bullet for its superb accuracy and excellent stopping power. Its special heavy jacket provides 80-85% weight retention. These bullets are favored for large or dangerous game.

Nosler® Partition®

This Nosler design is a proven choice for medium to large game animals. A partioned copper jacket allows the front half of the bullet to mushroom, while the rear core remains intact, driving forward for deep penetration and stopping power.

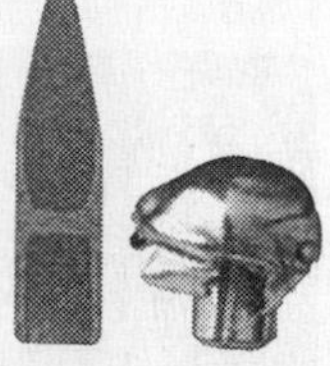

Nosler® Ballistic Tip®

With proven fast, flat-shooting wind-defying performance, it's specially designed for long-range shots at varmints, predators and small to medium game. A color-coded polycarbonate tip provides easy identification, prevents deformation in the magazine and drives back on impact for expansion and immediate energy transfer.

Speer® Grand Slam®

An excellent all-around choice for medium to large game. When hunting both woods and clearings, you need a bullet that handles any situation. The Speer Grand Slam features a slim profile, yet thicker metal on the jacket's shank and internal flutes at the bullet's tip. This gives you flat shooting capability, a tip that mushrooms perfectly on impact and a bullet that stays in one piece.

Speer® African Grand Slam®

For big, dangerous game, you need a bullet that penetrates deep without excessive expansion. That's precisely the nature of our African Grand Slam bullet. A massive solid gilding metal jacket helps the bullet maintain its length and weight, while a "stop shoulder" prevents tip rollback. The Hot-Cor is firmly held by multi-lock serrations which help lock the core to the jacket.

Speer® African Grand Slam® Solid

The African Grand Slam features a Tungsten-Carbide core to keep the weight up without making the bullet too long. A flat tip ensures stability and straight line penetration.

Speer® TNT®

Varmint hunters require two things from a bullet: tight groups and quick expansion. The Speer TNT gives you both. For rapid expansion, TNT jackets are fluted more than 90% of their length and have a dead-soft lead core.

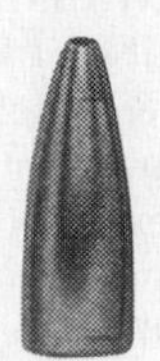

Bullets in Federal Ammunition

Classic® Centerfire Rifle

Hi-Shok® Soft Point

It's a proven performer on small game and thin-skinned medium game. It has an aerodynamic tip for a flat trajectory. The exposed soft point expands rapidly for hard hits, even as velocity slows at longer ranges.

Hi-Shok® Soft Point Round Nose

For generations, hunters have made this bullet the choice for deer and bear in heavy cover. Its large exposed tip, good weight retention and specially tapered jacket provide controlled expansion for deep penetration.

Hi-Shok® Soft Point Flat Nose

This is the bullet hunters traditionally choose when headed into thick cover. It expands reliably and penetrates deep on light to medium game. The flat nose prevents accidental discharge in tubular magazines.

Speer® Hot-Cor® Soft Point

For larger game, Vernon Speer recognized the importance of bullet integrity. Nearly 40 years ago, he developed the Hot-Cor®, a bullet with a molten lead core poured into the jacket. Today, this still gives you excellent bullet integrity, combining nearly 200% expansion with deep penetration.

Full Metal Jacket Boat-Tail

These accurate, non-expanding bullets give you a flat shooting trajectory, leave a small exit hole in game, and puts clean holes in paper - great for sharpening your shooting eye. And they're famous for smooth, reliable feeding into semi-automatics too.

Classic® Handgun Bullet Styles

Lead Round Nose

A great economical training round for practicing at the range. It dates back to the early part of this century. This bullet is 100% lead with no jacket. It provides excellent accuracy and is very economical.

Full Metal Jacket

A good choice for range practice and reducing lead fouling in the barrel. The jacket extends from the nose to the base, preventing bullet expansion and barrel leading. It is used primarily as military ammunition and for recreational shooting.

Hi-Shok® Jacketed Soft Point

It's a proven performer on small to medium-sized game.

Lead Semi-Wadcutter

The most popular all-around choice for target and personal defense. a versatile design which cuts clean holes in targets and efficiently transfers energy.

Hi-Shok® Jacketed Hollow Point

It's an ideal personal defense round in revolvers and semi-autos. Creates quick, positive expansion with proven accuracy. Specially designed jacket ensures smooth feeding into autoloading firearms.

Semi-Wadcutter Hollow Point

A good combination for both small game and personal defense. Hollow point design promotes uniform expansion.

Premium® Handgun Bullet Styles

Hydra-Shok®

The choice of law enforcement agencies nationwide. Federal's unique center-post design delivers controlled expansion, and the notched jacket provides efficient energy transfer to penetrate barriers while retaining stopping power. The deep penetration of this jacketed bullet satisfies even the FBI's stringent testing requirements.

Premium® Personal Defense®

We hope you never have to use our Premium Personal Defense ammunition in a critical situation. But, if you do, you'll appreciate the increased muzzle velocity and energy compared to standard loads, and the rapid bullet expansion that delivers instant stopping power. You'll also appreciate that recoil is significantly reduced. In addition, our unique clear packaging lets you see the ammo before you open the box.

Premium Expanding Full Metal Jacket

An ideal choice for agencies that don't permit hollow point ammunition, this revolutionary barrier-penetrating design combines a scored metal nose over an internal rubber tip that collapses on impact. It never fills with barrier material and assures expansion on every shot. A lead core at the base maintains weight retension.

CastCore

Premium CastCore gives you a heavyweight, flat nosed, hard cast-lead bullet that smashes through bone, without breaking apart.

Trophy Bonded Bear Claw

The Trophy Bonded Bear Claw handgun bullet has a fusion-bonded jacket and core for up to 95% weight retention, better penetration and more knockdown power.

Fiocchi Ammunition

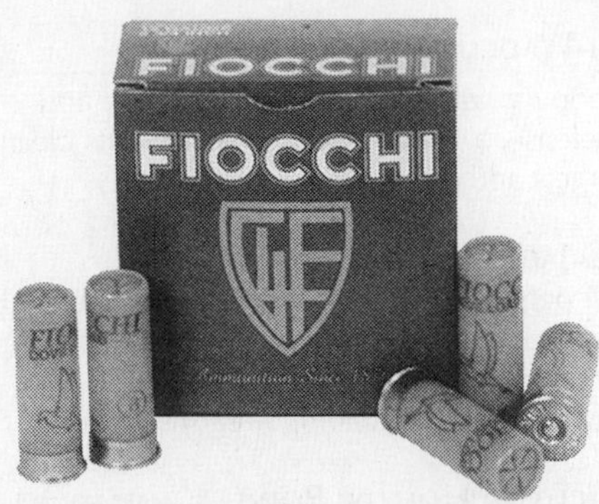

Known for its shotshells and .22 rimfire ammunition, Fiocchi also markets centerfire pistol and rifle cartridges. This Italian firm has been in business since 1876.

Fiocchi Target Loads offer you many choices to suit the shell to your game: Standard 1⅛-ounce loads for everything from registered trap and skeet to sporting clays. One-ounce loads that deliver superior performance with less recoil than a comparable 1⅛-ounce load. Also, a ⅞-ounce training load for new or recoil sensitive shooters. Fiocchi lilac-colored hulls are fully reloadable.

Stock #		Gauge	Shell Length	Dram. Equiv.	Muzzle Velocity	Shot Oz.	Shot Sizes	Rds./Box	Shot Type
Steel (Waterfowl Loads)									
1235ST	Speed Steel	12	3 1/2"	Max.	1460	1 3/8	T BBB BB 1	25	Treated Steel
1235SH	Heavy Steel	12	3 1/2"	Max.	1300	1 9/16	T BBB BB 1	25	Treated Steel
123ST	Speed Steel	12	3"	Max.	1475	1 1/8	BBB BB 1 2 3 4	25	Treated Steel
123S	Steel	12	3"	Max.	1320	1 1/4	T BBB BB 1 2 3 4	25	Treated Steel
123SH	Heavy Steel	12	3"	Max.	1350	1 3/8	BB 1 2 3 4	25	Treated Steel
12S78	Training Load	12	2 3/4"	Max.	1440	7/8	7	25	Treated Steel
12S1OZ	Upland Steel	12	2 3/4"	Max.	1400	1	4 6 7	25	Treated Steel
12S118	Steel	12	2 3/4"	Max.	1375	1 1/8	BB 1 2 3 4 6	25	Treated Steel
12S114	Heavy Steel	12	2 3/4"	Max.	1275	1 1/4	BB 1 2 3 4	25	Treated Steel
20S	Upland Steel	20	2 3/4"	Max.	1470	3/4	3 4 6 7	25	Treated Steel
203ST	Speed Steel	20	3"	Max.	1500	7/8	2 3 4	25	Treated Steel
Field Loads (Upland Game Loads)									
12HF	Heavy Field	12	2 3/4"	3 1/4	1225	1 1/4	6 7-12/ 8 9	25	Lead
12FLD	Field Load	12	2 3/4"	3 1/4	1255	1 1/8	6 7-1/2 8 9	25	Lead
16FLD	Field Load	16	2 3/4"	2 3/4	1185	1 1/8	6 7-12 8	25	Lead
20FLD	Field Load	20	2 3/4"	2 1/2	1165	1	6 7-1/2 8 9	25	Lead
Dove Loads									
12MS3	Multi-Sport	12	2 3/4"	3	1250	1	7-1/2 8 9	25	Lead
12GT1	Game & Target	12	2 3/4"	3 1/4	1290	1	6 7-1/2 8 9	25	Lead
12GT118	Game & Target	12	2 3/4"	3	1200	1 1/8	7-1/2 8	25	Lead
16GT	Game & Target	16	2 3/4"	2 1/2	1165	1	6 7-1/2 8 9	25	Lead
20GT	Game & Target	20	2 3/4"	2 1/2	1210	7/8	6 7-1/2 8 9	25	Lead
28GT	Game & Target	28	2 3/4"	2	1200	3/4	8 9	25	Lead
410GT	Game & Target	410	2 1/2"	Max	1200	1/2	8 9	25	Lead
Target Loads									
12TL	Target Light	12	2 3/4"	2 3/4	1150	1	7-1/2 8 8-1/2 9	25	Hi-Antimony Lead
12TH	Target Heavy	12	2 3/4"	3	1200	1	7-1/2 8 8-1/2	25	Hi-Antimony Lead
12TX	Little Rhino	12	2 3/4"	HDCP	1250	1	7-1/2 8 8-1/2	25	Hi-Antimony Lead
12CRSR	Crusher	12	2 3/4"	Max	1300	1	7-1/2 8 8-1/2 9	25	Hi-Antimony Lead
12LITE	Lite	12	2 3/4"	2 7/8	1165	1 1/8	7-1/2 8 9	25	Hi-Antimony Lead
12VIPL	VIP Light	12	2 3/4"	2 3/4	1150	1 1/8	7-1/2 8 9	25	Hi-Antimony Lead
12VIPH	VIP Heavy	12	2 3/4"	3	1200	1 1/8	7-1/2 8 9	25	Hi-Antimony Lead
12WRNO	White Rhino	12	2 3/4"	HDCP	1250	1 1/8	7-1/2 8 8-1/2 9	25	Hi-Antimony Lead
1278OZ	Training Load	12	2 3/4"	3	1200	7/8	7-1/2 8	25	Hi-Antimony Lead
12IN24	International	12	2 3/4"	Max	1350	24 grams	7-1/2 8 8-1/2	25	Hi-Antimony Lead
Sub-Gauge									
20VIP	VIP	20	2 3/4"	2 1/2	1200	7/8	7-1/2 8 9	25	Hi-Antimony Lead
28GT	Game & Target	28	2 3/4"	2	1200	3/4	8 9	25	Lead
28HV	High Velocity	28	2 3/4"	2 1/4	1285	3/4	6 7-1/2 8 9	25	Lead
410GT	Game & Target	410	2 1/2"	Max	1200	1/2	8 9	25	Lead
High Velocity									
12HV	High Velocity	12	2 3/4"	3 3/4	1330	1 1/4	4 5 6 7-1/2 8 9	25	Lead
16HV	High Velocity	16	2 3/4"	3 1/8	1300	1 1/8	4 6 7-1/2 8	25	Lead
20HV	High Velocity	20	2 3/4"	2 3/4	1220	1	4 5 6 7-1/2 8 9	25	Lead
28HV	High Velocity	28	2 3/4"	2 1/4	1285	3/4	6 7-1/2 8 9	25	Lead
410HV	High Velocity	410	3"	Max	1140	11/16	6 7-1/2 8 9	25	Lead

Fiocchi Ammunition

Shotshell Application Guide

Game	Lead Shot Size	Steel Shot Size	Recommended Loads
Geese	NA	T-BBB-BB-1	Heavy Steel, Speed Steel
Ducks	NA	BB-1-2-3-4-6	Heavy Steel, Speed Steel, Upland Steel
Pheasant	4-5-6	3-4-5-6	Golden Pheasant, HV, Speed Steel, Upland Steel, HVN
Turkey	4-5-6	4-5	Turkey Tunder, HV, HVN
Grouse/Partridge	5-6-7 1/2-8	4-6-7	Field Loads, Upland Steel, HV, HVN, HFN
Quail	7 1/2-8-9	7	Field Loads, HV, Upland Steel, HVN, HFN
Dove/Pigeon	6-7 1/2-8-9	6-7	Field Loads, GT, Dove, HV, HFN, HVN
Rabbit/Squirrel	4-5-6-7 1/2	6-7	Field Loads, HV, GT, Upland Steel, HFN, HVN
Deer/Boar	00-Slug	NA	12HV00BK, 12 Gauge Slug, 20 Gauge Slug
Trap	7 1/2-8-8 1/2	6-7	TL, TH, TX, VIP, LITE, WRNO, MS, TRAPH, TRAPL
Skeet	8-8 1/2-9	7	TL, TH, TX, VIP, LITE, WRNO, MS
Sporting Clays	7 1/2-8-8 1/2-9	7	TL, TH, TX, TIP, LITE, WRNO, MS
Steel Target			Upland Steel, Training Load

Shot Pellet Sizes

Size #	9	8-1/2	8	7-1/2	6	5	4	3	2	1	BB	BBB	T	#4	00
Dia.In.	.08	.085	.09	.095	.11	.12	.13	.14	.15	.16	.18	.19	.20	.24	.33
Dia.MM	2.03	2.16	2.29	2.41	279	3.05	3.30	3.56	3.81	4.06	4.57	4.83	5.08	6.10	8.38

Number of Lead Pellets in Various Loads

Lead Pellets		9	8-1/2	8	7-1/2	6	5	4
1 oz.		585	480	409	345	232	172	136
1 1/8 oz.	658	540	460	388	251	194	153	
1 1/4 oz.	731	600	511	431	276	215	170	
1 3/8 oz.	804	660	562	474	307	237	187	
1 3/4 oz.	-	-	-	-	395	304	239	

Number of Steel Pellets in Various Loads

Steel Pellets		7	6	4	3	2	1	BB	BBB	T
3/4 oz.		315	237	143	115	-	-	-	-	-
7/8 oz.		365	-	167	134	109	-	-	-	-
1 oz.		420	316	191	-	-	-	-	-	-
1 1/8 oz.	-	355	215	172	140	115	81	68	-	
1 1/4 oz.	-	-	239	191	151	128	90	-	-	
1 3/8 oz.	-	-	262	210	171	141	99	84	73	
1 9/16 oz.	-	-	-	-	-	161	113	95	83	

Note: When comparing steel shot to lead shot, increase shot size by two to get similar downrange results (i.e. Lead #4 to Steel #2). Check your shotgun and choke manufacturer for steel shot compatibility.

Fiocchi Ammunition

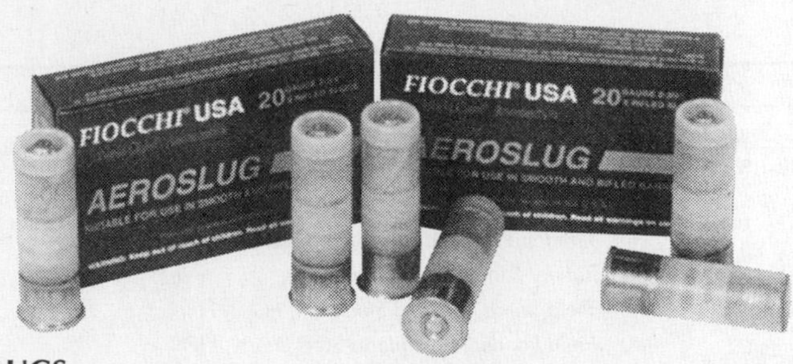

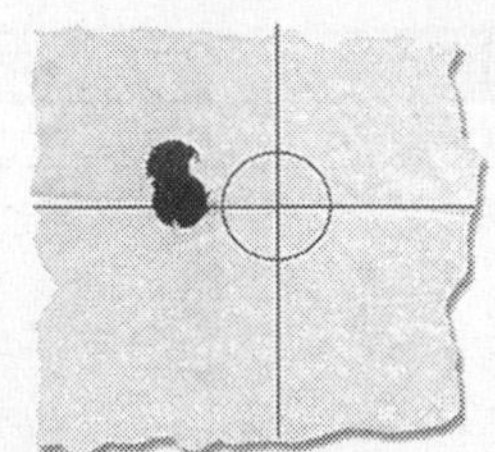

Slugs

Fiocchi's Slugs in both 12 and 20 gauge feature an attached wad profiled to provide in-flight stability and increased accuracy.

The three-shot group here measures .450 inches; it was fired at 50 yds. from a bench rest with a Mossberg 500 Crown Grade 24" fully rifled barrel and 4 power scope.

Stock #	Gauge	Shell Length	Dram. Equiv.	Muzzle Velocity	Pellet Ct.	Shot Sizes	Rds. Box	Shot Type
Buckshot								
12HV4BK Buckshot	12	2 3/4"	Max	1325	27 pell.	4 Buck	10	Hi-Antimony Nicke-Plated
12HV00BK Buckshot	12	2 3/4"	Max	1300	9 pell.	00 Buck	10	Hi-Antimony Nickel-Plated
12LE00BK Reduced Recoil*	12	2 3/4"	Max	1150	9 pell.	00 Buck	10	Hi-Antimony Nickel-Plated

Stock #		Gauge	Shell Length	MM	Dram. Equiv.	Muzzle Velocity	Shot Oz.	Shot Sizes	Rds. Box	Shot Type
Slugs										
12TS1	Trophy Slug	12	2 3/4"	70	Max	1560	1	Rifled Slug	5	Lead w/attached Wad
20TS78	Trophy Slug	20	2 3/4"	70	Max	1650	7/8	Rifled Slug	5	Lead w/attached Wad

Stock #	Gauge	Shell Length	Dram. Equiv.	Muzzle Velocity	Shot Oz.	Shot Sizes	Rds. Box	Shot Type
Nickel Plated Hunting Loads								
12HFN Live Bird Pigeon	12	2 3/4"	3 1/4	1225	1 1/4	7-1/2 8	25	Nickel-Plated Lead
12HVN High Velocity Nickel	12	2 3/4"	3 3/4	1330	1 1/4	4 5 6 7-1/2 8 9	25	Nickel-Plated Lead
12GP Golden Pheasant	12	2 3/4"	Max	1250	1 3/8	4 5 6	25	Nickel-Plated Lead
203GP Golden Pheasant 20	20	3"	Max	1200	1 1/4	4 5 6	25	Nickel-Plated Lead
12TT Turkey Thunder	12	2 3/4"	Max	1250	1 3/8	4 5 6	10	Nickel-Plated Lead
123TT Turkey Thunder	12	3	Max	1150	1 3/4	4 5 6	10	Nickel-Plated Lead
FITASC								
12HFN Live Bird Pigeon/FITASC	12	2 3/4"	3 1/4	1225	1 1/4	7-1/2 8	25	Nickel-Plated Lead
12HFN Heavy Field	12	2 3/4"	3 1/4	1225	1 1/4	7-1/2 8	25	Lead
Interceptor Spreader								
12CPTR Interceptor	12	2 3/4"	Max	1300	1	7-1/2 8 8-1/2 9	25	Lead
Sporting Clays Power Spreaders								
12SSCH Power Spreader	12	2 3/4"	3	1200	1 1/8	7-1/2 8 8-1/2 9	25	Lead
12SSCX Power Spreader	12	2 3/4"	Max	1250	1 1/8	8 8-1/2 9	25	Lead
Sporting Target Load								
12S78 Steel Target Load	12	2 3/4"	Max	1440	7/8	7	25	Steel
12S1OZ Steel Target Load	12	2 3/4"	Max	1400	1	6 7	25	Steel
20S Steel Target Load	20	2 3/4"	Max	1490	3/4	6 7	25	Steel
Ultra Low Recoil Loads								
1278OZ Trainer	12	2 3/4"	Lite	1200	7/8	7-1/2 8	25	Hi-Antimony Lead
MULTI-SPORT LOADS-GAME & TARGET								
12MS3 Multi-Sport	12	2 3/4"	3	1250	1	7-1/2 8 9	25	Lead
12GT Game & Target	12	2 3/4"	3 1/4	1290	1	6 7-1/2 8 9	25	Lead
12GT118 Game & Target	12	2 3/4"	3	1200	1 1/8	7-1/2 8	25	Lead
LOW RECOIL TRAP LOADS								
12TRAPL Low-Recoil Trap Light	12	2 3/4"	2 3/4	1140	1 1/8	7-1/2 8	25	Hi-Antimony Lead
12TRAPH Low-Recoil Trap Heavy	12	2 3/4"	3	1185	1 1/8	7-1/2 8	25	Hi-Antimony Lead

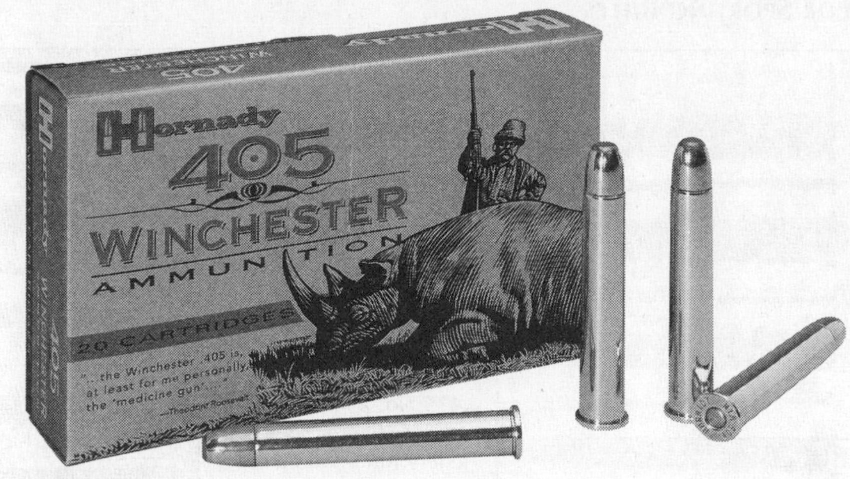

HORNADY .405 WINCHESTER
Hornady has brought the old warhorse favored by Teddy Roosevelt into the 21st century by designing a high-performance cartridge that delivers amazing power and accuracy from the .405 Winchester. The .405 Winchester cartridge is loaded with a 300-grain FP bullet from Hornady.

.444 MARLIN LIGHT MAG
When the .444 Marlin was born as a joint project between Marlin and Remington, shooters quickly fell in love with the combination of a high-performance cartridge in a lever-action rifle. Now, Hornady has gone the original one better by loading the .444 Marlin with the high-performance 265-grain bullet that has been a staple of the line since 1964.

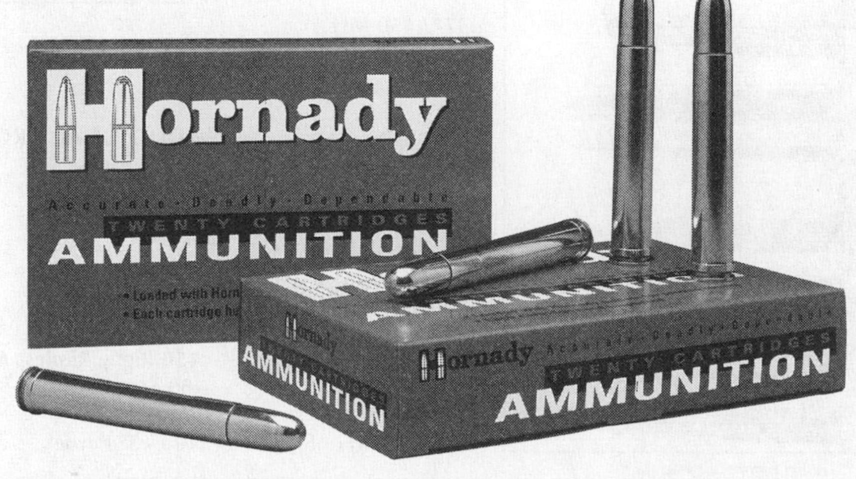

.458 LOTT
Developed by Jack Lott and a favorite of custom rifle builders and African hunters.

Kynoch

Nitro-Express-Sporting Ammunition

For Sporting Rifles

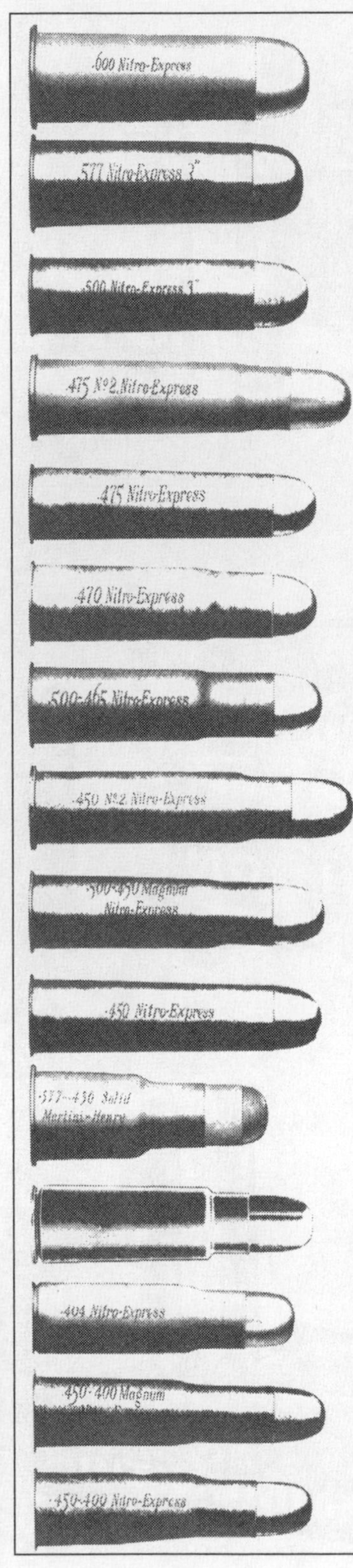

.600 NE
900 gr Solid or SN

.577 NE 3"
750 gr Solid or SN

.500 NE 3"
570 gr Solid or SN

.475 No. 2 NE
480 gr Solid or SN for Jeffery Rifles: 500 gr Solid or SN

.475 NE
480 gr Solid or SN

.470 NE
500 gr Solid or SN

.500/.465 NE
480 gr Solid or SN

.450 No. 2 NE
480 gr Solid or SN

.500/.450
Magnum NE
480 gr Solid or SN

.450 NE
480 gr Solid or SN

.577/.450 MH
480 gr Solid Lead

.416 Rigby
410 gr Solid or SN

.404 Rimless NE
400 gr Solid or SN

.450/.400
Magnum NE
400 gr Solid or SN

.450/.440 NE
400 gr Solid or SN

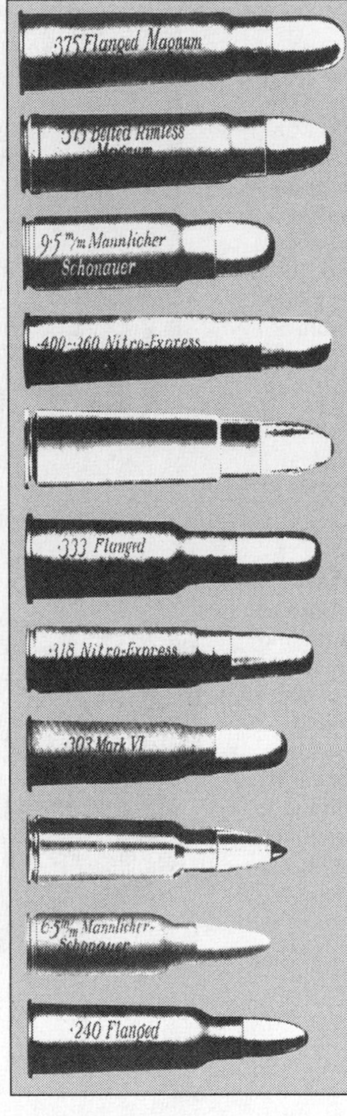

.375 Flanged Magnum
300, 270 or 235 gr Solid or SN

.375 Belted Magnum
300, 270 or 235 gr Solid or SN

9.5 mm Mannlicher
Schonauer 270 gr Solid or SN

.400/.360 NE for Purdey Rifles: 300 gr for Westley Richards: 314 gr. Solid or SN

.350 Rigby Magnum
225 gr or 250 gr, Solid or SN

.333 Jeffrey Flanged NE
300 gr Solid or SN

.318 Rimless NE
250 gr Solid or SN
180 gr SN

.303 British
215 gr Solid or SN

.275 Rigby Rimless
140 gr SN

6.5 m/m Mannlicher
Schonauer 160 gr SN

.240 H&H Flanged
100 gr SN

Additional Proprietary Calibers Available:

.700 NE
1000 gr Solid

.500 Jeffery
535 gr Solid or SN

.450 Rigby Rimless Magnum
480 gr Solid or SN

.400 - 3" Purdey
230 gr SN

.505 Gibbs Magnum
525 gr Solid or SN

.425 Westley Richards Magnum
410 gr Solid or SN

.300 H&H Flanged Magnum
220 gr Solid or SN

Magtech Ammunition

Magtech Ammunition Co. imports and distributes high-quality rifle and pistol cartridges manufactured by Companhia Brasileira de Cartuchos (CBC). in Sao Paulo, Brazil. Before 1976, it was owned and managed by Remington Arms and ICI - the UK's Imperial Chemical Company.

Symbol	Caliber	Bullet			Velocity						Energy						Mid-Range Trajectory				Test Barrel Length	
		Style	Weight		Muzzle		50m	50yd	100m	100yd	Muzzle		50m	50yd	100m	100yd	50m	50yd	100m	100yd		
			g	gr	m/s	fps	m/s	fps	m/s	fps	J	ft/lbs	J	ft/lbs	J	ft/lbs	cm	inch	cm	inch	cm	inch
GG357A	.357 Mag	JHP	8.10	125	420	1,378	353	1,170	307	1,020	714	527	505	381	382	289	1.5	0.5	7.5	2.5	10.2V	4-V
GG380A	.380 Auto+P	JHP	5.5	85	330	1,082	303	999	282	936	300	221	252	188	219	166	3.1	1.0	13.3	4.3	9.5	3¾
GG38A	.38 SPL+P	JHP	8.10	125	310	1,017	295	971	282	931	389	287	352	262	322	241	3.4	1.1	14.3	4.6	10.2	4
GG9A	9mm Luger+P	JHP	7.45	115	380	1,246	344	1,137	318	1,056	538	397	441	330	377	285	2.4	0.8	10.5	3.4	10.2	4
GG9B	9mm Luger	JHP	8.03	124	334	1,096	304	1,017	286	958	448	331	371	285	328	253	3.1	1.0	12.5	4.1	10.2	4
GG40A	.40 S&W	JHP	10.0	155	367	1,024	338	1,118	317	1,1052	677	500	596	430	523	381	2.5	0.8	10.9	3.5	10.2	4
GG40B	.40 S&W	JHP	11.66	180	302	990	282	938	268	891	532	392	463	352	419	318	3.7	1.2	13.4	4.5	10.2	4
GG45A	.45 Auto+P	JHP	12.0	185	350	1,148	323	1,066	303	1,005	735	540	626	467	551	415	2.7	0.9	11.8	3.8	12.7	5
GG45B	.45 Auto+P	JHP	14.90	230	307	1,007	290	965	279	927	702	518	626	475	580	440	4.0	1.3	12.5	4.0	12.7	5

PMC

PMC RIFLE CARTRIDGES

Precision Made Cartridges

PMC (Precision Made Cartridges) is the same firm as Eldorado Cartridge Company. It is a fast-growing enterprise whose product line continues to expand. The firm offers more than 50 handgun loads, from .25 Auto to .44 Magnum, including five specifically for Cowboy Action shooting. The centerfire rifle stable includes cowboy action loads in .30-30 and .45-70, plus a wide variety of hunting and match ammunition from .222 Remington to .375 H&H Magnum. The selection of .22 rimfire rounds features hunting, plinking and match loads.

PMC offers a broad choice of bullet styles. In pistol ammo, there's the quick-opening Starfire hollowpoint, a traditional jacketed hollowpoint, a jacketed softpoint and a full-metal-jacket (hardball) bullet — plus lead wadcutter, semi-wadcutter and round-nose options. Rifle bullets include the Barnes X-Bullet, .30-30 Starfire hollowpoint, Sierra boat-tail hollowpoint, Sierra boat-tail softpoint, pointed softpoint, softpoint, flat-nose softpoint and full metal jacket.

PMC also manufactures shotshells, from light dove and quail and target loads to heavy steel-shot loads for geese.

PMC also has a rural Nevada plant that offers test-firing opportunities out the back door.

PMC

CENTERFIRE RIFLE AMMUNITION

FIELD AND TARGET

LESS LETHAL RUBBER FIN BATON

LESS LETHAL RUBBER BUCK SHOT

PMC Gold Line Now Features The Barnes XLC Coated X-Bullet

Premier-performance PMC Gold Line rifle cartridges feature the Barnes SLC Coated X-Bullet. The solid-copper X-Bullet has a reputation for deep penetration and reliable expansion. The exclusive blue XLC coating is a high-tech, dry-film lubricant that will decrease the friction within the rifle bore. The barrel stays cooler and copper fouling is reduced.

PMC Field & Target Shotshells

The PMC Field & Target shell combines the dense patterning and target-smashing performance of a PMC Clay Target shell with the solid penetration necessary for taking lighter upland birds and small game. It's the perfect all-purpose load for shooters who wish to use the same load for clay targets and wing shooting. Features include clean-burning powder to keep your shotgun functioning smoothly, high antimony, chilled lead shot to give good penetration, reliable ignition primers and a tough, reloadable ribbed plastic hull.

PMC Less-Lethal Shotshells

PMC has a shotshell line for law enforcement and home defense. The rubber projectiles discourage home intruders when lethal force may not be desirable.

Fin-stabilized Rubber Baton

The rubber projectile in this shell utilizes canted fins and a bore-riding band, both of which contribute to stable flight and enhanced accuracy. It will produce groups of 2-4 inches at 20 yards. Available in 12 gauge only.

000 Rubber Buckshot

Low-energy shell loaded with twelve ⅜th-inch rubber balls. Available in 12 gauge only.

PREMIER® HEVI-SHOT MAGNUM TURKEY LOADS

If you're passionate about turkey hunting, new Premier Hevi-Shot is the load for you. This load won all event classes at the 2001 National Wild Turkey Federation Annual Turkey Shoot. It routinely achieves patterns in excess of 90%. Shot material alloy of tungsten, nickel and iron fea- tures a 10% higher density than lead, which yields denser patterns and higher energy - a lead improve-ment. A superior product for serious turkey hunters.

INDEX/ EDI NO.	GAUGE	SHELL LENGTH	POWDER DR. EQ.	VELOCITY (FT./SEC.@3 FT.)	OUNCES OF SHOT	SHOT SIZES
PREMIER® HEVI-SHOT® HIGH VELOCITY MAGNUM TURKEY BUFFERED LOADS						
PRHSHV12M	12	3"	Max	1300	1 1/2	4, 5, 6
PRHSHV1235M	12	3 1/2"	Max	1300	1 3/4	4, 5, 6
PREMIER® HEVI-SHOT® MAGNUM TURKEY BUFFERED LOADS						
PRHS12SM	12	2 3/4"	Max	1250	1 3/8	4, 5, 6
PRHS12HM	12	3"	Max	1225	1 5/8	4, 5, 6
PRHS1235M	12	3 1/2"	Max	1225	1 7/8	4, 5, 6

PREMIER® HEVI-SHOT NITRO MAGNUM WATERFOWL LOADS

Premier Hevi-Shot Nitro Magnums are manufactured of a non-toxic tungsten-nickel-iron alloy, Hevi-Shot is 10% denser than lead and an amazing 54% denser than steel. Shooting an equal payload and shot size, Hevi-Shot pel-lets have 25% more energy at 50 yards than steel pellets have at 30 yards. This allows you to drop down three shot sizes to maintain pattern energy and dramatically increase on-game pellet count. The resulting Hevi-Shot patterning, with full chokes, yields an average of 88% efficiency.

DENSITY COMPARISON	
Density Of Steel	7.8
Density Of Lead	10.9
Density Of Hevi-Shot	12.0

INDEX/ EDI NO.	GAUGE	SHELL LENGTH	POWDER DR. EQ.	VELOCITY (FT./SEC.@3 FT.)	OUNCES OF SHOT	SHOT SIZES
PREMIER® HEVI-SHOT® NITRO MAGNUM WATERFOWL LOADS						
PRHSN10M	10	3 1/2"	Magnum	1300	1 3/4	2,4
PRHSN12SM	12	2 3/4"	Magnum	1325	1 1/4	4, 6, 7 1/2
PRHSN12HM	12	3"	Magnum	1300	1 1/2	2, 4, 6
PRHSN1235	12	3 1/2"	Magnum	1300	1 3/4	2, 4, 6
PRHSN20M	20	3"	Magnum	1300	1 1/8	4, 6

AMMUNITION

Remington Ammunition

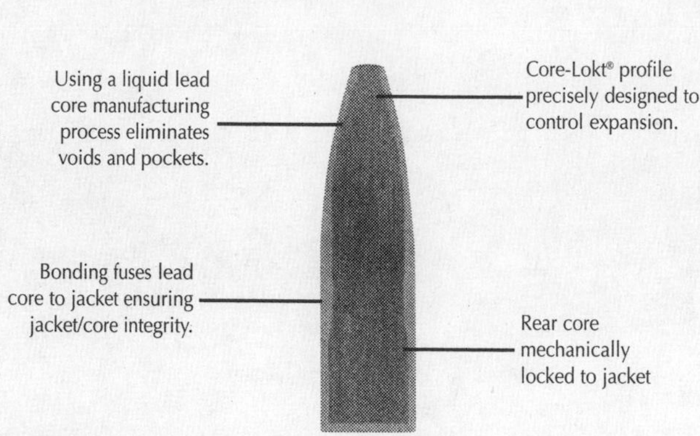

Using a liquid lead core manufacturing process eliminates voids and pockets.
Core-Lokt® profile precisely designed to control expansion.
Bonding fuses lead core to jacket ensuring jacket/core integrity.
Rear core mechanically locked to jacket

Remington
RIFLE CARTRIDGES
PREMIER SHORT ACTION ULTRA MAG
300 REMINGTON SA ULTRA MAG
NOSLER PARTITION

Premier Short-Action Ultra Mag

Long-action magnum performance is available in a short-action configuration. The Premier SA Ultra Mag cartridges feature a state-of-the-art design. The SA Ultra Mag cartridge headspaces off the shoulder of the case, rather than a belt, promoting more precise bore alignment and therefore improved accuracy. Furthermore, the highly efficient case design duplicates or exceeds belted magnum ballistics with less powder, which in turn means less felt recoil. Finally, the entire package achieves greater downrange velocity and energy than traditional 300 Win Mag and 7mm Remington Mag calibers. SA Ultra Mag ammo will be available to match Remington's Model Seven Magnum rifles in two popular calibers: 300 Remington SA Ultra Mag and 7mm Remington SA Ultra Mag.

Premier® Short Action Ultra Mag™

Caliber	Index/EDI No.	Bullet Weight	Bullet Type
7mm Rem. SA UM	PR7SM1	140	PSP Core-Lokt® Ultra
7mm Rem. SA UM	PR7SM2	150	PSP Core-Lokt®
7mm Rem. SA UM	PR7SM3	160	Nosler® Partition®
300 Rem. SA UM	PR300SM1	150	PSP Core-Lokt® Ultra
300 Rem. SA UM	PR300SM2	165	PSP Core-Lokt®
300 Rem. SA UM	PR300SM3	180	Nosler® Partition®

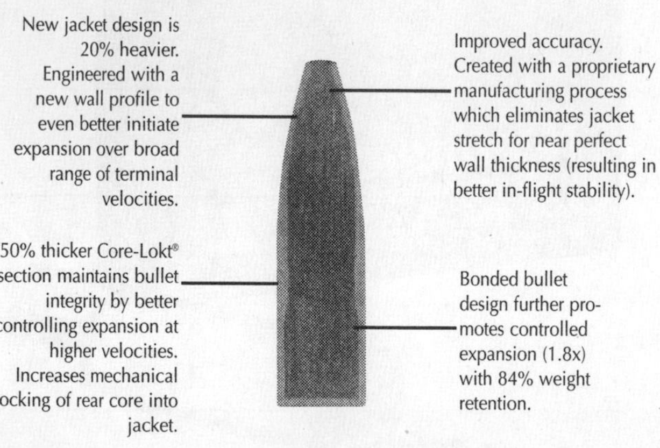

New jacket design is 20% heavier. Engineered with a new wall profile to even better initiate expansion over broad range of terminal velocities.
Improved accuracy. Created with a proprietary manufacturing process which eliminates jacket stretch for near perfect wall thickness (resulting in better in-flight stability).
50% thicker Core-Lokt® section maintains bullet integrity by better controlling expansion at higher velocities. Increases mechanical locking of rear core into jacket.
Bonded bullet design further promotes controlled expansion (1.8x) with 84% weight retention.

Remington
30-06 SPRINGFIELD
RIFLE CARTRIDGES
Remington
PREMIER CORE-LOKT ULTRA
20 CENTERFIRE RIFLE CARTRIDGES

Premier Core-Lokt Ultra

The Premier Core-Lokt Ultra's bonded bullet retains up to 90% of its original weight with maximum penetration and energy transfer. Featuring a progressively-tapered jacket design, the Core-Lokt Ultra bullet initiates and controls expansion up to 1.8X. The unique design of the bullet, combined with the bonded lead core, provides the hunter with a Premier bullet that yields unmatched performance from 50 yards to 500 yards and all yardages in between.

Premier® Core-Lokt® Ultra

Caliber	Index/EDI No.	Bullet Weight	Bullet Type
270 Win	PRC270WB	140	Core-Lokt® Ultra PSP
7mm Remington Mag	PRC7MMRA	140	Core-Lokt® Ultra PSP
30-06 Springfield	PRC3006C	180	Core-Lokt® Ultra PSP
300 Win Mag	PRC300WC	180	Core-Lokt® Ultra PSP
308 Winchester	PRC308WC	180	Core-Lokt® Ultra PSP

Rottweil Brenneke Cartridges

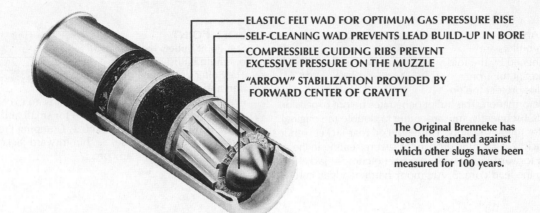

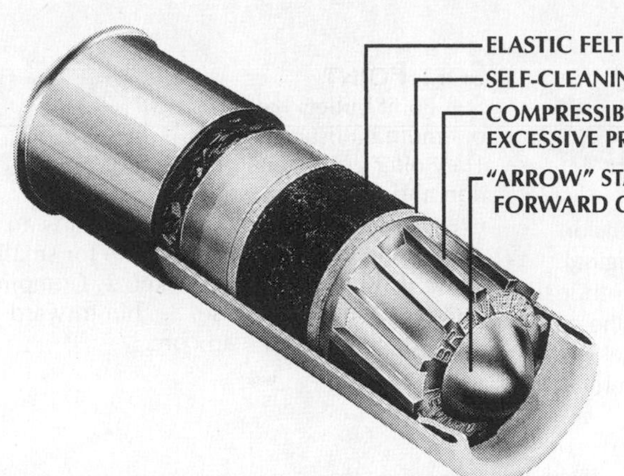
ELASTIC FELT WAD FOR OPTIMUM GAS PRESSURE RISE
SELF-CLEANING WAD PREVENTS LEAD BUILD-UP IN BORE
COMPRESSIBLE GUIDING RIBS PREVENT EXCESSIVE PRESSURE ON THE MUZZLE
"ARROW" STABILIZATION PROVIDED BY FORWARD CENTER OF GRAVITY

The Original Brenneke has been the standard against which other slugs have been measured for 100 years.

Specifications

Brenneke Load	Barrel	Distance (yds)	Velocity (ft./sec.)	Energy (ft./lbs.)	Trajectory (in)
SuperSabot 12 GA	Rifled only	Muzzle	1407	2157	-2.0
2¾"		25	1274	1770	+0.4
1⅛ oz		50	1165	1478	+1.6
		75	1080	1272	+1.1
		100	1017	1127	-1.3
SuperSabot 12 GA	Rifled only	Muzzle	1526	2536	-2.0
3"		25	1376	2064	+0.2
1⅛ oz		50	1248	1697	+1.2
		75	1144	1426	+0.9
		100	1065	1236	-1.1
K.O. Sabot 12 GA	Smooth or rifled	Muzzle	1509	2184	-2.0
2¾"		25	1344	1733	+0.3
1 oz		50	1206	1395	+1.3
		75	1101	1162	+0.9
		100	1024	1007	-1.3
K.O. Sabot 12 GA	Smooth or rifled	Muzzle	1673	2686	-2.0
3"		25	1487	2122	+0.0
1 oz		50	1325	1685	+1.0
		75	1191	1361	+0.7
		100	1090	1139	-1.1
Super Magnum 12 GA	Rifled only	Muzzle	1502	3014	-2.0
3"		25	1295	2241	+0.4
1⅜ oz		50	1136	1724	+1.6
		75	1030	1418	+1.0
		100	955	1219	-1.5
Black Magic	Smooth or rifled	Muzzle	1502	3014	-2.0
Magnum 12 GA		25	1295	2241	+0.4
3"		50	1136	1724	+1.6
1⅜ oz		75	1030	1418	+1.0
		100	955	1219	-1.5
Magnum 20 GA	Smooth or rifled	Muzzle	1476	2120	-2.0
3"		25	1322	1701	+0.4
1 oz		50	1193	1385	+1.5
		75	1094	1165	+1.2
		100	1022	1016	-1.0
K.O. 12 GA	Smooth or rifled	Muzzle	1600	2491	-2.0
2¾"		25	1377	1845	+0.3
1 oz		50	1199	1399	+1.5
		75	1072	1118	+1.2
		100	987	948	-1.0
Heavy Field Short	Smooth or rifled	Muzzle	1476	2538	-2.0
Magnum 12 GA		25	1310	2000	+0.4
2¾"		50	1174	1606	+1.5
1¼ oz		75	1075	1346	+1.0
		100	1002	1170	-1.4
Low Recoil	Smooth or rifled	Muzzle	1246	1511	-2.0
12 GA		25	1104	1186	+0.7
2¾"		50	1009	991	+1.6
1 oz		75	941	862	+0.4
		100	886	764	-3.2
Magnum .410	Smooth or rifled	Muzzle	1755	781	-2.0
3"		25	1427	517	+0.2
¼ oz		50	1179	352	+1.4
		75	1025	266	+1.0
		100	930	219	-1.4
Buckshot	Smooth only	Muzzle	N.A.		
2¾"					
1⅛ oz (9 pellets)					

AMMUNITION

RWS Centerfire Cartridges

Bullets and Ballistics for Norma

Vulkan

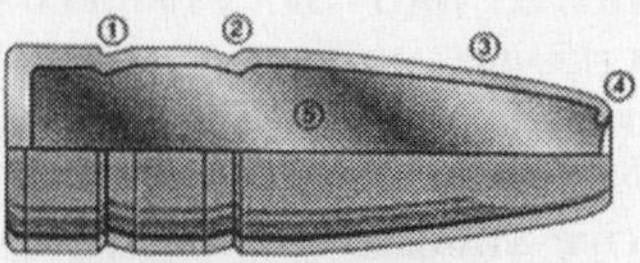

Vulkan bullets are strengthened by the folded jacket at the front. The folds protect the tip from deformation. The bullet penetrates before expansion starts. Subsequently, mushrooming to double the original diameter follows rapidly. 1. Reinforced rear jacket with lead core lock. 2. Crimping groove for secure seating in the case. 3. Thin forward jacket with internal notches. 4. Jacket folded into the lead core. 5. Antimony hardened lead core.

Soft Point

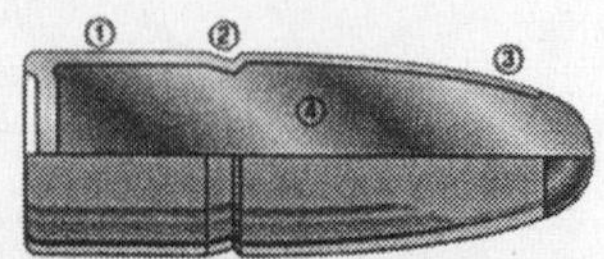

Soft Point bullets have optimum ballistic shape. They offer good penetration and mushroom well, even on smaller game. The Soft Point is an excellent all-around bullet particularly suitable for small and medium game. 1. Reinforced rear jacket. 2. Crimping groove for secure seating in the case. 3. Thin forward jacket. 4. Antimony hardened lead core.

DK

The design of the DK bullet is the result of Dynamit Nobel's extensive ballistics research.

Manufactured at considerable expense, DK bullets barely splinter, mushroom in a controlled manner, have a residue body of over 50 percent, and usually produce an exit hole. A true twin core that separates to perform two separate functions upon impact, penetration and a high degree of impact force, combine to give the DK a clear advantage over traditional bullets, especially for large game with heavy bones and muscles.

RWS

The RWS cone point bullet was designed and developed after exhaustive studies in the laboratory as well as in the field.

A carefully engineered matching of casing and core material and an aerodynamically favorable bullet shape have been paired to produce a controlled mushrooming to almost twice caliber size. The rear groove, which joins the lead core and casing, controls mushrooming and preserves effective residual body to give it killing power.

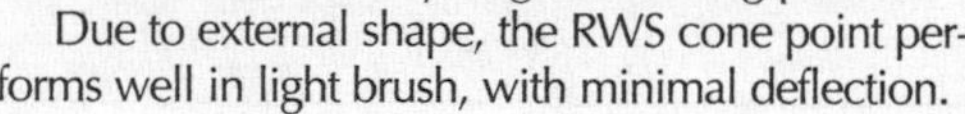

Due to external shape, the RWS cone point performs well in light brush, with minimal deflection.

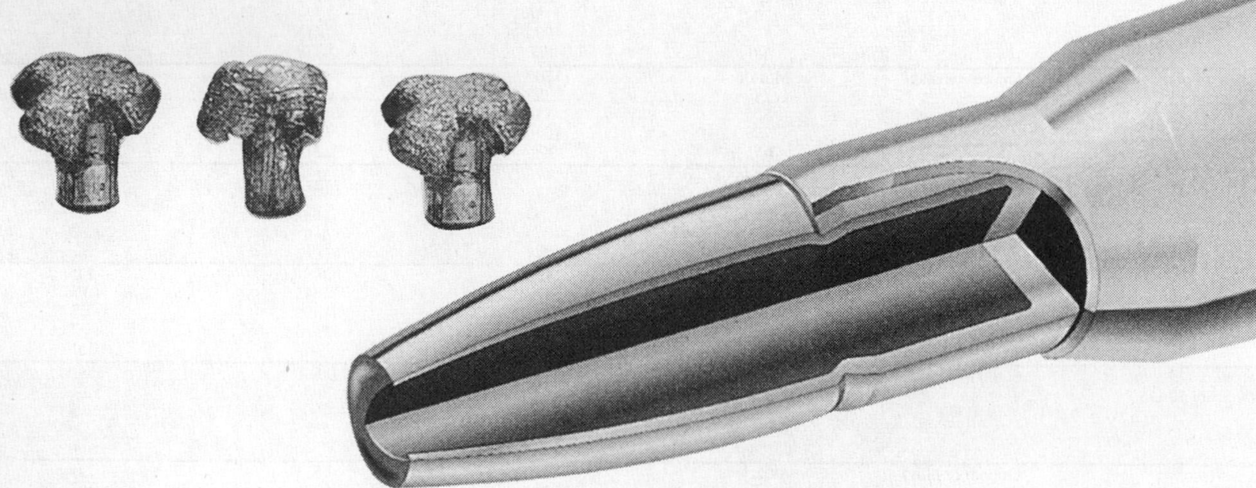

Norma Oryx

This bullet is designed to penetrate deep. The jacket and core are bonded together through a chemical process. This ensures a very high residual weight, even in tough targets. Despite the solid construction, mushrooming starts early. The Oryx bullet delivers excellent deep energy transfer and is suitable for big and medium sized game.

Price: box of 20 cartridges . . . . From $42-66

- Bonded bullet-lead core soldered into copper jacket
- Good penetration
- Exceptional expansion, combined with bonding, results in deep wound channel and minimal meat damage
- Very high weight retention

RWS Rimfire Cartridges

RWS .22 R50

For competitive shooters demanding the ultimate in precision. This cartridge has been used to establish several world records and is used by Olympic Gold Medalists. No finer cartridge can be bought at any price.

Price: $13/box

RWS .22 Short R25

Designed for world class Rapid Fire Pistol events, this cartridge provides the shooter with outstanding accuracy and minimal recoil. Manufactured to exacting standards, the shooter can be assured of consistent performance.

Price: $9/box

Technical Data

				Velocity (ft./sec.)			Energy (ft./lbs.)				Trajectory inches above (+) or below (-) line of sight								
Cartridges	Bullet Style	Bullet Weight (grains)	Max. Chamber Pressure (psi)	muzzle	50y	100y	muzzle	50y	100y	Open Sight At	25 yds	50 yds	75 yds	100yds	Scope sighted in at	25 yds	50 yds	75 yds	100 yds
.22 L.R. R 50	Lead	40	25.600	1.070	970	890	100	80	70	--	--	--	--	--	--	--	--	--	--
.22 Short R 25	Lead	28	18.500	560	490	---	20	15	--	--	--	--	--	--	--	--	--	--	--
.22 L.R. Rifle Match	Lead	40	25.600	1.035	945	860	95	80	65	50 yds.	+0.7		-3.2	-9.0	50 yds	+0.1		-2.6	-7.8
.22 L.R. Target Rifle	Lead	40	25.600	1.080	990	900	100	85	70	50 yds.	+0.6		-3.1	-8.7	50 yds	+0.1		-2.5	-7.5
.22 L.R. Subsonic	Hollow Point	40	25.600	1.000	915	835	90	75	60	50 yds.	+0.8		-3.4	-4.7	50 yds	+0.2		+2.8	-8.5
.22 L.R. HV	Lead	40	25.600	1.310	1.120	990	150	110	85		--	--	--	--	--	--	--	--	--
Hollow point	coppered																		
.22 Magnum	Soft Point	40	25.600	2.020	1.710	1.430	360	260	180	100 yds.	+0.6	+1.3	+1.1	0	100 yds	-0.3	+0.7	+0.8	0
.22 Magnum	Full Jacket	40	25.600	2.020	1.710	1.430	360	260	180	100 yds.	+0.6	+1.3	+1.1	0	100 yds	-0.3	+0.7	+0.8	0
.22 LR R100	Lead	40	25.600	1.175	1.065	970	100	80	70	100 yds.	+0.6	+13	+1.1	0	100 yds.	-0.3	+0.7	+0.8	0

RWS Rimfire Cartridges

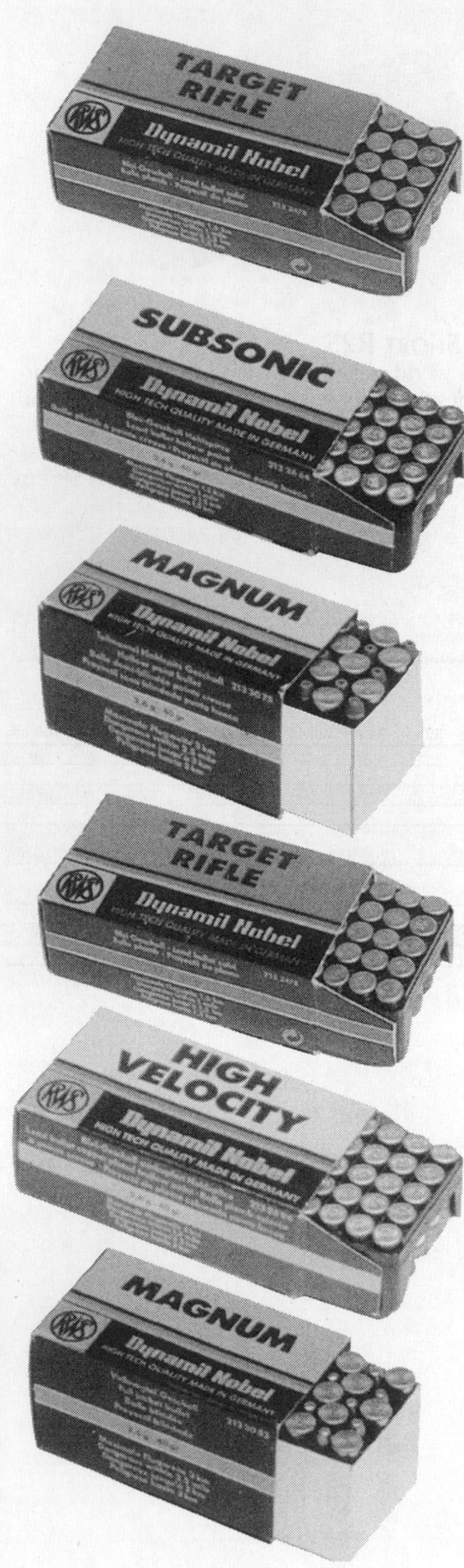

RWS .22 L.R. Rifle Match

Perfect for the club level target competitor. Accurate and affordable.

Price: **$8/box**

RWS .22 L.R. Subsonic Hollow Point

Subsonic ammunition is a favorite ammunition of shooters whose shooting range is limited to where the noise of a conventional cartridge would be a problem.

Price: **$5/box**

RWS .22 Magnum Hollow Point

The soft point allows good expansion on impact, while preserving the penetration characteristics necessary for larger vermin and game.

Price: **$24/box**

RWS .22 L.R. Target Rifle

An ideal training and field cartridge, the .22 Long Rifle Target also excels in informal competitions. The target .22 provides the casual shooter with accuracy at an economical price.

Price: **$4/box**

RWS .22 L.R. HV Hollow Point

A higher velocity hollow point offers the shooter greater shocking power in game, suitable for both small game and vermin.

Price: **$6/box**

RWS .22 Magnum Full Jacket

Outstanding penetration characteristics of this cartridge allow the shooter to easily tackle game where penetration is necessary.

Price: **$24/box**

Winchester Ammunition

Winchester Supreme & Super-X 270 WSM and 7mm WSM Winchester Short Magnum

Winchester's 300 WSM won the "Ammunition of the Year" in 2002. These cartridges deliver incredible accuracy as well as magnum energy and velocity performance in a short-action cartridge, all with lower perceived recoil in lighter-weight rifles.

Winchester Supreme Platinum Tip Hunting Ammunition

Winchester's Platinum Tip Hollow Point Hunting Ammunition is ideal for deer hunting. Available in 12 gauge sabot slug shotshell and as a 50-caliber Muzzleloading sabot bullet, the Platinum Tip Hollow Point bullet has a reverse taper jacket that delivers superior accuracy, uniform expansion and on-target energy delivery.

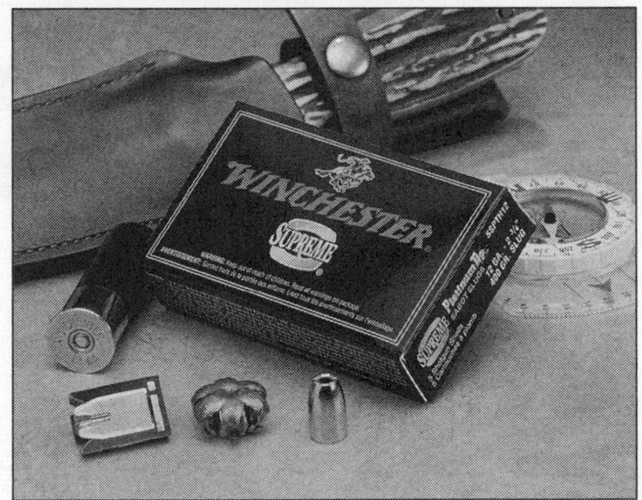

Winchester Super-X Drylok Hi-Velocity Steel Waterfowl Loads

Available in 12 gauge 3" and 3 ½", these steel shotshells give a performance boost, with 1550 feet-per-second muzzle velocity. Add the exclusive water-resistant Super-X Drylok wad system, and you have a traditional steel load delivering greater per-pellet energy on target for superior bird hunting in harsh conditions.

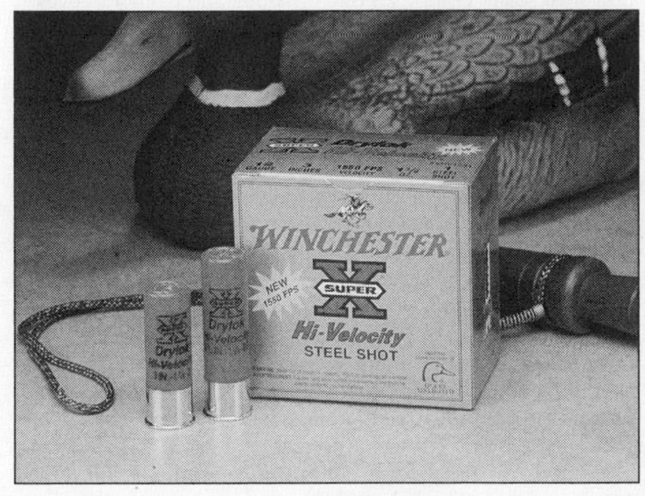

AMMUNITION

Z-Hat

Custom Dies and Ammunition

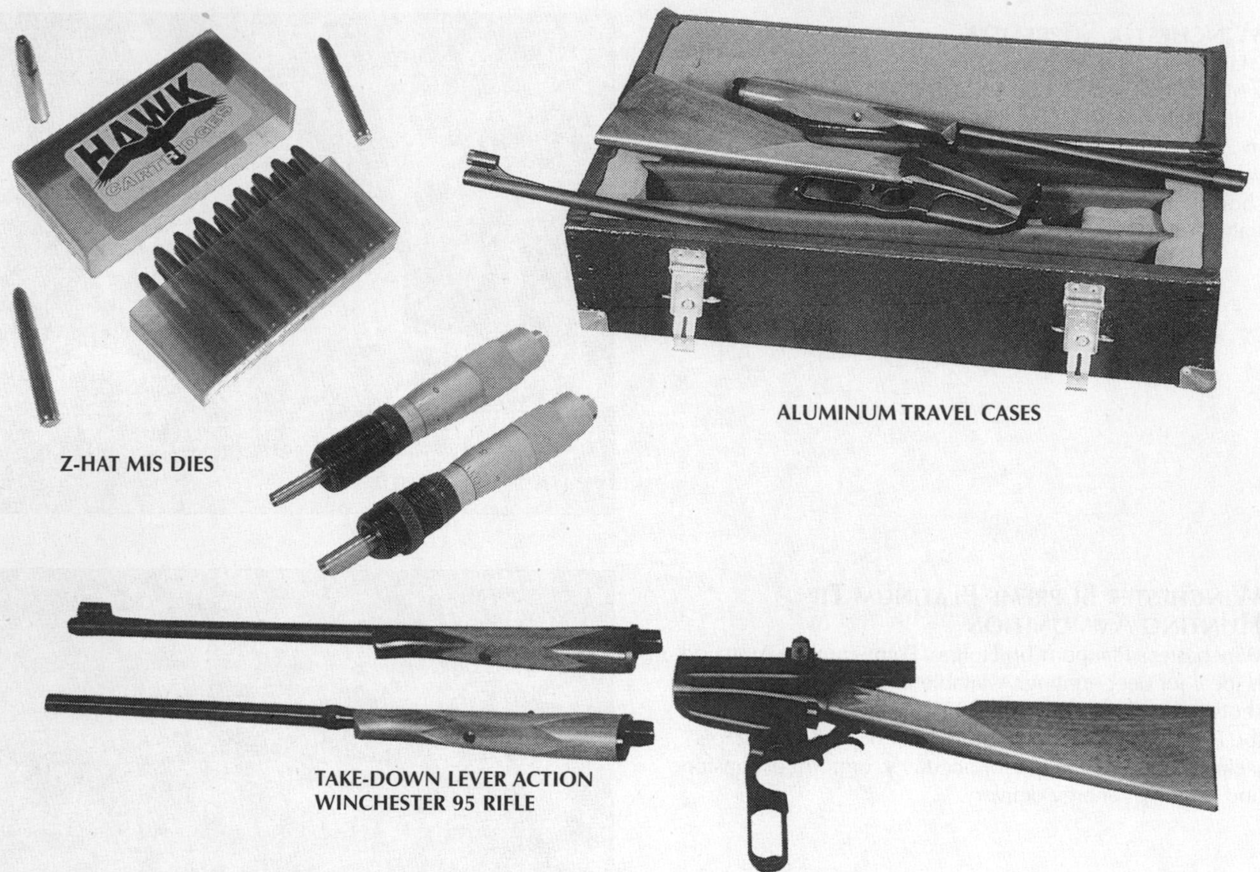

Z-HAT MIS DIES

ALUMINUM TRAVEL CASES

TAKE-DOWN LEVER ACTION WINCHESTER 95 RIFLE

Fred Zeglin's work with Hawk wildcat cartridges, and his experience as a gunsmith, have resulted in a business that includes building and servicing rifles, developing loads and marketing premium-quality brass for Hawk cartridges and supplying shooters with match-grade loading dies.

The Z-Hat Micrometer Inline Seating (MIS) die is a universal in line bullet seater, similar to a "Vickerman" die. The universal seater comprises one die body and caliber sleeves for any caliber. It works with wildcats and obsolete rounds, as well as standard cartridges.

The MIS indexes on the datum line of the case shoulder and on the give of the bullet. This allows use of the MIS die with any caliber, .22 through .378 Wby. and 411 Hawk. 17 caliber is available on special order.

The Z-Hat takedown rifle conversion is a full thread system based on the 100-year-old Thomas Bland design. Simplicity of design insures longevity. This takedown involves the installation of a heavy contact plate on the barrel assembly, so that the barrel will always index to the same point. The 95 Winchester or Browning actions are fitted to the plate/barrel assembly, and a simple lock screw holds the assembly tightly aligned. Mutliple barrels are possible, each with its own complete forearm assembly, making it easy to switch barrels and calibers. The original factory barrel can be converted, as can any new barrel. This system, like the ability to use various calibers, has sight systems setup on one gun. For instance, Express sights on one barrel and a Scout Scope on the other. Zeglin is developing a version of this takedown design for the Winchester Model 70 bolt-action.

Takedowns are normally shipped in a high-quality aluminum travel case. Charcoal is standard; other colors are available. These custom cases, designed specifically for takedown rifles, hold the rifle snugly in transit. At the same time they look more like tool boxes than gun cases, so are less likely to attract unwanted attention from baggage handlers. More conventional shotgun style cases are available too.

Hawk Cartridges:

240 Hawk • 257 Hawk • 264 Hawk • 270 Hawk • 284 Hawk • 300 Hawk • 8mm Hawk • 338 Hawk • 358 Hawk • 9.3 Hawk • 375 Hawk • 411 Hawk

Z-Hat offers formed brass for all 12 Hawk cartridges, at $29.95 per 20. Loaded rounds are available at $69.95 per box, in .338, .358 and .375 Hawk. Custom loads for your rifle can be developed at Z-Hat (www.Rifle.Builder @ Z-Hat.com, or phone 307-577-7443).

Fred also offers custom sizing dies with Z-Hat custom rifles, and he builds a ring die that can size standard bullets to fit obsolete bore diameters.

Prices:

In-Line Seater set up for one cartridge $99
Caliber inserts 17

BALLISTICS

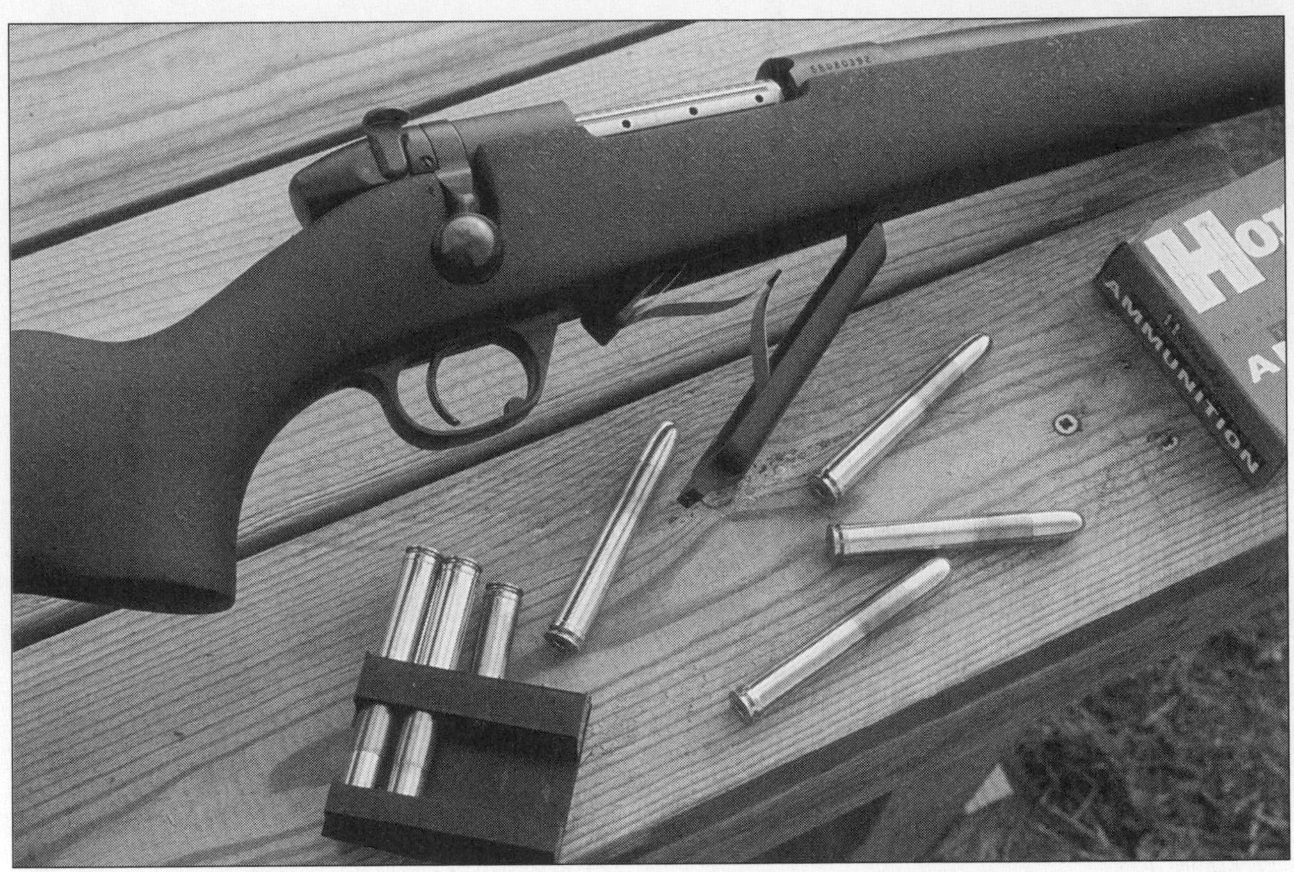

BALLISTICS

Centerfire Rifle Ballistics

Comprehensive Ballistics Tables for Currently Manufactured Sporting Rifle Cartridges

No more collecting catalogs and peering at microscopic print to find out what ammunition is offered for a cartridge, and how it performs relative to other factory loads! *Shooter's Bible* has assembled the data for you, in easy-to-read tables, by cartridge. Of course, this section will be updated every year to bring you the latest information.

Notes: Data is taken from manufacturers' charts; your chronograph readings may vary. Listings are current as of February the year *Shooter's Bible* appears (not the cover year). Listings are not intended as recommendations. For example, the data for the .44 Magnum at 400 yards shows its effective range is much shorter. The lack of data for a 285-grain .375 H&H bullet beyond 300 yards does not mean the bullet has no authority farther out. Besides ammunition, the rifle, sights, conditions and shooter ability all must be considered when contemplating a long shot. Accuracy and bullet energy both matter when big game is in the offing. Barrel length affects velocity, and at various rates depending on the load. As a rule, figure 50 fps per inch of barrel, plus or minus, if your barrel is longer or shorter than 22 inches. Bullets are given by make, weight (in grains) and type.

Most type abbreviations are self-explanatory: BTU=Boat-Tail, **FMJ**=Full Metal Jacket, **HP**=Hollow Point, **SP**=Soft Point – except in Hornady listings, where SP is the firm's Spire Point. **TNT** and **TXP** are trademarked designations of Speer and Norma. **XLC** identifies a coated Barnes X bullet. **HE** indicates a Federal High Energy load, similar to the Hornady **LM** (Light Magnum) and **HM** (Heavy Magnum) cartridges. **Arc** (trajectory) is based on a zero range published by the manufacturer, from 100 to 300 yards. If a zero does not fall in a yardage column, it lies halfway between – at 150 yards, for example, if the bullet's strike is "+" at 100 yards and "-" at 200.

.17 Remington to .222 Remington

CARTRIDGE BULLET	RANGE, YARDS:	0	100	200	300	400
.17 REMINGTON						
Rem. 25 HP Power-Lokt	velocity, fps:	4040	3284	2644	2086	1606
	energy, ft-lb:	906	599	388	242	143
	arc, inches:		+1.8	0	-3.3	-16.6
.218 BEE						
Win. 46 Hollow Point	velocity, fps:	2760	2102	1550	1155	961
	energy, ft-lb:	778	451	245	136	94
	arc, inches:		0	-7.2	-29.4	
.22 HORNET						
Hornady 35 V-Max	velocity, fps:	3100	2278	1601	1135	929
	energy, ft-lb:	747	403	199	100	67
	arc, inches:	+2.8	0	-16.9	-60.4	
Rem. 45 Pointed Soft Point	velocity, fps:	2690	2042	1502	1128	948
	energy, ft-lb:	723	417	225	127	90
	arc, inches:		0	-7.1	-30.0	
Rem. 45 Hollow Point	velocity, fps:	2690	2042	1502	1128	948
	energy, ft-lb:	723	417	225	127	90
	arc, inches:		0	-7.1	-30.0	
Win. 34 Jacketed HP	velocity, fps:	3050	2132	1415	1017	852
	energy, ft-lb:	700	343	151	78	55
	arc, inches:		0	-6.6	-29.9	
Win. 45 Soft Point	velocity, fps:	2690	2042	1502	1128	948
	energy, ft-lb:	723	417	225	127	90
	arc, inches:		0	-7.7	-31.3	
Win. 46 Hollow Point	velocity, fps:	2690	2042	1502	1128	948
	energy, ft-lb:	739	426	230	130	92
	arc, inches:		0	-7.7	-31.3	

CARTRIDGE BULLET	RANGE, YARDS:	0	100	200	300	400
.221 REMINGTON FIREBALL						
Rem. V-Max boat-tail	velocity, fps:	2995	2605	2247	1918	1622
	energy, ft-lb:	996	753	560	408	292
	arc, inches:		+1.8	0	-8.8	-27.1
.222 REMINGTON						
Federal 50 Hi-Shok	velocity, fps:	3140	2600	2120	1700	1350
	energy, ft-lb:	1095	750	500	320	200
	arc, inches:		+1.9	0	-9.7	-31.6
Federal 55 FMJ boat-tail	velocity, fps:	3020	2740	2480	2230	1990
	energy, ft-lb:	1115	915	750	610	484
	arc, inches:		+1.6	0	-7.3	-21.5
Hornady 40 V-Max	velocity, fps:	3600	3117	2673	2269	1911
	energy, ft-lb:	1151	863	634	457	324
	arc, inches:		+1.1	0	-6.1	-18.9
Hornady 50 V-Max	velocity, fps:	3140	2729	2352	2008	1710
	energy, ft-lb:	1094	827	614	448	325
	arc, inches:		+1.7	0	-7.9	-24.4
Norma 50 Soft Point	velocity, fps:	3199	2667	2193	1771	
	energy, ft-lb:	1136	790	534	348	
	arc, inches:		+1.7	0	-9.1	
Norma 50 FMJ	velocity, fps:	2789	2326	1910	1547	
	energy, ft-lb:	864	601	405	266	
	arc, inches:		+2.5	0	-12.2	
Norma 62 Soft Point	velocity, fps:	2887	2457	2067	1716	
	energy, ft-lb:	1148	831	588	405	
	arc, inches:		+2.1	0	-10.4	
PMC 50 Pointed Soft Point	velocity, fps:	3044	2727	2354	2012	1651
	energy, ft-lb:	1131	908	677	494	333
	arc, inches:		+1.6	0	-7.9	-24.5

Centerfire Rifle Ballistics

.222 Remington to .223 Remington

CARTRIDGE BULLET	RANGE, YARDS:	0	100	200	300	400
Rem. 50 Pointed Soft Point	velocity, fps:	3140	2602	2123	1700	1350
	energy, ft-lb:	1094	752	500	321	202
	arc, inches:		+1.9	0	-9.7	-31.7
Rem. 50 HP Power-Lokt	velocity, fps:	3140	2635	2182	1777	1432
	energy, ft-lb:	1094	771	529	351	228
	arc, inches:		+1.8	0	-9.2	-29.6
Rem. 50 V-Max boat-tail	velocity, fps:	3140	2744	2380	2045	1740
	energy, ft-lb:	1094	836	629	464	336
	arc, inches:		+1.6	0	-7.8	-23.9
Win. 40 Ballistic Silvertip	velocity, fps:	3370	2915	2503	2127	1786
	energy, ft-lb:	1009	755	556	402	283
	arc, inches:		+1.3	0	-6.9	-21.5
Win. 50 Pointed Soft Point	velocity, fps:	3140	2602	2123	1700	1350
	energy, ft-lb:	1094	752	500	321	202
	arc, inches:		+2.2	0	-10.0	-32.3

.223 Remington

CARTRIDGE BULLET	RANGE, YARDS:	0	100	200	300	400
Black Hills 40 Nosler B. Tip	velocity, fps:	3600				
	energy, ft-lb:	1150				
	arc, inches:					
Black Hills 50 V-Max	velocity, fps:	3300				
	energy, ft-lb:	1209				
	arc, inches:					
Black Hills 52 Match HP	velocity, fps:	3300				
	energy, ft-lb:	1237				
	arc, inches:					
Black Hills 55 Softpoint	velocity, fps:	3250				
	energy, ft-lb:	1270				
	arc, inches:					
Black Hills 60 SP or V-Max	velocity, fps:	3150				
	energy, ft-lb:	1322				
	arc, inches:					
Black Hills 60 Partition	velocity, fps:	3150				
	energy, ft-lb:	1322				
	arc, inches:					
Black Hills 68 Heavy Match	velocity, fps:	2850				
	energy, ft-lb:	1227				
	arc, inches:					
Black Hills 69 Sierra MK	velocity, fps:	2850				
	energy, ft-lb:	1245				
	arc, inches:					
Black Hills 73 Berger BTHP	velocity, fps:	2750				
	energy, ft-lb:	1226				
	arc, inches:					
Black Hills 75 Heavy Match	velocity, fps:	2750				
	energy, ft-lb:	1259				
	arc, inches:					
Black Hills 77 Sierra MKing	velocity, fps:	2750				
	energy, ft-lb:	1293				
	arc, inches:					
Federal 50 Jacketed HP	velocity, fps:	3400	2910	2460	2060	1700
	energy, ft-lb:	1285	940	675	470	320
	arc, inches:		+1.3	0	-7.1	-22.7
Federal 50 Speer TNT HP	velocity, fps:	3300	2860	2450	2080	1750
	energy, ft-lb:	1210	905	670	480	340
	arc, inches:		+1.4	0	-7.3	-22.6
Federal 52 Sierra MatchKing BTHP	velocity, fps:	3300	2860	2460	2090	1760
	energy, ft-lb:	1255	945	700	505	360
	arc, inches:		+1.4	0	-7.2	-22.4
Federal 55 Hi-Shok	velocity, fps:	3240	2750	2300	1910	1550
	energy, ft-lb:	1280	920	650	445	295
	arc, inches:		+1.6	0	-8.2	-26.1
Federal 55 FMJ boat-tail	velocity, fps:	3240	2950	2670	2410	2170
	energy, ft-lb:	1280	1060	875	710	575
	arc, inches:		+1.3	0	-6.1	-18.3
Federal 55 Sierra GameKing BTHP	velocity, fps:	3240	2770	2340	1950	1610
	energy, ft-lb:	1280	935	670	465	315
	arc, inches:		+1.5	0	-8.0	-25.3
Federal 55 Trophy Bonded	velocity, fps:	3100	2630	2210	1830	1500
	energy, ft-lb:	1175	845	595	410	275
	arc, inches:		+1.8	0	-8.9	-28.7
Federal 55 Nosler Bal. Tip	velocity, fps:	3240	2870	2530	2220	1920
	energy, ft-lb:	1280	1005	780	600	450
	arc, inches:		+1.4	0	-6.8	-20.8
Federal 55 Sierra BlitzKing	velocity, fps:	3240	2870	2520	2200	1910
	energy, ft-lb:	1280	1005	775	590	445
	arc, inches:		+-1.4	0	-6.9	-20.9
Federal 62 FMJ	velocity, fps:	3020	2650	2310	2000	1710
	energy, ft-lb:	1225	970	735	550	405
	arc, inches:		+1.7	0	-8.4	-25.5
Federal 64 Hi-Shok SP	velocity, fps:	3090	2690	2325	1990	1680
	energy, ft-lb:	1360	1030	770	560	400
	arc, inches:		+1.7	0	-8.2	-25.2
Federal 69 Sierra MatchKing BTHP	velocity, fps:	3000	2720	2460	2210	1980
	energy, ft-lb:	1380	1135	925	750	600
	arc, inches:		+1.6	0	-7.4	-21.9
Hornady 40 V-Max	velocity, fps:	3800	3305	2845	2424	2044
	energy, ft-lb:	1282	970	719	522	371
	arc, inches:		+0.8	0	-5.3	-16.6
Hornady 53 Hollow Point	velocity, fps:	3330	2882	2477	2106	1710
	energy, ft-lb:	1305	978	722	522	369
	arc, inches:		+1.7	0	-7.4	-22.7
Hornady 55 V-Max	velocity, fps:	3240	2859	2507	2181	1891
	energy, ft-lb:	1282	998	767	581	437
	arc, inches:		+1.4	0	-7.1	-21.4
Hornady 55 Urban Tactical	velocity, fps:	2970	2626	2307	2011	1739
	energy, ft-lb:	1077	842	650	494	369
	arc, inches:		+1.5	0	-8.1	-24.9
Hornady 60 Soft Point	velocity, fps:	3150	2782	2442	2127	1837
	energy, ft-lb:	1322	1031	795	603	450
	arc, inches:		+1.6	0	-7.5	-22.5
Hornady 60 Urban Tactical	velocity, fps:	2950	2619	2312	2025	1762
	energy, ft-lb:	1160	914	712	546	413
	arc, inches:		+1.6	0	-8.1	-24.7
Hornady 75 BTHP Match	velocity, fps:	2790	2554	2330	2119	1926
	energy, ft-lb:	1296	1086	904	747	617
	arc, inches:		+2.4	0	--8.8	-25.1
Hornady 75 BTHP Tactical	velocity, fps:	2630	2409	2199	2000	1814
	energy, ft-lb:	1152	966	805	666	548
	arc, inches:		-2.0	0	-9.2	-25.9
PMC 55 HP boat-tail	velocity, fps:	3240	2717	2250	1832	1473
	energy, ft-lb:	1282	901	618	410	265
	arc, inches:		+1.6	0	-8.6	-27.7
PMC 55 FMJ boat-tail	velocity, fps:	3195	2882	2525	2169	1843
	energy, ft-lb:	1246	1014	779	574	415
	arc, inches:		+1.4	0	-6.8	-21.1
PMC 55 Pointed Soft Point	velocity, fps:	3112	2767	2421	2100	1806
	energy, ft-lb:	1182	935	715	539	398
	arc, inches:		+1.5	0	-7.5	-22.9

Centerfire Rifle Ballistics

.223 Remington to .22-250 Remington

CARTRIDGE BULLET	RANGE, YARDS:	0	100	200	300	400
PMC 64 Pointed Soft Point	velocity, fps:	2775	2511	2261	2026	1806
	energy, ft-lb:	1094	896	726	583	464
	arc, inches:		+2.0	0	-8.8	-26.1
PMC 69 BTHP Match	velocity, fps:					
	energy, ft-lb:					
	arc, inches:					
Rem. 50 V-Max, boat-tail	velocity, fps:	3300	2889	2514	2168	1851
	energy, ft-lb:	1209	927	701	522	380
	arc, inches:		+1.4	0	-6.9	-21.2
Rem. 55 Pointed Soft Point	velocity, fps:	3240	2747	2304	1905	1554
	energy, ft-lb:	1282	921	648	443	295
	arc, inches:		+1.6	0	-8.2	-26.2
Rem. 55 HP Power-Lokt	velocity, fps:	3240	2773	2352	1969	1627
	energy, ft-lb:	1282	939	675	473	323
	arc, inches:		+1.5	0	-7.9	-24.8
Rem. 55 Metal Case	velocity, fps:	3240	2759	2326	1933	1587
	energy, ft-lb:	1282	929	660	456	307
	arc, inches:		+1.6	0	-8.1	-25.5
Rem. 62 HP Match	velocity, fps:	3025	2572	2162	1792	1471
	energy, ft-lb:	1260	911	643	442	298
	arc, inches:		+1.9	0	-9.4	-29.9
Win. 40 Ballistic Silvertip	velocity, fps:	3700	3166	2693	2265	1879
	energy, ft-lb:	1216	891	644	456	314
	arc, inches:		+1.0	0	-5.8	-18.4
Win. 45 JHP	velocity, fps:	3600				
	energy, ft-lb:	1295				
	arc, inches:					
Win. 50 Ballistic Silvertip	velocity, fps:	3410	2982	2593	2235	1907
	energy, ft-lb:	1291	987	746	555	404
	arc, inches:		+1.2	0	-6.4	-19.8
Win. 53 Hollow Point	velocity, fps:	3330	2882	2477	2106	1770
	energy, ft-lb:	1305	978	722	522	369
	arc, inches:		+1.7	0	-7.4	-22.7
Win. 55 Pointed Soft Point	velocity, fps:	3240	2747	2304	1905	1554
	energy, ft-lb:	1282	921	648	443	295
	arc, inches:		+1.9	0	-8.5	-26.7
Win. 55 Super Clean NT	velocity, fps:	3150	2520	1970	1505	1165
	energy, ft-lb:	1212	776	474	277	166
	arc, inches:		+2.8	0	-11.9	-38.9
Win. 55 FMJ	velocity, fps:	3240	2854			
	energy, ft-lb:	1282	995			
	arc, inches:					
Win. 55 Ballistic Silvertip	velocity, fps:	3240	2871	2531	2215	1923
	energy, ft-lb:	1282	1006	782	599	451
	arc, inches:		+1.4	0	-6.8	-20.8
Win. 64 Power-Point	velocity, fps:	3020	2656	2320	2009	1724
	energy, ft-lb:	1296	1003	765	574	423
	arc, inches:		+1.7	0	-8.2	-25.1
Win. 64 Power-Point Plus	velocity, fps:	3090	2684	2312	1971	1664
	energy, ft-lb:	1357	1024	760	552	393
	arc, inches:		+1.7	0	-8.2	-25.4

.5.6 x 52 R

CARTRIDGE BULLET	RANGE, YARDS:	0	100	200	300	400
Norma 71 Soft Point	velocity, fps:	2789	2446	2128	1835	
	energy, ft-lb:	1227	944	714	531	
	arc, inches:		+2.1	0	-9.9	

.22 PPC

CARTRIDGE BULLET	RANGE, YARDS:	0	100	200	300	400
A-Square 52 Berger	velocity, fps:	3300	2952	2629	2329	2049
	energy, ft-lb:	1257	1006	798	626	485
	arc, inches:		+1.3	0	-6.3	-19.1

.225 Winchester

CARTRIDGE BULLET	RANGE, YARDS:	0	100	200	300	400
Win. 55 Pointed Soft Point	velocity, fps:	3570	3066	2616	2208	1838
	energy, ft-lb:	1556	1148	836	595	412
	arc, inches:		+2.4	+2.0	-3.5	-16.3

.224 Weatherby Magnum

CARTRIDGE BULLET	RANGE, YARDS:	0	100	200	300	400
Wby. 55 Pointed Expanding	velocity, fps:	3650	3192	2780	2403	2056
	energy, ft-lb:	1627	1244	944	705	516
	arc, inches:		+2.8	+3.7	0	-9.8

.22-250 Remington

CARTRIDGE BULLET	RANGE, YARDS:	0	100	200	300	400
Federal 40 Sierra Varminter	velocity, fps:	4000	3320	2720	2200	1740
	energy, ft-lb:	1420	980	660	430	265
	arc, inches:		+0.8	0	-5.6	-18.4
Federal 55 Hi-Shok	velocity, fps:	3680	3140	2660	2220	1830
	energy, ft-lb:	1655	1200	860	605	410
	arc, inches:		+1.0	0	-6.0	-19.1
Federal 55 Sierra BlitzKing	velocity, fps:	3680	3270	2890	2540	2220
	energy, ft-lb:	1655	1300	1020	790	605
	arc, inches:		+0.9	0	-5.1	-15.6
Federal 55 Sierra GameKing BTHP	velocity, fps:	3680	3280	2920	2590	2280
	energy, ft-lb:	1655	1315	1040	815	630
	arc, inches:		+0.9	0	-5.0	-15.1
Federal 55 Trophy Bonded	velocity, fps:	3600	3080	2610	2190	1810
	energy, ft-lb:	1585	1155	835	590	400
	arc, inches:		+1.1	0	-6.2	-19.8
Hornady 40 V-Max	velocity, fps:	4150	3631	3147	2699	2293
	energy, ft-lb:	1529	1171	879	647	467
	arc, inches:		+0.5	0	-4.2	-13.3
Hornady 50 V-Max	velocity, fps:	3800	3349	2925	2535	2178
	energy, ft-lb:	1603	1245	950	713	527
	arc, inches:		+0.8	0	-5.0	-15.6
Hornady 53 Hollow Point	velocity, fps:	3680	3185	2743	2341	1974
	energy, ft-lb:	1594	1194	886	645	459
	arc, inches:		+1.0	0	-5.7	-17.8
Hornady 55 V-Max	velocity, fps:	3680	3265	2876	2517	2183
	energy, ft-lb:	1654	1302	1010	772	582
	arc, inches:		+0.9	0	-5.3	-16.1
Hornady 60 Soft Point	velocity, fps:	3600	3195	2826	2485	2169
	energy, ft-lb:	1727	1360	1064	823	627
	arc, inches:		+1.0	0	-5.4	-16.3
Norma 53 Soft Point	velocity, fps:	3707	3234	2809	1716	
	energy, ft-lb:	1618	1231	928	690	
	arc, inches:		+0.9	0	-5.3	
PMC 55 HP boat-tail	velocity, fps:	3680	3104	2596	2141	1737
	energy, ft-lb:	1654	1176	823	560	368
	arc, inches:		+1.1	0	-6.3	-20.2
PMC 55 Pointed Soft Point	velocity, fps:	3586	3203	2852	2505	2178
	energy, ft-lb:	1570	1253	993	766	579
	arc, inches:		+1.0	0	-5.2	-16.0
Rem. 50 V-Max boat-tail (also in EtronX)	velocity, fps:	3725	3272	2864	2491	2147
	energy, ft-lb:	1540	1188	910	689	512
	arc, inches:		+1.7	+1.6	-2.8	-12.8
Rem. 55 Pointed Soft Point	velocity, fps:	3680	3137	2656	2222	1832
	energy, ft-lb:	1654	1201	861	603	410
	arc, inches:		+1.9	+1.8	-3.3	-15.5
Rem. 55 HP Power-Lokt	velocity, fps:	3680	3209	2785	2400	2046
	energy, ft-lb:	1654	1257	947	703	511
	arc, inches:		+1.8	+1.7	-3.0	-13.7

Centerfire Rifle Ballistics

.22-250 Remington to .243 Winchester

BALLISTICS

CARTRIDGE BULLET	RANGE, YARDS:	0	100	200	300	400
Rem. 60 Nosler Partition	velocity, fps:	3500	3045	2634	2258	1914
(also in EtronX)	energy, ft-lb:	1632	1235	924	679	488
	arc, inches:		+2.1	+1.9	-3.4	-15.5
Win. 40 Ballistic Silvertip	velocity, fps:	4150	3591	3099	2658	2257
	energy, ft-lb:	1530	1146	853	628	453
	arc, inches:		+0.6	0	-4.2	-13.4
Win. 50 Ballistic Silvertip	velocity, fps:	3810	3341	2919	2536	2182
	energy, ft-lb:	1611	1239	946	714	529
	arc, inches:		+0.8	0	-4.9	-15.2
Win. 55 Pointed Soft Point	velocity, fps:	3680	3137	2656	2222	1832
	energy, ft-lb:	1654	1201	861	603	410
	arc, inches:		+2.3	+1.9	-3.4	-15.9
Win. 55 Ballistic Silvertip	velocity, fps:	3680	3272	2900	2558	2240
	energy, ft-lb:	1654	1307	1027	799	613
	arc, inches:		+0.9	0	-5.0	-15.4

.220 Swift

CARTRIDGE BULLET	RANGE, YARDS:	0	100	200	300	400
Federal 52 Sierra MatchKing	velocity, fps:	3830	3370	2960	2600	2230
BTHP	energy, ft-lb:	1690	1310	1010	770	575
	arc, inches:		+0.8	0	-4.8	-14.9
Federal 55 Sierra BlitzKing	velocity, fps:	3800	3370	2990	2630	2310
	energy, ft-lb:	1765	1390	1090	850	650
	arc, inches:		+0.8	0	-4.7	-14.4
Federal 55 Trophy Bonded	velocity, fps:	3700	3170	2690	2270	1880
	energy, ft-lb:	1670	1225	885	625	430
	arc, inches:		+1.0	0	-5.8	-18.5
Hornady 40 V-Max	velocity, fps:	4200	3678	3190	2739	2329
	energy, ft-lb:	1566	1201	904	666	482
	arc, inches:		+0.5	0	-4.0	-12.9
Hornady 50 V-Max	velocity, fps:	3850	3396	2970	2576	2215
	energy, ft-lb:	1645	1280	979	736	545
	arc, inches:		+0.7	0	-4.8	-15.1
Hornady 50 SP	velocity, fps:	3850	3327	2862	2442	2060
	energy, ft-lb:	1645	1228	909	662	471
	arc, inches:		+0.8	0	-5.1	-16.1
Hornady 55 V-Max	velocity, fps:	3680	3265	2876	2517	2183
	energy, ft-lb:	1654	1302	1010	772	582
	arc, inches:		+0.9	0	-5.3	-16.1
Hornady 60 Hollow Point	velocity, fps:	3600	3199	2824	2475	2156
	energy, ft-lb:	1727	1364	1063	816	619
	arc, inches:		+1.0	0	-5.4	-16.3
Norma 50 Soft Point	velocity, fps:	4019	3380	2826	2335	
	energy, ft-lb:	1794	1268	887	605	
	arc, inches:		+0.7	0	-5.1	
Rem. 50 Pointed Soft Point	velocity, fps:	3780	3158	2617	2135	1710
	energy, ft-lb:	1586	1107	760	506	325
	arc, inches:		+0.3	-1.4	-8.2	
Rem. 50 V-Max boat-tail	velocity, fps:	3780	3321	2908	2532	2185
(also in EtronX)	energy, ft-lb:	1586	1224	939	711	530
	arc, inches:		+0.8	0	-5.0	-15.4
Win. 40 Ballistic Silvertip	velocity, fps:	4050	3518	3048	2624	2238
	energy, ft-lb:	1457	1099	825	611	445
	arc, inches:		+0.7	0	-4.4	-13.9
Win. 50 Pointed Soft Point	velocity, fps:	3870	3310	2816	2373	1972
	energy, ft-lb:	1663	1226	881	625	432
	arc, inches:		+0.8	0	-5.2	-16.7

.223 WSSM

CARTRIDGE BULLET	RANGE, YARDS:	0	100	200	300	400
Win. 55 Ballistic Silvertip	velocity, fps:	3850	3438	3064	2721	2402
	energy, ft-lb:	1810	1444	1147	904	704
	arc, inches:		+0.7	0	-4.4	-13.6
Win. 55 Pointed Softpoint	velocity, fps:	3850	3367	2934	2541	2181
	energy, ft-lb:	1810	1384	1051	789	581
	arc, inches:		+0.8	0	-4.9	-15.1
Win. 64 Power-Point	velocity, fps:	3600	3144	2732	2356	2011
	energy, ft-lb:	1841	1404	1061	789	574
	arc, inches:		+1.0	0	-5.7	-17.7

6mm PPC

CARTRIDGE BULLET	RANGE, YARDS:	0	100	200	300	400
A-Square 68 Berger	velocity, fps:	3100	2751	2428	2128	1850
	energy, ft-lb:	1451	1143	890	684	516
	arc, inches:		+1.5	0	-7.5	-22.6

6x70 R

CARTRIDGE BULLET	RANGE, YARDS:	0	100	200	300	400
Norma 90 Nosler Bal. Tip	velocity, fps:	2461	2231	2013	1809	
	energy, ft-lb:	1211	995	810	654	
	arc, inches:		+2.7	0	-11.3	

.243 Winchester

CARTRIDGE BULLET	RANGE, YARDS:	0	100	200	300	400
Black Hills 55 Nosler B. Tip	velocity, fps:	3800				
	energy, ft-lb:	1763				
	arc, inches:					
Black Hills 90 Nosler B. Tip	velocity, fps:	2950				
	energy, ft-lb:	1836				
	arc, inches:					
Federal 70 Nosler Bal. Tip	velocity, fps:	3400	3070	2760	2470	2200
	energy, ft-lb:	1795	1465	1185	950	755
	arc, inches:		+1.1	0	-5.7	-17.1
Federal 70 Speer TNT HP	velocity, fps:	3400	3040	2700	2390	2100
	energy, ft-lb:	1795	1435	1135	890	685
	arc, inches:		+1.1	0	-5.9	-18.0
Federal 80 Sierra Pro-Hunter	velocity, fps:	3350	2960	2590	2260	1950
	energy, ft-lb:	1995	1550	1195	905	675
	arc, inches:		+1.3	0	-6.4	-19.7
Federal 85 Sierra GameKing	velocity, fps:	3320	3070	2830	2600	2380
BTHP	energy, ft-lb:	2080	1770	1510	1280	1070
	arc, inches:		+1.1	0	-5.5	-16.1
Federal 90 Trophy Bonded	velocity, fps:	3100	2850	2610	2380	2160
	energy, ft-lb:	1920	1620	1360	1130	935
	arc, inches:		+1.4	0	-6.1	-19.2
Federal 100 Hi-Shok	velocity, fps:	2960	2700	2450	2220	1990
	energy, ft-lb:	1945	1615	1330	1090	880
	arc, inches:		+1.6	0	-7.5	-22.0
Federal 100 Sierra GameKing	velocity, fps:	2960	2760	2570	2380	2210
BTSP	energy, ft-lb:	1950	1690	1460	1260	1080
	arc, inches:		+1.5	0	-6.8	-19.8
Federal 100 Nosler Partition	velocity, fps:	2960	2730	2510	2300	2100
	energy, ft-lb:	1945	1650	1395	1170	975
	arc, inches:		+1.6	0	-7.1	-20.9
Hornady 58 V-Max	velocity, fps:	3750	3319	2913	2539	2195
	energy, ft-lb:	1811	1418	1093	830	620
	arc, inches:		+1.2	0	-5.5	-16.4
Hornady 75 Hollow Point	velocity, fps:	3400	2970	2578	2219	1890
	energy, ft-lb:	1926	1469	1107	820	595
	arc, inches:		+1.2	0	-6.5	-20.3
Hornady 100 BTSP	velocity, fps:	2960	2728	2508	2299	2099
	energy, ft-lb:	1945	1653	1397	1174	979
	arc, inches:		+1.6	0	-7.2	-21.0
Hornady 100 BTSP LM	velocity, fps:	3100	2839	2592	2358	2138
	energy, ft-lb:	2133	1790	1491	1235	1014
	arc, inches:		+1.5	0	-6.8	-19.8

Centerfire Rifle Ballistics

.243 Winchester to .25-20 Winchester

CARTRIDGE BULLET	RANGE, YARDS:	0	100	200	300	400
Norma 80 FMJ	velocity, fps:	3117	2750	2412	2098	
	energy, ft-lb:	1726	1344	1034	782	
	arc, inches:		+1.5	0	-7.5	
Norma 100 FMJ	velocity, fps:	3018	2747	2493	2252	
	energy, ft-lb:	2023	1677	1380	1126	
	arc, inches:		+1.5	0	-7.1	
Norma 100 Soft Point	velocity, fps:	3018	2748	2493	2252	
	energy, ft-lb:	2023	1677	1380	1126	
	arc, inches:		+1.5	0	-7.1	
PMC 80 Pointed Soft Point	velocity, fps:	2940	2684	2444	2215	1999
	energy, ft-lb:	1535	1280	1060	871	709
	arc, inches:		+1.7	0	-7.5	-22.1
PMC 85 HP boat-tail	velocity, fps:	3275	2922	2596	2292	2009
	energy, ft-lb:	2024	1611	1272	991	761
	arc, inches:		+1.3	0	-6.5	-19.7
PMC 100 Pointed Soft Point	velocity, fps:	2743	2507	2283	2070	1869
	energy, ft-lb:	1670	1395	1157	951	776
	arc, inches:		+2.0	0	-8.7	-25.5
PMC 100 SP boat-tail	velocity, fps:	2960	2742	2534	2335	2144
	energy, ft-lb:	1945	1669	1425	1210	1021
	arc, inches:		+1.6	0	-7.0	-20.5
Rem. 75 V-Max boat-tail	velocity, fps:	3375	3065	2775	2504	2248
	energy, ft-lb:	1897	1564	1282	1044	842
	arc, inches:		+2.0	+1.8	-3.0	-13.3
Rem. 80 Pointed Soft Point	velocity, fps:	3350	2955	2593	2259	1951
	energy, ft-lb:	1993	1551	1194	906	676
	arc, inches:		+2.2	+2.0	-3.5	-15.8
Rem. 80 HP Power-Lokt	velocity, fps:	3350	2955	2593	2259	1951
	energy, ft-lb:	1993	1551	1194	906	676
	arc, inches:		+2.2	+2.0	-3.5	-15.8
Rem. 90 Nosler Bal. Tip	velocity, fps:	3120	2871	2635	2411	2199
(also in EtronX) or Scirocco	energy, ft-lb:	1946	1647	1388	1162	966
	arc, inches:		+1.4	0	-6.4	-18.8
Rem. 95 AccuTip	velocity, fps:	3120	2847	2590	2347	2118
	energy, ft-lb:	2053	1710	1415	1162	946
	arc, inches:		+1.5	0	-6.6	-19.5
Rem. 100 PSP Core-Lokt	velocity, fps:	2960	2697	2449	2215	1993
(also in EtronX)	energy, ft-lb:	1945	1615	1332	1089	882
	arc, inches:		+1.6	0	-7.5	-22.1
Rem. 100 PSP boat-tail	velocity, fps:	2960	2720	2492	2275	2069
	energy, ft-lb:	1945	1642	1378	1149	950
	arc, inches:		+2.8	+2.3	-3.8	-16.6
Speer 100 Grand Slam	velocity, fps:	2950	2684	2434	2197	
	energy, ft-lb:	1932	1600	1315	1072	
	arc, inches:		+1.7	0	-7.6	-22.4
Win. 55 Ballistic Silvertip	velocity, fps:	4025	3597	3209	2853	2525
	energy, ft-lb:	1978	1579	1257	994	779
	arc, inches:		+0.6	0	-4.0	-12.2
Win. 80 Pointed Soft Point	velocity, fps:	3350	2955	2593	2259	1951
	energy, ft-lb:	1993	1551	1194	906	676
	arc, inches:		+2.6	+2.1	-3.6	-16.2
Win. 95 Ballistic Silvertip	velocity, fps:	3100	2854	2626	2410	2203
	energy, ft-lb:	2021	1719	1455	1225	1024
	arc, inches:		+1.4	0	-6.4	-18.9
Win. 100 Power-Point	velocity, fps:	2960	2697	2449	2215	1993
	energy, ft-lb:	1945	1615	1332	1089	882
	arc, inches:		+1.9	0	-7.8	-22.6
Win. 100 Power-Point Plus	velocity, fps:	3090	2818	2562	2321	2092
	energy, ft-lb:	2121	1764	1458	1196	972
	arc, inches:		+1.4	0	-6.7	-20.0

6mm Remington

CARTRIDGE BULLET	RANGE, YARDS:	0	100	200	300	400
Federal 80 Sierra Pro-Hunter	velocity, fps:	3470	3060	2690	2350	2040
	energy, ft-lb:	2140	1665	1290	980	735
	arc, inches:		+1.1	0	-5.9	-18.2
Federal 100 Hi-Shok	velocity, fps:	3100	2830	2570	2330	2100
	energy, ft-lb:	2135	1775	1470	1205	985
	arc, inches:		+1.4	0	-6.7	-19.8
Federal 100 Nosler Partition	velocity, fps:	3100	2860	2640	2420	2220
	energy, ft-lb:	2135	1820	1545	1300	1090
	arc, inches:		+1.4	0	-6.3	-18.7
Hornady 100 SP boat-tail	velocity, fps:	3100	2861	2634	2419	2231
	energy, ft-lb:	2134	1818	1541	1300	1088
	arc, inches:		+1.3	0	-6.5	-18.9
Hornady 100 SPBT LM	velocity, fps:	3250	2997	2756	2528	2311
	energy, ft-lb:	2345	1995	1687	1418	1186
	arc, inches:		+1.6	0	-6.3	-18.2
Rem. 75 V-Max boat-tail	velocity, fps:	3400	3088	2797	2524	2267
	energy, ft-lb:	1925	1587	1303	1061	856
	arc, inches:		+1.9	+1.7	-3.0	-13.1
Rem. 100 PSP Core-Lokt	velocity, fps:	3100	2829	2573	2332	2104
	energy, ft-lb:	2133	1777	1470	1207	983
	arc, inches:		+1.4	0	-6.7	-19.8
Rem. 100 PSP boat-tail	velocity, fps:	3100	2852	2617	2394	2183
	energy, ft-lb:	2134	1806	1521	1273	1058
	arc, inches:		+1.4	0	-6.5	-19.1
Win. 100 Power-Point	velocity, fps:	3100	2829	2573	2332	2104
	energy, ft-lb:	2133	1777	1470	1207	983
	arc, inches:		+1.7	0	-7.0	-20.4

.243 WSSM

CARTRIDGE BULLET	RANGE, YARDS:	0	100	200	300	400
Win. 55 Ballistic Silvertip	velocity, fps:	4060	3628	3237	2880	2550
	energy, ft-lb:	2013	1607	1280	1013	794
	arc, inches:		+0.6	0	-3.9	-12.0
Win. 95 Ballistic Silvertip	velocity, fps:	3250	3000	2763	2538	2325
	energy, ft-lb:	2258	1898	1610	1359	1140
	arc, inches:		+1.2	0	5.7	16.9
Win. 100 Power Point	velocity, fps:	3110	2838	2583	2341	2112
	energy, ft-lb:	2147	1789	1481	1217	991
	arc, inches:		+1.4	0	-6.6	-19.7

.240 Weatherby Magnum

CARTRIDGE BULLET	RANGE, YARDS:	0	100	200	300	400
Wby. 87 Pointed Expanding	velocity, fps:	3523	3199	2898	2617	2352
	energy, ft-lb:	2397	1977	1622	1323	1069
	arc, inches:		+2.7	+3.4	0	-8.4
Wby. 90 Barnes-X	velocity, fps:	3500	3222	2962	2717	2484
	energy, ft-lb:	2448	2075	1753	1475	1233
	arc, inches:		+2.6	+3.3	0	-8.0
Wby. 95 Nosler Bal. Tip	velocity, fps:	3420	3146	2888	2645	2414
	energy, ft-lb:	2467	2087	1759	1475	1229
	arc, inches:		+2.7	+3.5	0	-8.4
Wby. 100 Pointed Expanding	velocity, fps:	3406	3134	2878	2637	2408
	energy, ft-lb:	2576	2180	1839	1544	1287
	arc, inches:		+2.8	+3.5	0	-8.4
Wby. 100 Partition	velocity, fps:	3406	3136	2882	2642	2415
	energy, ft-lb:	2576	2183	1844	1550	1294
	arc, inches:		+2.8	+3.5	0	-8.4

.25-20 Winchester

CARTRIDGE BULLET	RANGE, YARDS:	0	100	200	300	400
Rem. 86 Soft Point	velocity, fps:	1460	1194	1030	931	858
	energy, ft-lb:	407	272	203	165	141
	arc, inches:		0	-22.9	-78.9	-173.0

Centerfire Rifle Ballistics

.25-20 Winchester to 6.53 (.257) Scramjet

Cartridge Bullet	Range, yards:	0	100	200	300	400
Win. 86 Soft Point	velocity, fps:	1460	1194	1030	931	858
	energy, ft-lb:	407	272	203	165	141
	arc, inches:		0	-23.5	-79.6	-175.9

.25-35 Winchester

Cartridge Bullet	Range, yards:	0	100	200	300	400
Win. 117 Soft Point	velocity, fps:	2230	1866	1545	1282	1097
	energy, ft-lb:	1292	904	620	427	313
	arc, inches:		+2.1	-5.1	-27.0	-70.1

.250 Savage

Cartridge Bullet	Range, yards:	0	100	200	300	400
Rem. 100 Pointed SP	velocity, fps:	2820	2504	2210	1936	1684
	energy, ft-lb:	1765	1392	1084	832	630
	arc, inches:		+2.0	0	-9.2	-27.7
Win. 100 Silvertip	velocity, fps:	2820	2467	2140	1839	1569
	energy, ft-lb:	1765	1351	1017	751	547
	arc, inches:		+2.4	0	-10.1	-30.5

.257 Roberts

Cartridge Bullet	Range, yards:	0	100	200	300	400
Federal 120 Nosler Partition	velocity, fps:	2780	2560	2360	2160	1970
	energy, ft-lb:	2060	1750	1480	1240	1030
	arc, inches:		+1.9	0	-8.2	-24.0
Hornady 117 SP boat-tail	velocity, fps:	2780	2550	2331	2122	1925
	energy, ft-lb:	2007	1689	1411	1170	963
	arc, inches:		+1.9	0	-8.3	-24.4
Hornady 117 SP boat-tail LM	velocity, fps:	2940	2694	2460	2240	2031
	energy, ft-lb:	2245	1885	1572	1303	1071
	arc, inches:		+1.7	0	-7.6	-21.8
Rem. 117 SP Core-Lokt	velocity, fps:	2650	2291	1961	1663	1404
	energy, ft-lb:	1824	1363	999	718	512
	arc, inches:		+2.6	0	-11.7	-36.1
Win. 117 Power-Point	velocity, fps:	2780	2411	2071	1761	1488
	energy, ft-lb:	2009	1511	1115	806	576
	arc, inches:		+2.6	0	-10.8	-33.0

.25-06 Remington

Cartridge Bullet	Range, yards:	0	100	200	300	400
Black Hills 100 Nosler B. Tip	velocity, fps:	3200				
	energy, ft-lb:	2259				
	arc, inches:					
Black Hills 115 Barnes X	velocity, fps:	2975				
	energy, ft-lb:	2259				
	arc, inches:					
Federal 90 Sierra Varminter	velocity, fps:	3440	3040	2680	2340	2030
	energy, ft-lb:	2365	1850	1435	1100	825
	arc, inches:		+1.1	0	-6.0	-18.3
Federal 100 Barnes XLC	velocity, fps:	3210	2970	2750	2540	2330
	energy, ft-lb:	2290	1965	1680	1430	1205
	arc, inches:		+1.2	0	-5.8	-17.0
Federal 100 Nosler Bal. Tip	velocity, fps:	3210	2960	2720	2490	2280
	energy, ft-lb:	2290	1940	1640	1380	1150
	arc, inches:		+1.2	0	-6.0	-17.5
Federal 115 Nosler Partition	velocity, fps:	2990	2750	2520	2300	2100
	energy, ft-lb:	2285	1930	1620	1350	1120
	arc, inches:		+1.6	0	-7.0	-20.8
Federal 115 Trophy Bonded	velocity, fps:	2990	2740	2500	2270	2050
	energy, ft-lb:	2285	1910	1590	1310	1075
	arc, inches:		+1.6	0	-7.2	-21.1
Federal 117 Sierra Pro Hunt.	velocity, fps:	2990	2730	2480	2250	2030
	energy, ft-lb:	2320	1985	1645	1350	1100
	arc, inches:		+1.6	0	-7.2	-21.4
Federal 117 Sierra GameKing	velocity, fps:	2990	2770	2570	2370	2190
BTSP	energy, ft-lb:	2320	2000	1715	1465	1240
	arc, inches:		+1.5	0	-6.8	-19.9
Hornady 117 SP boat-tail	velocity, fps:	2990	2749	2520	2302	2096
	energy, ft-lb:	2322	1962	1649	1377	1141
	arc, inches:		+1.6	0	-7.0	-20.7
Hornady 117 SP boat-tail LM	velocity, fps:	3110	2855	2613	2384	2168
	energy, ft-lb:	2512	2117	1774	1476	1220
	arc, inches:		+1.8	0	-7.1	-20.3
PMC 117 PSP	velocity, fps:					
	energy, ft-lb:					
	arc, inches:					
Rem. 100 PSP Core-Lokt	velocity, fps:	3230	2893	2580	2287	2014
	energy, ft-lb:	2316	1858	1478	1161	901
	arc, inches:		+1.3	0	-6.6	-19.8
Rem. 120 PSP Core-Lokt	velocity, fps:	2990	2730	2484	2252	2032
	energy, ft-lb:	2382	1985	1644	1351	1100
	arc, inches:		+1.6	0	-7.2	-21.4
Speer 120 Grand Slam	velocity, fps:	3130	2835	2558	2298	
	energy, ft-lb:	2610	2141	1743	1407	
	arc, inches:		+1.4	0	-6.8	-20.1
Win. 90 Pos. Exp. Point	velocity, fps:	3440	3043	2680	2344	2034
	energy, ft-lb:	2364	1850	1435	1098	827
	arc, inches:		+2.4	+2.0	-3.4	-15.0
Win. 115 Ballistic Silvertip	velocity, fps:	3060	2825	2603	2390	2188
	energy, ft-lb:	2391	2038	1729	1459	1223
	arc, inches:		+1.4	0	-6.6	-19.2

.257 Weatherby Magnum

Cartridge Bullet	Range, yards:	0	100	200	300	400
Federal 115 Nosler Partition	velocity, fps:	3150	2900	2660	2440	2220
	energy, ft-lb:	2535	2145	1810	1515	1260
	arc, inches:		+1.3	0	-6.2	-18.4
Federal 115 Trophy Bonded	velocity, fps:	3150	2890	2640	2400	2180
	energy, ft-lb:	2535	2125	1775	1470	1210
	arc, inches:		+1.4	0	-6.3	-18.8
Wby. 87 Pointed Expanding	velocity, fps:	3825	3472	3147	2845	2563
	energy, ft-lb:	2826	2328	1913	1563	1269
	arc, inches:		+2.1	+2.8	0	-7.1
Wby. 100 Pointed Expanding	velocity, fps:	3602	3298	3016	2750	2500
	energy, ft-lb:	2881	2416	2019	1680	1388
	arc, inches:		+2.4	+3.1	0	-7.7
Wby. 115 Nosler Bal. Tip	velocity, fps:	3400	3170	2952	2745	2547
	energy, ft-lb:	2952	2566	2226	1924	1656
	arc, inches:		+3.0	+3.5	0	-7.9
Wby. 115 Barnes X	velocity, fps:	3400	3158	2929	2711	2504
	energy, ft-lb:	2952	2546	2190	1877	1601
	arc, inches:		+2.7	+3.4	0	-8.1
Wby. 117 RN Expanding	velocity, fps:	3402	2984	2595	2240	1921
	energy, ft-lb:	3007	2320	1742	1302	956
	arc, inches:		+3.4	+4.31	0	-11.1
Wby. 120 Nosler Partition	velocity, fps:	3305	3046	2801	2570	2350
	energy, ft-lb:	2910	2472	2091	1760	1471
	arc, inches:		+3.0	+3.7	0	-8.9

6.53 (.257) Scramjet

Cartridge Bullet	Range, yards:	0	100	200	300	400
Lazzeroni 85 Nosler Bal. Tip	velocity, fps:	3960	3652	3365	3096	2844
	energy, ft-lb:	2961	2517	2137	1810	1526
	arc, inches:		+1.7	+2.4	0	-6.0
Lazzeroni 100 Nosler Part.	velocity, fps:	3740	3465	3208	2965	2735
	energy, ft-lb:	3106	2667	2285	1953	1661
	arc, inches:		+2.1	+2.7	0	-6.7

Centerfire Rifle Ballistics

6.5x50 Japanese to .270 Winchester

BALLISTICS

CARTRIDGE BULLET	RANGE, YARDS:	0	100	200	300	400
6.5x50 Japanese						
Norma 156 Alaska	velocity, fps:	2067	1832	1615	1423	
	energy, ft-lb:	1480	1162	904	701	
	arc, inches:		+4.4	0	-17.8	
6.5x52 Carcano						
Norma 156 Alaska	velocity, fps:	2428	2169	1926	1702	
	energy, ft-lb:	2043	1630	1286	1004	
	arc, inches:		+2.9	0	-12.3	
6.5x55 Swedish						
Federal 140 Hi-Shok	velocity, fps:	2600	2400	2220	2040	1860
	energy, ft-lb:	2100	1795	1525	1285	1080
	arc, inches:		+2.3	0	-9.4	-27.2
Federal 140 Trophy Bonded	velocity, fps:	2550	2350	2160	1980	1810
	energy, ft-lb:	2020	1720	1450	1220	1015
	arc, inches:		+2.4	0	-9.8	-28.4
Federal 140 Sierra MatchKg. BTHP	velocity, fps:	2630	2460	2300	2140	2000
	energy, ft-lb:	2140	1880	1640	1430	1235
	arc, inches:		+16.4	+28.8	+33.9	+31.8
Hornady 129 SP LM	velocity, fps:	2770	2561	2361	2171	1994
	energy, ft-lb:	2197	1878	1597	1350	1138
	arc, inches:		+2.0	0	-8.2	-23.2
Hornady140 SP LM	velocity, fps:	2740	2541	2351	2169	1999
	energy, ft-lb:	2333	2006	1717	1463	1242
	arc, inches:		+2.4	0	-8.7	-24.0
Norma 139 Vulkan	velocity, fps:	2854	2569	2302	2051	
	energy, ft-lb:	2515	2038	1636	1298	
	arc, inches:		+1.8	0	-8.4	
Norma 140 Nosler Partition	velocity, fps:	2789	2592	2403	2223	
	energy, ft-lb:	2419	2089	1796	1536	
	arc, inches:		+1.8	0	-7.8	
Norma 156 TXP Swift A-Fr.	velocity, fps:	2526	2276	2040	1818	
	energy, ft-lb:	2196	1782	1432	1138	
	arc, inches:		+2.6	0	-10.9	
Norma 156 Alaska	velocity, fps:	2559	2245	1953	1687	
	energy, ft-lb:	2269	1746	1322	986	
	arc, inches:		+2.7	0	-11.9	
Norma 156 Vulkan	velocity, fps:	2644	2395	2159	1937	
	energy, ft-lb:	2422	1987	1616	1301	
	arc, inches:		+2.2	0	-9.7	
Norma 156 Oryx	velocity, fps:	2559	2308	2070	1848	
	energy, ft-lb:	2269	1845	1485	1183	
	arc, inches:		+2.5	0	-10.6	
PMC 139 Pointed Soft Point	velocity, fps:	2850	2560	2290	2030	1790
	energy, ft-lb:	2515	2025	1615	1270	985
	arc, inches:		+2.2	0	-8.9	-26.3
PMC 140 HP boat-tail	velocity, fps:	2560	2398	2243	2093	1949
	energy, ft-lb:	2037	1788	1563	1361	1181
	arc, inches:		+2.3	0	-9.2	-26.4
PMC 140 SP boat-tail	velocity, fps:	2560	2386	2218	2057	1903
	energy, ft-lb:	2037	1769	1529	1315	1126
	arc, inches:		+2.3	0	-9.4	-27.1
PMC 144 FMJ	velocity, fps:	2650	2370	2110	1870	1650
	energy, ft-lb:	2425	1950	1550	1215	945
	arc, inches:		+2.7	0	-10.5	-30.9
Rem. 140 PSP Core-Lokt	velocity, fps:	2550	2353	2164	1984	1814
	energy, ft-lb:	2021	1720	1456	1224	1023
	arc, inches:		+2.4	0	-9.8	-27.0
Speer 140 Grand Slam	velocity, fps:	2550	2318	2099	1892	
	energy, ft-lb:	2021	1670	1369	1112	
	arc, inches:		+2.5	0	-10.4	-30.6
Win. 140 Soft Point	velocity, fps:	2550	2359	2176	2002	1836
	energy, ft-lb:	2022	1731	1473	1246	1048
	arc, inches:		+2.4	0	-9.7	-28.1
.260 Remington						
Federal 140 Sierra GameKing BTSP	velocity, fps:	2750	2570	2390	2220	2060
	energy, ft-lb:	2350	2045	1775	1535	1315
	arc, inches:		+1.9	0	-8.0	-23.1
Federal 140 Trophy Bonded	velocity, fps:	2750	2540	2340	2150	1970
	energy, ft-lb:	2350	2010	1705	1440	1210
	arc, inches:		+1.9	0	-8.4	-24.1
Rem. 120 Nosler Bal. Tip	velocity, fps:	2890	2688	2494	2309	2131
	energy, ft-lb:	2226	1924	1657	1420	1210
	arc, inches:		+1.7	0	-7.3	-21.1
Rem. 120 AccuTip	velocity, fps:	2890	2697	2512	2334	2163
	energy, ft-lb:	2392	2083	1807	1560	1340
	arc, inches:		+1.6	0	-7.2	-20.7
Rem. 125 Nosler Partition	velocity, fps:	2875	2669	2473	2285	2105
	energy, ft-lb:	2294	1977	1697	1449	1230
	arc, inches:		+1.71	0	-7.4	-21.4
Rem. 140 PSP Core-Lokt	velocity, fps:	2750	2544	2347	2158	1979
	energy, ft-lb:	2351	2011	1712	1448	1217
	arc, inches:		+1.9	0	-8.3	-24.0
Speer 140 Grand Slam	velocity, fps:	2750	2518	2297	2087	
	energy, ft-lb:	2351	1970	1640	1354	
	arc, inches:		+2.3	0	-8.9	-25.8
6.5/284						
Norma 120 Nosler Bal. Tip	velocity, fps:	3117	2890	2674	2469	
	energy, ft-lb:	2589	2226	1906	1624	
	arc, inches:		+1.3	0	-6.2	
Norma 140 Nosler Part.	velocity, fps:	2953	2750	2557	2371	
	energy, ft-lb:	2712	2352	2032	1748	
	arc, inches:		+1.5	0	-6.8	
.264 Winchester Magnum						
Rem. 140 PSP Core-Lokt	velocity, fps:	3030	2782	2548	2326	2114
	energy, ft-lb:	2854	2406	2018	1682	1389
	arc, inches:		+1.5	0	-6.9	-20.2
Win. 140 Power-Point	velocity, fps:	3030	2782	2548	2326	2114
	energy, ft-lb:	2854	2406	2018	1682	1389
	arc, inches:		+1.8	0	-7.2	-20.8
.270 Winchester						
Black Hills 130 Barnes X	velocity, fps:	2950				
	energy, ft-lb:	2184				
	arc, inches:					
Black Hills 130 Nosler B. Tip	velocity, fps	2950				
	energy, ft-lb:	2184				
	arc, inches:					
Federal 130 Hi-Shok	velocity, fps:	3060	2800	2560	2330	2110
	energy, ft-lb:	2700	2265	1890	1565	1285
	arc, inches:		+1.5	0	-6.8	-20.0
Federal 130 Sierra Pro-Hunt.	velocity, fps:	3060	2830	2600	2390	2190
	energy, ft-lb:	2705	2305	1960	1655	1390
	arc, inches:		+1.4	0	-6.4	-19.0
Federal 130 Sierra GameKing	velocity, fps:	3060	2830	2620	2410	2220
	energy, ft-lb:	2700	2320	1980	1680	1420
	arc, inches:		+1.4	0	-6.5	-19.0

Centerfire Rifle Ballistics

.270 Winchester

CARTRIDGE BULLET	RANGE, YARDS:	0	100	200	300	400
Federal 130 Nosler Bal. Tip	velocity, fps:	3060	2840	2630	2430	2230
	energy, ft-lb:	2700	2325	1990	1700	1440
	arc, inches:		+1.4	0	-6.5	-18.8
Federal 130 Barnes XLC	velocity, fps:	3060	2840	2620	2420	2220
	energy, ft-lb:	2705	2320	1985	1690	1425
	arc, inches:		+1.4	0	-6.4	-18.9
Federal 130 Trophy Bonded	velocity, fps:	3060	2810	2570	2340	2130
	energy, ft-lb:	2705	2275	1905	1585	1310
	arc, inches:		+1.5	0	-6.7	-19.8
Federal 140 Trophy Bonded	velocity, fps:	2940	2700	2480	2260	2060
	energy, ft-lb:	2685	2270	1905	1590	1315
	arc, inches:		+1.6	0	-7.3	-21.5
Federal 140 Tr. Bonded HE	velocity, fps:	3100	2860	2620	2400	2200
	energy, ft-lb:	2990	2535	2140	1795	1500
	arc, inches:		+1.4	0	-6.4	-18.9
Federal 150 Hi-Shok RN	velocity, fps:	2850	2500	2180	1890	1620
	energy, ft-lb:	2705	2085	1585	1185	870
	arc, inches:		+2.0	0	-9.4	-28.6
Federal 150 Sierra GameKing	velocity, fps:	2850	2660	2480	2300	2130
	energy, ft-lb:	2705	2355	2040	1760	1510
	arc, inches:		+1.7	0	-7.4	-21.4
Federal 150 Sierra GameKing	velocity, fps:	3000	2800	2620	2430	2260
HE	energy, ft-lb:	2995	2615	2275	1975	1700
	arc, inches:		+1.5	0	-6.5	-18.9
Federal 150 Nosler Partition	velocity, fps:	2850	2590	2340	2100	1880
	energy, ft-lb:	2705	2225	1815	1470	1175
	arc, inches:		+1.9	0	-8.3	-24.4
Hornady 130 SST	velocity, fps:	3060	2845	2639	2442	2254
(or Interbond)	energy, ft-lb:	2700	2335	2009	1721	1467
	arc, inches:		+1.4	0	-6.6	-19.1
Hornady 130 SST LM	velocity, fps:	3215	2998	2790	2590	2400
(or Interbond)	energy, ft-lb:	2983	2594	2246	1936	1662
	arc, inches:		+1.2	0	-5.8	-17.0
Hornady 140 SP boat-tail	velocity, fps:	2940	2747	2562	2385	2214
	energy, ft-lb:	2688	2346	2041	1769	1524
	arc, inches:		+1.6	0	-7.0	-20.2
Hornady 140 SP boat-tail LM	velocity, fps:	3100	2894	2697	2508	2327
	energy, ft-lb:	2987	2604	2261	1955	1684
	arc, inches:		+1.4	0	6.3	-18.3
Hornady 150 SP	velocity, fps:	2800	2684	2478	2284	2100
	energy, ft-lb:	2802	2400	2046	1737	1469
	arc, inches:		+1.7	0	-7.4	-21.6
Norma 130 SP	velocity, fps:	3140	2862	2601	2354	
	energy, ft-lb:	2847	2365	1953	1600	
	arc, inches:	0	+1.3	0	-6.5	
Norma 150 SP	velocity, fps:	2799	2555	2323	2104	
	energy, ft-lb:	2610	2175	1798	1475	
	arc, inches:	0	+1.9	0	-8.3	
PMC 130 Barnes X	velocity, fps:	2910	2717	2533	2356	2186
	energy, ft-lb:	2444	2131	1852	1602	1379
	arc, inches:		+1.6	0	-7.1	-20.4
PMC 130 SP boat-tail	velocity, fps:	3050	2830	2620	2421	2229
	energy, ft-lb:	2685	2312	1982	1691	1435
	arc, inches:		+1.5	0	-6.5	-19.0
PMC 130 Pointed Soft Point	velocity, fps:	2816	2593	2381	2179	1987
	energy, ft-lb:	2288	1941	1636	1370	1139
	arc, inches:		+1.8	0	-8.0	-23.2
PMC 150 Barnes X	velocity, fps:	2700	2541	2387	2238	2095
	energy, ft-lb:	2428	2150	1897	1668	1461
	arc, inches:		+2.0	0	-8.1	-23.1
PMC 150 SP boat-tail	velocity, fps:	2850	2660	2477	2302	2134
	energy, ft-lb:	2705	2355	2043	1765	1516
	arc, inches:		+1.7	0	-7.4	-21.4
PMC 150 Pointed Soft Point	velocity, fps:	2547	2368	2197	2032	1875
	energy, ft-lb:	2160	1868	1607	1375	1171
	arc, inches:		+2.4	0	-9.5	-27.5
Rem. 100 Pointed Soft Point	velocity, fps:	3320	2924	2561	2225	1916
	energy, ft-lb:	2448	1898	1456	1099	815
	arc, inches:		+2.3	+2.0	-3.6	-16.2
Rem. 130 PSP Core-Lokt	velocity, fps:	3060	2776	2510	2259	2022
	energy, ft-lb:	2702	2225	1818	1472	1180
	arc, inches:		+1.5	0	-7.0	-20.9
Rem. 130 Bronze Point	velocity, fps:	3060	2802	2559	2329	2110
	energy, ft-lb:	2702	2267	1890	1565	1285
	arc, inches:		+1.5	0	-6.8	-20.0
Rem. 130 Swift Scirocco	velocity, fps:	3060	2838	2677	2425	2232
	energy, ft-lb:	2702	2325	1991	1697	1438
	arc, inches:		+1.4	0	-6.5	-18.8
Rem. 130 AccuTip BTU	velocity, fps:	3060	2845	2639	2442	2254
	energy, ft-lb:	2702	2336	2009	1721	1467
	arc, inches:		+1.4	0	-6.4	-18.6
Rem. 140 Swift A-Frame	velocity, fps:	2925	2652	2394	2152	1923
	energy, ft-lb:	2659	2186	1782	1439	1150
	arc, inches:		+1.7	0	-7.8	-23.2
Rem. 140 PSP boat-tail	velocity, fps:	2960	2749	2548	2355	2171
	energy, ft-lb:	2723	2349	2018	1724	1465
	arc, inches:		+1.6	0	-6.9	-20.1
Rem. 140 Nosler Bal. Tip	velocity, fps:	2960	2754	2557	2366	2187
	energy, ft-lb:	2724	2358	2032	1743	1487
	arc, inches:		+1.6	0	-6.9	-20.0
Rem. 140 PSP C-L Ultra	velocity, fps:	2925	2667	2424	2193	1975
	energy, ft-lb:	2659	2211	1826	1495	1212
	arc, inches:		+1.7	0	-7.6	-22.5
Rem. 150 SP Core-Lokt	velocity, fps:	2850	2504	2183	1886	1618
	energy, ft-lb:	2705	2087	1587	1185	872
	arc, inches:		+2.0	0	-9.4	-28.6
Rem. 150 Nosler Partition	velocity, fps:	2850	2652	2463	2282	2108
	energy, ft-lb:	2705	2343	2021	1734	1480
	arc, inches:		+1.7	0	-7.5	-21.6
Speer 130 Grand Slam	velocity, fps:	3050	2774	2514	2269	
	energy, ft-lb:	2685	2221	1824	1485	
	arc, inches:		+1.5	0	-7.0	-20.9
Speer 150 Grand Slam	velocity, fps:	2830	2594	2369	2156	
	energy, ft-lb:	2667	2240	1869	1548	
	arc, inches:		+1.8	0	-8.1	-23.6
Win. 130 Power-Point	velocity, fps:	3060	2802	2559	2329	2110
	energy, ft-lb:	2702	2267	1890	1565	1285
	arc, inches:		+1.8	0	-7.1	-20.6
Win. 130 Power-Point Plus	velocity, fps:	3150	2881	2628	2388	2161
	energy, ft-lb:	2865	2396	1993	1646	1348
	arc, inches:		+1.3	0	-6.4	-18.9
Win. 130 Silvertip	velocity, fps:	3060	2776	2510	2259	2022
	energy, ft-lb:	2702	2225	1818	1472	1180
	arc, inches:		+1.8	0	-7.4	-21.6
Win. 130 Ballistic Silvertip	velocity, fps:	3050	2828	2618	2416	2224
	energy, ft-lb:	2685	2309	1978	1685	1428
	arc, inches:		+1.4	0	-6.5	-18.9
Win. 140 Fail Safe	velocity, fps:	2920	2671	2435	2211	1999
	energy, ft-lb:	2651	2218	1843	1519	1242
	arc, inches:		+1.7	0	-7.6	-22.3

Centerfire Rifle Ballistics

.270 Winchester to 7mm-08 Remington

CARTRIDGE BULLET	RANGE, YARDS:	0	100	200	300	400
Win. 150 Power-Point	velocity, fps:	2850	2585	2336	2100	1879
	energy, ft-lb:	2705	2226	1817	1468	1175
	arc, inches:		+2.2	0	-8.6	-25.0
Win. 150 Power-Point Plus	velocity, fps:	2950	2679	2425	2184	1957
	energy, ft-lb:	2900	2391	1959	1589	1276
	arc, inches:		+1.7	0	-7.6	-22.6
Win. 150 Partition Gold	velocity, fps:	2930	2693	2468	2254	2051
	energy, ft-lb:	2860	2416	2030	1693	1402
	arc, inches:		+1.7	0	-7.4	-21.6

.270 Winchester Short Magnum

CARTRIDGE BULLET	RANGE, YARDS:	0	100	200	300	400
Win. 130 Bal. Silvertip	velocity, fps:	3275	3041	2820	2609	2408
	energy, ft-lb:	3096	2669	2295	1964	1673
	arc, inches:		+1.1	0	-5.5	-16.1
Win. 140 Fail Safe	velocity, fps:	3125	2865	2619	2386	2165
	energy, ft-lb:	3035	2550	2132	1769	1457
	arc, inches:		+1.4	0	-6.5	-19.0
Win. 150 Ballistic Silvertip	velocity, fps:	3120	2923	2734	2554	2380
	energy, ft-lb:	3242	2845	2490	2172	1886
	arc, inches:		+1.3	0	-5.9	-17.2
Win. 150 Power Point	velocity, fps:	3150	2867	2601	2350	2113
	energy, ft-lb:	3304	2737	2252	1839	1487
	arc, inches:		+1.4	0	-6.5	-19.4

.270 Weatherby Magnum

CARTRIDGE BULLET	RANGE, YARDS:	0	100	200	300	400
Federal 130 Nosler Partition	velocity, fps:	3200	2960	2740	2520	2320
	energy, ft-lb:	2955	2530	2160	1835	1550
	arc, inches:		+1.2	0	-5.9	-17.3
Federal 130 Sierra GameKing	velocity, fps:	3200	2980	2780	2580	2400
BTSP	energy, ft-lb:	2955	2570	2230	1925	1655
	arc, inches:		+1.2	0	-5.7	-16.6
Federal 140 Trophy Bonded	velocity, fps:	3100	2840	2600	2370	2150
	energy, ft-lb:	2990	2510	2100	1745	1440
	arc, inches:		+1.4	0	-6.6	-19.3
Wby. 100 Pointed Expanding	velocity, fps:	3760	3396	3061	2751	2462
	energy, ft-lb:	3139	2560	2081	1681	1346
	arc, inches:		+2.3	+3.0	0	-7.6
Wby. 130 Pointed Expanding	velocity, fps:	3375	3123	2885	2659	2444
	energy, ft-lb:	3288	2815	2402	2041	1724
	arc, inches:		+2.8	+3.5	0	-8.4
Wby. 130 Nosler Partition	velocity, fps:	3375	3127	2892	2670	2458
	energy, ft-lb:	3288	2822	2415	2058	1744
	arc, inches:		+2.8	+3.5	0	-8.3
Wby. 140 Nosler Bal. Tip	velocity, fps:	3300	3077	2865	2663	2470
	energy, ft-lb:	3385	2943	2551	2204	1896
	arc, inches:		+2.9	+3.6	0	-8.4
Wby. 140 Barnes X	velocity, fps:	3250	3032	2825	2628	2438
	energy, ft-lb:	3283	2858	2481	2146	1848
	arc, inches:		+3.0	+3.7	0	-8.7
Wby. 150 Pointed Expanding	velocity, fps:	3245	3028	2821	2623	2434
	energy, ft-lb:	3507	3053	2650	2292	1973
	arc, inches:		+3.0	+3.7	0	-8.7
Wby. 150 Nosler Partition	velocity, fps:	3245	3029	2823	2627	2439
	energy, ft-lb:	3507	3055	2655	2298	1981
	arc, inches:		+3.0	+3.7	0	-8.

7-30 Waters

CARTRIDGE BULLET	RANGE, YARDS:	0	100	200	300	400
Federal 120 Sierra GameKing	velocity, fps:	2700	2300	1930	1600	1330
BTSP	energy, ft-lb:	1940	1405	990	685	470
	arc, inches:		+2.6	0	-12.0	-37.6

7mm Mauser (7x57)

CARTRIDGE BULLET	RANGE, YARDS:	0	100	200	300	400
Federal 140 Sierra Pro-Hunt.	velocity, fps:	2660	2450	2260	2070	1890
	energy, ft-lb:	2200	1865	1585	1330	1110
	arc, inches:		+2.1	0	-9.0	-26.1
Federal 140 Nosler Partition	velocity, fps:	2660	2450	2260	2070	1890
	energy, ft-lb:	2200	1865	1585	1330	1110
	arc, inches:		+2.1	0	-9.0	-26.1
Federal 175 Hi-Shok RN	velocity, fps:	2440	2140	1860	1600	1380
	energy, ft-lb:	2315	1775	1340	1000	740
	arc, inches:		+3.1	0	-13.3	-40.1
Hornady 139 SP boat-tail	velocity, fps:	2700	2504	2316	2137	1965
	energy, ft-lb:	2251	1936	1656	1410	1192
	arc, inches:		+2.0	0	-8.5	-24.9
Hornady 139 SP boat-tail LM	velocity, fps:	2830	2620	2450	2250	2070
	energy, ft-lb:	2475	2135	1835	1565	1330
	arc, inches:		+1.8	0	-7.6	-22.1
Hornady 139 SP LM	velocity, fps:	2950	2736	2532	2337	2152
	energy, ft-lb:	2686	2310	1978	1686	1429
	arc, inches:		+2.0	0	-7.6	-21.5
Norma 150 Soft Point	velocity, fps:	2690	2479	2278	2087	
	energy, ft-lb:	2411	2048	1729	1450	
	arc, inches:		+2.0	0	-8.8	
PMC 140 Pointed Soft Point	velocity, fps:	2660	2450	2260	2070	1890
	energy, ft-lb:	2200	1865	1585	1330	1110
	arc, inches:		+2.4	0	-9.6	-27.3
PMC 175 Soft Point	velocity, fps:	2440	2140	1860	1600	1380
	energy, ft-lb:	2315	1775	1340	1000	740
	arc, inches:		+1.5	-3.6	-18.6	-46.8
Rem. 140 PSP Core-Lokt	velocity, fps:	2660	2435	2221	2018	1827
	energy, ft-lb:	2199	1843	1533	1266	1037
	arc, inches:		+2.2	0	-9.2	-27.4
Win. 145 Power-Point	velocity, fps:	2660	2413	2180	1959	1754
	energy, ft-lb:	2279	1875	1530	1236	990
	arc, inches:		+1.1	-2.8	-14.1	-34.4

7x57 R

CARTRIDGE BULLET	RANGE, YARDS:	0	100	200	300	400
Norma 150 FMJ	velocity, fps:	2690	2489	2296	2112	
	energy, ft-lb:	2411	2063	1756	1486	
	arc, inches:		+2.0	0	-8.6	
Norma 154 Soft Point	velocity, fps:	2625	2417	2219	2030	
	energy, ft-lb:	2357	1999	1684	1410	
	arc, inches:		+2.2	0	-9.3	

7mm-08 Remington

CARTRIDGE BULLET	RANGE, YARDS:	0	100	200	300	400
Federal 140 Nosler Partition	velocity, fps:	2800	2590	2390	2200	2020
	energy, ft-lb:	2435	2085	1775	1500	1265
	arc, inches:		+1.8	0	-8.0	-23.1
Federal 140 Nosler Bal. Tip	velocity, fps:	2800	2610	2430	2260	2100
	energy, ft-lb:	2440	2135	1840	1590	1360
	arc, inches:		+1.8	0	-7.7	-22.3
Federal 140 Tr. Bonded HE	velocity, fps:	2950	2660	2390	2140	1900
	energy, ft-lb:	2705	2205	1780	1420	1120
	arc, inches:		+1.7	0	-7.9	-23.2
Federal 150 Sierra Pro-Hunt.	velocity, fps:	2650	2440	2230	2040	1860
	energy, ft-lb:	2340	1980	1660	1390	1150
	arc, inches:		+2.2	0	-9.2	-26.7
Hornady 139 SP boat-tail LM	velocity, fps:	3000	2790	2590	2399	2216
	energy, ft-lb:	2777	2403	2071	1776	1515
	arc, inches:		+1.5	0	-6.7	-19.4
PMC 140 PSP	velocity, fps:					
	energy, ft-lb:					
	arc, inches:					

Centerfire Rifle Ballistics

7mm-08 Remington to .280 Remington

CARTRIDGE BULLET	RANGE, YARDS:	0	100	200	300	400
Rem. 120 Hollow Point	velocity, fps:	3000	2725	2467	2223	1992
	energy, ft-lb:	2398	1979	1621	1316	1058
	arc, inches:		+1.6	0	-7.3	-21.7
Rem. 140 PSP Core-Lokt	velocity, fps:	2860	2625	2402	2189	1988
	energy, ft-lb:	2542	2142	1793	1490	1228
	arc, inches:		+1.8	0	-7.8	-22.9
Rem. 140 PSP boat-tail	velocity, fps:	2860	2656	2460	2273	2094
	energy, ft-lb:	2542	2192	1881	1606	1363
	arc, inches:		+1.7	0	-7.5	-21.7
Rem. 140 Nosler Bal. Tip	velocity, fps:	2860	2670	2488	2313	2145
	energy, ft-lb:	2543	2217	1925	1663	1431
	arc, inches:		+1.7	0	-7.3	-21.2
Rem. 140 Nosler Partition	velocity, fps:	2860	2648	2446	2253	2068
	energy, ft-lb:	2542	2180	1860	1577	1330
	arc, inches:		+1.7	0	-7.6	-22.0
Speer 145 Grand Slam	velocity, fps:	2845	2567	2305	2059	
	energy, ft-lb:	2606	2121	1711	1365	
	arc, inches:		+1.9	0	-8.4	-25.5
Win. 140 Power-Point	velocity, fps:	2800	2523	2268	2027	1802
	energy, ft-lb:	2429	1980	1599	1277	1010
	arc, inches:		+2.0	0	-8.8	-26.0
Win. 140 Power-Point Plus	velocity, fps:	2875	2597	2336	2090	1859
	energy, ft-lb:	2570	1997	1697	1358	1075
	arc, inches:		+2.0	0	-8.8	26.0
Win. 140 Fail Safe	velocity, fps:	2760	2506	2271	2048	1839
	energy, ft-lb:	2360	1953	1603	1304	1051
	arc, inches:		+2.0	0	-8.8	-25.9
Win. 140 Ballistic Silvertip	velocity, fps:	2770	2572	2382	2200	2026
	energy, ft-lb:	2386	2056	1764	1504	1276
	arc, inches:		+1.9	0	-8.0	-23.8

7x64 Brenneke

CARTRIDGE BULLET	RANGE, YARDS:	0	100	200	300	400
Federal 160 Nosler Partition	velocity, fps:	2650	2480	2310	2150	2000
	energy, ft-lb:	2495	2180	1895	1640	1415
	arc, inches:		+2.1	0	-8.7	-24.9
Norma 154 Soft Point	velocity, fps:	2821	2605	2399	2203	
	energy, ft-lb:	2722	2321	1969	1660	
	arc, inches:		+1.8	0	-7.8	
Norma 170 Vulkan	velocity, fps:	2756	2501	2259	2031	
	energy, ft-lb:	2868	2361	1927	1558	
	arc, inches:		+2.0	0	-8.8	
Norma 170 Oryx	velocity, fps:	2756	2481	2222	1979	
	energy, ft-lb:	2868	2324	1864	1478	
	arc, inches:		+2.1	0	-9.2	
Norma 170 Plastic Point	velocity, fps:	2756	2519	2294	2081	
	energy, ft-lb:	2868	2396	1987	1635	
	arc, inches:		+2.0	0	-8.6	
Rem. 175 PSP Core-Lokt	velocity, fps:	2650	2445	2248	2061	1883
	energy, ft-lb:	2728	2322	1964	1650	1378
	arc, inches:		+2.2	0	-9.1	-26.4
Speer 160 Grand Slam	velocity, fps:	2600	2376	2164	1962	
	energy, ft-lb:	2401	2006	1663	1368	
	arc, inches:		+2.3	0	-9.8	-28.6
Speer 175 Grand Slam	velocity, fps:	2650	2461	2280	2106	
	energy, ft-lb:	2728	2353	2019	1723	
	arc, inches:		+2.4	0	-9.2	-26.2

7x65 R

CARTRIDGE BULLET	RANGE, YARDS:	0	100	200	300	400
Norma 170 Plastic Point	velocity, fps:	2625	2390	2167	1956	
	energy, ft-lb:	2602	2157	1773	1445	
	arc, inches:		+2.3	0	-9.7	
Norma 170 Vulkan	velocity, fps:	2657	2392	2143	1909	
	energy, ft-lb:	2666	2161	1734	1377	
	arc, inches:		+2.3	0	-9.9	
Norma 170 Oryx	velocity, fps:	2657	2378	2115	1871	
	energy, ft-lb:	2666	2135	1690	1321	
	arc, inches:		+2.3	0	-10.1	

.284 Winchester

CARTRIDGE BULLET	RANGE, YARDS:	0	100	200	300	400
Win. 150 Power-Point	velocity, fps:	2860	2595	2344	2108	1886
	energy, ft-lb:	2724	2243	1830	1480	1185
	arc, inches:		+2.1	0	-8.5	-24.8

.280 Remington

CARTRIDGE BULLET	RANGE, YARDS:	0	100	200	300	400
Federal 140 Sierra Pro-Hunt.	velocity, fps:	2990	2740	2500	2270	2060
	energy, ft-lb:	2770	2325	1940	1605	1320
	arc, inches:		+1.6	0	-7.0	-20.8
Federal 140 Trophy Bonded	velocity, fps:	2990	2630	2310	2040	1730
	energy, ft-lb:	2770	2155	1655	1250	925
	arc, inches:		+1.6	0	-8.4	-25.4
Federal 140 Tr. Bonded HE	velocity, fps:	3150	2850	2570	2300	2050
	energy, ft-lb:	3085	2520	2050	1650	1310
	arc, inches:		+1.4	0	-6.7	-20.0
Federal 150 Hi-Shok	velocity, fps:	2890	2670	2460	2260	2060
	energy, ft-lb:	2780	2370	2015	1695	1420
	arc, inches:		+1.7	0	-7.5	-21.8
Federal 150 Nosler Partition	velocity, fps:	2890	2690	2490	2310	2130
	energy, ft-lb:	2780	2405	2070	1770	1510
	arc, inches:		+1.7,	0	-7.2	-21.1
Federal 160 Trophy Bonded	velocity, fps:	2800	2570	2350	2140	1940
	energy, ft-lb:	2785	2345	1960	1625	1340
	arc, inches:		+1.9	0	-8.3	-24.0
Hornady 139 SPBT LMmoly	velocity, fps:	3110	2888	2675	2473	2280
	energy, ft-lb:	2985	2573	2209	1887	1604
	arc, inches:		+1.4	0	-6.5	-18.6
Norma 170 Vulkan	velocity, fps:	2592	2346	2113	1894	
	energy, ft-lb:	2537	2078	1686	1354	
	arc, inches:		+2.4	0	-10.2	
Norma 170 Oryx	velocity, fps:	2690	2416	2159	1918	
	energy, ft-lb:	2732	2204	1760	1389	
	arc, inches:		+2.2	0	-9.7	
Norma 170 Plastic Point	velocity, fps:	2707	2468	2241	2026	
	energy, ft-lb:	2767	2299	1896	1550	
	arc, inches:		+2.1	0	-9.1	
Rem. 140 PSP Core-Lokt	velocity, fps:	3000	2758	2528	2309	2102
	energy, ft-lb:	2797	2363	1986	1657	1373
	arc, inches:		+1.5	0	-7.0	-20.5
Rem. 140 PSP boat-tail	velocity, fps:	2860	2656	2460	2273	2094
	energy, ft-lb:	2542	2192	1881	1606	1363
	arc, inches:		+1.7	0	-7.5	-21.7
Rem. 140 Nosler Bal. Tip	velocity, fps:	3000	2804	2616	2436	2263
	energy, ft-lb:	2799	2445	2128	1848	1593
	arc, inches:		+1.5	0	-6.8	-19.0
Rem. 150 PSP Core-Lokt	velocity, fps:	2890	2624	2373	2135	1912
	energy, ft-lb:	2781	2293	1875	1518	1217
	arc, inches:		+1.8	0	-8.0	-23.6
Rem. 165 SP Core-Lokt	velocity, fps:	2820	2510	2220	1950	1701
	energy, ft-lb:	2913	2308	1805	1393	1060
	arc, inches:		+2.0	0	-9.1	-27.4
Speer 145 Grand Slam	velocity, fps:	2900	2619	2354	2105	
	energy, ft-lb:	2707	2207	1784	1426	
	arc, inches:		+2.1	0	-8.4	-24.7

Centerfire Rifle Ballistics

.280 Remington to 7mm Remington Magnum

CARTRIDGE BULLET	RANGE, YARDS:	0	100	200	300	400
Speer 160 Grand Slam	velocity, fps:	2890	2652	2425	2210	
	energy, ft-lb:	2967	2497	2089	1735	
	arc, inches:		+1.7	0	-7.7	-22.4
Win. 140 Fail Safe	velocity, fps:	3050	2756	2480	2221	1977
	energy, ft-lb:	2893	2362	1913	1533	1216
	arc, inches:		+1.5	0	-7.2	-21.5
Win. 140 Ballistic Silvertip	velocity, fps:	3040	2842	2653	2471	2297
	energy, ft-lb:	2872	2511	2187	1898	1640
	arc, inches:		+1.4	0	-6.3	-18.4

7mm Remington Magnum

CARTRIDGE BULLET	RANGE, YARDS:	0	100	200	300	400
A-Square 175 Monolithic Solid	velocity, fps:	2860	2557	2273	2008	1771
	energy, ft-lb:	3178	2540	2008	1567	1219
	arc, inches:		+1.92	0	-8.7	-25.9
Black Hills 140 Nos. Bal. Tip	velocity, fps:	3150				
	energy, ft-lb:	3084				
	arc, inches:					
Black Hills 140 Barnes X	velocity, fps:	3150				
	energy, ft-lb:	3084				
	arc, inches:					
Federal 140 Nosler Partition	velocity, fps:	3150	2930	2710	2510	2320
	energy, ft-lb:	3085	2660	2290	1960	1670
	arc, inches:		+1.3	0	-6.0	-17.5
Federal 140 Trophy Bonded	velocity, fps:	3150	2910	2680	2460	2250
	energy, ft-lb:	3085	2630	2230	1880	1575
	arc, inches:		+1.3	0	-6.1	-18.1
Federal 150 Hi-Shok	velocity, fps:	3110	2830	2570	2320	2090
	energy, ft-lb:	3220	2670	2200	1790	1450
	arc, inches:		+1.4	0	-6.7	-19.9
Federal 150 Sierra GameKing BTSP	velocity, fps:	3110	2920	2750	2580	2410
	energy, ft-lb:	3220	2850	2510	2210	1930
	arc, inches:		+1.3	0	-5.9	-17.0
Federal 150 Nosler Bal. Tip	velocity, fps:	3110	2910	2720	2540	2370
	energy, ft-lb:	3220	2825	2470	2150	1865
	arc, inches:		+1.3	0	-6.0	-17.4
Federal 160 Barnes XLC	velocity, fps:	2940	2760	2580	2410	2240
	energy, ft-lb:	3070	2695	2360	2060	1785
	arc, inches:		+1.5	0	-6.8	-19.6
Federal 160 Sierra Pro-Hunt.	velocity, fps:	2940	2730	2520	2320	2140
	energy, ft-lb:	3070	2640	2260	1920	1620
	arc, inches:		+1.6	0	-7.1	-20.6
Federal 160 Nosler Partition	velocity, fps:	2950	2770	2590	2420	2250
	energy, ft-lb:	3090	2715	2375	2075	1800
	arc, inches:		+1.5	0	-6.7	-19.4
Federal 160 Trophy Bonded	velocity, fps:	2940	2660	2390	2140	1900
	energy, ft-lb:	3070	2505	2025	1620	1280
	arc, inches:		+1.7	0	-7.9	-23.3
Federal 165 Sierra GameKing BTSP	velocity, fps:	2950	2800	2650	2510	2370
	energy, ft-lb:	3190	2865	2570	2300	2050
	arc, inches:		+1.5	0	-6.4	-18.4
Federal 175 Hi-Shok	velocity, fps:	2860	2650	2440	2240	2060
	energy, ft-lb:	3180	2720	2310	1960	1640
	arc, inches:		+1.7	0	-7.6	-22.1
Federal 175 Trophy Bonded	velocity, fps:	2860	2600	2350	2120	1900
	energy, ft-lb:	3180	2625	2150	1745	1400
	arc, inches:		+1.8	0	-8.2	-24.0
Hornady 139 SPBT	velocity, fps:	3150	2933	2727	2530	2341
	energy, ft-lb:	3063	2656	2296	1976	1692
	arc, inches:		+1.2	0	-6.1	-17.7
Hornady 139 SST (or Interbond)	velocity, fps:	3150	2948	2754	2569	2391
	energy, ft-lb:	3062	2681	2341	2037	1764
	arc, inches:		+1.1	0	-5.7	-16.7
Hornady 139 SST LM (or Interbond)	velocity, fps:	3250	3044	2847	2657	2475
	energy, ft-lb:	3259	2860	2501	2178	1890
	arc, inches:		+1.1	0	-5.5	-16.2
Hornady 139 SPBT HMmoly	velocity, fps:	3250	3041	2822	2613	2413
	energy, ft-lb:	3300	2854	2458	2106	1797
	arc, inches:		+1.1	0	-5.7	-16.6
Hornady 154 Soft Point	velocity, fps:	3035	2814	2604	2404	2212
	energy, ft-lb:	3151	2708	2319	1977	1674
	arc, inches:		+1.3	0	-6.7	-19.3
Hornady 154 SST (or Interbond)	velocity, fps:	3035	2850	2672	2501	2337
	energy, ft-lb:	3149	2777	2441	2139	1867
	arc, inches:		+1.4	0	-6.5	-18.7
Hornady 162 SP boat-tail	velocity, fps:	2940	2757	2582	2413	2251
	energy, ft-lb:	3110	2735	2399	2095	1823
	arc, inches:		+1.6	0	-6.7	-19.7
Hornady 175 SP	velocity, fps:	2860	2650	2440	2240	2060
	energy, ft-lb:	3180	2720	2310	1960	1640
	arc, inches:		+2.0	0	-7.9	-22.7
Norma 140 Nosler Bal. Tip	velocity, fps:	3150	2936	2732	2537	
	energy, ft-lb:	3085	2680	2320	2001	
	arc, inches:		+1.2	0	-5.9	
Norma 150 Scirocco	velocity, fps:	3117	2934	2758	2589	
	energy, ft-lb:	3237	2869	2535	2234	
	arc, inches:		+1.2	0	-5.8	
Norma 170 Vulkan	velocity, fps:	3018	2747	2493	2252	
	energy, ft-lb:	3439	2850	2346	1914	
	arc, inches:		+1.5	0	-2.8	
Norma 170 Oryx	velocity, fps:	2887	2601	2333	2080	
	energy, ft-lb:	3147	2555	2055	1634	
	arc, inches:		+1.8	0	-8.2	
Norma 170 Plastic Point	velocity, fps:	3018	2762	2519	2290	
	energy, ft-lb:	3439	2880	2394	1980	
	arc, inches:		+1.5	0	-7.0	
PMC 140 Barnes X	velocity, fps:	3000	2808	2624	2448	2279
	energy, ft-lb:	2797	2451	2141	1863	1614
	arc, inches:		+1.5	0	-6.6	18.9
PMC 140 Pointed Soft Point	velocity, fps:	3099	2878	2668	2469	2279
	energy, ft-lb:	2984	2574	2212	1895	1614
	arc, inches:		+1.4	0	-6.2	-18.1
PMC 140 SP boat-tail	velocity, fps:	3125	2891	2669	2457	2255
	energy, ft-lb:	3035	2597	2213	1877	1580
	arc, inches:		+1.4	0	-6.3	-18.4
PMC 160 Barnes X	velocity, fps:	2800	2639	2484	2334	2189
	energy, ft-lb:	2785	2474	2192	1935	1703
	arc, inches:		+1.8	0	-7.4	-21.2
PMC 160 Pointed Soft Point	velocity, fps:	2914	2748	2586	2428	2276
	energy, ft-lb:	3016	2682	2375	2095	1840
	arc, inches:		+1.6	0	-6.7	-19.4
PMC 160 SP boat-tail	velocity, fps:	2900	2696	2501	2314	2135
	energy, ft-lb:	2987	2582	2222	1903	1620
	arc, inches:		+1.7	0	-7.2	-21.0
PMC 175 Pointed Soft Point	velocity, fps:	2860	2645	2442	2244	2957
	energy, ft-lb:	3178	2718	2313	1956	1644
	arc, inches:		+2.0	0	-7.9	-22.7
Rem. 140 PSP Core-Lokt	velocity, fps:	3175	2923	2684	2458	2243
	energy, ft-lb:	3133	2655	2240	1878	1564
	arc, inches:		+2.2	+1.9	-3.2	-14.2

Centerfire Rifle Ballistics

7MM REMINGTON MAGNUM TO 7MM WEATHERBY MAGNUM

CARTRIDGE BULLET	RANGE, YARDS:	0	100	200	300	400
Rem. 140 PSP boat-tail	velocity, fps:	3175	2956	2747	2547	2356
	energy, ft-lb:	3133	2715	2345	2017	1726
	arc, inches:		+2.2	+1.6	-3.1	-13.4
Rem. 150 AccuTip	velocity, fps:	3110	2926	2749	2579	2415
	energy, ft-lb:	3221	2850	2516	2215	1943
	arc, inches:		+1.3	0	-5.9	-17.0
Rem. 150 PSP Core-Lokt	velocity, fps:	3110	2830	2568	2320	2085
	energy, ft-lb:	3221	2667	2196	1792	1448
	arc, inches:		+1.3	0	-6.6	-20.2
Rem. 150 Nosler Bal. Tip	velocity, fps:	3110	2912	2723	2542	2367
	energy, ft-lb:	3222	2825	2470	2152	1867
	arc, inches:		+1.2	0	-5.9	-17.3
Rem. 150 Swift Scirocco	velocity, fps:	3110	2927	2751	2582	2419
	energy, ft-lb:	3221	2852	2520	2220	1948
	arc, inches:		+1.3	0	-5.9	-17.0
Rem. 160 Swift A-Frame	velocity, fps:	2900	2659	2430	2212	2006
	energy, ft-lb:	2987	2511	2097	1739	1430
	arc, inches:		+1.7	0	-7.6	-22.4
Rem. 160 Nosler Partition	velocity, fps:	2950	2752	2563	2381	2207
	energy, ft-lb:	3091	2690	2333	2014	1730
	arc, inches:		+0.6	-1.9	-9.6	-23.6
Rem. 175 PSP Core-Lokt	velocity, fps:	2860	2645	2440	2244	2057
	energy, ft-lb:	3178	2718	2313	1956	1644
	arc, inches:		+1.7	0	-7.6	-22.1
Speer 145 Grand Slam	velocity, fps:	3140	2843	2565	2304	
	energy, ft-lb:	3174	2602	2118	1708	
	arc, inches:		+1.4	0	-6.7	
Speer 175 Grand Slam	velocity, fps:	2850	2653	2463	2282	
	energy, ft-lb:	3156	2734	2358	2023	
	arc, inches:		+1.7	0	-7.5	-21.7
Win. 140 Fail Safe	velocity, fps:	3150	2861	2589	2333	2092
	energy, ft-lb:	3085	2544	2085	1693	1361
	arc, inches:		+1.4	0	-6.6	-19.5
Win. 140 Ballistic Silvertip	velocity, fps:	3100	2889	2687	2494	2310
	energy, ft-lb:	2988	2595	2245	1934	1659
	arc, inches:		+1.3	0	-6.2	-17.9
Win. 150 Power-Point	velocity, fps:	3090	2812	2551	2304	2071
	energy, ft-lb:	3181	2634	2167	1768	1429
	arc, inches:		+1.5	0	-6.8	-20.2
Win. 150 Power-Point Plus	velocity, fps:	3130	2849	2586	2337	2102
	energy, ft-lb:	3264	2705	2227	1819	1472
	arc, inches:		+1.4	0	-6.6	-19.6
Win. 150 Ballistic Silvertip	velocity, fps:	3100	2903	2714	2533	2359
	energy, ft-lb:	3200	2806	2453	2136	1853
	arc, inches:		+1.3	0	-6.0	-17.5
Win. 160 Partition Gold	velocity, fps:	2950	2743	2546	2357	2176
	energy, ft-lb:	3093	2674	2303	1974	1682
	arc, inches:		+1.6	0	-6.9	-20.1
Win. 160 Fail Safe	velocity, fps:	2920	2678	2449	2331	2025
	energy, ft-lb:	3030	2549	2131	1769	1457
	arc, inches:		+1.7	0	-7.5	-22.0
Win. 175 Power-Point	velocity, fps:	2860	2645	2440	2244	2057
	energy, ft-lb:	3178	2718	2313	1956	1644
	arc, inches:		+2.0	0	-7.9	-22.7

7MM REMINGTON SHORT ULTRA MAG

CARTRIDGE BULLET	RANGE, YARDS:	0	100	200	300	400
Rem. 140 PSP C-L Ultra	velocity, fps:	3175	2934	2707	2490	2283
	energy, ft-lb:	3133	2676	2277	1927	1620
	arc, inches:		+1.3	0	-6.0	-17.7
Rem. 150 PSP Core-Lokt	velocity, fps:	3110	2828	2563	2313	2077
	energy, ft-lb:	3221	2663	2188	1782	1437
	arc, inches:		+2.5	+2.1	-3.6	-15.8
Rem. 160 Partition	velocity, fps:	2960	2762	2572	2390	2215
	energy, ft-lb:	3112	2709	2350	2029	1744
	arc, inches:		+2.6	+2.2	-3.6	-15.4

7MM WINCHESTER SHORT MAGNUM

CARTRIDGE BULLET	RANGE, YARDS:	0	100	200	300	400
Win. 140 Bal. Silvertip	velocity, fps:	3225	3008	2801	2603	2414
	energy, ft-lb:	3233	2812	2438	2106	1812
	arc, inches:		+1.2	0	-5.6	-16.4
Win. 150 Power Point	velocity, fps:	3200	2915	2648	2396	2157
	energy, ft-lb:	3410	2830	2335	1911	1550
	arc, inches:		+1.3	0	-6.3	-18.6
Win. 160 Fail Safe	velocity, fps:	2990	2744	2512	2291	2081
	energy, ft-lb:	3176	2675	2241	1864	1538
	arc, inches:		+1.6	0	-7.1	-20.8

7MM WEATHERBY MAG.

CARTRIDGE BULLET	RANGE, YARDS:	0	100	200	300	400
Federal 160 Nosler Partition	velocity, fps:	3050	2850	2650	2470	2290
	energy, ft-lb:	3305	2880	2505	2165	1865
	arc, inches:		+1.4	0	-6.3	-18.4
Federal 160 Sierra GameKing	velocity, fps:	3050	2880	2710	2560	2400
BTSP	energy, ft-lb:	3305	2945	2615	2320	2050
	arc, inches:		+1.4	0	-6.1	-17.4
Federal 160 Trophy Bonded	velocity, fps:	3050	2730	2420	2140	1880
	energy, ft-lb:	3305	2640	2085	1630	1255
	arc, inches:		+1.6	0	-7.6	-22.7
Hornady 154 Soft Point	velocity, fps:	3200	2971	2753	2546	2348
	energy, ft-lb:	3501	3017	2592	2216	1885
	arc, inches:		+1.2	0	-5.8	-17.0
Hornady 154 SST	velocity, fps:	3200	3009	2825	2648	2478
(or Interbond)	energy, ft-lb:	3501	3096	2729	2398	2100
	arc, inches:		+1.2	0	-5.7	-16.5
Hornady 175 Soft Point	velocity, fps:	2910	2709	2516	2331	2154
	energy, ft-lb:	3290	2850	2459	2111	1803
	arc, inches:		+1.6	0	-7.1	-20.6
Wby. 139 Pointed Expanding	velocity, fps:	3340	3079	2834	2601	2380
	energy, ft-lb:	3443	2926	2478	2088	1748
	arc, inches:		+2.9	+3.6	0	-8.7
Wby. 140 Nosler Partition	velocity, fps:	3303	3069	2847	2636	2434
	energy, ft-lb:	3391	2927	2519	2159	1841
	arc, inches:		+2.9	+3.6	0	-8.5
Wby. 150 Nosler Bal. Tip	velocity, fps:	3300	3093	2896	2708	2527
	energy, ft-lb:	3627	3187	2793	2442	2127
	arc, inches:		+2.8	+3.5	0	-8.2
Wby. 150 Barnes X	veloctiy, fps:	3100	2901	2710	2527	2352
	energy, ft-lb:	3200	2802	2446	2127	1842
	arc, inches:		+3.3	+4.0	0	-9.4
Wby. 154 Pointed Expanding	velocity, fps:	3260	3028	2807	2597	2397
	energy, ft-lb:	3634	3134	2694	2307	1964
	arc, inches:		+3.0	+3.7	0	-8.8
Wby. 160 Nosler Partition	velocity, fps:	3200	2991	2791	2600	2417
	energy, ft-lb:	3638	3177	2767	2401	2075
	arc, inches:		+3.1	+3.8	0	-8.9
Wby. 175 Pointed Expanding	velocity, fps:	3070	2861	2662	2471	2288
	energy, ft-lb:	3662	3181	2753	2373	2034
	arc, inches:		+3.5	+4.2	0	-9.9

Centerfire Rifle Ballistics

7mm Dakota to .30-30 Winchester

7mm Dakota

Cartridge Bullet	Range, Yards:	0	100	200	300	400
Dakota 140 Barnes X	velocity, fps:	3500	3253	3019	2798	2587
	energy, ft-lb:	3807	3288	2833	2433	2081
	arc, inches:		+2.0	+2.1	-1.5	-9.6
Dakota 160 Barnes X	velocity, fps:	3200	3001	2811	2630	2455
	energy, ft-lb:	3637	3200	2808	2456	2140
	arc, inches:		+2.1	+1.9	-2.8	-12.5

7mm STW

Cartridge Bullet	Range, Yards:	0	100	200	300	400
A-Square 140 Nos. Bal. Tip	velocity, fps:	3450	3254	3067	2888	2715
	energy, ft-lb:	3700	3291	2924	2592	2292
	arc, inches:		+2.2	+3.0	0	-7.3
A-Square 160 Nosler Part.	velocity, fps:	3250	3071	2900	2735	2576
	energy, ft-lb:	3752	3351	2987	2657	2357
	arc, inches:		+2.8	+3.5	0	-8.2
A-Square 160 SP boat-tail	velocity, fps:	3250	3087	2930	2778	2631
	energy, ft-lb:	3752	3385	3049	2741	2460
	arc, inches:		+2.8	+3.4	0	-8.0
Federal 140 Trophy Bonded	velocity, fps:	3330	3080	2850	2630	2420
	energy, ft-lb:	3435	2950	2520	2145	1815
	arc, inches:		+1.1	0	-5.4	-15.8
Federal 150 Trophy Bonded	velocity, fps:	3250	3010	2770	2560	2350
	energy, ft-lb:	3520	3010	2565	2175	1830
	arc, inches:		+1.2	0	-5.7	-16.7
Federal 160 Sierra GameKing	velocity, fps:	3200	3020	2850	2670	2530
BTSP	energy, ft-lb:	3640	3245	2890	2570	2275
	arc, inches:		+1.1	0	-5.5	-15.7
Rem. 140 PSP Core-Lokt	velocity, fps:	3325	3064	2818	2585	2364
	energy, ft-lb:	3436	2918	2468	2077	1737
	arc, inches:		+2.0	+1.7	-2.9	-12.8
Rem. 140 Swift A-Frame	velocity, fps:	3325	3020	2735	2467	2215
	energy, ft-lb:	3436	2834	2324	1892	1525
	arc, inches:		+2.1	+1.8	-3.1	-13.8
Speer 145 Grand Slam	velocity, fps:	3300	2992	2075	2435	
	energy, ft-lb:	3506	2882	2355	1909	
	arc, inches:		+1.2	0	-6.0	-17.8
Win. 140 Ballistic Silvertip	velocity, fps:	3320	3100	2890	2690	2499
	energy, ft-lb:	3427	2982	2597	2250	1941
	arc, inches:		+1.1	0	-5.2	-15.2
Win. 150 Power-Point	velocity, fps:	3250	2957	2683	2424	2181
	energy, ft-lb:	3519	2913	2398	1958	1584
	arc, inches:		+1.2	0	-6.1	-18.1
Win. 160 Fail Safe	velocity, fps:	3150	2894	2652	2422	2204
	energy, ft-lb:	3526	2976	2499	2085	1727
	arc, inches:		+1.3	0	-6.3	-18.5

7mm Remington Ultra Mag

Cartridge Bullet	Range, Yards:	0	100	200	300	400
Rem. 140 PSP Core-Lokt	velocity, fps:	3425	3158	2907	2669	2444
	energy, ft-lb:	3646	3099	2626	2214	1856
	arc, inches:		+1.8	+1.6	-2.7	-11.9
Rem. 140 Nosler Partition	velocity, fps:	3425	3184	2956	2740	2534
	energy, ft-lb:	3646	3151	2715	2333	1995
	arc, inches:		+1.7	+1.6	-2.6	-11.4
Rem. 160 Nosler Partition	velocity, fps:	3200	2991	2791	2600	2417
	energy, ft-lb:	3637	3177	2767	2401	2075
	arc, inches:		+2.1	+1.8	-3.0	-12.9

7.21 (.284) Firehawk

Cartridge Bullet	Range, Yards:	0	100	200	300	400
Lazzeroni 140 Nosler Part.	velocity, fps:	3580	3349	3130	2923	2724
	energy, ft-lb:	3985	3488	3048	2656	2308
	arc, inches:		+2.2	+2.9	0	-7.0
Lazzeroni 160 Swift A-Fr.	velocity, fps:	3385	3167	2961	2763	2574
	energy, ft-lb:	4072	3565	3115	2713	2354
	arc, inches:		+2.6	+3.3	0	-7.8

7.5x55 Swiss

Cartridge Bullet	Range, Yards:	0	100	200	300	400
Norma 180 Soft Point	velocity, fps:	2651	2432	2223	2025	
	energy, ft-lb:	2810	2364	1976	1639	
	arc, inches:		+2.2	0	-9.3	

7.62x39 Russian

Cartridge Bullet	Range, Yards:	0	100	200	300	400
Federal 123 Hi-Shok	velocity, fps:	2300	2030	1780	1550	1350
	energy, ft-lb:	1445	1125	860	655	500
	arc, inches:		0	-7.0	-25.1	
Federal 124 FMJ	velocity, fps:	2300	2030	1780	1560	1360
	energy, ft-lb:	1455	1135	875	670	510
	arc, inches:		+3.5	0	-14.6	-43.5
Norma 150 Soft Point	velocity, fps:	2953	2622	2314	2028	
	energy, ft-lb:	2905	2291	1784	1370	
	arc, inches:		+1.8	0	-8.3	
Norma 180 Soft Point	velocity, fps:	2575	2360	2154	1960	
	energy, ft-lb:	2651	2226	1856	1536	
	arc, inches:		+2.4	0	-9.9	
PMC 123 FMJ	velocity, fps:	2350	2072	1817	1583	1368
	energy, ft-lb:	1495	1162	894	678	507
	arc, inches:		0	-5.0	-26.4	-67.8
PMC 125 Pointed Soft Point	velocity, fps:	2320	2046	1794	1563	1350
	energy, ft-lb:	1493	1161	893	678	505
	arc, inches:		0	-5.2	-27.5	-70.6
Rem. 125 Pointed Soft Point	velocity, fps:	2365	2062	1783	1533	1320
	energy, ft-lb:	1552	1180	882	652	483
	arc, inches:		0	-6.7	-24.5	
Win. 123 Soft Point	velocity, fps:	2365	2033	1731	1465	1248
	energy, ft-lb:	1527	1129	818	586	425
	arc, inches:		+3.8	0	-15.4	-46.3

.30 Carbine

Cartridge Bullet	Range, Yards:	0	100	200	300	400
Federal 110 Hi-Shok RN	velocity, fps:	1990	1570	1240	1040	920
	energy, ft-lb:	965	600	375	260	210
	arc, inches:		0	-12.8	-46.9	
Federal 110 FMJ	velocity, fps:	1990	1570	1240	1040	920
	energy, ft-lb:	965	600	375	260	210
	arc, inches:		0	-12.8	-46.9	
Magtech 110 FMC	velocity, fps:	1990	1654			
	energy, ft-lb:	965	668			
	arc, inches:		0			
PMC 110 FMJ	velocity, fps:	1927	1548	1248		
	energy, ft-lb:	906	585	380		
	arc, inches:		0	-14.2		
Rem. 110 Soft Point	velocity, fps:	1990	1567	1236	1035	923
	energy, ft-lb:	967	600	373	262	208
	arc, inches:		0	-12.9	-48.6	
Win. 110 Hollow Soft Point	velocity, fps:	1990	1567	1236	1035	923
	energy, ft-lb:	967	600	373	262	208
	arc, inches:		0	-13.5	-49.9	

.30-30 Winchester

Cartridge Bullet	Range, Yards:	0	100	200	300	400
Federal 125 Hi-Shok HP	velocity, fps:	2570	2090	1660	1320	1080
	energy, ft-lb:	1830	1210	770	480	320
	arc, inches:		+3.3	0	-16.0	-50.9
Federal 150 Hi-Shok FN	velocity, fps:	2390	2020	1680	1400	1180
	energy, ft-lb:	1900	1355	945	650	460
	arc, inches:		+3.6	0	-15.9	-49.1

Centerfire Rifle Ballistics

.30-30 Winchester to .308 Winchester

CARTRIDGE BULLET	RANGE, YARDS:	0	100	200	300	400
Federal 170 Hi-Shok RN	velocity, fps:	2200	1900	1620	1380	1190
	energy, ft-lb:	1830	1355	990	720	535
	arc, inches:		+4.1	0	-17.4	-52.4
Federal 170 Sierra Pro-Hunt.	velocity, fps:	2200	1820	1500	1240	1060
	energy, ft-lb:	1830	1255	845	575	425
	arc, inches:		+4.5	0	-20.0	-63.5
Federal 170 Nosler Partition	velocity, fps:	2200	1900	1620	1380	1190
	energy, ft-lb:	1830	1355	990	720	535
	arc, inches:		+4.1	0	-17.4	-52.4
Hornady 150 Round Nose	velocity, fps:	2390	1973	1605	1303	1095
	energy, ft-lb:	1902	1296	858	565	399
	arc, inches:		0	-8.2	-30.0	
Hornady 170 Flat Point	velocity, fps:	2200	1895	1619	1381	1191
	energy, ft-lb:	1827	1355	989	720	535
	arc, inches:		0	-8.9	-31.1	
Norma 150 Soft Point	velocity, fps:	2329	2008	1716	1459	
	energy, ft-lb:	1807	1344	981	709	
	arc, inches:		+3.6	0	-15.5	
PMC 150 Starfire HP	velocity, fps:	2100	1769	1478		
	energy, ft-lb:	1469	1042	728		
	arc, inches:		0	-10.8		
PMC 150 Flat Nose	velocity, fps:	2159	1819	1554		
	energy, ft-lb:	1552	1102	804		
	arc, inches:		0	-9.0		
PMC 170 Flat Nose	velocity, fps:	1965	1680	1480		
	energy, ft-lb:	1457	1065	827		
	arc, inches:		0	-10.7		
Rem. 55 PSP (sabot)	velocity, fps:	3400	2693	2085	1570	1187
"Accelerator"	energy, ft-lb:	1412	886	521	301	172
	arc, inches:		+1.7	0	-9.9	-34.3
Rem. 150 SP Core-Lokt	velocity, fps:	2390	1973	1605	1303	1095
	energy, ft-lb:	1902	1296	858	565	399
	arc, inches:		0	-7.6	-28.8	
Rem. 170 SP Core-Lokt	velocity, fps:	2200	1895	1619	1381	1191
	energy, ft-lb:	1827	1355	989	720	535
	arc, inches:		0	-8.3	-29.9	
Rem. 170 HP Core-Lokt	velocity, fps:	2200	1895	1619	1381	1191
	energy, ft-lb:	1827	1355	989	720	535
	arc, inches:		0	-8.3	-29.9	
Speer 150 Flat Nose	velocity, fps:	2370	2067	1788	1538	
	energy, ft-lb:	1870	1423	1065	788	
	arc, inches:		+3.3	0	-14.4	-43.7
Win. 150 Hollow Point	velocity, fps:	2390	2018	1684	1398	1177
	energy, ft-lb:	1902	1356	944	651	461
	arc, inches:		0	-7.7	-27.9	
Win. 150 Power-Point	velocity, fps:	2390	2018	1684	1398	1177
	energy, ft-lb:	1902	1356	944	651	461
	arc, inches:		0	-7.7	-27.9	
Win. 150 Silvertip	velocity,fps:	2390	2018	1684	1398	1177
	energy, ft-lb:	1902	1356	944	651	461
	arc, inches:		0	-7.7	-27.9	
Win. 150 Power-Point Plus	velocity, fps:	2480	2095	1747	1446	1209
	energy, ft-lb:	2049	1462	1017	697	487
	arc, inches:		0	-6.5	-24.5	
Win. 170 Power-Point	velocity, fps:	2200	1895	1619	1381	1191
	energy, ft-lb:	1827	1355	989	720	535
	arc, inches:		0	-8.9	-31.1	
Win. 170 Silvertip	velocity, fps:	2200	1895	1619	1381	1191
	energy, ft-lb:	1827	1355	989	720	535
	arc, inches:		0	-8.9	-31.1	

.300 Savage

CARTRIDGE BULLET	RANGE, YARDS:	0	100	200	300	400
Federal 150 Hi-Shok	velocity, fps:	2630	2350	2100	1850	1630
	energy, ft-lb:	2305	1845	1460	1145	885
	arc, inches:		+2.4	0	-10.4	-30.9
Federal 180 Hi-Shok	velocity, fps:	2350	2140	1940	1750	1570
	energy, ft-lb:	2205	1825	1495	1215	985
	arc, inches:		+3.1	0	-12.4	-36.1
Rem. 150 PSP Core-Lokt	velocity, fps:	2630	2354	2095	1853	1631
	energy, ft-lb:	2303	1845	1462	1143	806
	arc, inches:		+2.4	0	-10.4	-30.9
Rem. 180 SP Core-Lokt	velocity, fps:	2350	2025	1728	1467	1252
	energy, ft-lb:	2207	1639	1193	860	626
	arc, inches:		+1.5	-4.0	-21.3	-54.8
Win. 150 Power-Point	velocity, fps:	2630	2311	2015	1743	1500
	energy, ft-lb:	2303	1779	1352	1012	749
	arc, inches:		+2.8	0	-11.5	-34.4

.307 Winchester

CARTRIDGE BULLET	RANGE, YARDS:	0	100	200	300	400
Win. 180 Power-Point	velocity, fps:	2510	2179	1874	1599	1362
	energy, ft-lb:	2519	1898	1404	1022	742
	arc, inches:		+1.5	-3.6	-18.6	-47.1

.30-40 Krag

CARTRIDGE BULLET	RANGE, YARDS:	0	100	200	300	400
Rem. 180 PSP Core-Lokt	velocity, fps:	2430	2213	2007	1813	1632
	energy, ft-lb:	2360	1957	1610	1314	1064
	arc, inches, s:		0	-5.6	-18.6	
Win. 180 Power-Point	velocity, fps:	2430	2099	1795	1525	1298
	energy, ft-lb:	2360	1761	1288	929	673
	arc, inches, s:		0	-7.1	-25.0	

.308 Winchester

CARTRIDGE BULLET	RANGE, YARDS:	0	100	200	300	400
Black Hills 150 Nosler B. Tip	velocity, fps:	2800				
	energy, ft-lb:	2611				
	arc, inches:					
Black Hills 165 Nosler B. Tip	velocity, fps:	2650				
(and SP)	energy, ft-lb:	2573				
	arc, inches:					
Black Hills 168 Barnes X	velocity, fps:	2650				
(and Match)energy, ft-lb:	2620					
	arc, inches:					
Black Hills 175 Match	velocity, fps:	2600				
	energy, ft-lb:	2657				
	arc, inches:					
Federal 150 Hi-Shok	velocity, fps:	2820	2530	2260	2010	1770
	energy, ft-lb:	2650	2140	1705	1345	1050
	arc, inches:		+2.0	0	-8.8	-26.3
Federal 150 Nosler Bal. Tip.	velocity, fps:	2820	2610	2410	2220	2040
	energy, ft-lb:	2650	2270	1935	1640	1380
	arc, inches:		+1.8	0	-7.8	-22.7
Federal 150 FMJ boat-tail	velocity, fps:	2820	2620	2430	2250	2070
	energy, ft-lb:	2650	2285	1965	1680	1430
	arc, inches:		+1.8	0	-7.7	-22.4
Federal 150 Barnes XLC	velocity, fps:	2820	2610	2400	2210	2030
	energy, ft-lb:	2650	2265	1925	1630	1370
	arc, inches:		+1.8	0	-7.8	-22.9
Federal 155 Sierra MatchKg.	velocity, fps:	2950	2740	2540	2350	2170
BTHP	energy, ft-lb:	2995	2585	2225	1905	1620
	arc, inches:		+13.2	+23.3	+28.1	+26.5
Federal 165 Sierra GameKing	velocity, fps:	2700	2520	2330	2160	1990
BTSP	energy, ft-lb:	2670	2310	1990	1700	1450
	arc, inches:		+2.0	0	-8.4	-24.3

Centerfire Rifle Ballistics

.308 WINCHESTER

CARTRIDGE BULLET	RANGE, YARDS:	0	100	200	300	400
Federal 165 Trophy Bonded	velocity, fps:	2700	2440	2200	1970	1760
	energy, ft-lb:	2670	2185	1775	1425	1135
	arc, inches:		+2.2	0	-9.4	-27.7
Federal 165 Tr. Bonded HE	velocity, fps:	2870	2600	2350	2120	1890
	energy, ft-lb:	3020	2485	2030	1640	1310
	arc, inches:		+1.8	0	-8.2	-24.0
Federal 168 Sierra MatchKg.	velocity, fps:	2600	2410	2230	2060	1890
BTHP	energy, ft-lb:	2520	2170	1855	1580	1340
	arc, inches:		+17.7	+31.0	+37.2	+35.4
Federal 180 Hi-Shok	velocity, fps:	2620	2390	2180	1970	1780
	energy, ft-lb:	2745	2290	1895	1555	1270
	arc, inches:		+2.3	0	-9.7	-28.3
Federal 180 Sierra Pro-Hunt.	velocity, fps:	2620	2410	2200	2010	1820
	energy, ft-lb:	2745	2315	1940	1610	1330
	arc, inches:		+2.3	0	-9.3	-27.1
Federal 180 Nosler Partition	velocity, fps:	2620	2430	2240	2060	1890
	energy, ft-lb:	2745	2355	2005	1700	1430
	arc, inches:		+2.2	0	-9.2	-26.5
Federal 180 Nosler Part. HE	velocity, fps:	2740	2550	2370	2200	2030
	energy, ft-lb:	3000	2600	2245	1925	1645
	arc, inches:		+1.9	0	-8.2	-23.5
Hornady 110 Urban Tactical	velocity, fps:	3170	2825	2504	2206	1937
	energy, ft-lb:	2454	1950	1532	1189	916
	arc, inches:		+1.5	0	-7.2	-21.2
Hornady 150 SP boat-tail	velocity, fps:	2820	2560	2315	2084	1866
	energy, ft-lb:	2648	2183	1785	1447	1160
	arc, inches:		+2.0	0	-8.5	-25.2
Hornady 150 SST	velocity, fps:	2820	2593	2378	2174	1984
(or Interbond)	energy, ft-lb:	2648	2240	1884	1574	1311
	arc, inches:		+1.9	0	-8.1	-22.9
Hornady 150 SST LM	velocity, fps:	3000	2765	2541	2328	2127
(or Interbond)	energy, ft-lb:	2997	2545	2150	1805	1506
	arc, inches:		+1.5	0	-7.1	-20.6
Hornady 150 SP LM	velocity, fps:	2980	2703	2442	2195	1964
	energy, ft-lb:	2959	2433	1986	1606	1285
	arc, inches:		+1.6	0	-7.5	-22.2
Hornady 155 A-Max	velocity, fps:	2815	2610	2415	2229	2051
	energy, ft-lb:	2727	2345	2007	1709	1448
	arc, inches:		+1.9	0	-7.9	-22.6
Hornady 165 SP boat-tail	velocity, fps:	2700	2496	2301	2115	1937
	energy, ft-lb:	2670	2283	1940	1639	1375
	arc, inches:		+2.0	0	-8.7	-25.2
Hornady 165 SPBT LM	velocity, fps:	2870	2658	2456	2283	2078
	energy, ft-lb:	3019	2589	2211	1877	1583
	arc, inches:		+1.7	0	-7.5	-21.8
Hornady 165 SST LM	velocity, fps:	2880	2672	2474	2284	2103
(or Interbond)	energy, ft-lb:	3038	2616	2242	1911	1620
	arc, inches:		+1.6	0	-7.3	-21.2
Hornady 168 BTHP Match	velocity, fps:	2700	2524	2354	2191	2035
	energy, ft-lb:	2720	2377	2068	1791	1545
	arc, inches:		+2.0	0	-8.4	-23.9
Hornady 168 BTHP Match	velocity, fps:	2640	2630	2429	2238	2056
LM	energy, ft-lb:	3008	2579	2201	1868	1577
	arc, inches:		+1.8	0	-7.8	-22.4
Hornady 168 A-Max Match	velocity fps:	2620	2446	2280	2120	1972
	energy, ft-lb:	2560	2232	1939	1677	1450
	arc, inches:		+2.6	0	-9.2	-25.6
Hornady 168 A-Max	velocity, fps:	2700	2491	2292	2102	1921
	energy, ft-lb:	2719	2315	1959	1648	1377
	arc, inches:		+2.4	0	-9.0	-25.9
Hornady 178 A-Max	velocity, fps:	2965	2778	2598	2425	2259
	energy, ft-lb:	3474	3049	2666	2323	2017
	arc, inches:		+1.6	0	-6.9	-19.8
Hornady 180 A-Max Match	velocity, fps:	2550	2397	2249	2106	1974
	energy, ft-lb:	2598	2295	2021	1773	1557
	arc, inches:		+2.7	0	-9.5	-26.2
Norma 150 Nosler Bal. Tip	velocity, fps:	2822	2588	2365	2154	
	energy, ft-lb:	2653	2231	1864	1545	
			+1.6	0	-7.1	
Norma 150 Soft Point	velocity, fps:	2861	2537	2235	1954	
	energy, ft-lb:	2727	2144	1664	1272	
	arc, inches:		+2.0	0	-9.0	
Norma 165 TXP Swift A-Fr.	velocity, fps:	2700	2459	2231	2015	
	energy, ft-lb:	2672	2216	1824	1488	
	arc, inches:		+2.1	0	-9.1	
Norma 180 Plastic Point	velocity, fps:	2612	2365	2131	1911	
	energy, ft-lb:	2728	2235	1815	1460	
	arc, inches:		+2.4	0	-10.1	
Norma 180 Nosler Partition	velocity, fps:	2612	2414	2225	2044	
	energy, ft-lb:	2728	2330	1979	1670	
	arc, inches:		+2.2	0	-9.3	
Norma 180 Alaska	velocity, fps:	2612	2269	1953	1667	
	energy, ft-lb:	2728	2059	1526	1111	
	arc, inches:		+2.7	0	-11.9	
Norma 180 Vulkan	velocity, fps:	2612	2325	2056	1806	
	energy, ft-lb:	2728	2161	1690	1304	
	arc, inches:		+2.5	0	-10.8	
Norma 180 Oryx	velocity, fps:	2612	2305	2019	1755	
	energy, ft-lb:	2728	2124	1629	1232	
	arc, inches:		+2.5	0	-11.1	
Norma 200 Vulkan	velocity, fps:	2461	2215	1983	1767	
	energy, ft-lb:	2690	2179	1747	1387	
	arc, inches:		+2.8	0	-11.7	
PMC 147 FMJ boat-tail	velocity, fps:	2751	2473	2257	2052	1859
	energy, ft-lb:	2428	2037	1697	1403	1150
	arc, inches:		+2.3	0	-9.3	-27.3
PMC 150 Barnes X	velocity, fps:	2700	2504	2316	2135	1964
	energy, ft-lb:	2428	2087	1786	1518	1284
	arc, inches:		+2.0	0	-8.6	-24.7
PMC 150 Pointed Soft Point	velocity, fps:	2643	2417	2203	1999	1807
	energy, ft-lb:	2326	1946	1615	1331	1088
	arc, inches:		+2.2	0	-9.4	-27.5
PMC 150 SP boat-tail	velocity, fps:	2820	2581	2354	2139	1935
	energy, ft-lb:	2648	2218	1846	1523	1247
	arc, inches:		+1.9	0	-8.2	-24.0
PMC 165 Barnes X	velocity, fps:	2600	2425	2256	2095	1940
	energy, ft-lb:	2476	2154	1865	1608	1379
	arc, inches:		+2.2	0	-9.0	-26.0
PMC 168 HP boat-tail	velocity, fps:	2650	2460	2278	2103	1936
	energy, ft-lb:	2619	2257	1935	1649	1399
	arc, inches:		+2.1	0	--8.8	-25.6
PMC 180 Pointed Soft Point	velocity, fps:	2410	2223	2044	1874	1714
	energy, ft-lb:	2320	1975	1670	1404	1174
	arc, inches:		+2.8	0	-11.1	-32.0
PMC 180 SP boat-tail	velocity, fps:	2620	2446	2278	2117	1962
	energy, ft-lb:	2743	2391	2074	1790	1538
	arc, inches:		+2.2	0	-8.9	-25.4
Rem. 150 PSP Core-Lokt	velocity, fps:	2820	2533	2263	2009	1774
	energy, ft-lb:	2648	2137	1705	1344	1048
	arc, inches:		+2.0	0	-8.8	-26.2

Centerfire Rifle Ballistics

.308 Winchester to .30-06 Springfield

CARTRIDGE BULLET	RANGE, YARDS:	0	100	200	300	400
Rem. 150 PSP C-L Ultra	velocity, fps:	2620	2404	2198	2002	1818
	energy, ft-lb:	2743	2309	1930	1601	1320
	arc, inches:		+2.3	0	-9.5	-26.4
Rem. 150 Swift Scirocco	velocity, fps:	2820	2611	2410	2219	2037
	energy, ft-lb:	2648	2269	1935	1640	1381
	arc, inches:		+1.8	0	-7.8	-22.7
Rem. 165 AccuTip	velocity, fps:	2700	2501	2311	2129	1958
	energy, ft-lb:	2670	2292	1957	1861	1401
	arc, inches:		+2.0	0	-8.6	-24.8
Rem. 165 PSP boat-tail	velocity, fps:	2700	2497	2303	2117	1941
	energy, ft-lb:	2670	2284	1942	1642	1379
	arc, inches:		+2.0	0	-8.6	-25.0
Rem. 165 Nosler Bal. Tip	velocity, fps:	2700	2613	2333	2161	1996
	energy, ft-lb:	2672	2314	1995	1711	1460
	arc, inches:		+2.0	0	-8.4	-24.3
Rem. 165 Swift Scirocco	velocity, fps:	2700	2513	2233	2161	1996
	energy, fps:	2670	2313	1994	1711	1459
	arc, inches:		+2.0	0	-8.4	-24.3
Rem. 168 HPBT Match	velocity, fps:	2680	2493	2314	2143	1979
	energy, ft-lb:	2678	2318	1998	1713	1460
	arc, inches:		+2.1	0	-8.6	-24.7
Rem. 180 SP Core-Lokt	velocity, fps:	2620	2274	1955	1666	1414
	energy, ft-lb:	2743	2066	1527	1109	799
	arc, inches:		+2.6	0	-11.8	-36.3
Rem. 180 PSP Core-Lokt	velocity, fps:	2620	2393	2178	1974	1782
	energy, ft-lb:	2743	2288	1896	1557	1269
	arc, inches:		+2.3	0	-9.7	-28.3
Rem. 180 Nosler Partition	velocity, fps:	2620	2436	2259	2089	1927
	energy, ft-lb:	2743	2371	2039	1774	1485
	arc, inches:		+2.2	0	-9.0	-26.0
Speer 150 Grand Slam	velocity, fps:	2900	2599	2317	2053	
	energy, ft-lb:	2800	2249	1788	1404	
	arc, inches:		+2.1	0	-8.6	-24.8
Speer 165 Grand Slam	velocity, fps:	2700	2475	2261	2057	
	energy, ft-lb:	2670	2243	1872	1550	
	arc, inches:		+2.1	0	-8.9	-25.9
Speer 180 Grand Slam	velocity, fps:	2620	2420	2229	2046	
	energy, ft-lb:	2743	2340	1985	1674	
	arc, inches:		+2.2	0	-9.2	-26.6
Win. 150 Power-Point	velocity, fps:	2820	2488	2179	1893	1633
	energy, ft-lb:	2648	2061	1581	1193	888
	arc, inches:		+2.4	0	-9.8	-29.3
Win. 150 Power-Point Plus	velocity, fps:	2900	2558	2241	1946	1678
	energy, ft-lb:	2802	2180	1672	1262	938
	arc, inches:		+1.9	0	-8.9	-27.0
Win. 150 Partition Gold	velocity, fps:	2900	2645	2405	2177	1962
	energy, ft-lb:	2802	2332	1927	1579	1282
	arc, inches:		+1.7	0	-7.8	-22.9
Win. 150 Ballistic Silvertip	velocity, fps:	2810	2601	2401	2211	2028
	energy, ft-lb:	2629	2253	1920	1627	1370
	arc, inches:		+1.8	0	-7.8	-22.8
Win. 150 Fail Safe	velocity, fps:	2820	2533	2263	2010	1775
	energy, ft-lb:	2649	2137	1706	1346	1049
	arc, inches:		+2.0	0	-8.8	-26.2
Win. 168 Ballistic Silvertip	velocity, fps:	2670	2484	2306	2134	1971
	energy, ft-lb:	2659	2301	1983	1699	1449
	arc, inches:		+2.1	0	-8.6	-24.8
Win. 168 HP boat-tail Match	velocity, fps:	2680	2485	2297	2118	1948
	energy, ft-lb:	2680	2303	1970	1674	1415
	arc, inches:		+2.1	0	-8.7	-25.1
Win. 180 Power-Point	velocity, fps:	2620	2274	1955	1666	1414
	energy, ft-lb:	2743	2066	1527	1109	799
	arc, inches:		+2.9	0	-12.1	-36.9
Win. 180 Silvertip	velocity, fps:	2620	2393	2178	1974	1782
	energy, ft-lb:	2743	2288	1896	1557	1269
	arc, inches:		+2.6	0	-9.9	-28.9

.30-06 Springfield

CARTRIDGE BULLET	RANGE, YARDS:	0	100	200	300	400
A-Square 180 M & D-T	velocity, fps:	2700	2365	2054	1769	1524
	energy, ft-lb:	2913	2235	1687	1251	928
	arc, inches:		+2.4	0	-10.6	-32.4
A-Square 220 Monolythic Solid	velocity, fps:	2380	2108	1854	1623	1424
	energy, ft-lb:	2767	2171	1679	1287	990
	arc, inches:		+3.1	0	-13.6	-39.9
Black Hills 150 Nosler B. Tip	velocity, fps:	2900				
	energy, ft-lb:	2770				
	arc, inches:					
Black Hills 165 Nosler B. Tip	velocity, fps:	2750				
	energy, ft-lb:	2770				
	arc, inches:					
Black Hills 168 Hor. Match	velocity, fps:	2700				
	energy, ft-lb:	2718				
	arc, inches:					
Black Hills 180 Barnes X	velocity, fps:	2650				
	energy, ft-lb:	2806				
	arc, inches:					
Federal 125 Sierra Pro-Hunt.	velocity, fps:	3140	2780	2450	2140	1850
	energy, ft-lb:	2735	2145	1660	1270	955
	arc, inches:		+1.5	0	-7.3	-22.3
Federal 150 Hi-Shok	velocity, fps:	2910	2620	2340	2080	1840
	energy, ft-lb:	2820	2280	1825	1445	1130
	arc, inches:		+1.8	0	-8.2	-24.4
Federal 150 Sierra Pro-Hunt.	velocity, fps:	2910	2640	2380	2130	1900
	energy, ft-lb:	2820	2315	1880	1515	1205
	arc, inches:		+1.7	0	-7.9	-23.3
Federal 150 Sierra GameKing BTSP	velocity, fps:	2910	2690	2480	2270	2070
	energy, ft-lb:	2820	2420	2040	1710	1430
	arc, inches:		+1.7	0	-7.4	-21.5
Federal 150 Nosler Bal. Tip	velocity, fps:	2910	2700	2490	2300	2110
	energy, ft-lb:	2820	2420	2070	1760	1485
	arc, inches:		+1.6	0	-7.3	-21.1
Federal 150 FMJ boat-tail	velocity, fps:	2910	2710	2510	2320	2150
	energy, ft-lb:	2820	2440	2100	1800	1535
	arc, inches:		+1.6	0	-7.1	-20.8
Federal 165 Sierra Pro-Hunt.	velocity, fps:	2800	2560	2340	2130	1920
	energy, ft-lb:	2875	2410	2005	1655	1360
	arc, inches:		+1.9	0	-8.3	-24.3
Federal 165 Sierra GameKing BTSP	velocity, fps:	2800	2610	2420	2240	2070
	energy, ft-lb:	2870	2490	2150	1840	1580
	arc, inches:		+1.8	0	-7.8	-22.4
Federal 165 Sierra GameKing HE	velocity, fps:	3140	2900	2670	2450	2240
	energy, ft-lb:	3610	3075	2610	2200	1845
	arc, inches:		+1.5	0	-6.9	-20.4
Federal 165 Nosler Bal. Tip	velocity, fps:	2800	2610	2430	2250	2080
	energy, ft-lb:	2870	2495	2155	1855	1585
	arc, inches:		+1.8	0	-7.7	-22.3
Federal 165 Trophy Bonded	velocity, fps:	2800	2540	2290	2050	1830
	energy, ft-lb:	2870	2360	1915	1545	1230
	arc, inches:		+2.0	0	-8.7	-25.4

Centerfire Rifle Ballistics

.30-06 Springfield

CARTRIDGE BULLET	RANGE, YARDS:	0	100	200	300	400
Federal 165 Tr. Bonded HE	velocity, fps:	3140	2860	2590	2340	2100
	energy, ft-lb:	3610	2990	2460	2010	1625
	arc, inches:		+1.6	0	-7.4	-21.9
Federal 168 Sierra MatchKg.	velocity, fps:	2700	2510	2320	2150	1980
BTHP	energy, ft-lb:	2720	2350	2010	1720	1460
	arc, inches:		+16.2	+28.4	+34.1	+32.3
Federal 180 Hi-Shok	velocity, fps:	2700	2470	2250	2040	1850
	energy, ft-lb:	2915	2435	2025	1665	1360
	arc, inches:		+2.1	0	-9.0	-26.4
Federal 180 Sierra Pro-Hunt.	velocity, fps:	2700	2350	2020	1730	1470
RN	energy, ft-lb:	2915	2200	1630	1190	860
	arc, inches:		+2.4	0	-11.0	-33.6
Federal 180 Nosler Partition	velocity, fps:	2700	2500	2320	2140	1970
	energy, ft-lb:	2915	2510	2150	1830	1550
	arc, inches:		+2.0	0	-8.6	-24.6
Federal 180 Nosler Part. HE	velocity, fps:	2880	2690	2500	2320	2150
	energy, ft-lb:	3315	2880	2495	2150	1845
	arc, inches:		+1.7	0	-7.2	-21.0
Federal 180 Sierra GameKing	velocity, fps:	2700	2540	2380	2220	2080
BTSP	energy, ft-lb:	2915	2570	2260	1975	1720
	arc, inches:		+1.9	0	-8.1	-23.1
Federal 180 Barnes XLC	velocity, fps:	2700	2530	2360	2200	2040
	energy, ft-lb:	2915	2550	2220	1930	1670
	arc, inches:		+2.0	0	-8.3	-23.8
Federal 180 Trophy Bonded	velocity, fps:	2700	2460	2220	2000	1800
	energy, ft-lb:	2915	2410	1975	1605	1290
	arc, inches:		+2.2	0	-9.2	-27.0
Federal 180 Tr. Bonded HE	velocity, fps:	2880	2630	2380	2160	1940
	energy, ft-lb:	3315	2755	2270	1855	1505
	arc, inches:		+1.8	0	-8.0	-23.3
Federal 220 Sierra Pro-Hunt.	velocity, fps:	2410	2130	1870	1630	1420
RN	energy, ft-lb:	2835	2215	1705	1300	985
	arc, inches:		+3.1	0	-13.1	-39.3
Hornady 150 SP	velocity, fps:	2910	2617	2342	2083	1843
	energy, ft-lb:	2820	2281	1827	1445	1131
	arc, inches:		+2.1	0	-8.5	-25.0
Hornady 150 SP LM	velocity, fps:	3100	2815	2548	2295	2058
	energy, ft-lb:	3200	2639	2161	1755	1410
	arc, inches:		+1.4	0	-6.8	-20.3
Hornady 150 SP boat-tail	velocity, fps:	2910	2683	2467	2262	2066
	energy, ft-lb:	2820	2397	2027	1706	1421
	arc, inches:		+2.0	0	-7.7	-22.2
Hornady 150 SST	velocity, fps:	2910	2802	2599	2405	2219
(or Interbond)	energy, ft-lb:	3330	2876	2474	2118	1803
	arc, inches:		+1.5	0	-6.6	-19.3
Hornady 150 SST LM	velocity, fps:	3100	2860	2631	2414	2208
	energy, ft-lb:	3200	2724	2306	1941	1624
	arc, inches:		+1.4	0	-6.6	-19.2
Hornady 165 SP boat-tail	velocity, fps:	2800	2591	2392	2202	2020
	energy, ft-lb:	2873	2460	2097	1777	1495
	arc, inches:		+1.8	0	-8.0	-23.3
Hornady 165 SPBT LM	velocity, fps:	3015	2790	2575	2370	2176
	energy, ft-lb:	3330	2850	2428	2058	1734
	arc, inches:		+1.6	0	-7.0	-20.1
Hornady 165 SST	velocity, fps:	2800	2598	2405	2221	2046
(or Interbond)	energy, ft-lb:	2872	2473	2119	1808	1534
	arc, inches:		+1.9	0	-8.0	-22.8
Hornady 165 SST LM	velocity, fps:	3015	2802	2599	2405	2219
	energy, ft-lb:	3330	2878	2474	2118	1803
	arc, inches:		+1.5	0	-6.5	-19.3
Hornady 168 HPBT Match	velocity, fps:	2790	2620	2447	2280	2120
	energy, ft-lb:	2925	2561	2234	1940	1677
	arc, inches:		+1.7	0	-7.7	-22.2
Hornady 180 SP	velocity, fps:	2700	2469	2258	2042	1846
	energy, ft-lb:	2913	2436	2023	1666	1362
	arc, inches:		+2.4	0	-9.3	-27.0
Hornady 180 SPBT LM	velocity, fps:	2880	2676	2480	2293	2114
	energy, ft-lb:	3316	2862	2459	2102	1786
	arc, inches:		+1.7	0	-7.3	-21.3
Norma 150 Nosler Bal. Tip	velocity, fps:	2936	2713	2502	2300	
	energy, ft-lb:	2872	2453	2085	1762	
	arc, inches:		+1.6	0	-7.1	
Norma 150 Soft Point	velocity, fps:	2972	2640	2331	2043	
	energy, ft-lb:	2943	2321	1810	1390	
	arc, inches:		+1.8	0	-8.2	
Norma 180 Alaska	velocity, fps:	2700	2351	2028	1734	
	energy, ft-lb:	2914	2209	1645	1202	
	arc, inches:		+2.4	0	-11.0	
Norma 180 Nosler Partition	velocity, fps:	2700	2494	2297	2108	
	energy, ft-lb:	2914	2486	2108	1777	
	arc, inches:		+2.1	0	-8.7	
Norma 180 Plastic Point	velocity, fps:	2700	2455	2222	2003	
	energy, ft-lb:	2914	2409	1974	1603	
	arc, inches:		+2.1	0	-9.2	
Norma 180 Vulkan	velocity, fps:	2700	2416	2150	1901	
	energy, ft-lb:	2914	2334	1848	1445	
	arc, inches:		+2.2	0	-9.8	
Norma 180 Oryx	velocity, fps:	2700	2387	2095	1825	
	energy, ft-lb:	2914	2278	1755	1332	
	arc, inches:		+2.3	0	-10.2	
Norma 180 TXP Swift A-Fr.	velocity, fps:	2700	2479	2268	2067	
	energy, ft-lb:	2914	2456	2056	1708	
	arc, inches:		+2.0	0	-8.8	
Norma 200 Vulkan	velocity, fps:	2641	2385	2143	1916	
	energy, ft-lb:	3098	2527	2040	1631	
	arc, inches:		+2.3	0	-9.9	
Norma 200 Oryx	velocity, fps:	2625	2362	2115	1883	
	energy, ft-lb:	3061	2479	1987	1575	
	arc, inches:		+2.3	0	-10.1	
PMC 150 X-Bullet	velocity, fps:	2750	2552	2361	2179	2005
	energy, ft-lb:	2518	2168	1857	1582	1339
	arc, inches:		+2.0	0	-8.2	-23.7
PMC 150 Pointed Soft Point	velocity, fps:	2773	2542	2322	2113	1916
	energy, ft-lb:	2560	2152	1796	1487	1222
	arc, inches:		+1.9	0	-8.4	-24.6
PMC 150 SP boat-tail	velocity, fps:	2900	2657	2427	2208	2000
	energy, ft-lb:	2801	2351	1961	1623	1332
	arc, inches:		+1.7	0	-7.7	-22.5
PMC 150 FMJ	velocity, fps:	2773	2542	2322	2113	1916
	energy, ft-lb:	2560	2152	1796	1487	1222
	arc, inches:		+1.9	0	-8.4	-24.6
PMC 165 Barnes X	velocity, fps:	2750	2569	2395	2228	2067
	energy, ft-lb:	2770	2418	2101	1818	1565
	arc, inches:		+1.9	0	-8.0	-23.0
PMC 180 Barnes X	velocity, fps:	2650	2487	2331	2179	2034
	energy, ft-lb:	2806	2472	2171	1898	1652
	arc, inches:		+2.1	0	-8.5	-24.3
PMC 180 Pointed Soft Point	velocity, fps:	2550	2357	2172	1996	1829
	energy, ft-lb:	2598	2220	1886	1592	1336
	arc, inches:		+2.4	0	-9.7	-28.2

Centerfire Rifle Ballistics

.30-06 Springfield to .300 H&H Magnum

CARTRIDGE BULLET	RANGE, YARDS:	0	100	200	300	400
PMC 180 SP boat-tail	velocity, fps:	2700	2523	2352	2188	2030
	energy, ft-lb:	2913	2543	2210	1913	1646
	arc, inches:		+2.0	0	-8.3	-23.9
Rem. 55 PSP (sabot)	velocity, fps:	4080	3484	2964	2499	2080
"Accelerator"	energy, ft-lb:	2033	1482	1073	763	528
	arc, inches:		+1.4	+1.4	-2.6	-12.2
Rem. 125 Pointed Soft Point	velocity, fps:	3140	2780	2447	2138	1853
	energy, ft-lb:	2736	2145	1662	1269	953
	arc, inches:		+1.5	0	-7.4	-22.4
Rem. 150 AccuTip	velocity, fps:	2910	2686	2473	2270	2077
	energy, ft-lb:	2820	2403	2037	1716	1436
	arc, inches:		+1.8	0	-7.4	-21.5
Rem. 150 PSP Core-Lokt	velocity, fps:	2910	2617	2342	2083	1843
	energy, ft-lb:	2820	2281	1827	1445	1131
	arc, inches:		+1.8	0	-8.2	-24.4
Rem. 150 Bronze Point	velocity, fps:	2910	2656	2416	2189	1974
	energy, ft-lb:	2820	2349	1944	1596	1298
	arc, inches:		+1.7	0	-7.7	-22.7
Rem. 150 Nosler Bal. Tip	velocity, fps:	2910	2696	2492	2298	2112
	energy, ft-lb:	2821	2422	2070	1769	1485
	arc, inches:		+1.6	0	-7.3	-21.1
Rem. 150 Swift Scirocco	velocity, fps:	2910	2696	2492	2298	2111
	energy, ft-lb:	2820	2421	2069	1758	1485
	arc, inches:		+1.6	0	-7.3	-21.1
Rem. 165 AccuTip	velocity, fps:	2800	2597	2403	2217	2039
	energy, ft-lb:	2872	2470	2115	1800	1523
	arc, inches:		+1.8	0	-7.9	-22.8
Rem. 165 PSP Core-Lokt	velocity, fps:	2800	2534	2283	2047	1825
	energy, ft-lb:	2872	2352	1909	1534	1220
	arc, inches:		+2.0	0	-8.7	-25.9
Rem. 165 PSP boat-tail	velocity, fps:	2800	2592	2394	2204	2023
	energy, ft-lb:	2872	2462	2100	1780	1500
	arc, inches:		+1.8	0	-7.9	-23.0
Rem. 165 Nosler Bal. Tip	velocity, fps:	2800	2609	2426	2249	2080
	energy, ft-lb:	2873	2494	2155	1854	1588
	arc, inches:		+1.8	0	-7.7	-22.3
Rem. 180 SP Core-Lokt	velocity, fps:	2700	2348	2023	1727	1466
	energy, ft-lb:	2913	2203	1635	1192	859
	arc, inches:		+2.4	0	-11.0	-33.8
Rem. 180 PSP Core-Lokt	velocity, fps:	2700	2469	2250	2042	1846
	energy, ft-lb:	2913	2436	2023	1666	1362
	arc, inches:		+2.1	0	-9.0	-26.3
Rem. 180 PSP C-L Ultra	velocity, fps:	2700	2480	2270	2070	1882
	energy, ft-lb:	2913	2457	2059	1713	1415
	arc, inches:		+2.1	0	-8.9	-25.8
Rem. 180 Bronze Point	velocity, fps:	2700	2485	2280	2084	1899
	energy, ft-lb:	2913	2468	2077	1736	1441
	arc, inches:		+2.1	0	-8.8	-25.5
Rem. 180 Swift A-Frame	velocity, fps:	2700	2465	2243	2032	1833
	energy, ft-lb:	2913	2429	2010	1650	1343
	arc, inches:		+2.1	0	-9.1	-26.6
Rem. 180 Nosler Partition	velocity, fps:	2700	2512	2332	2160	1995
	energy, ft-lb:	2913	2522	2174	1864	1590
	arc, inches:		+2.0	0	-8.4	-24.3
Rem. 220 SP Core-Lokt	velocity, fps:	2410	2130	1870	1632	1422
	energy, ft-lb:	2837	2216	1708	1301	988
	arc, inches, s:		0	-6.2	-22.4	
Speer 150 Grand Slam	velocity, fps:	2975	2669	2383	2114	
	energy, ft-lb:	2947	2372	1891	1489	
	arc, inches:		+2.0	0	-8.1	-24.1
Speer 165 Grand Slam	velocity, fps:	2790	2560	2342	2134	
	energy, ft-lb:	2851	2401	2009	1669	
	arc, inches:		+1.9	0	-8.3	-24.1
Speer 180 Grand Slam	velocity, fps:	2690	2487	2293	2108	
	energy, ft-lb:	2892	2472	2101	1775	
	arc, inches:		+2.1	0	-8.8	-25.1
Win. 125 Pointed Soft Point	velocity, fps:	3140	2780	2447	2138	1853
	energy, ft-lb:	2736	2145	1662	1269	953
	arc, inches:		+1.8	0	-7.7	-23.0
Win. 150 Power-Point	velocity, fps:	2920	2580	2265	1972	1704
	energy, ft-lb:	2839	2217	1708	1295	967
	arc, inches:		+2.2	0	-9.0	-27.0
Win. 150 Power-Point Plus	velocity, fps:	3050	2685	2352	2043	1760
	energy, ft-lb:	3089	2402	1843	1391	1032
	arc, inches:		+1.7	0	-8.0	-24.3
Win. 150 Silvertip	velocity, fps:	2910	2617	2342	2083	1843
	energy, ft-lb:	2820	2281	1827	1445	1131
	arc, inches:		+2.1	0	-8.5	-25.0
Win. 150 Partition Gold	velocity, fps:	2960	2705	2464	2235	2019
	energy, ft-lb:	2919	2437	2022	1664	1358
	arc, inches:		+1.6	0	-7.4	-21.7
Win. 150 Ballistic Silvertip	velocity, fps:	2900	2687	2483	2289	2103
	energy, ft-lb:	2801	2404	2054	1745	1473
	arc, inches:		+1.7	0	-7.3	-21.2
Win. 150 Fail Safe	velocity, fps:	2920	2625	2349	2089	1848
	energy, ft-lb:	2841	2296	1838	1455	1137
	arc, inches:		+1.8	0	-8.1	-24.3
Win. 165 Pointed Soft Point	velocity, fps:	2800	2573	2357	2151	1956
	energy, ft-lb:	2873	2426	2036	1696	1402
	arc, inches:		+2.2	0	-8.4	-24.4
Win. 165 Fail Safe	velocity, fps:	2800	2540	2295	2063	1846
	energy, ft-lb:	2873	2365	1930	1560	1249
	arc, inches:		+2.0	0	-8.6	-25.3
Win. 168 Ballistic Silvertip	velocity, fps:	2790	2599	2416	2240	2072
	energy, ft-lb:	2903	2520	2177	1872	1601
	arc, inches:		+1.8	0	-7.8	-22.5
Win. 180 Ballistic Silvertip	velocity, fps:	2750	2572	2402	2237	2080
	energy, ft-lb:	3022	2644	2305	2001	1728
	arc, inches:		+1.9	0	-7.9	-22.8
Win. 180 Power-Point	velocity, fps:	2700	2348	2023	1727	1466
	energy, ft-lb:	2913	2203	1635	1192	859
	arc, inches:		+2.7	0	-11.3	-34.4
Win. 180 Power-Point Plus	velocity, fps:	2770	2563	2366	2177	1997
	energy, ft-lb:	3068	2627	2237	1894	1594
	arc, inches:		+1.9	0	-8.1	-23.6
Win. 180 Silvertip	velocity, fps:	2700	2469	2250	2042	1846
	energy, ft-lb:	2913	2436	2023	1666	1362
	arc, inches:		+2.4	0	-9.3	-27.0
Win. 180 Partition Gold	velocity, fps:	2790	2581	2382	2192	2010
	energy, ft-lb:	3112	2664	2269	1920	1615
	arc, inches:		+1.9	0	-8.0	-23.2
Win. 180 Fail Safe	velocity, fps:	2700	2486	2283	2089	1904
	energy, ft-lb:	2914	2472	2083	1744	1450
	arc, inches:		+2.1	0	-8.7	-25.5

.300 H&H Magnum

CARTRIDGE BULLET	RANGE, YARDS:	0	100	200	300	400
Federal 180 Nosler Partition	velocity, fps:	2880	2620	2380	2150	1930
	energy, ft-lb:	3315	2750	2260	1840	1480
	arc, inches:		+1.8	0	-8.0	-23.4

Centerfire Rifle Ballistics

.300 H&H Magnum to .300 Winchester Magnum

CARTRIDGE BULLET	RANGE, YARDS:	0	100	200	300	400
Win. 180 Fail Safe	velocity, fps:	2880	2628	2390	2165	1952
	energy, ft-lb:	3316	2762	2284	1873	1523
	arc, inches:		+1.8	0	-7.9	-23.2

.308 Norma Magnum

CARTRIDGE BULLET	RANGE, YARDS:	0	100	200	300	400
Norma 180 TXP Swift A-Fr.	velocity, fps:	2953	2704	2469	2245	
	energy, ft-lb:	3486	2924	2437	2016	
	arc, inches:		+1.6	0	-7.3	
Norma 200 Vulkan	velocity, fps:	2903	2624	2361	2114	
	energy, ft-lb:	3744	3058	2476	1985	
	arc, inches:	0	+1.8	0	-8.0	

.300 Winchester Magnum

CARTRIDGE BULLET	RANGE, YARDS:	0	100	200	300	400
A-Square 180 Dead Tough	velocity, fps:	3120	2756	2420	2108	1820
	energy, ft-lb:	3890	3035	2340	1776	1324
	arc, inches:		+1.6	0	-7.6	-22.9
Black Hills 180 Nosler B. Tip	velocity, fps:	3100				
	energy, ft-lb:	3498				
	arc, inches:					
Black Hills 180 Barnes X	velocity, fps:	2950				
	energy, ft-lb:	3498				
	arc, inches:					
Black Hills 190 Match	velocity, fps:	2950				
	energy, ft-lb:	3672				
	arc, inches:					
Federal 150 Sierra Pro Hunt.	velocity, fps:	3280	3030	2800	2570	2360
	energy, ft-lb:	3570	3055	2600	2205	1860
	arc, inches:		+1.1	0	-5.6	-16.4
Federal 150 Trophy Bonded	velocity, fps:	3280	2980	2700	2430	2190
	energy, ft-lb:	3570	2450	2420	1970	1590
	arc, inches:		+1.2	0	-6.0	-17.9
Federal 180 Sierra Pro Hunt.	velocity, fps:	2960	2750	2540	2340	2160
	energy, ft-lb:	3500	3010	2580	2195	1860
	arc, inches:		+1.6	0	-7.0	-20.3
Federal 180 Barnes XLC	velocity, fps:	2960	2780	2600	2430	2260
	energy, ft-lb:	3500	3080	2700	2355	2050
	arc, inches:		+1.5	0	-6.6	-19.2
Federal 180 Trophy Bonded	velocity, fps:	2960	2700	2460	2220	2000
	energy, ft-lb:	3500	2915	2410	1975	1605
	arc, inches:		+1.6	0	-7.4	-21.9
Federal 180 Tr. Bonded HE	velocity, fps:	3100	2830	2580	2340	2110
	energy, ft-lb:	3840	3205	2660	2190	1790
	arc, inches:		+1.4	0	-6.6	-19.7
Federal 180 Nosler Partition	velocity, fps:	2960	2700	2450	2210	1990
	energy, ft-lb:	3500	2905	2395	1955	1585
	arc, inches:		+1.6	0	-7.5	-22.1
Federal 190 Sierra MatchKg. BTHP	velocity, fps:	2900	2730	2560	2400	2240
	energy, ft-lb:	3550	3135	2760	2420	2115
	arc, inches:		+12.9	+22.5	+26.9	+25.1
Federal 200 Sierra GameKing BTSP	velocity, fps:	2830	2680	2530	2380	2240
	energy, ft-lb:	3560	3180	2830	2520	2230
	arc, inches:		+1.7	0	-7.1	-20.4
Federal 200 Nosler Part. HE	velocity, fps:	2930	2740	2550	2370	2200
	energy, ft-lb:	3810	3325	2885	2495	2145
	arc, inches:		+1.6	0	-6.9	-20.1
Federal 200 Trophy Bonded	velocity, fps:	2800	2570	2350	2150	1950
	energy, ft-lb:	3480	2935	2460	2050	1690
	arc, inches:		+1.9	0	-8.2	-23.9
Hornady 150 SP boat-tail	velocity, fps:	3275	2988	2718	2464	2224
	energy, ft-lb:	3573	2974	2461	2023	1648
	arc, inches:		+1.2	0	-6.0	-17.8
Hornady 150 SST (and Interbond)	velocity, fps:	3275	3027	2791	2565	2352
	energy, ft-lb:	3572	3052	2593	2192	1842
	arc, inches:		+1.2	0	-5.8	-17.0
Hornady 165 SP boat-tail	velocity, fps:	3100	2877	2665	2462	2269
	energy, ft-lb:	3522	3033	2603	2221	1887
	arc, inches:		+1.3	0	-6.5	-18.5
Hornady 165 SST	velocity, fps:	3100	2885	2680	2483	2296
	energy, ft-lb:	3520	3049	2630	2259	1930
	arc, inches:		+1.4	0	-6.4	-18.6
Hornady 180 SP boat-tail	velocity, fps:	2960	2745	2540	2344	2157
	energy, ft-lb:	3501	3011	2578	2196	1859
	arc, inches:		+1.9	0	-7.3	-20.9
Hornady 180 SST	velocity, fps:	2960	2764	2575	2395	2222
	energy, ft-lb:	3501	3052	2650	2292	1974
	arc, inches:		+1.6	0	-7.0	-20.1
Hornady 180 SPBT HM	velocity, fps:	3100	2879	2668	2467	2275
	energy, ft-lb:	3840	3313	2845	2431	2068
	arc, inches:		+1.4	0	-6.4	-18.7
Hornady 190 SP boat-tail	velocity, fps:	2900	2711	2529	2355	2187
	energy, ft-lb:	3549	3101	2699	2340	2018
	arc, inches:		+1.6	0	-7.1	-20.4
Norma 150 Nosler Bal. Tip	velocity, fps:	3250	3014	2791	2578	
	energy, ft-lb:	3519	3027	2595	2215	
	arc, inches:		+1.1	0	-5.6	
Norma 165 Scirocco	velocity, fps:	3117	2921	2734	2554	
	energy, ft-lb:	3561	3127	2738	2390	
	arc, inches:		+1.2	0	-5.9	
Norma 180 Soft Point	velocity, fps:	3018	2780	2555	2341	
	energy, ft-lb:	3641	3091	2610	2190	
	arc, inches:		+1.5	0	-7.0	
Norma 180 Plastic Point	velocity, fps:	3018	2755	2506	2271	
	energy, ft-lb:	3641	3034	2512	2062	
	arc, inches:		+1.6	0	-7.1	
Norma 180 TXP Swift A-Fr.	velocity, fps:	2920	2688	2467	2256	
	energy, ft-lb:	3409	2888	2432	2035	
	arc, inches:		+1.7	0	-7.4	
Norma 200 Vulkan	velocity, fps:	2887	2609	2347	2100	
	energy, ft-lb:	3702	3023	2447	1960	
	arc, inches:		+1.8	0	-8.2	
Norma 200 Oryx	velocity, fps:	3018	2755	2506	2271	
	energy, ft-lb:	4046	3371	2791	2292	
	arc, inches:		+1.5	0	-7.0	
PMC 150 Barnes X	velocity, fps:	3135	2918	2712	2515	2327
	energy, ft-lb:	3273	2836	2449	2107	1803
	arc, inches:		+1.3	0	-6.1	-17.7
PMC 150 Pointed Soft Point	velocity, fps:	3150	2902	2665	2438	2222
	energy, ft-lb:	3304	2804	2364	1979	1644
	arc, inches:		+1.3	0	-6.2	-18.3
PMC 150 SP boat-tail	velocity, fps:	3250	2987	2739	2504	2281
	energy, ft-lb:	3517	2970	2498	2088	1733
	arc, inches:		+1.2	0	-6.0	-17.4
PMC 180 Barnes X	velocity, fps:	2910	2738	2572	2412	2258
	energy, ft-lb:	3384	2995	2644	2325	2037
	arc, inches:		+1.6	0	-6.9	-19.8
PMC 180 PSP	velocity, fps:	2853	2643	2446	2258	2077
	energy, ft-lb:	3252	2792	2391	2037	1724
	arc, inches:		+1.7	0	-7.5	-21.9
PMC 180 SP boat-tail	velocity, fps:	2900	2714	2536	2365	2200
	energy, ft-lb:	3361	2944	2571	2235	1935
	arc, inches:		+1.6	0	-7.1	-20.3

Centerfire Rifle Ballistics

.300 Winchester Magnum to .300 Weatherby Magnum

CARTRIDGE BULLET	RANGE, YARDS:	0	100	200	300	400
Rem. 150 PSP Core-Lokt	velocity, fps:	3290	2951	2636	2342	2068
	energy, ft-lb:	3605	2900	2314	1827	1859
	arc, inches:		+1.6	0	-7.0	-20.2
Rem. 180 AccuTip	velocity, fps:	2960	2764	2577	2397	2224
	energy, ft-lb:	3501	3053	2653	2295	1976
	arc, inches:		+1.5	0	-6.8	-19.6
Rem. 180 PSP Core-Lokt	velocity, fps:	2960	2745	2540	2344	2157
	energy, ft-lb:	3501	3011	2578	2196	1424
	arc, inches:		+2.2	+1.9	-3.4	-15.0
Rem. 180 PSP C-L Ultra	velocity, fps:	2960	2727	2505	2294	2093
	energy, ft-lb:	3501	2971	2508	2103	1751
	arc, inches:		+2.7	+2.2	-3.8	-16.4
Rem. 180 Nosler Partition	velocity, fps:	2960	2725	2503	2291	2089
	energy, ft-lb:	3501	2968	2503	2087	1744
	arc, inches:		+1.6	0	-7.2	-20.9
Rem. 180 Nosler Bal. Tip	velocity, fps:	2960	2774	2595	2424	2259
	energy, ft-lb:	3501	3075	2692	2348	2039
	arc, inches:		+1.5	0	-6.7	-19.3
Rem. 180 Swift Scirocco	velocity, fps:	2960	2774	2595	2424	2259
	energy, ft-lb:	3501	3075	2692	2348	2039
	arc, inches:		+1.5	0	-6.7	-19.3
Rem. 190 PSP boat-tail	velocity, fps:	2885	2691	2506	2327	2156
	energy, ft-lb:	3511	3055	2648	2285	1961
	arc, inches:		+1.6	0	-7.2	-20.8
Rem. 200 Swift A-Frame	velocity, fps:	2825	2595	2376	2167	1970
	energy, ft-lb:	3544	2989	2506	2086	1722
	arc, inches:		+1.8	0	-8.0	-23.5
Speer 180 Grand Slam	velocity, fps:	2950	2735	2530	2334	
	energy, ft-lb:	3478	2989	2558	2176	
	arc, inches:		+1.6	0	-7.0	-20.5
Speer 200 Grand Slam	velocity, fps:	2800	2597	2404	2218	
	energy, ft-lb:	3481	2996	2565	2185	
	arc, inches:		+1.8	0	-7.9	-22.9
Win. 150 Power-Point	velocity, fps:	3290	2951	2636	2342	2068
	energy, ft-lb:	3605	2900	2314	1827	1424
	arc, inches:		+2.6	+2.1	-3.5	-15.4
Win. 150 Fail Safe	velocity, fps:	3260	2943	2647	2370	2110
	energy, ft-lb:	3539	2884	2334	1871	1483
	arc, inches:		+1.3	0	-6.2	-18.7
Win. 165 Fail Safe	velocity, fps:	3120	2807	2515	2242	1985
	energy, ft-lb:	3567	2888	2319	1842	1445
	arc, inches:		+1.5	0	-7.0	-20.0
Win. 180 Power-Point	velocity, fps:	2960	2745	2540	2344	2157
	energy, ft-lb:	3501	3011	2578	2196	1859
	arc, inches:		+1.9	0	-7.3	-20.9
Win. 180 Power-Point Plus	velocity, fps:	3070	2846	2633	2430	2236
	energy, ft-lb:	3768	3239	2772	2361	1999
	arc, inches:		+1.4	0	-6.4	-18.7
Win. 180 Ballistic Silvertip	velocity, fps:	2950	2764	2586	2415	2250
	energy, ft-lb:	3478	3054	2673	2331	2023
	arc, inches:		+1.5	0	-6.7	-19.4
Win. 180 Fail Safe	velocity, fps:	2960	2732	2514	2307	2110
	energy, ft-lb:	3503	2983	2528	2129	1780
	arc, inches:		+1.6	0	-7.1	-20.7
Win. 180 Partition Gold	velocity, fps:	3070	2859	2657	2464	2280
	energy, ft-lb:	3768	3267	2823	2428	2078
	arc, inches:		+1.4	0	-6.3	-18.3

.300 Remington Short Ultra Mag

CARTRIDGE BULLET	RANGE, YARDS:	0	100	200	300	400
Rem. 150 PSP C-L Ultra	velocity, fps:	3200	2901	2672	2359	2112
	energy, ft-lb:	3410	2803	2290	1854	1485
	arc, inches:		+1.3	0	-6.4	-19.1
Rem. 165 PSP Core-Lokt	velocity, fps:	3075	2792	2527	2276	2040
	energy, ft-lb:	3464	2856	2339	1828	1525
	arc, inches:		+1.5	0	-7.0	-20.7
Rem. 180 Partition	velocity, fps:	2960	2761	2571	2389	2214
	energy, ft-lb:	3501	3047	2642	2280	1959
	arc, inches:		+1.5	0	-6.8	-19.7

.300 Winchester Short Magnum

CARTRIDGE BULLET	RANGE, YARDS:	0	100	200	300	400
Federal 150 Nosler Bal. Tip	velocity, fps:	3200	2970	2755	2545	2345
	energy, ft-lb:	3410	2940	2520	2155	1830
	arc, inches:		+1.2	0	-5.8	-17.0
Federal 180 Grand Slam	velocity, fps:	2970	2740	2530	2320	2130
	energy, ft-lb:	3525	3010	2555	2155	1810
	arc, inches:		+1.5	0	-7.0	-20.5
Federal 180 Trophy Bonded	velocity, fps:	2970	2730	2500	2280	2080
	energy, ft-lb:	3525	2975	2500	2085	1725
	arc, inches:		+1.5	0	-7.2	-21.0
Federal 180 Nosler Partition	velocity, fps:	2975	2750	2535	2290	2126
	energy, ft-lb:	3540	3025	2570	2175	1825
	arc, inches:		+1.5	0	-7.0	-20.3
Federal 180 Hi-Shok SP	velocity, fps:	2970	2520	2115	1750	1430
	energy, ft-lb:	3525	2540	1785	1220	820
	arc, inches:		+2.2	0	-9.9	-31.4
Win. 150 Ballistic Silvertip	velocity, fps:	3300	3061	2834	2619	2414
	energy, ft-lb:	3628	3121	2676	2285	1941
	arc, inches:		+1.1	0	-5.4	-15.9
Win. 180 Ballistic Silvetip	velocity, fps:	3010	2822	2641	2468	2301
	energy, ft-lb:	3621	3182	2788	2434	2116
	arc, inches:		+1.4	0	-6.4	-18.6
Win. 180 Fail Safe	velocity, fps:	2970	2741	2524	2317	2120
	energy, ft-lb:	3526	3005	2547	2147	1797
	arc, inches:		+1.6	0	-7.0	-20.5
Win. 180 Power Point	velocity, fps:	2970	2755	2549	2353	2166
	energy, ft-lb:	3526	3034	2598	2214	1875
	arc, inches:		+1.5	0	-6.9	-20.1

.300 Weatherby Magnum

CARTRIDGE BULLET	RANGE, YARDS:	0	100	200	300	400
A-Square 180 Dead Tough	velocity, fps:	3180	2811	2471	2155	1863
	energy, ft-lb:	4041	3158	2440	1856	1387
	arc, inches:		+1.5	0	-7.2	-21.8
A-Square 220 Monolythic Solid	velocity, fps:	2700	2407	2133	1877	1653
	energy, ft-lb:	3561	2830	2223	1721	1334
	arc, inches:		+2.3	0	-9.8	-29.7
Federal 180 Sierra GameKing BTSP	velocity, fps:	3190	3010	2830	2660	2490
	energy, ft-lb:	4065	3610	3195	2820	2480
	arc, inches:		+1.2	0	-5.6	-16.0
Federal 180 Trophy Bonded	velocity, fps:	3190	2950	2720	2500	2290
	energy, ft-lb:	4065	3475	2955	2500	2105
	arc, inches:		+1.3	0	-5.9	-17.5
Federal 180 Tr. Bonded HE	velocity, fps:	3330	3080	2850	2750	2410
	energy, ft-lb:	4430	3795	3235	2750	2320
	arc, inches:		+1.1	0	-5.4	-15.8
Federal 180 Nosler Partition	velocity, fps:	3190	2980	2780	2590	2400
	energy, ft-lb:	4055	3540	3080	2670	2305
	arc, inches:		+1.2	0	-5.7	-16.7

Centerfire Rifle Ballistics

.338 Winchester Magnum to 7.65x53 Argentine

CARTRIDGE BULLET	RANGE, YARDS:	0	100	200	300	400
Federal 180 Nosler Part. HE	velocity, fps:	3330	3110	2810	2710	2520
	energy, ft-lb:	4430	3875	3375	2935	2540
	arc, inches:		+1.0	0	-5.2	-15.1
Federal 200 Trophy Bonded	velocity, fps:	2900	2670	2440	2230	2030
	energy, ft-lb:	3735	3150	2645	2200	1820
	arc, inches:		+1.7	0	-7.6	-22.2
Hornady 150 SST	velocity, fps:	3375	3123	2882	2652	2434
(or Interbond)	energy, ft-lb:	3793	3248	2766	2343	1973
	arc, inches:		+1.0	0	-5.4	-15.8
Hornady 180 SP	velocity, fps:	3120	2891	2673	2466	2268
	energy, ft-lb:	3890	3340	2856	2430	2055
	arc, inches:		+1.3	0	-6.2	-18.1
Hornady 180 SST	velocity, fps:	3120	2911	2711	2519	2335
	energy, ft-lb:	3890	3386	2936	2535	2180
	arc, inches:		+1.3	0	-6.2	-18.1
Rem. 180 PSP Core-Lokt	velocity, fps:	3120	2866	2627	2400	2184
	energy, ft-lb:	3890	3284	2758	2301	1905
	arc, inches:		+2.4	+2.0	-3.4	-14.9
Rem. 190 PSP boat-tail	velocity, fps:	3030	2830	2638	2455	2279
	energy, ft-lb:	3873	3378	2936	2542	2190
	arc, inches:		+1.4	0	-6.4	-18.6
Rem. 200 Swift A-Frame	velocity, fps:	2925	2690	2467	2254	2052
	energy, ft-lb:	3799	3213	2701	2256	1870
	arc, inches:		+2.8	+2.3	-3.9	-17.0
Speer 180 Grand Slam	velocity, fps:	3185	2948	2722	2508	
	energy, ft-lb:	4054	3472	2962	2514	
	arc, inches:		+1.3	0	-5.9	-17.4
Wby. 150 Pointed Expanding	velocity, fps:	3540	3225	2932	2657	2399
	energy, ft-lb:	4173	3462	2862	2351	1916
	arc, inches:		+2.6	+3.3	0	-8.2
Wby. 150 Nosler Partition	velocity, fps:	3540	3263	3004	2759	2528
	energy, ft-lb:	4173	3547	3005	2536	2128
	arc, inches:		+2.5	+3.2	0	-7.7
Wby. 165 Pointed Expanding	velocity, fps:	3390	3123	2872	2634	2409
	energy, ft-lb:	4210	3573	3021	2542	2126
	arc, inches:		+2.8	+3.5	0	-8.5
Wby. 165 Nosler Bal. Tip	velocity, fps:	3350	3133	2927	2730	2542
	energy, ft-lb:	4111	3596	3138	2730	2367
	arc, inches:		+2.7	+3.4	0	-8.1
Wby. 180 Pointed Expanding	velocity, fps:	3240	3004	2781	2569	2366
	energy, ft-lb:	4195	3607	3091	2637	2237
	arc, inches:		+3.1	+3.8	0	-9.0
Wby. 180 Barnes X	velocity, fps:	3190	2995	2809	2631	2459
	energy, ft-lb:	4067	3586	3154	2766	2417
	arc, inches:		+3.1	+3.8	0	-8.7
Wby. 180 Nosler Partition	velocity, fps:	3240	3028	2826	2634	2449
	energy, ft-lb:	4195	3665	3193	2772	2396
	arc, inches:		+3.0	+3.7	0	-8.6
Wby. 200 Nosler Partition	velocity, fps:	3060	2860	2668	2485	2308
	energy, ft-lb:	4158	3631	3161	2741	2366
	arc, inches:		+3.5	+4.2	0	-9.8
Wby. 220 RN Expanding	velocity, fps:	2845	2543	2260	1996	1751
	energy, ft-lb:	3954	3158	2495	1946	1497
	arc, inches:		+4.9	+5.9	0	-14.6

.300 Dakota

CARTRIDGE BULLET	RANGE, YARDS:	0	100	200	300	400
Dakota 165 Barnes X	velocity, fps:	3200	2979	2769	2569	2377
	energy, ft-lb:	3751	3251	2809	2417	2070
	arc, inches:		+2.1	+1.8	-3.0	-13.2
Dakota 200 Barnes X	velocity, fps:	3000	2824	2656	2493	2336
	energy, ft-lb:	3996	3542	3131	2760	2423
	arc, inches:		+2.2	+1.5	-4.0	-15.2

.300 Pegasus

CARTRIDGE BULLET	RANGE, YARDS:	0	100	200	300	400
A-Square 180 SP boat-tail	velocity, fps:	3500	3319	3145	2978	2817
	energy, ft-lb:	4896	4401	3953	3544	3172
	arc, inches:		+2.3	+2.9	0	-6.8
A-Square 180 Nosler Part.	velocity, fps:	3500	3295	3100	2913	2734
	energy, ft-lb:	4896	4339	3840	3392	2988
	arc, inches:		+2.3	+3.0	0	-7.1
A-Square 180 Dead Tough	velocity, fps:	3500	3103	2740	2405	2095
	energy, ft-lb:	4896	3848	3001	2312	1753
	arc, inches:		+1.1	0	-5.7	-17.5

.300 Remington Ultra Mag

CARTRIDGE BULLET	RANGE, YARDS:	0	100	200	300	400
Federal 180 Trophy Bonded	velocity, fps:	3250	3000	2770	2550	2340
	energy, ft-lb:	4220	3605	3065	2590	2180
	arc, inches:		+1.2	0	-5.7	-16.8
Rem. 150 Swift Scirocco	velocity, fps:	3450	3208	2980	2762	2556
	energy, ft-lb:	3964	3427	2956	2541	2175
	arc, inches:		+1.7	+1.5	-2.6	-11.2
Rem. 180 Nosler Partition	velocity, fps:	3250	3037	2834	2640	2454
	energy, ft-lb:	4221	3686	3201	2786	2407
	arc, inches:		+2.4	+1.8	-3.0	-12.7
Rem. 180 Swift Scirocco	velocity, fps:	3250	3048	2856	2672	2495
	energy, ft-lb:	4221	3714	3260	2853	2487
	arc, inches:		+2.0	+1.7	-2.8	-12.3
Rem. 180 PSP Core-Lokt	velocity, fps:	3250	2988	2742	2508	2287
	energy, ft-lb:	3517	2974	2503	2095	1741
	arc, inches:		+2.1	+1.8	-3.1	-13.6
Rem. 200 Nosler Partition	velocity, fps:	3025	2826	2636	2454	2279
	energy, ft-lb:	4063	3547	3086	2673	2308
	arc, inches:		+2.4	+2.0	-3.4	-14.6

.30-378 Weatherby Magnum

CARTRIDGE BULLET	RANGE, YARDS:	0	100	200	300	400
Wby. 165 Nosler Bal. Tip	velocity, fps:	3500	3275	3062	2859	2665
	energy, ft-lb:	4488	3930	3435	2995	2603
	arc, inches:		+2.4	+3.0	0	-7.4
Wby. 180 Barnes X	velocity, fps:	3450	3243	3046	2858	2678
	energy, ft-lb:	4757	4204	3709	3264	2865
	arc, inches:		+2.4	+3.1	0	-7.4
Wby. 200 Nosler Partition	velocity, fps:	3160	2955	2759	2572	2392
	energy, ft-lb:	4434	3877	3381	2938	2541
	arc, inches:		+3.2	+3.9	0	-9.1

7.82 (.308) Warbird

CARTRIDGE BULLET	RANGE, YARDS:	0	100	200	300	400
Lazzeroni 150 Nosler Part.	velocity, fps:	3680	3432	3197	2975	2764
	energy, ft-lb:	4512	3923	3406	2949	2546
	arc, inches:		+2.1	+2.7	0	-6.6
Lazzeroni 180 Nosler Part.	velocity, fps:	3425	3220	3026	2839	2661
	energy, ft-lb:	4689	4147	3661	3224	2831
	arc, inches:		+2.5	+3.2	0	-7.5
Lazzeroni 200 Swift A-Fr.	velocity, fps:	3290	3105	2928	2758	2594
	energy, ft-lb:	4808	4283	3808	3378	2988
	arc, inches:		+2.7	+3.4	0	-7.9

7.65x53 Argentine

CARTRIDGE BULLET	RANGE, YARDS:	0	100	200	300	400
Norma 180 Soft Point	velocity, fps:	2592	2386	2189	2002	
	energy, ft-lb:	2686	2276	1916	1602	
	arc, inches:		+2.3	0	-9.6	

.303 British

CARTRIDGE BULLET	RANGE, YARDS:	0	100	200	300	400
Federal 150 Hi-Shok	velocity, fps:	2690	2440	2210	1980	1780
	energy, ft-lb:	2400	1980	1620	1310	1055
	arc, inches:		+2.2	0	-9.4	-27.6
Federal 180 Sierra Pro-Hunt.	velocity, fps:	2460	2230	2020	1820	1630
	energy, ft-lb:	2420	1995	1625	1315	1060
	arc, inches:		+2.8	0	-11.3	-33.2
Federal 180 Tr. Bonded HE	velocity, fps:	2590	2350	2120	1900	1700
	energy, ft-lb:	2680	2205	1795	1445	1160
	arc, inches:		+2.4	0	-10.0	-30.0
Hornady 150 Soft Point	velocity, fps:	2685	2441	2210	1992	1787
	energy, ft-lb:	2401	1984	1627	1321	1064
	arc, inches:		+2.2	0	-9.3	-27.4
Hornady 150 SP LM	velocity, fps:	2830	2570	2325	2094	1884
	energy, ft-lb:	2667	2199	1800	1461	1185
	arc, inches:		+2.0	0	-8.4	-24.6
Norma 150 Soft Point	velocity, fps:	2723	2438	2170	1920	
	energy, ft-lb:	2470	1980	1569	1228	
	arc, inches:		+2.2	0	-9.6	
PMC 180 SP boat-tail	velocity, fps:	2450	2276	2110	1951	1799
	energy, ft-lb:	2399	2071	1779	1521	1294
	arc, inches:		+2.6	0	-10.4	-30.1
Rem. 180 SP Core-Lokt	velocity, fps:	2460	2124	1817	1542	1311
	energy, ft-lb:	2418	1803	1319	950	687
	arc, inches, s:		0	-5.8	-23.3	
Win. 180 Power-Point	velocity, fps:	2460	2233	2018	1816	1629
	energy, ft-lb:	2418	1993	1627	1318	1060
	arc, inches, s:		0	-6.1	-20.8	

7.7x58 Japanese Arisaka

CARTRIDGE BULLET	RANGE, YARDS:	0	100	200	300	400
Norma 180 Soft Point	velocity, fps:	2493	2291	2099	1916	
	energy, ft-lb:	2485	2099	1761	1468	
	arc, inches:		+2.6	0	-10.5	

.32-20 Winchester

CARTRIDGE BULLET	RANGE, YARDS:	0	100	200	300	400
Rem. 100 Lead	velocity, fps:	1210	1021	913	834	769
	energy, ft-lb:	325	231	185	154	131
	arc, inches:		0	-31.6	-104.7	
Win. 100 Lead	velocity, fps:	1210	1021	913	834	769
	energy, ft-lb:	325	231	185	154	131
	arc, inches:		0	-32.3	-106.3	

.32 Winchester Special

CARTRIDGE BULLET	RANGE, YARDS:	0	100	200	300	400
Federal 170 Hi-Shok	velocity, fps:	2250	1920	1630	1370	1180
	energy, ft-lb:	1910	1395	1000	710	520
	arc, inches:		0	-8.0	-29.2	
Rem. 170 SP Core-Lokt	velocity, fps:	2250	1921	1626	1372	1175
	energy, ft-lb:	1911	1393	998	710	521
	arc, inches:		0	-8.0	-29.3	
Win. 170 Power-Point	velocity, fps:	2250	1870	1537	1267	1082
	energy, ft-lb:	1911	1320	892	606	442
	arc, inches:		0	-9.2	-33.2	

8mm Mauser (8x57)

CARTRIDGE BULLET	RANGE, YARDS:	0	100	200	300	400
Federal 170 Hi-Shok	velocity, fps:	2360	1970	1620	1330	1120
	energy, ft-lb:	2100	1465	995	670	475
	arc, inches:		0	-7.6	-28.5	
Hornady 195 SP	velocity, fps:	2550	2343	2146	1959	1782
	energy, ft-lb:	2815	2377	1994	1861	1375
	arc, inches:	+2.3	0	-9.9	-28.8	-58.8
Norma 196 Alaska	velocity, fps:	2395	2112	1850	1611	
	energy, ft-lb:	2714	2190	1754	1399	
	arc, inches:		0	-6.3	-22.9	
Norma 196 Soft Point (JS)	velocity, fps:	2526	2244	1981	1737	
	energy, ft-lb:	2778	2192	1708	1314	
	arc, inches:	+2.7	0	-11.6		
Norma 196 Vulkan (JS)	velocity, fps:	2526	2276	2041	1821	
	energy, ft-lb:	2778	2256	1813	1443	
	arc, inches:	+2.6	0	-11.0		
PMC 170 Pointed Soft Point	velocity, fps:	2360	1969	1622	1333	1123
	energy, ft-lb:	2102	1463	993	671	476
	arc, inches:	+1.8	0	-4.5	-24.3	-63.8
Rem. 170 SP Core-Lokt	velocity, fps:	2360	1969	1622	1333	1123
	energy, ft-lb:	2102	1463	993	671	476
	arc, inches:		0	-7.6	-28.6	
Win. 170 Power-Point	velocity, fps:	2360	1969	1622	1333	1123
	energy, ft-lb:	2102	1463	993	671	476
	arc, inches:		0	-8.2	-29.8	

8mm Remington Magnum

CARTRIDGE BULLET	RANGE, YARDS:	0	100	200	300	400
A-Square 220 Monolythic Solid	velocity, fps:	2800	2501	2221	1959	1718
	energy, ft-lb:	3829	3055	2409	1875	1442
	arc, inches:		+2.1	0	-9.1	-27.6
Rem. 200 Swift A-Frame	velocity, fps:	2900	2623	2361	2115	1885
	energy, ft-lb:	3734	3054	2476	1987	1577
	arc, inches:		+1.8	0	-8.0	-23.9

.338-06

CARTRIDGE BULLET	RANGE, YARDS:	0	100	200	300	400
A-Square 200 Nos. Bal. Tip	velocity, fps:	2750	2553	2364	2184	2011
	energy, ft-lb:	3358	2894	2482	2118	1796
	arc, inches:		+1.9	0	-8.2	-23.6
A-Square 250 SP boat-tail	velocity, fps:	2500	2374	2252	2134	2019
	energy, ft-lb:	3496	3129	2816	2528	2263
	arc, inches:		+2.4	0	-9.3	-26.0
A-Square 250 Dead Tough	velocity, fps:	2500	2222	1963	1724	1507
	energy, ft-lb:	3496	2742	2139	1649	1261
	arc, inches:		+2.8	0	-11.9	-35.5

.338 Winchester Magnum

CARTRIDGE BULLET	RANGE, YARDS:	0	100	200	300	400
A-Square 250 SP boat-tail	velocity, fps:	2700	2568	2439	2314	2193
	energy, ft-lb:	4046	3659	3302	2972	2669
	arc, inches:		+4.4	+5.2	0	-11.7
A-Square 250 Triad	velocity, fps:	2700	2407	2133	1877	1653
	energy, ft-lb:	4046	3216	2526	1956	1516
	arc, inches:		+2.3	0	-9.8	-29.8
Federal 210 Nosler Partition	velocity, fps:	2830	2600	2390	2180	1980
	energy, ft-lb:	3735	3160	2655	2215	1835
	arc, inches:		+1.8	0	-8.0	-23.3
Federal 225 Sierra Pro-Hunt.	velocity, fps:	2780	2570	2360	2170	1980
	energy, ft-lb:	3860	3290	2780	2340	1960
	arc, inches:		+1.9	0	-8.2	-23.7
Federal 225 Trophy Bonded	velocity, fps:	2800	2560	2330	2110	1900
	energy, ft-lb:	3915	3265	2700	2220	1800
	arc, inches:		+1.9	0	-8.4	-24.5
Federal 225 Tr. Bonded HE	velocity, fps:	2940	2690	2450	2230	2010
	energy, ft-lb:	4320	3610	3000	2475	2025
	arc, inches:		+1.7	0	-7.5	-22.0
Federal 225 Barnes XLC	velocity, fps:	2800	2610	2430	2260	2090
	energy, ft-lb:	3915	3405	2950	2545	2190
	arc, inches:		+1.8	0	-7.7	-22.2

Centerfire Rifle Ballistics

.338 Winchester Magnum to .338-378 Weatherby Magnum

BALLISTICS

CARTRIDGE BULLET	RANGE, YARDS:	0	100	200	300	400
Federal 250 Nosler Partition	velocity, fps:	2660	2470	2300	2120	1960
	energy, ft-lb:	3925	3395	2925	2505	2130
	arc, inches:		+2.1	0	-8.8	-25.1
Federal 250 Nosler Part HE	velocity, fps:	2800	2610	2420	2250	2080
	energy, ft-lb:	4350	3775	3260	2805	2395
	arc, inches:		+1.8	0	-7.8	-22.5
Hornady 225 Soft Point HM	velocity, fps:	2920	2678	2449	2232	2027
	energy, ft-lb:	4259	3583	2996	2489	2053
	arc, inches:		+1.8	0	-7.6	-22.0
Norma 225 TXP Swift A-Fr.	velocity, fps:	2740	2507	2286	2075	
	energy, ft-lb:	3752	3141	2611	2153	
	arc, inches:		+2.0	0	-8.7	
Norma 250 Nosler Partition	velocity, fps:	2657	2470	2290	2118	
	energy, ft-lb:	3920	3387	2912	2490	
	arc, inches:		+2.1	0	-8.7	
PMC 225 Barnes X	velocity, fps:	2780	2619	2464	2313	2168
	energy, ft-lb:	3860	3426	3032	2673	2348
	arc, inches:		+1.8	0	-7.6	-21.6
Rem. 200 Nosler Bal. Tip	velocity, fps:	2950	2724	2509	2303	2108
	energy, ft-lb:	3866	3295	2795	2357	1973
	arc, inches:		+1.6	0	-7.1	-20.8
Rem. 210 Nosler Partition	velocity, fps:	2830	2602	2385	2179	1983
	energy, ft-lb:	3734	3157	2653	2214	1834
	arc, inches:		+1.8	0	-7.9	-23.2
Rem. 225 PSP Core-Lokt	velocity, fps:	2780	2572	2374	2184	2003
	energy, ft-lb:	3860	3305	2815	2383	2004
	arc, inches:		+1.9	0	-8.1	-23.4
Rem. 225 Swift A-Frame	velocity, fps:	2785	2517	2266	2029	1808
	energy, ft-lb:	3871	3165	2565	2057	1633
	arc, inches:		+2.0	0	-8.8	-25.2
Rem. 250 PSP Core-Lokt	velocity, fps:	2660	2456	2261	2075	1898
	energy, ft-lb:	3927	3348	2837	2389	1999
	arc, inches:		+2.1	0	-8.9	-26.0
Speer 250 Grand Slam	velocity, fps:	2645	2442	2247	2062	
	energy, ft-lb:	3883	3309	2803	2360	
	arc, inches:		+2.2	0	-9.1	-26.2
Win. 200 Power-Point	velocity, fps:	2960	2658	2375	2110	1862
	energy, ft-lb:	3890	3137	2505	1977	1539
	arc, inches:		+2.0	0	-8.2	-24.3
Win. 200 Ballistic Silvertip	velocity, fps:	2950	2724	2509	2303	2108
	energy, ft-lb:	3864	3294	2794	2355	1972
	arc, inches:		+1.6	0	-7.1	-20.8
Win. 230 Fail Safe	velocity, fps:	2780	2573	2375	2186	2005
	energy, ft-lb:	3948	3382	2881	2441	2054
	arc, inches:		+1.9	0	-8.1	-23.4
Win. 250 Partition Gold	velocity, fps:	2650	2467	2291	2122	1960
	energy, ft-lb:	3899	3378	2914	2520	2134
	arc, inches:		+2.1	0	-8.7	-25.2

.340 Weatherby Magnum

CARTRIDGE BULLET	RANGE, YARDS:	0	100	200	300	400
A-Square 250 SP boat-tail	velocity, fps:	2820	2684	2552	2424	2299
	energy, ft-lb:	4414	3999	3615	3261	2935
	arc, inches:		+4.0	+4.6	0	-10.6
A-Square 250 Triad	velocity, fps:	2820	2520	2238	1976	1741
	energy, ft-lb:	4414	3524	2781	2166	1683
	arc, inches:		+2.0	0	-9.0	-26.8
Federal 225 Trophy Bonded	velocity, fps:	3100	2840	2600	2370	2150
	energy, ft-lb:	4800	4035	3375	2800	2310
	arc, inches:		+1.4	0	-6.5	-19.4
Wby. 200 Pointed Expanding	velocity, fps:	3221	2946	2688	2444	2213
	energy, ft-lb:	4607	3854	3208	2652	2174
	arc, inches:		+3.3	+4.0	0	-9.9
Wby. 200 Nosler Bal. Tip	velocity, fps:	3221	2980	2753	2536	2329
	energy, ft-lb:	4607	3944	3364	2856	2409
	arc, inches:		+3.1	+3.9	0	-9.2
Wby. 210 Nosler Partition	velocity, fps:	3211	2963	2728	2505	2293
	energy, ft-lb:	4807	4093	3470	2927	2452
	arc, inches:		+3.2	+3.9	0	-9.5
Wby. 225 Pointed Expanding	velocity, fps:	3066	2824	2595	2377	2170
	energy, ft-lb:	4696	3984	3364	2822	2352
	arc, inches:		+3.6	+4.4	0	-10.7
Wby. 225 Barnes X	velocity, fps:	3001	2804	2615	2434	2260
	energy, ft-lb:	4499	3927	3416	2959	2551
	arc, inches:		+3.6	+4.3	0	-10.3
Wby. 250 Pointed Expanding	velocity, fps:	2963	2745	2537	2338	2149
	energy, ft-lb:	4873	4182	3572	3035	2563
	arc, inches:		+3.9	+4.6	0	-11.1
Wby. 250 Nosler Partition	velocity, fps:	2941	2743	2553	2371	2197
	energy, ft-lb:	4801	4176	3618	3120	2678
	arc, inches:		+3.9	+4.6	0	-10.9

.330 Dakota

CARTRIDGE BULLET	RANGE, YARDS:	0	100	200	300	400
Dakota 200 Barnes X	velocity, fps:	3200	2971	2754	2548	2350
	energy, ft-lb:	4547	3920	3369	2882	2452
	arc, inches:		+2.1	+1.8	-3.1	-13.4
Dakota 250 Barnes X	velocity, fps:	2900	2719	2545	2378	2217
	energy, ft-lb:	4668	4103	3595	3138	2727
	arc, inches:		+2.3	+1.3	-5.0	-17.5

.338 Remington Ultra Mag

CARTRIDGE BULLET	RANGE, YARDS:	0	100	200	300	400
Federal 210 Nosler Partition	velocity, fps:	3025	2800	2585	2385	2190
	energy, ft-lb:	4270	3655	3120	2645	2230
	arc, inches:		+1.5	0	-6.7	-19.5
Federal 250 Trophy Bonded	velocity, fps:	2860	2630	2420	2210	2020
	energy, ft-lb:	4540	3850	3245	2715	2260
	arc, inches:		+0.8	0	-7.7	-22.6
Rem. 250 Swift A-Frame	velocity, fps:	2860	2645	2440	2244	2057
	energy, ft-lb:	4540	3882	3303	2794	2347
	arc, inches:		+1.7	0	-7.6	-22.1
Rem. 250 PSP Core-Lokt	velocity, fps:	2860	2647	2443	2249	2064
	energy, ft-lb:	4540	3888	3314	2807	2363
	arc, inches:		+1.7	0	-7.6	-22.0

.338 Lapua

CARTRIDGE BULLET	RANGE, YARDS:	0	100	200	300	400
Black Hills 250 Sierra MKing	velocity, fps:	2950				
	energy, ft-lb:	4831				
	arc, inches:					
Black Hills 300 Sierra MKing	velocity, fps:	2800				
	energy, ft-lb:	5223				
	arc, inches:					

.338-378 Weatherby Magnum

CARTRIDGE BULLET	RANGE, YARDS:	0	100	200	300	400
Wby. 200 Nosler Bal. Tip	velocity, fps:	3350	3102	2868	2646	2434
	energy, ft-lb:	4983	4273	3652	3109	2631
	arc, inches:	0	+2.8	+3.5	0	-8.4
Wby. 225 Barnes X	velocity, fps:	3180	2974	2778	2591	2410
	energy, ft-lb:	5052	4420	3856	3353	2902
	arc, inches:	0	+3.1	+3.8	0	-8.9
Wby. 250 Nosler Partition	velocity, fps:	3060	2856	2662	2475	2297
	energy, ft-lb:	5197	4528	3933	3401	2927
	arc, inches:	0	+3.5	+4.2	0	-9.8

CARTRIDGE BULLET	RANGE, YARDS:	0	100	200	300	400
8.59 (.338) TITAN						
Lazzeroni 200 Nos. Bal. Tip	velocity, fps:	3430	3211	3002	2803	2613
	energy, ft-lb:	5226	4579	4004	3491	3033
	arc, inches:		+2.5	+3.2	0	-7.6
Lazzeroni 225 Nos. Partition	velocity, fps:	3235	3031	2836	2650	2471
	energy, ft-lb:	5229	4591	4021	3510	3052
	arc, inches:		+3.0	+3.6	0	-8.6
Lazzeroni 250 Swift A-Fr.	velocity, fps:	3100	2908	2725	2549	2379
	energy, ft-lb:	5336	4697	4123	3607	3143
	arc, inches:		+3.3	+4.0	0	-9.3
.338 A-SQUARE						
A-Square 200 Nos. Bal. Tip	velocity, fps:	3500	3266	3045	2835	2634
	energy, ft-lb:	5440	4737	4117	3568	3081
	arc, inches:		+2.4	+3.1	0	-7.5
A-Square 250 SP boat-tail	velocity, fps:	3120	2974	2834	2697	2565
	energy, ft-lb:	5403	4911	4457	4038	3652
	arc, inches:		+3.1	+3.7	0	-8.5
A-Square 250 Triad	velocity, fps:	3120	2799	2500	2220	1958
	energy, ft-lb:	5403	4348	3469	2736	2128
	arc, inches:		+1.5	0	-7.1	-20.4
.338 EXCALIBER						
A-Square 200 Nos. Bal. Tip	velocity, fps:	3600	3361	3134	2920	2715
	energy, ft-lb:	5755	5015	4363	3785	3274
	arc, inches:		+2.2	+2.9	0	-6.7
A-Square 250 SP boat-tail	velocity, fps:	3250	3101	2958	2684	2553
	energy, ft-lb:	5863	5339	4855	4410	3998
	arc, inches:		+2.7	+3.4	0	-7.8
A-Square 250 Triad	velocity, fps:	3250	2922	2618	2333	2066
	energy, ft-lb:	5863	4740	3804	3021	2370
	arc, inches:		+1.3	0	-6.4	-19.2
.348 WINCHESTER						
Win. 200 Silvertip	velocity, fps:	2520	2215	1931	1672	1443
	energy, ft-lb:	2820	2178	1656	1241	925
	arc, inches:		0	-6.2	-21.9	
.357 MAGNUM						
Federal 180 Hi-Shok HP	velocity, fps:	1550	1160	980	860	770
Hollow Point	energy, ft-lb:	960	535	385	295	235
	arc, inches:		0	-22.8	-77.9	-173.8
Win. 158 Jacketed SP	velocity, fps:	1830	1427	1138	980	883
	energy, ft-lb:	1175	715	454	337	274
	arc, inches:		0	-16.2	-57.0	-128.3
.35 REMINGTON						
Federal 200 Hi-Shok	velocity, fps:	2080	1700	1380	1140	1000
	energy, ft-lb:	1920	1280	840	575	445
	arc, inches:		0	-10.7	-39.3	
Rem. 150 PSP Core-Lokt	velocity, fps:	2300	1874	1506	1218	1039
	energy, ft-lb:	1762	1169	755	494	359
	arc, inches:		0	-8.6	-32.6	
Rem. 200 SP Core-Lokt	velocity, fps:	2080	1698	1376	1140	1001
	energy, ft-lb:	1921	1280	841	577	445
	arc, inches:		0	-10.7	-40.1	
Win. 200 Power-Point	velocity, fps:	2020	1646	1335	1114	985
	energy, ft-lb:	1812	1203	791	551	431
	arc, inches:		0	-12.1	-43.9	
.356 WINCHESTER						
Win. 200 Power-Point	velocity, fps:	2460	2114	1797	1517	1284
	energy, ft-lb:	2688	1985	1434	1022	732
	arc, inches:		+1.6	-3.8	-20.1	-51.2
.358 WINCHESTER						
Win. 200 Silvertip	velocity, fps:	2490	2171	1876	1610	1379
	energy, ft-lb:	2753	2093	1563	1151	844
	arc, inches:		+1.5	-3.6	-18.6	-47.2
.35 WHELEN						
Federal 225 Trophy Bonded	velocity, fps:	2600	2400	2200	2020	1840
	energy, ft-lb:	3375	2865	2520	2030	1690
	arc, inches:		+2.3	0	-9.4	-27.3
Rem. 200 Pointed Soft Point	velocity, fps:	2675	2378	2100	1842	1606
	energy, ft-lb:	3177	2510	1958	1506	1145
	arc, inches:		+2.3	0	-10.3	-30.8
Rem. 250 Pointed Soft Point	velocity, fps:	2400	2197	2005	1823	1652
	energy, ft-lb:	3197	2680	2230	1844	1515
	arc, inches:		+1.3	-3.2	-16.6	-40.0
.358 NORMA MAGNUM						
A-Square 275 Triad	velocity, fps:	2700	2394	2108	1842	1653
	energy, ft-lb:	4451	3498	2713	2072	1668
	arc, inches:		+2.3	0	-10.1	-29.8
Norma 250 TXP Swift A-Fr.	velocity, fps:	2723	2467	2225	1996	
	energy, ft-lb:	4117	3379	2748	2213	
	arc, inches:		+2.1	0	-9.1	
Norma 250 Woodleigh	velocity, fps:	2799	2442	2112	1810	
	energy, ft-lb:	4350	3312	2478	1819	
	arc, inches:		+2.2	0	-10.0	
.358 STA						
A-Square 275 Triad	velocity, fps:	2850	2562	2292	2039	1764
	energy, ft-lb:	4959	4009	3208	2539	1899
	arc, inches:		+1.9	0	-8.6	-26.1
9.3x57						
Norma 232 Vulkan	velocity, fps:	2329	2031	1757	1512	
	energy, ft-lb:	2795	2126	1591	1178	
	arc, inches:		+3.5	0	-14.9	
Norma 286 Alaska	velocity, fps:	2067	1857	1662	1484	
	energy, ft-lb:	2714	2190	1754	1399	
	arc, inches:		+4.3	0	-17.0	
9.3x62						
A-Square 286 Triad	velocity, fps:	2360	2089	1844	1623	1369
	energy, ft-lb:	3538	2771	2157	1670	1189
	arc, inches:		+3.0	0	-13.1	-42.2
Norma 232 Vulkan	velocity, fps:	2625	2327	2049	1792	
	energy, ft-lb:	3551	2791	2164	1655	
	arc, inches:		+2.5	0	-10.8	
Norma 232 Oryx	velocity, fps:	2625	2294	1988	1708	
	energy, ft-lb:	3535	2700	2028	1497	
	arc, inches:		+2.5	0	-11.4	
Norma 286 Plastic Point	velocity, fps:	2362	2141	1931	1736	
	energy, ft-lb:	3544	2911	2370	1914	
	arc, inches:		+3.1	0	-12.4	
Norma 286 Alaska	velocity, fps:	2362	2135	1920	1720	
	energy, ft-lb:	3544	2894	2342	1879	
	arc, inches:		+3.1	0	-12.5	

Centerfire Rifle Ballistics

9.3x64 to .375 JRS

9.3x64

Cartridge Bullet	Range, yards:	0	100	200	300	400
A-Square 286 Triad	velocity, fps:	2700	2391	2103	1835	1602
	energy, ft-lb:	4629	3630	2808	2139	1631
	arc, inches:		+2.3	0	-10.1	-30.8

9.3x74 R

Cartridge Bullet	Range, yards:	0	100	200	300	400
A-Square 286 Triad	velocity, fps:	2360	2089	1844	1623	
	energy, ft-lb:	3538	2771	2157	1670	
	arc, inches:		+3.6	0	-14.0	
Norma 232 Vulkan	velocity, fps:	2625	2327	2049	1792	
	energy, ft-lb:	3551	2791	2164	1655	
	arc, inches:		+2.5	0	-10.8	
Norma 232 Oryx	velocity, fps:	2526	2191	1883	1605	
	energy, ft-lb:	3274	2463	1819	1322	
	arc, inches:		+2.9	0	-12.8	
Norma 286 Alaska	velocity, fps:	2362	2135	1920	1720	
	energy, ft-lb:	3544	2894	2342	1879	
	arc, inches:		+3.1	0	-12.5	
Norma 286 Plastic Point	velocity, fps:	2362	2135	1920	1720	
	energy, ft-lb:	3544	2894	2342	1879	
	arc, inches:		+3.1	0	-12.5	

.375 Winchester

Cartridge Bullet	Range, yards:	0	100	200	300	400
Win. 200 Power-Point	velocity, fps:	2200	1841	1526	1268	1089
	energy, ft-lb:	2150	1506	1034	714	
	arc, inches:		0	-9.5	-33.8	

.375 H&H Magnum

Cartridge Bullet	Range, yards:	0	100	200	300	400
A-Square 300 SP boat-tail	velocity, fps:	2550	2415	2284	2157	2034
	energy, ft-lb:	4331	3884	3474	3098	2755
	arc, inches:		+5.2	+6.0	0	-13.3
A-Square 300 Triad	velocity, fps:	2550	2251	1973	1717	1496
	energy, ft-lb:	4331	3375	2592	1964	1491
	arc, inches:		+2.7	0	-11.7	-35.1
Federal 250 Trophy Bonded	velocity, fps:	2670	2360	2080	1820	1580
	energy, ft-lb:	3955	3100	2400	1830	1380
	arc, inches:		+2.4	0	-10.4	-31.7
Federal 270 Hi-Shok	velocity, fps:	2690	2420	2170	1920	1700
	energy, ft-lb:	4340	3510	2810	2220	1740
	arc, inches:		+2.4	0	-10.9	-33.3
Federal 300 Hi-Shok	velocity, fps:	2530	2270	2020	1790	1580
	energy, ft-lb:	4265	3425	2720	2135	1665
	arc, inches:		+2.6	0	-11.2	-33.3
Federal 300 Nosler Partition	velocity, fps:	2530	2320	2120	1930	1750
	energy, ft-lb:	4265	3585	2995	2475	2040
	arc, inches:		+2.5	0	-10.3	-29.9
Federal 300 Trophy Bonded	velocity, fps:	2530	2280	2040	1810	1610
	energy, ft-lb:	4265	3450	2765	2190	1725
	arc, inches:		+2.6	0	-10.9	-32.8
Federal 300 Tr. Bonded HE	velocity, fps:	2700	2440	2190	1960	1740
	energy, ft-lb:	4855	3960	3195	2550	2020
	arc, inches:		+2.2	0	-9.4	-28.0
Federal 300 Trophy Bonded Sledgehammer Solid	velocity, fps:	2530	2160	1820	1520	1280
	energy, ft-lb:	4265	3105	2210	1550	1090
	arc, inches, s:		0	-6.0	-22.7	-54.6
Hornady 270 SP HM	velocity, fps:	2870	2620	2385	2162	1957
	energy, ft-lb:	4937	4116	3408	2802	2296
	arc, inches:		+2.2	0	-8.4	-23.9
Hornady 300 FMJ RN HM	velocity, fps:	2705	2376	2072	1804	1560
	energy, ft-lb:	4873	3760	2861	2167	1621
	arc, inches:		+2.7	0	-10.8	-32.1
Norma 300 Soft Point	velocity, fps:	2549	2211	1900	1619	
	energy, ft-lb:	4329	3258	2406	1747	
	arc, inches:		+2.8	0	-12.6	
Norma 300 TXP Swift A-Fr.	velocity, fps:	2559	2296	2049	1818	
	energy, ft-lb:	4363	3513	2798	2203	
	arc, inches:		+2.6	0	-10.9	
Norma 300 Barnes Solid	velocity, fps:	2493	2061	1677	1356	
	energy, ft-lb:	4141	2829	1873	1234	
	arc, inches:		+3.4	0	-16.0	
PMC 270 PSP	velocity, fps:					
	energy, ft-lb:					
	arc, inches:					
PMC 270 Barnes X	velocity, fps:	2690	2528	2372	2221	2076
	energy, ft-lb:	4337	3831	3371	2957	2582
	arc, inches:		+2.0	0	-8.2	-23.4
PMC 300 Barnes X	velocity, fps:	2530	2389	2252	2120	1993
	energy, ft-lb:	4263	3801	3378	2994	2644
	arc, inches:		+2.3	0	-9.2	-26.1
Rem. 270 Soft Point	velocity, fps:	2690	2420	2166	1928	1707
	energy, ft-lb:	4337	3510	2812	2228	1747
	arc, inches:		+2.2	0	-9.7	-28.7
Rem. 300 Swift A-Frame	velocity, fps:	2530	2245	1979	1733	1512
	energy, ft-lb:	4262	3357	2608	2001	1523
	arc, inches:		+2.7	0	-11.7	-35.0
Speer 285 Grand Slam	velocity, fps:	2610	2365	2134	1916	
	energy, ft-lb:	4310	3540	2883	2323	
	arc, inches:		+2.4	0	-9.9	
Speer 300 African GS Tungsten Solid	velocity, fps:	2609	2277	1970	1690	
	energy, ft-lb:	4534	3453	2585	1903	
	arc, inches:		+2.6	0	-11.7	-35.6
Win. 270 Fail Safe	velocity, fps:	2670	2447	2234	2033	1842
	energy, ft-lb:	4275	3590	2994	2478	2035
	arc, inches:		+2.2	0	-9.1	-28.7
Win. 300 Fail Safe	velocity, fps:	2530	2336	2151	1974	1806
	energy, ft-lb:	4265	3636	3082	2596	2173
	arc, inches:		+2.4	0	-10.0	-26.9

.375 Dakota

Cartridge Bullet	Range, yards:	0	100	200	300	400
Dakota 270 Barnes X	velocity, fps:	2800	2617	2441	2272	2109
	energy, ft-lb:	4699	4104	3571	3093	2666
	arc, inches:		+2.3	+1.0	-6.1	-19.9
Dakota 300 Barnes X	velocity, fps:	2600	2316	2051	1804	1579
	energy, ft-lb:	4502	3573	2800	2167	1661
	arc, inches:		+2.4	-0.1	-11.0	-32.7

.375 Weatherby

Cartridge Bullet	Range, yards:	0	100	200	300	400
A-Square 300 SP boat-tail	velocity, fps:	2700	2560	2425	2293	2166
	energy, ft-lb:	4856	4366	3916	3503	3125
	arc, inches:		+4.5	+5.2	0	-11.9
A-Square 300 Triad	velocity, fps:	2700	2391	2103	1835	1602
	energy, ft-lb:	4856	3808	2946	2243	1710
	arc, inches:		+2.3	0	-10.1	-30.8

.375 JRS

Cartridge Bullet	Range, yards:	0	100	200	300	400
A-Square 300 SP boat-tail	velocity, fps:	2700	2560	2425	2293	2166
	energy, ft-lb:	4856	4366	3916	3503	3125
	arc, inches:		+4.5	+5.2	0	-11.9
A-Square 300 Triad	velocity, fps:	2700	2391	2103	1835	1602
	energy, ft-lb:	4856	3808	2946	2243	1710
	arc, inches:		+2.3	0	-10.1	-30.8

Centerfire Rifle Ballistics

.375 Remington Ultra Magnum to .416 Rimmed

.375 Remington Ultra Mag

Cartridge Bullet	Range, Yards:	0	100	200	300	400
Rem. 270 Soft Point	velocity, fps:	2900	2558	2241	1947	1678
	energy, fps:	5041	3922	3010	2272	1689
	arc, inches:		+1.9	0	-9.2	-27.8
Rem. 300 Swift A-Frame	velocity, fps:	2760	2505	2263	2035	1822
	energy, fps:	5073	4178	3412	2759	2210
	arc, inches:		+2.0	0	-8.8	-26.1

.375 A-Square

Cartridge Bullet	Range, Yards:	0	100	200	300	400
A-Square 300 SP boat-tail	velocity, fps:	2920	2773	2631	2494	2360
	energy, ft-lb:	5679	5123	4611	4142	3710
	arc, inches:		+3.7	+4.4	0	-9.8
A-Square 300 Triad	velocity, fps:	2920	2596	2294	2012	1762
	energy, ft-lb:	5679	4488	3505	2698	2068
	arc, inches:		+1.8	0	-8.5	-25.5

.378 Weatherby

Cartridge Bullet	Range, Yards:	0	100	200	300	400
A-Square 300 SP boat-tail	velocity, fps:	2900	2754	2612	2475	2342
	energy, ft-lb:	5602	5051	4546	4081	3655
	arc, inches:		+3.8	+4.4	0	-10.0
A-Square 300 Triad	velocity, fps:	2900	2577	2276	1997	1747
	energy, ft-lb:	5602	4424	3452	2656	2034
	arc, inches:		+1.9	0	-8.7	-25.9
Wby. 270 Pointed Expanding	velocity, fps:	3180	2921	2677	2445	2225
	energy, ft-lb:	6062	5115	4295	3583	2968
	arc, inches:		+1.3	0	-6.1	-18.1
Wby. 270 Barnes X	velocity, fps:	3150	2954	2767	2587	2415
	energy, ft-lb:	5948	5232	4589	4013	3495
	arc, inches:		+1.2	0	-5.8	-16.7
Wby. 300 RN Expanding	velocity, fps:	2925	2558	2220	1908	1627
	energy, ft-lb:	5699	4360	3283	2424	1764
	arc, inches:		+1.9	0	-9.0	-27.8
Wby. 300 FMJ	velocity, fps:	2925	2591	2280	1991	1725
	energy, ft-lb:	5699	4470	3461	2640	1983
	arc, inches:		+1.8	0	-8.6	-26.1

.38-40 Winchester

Cartridge Bullet	Range, Yards:	0	100	200	300	400
Win. 180 Soft Point	velocity, fps:	1160	999	901	827	
	energy, ft-lb:	538	399	324	273	
	arc, inches:		0	-23.4	-75.2	

.38-55 Winchester

Cartridge Bullet	Range, Yards:	0	100	200	300	400
Black Hills 255 FN Lead	velocity, fps:	1250				
	energy, ft-lb:	925				
	arc, inches:					
Win. 255 Soft Point	velocity, fps:	1320	1190	1091	1018	
	energy, ft-lb:	987	802	674	587	
	arc, inches:		0	-33.9	-110.6	

.41 Magnum

Cartridge Bullet	Range, Yards:	0	100	200	300	400
Win. 240 Platinum Tip	velocity, fps:	1830	1488	1220	1048	
	energy, ft-lb:	1784	1180	792	585	
	arc inches:		0	-15.0	-53.4	

.450/.400 (3")

Cartridge Bullet	Range, Yards:	0	100	200	300	400
A-Square 400 Triad	velocity, fps:	2150	1910	1690	1490	
	energy, ft-lb:	4105	3241	2537	1972	
	arc, inches:		+4.4	0	-16.5	

.450/.400 (3¼")

Cartridge Bullet	Range, Yards:	0	100	200	300	400
A-Square 400 Triad	velocity, fps:	2150	1910	1690	1490	
	energy, ft-lb:	4105	3241	2537	1972	
	arc, inches:		+4.4	0	-16.5	

.404 Jeffery

Cartridge Bullet	Range, Yards:	0	100	200	300	400
A-Square 400 Triad	velocity, fps:	2150	1901	1674	1468	1299
	energy, ft-lb:	4105	3211	2489	1915	1499
	arc, inches:		+4.1	0	-16.4	-49.1

.405 Winchester

Cartridge Bullet	Range, Yards:	0	100	200	300	400
Hornady 300 Flatpoint	velocity, fps:	2200	1851	1545	1296	
	energy, ft-lb:	3224	2282	1589	1119	
	arc, inches:		+4.6	0	-19.5	

.416 Taylor

Cartridge Bullet	Range, Yards:	0	100	200	300	400
A-Square 400 Triad	velocity, fps:	2350	2093	1853	1634	1443
	energy, ft-lb:	4905	3892	3049	2371	1849
	arc, inches:		+3.2	0	-13.6	-39.8

.416 Hoffman

Cartridge Bullet	Range, Yards:	0	100	200	300	400
A-Square 400 Triad	velocity, fps:	2380	2122	1879	1658	1464
	energy, ft-lb:	5031	3998	3136	2440	1903
	arc, inches:		+3.1	0	-13.1	-38.7

.416 Remington Magnum

Cartridge Bullet	Range, Yards:	0	100	200	300	400
A-Square 400 Triad	velocity, fps:	2380	2122	1879	1658	1464
	energy, ft-lb:	5031	3998	3136	2440	1903
	arc, inches:		+3.1	0	-13.2	-38.7
Federal 400 Trophy Bonded	velocity, fps:	2400	2150	1920	1700	1500
Sledgehammer Solid	energy, ft-lb:	5115	4110	3260	2565	2005
	arc, inches:		0	-6.0	-21.6	-49.2
Federal 400 Trophy Bonded	velocity, fps:	2400	2180	1970	1770	1590
	energy, ft-lb:	5115	4215	3440	2785	2245
	arc, inches:		0	-5.8	-20.6	-46.9
Rem. 400 Swift A-Frame	velocity, fps:	2400	2175	1962	1763	1579
	energy, ft-lb:	5115	4201	3419	2760	2214
	arc, inches:		+1.3	-3.3	-17.0	-41.9

.416 Rigby

Cartridge Bullet	Range, Yards:	0	100	200	300	400
A-Square 400 Triad	velocity, fps:	2400	2140	1897	1673	1478
	energy, ft-lb:	5115	4069	3194	2487	1940
	arc, inches:		+3.0	0	-12.9	-38.0
Federal 400 Trophy Bonded	velocity, fps:	2370	2150	1940	1750	1570
	energy, ft-lb:	4990	4110	3350	2715	2190
	arc, inches:		0	-6.0	-21.3	-48.1
Federal 400 Trophy Bonded	velocity, fps:	2370	2120	1890	1660	1460
Sledgehammer Solid	energy, ft-lb:	4990	3975	3130	2440	1895
	arc, inches:		0	-6.3	-22.5	-51.5
Federal 410 Woodleigh	velocity, fps:	2370	2110	1870	1640	1440
Weldcore	energy, ft-lb:	5115	4050	3165	2455	1895
	arc, inches:		0	-7.4	-24.8	-55.0
Federal 410 Solid	velocity, fps:	2370	2110	2870	1640	1440
	energy, ft-lb:	5115	4050	3165	2455	1895
	arc, inches:		0	-7.4	-24.8	-55.0
Norma 400 TXP Swift A-Fr.	velocity, fps:	2350	2127	1917	1721	
	energy, ft-lb:	4906	4021	3266	2632	
	arc, inches:		+3.1	0	-12.5	
Norma 400 Barnes Solid	velocity, fps:	2297	1930	1604	1330	
	energy, ft-lb:	4687	3310	2284	1571	
	arc, inches:		+3.9	0	-17.7	

.416 Rimmed

Cartridge Bullet	Range, Yards:	0	100	200	300	400
A-Square 400 Triad	velocity, fps:	2400	2140	1897	1673	
	energy, ft-lb:	5115	4069	3194	2487	
	arc, inches:		+3.3	0	-13.2	

Centerfire Rifle Ballistics

.416 Dakota to .458 Winchester Magnum

Cartridge Bullet	Range, yards:	0	100	200	300	400
.416 Dakota						
Dakota 400 Barnes X	velocity, fps:	2450	2294	2143	1998	1859
	energy, ft-lb:	5330	4671	4077	3544	3068
	arc, inches:		+2.5	-0.2	-10.5	-29.4
.416 Weatherby						
A-Square 400 Triad	velocity, fps:	2600	2328	2073	1834	1624
	energy, ft-lb:	6004	4813	3816	2986	2343
	arc, inches:		+2.5	0	-10.5	-31.6
Wby. 350 Barnes X	velocity, fps:	2850	2673	2503	2340	2182
	energy, ft-lb:	6312	5553	4870	4253	3700
	arc, inches:		+1.7	0	-7.2	-20.9
Wby. 400 Swift A-Fr.	velocity, fps:	2650	2426	2213	2011	1820
	energy, ft-lb:	6237	5227	4350	3592	2941
	arc, inches:		+2.2	0	-9.3	-27.1
Wby. 400 RN Expanding	velocity, fps:	2700	2417	2152	1903	1676
	energy, ft-lb:	6474	5189	4113	3216	2493
	arc, inches:		+2.3	0	-9.7	-29.3
Wby. 400 Monolithic Solid	velocity, fps:	2700	2411	2140	1887	1656
	energy, ft-lb:	6474	5162	4068	3161	2435
	arc, inches:		+2.3	0	-9.8	-29.7
10.57 (.416) Meteor						
Lazzeroni 400 Swift A-Fr.	velocity, fps:	2730	2532	2342	2161	1987
	energy, ft-lb:	6621	5695	4874	4147	3508
	arc, inches:		+1.9	0	-8.3	-24.0
.425 Express						
A-Square 400 Triad	velocity, fps:	2400	2136	1888	1662	1465
	energy, ft-lb:	5115	4052	3167	2454	1906
	arc, inches:		+3.0	0	-13.1	-38.3
.44-40 Winchester						
Rem. 200 Soft Point	velocity, fps:	1190	1006	900	822	756
	energy, ft-lb:	629	449	360	300	254
	arc, inches:		0	-33.1	-108.7	-235.2
Win. 200 Soft Point	velocity, fps:	1190	1006	900	822	756
	energy, ft-lb:	629	449	360	300	254
	arc, inches:		0	-33.3	-109.5	-237.4
.44 Remington Magnum						
Federal 240 Hi-Shok HP	velocity, fps:	1760	1380	1090	950	860
	energy, ft-lb:	1650	1015	640	485	395
	arc, inches:		0	-17.4	-60.7	-136.0
Rem. 210 Semi-Jacketed HP	velocity, fps:	1920	1477	1155	982	880
	energy, ft-lb:	1719	1017	622	450	361
	arc, inches:		0	-14.7	-55.5	-131.3
Rem. 240 Soft Point	velocity, fps:	1760	1380	1114	970	878
	energy, ft-lb:	1650	1015	661	501	411
	arc, inches:		0	-17.0	-61.4	-143.0
Rem. 240 Semi-Jacketed Hollow Point	velocity, fps:	1760	1380	1114	970	878
	energy, ft-lb:	1650	1015	661	501	411
	arc, inches:		0	-17.0	-61.4	-143.0
Rem. 275 JHP Core-Lokt	velocity, fps:	1580	1293	1093	976	896
	energy, ft-lb:	1524	1020	730	582	490
	arc, inches:		0	-19.4	-67.5	-210.8
Win. 210 Silvertip HP	velocity, fps:	1580	1198	993	879	795
	energy, ft-lb:	1164	670	460	361	295
	arc, inches:		0	-22.4	-76.1	-168.0
Win. 240 Hollow Soft Point	velocity, fps:	1760	1362	1094	953	861
	energy, ft-lb:	1650	988	638	484	395
	arc, inches:		0	-18.1	-65.1	-150.3
Win. 250 Platinum Tip	velocity, fps:	1830	1475	1201	1032	931
	energy, ft-lb:	1859	1208	801	591	481
	arc, inches:		0	-15.3	-54.7	-126.6
.444 Marlin						
Rem. 240 Soft Point	velocity, fps:	2350	1815	1377	1087	941
	energy, ft-lb:	2942	1755	1010	630	472
	arc, inches:		+2.2	-5.4	-31.4	-86.7
Hornady 265 FP LM	velocity, fps:	2335	1913	1551	1266	
	energy, ft-lb:	3208	2153	1415	943	
	arc, inches:		+ 2.0	-4.9	-26.5	
.45-70 Government						
Black Hills 405 FPL	velocity, fps:	1250				
	energy, ft-lb:					
	arc, inches:					
Federal 300 Sierra Pro-Hunt. HP FN	velocity, fps:	1880	1650	1430	1240	1110
	energy, ft-lb:	2355	1815	1355	1015	810
	arc, inches:		0	-11.5	-39.7	-89.1
PMC 350 FNSP	velocity, fps:					
	energy, ft-lb:					
	arc, inches:					
Rem. 300 Jacketed HP	velocity, fps:	1810	1497	1244	1073	969
	energy, ft-lb:	2182	1492	1031	767	625
	arc, inches:		0	-13.8	-50.1	-115.7
Rem. 405 Soft Point	velocity, fps:	1330	1168	1055	977	918
	energy, ft-lb:	1590	1227	1001	858	758
	arc, inches:		0	-24.0	-78.6	-169.4
Win. 300 Jacketed HP	velocity, fps:	1880	1650	1425	1235	1105
	energy, ft-lb:	2355	1815	1355	1015	810
	arc, inches:		0	-12.8	-44.3	-95.5
Win. 300 Partition Gold	velocity, fps:	1880	1558	1292	1103	988
	energy, ft-lb:	2355	1616	1112	811	651
	arc, inches:		0	-12.9	-46.0	-104.9
.450 Nitro Express (3¼")						
A-Square 465 Triad	velocity, fps:	2190	1970	1765	1577	
	energy, ft-lb:	4952	4009	3216	2567	
	arc, inches:		+4.3	0	-15.4	
.450 #2						
A-Square 465 Triad	velocity, fps:	2190	1970	1765	1577	
	energy, ft-lb:	4952	4009	3216	2567	
	arc, inches:		+4.3	0	-15.4	
.458 Winchester Magnum						
A-Square 465 Triad	velocity, fps:	2220	1999	1791	1601	1433
	energy, ft-lb:	5088	4127	3312	2646	2121
	arc, inches:		+3.6	0	-14.7	-42.5
Federal 350 Soft Point	velocity, fps:	2470	1990	1570	1250	1060
	energy, ft-lb:	4740	3065	1915	1205	870
	arc, inches:		0	-7.5	-29.1	-71.1
Federal 400 Trophy Bonded	velocity, fps:	2380	2170	1960	1770	1590
	energy, ft-lb:	5030	4165	3415	2785	2255
	arc, inches:		0	-5.9	-20.9	-47.1
Federal 500 Solid	velocity, fps:	2090	1870	1670	1480	1320
	energy, ft-lb:	4850	3880	3085	2440	1945
	arc, inches:		0	-8.5	-29.5	-66.2
Federal 500 Trophy Bonded	velocity, fps:	2090	1870	1660	1480	1310
	energy, ft-lb:	4850	3870	3065	2420	1915
	arc, inches:		0	-8.5	-29.7	-66.8

CARTRIDGE BULLET	RANGE, YARDS:	0	100	200	300	400
Federal 500 Trophy Bonded Sledgehammer Solid	velocity, fps:	2090	1860	1650	1460	1300
	energy, ft-lb:	4850	3845	3025	2365	1865
	arc, inches:		0	-8.6	-30.0	-67.8
Federal 510 Soft Point	velocity, fps:	2090	1820	1570	1360	1190
	energy, ft-lb:	4945	3730	2790	2080	1605
	arc, inches:		0	-9.1	-32.3	-73.9
Hornady 500 FMJ-RN HM	velocity, fps:	2260	1984	1735	1512	
	energy, ft-lb:	5670	4368	3341	2538	
	arc, inches:		0	-7.4	-26.4	
Norma 500 TXP Swift A-Fr.	velocity, fps:	2116	1903	1705	1524	
	energy, ft-lb:	4972	4023	3228	2578	
	arc, inches:		+4.1	0	-16.1	
Norma 500 Barnes Solid	velocity, fps:	2067	1750	1472	1245	
	energy, ft-lb:	4745	3401	2405	1721	
	arc, inches:		+4.9	0	-21.2	
Rem. 450 Swift A-Frame PSP	velocity, fps:	2150	1901	1671	1465	1289
	energy, ft-lb:	4618	3609	2789	2144	1659
	arc, inches:		0	-8.2	-28.9	
Speer 500 African GS Tungsten Solid	velocity, fps:	2120	1845	1596	1379	
	energy, ft-lb:	4989	3780	2828	2111	
	arc, inches:		0	-8.8	-31.3	
Speer African Grand Slam	velocity, fps:	2120	1853	1609	1396	
	energy, ft-lb:	4989	3810	2875	2163	
	arc, inches:		0	-8.7	-30.8	
Win. 510 Soft Point	velocity, fps:	2040	1770	1527	1319	1157
	energy, ft-lb:	4712	3547	2640	1970	1516
	arc, inches:		0	-10.3	-35.6	
.458 Lott						
A-Square 465 Triad	velocity, fps:	2380	2150	1932	1730	1551
	energy, ft-lb:	5848	4773	3855	3091	2485
	arc, inches:		+3.0	0	-12.5	-36.4
Hornady 500 RN	velocity, fps:	2300	2022	1776	1551	
	energy, ft-lb:	5872	4537	3502	2671	
	arc, inches:		+3.4	0	-1.43	
.450 Ackley						
A-Square 465 Triad	velocity, fps:	2400	2169	1950	1747	1567
	energy, ft-lb:	5947	4857	3927	3150	2534
	arc, inches:		+2.9	0	-12.2	-35.8
.460 Short A-Square						
A-Square 500 Triad	velocity, fps:	2420	2198	1987	1789	1613
	energy, ft-lb:	6501	5362	4385	3553	2890
	arc, inches:		+2.9	0	-11.6	-34.2
.450 Dakota						
Dakota 500 Barnes Solid	velocity, fps:	2450	2235	2030	1838	1658
	energy, ft-lb:	6663	5544	4576	3748	3051
	arc, inches:		+2.5	-0.6	-12.0	-33.8
.460 Weatherby Magnum						
A-Square 500 Triad	velocity, fps:	2580	2349	2131	1923	1737
	energy, ft-lb:	7389	6126	5040	4107	3351
	arc, inches:		+2.4	0	-10.0	-29.4
Wby. 450 Barnes X	velocity, fps:	2700	2518	2343	2175	2013
	energy, ft-lb:	7284	6333	5482	4725	4050
	arc, inches:		+2.0	0	-8.4	-24.1
Wby. 500 RN Expanding	velocity, fps:	2600	2301	2022	1764	1533
	energy, ft-lb:	7504	5877	4539	3456	2608
	arc, inches:		+2.6	0	-11.1	-33.5
Wby. 500 FMJ	velocity, fps:	2600	2309	2037	1784	1557
	energy, ft-lb:	7504	5917	4605	3534	2690
	arc, inches:		+2.5	0	-10.9	-33.0
.500/.465						
A-Square 480 Triad	velocity, fps:	2150	1928	1722	1533	
	energy, ft-lb:	4926	3960	3160	2505	
	arc, inches:		+4.3	0	-16.0	
.470 Nitro Express						
A-Square 500 Triad	velocity, fps:	2150	1912	1693	1494	
	energy, ft-lb:	5132	4058	3182	2478	
	arc, inches:		+4.4	0	-16.5	
Federal 500 Woodleigh Weldcore	velocity, fps:	2150	1890	1650	1440	1270
	energy, ft-lb:	5130	3965	3040	2310	1790
	arc, inches:		0	-9.3	-31.3	-69.7
Federal 500 Woodleigh Weldcore Solid	velocity, fps:	2150	1890	1650	1440	1270
	energy, ft-lb:	5130	3965	3040	2310	1790
	arc, inches:		0	-9.3	-31.3	-69.7
Federal 500 Trophy Bonded	velocity, fps:	2150	1940	1740	1560	1400
	energy, ft-lb:	5130	4170	3360	2695	2160
	arc, inches:		0	-7.8	-27.1	-60.8
Federal 500 Trophy Bonded Sledgehammer Solid	velocity, fps:	2150	1940	1740	1560	1400
	ft-lb:	5130	4170	3360	2695	2160
	arc, inches:		0	-7.8	-27.1	-60.8
.470 Capstick						
A-Square 500 Triad	velocity, fps:	2400	2172	1958	1761	1553
	energy, ft-lb:	6394	5236	4255	3445	2678
	arc, inches:		+2.9	0	-11.9	-36.1
475 #2						
A-Square 480 Triad	velocity, fps:	2200	1964	1744	1544	
	energy, ft-lb:	5158	4109	3240	2539	
	arc, inches:		+4.1	0	-15.6	
.475 #2 Jeffery						
A-Square 500 Triad	velocity, fps:	2200	1966	1748	1550	
	energy, ft-lb:	5373	4291	3392	2666	
	arc, inches:		+4.1	0	-15.6	
.495 A-Square						
A-Square 570 Triad	velocity, fps:	2350	2117	1896	1693	1513
	energy, ft-lb:	6989	5671	4552	3629	2899
	arc, inches:		+3.1	0	-13.0	-37.8
.500 Nitro Express (3")						
A-Square 570 Triad	velocity, fps:	2150	1928	1722	1533	
	energy, ft-lb:	5850	4703	3752	2975	
	arc, inches:		+4.3	0	-16.1	
.500 A-Square						
A-Square 600 Triad	velocity, fps:	2470	2235	2013	1804	1620
	energy, ft-lb:	8127	6654	5397	4336	3495
	arc, inches:		+2.7	0	-11.3	-33.5
.505 Gibbs						
A-Square 525 Triad	velocity, fps:	2300	2063	1840	1637	
	energy, ft-lb:	6166	4962	3948	3122	
	arc, inches:		+3.6	0	-14.2	
.577 Nitro Express						
A-Square 750 Triad	velocity, fps:	2050	1811	1595	1401	
	energy, ft-lb:	6998	5463	4234	3267	
	arc, inches:		+4.9	0	-18.5	

Centerfire Rifle Ballistics

.577 Tyrannosaur to 700 Nitro Express

CARTRIDGE BULLET	RANGE, YARDS:	0	100	200	300	400
.577 Tyrannosaur						
A-Square 750 Triad	velocity, fps:	2460	2197	1950	1723	1516
	energy, ft-lb:	10077	8039	6335	4941	3825
	arc, inches:		+2.8	0	-12.1	-36.0
.600 Nitro Express						
A-Square 900 Triad	velocity, fps:	1950	1680	1452	1336	
	energy, ft-lb:	7596	5634	4212	3564	
	arc, inches:		+5.6	0	-20.7	
.700 Nitro Express						
A-Square 1000 Monolithic Solid	velocity, fps:	1900	1669	1461	1288	
	energy, ft-lb:	8015	6188	4740	3685	
	arc, inches:		+5.8	0	-22.2	

Centerfire Handgun Ballistics

Centerfire Handgun Ballistics

Data shown here is taken from manufacturers' charts; your chronograph readings may vary. Barrel lengths for pistol data vary, and depend in part on which pistols are typically chambered in a given cartridge. Velocity variations due to barrel length depend on the baseline bullet speed and the load. Velocity for the .30 Carbine, normally a rifle cartridge, was determined in a pistol barrel. Listings are current as of February the year *Shooter's Bible* appears (not the cover year). Listings are not intended as recommendations. For example, the data for the .25 Auto gives velocity and energy readings to 100 yards. Few handgunners would call the little .25 a 100-yard cartridge.

Abbreviations: Bullets are designated by loading company, weight (in grains) and type, with these abbreviations for shape and construction: **BJHP**=Brass-Jacketed Hollowpoint; **FN**=Flat Nose; **FMC**=Full Metal Case; **FMJ**=Full Metal Jacket; **HP**=Hollowpoint; **L**=Lead; **LF**=Lead-Free; **+P**=a more powerful load than traditionally manufactured for that round; **RN**=Round Nose; **SFHP**=Starfire (PMC) Hollowpoint; **SP**=Softpoint; **SWC**=Semi Wadcutter; **TMJ**=Totally Metal Jacket (Speer); **WC**=Wadcutter; **CEPP**, **SXT** and **XTP** are trademarked designations of Lapua, Winchester and Hornady, respectively.

.25 Auto to .32 S&W Long

CARTRIDGE BULLET	RANGE, YARDS:	0	25	50	75	100
.25 AUTO						
Federal 50 FMJ	velocity, fps:	760	750	730	720	700
	energy, ft-lb:	65	60	60	55	55
Hornady 35 JHP/XTP	velocity, fps:	900		813		742
	energy, ft-lb:	63		51		43
Magtech 50 FMC	velocity, fps:	760		707		659
	energy, ft-lb:	64		56		48
PMC 50 FMJ	velocity, fps:	754	730	707	685	663
	energy, ft-lb:	62				
Rem. 50 Metal Case	velocity, fps:	760		707		659
	energy, ft-lb:	64		56		48
Speer 35 Gold Dot	velocity, fps:	900		816		747
	energy, ft-lb:	63		52		43
Speer 50 TMJ (and Blazer)	velocity, fps:	760		717		677
	energy, ft-lb:	64		57		51
Win. 45 Expanding Point	velocity, fps:	815		729		655
	energy, ft-lb	66		53		42
Win. 50 FMJ	velocity, fps:	760		707		
	energy, ft-lb	64		56		
.30 LUGER						
Win. 93 FMJ	velocity, fps:	1220		1110		1040
	energy, ft-lb	305		255		225
.30 CARBINE						
Win. 110 Hollow SP	velocity, fps:	1790		1601		1430
	energy, ft-lb	783		626		500
.32 AUTO						
Federal 65 Hydra-Shok JHP	velocity, fps:	950	920	890	860	830
	energy, ft-lb:	130	120	115	105	100
Federal 71 FMJ	velocity, fps:	910	880	860	830	810
	energy, ft-lb:	130	120	115	110	105
Hornady 60 JHP/XTP	velocity, fps:	1000		917		849
	energy, ft-lb:	133		112		96
Hornady 71 FMJ-RN	velocity, fps:	900		845		797
	energy, ft-lb:	128		112		100

CARTRIDGE BULLET	RANGE, YARDS:	0	25	50	75	100
Magtech 71 FMC	velocity, fps:	905		855		810
	energy, ft-lb:	129		115		103
Magtech 71 JHP	velocity, fps:	905		855		810
	energy, ft-lb:	129		115		103
PMC 60 JHP	velocity, fps:	980	849	820	791	763
	energy, ft-lb:	117				
PMC 71 FMJ	velocity, fps:	870	841	814	791	763
	energy, ft-lb:	119				
Rem. 71 Metal Case	velocity, fps:	905		855		810
	energy, ft-lb:	129		115		97
Speer 60 Gold Dot	velocity, fps:	960		868		796
	energy, ft-lb:	123		100		84
Speer 71 TMJ (and Blazer)	velocity, fps:	900		855		810
	energy, ft-lb:	129		115		97
Win. 60 Silvertip HP	velocity, fps:	970		895		835
	energy, ft-lb	125		107		93
Win. 71 FMJ	velocity, fps:	905		855		
	energy, ft-lb	129		115		
.32 S&W						
Rem. 88 LRN	velocity, fps:	680		645		610
	energy, ft-lb:	90		81		73
Win. 85 LRN	velocity, fps:	680		645		610
	energy, ft-lb	90		81		73
.32 S&W LONG						
Federal 98 LWC	velocity, fps:	780	700	630	560	500
	energy, ft-lb:	130	105	85	70	55
Federal 98 LRN	velocity, fps:	710	690	670	650	640
	energy, ft-lb:	115	105	100	95	90
Lapua 83 LWC	velocity, fps:	240		189		149
	energy, ft-lb:	154		95		59
Lapua 98 LWC	velocity, fps:	240		202		171
	energy, ft-lb:	183		130		93
Magtech 98 LRN	velocity, fps:	705		670		635
	energy, ft-lb:	108		98		88

Centerfire Handgun Ballistics

.32 S&W Long to 9mm Luger

Cartridge Bullet	Range, Yards:	0	25	50	75	100
Magtech 98 LWC	velocity, fps:	682		579		491
	energy, ft-lb:	102		73		52
Norma 98 LWC	velocity, fps:	787	759	732		683
	energy, ft-lb:	136	126	118		102
PMC 98 LRN	velocity, fps:	789	770	751	733	716
	energy, ft-lb:	135				
PMC 100 LWC	velocity, fps:	683	652	623	595	569
	energy, ft-lb:	102				
Rem. 98 LRN	velocity, fps:	705		670		635
	energy, ft-lb:	115		98		88
Win. 98 LRN	velocity, fps:	705		670		635
		115		98		88

.32 Short Colt

Cartridge Bullet	Range, Yards:	0	25	50	75	100
Win. 80 LRN	velocity, fps:	745		665		590
	energy, ft-lb	100		79		62

.32-20

Cartridge Bullet	Range, Yards:	0	25	50	75	100
Black Hills 115 FPL	velocity, fps:	800				
	energy, ft-lb:					

.32 H&R Magnum

Cartridge Bullet	Range, Yards:	0	25	50	75	100
Black Hills 85 JHP	velocity, fps	1100				
	energy, ft-lb	228				
Black Hills 90 FPL	velocity, fps	750				
	energy, ft-lb					
Black Hills 115 FPL	velocity, fps	800				
	energy, ft-lb					
Federal 85 Hi-Shok JHP	velocity, fps:	1100	1050	1020	970	930
	energy, ft-lb:	230	210	195	175	165
Federal 95 LSWC	velocity, fps:	1030	1000	940	930	900
	energy, ft-lb:	225	210	195	185	170

9mm Makarov

Cartridge Bullet	Range, Yards:	0	25	50	75	100
Federal 90 Hi-Shok JHP	velocity, fps:	990	950	910	880	850
	energy, ft-lb:	195	180	165	155	145
Federal 90 FMJ	velocity, fps:	990	960	920	900	870
	energy, ft-lb:	205	190	180	170	160
Hornady 95 JHP/XTP	velocity, fps:	1000		930		874
	energy, ft-lb:	211		182		161
Speer 95 TMJ Blazer	velocity, fps:	1000		928		872
	energy, ft-lb:	211		182		161

9mm Luger

Cartridge Bullet	Range, Yards:	0	25	50	75	100
Black Hills 115 JHP +P	velocity, fps:	1300				
	energy, ft-lb:	431				
Black Hills 115 FMJ	velocity, fps:	1150				
	energy, ft-lb:	336				
Black Hills 115 EXP JHP	velocity, fps:	1250				
	energy, ft-lb:	400				
Black Hills 124 JHP +P	velocity, fps:	1250				
	energy, ft-lb:	430				
Black Hills 124 JHP	velocity, fps:	1150				
	energy, ft-lb:	363				
Black Hills 147 JHP subsonic	velocity, fps:	975				
	energy, ft-lb:	309				
Black Hills 147 FMJ subsonic	velocity, fps:	975				
	energy, ft-lb:	309				
Federal 105 EFMJ	velocity, fps:	1225	1160	1105	1060	1025
	energy, ft-lb:	350	315	285	265	245
Federal 115 Hi-Shok JHP	velocity, fps:	1160	1100	1060	1020	990
	energy, ft-lb:	345	310	285	270	250
Federal 115 FMJ	velocity, fps:	1160	1100	1060	1020	990
	energy, ft-lb:	345	310	285	270	250
Federal 124 FMJ	velocity, fps:	1120	1070	1030	990	960
	energy, ft-lb:	345	315	290	270	255
Federal 124 Hydra-Shok JHP	velocity, fps:	1120	1070	1030	990	960
	energy, ft-lb:	345	315	290	270	255
Federal 124 TMJ TMF Primer	velocity, fps:	1120	1070	1030	990	960
	energy, ft-lb:	345	315	290	270	255
Federal 124 Truncated FMJ	velocity, fps:	1120	1070	1030	990	960
Match	energy, ft-lb:	345	315	290	270	255
Federal 124 Nyclad HP	velocity, fps:	1120	1070	1030	990	960
	energy, ft-lb:	345	315	290	270	255
Federal 124 FMJ +P	velocity, fps:	1120	1070	1030	990	960
	energy, ft-lb:	345	315	290	270	255
Federal 135 Hydra-Shok JHP	velocity, fps:	1050	1030	1010	980	970
	energy, ft-lb:	330	315	300	290	280
Federal 147 Hydra-Shok JHP	velocity, fps:	1000	960	920	890	860
	energy, ft-lb:	325	300	275	260	240
Federal 147 Hi-Shok JHP	velocity, fps:	980	950	930	900	880
	energy, ft-lb:	310	295	285	265	255
Federal 147 FMJ FN	velocity, fps:	960	930	910	890	870
	energy, ft-lb:	295	280	270	260	250
Federal 147 TMJ TMF Primer	velocity, fps:	960	940	910	890	870
	energy, ft-lb:	300	285	270	260	245
Hornady 115 JHP/XTP	velocity, fps:	1155		1047		971
	energy, ft-lb:	341		280		241
Hornady 124 JHP/XTP	velocity, fps:	1110		1030		971
	energy, ft-lb:	339		292		259
Hornady 147 JHP/XTP	velocity, fps:	975		935		899
	energy, ft-lb:	310		285		264
Lapua 116 FMJ	velocity, fps:	365		319*		290*
	energy, ft-lb:	500		381*		315*
Lapua 120 FMJ CEPP Super	velocity, fps:	360		316*		288*
	energy, ft-lb:	505		390*		324*
Lapua 120 FMJ CEPP Extra	velocity, fps:	360		316*		288*
	energy, ft-lb:	505		390*		324*
Lapua 123 HP Megashock	velocity, fps:	355		311*		284*
	energy, ft-lb:	504		388*		322*
Lapua 123 FMJ	velocity, fps:	320		292*		272*
	energy, ft-lb:	410		342*		295*
Lapua 123 FMJ Combat	velocity, fps:	55		315*		289*
	energy, ft-lb:	504		397*		333*
Magtech 115 JHP +P	velocity, fps:	1246		1137		1056
	energy, ft-lb:	397		330		285
Magtech 115 FMC	velocity, fps:	1135		1027		961
	energy, ft-lb:	330		270		235
Magtech 115 JHP	velocity, fps:	1155		1047		971
	energy, ft-lb:	340		280		240
Magtech 124 FMC	velocity, fps:	1109		1030		971
	energy, ft-lb:	339		292		259
Norma 123 Full jacket	velocity, fps:	1099	1032	980		899
	energy, ft-lb:	331	292	263		221
Norma 123 Full jacket	velocity, fps:	1280	1170	1086		972
	energy, ft-lb:	449	375	323		259
PMC 95 SFHP	velocity, fps:	1250	1239	1228	1217	1207
	energy, ft-lb:	330				
PMC 115 FMJ	velocity, fps:	1157	1100	1053	1013	979
	energy, ft-lb:	344				
PMC 115 JHP	velocity, fps:	1167	1098	1044	999	961
	energy, ft-lb:	350				

Centerfire Handgun Ballistics

9mm Luger to .380 Auto

CARTRIDGE BULLET	RANGE, YARDS:	0	25	50	75	100
PMC 124 SFHP	velocity, fps:	1090	1043	1003	969	939
	energy, ft-lb:	327				
PMC 124 FMJ	velocity, fps:	1110	1059	1017	980	949
	energy, ft-lb:	339				
Rem. 101 Lead Free Frangible	velocity, fps:	1220		1092		1004
	energy, ft-lb:	334		267		226
Rem. 115 FN Enclosed Base	velocity, fps:	1135		1041		973
	energy, ft-lb:	329		277		242
Rem. 115 Metal Case	velocity, fps:	1135		1041		973
	energy, ft-lb:	329		277		242
Rem. 115 JHP	velocity, fps:	1155		1047		971
	energy, ft-lb:	341		280		241
Rem. 115 JHP +P	velocity, fps:	1250		1113		1019
	energy, ft-lb:	399		316		265
Rem. 124 JHP	velocity, fps:	1120		1028		960
	energy, ft-lb:	346		291		254
Rem. 124 FNEB	velocity, fps:	1100		1030		971
	energy, ft-lb:	339		292		252
Rem. 124 BJHP	velocity, fps:	1125		1031		963
	energy, ft-lb:	349		293		255
Rem. 124 BJHP +P	velocity, fps:	1180		1089		1021
	energy, ft-lb:	384		327		287
Rem. 124 Metal Case	velocity, fps:	1110		1030		971
	energy, ft-lb:	339		292		259
Rem. 147 JHP subsonic	velocity, fps:	990		941		900
	energy, ft-lb:	320		289		264
Rem. 147 BJHP	velocity, fps:	990		941		900
	energy, ft-lb:	320		289		264
Speer 90 Frangible	velocity, fps:	1350		1132		1001
	energy, ft-lb:	364		256		200
Speer 115 JHP Blazer	velocity, fps:	1145		1024		943
	energy, ft-lb:	335		268		227
Speer 115 FMJ Blazer	velocity, fps:	1145		1047		971
	energy, ft-lb:	341		280		241
Speer 115 FMJ	velocity, fps:	1200		1060		970
	energy, ft-lb:	368		287		240
Speer 115 Gold Dot HP	velocity, fps:	1200		1047		971
	energy, ft-lb:	341		280		241
Speer 124 FMJ Blazer	velocity, fps:	1090		989		917
	energy, ft-lb:	327		269		231
Speer 124 FMJ	velocity, fps:	1090		987		913
	energy, ft-lb:	327		268		230
Speer 124 TMJ-CF (and Blazer)	velocity, fps:	1090		989		917
	energy, ft-lb:	327		269		231
Speer 124 Gold Dot HP	velocity, fps:	1150		1030		948
	energy, ft-lb:	367		292		247
Speer 124 Gold Dot HP+P	velocity, ft-lb:	1220		1085		996
	energy, ft-lb:	410		324		273
Speer 147 TMJ Blazer	velocity, fps:	950		912		879
	energy, ft-lb:	295		272		252
Speer 147 TMJ	velocity, fps:	985		943		906
	energy, ft-lb:	317		290		268
Speer 147 TMJ-CF (and Blazer)	velocity, fps:	985		960		924
	energy, ft-lb:	326		300		279
Speer 147 Gold Dot	velocity, fps:	985		960		924
	energy, ft-lb:	326		300		279
Win. 105 Jacketed FP	velocity, fps:	1200		1074		989
	energy, ft-lb:	336		269		228
Win. 115 Silvertip HP	velocity, fps:	1225		1095		1007
	energy, ft-lb:	383		306		259
Win. 115 Jacketed HP	velocity, fps:	1225		1095		
	energy, ft-lb:	383		306		
Win. 115 FMJ	velocity, fps:	1190		1071		
	energy, ft-lb:	362		293		
Win. 115 Brass Enclosed Base	velocity, fps:	1190		1088		
WinClean	energy, ft-lb:	362		302		
Win. 124 FMJ	velocity, fps:	1140		1050		
	energy, ft-lb:	358		303		
Win. 124 Brass Enclosed Base	velocity, fps:	1130		1049		
WinClean	energy, ft-lb:	352		303		
Win. 147 FMJ FN	velocity, fps:	990		945		
	energy, ft-lb:	320		292		
Win. 147 SXT	velocity, fps:	990		947		909
	energy, ft-lb:	320		293		270
Win. 147 Silvertip HP	velocity, fps:	1010		962		921
	energy, ft-lb:	333		302		277
Win. 147 JHP	velocity, fps:	990		945		
	energy, ft-lb:	320		291		
Win. 147 Brass Enclosed Base	velocity, fps:	990		945		
WinClean	energy, ft-lb:	320		291		

9 x 23 Winchester

CARTRIDGE BULLET	RANGE, YARDS:	0	25	50	75	100
Win. 124 Jacketed FP	velocity, fps:	1460		1308		
	energy, ft-lb:	587		471		
Win. 125 Silvertip HP	velocity, fps:	1450		1249		1103
	energy, ft-lb:	583		433		338

.38 S&W

CARTRIDGE BULLET	RANGE, YARDS:	0	25	50	75	100
Rem. 146 LRN	velocity, fps:	685		650		620
	energy, ft-lb:	150		135		125
Win. 145 LRN	velocity, fps:	685		650		620
	energy, ft-lb:	150		135		125

.38 Short Colt

CARTRIDGE BULLET	RANGE, YARDS:	0	25	50	75	100
Rem. 125 LRN	velocity, fps:	730		685		645
	energy, ft-lb:	150		130		115

.38 Long Colt

CARTRIDGE BULLET	RANGE, YARDS:	0	25	50	75	100
Black Hills 158 RNL	velocity, fps:	650				
	energy, ft-lb:					

.380 Auto

CARTRIDGE BULLET	RANGE, YARDS:	0	25	50	75	100
Black Hills 90 JHP	velocity, fps:	1000				
	energy, ft-lb:	200				
Black Hills 95 FMJ	velocity, fps:	950				
	energy, ft-lb:	190				
Federal 90 Hi-Shok JHP	velocity, fps:	1000	940	890	840	800
	energy, ft-lb:	200	175	160	140	130
Federal 90 Hydra-Shok JHP	velocity, fps:	1000	940	890	840	800
	energy, ft-lb:	200	175	160	140	130
Federal 95 FMJ	velocity, fps:	960	910	870	830	790
	energy, ft-lb:	190	175	160	145	130
Hornady 90 JHP/XTP	velocity, fps:	1000		902		823
	energy, ft-lb:	200		163		135
Magtech 85 JHP + P	velocity, fps:	1082		999		936
	energy, ft-lb:	221		188		166
Magtech 95 FMC	velocity, fps:	951		861		781
	energy, ft-lb:	190		156		128
Magtech 95 JHP	velocity, fps:	951		861		781
	energy, ft-lb:	190		156		128
PMC 90 FMJ	velocity, fps:	910	872	838	807	778
	energy, ft-lb:	165				

Centerfire Handgun Ballistics

.380 Auto to .38 Special

CARTRIDGE BULLET	RANGE, YARDS:	0	25	50	75	100
PMC 90 JHP	velocity, fps:	917	878	844	812	782
	energy, ft-lb:	168				
PMC 95 SFHP	velocity, fps:	925	884	847	813	783
	energy, ft-lb:	180				
Rem. 88 JHP	velocity, fps:	990		920		868
	energy, ft-lb:	191		165		146
Rem. 95 FN Enclosed Base	velocity, fps:	955		865		785
	energy, ft-lb:	190		160		130
Rem. 95 Metal Case	velocity, fps:	955		865		785
	energy, ft-lb:	190		160		130
Rem. 102 BJHP	velocity, fps:	940		901		866
	energy, ft-lb:	200		184		170
Speer 88 JHP Blazer	velocity, fps:	950		920		870
	energy, ft-lb:	195		164		148
Speer 90 Gold Dot	velocity, fps:	990		907		842
	energy, ft-lb:	196		164		142
Speer 95 TMJ Blazer	velocity, fps:	945		865		785
	energy, ft-lb:	190		160		130
Speer 95 TMJ	velocity, fps:	950		877		817
	energy, ft-lb:	180		154		133
Win. 85 Silvertip HP	velocity, fps:	1000		921		860
	energy, ft-lb:	189		160		140
Win. 95 SXT	velocity, fps:	955		889		835
	energy, ft-lb:	192		167		147
Win. 95 FMJ	velocity, fps:	955		865		
	energy, ft-lb:	190		160		
Win. 95 Brass Enclosed Base	velocity, fps:	955		881		
WinClean	energy, ft-lb:	192		164		

.38 Special

CARTRIDGE BULLET	RANGE, YARDS:	0	25	50	75	100
Black Hills 125 JHP +P	velocity, fps:	1050				
	energy, ft-lb:	306				
Black Hills 158 CNL	velocity, fps:	800				
	energy, ft-lb:					
Federal 110 Hydra-Shok JHP	velocity, fps:	1000	970	930	910	880
	energy, ft-lb:	245	225	215	200	190
Federal 110 Hi-Shok JHP +P	velocity, fps:	1000	960	930	900	870
	energy, ft-lb:	240	225	210	195	185
Federal 125 Nyclad HP	velocity, fps:	830	780	730	690	650
	energy, ft-lb:	190	170	150	130	115
Federal 125 Hi-Shok JSP +P	velocity, fps:	950	920	900	880	860
	energy, ft-lb:	250	235	225	215	205
Federal 125 Hi-Shok JHP +P	velocity, fps:	950	920	900	880	860
	energy, ft-lb:	250	235	225	215	205
Federal 125 Nyclad HP +P	velocity, fps:	950	920	900	880	860
	energy, ft-lb:	250	235	225	215	205
Federal 129 Hydra-	velocity, fps:	950	930	910	890	870
Shok JHP+P	energy, ft-lb:	255	245	235	225	215
Federal 130 FMJ	velocity, fps:	950	920	890	870	840
	energy, ft-lb:	260	245	230	215	205
Federal 148 LWC Match	velocity, fps:	710	670	630	600	560
	energy, ft-lb:	165	150	130	115	105
Federal 158 LRN	velocity, fps:	760	740	720	710	690
	energy, ft-lb:	200	190	185	175	170
Federal 158 LSWC	velocity, fps:	760	740	720	710	690
	energy, ft-lb:	200	190	185	175	170
Federal 158 Nyclad RN	velocity, fps:	760	740	720	710	690
	energy, ft-lb:	200	190	185	175	170
Federal 158 SWC HP +P	velocity, fps:	890	870	860	840	820
	energy, ft-lb:	280	265	260	245	235
Federal 158 LSWC +P	velocity, fps:	890	870	860	840	820
	energy, ft-lb:	270	265	260	245	235
Federal 158 Nyclad	velocity, fps:	890	870	860	840	820
SWC-HP+P	energy, ft-lb:	270	265	260	245	235
Hornady 125 JHP/XTP	velocity, fps:	900		856		817
	energy, ft-lb:	225		203		185
Hornady 140 JHP/XTP	velocity, fps:	825		790		757
	energy, ft-lb:	212		194		178
Hornady 140 Cowboy	velocity, fps:	800		767		735
	energy, ft-lb:	199		183		168
Hornady 148 HBWC	velocity, fps:	800		697		610
	energy, ft-lb:	210		160		122
Hornady 158 JHP/XPT	velocity, fps:	800		765		731
	energy, ft-lb:	225		205		188
Lapua 123 HP Megashock	velocity, fps:	355		311		284
	energy, ft-lb:	504		388		322
Lapua 148 LWC	velocity, fps:	230		203		181
	energy, ft-lb:	254		199		157
Lapua 150 SJFN	velocity, fps:	325		301		283
	energy, ft-lb:	512		439		388
Lapua 158 FMJLF	velocity, fps:	255		243		232
	energy, ft-lb:	332		301		275
Lapua 158 LRN	velocity, fps:	255		243		232
	energy, ft-lb:	332		301		275
Magtech 125 JHP +P	velocity, fps:	1017		971		931
	energy, ft-lb:	287		262		241
Magtech 148 LWC	velocity, fps:	710		634		566
	energy, ft-lb:	166		132		105
Magtech 158 LRN	velocity, fps:	755		728		693
	energy, ft-lb:	200		183		168
Magtech 158 LFN	velocity, fps:	800		776		753
	energy, ft-lb:	225		211		199
Magtech 158 SJHP	velocity, fps:	807		779		753
	energy, ft-lb:	230		213		199
Magtech 158 LSWC	velocity, fps:	755		721		689
	energy, ft-lb:	200		182		167
Magtech 158 FMC-Flat	velocity, fps:	807		779		753
	energy, ft-lb:	230		213		199
PMC 125 SFHP +P	velocity, fps:	950	918	889	863	838
	energy, ft-lb:	251				
PMC 125 JHP +P	velocity, fps:	974	938	906	878	851
	energy, ft-lb:	266				
PMC 132 FMJ	velocity, fps:	841	820	799	780	761
	energy, ft-lb:	206				
PMC 148 LWC	velocity, fps:	728	694	662	631	602
	energy, ft-lb:	175				
PMC 158 LRN	velocity, fps:	820	801	783	765	749
	energy, ft-lb:	235				
PMC 158 JSP	velocity, fps:	835	816	797	779	762
	energy, ft-lb:	245				
PMC 158 LFP	velocity, fps:	800		761		725
	energy, ft-lb:	225		203		185
Rem. 101 Lead Free Frangible	velocity, fps:	950		896		850
	energy, ft-lb:	202		180		162
Rem. 110 SJHP	velocity, fps:	950		890		840
	energy, ft-lb:	220		194		172
Rem. 110 SJHP +P	velocity, fps:	995		926		871
	energy, ft-lb:	242		210		185
Rem. 125 SJHP +P	velocity, ft-lb:	945		898		858
	energy, ft-lb:	248		224		204

Centerfire Handgun Ballistics

.38 Special to .357 Magnum

CARTRIDGE BULLET	RANGE, YARDS:	0	25	50	75	100
Rem. 125 FN Enclosed Base	velocity, fps:	1025		976		935
	energy, ft-lb:	292		264		243
Rem. 125 BJHP	velocity, fps:	975		929		885
	energy, ft-lb:	264		238		218
Rem. 130 Metal Case	velocity, fps:	950		913		879
	energy, ft-lb:	261		240		223
Rem. 148 LWC Match	velocity, fps:	710		634		566
	energy, ft-lb:	166		132		105
Rem. 158 LRN	velocity, fps:	755		723		692
	energy, ft-lb:	200		183		168
Rem. 158 SWC +P	velocity, fps:	890		855		823
	energy, ft-lb:	278		257		238
Rem. 158 SWC	velocity, fps:	755		723		692
	energy, ft-lb:	200		183		168
Rem. 158 LHP +P	velocity, fps:	890		855		823
	energy, ft-lb:	278		257		238
Speer 125 JHP +P Blazer	velocity, fps:	945		898		858
	energy, ft-lb:	248		224		204
Speer 125 Gold Dot +P	velocity, fps:	945		898		858
	energy, ft-lb:	248		224		204
Speer 158 TMJ +P	velocity, fps:	900		852		818
(and Blazer)	energy, ft-lb:	278		255		235
Speer 158 LRN Blazer	velocity, fps:	755		723		692
	energy, ft-lb:	200		183		168
Speer 158 Trail Blazer LFN	velocity, fps:	800		761		725
	energy, ft-lb:	225		203		184
Speer 158 TMJ-CF +P	velocity, fps:	900		852		818
(and Blazer)	energy, ft-lb:	278		255		235
Win. 110 Silvertip HP	velocity, fps:	945		894		850
	energy, ft-lb:	218		195		176
Win. 110 Jacketed FP	velocity, fps:	975		906		849
	energy, ft-lb:	232		201		176
Win. 125 Jacketed HP	velocity, fps:	945		898		
	energy, ft-lb:	248		224		
Win. 125 Jacketed HP +P	velocity, fps:	945		898		858
	energy, ft-lb:	248		224		204
Win. 125 Jacketed FP	velocity, fps:	850		804		
	energy, ft-lb:	201		179		
Win. 125 Silvertip HP + P	velocity, fps:	945		898		858
	energy, ft-lb:	248		224		204
Win. 125 Jacketed FP	velocity, fps:	775		742		
WinClean	energy, ft-lb:	167		153		
Win. 130 FMJ	velocity, fps:	800		765		
	energy, ft-lb:	185		169		
Win. 130 SXT +P	velocity, fps:	925		887		852
	energy, ft-lb:	247		227		210
Win. 148 LWC Super Match	velocity, fps:	710		634		566
	energy, ft-lb:	166		132		105
Win. 150 Lead	velocity, fps:	845		812		
	energy, ft-lb:	238		219		
Win. 158 Lead	velocity, fps:	800		761		725
	energy, ft-lb:	225		203		185
Win. 158 LRN	velocity, fps:	755		723		693
	energy, ft-lb:	200		183		168
Win. 158 LSWC	velocity, fps:	755		721		689
	energy, ft-lb:	200		182		167
Win. 158 LSWC HP +P	velocity, fps:	890		855		823
	energy, ft-lb:	278		257		238

.38-40

CARTRIDGE BULLET	RANGE, YARDS:	0	25	50	75	100
Black Hills 180 FPL	velocity, fps:	800				
	energy, ft-lb:					

.38 Super

CARTRIDGE BULLET	RANGE, YARDS:	0	25	50	75	100
Federal 130 FMJ +P	velocity, fps:	1200	1140	1100	1050	1020
	energy, ft-lb:	415	380	350	320	300
PMC 115 JHP	velocity, fps:	1116	1052	1001	959	923
	energy, ft-lb:	318				
PMC 130 FMJ	velocity, fps:	1092	1038	994	957	924
	energy, ft-lb:	348				
Rem. 130 Metal Case	velocity, fps:	1215		1099		1017
	energy, ft-lb:	426		348		298
Win. 125 Silvertip HP +P	velocity, fps:	1240		1130		1050
	energy, ft-lb:	427		354		306
Win. 130 FMJ +P	velocity, fps:	1215		1099		
	energy, ft-lb:	426		348		

.357 Sig

CARTRIDGE BULLET	RANGE, YARDS:	0	25	50	75	100
Federal 125 FMJ	velocity, fps:	1350	1270	1190	1130	1080
	energy, ft-lb:	510	445	395	355	325
Federal 125 JHP	velocity, fps:	1350	1270	1190	1130	1080
	energy, ft-lb:	510	445	395	355	325
Federal 150 JHP	velocity, fps:	1130	1080	1030	1000	970
	energy, ft-lb:	420	385	355	330	310
Hornady 124 JHP/XTP	velocity, fps:	1350		1208		1108
	energy, ft-lb:	502		405		338
Hornady 147 JHP/XTP	velocity, fps:	1225		1138		1072
	energy, ft-lb:	490		422		375
PMC 124 SFHP	velocity, fps:	1350	1263	1190	1132	1083
	energy, ft-lb:	502				
PMC 124 FMJ/FP	velocity, fps:	1350	1242	1158	1093	1040
	energy, ft-lb:	512				
Rem. 104 Lead Free Frangible	velocity, fps:	1400		1223		1094
	energy, ft-lb:	453		345		276
Rem. 125 Metal Case	velocity, fps:	1350		1146		1018
	energy, ft-lb:	506		422		359
Rem. 125 JHP	velocity, fps:	1350		1157		1032
	energy, ft-lb:	506		372		296
Speer 125 TMJ (and Blazer)	velocity, fps:	1350		1177		1057
	energy, ft-lb:	502		381		307
Speer 125 TMJ-CF	velocity, fps:	1350		1177		1057
	energy, ft-lb:	502		381		307
Speer 125 Gold Dot	velocity, fps:	1375		1203		1079
	energy, ft-lb:	525		402		323
Win. 105 JFP	velocity, fps:	1370		1179		1050
	energy, ft-lb	438		324		257
Win. 125 FMJ FN	velocity, fps:	1350		1185		
	energy, ft-lb	506		390		

.357 Magnum

CARTRIDGE BULLET	RANGE, YARDS:	0	25	50	75	100
Black Hills 125 JHP	velocity, fps:	1500				
	energy, ft-lb:	625				
Black Hills 158 CNL	velocity, fps:	800				
	energy, ft-lb:					
Federal 110 Hi-Shok JHP	velocity, fps:	1300	1180	1090	1040	990
	energy, ft-lb:	410	340	290	260	235
Federal 125 Hi-Shok JHP	velocity, fps:	1450	1350	1240	1160	1100
	energy, ft-lb:	580	495	430	370	335
Federal 130 Hydra-Shok JHP	velocity, fps:	1300	1210	1130	1070	1020
	energy, ft-lb:	490	420	370	330	300

Centerfire Handgun Ballistics

.357 Magnum to .40 S&W

CARTRIDGE BULLET	RANGE, YARDS:	0	25	50	75	100
Federal 158 Hi-Shok JSP	velocity, fps:	1240	1160	1100	1060	1020
	energy, ft-lb:	535	475	430	395	365
Federal 158 JSP	velocity, fps:	1240	1160	1100	1060	1020
	energy, ft-lb:	535	475	430	395	365
Federal 158 LSWC	velocity, fps:	1240	1160	1100	1060	1020
	energy, ft-lb:	535	475	430	395	365
Federal 158 Hi-Shok JHP	velocity, fps:	1240	1160	1100	1060	1020
	energy, ft-lb:	535	475	430	395	365
Federal 158 Hydra-Shok JHP	velocity, fps:	1240	1160	1100	1060	1020
	energy, ft-lb:	535	475	430	395	365
Federal 180 Hi-Shok JHP	velocity, fps:	1090	1030	980	930	890
	energy, ft-lb:	475	425	385	350	320
Federal 180 Castcore	velocity, fps:	1250	1200	1160	1120	1080
	energy, ft-lb:	625	575	535	495	465
Hornady 125 JHP/XTP	velocity, fps:	1500		1314		1166
	energy, ft-lb:	624		479		377
Hornady 125 JFP/XTP	velocity, fps:	1500		1311		1161
	energy, ft-lb:	624		477		374
Hornady 140 Cowboy	velocity, fps:	800		767		735
	energy, ft-lb:	199		183		168
Hornady 140 JHP/XTP	velocity, fps:	1400		1249		1130
	energy, ft-lb:	609		485		397
Hornady 158 JHP/XTP	velocity, fps:	1250		1150		1073
	energy, ft-lb:	548		464		404
Hornady 158 JFP/XTP	velocity, fps:	1250		1147		1068
	energy, ft-lb:	548		461		400
Lapua 150 FMJ CEPP Super	velocity, fps:	370		527		303
	energy, ft-lb:	664		527		445
Lapua 150 SJFN	velocity, fps:	385		342		313
	energy, ft-lb:	719		569		476
Lapua 158 SJHP	velocity, fps:	470		408		359
	energy, ft-lb:	1127		850		657
Magtech 158 SJSP	velocity, fps:	1235		1104		1015
	energy, ft-lb:	535		428		361
Magtech 158 SJHP	velocity, fps:	1235		1104		1015
	energy, ft-lb:	535		428		361
PMC 125 JHP	velocity, fps:	1194	1117	1057	1008	967
	energy, ft-lb:	399				
PMC 150 JHP	velocity, fps:	1234	1156	1093	1042	1000
	energy, ft-lb:	512				
PMC 150 SFHP	velocity, fps:	1205	1129	1069	1020	980
	energy, ft-lb:	484				
PMC 158 JSP	velocity, fps:	1194	1122	1063	1016	977
	energy, ft-lb:	504				
PMC 158 LFP	velocity, fps:	800		761		725
	energy, ft-lb:	225		203		185
Rem. 110 SJHP	velocity, fps:	1295		1094		975
	energy, ft-lb:	410		292		232
Rem. 125 SJHP	velocity, fps:	1450		1240		1090
	energy, ft-lb:	583		427		330
Rem. 125 BJHP	velocity, fps:	1220		1095		1009
	energy, ft-lb:	413		333		283
Rem. 125 FNEB	velocity, fps:	1450		1240		1090
	energy, ft-lb:	583		427		330
Rem. 158 SJHP	velocity, fps:	1235		1104		1015
	energy, ft-lb:	535		428		361
Rem. 158 SP	velocity, fps:	1235		1104		1015
	energy, ft-lb:	535		428		361
Rem. 158 SWC	velocity, fps:	1235		1104		1015
	energy, ft-lb:	535		428		361
Rem. 165 JHP Core-Lokt	velocity, fps:	1290		1189		1108
	energy, ft-lb:	610		518		450
Rem. 180 SJHP	velocity, fps:	1145		1053		985
	energy, ft-lb:	542		443		388
	energy, ft-lb:	542		443		388
Speer 125 Gold Dot	velocity, fps:	1450		1240		1090
	energy, ft-lb:	583		427		330
Speer 158 JHP Blazer	velocity, fps:	1150		1104		1015
	energy, ft-lb:	535		428		361
Speer 158 Gold Dot	velocity, fps:	1235		1104		1015
	energy, ft-lb:	535		428		361
Speer 170 Gold Dot SP	velocity, fps:	1180		1089		1019
	energy, ft-lb:	525		447		392
Win. 110 JFP	velocity, fps:	1275		1105		998
	energy, ft-lb:	397		298		243
Win. 110 JHP	velocity, fps:	1295		1095		
	energy, ft-lb:	410		292		
Win. 125 JFP WinClean	velocity, fps:	1370		1183		
	energy, ft-lb:	521		389		
Win. 145 Silvertip HP	velocity, fps:	1290		1155		1060
	energy, ft-lb:	535		428		361
Win. 158 JHP	velocity, fps:	1235		1104		1015
	energy, ft-lb:	535		428		361
Win. 158 JSP	velocity, fps:	1235		1104		1015
	energy, ft-lb:	535		428		361
Win. 180 Partition Gold	velocity, fps:	1180		1088		1020
	energy, ft-lb:	557		473		416

.40 S&W

CARTRIDGE BULLET	RANGE, YARDS:	0	25	50	75	100
Black Hills 155 JHP	velocity, fps:	1150				
	energy, ft-lb:	450				
Black Hills 165 EXP JHP	velocity, fps:	1150				
	energy, ft-lb:	483				
Black Hills 180 JHP	velocity, fps:	1000				
	energy, ft-lb:	400				
Federal 135 Hydra-Shok JHP	velocity, fps:	1190	1050	970	900	850
	energy, ft-lb:	420	330	280	245	215
Federal 155 FMJ Ball	velocity, fps:	1140	1080	1030	990	960
	energy, ft-lb:	445	400	365	335	315
Federal 155 Hi-Shok JHP	velocity, fps:	1140	1080	1030	990	950
	energy, ft-lb:	445	400	365	335	315
Federal 155 Hydra-Shok JHP	velocity, fps:	1140	1080	1030	990	950
	energy, ft-lb:	445	400	365	335	315
Federal 165 EFMJ	velocity, fps:	1190	1060	970	905	850
	energy, ft-lb:	520	410	345	300	265
Federal 165 FMJ	velocity, fps:	1050	1020	990	960	935
	energy, ft-lb:	405	380	355	335	320
Federal 165 FMJ Ball	velocity, fps:	980	950	920	900	880
	energy, ft-lb:	350	330	310	295	280
Federal 165 Hydra-Shok JHP	velocity, fps:	980	950	930	910	890
Federal 180 High	velocity, fps:	990	960	930	910	890
Antim. Lead	energy, ft-lb:	390	365	345	330	315
Federal 180 TMJ TMF Primer	velocity, fps:	990	960	940	910	890
	energy, ft-lb:	390	370	350	330	315
Federal 180 FMJ Ball	velocity, fps:	990	960	940	910	890
	energy, ft-lb:	390	370	350	330	315
Federal 180 Hi-Shok JHP	velocity, fps:	990	960	930	910	890
	energy, ft-lb:	390	365	345	330	315
Federal 180 Hydra-Shok JHP	velocity, fps:	990	960	930	910	890
	energy, ft-lb:	390	365	345	330	315

Centerfire Handgun Ballistics

.40 S&W to .44 Colt

CARTRIDGE BULLET	RANGE, YARDS:	0	25	50	75	100
Hornady 155 JHP/XTP	velocity, fps:	1180		1061		980
	energy, ft-lb:	479		388		331
Hornady 180 JHP/XTP	velocity, fps:	950		903		862
	energy, ft-lb:	361		326		297
Magtech 155 JHP	velocity, fps:	1025		1118		1052
	energy, ft-lb:	500		430		381
Magtech 180 JHP	velocity, fps:	990		933		886
	energy, ft-lb:	390		348		314
Magtech 180 FMC	velocity, fps:	990		933		886
	energy, ft-lb:	390		348		314
PMC 155 SFHP	velocity, fps:	1160	1092	1039	994	957
	energy, ft-lb:	463				
PMC 165 JHP	velocity, fps:	1040	1002	970	941	915
	energy, ft-lb:	396				
PMC 165 FMJ	velocity, fps:	1010	977	948	922	899
	energy, ft-lb:	374				
PMC 180 FMJ/FP	velocity, fps:	985	957	931	908	885
	energy, ft-lb:	388				
PMC 180 SFHP	velocity, fps:	985	958	933	910	889
	energy, ft-lb:	388				
Rem. 141 Lead Free	velocity, fps:	1135		1056		996
Frangible	energy, ft-lb:	403		349		311
Rem. 155 JHP	velocity, fps:	1205		1095		1017
	energy, ft-lb:	499		413		356
Rem. 165 BJHP	velocity, fps:	1150		1040		964
	energy, ft-lb:	485		396		340
Rem. 180 JHP	velocity, fps:	1015		960		914
	energy, ft-lb:	412		368		334
Rem. 180 FN Enclosed Base	velocity, fps:	985		936		893
	energy, ft-lb:	388		350		319
Rem. 180 Metal Case	velocity, fps:	985		936		893
	energy, ft-lb:	388		350		319
Rem. 180 BJHP	velocity, fps:	1015		960		914
	energy, ft-lb:	412		368		334
Speer 105 Frangible	velocity, fps:	1380		1128		985
	energy, ft-lb:	444		297		226
Speer 155 TMJ Blazer	velocity, fps:	1175		1047		963
	energy, ft-lb:	475		377		319
Speer 155 TMJ	velocity, fps:	1200		1065		976
	energy, ft-lb:	496		390		328
Speer 155 Gold Dot	velocity, fps:	1200		1063		974
	energy, ft-lb:	496		389		326
Speer 165 TMJ Blazer	velocity, fps:	1100		1006		938
	energy, ft-lb:	443		371		321
Speer 165 TMJ	velocity, fps:	1150		1040		964
	energy, ft-lb:	484		396		340
Speer 165 Gold Dot	velocity, fps:	1150		1043		966
	energy, ft-lb:	485		399		342
Speer 180 HP Blazer	velocity, fps:	985		951		909
	energy, ft-lb:	400		361		330
Speer 180 FMJ Blazer	velocity, fps:	1000		937		886
	energy, ft-lb:	400		351		313
Speer 180 FMJ	velocity, fps:	1000		951		909
	energy, ft-lb:	400		361		330
Speer 180 TMJ-CF	velocity, fps:	1000		951		909
(and Blazer)	energy, ft-lb:	400		361		330
Speer 180 Gold Dot	velocity, fps:	1025		957		902
	energy, ft-lb:	420		366		325
Win. 140 JFP	velocity, fps:	1155		1039		960
	energy, ft-lb:	415		336		286
Win. 155 Silvertip HP	velocity, fps:	1205		1096		1018
	energy, ft-lb	500		414		357
Win. 165 SXT	velocity, fps:	1130		1041		977
	energy, ft-lb:	468		397		349
Win. 165 FMJ FN	velocity, fps:	1060		1001		
	energy, ft-lb:	412		367		
Win. 165 Brass Enclosed Base	velocity, fps:	1130		1054		
WinClean	energy, ft-lb:	468		407		
Win. 180 JHP	velocity, fps:	1010		954		
	energy, ft-lb:	408		364		
Win. 180 FMJ	velocity, fps:	990		936		
	energy, ft-lb:	390		350		
Win. 180 SXT	velocity, fps:	1010		954		909
	energy, ft-lb:	408		364		330
Win. 180 Brass Enclosed Base	velocity, fps:	990		943		
WinClean	energy, ft-lb:	392		356		

10 mm Auto

CARTRIDGE BULLET	RANGE, YARDS:	0	25	50	75	100
Federal 155 Hi-Shok JHP	velocity, fps:	1330	1230	1140	1080	1030
	energy, ft-lb:	605	515	450	400	360
Federal 180 Hi-Shok JHP	velocity, fps:	1030	1000	970	950	920
	energy, ft-lb:	425	400	375	355	340
Federal 180 Hydra-Shok JHP	velocity, fps:	1030	1000	970	950	920
	energy, ft-lb:	425	400	375	355	340
Federal 180 High Antim. Lead	velocity, fps:	1030	1000	970	950	920
	energy, ft-lb:	425	400	375	355	340
Federal 180 FMJ	velocity, fps:	1060	1025	990	965	940
	energy, ft-lb:	400	370	350	330	310
Hornady 155 JHP/XTP	velocity, fps:	1265		1119		1020
	energy, ft-lb:	551		431		358
Hornady 180 JHP/XTP	velocity, fps:	1180		1077		1004
	energy, ft-lb:	556		464		403
Hornady 200 JHP/XTP	velocity, fps:	1050		994		948
	energy, ft-lb:	490		439		399
PMC 170 JHP	velocity, fps:	1200	1117	1052	1000	958
	energy, ft-lb:	543				
PMC 180 SFHP	velocity, fps:	950	926	903	882	862
	energy, ft-lb:	361				
PMC 200 TC-FMJ	velocity, fps:	1050	1008	972	941	912
	energy, ft-lb:	490				
Rem. 180 Metal Case	velocity, fps:	1150		1063		998
	energy, ft-lb:	529		452		398
Speer 200 TMJ Blazer	velocity, fps:	1050		966		952
	energy, ft-lb:	490		440		402
Win. 175 Silvertip HP	velocity, fps:	1290		1141		1037
	energy, ft-lb:	649		506		418

.41 Remington Magnum

CARTRIDGE BULLET	RANGE, YARDS:	0	25	50	75	100
Federal 210 Hi-Shok JHP	velocity, fps:	1300	1210	1130	1070	1030
	energy, ft-lb:	790	680	595	540	495
PMC 210 TCSP	velocity, fps:	1290	1201	1128	1069	1021
	energy, ft-lb:	774				
Rem. 210 SP	velocity, fps:	1300		1162		1062
	energy, ft-lb:	788		630		526
Win. 175 Silvertip HP	velocity, fps:	1250		1120		102
	energy, ft-lb:	607		488		412
Win. 240 Platinum Tip	velocity, ft-lb:	1250		1151		1075
	energy, ft-lb:	833		706		616

.44 Colt

CARTRIDGE BULLET	RANGE, YARDS:	0	25	50	75	100
Black Hills 230 FPL	velocity, fps:	730				
	energy, ft-lb:					

Centerfire Handgun Ballistics

.44 Russian to .45 Automatic (ACP)

CARTRIDGE BULLET	RANGE, YARDS:	0	25	50	75	100
.44 RUSSIAN						
Black Hills 210 FPL	velocity, fps:	650				
	energy, ft-lb:					
.44 SPECIAL						
Black Hills 210 FPL	velocity, fps:	700				
	energy, ft-lb:					
Federal 200 SWC HP	velocity, fps:	900	860	830	800	770
	energy, ft-lb:	360	330	305	285	260
Federal 250 CastCore	velocity, fps:	1250	1200	1150	1110	1080
	energy, ft-lb:	865	795	735	685	645
Hornady 180 JHP/XTP	velocity, fps:	1000		935		882
	energy, ft-lb:	400		350		311
Magtech 240 LFN	velocity, fps:	750		722		696
	energy, ft-lb:	300		278		258
PMC 180 JHP	velocity, fps:	980	938	902	869	839
	energy, ft-lb:	383				
PMC 240 SWC-CP	velocity, fps:	764	744	724	706	687
	energy, ft-lb:	311				
PMC 240 LFP	velocity, fps:	750		719		690
	energy, ft-lb:	300		275		253
Rem. 246 LRN	velocity, fps:	755		725		695
	energy, ft-lb:	310		285		265
Speer 200 HP Blazer	velocity, fps:	875		825		780
	energy, ft-lb:	340		302		270
Speer 200 Trail Blazer LFN	velocity, fps:	750		714		680
	energy, ft-lb:	250		226		205
Speer 200 Gold Dot	velocity, fps:	875		825		780
	energy, ft-lb:	340		302		270
Win. 200 Silvertip HP	velocity, fps:	900		860		822
	energy, ft-lb:	360		328		300
Win. 240 Lead	velocity, fps:	750		719		690
	energy, ft-lb	300		275		253
Win. 246 LRN	velocity, fps:	755		725		695
	energy, ft-lb:	310		285		265
.44 REMINGTON MAGNUM						
Black Hills 240 JHP	velocity, fps:	1260				
	energy, ft-lb:	848				
Black Hills 300 JHP	velocity, fps:	1150				
	energy, ft-lb:	879				
Federal 180 Hi-Shok JHP	velocity, fps:	1610	1480	1370	1270	1180
	energy, ft-lb:	1035	875	750	640	555
Federal 240 Hi-Shok JHP	velocity, fps:	1180	1130	1080	1050	1010
	energy, ft-lb:	740	675	625	580	550
Federal 240 Hydra-Shok JHP	velocity, fps:	1180	1130	1080	1050	1010
	energy, ft-lb:	740	675	625	580	550
Federal 240 JHP	velocity, fps:	1180	1130	1080	1050	1010
	energy, ft-lb:	740	675	625	580	550
Federal 300 CastCore	velocity, fps:	1250	1200	1160	1120	1080
	energy, ft-lb:	1040	960	885	825	775
Hornady 180 JHP/XTP	velocity, fps:	1550		1340		1173
	energy, ft-lb:	960		717		550
Hornady 200 JHP/XTP	velocity, fps:	1500		1284		1128
	energy, ft-lb:	999		732		565
Hornady 240 JHP/XTP	velocity, fps:	1350		1188		1078
	energy, ft-lb:	971		753		619
Hornady 300 JHP/XTP	velocity, fps:	1150		1084		1031
	energy, ft-lb:	881		782		708
Magtech 240 SJSP	velocity, fps:	1180		1081		1010
	energy, ft-lb:	741		632		623
PMC 180 JHP	velocity, fps:	1392	1263	1157	1076	1015
	energy, ft-lb:	772				
PMC 240 JHP	velocity, fps:	1301	1218	1147	1088	1041
	energy, ft-lb:	900				
PMC 240 TC-SP	velocity, fps:	1300	1216	1144	1086	1038
	energy, ft-lb:	900				
PMC 240 SFHP	velocity, fps:	1300	1212	1138	1079	1030
	energy, ft-lb:	900				
PMC 240 LSWC-GCK	velocity, fps:	1225	1143	1077	1025	982
	energy, ft-lb:	806				
Rem. 180 JSP	velocity, fps:	1610		1365		1175
	energy, ft-lb:	1036		745		551
Rem. 210 Gold Dot HP	velocity, fps:	1450		1276		1140
	energy, ft-lb:	980		759		606
Rem. 240 SP	velocity, fps:	1180		1081		1010
	energy, ft-lb:	721		623		543
Rem. 240 SJHP	velocity, fps:	1180		1081		1010
	energy, ft-lb:	721		623		543
Rem. 275 JHP Core-Lokt	velocity, fps:	1235		1142		1070
	energy, ft-lb:	931		797		699
Speer 240 JHP Blazer	velocity, fps:	1200		1092		1015
	energy, ft-lb:	767		636		549
Speer 240 Gold Dot HP	velocity, fps:	1400		1255		1139
	energy, ft-lb:	1044		839		691
Speer 270 Gold Dot SP	velocity, fps:	1250		1142		1060
	energy, ft-lb:	937		781		674
Win. 210 Silvertip HP	velocity, fps:	1250		1106		1010
	energy, ft-lb:	729		570		475
Win. 240 Hollow SP	velocity, fps:	1180		1081		1010
	energy, ft-lb:	741		623		543
Win. 240 JSP	velocity, fps:	1180		1081		
	energy, ft-lb:	741		623		
Win. 250 Partition Gold	velocity, fps:	1230		1132		1057
	energy, ft-lb:	840		711		620
Win. 250 Platinum Tip	velocity, fps:	1250		1148		1070
	energy, ft-lb:	867		732		635
.44-40						
Black Hills 200 RNFP	velocity, fps:	800				
	energy, ft-lb:					
Hornady 205 Cowboy	velocity, fps:	725		697		670
	energy, ft-lb:	239		221		204
Magtech 225 LFN	velocity, fps:	725		703		681
	energy, ft-lb:	281		247		232
PMC 225 LFP	velocity, fps:	725		723		695
	energy, ft-lb:	281		261		242
Win. 225 Lead	velocity, fps:	750		723		695
	energy, ft-lb:	281		261		242
.45 AUTOMATIC (ACP)						
Black Hills 185 JHP	velocity, fps:	1000				
	energy, ft-lb:	411				
Black Hills 200 Match SWC	velocity, fps:	875				
	energy, ft-lb:	340				
Black Hills 230 FMJ	velocity, fps:	850				
	energy, ft-lb:	368				
Black Hills 230 JHP	velocity, fps:	850				
	energy, ft-lb:	368				
Black Hills 230 JHP +P	velocity, fps:	950				
	energy, ft-lb:	460				
Federal 165 Hydra-Shok JHP	velocity, fps:	1060	1020	980	950	920
	energy, ft-lb:	410	375	350	330	310

Centerfire Handgun Ballistics

.45 Automatic (ACP) to .45 Colt

CARTRIDGE BULLET	RANGE, YARDS:	0	25	50	75	100
Federal 165 EFMJ	velocity, fps:	1090	1045	1005	975	942
	energy, ft-lb:	435	400	370	345	325
Federal 185 Hi-Shok JHP	velocity, fps:	950	920	900	880	860
	energy, ft-lb:	370	350	335	315	300
Federal 185 FMJ-SWC Match	velocity, fps:	780	730	700	660	620
	energy, ft-lb:	245	220	200	175	160
Federal 200 Exp. FMJ	velocity, fps:	1030	1000	970	940	920
	energy, ft-lb:	470	440	415	395	375
Federal 230 FMJ	velocity, fps:	850	830	810	790	770
	energy, ft-lb:	370	350	335	320	305
Federal 230 FMJ Match	velocity, fps:	855	835	815	795	775
	energy, ft-lb:	375	355	340	325	305
Federal 230 Hi-Shok JHP	velocity, fps:	850	830	810	790	770
	energy, ft-lb:	370	350	335	320	300
Federal 230 Hydra-Shok JHP	velocity, fps:	850	830	810	790	770
	energy, ft-lb:	370	350	335	320	305
Federal 230 FMJ	velocity, fps:	850	830	810	790	770
	energy, ft-lb:	370	350	335	320	305
Federal 230 TMJ TMF Primer	velocity, fps:	850	830	810	790	770
	energy, ft-lb:	370	350	335	315	305
Hornady 185 JHP/XTP	velocity, fps:	950		880		819
	energy, ft-lb:	371		318		276
Hornady 200 JHP/XTP	velocity, fps:	900		855		815
	energy, ft-lb:	358		325		295
Hornady 200 HP/XTP +P	velocity, fps:	1055		982		925
	energy, ft-lb:	494		428		380
Hornady 230 FMJ/RN	velocity, fps:	850		809		771
	energy, ft-lb:	369		334		304
Hornady 230 FMJ/FP	velocity, fps:	850		809		771
	energy, ft-lb:	369		334		304
Hornady 230 HP/XTP +P	velocity, fps:	950		904		865
	energy, ft-lb:	462		418		382
Magtech 185 JHP +P	velocity, fps:	1148		1066		1055
	energy, ft-lb:	540		467		415
Magtech 200 LSWC	velocity, fps:	950		910		874
	energy, ft-lb:	401		368		339
Magtech 230 FMC	velociy, fps:	837		800		767
	energy, ft-lb:	356		326		300
Magtech 230 FMC-SWC	velocity, fps:	780		720		660
	energy, ft-lb:	310		265		222
PMC 185 JHP	velocity, fps:	903	870	839	811	785
	energy, ft-lb:	339				
PMC 200 FMJ-SWC	velocity, fps:	850	818	788	761	734
	energy, ft-lb:	321				
PMC 230 SFHP	velocity, fps:	850	830	811	792	775
	energy, ft-lb:	369				
PMC 230 FMJ	velocity, fps:	830	809	789	769	749
	energy, ft-lb:	352				
Rem. 175 Lead Free Frangible	velocity, fps:	1020		923		851
	energy, ft-lb:	404		331		281
Rem. 185 JHP	velocity, fps:	1000		939		889
	energy, ft-lb:	411		362		324
Rem. 185 BJHP	velocity, fps:	1015		951		899
	energy, ft-lb:	423		372		332
Rem. 185 BJHP +P	velocity, fps:	1140		1042		971
	energy, ft-lb:	534		446		388
Rem. 185 MC	velocity, fps:	1015		955		907
	energy, ft-lb:	423		375		338
Rem. 230 FN Enclosed Base	velocity, fps:	835		800		767
	energy, ft-lb:	356		326		300
Rem. 230 Metal Case	velocity, fps:	835		800		767
	energy, ft-lb:	356		326		300
Rem. 230 JHP	velocity, fps:	835		800		767
	energy, ft-lb:	356		326		300
Rem. 230 BJHP	velocity, fps:	875		833		795
	energy, ft-lb:	391		355		323
Speer 140 Frangible	velocity, fps:	1200		1029		928
	energy, ft-lb:	448		329		268
Speer 185 Gold Dot	velocity, fps:	1050		956		886
	energy, ft-lb:	453		375		322
Speer 185 TMJ/FN	velocity, fps:	1000		909		839
	energy, ft-lb:	411		339		289
Speer 200 JHP Blazer	velocity, fps:	975		917		860
	energy, ft-lb:	421		372		328
Speer 200 Gold Dot +P	velocity, fps:	1080		994		930
	energy, ft-lb:	518		439		384
Speer 200 TMJ/FN	velocity, fps:	975		897		834
	energy, ft-lb:	422		357		309
Speer 230 FMJ (and Blazer)	velocity, fps:	845		804		775
	energy, ft-lb:	363		329		304
Speer 230 TMJ-CF (and Blazer)	velocity, fps:	845		804		775
	energy, ft-lb:	363		329		304
Speer 230 Gold Dot	velocity, fps:	890		845		805
	energy, ft-lb:	405		365		331
Win. 170 JFP	velocity, fps:	1050		982		928
	energy, ft-lb:	416		364		325
Win. 185 Silvertip HP	velocity, fps:	1000		938		888
	energy, ft-lb:	411		362		324
Win. 185 FMJ FN	velocity, fps:	910		861		
	energy, ft-lb:	340		304		
Win. 185 Brass Enclosed Base	velocity, fps:	910		835		
WinClean	energy, ft-lb:	340		286		
Win. 230 JHP	velocity, fps:	880		842		
	energy, ft-lb:	396		363		
Win. 230 FMJ	velocity, fps:	835		800		
	energy, ft-lb:	356		326		
Win. 230 SXT	velocity, fps:	880		846		816
	energy, ft-lb:	396		366		340
Win. 230 JHP subsonic	velocity, fps:	880		842		808
	energy, ft-lb:	396		363		334
Win. 230 Brass Enclosed Base	velocity, fps:	835		802		
WinClean	energy, ft-lb:	356		329		
.45 Winchester Magnum						
Win. 260 Partition Gold	velocity, fps:	1200		1105		1033
	energy, ft-lb:	832		705		616
Win. 260 JHP	velocity, fps:	1200		1099		1026
	energy, ft-lb:	831		698		607
.45 Schofield						
Black Hills 180 FNL	velocity, fps:	730				
	energy, ft-lb:					
Black Hills 230 RNFP	velocity, fps:	730				
	energy, ft-lb:					
.45 Colt						
Black Hills 250 RNFP	velocity, fps:	725				
	energy, ft-lb:					
Federal 225 SWC HP	velocity, fps:	900	880	860	840	820
	energy, ft-lb:	405	385	370	355	340

Centerfire Handgun Ballistics

.45 Colt to .50 Action Express

CARTRIDGE BULLET	RANGE, YARDS:	0	25	50	75	100
Hornady 255 Cowboy	velocity, fps:	725		692		660
	energy, ft-lb:	298		271		247
Magtech 250 LFN	velocity, fps:	750		726		702
	energy, ft-lb:	312		293		274
PMC 250 LFP	velocity, fps:	800		767		736
	energy, ft-lb:	355		331		309
Rem. 225 SWC	velocity, fps:	960		890		832
	energy, ft-lb:	460		395		346
Rem. 250 RLN	velocity, fps:	860		820		780
	energy, ft-lb:	410		375		340
Speer 200 FMJ Blazer	velocity, fps:	1000		938		889
	energy, ft-lb:	444		391		351
Speer 230 Trail Blazer LFN	velocity, fps:	750		716		684
	energy, ft-lb:	287		262		239
Speer 250 Gold Dot	velocity, fps:	900		860		823
	energy, ft-lb:	450		410		376
Win. 225 Silvertip HP	velocity, fps:	920		877		839
	energy, ft-lb:	423		384		352
Win. 255 LRN	velocity, fps:	860		820		780
	energy, ft-lb:	420		380		345

.454 Casull

CARTRIDGE BULLET	RANGE, YARDS:	0	25	50	75	100
Federal 300 Trophy Bonded	velocity, fps:	1630	1540	1450	1380	1300
	energy, ft-lb:	1760	1570	1405	1260	1130
Federal 360 CastCore	velocity, fps:	1500	1435	1370	1310	1255
	energy, ft-lb:	1800	1640	1500	1310	1260
Hornady 240 XTP-MAG	velocity, fps:	1900		1679		1483
	energy, ft-lb:	1923		1502		1172
Hornady 300 XTP-MAG	velocity, fps:	1650		1478		1328
	energy, ft-lb:	1813		1455		1175
Magtech 260 SJSP	velocity, fps:	1800		1577		1383
	energy, ft-lb:	1871		1437		1104
Rem. 300 Core-Lokt Ultra	velocity, fps:	1625		1472		1335
	energy, ft-lb:	1759		1442		1187
Speer 300 Gold Dot HP	velocity, fps:	1625		1477		1343
	energy, ft-lb:	1758		1452		1201
Win. 250 JHP	velocity, fps:	1300		1151		1047
	energy, ft-lb:	938		735		608
Win. 260 Partition Gold	velocity, fps:	1800		1605		1427
	energy, ft-lb:	1871		1485		1176
Win. 260 Platinum Tip	velocity, fps:	1800		1596		1414
	eneryg, ft-lb:	1870		1470		1154
Win. 300 JFP	velocity, fps:	1625		1451		1308
	energy, ft-lb:	1759		1413		1141

.475 Linebaugh

CARTRIDGE BULLET	RANGE, YARDS:	0	25	50	75	100
Hornady 400 XTP-MAG	velocity, fps:	1300		1179		1093
	energy, ft-lb:	1501		1235		1060

.480 Ruger

CARTRIDGE BULLET	RANGE, YARDS:	0	25	50	75	100
Hornady 325 XTP-MAG	velocity, fps:	1350		1191		1076
	energy, ft-lb:	1315		1023		835
Speer 275 Gold Dot HP	velocity, fps:	1450		1284		1152
	energy, ft-lb:	1284		1007		810
Speer 325 SP	velocity, fps:	1350		1224		1124
	energy, ft-lb:	1315		1082		912

.50 Action Express

CARTRIDGE BULLET	RANGE, YARDS:	0	25	50	75	100
Speer 300 Gold Dot HP	velocity, fps:	1550		1361		1207
	energy, ft-lb:	1600		1234		970
Speer 325 UCHP	velocity, fps:	1400		1232		1106
	energy, ft-lb:	1414		1095		883

HANDLOADING

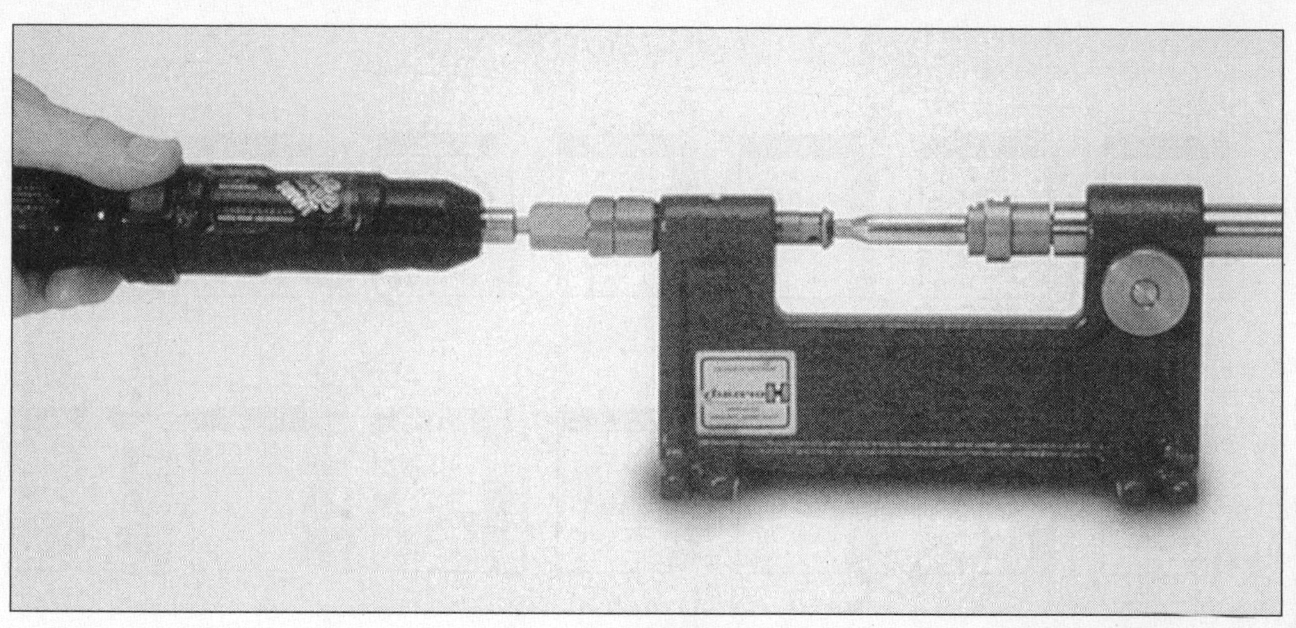

Barnes Bullets

The All Copper Barnes X-Bullet

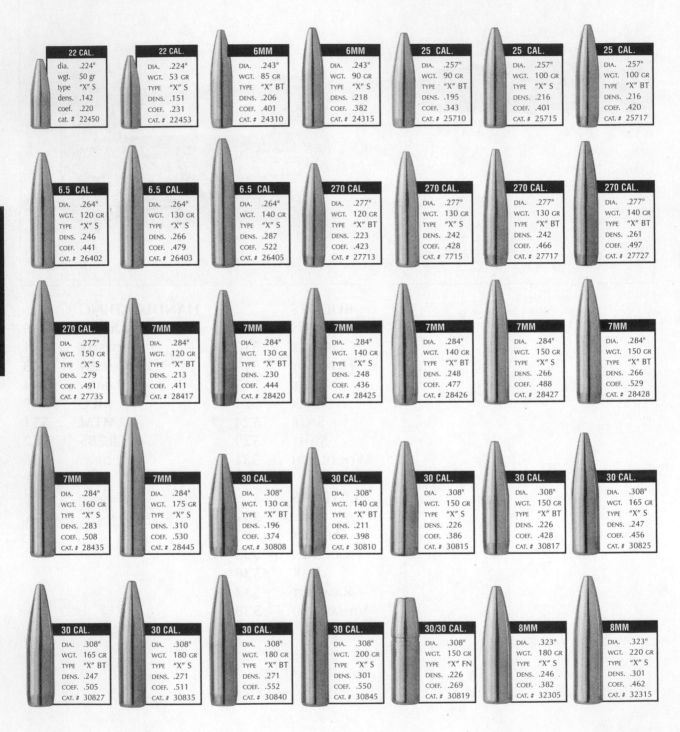

Caliber	Dia.	Wgt.	Type	Dens.	Coef.	Cat. #
22 CAL.	.224"	50 gr	"X" S	.142	.220	22450
22 CAL.	.224"	53 GR	"X" S	.151	.231	22453
6MM	.243"	85 GR	"X" BT	.206	.401	24310
6MM	.243"	90 GR	"X" S	.218	.382	24315
25 CAL.	.257"	90 GR	"X" BT	.195	.343	25710
25 CAL.	.257"	100 GR	"X" S	.216	.401	25715
25 CAL.	.257"	100 GR	"X" BT	.216	.420	25717
6.5 CAL.	.264"	120 GR	"X" S	.246	.441	26402
6.5 CAL.	.264"	130 GR	"X" S	.266	.479	26403
6.5 CAL.	.264"	140 GR	"X" S	.287	.522	26405
270 CAL.	.277"	120 GR	"X" BT	.223	.423	27713
270 CAL.	.277"	130 GR	"X" S	.242	.428	7715
270 CAL.	.277"	130 GR	"X" BT	.242	.466	27717
270 CAL.	.277"	140 GR	"X" BT	.261	.497	27727
270 CAL.	.277"	150 GR	"X" S	.279	.491	27735
7MM	.284"	120 GR	"X" BT	.213	.411	28417
7MM	.284"	130 GR	"X" BT	.230	.444	28420
7MM	.284"	140 GR	"X" S	.248	.436	28425
7MM	.284"	140 GR	"X" BT	.248	.477	28426
7MM	.284"	150 GR	"X" S	.266	.488	28427
7MM	.284"	150 GR	"X" BT	.266	.529	28428
7MM	.284"	160 GR	"X" S	.283	.508	28435
7MM	.284"	175 GR	"X" S	.310	.530	28445
30 CAL.	.308"	130 GR	"X" BT	.196	.374	30808
30 CAL.	.308"	140 GR	"X" BT	.211	.398	30810
30 CAL.	.308"	150 GR	"X" S	.226	.386	30815
30 CAL.	.308"	150 GR	"X" BT	.226	.428	30817
30 CAL.	.308"	165 GR	"X" S	.247	.456	30825
30 CAL.	.308"	165 GR	"X" BT	.247	.505	30827
30 CAL.	.308"	180 GR	"X" S	.271	.511	30835
30 CAL.	.308"	180 GR	"X" BT	.271	.552	30840
30 CAL.	.308"	200 GR	"X" S	.301	.550	30845
30/30 CAL.	.308"	150 GR	"X" FN	.226	.269	30819
8MM	.323"	180 GR	"X" S	.246	.382	32305
8MM	.323"	220 GR	"X" S	.301	.462	32315

Barnes Bullets

The All Copper Barnes X-Bullet

CAL.	DIA.	WGT.	TYPE	DENS.	COEF.	CAT. #
338 CAL.	.338"	160 GR	"X" S	.200	.337	33878
338 CAL.	.338"	175 GR	"X" S	.218	.392	33880
338 CAL.	.338"	185 GR	"X" BT	.231	.437	33881
338 CAL.	.338"	200 GR	"X" S	.250	.440	33882
338 CAL.	.338"	210 GR	"X" BT	.263	.471	33883
338 CAL.	.338"	225 GR	"X" S	.281	.482	33885
338 CAL.	.338"	250 GR	"X" S	.313	.521	33890
348 WIN.	.348"	200 GR	"X" FN	.234	.291	34800
348 WIN.	.348"	220 GR	"X" FN	.260	.315	34802
35 CAL.	.358"	180 GR	"X" S	.201	.298	35810
35 CAL.	.358"	200 GR	"X" S	.223	.346	35815
35 CAL.	.358"	250 GR	"X" S	.279	.458	35835
9.3 CAL.	.366"	250 GR	"X" S	.267	.428	36605
9.3 CAL.	.366"	286 GR	"X" S	.305	.468	36615
375 CAL.	.375"	210 GR	"X" S	.213	.341	37575
375 CAL.	.375"	250 GR	"X" S	.254	.450	37582
375 CAL.	.375"	270 GR	"X" S	.275	.503	37585
375 CAL.	.375"	300 GR	"X" S	.305	.555	37590
405 WIN.	.411"	300 GR	"X" S	.254	.313	41178
416 CAL.	.416"	300 GR	"X" S	.247	.394	41680
416 CAL.	.416"	350 GR	"X" S	.289	.521	41685
416 CAL.	.416"	400 GR	"X" S	.330	.546	41690
404 JEFF 425 EXP	.423"	400 GR	"X" S	.319	.537	42385
458 MAG	.458"	300 GR	"X" S	.204	.340	45802
458 MAG	.458"	350 GR	"X" S	.283	.402	45805
458 MAG	.458"	450 GR	"X" S	.306	.488	45818
458 MAG	.458"	500 GR	"X" S	.341	.526	45822
45/70 CAL.	.458"	250 GR	"X" FN	.170	.172	45831
45-70 CAL.	.458"	300 GR	"X" FN	.206	.204	45832

Barnes Bullets

Triple-Shock and Expander MZ Muzzleloader Bullets

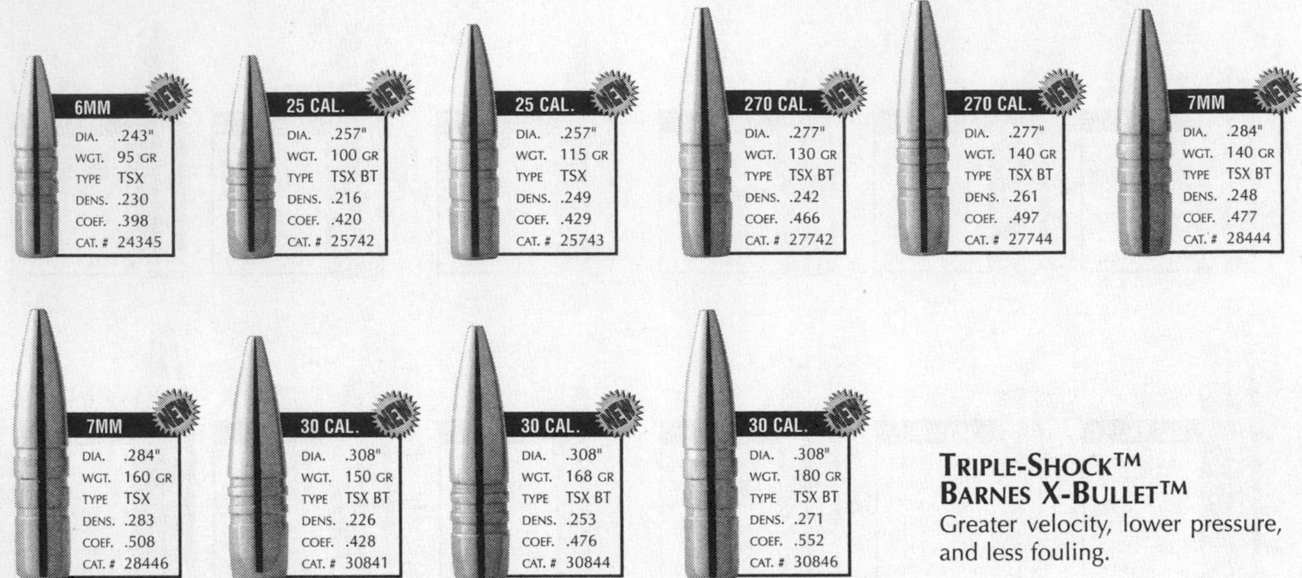

TRIPLE-SHOCK™ BARNES X-BULLET™

Greater velocity, lower pressure, and less fouling.

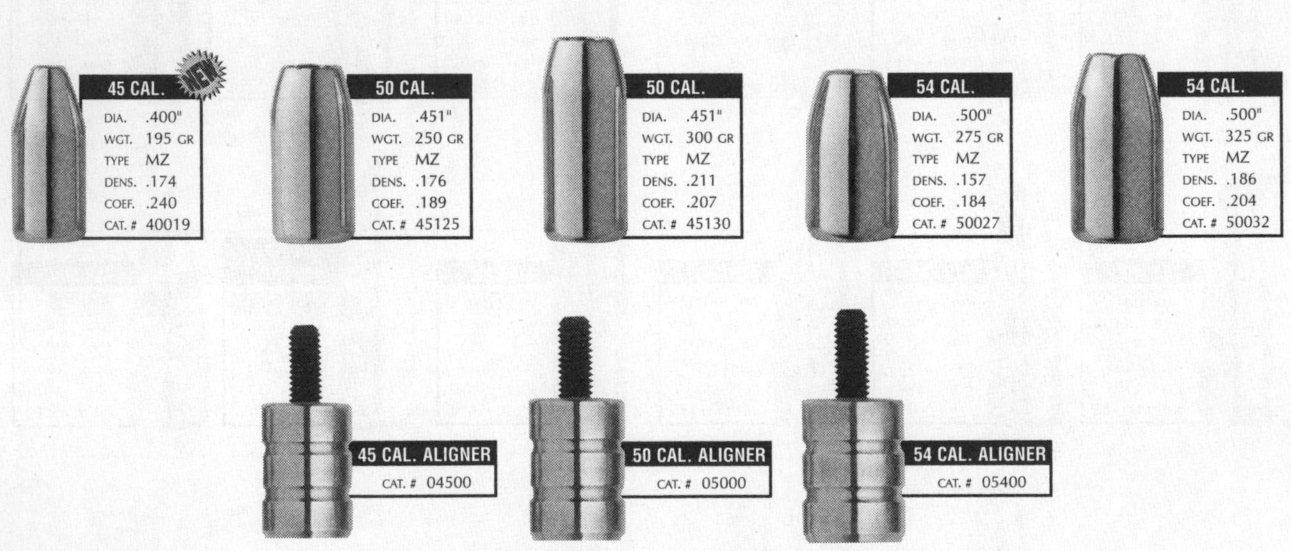

EXPANDER MZ™ MUZZLELOADER BULLETS

With only one shot available, it better be with the best.

Barnes Bullets
XLC Coated X-Bullets

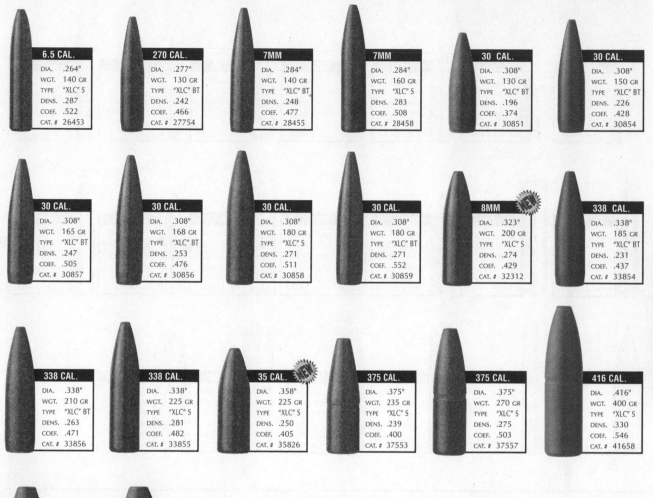

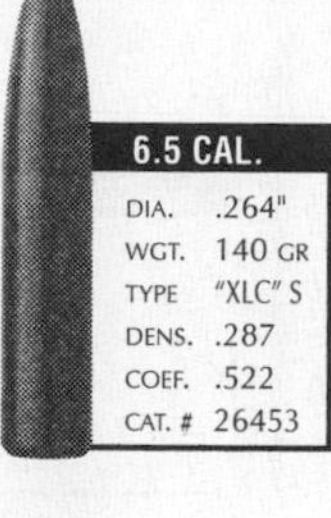

6.5 CAL.
DIA. .264"
WGT. 140 GR
TYPE "XLC" S
DENS. .287
COEF. .522
CAT. # 26453

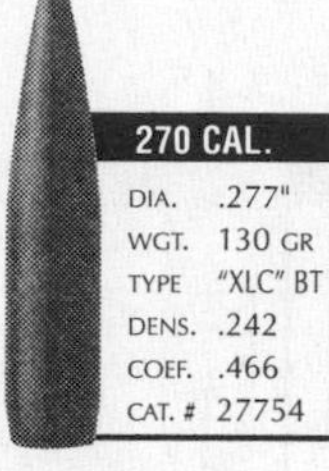

270 CAL.
DIA. .277"
WGT. 130 GR
TYPE "XLC" BT
DENS. .242
COEF. .466
CAT. # 27754

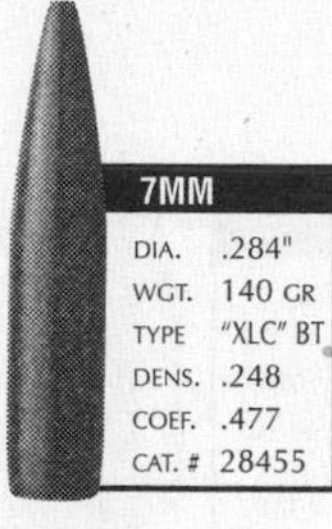

7MM
DIA. .284"
WGT. 140 GR
TYPE "XLC" BT
DENS. .248
COEF. .477
CAT. # 28455

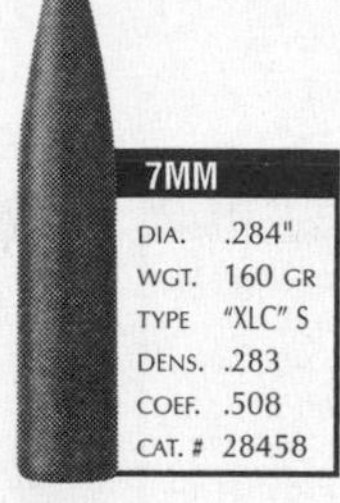

7MM
DIA. .284"
WGT. 160 GR
TYPE "XLC" S
DENS. .283
COEF. .508
CAT. # 28458

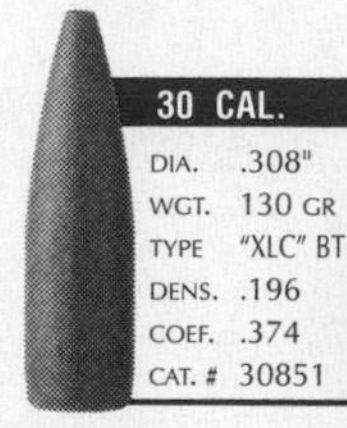

30 CAL.
DIA. .308"
WGT. 130 GR
TYPE "XLC" BT
DENS. .196
COEF. .374
CAT. # 30851

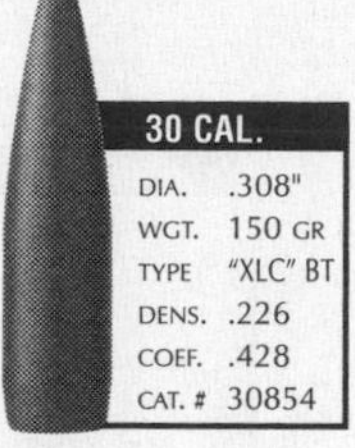

30 CAL.
DIA. .308"
WGT. 150 GR
TYPE "XLC" BT
DENS. .226
COEF. .428
CAT. # 30854

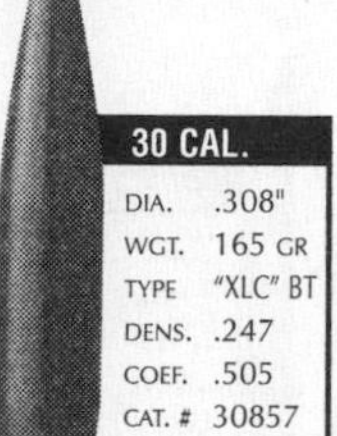

30 CAL.
DIA. .308"
WGT. 165 GR
TYPE "XLC" BT
DENS. .247
COEF. .505
CAT. # 30857

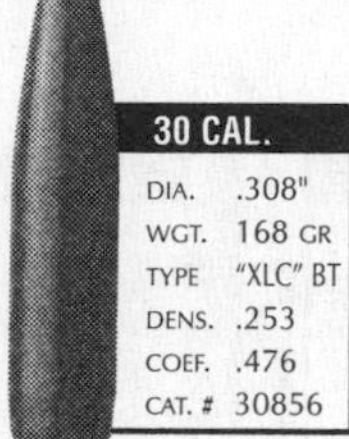

30 CAL.
DIA. .308"
WGT. 168 GR
TYPE "XLC" BT
DENS. .253
COEF. .476
CAT. # 30856

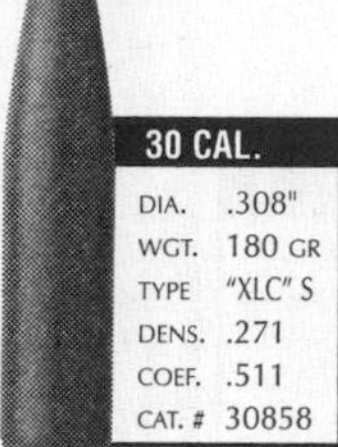

30 CAL.
DIA. .308"
WGT. 180 GR
TYPE "XLC" S
DENS. .271
COEF. .511
CAT. # 30858

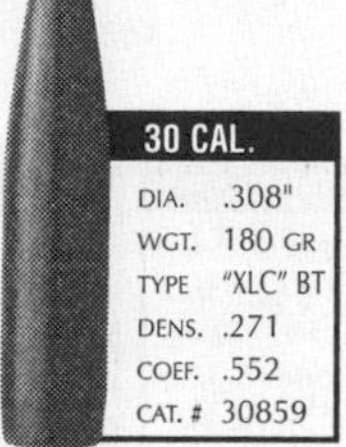

30 CAL.
DIA. .308"
WGT. 180 GR
TYPE "XLC" BT
DENS. .271
COEF. .552
CAT. # 30859

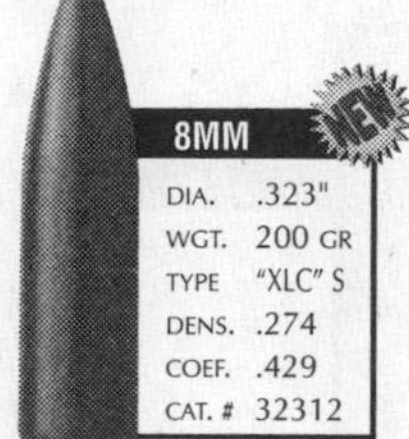

8MM
NEW
DIA. .323"
WGT. 200 GR
TYPE "XLC" S
DENS. .274
COEF. .429
CAT. # 32312

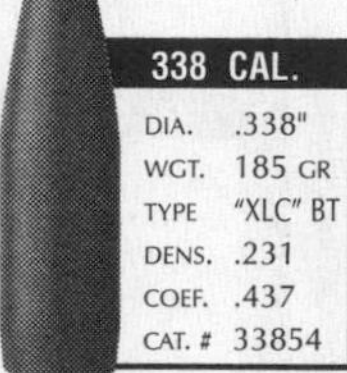

338 CAL.
DIA. .338"
WGT. 185 GR
TYPE "XLC" BT
DENS. .231
COEF. .437
CAT. # 33854

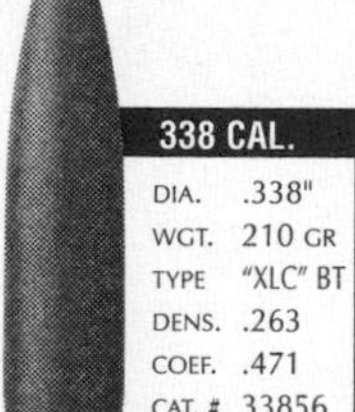

338 CAL.
DIA. .338"
WGT. 210 GR
TYPE "XLC" BT
DENS. .263
COEF. .471
CAT. # 33856

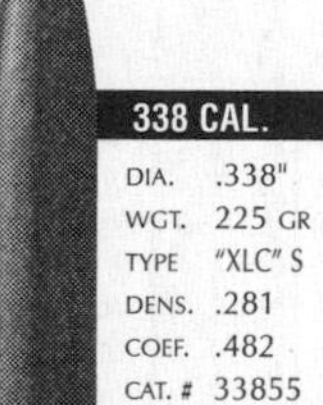

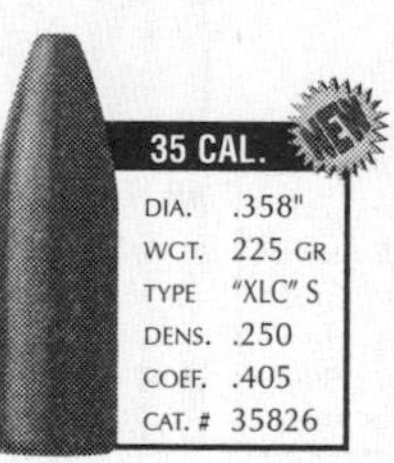

35 CAL.
NEW
DIA. .358"
WGT. 225 GR
TYPE "XLC" S
DENS. .250
COEF. .405
CAT. # 35826

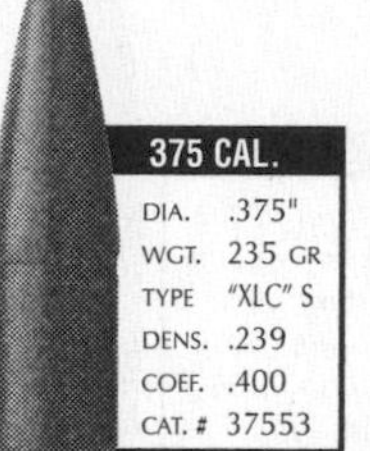

375 CAL.
DIA. .375"
WGT. 235 GR
TYPE "XLC" S
DENS. .239
COEF. .400
CAT. # 37553

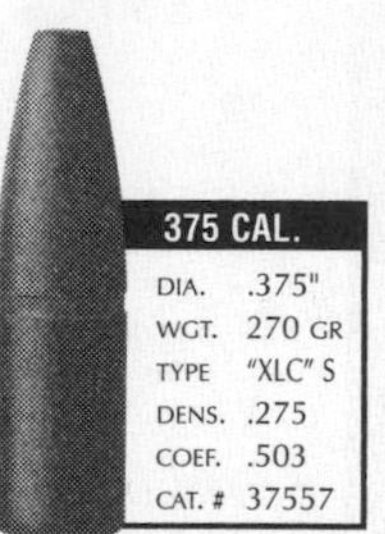

375 CAL.
DIA. .375"
WGT. 270 GR
TYPE "XLC" S
DENS. .275
COEF. .503
CAT. # 37557

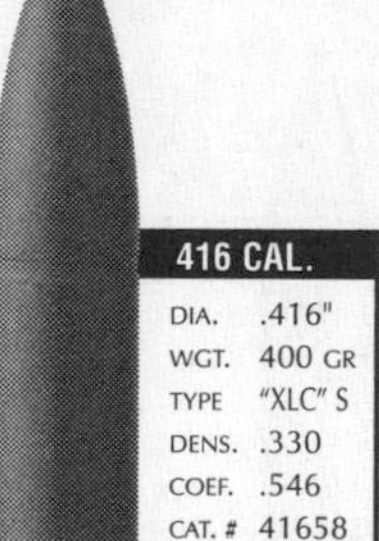

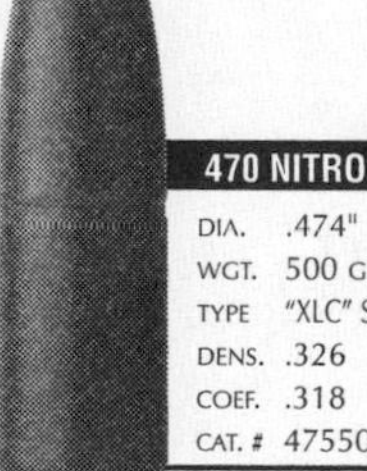

470 NITRO
DIA. .474"
WGT. 500 GR
TYPE "XLC" S
DENS. .326
COEF. .318
CAT. # 47550

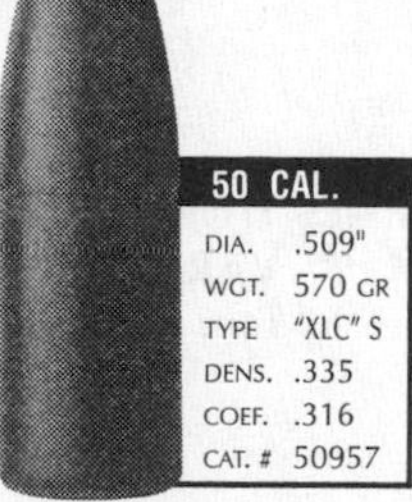

50 CAL.
DIA. .509"
WGT. 570 GR
TYPE "XLC" S
DENS. .335
COEF. .316
CAT. # 50957

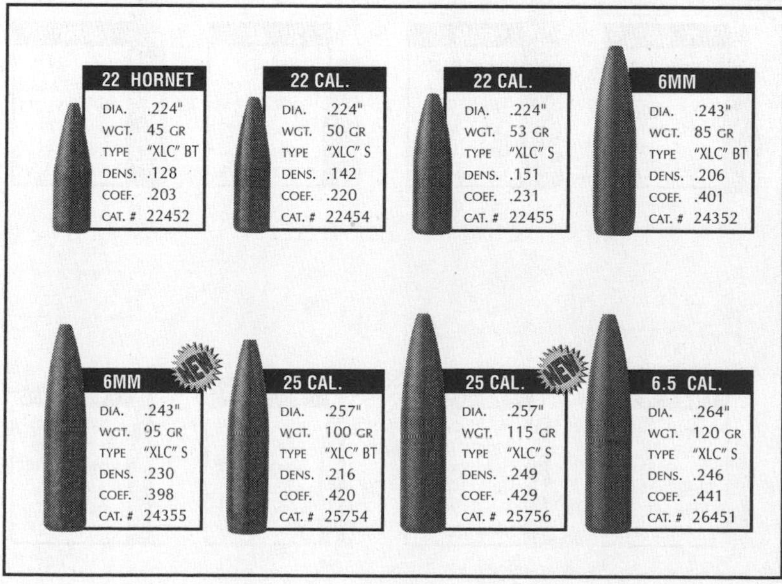

22 HORNET
DIA. .224"
WGT. 45 GR
TYPE "XLC" BT
DENS. .128
COEF. .203
CAT. # 22452
22 CAL.
DIA. .224"
WGT. 50 GR
TYPE "XLC" S
DENS. .142
COEF. .220
CAT. # 22454
22 CAL.
DIA. .224"
WGT. 53 GR
TYPE "XLC" S
DENS. .151
COEF. .231
CAT. # 22455
6MM
DIA. .243"
WGT. 85 GR
TYPE "XLC" BT
DENS. .206
COEF. .401
CAT. # 24352
6MM
NEW
DIA. .243"
WGT. 95 GR
TYPE "XLC" S
DENS. .230
COEF. .398
CAT. # 24355
25 CAL.
DIA. .257"
WGT. 100 GR
TYPE "XLC" BT
DENS. .216
COEF. .420
CAT. # 25754
25 CAL.
NEW
DIA. .257"
WGT. 115 GR
TYPE "XLC" S
DENS. .249
COEF. .429
CAT. # 25756
6.5 CAL.
DIA. .264"
WGT. 120 GR
TYPE "XLC" S
DENS. .246
COEF. .441
CAT. # 26451

Barnes Bullets

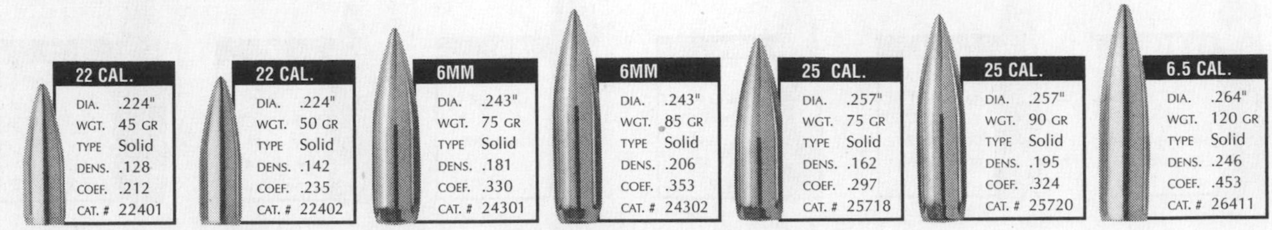

	22 CAL.	22 CAL.	6MM	6MM	25 CAL.	25 CAL.	6.5 CAL.
DIA.	.224"	.224"	.243"	.243"	.257"	.257"	.264"
WGT.	45 GR	50 GR	75 GR	85 GR	75 GR	90 GR	120 GR
TYPE	Solid	Solid	Solid	Solid	Solid	Solid	Solid
DENS.	.128	.142	.181	.206	.162	.195	.246
COEF.	.212	.235	.330	.353	.297	.324	.453
CAT. #	22401	22402	24301	24302	25718	25720	26411

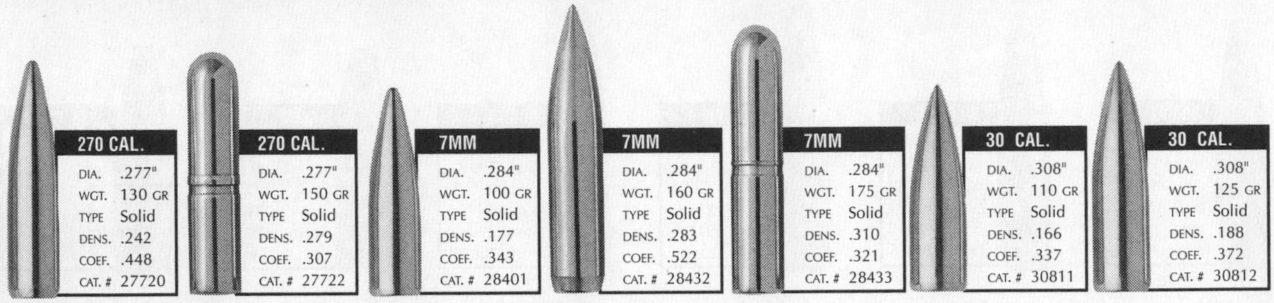

	270 CAL.	270 CAL.	7MM	7MM	7MM	30 CAL.	30 CAL.
DIA.	.277"	.277"	.284"	.284"	.284"	.308"	.308"
WGT.	130 GR	150 GR	100 GR	160 GR	175 GR	110 GR	125 GR
TYPE	Solid	Solid	Solid	Solid	Solid	Solid	Solid
DENS.	.242	.279	.177	.283	.310	.166	.188
COEF.	.448	.307	.343	.522	.321	.337	.372
CAT. #	27720	27722	28401	28432	28433	30811	30812

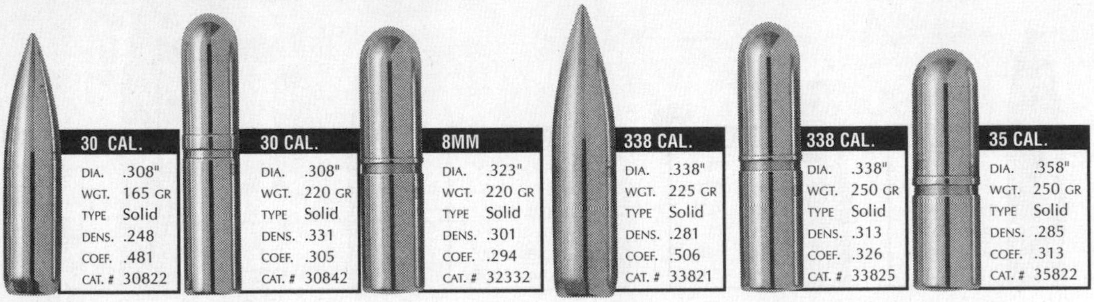

	30 CAL.	30 CAL.	8MM	338 CAL.	338 CAL.	35 CAL.
DIA.	.308"	.308"	.323"	.338"	.338"	.358"
WGT.	165 GR	220 GR	220 GR	225 GR	250 GR	250 GR
TYPE	Solid	Solid	Solid	Solid	Solid	Solid
DENS.	.248	.331	.301	.281	.313	.285
COEF.	.481	.305	.294	.506	.326	.313
CAT. #	30822	30842	32332	33821	33825	35822

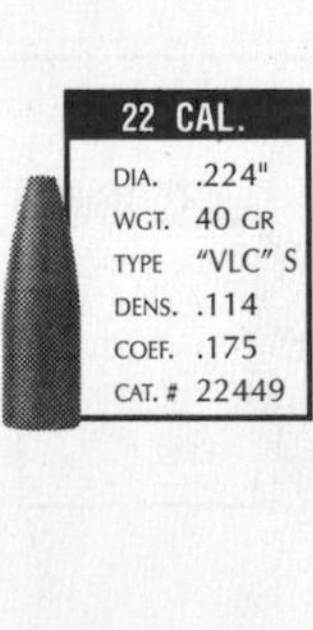

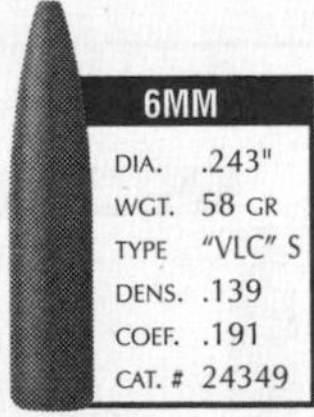

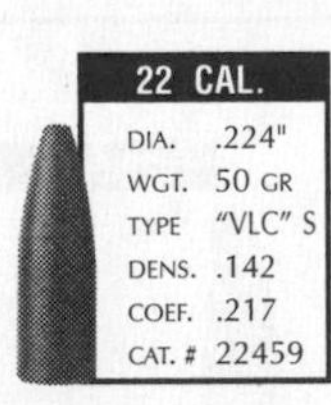

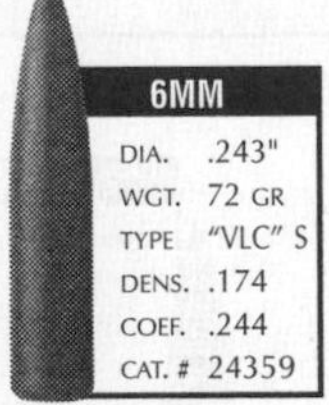

	22 CAL.	6MM	22 CAL.	6MM
DIA.	.224"	.243"	.224"	.243"
WGT.	40 GR	58 GR	50 GR	72 GR
TYPE	"VLC" S	"VLC" S	"VLC" S	"VLC" S
DENS.	.114	.139	.142	.174
COEF.	.175	.191	.217	.244
CAT. #	22449	24349	22459	24359

BARNES BURNER™ VLC™ VARMINT BULLET

Solid dry film for ultra-high velocity firing.

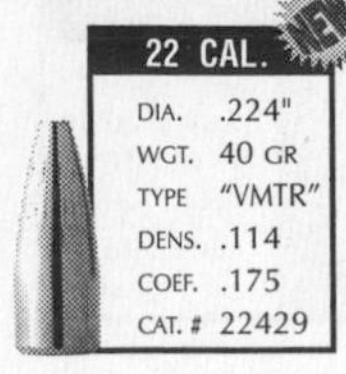

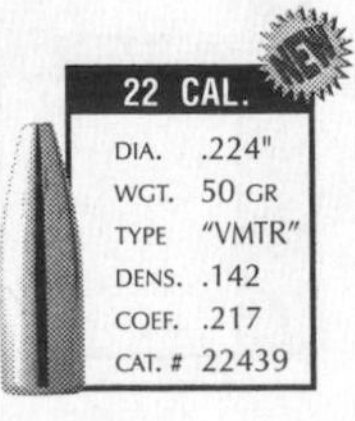

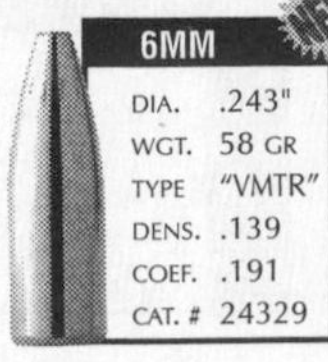

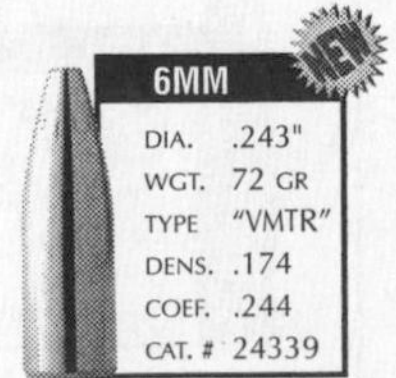

	22 CAL. (NEW)	22 CAL. (NEW)	6MM (NEW)	6MM (NEW)
DIA.	.224"	.224"	.243"	.243"
WGT.	40 GR	50 GR	58 GR	72 GR
TYPE	"VMTR"	"VMTR"	"VMTR"	"VMTR"
DENS.	.114	.142	.139	.174
COEF.	.175	.217	.191	.244
CAT. #	22429	22439	24329	24339

BARNES BURNER™ VARMIN-A-TOR™ BULLET

Taking varmint hunting to new extremes in explosive accuracy.

Barnes Bullets

COPPER-JACKET/LEAD CORE BARNES ORIGINAL

The preferred bullet of discriminating hunters for more than 65 years.

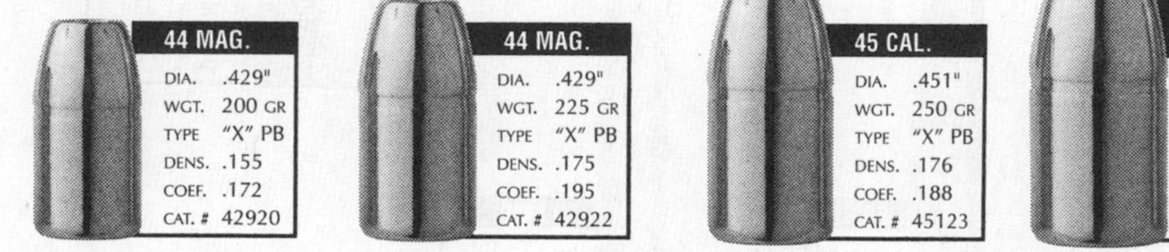

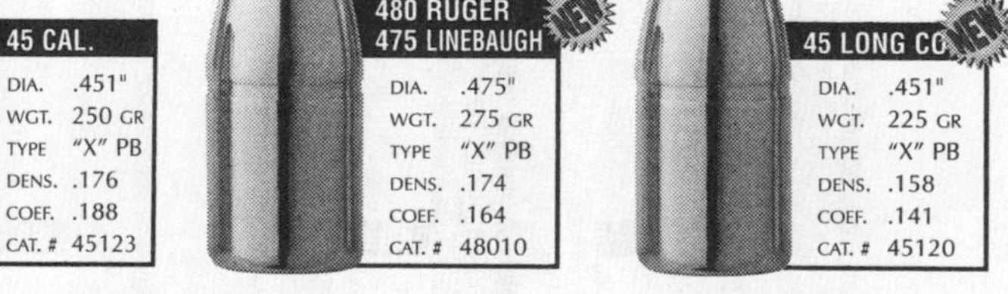

480 RUGER
475 LINEBAUGH
NEW
DIA. .475"
WGT. 275 GR
TYPE "X" PB
DENS. .174
COEF. .164
CAT. # 48010
45 LONG CO
NEW
DIA. .451"
WGT. 225 GR
TYPE "X" PB
DENS. .158
COEF. .141
CAT. # 45120

BARNES XPB PISTOL BULLETS

HANDLOADING

Barnes Bullets

Barnes Solids

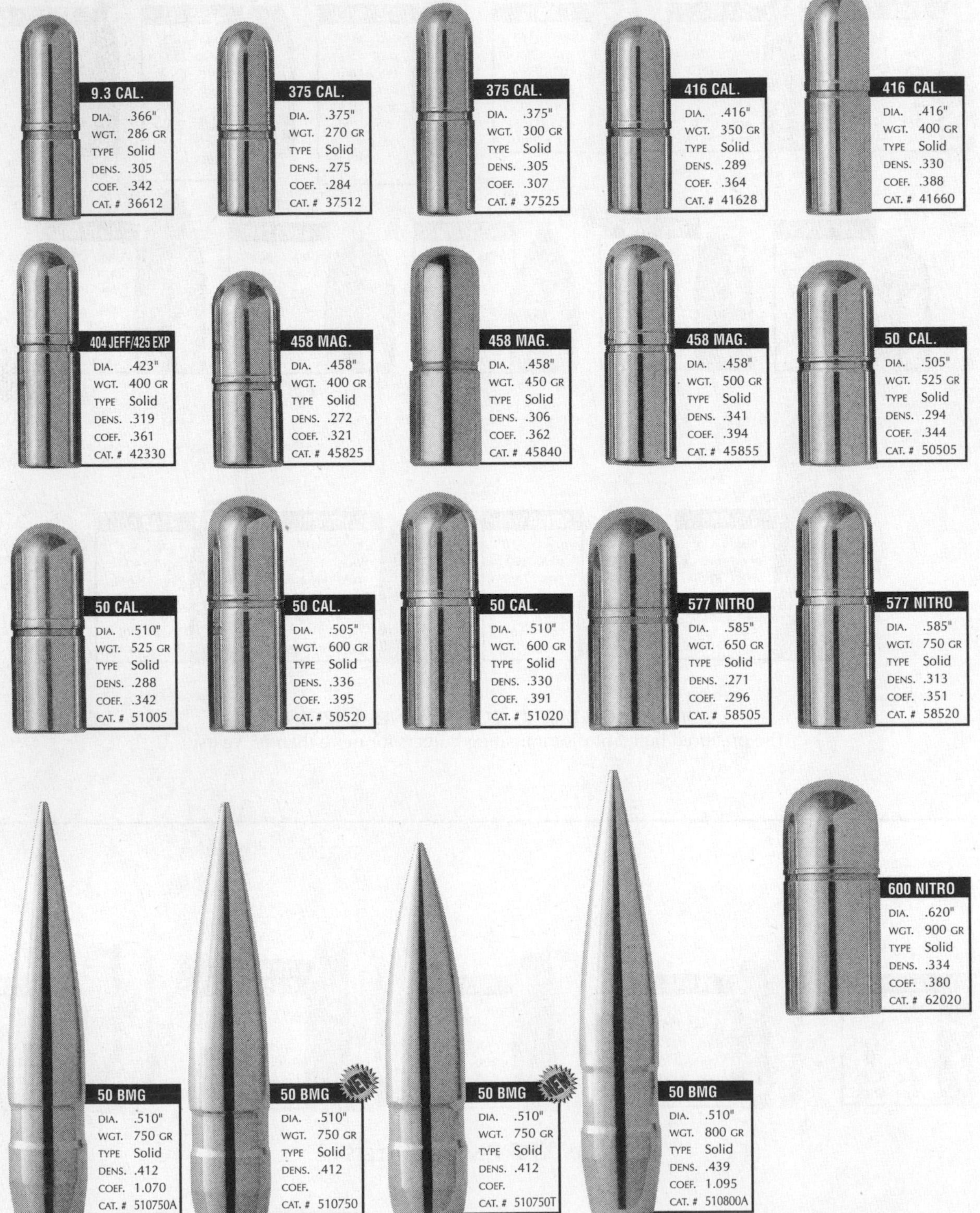

Berger Bullets

Berger's match bullets are well-known for their superior performance in benchrest matches. Now Berger offers a variety of bullets from .17 to .30. All feature J4 jackets with wall concentricity tolerance of .0003. Lead cores are 99.9% pure and swaged in dies to within .0001 of round. Berger's line includes several profiles: Low Drag, Very Low Drag, Length Tolerant, Maximum-Expansion, besides standard flat-base and standard boat-tail.

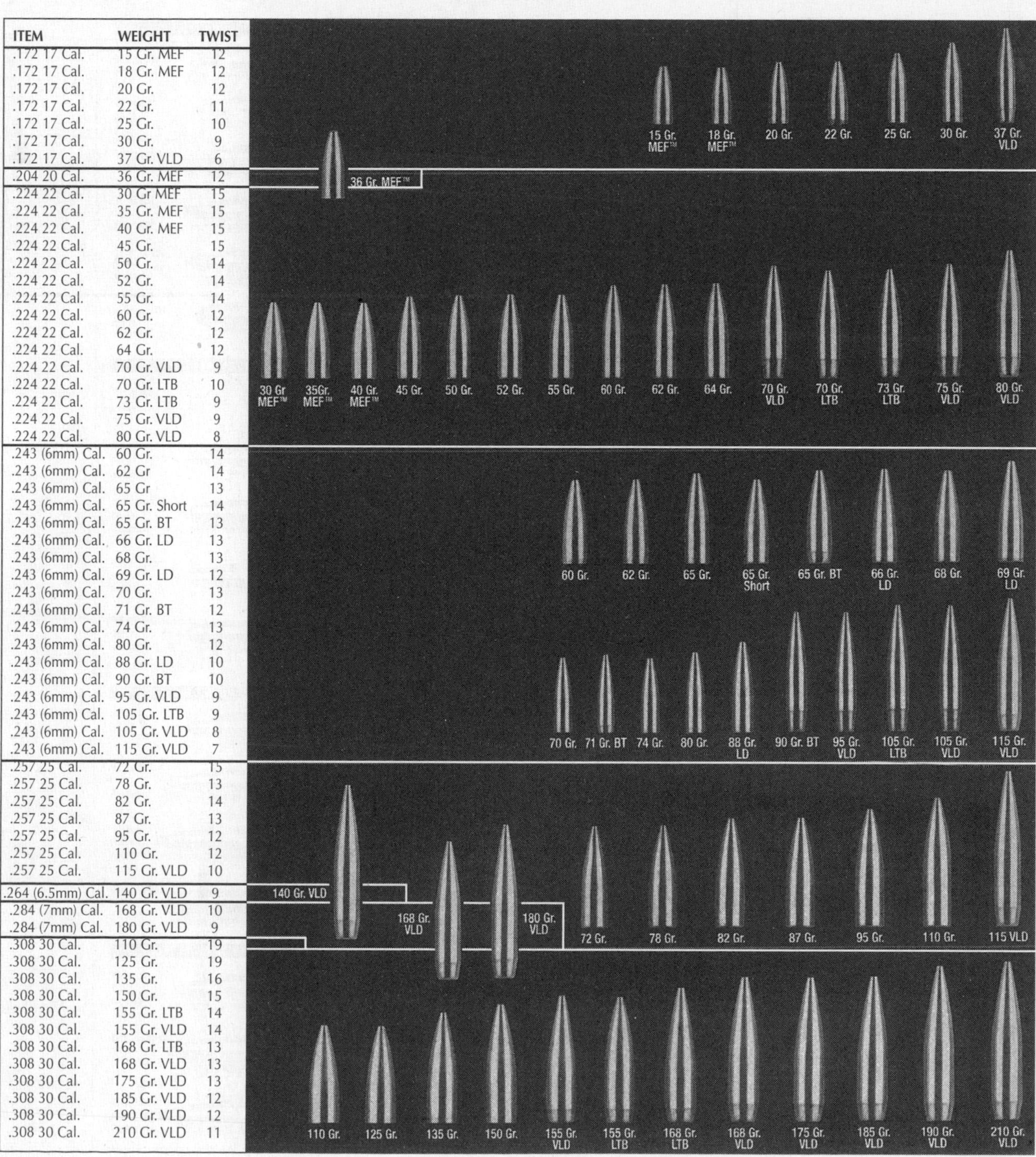

ITEM	WEIGHT	TWIST
.172 17 Cal.	15 Gr. MEF	12
.172 17 Cal.	18 Gr. MEF	12
.172 17 Cal.	20 Gr.	12
.172 17 Cal.	22 Gr.	11
.172 17 Cal.	25 Gr.	10
.172 17 Cal.	30 Gr.	9
.172 17 Cal.	37 Gr. VLD	6
.204 20 Cal.	36 Gr. MEF	12
.224 22 Cal.	30 Gr MEF	15
.224 22 Cal.	35 Gr. MEF	15
.224 22 Cal.	40 Gr. MEF	15
.224 22 Cal.	45 Gr.	15
.224 22 Cal.	50 Gr.	14
.224 22 Cal.	52 Gr.	14
.224 22 Cal.	55 Gr.	14
.224 22 Cal.	60 Gr.	12
.224 22 Cal.	62 Gr.	12
.224 22 Cal.	64 Gr.	12
.224 22 Cal.	70 Gr. VLD	9
.224 22 Cal.	70 Gr. LTB	10
.224 22 Cal.	73 Gr. LTB	9
.224 22 Cal.	75 Gr. VLD	9
.224 22 Cal.	80 Gr. VLD	8
.243 (6mm) Cal.	60 Gr.	14
.243 (6mm) Cal.	62 Gr	14
.243 (6mm) Cal.	65 Gr	13
.243 (6mm) Cal.	65 Gr. Short	14
.243 (6mm) Cal.	65 Gr. BT	13
.243 (6mm) Cal.	66 Gr. LD	13
.243 (6mm) Cal.	68 Gr.	13
.243 (6mm) Cal.	69 Gr. LD	12
.243 (6mm) Cal.	70 Gr.	13
.243 (6mm) Cal.	71 Gr. BT	12
.243 (6mm) Cal.	74 Gr.	13
.243 (6mm) Cal.	80 Gr.	12
.243 (6mm) Cal.	88 Gr. LD	10
.243 (6mm) Cal.	90 Gr. BT	10
.243 (6mm) Cal.	95 Gr. VLD	9
.243 (6mm) Cal.	105 Gr. LTB	9
.243 (6mm) Cal.	105 Gr. VLD	8
.243 (6mm) Cal.	115 Gr. VLD	7
.257 25 Cal.	72 Gr.	15
.257 25 Cal.	78 Gr.	13
.257 25 Cal.	82 Gr.	14
.257 25 Cal.	87 Gr.	13
.257 25 Cal.	95 Gr.	12
.257 25 Cal.	110 Gr.	12
.257 25 Cal.	115 Gr. VLD	10
.264 (6.5mm) Cal.	140 Gr. VLD	9
.284 (7mm) Cal.	168 Gr. VLD	10
.284 (7mm) Cal.	180 Gr. VLD	9
.308 30 Cal.	110 Gr.	19
.308 30 Cal.	125 Gr.	19
.308 30 Cal.	135 Gr.	16
.308 30 Cal.	150 Gr.	15
.308 30 Cal.	155 Gr. LTB	14
.308 30 Cal.	155 Gr. VLD	14
.308 30 Cal.	168 Gr. LTB	13
.308 30 Cal.	168 Gr. VLD	13
.308 30 Cal.	175 Gr. VLD	13
.308 30 Cal.	185 Gr. VLD	12
.308 30 Cal.	190 Gr. VLD	12
.308 30 Cal.	210 Gr. VLD	11

Hornady Rifle Bullets

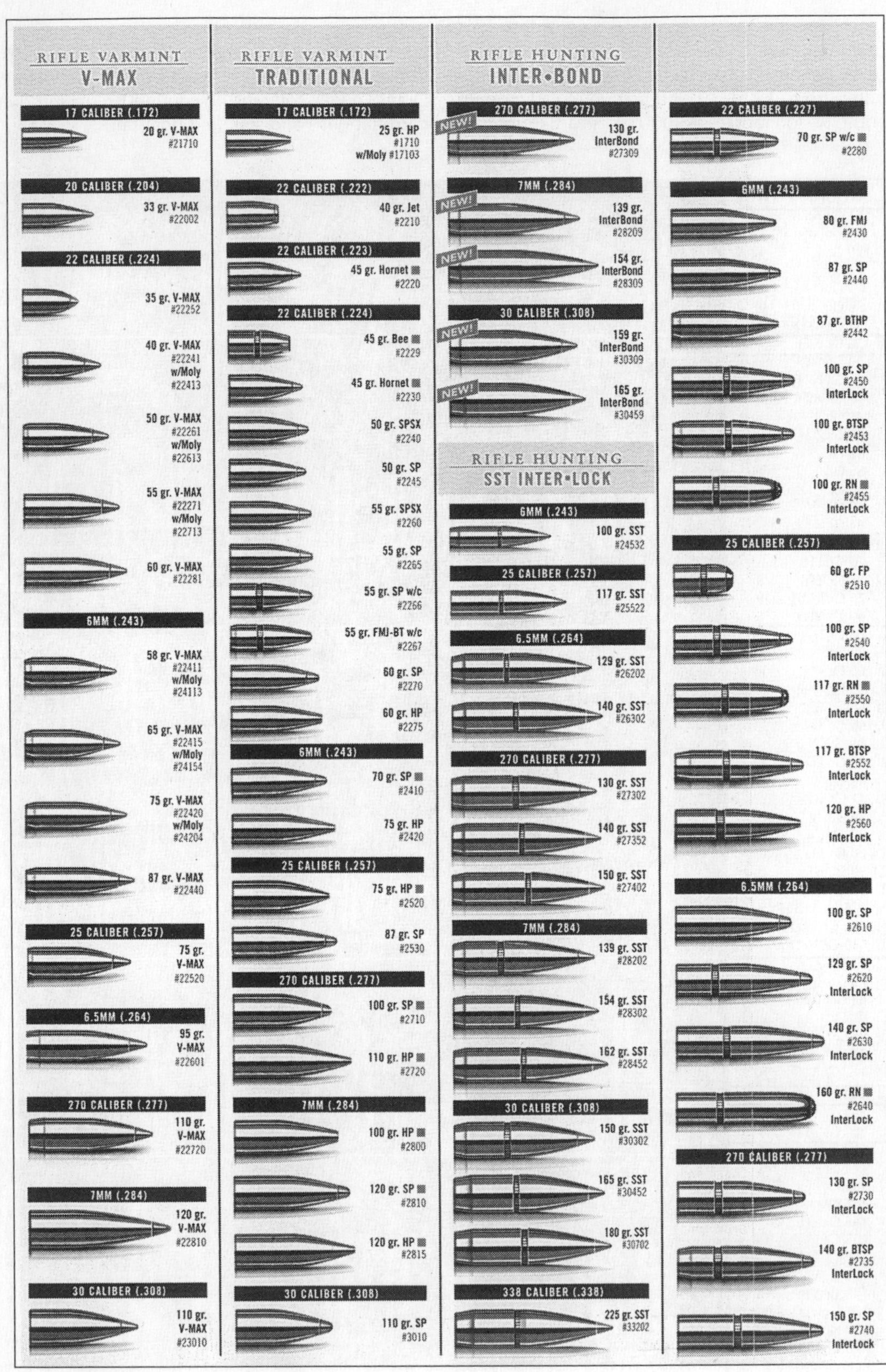

RIFLE VARMINT
V-MAX
17 CALIBER (.172)
20 gr. V-MAX #21710
20 CALIBER (.204)
33 gr. V-MAX #22002
22 CALIBER (.224)
35 gr. V-MAX #22252
40 gr. V-MAX #22241 w/Moly #22413
50 gr. V-MAX #22261 w/Moly #22613
55 gr. V-MAX #22271 w/Moly #22713
60 gr. V-MAX #22281
6MM (.243)
58 gr. V-MAX #22411 w/Moly #24113
65 gr. V-MAX #22415 w/Moly #24154
75 gr. V-MAX #22420 w/Moly #24204
87 gr. V-MAX #22440
25 CALIBER (.257)
75 gr. V-MAX #22520
6.5MM (.264)
95 gr. V-MAX #22601
270 CALIBER (.277)
110 gr. V-MAX #22720
7MM (.284)
120 gr. V-MAX #22810
30 CALIBER (.308)
110 gr. V-MAX #23010
RIFLE VARMINT
TRADITIONAL
17 CALIBER (.172)
25 gr. HP #1710 w/Moly #17103
22 CALIBER (.222)
40 gr. Jet #2210
22 CALIBER (.223)
45 gr. Hornet #2220
22 CALIBER (.224)
45 gr. Bee #2229
45 gr. Hornet #2230
50 gr. SPSX #2240
50 gr. SP #2245
55 gr. SPSX #2260
55 gr. SP #2265
55 gr. SP w/c #2266
55 gr. FMJ-BT w/c #2267
60 gr. SP #2270
60 gr. HP #2275
6MM (.243)
70 gr. SP #2410
75 gr. HP #2420
25 CALIBER (.257)
75 gr. HP #2520
87 gr. SP #2530
270 CALIBER (.277)
100 gr. SP #2710
110 gr. HP #2720
7MM (.284)
100 gr. HP #2800
120 gr. SP #2810
120 gr. HP #2815
30 CALIBER (.308)
110 gr. SP #3010
RIFLE HUNTING
INTER•BOND
270 CALIBER (.277)
NEW!
130 gr. InterBond #27309
7MM (.284)
NEW!
139 gr. InterBond #28209
NEW!
154 gr. InterBond #28309
30 CALIBER (.308)
NEW!
159 gr. InterBond #30309
NEW!
165 gr. InterBond #30459
RIFLE HUNTING
SST INTER•LOCK
6MM (.243)
100 gr. SST #24532
25 CALIBER (.257)
117 gr. SST #25522
6.5MM (.264)
129 gr. SST #26202
140 gr. SST #26302
270 CALIBER (.277)
130 gr. SST #27302
140 gr. SST #27352
150 gr. SST #27402
7MM (.284)
139 gr. SST #28202
154 gr. SST #28302
162 gr. SST #28452
30 CALIBER (.308)
150 gr. SST #30302
165 gr. SST #30452
180 gr. SST #30702
338 CALIBER (.338)
225 gr. SST #33202
22 CALIBER (.227)
70 gr. SP w/c #2280
6MM (.243)
80 gr. FMJ #2430
87 gr. SP #2440
87 gr. BTHP #2442
100 gr. SP #2450 InterLock
100 gr. BTSP #2453 InterLock
100 gr. RN #2455 InterLock
25 CALIBER (.257)
60 gr. FP #2510
100 gr. SP #2540 InterLock
117 gr. RN #2550 InterLock
117 gr. BTSP #2552 InterLock
120 gr. HP #2560 InterLock
6.5MM (.264)
100 gr. SP #2610
129 gr. SP #2620 InterLock
140 gr. SP #2630 InterLock
160 gr. RN #2640 InterLock
270 CALIBER (.277)
130 gr. SP #2730 InterLock
140 gr. BTSP #2735 InterLock
150 gr. SP #2740 InterLock

HANDLOADING

Hornady Rifle Bullets

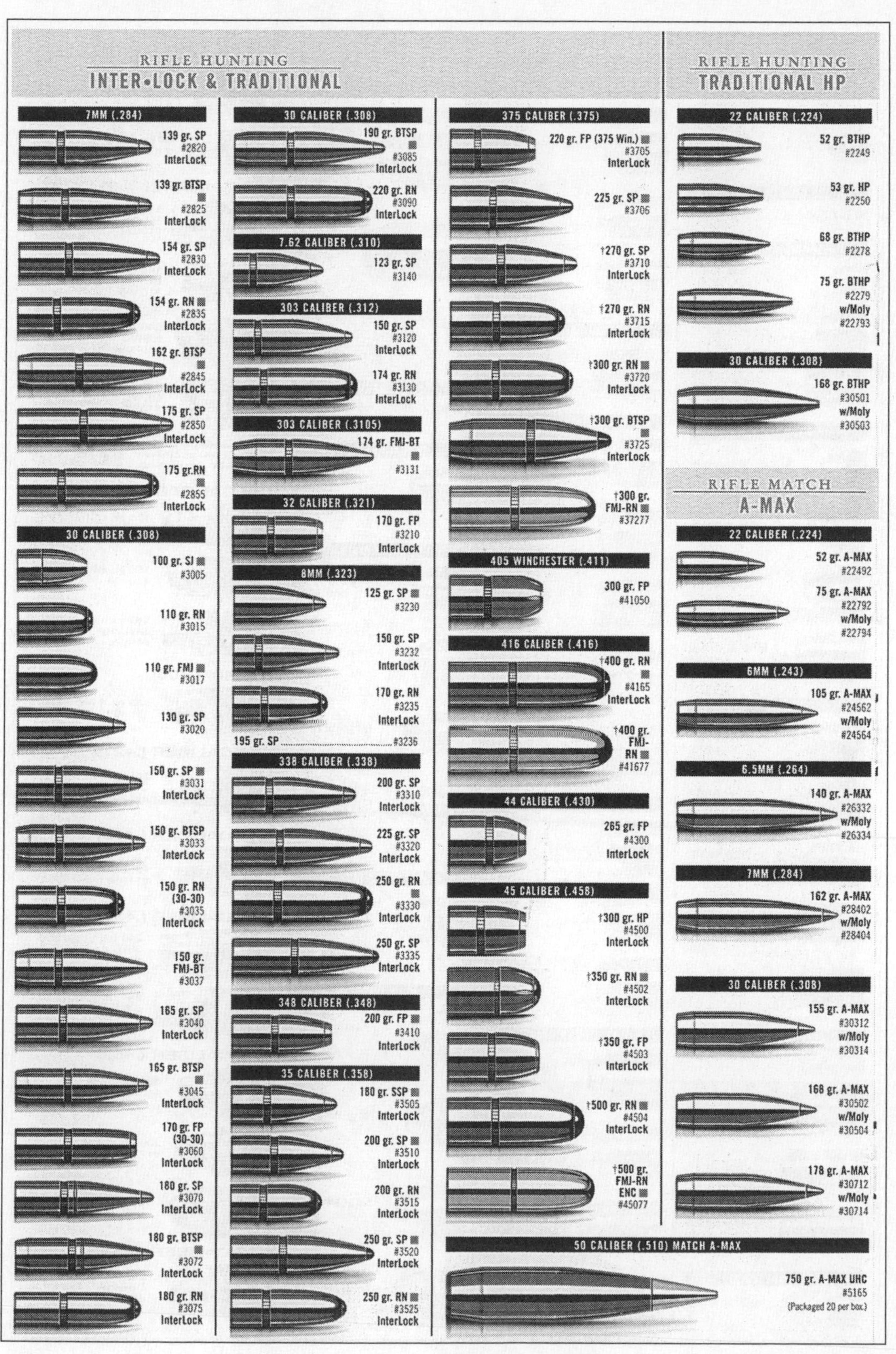

RIFLE HUNTING
INTER•LOCK & TRADITIONAL
7MM (.284)
139 gr. SP #2820 InterLock
139 gr. BTSP #2825 InterLock
154 gr. SP #2830 InterLock
154 gr. RN #2835 InterLock
162 gr. BTSP #2845 InterLock
175 gr. SP #2850 InterLock
175 gr.RN #2855 InterLock
30 CALIBER (.308)
100 gr. SJ #3005
110 gr. RN #3015
110 gr. FMJ #3017
130 gr. SP #3020
150 gr. SP #3031 InterLock
150 gr. BTSP #3033 InterLock
150 gr. RN (30-30) #3035 InterLock
150 gr. FMJ-BT #3037
165 gr. SP #3040 InterLock
165 gr. BTSP #3045 InterLock
170 gr. FP (30-30) #3060 InterLock
180 gr. SP #3070 InterLock
180 gr. BTSP #3072 InterLock
180 gr. RN #3075 InterLock
30 CALIBER (.308)
190 gr. BTSP #3085 InterLock
220 gr. RN #3090 InterLock
7.62 CALIBER (.310)
123 gr. SP #3140
303 CALIBER (.312)
150 gr. SP #3120 InterLock
174 gr. RN #3130 InterLock
303 CALIBER (.3105)
174 gr. FMJ-BT #3131
32 CALIBER (.321)
170 gr. FP #3210 InterLock
8MM (.323)
125 gr. SP #3230
150 gr. SP #3232 InterLock
170 gr. RN #3235 InterLock
195 gr. SP .... #3236
338 CALIBER (.338)
200 gr. SP #3310 InterLock
225 gr. SP #3320 InterLock
250 gr. RN #3330 InterLock
250 gr. SP #3335 InterLock
348 CALIBER (.348)
200 gr. FP #3410 InterLock
35 CALIBER (.358)
180 gr. SSP #3505 InterLock
200 gr. SP #3510 InterLock
200 gr. RN #3515 InterLock
250 gr. SP #3520 InterLock
250 gr. RN #3525 InterLock
375 CALIBER (.375)
220 gr. FP (375 Win.) #3705 InterLock
225 gr. SP #3706
†270 gr. SP #3710 InterLock
†270 gr. RN #3715 InterLock
†300 gr. RN #3720 InterLock
†300 gr. BTSP #3725 InterLock
†300 gr. FMJ-RN #37277
405 WINCHESTER (.411)
300 gr. FP #41050
416 CALIBER (.416)
†400 gr. RN #4165 InterLock
†400 gr. FMJ-RN #41677
44 CALIBER (.430)
265 gr. FP #4300 InterLock
45 CALIBER (.458)
†300 gr. HP #4500 InterLock
†350 gr. RN #4502 InterLock
†350 gr. FP #4503 InterLock
†500 gr. RN #4504 InterLock
†500 gr. FMJ-RN ENC #45077
RIFLE HUNTING
TRADITIONAL HP
22 CALIBER (.224)
52 gr. BTHP #2249
53 gr. HP #2250
68 gr. BTHP #2278
75 gr. BTHP #2279 w/Moly #22793
30 CALIBER (.308)
168 gr. BTHP #30501 w/Moly #30503
RIFLE MATCH
A-MAX
22 CALIBER (.224)
52 gr. A-MAX #22492
75 gr. A-MAX #22792 w/Moly #22794
6MM (.243)
105 gr. A-MAX #24562 w/Moly #24564
6.5MM (.264)
140 gr. A-MAX #26332 w/Moly #26334
7MM (.284)
162 gr. A-MAX #28402 w/Moly #28404
30 CALIBER (.308)
155 gr. A-MAX #30312 w/Moly #30314
168 gr. A-MAX #30502 w/Moly #30504
178 gr. A-MAX #30712 w/Moly #30714
50 CALIBER (.510) MATCH A-MAX
750 gr. A-MAX UHC #5165 (Packaged 20 per box.)

Hornady Handguns Bullets

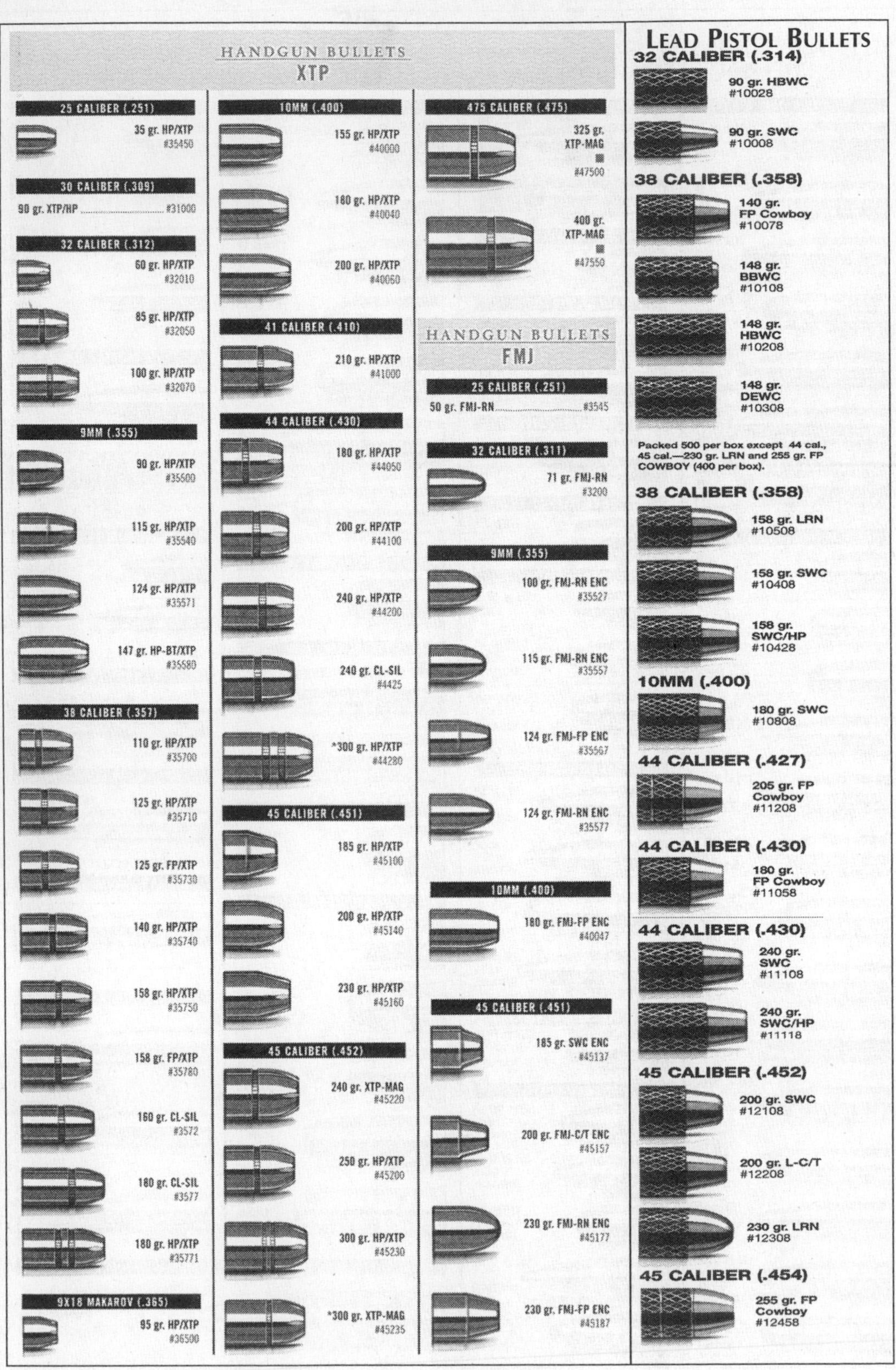

HANDGUN BULLETS
XTP
25 CALIBER (.251)
35 gr. HP/XTP #35450
30 CALIBER (.309)
90 gr. XTP/HP #31000
32 CALIBER (.312)
60 gr. HP/XTP #32010
85 gr. HP/XTP #32050
100 gr. HP/XTP #32070
9MM (.355)
90 gr. HP/XTP #35500
115 gr. HP/XTP #35540
124 gr. HP/XTP #35571
147 gr. HP-BT/XTP #35580
38 CALIBER (.357)
110 gr. HP/XTP #35700
125 gr. HP/XTP #35710
125 gr. FP/XTP #35730
140 gr. HP/XTP #35740
158 gr. HP/XTP #35750
158 gr. FP/XTP #35780
160 gr. CL-SIL #3572
180 gr. CL-SIL #3577
180 gr. HP/XTP #35771
9X18 MAKAROV (.365)
95 gr. HP/XTP #36500
10MM (.400)
155 gr. HP/XTP #40000
180 gr. HP/XTP #40040
200 gr. HP/XTP #40060
41 CALIBER (.410)
210 gr. HP/XTP #41000
44 CALIBER (.430)
180 gr. HP/XTP #44050
200 gr. HP/XTP #44100
240 gr. HP/XTP #44200
240 gr. CL-SIL #4425
*300 gr. HP/XTP #44280
45 CALIBER (.451)
185 gr. HP/XTP #45100
200 gr. HP/XTP #45140
230 gr. HP/XTP #45160
45 CALIBER (.452)
240 gr. XTP-MAG #45220
250 gr. HP/XTP #45200
300 gr. HP/XTP #45230
*300 gr. XTP-MAG #45235
475 CALIBER (.475)
325 gr. XTP-MAG #47500
400 gr. XTP-MAG #47550
HANDGUN BULLETS
FMJ
25 CALIBER (.251)
50 gr. FMJ-RN #3545
32 CALIBER (.311)
71 gr. FMJ-RN #3200
9MM (.355)
100 gr. FMJ-RN ENC #35527
115 gr. FMJ-RN ENC #35557
124 gr. FMJ-FP ENC #35567
124 gr. FMJ-RN ENC #35577
10MM (.400)
180 gr. FMJ-FP ENC #40047
45 CALIBER (.451)
185 gr. SWC ENC #45137
200 gr. FMJ-C/T ENC #45157
230 gr. FMJ-RN ENC #45177
230 gr. FMJ-FP ENC #45187
LEAD PISTOL BULLETS
32 CALIBER (.314)
90 gr. HBWC #10028
90 gr. SWC #10008
38 CALIBER (.358)
140 gr. FP Cowboy #10078
148 gr. BBWC #10108
148 gr. HBWC #10208
148 gr. DEWC #10308
Packed 500 per box except 44 cal., 45 cal.—230 gr. LRN and 255 gr. FP COWBOY (400 per box).
38 CALIBER (.358)
158 gr. LRN #10508
158 gr. SWC #10408
158 gr. SWC/HP #10428
10MM (.400)
180 gr. SWC #10808
44 CALIBER (.427)
205 gr. FP Cowboy #11208
44 CALIBER (.430)
180 gr. FP Cowboy #11058
44 CALIBER (.430)
240 gr. SWC #11108
240 gr. SWC/HP #11118
45 CALIBER (.452)
200 gr. SWC #12108
200 gr. L-C/T #12208
230 gr. LRN #12308
45 CALIBER (.454)
255 gr. FP Cowboy #12458

HANDLOADING

Nosler Bullets

NOSLER CUSTOM COMPETITION

Nosler has blended the renowned accuracy of the J4 bullet jacket with its own ultra-precise lead alloy cores to create a new performance standard for the popular .30 caliber match bullets.

Cal. Dia.	BULLET WEIGHT AND STYLE	SECT. DENS.	BAL. COEF.	PART#
22 .224"	NEW! 69 GR. HPBT 250 QUANTITY BULK PACK	.196	.359	53065
	NEW! 80 GR. HPBT 250 QUANTITY BULK PACK	.228	.440	53080
30 .308"	155 GR. HPBT 250 QUANTITY BULK PACK	.233	.450	53155 53169
	168 GR. HPBT 250 QUANTITY BULK PACK	.253	.462	53164 53168

Custom Competition™ formerly J4™ Competition

Cal. Dia.	BULLET WEIGHT AND STYLE	SECT. DENS.	BAL. COEF.	PART#
22 .224"	69 GR. HPBT 250 QUANTITY BULK PACK	.196	.359	17101 53065
	NEW! 77 GR. HPBT 250 QUANTITY BULK PACK	.219	.340	22421 53064
	80 GR. HPBT 250 QUANTITY BULK PACK	.228	.440	25116 53080
30 .308"	155 GR. HPBT 250 QUANTITY BULK PACK	.233	.450	53155 53169
	168 GR. HPBT 250 QUANTITY BULK PACK	.253	.462	53164 53168

Bullets for Pistols

Cal. Dia.	BULLET WEIGHT AND STYLE	SECT. DENS.	BAL. COEF.	PART#
9mm .355"	115 GR. HOLLOW POINT 250 QUANTITY BULK PACK	.130	.110	44848
38 .357"	115 GR. HOLLOW POINT PRACTICAL PISTOL™ 250 QUANTITY BULK PACK	.129	.110	44835
	135 GR. PRACTICAL PISTOL™ 250 QUANTITY BULK PACK	.151	.149	44836
10mm .400"	135 GR. HOLLOW POINT 250 QUANTITY BULK PACK	.121	.093	44852
	150 GR. HOLLOW POINT 250 QUANTITY BULK PACK	.134	.106	44860
45 .451"	185 GR. HOLLOW POINT 250 QUANTITY BULK PACK	.130	.142	44847
	230 GR. FULL METAL JACKET	.162	.183	42064

Bullets for Revolvers

Cal. Dia.	BULLET WEIGHT AND STYLE	SECT. DENS.	BAL. COEF.	PART#
38 .357"	125 GR. HOLLOW POINT 250 QUANTITY BULK PACK	.140	.143	44840
	158 GR. HOLLOW POINT 250 QUANTITY BULK PACK	.177	.182	44841
	180 GR. SILHOUETTE 250 QUANTITY BULK PACK	.202	.210	44851
41 .410"	210 GR. HOLLOW POINT	.178	.170	43012
44 .429"	200 GR. HOLLOW POINT 250 QUANTITY BULK PACK	.155	.151	44846
	240 GR. HOLLOW POINT 250 QUANTITY BULK PACK	.186	.173	44842
	240 GR. SOFT POINT 250 QUANTITY BULK PACK	.186	.177	44868
	300 GR. HOLLOW POINT	.233	.206	42069
45 Colt .451"	250 GR. HOLLOW POINT	.176	.177	43013

Partition-HG™

50 cal/250 GR. JHP	.429"	50441
50 cal/260 GR. JHP	.451"	50260
54 cal/260 GR. JHP	.451"	54261
50 cal/300 GR. JPP	.451"	50281
54 cal/300 GR. JPP	.451"	54281

S.H.O.T.S.™

50 cal/250 grain JHP	.451"	50251
50 cal/300 grain JHP	.429"	50301
54 cal/250 grain JHP	.451"	54251

High volume shooters can now get Nosler's specially designed plastic muzzleloading sabots in 50-count Bulk Packs:

50 cal. sabots for 44 cal. bullets	50095
50 cal. sabots for 45 cal. bullets	50096
54 cal. sabots for 45 cal. bullets	50097

Nosler Bullets

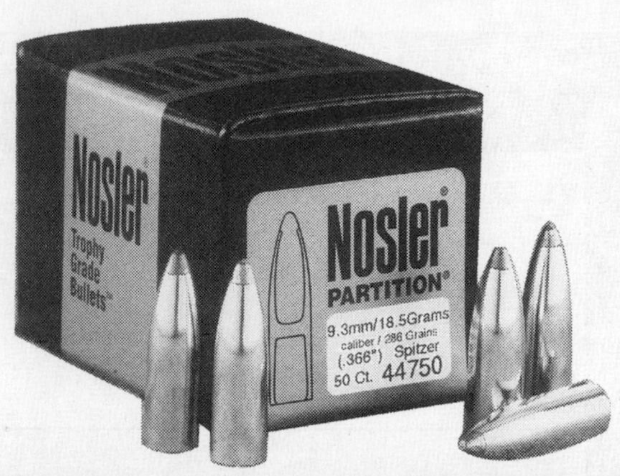

Nosler Partition® Bullets

The Nosler Partition® bullet earned its reputation among professional guides and serious hunters for one reason: it doesn't fail. The patented Partition® design offers a dual core that is unequalled in mushrooming, weight retention and hydrostatic shock.

Cal. Dia.	Bullet Weight and Style	Sect. Dens.	Bal. Coef.	Part#
22 .224"	60 GR. SPITZER	.171	.228	16316
6mm .243"	85 GR. SPITZER	.206	.315	16314
	95 GR. SPITZER	.230	.365	16315
	100 GR. SPITZER	.242	.384	35642
25 .257"	100 GR. SPITZER	.216	.377	16317
	115 GR. SPITZER	.249	.389	16318
	120 GR. SPITZER	.260	.391	35643
6.5mm .264"	100 GR. SPITZER	.205	.326	16319
	125 GR. SPITZER	.256	.449	16320
	140 GR. SPITZER	.287	.490	16321
270 .277"	130 GR. SPITZER	.242	.416	16322
	NEW! 140 GR. SPITZER	.261	.432	35200
	150 GR. SPITZER	.279	.465	16323
	160 GR. SEMI SPITZER	.298	.434	16324
7mm .284"	140 GR. SPITZER	.248	.434	16325
	150 GR. SPITZER	.266	.456	16326
	160 GR. SPITZER	.283	.475	16327
	175 GR. SPITZER	.310	.519	35645
30 .308"	150 GR. SPITZER	.226	.387	16329
	165 GR. SPITZER	.248	.410	16330
	170 GR. ROUND NOSE	.256	.252	16333
	180 GR. PROTECTED POINT	.271	.361	25396
	180 GR. SPITZER	.271	.474	16331
	200 GR. SPITZER	.301	.481	35626
	220 GR. SEMI SPITZER	.331	.351	16332
8mm .323"	200 GR. SPITZER	.274	.426	35277
338 .338"	210 GR. SPITZER	.263	.400	16337
	225 GR. SPITZER	.281	.454	16336
	250 GR. SPITZER	.313	.473	35644
35 .358"	225 GR. SPITZER	.251	.430	44800
	250 GR. SPITZER	.279	.446	44801
9.3mm .366"	286 GR. SPITZER (18.5 GRAM)	.307	.482	44750
375 .375"	260 GR. SPITZER	.264	.314	44850
	300 GR. SPITZER	.305	.398	44845
416 .416"	400 GR. SPITZER	.330	.390	45200
45-70 .458"	300 GR. PROTECTED POINT	.204	.199	45325
PARTITION-HG™ 38 .357"	180 GR. HOLLOW POINT	.202	.201	35180
PARTITION-HG™ 44 .429"	250 GR. HOLLOW POINT	.194	.200	44250
PARTITION-HG™ 45 .451"	260 GR. HOLLOW POINT	.182	.174	45260
	300 GR. PROTECTED POINT	.211	.199	45350

Nosler Bullets

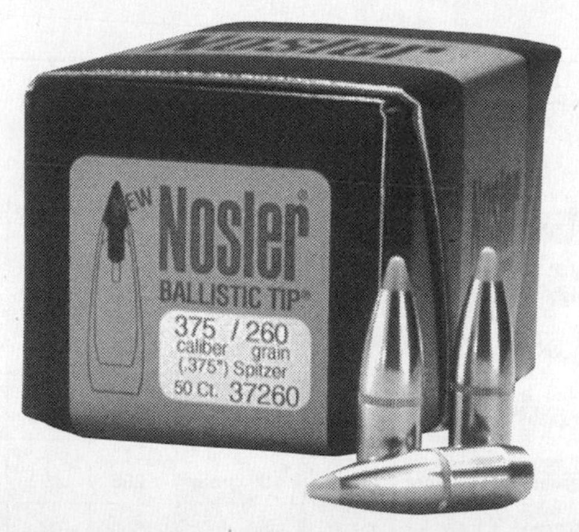

Nosler Ballistic Tip® Hunting Bullets

Nosler has replaced the familiar lead point of the Spitzer with a tough polycarbonate tip. The purpose of this new Ballistic Tip® is to resist deforming in the magazine and feed ramp of many rifles. The Solid Base® design produces controlled expansion for excellent mushrooming and exceptional accuracy.

Varmint Bullets

Cal. Dia.	Bullet Weight and Style	Sect. Dens.	Bal. Coef.	Part#
22 .224"	40 GR. SPITZER (ORANGE TIP) 250 CT. VARMINT PAK™	.114	.221	39510 39555
	45 GR. HORNET (SOFT LEAD TIP)	.128	.144	35487
	50 GR. SPITZER (ORANGE TIP) 250 CT. VARMINT PAK™	.142	.238	39522 39557
	55 GR. SPITZER (ORANGE TIP) 250 CT. VARMINT PAK™	.157	.267	39526 39560
6mm .243"	55 GR. SPITZER (PURPLE TIP) 250 CT. VARMINT PAK™	.133	.276	24055 39565
	70 GR. SPITZER (PURPLE TIP) 250 CT. VARMINT PAK™	.169	.310	39532 39570
	80 GR. SPITZER (PURPLE TIP)	.194	.339	24080
25 .257"	85 GR. SPITZER (BLUE TIP)	.183	.331	43004

Hunting Bullets

Cal. Dia.	Bullet Weight and Style	Sect. Dens.	Bal. Coef.	Part#
6mm .243"	90 GR. SPITZER (PURPLE TIP)	.218	.365	24090
	95 GR. SPITZER (PURPLE TIP)	.230	.379	24095
25 .257"	100 GR. SPITZER (BLUE TIP)	.216	.393	25100
	115 GR. SPITZER (BLUE TIP)	.249	.453	25115
6.5mm .264"	100 GR. SPITZER (BROWN TIP)	.205	.350	26100
	120 GR. SPITZER (BROWN TIP)	.246	.458	26120
270 .277"	130 GR. SPITZER (YELLOW TIP)	.242	.433	27130
	140 GR. SPITZER (YELLOW TIP)	.261	.456	27140
	150 GR. SPITZER (YELLOW TIP)	.279	.496	27150
7mm .284"	120 GR. FLAT POINT (SOFT LEAD TIP)	.213	.195	28121
	120 GR. SPITZER (RED TIP)	.213	.417	28120
	140 GR. SPITZER (RED TIP)	.248	.485	28140
	150 GR. SPITZER (RED TIP)	.266	.493	28150
30 .308"	125 GR. SPITZER (GREEN TIP)	.188	.366	30125
	150 GR. SPITZER (GREEN TIP)	.226	.435	30150
	165 GR. SPITZER (GREEN TIP)	.248	.475	30165
	180 GR. SPITZER (GREEN TIP)	.271	.507	30180
8mm .323"	180 GR. SPITZER (GUNMETAL TIP)	.247	.394	32180
338 .338"	180 GR. SPITZER (MAROON TIP)	.225	.372	33180
	200 GR. SPITZER (MAROON TIP)	.250	.414	33200
35 .358"	225 GR. WHELEN (BUCKSKIN TIP)	.251	.421	35225
9.3mm .366"	250 GR. SPITZER (OLIVE TIP) *Available Mid-year*	.267	.494	36250
375 .375"	NEW! 260 GR. SPITZER (SAFARI TIP)	.264	.473	37260

HANDLOADING

Nosler Bullets

BALLISTIC SILVERTIP

Cal.	Dia.	Bullet Weight	Sect. Dens.	Bal. Coef.	Part #
22	.224"	40 grain	.114	.221	51005
22	.224"	50 grain	.142	.238	51010
22	.224"	55 grain	.157	.267	51031
6mm	.243"	55 grain	.133	.276	51030
6mm	.243"	95 grain	.230	.379	51040
25	.257"	85 grain	.183	.331	51045
25	.257"	115 grain	.249	.453	51050

BALLISTIC SILVERTIP

Cal.	Dia.	Bullet Weight	Sect. Dens.	Bal. Coef.	Part #
270	.277"	130 grain	.242	.433	51075
270 (NEW!)	.277"	150 grain	.279	.496	51100
270	.277"	130 grain	.242	.433	51075
7mm	.284"	140 grain	.248	.485	51105
7mm	.284"	150 grain	.266	.493	51110
30	.308"	150 grain	.226	.435	51150
30	.308"	168 grain	.253	.490	51160
30	.308"	180 grain	.271	.507	51170
338	.338"	200 grain	.250	.414	51200

FAIL SAFE

Cal.	Dia.	Bullet Weight	Sect. Dens.	Bal. Coef.	Part #
270	.277"	140 grain	.261	.322	53140
7mm	.284"	140 grain	.248	.323	53150
7mm	.284"	160 grain	.283	.382	53160
30	.308"	150 grain	.226	.308	53170
30	.308"	165 grain	.248	.314	53175
30	.308"	180 grain	.271	.391	53180
338	.338"	230 grain	.288	.436	53230
375	.375"	270 grain	.274	.393	53350
375	.375"	300 grain	.305	.441	53360

PARTITION GOLD

Cal.	Dia.	Bullet Weight	Sect. Dens.	Bal. Coef.	Part #
270	.277"	150 grain	.279	.465	52100
7mm	.284"	160 grain	.283	.475	52150
30	.308"	150 grain	.226	.387	52200
30	.308"	180 grain	.271	.474	52230
338	.338"	250 grain	.313	.473	52280

PARTITION GOLD MOLY-FREE

Cal.	Dia.	Bullet Weight	Sect. Dens.	Bal. Coef.	Part #
270	.277"	150 grain	.279	.465	52101
7mm	.284"	160 grain	.283	.475	52151
30	.308"	150 grain	.226	.387	52201
30	.308"	180 grain	.271	.474	52231
338	.338"	250 grain	.313	.473	52281

Ballistic Silvertip, Fail Safe and Partition Gold bullets are made by Nosler for loading in Winchester ammunition in a project known as Combined Technology.

Sierra Bullets

Rifle Bullets

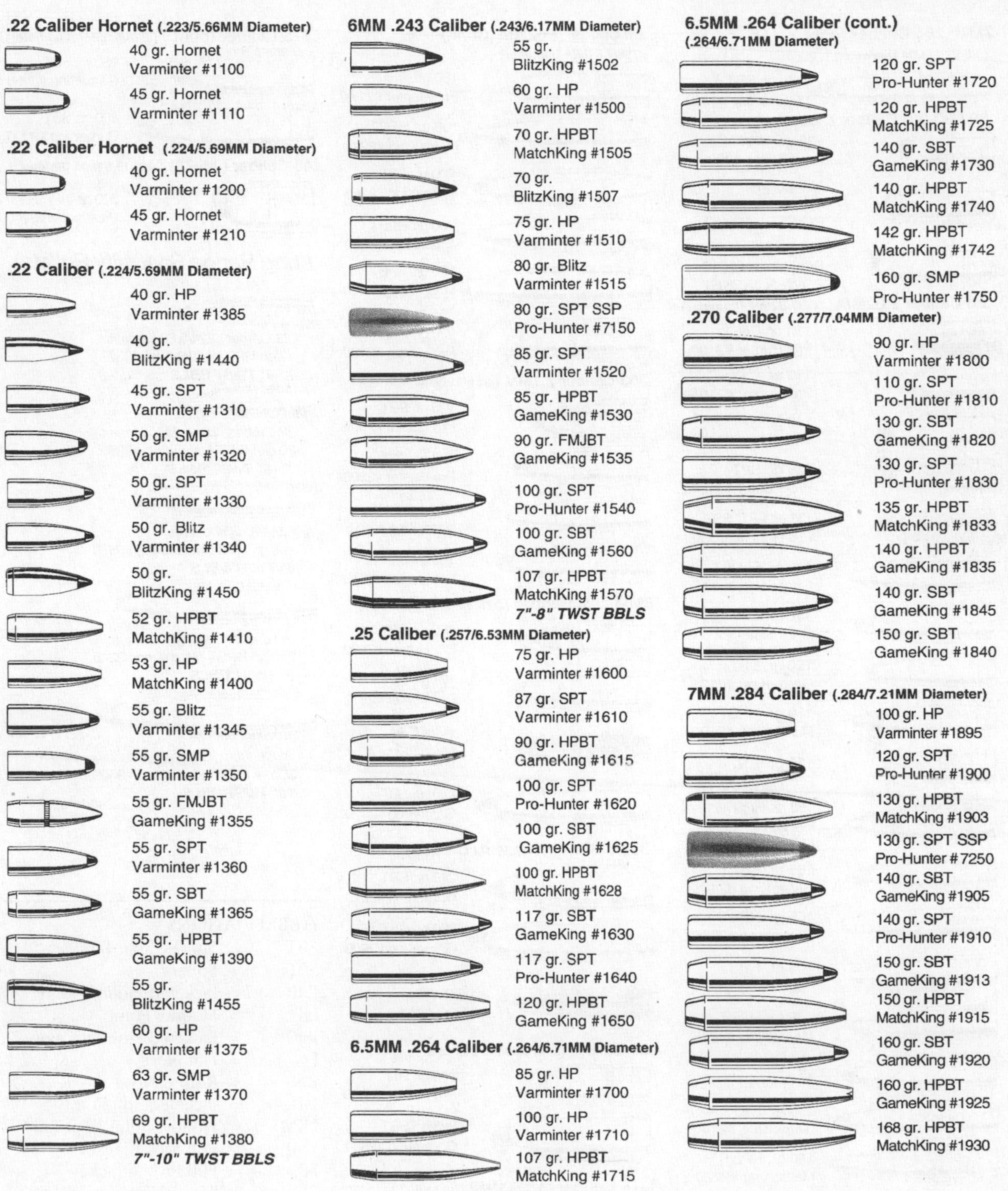

.22 Caliber Hornet (.223/5.66MM Diameter)
40 gr. Hornet Varminter #1100
45 gr. Hornet Varminter #1110
.22 Caliber Hornet (.224/5.69MM Diameter)
40 gr. Hornet Varminter #1200
45 gr. Hornet Varminter #1210
.22 Caliber (.224/5.69MM Diameter)
40 gr. HP Varminter #1385
40 gr. BlitzKing #1440
45 gr. SPT Varminter #1310
50 gr. SMP Varminter #1320
50 gr. SPT Varminter #1330
50 gr. Blitz Varminter #1340
50 gr. BlitzKing #1450
52 gr. HPBT MatchKing #1410
53 gr. HP MatchKing #1400
55 gr. Blitz Varminter #1345
55 gr. SMP Varminter #1350
55 gr. FMJBT GameKing #1355
55 gr. SPT Varminter #1360
55 gr. SBT GameKing #1365
55 gr. HPBT GameKing #1390
55 gr. BlitzKing #1455
60 gr. HP Varminter #1375
63 gr. SMP Varminter #1370
69 gr. HPBT MatchKing #1380
7"-10" TWST BBLS
6MM .243 Caliber (.243/6.17MM Diameter)
55 gr. BlitzKing #1502
60 gr. HP Varminter #1500
70 gr. HPBT MatchKing #1505
70 gr. BlitzKing #1507
75 gr. HP Varminter #1510
80 gr. Blitz Varminter #1515
80 gr. SPT SSP Pro-Hunter #7150
85 gr. SPT Varminter #1520
85 gr. HPBT GameKing #1530
90 gr. FMJBT GameKing #1535
100 gr. SPT Pro-Hunter #1540
100 gr. SBT GameKing #1560
107 gr. HPBT MatchKing #1570
7"-8" TWST BBLS
.25 Caliber (.257/6.53MM Diameter)
75 gr. HP Varminter #1600
87 gr. SPT Varminter #1610
90 gr. HPBT GameKing #1615
100 gr. SPT Pro-Hunter #1620
100 gr. SBT GameKing #1625
100 gr. HPBT MatchKing #1628
117 gr. SBT GameKing #1630
117 gr. SPT Pro-Hunter #1640
120 gr. HPBT GameKing #1650
6.5MM .264 Caliber (.264/6.71MM Diameter)
85 gr. HP Varminter #1700
100 gr. HP Varminter #1710
107 gr. HPBT MatchKing #1715
6.5MM .264 Caliber (cont.) (.264/6.71MM Diameter)
120 gr. SPT Pro-Hunter #1720
120 gr. HPBT MatchKing #1725
140 gr. SBT GameKing #1730
140 gr. HPBT MatchKing #1740
142 gr. HPBT MatchKing #1742
160 gr. SMP Pro-Hunter #1750
.270 Caliber (.277/7.04MM Diameter)
90 gr. HP Varminter #1800
110 gr. SPT Pro-Hunter #1810
130 gr. SBT GameKing #1820
130 gr. SPT Pro-Hunter #1830
135 gr. HPBT MatchKing #1833
140 gr. HPBT GameKing #1835
140 gr. SBT GameKing #1845
150 gr. SBT GameKing #1840
7MM .284 Caliber (.284/7.21MM Diameter)
100 gr. HP Varminter #1895
120 gr. SPT Pro-Hunter #1900
130 gr. HPBT MatchKing #1903
130 gr. SPT SSP Pro-Hunter #7250
140 gr. SBT GameKing #1905
140 gr. SPT Pro-Hunter #1910
150 gr. SBT GameKing #1913
150 gr. HPBT MatchKing #1915
160 gr. SBT GameKing #1920
160 gr. HPBT GameKing #1925
168 gr. HPBT MatchKing #1930

Sierra Bullets

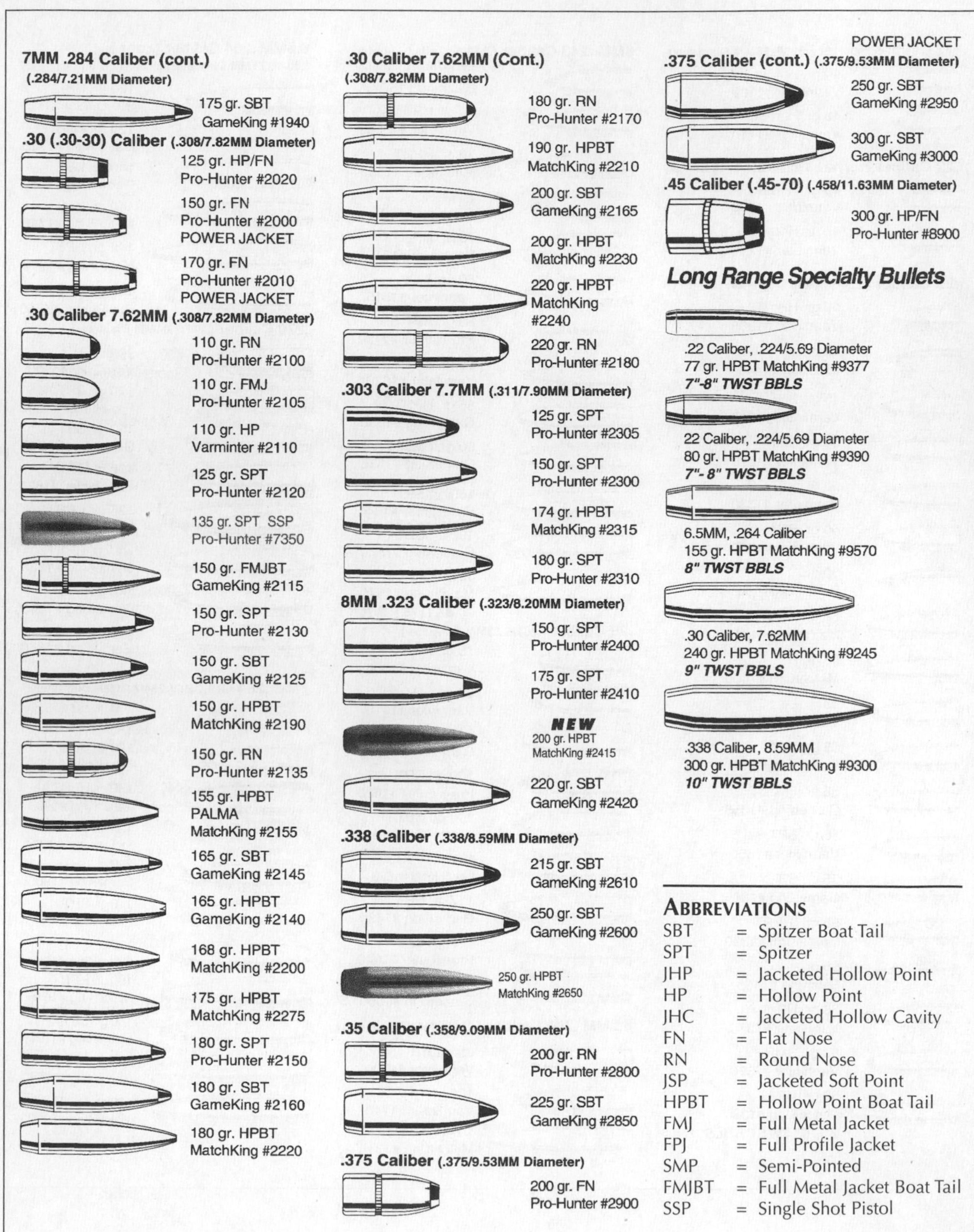
7MM .284 Caliber (cont.)
(.284/7.21MM Diameter)
175 gr. SBT GameKing #1940
.30 (.30-30) Caliber (.308/7.82MM Diameter)
125 gr. HP/FN Pro-Hunter #2020
150 gr. FN Pro-Hunter #2000 POWER JACKET
170 gr. FN Pro-Hunter #2010 POWER JACKET
.30 Caliber 7.62MM (.308/7.82MM Diameter)
110 gr. RN Pro-Hunter #2100
110 gr. FMJ Pro-Hunter #2105
110 gr. HP Varminter #2110
125 gr. SPT Pro-Hunter #2120
135 gr. SPT SSP Pro-Hunter #7350
150 gr. FMJBT GameKing #2115
150 gr. SPT Pro-Hunter #2130
150 gr. SBT GameKing #2125
150 gr. HPBT MatchKing #2190
150 gr. RN Pro-Hunter #2135
155 gr. HPBT PALMA MatchKing #2155
165 gr. SBT GameKing #2145
165 gr. HPBT GameKing #2140
168 gr. HPBT MatchKing #2200
175 gr. HPBT MatchKing #2275
180 gr. SPT Pro-Hunter #2150
180 gr. SBT GameKing #2160
180 gr. HPBT MatchKing #2220
.30 Caliber 7.62MM (Cont.)
(.308/7.82MM Diameter)
180 gr. RN Pro-Hunter #2170
190 gr. HPBT MatchKing #2210
200 gr. SBT GameKing #2165
200 gr. HPBT MatchKing #2230
220 gr. HPBT MatchKing #2240
220 gr. RN Pro-Hunter #2180
.303 Caliber 7.7MM (.311/7.90MM Diameter)
125 gr. SPT Pro-Hunter #2305
150 gr. SPT Pro-Hunter #2300
174 gr. HPBT MatchKing #2315
180 gr. SPT Pro-Hunter #2310
8MM .323 Caliber (.323/8.20MM Diameter)
150 gr. SPT Pro-Hunter #2400
175 gr. SPT Pro-Hunter #2410
NEW
200 gr. HPBT MatchKing #2415
220 gr. SBT GameKing #2420
.338 Caliber (.338/8.59MM Diameter)
215 gr. SBT GameKing #2610
250 gr. SBT GameKing #2600
250 gr. HPBT MatchKing #2650
.35 Caliber (.358/9.09MM Diameter)
200 gr. RN Pro-Hunter #2800
225 gr. SBT GameKing #2850
.375 Caliber (.375/9.53MM Diameter)
200 gr. FN Pro-Hunter #2900
POWER JACKET
.375 Caliber (cont.) (.375/9.53MM Diameter)
250 gr. SBT GameKing #2950
300 gr. SBT GameKing #3000
.45 Caliber (.45-70) (.458/11.63MM Diameter)
300 gr. HP/FN Pro-Hunter #8900
Long Range Specialty Bullets
.22 Caliber, .224/5.69 Diameter
77 gr. HPBT MatchKing #9377
7"-8" TWST BBLS
22 Caliber, .224/5.69 Diameter
80 gr. HPBT MatchKing #9390
7"- 8" TWST BBLS
6.5MM, .264 Caliber
155 gr. HPBT MatchKing #9570
8" TWST BBLS
.30 Caliber, 7.62MM
240 gr. HPBT MatchKing #9245
9" TWST BBLS
.338 Caliber, 8.59MM
300 gr. HPBT MatchKing #9300
10" TWST BBLS
ABBREVIATIONS
SBT = Spitzer Boat Tail
SPT = Spitzer
JHP = Jacketed Hollow Point
HP = Hollow Point
JHC = Jacketed Hollow Cavity
FN = Flat Nose
RN = Round Nose
JSP = Jacketed Soft Point
HPBT = Hollow Point Boat Tail
FMJ = Full Metal Jacket
FPJ = Full Profile Jacket
SMP = Semi-Pointed
FMJBT = Full Metal Jacket Boat Tail
SSP = Single Shot Pistol

Sierra Bullets
Handgun Bullets

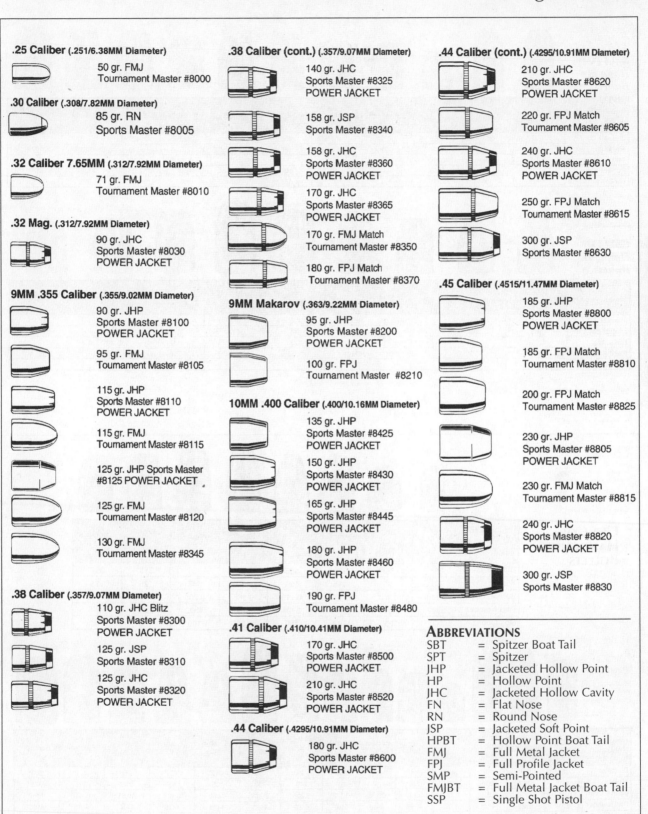

.25 Caliber (.251/6.38MM Diameter)

50 gr. FMJ
Tournament Master #8000

.30 Caliber (.308/7.82MM Diameter)

85 gr. RN
Sports Master #8005

.32 Caliber 7.65MM (.312/7.92MM Diameter)

71 gr. FMJ
Tournament Master #8010

.32 Mag. (.312/7.92MM Diameter)

90 gr. JHC
Sports Master #8030
POWER JACKET

9MM .355 Caliber (.355/9.02MM Diameter)

90 gr. JHP
Sports Master #8100
POWER JACKET

95 gr. FMJ
Tournament Master #8105

115 gr. JHP
Sports Master #8110
POWER JACKET

115 gr. FMJ
Tournament Master #8115

125 gr. JHP Sports Master
#8125 POWER JACKET

125 gr. FMJ
Tournament Master #8120

130 gr. FMJ
Tournament Master #8345

.38 Caliber (.357/9.07MM Diameter)

110 gr. JHC Blitz
Sports Master #8300
POWER JACKET

125 gr. JSP
Sports Master #8310

125 gr. JHC
Sports Master #8320
POWER JACKET

.38 Caliber (cont.) (.357/9.07MM Diameter)

140 gr. JHC
Sports Master #8325
POWER JACKET

158 gr. JSP
Sports Master #8340

158 gr. JHC
Sports Master #8360
POWER JACKET

170 gr. JHC
Sports Master #8365
POWER JACKET

170 gr. FMJ Match
Tournament Master #8350

180 gr. FPJ Match
Tournament Master #8370

9MM Makarov (.363/9.22MM Diameter)

95 gr. JHP
Sports Master #8200
POWER JACKET

100 gr. FPJ
Tournament Master #8210

10MM .400 Caliber (.400/10.16MM Diameter)

135 gr. JHP
Sports Master #8425
POWER JACKET

150 gr. JHP
Sports Master #8430
POWER JACKET

165 gr. JHP
Sports Master #8445
POWER JACKET

180 gr. JHP
Sports Master #8460
POWER JACKET

190 gr. FPJ
Tournament Master #8480

.41 Caliber (.410/10.41MM Diameter)

170 gr. JHC
Sports Master #8500
POWER JACKET

210 gr. JHC
Sports Master #8520
POWER JACKET

.44 Caliber (.4295/10.91MM Diameter)

180 gr. JHC
Sports Master #8600
POWER JACKET

.44 Caliber (cont.) (.4295/10.91MM Diameter)

210 gr. JHC
Sports Master #8620
POWER JACKET

220 gr. FPJ Match
Tournament Master #8605

240 gr. JHC
Sports Master #8610
POWER JACKET

250 gr. FPJ Match
Tournament Master #8615

300 gr. JSP
Sports Master #8630

.45 Caliber (.4515/11.47MM Diameter)

185 gr. JHP
Sports Master #8800
POWER JACKET

185 gr. FPJ Match
Tournament Master #8810

200 gr. FPJ Match
Tournament Master #8825

230 gr. JHP
Sports Master #8805
POWER JACKET

230 gr. FMJ Match
Tournament Master #8815

240 gr. JHC
Sports Master #8820
POWER JACKET

300 gr. JSP
Sports Master #8830

Abbreviations

SBT = Spitzer Boat Tail
SPT = Spitzer
JHP = Jacketed Hollow Point
HP = Hollow Point
JHC = Jacketed Hollow Cavity
FN = Flat Nose
RN = Round Nose
JSP = Jacketed Soft Point
HPBT = Hollow Point Boat Tail
FMJ = Full Metal Jacket
FPJ = Full Profile Jacket
SMP = Semi-Pointed
FMJBT = Full Metal Jacket Boat Tail
SSP = Single Shot Pistol

HANDLOADING

Speer Handgun Bullets

Gold Dot Handgun Bullets

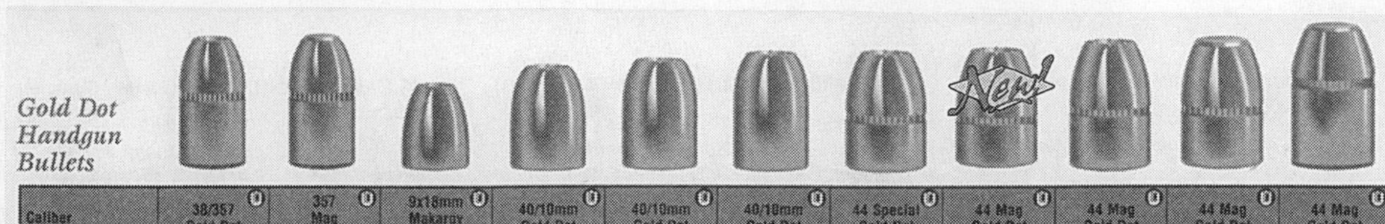

Caliber & Type	38/357 Gold Dot HP	357 Mag Gold Dot SP	9x18mm Makarov Gold Dot HP	40/10mm Gold Dot HP	40/10mm Gold Dot HP	40/10mm Gold Dot HP	44 Special Gold Dot HP	44 Mag Gold Dot HP	44 Mag Gold Dot HP	44 Mag Gold Dot SP	44 Mag Gold Dot SP
Diameter	.357"	.357"	.364"	.400"	.400"	.400"	.429"	.429"	.429"	.429"	.429"
Weight (grs.)	158	170	90	155	165	180	200	210	240	240	270
Ballist. Coef.	0.168	0.185	0.107	0.123	0.138	0.143	0.145	0.154	0.175	0.175	0.193
Part Number	4215	4230	3999	4400	4397	4406	4427	4428	4455	4456	4461
Box Count	100	100	100	100	100	100	100	100	100	100	50

Gold Dot Handgun Bullets

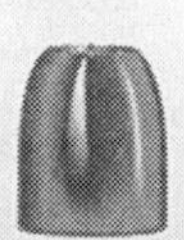

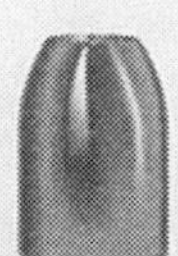

Caliber & Type	45 Auto Gold Dot HP	45 Auto Gold Dot HP	45 Auto Gold Dot HP	45 Colt Gold Dot HP	454 Casull Gold Dot HP	475 Linebaugh® Gold Dot SP	480 Ruger Gold Dot SP	480 Ruger Gold Dot HP	50 Action Express Gold Dot HP
Diameter	.451"	.451"	.451"	.452"	.452"	.475"	.475"	.475"	.500"
Weight (grs.)	185	200	230	250	300	400	325	275	300
Ballist. Coef.	0.109	0.138	0.143	0.165	0.233	0.242	0.191	0.162	0.155
Part Number	4470	4478	4483	4484	3974	3976	3978	3973	4493
Box Count	100	100	100	100	50	50	50	50	50

UNI-COR HANDGUN BULLETS

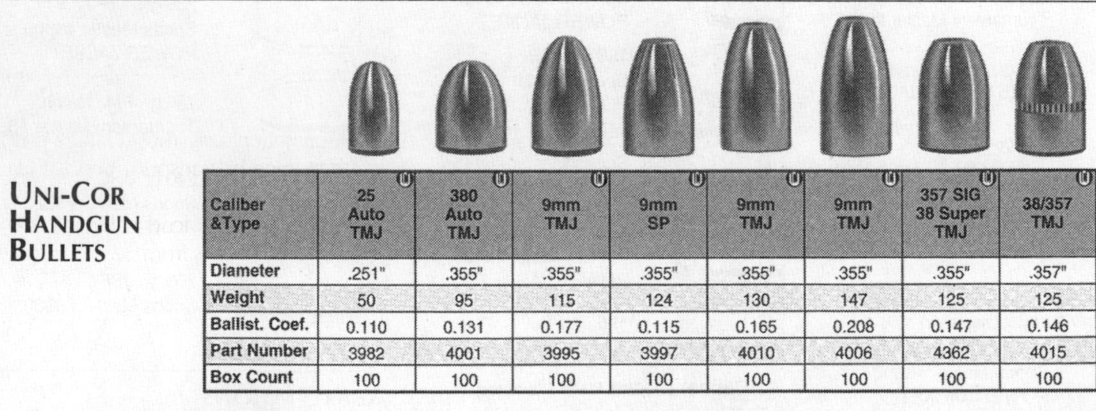

Caliber &Type	25 Auto TMJ	380 Auto TMJ	9mm TMJ	9mm SP	9mm TMJ	9mm TMJ	357 SIG 38 Super TMJ	38/357 TMJ
Diameter	.251"	.355"	.355"	.355"	.355"	.355"	.355"	.357"
Weight	50	95	115	124	130	147	125	125
Ballist. Coef.	0.110	0.131	0.177	0.115	0.165	0.208	0.147	0.146
Part Number	3982	4001	3995	3997	4010	4006	4362	4015
Box Count	100	100	100	100	100	100	100	100

Caliber &Type	38/357 TMJ	357 Mag Sil. Match TMJ	357 Mag Sil. Match TMJ	9x18mm Makarov TMJ	40/10mm TMJ	40/10mm TMJ	40/10mm TMJ	44 Mag Sil. Match TMJ	44 Mag SP	45 Match TMJ	45 Match TMJ	45 Auto TMJ	45 Colt 454 Casull SP	50 Action Express HP
Diameter	.357"	.357"	.357"	.364"	.400"	.400"	.400"	.429"	.429"	.451"	.451"	.451"	.451"	.500"
Weight	158	180	200	95	155	165	180	240	300	185	200	230	300	325
Ballist. Coef.	0.173	0.230	0.236	0.127	0.125	0.135	0.143	0.206	0.213	0.090	0.128	0.153	0.199	0.149
Part Number	4207	4229	4231	4375	4399	4410	4402	4459	4463	4473	4475	4480	4485	4495
Box Count	100	100	100	100	100	100	100	100	50	100	100	100	50	50

Speer Handgun Bullets

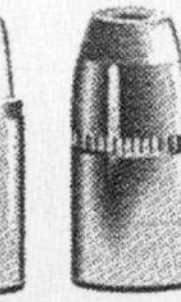

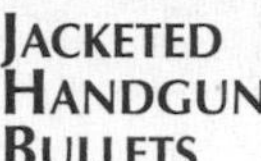

Jacketed Handgun Bullets

Caliber &Type	32 JHP	32 JHP	38/357 JHP	38/357 JSP	38/357 JHP	38/357 JHP	38/357 JHP-SWC	38/357 JHP
Diameter	.312"	.312"	.357"	.357"	.357"	.357"	.357"	.357"
Weight	85	100	110	125	125	140	146	158
Ballist. Coef.	0.121	0.167	0.122	0.140	0.135	0.152	0.159	0.158
Part Number	3987	3981	4007	4011	4013	4203	4205	4211
Box Count	100	100	100	100	100	100	100	100

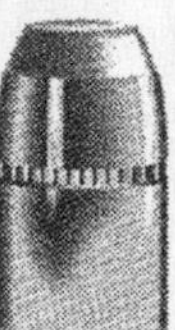

Caliber &Type	38/357 JSP	41 Mag JHP-SWC	41 Mag JSP-SWC	44 Mag JHP	44 Mag JHP-SWC	44 Mag JSP-SWC	44 Mag JHP	44 Mag JSP	45 JHP	45 JHP
Diameter	.357"	.410"	.410"	.429"	.429"	.429"	.429"	.429"	.451"	.451"
Weight	158	200	220	200	225	240	240	240	225	260
Ballist. Coef.	0.158	0.113	0.137	0.122	0.146	0.157	0.165	0.164	0.169	0.183
Part Number	4217	4405	4417	4425	4435	4447	4453	4457	4479	4481
Box Count	100	100	100	100	100	100	100	100	100	100

Lead Handgun Bullets

All Speer lead bullets now feature our hi-tech, multilayer lube system first introduced in our Idaho Territory lead bullets. This great lube is, simplet stated, the best thing in lead bullets. It stays with the bullet instead of burning off, virtually eliminating the gas cutting that causes most leading problems. It won't melt-off in storage or transport, and is clean and dry to the touch.

For target shooting or plinking, Speer lead bullets are now even a better value. Available in calibers from 32 through 45.

Lead Handgun Bullets

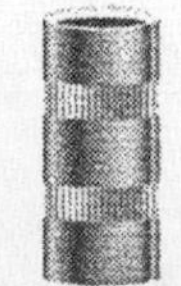

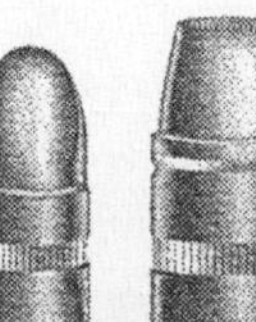

Caliber & Type	32 HB-WC	9mm RN	38 BB-WC	38 DE-WC	38 HB-WC	38 SWC	38 HP-SWC	38 RN	44 SWC	45 SWC	45 RN	45 SWC
Diameter	.314"	.356"	.358"	.358"	.358"	.358"	.358"	.358"	.430"	.452"	.452"	.452"
Weight (grs.)	98	125	148	148	148	158	158	158	240	200	230	250
Part Number	--	4601	4605	--	4617	4623	4627	4647	4660	4677	4690	4683
Bulk Part No.	4600	4602	4606	4611	4618	4624	4628	4648	4661	4678	4691	4684

Speer Rifle Bullets

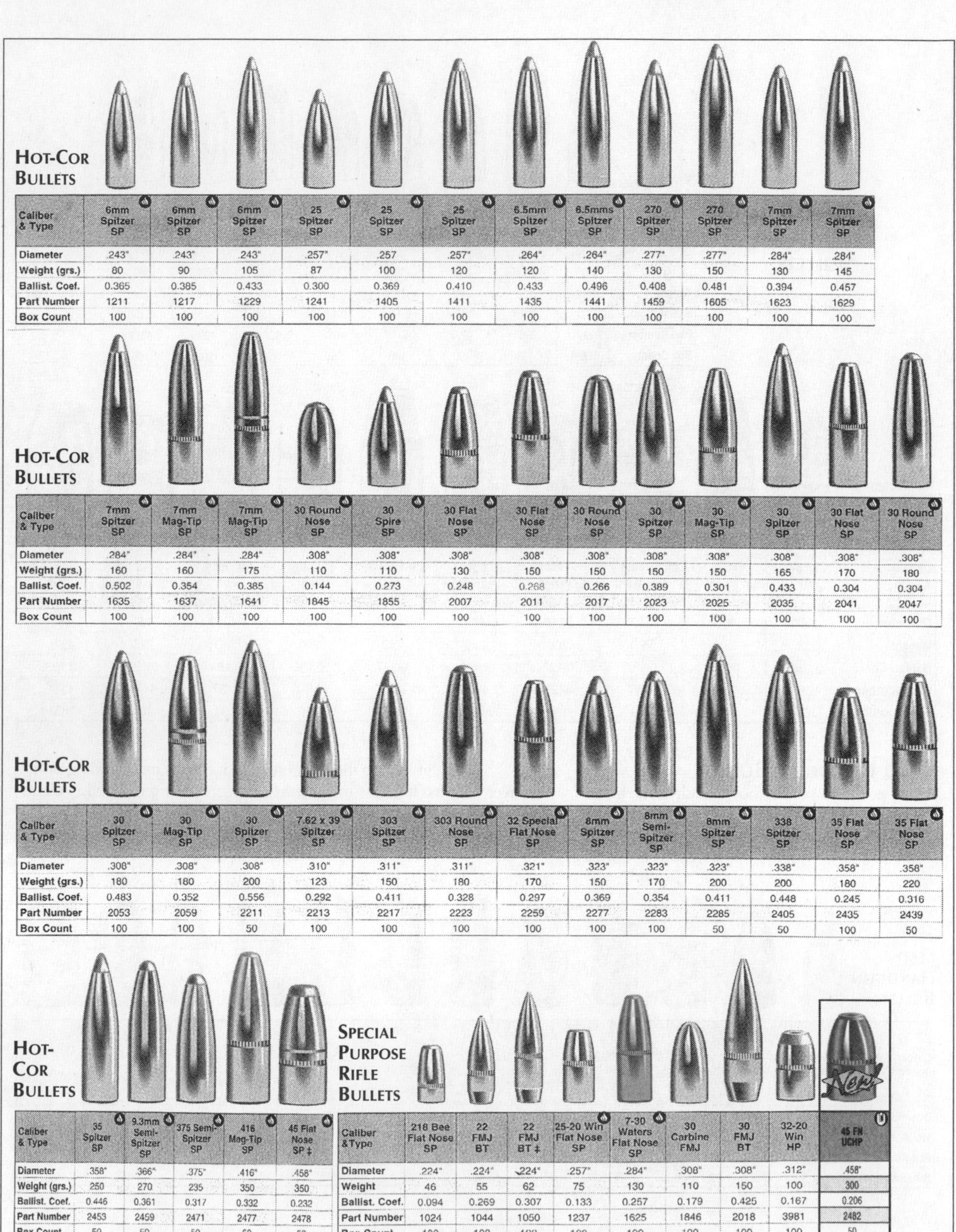

Hot-Cor Bullets

Caliber & Type	6mm Spitzer SP	6mm Spitzer SP	6mm Spitzer SP	25 Spitzer SP	25 Spitzer SP	25 Spitzer SP	6.5mm Spitzer SP	6.5mms Spitzer SP	270 Spitzer SP	270 Spitzer SP	7mm Spitzer SP	7mm Spitzer SP
Diameter	.243"	.243"	.243"	.257"	.257	.257"	.264"	.264"	.277"	.277"	.284"	.284"
Weight (grs.)	80	90	105	87	100	120	120	140	130	150	130	145
Ballist. Coef.	0.365	0.385	0.433	0.300	0.369	0.410	0.433	0.496	0.408	0.481	0.394	0.457
Part Number	1211	1217	1229	1241	1405	1411	1435	1441	1459	1605	1623	1629
Box Count	100	100	100	100	100	100	100	100	100	100	100	100

Hot-Cor Bullets

Caliber & Type	7mm Spitzer SP	7mm Mag-Tip SP	7mm Mag-Tip SP	30 Round Nose SP	30 Spire SP	30 Flat Nose SP	30 Flat Nose SP	30 Round Nose SP	30 Spitzer SP	30 Mag-Tip SP	30 Spitzer SP	30 Flat Nose SP	30 Round Nose SP
Diameter	.284"	.284"	.284"	.308"	.308"	.308"	.308"	.308"	.308"	.308"	.308"	.308"	.308"
Weight (grs.)	160	160	175	110	110	130	150	150	150	150	165	170	180
Ballist. Coef.	0.502	0.354	0.385	0.144	0.273	0.248	0.268	0.266	0.389	0.301	0.433	0.304	0.304
Part Number	1635	1637	1641	1845	1855	2007	2011	2017	2023	2025	2035	2041	2047
Box Count	100	100	100	100	100	100	100	100	100	100	100	100	100

Hot-Cor Bullets

Caliber & Type	30 Spitzer SP	30 Mag-Tip SP	30 Spitzer SP	7.62 x 39 Spitzer SP	303 Spitzer SP	303 Round Nose SP	32 Special Flat Nose SP	8mm Spitzer SP	8mm Semi-Spitzer SP	8mm Spitzer SP	338 Spitzer SP	35 Flat Nose SP	35 Flat Nose SP
Diameter	.308"	.308"	.308"	.310"	.311"	.311"	.321"	.323"	.323"	.323"	.338"	.358"	.358"
Weight (grs.)	180	180	200	123	150	180	170	150	170	200	200	180	220
Ballist. Coef.	0.483	0.352	0.556	0.292	0.411	0.328	0.297	0.369	0.354	0.411	0.448	0.245	0.316
Part Number	2053	2059	2211	2213	2217	2223	2259	2277	2283	2285	2405	2435	2439
Box Count	100	100	50	100	100	100	100	100	100	50	50	100	50

Hot-Cor Bullets

Caliber & Type	35 Spitzer SP	9.3mm Semi-Spitzer SP	375 Semi-Spitzer SP	416 Mag-Tip SP	45 Flat Nose SP ‡
Diameter	.358"	.366"	.375"	.416"	.458"
Weight (grs.)	250	270	235	350	350
Ballist. Coef.	0.446	0.361	0.317	0.332	0.232
Part Number	2453	2459	2471	2477	2478
Box Count	50	50	50	50	50

‡ Not recommended for lever-action rifles.

Special Purpose Rifle Bullets

New

Caliber & Type	218 Bee Flat Nose SP	22 FMJ BT	22 FMJ BT ‡	25-20 Win Flat Nose SP	7-30 Waters Flat Nose SP	30 Carbine FMJ	30 FMJ BT	32-20 Win HP	45 FN UCHP
Diameter	.224"	.224"	.224"	.257"	.284"	.308"	.308"	.312"	.458"
Weight	46	55	62	75	130	110	150	100	300
Ballist. Coef.	0.094	0.269	0.307	0.133	0.257	0.179	0.425	0.167	0.206
Part Number	1024	1044	1050	1237	1625	1846	2018	3981	2482
Box Count	100	100	100	100	100	100	100	100	50

‡ Recommended for twist rates of 1 in 10" or faster.

Speer Rifle Bullets

BOAT-TAIL RIFLE BULLETS

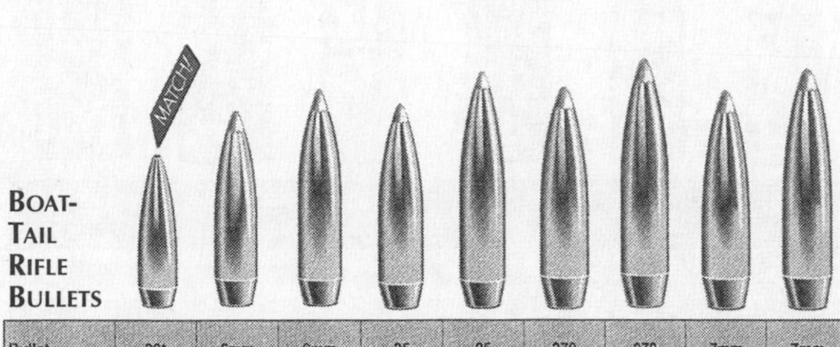

Bullet Caliber & Type	22* Match HPBT	6mm Spitzer SPBT	6mm Spitzer SPBT	25 Spitzer SPBT	25 Spitzer SPBT	270 Spitzer SPBT	270 Spitzer SPBT	7mm Spitzer SPBT	7mm Spitzer SPBT
Diameter	.224"	.243"	.243"	.257"	.257"	.277"	.277"	.284"	.284"
Weight (grs.)	52	85	100	100	120	130	150	130	145
Ballist. Coef.	0.253	0.404	0.430	0.393	0.435	0.449	0.496	0.411	0.502
Part Number	1036	1213	1220	1408	1410	1458	1604	1624	1628
Box Count	100	100	100	100	100	100	100	100	100

MHP RIFLE BULLETS

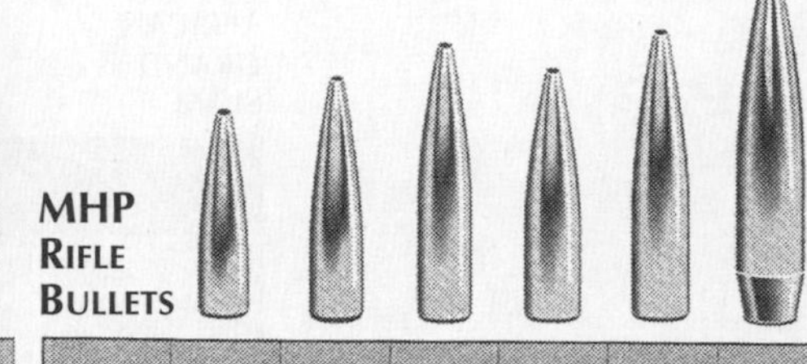

Caliber &Type	22 MHP HP	6mm MHP HP	25 MHP HP	270 MHP HP	7mm MHP HP	30 MHP Match HPBT
Diameter	.224"	.243"	.257"	.277"	.284"	.308"
Weight	50	70	87	90	110	168
Ballist. Coef.	0.234	0.296	0.325	0.289	0.355	0.504
Part Number	1031	1207	1247	1457	1615	2039
Box Count	100	100	100	100	100	100

BOAT-TAIL RIFLE BULLETS

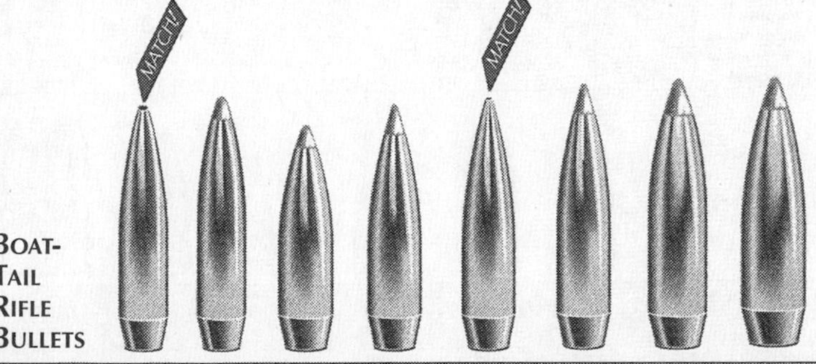

Bullet Caliber & Type	7mm* Match HPBT	7mm Spitzer SPBT	30 Spitzer SPBT	30 Spitzer SPBT	30* Match HPBT	30 Spitzer SPBT	338 Spitzer SPBT	375 Spitzer SPBT
Diameter	.284"	.284"	.308"	.308"	.308"	.308"	.338"	.375"
Weight (grs.)	145	160	150	165	168	180	225	270
Ballist. Coef.	0.465	0.556	0.423	0.477	0.480	0.540	0.484	0.429
Part Number	1631	1634	2022	2034	2040	2052	2406	2472
Box Count	100	100	100	100	100	100	50	50

*Match bullets are not recommended for use on game animals.

GRAND SLAM

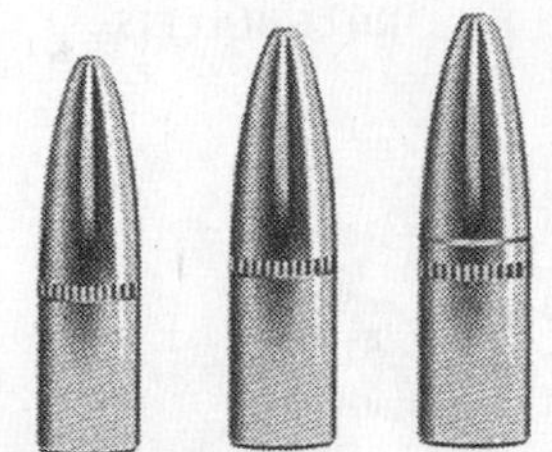

Bullet Caliber & Type	6mm GS SP	25 GS SP	6.5mm GS SP
Diameter	.243"	.257"	.264"
Weight (grs.)	100	120	140
Ballist. Coef.	0.351	0.328	0.385
Part Number	1222	1415	1444
Box Count	50	50	50

GRAND SLAM

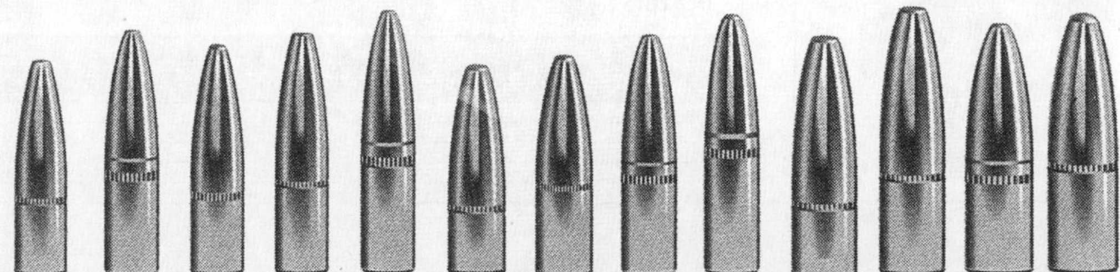

Bullet Caliber & Type	270 Grand Slam SP	270 Grand Slam SP	7mm Grand Slam SP	7mm Grand Slam SP	7mm Grand Slam SP	30 Grand Slam SP	30 Grand Slam SP	30 Grand Slam SP	30 Grand Slam SP	338 Grand Slam SP	338 Grand Slam SP	35 Grand Slam SP	375 Grand Slam SP
Diameter	.277"	.277"	.284"	.284"	.284"	.308"	.308"	.308"	.308"	.338"	.338"	.358"	.375"
Weight (grs.)	130	150	145	160	175	150	165	180	200	225	250	250	285
Ballist. Coef.	0.345	0.385	0.327	0.387	0.465	0.305	0.393	0.416	0.448	.0382	0.431	0.335	0.354
Part Number	1465	1608	1632	1638	1643	2026	2038	2063	2212	2407	2408	2455	2473
Box Count	50	50	50	50	50	50	50	50	50	50	50	50	50

Speer Rifle Bullets

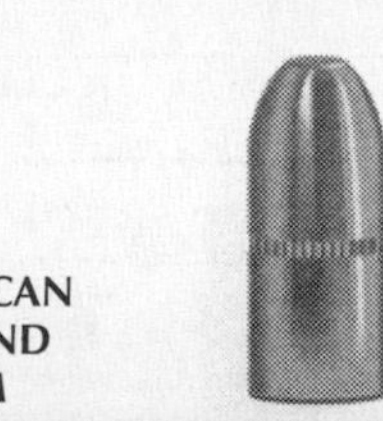
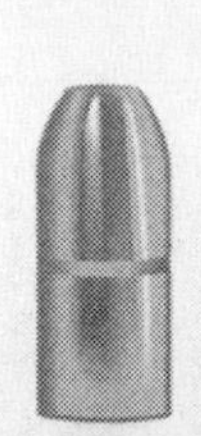

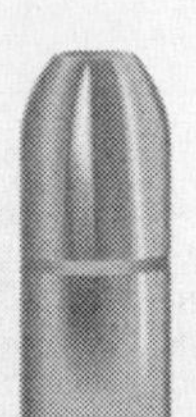

AFRICAN GRAND SLAM

Bullet Caliber & Type	375 AGS SP	375 AGS Tungsten Solid	416 AGS SP	416 AGS Tungsten Solid	45 AGS SP	45 AGS Tungsten Solid
Diameter	.375"	.375"	.416"	.416"	.458"	.458"
Weight (grs.)	300	300	400	400	500	500
Ballist. Coef.	0.323	0.258	0.318	0.262	0.285	0.277
Part Number	2470	2474	2475	2476	2485	2486
Box Count	25	25	25	25	25	25

JACKETED RIFLE BULLETS

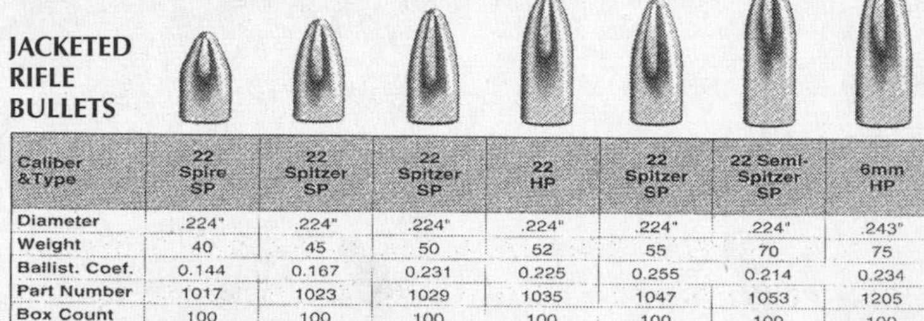

Caliber &Type	22 Spire SP	22 Spitzer SP	22 Spitzer SP	22 HP	22 Spitzer SP	22 Semi-Spitzer SP	6mm HP
Diameter	.224"	.224"	.224"	.224"	.224"	.224"	.243"
Weight	40	45	50	52	55	70	75
Ballist. Coef.	0.144	0.167	0.231	0.225	0.255	0.214	0.234
Part Number	1017	1023	1029	1035	1047	1053	1205
Box Count	100	100	100	100	100	100	100

JACKETED RIFLE BULLETS

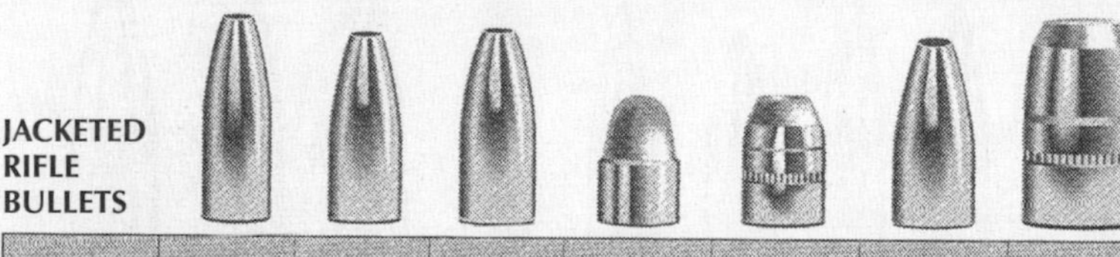

Caliber &Type	25 HP	270 HP	7mm HP	30 Plinker RN SP	30 HP	30 HP	45 Flat Nose SP
Diameter	.257"	.277"	.284"	.308"	.308"	.308"	.458"
Weight	100	100	115	100	110	130	400
Ballist. Coef.	0.255	0.225	0.257	0.124	0.136	0.263	0.214
Part Number	1407	1447	1617	1805	1835	2005	2479
Box Count	100	100	100	100	100	100	50

TNT RIFLE BULLETS

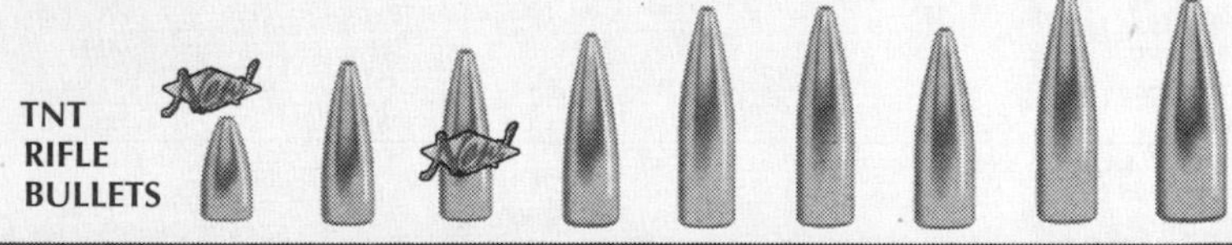

Caliber &Type	22 Hornet TNT HP	22 TNT HP	22 TNT HP (HV)	6mm TNT HP	25 TNT HP	6.5mm TNT HP	270 TNT HP	7mm TNT HP	30 TNT HP
Diameter	.224"	.224"	.224"	.243"	.257"	.264"	.277"	.284"	.308"
Weight	33	50	55	70	87	90	90	110	125
Ballist. Coef.	0.112	0.223	0.233	0.282	0.310	0.281	0.275	0.338	0.326
Part Number	1014	1030	1032	1206	1246	1445	1446	1616	1986
Box Count	100	100	100	100	100	100	100	100	100

Deep-Shok® Rifle Bullets

- Compound-profile, fluted jacket
  Reliable, controlled expansion over a wide range of hunting conditions
- Boat Tail design
  Higher ballistic coefficient for better energy retention at long range
- Hot-Cor
  Eliminates oxide layers that lead to core slippage
- Large heel lock
  Mechanically locks the core to the jacket
- Available in 165 gr. and 180 gr. - 30 cal.

Trophy Bonded® Bear Claw® Rifle Bullets

- Fusion-bonded core
  Fusion bonding ensures retained weights in excess of 95 percent.
- Solid copper shank
  Ensures deep penetration
- Protected soft point
  Long jacket protects lead tip against recoil damage
- Available from .224 55 gr. to .458 500 gr.

Swift

A-Frame and Scirocco Bullets

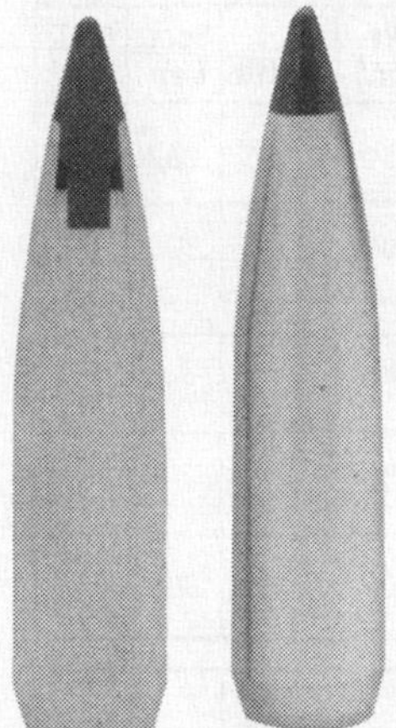

SWIFT SCIROCCO™ BONDED 30 CAL. (.308") 180-GR. POLYMER TIP/BOAT TAIL SPITZER

Tapered jacket and proprietary bonding process produce controlled mushrooming with high weight retention. Ideally suited to fast, flat-shooting calibers.

SCIROCCO™ RIFLE BULLETS

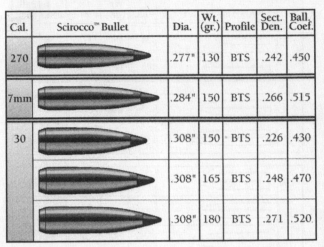

Cal.	Scirocco™ Bullet	Dia.	Wt. (gr.)	Profile	Sect. Den.	Ball. Coef.
270		.277"	130	BTS	.242	.450
7mm		.284"	150	BTS	.266	.515
30		.308"	150	BTS	.226	.430
		.308"	165	BTS	.248	.470
		.308"	180	BTS	.271	.520

BTS=Boat Tail Spitzer

THE SWIFT BULLET COMPANY

The Swift Bullet Company has two types of big game bullets.

The **Scirocco** design starts with a tough, pointed, polymer tip that reduces air resistance, prevents tip deformation, and blends symmetrically into the curved radius of its secant ogive nose section. A moderate 15-degree boat-tail base reduces drag and eases seating. The thick base prevents bullet deformation during launch. **Scirocco's** shape creates two other significant advantages. One is an extremely high ballistic coefficient. The other, derived from the secant ogive nose, is a comparatively long bearing surface for a sharply pointed bullet, a feature that improves rotational stability.

Inside, the **Scirocco** has a bonded-core construction with a pure lead core encased in a tapered, progressively thickening jacket of pure copper. Pure copper was selected because it is more malleable and less brittle than less expensive gilding metal. Both jacket and core are bonded together by Swift's proprietary bonding process so that the bullet expands without break-up as if the two parts were the same metal. In tests, the new bullet mushroomed effectively at velocities as low as 1440 fps, yet stayed together at velocities in excess of 3,000 fps, with over 70 percent weight retention.

Swift's **A-Frame** bullet, with its mid-section wall of copper, is still earning praise for its deep-driving dependability in tough game. Less aerodynamic than the Scirocco, it produces a broad mushroom while carrying almost all its weight through muscle and bone. Available in a wide range of weights and diameters, it is also a bonded-core bullet.

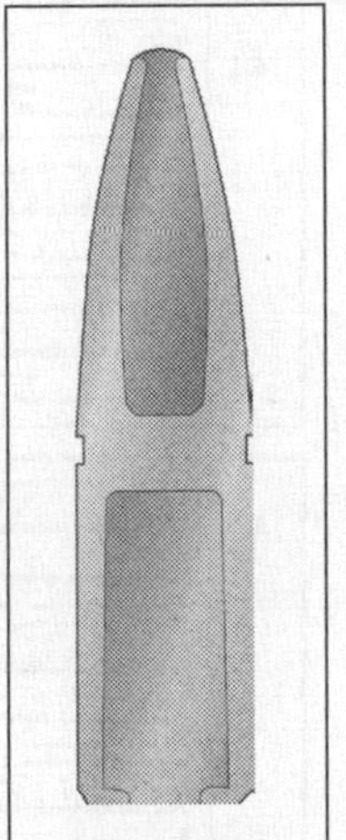

A-Frame Bullet Design

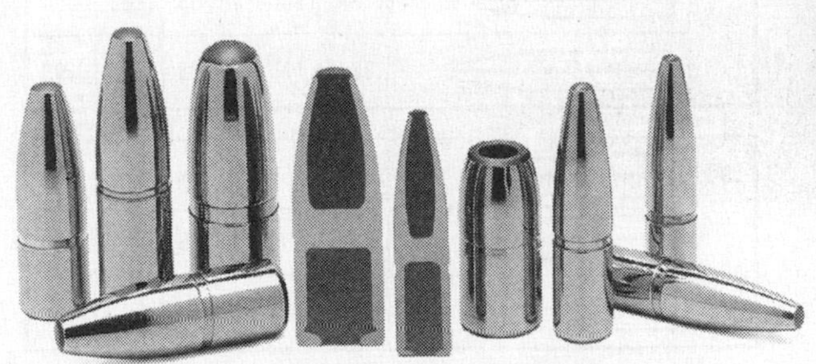

The Swift A-Frame, noted for deep penetration in tough game, is loaded in Remington Premier ammunition.

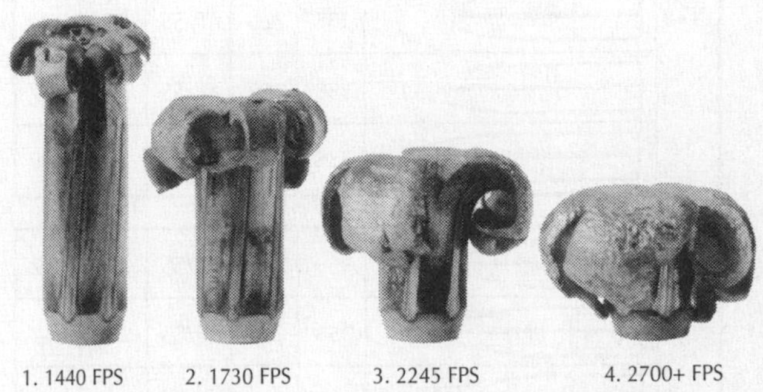

Swift SciroccoTM Expands dependably over a wide range of velocities, and maintains high jacket/core integrity.

HANDLOADING

Swift

A-Frame Rifle Bullet Specifications

Cal.	A-Frame™ Bullet	Dia.	Wt. (gr.)	Profile	Sect. Den.	Ball. Coef.
.25		.257″	100	AF/SS	.216	.318
		.257″	120	AF/SS	.260	.382
6.5 mm		.264″	120	AF/SS	.246	.344
		.264″	140	AF/SS	.287	.401
.270		.277″	130	AF/SS	.242	.323
		.277″	140	AF/SS	.261	.414
		.277″	150	AF/SS	.279	.444
7mm		.284″	140	AF/SS	.248	.335
		.284″	160	AF/SS	.283	.450
		.284″	175	AF/SS	.310	.493
.30		.308″	165	AF/SS	.249	.367
		.308″	180	AF/SS	.271	.400
		.308″	200	AF/SS	.301	.444
8mm		.323″	200	AF/SS	.274	.357
		.323″	220	AF/SS	.301	.393
.338		.338″	225	AF/SS	.281	.384
		.338″	250	AF/SS	.313	.427
		.338″	275	AF/SS	.344	.469
.35		.358″	225	AF/SS	.251	.312
		.358″	250	AF/SS	.279	.347
		.358″	280	AF/SS	.312	.388
9.3 mm		.366″	250	AF/SS	.267	.285
		.366″	300	AF/SS	.320	.342
.375		.375″	250	AF/SS	.254	.271
		.375″	270	AF		
		.375″	300	AF/SS	.305	.325
.416		.416″	350	AF/SS	.289	.321
		.416″	400	AF/SS	.330	.367
.458		.458″	400	AF/FN	.272	.258
		.458″	450	AF/SS	.307	.325
		.458″	500	AF/SS	.341	.361
.470		.475″	500	AF/RN	.329	.364

Handgun Bullet Specifications

Cal.	A-Frame™ Bullet	Dia.	Wt. (gr.)	Profile	Sect. Den.	Ball. Coef.
.44		.430″	240	AF/HP	.185	.119
		.430″	280	AF/HP	.216	.139
		.430″	300	AF/HP	.232	.147
.45		.452″	265	AF	.210	.135
		.452″	300	AF/HP	.210	.135
		.452″	325	AF	.210	.135

HANDLOADING

Woodleigh Premium Bullets

Weldcore Soft Nose

Woodleigh Weldcore Soft Nose bullets are made from 90/100 gilding metal (90% copper: 10% zinc) 1.6 mm thick. Maximum retained weight is obtained by fusing the pure lead to the gilding metal jacket, hence the name "Weldcore."

Full Metal Jacket

Made from gilding metal-clad steel 2mm thick, jackets on fmj bullets are heavy at the nose for extra impact resistance. The jacket then tapers towards the base to assist rifling engraving.

Calibre Diameter	Type	Weight Grain	SD	BC
700 Nitro	SN	1000	.292	.340
.700″	FMJ	1000	.292	.340
600 Nitro	SN	900	.334	.371
.620″	FMJ	900	.334	.334
577 Nitro	SN	750	.313	.346
.585″	FMJ	750	.313	.351
	SN	650	.271	.292
	FMJ	650	.271	.292
577 B.P. .585″	SN	650	.271	.320
500 Nitro	SN	570	.313	.474
.510″	FMJ	570	.313	.434
500 B.P. .510″	SN	440	.242	.336
500	PP	535	.304	.460
Jeffery	SN	535	.304	.460
.510″	FMJ	535	.304	.422
	PP	600	.330	.423
	FMJ	600	.330	.330
505	PP	600	.336	.450
Gibbs	SN	525	.294	.445
.505″	FMJ	525	.294	.408
	FMJ	600	.366	.450
475 No2	SN	500	.300	.420
Jeffery .488″	FMJ	500	.300	.416
475 No2	SN	480	.303	.400
.483″	FMJ	480	.303	.410
476 W.R.	SN	520	.328	.420
.476″	FMJ	520	.328	.455
475 Nitro	SN	480	.227	.307
.476″	FMJ	480	.227	.257
470 Nitro	SN	500	.318	.411
.474″	FMJ	500	.318	.410
465 Nitro	SN	480	.318	.410
.468″	FMJ	480	.318	.407
450 Nitro	SN	480	.327	.419
.458″	FMJ	480	.327	.410
458 Mag.	SN	500	.341	.430
.458″	SN	550	.375	.480
	FMJ	500	.341	.405
	FMJ	550	.375	.426
	PP	400	.272	.420
	RN	350	.238	.305
45/70 .458″	FN	405	.276	.250
11.3x62 Schuler .440″	SN	401	.296	.411
425 W.R.	SN	410	.310	.344
.435″	FMJ	410	.310	.336
404	SN	400	.319	.354
Jeffery	FMJ	400	.319	.358
.423″	SN	350	.279	.357
10.75x68mm	SN	347	.277	.355
.423″	FMJ	347	.277	.307
416	SN	410	.338	.375
Rigby	FMJ	410	.338	.341
.416″	PP	340	.281	.425
	SN	450	.372	.402
450/400	SN	400	.338	.384
Nitro .411″ or .408″	FMJ	400	.338	.433

Calibre Diameter	Type	Weight Grain	SD	BC
.408	SN	400	.338	.384
.408	FMJ	400	.338	.433
375 Mag.	PP	235	.239	.331
.375″	RN	270	.275	.305
	SP	270	.275	.380
	PP	270	.275	.352
	RN	300	.305	.340
	SP	300	.305	.425
	PP	300	.305	.420
	FMJ	300	.305	.307
	RN	350	.354	.354
	PP	350	.354	.440
	FMJ	350	.354	.372
405 Win., .411″	SN	300	.254	.194
9.3mm	SN	286	.305	.331
.366″	PP	286	.305	.381
	FMJ	286	.305	.324
	SN	250	.267	.296
360 No2	SN	320	.341	.378
.366″	FMJ	320	.341	.362
	PP	320	.343	.428
358 Cal	SN	225	.250	.277
.358″	FMJ	225	.250	.298
	SN	250	.285	.365
	SN	310	.346	.400
	FMJ	310	.346	.378
338 Mag	PP	225	.281	.425
.338″	SN	250	.313	.332
	PP	250	.313	.470
	FMJ	250	.313	.326
	SN	300	.375	.416
	FMJ	300	.375	.398
333	SN	250	.328	.400
Jeffery	SN	300	.386	.428
.333″	FMJ	300	.386	.419
318 W.R.	SN	250	.328	.420
.330″	FMJ	250	.328	.364
8mm	SN	196	.268	.370
.323″	SN	220	.302	.363
	SN	250	.343	.389
8X57	SN	200	.282	.370
303	SN	174	.257	.342
British .312	PP	215	.316	.359
308 Cal	FMJ	220	.331	.359
.308″	RN	220	.331	.367
	PP	180	.273	.376
	PP	165	.250	.320
	PP	150	.226	.301
Win Mag.	PP	180	.273	.435
	PP	200	.301	.450
275 H&H	PP	160	.275	.474
.287″	PP	175	.301	.518
7mm	PP	140	.247	.436
.284″	PP	160	.282	.486
	PP	175	.312	.530
270 Win	PP	130	.241	.409
.277″	PP	150	.278	.463

SP = Semi-point • PP = Protected Point • FN = Flat Nose • RN = Round Nose • FMJ = Full Metal Jacket
All PP, FN, RN, SP, SN bullets are Weldcore Softnose

98% & 95% RETAINED WEIGHT 300 WIN MAG 180GR PP

458 X 500GN SN RECOVERED FROM BUFFALO

270 WIN 150GN PP 86% RETAINED WEIGHT

94% RETAINED WEIGHT 300 WIN MAG 180GR PP

500/465 RECOVERED FROM BUFFALO

Accurate Powder

Accurate Powder Specifications

	NG*	Avg. Length/Thickness		Avg. Diameter		Bulk Density**	VMD	Comparative Powders***	
		inches	mm	Inches	mm	Gram/cc	cc/grain	Ball	Extruded
Ball Propellants									
Handguns/Shotshell									
No.2 Imp.	14.0			0.018	0.457	0.650	0.100	WIN 231	Bullseye
No. 5	18.0			0.027	0.686	0.950	0.068	WIN 540	
No. 7	12.0			0.012	0.305	0.985	0.066	WIN 630	
No. 9	10.0			1.015	0.381	0.935	0.069	WIN 296	
AA 1680	10.0			0.014	0.356	0.950	0.068	WIN 680	
Solo 4100	10.0			0.011	0.279	0.960	0.068	WIN 296	
Rifle									
AA 2230	10.0			0.022	0.559	0.980	0.066	BL C2, WIN 748	
AA 2460	10.0			0.022	0.559	0.990	0.065	BL C2, WIN 748	
AA2520	10.0			0.022	0.559	0.970	0.067		
AA2700	10.0			0.022	0.559	0.960	0.068	WIN 760	
MAGPRO	9.0			0.030	0.762	0.970	0.067		
AA 8700	10.0			0.030	0.762	0.960	0.068	H870	
Extruded Propellants									
Shotshell/Handguns									
Nirto 100	21.0	0.010	0.254	0.058	1.473	0.505	0.128		700X, Red Dot
Solo 1000		0.010	0.254	0.052	1.321	0.510	0.127		Green Dot
Solo 1250		0.013	0.033	0.051	1.295	0.550	0.118		PB
Rifle/handgun									
XMP-5744	20.00	0.048	1.219	0.033	0.838	0.880	0.074		No Equiv.
Rifle									
XMR-2015		0.039	0.991	0.031	0.787	0.880	0.074		H322,N201 IMR 4198
XMR-2495		0.068	1.727	0.029	0.737	0.880	0.074		IMR 4895
XMR-4064		0.050	1.270	0.035	0.889	0.890	0.072		IMR 4064
XMR-4350		0.083	0.038	0.038	0.965	0.890	0.072		IMR 4350
XMR-3100		0.083	0.038	0.038	0.965	0.920	0.070		IMR 4831

*NG-NItroglycerin (glyceryl trinitrate) **glcc ***For comparison only, not a loading recommendation

Alliant Smokeless Powders

Alliant Rifle, Shotgun and Pistol Powders

Powder	Relative Quickness	Principal Purpose	Secondary Uses
Bullseye®	100%	Handgun Loads	12 ga. Light Target Loads
Red Dot®	94.1%	Light & Standard 12 & 16 ga. Target Loads	Handgun Loads
American Select®	81.0%	12 ga. Target Loads	Cowboy Action Handgun Loads
Green Dot®	77.9%	Handicap Trap Loads	20 & 28 ga. Target Loads
Unique®	61.6%	All-around Shotshell Powder, 12, 16 & 20 ga.	Handgun Loads
Power Pistol®	58.6%	High Performance 9mm, .40 S&W & 10mm	Moderate Pistol Cartridges
Herco®	56.1%	Heavy Shotshell Loads 10, 12 16, 20 & 28 ga.	Heavy Handgun Loads
Blue Dot®	37.8%	Magnum Shotshell Loads 10, 12, 16, 20 & 28 ga.	Magnum Handgun Loads
Steel™	34.0%	Non-Toxic Hunting Shotshell	2 oz. Turkey Loads
2400®	27.00%	Magnum Handgun Loads	.22 Hornet & 218 Bee
Reloader® 7	19.4%	Light Rifle	45-70 Gov't
Reloader® 15	13.7%	Medium Rifle	Silhouette Rifle
Reloader® 19	11.3%	Standard Rifle	Light Magnum Rifle
Reloader® 22	11.1%	Magnum Rifle	Heavy Bullet Stand Rifle
Reloader® 25	10.5%	Heavy Magnum Rifle	Magnum Rifle

Hodgdon Smokeless Powder

Pyrodex Pellets
Both rifle and pistol pellets eliminate powder measures, speeds shooting for black powder enthusiasts.

Extreme H4198
H4198 was developed especially for small and medium capacity cartridges.

Extreme H322
This powder fills the gap between H4198 and BL-C9(2). Performs best in small to medium capacity cases.

Extreme Benchmark
A fine choice for small rifle cases like the .223 Rem and PPC competition rounds. Appropriate also for the 300-30 and 7x57.

Spherical BL-C2
Best performance is in the 222, .308 other cases smaller than 30/06.

Spherical H335®
Similar to BL-C(2), H335 is popular for its performance in medium capacity cases, especially in 222 and 308 Winchester.

Extreme Varget
Features small extruded grain powder for uniform metering, plus higher velocities/normal pressures in such calibers as .223, 22-250, 306, 30-06, 375 H&H

Extreme H4895®
4895 gives desirable performance in almost all cases from 222 Rem. to 458 Win. Reduced loads, to as low as 3/5 maximum, still give target accuracy.

Spherical H380®
This number fills a gap between 4320 and 4350. It is excellent in 22/250, 220 Swift, the 6mm's, 257 and 30/06.

Spherical H414®
In many popular medium to medium-large calibers, pressure velocity relationship is better.

Extreme H4350
This powder gives superb accuracy at optimum velocity for many large capacity metallic rifle cartridges.

Extreme H4831®
Outstanding performance with medium and heavy bullets in the 6mm's, 25/06, 270 and Magnum calibers. Also available with shortened grains (H4831SC) for easy metering.

Extreme H1000 Extruded Powder
Fills the gap between H4831 and H870. Works especially well in overbore capacity cartridges (1,000-yard shooters take note).

Extreme H50 BMG
Designed for the 50 Browning Machine Gun cartridge. Highly insensitive to extreme temperature changes.

Clays
Tailored for use in 12 ga., 7/8, 1-oz. and 1 1/8-oz. loads. Also performs well in many handgun applications, including .38 Special, .40 S&W and 45 ACP. Perfect for 1 1/8 and 1 oz. loads.

RETUMBO
A true magnum rifle powder, designed for such cartridges as the 300 Rem. Ultra Mag., 30-378 Weatherby, the 7mm STW and other cases with large capacities and small bores. Shooters can expect up to 40-100 feet per second more velocity than other magnum powders.

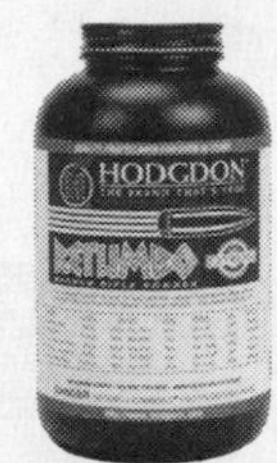

Triple Seven
A muzzleloading propellant that does not use sulfur, keeping shooter's hand clean. No offensive odor and cleaning is as easy as running a water soaked patch down the barrel followed by 3 or 4 dry patches!

Universal Clays
Loads nearly all of the straight-wall pistol cartridges as well as 12 ga. 1.25 oz. thru 28 ga. 3/4 oz. target loads.

International Clays
Ideal for 12 and 20 ga. autoloaders who want reduced recoil.

Titewad
This 12 ga. flattened spherical shotgun powder is ideal for 7/8, 1 and 1 1/8 oz. loads, with minimum recoil and mild muzzle report.

HS-6 and HS-7
HS-6 and HS-7 for Magnum field loads are unsurpassed, since they do not pack in the measure. They deliver uniform charges and are dense to allow sufficient wad column for best patterns.

Longshot
A new spherical powder for heavy shotgun loads.

HP38
A fast pistol powder for most pistol loading. Especially recommended for mid-range 38 specials.

Titegroup
Excellent for most straight-walled pistol cartridges, incl. 38 Spec., 44 Spec., 45 ACP. Low charge weights, clean burning; position insensitive and flawless ignition.

H110
A spherical powder made especially for the 30 M1 carbine. H110 also does very well in 357, 44 spec., 44 Mag. or 410 ga. shotshell. Magnum primers are recommended for consistent ignition.

H4227
An extruded powder similar to H110, it is the fastest burning in Hodgdon's line. Recommended for the 22 Hornet and some specialized loading in the 45-70 caliber. Also excellent in magnum pistol and .410 shotgun.

Lil' Gun
This powder was developed specifically for the .410 shotgun but works very well in rifle cartridges like the .22 Hornet and in the .44 magnum.

HANDLOADING

IMR Powders

E.I. DuPont de Nemours began its corporate life in 1802, on Delaware's Brandywine River. The varied product line that evolved over the next couple of centuries could hardly have been imagined by its founder, French immigrant Eleuthere Irenee DuPont.

"I can make better black powder than what your country has in its magazines," DuPont told Alexander Hamilton. The enterprising engineer got the help he needed to build a plant in Wilmington. The new propellant satisfied U.S. ordnance officers, and DuPont put down roots. Gunpowder was the firm's primary product for most of the 19th century. In the 1880s, DuPont built a plant at Carney's Point to boost capacity. During World War I, 25,000 people went to work at this facility on the Brandywine, providing more than 80 percent of the military powders used by the Allies (the British, French, Danes, and Russians as well as U.S. troops.

Soon after the transition from black to smokeless powders at the close of the 19th century, "MR" began appearing on canisters of DuPont powders. It meant "military rifle." The IMR line of "improved military rifle" powders came along in the 1920s, when four-digit numbers replaced two-digit numbers in DuPont designations. MR 10 and the like died out. IMR fuels, beginning with 4198, supplanted them. The first had relatively fast burn rates, because in those days, rifle cartridges were small. In 1934, DuPont introduced IMR 4227. In the early 1940s, IMR 4895 came along, specifically for the .30-06 in the M1 Garand service rifle. About that time the first slow IMR propellant made its debut. Developed for 20mm cannons, IMR 4831 would become one of the most popular powders for high-capacity rifle cartridges developed by wildcatters like Roy Weatherby and P.O. Ackley. Incidentally, label numbers have nothing to do with burning rate. According to long-time DuPont engineer Larry Werner, powder is labeled chronologically. The highest numbers indicate the most recent propellants.

You'll find differences in charts ranking the burn rates of IMR and other smokeless powders. The reason: powders can behave differently as you change case shape and bore diameter, fuel charge and bullet weight. IMR gives all its powders a Relative Quickness value, assigning IMR 4350 an arbitrary value of 100. According to Larry Werner, quick-burning IMR 4227 has an RQ of 180; IMR 4198 comes in at 165 and IMR 3031 at 135. IMR 4064, 4320 and 4895 are listed at 120, 115 and 110 respectively, though some loading manuals suggest a different order. IMR 4831 and 7828 burn more slowly. "Closed bomb" tests are used to gauge burn rate. A unit charge of powder ignited in a chamber of known volume produces a pressure curve that's then compared to the curves from other propellants.

DuPont's MR line included single-base (nitrocellulose) and double-base (nitrocellulose with nitroglycerine) powders. "The nitro gives you more energy per grain," explains Larry, "and it reduces the tendency for the grains to pick up moisture. Its drawback is more residue. Double-base powders generally don't burn as clean. To get the full effect of nitroglycerine, you really need 8 to 12 percent in the mix, but some powders claimed to be double-base contain less." All commercial ball powders are double-base, he says. The current IMR line includes only single-base propellants.

IMR powders are no longer made by DuPont. The IMR trademark belongs to EXPRO, another chemical firm. The transfer has its roots in the Depression, which DuPont weathered. But scathing political attacks from certain U.S. senators accused the company of war-mongering. As Hitler tuned his war machine and the U.S. prepared to re-arm, DuPont boosted its production capacity. "But the company was fed up with the treatment it had received from Congress," Larry remembers. Rather than build new plants, it contracted to operate government facilities for one dollar a year. That way, it could not be said to have had a stake in the hostilities. Of course, the government had no powder works that could match DuPont's, so the firm supervised construction of seven factories modeled on the Carney's Point plant. Another was built in Canada. At the height of the Second World War, these facilities shipped a million pounds of powder a day.

In the summer of 1978, DuPont contracted with Valleyfield Chemical Products in Quebec to produce its commercial smokeless propellants. (The Valleyfield plant was the Canadian factory built during World War II. It had been operated by CIL, or Canadian Industries, Ltd., a branch of the government.) In 1982, Valleyfield Chemical sold to Welland Chemical, which became EXPRO.

In December, 1986, DuPont sold its smokeless powder business to EXPRO. The IMR Powder Company became a testing and marketing firm for EXPRO propellants. IMR's laboratory and offices in Plattsburg, New York, now develop ballistics data for IMR powders and package and distribute them to dealers. EXPRO, with an annual manufacturing capacity of more than 10 million pounds, also makes other powders, including Alliant. Though DuPont owned 70 percent of Remington for decades, it has from time to time provided powder for competing ammunition firms.

Powders sold with the IMR label have changed since the 1940s, and America's powder industry is nothing like E.I. DuPont de Nemours found it back in 1802. Still, target shooters and hunters remain indebted to the enterprise of the young French immigrant – and to those men and women who have made and used MR and IMR powders in our country's defense.

Ramshot Powders

Western Powders, Inc. Ramshot powders are all double-base propellants, meaning they contain nitrocellulose and nitroglycerine. While some spherical or ball powders are known for leaving plenty of residue in barrels, Ramshots people say these new fuels burn very clean. They meter easily, as do all ball powders. Plastic cannisters are designed for spill-proof use and include basic loading data on the labels.

Ramshot Competition is for the clay target shooter. A fast-burning powder comparable to 700-X or Red Dot it performs well in a variety of 12-gauge target loads, offering low recoil, consistent pressures and clean combustion.

Ramshot True Blue was designed for small to medium-size handgun cartridges. Similar to Winchester 231 and Hodgdon HP-38, it has enough bulk to nearly fill most cases, thereby better positioning the powder for ignition.

Ramshot Zip, a fast-burning target powder for cartridges like the .38 Special and .45 ACP, gives competitors uniform velocities.

Ramshot Silhouette is ideal for the 9mm handgun cartridge, from light to heavy loads. It also works well in the .40 Smith & Wesson and combat loads for the .45 Auto.

Ramshot Enforcer is a match for high-performance handgun hulls like the .40 Smith & Wesson. It is designed for full-power loading and high velocities.Ramshot X-Terminator, a fast-burning rifle powder, excels in small-caliber, medium-capacity cartridges. It has the versatility to serve in both target and high-performance varmint loads.

Ramshot TAC was formulated for tactical rifle cartridges, specifically the .223 and .308. It has produced exceptional accuracy with a variety of bullets and charge weights.

Ramshot Big Game is a versatile propellant for cartridges as diverse as the .30-06 and the .338 Winchester, and for light-bullet loads in small-bore magnums.

Ramshot Magnum is the slowest powder of the Western line, and does its best work in cartridges with lots of case volume and small to medium bullet diameter. It is the powder of choice in 7mm and .30 Magnums.

Ramshot X-terminator is a clean burning powder designed for the .222 Rem., 223 Rem., and .22 Benchrest calibers.

www.ramshot.com

HANDLOADING

Vihtavuori

HANDLOADING

Kaltron-Pettibone imports Vihtavuori propellants (and Lapua ammunition in the U.S.) The powders, only recently available Stateside, have become popular with American shooters, who applaud their consistency. Their burning rates complement those of powders from IMR, Accurate, Hodgdon and Alliant (the ReLoder series). Here's a synopsis. Note that "similar" in these descriptions does NOT connote interchangeability!

N11O: very fast, for rifle cartridges like the .22 Hornet and .25-20, and for powerful handgun rounds like the .357 and .44 Magnums; similar powders include H110, Winchester 296, Alliant 2400.

N120: a fast powder that requires high pressure for complete and efficient burn; similar to IMR 4227 and best used in small-capacity .22 centerfires.

N130: a bit slower than 4227 but still quick; a standard propellant in the .22 and 6mm PPC.

N133: slow enough for use in medium-capacity .22 cartridges like the .223; also useful in the .45-70 and similar cartridges with little or no neck restriction; similar to IMR 4198.

N135: a versatile powder of medium burn rate, ideal in the .308 and close derivatives, as well as the .30-06; applications from the various 17-calibers to the .458 Winchester; similar to RL-12.

N140: . . slightly slower than N135, but useful in the same cartridges and any that would be served with RL-15 or IMR 4320; a fine choice for the .30-06 and .375 H&H.

N150: a medium-slow powder for light-bullet loads in the .270 and the 30-caliber magnums; an excellent alternative to Winchester 760, Hodgdon H414, IMR 4350.

N160: a workhorse powder for magnum cases and high-velocity rounds on the .308 and .30-06 hulls; similar to RL-19, IMR 4831, Accurate 3100; useful in the .243, .270, 7mm Remington and .300 and .338 Winchester Magnums.

N165: a slow powder for "overbore" magnum cases and for heavy-bullet loads in the medium-bore magnums; ideal for high-performance .300s with all bullet weights; similar to H4831 and RL-22.

N170: the slowest-burning of Vihtavuori's propellants, for small-bore magnums like the .257 Weatherby and .264 Winchester; similar to H1000 and RL-25.

Unlike the single-base (nitrocellulose) N100 series, the N500 series of Vihtavuori powders has a nitroglycerol component (up to 25 percent, by impregnation). There's also a special stabilizer, a flame reducing agent, a wear-reducing agent and coating agents that ensure progressive burning in the case to provide uniform and efficient pressure curves. These high-energy double-base powders are available in three burning rates, equivalent to the 100-series powders with the same last digits. N540 is applicable in the same cartridges as N140. N550 is a match for N150. N560 is the slowest, an ideal propellant for the .270 Winchester and 6.5x55 Swedish Mauser.

Vihtavuori also makes single-base powders for the .50 BMG. The 24N41 is slightly faster than the 20N29. Eight Vihtavuori pistol powders complete the 2003 line:

N310: as fast as Bullseye, for small-capacity cartridges like the .25 ACP up to the 9mm Luger.

N320: slightly faster than Winchester 231, a versatile powder for the most popular of pistol rounds, including the .38 Special, .357 Magnum, .45 ACP, .44 Magnum and .45 Long Colt.

N330: useful in medium- to large-capacity cases from the .38 Special to the various .44s and .45s; similar to Green Dot.

N340: slow enough for high-performance loads in the .357 and .44 Magnums, also useful in the .38 Super and .30 Luger; similar to Winchester 540.

N350: a slow powder for magnum and heavy-bullet handgun loads; burning rate like that of Blue Dot or Hi-Skor 800-X.

3N37: between N340 and N350 in burn rate; recommended for competitive shooters.

3N38: a competition powder specifically for high-speed loads in the .38 Super and 9mm Luger.

N105 Super Magnum: a very slow pistol powder for heavy-bullet loads in magnum cases; almost as slow as N110.

Dillon Precision Reloaders

Dillon Precision is a leader in the shotgun shooting sports market with its SL 900 progressive shotshell reloader. Based on Dillon's proven XL 650 O-frame design, it incorporates the same powerful compound linkage. The automatic case insert system, fed by an electric case collator, ranks high among the new features of this reloader. Adjustable shot and powder bars come as standard equipment. Both the powder and shot bars are case-activated, so no powder or shot can spill when no shell is at that station. Should the operator forget to insert a wad during the reloading process, the SL 900 will not dispense shot into the powder-charged hull. Both powder and shot systems are based on Dillon's adjustable powder bar design, which is accurate to within a few tenths of a grain. These systems also eliminate the need for fixed-volume bushings. Simply adjust the measures to dispense the exact charges required.

The Dillon SL 900 is the first progressive shotshell loader on which it is practical to change gauges. An interchangeable toolhead makes it quick and easy to change from one gauge to another. The SL 900 also has an extra large, remote shot hopper that holds an entire 25-pound bag of shot, making it easy to fill with a funnel. The unique shot reservoir/dispenser helps ensure that a consistent volume of shot is delivered to each shell.

For shotgunners who shoot and load for multiple gauges or different kinds of shooting, the SL 900's interchangeable toolhead feature makes quick work of changing from one gauge to another. It uses a collet-type sizing die that re-forms the base of the shotshell to factory specifications—a feature that ensures reliable feeding in all shotguns. The heat-treated steel crimp die forms and folds the hull before the final taper crimp die radiuses and blends the end of the hull and locks the crimp into place.

Model RL550B Progressive Loader

- Accommodates over 120 calibers
- Interchangeable toolhead assembly
- Auto/Powder priming systems
- Uses standard ⅞" by 14 dies
- Loading rate: 500-600 rounds per hour

Price:. $326

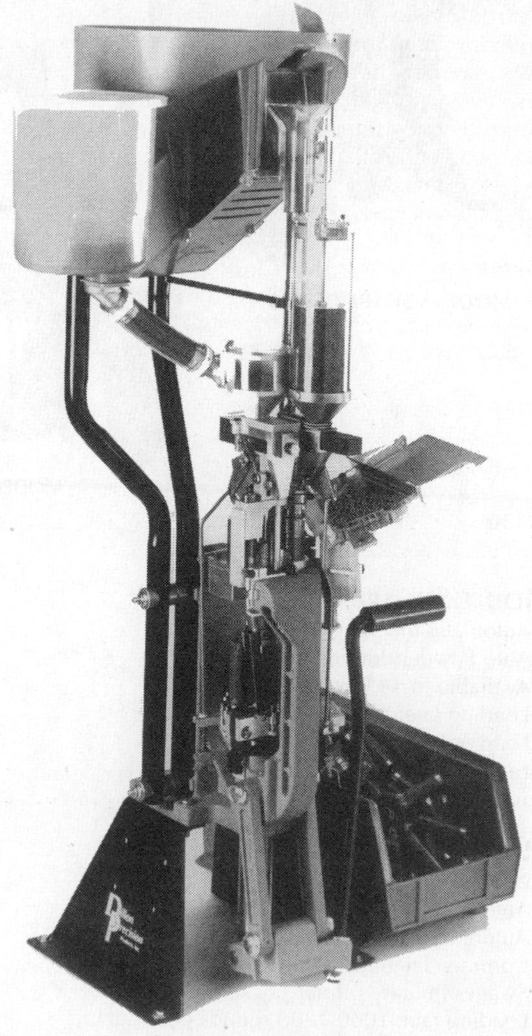

Model SL900

Price: $820

Dillon Precision Reloaders

MODEL AT-500

MODEL SQUARE DEAL B

MODEL SUPER 1050 AND RL 1050

MODEL XL 650

Model Square Deal B

- Automatic Indexing
- Auto Powder/Priming Systems
- Available in 14 handgun calibers
- Loading rate: 400-500 rounds per hour
- Loading dies standard
- Factory adjusted, ready-to-use

Price: **$278**

Model Super 1050 and RL 1050

- Automatic indexing
- Auto powder/priming systems
- Automatic casefeeder
- Commercial grade machine
- Swages military primer pockets
- Loading rate: 1000-1200 rounds per hour
- Weighs 54 lbs.
- Eight stations

Price: **1399**

Model XL 650

- Rotary indexing plate for primers
- Automatic indexing
- Uses standard 7/8" x 14 dies
- Loading rate: 800-1000 rounds per hour
- Five-station interchangeable toolhead

Price: **$444**

Model AT-500

- Loads over 40 calibers
- Uses standard 7/8" by 14 dies
- Upgradeable to Model RL 550B
- Interchangeable toolhead
- Switch from one caliber to another in 30 seconds
- Universal shellplate

Price: **194**

Forster Reloading

CO-AX® BENCH REST® RIFLE DIES

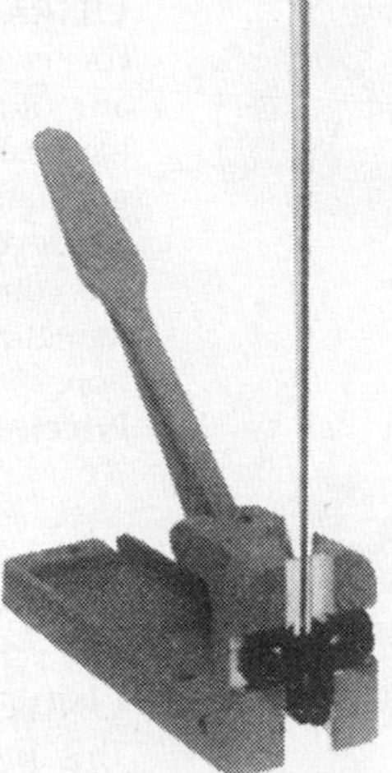

PRIMER SEATER

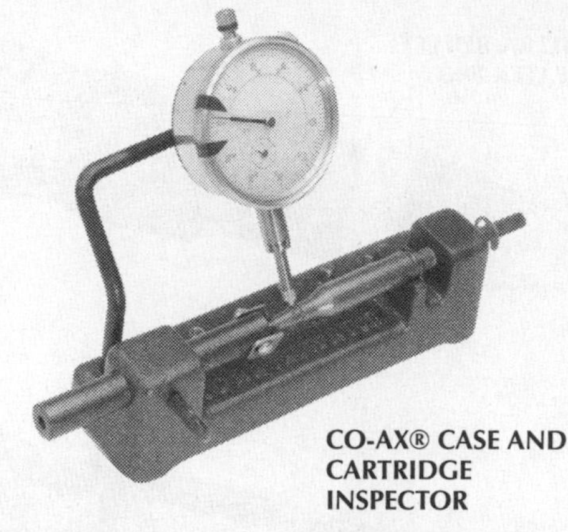

CO-AX® CASE AND CARTRIDGE INSPECTOR

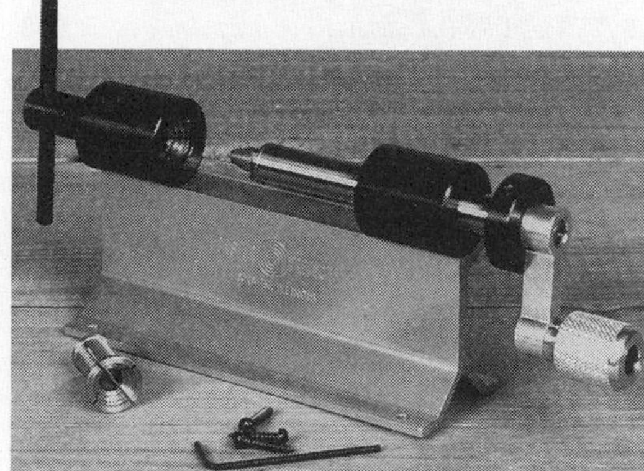

HAND CASE TRIMMER

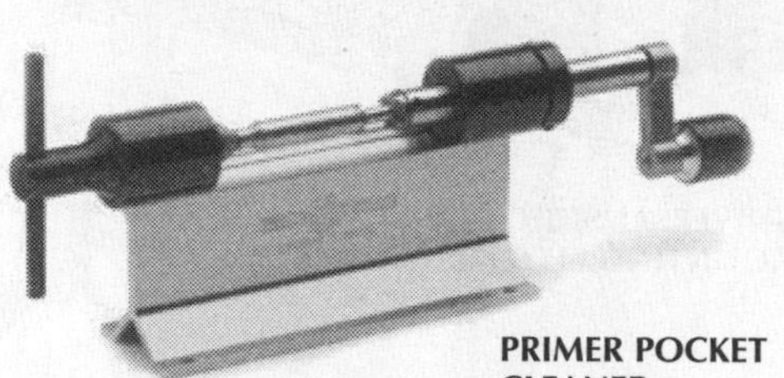

PRIMER POCKET CLEANER

CO-AX® Bench Rest® Rifle Dies

Bench Rest Rifle Dies are glass-hard and polished mirror-smooth with special attention given to headspace, tapers and diameters. Sizing die has an elevated expander button to ensure better alignment of case and neck.

Bench Rest® Die Set $76
Ultra Bench Rest Die Set $103
Full Length Sizer $35
Bench Rest Seating Die. $42

Hand Case Trimmer

Shell holder is a Brown & Sharpe-type collet. Case and cartridge conditioning accessories include inside neck reamer, outside neck turner, deburring tool, hollow pointer and primer pocket cleaners. The case trimmer trims all cases, ranging from 17 to 458 Winchester caliber.

Price:. $64

Primer Seater With "E-Z-Just" Shellholder

The Bonanza Primer Seater is designed so that primers are seated co-axially (primer in line with primer pocket). Mechanical leverage allows primers to be seated fully without crushing. With the addition of one extra set of disc shell holders and one extra Primer Unit, all modern cases, rim or rimless, from 222 up to 458 Magnum, can be primed. Shell holders are easily adjusted to any case by rotating to contact rim or cannelure of the case.

Primer Seater $75

"Classic 50" Case Trimmer (not shown)

Handles more than 100 different big bore calibers–500 Nitro Express, 416 Rigby, 50 Sharps, 475 H&H, etc. Also available: .50 BMG Case Trimmer, designed specifically for reloading needs of .50 Cal. BMG shooters.

Price: "Classic 50" Case Trimmer $91
.50 BMG Case Trimmer $96

CO-AX® Case and Cartridge Inspector

One tool to perform three vital measurements. Accurate performance from ammunition is absolutely dependent on uniformity of both the bullet and the case. Forster's exclusive Co-Ax® Case & Cartridge Inspector provides the ability to ensure uniformity by measuring three critical dimensions: • Neck wall thickness • Case neck concentricity • Bullet runout.

Measurements are in increments of one-thousandth of an inch. The Inspector is unique because it checks both the bullet and case alignment in relation to the centerline (axis) of the entire cartridge or case.

Price:. $87

Primer Pocket Cleaner

The Primer Pocket Cleaner helps ensure consistent ignition and reduce the incidence of misfires by removing powder and primer residue frm the primer pockets of your cases. This simple took is easy to use: Just hold the case mouth over the Primer Pocket Center with one hand while you quickly and easily clean the primer pockets by turning the Case Trimmer Handle.

Price:. $8

Forster Reloading

ULTRA BULLET SEATER DIE

UNIVERSAL SIGHT MOUNTING FIXTURE

CO-AX LOADING PRESS B-2

BENCH REST POWDER MEASURE

Ultra Bullet Seater Die

Forster's new Ultra Die is available in 56 calibers, more than any other brand of micrometer-style seater. Adjustment is identical to that of a precision micrometer—the head is graduated to .001" increments with .025" bullet movement per revolution. The cartridge case, bullet and seating stem are completely supported and perfectly aligned in a close-fitting chamber before and during the bullet seating operation.

Price:. $68

Universal Sight Mounting Fixture

This product fills the exacting requirements needed for drilling and tapping holes for the mounting of scopes, receiver sights, shotgun beads, etc. The fixture handles any single-barrel gun—bolt-action, lever-action or pump-action—as long as the barrel can be laid into the "V" blocks of the fixture. Rifles with tube magazines are drilled in the same manner by removing the magazine tube. The fixture's main body is made of aluminum casting. The two "V" blocks are adjustable for height and are made of hardened steel ground accurately on the "V" as well as the shaft.

Price:. 384

CO-AX® Loading Press Model B-2

Designed to make reloading easier and more accurate, this press offers the following features: Snap-in and snap-out die change • Positive spent primer catcher • Automatic self-acting shell holder • Floating guide rods • Working room for right- or left-hand operators • Top priming device seats primers to factory specifications • Uses any standard 7/8" x 14 dies • No torque on the head • Perfect alignment of die and case • Three times the mechanical advantage of a "C" press

Price:. 309

Bench Rest Powder Measure

When operated uniformly, this measure will throw uniform charges from 2½ grains Bullseye to 95 grains #4320. No extra drums are needed. Powder is metered from the charge arm, allowing a flow of powder without extremes in variation while minimizing powder shearing. Powder flows through its own built-in baffle, entering the charge arm uniformly.

Price:. 117

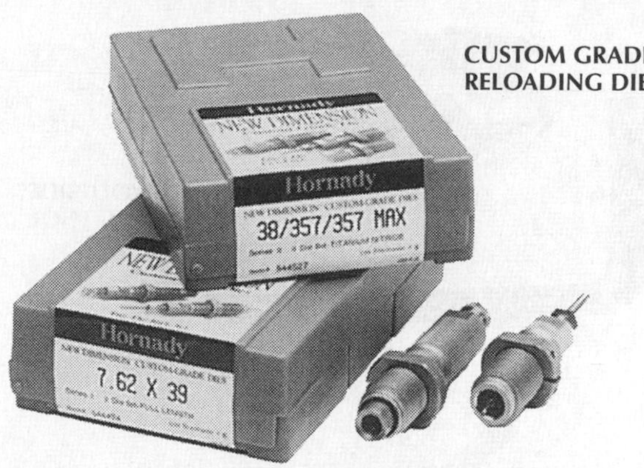

CUSTOM GRADE RELOADING DIES

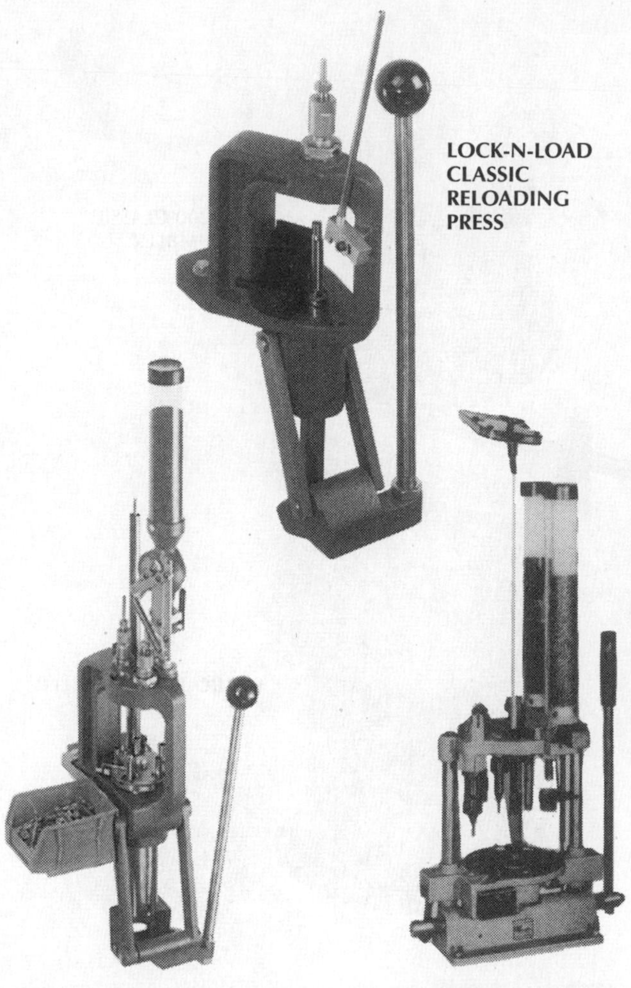

LOCK-N-LOAD CLASSIC RELOADING PRESS

LOCK-N-LOAD

MODEL 366

Custom Grade Reloading Dies

Features an Elliptical Expander that minimizes friction and reduces case neck stretch, plus the need for a tapered expander for "necking up" to the next larger caliber. Other recent design changes include a hardened steel decap pin that will not break, bend or crack even when depriming stubborn military cases. A bullet seater alignment sleeve guides the bullet and case neck into the die for in-line benchrest alignment. All New Dimension Reloading Dies include: collar and collar lock to center expander precisely; one-piece expander spindle with tapered bottom for easy cartridge insertion; wrench flats on die body, Sure-Loc™ lock rings and collar lock for easy tightening; and built-in crimper.

Prices:
New Dimension Custom Grade Reloading Dies:
Series II Three-die Rifle Set $32
Series III 40
Match Grade 39

Lock-N-Load Classic Press

Lock-N-Load is available on Hornady's single stage and progressive reloader models. This bushing system locks the die into the press like a rifle bolt. Instead of threading dies in and out of the press, you simply lock and unlock them with a slight twist. Dies are held firmly in a die bushing that stays with the die and retains the die setting. The Lock-N-Load Classic Press features an easy-grip handle, an O-style frame made of high-strength alloy, and a positive priming system that feeds, aligns and seats the primer smoothly and automatically.

Prices: Lock-N-Load Press $123
Lock-N-Load Classic Press Kit 292
Also Available: Lock-N-Load
50 BMG Press 353
50 BMG Press Kit 575

Lock-N-Load Auto Progressive Press

The Lock-N-Load Automatic Progressive reloading press featuring the Lock-N-Load bushing system offers the flexibility to add a roll or taper crimp die. Dies and powder measure are inserted into Lock-N-Load die bushings, which lock securely into the press. The bushings remain with the die and powder measure and can be removed in seconds. They also fit on other presses. Other features include: deluxe powder measure, automatic indexing, off-set handle, power-pac linkage, case ejector.

Price:
Lock-N-Load Auto Progressive Press (includes five die bushings, shellplate, primer catcher, Positive Priming System, powder drop, Deluxe Powder Measure, automatic primer feed) $397

Model 366 Auto Shotshell Reloader

The 366 Auto features full-length resizing with each stroke, automatic primer feed, swing-out wad guide, three-state crimping featuring Taper-Loc for factory tapered crimp, automatic advance to the next station and automatic ejection. The turntable holds 8 shells for 8 operations with each stroke. Automatic charge bar loads shot and powder, dies and crimp starters for 6 point, 8 point and paper crimps.

Price:
Model 366 Auto Shotshell Reloader:
12, 20, 28 gauge or .410 bore 523

Lyman Reloading Tools

MODEL 1200 CLASSIC TURBO TUMBLER

"IINSIDE/OUTSIDE" DEBURRING TOOL

TURBO TWIN TUMBLER

MASTER CASTING KIT

Model 1200 Classic Turbo Tumbler

This sturdy case tumbler features a redesigned base and drive system, plus a stronger suspension system and built-in exciters for better tumbling action and faster cleaning

Model 1200 Classic **$100**
Model 1200 Auto-Flo **100**
Also available:
Model 600 . . . . **70**
Model 2200 Auto-Flo **125**
Model 3200 Auto-Flo **185**

"Iinside/Outside" Deburring Tool

This tool features an adjustable cutting blade that adapts easily to the mouth of any rifle or pistol case from 22 caliber to 45 caliber with a simple hex wrench adjustment. Inside deburring is completed by a conical internal section with slotted cutting edges, thus providing uniform inside and outside deburring in one simple operation. The deburring tool is mounted on an anodized aluminum handle that is machine-knurled for a sure grip.

Deburring Tool **14**

Turbo Twin Tumbler

The Twin features Lyman 1200 Pro Tumbler with an extra, 600 bowl system. Reloaders may use each bowl interchangeably for small or large capacity loads. 1200 Pro Bowl System has a built-in sifter lid for easy sifting of cases and media at the end of the polishing cycle. The Twin Tumbler features the Lyman Hi-Profile base design with built-in exciters and anti-rotation pads for faster, more consistent tumbling action.

Turbo Twin Tumbler 110V **$80**

Master Casting Kit

Designed especially to meet the needs of blackpowder shooters, this kit features Lyman's combination round ball and maxi ball mould blocks. It also contains a combination double cavity mould, mould handle, mini-mag furnace, lead dipper, bullet lube, a user's manual and a cast bullet guide. Kits are available in 45, 50 and 54 caliber.

Master Casting Kit **170**

Lyman Reloading Tools

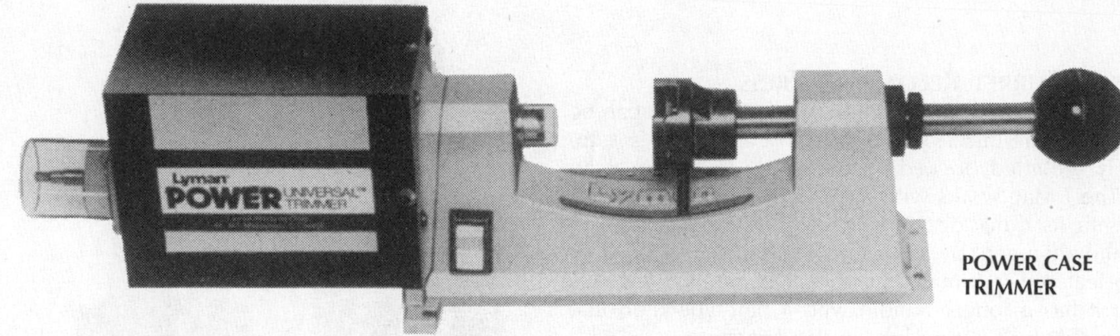

POWER CASE TRIMMER

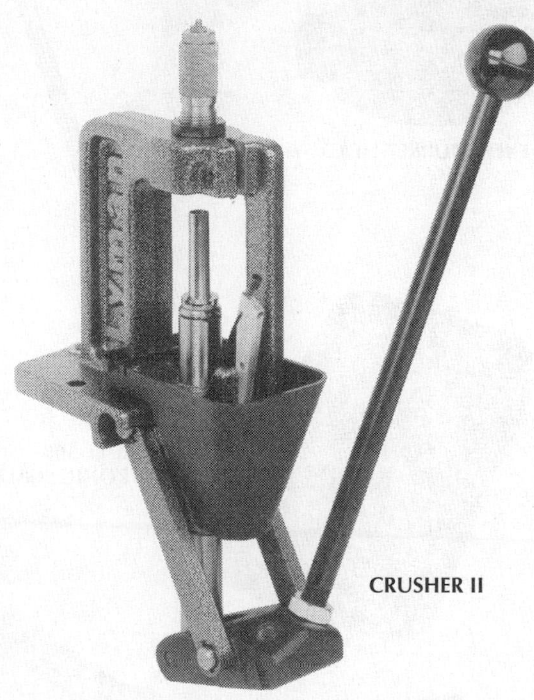

CRUSHER II

Acculine Outside Neck Turner (not shown)

To obtain perfectly concentric case necks, Lyman's Outside Neck Turner assures reloaders of uniform neck wall thickness and outside neck diameter. The unit fits Lyman's Universal Trimmer and AccuTrimmer. In use, each case is run over a mandrel, which centers the case for the turning operation. The cutter is carefully adjusted to remove a minimum amount of brass. Rate of feed is adjustable and a mechanical stop controls length of cut. Mandrels are available for calibers from .17 to .375; cutter blade can be adjusted for any diameter from .195″ to .405".

Outside Neck Turner w/extra blade, 6 mandrels $30
Individual Mandrels 4

Crusher II Pro Kit

Includes press, loading block, case lube kit, primer tray, Model 500 Pro scale, powder funnel and Lyman Reloading Handbook.

Starter Kit 165

Lyman Crusher II Reloading Press

The only press for rifle or pistol cartridges that offers the advantage of powerful compound leverage combined with a true Magnum press opening. A unique handle design transfers power easily to the center of the ram. A 4½-inch press opening accommodates even the largest cartridges.

Crusher II Press

With Priming Arm and Catcher 117

Power Case Trimmer

The Lyman Power Trimmer is powered by a fan-cooled electric motor designed to withstand the severe demands of case trimming. The unit, which features the Universal™ Chuckhead, allows cases to be positioned for trimming or removed with fingertip ease. The Power Trimmer package includes Nine-Pilot Multi-Pack. Two cutter heads and a pair of wire end brushes for cleaning primer pockets are included. Other features include safety guards, on-off rocker switch, heavy cast base with receptacles for nine pilots, and bolt holes for mounting on a work bench. Available for 110 V or 220 V systems.

Prices: 110 V Model $200
220 V Model 200

Lyman Reloading Tools

T-Mag II Turret Reloading Press

With the T-Mag II, up to six different reloading dies can be mounted on one turret. This means all dies can be set up, precisely mounted, locked in and ready to reload at all times. The T-Mag works with all 7/8 x 14 dies. The T-Mag II turret with its quick-disconnect release system is held in rock-solid alignment by a 3/4-inch steel stud.

Also featured is Lyman's Crusher II compound leverage system. It has a longer handle with a ball-type knob that mounts easily for right- or left-handed operation.

T-Mag II Press w/Priming Arm & Catcher $165
Extra Turret Head 38
Also available:
Expert Kit that includes T-MAG II Press, Universal Case Trimmer and pilot Multi-Pak, Model 500 powder scale and Model 50 powder measure, plus accessories and Reloading Manual. Available in calibers 30-06,270 and 308
Price:. 365

Electronic Scale Model LE-1000

Accurate to 1/10 grain, Lyman's LE: 1000 measures up to 1000 grains of powder and easily converts to the gram mode for metric measurements. The push-button automatic calibration feature eliminates the need for calibrating with a screwdriver. The scale works off a single 9V battery or AC power adapter (included with each scale). Its compact design allows the LE-1000 to be carried to the field easily. A sculpted carrying case is optional. 110 Volt or 220 Volt.

Model LE-1000 Electronic Scale 260
Model LE-300 Electronic Scale 167
Model LE-500 Electric Scale 184

55 Classic Black Powder Measure

Lyman's 55 Classic Powder Measure is ideal for the Cowboy Action Competition or the growing number of black powder cartridge shooters. The one-pound-capacity aluminum reservoir and brass powder meter eliminate static. The internal powder baffel assures highly accurate and consistent charges. The 24" powder compacting drop tube allows the maximum charge in each cartridge. Drop tube works on calibers 38 through 50 and mounts easily to the bottom of the measure. Clamp on back allows easy mounting of the measure at a convenient height, when using long drop tubes.

55 Classic Powder Measure (std model-no tubes). . . . 108
55 Classic Powder Measure (with drop tubes) 125
Powder Drop Tubes Only 29

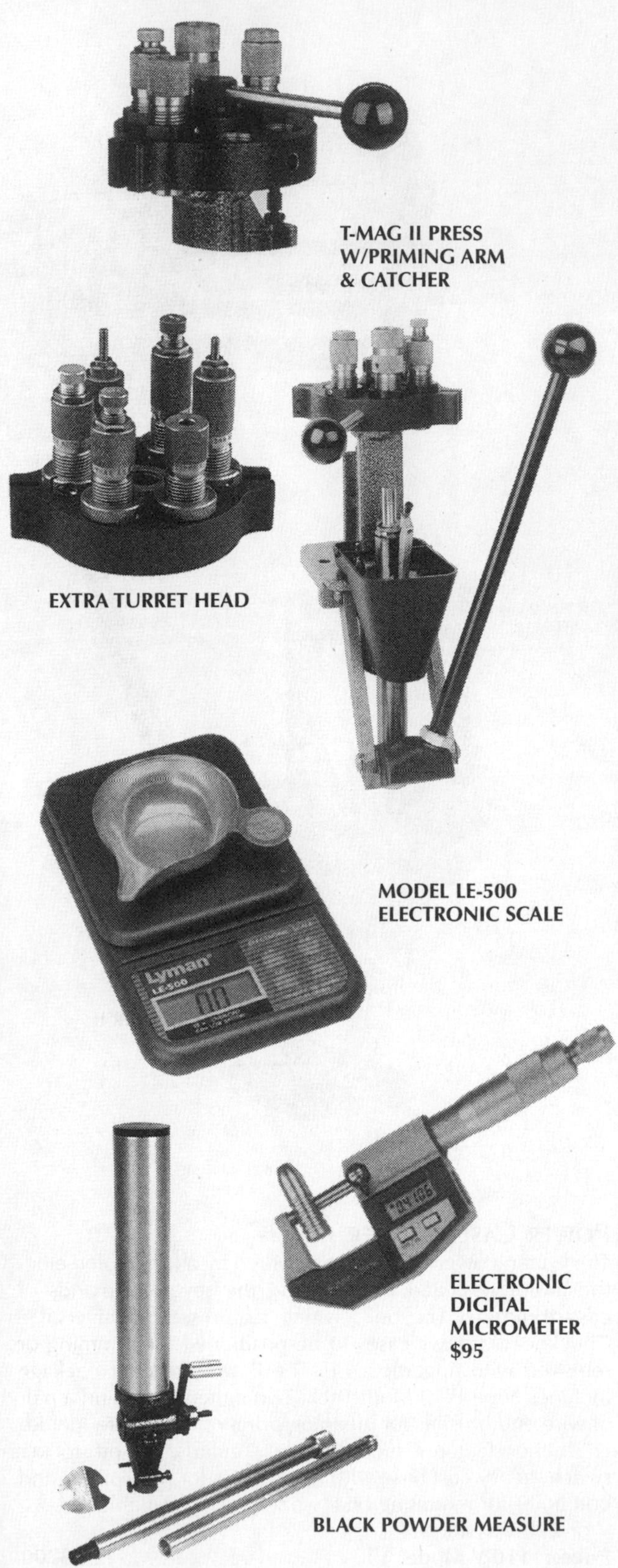

T-MAG II PRESS W/PRIMING ARM & CATCHER

EXTRA TURRET HEAD

MODEL LE-500 ELECTRONIC SCALE

ELECTRONIC DIGITAL MICROMETER $95

BLACK POWDER MEASURE

Lyman Reloading Tools

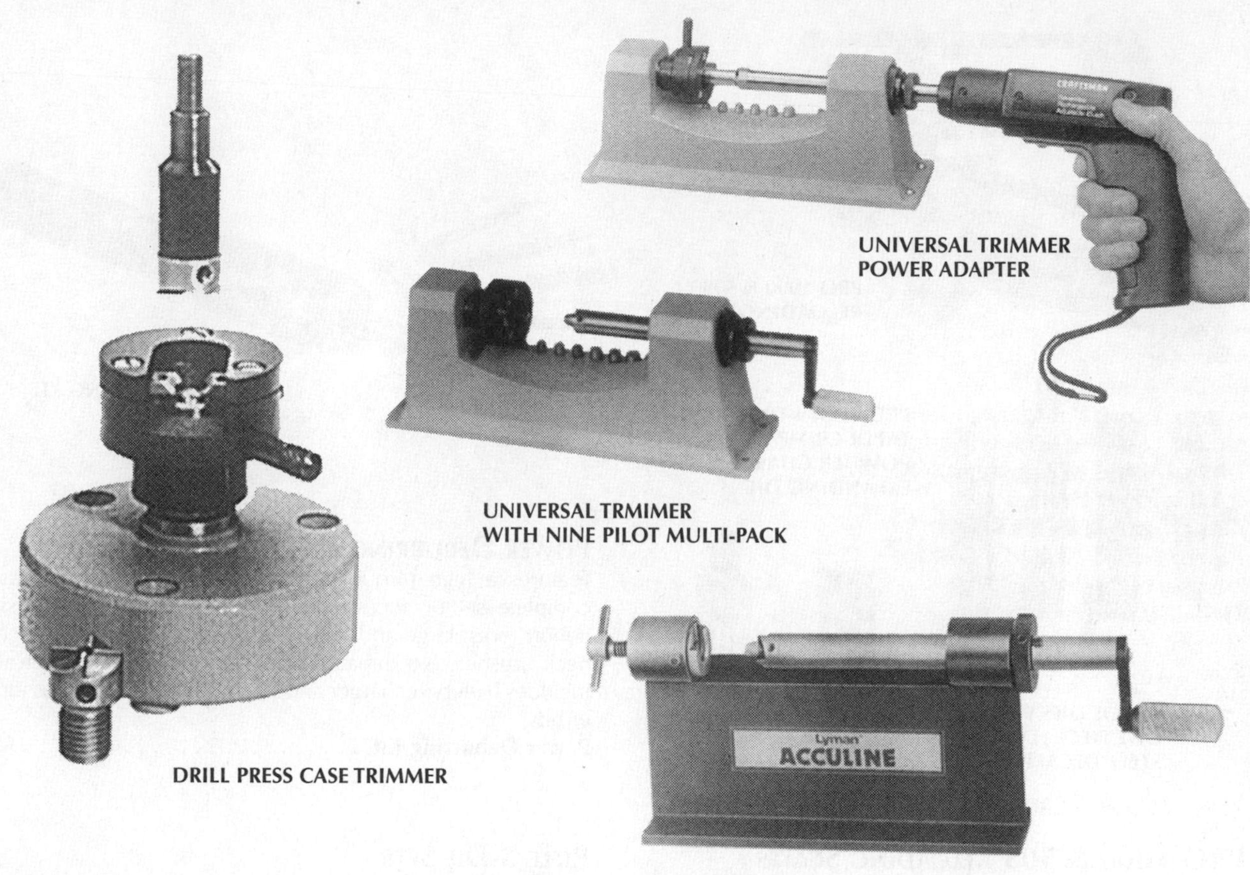

UNIVERSAL TRIMMER POWER ADAPTER

UNIVERSAL TRMIMER WITH NINE PILOT MULTI-PACK

DRILL PRESS CASE TRIMMER

ACCU-TRIMMER

Drill Press Case Trimmer

Intended for competitive shooters, varmint hunters, and other sportsmen who use large quantities of reloaded ammunition, this drill press case trimmer consists of the Universal™ Chuckhead, a cutter shaft adapted for use in a drill press, and two quick-change cutter heads. Its two major advantages are speed and accuracy. An experienced operator can trim several hundred cases an hour, and each will be trimmed to a precise length.

Drill Press Case Trimmer $50

Accu-Trimmer

Lyman's Accu Trimmer can be used for all rifle and pistol cases from 22 to 458 Winchester Magnum. Standard shellholders are used to position the case, and the trimmer incorporates standard Lyman cutter heads and pilots. Mounting options include bolting to a bench, C-clamp or vise.

Accu Trimmer w/9-pilot multi-pak 45

Universal Trmimer with Nine Pilot Multi-Pack

This trimmer with patented chuckhead accepts all metallic rifle or pistol cases, regardless of rim thickness. To change calibers, simply change the case head pilot. Other features include coarse and fine cutter adjustments, an oil-impregnated bronze bearing, and a rugged cast base to assure precision alignment and years of service. Optional carbide cutter available. Trimmer Stop Ring includes 20 indicators as reference marks.

Trimmer Multi-Pack (incl. 9 pilots: 22, 24, 27, 28/7mm, 30, 9mm, 35, 44 and 4A 68
Nine Pilot Multi-Pack 12
Power Pack Trimmer 78
Universal Trimmer Power Adapter 20

Electronic Digital Caliper (NOT SHOWN)

Lyman's 6″ electronic caliper gives a direct digital readout for both inches and millimeters and can perform both inside and outside depth measurements. Its zeroing function allows the user to select zeroing dimensions and sort parts or cases by their plus or minus variation. The caliper works on a single, standard 1.5 volt silver oxide battery and comes with a fitted wooden storage case.

Electronic Caliper. 100
Also Available:
4″ Pocket Electronic Caliper. 83

Lyman Reloading Tools

PRO 1000 & 505 RELOADING SCALES

PREMIUM 4-DIE SET WITH TAPER CRIMP AND POWDER CHARGE EXPANDING DIE

PISTOL DIES FEATURE ONE PIECE HARDENED STEEL DECAPPING ROD

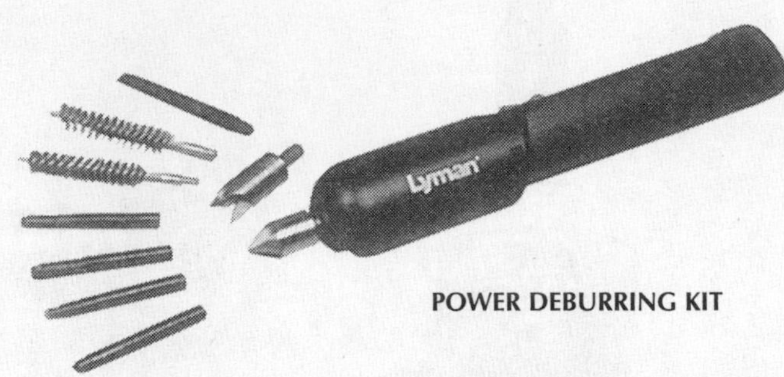

POWER DEBURRING KIT

Power Deburring Kit

Features a high torque, rechargeable power driver plus a complete set of accessories, including inside and outside deburr tools, large and small reamers and cleaners and case neck brushes. No threading or chucking required. Set also includes battery recharger and standard flat and phillips driver bits.

Power Deburring Kit **$55**

PRO 1000 & 505 Reloading Scales

Features include improved platform system; hi-tech base design of high-impact styrene; extra-large, smooth leveling wheel; dual agate bearings; larger damper for fast zeroing; built-in counter weight compartment; easy-to-read beam.

Pro 1000 Scale **$63**
Pro 500 Scale **45**

Rifle Die Sets

Lyman precision rifle dies are manufactured on computer controlled equipment ensuring that each die is chambered perfectly and has a smooth finish. Each sizing die for bottlenecked rifle cartridges is then carefully vented. This vent hole is precisely placed to prevent air traps that can damage cartridge cases. Each sizing die is polished, then heat treated for toughness. It receives a final hand polish for extra smoothness. Fine adjustment threads on the bullet seating stem allow for precision adjustments of bullet seating depth. Lyman dies fit all popular presses using industry standard 7/8 x 14 threads, including RCBS, Lee, Hornady, Dillon, Redding and others.

Rifle 2-Die Sets

Set consists of a full length resizing die with decapping stem and neck expanding button and a bullet seating die for loading jacketed bullets in bottlenecked rifle cases. For those who load cast bullets, use a neck expanding die, available separately.

Price: **30**

Rifle 3-Die Sets

Straight wall rifle cases require these three die sets consisting of a full length resizing die with decapping stem, a two step neck expanding (M) die and a bullet seating die. These sets are ideal for loading cast bullets due to the inclusion of the neck expanding die.

Price: **40**
Classic Calibers **50**
Classic Neck Size Dies **32**

Premium Carbide 4-die sets for pistols

Lyman 4-Die Sets feature a separate taper crimp die and powder charge/expanding die. The powder charge/expand die has a special hollow 2-step neck expanding plug which allows powder to flow through the die from a powder measure directly into the case. The powder charge/expanding die has a standard 7/8 x 14 thread and will accept Lyman's 55 Powder Measure, or most other powder measures.

Price: **54**

3-die carbide pistol die sets

Lyman originated the Tungsten Carbide (T-C) sizing die and the addition of extra seating screws for pistol die sets and the two step neck expanding die. Multi-Deluxe Die sets offer these features; a one-piece hardened steel decapping rod and extra seating screws for all popular bullet nose shapes; all-steel construction.

Price: **42**

MEC Shotshell Reloaders

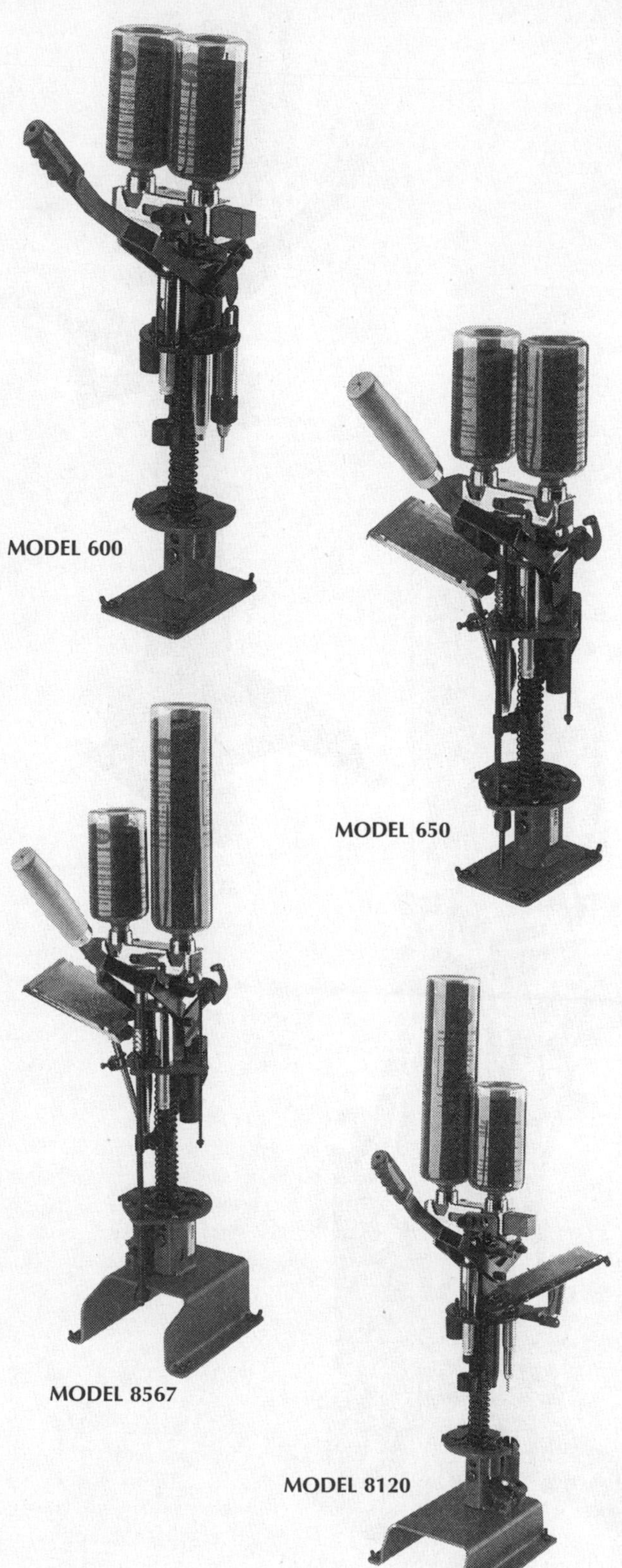

MODEL 600 JR. MARK V

This single-stage reloader features a cam-action crimp die to ensure that each shell returns to its original condition. MEC's 600 Jr. Mark 5 can load 6 to 8 boxes per hour and can be updated with the 285 CA primer feed. Press is adjustable for 3" shells.

Price: **$112**

MODEL 650

This reloader works on 6 shells at once. A reloaded shell is completed with every stroke. The MEC 650 does not resize except as a separate operation. Automatic Primer feed is standard. Simply fill it with a full box of primers and it will do the rest. Reloader has 3 crimping stations: the first one starts the crimp, the second closes the crimp, and the third places a taper on the shell. Available in 12, 16, 20 and 28 gauge and .410 bore. No die sets are available.

Price: **213**

MODEL 8567 GRABBER

This reloader features 12 different operations at all 6 stations, producing finished shells with each stroke of the handle. It includes a fully automatic primer feed and Auto-Cycle charging, plus MEC's exclusive 3-stage crimp. The "Power Ring" resizer ensures consistent, accurately sized shells without interrupting the reloading sequence. Simply put in the wads and shell casings, then remove the loaded shells with each pull of the handle. Optional kits to load 3" shells and steel shot make this reloader tops in its field. Resizes high and low base shells. Available in 12, 16, 20, 28 gauge and .410 bore. No die sets are available.

Price: **306**

MODEL 8120 SIZEMASTER

Sizemaster's "Power Ring" collet resizer returns each base to factory specifications. This generation resizing station handles brass or steel heads, both high and low base. An 8-fingered collet squeezes the base back to original dimensions, then opens up to release the shell easily. The E-Z Prime auto primer feed is standard equipment (not offered in .410 bore). Press is adjustable for 3" shells and is available in 10, 12, 16, 20, 28 gauge and .410 bore. Die sets are available at: $88.67 ($104.06 in 10 ga.)

Price: **170**

HANDLOADING

MEC Reloading

Steelmaster Single State

The only shotshell reloader equipped to load steel shotshells as well as lead ones. Every base is resized to factory specs by a precision "power ring" collet. Handles brass or steel heads in high or low base. The E-Z prime auto primer feed dispenses primers automatically and is standard equipment. Separate presses are available for 12 gauge 2¾", 3", 12 gauge 3½" and 10 gauge.

8639 Steelmaster 10 &12 ga 184
8755 Steelmaster 12 ga. 3½" only 206

MEC 9000 Series Shotshell Reloader

MEC's 9000 Series features automatic indexing and finished shell ejection for quicker and easier reloading. The factory set speed provides uniform movement through every reloading stage. Dropping the primer into the reprime station no longer requires operator "feel." The reloader requires only a minimal adjustment from low to high brass domestic shells, any one of which can be removed for inspection from any station. Can be set up for automatic or manual indexing. Available in 12, 16, 20 and 28 gauge and .410 bore. No die sets are available.

MEC 9000H 897
MEC 9000H without pump 485
MEC 9000G Series 372
Also Available: MEC Super Sizer
Resize shotgun shells back to factory specs!
Price: 64

STEEL MASTER

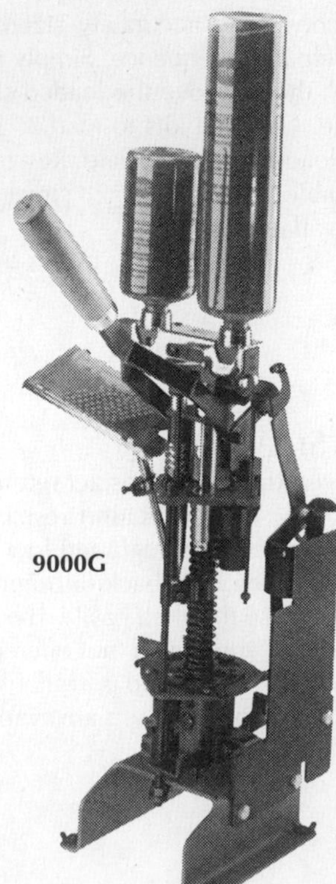

9000G

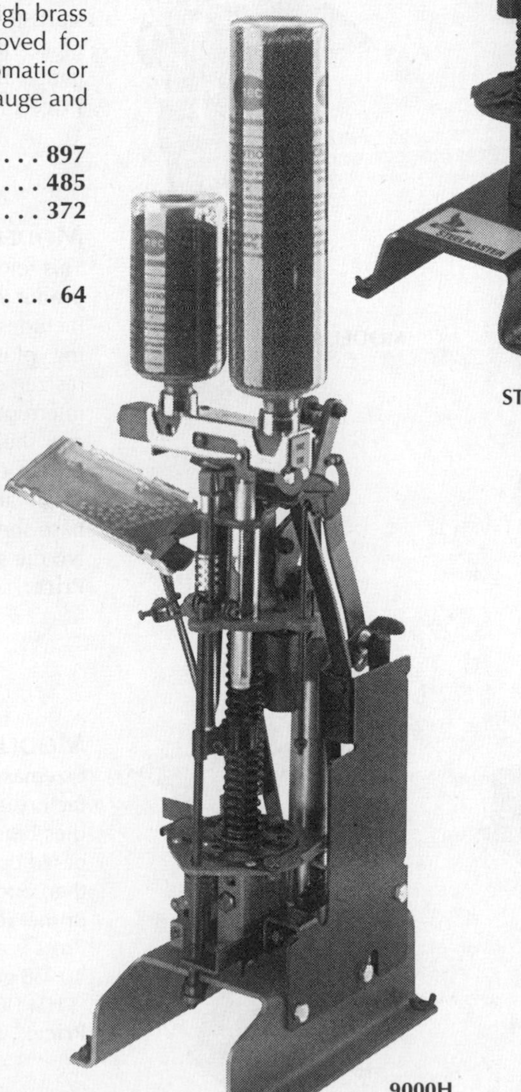

9000H

MTM Reloading

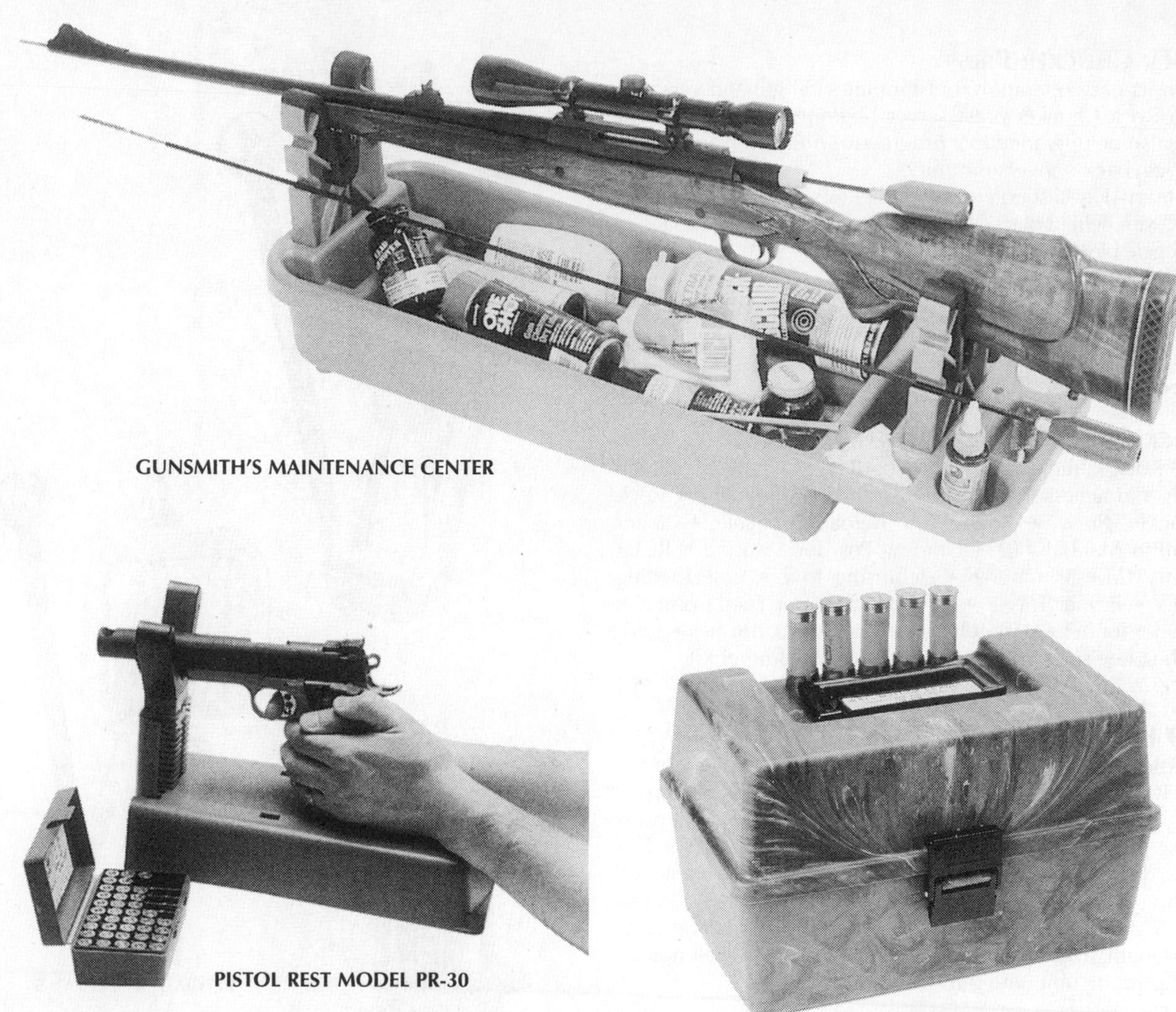

GUNSMITH'S MAINTENANCE CENTER

PISTOL REST MODEL PR-30

CASE-GARD IN WILD CAMO

Gunsmith's Maintenance Center

MTM's Gunsmiths Maintenance Center (RMC-5) is designed for mounting scopes and swivels, bedding actions or for cleaning rifles and shotguns. Multi-positional forks allow for eight holding combinations, making it possible to service firearm level, upright or upside down. The large middle section keeps tools and cleaning supplies in one area. Individual solvent compartments help to eliminate accidental spills. Cleaning rods stay where they are needed with the two built-in holders provided. Both forks (covered with a soft molded-on rubber pad) grip and protect the firearm. The RMC-5 is made of engineering- grade plastic for years of rugged use. Not Shown: Extensive line of plastic ammo boxes, reloading trays, pistol cases, target holders, clay target throwers, arrow and tackle boxes.

Dimensions: 29.5" X 9.5"

Model RMC-5-30 . . . . **$31**

Pistol Rest Model PR-30

MTM's PR-30 Pistol Rest will accommodate any size handgun, from a Derringer to a 14" Contender. A locking front support leg adjusts up or down, allowing 20 different positions. Rubber padding molded to the tough polypropylene fork protects firearms from scratches. Fork clips into the base when not in use for compact storage.

Dimensions: 6" x 11" x 2.5

Pistol Rest Model PR-30 . . . . **$17**

Case-Gard in Wild Camo

The CASE-GARD SF-100 holds 100 shotshells in two removable trays. Designed primarily for hunters, this dust and moisture resistant carrier features a heavy-duty latch, fold-down handle, integral hinge and textured finish.

Price: SF-100 12 or 20 ga.

Wild Camo Shotshell Box **17**

RCBS Reloading Tools

Rock Chucker Press

With its easy operation, outstanding strength and versatility, a Rock Chucker press serves beginner and pro alike. It can also be upgraded to a progressive press with an optional Piggyback conversion unit.

- Heavy-duty cast iron for easy case-resizing
- 1″ ram held in place by 12.5 sq. in. of rambearing surface
- Toggle blocks of ductile iron
- Compound leverage system
- 7/8"-14 thread for all standard reloading dies and accessories
- Milled slot and set screws accept optional RCBS automatic primer feed

Price:. $151

Rock Chucker Master Reloading Kit

The Rock Chucker Master Reloading Kit includes all the tools and accessories needed to start handloading: • Rock Chucker Press • RCBS 505 Reloading Scale • Speer TrimPro Manual #12 • Uniflow Powder Measure • RCBS Rotary Case Trimmer-2 • deburring tool • case loading block • Primer Tray-2 • Automatic Primer Feed Combo • powder funnel • case lube pad • case neck brushes • fold-up hex key set • Trim Pro Manual Case Trimmer Kit

Price:. 394

.50 BMG Pack

Shooters who favor the .50 BMG have all they need in the .50 BMG Pack from RCBS®. The Pack includes the press, dies, and accessory items needed, all in one box. The press is the powerful Ammo Master® Single Stage rigged for 1.5-inch dies. It has a massive 1.5-inch solid steel ram and plenty of height for the big .50. The kit also has a set of RCBS .50 BMG, 1.5-inch reloading dies, including both full-length sizer and seater. Other items are a shell holder, ram priming unit, and a trim die.

Price:. 581

AmmoMaster Reloading System

The AmmoMaster offers any handloader the freedom to configure a press to his particular needs and preferences. It covers the complete spectrum of reloading, from single stage through fully automatic pro-gressive reloading, from .25 Auto to .50 caliber. The AmmoMaster Auto has all the features of a five-station press.

Single Stage 220

Reloader Special-5

The Reloader Special press features a comfortable ball handle and a primer arm so that cases can be primed and resized at the same time.

- Compound leverage system
- Solid aluminum black "O" frame offset for unobstructed access
- Corrosion-resistant baked-powder finish
- Can be upgraded to progressive reloading with an optional Piggyback II conversion unit
- 7/8" - 14 thread for all standard reloading dies and accessories

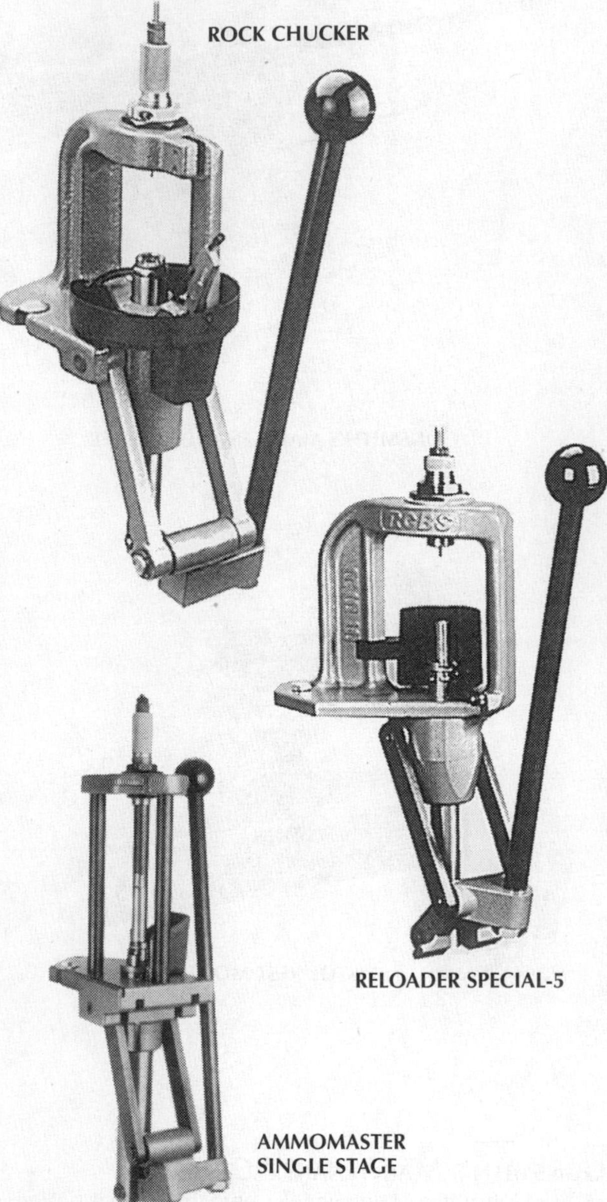

ROCK CHUCKER

RELOADER SPECIAL-5

AMMOMASTER SINGLE STAGE

Price:. $120
Reloading Starter Kit 281

Piggyback III Conversion Kit (NOT SHOWN)

- The Piggyback III conversion unit moves from single-stage reloading to 5-station, manual-indexing, progressive reloading in one step
- Increases output from 50 rounds an hour to well over 400

The Piggyback III will work with the RCBS Rock Chucker, Reloader Special-3, and Reloader Special-5.

Price:. 298

RCBS Reloading Tools

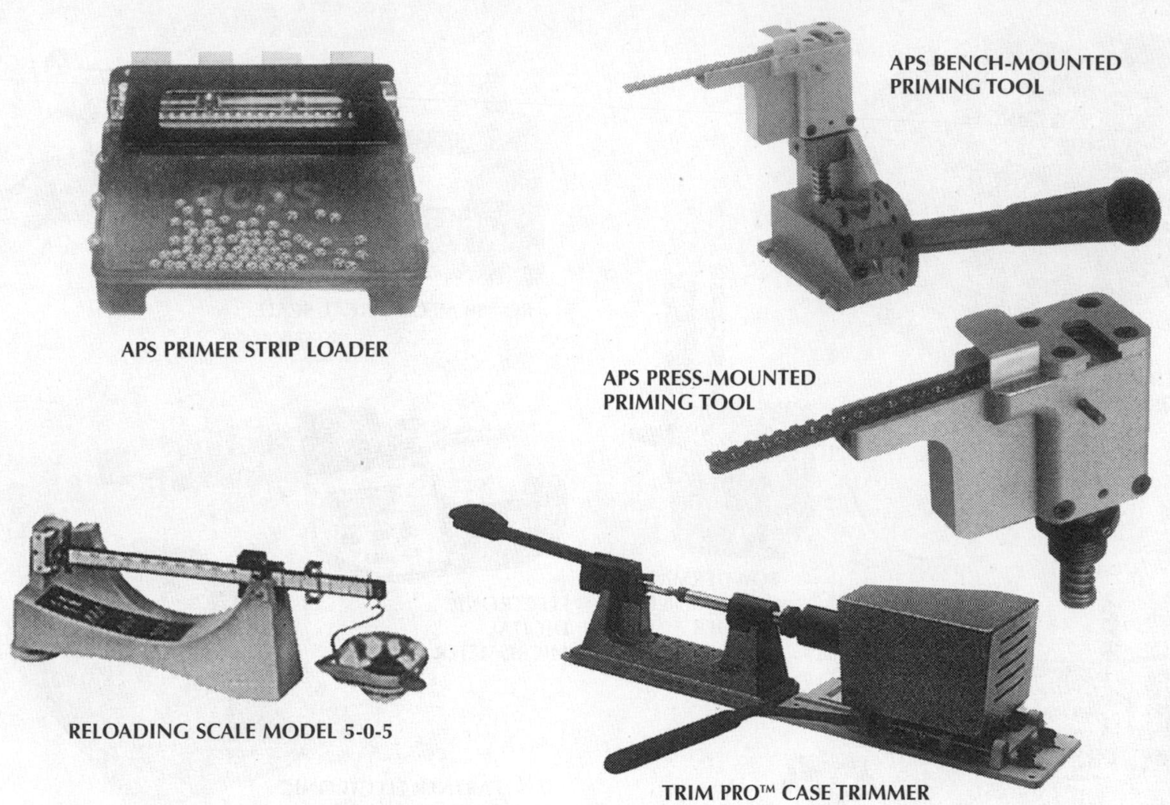
APS BENCH-MOUNTED PRIMING TOOL

APS PRIMER STRIP LOADER

APS PRESS-MOUNTED PRIMING TOOL

RELOADING SCALE MODEL 5-0-5

TRIM PRO™ CASE TRIMMER

APS Bench-Mounted Priming Tool

The APS Bench-Mounted Priming Tool was created for reloaders who prefer a separate, specialized tool dedicated to priming only. The handle of the bench-mounted tool is designed to provide hours of comfortable loading. Handle position can be adjusted for bench height.

Price: **$99**

APS Primer Strip Loader

For those who keep a supply of CCI primers in conventional packaging, the APS primer strip loader allows quick filling of empty strips. Each push of the handle seats 25 primers.

Price: **29**

Pow'r Pull Bullet Puller (not shown)

The RCBS Pow'r Pull bullet puller features a three-jaw chuck that grips the case rim—just rap it on any solid surface like a hammer, and powder and bullet drop into the main chamber for re-use. A soft cushion protects bullets from damage. Works with most centerfire cartridges from .22 to .45 (not for use with rimfire cartridges).

Price: **30**

Reloading Scale Model 5-0-5

This 511-grain capacity scale has a three-poise system with widely spaced, deep beam notches to keep them in place. Two smaller poises on right side adjust from 0.1 to 10 grains, larger one on left side adjusts in full 10-grain steps. The first scale to use magnetic dampening to eliminate beam oscillation, the 5-0-5 also has a sturdy die-cast base with large leveling legs for stability. Self-aligning agate bearings support the hardened steel beam pivots for a guaranteed sensitivity to 0.1 grains.

Price: **$91**

APS Press-MountedPriming Tool

This APS press-mounted priming tool provides the same features as the bench-mounted tool, except it attaches to any single-stage press that accepts standard 7/8″ x 14 dies.

Price: **63**

Trim Pro™ Case Trimmer

Cartridge cases are trimmed quickly and easily with a few turns of the RCBS Trim Pro case trimmer. The lever-type handle is more accurate to use than draw collet systems. A flat plate shell holder keeps cases locked in place and aligned. A micrometer fine adjustment bushing offers trimming accuracy to within .001″. Made of die-cast metal with hardened cutting blades. The power model is like having a personal lathe, delivering plenty of torque. Positive locking handle and in-line power switch make it simple and safe.

Price: Power 110 Vac Kit **254**

Manual **97**

Also available:

Trim Pro Case Trimmer Stand **19**

Case Holder Accessory **41**

RCBS Reloading Tools

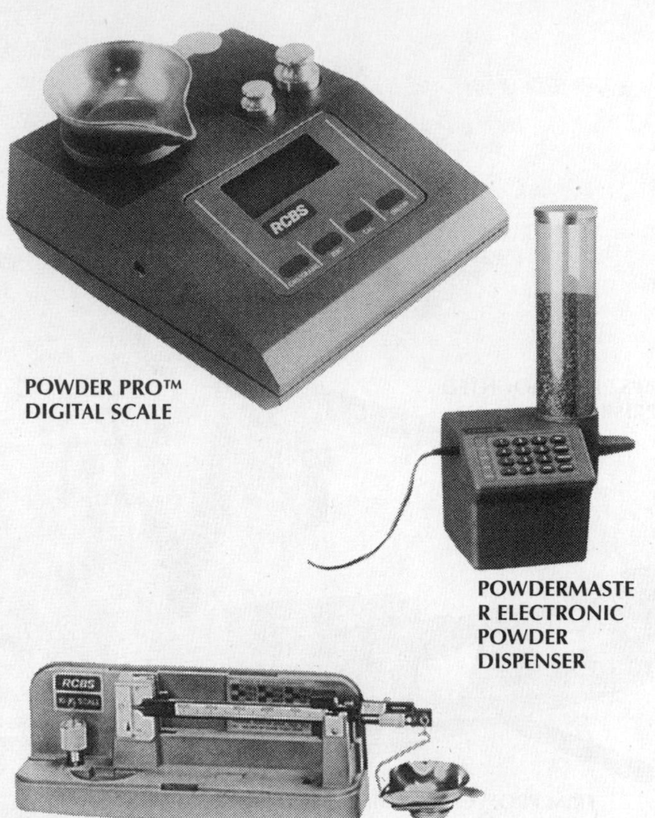

POWDER PRO™ DIGITAL SCALE

POWDERMASTER ELECTRONIC POWDER DISPENSER

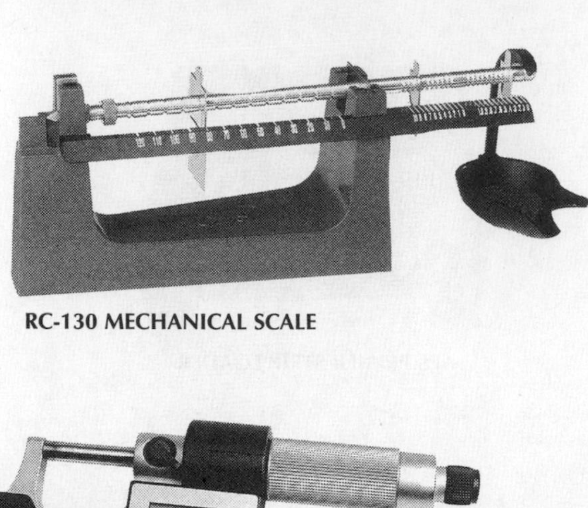

RC-130 MECHANICAL SCALE

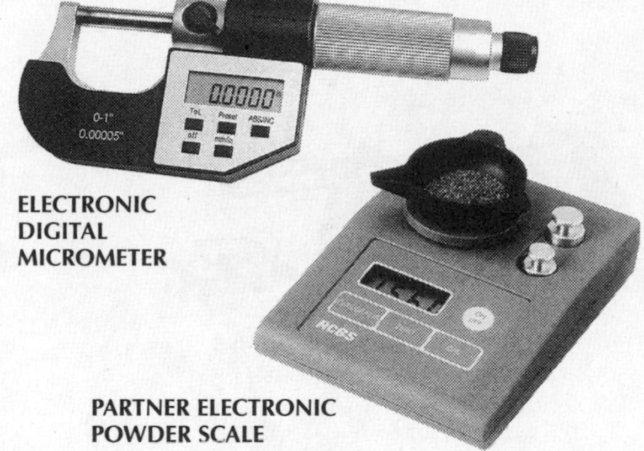

ELECTRONIC DIGITAL MICROMETER

PARTNER ELECTRONIC POWDER SCALE

RELOADING SCALE MODEL 10-10 UP TO 1010 GRAIN CAPACITY

Powder Pro™ Digital Scale

The RCBS Powder Pro Digital Scale has a 1500-grain capacity. Powder, bullets, even cases can be weighed with accuracy of 0.1 grain. Includes infra-red data port for transferring information to the Powdermaster Electronic Powder Dispenser and electronic powder trickler.

Price: 110 VAC **$246**

Powdermaster Electronic Powder Dispenser

Works in combination with the RCBS Powder Pro Digital Scale and with all types of smokeless powder. Can be used as a power trickler as well as a powder dispenser. Accurate to one-tenth of a grain.

Price: **264**

Reloading Scale Model 10-10 Up to 1010 Grain Capacity

Normal capacity is 510 grains, which can be increased without loss of sensitivity by attaching the included extra weight. Features include micrometer poise for quick, precise weighing, special approach-to-weight indicator, easy-to-read graduation, magnetic dampener, agate bearings, anti-tip pan, and dustproof lid snaps on to cover scale for storage. Sensitivity is guaranteed to 0.1 grains.

Price: **145**

RC-130 Mechanical Scale

The RC130 features a 130 grain capacity and maintenance-free movement, plus a magnetic dampening system for fast readings. A 3-poise design incorporates easy adjustments with a beam that is graduated in increments of 10 grains and one grain. A micrometer poise measures in 0.1 grain increments with acuracy to ±0.1 grain.

Price: **$41**

Electronic Digital Micrometer

•Instant reading • Large, easy to read numbers for error reduction with instant inch/millimeter conversion • Zero adjust at any position • thimble lock for measuring like objects • replaceable silver oxide cell – 1.55 Volt • auto off after 5 minutes for longer battery life • adjustment wrench included • fitted wooden storage cases

Price: **107**

Partner Electronic Powder Scale

Accurate for +/- one-tenth of a grain up to 350 grains and +/- two-tenths from 350 to 750 grains. Large LCD display is angled for easy reading over a wide range of positions. Powered by 9-volt battery.

Price: **177**

RCBS Reloading Tools

RCBS Turret Press

Handloaders who want to speed up the loading process without giving up the level of control offered by a single-stage press can boost their output fourfold with the RCBS Turret Press. With pre-set dies in the six-station turret head, the Turret Press can increase production from 50 to 200 rounds per hour with a simple manual operation.

The frame, links, and toggle block of the press are constructed of strong, reliable, cast iron. The handle offers compound leverage for full-length sizing of any caliber from .25 ACP to .460 Wea-therby Magnum. Priming is accomplished with a reliable tube feed priming system.

Six stations allow the handloader to customize his set-up with the options of using a lube die in station one and seating and crimping bullets in separate operations. The quick-change turret head makes caliber changes fast and easy. Dies can be left in the turret head to eliminate set-up and tear-down time. This press accepts all standard 7/8 - 14 dies and shell holders and comes with the RCBS lifetime warranty.

Price: RCBS Turret Press $208
Turret Deluxe Reloading Kit 402

RCBS Pro 2000 Progressive Press

Constructed of strong and reliable cast iron, the Pro 2000 features five reloading stations. It can be set up with a lube die in station one, sizing dies in station two and three, a Powder Checker or Lock Out Die in station four and seating die in station five. Bullet seating and crimping can also be done in separate operations in station four and five.

The case-actuated powder measure assures repeatability of dispensing powder and eliminates spillage. A Micrometer Adjustment Screw allows precise return to previously recorded powder charges. All dies are standard 7/8-14, including the Expander Die.

The press incorporates RCBS's exclusive APS Priming System. Using preloaded plastic priming strips, it eliminates handling of primers and loading tube priming. Compound leverage in the press allows effortless full-length sizing in any caliber, from .32 Auto to the .460 Weatherby Magnum. The press is covered by the RCBS Lifetime Warranty.

Prices:
RCBS Pro 2000 Progressive Press 517
Pro 2000 Deluxe Reloading Kit................. 886

RCBS Grand Shotshell Press

Features: The combination of the Powder system and shot system and Case Holders allows the user to reload shells without fear of spillage. The powder system is case-actuated: no hull, no powder. Cases are easily removed with universal 12 and 20 gauge case holders allowing cases to be sized down to the rim. **Priming system:** Only one primer feeds at a time. Steel size ring: Provides complete resizing of high and low base hulls. Holds 25 lbs of shot and 1½ lbs. of powder. Lifetime warranty.

Price 689

HANDLOADING

Redding Reloading Tools

HANDLOADING

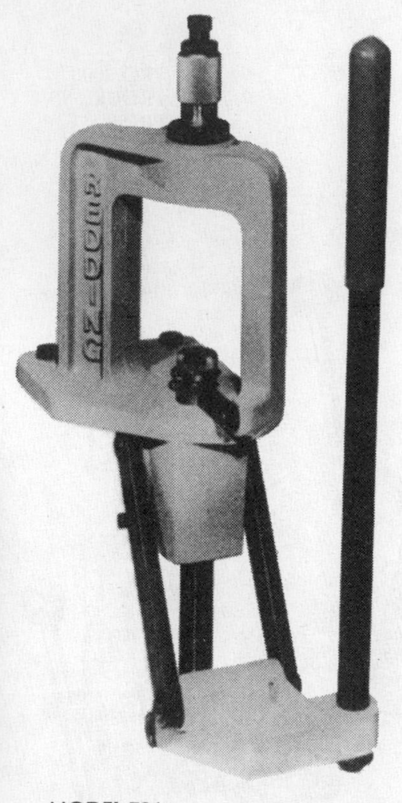

MODEL 721

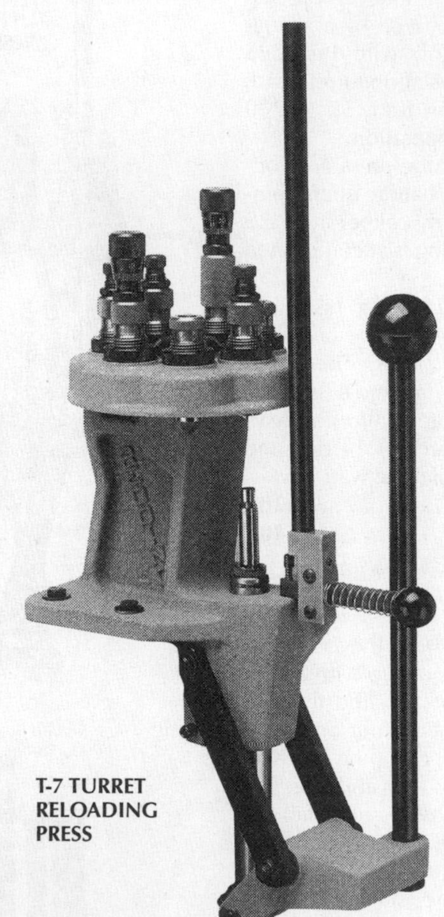
T-7 TURRET RELOADING PRESS

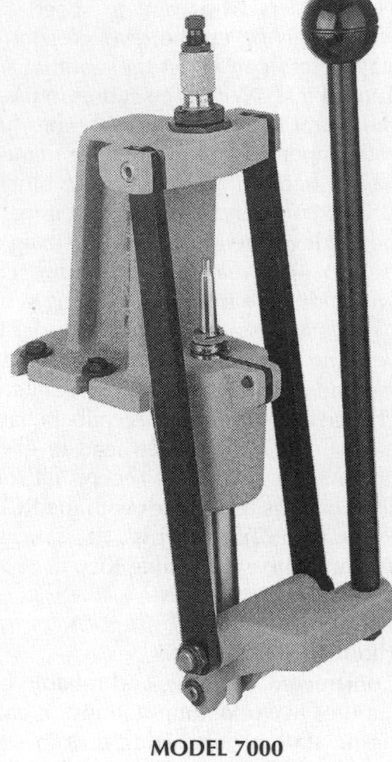
MODEL 7000

Model 721 "The Boss" Press

This "O" type reloading press features a rigid cast iron frame whose 36° offset provides the best visibility and access of comparable presses. Its "Smart" primer arm moves in and out of position automatically with ram travel. The priming arm is positioned at the bottom of ram travel for lowest leverage and best feel. Model 721 accepts all standard 7/8-14 threaded dies and universal shell holders.

Model 721 "The Boss" $140
With Shellholder and 10A Dies 180

Also available:

Boss Pro-Pak Reloading Kit.
Includes Boss Reloading Press, #2 Powder and Bullet Scale, Powder Trickler, Reloading Dies 375
w/o dies and shellholder 324

Boss Deluxe Reloading Kit.
Includes all items in the Pro-Pak plus: Match-Grade Model 3BR Powder Measure and Model 1400 case trimmer 579

Big Boss Reloading Press.
All the features of the Boss with a heavier frame. . . . 170

Ultramag Model 7000

Unlike other reloading presses that connect the linkage to the lower half of the press, the Ultramag's compound leverage system is connected at the top of the press frame. This allows the reloader to develop tons of pressure without the usual concern about press frame deflection. Huge frame opening will handle 50 x 3¼-inch Sharps with ease.

No. 700 Press, complete $315
No. 700K Kit, includes shell holder and one set of dies 356

T-7 Turret Reloading Press

Features: 7 station turret head, heavy duty cast iron frame, 1" diameter ram, optional "Slide Bar Automatic Primer Feeder System". This feeder eliminates handling of primers during sizing and speeds up reloading operations.

T-7 Turret Press 299
Kit, including press, shellholder and dies. 339
Slide Bar Automatic Primer Feeder System 39

Redding Reloading Dies

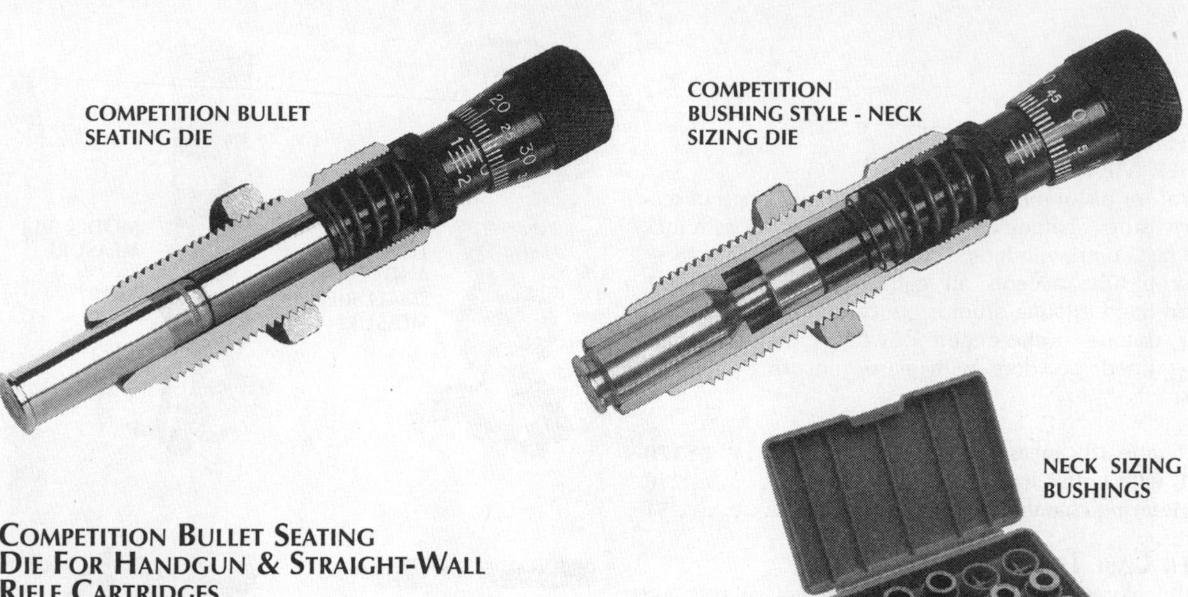

Competition Bullet Seating Die For Handgun & Straight-Wall Rifle Cartridges

Advanced Bullet Alignment

Positive alignment between the bullet and cartridge case prior to bullet seating is essential to fine accuracy. Here is how this die works:

The precision fitting seating stem is allowed to move well down into the chamber of the die to accomplish early bullet contact. The spring loading of the seating stem provides the positive alignment bias between its tapered nose and the bullet ogive. Thus spring loading and bullet alignment are maintained as the bullet and cartridge case move upward until the actual seating of the bullet begins.

Micrometer Adjustment

The micrometer adjustment simplifies setting and recording bullet seating depth. By recording the micrometer setting of reloads one can return to that same overall length by simply "dialing it in." The micrometer is calibrated in .001" increments, is infinitely adjustable and has a "zero" set feature that allows setting desired load to zero if desired.

Separate Crimp

Competition shooters generally prefer bullet crimping as a separate operation from bullet seating. A superior crimp will be acomplished by using a Redding "Profile Crimp" or "Taper Crimp" die.

Progressive Press Compatible

The Competition Seating Die for straight-wall cartridges has been made compatible with all popular progressive reloading presses. The industry standard ⅞ x 14 threaded die bodies have been slightly extended to allow full thread engagement of the lock ring. An oversize bell-mouth chamfer with smooth radius has been added to the bottom of the die to ease case and bullet entry in progressive presses.

Price: **$82**

Competition bullet seating dies for bottleneck cases

Category I **108**

Category II **132**

Competition Bushing Style - Neck Sizing Die

This die allows you to fit the neck of your case perfectly in the chamber. As in the Competition Seating Die, the cartridge case is completely supported and aligned with the sizing bushing and remains supported in the sliding sleeve as it moves upward while the resizing bushing self-centers on the case neck.

The micrometer adjustment of the bushing position delivers precise control to the desired neck length. All dies are supplied without bushings.

Category I **$108**

Category II **132**

Redding Neck Sizing Bushings

Redding Neck Sizing Bushings are available in two styles. Both share the same external dimensions (½" O.D. x ⅜" long) and freely interchange in all Redding Bushing style Neck Sizing Dies.

They are available in .001" size increments throughout the range of .185" thru .365", covering all calibers from .17 to .338.

By selecting the correct bushing, the right amount of neck tension is provided to properly hold the bullet.

Part No. 73185 thru 73365 . . . . **14**

Heat treated steel. The sizing diameters are hand-polished with a surface hardness of Rc 60-62 to reduce sizing effort.

Part No. 76185 thru 76365 . . . . **24**

Heat treated steel as above but with the addition of a Titanium Nitride surface treatment to further increase the effective surface hardness and reduce sizing friction.

Redding Reloading Tools

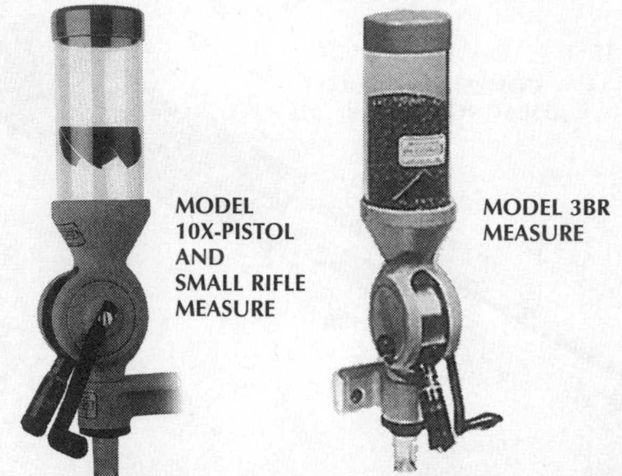

Match-Grade Powder Measure Model 3BR

Universal- or pistol-metering chambers interchange in seconds. Measures charges 100 grains. Unit is fitted with lock ring for fast dump with large "clear" plastic reservoir. "See-thru" drop tube accepts all calibers from 22 to 600. Precision-fitted rotating drum is critically honed to prevent powder escape. Knife-edged powder chamber shears coarse-grained powders with ease, ensuring accurate charges.

Prices:
Match Grade 3BR measure $170
3BR Kit, with both Chambers 210
Pistol Metering chamber (0-10 grains)............ 51

Master Case Trimmer Model 1400

This unit features a universal collet that accepts all rifle and pistol cases. The frame is cast iron with storage holes in the base for extra pilots. Coarse and fine adjustments are provided for case length.

- Six pilots (22, 6mm, 25, 270, 7mm and 30 cal.)
- Universal collet
- Two neck cleaning brushes (22 thru 30 cal.)
- Two primer pocket cleaners (large and small)
- Tin coated replaceable cutter
- Accessory power screwdriver adaptor

Prices:
No. 1400 Master Case Trimmer complete 99
No. 1500 Pilots 5

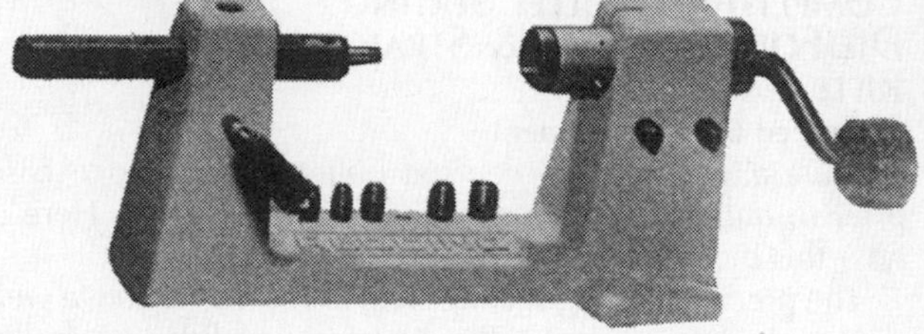

MODEL 1400 TRIMMER

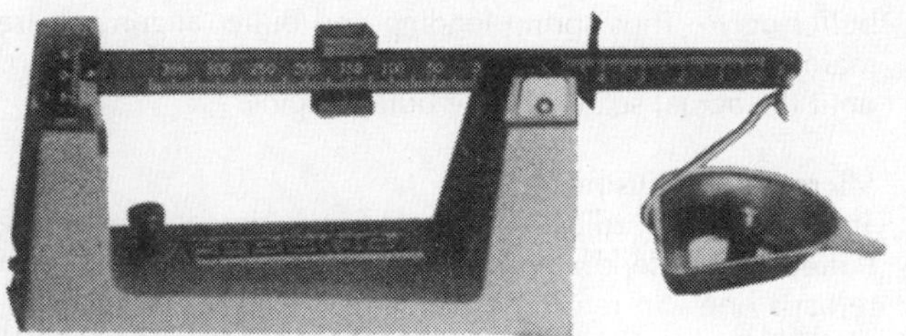

MODEL RS-1 SCALE

Competition Model BR-30 Powder Measure (not shown)

This powder measure features a drum and micrometer that limit the overall charging range from a low of 10 grains to a maximum of 50 grains. The diameter of Model 3BR's metering cavity has been reduced, and the metering plunger has a unique hemispherical shape, creating a powder cavity that resembles the bottom of a test tube. The result: irregular powder settling is alleviated and charge-to-charge uniformity is enhanced.

Price:
Competition Model BR-30 Powder Measure 204

Standard Powder And Bullet Scale Model RS-1

For the beginner or veteran reloader. Only two counterpoises need to be moved to obtain the full capacity range of 1/10 grain to 380 grains.

Model No. RS-1 57
Also available:
Master Powder & Bullet Scale.
Same as standard model, but includes a magnetic dampened beam swing for extra fast readings.
Price:
505-grain capacity 87

Competition Model 10X-Pistol And Small Rifle Powder Measure

This powder measure uses all of the special features of Competition Model BR-30, combined with new drum and metering unit designed to provide the most uniform metering of small charge weights. To achieve the best metering possible at the targeted charge weight of approximately 10 grains, the diameter of the metering cavity is reduced and the metering plunger is given a unique hemispherical shape. Charge range: 1 to 25 grains.

To provide increased versatility, the 10X-Pistol Powder Measure has a drum assembly that can be easily changed from right to left-handed operation. In addition to offering left-handed reloaders increased ease of operation, this feature adapts the 10X-Pistol Powder Measure to progressive reloading presses.

No. 03400 Competition Model 10X-Pistol
Price: Powder Measure $204

Redding Reloading Accessories

"Instant Indicator" Headspace And Bullet Comparator

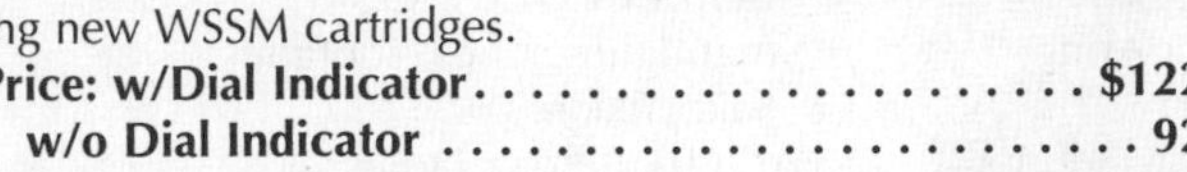

The Instant Indicator checks the headspace from the case shoulder to the base. Bullet seating depths can be compared and bullets can be sorted by checking the base of bullet to give dimension. Case length can be measured. Available for 33 cartridges from .222 Rem to .338 Win. Mag., including new WSSM cartridges.

Price: w/Dial Indicator **$122**
w/o Dial Indicator **92**

"EZ Feed" Shellholders

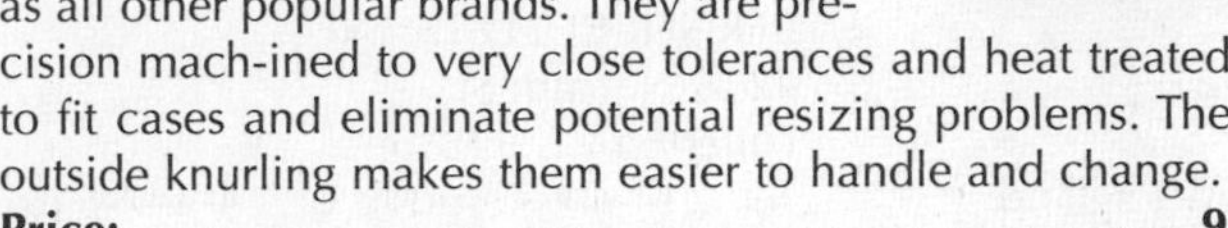

Redding shellholders are of a Universal "snap-in" design recommended for use with all Redding dies and presses, as well as all other popular brands. They are precision mach-ined to very close tolerances and heat treated to fit cases and eliminate potential resizing problems. The outside knurling makes them easier to handle and change.

Price: **9**

Form & Trim Dies

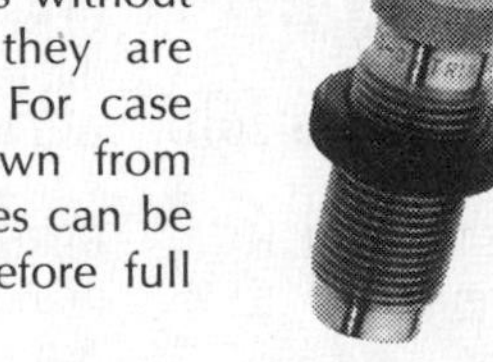

Redding trim dies file trim cases without unnecessary resizing because they are made to chamber dimensions. For case forming and necking brass down from another caliber, Redding trim dies can be the perfect intermediate step before full length resizing.

Prices:
Series A **29**
Series B **39**
Series C **47**
Series D **54**

Neck Sizing Dies

These dies size only the necks of bottleneck cases to prolong brass life and improve accuracy. These dies size only the neck and not the shoulder or body, fired cases should not be interchanged between rifles of the same caliber. Available individually or in Deluxe Die Sets.

Prices:
Series A **34**
Series B **45**
Series C **56**
Series D **63**

Pistol Trim Dies

Redding trim dies for pistol calibers allow trimming cases without excessive resizing. Pistol trim dies require extended shellholders.

Series A **29**
Series B **39**
Series C **47**
Series D **54**

Profile Crimp Dies

For handgun cartridges which do not headspace on the case mouth. These dies were designed for those who want the best possible crimp. Profile crimp dies provide a tighter, more uniform roll type crimp, and require the bullet to be seated to the correct depth in a previous operation.

Series A **27**
Series B **33**
Series C **38**
Series D **42**

Carbide Size Button Kits

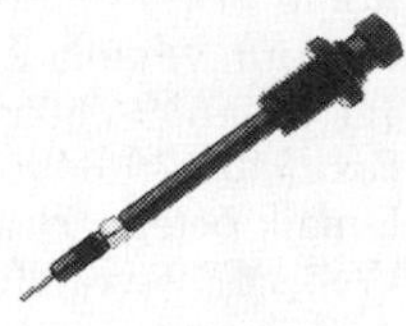

Make inside neck sizing smoother and easier without lubrication. Now die sets can be upgraded with a carbide size button kit. Available for bottleneck cartridges 22 thru 338 cal. The carbide size button is free-floating on the decap rod, allowing it to self-center in the case neck. Kits contain: carbide size button, retainer and spare decapping pin. These kits also fit all Type-S dies

Price: **25**

Extended Shell Holders

Extended shellholders are required when trimming short cases under 1½" O.A.L. They are machined to the same tolerances as standard shellholders except they're longer.

Price: **14**

Taper And Crimp Dies

Designed for handgun cartridges which headspace on the case mouth where conventional roll crimping is undesirable. Also available for some revolver cartridges, for those who prefer the uniformity of a taper crimp. Now available in the following rifle calibers: 223 Rem., 7.62MM x 39, 30-30, 308 Win, 30-06, 300, Win Mag

Prices:
Series A **27**
Series B **33**
Series C **38**
Series D **42**

Directory of Manufacturers & Suppliers

The following manufacturers, suppliers and distributors of firearms, reloading equipment, sights, scopes, ammo and accessories all appear with their products in the "Specifications" and/or "Manufacturers' Showcase" sections of this edition of Shooter's Bible.

ACCURATE ARMS CO., INC.
(gunpowder, reloading)
5891 Hwy. 230 W
McEwen, Tennessee 37101
Tel: 931-729-4207; 800-416-3006
Fax: 931-729-4211
Web Site: www.accuratepowder.com

AIMPOINT INC.
(sights, scopes, mounts)
3989 HWY 62 West
Berryville, AR 72616, USA
Tel: 870-423-3398
Fax: 870-423-2960
Web Site: www.aimpoint.com
E-mail: info@aimpoint.com

ALLIANT POWDER
(gunpowder)
Route 114, P.O. Box 6 Bldg. 229
Radford, Virginia 24143-0096
Tel: 540-639-7805; 800-276-9337
Fax: 540-639-8496
E-mail: peter_jackson@atk.com
Web site: www.alliant_powder.com

AMERICAN DERRINGER CORP.
(handguns)
127 North Lacy Drive
Waco, Texas 76705
Tel: 817-799-9111 Fax: 817-799-7935
Web site: www.amderringer.com

AMERICAN HUNTING RIFLES, INC.
(AHR rifles)
P.O. Box 300
Hamilton, MT 59840
Tel: 406-961-1410
Web site: www.hunting-rifles.com

A.G. ANSCHUTZ GmbH
(rifles, pistols)
Web site: www.anschutz-sporters.com
Available through Tristar Sporting Arms

AO SIGHT SYSTEMS
2401 Ludelle St.
Forth Worth, Texas 76105
Tel: 817-536-0136; 888-744-4880
Fax: 800-734-7939
Web site: www.xsights.com

AUSTIN & HALLECK
2150 South 950 East
Provo UT 84606-6285
Tel: 801-371-0412 Fax: 801-374-9998
www.austinhalleck.com

AUTO-ORDNANCE CORP.
Available through Kahr Arms

AXTELL RIFLE CO.
The Riflesmith
353 Mill Creek Rd.
Sheridan MT 59749
Tel: 406-842-5814
Website: www.riflesmith.com

AYA
(shotguns)
Available through New England Custom Gun Service

LES BAER CUSTOM, INC.
29601 34th St.
Hillsdale IL 61257
Tel: 309-658-2716 Fax: 309-658-2610

BANSNER'S ULTIMATE RIFLES L.L.C.
Mark Bansner (custom guns)
P.O. Box 839
261 East Main St.
Adamstown PA 19501
Tel: 717-484-2370 Fax: 717-484-0523
Website: www.bansnersrifle.com

BARNES BULLETS
P.O. Box 215
750 N. 2600 W.
American Fork, Utah 84003
Lindon, Utah 84042
Tel: 385-756-4222; 800-574-9200
Fax: 385-756-2465
E-mail: email@barnesbullets.com
Web site: www.barnesbullets.com

BATTENFIELD TECHNOLOGIES, INC.
(reloading equipment)
5885 West Van Horn Tavery Rd.
Columbia, Missouri 65203
Tel:877-509-9160 Fax: 573-446-6606
Web site: www.midwayusa.com

BENELLI U.S.A. CORP.
(shotguns)
17603 Indian Head Hwy, Suite 200
Accokeek, Maryland 20607-2501
Tel: 301-283-6981 Fax: 301-283-6988
Web site: www.benelliusa.com
E-mail benusa1@aol.com

BERETTA U.S.A. CORP.
(handguns, rifles, shotguns; Sako,Tikka)
17601 Beretta Drive
Accokeek, Maryland 20607
Tel: 301-283-2191 Fax: 301-283-0189
Web site: www.berettausa.com
E-mail: cwilliams@berettausa.com

BERGER BULLETS, INC.
4275 N. Palm St.
Fullerton CA 92835
Tel: 714-447-5456 Fax: 714-447-5407
www.bergerbullets.com
Web site: www.bergerbullets.com

BERNARDELLI
(handguns, shotguns)
Available through Armsport

BERSA
(handguns)
Available through Eagle Imports Inc.

ROGER BIESEN
(custom guns)
W. 5021 Rosewood
Spokane, Washington 99208
Tel: 509-328-9340

BLACK HILLS AMMUNITION
P.O. Box 3090
3050 Eglin
Rapid City, South Dakota 57709-3090
Tel: 605-348-5150 Fax: 605-348-9827
Web site www.black-hills.com
E-mail: black-hills.com

BLACKPOWDER PRODUCTS, INC.
(CVA & Winchester Blackpowder)
5988 Peachtree Corners East
Norcross GA 30071
Tel: 770-449-4687 Fax: 770-242-8546
www.bpiguns.com

BLASER USA, INC.
(rifles) Available through Sig Arms

REFERENCE

Directory of Manufacturers & Suppliers

BONANZA
(reloading tools)
See Forster Products

BOND ARMS INC.
(handguns)
204 Alpha Lane
P.O. Box 1296
Granbury, Texas 76048
Tel: 817-573-4445 Fax: 817-573-5636
(see p. 76 in Manufacturers' Showcase)

KENT BOWERLY
(custom guns)
710 Golden Pheasant Drive
Redmond, Oregon 97756
Tel: 541-923-3501

BRENNEKE OF AMERICA LTD.
(ammunition)
P.O. Box 1481
Clinton, Iowa 52733-1481
Tel.: 800-753-9733
Fax: (563) 244 7421
Web site: www.brennekeusa.com

ED BROWN PRODUCTS, INC.
(rifles, handguns)
P.O. Box 492
Perry, Missouri 63462
Tel: 573-565-3261 Fax: 573-565-2791
Web site: www.edbrown.com

BROWNING
(handguns, rifles, shotguns, blackpowder guns)
One Browning Place
Morgan, Utah 84050
Tel: 801-876-2711 Fax: 801-876-3331
Web site: www.browning.com

BROWN PRECISION, INC.
(custom rifles)
7786 Molinos Avenue P.O. Box 270 W.
Los Molinos, California 96055
Tel: 530-384-2506 Fax: 530-384-1638

BSA OPTICS, INC.
3911 SW 47th Ave., Ste 914
Ft. Lauderdale, Florida 33314
Tel: 954-581-2144 Fax: 954-581-3165
Web site: www.bsa.optic.com
E-mail: bsaoptic@bellsouth.net

BURRIS COMPANY, INC.
(scopes)
331 East Eighth Street P.O. Box 1899
Greeley, Colorado 806321-1899
Tel: 970-356-1670; 888-228-7747
Fax: 970-356-8702
Web site: www.burrisoptics.com

BUSHNELL
(scopes, Tasco scopes)
Performance Optics
9200 Cody
Overland Park, Kansas 66214
Tel: 913-752-3400 Fax: 913-752-3550
Web site: www.bushnell.com

CABELA'S INC.
(blackpowder rifles)
One Cabella Drive
Sidney, Nebraska 69160
Tel: 308-254-5505 Fax: 308-254-6669

CCI/SPEER-BLOUNT, INC.
(ammunition, bullets)
2299 Snake River Ave., P.O. Box 856
Lewiston, Idaho 83501
Tel: 208-746-2351 Fax: 208-746-3904
Web site: www.cci-ammunition.com
www.speer-bullets.com

CHRISTENSEN ARMS
(rifles)
192 E. 100 N.
Fayette, Utah 84630
Tel: 801-528-7199
Web site: www.christensenarms.com

DAVID CHRISTMAN, JR.
(custom gunmaker)
216 Rundell Loop Rd.
Delhi LA 71232
Tel: 318-878-1395

CIMARRON FIREARMS CO.
(revolvers, rifles)
Wed site: www.cimarron-firearms.com
E-mail:cimarron@fbg.net

CLARK CUSTOM GUNS INC.
Jim Clark, Jr.
336 Shootout Lane
Princeton LA 71067
Tel: 888-458-4126
www.clarkcustomguns.com

COLT BLACKPOWDER ARMS CO.
(handguns)
110 8th street
Brooklyn, New York 11215
Tel: 718-499-4678 Fax: 718-768-8056

COLT'S MANUFACTURING CO., INC.
(handguns, rifles)
P.O. Box 1868
Hartford, Connecticut 06144-1868
Tel: 800-962-COLT Fax: 860-244-1467
Web site: www.colt.com

CONNECTICUT SHOTGUN MFG. CO.
(A.H. Fox shotguns)
35 Woodland Street, P.O. Box 1692
New Britain, Connecticut 06051-1692
Tel: 860-225-6581 Fax: 860-832-8707

COOPER FIREARMS of Montana, Inc.
P.O. Box 114
Stevensville, Montana 59870
Tel: 406-777-5534
Web site: www.cooperfirearms.com

CVA
(blackpowder arms)
5988 Peachtree Corners East
Norcross, Georgia 30071
Tel: 800-320-8767 Fax: 770-242-8546
Web site: www.cva.com
E-mail: sales@cva.com

CZ-USA
(pistols, rifles)
P.O. Box 171073
Kansas City, Kansas 66117-0073
Tel: 913-321-1811; 800-955-4486
Fax: 913-321-2251
Web site: www.cz-usa.com
E-mail: cz-usa@qvl.net

DAKOTA ARMS
(rifles, shotguns)
1310 Industry Road
Sturgis, South Dakota 57785
Tel:605-347-4686 Fax: 605-347-4459; 508-302-4784
Web site: www.dakotarms.com
E-mail: dakarms@sturgis.com
CHARLES DALY (pistols, shotguns)
Available through K.B.I., Inc.

DESERT EAGLE
(handguns)
Available through Magnum Research Inc.

DGS, INC.
(Dale A. Storey custom guns)
1117 E. 12th Street
Casper, Wyoming 82601
Tel: 307-237-2414

Directory of Manufacturers & Suppliers

DILLON PRECISION PRODUCTS, INC. (reloading equipment)
8009 East Dillon's Way
Scottsdale, Arizona 85260-9865
Tel: 800-223-4570; 602-948-8009
Fax: 602-998-2786
Web site: www.dillonprecision.com

DIXIE GUN WORKS
(blackpowder guns)
P.O. Box 130
Union City, Tennessee 38281
Tel: 800-238-6785
Fax: 901-885-0440 info: 901-885-0700
Web site: www.dixiegun.com

DOCTER SCOPES
Available through Eldorado Cartridge Corp.

DOWNSIZER CORPORATION
(handguns)
P.O. Box 710316
Santee, California 92072-0316
Tel: 619-448-5510 Fax: 619-448-5780
Web site: www.downsizer.com

DYNAMIT NOBEL/RWS
(Rottweil shotguns and ammunition, Steyr Mannlicher)
81 Ruckman Road
Closter, New Jersey 07624
Tel: 201-767-1995 Fax: 201-767-1589

EAGLE IMPORTS, INC.
(Bersa, Comanche, Llama and Firestorm handguns)
1750 Brielle Avenue, Unit B1
Wanamassa, New Jersey 07712
Tel: 732-493-0302 Fax: 732-493-0301

D'ARCY ECHOLS
(custom rifles)
98 West 300 South, P.O. Box 421
Millville, Utah 84326
Tel: 435-755-6842

ELDORADO CARTRIDGE CORP.
(PMC ammo, Docter scopes and Verona shotguns)
PO Box 62508
Boulder City NV 89005
Tel: 702-294-0025 Fax: 702-294-0121
www.pmcammo.com

E.M.F. COMPANY, INC.
(Dakota handguns; Uberti handguns, blackpower arms, rifles)
1900 East Warner Avenue, Suite 1-D
Santa Ana, California 92705
Tel: 714-261-6611 Fax: 714-756-0133
Web site: www.emf-company.com

ENTRÉPRISE ARMS
(handguns)
15861 Busines Center Drive
Irwindale, California 91706-2062
Tel: 626-962-8712 Fax: 626-962-4692
Web site: www.entreprise.com

EUROARMS OF AMERICA INC.
(blackpowder arms)
P.O. Box 3277
Winchester, Virginia 22604
Tel: 540-662-1863

EUROPEAN AMERICAN ARMORY CORP.
(E.A.A. handguns, rifles)
P.O. Box 1299
Sharpes, Florida 32959
Tel: 800-536-4442 Tel: 321-639-4942
Fax: 321-639-7006
Web site: www.eaacorp.com

FABARMS
(shotguns)
Available through Heckler & Koch

FEDERAL CARTRIDGE CO.
(ammunition, ballistics)
900 Ehlen Drive
Anoka, Minnesota 55303-7503
Tel: 800-322-2342; 763-323-2300
Fax: 763-323-2506
Web site: www.federalcartridge.com

KENT "BUZZ" FLETCHER
(custom gunmaker)
117 Siler Rd.
Taos NM 87571
Tel: 505-758-3486

FLODMAN GUNS SWEDEN
640 60 Akers styckebruk
Jarsta, Sweden
Tel: 46 159308 61 Fax: 46 159300 61
www.flodman.com

FIRESTORM PISTOLS
Available through Eagle Imports

FIOCCHI OF AMERICA
(ammunition)
6930 Fremont Rd.
Ozark, Missouri 65721
Tel: 800-721-AMMO; 417-725-4118
Fax: 417-725-1039
Web Site: www.fiocchiusa.com

FLINTLOCKS, ETC.
(Pedersoli replica rifles)
160 Rossiter Road, P.O. Box 181
Richmond, Massachusetts 01254
Tel: 413-698-3822 Fax: 1-888-GUNCLIP
Web site: www.GUNMAGS.com

FORSTER PRODUCTS
(reloading)
310 East Lanark Avenue
Lanark, Illinois 61046
Tel: 815-493-6360 Fax: 815-493-2371
Web site: forsterproducts.com
E-mail: infor@forsterproducts.com

A.H. FOX (shotguns)
Available through Connecticut Shotgun Mfg. Co.

FRANCHI
(shotguns)
Available through Beretta

FREEDOM ARMS
(handguns)
314 Hyw. 239, P.O. Box 150
Freedom, Wyoming 83120-0150
Tel: 307-883-2468 Fax: 307-883-2005
Web site: www.freedomarms.com
E-mail: freedom@freedomarms.com

GIBBS RIFLE COMPANY
211 Lawn Street
Martinsburg, West Virginia 25401
Tel: 304-262-1651 Fax: 304-262-1658
E-mail: support@gibbsrifle.com

GLOCK, INC.
(pistols)
6000 Highland Parkway
Smyrna, Georgia 30082
Tel: 770-432-1202 Fax: 770-433-8719

GARY GOUDY
(custom gunmaker)
1512 S. 5th St.
Dayton WA 99328
Tel: 509-382-2726

CHARLES GRACE
(custom gunmaker)
1006 Western Avenue
Trinidad, Colorado 81081
Tel: 719-846-9435

REFERENCE

Directory of Manufacturers & Suppliers

GSI (GUN SOUTH INC.)
(Mauser rifles; Merkel shotguns)
7661 Commerce Lane, P.O. Box 129
Trussville, Alabama 35173
Tel: 800-821-3021; 205-655-8299
Fax: 205-655-7078
Web site: www.gsifirearms.com
E-mail: infor@gsifirearms.com

H&R 1871 INC.
Available through New England Firearms
www.hr1871.com

H-S PRECISION
(rifles, pistols)
1301 Turbine Drive
Rapid City, South Dakota 57703
Tel: 605-341-3006 Fax: 605-342-8964
Web site: www.hsprecision.com

HAMMERLI U.S.A.
(handguns)
19296 Oak Grove Circle
Groveland, California 95321
Tel: 209-962-5311 Fax: 209-962-5931

HECKLER & KOCH
(handguns, rifles; and Fabarms shotguns)
21480 Pacific Blvd.
Sterling, Virginia 20166
Tel: 703-450-1900 Fax: 703-450-8160
Web site: www.hecklerkoch-usa.com

HENRY REPEATING ARMS CO.
(rifles)
110 8th Street
Brooklyn, New York 11215
Tel: 718-499-5600 Fax: 718-768-8056
Web site: www.henryrepeatingcom

DARWIN HENSLEY
(custom rifles)
63133 E. Barlow Trail Rd.
Brightwood, Oregon 97011
Tel: 503-622-5411

HERITAGE MANUFACTURING
(handguns)
4600 NW 135 St.
Opa Locka, Florida 33054
Tel: 305-685-5966 Fax: 305-687-6721
Web site: www.heritagemfg.com

HI-POINT FIREARMS
(handguns)
MKS Supply, Inc.
8611-A North Dixie Drive
Dayton, Ohio 45414
Tel/Fax: 877-425-48671
Web site: www.hi-pointfirearms.com

HIGH STANDARD MFG. CO., INC.
5200 Mitchelldale Suite E-17
Houston TX 77092
Tel: 800-272-7816; 713-462-4200
Fax: 713-681-5665

HILL COUNTRY RIFLE CO.
5726 Morningside Dr.
New Braunfels, Texas 78132
Tel: 830-609-3139
Web site: www.hillcountryrifle.com

BOB HISSERICH
(custom gunmaker)
StockWorks Rifles
1843 S. Los Alamos
Mesa, Arizona 85204
Tel: 480-545-2994 Fax: 480-507-7560
Web site: www.stockworks.net

HODGDON POWDER CO., INC.
(gunpowder)
6231 Robinson, P.O. Box 2932
Shawnee Mission, Kansas 66201
Tel: 913-362-9455 Fax: 913-362-1307
Web site: www.hodgdon.com
E-mail: info@hodgdon.com

PATRICK HOLEHAN
(custom rifles)
5758 E. 34th St.
Tucson, Arizona 85711
Tel: 520-745-0622
E-mail: plholehan@juno.com

HORNADY MFG. CO.
(ammunition, reloading)
P.O. Box 1848; 3625 Old Potash Hwy.
Grand Island, Nebraska 68803
Tel: 308-382-1390 Fax: 308-382-5761
Web site: www.hornady.com

HOWA
(rifles)
Available through Legacy Sports

STEVEN DODD HUGHES
(custom rifles)
P.O. Box 545
Livingston, Montana 59047
Tel: 406-222-9377

IMR POWDER CO. INC.
1080 Military Turnpike, Suite 2,
Plattsburgh, NY 12901
Tel: 877-IMR-DATA
www.imrpowder.com

ITHACA GUN CO.
(shotguns)
901 Route 34-B
Kings Ferry, New York 13081
Tel: 315-364-7171 Fax: 315-364-5134
Web site: www.ithacagun.com

JARRETT RIFLES INC.
(custom rifles)
383 Brown Road
Jackson, South Carolina 29831
Tel: 803-471-3616 Fax: 803-471-9246
Web site: www.jarrettrifles.com

KAHLES
(scopes)
2 Slater Rd.
Cranston, Rhode Island 02920
Tel: 800-426-3089
Web site: www.kahlesoptics.com
Fax: 401-734-5888

KAHR ARMS
(handguns, Auto-Ordnance)
630 Route 303, POB 220
Blauvelt, New York 10913
Tel: 508-795-3919 Fax: 508-795-7046
Web site: www.kahr.com

K.B.I., INC.
(rifles, handguns, shotguns; Charles Daly rifles, shotguns; FEG handguns)
P.O. box 6625
Harrisburg, Pennsylvania 17112-0625
Tel: 717-540-8518
Fax: 717-540-8567
Web site: www.kbi-inc.com or www.charlesdaly.com
E-mail: sales @kbi-inc.com

KEL-TEC CNC IND INC.
(handguns)
P.O. Box 236009
Cocoa, Florida 32926
Tel: 321-631-0068 Fax: 231-631-1169
Web site: www.kel-tec.com
E-mail: aimkeltec@aol.com

KIMBER MANUFACTURING, INC.
(handguns, rifles)
1 Lawton Street
Yonkers, New York 10705
Tel: 914-964-0771; 888-243-4522
E-mail: info@kimberamerica.com

Directory of Manufacturers & Suppliers

KNIGHT RIFLES
(blackpowder rifles)
P.O. Box 130, 21852 Hwy. J46
Centerville, Iowa 52544-0130
Tel: 515-856-2626 Fax: 515-856-2628
Web site: www.knightrifles.com
E-mail: knightrifles@lisco.net

KRIEGHOFF INTERNATIONAL INC.
(rifles, shotguns)
337A Route 611, P.O. Box 549
Ottsville, Pennsylvania 18942
Tel: 610-847-5173 Fax: 610-847-8691

KYNOCH AMMUNITION
Kynamco Limited -
The Old Railway Station
Mildenhall, IP28 7DT England
Tel: +44 (0) 1638 711999
Fax: +44 (0) 1638 515251

L.A.R. MANUFACTURING, INC.
(Grizzly rifles)
4133 West Farm Rd.
West Jordan, Utah 84088-4997
Tel: 801-280-3505 Fax: 801-280-1972
Web site: www.largrizzly.com
E-mail: guns@largrizzly.com

LASERAIM TECHNOLOGIES INC.
(sights)
721 Main St., P.O. Box 3548
Little Rock, Arkansas 72203-3548
Tel: 501-375-2227 Fax: 501-372-1445

LEGACY SPORTS INTL.
(Howa & Mauser rifles)
206 S. Union St.
Alexandria VA 22314
Tel: 703-548-4837 Fax: 703-549-7826
www.legacysports.com

LENARTZ MUZZLOADING
(blackpowder guns)
8001 Whitneyville Rd.
Alto, Michigan 49302

LEUPOLD & STEVENS, INC.
(scopes, mounts)
14400 N.W. Greenbriar Parkway,
P.O. Box 688
Beaverton, Oregon 97075
Tel: 503-646-9171 Fax: 503-526-1475
Web site: www.leupold.com

LLAMA
(handguns)
Available through Eagle Imports

LONE STAR RIFLE CO., INC.
11231 Rose Road
Conroe, Texas 77303
Tel: 409-856-3363
Web site: www.lonstarrifle.com

LYMAN PRODUCTS CORP.
(blackpowder guns, reloading tools)
475 Smith Street
Middletown, Connecticut 06457
Tel: 800-225-9626; 860-632-2020
Fax: 860-632-1699
Web site: www.lymanproducts.com
E-mail: lymansales@cshore.com

MAGNUM RESEARCH INC.
(handguns, rifles, Desert Eagle)
7110 University Avenue N.E.
Minneapolis, Minnesota 55432
Tel: 612-574-1868 Fax: 612-574-0109
Web site: www.magnumresearch.com

MAGTECH AMMUNITION CO.INC
6845 20th Ave. South
Suite 120
Centerville MN 55038
Tel: 800-466-7191 Fax: 651-429-9485

MARKESBERY MUZZLELOADERS, INC. (blackpowder guns)
7785 Foundation Drive, Suite 6
Florence, Kentucky 41042
Tel: 606-342-5553 Fax: 606-342-2380
Web site: www.markesbery.com

MARLIN FIREARMS COMPANY
(rifles, shotguns, blackpowder)
100 Kenna Drive, P.O. Box 248
North Haven, Connecticut 06473
Tel: 203-239-5621 Fax: 203-234-7991
Web site: www.marlinfirearms.com

MAROCCHI
(Conquista shotguns)
Available through Precision Sales Int'l.

MEC INC.
(reloading tools)
c/o Mayville Engineering Co.
715 South Street
Mayville, Wisconsin 53050
Tel: 800-797-4MEC; 920-387-4500
Fax: 920-387-5802
Web site: www.mecreloaders.com
E-mail: reloaders@mayvl.com

MERKEL
(shotguns, rifles)
Available through GSI (Gun South Inc.)
Web site: www.gsifirearms.com

DAVID MILLER
(custom rifles)
3131 E. Greenlee Rd.
Tucson, AZ 85716

M.O.A. CORP.
(handguns)
2451 Old Camden Pike
Eaton, Ohio 45302
Tel: 937-456-3669 Fax: 937-456-9331
Web site: moaguns.com

O.F. MOSSBERG & SONS, INC.
(shotguns, rifles)
7 Grasso Avenue, P.O. Box 497
North Haven, Connecticut 06473
Tel: 203-230-5300 Fax: 203-230-5420
Web site: www.mossberg.com

MTM MOLDED PRODUCTS
(cases, reloading accessories)
P.O. Box 13117
Dayton, Ohio 45413
Tel: 937-890-7461 Fax: 937-890-1747
Web site: www.intmcase-grad.com
(see also p. 80 in Manufacturers' showcase)

NAVY ARMS COMPANY, INC.
(handguns, rifles, blackpowder guns)
815 22nd. Street
Union City, NJ 07087
Tel: 201-863-7100 Fax: (201) 863-8770
Web site: www.navyarms.com

NELSON'S CUSTOM GUNS, INC.
Stephen Nelson
7430 NW Valley View Dr.
Corvallis OR 97330
Tel: 541-745-5232

NEW ENGLAND ARMS CORP./FAIR TECHNI MEC
6 Lawrence Lane, P.O. Box 278
Kittery Point, Maine 03905
Tel: 207-439-0593 Fax: 207-439-6726

NEW ENGLAND CUSTOM GUN LTD.
(AYA shotguns and Schmidt-Bender Scopes)

Directory of Manufacturers & Suppliers

438 Willow Brook Rd.
Plainfield, NH 03781
Tel: 603-469-3450 Fax 603-469-3471

NEW ENGLAND FIREARMS CO. INC.
(handguns, rifles, shotguns, H&R 1871)
60 Industrial Rowe
Gardner, Massachusetts 01440
Tel: 978-632-9393 Fax: 978-632-2300

NEW ULTRA LIGHT ARMS, LLC
1024 Grafton Road
Morgantown, West Virginia 26508
Tel: 304-292-0600 Fax: 304-292-9662
E-mail: newultralightarm@cs.com

NIKON INC.
(scopes)
1300 Walt Whitman Road
Melville, New York 11747-3064
Tel: 631-547-4200 Fax: 631-547-4040
Web site: www.nikonusa.com

DAVE NORIN
(custom gunmaker)
2010 Washington St.
Waukegan IL 60085
Tel: 847-662-4034

NORTH AMERICAN ARMS
(handguns)
2150 South 950 East
Provo, Utah 84606-6285
Tel: 800-821-5783; 801-374-9990
Fax: 801-374-9998
Web site: www.naaminis.com

NOSLER BULLETS, INC.
(bullets)
P.O. Box 671, 107 SW Columbia
Bend, Oregon 97709
Tel: 541-382-3921 Fax: 541-388-4667
Web site: www.nosler.com

OLIN/WINCHESTER
(ammunition, primers, cases)
427 No. Shamrock St.
East Alton, Illinois 62024-1174
Tel: 618-258-3692 Fax: 618-258-3609
Web site: www.winchester.com

PARA-ORDNANCE MFG, INC.
(handguns)
PO Box 1
Oakhurst, CA 93644
Tel: 559-683-3060Fax: 559-683-3061
Web site: www.paraord.com
E-mail: info@paraord.com

PEDERSOLI, DAVIDE
(replica arms)
Available through Flintlocks Etc.
Web site: www.davide-pedersoli.com

PENTAX
(scopes)
P.O. Box 6509 (80155)
35 Inverness Drive East
Englewood, Colorado 80112
Tel: 303-799-8000 Fax: 303-790-1131
Web site: www.pentax.com

PERAZZI U.S.A.
1010 W. 10th St.
Azusa CA 91702
Tel: 626-334-1234 Fax: 626-334-0344
PerazziUSA@aol.com

PMC CARTRIDGES
Available through Eldorado Cartridge Corp.
www.pmcammo.com

PRAIRIE GUN WORKS
(rifles)
1-761 Marion St.
Winnipeg, Manitoba, Canada R2J0K6
Tel: 204-231-2976 Fax: 204-231-8566
Web site: www.prairiegunworks.com

PRECISION SALES INTERNATIONAL
(Marocchi shotguns)
P.O. Box 1776
Westfield, Massachusetts 01086
Tel: 413-562-5055 Fax: 413-562-5056
Web site: www.precision-sales.com

RAMSHOT PROPELLANT
(gunpowder)
Western Powders, P.O. Box 158
Miles City, Montana 59301
Tel: 406-232-0422 Fax: 406-232-0430
Web site: www.westernpowders.com

RCBS
(reloading equipment)
605 Oro Dam Blvd.
Oroville, California 95965
Tel: 916-533-5191 Fax: 916-533-1647
Web site: www.rcbs.com

REDDING RELOADING EQUIPMENT
(reloading tools)
1089 Starr Road
Cortland, New York 13045
Tel: 607-753-3331 Fax: 607-756-8445
Web site: www.redding-reloading.com
E-mail: techline@redding-reloading.com

REDFIELD
Available through Simmons
(scopes)
P.O. Box 38
Onalaska, Wisconsin 54650
Tel: 608-781-5800 Fax: 608-781-0368
Web site: www.redfieldoptics.com

REMINGTON ARMS COMPANY, INC.
(rifles, shotguns, blackpowder arms, ammunition)
870 Remington Drive, P.O. Box 700
Madison, North Carolina 27025-0700
Tel: 800-243-9700 Fax: 336-548-7741
Web site: www.remington.com

RIFLES, INC.
3580 Leal Rd.
Pleasanton TX 78064
Tel: 830-569-2055 Fax: 830-569-2297

RAY RIGANIAN
(custom gunmaker)
324 N. Central Ave., Unit B
Glendale CA 91203
Tel: 818-502-2678

RIZZINI
(shotguns)
Available through Traditions Firearms
Web site: www.rizzini.it

ROSSI FIREARMS
(handguns, rifles, shotguns)
BrazTech Intl.
16175 NW 49th Ave.
Miami,Florida 33014
Tel: 305-624-1115 Fax: 305-623-7506
Web site: www.rossiusa.com

ROTTWEIL BRENNEKE
(see Brenneke)

RUGER
(handguns, rifles, shotguns, blackpowder guns) See Sturm, Ruger & Co., Inc.

RWS
Available through Dynamit Nobel

SAFARI ARMS
(handguns)

REFERENCE

Directory of Manufacturers & Suppliers

c/o Olympic Arms, Inc.
624 Old Pacific Hwy SE
Olympia, Washington 98513
Tel: 360-459-7940 Fax: 360-491-3447
Web site: www.olyarms.com
800-228-3471

SAKO
(rifles, actions, scope mounts, ammo)
Available through Beretta U.S.A. Corp.

SAUER
(rifles)
c/o Paul Company, Inc.
27385 Pressonville Road
Wellsville, Kansas 66092
Tel: 913-883-4444 Fax: 913-883-1515

SAVAGE ARMS
(handguns, rifles, shotguns)
Savage Arms, Inc.
100 Springdale Road
Westfield, MA 01085
Tel: 413-568-7001
Fax: 413-562-7764
Web site: www.savagearms.com

SCHMIDT AND BENDER INC.
(scopes)
Schmidt & Bender U.S.A.
P.O. Box 134
Meriden, New Hampshire 03770
Tel: 800-468-3450 Fax: 603-469-3471
Web site: www.schmidt-bender.de

ANTHONY SCHUELKE
(custom guns)
1606 N. Baxter Ave.
Glencoe, Minnesota 55336
Tel: 320-864-3905

SHILOH RIFLE MANUFACTURING
(Blackpowder guns)
PO Box 279
Big Timber MT 59011
Tel: 406-932-4454 Fax: 406-932-5627
Shilohrifle@men.net

SIERRA BULLETS
(bullets)
P.O. Box 818
1400 West Henry Steet
Sedalia, Missouri 65301
Tel: 888-223-3006; 660-827-6300
Fax: 660-827-4999
Web site: www.sierrabullets.com
E-mail: sierra@sierrabullets.com

SIGARMS INC.
(Sig-Sauer shotguns, handguns, Blaser rifles)
18 Industrial Dr.
Exeter, New Hampshire 03833
Tel: 603-772-2302 Fax: 603-772-1481
Web site: www.sigarms.com

SIGHTRON, INC.
(scopes)
100 Jeffrey Way, Suite A
Youngville NC 27596
Tel: 919-562-3000 Fax: 919-556-0157
www.sightron.com

GENE SIMILLION
(custom guns)
220 S. Wisconsin
Gunnison, Colorado 81230
Tel: 970-641-1126

SIMMONS Outdoor corp.
(scopes, Weaver, Redfield)
201 Plantation Oak Drive
Thomasville, GA 31792
Tel: 229-227-9053 Fax: 229-227-6454
Web site: www.simmonsoptics.com

SISK RIFLES
(cusom rifles)
Charlie Sisk
16607 Port O'Call
Crosby, Texas 77532
Tel: 281-328-5458

SKB SHOTGUNS
(shotguns)
4325 S. 120th Street
Omaha, Nebraska 68137-1253
Tel: 800-752-2767 Fax: 402-330-8040
Web site: www.skbshotguns.com
E-mail: SKB@radiks.net

SMITH & WESSON
(handguns)
2100 Roosevelt Avenue, P.O. Box 2208
Springfield, Massachusetts 01102-2208
Tel: 413-781-8300; 800-331-0852
Fax: 413-747-3317
Web site: www.smith-wesson.com

SPEER
(bullets)
Available through CCI/Speer-Blount, Inc.

SPRINGFIELD INC.
(handguns, rifles, Aimpoint scopes, & sights)
420 West Main Street
Geneseo, Illinois 61254
Tel: 800-680-6866; 309-944-5631
Fax: 309-944-3676
Web site: www.springfield-armory.com

STEYR-MANNLICHER
(rifles)
Available throughDynamit/Nobel
Web site: www.dnrws.com

STOEGER INDUSTRIES
(shotguns)
17603 Indian Head Hwy., Suite 200
Accokeek, Maryland 20607
Tel: 301-283-6300 Fax: 301-283-6586
Web site:
jtroiani@stoegerindustries.com

DALE STOREY
(custom gunmaker) (See DGS, Inc.)

MARK STRATTON
(custom gunmaker)
Mukilteo, Washington 98037
Tel: 425-745-8309
Web Site: www.gunmaker.net
E-mail: octbarrel@aol.com

STURM, RUGER AND COMPANY, INC.
(Ruger handguns, rifles, shotguns, blackpower, revolvers)
200 Ruger Road
Prescott, Arizona 86301
Tel: 520-541-8820 Fax: 520-541-8850
Web site: www.ruger-firearms.com

SWAROVSKI OPTIK NORTH AMERICA
(scopes)
2 Slater Road
Cranston, Rhode Island 02920
Tel: 800-426-3089; 401-734-1800
Fax: 401-734-5888; 877-287-8517
Web site: www.swarovskioptik.com

SWIFT BULLET CO.
(bullets)
201 Main Street
P.O. Box 27
Quinter, Kansas 67752
Tel: 785-754-3959 Fax: 785-754-2359

SWIFT INSTRUMENTS, INC.
(scopes, mounts)
952 Dorchester Avenue
Boston, Massachusetts 02125

Directory of Manufacturers & Suppliers

Tel: 800-446-1116 Fax: 617-436-3232
Web site: www.swift-optics.com

SZECSEI & FUCHS
(custom rifles)
450 Charles Street
Windsor, Ontario N8X 371 Canada
Tel: 001 519 966 1234

TASCO WORLDWIDE, INC.
See Bushnell
(scopes, mounts)
Web site: www.tasco.com

TAURUS INT'L, INC.
(handguns)
16175 N.W. 49th Avenue
Miami, Florida 33014-6314
Tel: 800-327-3776; 305-624-1115
Fax: 305-623-7506
Web site: www.taurususa.com

TAYLOR'S & CO. INC.
(rifles, carbines)
304 Lenoir Drive
Winchester, Virginia 22603
Tel: 540-722-2017 Fax: 540-722-2018
Web site: www.taylorsfirearms.com
E-mail: info@taylorsfirearms.com

THOMPSON & CAMPBELL
(custom rifles)
Cromarty – The Black Isle
Ross-Shire IV11 8YB Scotland
Tel: +44 (0) 1381 600 536
Fax: +44 (0) 1381 600 767

THOMPSON/CENTER ARMS
(handguns, rifles, reloading,
blackpowder arms)
Farmington Road, P.O. Box 5002
Rochester, New Hampshire 03867
Tel: 603-332-2394 Fax: 603-332-5133
Web site: www.tcarms.com

TIKKA
(rifles, shotguns))
Available through Beretta U.S.A.

TRADITIONS PERFORMANCE-FIREARMS
(blackpowder arms, rizzini Shotguns)
1375 Boston Post Road
P.O. Box 776
Old Saybrook, Connecticut 06475-0776
Tel: 860-388-4656 Fax: 860-388-4657
Web site: www.traditionfirearms.com
E-mail: info@traditionsfirearms.com

TRIJICON
(rifle scopes)
49385 Shafer Ave. P.O. Box 930059
Wixom, Michigan 48393
Tel: 248-960-7700; 800-338-0563
Fax: 248-960-7725
Web site: www.trijikon-inc.com

UBERTI USA, INC.
(handguns, rifles, blackpowder guns)
Stoeger Industries
17603 Indian Head Hwy, Suite 200
Accokeek, MD 20607
Tel: 301-283-6300

U.S. REPEATING ARMS CO.
(Winchester rifles, shotguns)
275 Winchester Ave.
Morgan, Utah 84050-9326
Tel: 801-876-3440 Fax: 801-876-3737
Web site: www.winchesterguns.com

VERONA SHOTGUNS
Available through Eldorado Cartridge

VIHTAVUORI POWDER
1241 Ellis St.
Bensenville IL 60106
Tel: 630-350-1116 Fax: 630-350-1606

WALTHER U.S.A.
(handguns)
2100 Roosevelt Ave.
Springfield, Massachusetts 01104
Tel: 800-372-6454 Fax: 413-747-3592
Web site: www.walther-usa.com

WEATHERBY, INC.
(rifles, shotguns, ammunition)
3100 El Camino Real
Atascadero, California 93422
Tel: 800-227-2016; 805-466-1767
Fax: 805-466-2527
Web Site: www.weatherby.com

WEAVER
(scopes)
Available through Simmons
Wev site: www.weaveroptics.com

WILDEY F.A. INC.
(handguns)
45 Angevine Road
Warren, Connecticut 06754
Tel: 860-355-9000 Fax: 860-354-7759
Web site: www.wildeyguns.com

WILD WEST GUNS, INC.
(Summit rifles)
7521 Old Seward Hwy., Unit A
Anchorage, Alaska 99518
Tel: 800-992-4570 Fax: 907-344-4005
Web site: www.wildwestguns.com
E-mail: wwguns@ak.net

WILLIAMS GUN SIGHT CO.
7389 Lapeer Road
P.O. Box 329
Davison, Michigan 48423
Tel: 800-530-9028; 810-653-2131
Fax: 810-658-2140
Web site: www.williamsgunsight.com

WINCHESTER
(ammunition, primers,
cases, ballistics)
Available through Olin/Winchester
Web site: www.winchester.com

WINCHESTER FIREARMS
(rifles, shotguns)
Available through U.S. Repeating
Arms Co.
Web site: www.winchester-guns.com

WINCHESTER MUZZLELOADING
Available through Blackpowder Prods.

WOODLEIGH BULLETS
Huntingtons
POB 991
601 Oro Dam Blvd.
Oroville CA 95965
Fax: 530-534-1212

CARL ZEISS OPTICAL, INC.
13017 N. Kingston Ave.
Chester VA 23836
Tel: 804-530-8300
Fax: 804-530-8325

Z-HAT CUSTOM DIES
(reloading)
4010A S. Poplar, Suite 72
Casper, Wyoming 82601
Tel: 307-577-7443
Web site: www.z-hat.com
E-mail: RifleBuilder@z-hat.com

Gunfinder Index

To help you find the model of your choice, the following index includes every firearm found in the Shooter's Bible 2004, listed by type of gun.

RIFLES

Centerfire Bolt Action

REFERENCE

Gunfinder Index

Gunfinder Index

REFERENCE

Gunfinder Index

REFERENCE

Gunfinder Index

REFERENCE

Gunfinder Index

REFERENCE

Gunfinder Index

REFERENCE

Gunfinder Index

REFERENCE

REFERENCE